PAGE
32

ON THE ROAD

YOUR COMPLETE DESTINATION GUIDE
In-depth reviews, detailed listings
and insider tips

Poland
p387

Germany
p167

Czech Republic
p97

Slovakia
p473

Liechtenstein
p381

Austria
p34

Hungary
p313

Switzerland
p561

Slovenia
p521

THIS EDITION WRITTEN AND RESEARCHED BY

Lisa Dunford
Brett Atkinson, Mark Baker, Kerry Christiani,
Steve Fallon, Tim Richards, Caroline Sieg,
Ryan Ver Berkmoes

914.304
CEN

Welcome to Central Europe

Old-World Appeal

Teutonic half-timbered villages, sgraffito-decorated Renaissance squares, medieval walled towns...if you're looking for old-world appeal, you've come to the right place. Wander the darkly Gothic alleyways of Prague, admire the baroque excess of Salzburg or take in the colourful old-Venetian influence on the Slovenian port of Piran. Poland and the Czech Republic seem to have more than their fair share of medieval masterpieces, but you can find narrow lanes and quaint townscapes throughout the region – from Bern, Switzerland to Bardejov, Slovakia. Smaller gems such as Bamberg, Germany are often far from the tourist radar. On mornings when the mists lie heavy and crowds are few, you might imagine yourself in an earlier century.

Atmospheric Eating & Drinking

Nourishing yourself is more fun in a great atmosphere, and Central Europe's abundance of outdoor cafes, beer halls and coffee houses offer just that. When the temperatures rise in spring, outdoor tables proliferate along with the daffodils and tulips. Enjoy a plate of pasta while admiring the Slovenian coast, nosh *pierogi* (dumplings) on a Polish cobblestone street

At once natural and refined, folksy and cultured: the combination of mountain rusticity with old-world élan captivates in Central Europe.

(above) Ride the cable car up Petřín Hill (p111) and admire the view of Prague, Czech Republic (below) Cyclists chasing their shadows along the embankment of Bremen's Old Town (p279), Germany

or dip into fondue lakeside in Switzerland. Beer gardens across the region offer an opportunity to enjoy hearty food, a convivial atmosphere and a good brew alfresco. Once the weather cools, move inside to a boisterous beer hall. Or, for something a little sweeter, try a cake at a coffee house or pastry cafe. The most famous are in Vienna and Budapest, but you'll find many options – and other interesting places to eat and drink – all across the region.

Outdoor Adventure

With mountains covering so many Central European states, it's no wonder that the outdoors holds such an attraction in the region. The Alps rise to their highest in Switzerland, with jagged, Toblerone-like peaks such as the Matterhorn, and continue on through very southern Germany, across Austria and south into Slovenia. You can hike, bike, ski or just ride the gondolas and funiculars to enjoy the Alpine views. Other mountains, like the Swiss Jura and the Polish–Slovak Tatras, offer no less adventure. There are also sculptural sandstone 'rock towns' in the Czech Republic to climb, waterfall-filled gorges in Slovakia and Slovenia to hike and the bucolic Black Forest to walk in Germany. It seems that around every corner there is a new part of nature to explore.

› Central Europe

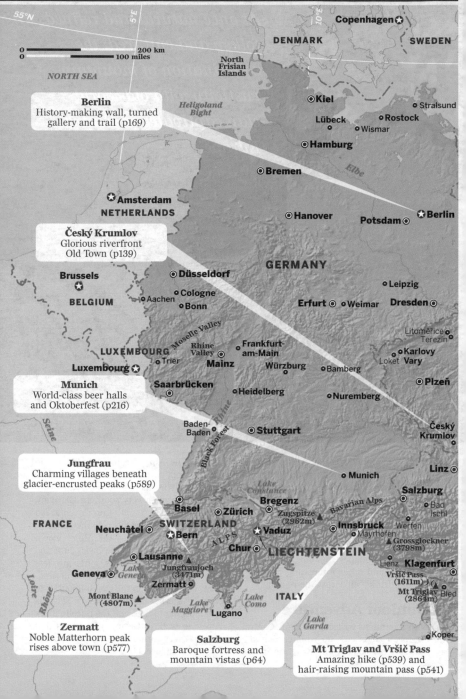

Berlin
History-making wall, turned gallery and trail (p169)

Český Krumlov
Glorious riverfront Old Town (p139)

Munich
World-class beer halls and Oktoberfest (p216)

Jungfrau
Charming villages beneath glacier-encrusted peaks (p589)

Zermatt
Noble Matterhorn peak rises above town (p577)

Salzburg
Baroque fortress and mountain vistas (p64)

Mt Triglav and Vršič Pass
Amazing hike (p539) and hair-raising mountain pass (p541)

NORTH SEA

DENMARK
SWEDEN

Copenhagen

North Frisian Islands

Heligoland Bight

Kiel
Stralsund
Lübeck
Rostock
Wismar
Hamburg

Bremen

Amsterdam
NETHERLANDS

Hanover
Potsdam
Berlin

GERMANY

Brussels
BELGIUM

Düsseldorf
Aachen
Cologne
Bonn

Leipzig

Erfurt
Weimar
Dresden

Litoměřice
Terezín

Moselle Valley

Rhine Valley
Trier

Frankfurt-am-Main
Mainz
Würzburg
Bamberg

Karlovy Vary
Loket

Plzeň

LUXEMBOURG
Luxembourg

Saarbrücken
Heidelberg

Nuremberg

Český Krumlov

Seine

Baden-Baden

Black Forest

Stuttgart

Munich

Linz

Salzburg
Bad Ischl

Jungfrau

Lake Constance

Bregenz
Zugspitze (2962m)

Bavarian Alps

Werfen

Basel
Zürich

FRANCE

Neuchâtel

SWITZERLAND
Bern

Lausanne

Geneva

Lake Geneva

Jungfraujoch (3471m)
Zermatt

Mont Blanc (4807m)

Vaduz

Chur

Innsbruck
Mayrhofen

Grossglockner (3798m)

LIECHTENSTEIN

Lienz

Klagenfurt

Vršič Pass (1611m)

Mt Triglav (2864m)
Bled

ALPS

Rhône

Loire

Lake Maggiore

Lago Lugano

Lake Como

ITALY

Lake Garda

Koper

55°N
5°E
10°E

0 ——— 200 km
0 ——— 100 miles

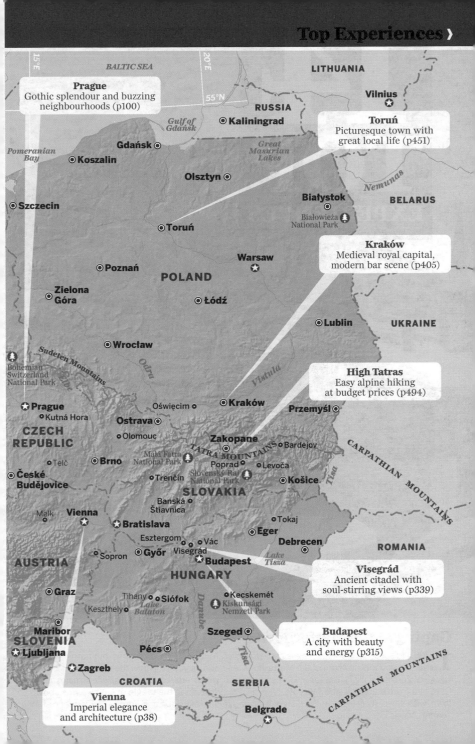

Prague
Gothic splendour and buzzing neighbourhoods (p100)

Toruń
Picturesque town with great local life (p451)

Kraków
Medieval royal capital, modern bar scene (p405)

High Tatras
Easy alpine hiking at budget prices (p494)

Visegrád
Ancient citadel with soul-stirring views (p339)

Budapest
A city with beauty and energy (p315)

Vienna
Imperial elegance and architecture (p38)

14 TOP EXPERIENCES

Gaping at the Matterhorn

1 Sure, it graces Toblerone packages and evokes stereotypical 'Heidi' scenes, but nothing prepares you for the allure of the Matterhorn. As soon as you step into the timber-chalet-filled village of Zermatt (p577), this loner looms above you, mesmerising with its chiselled, majestic peak. Gaze at it from a tranquil sidewalk cafe, hike in its shadow along the tangle of Alpine paths above town, with cowbells clinking in the distance, or pause on a ski slope and admire its magnetic stance. Zermatt, Valais, Switzerland

Singing in Salzburg

2 A fortress on a hill, 17th-century cobbled streets, Mozart, the ultimate singalong: if Salzburg (p64) didn't exist, someone would have to invent it just to keep all the acolytes who visit each year happy. It's hard to say what's more popular, but you just have to see all the DVDs for sale to know that this is Sound of Music country. Faster than you can say 'Do-Re-Mi' you can be whisked into the gorgeous steep hills that are alive with tour groups year-round.

Beer-Drinking in Munich

3 It's not just the idea that you can drink beer in Munich (p216) – everybody knows you can. It's the variety of places where you can drink that astounds and makes this a must-stop. There's Oktoberfest, of course, and then there are the famous beer halls, from the huge and infamous (Hofbräuhaus) to the huge and merely wonderful (Augustiner Bräustuben). And why stay inside for your frothy, refreshing litre of lager? You can drink it in a park (Chinesischer Turm) or in the city centre (Viktualienmarkt) – or really just about anywhere.

Exploring Prague

4 Prague Castle and Old Town Square are highlights of the Czech capital (p100), but for a more insightful look at life two decades after the Velvet Revolution, head to local neighbourhoods around the centre. Working-class Žižkov and energetic Smíchov are crammed with pubs, while elegant, tree-lined Vinohrady features a diverse menu of cosmopolitan restaurants. Gritty Holešovice showcases many forms of art, from iconic works from the last century to more recent but equally challenging pieces. Staroměstské nám (Old Town Square), Prague, Czech Republic

Discovering Kraków

5 As popular as it is, Poland's former royal capital (p405) never disappoints. It's hard to pinpoint exactly why it's so special, but there's a satisfying aura of history radiating from the sloping stone buttresses of the medieval buildings in the Old Town that makes its streets seem, well, just right. Add to that the extremes of a spectacular castle and the low-key, oh-so-cool bar scene situated within the tiny worn buildings of the Kazimierz backstreets, and it's a city you want to seriously get to know. Main Market Square (Rynek Główny), Kraków, Poland

Admiring Imperial Vienna

6 Imagine having unlimited riches and top architects at your hands for 640 years – that's the Vienna (p38) of the Habsburgs. The monumentally graceful Hofburg (p39) whisks you back to the age of empires as you marvel at the treasury's imperial crowns, the equine ballet of the Spanish Riding School and the chandelier-lit apartments fit for Empress Elisabeth. The palace is rivalled in grandeur only by the 1441-room Schloss Schönbrunn (p42), a Unesco World Heritage site, and the baroque Schloss Belvedere (p43), both set in exquisite landscaped gardens. Schloss Schönbrunn, Austria

Climbing Mt Triglav & Vršič Pass

7 They say you're not really a Slovene until you've climbed Mt Triglav (p539). There's no rule about which particular route to take – there are about 20 ways up – but if you're a novice, ascend with a guide from the Pokljuka Plateau north of Bohinj. If time is an issue and you're driving, head for the Vršič Pass (p541), which stands (literally) head and shoulders above the rest. It leads from Alpine Gorenjska, past Mt Triglav itself and down to sunny Primorska and the bluer-than-blue Soča River in one hair-raising, spine-tingling hour. Julian Alps, Triglav National Park, Slovenia

Checking out Český Krumlov

8 Showcasing quite possibly Europe's most glorious Old Town, Český Krumlov (p139) is, for many travellers, a popular day trip from Prague. But a rushed few hours navigating the town's meandering lanes and clifftop castle sells short the CK experience. Stay at least one night to lose yourself in the Old Town's after-dark shadows, and get cosy in riverside restaurants, cafes and pubs. The following morning go rafting or canoeing on the Vltava River before exploring the nearby Newcastle mountains by horse or mountain bike.

Remembering the Wall, Berlin

9 It's hard to believe, 20 years on, that the Berlin Wall really cut through this city. The best way to examine its role in Berlin (p169) is to make your way – on foot or by bike – along the Berlin Wall Trail (p177). Passing the Brandenburg Gate (p173), analysing graffiti at the East Side Gallery or learning about its history at the Documentation Centre: the path brings it all into context. It's heartbreaking, hopeful and sombre, and integral to trying to understand Germany's capital. Berliner Mauerweg (Berlin Wall Trail), Germany

RICHARD I'ANSON/LONELY PLANET IMAGES ©

Appreciating Budapest

10 Hungary's capital (p315) has cleaned up its act in recent years. Gone are those old Soviet-era cars that used to spew their choking blue haze over the flat landscape of Pest. Now, the hills on the Buda side of the city are gleaming, and Pest itself is teeming with energy and life. It's no stretch to say that these days Budapest combines the beauty of Prague and buzz of Berlin into something that's uniquely Hungarian. St Stephen's Basilica, Budapest, Hungary

STEPHEN SAKS/LONELY PLANET IMAGES ©

Viewing Visegrád

11 A lonely, abandoned fortress (p339) high atop the Danube River marks what was once the northern border of the Roman Empire. Long after the Romans decamped, the ancient Hungarian kings, the Ottoman Turks and the Austrian Habsburgs in turn all marked this turf as their own. Climb to the top for some soul-stirring vistas over the surrounding countryside and ponder for a moment the kingdoms and peoples who have come and gone over 16 centuries of history. Danube Bend and Visegrád, Hungary

Hiking the High Tatras

12 The rocky, alpine peaks of the High Tatras (p494) in Slovakia are the highest in the Carpathians, with 25 peaks over 2500m. But hiking this impressive little range needn't require an Olympian effort. In the morning, ride a cable car up to 1800m and you can hike along mid elevation trails, stopping at a log-cabin hikers' hut, with a restaurant, for lunch. A few hours more and you're at a funicular terminus that will take you down to a turn-of-the-20th-century resort village below, well in time for dinner. View of High Tatras, Slovakia, from Tatra National Park

WAYNE WALTON/LONELY PLANET IMAGES ©

WITOLD SKRYPCZAK/LONELY PLANET IMAGES ©

Visiting Jungfrau Villages

14 Three of Europe's most impressive, glacier-encrusted peaks form the backdrop to the quaint towns and ski villages throughout Switzerland's Jungfrau region (p589). By day, take advantage of 200km worth of ski and snowboard pistes (and hundreds more kilometres of hiking trails). By night, return to an atmospheric chalet in resort towns like bustling Grindelwald or car-free Mürren. Here every home and hostel has a postcard-worthy view, and cowbells echo in the valleys. This is storybook Switzerland at its best. Mürren, Switzerland, below

GLENN VAN DER KNIJFF/LONELY PLANET IMAGES ©

Touring Toruń

13 This beautiful Gothic city (p451) has just the right balance between sightseeing and relaxing. Grab a zapiekanka (a Polish snack consisting of a toasted roll with mushrooms, cheese and tomato sauce) from the window of the milk bar just off the main square, then saunter past the locals to check out the curious statuary around the square's edge, including a monument to local hero Copernicus. Finish the day at one of the fancy beer-garden decks perched on the cobblestones. Copernicus statue in front of Old Town Hall, Toruń, Poland, above

need to know

Buses

» For travel in the mountains or between villages.

Trains

» Go almost everywhere; fastest connections are in the west.

When to Go

Warm to hot summers, mild winters
Warm to hot summers, cold winters
Mild summers, cold winters
Cold climate

Gdańsk
GO Jul-Aug

Berlin
GO Jun-Aug

Tatra Mountains
GO Jul-Sep

Zürich
• **GO** May-Sep

Budapest
GO May-Sep

The Alps
GO Dec-Mar
& Jul-Aug

Ljubljana
GO Apr-Jun & Sep

Set Your Budget

Less than

€60

» Dorm beds: €12–30

» Fresh-food markets and cheap eats available

» Camping, hiking and free museum days keep costs down

Midrange

€60– 180

» Double room in a pension or guesthouse: €60–100

» Double room in a small hotel with restaurant: €90–180

» Great value daily lunch menus at top restaurants

Top End over

€180

» International and boutique hotels: €180 and up

» Expect exorbitant rates in Switzerland, Berlin and Prague

» Hire a car (from €30 per day) for independent travel

High Season (Jul–Aug)

» Expect crowds at major attractions; book hotels ahead.

» Temperatures soar, especially in Hungary and Slovenia.

» Higher-elevation hiking trails become accessible.

Shoulder (May– Jun & Sep–Oct)

» Prices remain peak, but crowds ease off.

» Moderate weather.

» Village museums and castles remain open.

» Bad timing for Alpine hiking or skiing.

Low Season (Nov–Mar)

» Outside the holidays, prices drop 30% to 50%.

» Christmas markets light up cities in late November and December.

» Ski season kicks in.

» Some attractions close.

Driving
» Car hire readily available at airports throughout Central Europe; roads are quite good.

Ferries
» Travel by sea between Poland or Germany and Scandinavia, or from Slovenia to Italy.

Bicycles
» Beware of mountainous terrain and bring bike locks for the cities; the west has more dedicated cycle paths than the east.

Planes
» Budget airlines connect with many destinations in Western Europe and the UK.

Websites
» **Central Europe Experience** (www.gotocentraleurope.com) Regional activities info

» **Deutsche Bahn** (www.bahn.de) Best online train timetable for the region

» **In Your Pocket** (www.inyourpocket.com) Event listings for some cities

» **Lonely Planet** (www.lonelyplanet.com) Destination coverage, hotel booking and travellers forum

» **Real Beer** (www.realbeer.com/edu/central_europe) Czech and German beer dominate

Money
See individual country chapters for more information on specific currencies and exchange rates.

» **Crown** Czech Republic (Koruna česká; Kč)

» **Euro** Germany, Austria, Slovenia and Slovakia use the euro (€)

» **Forint** Hungary (HUF; Ft)

» **Swiss Franc** Leichtenstein, Switzerland (Sfr)

» **Złoty** Poland (PLN; zł)

Visas
» Visitors from Australia, New Zealand, Canada, Japan and the US can travel visa-free in Central Europe for 90 days.

» All countries in this book are part of the Schengen Agreement, therefore considered one 'country' in terms of your 90-day stay.

» As part of the Schengen Agreement, EU citizens generally do not need visas and may be able to work across the region.

Arriving in Central Europe
For more see the Survival Guide (p629) and individual country Getting There & Away sections.

» **Berlin Tegel Airport** Bus – 30 minutes to centre; frequent service

» **Frankfurt airport** Trains – 15 minutes to centre; several hourly

» **Vienna International Airport** Trains – 15–25 minutes to centre; every 30 minutes

» **Zürich airport** Trains – 10–15 minutes to main train station; frequent service

What to Take
» **Earplugs** Helpful for sleeping at hostels, and in busy cities
» **Ecofriendly shopping bag** To use at all the fruit and vegetable markets
» **Extra ziptop bags** Keep products from leaking and wet clothes separate from dry
» **Hiking boots** For conquering the Alps or the Tatra Mountains
» **Lonely Planet's** *Central Europe Phrasebook*
» **Pocket knife with bottle-opener** For picnics on trains (but check it with your luggage on planes)
» **Sandals or thongs (flip-flops)** Useful at Baltic beaches and Hungarian spas
» **Two-pin plug adaptors** If you're coming from the UK, North America or Down Under
» **Waterproof jacket or umbrella** For travel during the rainy shoulder season

if you like...

World Heritage Sites

Unesco's World Heritage list contains more than 80 of Central Europe's cultural and natural gems. Following their trail would take you to all of the region's states but one (alas, little Liechtenstein has yet to garner recognition). A sampling...

Škocjan Caves There's an unimaginably deep chasm to cross by footbridge while exploring these Slovenian caves (p544)

Wartburg A timber-and-stone edifice where Bach was born is the only German castle to make the list (p204)

Kutná Hora A 14th-century townscape built outside Prague by silver-mining interests (p123)

Białowieża National Park In the furthest eastern reaches of Poland, the drawcard here is the magnificent European bison (p403)

Bardejov Slovakia's best-preserved Gothic-Renaissance town square, surrounded by 15th-century walls (p512)

Pannonhalma Abbey Buildings in northeastern Hungary's most ancient abbey date to the 13th century, but the library boasts even older treasures (p345)

Hiking

Icy blue glacial lakes, crashing waterfalls, technical ascents...with so much striking mountain scenery, hiking in Central Europe is almost always a superlative – and challenging – experience.

Slovenský Raj National Park, Slovakia Ladders and chain-assists line the trails of the waterfall-filled gorge hikes in this national park (p506)

Zakopane, Poland Southern Poland's Tatra Mountain trails lead to emerald-green lakes like Morskie Oko (p427)

Fürstensteig trail, Liechtenstein The most famous, and most precipitous, of 400km of hiking trails through this tiny country (p384)

Swiss National Park, Switzerland In addition to sparkling glaciers, you may get to see ibex or eagles along the trails in this country's only national park (p607)

Black Forest, Germany Seemingly endless paths lead from bucolic villages to misty peaks and crags (p248)

Kitzbühel Alps, Austria Peak-to-peak hiking here is well-served by cable cars, with plenty of alpine accommodation to boot (p83)

Castles

Defence was long a priority here at the crossroads of Europe. In some countries it seems that at the top of any craggy cliff you'll find a castle ruin. Stony fortresses typically date from the 12th to the 17th century. Then, as peace reigned, ruling families expanded and constructed chateaux and ornate palaces.

Karlštejn Castle, Czech Republic A finely restored, high Gothic castle built by Emperor Charles IV in the 14th century (p122)

Spiš Castle, Slovakia Impressive fortress ruins sprawl over more than four hilltop hectares (p505)

Neuschwanstein, Germany Mad King Ludwig's over-the-top castle inspired Walt Disney to create Fantasyland (p236)

Wawel Castle, Poland Kraków's town castle contains a large cathedral and is an enduring symbol of the country (p405)

Vienna's palaces, Austria The Hofburg palace (p39) served as the imperial Habsburg home for six centuries, Schönbrunn (p42) was their ornate summer residence

RICHARD I'ANSON/LONELY PLANET IMAGES ©

» Communist-era statue at Memento Park (p317), Budapest, Hungary

Nightlife

Just about every one of the larger capitals in Central Europe, such as Prague and Budapest, will have a club scene, plus some live music. Smaller towns like Ljubljana and Bratislava rely on a calmer cafe culture for their evening's entertainment. Your choice: dancing until dawn or a quiet, alfresco conversation with friends. Top cities for stepping out...

Berlin With more cutting-edge clubs than seems possible, Berlin is where DJs experiment with the sounds of tomorrow (p188)

Zürich Trendy waterside bars, design-driven nightclubs and plush lounges – the city's scene is uber chic and stylish (p597)

Warsaw There's no shortage of good dance clubs in Warsaw, but go out for the live jazz venues, too (p399)

St Moritz, Switzerland The rich and richer fill up the many bars that pulse here après-ski (p607)

Sacred Spaces

Christianity, Judaism and Islam have all influenced Central Europe. Impressive cathedrals inhabit many of the town castles and squares, and other sacred sites are scattered around the countries.

Old Jewish Cemetery The approximately 12,000 ancient graves here date from 1439; it's an evocative setting that is just one of the many sacred Jewish sights in Prague (p100)

Mosque Church Originally constructed during the 16th-century Turkish occupation of Hungary, this mosque-turned-church retains several Islamic elements (p355)

Wooden churches of Slovakia The onion domes on the nail-less village churches reflect the eastern-facing faith in the Slovakian hinterland (p514)

Weiskirche A jaw-dropping example of 18th-century rococo excess, covered with gilt decorations and hand-painted stucco, sits in a peaceful German valley (p237)

Church of the Assumption This tiny church on a tinier island in an Alpine lake is perhaps Slovenia's most picturesque sacred space (p537)

History

We can learn a lot from history in a region that was ripped apart by several world wars – both hot and cold.

Berlin Wall, Germany Reverberations were felt across Europe when the wall dividing East and West Germany came down in 1989; what remains is part outdoor art gallery, part walking trail (p177)

Memento Park, Budapest An amazing collection of Hungary's socialist and Soviet-inspired statues that were removed from public spaces after the fall of communism (p317)

Auschwitz-Birkenau, Poland Two of the most infamous Nazi concentration camps remain partially standing as a heart-wrenching memorial and museum (p416)

Eagle's Nest, Germany Hitler's mountaintop lodge is now a major attraction; tours cover the war years in detail (p237)

Terezín, Czech Republic A fortress 'community' that was actually a waypoint for Nazi death camps; exhibits include poignant pictures and poems by children once held there (p125)

» Ogle the colourful and eccentric Hundertwasserhaus (p43) in Vienna, Austria

KRZYSZTOF DYDYNSKI/LONELY PLANET IMAGES ©

Artistic Haunts

With so many cultural capitals located in the central region, it's easy to follow in the footsteps of a favourite author or musician. Read or listen to their works as you experience their home cities.

Salzburg Native son Wolfgang Mozart's music resonates in all corners of this Austrian Alpine town – as does *The Sound of Music* (p64)

Weimar, Germany Bach, Liszt, Goethe and Nietzsche were just some of the luminaries who lived and worked here (p204)

Prague Postmodern authors Milan Kundera and Franz Kafka both left their mark on the Old Town streets of Prague (p100)

Warsaw Nobel Laureate and poet Czeslaw Milosz spent WWII attending underground lectures in Poland's capital city (p390)

Vienna As the cultural capital of the Austro-Hungarian empire, Vienna attracted the likes of Ludwig van Beethoven, Joseph Haydn and Béla Bartók; their classical music can still be heard at venues today (p38)

Old Towns

Central Europe's Old Towns are legendary. You'll hardly turn a corner without bumping into a Gothic arch or a medieval buttress. The ancient aura is perhaps best experienced in the more compact pedestrian centres.

Český Krumlov A stunning castle, baroque buildings and the winding Vltava River make this one of the Czech Republic's most charming Old Towns (p139)

Bratislava The rabbit warren-like streets in the Slovakian capital are studded with more outdoor cafes than you can shake a drink at (p476)

Ljubljana, Slovenia A hilltop castle perches above narrow streets and riverfront plazas where street musicians entertain in this lovely town (p523)

Kraków, Poland The stunning medieval centre escaped the ravages of WWII and, as such, is one of the region's best preserved (p405)

Salzburg 'If it's baroque, don't fix it' seems to be the motto in this incredible Old Town in the Austrian Alps (p64)

Drinks

Definitely don't miss the dark, light, sweet and wheat beers crafted in Germany. After that, if your liver can take it, there's plenty more regional imbibing to do.

Bison vodka, Poland Locals claim vodka was invented in Poland; try it here, flavoured with cherries, berries – or with grass from the bison fields (p485)

New wine, Austria In autumn when an evergreen branch appears over the *Heurigen* (wine tavern) door, you know effervescent new wine is available (p90)

Budvar, Czech Republic The original 'Budweiser' beer is still made today in České Budějovice; tour the factory (p136) or taste it at a beer hall

Absinthe, Switzerland This wormwood-aged, aniseed liqueur was once illegal; enjoy a modern version today in its birthplace, the Val de Travers (p575)

Fruit brandy, everywhere Look for fruit-flavoured firewater (OK, they usually call it 'brandy') all across the region. *Slivovice* is flavoured with plums, *pálinka* with apricots...

If you like... extreme sports

The Jungfrau region around Switzerland's Interlaken (p587) is an adventure sports mecca Go canyoning, parasailing or hydro-speed rafting in Bovec, Slovenia (p541) Try rock climbing, rafting or paragliding in the Zillertal valley in Austria (p83)

Modern Architecture

Sure, Central Europe is known for age-old architecture. But there's also a more modern side to the region.

Elbphilharmonie, Hamburg Pritzker prize–winning Swiss architects Jacques Herzog and Pierre de Meuron designed this modern glass facade in an old warehouse district (p283)

Hundertwassershaus, Vienna A colourful mish-mash of uneven floors, misshapen windows and industrial materials make up this apartment house (p43)

Bauhaus school, Germany Examples of the less-is-more, early-1900s design school aesthetic can be found in Weimar (p204), Dessau (p208) and Berlin (p169)

Museum of Czech Cubism, Prague A monument of the indigenous cubist style (p101)

Slovenian Mountaineering Museum, Mojstrana A modernist interpretation of the mountain surrounds (p541)

Secessionist style, Austria and Hungary Austro-Hungarian secessionist style emerged at the turn of the 20th century; examples include Vienna's Secession Building (p43) and Kecskemét's Ornamental Palace (p359)

Off the Beaten Track

Everyone's heard of Berlin and Budapest. If you feel you've been there, done that, then why not explore smaller, off-the-beaten-track towns? You're likely to have a more local experience as you discover these gems.

Toruń, Poland A beautiful Gothic city with curious statuary and plenty of beer gardens to enjoy (p451)

Kecskemét, Hungary Full of art nouveau architecture and small museums, the town itself is worth visiting before you set off to see the famous horses in the adjacent national park (p359)

Bern, Switzerland Often underrated, this capital city has a melange of medieval charm, folkloric fountains and a pulsating party scene (p579)

Piran, Slovenia There are Venetian alleyways to explore and fresh seafood to eat at this port town on the tip of a peninsula (p548)

Bamberg, Germany Cute little bridges span the canal that bisects one of Germany's best small towns; they also have smoked beer (p229)

Bathing

Opportunities abound in Central Europe if you enjoy a good soak. Thermal mineral waters bubble under parts of Germany and the Czech Republic and beneath all of Hungary and Slovakia. We list the main sites, but many smaller spas exist across these countries.

Budapest The queen of the spa towns, Budapest has thermal bathhouses dating back to Turkish times; the two most popular are ginormous Széchenyi Baths (p320) and the more intimate Gellért Baths (p317)

Piešťany, Slovakia A neoclassical thermal spa where you can be wrapped naked in hot mud or soak in a 'mirror pool' (p487)

Baden-Baden, Germany A 16-step Roman bathing experience is on offer in Germany's ritzy spa town (p247)

Karlovy Vary, Czech Republic Book a steam inhalation or a soak among the international set at the Czech answer to Baden-Baden (p128)

month by month

January

Sure it's cold, but what better time to go skiing? While the rest of the region is quiet, the mountains buzz with crowded runs, full cable cars and aprés-ski activities.

☆ Ball Season in Vienna

More than 300 balls take place in Austria's capital during January and February, including the season's highlight, the Opera Ball. Expect men in full tails and women in dazzling dresses gliding elegantly around the polished dance floor.

February

Frigid temperatures and prime ski conditions continue, but an abundance of pre-Lenten festivals start to warm things up in towns big and small across the region.

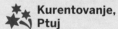 Kurentovanje, Ptuj

Parades of horned and feathered Carnival characters wearing painted masks and sheepskins highlight the 10-day festival leading up to Shrove Tuesday in Slovenia. This ethnographic tradition, which includes bonfires and performances, has taken place for more than 50 years. (p553)

Karneval/ Fasching, Germany

Towns in the traditional Catholic regions of Germany – Bavaria, along the Rhine and deep in the Black Forest – celebrate Carnival with costumed parties and parades in the week leading up to Lent.

☆ Fasnacht, Switzerland

At least six days of celebrating precede Fat Tuesday in Switzerland. The towns of Basel and Lucerne, in particular, live it up: masked revellers party to bands in the streets and bars stay open all night long.

March

As the first green shoots emerge in the lowlands, snow still lies heavy in the mountains above. Concert seasons start and continue until autumn.

☆ Budapest Spring Festival

Classical music is king late in March when Hungary's capital hosts two weeks of world-renowned opera, symphonic music and ballet performances. Venues include gilt concert halls and open-air stages set up on pedestrian squares. (p321)

☆ Polish Music Festivals

A number of towns in Poland have small spring music festivals. In Kraków the focus is organ concerts; in Wrocław jazz takes centre stage for three days when performances are held on the Odra River.

April

The proliferation of outdoor cafe tables proves that spring has well and truly sprung. Thankfully, high season hasn't arrived yet; prices remain low and crowds relatively few.

☆ Sechseläuten, Zürich

On the third Monday in April, Zürich, Switzerland, celebrates spring with a costumed parade and ceremonial burning of the snowman (Böögg). At 6pm a fire is lit under the 4m-high effigy; when the fireworks in his head explode, winter is finished. (p595)

 Festival of Sacred Music, Brno

During the weeks leading up to Easter, six ancient churches in the Czech Republic serve as a blessed backdrop for Lenten concerts. Events include the likes of the Prague Philharmonic performing Beethoven's celebrated mass, *Missa Solemnis*. (p147)

May

Asparagus season is in full swing; look for seasonal menus that include the much-prized white variety. Castles and outdoor village museums are now fully open, but it's too soon for high-altitude hiking.

Prague Spring

Czech composer Bedřich Smetana inspired Prague's most famous classical-music festival, which lasts from mid-May into June. It kicks off with a parade from Smetana's grave to the performance hall where his opera *Má Vlast* is staged. (p111)

Czech Beer Festival, Prague

Also in Prague, for two weeks from mid- to late May, the Czech Beer Festival pours more than 70 brews from around the country. It may be mild compared to Germany's Oktoberfest, but the three big exhibition-ground tents do give off a similar vibe. (p111)

Druga Godba, Ljubljana

In mid-May, Ljubljana, Slovenia, hosts a week-long festival of alternative and world music with bands from around the globe. The venue, a sprawling 18th-century monastic complex, is in rich contrast to the modern sounds. (p525)

June

Frequent rains help the alpine wildflowers bloom, and more and more hikers head to the hills – the lower ranges especially. It's strawberry season, so watch for little red morsels of joy.

Christopher Street Day, Berlin

First held in 1978, this German event in late June is one of the oldest gay and lesbian festivals in the world. Pride-related activities go on all week, culminating with floats and walking GLBT groups parading through the streets and the Tiergarten. (p181)

Jodler Fest Luzern

Lucerne, Switzerland, is at its Alpine best for three days in June, when 12,000 yodellers and alphorn players come to town. With a variety of colourful national costumes, the performances are wonderful to see as well as hear. (p585)

Olomouc Beer Festival

More than 20 breweries participate in this three-day outdoor festival in the eastern Czech Republic. In addition to beers to sample, there are beer souvenirs to buy and more than 40 folk and rock bands to listen to. (p151)

Wrocław Non Stop

For 10 days in late June, quirky art installations, alternative movies and music, experimental theatre and dance take centre stage in Wrocław, Poland. Public squares become art galleries and concert halls as the whole town gets in on the act.

July

Summer crowds arrive in earnest, so be sure to book lodging and hikers' huts ahead. It seems like every town and village is celebrating something with outdoor food stands and frivolities.

Jewish Culture Festival, Kraków

Concerts, films, theatre performances and scholarly lectures are all part of the early July, week-long celebration of Jewish culture in Kraków, Poland. Join local tours and excursions to towns in the area for art and memorial sightseeing. (p411)

Karlovy Vary International Film Festival

International celebrities often appear at this Czech Republic festival (www. kviff.com), which screens more than 200 films each year. Tickets are easy to get and concurrent outdoor events add to the energetic atmosphere. (p128)

☆ Montreux Jazz Festival

For two weeks in early to mid-July, a distinct air of glamour surrounds this fabulous Swiss festival in Montreux. The world's biggest names in jazz play to rapt audiences who have paid well for the tickets. There are also free outdoor performances to enjoy. (p614)

 B-Parade, Berlin

Enormous trucks filled with speakers literally make the earth move for the hundreds of thousands of partiers who line the route, dancing the entire time. This huge German techno street parade is usually held on the second weekend of July.

☆ More Music, Music Everywhere

Musical festivals abound across the region in July. Geneva, Vienna, Warsaw, Ljubljana, Bratislava and Kraków are just a few of the other towns that have concerts and cultural events.

☆ Salzburg Festival

In late July some 250,000 people crowd into this quaint Austrian city for a month-long, world-renowned festival of music, theatre and opera. Book tickets ahead: as one of Europe's largest classical events, first held in 1920, it's not unknown. (p68)

August

The year's hottest month is also the busiest. Despite the throngs, this is a good time to visit if you want plenty to do. City-planned events continue and thermal waterparks open for extended hours.

Zürich Street Parade

In early August 'love mobiles' (giant floats filled with revellers) cruise along the streets of Zürich in Switzerland blasting techno music. Hundreds of thousands of ravers dance in the streets in celebration of life, love and a good beat. (p614)

☆ Sziget Music Festival, Budapest

The week-long outdoor international-music bash in late July/early August is quite the party. Camp on Hungary's Óbuda Shipbuilding Island in central Budapest and listen to world music including rock, ska, hip hop and Romani – a little of everything, with an indie edge. (p322)

Motor Sports

Hotels fill up early during the Moto Grand Prix, a famous motorcycle race in Brno, Czech Republic. But that's nothing compared to the popularity of the Formula One Grand Prix auto race held 24km north of Budapest, Hungary in late July/early August.

Folk Festivals

Keep an eye out for placards advertising small summer folk festivals at weekends. These festivals usually include all kinds of revelry such as folk dances, music, food and drink. Towns and villages in Slovakia, Czech Republic, Poland and Hungary, especially, have them.

September

While some warmth may linger, autumn has already arrived in the mountains. Weather is unpredictable, but often a week or so of 'Indian summer' in late September provides excellent hiking potential.

Cows' Ball in Bohinj

On a mid-September weekend, the residents of Bohinj, Slovenia, mark the return of their cows from high pastures to the valleys by parading wreath-laden bovines through town. Food and folk music are part of the fun that culminates in a town dance. (p540)

🍷 Oktoberfest in Munich, Germany

Six million people guzzle 5 million litres of beer and 400,000 sausages each year at what may be one of the biggest festivals in the world. But don't show up in October, the carousing takes place on the last 15 days in *September*. (p222)

🏃 Mushroom Picking

Locals know that September is prime time for picking mushrooms in the hilly forests of Central Europe. Go with a local or a reliable field guide – the prettiest specimens are often the most poisonous.

October

You're likely to have the museums and castles to yourself if you travel in mild October, but don't forget a raincoat. Avoid the higher altitudes,

which are usually wetter and more sloshy than beautifully snow covered.

Viennale, Vienna

Austria's largest film festival takes place for two weeks in mid- to late October. The screenings have a decidedly independent, fringe-like feel, which attracts a youthful audience. Parties and related events are suitably cool and urban. (p47)

New Wine

From September into October, the new wines (unaged, usually light and effervescent) become available. Buy them at the local markets and vintners cellars, or attend town wine festivals in places like Budapest and Kecskemét, Hungary, and Neuchâtel and Lugano, Switzerland.

November

The best we can say is that prices are low and tourists scarce in this way off-season. Outdoor attractions close, a chill hangs about and places lack the holiday and ski season charm to come.

Onion Market in Bern

Traditionally, on the fourth Monday in November, this Swiss town held a market where you could stock up on stores for winter. Today you can also buy braided onion strands, onion dolls and onion advent wreaths. The carnival atmosphere ends with a giant confetti battle. (p614)

December

Twinkly lights and mulled wine spice up long, cold winter nights in December. Christmas markets and city-wide decorations create a festive atmosphere across the region. Avoid the holiday itself and prices remain remarkably low.

Christkindlmärkte, Vienna, Austria

Vienna's much-loved Christmas market begins in mid-November, continuing until Christmas Day. Wander among hundreds of craft and food stands beneath themed lights, then ice skate on the rink in front of the beautifully illuminated City Hall. (p47)

Christkindlesmarkt, Nuremberg

More than two million people attend Germany's most popular Christmas market, which fills most of Nuremberg's centre. Look for the Christmas angel and handmade ornaments, and don't miss the chance to eat *Lebkuchen* (large, soft gingerbread cookies). (p234)

Yet More Christmas Markets

Austria and Germany may have the largest fairs, but many towns across the region put up craft booths and decorations, sell hot food and wine, and hold outdoor concerts. Check what's going on in your city.

Escalade in Geneva

On December 11, Geneva, Switzerland, celebrates a foiled 15th-century invasion by parading in historic costumes, running races around an old town square and smashing symbolic chocolate pots. Once they're cracked open, make sure you get some of the marzipan candy inside. (p614)

itineraries

Whether you've got six days or 60, these itineraries provide a starting point for the trip of a lifetime. Want more inspiration? Head online to lonelyplanet.com/thorntree to chat with other travellers.

Two Weeks
Top Capital Tour

Spending two to three days per capital will give you a great overview of the region. Start your trip in the dynamic, delightfully idiosyncratic **Berlin**. The history-filled capital of reunited Germany is also something of a party place. Then ride the rails to sprawling **Warsaw**, with a reconstructed Old Town that became the capital of the Commonwealth of Poland and Lithuania back in the mid-16th century. After a few days, continue south to mystical **Prague**. The Czech seat of power is famous for its fantasyland of Gothic architecture – and for great beer. Next? **Bratislava** is a fascinating mix of Old Town charm and new development. The imperial opulence of the long-reigning Habsburg empire is still evident in Austria's capital, **Vienna**. Just don't satiate yourself on coffee house culture there; you have more cafes to visit in one-time cocapital **Budapest**. Today Hungary's main city is abuzz, a mix of the modern and the historic. If you have time, detour to **Ljubljana** in Slovenia and tiny **Vaduz** in Liechtenstein; otherwise World Heritage–listed **Bern**, the Swiss capital fought over by Holy Roman and Habsburg Empires alike, is your final stop. It's so beautiful, it's no wonder everyone wanted a piece of it.

Two Months
Central Europe In-Depth

With two months, you can cover the entire region, but it will still be a bit of a 'Best of' trip. Skyscraper-filled **Frankfurt-am-Main**, Germany, is most useful as an air hub, but you may want to spend a night. From there, shake off jet lag at the chi-chi spa centre **Baden-Baden** before exploring the bucolic towns of the **Black Forest**. Just across the Swiss border, the cobblestone streets and cafes of **Basel** await. Move on to the modern art and ancient architecture of the capital, **Bern**.

Soon the Alps beckon: **Interlaken** and the Jungfrau Region have some of the most extreme mountain scenery around. Check out the club scene of **Zürich** before crossing the spine of the Alps and getting ready to imbibe in the beer halls of **Munich**. Spend a few days, so you can bus it along the Romantic Road and see the fantasyland-like Neuschwanstein castle in **Füssen**. Next stop is the baroque, music-filled city of **Salzburg**. Then it's south into the Julian Alps and picture-postcard, lakeside **Bled**, Slovenia.

The lovely little capital of **Ljubljana** is also worth a stop before you ride the rails on to impressively imperial **Vienna**, Austria, for a couple of nights. A riverboat ride along the vineyard-laden **Danube Valley** is a worthy detour before travelling downstream to the bathhouses and bars of **Budapest**, Hungary. To the south, the architecture in **Pécs** retains some remarkable Turkish relics.

Heading north again, myriad Old Town cafes in **Bratislava**, Slovakia, make a good pit stop en route to the **Tatra Mountains**. On the Slovak side, the most atmospheric mid-mountain village is Ždiar, in Poland, it's Zakopane. Hike rugged area trails before you continue to **Kraków**, one of Europe's prettiest Old Towns, near the notorious Auschwitz concentration camp. A local favourite and another lively Old Town, **Wrocław** is next, then **Dresden**, Germany, a restored city that exhibits some impressive art.

The whole of **Prague** is like a museum, so you'll want to take several days wandering its neighbourhoods, or side trip to spend a night in even more medieval **Český Krumlov**. From Prague, you can return to catch a flight in Frankfurt-am-Main (7½ hours by train), or exciting and edgy Berlin is only three hours north by fast train.

Three Weeks
Northern Route

Mild weather makes summer the best time for seeing the most northern reaches of Germany and Poland. Start by spending a few nights in multicultural **Cologne**. Pass two days touring the country's most massive cathedral and several small museums. By evening heft a glass of locally brewed *Kölsch* beer in one of the town's lively beer halls and bars. From there day-trip over to character-filled **Aachen**, where you can float in bubbling thermal baths before wandering the quirky cobblestone streets. Moving on to charming **Bremen** for a night or two, you'll explore art nouveau alleyways and an ornate market hall before winding up at a cafe on the waterfront promenade.

Next, Germany's most energetic port town, **Hamburg**, will keep you entertained for at least three days. You'll enjoy the maritime history, the old brick warehouse district and the new glass-encased philharmonic hall. Take the ferry out to the windswept beaches and seafood restaurants of Germany's northernmost point, the **North Frisian Islands**.

Back on the mainland, **Lübeck** is a 12th-century, Unesco-recognised townscape of medieval merchants' houses and towers that is well worth a stopover. Save at least three days – and nights – for the rich history, museums, bars and clubs of **Berlin**. The Brandenburg Gate, Holocaust Memorial and East Side Gallery at the Berlin Wall are must-sees. In the evening you have your choice of subdued-but-happening nightlife in Prenzlauer Berg, the hipster havens in Friedrichshain or alternative clubs in slightly grungy Kreuzberg.

Entering Poland, make the Old Town of **Poznań**, where the lively university population keeps the ancient centre buzzing, the first overnight stop. Two days in the impressively Gothic, church-filled **Toruń** has a much slower pace. To the north, **Gdańsk** is Poland's largest Baltic Sea port town. You can easily spend a few days wandering the waterfront, taking boat excursions and exploring resorts like Sopot.

Five hours or so south, **Warsaw** may not be the prettiest city, but it has loads of history hidden among the big city sprawl. Take two days exploring the Old Town and war monuments. End your tour with an outing to **Białowieża National Park**, a biosphere reserve where the once nearly extinct European bison roams. The small village has plenty of places to stay overnight before your journey onward.

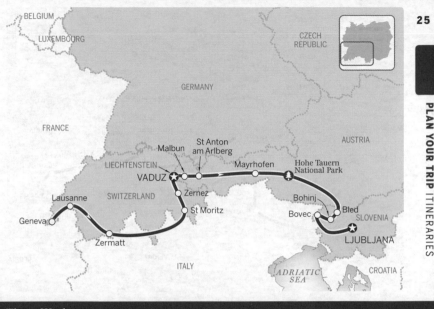

Three Weeks
Alpine Adventure

> Getting up close and personal with the Alps takes time; connections are almost never direct. Allow at least three to four days per region.

Starting out in **Geneva**, take a day and night to enjoy the city's cosmopolitan lakefront, cafes and fountains. If you want to gain altitude immediately, transfer on to quainter, also-lakeside **Lausanne** – part former fishing village with a summer beach-resort feel, part upscale, elegant shopping and dining town.

Next, explore Valais and Switzerland's 10 tallest peaks. Don your stylish togs and base yourself beneath the Matterhorn in the ritzy 19th-century resort town of **Zermatt**. Nearby, cogwheel trains and cable cars provide access to amazing hiking, skiing and mountain-seeing.

From Zermatt take the 7½-hour Glacier Express train ride over stunning high mountain passes to **St Moritz** in Graubünden. This region has 11,000km of hiking trails and incredible black diamond ski runs – and the town has fab nightlife to boot.

To the north, the Swiss National Park area is a quieter, more peaceful stop with rugged dolomite peaks, sprawling larch woodlands and untouched, topaz lakes. Stay in the village of **Zernez** or in the park itself.

Continuing on to the Liechtenstein Alps, you'll have to connect through **Vaduz** to get to end-of-the-road **Malbun**. Don't forget to snap a shot of the town's famous hilltop castle.

Neighbouring Austria's wild and beautiful Arlberg region is home to **St Anton am Arlberg**, a huge draw for skiers and boarders, with an active party scene.

The Tyrolean Zillertal Valley is as much a summer playground as a winter one. Set off from the town of **Mayrhofen** to go cycling, hiking, rock climbing or rafting.

One of the best drives in the Alps awaits you in **Hohe Tauern National Park**, a nearly 1800-sq-km wilderness with 3000 peaks. You'll undoubtedly pass over Grossglockner Road, a 1930s engineering marvel with 36 switchbacks.

South in Slovenia, Triglav National Park encompasses almost all of the Julian Alps. A postcard-perfect mountain setting and cute village make **Bled** the most popular base. But you should also check out the larger, less-crowded lake at **Bohinj** or adventure sports–oriented **Bovec** before connecting on from the capital, **Ljubljana**.

| Blue Danube |
| Seven-Day Sprint |

One Week
Seven-Day Sprint

Only have a week to spend? You don't actually have to run far. The picture-perfect towns close to the borders of Switzerland, Austria and Germany are tailor-placed for a quick highlights tour. Fly into **Zürich**, and spend a night in the lively urban centre that retains an Old World heart; don't miss hip Züri-West. From there, head up the mountains to the ever-idyllic lakeside city of **Lucerne**, where iconic half-timbered bridges cross glacier-cold waters.

Leave Switzerland for its immediate neighbour to the east, Austria. **Innsbruck** has hosted the Winter Olympics twice and is a great mountain base; from there you can ski or hike, taking sustenance in mountain huts. The beer halls of **Munich** are a short hop away. This atmospheric Bavarian town with good museums is worth a couple of days; when it's clear, you can see the Alps. A short final jaunt brings you to the perfect combination of hills and music: **Salzburg**. Mozart's one-time home has an abundance of old architecture, including an impressive castle, surrounded by mountains and Alpine lakes.

10 Days
Blue Danube

Build on Johann Strauss' classical attempt to capture the mood of Central Europe by exploring the region around the 'Blue Danube' river. Start with a water-view meal in Germany's **Regensburg**, a city replete with historical constructions. Then visit **Linz** and its stunning riverside art gallery before boarding a tour boat. Cruises stop in pretty **Melk**, dominated by an intimidating Benedictine monastery. After that is the **Danube Valley**, crowded with castles and vineyards, and best seen by water. On the northern bank of the Danube, **Krems an der Donau** has a pretty cobblestone centre.

Meander on by train to **Vienna**. Take a couple of days to tour the city before going by boat, train or bus to spend a night in the Slovakian capital, **Bratislava**, with its interesting mix of ancient Old Town and communist concrete. From there you can cruise along, following the Danube east into Hungary. Look up at **Esztergom** to see the awesome walled basilica high above. Finish with a few days in **Budapest**, where renting a bike and tootling around midriver Margaret Island caps off your Danube adventure.

» (above) Stroll over Reuss River on the Chapel Bridge (p584), Lucerne, Switzerland
» (left) Admire the ceiling of Mirror Hall at the baroque Benedictine Monastery (p57) in Melk, Austria

Coast to Coast
Far East

Two Weeks
Coast to Coast

From the Adriatic to the Baltic, going coast to coast takes you right up the centre of Central Europe. Connect to Slovenia through capital **Ljubljana**, and make your way to the water. Divide several days among the modern-day port of **Koper**, less-crowded **Izola** and the old Venetian gem **Piran**. Backtracking north, a side trip to the colossal **Škocjan Caves** is in order before you head into Austria.

From Ljubljana, you go through **Salzburg** (and may want to stop) en route to boating, bobbing and nature walking in the Lake District, **Salzkammergut**. Next, it's avant-garde and arty **Linz**. North in Germany, medieval **Regensburg** lies on the Danube riverfront. From there head north to **Würzburg** to taste the wines of the valley (or to oh-so-cute **Bamberg** for smoked beer). Spend a couple of days of cultural pursuit in **Weimar** – like Goethe, Liszt and Nietzsche before you. You might detour to see **Erfurt** and the nearby castle, or Buchenwald concentration camp. Transferring on to happening **Hamburg**, you've reached the coast and a lively last port of call.

One Month
Far East

Taking an eastern tack you'll be travelling through former communist countries, but you'd hardly know it today. Start in **Berlin**, where, instead of a wall dividing the city, you'll find an art gallery and walking path. Then travel to the dynamic East German city of **Leipzig**, where Bach and Wagner once lived. Make a stop in reconstructed baroque **Dresden** before staying a few days in tourist-filled **Prague**. You'll have a more authentic experience in a smaller, Unesco-recognised town like **Telč**. Then see modern Moravian life in upbeat **Brno**, and head east for another astronomical clock in laid-back **Olomouc**. If you like medieval construction, you'll love **Kraków**, Poland. To get to Slovakia, you pass through the **Tatra Mountains**, so you may as well stop. Below the mountains, the walled city of **Levoča** is close to the impressive Spiš Castle ruins. A musical fountain and Gothic cathedral highlight **Košice**. Thirsty? Because little **Tokaj**, Hungary, has been producing great dessert wines for ages. Vineyards also cover the hills surrounding the old town of **Eger** and its walkable wine-tasting valley. From there **Budapest** – and your onward journey – are not far west.

countries at a glance

Central Europe's charm lies in the common characteristics shared by some of its nations, juxtaposed with each country's individual attractions. Tuck into veal schnitzel and raise a stein to toast *Prost!* in Germany, Austria and Switzerland. Study communist history and Slavic cultures in Poland, Slovakia, Slovenia and the Czech Republic. Hike scenic trails and wander ancient Old Town streets all across the region.

For more country-specific pursuits, soak up the warm coastal sun at Slovenian ports or ski the continent's most extreme slopes in Switzerland. For high art and opera, visit Austria. Into WWII history? Poland has numerous well-preserved sites. For great brews, choose between German stouts and Czech Republic pilsners. Hungary boasts countless thermal spas; Slovakia has castles galore. Exploring the contrasts and commonalities of this intriguing region could well consume a lifetime.

Austria

Culture ✓✓✓
Mountains ✓✓✓
Architecture ✓✓

Music, Opera & Art
The capital, Vienna, is home to a cultural scene that includes world-class opera and art. But you'll also find Mozart's music resounding in Salzburg, modern art in Linz, and plays and festivals wherever you go.

Mountains
The Austrian Alps have hiking and skiing galore, and upland lakes serve as a summer playground. Whether swimming in Salzkammergut, climbing in Kitzbühel or driving over Grossglockner Road, the mountains offer quite a high.

Architecture
Ornate palaces, baroque castles and wacky modern constructs – Austria has it all. Look for impressive architecture in the cities and picture-perfect villages in the hills.

p34

Czech Republic

Old Towns ✓✓✓
Outdoors ✓✓
Beer ✓✓

Old Towns
The Czech Republic has more than its share of Central Europe's beautiful Old Towns. Prague tops the list, just don't miss Telč, Český Krumlov or Olomouc either.

Great Outdoors
The interesting landscapes around the country can inspire and amuse. Pinnacles, spires and other sandstone shapes punctuate Bohemian Switzerland National Park and 'rock towns' like Adršpach and Teplice.

Beer
Czech brews are enjoyed the world over; why not go straight to the source? Throw back a Pilsner in Plzeň and a Budvar in České Budějovice before you indulge in the emerging microbrewery scene.

p97

Germany

History ✓✓✓
Entertainment ✓✓
Culture ✓✓✓

History

Events in Germany have often dominated the Central European stage, especially during the two world wars. Travelling through the country, you'll feel the weight of history in places like Berlin, Weimar, Dachau and beyond.

Party On

Oktoberfest in Munich is perhaps the world's biggest party, and it's just one of the country's many festivals. At less celebratory times of year, check out the pulsing club scene in cities like Berlin.

Culture

The Bavarian culture, from oompah bands to beer halls, is enough reason to visit. You can also shop for cuckoo clocks in the Black Forest, or just admire the Teutonic half-timbered buildings as you go.

p167

Hungary

Spas ✓✓✓
Architecture ✓✓
Gastronomy ✓✓

Soaking in Spas

Sure, the thermal baths scattered across Hungary are recuperative, but they're also just plain fun. Try the big ones in Budapest then move on to the bubbles and squirts of smaller spas countrywide.

Architecture

Art nouveau in Budapest and Kecskemét, Moorish elements in Pécs and Eger...Hungary has a different style to much of Central Europe.

Gastronomy

From the country that made paprika famous comes a variety of delicious stews and sauces flavoured with this 'red gold'. Savour it with a glass of noteworthy Bull's Blood red or Tokaj white wine.

p313

Liechtenstein

Size ✓✓✓
Castle ✓
Hiking ✓

Size

Saying you've been to this pea-size principality (6km by 25km) is a claim to fame in itself. The sixth-smallest country in the world does a heck of a business in passport stamps and postcards – to prove that people have 'been there, done that'.

Castle-Dominated Capital

The capital, Vaduz, is barely a city (population 5160), and has a romantic appeal. It's dominated by the hillside royal castle and surrounded by alpine mountain peaks.

Hiking

Lacing the mountainous countryside are more than 400km of paths. The esteemed Fürstensteig trail is quite the course, with rope handholds to keep you from sharp drops.

p381

Poland

History ✓✓✓
Old Towns ✓✓
Mountains ✓

History

WWII history is ever present, whether you're at the Warsaw Rising Museum or the infamous Auschwitz concentration camp in Oświęcim. It can be both enlightening and emotionally challenging.

Old Towns

Well-preserved towns like Kraków, Toruń and Wrocław will wow you. But even big cities like Warsaw and Gdańsk have compact Old Town centres worth exploring.

Tatra Mountains

In the south of the country, the surprisingly tall peaks of the compact Tatra Mountains provide hiking, lodging and lower prices than the Central European Alps to the west.

p387

Slovakia

Hiking ✓✓✓
Castles ✓✓
Old Towns ✓

Hiking
More than 20% of this country is reserved parkland, but the whole thing is covered with trails. Hike the alpine peaks of the High Tatras, climb up waterfall-filled gorges in Slovensky Raj and traverse forests in the Malá Fatra.

Castles
Of the hundreds of fortress ruins in Slovakia, the 4-hectare Spiš Castle is the most impressive. More complete, fairytale-worthy castles include those in Trenčín, Devín and Bojnice.

Old Towns
The rabbit-warren Old Town of capital Bratislava is worth a wander before you explore the medieval walled town of Levoča, the perfect Renaissance square in Bardejov and a Middle Ages mining town, Banská Štiavnica.

p473

Slovenia

Mountains ✓✓
Coast ✓✓✓
Wine ✓

Julian Alps
Whether hiking up Mt Triglav, crossing Vršič Pass or rowing on Lake Bled, the Slovenian mountain scenery is truly impressive. Towns like Bovec and Bohinj serve as both summer and winter sports central.

Coast
The Adriatic coast of Slovenia is reminiscent of neighbouring Italy. The narrow old Venetian alleyways of Piran attract hordes of summer visitors. Avoid the crowds by seeking out other port towns like Koper and Izola.

Wine
Distinct Slovenian wines include peppery reds and dry rosés. Because exports are limited, the best local vintages can often be had nowhere but here.

p521

Switzerland

Mountains ✓✓✓
Skiing ✓✓✓
Nightlife ✓✓

Mountain Scenery
More than 65% of Switzerland is mountainous. The different regions of Valais, Jungfrau and the Jura each have their own character, but all offer spectacular vistas. Admire the views from cable cars, trains and the towns below.

Skiing
Some of the top skiing in the world is to be had on the Swiss slopes. Klein Matterhorn has Europe's highest runs and extensive summer skiing. Beginners can try one of more than 200 ski schools.

Nightlife
Zürich and Bern are well known for lively club scenes. Outside the cities, aprés-ski provides vibrant nightlife in mountain towns like chi-chi Zermatt and St Moritz.

p561

Look out for these icons:

 TOP CHOICE Our author's recommendation

A green or sustainable option

FREE No payment required

See the Index for a full list of destinations covered in this book.

On the Road

Austria

Includes »

Best Places to Eat

» Figlmüller (p49)
» Deuring-Schlössle (p86)
» Chez Nico (p81)
» Aiola Upstairs (p62)
» Alter Fuchs (p70)

Best Places to Stay

» Hotel Kaertnerhof (p48)
» Villa Trapp (p69)
» Nepomuks (p80)
» Hotel Schloss Dürnstein (p57)
» Seehotel Grüner Baum (p75)

Why Go?

For such a small country, Austria has made it big. This is, after all, the land where Mozart was born, Strauss taught the world to waltz and Julie Andrews grabbed the spotlight with her twirling entrance in the *Sound of Music*. This is where the Habsburgs built their 600-year empire, and where past glories still shine in the resplendent baroque palaces and chandelier-lit coffee houses of Vienna, Innsbruck and Salzburg. This is a perfectionist of a country and whatever it does – mountains, classical music, new media, castles, cake, you name it – it does exceedingly well.

Beyond its grandiose cities, Austria's allure lies outdoors. And whether you're schussing down the legendary slopes of Kitzbühel, climbing high in the Alps of Tirol or pedalling along the banks of the sprightly Danube, you'll find the kind of inspiring landscapes that no well-orchestrated symphony, camera lens or singing nun could ever quite do justice.

When to Go
Vienna

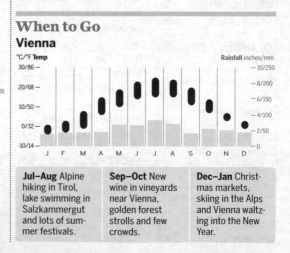

Jul–Aug Alpine hiking in Tirol, lake swimming in Salzkammergut and lots of summer festivals.

Sep–Oct New wine in vineyards near Vienna, golden forest strolls and few crowds.

Dec–Jan Christmas markets, skiing in the Alps and Vienna waltzing into the New Year.

Connections

Bang in the heart of Europe, Austria has speedy connections to its eight neighbouring countries. Trains (p96) from Vienna run to many Eastern European destinations, including Bratislava, Budapest, Prague and Warsaw; there are also connections south to Italy via Klagenfurt and north to Berlin. Salzburg is within sight of the Bavarian border, and there are many trains Munich-bound and beyond from the baroque city. Innsbruck is on the main rail line from Vienna to Switzerland, and two routes also lead to Munich. Look out for the fast, comfortable RailJet services to Germany and Switzerland.

ITINERARIES

Two Days

Spend this entire time in Vienna, making sure to visit the Habsburg palaces and Stephansdom before cosying up in a *Kaffeehäus* (coffee house). At night, check out the pumping bar scene.

One Week

Spend two days in Vienna, plus another day exploring the Wachau wine region, a day each in Salzburg and Innsbruck, one day exploring the Salzkammergut lakes, and finally one day in St Anton am Arlberg or Kitzbühel hiking or skiing (depending on the season).

Essential Food & Drink

» **Make it meaty** Go for a classic Wiener schnitzel, *Tafelspitz* (boiled beef with horseradish sauce) or *Schweinebraten* (pork roast). The humble wurst (sausage) comes in various guises.

» **On the side** Lashings of potatoes, either fried (*Pommes*), roasted (*Bratkartoffeln*), in a salad (*Erdapfelsalat*) or boiled in their skins (*Quellmänner*); *Knödel* (dumplings) and *Nudeln* (flat egg noodles).

» **Kaffee und Kuchen** Coffee and cake is Austria's sweetest tradition. Must-trys: flaky apple strudel, rich, chocolaty *Sacher Torte* and *Kaiserschmarrn* (sweet pancakes with raisins).

» **Wine at the source** Jovial locals gather in rustic *Heurigen* (wine taverns) in the wine-producing east, identified by an evergreen branch above the door. Sip crisp Grüner Veltiner whites and spicy Blaufränkisch wines.

» **Cheese fest** Dig into gooey *Käsnudeln* (cheese noodles) in Carinthia, *Kaspressknodel* (fried cheese dumplings) in Tirol and *Käsekrainer* (cheesy sausages) in Vienna. The hilly Bregenzerwald is studded with dairies.

AT A GLANCE

» **Currency** euro (€)

» **Language** German

» **Money** ATMs widely available; banks open Mon-Fri

» **Visas** Schengen rules apply

Fast Facts

» **Area** 83,855 sq km

» **Population** 8,217,280

» **Capital** Vienna

» **Telephone** country code ☑43; international access code ☑00

» **Emergency** ☑112

Exchange Rates

Australia	A$1	€0.74
Canada	C$1	€0.74
Japan	¥100	€0.87
New Zealand	NZ$1	€0.56
UK	UK£1	€1.16
USA	US$1	€0.67

Set Your Budget

» **Budget hotel room** €50

» **Two-course dinner** €15

» **Museum entrance** €7

» **Beer** €3

» **City transport ticket** €2

Resources

» **ÖAV** (www.alpenverein.at, in German) Austrian Alpine Club

» **ÖBB** (www.oebb.at) Austrian Federal Railways

» **Österreich Werbung** (www.austria.info) National tourism authority

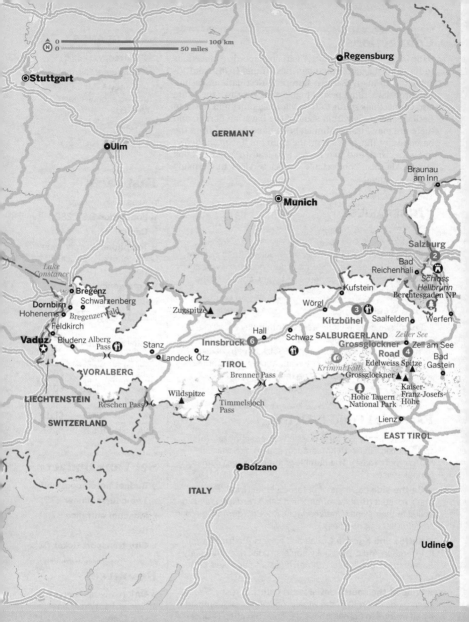

Austria Highlights

1 Discover the opulent Habsburg palaces, coffee houses and cutting-edge galleries of **Vienna** (p38)

2 Survey the baroque cityscape of **Salzburg** (p64) from the giddy height of 900-year-old Festung Hohensalzburg

3 Send your spirits soaring from peak to peak hiking and skiing in **Kitzbühel** (p83)

4 Buckle up for a rollercoaster ride of Alps and glaciers on the **Grossglockner Road** (p85), one of Austria's greatest drives

5 Dive into the crystal clear lakes of **Salzkammergut** (p72), Austria's summer playground

6 Whiz up to the Tyrolean Alps in Zaha Hadid's space-age funicular from picture-perfect **Innsbruck** (p77)

7 Explore the romantic Wachau and technology trailblazer Linz in the **Danube Valley** (p56)

VIENNA

♪01 / POP 1.68 MILLION

Few cities in the world glide so effortlessly between the present and the past like Vienna. Its splendid historical face is easily recognised: grand imperial palaces and bombastic baroque interiors, museums flanking magnificent squares.

But Vienna is also one of Europe's most dynamic urban spaces. A stone's throw from Hofburg (the Imperial Palace), the MuseumsQuartier houses some of the world's most provocative contemporary art behind a striking basalt facade. Outside, a courtyard buzzes on summer evenings with throngs of Viennese drinking and chatting.

The city of Mozart is also the Vienna of Falco, who immortalised its urban textures in song. It's a city where sushi and Austro-Asian fusion restaurants stand alongside the traditional *Beisl* (small taverns). In this Vienna, it's OK to mention poetry slam and Stephansdom in one breath.

Throw in the mass of green space within the confines of the city limits (almost half the city expanse is given over to parkland) and the 'blue' Danube cutting a path east of the historical centre, and this a capital that is distinctly Austrian.

History

Vienna was probably an important trading post for the Celts when the Romans arrived around 15 BC. They set up camp and named it Vindobona, after the Celtic tribe Vinid, and by the 3rd century it had developed into a town and vineyards were introduced to the area. It was first officially recorded as 'Wenia' in 881 and became a Babenberg stronghold in the 11th century. The Babenberg's ruled for 200 years, until the Habsburgs took control of the city's reins and held them firm until the end of WWI.

Over the centuries Vienna suffered Ottoman sieges in 1529 and 1683, and occupation in 1805 and 1809 by Napoleon and his armies. In the years in between, it received a major baroque makeover, the remnants of which can be seen in many buildings throughout the city. The mid-19th century saw Vienna blossom again, and the royal coffers were emptied to build the celebrated Ringstrasse and accompanying buildings.

Between the two world wars Vienna's political pendulum swung from one extreme to the other – the 1920s saw the influx of socialism and the 1930s the rise of fascism. Vienna suffered heavily under Allied bombing, and on 11 April 1945 advancing Russian troops liberated the city. The Allies joined them until Austria became independent in 1955, and since then it has gone from the razor's edge of Cold War to the focal point between new and old EU member nations.

◎ Sights

Vienna's stately buildings and beautifully tended parks are made for the aimless ambler. Humming with street entertainers, pedestrian-only shopping lanes in the Innere Stadt (inner city) like Kärntner Strasse and Graben are great for a shop 'n' stroll.

Some former homes of the great composers, including those of Mozart and Beethoven, are open to the public; ask at the tourist office.

Many of the following sights and attractions open slightly later in July and August, and close earlier from November to March.

FREE **Stephansdom** CHURCH
(Map p44; www.stephanskirche.at; 01, Stephansplatz; ☉6am-10pm Mon-Sat, 7am-10pm

ⓘ ADDRESSES & ORIENTATION

Many of the historic sights such as Stephansdom (St Stephen's Cathedral) are in Vienna's walkable heart, the Innere Stadt (inner city; 1st District), south of the river on a diversion of the Danube, the Danube Canal (Donaukanal). It's encircled on three sides by the Ringstrasse, a series of broad boulevards sporting an extravaganza of architectural delights.

In terms of addresses, Vienna is divided into 23 *Bezirke* (districts), fanning out in approximate numerical order clockwise around the Innere Stadt. Note that when reading addresses, the number of a building within a street *follows* the street name. Any number *before* the street name denotes the district. The middle two digits of postcodes correspond to the district. Thus a postcode of 1010 means the place is in district one, and 1230 refers to district 23.

One Day

Jump on tram 1 or 2 and circle the **Ringstrasse** (Ring road) for a brief but rewarding tour of the boulevard's buildings. Get out at Kärntner Strasse and wander towards the Gothic **Stephansdom** before heading to the **Hofburg** and the breathtaking art collection of the **Kunsthistorisches Museum**. Dine at an **Innere Stadt restaurant** before a night at the **Staatsoper**.

Two Days

On day two, visit imperial palace **Schönbrunn** before a feast of Austrian art at the **Leopold Museum**. Eat at Vienna's celebrated **Naschmarkt**, then cross the city for a twilight ride on the **Riesenrad**. Finish the day with local wine and food at a **Heuriger**.

Sun) Rising high and mighty above Vienna with its dazzling mosaic tiled roof is Stephansdom, or Steffl (little Stephen) as the Viennese call it. The cathedral was built on the site of a 12th-century church but its most distinctive features are Gothic.

Taking centre stage inside is the magnificent Gothic **stone pulpit**, fashioned in 1515 by Anton Pilgram. The baroque **high altar** in the main chancel depicts the stoning of St Stephen; the left chancel contains a winged altarpiece from Wiener Neustadt, dating from 1447; the right chancel houses the Renaissance-style red marble tomb of Friedrich III.

Dominating the cathedral is the skeletal, 136.7m-high Südturm (adult/child €3.50/1; ☉9am-5.30pm). Negotiating 343 steps brings you to a cramped viewing platform for a stunning panorama of Vienna. You can also explore the cathedral's **Katakomben** (catacombs; tours adult/child €4/1.50; ☉10-11.30am & 1.30-4.30pm Mon-Sat, 1.30-4.30pm Sun), housing the remains of plague victims in a bone house and urns containing some of the organs of Habsburg rulers – gripping stuff.

TOP CHOICE Hofburg   PALACE
(Imperial Palace; www.hofburg-wien.at) Nothing symbolises the culture and heritage of Austria more than its Hofburg, home base of the Habsburgs for six centuries, from the first emperor (Rudolf I in 1273) to the last (Karl I in 1918). The Hofburg owes its size and architectural diversity to plain old one-upmanship; the oldest section is the 13th-century **Schweizerhof** (Swiss Courtyard; Map p44).

The **Kaiserappartements** (Imperial Apartments; Map p44; adult/child €9.90/5.90; ☉9.30am-5.30pm), once occupied by Franz Josef I and Empress Elisabeth, are extra-ordinary for their chandelier-lit opulence. Included in the entry price, the **Sisi Museum** (Map p44) is devoted to the life of Austria's beauty-obsessed Empress Elisabeth, nicknamed 'Sisi'. Highlights include a reconstruction of her luxurious coach and the dress she wore on the eve of her wedding. A ticket to the Kaiserappartements also includes entry to the **Silberkammer** (Silver Chamber; Map p44), showcasing fine silverware and porcelain.

Among several other points of interest within the Hofburg you'll find the **Burgkapelle** (Royal Chapel; Map p44), where the Vienna Boys' Choir performs; the **Spanische Hofreitschule** (Spanish Riding School; Map p44; see p53); and the **Schatzkammer** (Imperial Treasury; Map p44; 01, Schweizerhof; adult/child €12/free; ☉10am-6pm Wed-Mon), which holds all manner of wonders including the 10th-century Imperial Crown, a 2860-carat Columbian emerald and even a thorn from Christ's crown.

ℹ MORE FOR YOUR MONEY

If you're planning on doing a lot of sightseeing, consider purchasing the Wien-Karte (Vienna Card; €18.50) for 72 hours of unlimited travel plus discounts at selected museums, attractions, cafes and shops. It's available from hotels and ticket offices.

The City of Vienna runs some 20 municipal museums (www.museum.vienna.at), which are included in a free booklet available at the Rathaus. Permanent exhibitions in all are free on Sundays.

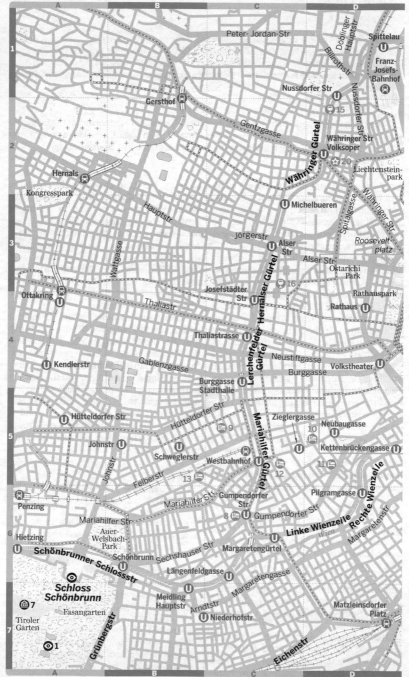

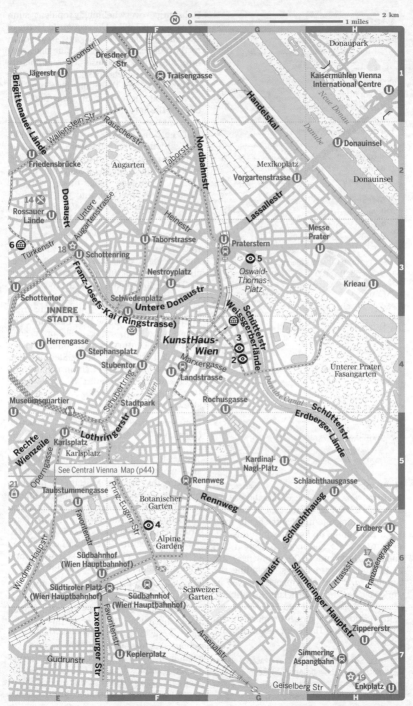

0 — 2 km
0 — 1 miles

Donaupark

Dresdner Str

Traisengasse

Jägerstr Ⓤ

Brigittenauer Lände

Kaisermühlen Vienna International Centre Ⓤ

Stromstr

Handelskai

Neue Donau

Wallenstein Str

Rauscherstr

Nordbahnstr

Taborstr

Danube

Friedensbrücke Ⓤ

Augarten

Mexikoplatz

Donauinsel Ⓤ

Donaust

Untere Augartenstrasse

Heinestr

Vorgartenstrasse Ⓤ

Donauinsel

14 Ⓗ

Rossauer Lände

Lassallestr

6 🏛

Türkenstr

Taborstrasse Ⓤ

Messe Prater Ⓤ

18 ★

Schottenring Ⓤ

Praterstern Ⓤ

Franz-Josefs-Kai (Ringstrasse)

Nestroyplatz Ⓤ

● 5

Oswald-Thomas-Platz

Krieau Ⓤ

Schottentor Ⓤ

Schwedenplatz Ⓤ

Untere Donaustr

Schüttelstr

Weissgerberlände

INNERE STADT 1

Herrengasse Ⓤ

KunstHaus-Wien

🏛

Stephansplatz Ⓤ

3 ◉

Unterer Prater Fasangarten

Stubentor Ⓤ

Marxergasse

2 ◉

Schubertring

Landstrasse Ⓤ

Museumsquartier Ⓤ

Stadtpark

Rochusgasse Ⓤ

Danube Canal

Schüttelstr

Erdberger Lände

Rechte Wienzeile

Lothringerstr

Wien

Karlsplatz Ⓤ

Karlsplatz

21 🔒

Operngasse

Taubstummengasse Ⓤ

Rennweg 🚊

Kardinal-Nagl-Platz Ⓤ

Schlachthausgasse Ⓤ

Schlachthausg

Botanischer Garten

Rennweg

Wiedner Hauptstr

Prinz-Eugen-Str

Favoritenstr

● 4

Alpine Garden

Erdberg Ⓤ

17 ★

Landstr

Littfassstr

Franzosengraben

Südbahnhof (Wien Hauptbahnhof)

Schweizer Garten

Simmeringer Hauptstr

Südtiroler Platz (Wien Hauptbahnhof) 🚊

Südbahnhof (Wien Hauptbahnhof)

Zippererstr Ⓤ

Laxenburger Str

Favoritenstr

Arsenalstr

Gudrunstr

Keplerplatz Ⓤ

Simmering Aspangbahn 🚊

19 ★

Geiselberg Str

Enkplatz Ⓤ

See Central Vienna Map (p44)

Vienna

Albertina   ART MUSEUM
(Map p44; www.albertina.at; 01, Albertinaplatz 3; adult/child €9.50/free; ◷10am-6pm, to 9pm Wed) Simply reading the highlights should have any art fan lining up for entry into this gallery. Among its enormous collection (1.5 million prints and 50,000 drawings) are 70 Rembrandts, 145 Dürers (including the famous *Hare*) and 43 Raphaels, as well as works by da Vinci, Michelangelo, Rubens, Cézanne, Picasso, Klimt and Kokoschka.

In addition to the mostly temporary exhibitions, a series of Habsburg staterooms are always open.

Schloss Schönbrunn   PALACE, MUSEUM
(Map p40; www.schoenbrunn.at; 13, Schönbrunner Schlossstrasse 47; Imperial Tour with audioguide adult/child €9.50/6.50; ◷8.30am-5pm) The

Habsburgs' overwhelmingly opulent summer palace is now a Unesco World Heritage site. Of the palace's 1441 rooms, 40 are open to the public; the Imperial Tour takes you into 26 of these. Because of the popularity of the palace, tickets are stamped with a departure time and there may be a time lag, so buy your ticket straight away and then explore the gardens.

Fountains dance in the French-style formal **gardens** (admission free; ◷6am-dusk). The gardens harbour the world's oldest zoo, the **Tiergarten** (Map p40; www.zoovienna.at; adult/child €14/6; ◷9am-6.30pm), founded in 1752; a 630m-long hedge **maze** (adult/child €2.90/1.70; ◷9am-6pm); and the **Gloriette** (Map p40; adult/child €2/1.40; ◷9am-6pm), whose roof offers a wonderful view over the palace grounds and beyond.

Kaisergruft   CHURCH
(Imperial Burial Vault; Map p44; www.kapuziner.at/wien, in German; 01 Neuer Markt; adult/child €4/1.50; ◷10am-6pm) Beneath the Kapuzinerkirche (Church of the Capuchin Friars), the high-peaked Kaisergruft is the final resting place of most of the Habsburg elite. The tombs range from simple to elaborate, such as the 18th-century baroque double casket of Maria Theresia and Franz Stephan. Empress Elisabeth's ('Sissi') coffin receives the most attention, however: lying alongside that of her husband, Franz Josef, it is often strewn with fresh flowers.

Kunsthistorisches Museum   ART MUSEUM
(Museum of Fine Arts; Map p44; www.khm.at; 01, Burgring 5; adult/child €12/free; ◷10am-6pm Tue-Sun, to 9pm Thu) When it comes to classical works of art, nothing comes close to the Kunsthistorisches Museum. It houses a huge range of art amassed by the Habsburgs and includes works by Rubens, Van Dyck, Holbein and Caravaggio. Paintings by Peter Brueghel the Elder, including *Hunters in the Snow,* also feature. There is an entire wing of ornaments, clocks and glassware, and Greek, Roman and Egyptian antiquities.

MuseumsQuartier   MUSEUM COMPLEX
(Museum Quarter; www.mqw.at; 07, Museumsplatz 1, ◷information & ticket centre 10am-7pm) Small books have been written on this popular site, so only a taste can be given here. This remarkable ensemble of museums, cafes, restaurants and bars occupies the former imperial stables designed by Fischer von Erlach. Spanning 60,000 sq metres, it's one of the world's most ambitious cultural spaces.

The highpoint is undoubtedly the **Leopold Museum** (Map p44; www.leopoldmuseum.org; adult/child €10/free; ⊙10am-6pm, to 9pm Thu), which showcases the world's largest collection of Egon Schiele paintings, alongside some fine works by Austrian artists like Klimt, Kokoschka and Albin Egger-Lienz.

The dark basalt **MUMOK** (Map p44; www.mumok.at; 07, Museumsplatz 1; adult/child €9/free; ⊙10am-6pm, to 9pm Thu) is alive with Vienna's premier collection of 20th-century art, centred on fluxus, nouveau realism, pop art and photo-realism.

Schloss Belvedere   PALACE, ART MUSEUM
(Map p44; www.belvedere.at; combined ticket adult/child €13.50/free) Belvedere is a masterpiece of total art and one of the world's finest baroque palaces, designed by Johann Lukas von Hildebrandt (1668–1745).

The first of the palace's two main buildings is the **Oberes Belvedere** (Upper Belvedere; Map p40; 03, Prinz-Eugen-Strasse 27; adult/child €9.50/free; ⊙10am-6pm). Pride and joy of the gallery is Gustav Klimt's rich gold *The Kiss* (1908), which perfectly embodies Viennese art nouveau, accompanied by other late-19th- to early-20th-century Austrian works. The second is the grandiose **Unteres Belvedere** (Lower Belvedere; Map p44; 03, Rennweg 6; adult/child €9.50/free; ⊙10am-6pm Thu-Tue, to 9pm Wed), which contains a baroque museum. The buildings sit at opposite ends of a manicured garden.

KunstHausWien   MUSEUM
(Map p40; www.kunsthauswien.com; 03, Untere Weissgerberstrasse 13; adult/child €9/4.50) Like something out of a toy shop, this gallery was designed by eccentric Viennese artist and architect Friedensreich Hundertwasser (1928–2000), whose love of uneven floors, colourful mosaic ceramics, irregular corners and rooftop greenery shines through. The permanent collection is a tribute to Hundertwasser, showcasing his paintings, graphics and philosophy on ecology and architecture.

Down the road there's a block of residential flats by Hundertwasser, the **Hundertwasserhaus** (Map p40; cnr Löwengasse &Kegelgasse). It's not possible to see inside, but you can visit the **Kalke Village** (Map p40; www.kalke-village.at; ⊙9am-7pm), also the handiwork of Hundertwasser, created from an old Michelin factory. It contains overpriced cafes, souvenir shops and art shops, all in typical Hundertwasser fashion with a distinct absence of straight lines.

FREE Prater   AMUSEMENT PARK
(Map p40; www.wien-prater.at; 02) This large park encompasses grassy meadows, woodlands, an amusement park known as the **Würstelprater** and one of the city's icons, the **Riesenrad** (www.wienerriesenrad.com; 02, Prater 90; adult/child €8.50/3.50; ⊙9am-11.45pm). Built in 1897, this 65m-high Ferris wheel takes about 20 minutes to rotate its 430-tonne weight, offering far-reaching views of Vienna. It achieved celluloid fame in *The Third Man*.

Palais Liechtenstein   ART MUSEUM
(www.liechtensteinmuseum.at; 09, Fürstengasse 1; adult/child €10/free; ⊙10am-5pm Fri-Tue) The collection of Duke Hans-Adam II of Liechtenstein is on show at Vienna's gorgeous baroque Liechtenstein Palace. It's one of the largest private collections in the world, and presents a feast of classical paintings including Raphael's *Portrait of a Man* (1503) and Rubens' *Decius Mus* cycle (1618).

Secession Building   LANDMARK
(Map p44; www.secession.at; 01, Friedrichstrasse 12; exhibition & frieze adult/child €8.50/5; ⊙10am-6pm Tue-Sun) This popular art nouveau 'temple of art' building was built in 1898 and bears an intricately woven gilt dome that the Viennese nickname the 'golden cabbage'. The highlight inside is the 34m-long *Beethoven Frieze* by Klimt.

Haus der Musik   MUSEUM
(Map p44; www.hdm.at; 01, Seilerstätte 30; adult/child €10/5.50; ⊙10am-10pm) Delving into the physics of sounds and paying tribute to Austria's great composers, this interactive museum is a fascinating journey through music. Most fun of all is the room where you can virtually conduct the Vienna Philharmonic.

Pestsäule   MEMORIAL
(Map p44; Plague Column; 01, Graben) Graben is dominated by the knobbly outline of

---

WANT MORE?

For in-depth information, reviews and recommendations at your fingertips, head to the Apple App Store to purchase Lonely Planet's *Vienna City Guide* iPhone app.

Alternatively, head to **Lonely Planet** (www.lonelyplanet.com/austria/vienna) for planning advice, author recommendations, traveller reviews and insider tips.

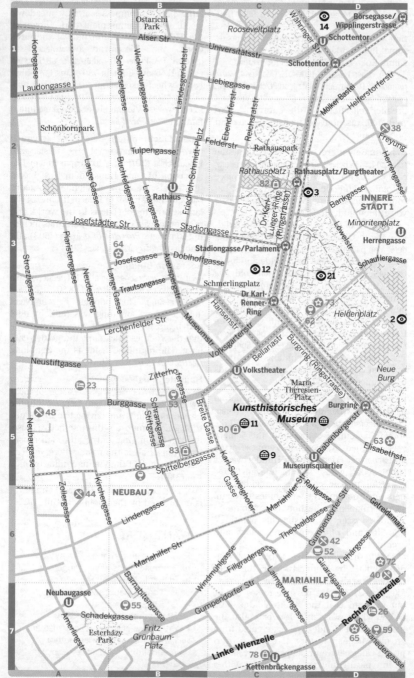

AUSTRIA VIENNA

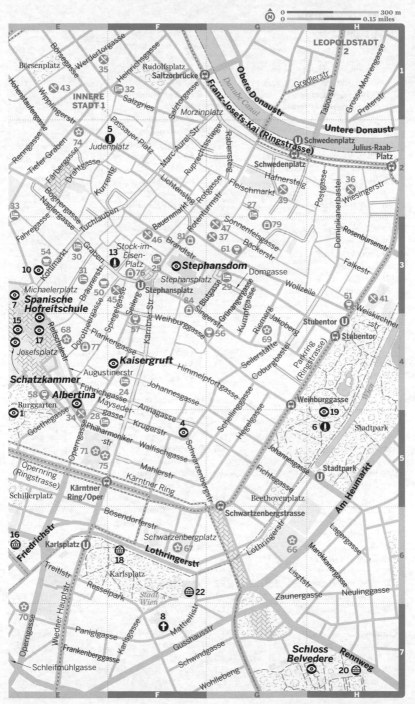

0 300 m
0 0.15 miles

LEOPOLDSTADT 2

INNERE STADT 1

Börsegasse
Werdertorgasse
Heinrichsgasse
Rudolfsplatz
Saltzorbrücke
Franz-Josefs-Kai (Ringstrasse)
Obere Donaustr
Danube Canal
Gredlerstr
Grosse Mohrengasse
Taborstr
Praterstr

Börseplatz
43
35
32
Salzgries
Salztorgasse
Morzinplatz
Untere Donaustr
Wipplingerstr
Hohenstaufengasse

Renngasse
Tiefer Graben
Farbergasse
Drahtgasse
Passauer Platz
Judenplatz
5
74
Marc-Aurel-Str
Ruprechtsstiege
Rabensteig
Schwedenplatz
Julius-Raab-Platz
Schwedenplatz

Bognergasse
Naglergasse
Tuchlauben
Fahregasse
Kurrentg
Lichtensteg
Rotgasse
Rotenturmstr
Fleischmarkt
Hafnersteig
Bauernmarkt
36
Wiesingerstr
39
27
Postgasse
Dominikanerbastei
Rosenbursenstr

33
Fahregasse
Graben
30
31
54
Kohlmarkt
13
Stock-im-Eisen-Platz
46
Brandstr
81
47
37
61
79
Sonnenfelsgasse
Bäckerstr
Falkestr

10
Braunerstr
50
45
25
76
Stephansplatz
Stephansdom
Domgasse
Wollzeile
51
41
Weiskirchnerstr

7
Spanische Hofreitschule
Michaelerplatz
Stephansplatz
84
Schulerstr
Grünangergasse
Singerstr
Blutgasse
29
Kumpfgasse
Riemerg
Jakoberg
Stubentor
Stubentor

15
17
68
77
Reitschulstr
Dorotheergasse
Plankengasse
Spiegelg
Seilerg
Kärntner-Str
Weihburggasse
57
56
69
Sellerstätte
Coburgbastei
Parkring (Ringstrasse)

Josefsplatz

Kaisergruft
Augustinerstr
Himmelpfortgasse
Johannesgasse
Hegelgasse
Schellinggasse

Schatzkammer
Führichgasse
24
Maysedergasse
Annagasse
Krugerstr
4
Walfischgasse
Schwarzenbergstr
Weihburggasse
19
6
Stadtpark

58
Albertina
1
Burggarten
Goethegasse
34
28
Philharmoniker-str
71
75
Mahlerstr
Opperngasse
Kärntner Ring
Johannesgasse
Fichtegasse
Stadtpark
Am Heumarkt
Lagergasse

Opernring (Ringstrasse)
Kärntner Ring/Oper
Bösendorferstr
Schwartzenbergstrasse
Lothringerstr
66
Marokkanergasse
Neulinggasse

Schillerplatz
16
Friedrichstr
Karlsplatz
18
Schwarzenbergplatz
67
Zaunergasse
Lisztstr

70
Opperngasse
Treitlstr
Wiedner Hauptstr
Resselpark
Karlsplatz
Stadt Wien
22
8
Mattiellistr

Paniglgasse
Frankenberggasse
Karlsgasse
Gusshausstr
Schwindgasse
Schloss Belvedere
20
Rennweg

Schleifmühlgasse
Wohllebeng

this memorial, designed by Fischer von Erlach in 1693 to commemorate the 75,000 victims of the Black Death.

Holocaust Memorial
MEMORIAL

(Map p44; 01, Judenplatz) This is Austria's first Holocaust memorial, the 'Nameless Library'. This squat, boxlike structure pays homage to the 65,000 Austrian Jews who were killed during the Holocaust.

Sigmund Freud Museum
MUSEUM

(Map p40; www.freud-museum.at; 09, Berggasse 19; adult/child €7/2.50; ⊙9am-5pm) Former house of the famous psychologist, now housing a small museum featuring some of his personal belongings.

Wien Museum
MUSEUM

(Map p44; www.museum.vienna.at, in German; 04, Karlsplatz 5; adult/child €6/free; ⊙10am-6pm Tue-Sun) Provides a snapshot of the city's history, and contains a handsome art collection with paintings by Klimt and Schiele.

Loos Haus
LANDMARK

(Map p44; 01, Michaelerplatz) A perfect example of the clean lines of Loos' work. Franz Josef hated it and described the windows, which lack lintels, as 'windows without eyebrows'.

Stadtbahn Pavilions
LANDMARK

(Map p44; 04, Karlsplatz; adult/child €2/1; ⊙10am-6pm Tue-Sun Apr-Oct) Jugendstil pavilions designed by Otto Wagner for Vienna's first public transport system.

☆ Activities

Dividing the Danube from the Neue Donau is the svelte Donauinsel (Danube Island), which stretches some 21.5km from opposite Klosterneuburg in the north to the Nationalpark Donau-Auen in the south. The island features long sections of **swimming** areas, concrete paths for **walking** and **cycling**, and restaurants and snack bars. The Alte Donau is a landlocked arm of the Danube, a favourite of **sailing** and boating enthusiasts, swimmers, walkers, fisherfolk and, in winter (when it's cold enough), for **ice skating**.

☞ Tours

The tourist office publishes a monthly list of guided walks, *Wiener Spaziergänge,* and can advise on bus tours and river cruises.

Vienna Tour Guides
WALKING TOURS

(www.wienguide.at; adult/child €14/7) Conducts 60 different guided walking tours, some of which are in English, from art nouveau architecture to Jewish traditions and the ever-popular *Third Man* Tour.

✵ Festivals & Events

Pick up a copy of the monthly booklet of events from the tourist office. Tickets for many events are available at **Wien-Ticket Pavillon** (Map p44) in the hut by the Staatsoper.

Opernball (01, Staatsoper) Of the 300 or so balls held in January and February, the Opernball (Opera Ball) is the ultimate. It's a supremely lavish affair, with the men in tails and women in shining white gowns.

Wiener Festwochen (www.festwochen. or.at) Wide-ranging program of arts from around the world, from May to mid-June.

Donauinselfest Free three-day festival of rock, pop, hardcore, folk and country music on the Donauinsel in June.

Musikfilm Festival (01, Rathausplatz) Screenings of operas, operettas and concerts outside the Rathaus in July and August.

Viennale (www.viennale.at) The country's biggest and best film festival, featuring fringe and independent films from around the world in October.

Christkindlmärkte Vienna's much-loved Christmas market season runs from mid-November to Christmas Day.

🛏 Sleeping

Cosy guesthouses, minimalist-chic hotels, funky hostels – it's all in the mix in Vienna.

> **WORTH A TRIP**
>
> ### LATE GREATS
>
> The **Zentralfriedhof** (11, Simmeringer Hauptstrasse 232-244; admission free; ⊙7am-7pm May-Aug, to 6pm Mar, Apr, Sep & Oct, 8am-5pm Nov-Feb; 🚊6 or 71 to Zentralfriedhof), about 4km southeast of the city centre, is one of Europe's largest cemeteries. With two and a half million graves, it has more 'residents' than Vienna. Beethoven, Schubert and Brahms have memorial tombs here, and in addition to the clump of famous composers, those pushing up daisies include architect Adolf Loos and the man of Austrian Pop, Falco.

SPIN OF THE RING

The Ringstrasse, often just called the Ring, is a wide, tree-lined boulevard encircling much of the Innere Stadt. The best way to see its monumental buildings is by jumping on tram 1 or 2 for a brief but rewarding self-guided tour. For the price of a single ticket you'll take in the neo-Gothic **Rathaus** (city hall; Map p44), the Greek Revival-style **Parliament** (Map p44), the 19th-century **Burgtheater** (Map p44) and the baroque **Karlskirche** (St Charles' Church; Map p44), among others.

Or hop off to relax in one of the Ring's three parks: flower-strewn **Burggarten** (Map p44), **Volksgarten** (Map p44) and **Stadtpark** (Map p44) with its **gold statue of Johann Strauss**.

Central Vienna is first to fill up, especially in summer, so book well ahead if you're keen to be close to the major sights.

TOP CHOICE **Hotel Kaertnerhof** HOTEL €€
(Map p44; ☎512 19 23; www.karntnerhof. com; 01, Grashofgasse 4; s/d from €95/140; @🖥) Tucked away from the bustle, this treasure oozes old Vienna charm, from the period paintings to the wood- and frosted-glass-panelled lift to the roof terrace. Rooms mix a few plain pieces with antiques, chandeliers and elegant curtains. With Stephansplatz less than five minutes away, this place is a steal.

Pension Hargita PENSION €
(Map p40; ☎526 19 28; www.hargita.at; 07, Andreas-gasse 1; s/d from €57/68; 🖥) Ignore the bland exterior – stepping into the wood-panelled lobby is like entering a mountain chalet. This Hungarian–Austrian family-operated space is tasteful simplicity. Fresh colours and flowers decorate the homey rooms, and the breakfast room has a country feel.

🍃 **Schweizer Pension** PENSION €
(Map p44; ☎533 81 56; www.schweizerpen sion.com; 01, Heinrichsgasse 2; s/d from €48/65; 🖥) This small, family-run pension is a superb deal, with homely touches and eco credentials. Book in advance, though, as it has only 11 rooms and is popular among those on squeezed budgets. Wi-fi is only available in the common areas.

🍃 **Boutiquehotel Stadthalle** HOTEL €€
(Map p40; ☎982 42 72; www.hotelstadthalle. at; 15, Hackengasse 20; s/d from €68/98) Welcome to Vienna's most sustainable hotel, which makes the most of solar power, rainwater collection and LED lighting. Rooms are a blend of modern with polished antiques. You'll get a 10% discount if you arrive by bike or train.

Hotel Sacher HOTEL €€€
(Map p44; ☎514 56-0; www.sacher.com; 01, Philharmonikerstrasse 4; d from €375; @🖥) Walking into the Sacher is like turning back the clock a hundred years. The reception, with its dark-wood panelling, deep red shades and heavy gold chandelier, recalls an expensive *fin-de-siècle* bordello. All rooms boast baroque furnishings and 19th-century oil paintings, and the top-floor spa pampers with chocolate treatments.

Altstadt PENSION €€
(Map p44; ☎522 66 66; www.altstadt.at; 07, Kirchengasse 41; s/d from €149/249; @🖥) One of Vienna's finest pensions, Altstadt has charming, individually decorated rooms, with high ceilings, plenty of space and a cosy lounge with free afternoon tea and cakes. Staff are genuinely affable and artworks are from the owner's personal collection.

Wombat's HOSTEL €
(Map p40; ☎897 36 23; www.wombats.at; 05, Mariahilfer Strasse 137; dm/r €20/56; @🖥) For a relaxed Aussie hostel vibe in central Vienna, it has to be Wombat's. Interiors are rainbow bright, dorms modern with en suite, and common areas include a bar and pool tables. Bike rental is also available.

Pension Nossek PENSION €€
(Map p44; ☎533 70 41-0; www.pension-nossek.at, in German; 01, Graben 17; s/d from €65/120; 🖥) Overlooking the Graben and just steps from Stephansdom, Nossek has an enviable location and polite service. Rooms are spacious, spotless and enhanced with baroque-style furnishings. Credit cards are not accepted.

Altwienerhof HOTEL €€
(Map p40; ☎892 60 00; www.altwienerhof.at; 15, Herklotzgasse 6; s/d €79/99) This pseudo-plush family-run hotel, just outside the Gürtel ring, offers ridiculously romantic abodes –

think miniature chandeliers, antique pieces, floral bedding and lace tablecloths. Breakfast is taken in the conservatory or large inner courtyard.

Aviano
PENSION €€
(Map p44; ☑512 83 30; www.secrethomes.at; 01, Marco-d'Aviano-Gasse 1; s/d €104/148; ☎) Aviano is a supremely central, good-value choice. The small high-ceilinged rooms feature whitewashed antique furnishings and decorative moulding. In summer, the sunny breakfast room opens onto a small balcony.

Pension Pertschy
PENSION €€
(Map p44; ☑534 49-0; www.pertschy.com; 01, Habsburgergasse 5; s/d €79/119; ☎⌖) This quiet pension, just off the Graben, is hard to beat. The spacious rooms sport bright colours and period pieces, the staff are friendly, and children are welcomed with gusto (toys and highchairs are available).

Westend City Hostel
HOSTEL €
(Map p40; ☑597 67 29; www.westendhostel.at; 06, Fügergasse 3; dm/s/d €20.50/52/62; @☎) This independent hostel received a bright and funky head-to-toe revamp in 2009. All of the spacious dorms are en suite and the ivy-clad inner courtyard is superb.

Hotel Drei Kronen
PENSION €€
(Map p44; ☑587 32 89; www.hotel3kronen.at; 04, Schleifmühlegasse 25; s/d €79/100; @☎) A sweet family-run abode near the Naschmarkt, with rooms decked out in Jugendstil furnishings. There's even free *Sekt* (sparkling wine) at breakfast.

Pension Kraml
PENSION €
(Map p40; ☑587 85 88; www.pensionkraml.at; 06, Brauergasse 5; s/d from €35/76, apt from €99; ☎) A quiet and cosy family-run pension, where old-school politeness and comfort are paramount. Rooms are large (if a little dated).

König von Ungarn
HOTEL €€
(Map p44; ☑515 84-0; www.kvu.at; 01, Schulerstrasse 10; s/d €150/219; ☎) Vienna's oldest hotel (1746) balances class and informality. Rooms are individually furnished with antiques (the best face Domgasse) and the inner courtyard is wonderful.

✖ Eating

Vienna has thousands of restaurants covering all budgets and styles of cuisine, but dining doesn't stop there. *Kaffeehäuser* (coffee houses), *Beisl* (small taverns) and *Heurigen* (wine taverns) are just as fine for a good meal. *Würstel Stande* (sausage stands) are conveniently located on street corners and squares.

TOP CHOICE Figlmüller
BEISL €€
(Map p44; ☑512 61 77; 01, Wollzeile 5; mains €7-15; ⊙lunch & dinner, closed Aug) This famous *Beisl* serves some of the biggest (and best) schnitzels in town. Sure, the rural decor is contrived and beer isn't served (only wine from the owner's own vineyard), but it doesn't get more Viennese than this.

Stomach
AUSTRIAN €€
(Map p40; ☑310 20 99; 09, Seegasse 26; mains €10-18; ⊙dinner Wed-Sat, lunch & dinner Sun) Once a butcher's shop, Stomach serves seriously good Austrian food, from Styrian roast beef to pumpkin soup. The interior is rural Austrian, and the overgrown garden creates a picturesque backdrop. Reservations are recommended.

Griechenbeisl
BEISL €€
(Map p44; ☑533 19 77; 01, Fleischmarkt 11; mains €11-24; ⊙11am-1am) This is Vienna's oldest *Beisl* (dating from 1447), once frequented by the likes of Beethoven, Schubert and Brahms. The vaulted, wood-panelled rooms are a cosy setting for classic Viennese dishes. Bag a spot in the front garden in summer.

Wrenkh
VEGETARIAN €€
(Map p44; ☑533 15 26; 01, Bauernmarkt 10; lunch menus €9.50-10.50, mains €8.50-19.50; ⊙lunch & dinner Mon-Fri, dinner Sat; ⊕✖) Glass-walled Wrenkh serves beautifully presented vegetarian food prepared with organic produce. The sleek-looking customers come for the lip-smacking fare that ranges from risotto to tofu.

DESIGNER SPLURGE

Vienna is making architectural waves with its ultra-sleek design hotels, including these two favourites:

DO & CO
HOTEL €€€
(Map p44; ☑241 88; www.doco.com; 01, Stephansplatz 12; r from €310) Swanky & sexy with views of Stephansdom.

Style Hotel
HOTEL €€€
(Map p44; ☑22 780 0; www.stylehotel. at; 01, Herrengasse 12; r from €250) Top contender for the title of Vienna's most fashionable hotel, with art nouveau and art deco overtones.

Zu den Zwei Liesln
BEISL €

(Map p44; ☑523 32 82; 07, Burggasse 63; lunch menus €4.90-5.30, mains €6-11.90) Six varieties of schnitzel crowd the menu at this classic budget *Beisl* of legendary status. The quaint and cosy wood-panelled interior is complemented by a tree-shaded inner courtyard.

En
JAPANESE €€

(Map p44; ☑532 44 90; 01, Werdertorgasse 8; lunch menus €8.20-9.70, mains €9-23; ⊗closed Sun) En offers some of the best sushi in Vienna, and its lunch menus are a bargain considering the quality. Outdoor seating is available in summer; in winter sit at the bar and watch the skilled sushi-makers prepare your meal.

St Josef
VEGETARIAN €

(Map p44; ☑526 68 18; 07, Mondscheingasse 10; small/large plates €6.80/8.20; ⊗breakfast & lunch Mon-Sat; ☺☑) This canteen-like vegetarian place that cooks to a theme each day (Indian, for instance) has a sparse, industrial character and super-friendly staff.

Expedit
ITALIAN €€

(Map p44; ☑512 33 13 23; 01, Wiesingerstrasse 6; mains €8-25; ⊗10am-1am Mon-Sat, to 10pm Sun) Expedit has moulded itself on a Ligurian *osteria*. Its warehouse decor creates a busy yet informal atmosphere and a clean, smart look. Every day brings new, seasonal dishes to the menu. Reservations are recommended.

Österreicher im MAK
AUSTRIAN €€

(Map p44; ☑7140 121; 01, Stubenring 5; lunch €6.40, mains €14.50-20.80; ⊗8.30am-1am) This is the brainchild of Helmut Österreicher, one of Austria's leading chefs. He jazzes up back-to-the-roots Austrian dishes such as *Tafelspitz* with exotic or nonregional ingredients. Sleek architectural lines create a modern flourish.

Ra'mien
ASIAN €€

(Map p44; ☑585 47 98; 06, Gumpendorfer Strasse 9; mains €7-16; ⊗Tue-Sun, closed Aug) Bright young things gravitate towards this minimalist-chic noodle bar, with a choice of Thai, Japanese, Chinese and Vietnamese noodle soups and rice dishes. The lounge bar downstairs has regular DJs and stays open until at least 2am.

Bitzinger Würstelstand am Albertinaplatz
SAUSAGE STAND €

(Map p44; 01, Albertinaplatz; sausages €2.80-3.50; ⊗24hr) Located behind the Staatsoper, this is one of Vienna's best sausage stands. Watch ladies and gents dressed to the nines while enjoying your wurst and a beer.

Trzesniewski
SANDWICHES €

(Map p44; Dorotheergasse 1; sandwiches from €2.80; ⊗8.30am-7.30pm Mon-Fri, 9am-5pm Sat) Possibly Austria's finest sandwich shop, with 21 delectably thick spreads, from tuna with egg to Swedish herring. Plan on sampling a few; two bites and they're gone.

Soupkultur
SOUP & SALAD €

(Map p44; Wipplingerstrasse 32; soups €3.90-4.50, salads €5.80-7.20; ⊗lunch Mon-Fri) Organic produce and aromatic spices are used to create eight different soups and eight varieties of salads each week.

Zanoni & Zanoni
ICE CREAM €

(Map p44; Lugeck 7; ice cream from €2; ⊗7am-midnight) An Italian gelataria and *pasticceria* open 365 days a year. Great for creamy gelati and late-night desserts.

Quick Eats & Self-Catering

Self-caterers can stock up at the Hofer, Billa and Spar **supermarkets** in the centre. Some have well-stocked delis that make sandwiches to order – the perfect cheap lunch on the run. The city is also dotted with markets.

Freyung Market
MARKET

(Map p44; 01, Freyung; ⊗9am-6pm Fri & Sat 1st & 3rd weekend of month) Sells fresh organic produce.

⚲ Drinking

Vienna is riddled with late-night drinking dens, with concentrations of pulsating bars north and south of the Naschmarkt, around Spittelberg (many double as restaurants) and along the Gürtel (mainly around the U6 stops of Josefstädter Strasse and Nussdorfer Strasse). The Bermuda Dreieck (Bermuda Triangle), near the Danube Canal in the Innere Stadt, also has many bars, but they are more touristy.

Vienna's age-old *Heurigen* are identified by a *Busch'n* (a green wreath or branch) hanging over the door; many have outside tables in large gardens or courtyards, while inside the atmosphere is rustic. Some serve a hot or cold buffet. *Heurigen* cluster in the wine-growing suburbs to the north, southwest, west and northwest of the city. Opening times are approximately from 4pm to 11pm, and wine costs around €2.50 per *Viertel* (250mL).

Palmenhaus BAR, CAFE

TOP CHOICE (Map p44; 01, Burggarten; ⊘10am-2am, closed Mon & Tue Jan-Feb) Housed in a beautifully restored Victorian palm house, the Palmenhaus has a relaxed vibe. In summer, tables spill out onto the pavement overlooking the green of the Burggarten, and there are occasional club nights.

Das Möbel BAR, CAFE

(Map p44; 07, Burggasse 10; ⊘10am-1am; ☏) The interior is never dull at this bar near the MuseumsQuartier. It's remarkable for its funky decor and furniture – cube stools, assorted moulded lamps – and everything is up for sale.

Vis-à-vis WINE BAR

(Map p44; 01, Wollzeile 5; ⊘4.30-10.30am Tue-Sat) Hidden down a narrow, atmospheric passage is this wee wine bar – it may only seat close to 10 but it makes up for it with over 350 wines on offer (strong emphasis on Austrian faves) and great antipasti.

Loos American Bar COCKTAIL BAR

(Map p44; 01, Kärntner Durchgang 10; ⊘noon-4am Sun-Wed, to 5am Thu-Sat) Designed by Adolf Loos in 1908, this tiny box decked head-to-toe in onyx is *the* spot for a classic cocktail in the Innere Stadt, expertly whipped up by talented mixologists.

10er Marie HEURIGER

(16, Ottakringerstrasse 222-224; ⊘3pm-midnight Mon-Sat) Vienna's oldest *Heuriger* has been going strong since 1740 – Schubert, Strauss and Crown Prince Rudolf all kicked back a glass or three here. The usual buffet is available.

Wein & Wasser WINE BAR

(Map p40; 08, Laudongasse 57; ⊘6pm-1am Mon-Sat) At 'Wine & Water', the staff warmly guide you through the lengthy list, including over 20 Austrian wines served by the glass. The brick arches, lit by flickering candles, create a cosy space for imbibing.

Halbestadt Bar COCKTAIL BAR

(Map p40; 09, Stadtbogen 155; ⊘6pm-2am Mon-Thu, 7pm-2am Fri, to 4am Sat & Sun) Impeccable hospitality, with no trace of snobbery, is what this sleek little bar under the subway arches is about. Mixologists hold court creating tongue-enticing works of art with glasses to match.

Futuregarden Bar & Art Club BAR, CLUB

(Map p44; 06, Schadekgasse 6; ⊘6pm-2am Mon-Sat, from 8pm Sun) A white, spartan space

NASCHMARKT NIBBLES

The sprawling **Naschmarkt** (Map p44; 06, Linke & Rechte Wienzeile; ⊘6am-6.30pm Mon-Fri, to 5pm Sat) is *the* place to *nasch* (snack) in Vienna. Big and bold, the market is a foodie's dream. The food stalls selling meats, fruits, vegetables, cheeses and spices are perfect for assembling your own picnic. There are also plenty of people-watching cafes, restaurants dishing up good-value lunches, delis and takeaway stands where you can grab a falafel or baguette.

with a cool atmosphere and up-to-the-minute electronic tracks.

Siebensternbräu PUB

(Map p44; www.7stern.at; 07, Siebensterngasse 19; ⊘10am-midnight) Large brewery with all the main varieties, plus hemp beer, chilli beer and smoky beer. The hidden back garden is sublime in summer.

Schikaneder BAR

(Map p44; 04, Margareten Strasse 22-24; ⊘6pm-4am) A grungy bar with a buzzing vibe that attracts students and an arty crowd. Also hosts movie nights.

Volksgarten Pavillon BAR

(Map p44; 01, Burgring 1; ⊘11am-2am Apr–mid-Sep) A lovely 1950s-style pavilion with views of Heldenplatz and an ever-popular garden.

☆ Entertainment

Vienna is, and probably will be till the end of time, the European capital of opera and classical music. The program of music events is never-ending and even the city's buskers are often classically trained musicians. The tourist office produces a handy monthly listing of concerts and other events.

Flex CLUB

(Map p40; www.flex.at; 01, Donaukanal, Augartenbrücke; ⊘6pm-4am) Vienna's most celebrated low-life club, Flex has one of the best sound systems in Europe, puts on great shows and features the top DJs from Vienna and abroad. Messed Up (techno) on Monday and London Calling (alternative and indie) on Wednesday and Friday are always popular.

COFFEE HOUSE CULTURE

Vienna's legendary *Kaffeehäuser* (coffee houses) are wonderful places for people-watching, daydreaming and catching up on gossip or world news. Most serve light meals alongside a mouth-watering array of cakes and tortes. Expect to pay around €7 for a coffee with a slice of cake. These are just some of our favourites.

Café Sperl
CAFE

(Map p44; 06, Gumpendorfer Strasse 11; ⊙7am-11pm Mon-Sat, 11am-8pm Sun, closed Sun in summer; 🔊) With its gorgeous Jugendstil fittings, grand dimensions, cosy booths and unhurried air, Sperl is one of Vienna's finest coffee houses. The must-try is *Sperl Torte* – an almond and chocolate cream dream.

Café Hawelka
CAFE

(Map p44; 01, Dorotheergasse 6; ⊙8am-2am Mon & Wed-Sat, from 10am Sun) A traditional haunt for artists and writers, this shabby-chic coffee house attracts the gamut of Viennese society. There's a convivial vibe between friends and complete strangers.

Café Sacher
CAFE

(Map p44; 01, Philharmonikerstrasse 4; ⊙8am-11:30pm) This opulent coffee house is celebrated for its *Sacher Torte* (€4), a rich chocolate cake with apricot jam once favoured by Emperor Franz Josef.

Café Prückel
CAFE

(Map p44; 01, Stubenring 24; ⊙8.30am-10pm) Intimate booths, strong coffee and diet-destroying cakes are all attractions at this 1950s gem. There's live piano music from 7pm to 10pm Monday, Wednesday and Friday.

Demel
CAFE

(Map p44; 01, Kohlmarkt 14; ⊙10am-7pm) An elegant, regal cafe near the Hofburg. Demel's speciality is the *Anna Torte,* a chocolate and nougat calorie-bomb.

Café Drechsler
CAFE

(Map p44; 06, Linke Wienzeile 22; ⊙8am-2am Mon, 3am-2am Tue-Sat, 3am-midnight Sun) Sir Terence Conran revamped this stylish yet distinctly Viennese cafe. Its goulash is legendary, as are the DJ tunes that keep the vibe hip and upbeat.

Kleines Café
CAFE

(Map p44; 01, Franziskanerplatz 3; ⊙10am-2am) Tiny bohemian cafe with wonderful summer seating on Franziskanerplatz.

Staatsoper
CONCERT VENUE

(Map p44; 📞514 44 7880; www.wiener-staatsoper.at; 01, Opernring 2; ⊙box office closed Sun) Performances at Vienna's premier opera and classical music venue are lavish, formal affairs, where people dress up. Standing-room tickets (€3 to €4) are sold 80 minutes before performances begin.

Musikverein
CONCERT VENUE

(Map p44; 📞505 81 90; www.musikverein.at; 01, Bösendorferstrasse 12; ⊙box office closed Sun) The opulent Musikverein, home to the Vienna Philharmonic Orchestra, is celebrated for its acoustics. Standing-room tickets in the main hall cost €4 to €6.

Porgy & Bess
JAZZ CLUB

(Map p44; www.porgy.at; 01, Riemergasse 11; ⊙7pm-late) Quality is the cornerstone of Porgy & Bess' popularity. The sophisticated club presents a top-drawer line-up of modern jazz acts and DJs fill spots on weekends.

Volksoper
CONCERT VENUE

(People's Opera; Map p40; 📞514 44 3670; www.volksoper.at; 09, Währinger Strasse 78; ⊙box office closed Sun) Vienna's second opera house features operettas, dance and musicals. Standing tickets go for as little as €2 to €6.

Szene Wien
LIVE MUSIC VENUE

(Map p40; www.szenewien.at; 11, Hauffgasse 26; ⊙7.30pm-late) Good things happen in small places – this small venue hauls out a mixed bag that includes rock, reggae, funk, jazz and world music.

Roxy
CLUB

(Map p44; www.sunshine.at; 04, Operngasse 24; ⊙11pm-4am Thu-Sat) Roxy's tiny dance floor reaches bursting point when DJs from the electronic scene guest here, though everything from Brazilian to jazzy grooves can be heard.

Konzerthaus
CONCERT VENUE

(Map p44; ☎242 002; www.konzerthaus.at; 03, Lothringerstrasse 20; ⊙box office closed Sun) This is a major venue in classical music circles, but throughout the year ethnic music, rock, pop or jazz can also be heard in its hallowed halls.

Volksgarten
CLUB

(Map p44; 01, Burgring 1; ⊙Tue-Sat) This club attracts a well-dressed crowd, keen to strut their stuff and scan for talent from the long bar. The quality sound system pumps out an array of music styles.

Theater an der Wien
THEATRE

(Map p44; www.musicalvienna.at; 06, Linke Wienzeile 6). Once the host of monumental premiers such as Mozart's *Die Zauberflöte*, this theatre now showcases opera, dance and concerts. Tickets start from €7 for standing room.

Palais Palffy
CLUB

(Map p44; www.palais-palffy.at; 01, Josefsplatz 6; ⊙from 9pm Thu-Sat) DJs spin electro, pop, house and oldies at this club housed in an illustrious old building. The 1st-floor lounge bar glitters under an enormous Swarovski crystal chandelier.

Burg Kino
CINEMA

(Map p44; www.burgkino.at; 01, Opernring 19) English films; has regular screenings of *The Third Man*.

Goodmann
CLUB

(Map p44; www.goodmann.at, in German; 04, Rechte Wienzeile 23; ⊙3am-10am Mon-Sat) This is where clubbers go for a snack when the clubs close (food is served till 8am).

English Theatre
THEATRE

(Map p44; www.englishtheatre.at; 08, Josefsgasse 12; ⊙box office closed Sun) Stages performances in English.

Why Not?
CLUB

(Map p44; www.why-not.at; 01, Tiefer Graben 22; ⊙10pm-4am Fri & Sat) This small, central club fills quickly mainly with young gay guys on weekends.

Arena
LIVE MUSIC

(Map p40; www.arena.co.at, in German; 03, Baumgasse 80; ⊙2pm-late) Hard rock and metal in a former slaughterhouse. Arena also shows films outdoors in summer.

🔒 Shopping

The Innere Stadt sells designer labels, sweets and jewellery; head to Mariahilfer Strasse for high-street brands. Idiosyncratic local stores cluster in Neubau, and Neubaugasse is good for secondhand hunters. Josefstädter Strasse has a quaint, old-fashioned shopping experience.

Wie Wien
GIFTS

(Map p40; www.wiewien.at; 05, Kettenbrückegasse 5; ⊙2-7pm Mon-Fri, 11am-6pm Sat) A Vienna concept store like no other – each piece in the shop represents the city in some way, from delicate ceramics with a picture of the Riesenrad to T-shirts depicting the Naschmarkt.

DON'T MISS

IMPERIAL ENTERTAINMENT

Founded over five centuries ago by Maximilian I as the imperial choir, the world-famous **Vienna Boys' Choir** (Wiener Sängerknaben; www.wsk.at) is the original boy band. These cherubic angels in sailor suits still hold a fond place in Austrian hearts. **Tickets** (☎533 99 27; www.bmbwk.gv.at, in German) for their Sunday performances at 9.15am (October to June) in the Burgkapelle (Royal Chapel) in the Hofburg should be booked around six weeks in advance. The group also performs regularly in the Musikverein.

Another throwback to the Habsburg glory days is the **Spanische Hofreitschule** (Spanish Riding School; Map p44; ☎533 90 31; www.srs.at; 01, Michaelerplatz 1; ⊙performances 11am Sat & Sun mid-Feb–Jun & late Aug-Dec). White Lipizzaner stallions gracefully perform equine ballet to classical music, while chandeliers shimmer from above and the audience cranes to see from pillared balconies. Tickets, costing between €23 and €143, are ordered through the website, but be warned that performances usually sell out months in advance. Unclaimed tickets are sold about two hours before performances). **Morning Training** (adult/child/family €12/6/24; ⊙10am-noon Tue-Sat Feb-Jun & mid-Aug–Dec) sameday tickets are available at the **visitor centre** (⊙9am-4pm Tue-Fri) on Michaelerplatz.

DON'T MISS

TO MARKET

Vienna's atmospheric **Flohmarkt** (flea market; Map p44; 05, Kettenbrück-engasse; ☉dawn-4pm Sat) shouldn't be missed, with goods piled up in apparent chaos on the walkway. Books, clothes, records, ancient electrical goods, old postcards, ornaments, carpets...you name it, it's all here. Come prepared to haggle.

From mid-November, *Christ-kindlmärkte* (Christmas markets) bring festive sparkle to Vienna, their stalls laden with gifts, *glühwein* (mulled wine) and *Maroni* (roasted chestnuts). Some of the best include the pretty but touristy **Rathausplatz market** (Map p44), the traditional **Spittelberg market** (Map p44) in Spittelberg's cobbled streets, where you can pick up quality crafts, and the authentic, oft-forgotten **Heiligenkreuzerhof market** (Map p44).

Dorotheum   AUCTION HOUSE
(Map p44; www.dorotheum.com; 01, Dorotheer-gasse 17; ☉10am-6pm Mon-Fri, 9am-5pm Sat) One of Europe's largest auction houses, where surprisingly not every item is priced out of this world. Stop by and simply browse – it's as entertaining as visiting many of Vienna's museums.

Lomoshop   PHOTOGRAPHY
(Map p44; 07, Museumsplatz 1; ☉11am-7pm Mon-Sun) Cult Lomo cameras, gadgets and accessories in the MuseumsQuartier.

Manner   CONFECTIONERY
(Map p44; www.manner.com; 01, Stephansplatz 7; ☉10am-6.30pm Sun-Fri, 9.30am-8.30pm Sat) One bite and you'll be hooked on the *Manner Schnitten* (wafers filled with hazelnut cream) sold at this old-world confectionery store since 1898.

Woka   PORCELAIN
(Map p44; www.woka.at; 01, Singerstrasse 16) Accurate re-creations of Wiener Werkstätte lamps are the hallmark of Woka.

Altmann & Kühne   PORCELAIN
(Map p44; Graben 30) Altmann & Kühne have been producing handmade bonbons for over 100 years using a well-kept secret recipe. The packaging is designed by Wiener Werkstätte.

ℹ Information

Many cafes and bars offer free wi-fi for their customers.

Airport Information Office (☉6am-11pm) Located in the arrival hall.

Allgemeines Krankenhaus (☏404 00; 09, Währinger Gürtel 18-20) Hospital with a 24-hour casualty ward.

Jugendinfo (Vienna Youth Information; ☏1799; www.jugendinfowien.at; 01, Babenberger-strasse 1; ☉noon-7pm Mon-Sat) Offers various reduced-price tickets for 14- to 26-year-olds.

Main post office (01, Fleischmarkt 19; ☉6am-10pm)

Police station (☏313 10; 01, Deutschmeister-platz 3)

Tourist Info Wien (☏211 14-555; www.wien.info; 01, Albertinaplatz; ☉9am-7pm) Vienna's main tourist office, with a ticket agency, hotel booking service, free maps and every brochure you could ever wish for.

ℹ Getting There & Away

Air

Vienna is the main centre for Austrian international flights. Although there are frequent flights to Graz, Klagenfurt, Salzburg, Linz and Innsbruck with **Austrian Airlines** (www.austrian.com) from Vienna, flying domestic routes offers few benefits over trains. Book early for the cheapest fares. For further details, see p93.

Boat

Fast hydrofoils travel eastwards to Bratislava (one way €19 to €31, return €38 to €62, 1¼ hours) daily from April to October and on Saturdays and Sundays in March. They also travel daily to Budapest (one way/return €89/109, 5½ hours). Bookings can be made through **DDSG Blue Danube** (☏58 880-0; www.ddsg-blue-danube.at; 02, Handelskai 265).

Heading west, a series of boats ply the Danube between Krems and Melk, with a handful of services originating in Vienna. Two respectable operators include DDSG Blue Danube and **Brandner** (☏07433-25 90; www.brandner.at), the latter located in Wallsee. Both run trips from April through October that start at around €11 one way. For trips into Germany, contact **Donauschiffahrt Wurm + Köck** (☏0732 783607; www.donauschiffahrt.de; Untere Donaulände 1, Linz).

Bus

Vienna currently has no central bus station. National Bundesbuses arrive and depart from several different locations, depending on the destination. Bus lines serving Vienna include **Eurolines** (www.eurolines.com).

Car & Motorcycle

The Gürtel is an outer ring road that joins up with the A22 on the north bank of the Danube and the A23 southeast of town. All the main road routes intersect with this system, including the A1 from Linz and Salzburg, and the A2 from Graz.

Train

Vienna is one of central Europe's main rail hubs. **Österreiche Bundesbahn** (ÖBB; Austrian Federal Railway; www.oebb.at) is the main operator. There are direct services and connections to many European cities. Sample destinations include Berlin (nine to 10 hours), Budapest (2¾ to four hours), Munich (four to five hours), Paris (12 to 13 hours), Prague (4½ to 5½ hours) and Venice (eight to nine hours).

Vienna has multiple train stations. At press time, a massive construction project was in progress at Vienna's former Südbahnhof: essentially the station was shut but an eastern section had been set up as a temporary station to serve some regional trains to/from the east, including Bratislava. The complex is due to reopen as Hauptbahnhof Wien (Vienna Central Station) in late 2012/early 2013, and as the main station it will receive international trains. As a result, all long-distance trains are being rerouted among the rest of Vienna's train stations. Additionally, Westbahnhof is undergoing major renovation; at press time, a provisional station had been created so that the station could remain in operation – it is slated to re-open in late 2011. Further train stations include Franz-Josefs-Bahnhof (which handles trains to/from the Danube Valley), Wien Mitte, Wien Nord and Meidling.

ℹ Getting Around

To/From the Airport

It is 19km from the city centre to **Vienna International Airport** (VIE; www.viennaairport.com) in Schwechat. The **City Airport Train** (CAT; www.cityairporttrain.com; return adult/child €18/free; ☺5.38am-11.08pm) runs every 30 minutes and takes 16 minutes between the airport and Wien Mitte; book online for a €2 discount. The **S-Bahn (S7)** does the same journey (single €3.60) but in 26 minutes.

Buses run every 20 or 30 minutes, between 5am and 11pm, from the airport (one way/return €6/11). Services run to Meidling, Westbahnhof and Schwedenplatz.

Taxis cost about €35. **C&K Airport Service** (☏44 444) charges €33 one way for shared vans.

Bicycle

Cycling is an excellent way to get around and explore the city – over 800km of cycle tracks criss-cross the capital. Popular cycling areas include the 7km path around the Ringstrasse, the Donauinsel, the Prater and along the Donaukanal (Danube Canal).

Vienna's city bike scheme is called **Vienna City Bike** (www.citybikewien.at, in German; 1st/2nd/3rd hour free/€1/2, per hour thereafter €4), with more than 60 bicycle stands across the city. A credit card is required to rent bikes – just swipe your card in the machine and follow the instructions (in a number of languages).

Car & Motorcycle

Due to a system of one-way streets and expensive parking, you're better off using the excellent public transport system. If you do plan to drive in the city, take special care of the trams; they always have priority and vehicles must wait behind trams when they stop to pick up or set down passengers.

Fiakers

More of a tourist novelty than anything else, a *Fiaker* is a traditional-style horse-drawn carriage. Bowler-hatted drivers generally speak English and point out places of interest en route. Expect to pay a cool €65/95 for a 40-/60-minute ride from Stephansplatz, Albertinaplatz or Heldenplatz.

Public Transport

Vienna has a unified public transport network that encompasses trains, trams, buses, and underground (U-Bahn) and suburban (S-Bahn) trains. Free maps and information pamphlets are available from **Wiener Linien** (www.wienerlinien.at, in German).

Before use, all tickets must be validated at the entrance to U-Bahn stations and on buses and trams (except for weekly and monthly tickets). Tickets are cheaper to buy from ticket machines

---

ℹ MEDIA

Tune into Vienna's cultural scene on the following websites:

» **About Vienna** (www.aboutvienna.org) General website with cultural and sightseeing information.

» **City of Vienna** (www.wien.gv.at) Comprehensive government-run website.

» **Falter** (www.falter.at, in German) Online version of the ever-popular Falter magazine.

» **Vienna Online** (www.vienna.at, in German) Site with info on parties, festivals and news.

in U-Bahn stations and in *Tabak* (tobacconist) shops, where singles cost €1.80. On board, they cost €2.20. Singles are valid for an hour, and you may change lines on the same trip.

A 24-hour ticket costs €5.70, a 48-hour ticket €10, a 72-hour ticket €13.60 and an eight-day ticket €28.80 (validate the ticket once per day as and when you need it). Weekly tickets (valid Monday to Sunday) cost €14; the Vienna Card (€18.50) includes travel on public transport for up to three days. The Strip Ticket (*Streifenkarte*) costs €7.20 and gives you four single tickets.

Ticket inspection is infrequent, but fare dodgers pay an on-the-spot fine of €62.

Taxi

Taxis are metered for city journeys and cost €2.60 flag fall during the day and €2.70 at night, plus a small per km fee. It's safe to hail taxis from the street, and there's generally an abundance of choice.

THE DANUBE VALLEY

The stretch of Danube between Krems and Melk, known locally as the Wachau, is arguably the loveliest along the entire length of the mighty river. Both banks are dotted with ruined castles and medieval towns, and lined with terraced vineyards. Further upstream is the industrial city of Linz, Austria's avant-garde art and new technology trailblazer.

Krems an der Donau

☑02732 / POP 23,800

Sitting on the northern bank of the Danube against a backdrop of terraced vineyards, Krems marks the beginning of the Wachau. It has an attractive cobbled centre, a small university, some good restaurants and the gallery-dotted Kunstmeile (Art Mile).

⊙ Sights & Activities

It's a pleasure to wander the cobblestone streets of Krems and Stein, especially at night – don't miss the baroque treasures of Schürerplatz and Rathausplatz squares in Stein.

Kunsthalle   ART MUSEUM
(www.kunsthalle.at; Franz-Zeller-Platz 3; adult/child €9/3.50; ⊙10am-6pm) The flagship of Krems' **Kunstmeile** (www.kunstmeile-krems.at), an eclectic collection of galleries and museums, the Kunsthalle has a program of small but excellent changing exhibitions.

🍴 Sleeping & Eating

Arte Hotel Krems   HOTEL €€
(☑711 23; www.arte-hotel.at, in German; Dr-Karl-Dorrek-Strasse 23; s €89-105, d €128-162; P🖳🕸🛜) This comfortable new art hotel close to the university has large, well-styled rooms in bright colours and with open-plan bathrooms.

Jugendherberge   HOSTEL €
(☑834 52; oejhv.noe.krems@aon.at; Ringstrasse 77; dm €18; ⊙closed Nov-Mar; P🖳) This popular HI (Hostelling International) hostel close to the tourist office is well geared for cyclists; it features a climbing wall, a garage for bicycles and packed lunches.

Mörwald Kloster Und   AUSTRIAN €€
(☑704 930; www.moerwald.at; Undstrasse 6; mains €20-33, 5-course menu €85, 3-course lunch €25; ⊙closed Sun & Mon; 🖳) Run by celebrity chef and winemaker Toni Mörwald, this is one of the Wachau's best restaurants. Delicacies from roast pigeon breast to fish dishes with French touches are married with top wines. There's a lovely garden.

ⓘ Information

Krems Tourismus (☑826 76; www.krems.info; Utzstrasse 1; ⊙9am-6pm Mon-Fri, 11am-5pm Sat, 11am-4pm Sun, closed Sat & Sun Nov-Apr) Has excellent city walk and vineyard maps, and stocks a *Heurigen* calendar.

ⓘ Getting There & Away

Frequent daily trains connect Krems with Vienna's Franz-Josefs-Bahnhof (€13.90, one hour). The quickest way to Melk is by train to Spitz, continuing by bus (€7.30, one hour, five times

---

WORTH A TRIP

THROUGH THE GRAPEVINE

The 830km **Weinstrasse Niederösterreich** (Lower Austria Wine Rd; www.weinstrassen.at) wends through eight wine-producing regions in Lower Austria, including the Kremstal, Kamptal and Weinviertel, passing beautiful terraced vineyards, bucolic villages, castles and abbeys. Visit the website for the low-down on local wineries (some with accommodation), wine shops and rustic *Heurigen* (wine taverns) where you can taste the region's pinot blanc (Weissburgunder), grüner veltliner, Riesling and red wines. Autumn is the time for semifermented *Sturm* (new wine).

daily). The boat station is near Donaustrasse, about 2km west of the train station.

Dürnstein

📞 02711 / POP 900

The pretty town of Dürnstein, on a supple curve in the Danube, is not only known for its beautiful buildings but also for the castle above the town where Richard I (the Lionheart) of England was imprisoned in 1192. His unscheduled stopover on the way home from the Crusades came courtesy of Austrian archduke Leopold V, whom he had insulted.

There's not much left of **Kuenringerburg castle** today. It's basically just a pile of rubble. Still, it's worth snapping a picture and the views from the top are breathtaking.

🛏 Sleeping & Eating

The tourist office has a list of private rooms and *Gasthöfe* (guesthouses) in Dürnstein.

TOP CHOICE Hotel Schloss Dürnstein   HOTEL €€€
(📞 212; www.schloss.at; Dürnstein 2; s €166, d €198-276, apt €355-380; P ❄ ☀) This castle is the last word in luxury in town, with antique-furnished rooms, a sauna and a high-end restaurant (mains €16 to €30) with staggering views over the river.

Hotel Sänger Blondel   HOTEL €€
(📞 253; www.saengerblondel.at; Klosterplatz/Dürnstein 64; s €68, d €86-112; P ❄ @) This hotel's good-sized rooms have views to the Danube, castle or garden.

Pension Böhmer   GUESTHOUSE €
(📞 239; Hauptstrasse 22; s/d €42/62; P) A small, reasonably priced guesthouse in the heart of town and just a quick hop from the castle.

Restaurant Loibnerhof   AUSTRIAN €€
(📞 828 90; Unterloiben 7; mains €15-26, 3- & 4-course menu €26-52; ⊙ closed Mon & Tue) Situated 1.5km east of Dürnstein in Unterloiben, this family-run restaurant inside a 400-year-old building has a leafy garden for enjoying local specialities such as *Kalbsbeuschel* (veal lights).

ℹ Information

For more about Dürnstein, contact the **tourist office** (📞 200; www.duernstein.at; ⊙ 9am-5pm) in the train station.

ℹ Getting There & Away

Dürnstein can be reached from Krems by train (€2, 11 minutes, hourly).

ℹ ON YOUR BIKE

Many towns in the Danube Valley are part of a bike hire network called **Leihradl**. After registering using a credit card (either by calling the hotline on 📞 02742-229 901 or on the website www.leihradl.at, in German), a refunded €1 is deducted and you can begin renting bicycles for €1/5 per hour/24 hours.

Melk

📞 02752 / POP 5200

With its sparkling and majestic abbey-fortress, Melk is a highlight of any visit to the Danube Valley. Many visitors cycle here for the day – wearily pushing their bikes through the cobblestone streets.

◎ Sights

Stift Melk   ABBEY
(Benedictine Abbey of Melk; 📞 5550; www.stift melk.at; Abt Berthold Dietmayr Strasse 1; adult/child/family €7.70/4.50/15.40, with guided tour €9.50/6.30/19; ⊙ 9am-5.30pm) Rising like a vision on a hill overlooking the town, Stift Melk is Austria's most famous abbey. It has been home to Benedictine monks since the 11th century, though it owes its current good looks to 18th-century mastermind Jakob Prandtauer.

The interior of the twin-spired monastery church is baroque gone barmy, with endless prancing angels and gold twirls. Other highlights include the **Bibliothek** (Library) and the **Marmorsaal** (Marble Hall); the trompe l'oeil on the ceiling (by Paul Troger) gives the illusion of greater height. Eleven of the imperial rooms, where dignitaries (including Napoleon) stayed, now house a **museum**.

From around November to March, the monastery can only be visited by guided tour (11am and 2pm daily). Always phone ahead to ensure you get an English-language tour.

🛏 Sleeping & Eating

Restaurants and cafes with alfresco seating line the Rathausplatz.

Hotel Restaurant zur Post   HOTEL €€
(📞 523 45; www.post-melk.at, in German; Linzer Strasse 1; s €61-71, d €98-112, apt €155-210; P @ ☎) This bright hotel in the heart of

town has large, comfortable rooms. There's a sauna, free bike use for guests and a decent restaurant serving Austrian classics.

Hotel Wachau HOTEL €€
(☎525 31; www.hotel-wachau.at; Am Wachberg 3; s €65, d €95-125;) For comfortable, modern rooms, try this hotel 2km southeast of the train station. The restaurant (mains €12 to €20, gourmet menu €45) is open for dinner Monday to Saturday and specialises in well-prepared regional cuisine.

Information

The **tourist office** (☎523 07-410; www.niederoesterreich.at/melk; Babenbergerstrasse 1; 9am-noon & 2-6pm Mon-Fri, 10am-noon Sat & Sun), east of Rathausplatz, has maps and plenty of useful information.

Getting There & Away

Boats leave from the canal by Pionierstrasse, 400m north of the abbey. There are hourly trains to Vienna (€15.70, 1¼ hours).

Linz

☎0732 / POP 189,000

In Linz beginnt's (It begins in Linz) goes the Austrian saying, and it's spot on. Linz is blessed with a leading-edge cyber centre and world-class contemporary-art gallery, both signs that Upper Austria kick-started the country's technological industry. Beyond the industrial outskirts you'll find plenty of culture, so much so that it gained the title of European Capital of Culture 2009.

Sights & Activities

Linz' baroque Hauptplatz and sculpture-strewn Danube Park are made for aimless ambling. The **Linz Card**, giving entry to major sights and unlimited use of public transport, costs €15/25 for one/three days.

Ars Electronica Center MUSEUM
(www.aec.at; Ars Electronica Strasse 1; adult/child €7/4; 9am-5pm Wed-Fri, to 9pm Thu, 10am-6pm Sat & Sun) Ars Electronica Center zooms in on tomorrow's technology, science and digital media. In themed labs you can interact with robots, animate digital objects and (virtually) travel the world. The shipshape centre kaleidoscopically changes colour after dark.

Lentos ART MUSEUM
(www.lentos.at; Ernst-Koref-Promenade 1; adult/child €6.50/4.50; 10am-6pm Wed-Mon, to 9pm Thu) Ars Electronica's rival icon across the Danube is the rectangular glass-and-steel Lentos, also strikingly illuminated by night. The gallery guards one of Austria's finest modern art collections, including works by Warhol, Schiele and Klimt, which sometimes feature in the large-scale exhibitions.

Neuer Dom CHURCH
(New Cathedral; Herrenstrasse 26; 8am-7pm) This neo-Gothic giant of a cathedral was designed in the mid-19th century by Vinzenz Statz of Cologne Dom fame. The tower's height was restricted to 134m, so as not to outshine Stephansdom in Vienna.

Landesgalerie ART MUSEUM
(State Museum; www.landesgalerie.at; Museumstrasse 14; adult/child €6.50/4.50; 9am-6pm Tue-Fri, to 9pm Thu, 10am-5pm Sat & Sun) Cutting-edge art exhibitions in neoclassical surrounds and a sculpture garden.

Schlossmuseum MUSEUM
(Castle Museum; www.schlossmuseum.at; Schlossberg 1; adult/child €6.50/4.50; 9am-6pm Tue-Fri, to 9pm Thu, 10am-5pm Sat & Sun) Linz' hilltop castle is a treasure trove of art and history. The Gothic ecclesiastical paintings are a highlight.

Festivals & Events

The **Ars Electronica Festival** (www.aec.at) in early September showcases cyber-art, computer music, and other marriages of technology and art. This leads into the **Brucknerfest** (www.brucknerhaus.at), which pays homage to native son Anton Bruckner with a month of classical music between

> DON'T MISS
>
> **RECORD-BREAKING RAILWAY**
>
> From Linz' Hauptplatz, the narrow-gauge **Pöstlingbergbahn** (adult/child €5.60/2.80; 6am-10pm Mon-Sat, 7.30am-10pm Sun) hauls you up to Pöstlingberg (537m), departing every 30 minutes. This gondola features in the Guinness Book of Records as the world's steepest mountain railway – quite some feat for such a low-lying city! Far-reaching city and Danube views await at the summit, and kids love to take a spin on the century-old fairytale train.

mid-September and early October. Be sure to book early.

🛏 Sleeping & Eating

The tourist office offers a free accommodation-booking service, but only face-to-face and not over the phone.

Pavement cafes, bistros and lively bars line up on and around Hauptplatz, on the main shopping thoroughfare Landstrasse and the cobbled Altstadt.

Spitz Hotel   HOTEL €€
(📞73 37 33; www.spitzhotel.at; Fiedlerstrasse 6; r €130-250; P@🛜) Much-lauded Austrian architect Isa Stein has left her avant-garde imprint on the Spitz. Each of the hotel's rooms has unique artworks. Minimalism rules here, with clean lines, open-plan bathrooms and hardwood floors.

Hotel am Domplatz   HOTEL €€
(📞77 30 00; www.hotelamdomplatz.at; Stifterstrasse 4; s €120-140, d €150-180; P❄@) Sidling up to the Neuer Dom, this glass-and-concrete design hotel reveals light, streamlined interiors. Wind down with a view at the rooftop spa.

Wolfinger   HISTORIC HOTEL €€
(📞77 32 91; www.hotelwolfinger.at; Hauptplatz 19; s/d €85/126; P@) This 500-year-old hotel, located on the main square, has an air of old-world grandeur. Archways, stuccowork and period furniture give the rooms some character.

Sommerhaus Hotel   HOTEL €
(📞24 57 376; www.sommerhaus-hotel.at; Julius-Raab-Strasse 10; s/d €49/74; P@) Sitting between the city and open fields, this revamped uni hotel has simple, comfy rooms and a big indoor pool. Take tram 1 or 2 to Schumpeterstrasse and walk five minutes.

k.u.k. Hofbäckerei   CAFE €
(Pfarrgasse 17; coffee & cake €3-6; ⊙6.30am-6pm Mon-Fri, 7am-12.30pm Sat) The empire lives on at this gloriously stuck-in-time cafe. Here Fritz Rath bakes *the* best *Linzer Torte* in town – rich, spicy and with lattice pastry that crumbles just so.

Cubus   FUSION €€
(Ars-Electronica-Strasse 1; mains €8.50-14.50; ⊙9am-1am Mon-Sat, to 6pm Sun; 🛜) On the 3rd floor of the Ars Electronica Center, this glass cube has stellar Danube views. The menu is strictly fusion and the two-course lunch a snip at €7.

Alte Welt   AUSTRIAN €€
(📞77 00 53; www.altewelt.at, in German; Hauptplatz 4; mains €9-16; ⊙lunch Mon-Sat, dinner daily) Set around an arcaded inner courtyard, Alte Welt serves hearty fare like roast pork and beef ragout, and a good-value two-course lunch for €6.50. It sometimes hosts live jazz and jam sessions.

ℹ Information

Atlas Media (Graben 17; internet per hour €2.50; ⊙9.30am-11pm Mon-Sat, 1-11pm Sun) Internet and discount international calls.

Hotspot Linz (www.hotspotlinz.at, in German) Free wi-fi at 120 hotspots in the city, including Ars Electronica Center and Lentos.

Post office (Domgasse 1; ⊙8am-6pm Mon-Fri, 9am-noon Sat) Handy to the centre.

Tourist Information Linz (📞7070 2009; www.linz.at; Hauptplatz 1; ⊙9am-7pm Mon-Sat, 10am-7pm Sun, shorter hours winter) Free city maps and room reservation service.

ℹ Getting There & Around

AIR Austrian Airlines, Lufthansa, Ryanair and Air Berlin fly to the **Blue Danube Airport** (www.linz-airport.at), 13km southwest of Linz. An hourly shuttle bus (€2.60, 20 minutes) links the airport to the main station from Monday to Saturday.

WORTH A TRIP

ST FLORIAN

One of Austria's finest Augustinian abbeys is St Florian's **Augustiner Chorherrenstift** (www.stift-st-florian.at; Stiftstrasse 1; tours adult/child €8/5; ⊙tours 11am, 1pm, 3pm May-Sep), 18km southeast of Linz. The abbey dates back to at least 819 but is now overwhelmingly baroque in style. A guided tour leads you through the opulent library, Marble Hall and the Altdorfer Gallery, displaying 14 paintings by Albrecht Altdorfer (1480–1538) of the Danube School. A vision of pink marble and gilding, the resplendent abbey church harbours the huge 18th-century organ upon which famous Romantic composer Anton Bruckner played during his stint as organist (1850 to 1855).

Buses run frequently between St Florian and Linz Hauptbahnhof (€2.60, 22 minutes); there is a reduced service on Sunday.

PUBLIC TRANSPORT Bus and tram tickets are bought before you board from pavement dispensers or *Tabak* (tobacconist) shops. Single tickets cost €1.80 and day passes €3.60. Some of the bus services stop early in the evening.

TRAIN Linz is halfway between Salzburg and Vienna on the main road and rail routes. Trains to Salzburg (€22, 1¼ hours) and Vienna (€31.20, 1½ hours) leave approximately twice hourly.

THE SOUTH

Austria's two main southern states, Styria (Steiermark) and Carinthia (Kärnten), often feel worlds apart from the rest of the country, both in climate and attitude. Styria is a blissful amalgamation of genteel architecture, rolling green hills, vine-covered slopes and soaring mountains. Its capital, Graz, is one of Austria's most attractive cities.

A jet-setting, fashion-conscious crowd heads to sun-drenched Carinthia for summer holidays. The region (which is right on the border with Italy) exudes an atmosphere that's as close to Mediterranean as this staunch country gets.

Graz

☎ 0316 / POP 257,350

Austria's second-largest city is probably its most relaxed and, after Vienna, its liveliest for after-hours pursuits. It's an attractive place with bristling green parkland, red rooftops and a small, fast-flowing river gushing through its centre. Architecturally, it has Renaissance courtyards and provincial baroque palaces complemented by innovative modern designs.

The surrounding countryside, a mixture of vineyards, mountains, forested hills and thermal springs, is within easy striking distance, and Graz has a beautiful bluff connected to the centre by steps, a funicular and a glass lift. Last but not least, a large student population (some 50,000) propels

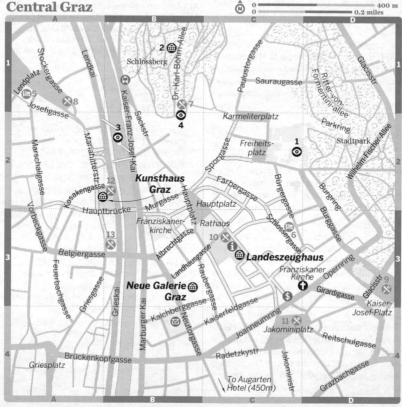

Central Graz

the nightlife and vibrant arts scene, creating a loveable and liveable city.

◉ Sights & Activities

Graz is a city easily enjoyed by simply wandering aimlessly. Admission to all of the major museums with a 24-hour ticket costs €11/14 for adults/children.

Universalmuseum Joanneum　　　MUSEUM
(www.museum-joanneum.at; Raubergasse 10) With its 19 locations, this ensemble of museums is the gardener of Graz' rich cultural landscape. Until work is completed, some museums will be closed until late 2011, including **Neue Galerie Graz** (adult/child €8/3; 10am-6pm, closed Mon), Styria's most important historical and contemporary art collection.

Kunsthaus Graz　　　ART MUSEUM
(www.kunsthausgraz.at; Lendkai 1; adult/child €7/3; ⊙10am-6pm, closed Mon) Designed by British architects Peter Cook and Colin Fournier, this world-class contemporary art space looks something like a space-age sea slug. Exhibitions change every three to four months.

Schloss Eggenberg　　　PALACE
(Eggenberger Allee 90; adult/child €7/3; ⊙10am-5pm, closed Mon & Nov-Palm Sunday) A blend

of gothic, Renaissance and baroque styles, this beautiful palace can be reached by tram 1 from Hauptplatz. Admission includes a guided tour (from 10am to 4pm on the hour except at 1pm), taking in 24 *Prunkräume* (staterooms), which are based around astronomy, the zodiac and classical or religious mythology.

FREE **Murinsel**　　　BRIDGE
This artificial island-cum-bridge in the River Mur is an open seashell of glass, concrete and steel, by New York artist Vito Acconci. It houses a trendy cafe-bar in aqua blue and a small stage. In summer, further downstream a beach bar is set up.

Schlossberg　　　VIEWPOINT
The wooded slopes of Schlossberg (473m) can be reached on foot, with the funicular **Schlossbergbahn** (Castle Hill Railway; 1hr ticket €1.90) from Kaiser-Franz-Josef-Kai, or by **Glass Lift** (1hr ticket €1.90) from Schlossbergplatz. Napoleon was hard-pressed to raze this fortress, but raze it he did. Today the medieval **Uhrturm** (Clock Tower) and a small **Garrison Museum** (Schlossberg 5a; adult/child €1/free; ⊙10am-4pm, closed Mon-Wed & Nov–mid-May) are the legacy.

Landeszeughaus　　　ARMOURY
(www.zeughaus.at; Herrengasse 16; adult/child €7/3; ⊙10am-6pm) A must-see for fans of armour and weapons, housing an astounding array of 30,000 gleaming exhibits.

FREE **Burg**　　　CASTLE, PARK
(Hofgasse) At the far end of Graz' 15th-century castle is an ingenious **double staircase** (1499). Adjoining it is the **Stadtpark**, the city's largest green space.

🛏 Sleeping

Hotel Daniel　　　HOTEL €€
(☏711 080; www.hoteldaniel.com; Europaplatz 1; r €59-79, breakfast €9 per person; ⓟ⊝✳@) Perched at the top of Annenstrasse, the Daniel is an exclusive design hotel. All rooms are tastefully furnished in minimalist designs; you can rent a Vespa (€15 per day) and there's a 24-hour espresso bar.

Hotel Strasser　　　HOTEL €
(☏71 39 77; www.hotel-strasser.at; Eggenberger Gürtel 11; s/d/tr/apt €45/65/93/180; ⓟ@☏) Strasser has some fascinating pseudo-neoclassical and Mediterranean touches, with Tuscan gold blending with mirrors and cast-iron balustrades. It's handy to the train station.

HUNDERTWASSER SPA

East Styria is famed for its thermal springs. Fans of Friedensreich Hundertwasser's playful architectural style won't want to miss the surreal **Rogner-Bad Blumau** (☑03383-51 00-0; www.blumau.com; adult/child €39/21; ☉9am-11pm), 50km east of Graz. The spa has all the characteristics of his art, including uneven rooms, grass on the roof, colourful ceramics and golden spires. Overnight accommodation includes entry to the spa. Call ahead to book treatments from sound meditation to invigorating Styrian elderberry wraps.

Hotel zum Dom HOTEL €€
(☑82 48 00; www.domhotel.co.at; Bürgergasse 14; s €83-93, d €170-220, ste €227-332; P☺) Hotel zum Dom's individually furnished rooms come with power showers or whirlpools, and one suite even has a terrace whirlpool.

Augarten Hotel HOTEL €€
(☑20 800; www.augartenhotel.at; Schönaugasse 53; s/d €115-165, d €140-190; P☀☺≋) The arty Augarten is decorated with the owner's private collection. All rooms are bright and modern, and the pool and sauna round off an excellent option.

Gasthof-Pension zur Steirer-Stub'n
GUESTHOUSE €
(☑71 68 55; www.pension-graz.at; Lendplatz 8; s/d €43/78, apt €110-160; ☺) A bright and breezy guesthouse where many of the good-sized rooms have patios overlooking Lendplatz.

Jugend und Familiengästehaus Graz HOSTEL €
(☑70 83 210; graz@jufa.at, Idlhofgasse 74; dm €22, s €39-46.50, d €64-77; P@☺) Take bus 31, 32 or 33 from Jakominiplatz for this HI hostel about 800m south of the main train station.

✗ Eating

With leafy salads dressed in delicious pumpkin-seed oil, fish specialities and *Pfand'l* (pan-grilled) dishes, Styrian cuisine is Austrian cooking at its light and healthy best.

Aside from the following listings, there are plenty of cheap eats near Universität Graz, particularly on Halbärthgasse, Zinzendorfgasse and Harrachgasse.

Stock up for a picnic at the **farmers markets** (☉4.30am-1pm, closed Sun) on Kaiser-Josef-Platz and Lendplatz. For **fast-food stands**, head for Hauptplatz and Jakominiplatz.

TOP CHOICE **Aiola Upstairs** INTERNATIONAL €€
(www.aiola.at, in German; Schlossberg 2; pasta €9.50-15, mains €17.50-25; ☉9am-midnight, closed Sun) This wonderful restaurant on Schlossberg has great views, delicious international flavours, a superb wine list, spot-on cocktails and very chilled music.

Der Steirer BEISL €€
(www.dersteirer.at, in German; Belgiergasse 1; mains €9-18.50, tapas €2, lunch menu €6.90; ☉11am-midnight) This Styrian neo-*Beisl* and wine bar has a small but excellent selection of local dishes and a large choice of wines. The goulash with fried polenta is easily one of the best in the country.

Mangolds VEGETARIAN €
(www.mangolds.at, in German; Griesgasse 11; meals €5-10; ☉11am-7pm Mon-Fri, to 4pm Sat; ☑) Tasty patties, rice dishes and over 40 different salads are served at this pay-by-weight vegetarian cafeteria.

iku INTERNATIONAL €
(☑8017 9292; www.iku-graz.at, in German; Lendkai 1; lunch menu €7; ☉9am-1am) This sleek restaurant inside the surrealistic Kunsthaus does great breakfasts, salads and lunch specials (11.30am to 3pm). Reserve ahead for the Sunday brunch with music.

♟ Drinking & Entertainment

The bar scene in Graz is split between three main areas: around the university; adjacent to the Kunsthaus; and on Mehlplatz and Prokopigasse (dubbed the 'Bermuda Triangle').

Insel Café CAFE
(Murinsel; ☉9.30am-midnight) This cafe offers a unique experience – you can sip on your drink as the Mur River splashes below your feet.

Orange BAR/CLUB
(www.cafe-bar-orange.at, in German; Elisabethstrasse 30; ☉8pm-3am) A student crowd flocks to this modern bar and club, with a patio for summer evenings. DJs spin regularly here.

Kulturhauskeller BAR, BEISL
(Elisabethstrasse 30; ☉9pm-5am, closed Sun & Mon) Next to Orange, the Kulturhauskeller is a cavernous cellar bar that heaves with

raunchy students on weekends. After 11pm admission is €3.

❶ Information

Graz Tourismus (☏80 75-0; www.graztour ismus.at; Herrengasse 16; ☉10am-6pm) Graz' main tourist office, with loads of free information on the city. Inside the train station is an information stand and terminal, and free hotline to the tourist office.

High Speed Internet-Selfstore (Herrengasse 3; per 30min €1; ☉7am-10pm) A coin-operated internet space inside the passage.

Main post office (Neutorgasse 46; ☉8am-7pm Mon-Fri, 9am-noon Sat)

❶ Getting There & Away

AIR Ryanair (www.ryanair.com) has regular flights from London Stansted to **Graz airport** (☏290 20; www.flughafen-graz.at), 10km south of the centre, while **Air Berlin** (www.airberlin. com) connects the city with Berlin.

BICYCLE Bicycle rental is available from **Bicycle** (☏68 86 45; Körösistrasse 5; per 24hr €10; ☉7am-1pm & 2-6pm, closed Sat & Sun).

PUBLIC TRANSPORT Single tickets (€1.90) for buses, trams and the Schlossbergbahn are valid for one hour, but you're usually better off buying a 24-hour pass (€4.10).

TRAIN Trains to Vienna depart hourly (€34, 2½ hours), and six daily go to Salzburg (€48, four hours). International train connections from Graz include Ljubljana (€34, 3½ hours) and Budapest (€46, 5½ hours).

Klagenfurt

☏0463 / POP 94,000

With its salacious location on Wörthersee and more Renaissance than baroque beauty, Carinthia's capital Klagenfurt has a distinct Mediterranean feel. While there isn't a huge amount here to see, it makes a handy base for exploring Wörthersee's lakeside villages and elegant medieval towns to the north.

◉ Sights & Activities

Boating and swimming are usually possible from May to September.

Wörthersee   LAKE

Owing to its thermal springs, the Wörthersee is one of the region's warmer lakes (an average 21°C in summer) and is great for swimming, lakeshore frolicking and water sports. The 50km **cycle path** around the lake is one of the 'Top 10' in Austria. In summer the tourist office cooperates with a hire com-

pany for bicycles (per 24 hours €10 to €19), which can also be picked up and dropped off at various points around the lake.

Europapark   PARK

The green expanse and its *Strandbad* (beach) on the shores of the Wörthersee are centres for splashy fun, and especially good for kids. The park's biggest draw is **Minimundus** (www. minimundus.at; Villacher Strasse 241; adult/child €12/7; ☉9am-6pm), a 'miniature world' with 140 replicas of the world's architectural icons, downsized to a scale of 1:25. To get there, take bus 10, 11, 12 or 22 from Heiligengeistplatz.

🍴 Sleeping & Eating

When you check into accommodation in Klagenfurt, ask for a *Gästekarte* (guest card), entitling you to discounts.

Arcotel Moser Verdino   HOTEL €€

(☏578 78; www.arcotel.at/moserverdino; Domgasse 2; s €80-144, d €104-256, ste €128-180, apt €148-1920; ❄@🛜) This excellent pick has high-quality modern rooms with flair, very helpful staff and often discounted rates.

Hotel Liebetegger   HOTEL €€

(☏569 35; www.liebetegger.com, in German; Völkermarkter Strasse 8; s €60, d €85-95, apt €110-200; P❄@🛜) Original artwork spruces up this hotel. The apartments can sleep up to four guests and it offers free use of bikes.

Jugendgästehaus Klagenfurt   HOSTEL €

(☏23 00 20; www.oejhv.or.at; Neckheimgasse 6; dm/s/d €20.50/28.50/49; P❄@) This modern HI hostel near Europapark is reached by bus 10, 12, 13 or 22.

Restaurant Maria Loretto   AUSTRIAN €€

(☏244 65; Lorettoweg 54; mains €15-25; ☉lunch & dinner Mar-Dec; P❄❄) A wonderful restaurant situated on a headland above Wörthersee near the *Strandbad*. Reserve for evenings or an outside table.

Zauberhutt'n   ITALIAN/AUSTRIAN €€

(Osterwitzgasse 6; mains €10-17; ☉Mon-Sat, closed lunch Sat; ❄) Pasta, pizza, delicious

---

❶ **FREE GUIDED WALKS**

Tailor your own Klagenfurt walking tour by picking up the brochure in English from the tourist office. It has a map and descriptions of monuments, historic buildings and hidden courtyards. Free guided tours depart from the tourist office at 10am during July and August.

grilled squid and classic meat dishes all feature at this inexpensive, family-run restaurant.

ℹ Information

Café-bar G@tes (Waagplatz 7; per 10min €1; ⏰9am-1am Mon-Fri, 7pm-1am Sat & Sun; 🛜) Wi-fi is free if you buy a drink.

Tourist office (📞53 722 23; www.info.klagen-furt.at; Rathaus, Neuer Platz 1; ⏰8am-6pm Mon-Fri, 10am-5pm Sat, 10am-3pm Sun) Sells Kärnten cards and books accommodation.

ℹ Getting There & Around

AIR Klagenfurt's **airport** (www.klagenfurt-airport.com; Flughafenstrasse 60-66) is served by Ryanair from London Stansted and Frankfurt-am-Main, and **TUIfly** (www.tuifly.com) from major German cities.

BUS Bus drivers sell single tickets (€1.80) and 24-hour passes (€4.20). To get to the airport, take bus 40 from the main train station to Annabichl (€1.80, 25 minutes, four times hourly), then change to bus 45 (10 minutes).

TRAIN Two hourly direct trains run from Klagenfurt to Vienna (€48, 3¾ hours) and Salzburg (€35.50, three hours). Trains to Graz depart every two to three hours (€35.50, 2¾ hours). Trains to western Austria, Italy, Slovenia and Germany go via Villach (€7.20, 30 to 40 minutes, two to four per hour).

SALZBURG

📞0662 / POP 147,600

The joke 'If it's baroque, don't fix it' is a perfect maxim for Salzburg; the tranquil Old Town burrowed below steep hills looks much as it did when Mozart lived here 250 years ago. Second only to Vienna in numbers of visitors, this compact city is centred on a tight grouping of narrow, cobbled streets overshadowed by ornate 17th-century buildings, which are in turn dominated by the medieval Hohensalzburg fortress from high above. Across the fast-flowing Salzach River rests the baroque Schloss Mirabell, surrounded by gorgeous manicured gardens.

If this doesn't whet your appetite, then bypass the grandeur and head straight for kitsch-country by joining a tour of *The Sound of Music* film locations.

◉ Sights

Old Town   HISTORIC AREA

A Unesco World Heritage site, Salzburg's Old Town centre is equally entrancing whether viewed from ground level or the hills above.

The grand **Residenzplatz**, with its horse-drawn carriages and mythical fountain, is a good starting point for a wander. The overwhelmingly baroque **Dom** (cathedral; Domplatz; admission free; ⏰8am-7pm Mon-Sat, 1-7pm Sun), slightly south, is entered via bronze doors symbolising faith, hope and charity. The adjacent **Dommuseum** (adult/child €6/2; ⏰10am-5pm Mon-Sat, 11am-6pm Sun) is a treasure-trove of ecclesiastical art.

From here, head west along Franziskanergasse and turn left into a courtyard for **Stiftskirche St Peter** (St Peter Bezirk 1/2; admission free; ⏰8.30am-noon & 2.30-6.30pm), an abbey church founded around 700. Among the lovingly tended graves in the grounds you'll find the **Katakomben** (catacombs; adult/student €1/0.60; ⏰10.30am-5pm Tue-Sun).

The western end of Franziskanergasse opens out into Max Reinhardt Platz, where you'll see the back of Fisher von Erlach's **Kollegienkirche** (Universitätsplatz; admission free; ⏰8am-6pm), another outstanding example of baroque architecture. The **Stift Nonnberg** (Nonnberg Convent; admission free; ⏰7am-dusk), where Maria first appears in *The Sound of Music*, is back in the other direction, a short climb up the hill to the east of the Festung Hohensalzburg.

TOP CHOICE **Festung Hohensalzburg**   FORTRESS (www.salzburg-burgen.at; Mönchsberg 34; adult with/without funicular €10.50/7.40, child €6/4.20; ⏰9am-8pm) Salzburg's most visible icon is this mighty clifftop fortress, one of the best preserved in Europe. Built in 1077, it was home to many prince-archbishops who ruled Salzburg from 798. Inside are the impressively ornate staterooms, torture chambers and two museums.

It takes 15 minutes to walk up the hill to the fortress, or you can catch the **Festungsbahn funicular** (Festungsgasse 4; adult/child one way €3.60/1.80, return €6/3.20; ⏰9am-8pm).

ℹ SALZBURG CARD

The money-saving **Salzburg Card** (1-/2-/3-day card €25/33/38) gets you entry to all of the major sights and attractions, a free river cruise, unlimited use of public transport (including cable cars) plus numerous discounts on tours and events. The card is half-price for children and €3 cheaper in the low season.

Salzburg Museum
MUSEUM

(www.smca.at; Mozartplatz 1; adult/child €7/3; ⊙9am-5pm Tue-Sun, to 8pm Thu) Housed in the baroque Neue Residenz palace, Salzburg's flagship museum hosts contemporary art exhibitions and celebrates the city's famous citizens, like 16th-century physician Paracelsus, in an interactive way. Salzburg's famous 35-bell **glockenspiel**, which chimes daily at 7am, 11am and 6pm, is on the palace's western flank.

Schloss Mirabell
PALACE

(⊙dawn-dusk) Prince-Archbishop Wolf Dietrich built this splendid palace in 1606 for his beloved mistress Salome Alt. The only way to see the sublime baroque interior is by attending an evening concert in the **Marmorsaal** (Marble Hall).

It's free to visit the manicured, fountaindotted **gardens**, which are less overrun first thing in the morning and early evening. The *Tänzerin* (dancer) sculpture is a great spot from which to take photographs. *Sound of Music* fans will of course recognise the Pegasus statue, the gnomes and the steps where the mini von Trapps practised 'Do-Re-Mi'.

Mozarts Geburtshaus
MUSEUM

(Mozart's Birthplace; www.mozarteum.at; Getreidegasse 9; adult/child €7/2.50; ⊙9am-5.30pm) Mozart was born in this bright-yellow townhouse in 1756 and spent the first 17 years of his life here. The museum today harbours a collection of memorabilia, including the miniature violin the child prodigy played, plus a lock of his hair and buttons from his jacket.

Mozart-Wohnhaus
MUSEUM

(Mozart's Residence; www.mozarteum.at; Makartplatz 8; adult/child €7/2.50; ⊙9am-5.30pm) The Mozart family moved to this more spacious abode in 1773, where a prolific Mozart composed works such as the *Shepherd King* and *Idomeneo*. Alongside family portraits and documents, you'll find Mozart's original fortepiano.

The museum also houses the free **Mozart Ton-und Filmmuseum** (⊙9am-1pm Mon, Tue & Fri, 1-5pm Wed & Thu), a film and music archive for the ultra-enthusiast.

Residenz
PALACE, ART MUSEUM

(www.residenzgalerie.at; Residenzplatz 1; adult/child €8.50/2.70; ⊙10am-5pm Tue-Sun) This resplendent baroque palace is where the princearchbishops held court until the 19th century. You can visit their opulently frescoed

WANT MORE?

Head to **Lonely Planet** (www.lonely planet.com/austria/salzburg) for planning advice, author recommendations, traveller reviews and insider tips.

staterooms, while the gallery spotlights Dutch and Flemish masters of the Rubens and Rembrandt ilk.

Museum der Moderne
ART MUSEUM

(www.museumdermoderne.at; Mönchsberg 32; adult/child €8/6; ⊙10am-6pm, to 8pm Wed) Straddling Mönchsberg's cliffs, this ultramodern gallery shows first-rate modern art exhibitions. The works of Gerhard Richter, Max Ernst and Hiroshi Sugimoto have previously featured.

The **Mönchsberg Lift** (Gstättengasse 13; with/without gallery ticket return €1.70/2.90; ⊙8am-7pm, to 9pm Wed) whizzes up to the gallery year-round.

FREE ## Friedhof St Sebastian
CEMETERY

(Nonnberggasse 2; ⊙7am-dusk) Tucked away behind the baroque St Sebastian's Church, this peaceful cemetery is the final resting place of Mozart family members and 16th-century physician Paracelsus. Outpomping them all, though, is Prince-Archbishop Wolf Dietrich von Raitenau's mosaictiled **mausoleum**, an elaborate memorial to himself.

☞ Tours

The horse-drawn carriages (*Fiaker*) in front of Residenz do guided Altstadt (Old Town) tours; prices depend on your itinerary.

One-hour guided tours of the historic centre depart daily at 12.15pm and 2pm on Mozartplatz and cost €9. You can borrow a two-hour iGuide from the tourist office (€7.50) to take in the sights at your own speed.

How much fun you have on a *Sound of Music* tour depends on whether your group gets into the yodel-eh-hee-hee spirit of things. If you can, try to get together your own little posse.

Fräulein Maria's Bicycle Tours
BICYCLE TOURS

(www.mariasbicycletours.com; adult/child incl bike hire €24/15; ⊙9.30am May-Sep) Wannabe Marias on bicycles. No booking is required; just turn up at the Mirabellplatz meeting point.

Salzburg

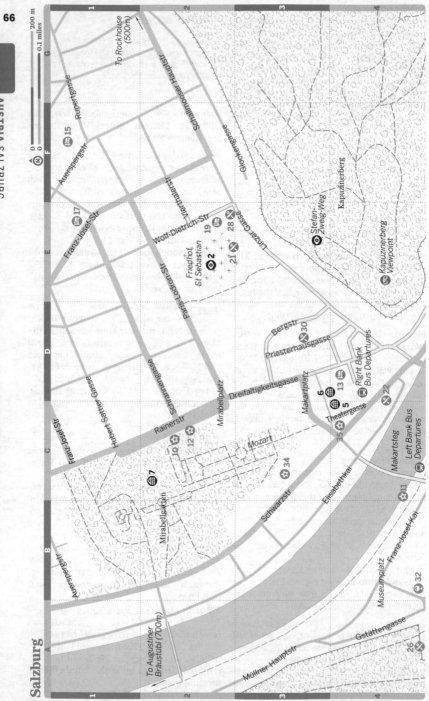

200 m
0.1 miles

To Rockhouse
(500m)

To Augustiner
Bräustübl (700m)

Rupertgasse
Auerspergstr
Schallmooser Hauptstr
Glockengasse
Kapuzinerberg
Stefan-Zweig-Weg
Kapuzinerberg
Viewpoint
Franz-Josef-Str
Paris-Lodron-Str
Vierthalerstr
Wolf-Dietrich-Str
Linzer Gasse
Friedhof
St Sebastian
Bergstr
Priesterhausgasse
Dreifaltigkeitsgasse
Makartplatz
Right Bank
Bus Departures
Theatergasse
Hubert Sattler Gasse
Schrannengasse
Rainerstr
Mirabellplatz
Mozart
Mirabellgarten
Schwarzstr
Elisabethkai
Makartsteg
Left Bank Bus
Departures
Franz-Josef-Kai
Museumplatz
Müllner Hauptstr
Gstättengasse
Auerspergstr
Franz-Josef-Str

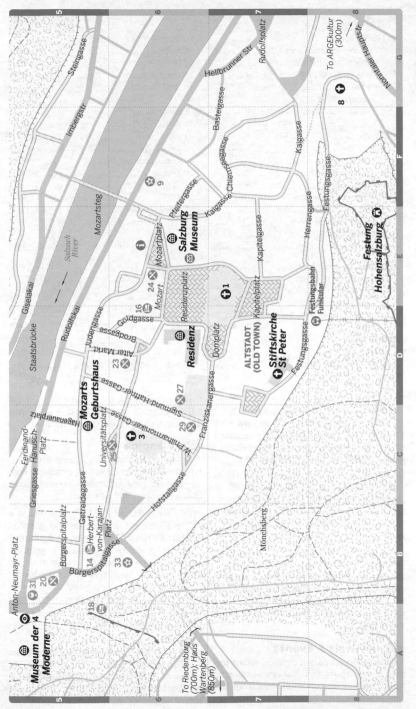

Steingasse

Imbergstr

Steingasse

Hellbrunner Str

Rudolfsplatz

To ARGEkultur (300m)

Nonntaler Hauptstr

Basteigasse

Kaigasse

Chiemseegasse

8

Kaigasse

Salzach River

Giselakai

Mozartsteg

Pfeifergasse

9

Kaigasse

Festungsgasse

Herrengasse

Festungsgasse

Festung Hohensalzburg

Staatsbrücke

Rudolfskai

Mozartplatz

Salzburg Museum

Mozartplatz

i

Residenzplatz

1

Kapitelgasse

Kapitelplatz

Festungsbahn Funicular

Goldgasse

Brodgasse

Judengasse

24

Mozart

16

Alter Markt

Residenzplatz

Residenz

Domplatz

ALTSTADT (OLD TOWN)

Stiftskirche St Peter

Festungsgasse

Hagenauerplatz

Sigmund-Haffner-Gasse

23

27

Franziskanergasse

Ferdinand-Hanusch-Platz

Griesgasse

Mozarts Geburtshaus

W Philharmoniker-Gasse

29

Hofstallgasse

Mönchsberg

Universitätsplatz

3

25

Getreidegasse

Herbert-von-Karajan-Platz

Bürgerspitalgasse

14

33

Bürgerspitalplatz

18

To Riedenburg (700m); Haus Wartenberg (850m)

Anton-Neumayr-Platz

Museum der Moderne

4

31

20

Bob's Special Tours   COACH TOURS
(☏849 511; www.bobstours.com; Rudolfskai 38; ⊙office 10am-3pm Mon-Fri, noon-2pm Sat & Sun) Minibus tours to *Sound of Music* locations (€40), the Bavarian Alps (€40) and Grossglockner (€80). Reservations essential.

Salzburg Sightseeing Tours   COACH TOURS
(☏881 616; www.salzburg-sightseeingtours.at; Mirabellplatz 2; adult/child €20/7; ⊙office 8am-6pm) Sells a 24-hour ticket for a multilingual hop-on, hop-off bus tour of the city and *Sound of Music* locations.

Salzburg Schiffsfahrt   RIVER CRUISES
(www.salzburgschifffahrt.at; adult/child €13/7, to Schloss Hellbrunn €16/10; ⊙Apr-Oct) Hour-long cruises depart from Makartsteg bridge, with some chugging on to Schloss Hellbrunn (the ticket price does not cover entry to the palace).

🎉 Festivals & Events

Austria's most renowned classical music festival, the **Salzburg Festival** (www.salzburgfestival.at) attracts international stars from late July to late August. Book on its website be-

fore January, or ask the **ticket office** (☏804 5-500; Herbert-von- Karajan-Platz 11; ⊙10am-6pm) about cancellations during the festival.

🛏 Sleeping

Ask for the tourist office's hotel brochure, which gives prices for hotels, pensions, hostels and camping grounds. Accommodation is at a premium during festivals.

[TOP CHOICE] **Haus Reichl**   GUESTHOUSE €
(☏826 248; www.privatzimmer.at; Reiterweg 52; s €30-35, d €48-52, tr €66-72; ℗) Expect a heartfelt welcome at this terrific pension, surrounded by meadows and mountains. Nothing is too much trouble for the kindly Reichls – a pick-up from the station, free bicycle hire, sightseeing tips, homemade pastries at breakfast, you name it. Bus 21 frequently trundles into the centre, 2km away.

YOHO Salzburg   HOSTEL €
(☏879 649; www.yoho.at; Paracelsusstrasse 9; dm €19-21, d €50; @🛜) Comfy bunks, free wi-fi, plenty of cheap beer – what more could a backpacker ask for? Except, perhaps, a merry sing-along with the *Sound of Music*

screened at 10.30am daily (yes, *every* day). The friendly crew can arrange tours, adventure sports and bike hire.

Arte Vida
GUESTHOUSE €€
(☑873 185; www.artevida.at; Dreifaltigkeitsgasse 9; s €50-110, d €70-120; 🛜) Arte Vida has the boho-chic feel of a Marrakesh riad, with its lantern-lit salon, communal kitchen and individually designed rooms done out in rich colours and fabrics. Markus arranges yoga sessions in the quiet garden, and outdoor activities.

Haus Wartenberg
GUESTHOUSE €€
(☑848 400; www.hauswartenberg.com; Riedenburgerstrasse 2; s/d €65/95; P@) Set in vine-strewn gardens, this 17th-century chalet guesthouse is a 10-minute stroll from the Altstadt. Country-style rooms done out in chunky pinewood and florals are in keeping with the character of the place.

Hotel & Villa Auersperg
HOTEL €€
(☑889 440; www.auersperg.at; Auerspergstrasse 61; s €109-139, d €145-188, ste €205; P@🛜) This charismatic villa-hotel hybrid fuses late-19th-century flair with contemporary design. Relax by the lily pond in the garden or in the rooftop wellness area with mountain views. Free bike hire is a bonus.

Hotel am Dom
HOTEL €€
(☑842 765; www.hotelamdom.at; Goldgasse 17; s €90-180, d €140-260; ✳@🛜) Antique meets boutique at this Altstadt hotel, where the original vaults and beams of the 800-year-old building contrast with razor-sharp design features. Artworks inspired by the Salzburg Festival grace the strikingly lit rooms.

Hotel Schloss Mönchstein
HISTORIC HOTEL €€€
(☑848 555-0; www.monchstein.at; Mönchsberg Park 26; d €335-445, ste €595-1450; P✳🛜) On a fairytale perch atop Mönchsberg, this 16th-century castle is honeymoon (and second mortgage) material. Rooms are lavishly decorated with Persian rugs and oil paintings. A massage in the spa, a candlelit tower dinner for two, a helicopter ride – just say the word.

Arthotel Blaue Gans
HISTORIC HOTEL €€
(☑842 491-50; www.hotel-blaue-gans-salzburg.at; Getreidegasse 43; s €120-140, d €140-200; ✳🛜) Contemporary design blends harmoniously with the original vaulting and beams of this 650-year-old hotel, with sleek yet comfortable rooms.

Wolf Dietrich
HISTORIC HOTEL €€
(☑871 275; www.salzburg-hotel.at; Wolf-Dietrich-Strasse 7; s/d €130/190; P@✳) Old-world elegance in the rooms, plus an ultramodern spa and pool. Organic produce is served at breakfast.

Hotel Mozart
HISTORIC HOTEL €€
(☑872 274; www.hotel-mozart.at; Franz-Josef-Strasse 27; s/d/tr/q €95/140/160/180; P🛜) An antique-filled lobby gives way to spotless rooms with comfy beds and sizeable bathrooms. Breakfast is worth the extra €10.

Stadtalm
HOSTEL €
(☑841 729; www.diestadtalm.com; dm €19) A recently revamped hostel atop Mönchsberg, where the big draw is the incredible view over Salzburg.

Camping Schloss Aigen
CAMPING GROUND €
(☑622 079; www.campingparadies.at; Weberbartlweg 20; campsites per adult/child/tent €5/3/4.60; ☺May-Sep) A leafy camping ground overlooking Gaisberg mountain, with a playground, minimarket and restaurant. Bus 10 runs into town from the stop 700m away.

✗ Eating

Old-fashioned taverns, world flavours, kitschy Mozart dinners – you'll find the lot in the Altstadt. Sidestep Getreidegasse's crowds and head for right-bank Linzer Gasse and its tributaries, and quieter right-bank backstreets such as those east of Residenzplatz.

If you're on a budget, go for the lunchtime *Tagesmenü* (fixed menu) served at most places. The Altstadt's mazy streets are scattered with delis, supermarkets and sausage stands. Self-caterers can find picnic fixings at the **Grüner Markt** (Universitätsplatz; ☺Mon-Sat).

DON'T MISS

NO TOURIST TRAPP

Did you know that there were 10 (not seven) von Trapp children? Or that Rupert was the eldest (so long Liesl) and the captain a gentle-natured man? For the truth behind the Hollywood legend, stay at **Villa Trapp** (☑63 08 60; www.villa-trapp.com; Traunstrasse 34; d €109-500) in Aigen district, 3km from the Altstadt. Marianne and Christopher have transformed the von Trapp's elegant 19th-century villa into a beautiful guesthouse, brimming with family heirlooms and snapshots. The villa sits in Salzburg's biggest private park.

DON'T MISS

COFFEE BREAK

Get *gemütlich* (comfy) over coffee, cake and people-watching in Salzburg's grandest cafes:

Demel   CAFE
(www.demel.at; Mozartplatz 2; ⊗9am-8pm; 🛜) Demel's 1st-floor balcony has a prime view of Mozartplatz. The must-try here is the *Anna Torte*: a moist chocolate sponge with a splash of orange liqueur, topped with a chocolate-nougat swirl.

Café Bazar   CAFE
(www.cafe-bazar.at; Schwarzstrasse 3; ⊗7.30am-11pm Mon-Sat, 9am-6pm Sat) All chandeliers, polished wood and intelligent conversation. Enjoy breakfast or a cream-filled torte on the terrace overlooking the Salzach River.

Café Tomaselli   CAFE
(www.tomaselli.at, in German; Alter Markt 9; ⊗7am-9pm) Going strong since 1705, this marble and wood-panelled cafe is a former Mozart haunt. It's famous for having Salzburg's flakiest strudels, best *Einspänner* (coffee with whipped cream) and grumpiest waiters.

Alter Fuchs   AUSTRIAN €
(📞882 022; Linzer Gasse 47-49; mains €9-16; ⊗Mon-Sat) This old fox prides itself on serving up old-fashioned Austrian fare, such as schnitzels fried to golden perfection. Foxes clad in bandanas guard the bar in the vaulted interior and there's a courtyard for good-weather dining.

Afro Café   AFRICAN €€
(📞844 888; Bürgerspitalplatz 5; lunch €6.90, mains €10-14; ⊗10am-midnight Mon-Sat) Hot-pink walls, beach-junk art and *big* hair...this afro-chic cafe keeps the good vibes and food coming. Fruity cocktails wash down favourites like grilled chicken with honey-lime glaze.

Riedenburg   GOURMET €€€
(📞830 815; www.riedenburg.at, in German; Neutorstrasse 31; lunch €18, mains €26-35; ⊗Tue-Sat) At this romantic Michelin-starred pick, Richard Brunnauer's creative Austrian signatures, such as venison and guinea fowl crêpes with wild herbs, are expertly matched with top wines.

zum Fidelen Affen   AUSTRIAN €€
(📞877 361; Priesterhausgasse 8; mains €10.50-16.50; ⊗dinner Mon-Sat) At the jovial monkey you'll dine heartily on Austrian classics like goulash and sweet curd dumplings in the vaulted interior or on the pavement terrace. Reservations are recommended.

M32   FUSION €€
(📞841 000; www.m32.at, in German; Mönchsberg 32; mains €14-26; ⊗9am-1am Tue-Sun) Bold colours and a forest of stag antlers reveal architect Matteo Thun's imprint at Museum der Moderne's glass-walled restaurant. The seasonal food and views are fantastic.

Triangel   AUSTRIAN €€
(📞842 229; www.triangel-salzburg.at; Wiener-Philharmoniker-Gasse 7; mains €9-20) Arty bistro near the Festspielhaus, with a market-fresh menu.

Mensa Toskana   INTERNATIONAL €
(Sigmund-Haffner-Gasse 11; lunch €4.20-5.10; ⊗lunch Mon-Fri) Atmospheric university cafe in the Altstadt, with a sunny terrace and decent lunches.

🌿 **Spicy Spices**   INDIAN €
(Wolf-Dietrich-Strasse 1; mains €6.50; 📶) 'Healthy heart, lovely soul' is the mantra of this all-organic, all-vegetarian haunt.

🍷 Drinking

Nobody's pretending Salzburg is rave city, but the days of lights out by 11pm are long gone. You'll find the biggest concentration of bars along both banks of the Salzach and the hippest around Gstättengasse and Anton-Neumayr-Platz.

TOP CHOICE **Augustiner Bräustübl**   BREW PUB
(Augustinergasse 4-6; ⊗3-11pm Mon-Fri, 2.30-11pm Sat & Sun) Who says monks can't enjoy themselves? This hillside complex of beer halls and gardens is not to be missed. The local monks' brew keeps the huge crowd of up to 2800 humming.

Republic   BAR
(Anton-Neumayr-Platz 2; ⊗8am-1am Sun-Thu, 8am-4am Fri & Sat) One of Salzburg's most happening haunts, with regular DJs and free events from tango on Sundays to salsa on Tuesdays.

Humboldt Stub'n   BAR
(Gstättengasse 4-6; ⊗10am-4am) A nail-studded Mozart punk guards this upbeat bar opposite Republic. Try a sickly Mozart cocktail (liqueur, cherry juice, cream and choco-

late). Beers are €2.50 at Wednesday's student night.

☆ Entertainment

Some of the high-brow venues include the **Schlosskonzerte** (☑848 586; www.salzburger -schlosskonzerte.at), in Schloss Mirabell's sublime baroque Marble Hall, and the **Mozarteum** (www.mozarteum.at; Schwarzstrasse 26). Marionettes bring the *Sound of Music* and Mozart's operas magically to life at **Salzburger Marionettentheater** (☑87 24 06; www.marionetten.at; Schwarzstrasse 24; ⊙May-Sep, Christmas, Easter).

Most bands with a modern bent will invariably play at either the **Rockhouse** (www. rockhouse.at, in German; Schallmooser Hauptstrasse 46) or **ARGEkultur** (www.argekultur.at, in German; Josef-Preis-Allee 16); both double as popular bars.

ⓘ Information

Many hotels and bars offer free wi-fi, and there are several cheap internet cafes near the train station. Bankomaten (ATMs) are all over the place; there are also exchange booths at the airport and downtown, but beware of high commission rates.

Hospital (☑44 82; Müllner Hauptstrasse 48) Just north of Mönchsberg.

International Telephone Discount (Kaiserschützenstrasse 8; internet per hour €2; ⊙9am-8pm Mon-Sat, 1-8pm Sun) Near the station. Also offers discount calls.

Police headquarters (☑63 83; Alpenstrasse 90)

Post office Main branch (Residenzplatz 9); station (Südtiroler Platz 1)

STA Travel (www.statravel.at; Rainerstrasse 2) Student and budget travel agency.

Tourist office (☑889 87-330; www.salzburg. info; Mozartplatz 5; ⊙9am-7pm) Has plenty of information about the city and its immediate surrounds; there's a ticket booking agency in the same building. For information on the rest of the province, visit the **Salzburgerland Tourismus** (www.salzburgerland.com) website.

Western Union (⊙8am-8.30pm Mon-Fri, to 2pm Sat, 1-6pm Sun) Changes money at its branch in the station post office.

ⓘ Getting There & Away

Air

Salzburg airport (www.salzburg-airport.com), a 20-minute bus ride from the centre, has regular scheduled flights to destinations all over Austria and Europe. Low-cost flights from the UK are provided by **Ryanair** (www.ryanair.com) and **easyJet** (www.easyjet.com). Other airlines include **British Airways** (www.britishairways. com) and **KLM** (www.klm.com).

Bus

Buses depart from just outside the Hauptbahnhof on Südtiroler Platz, where timetables are displayed. Bus information and tickets are available from the information points on the main concourse.

Hourly buses leave for the Salzkammergut including Bad Ischl (€9.10, 1½ hours), Mondsee (€5.70, 50 minutes), St Wolfgang (€8.40, 1¾ hours) and St Gilgen (€5.70, 50 minutes). For more information on buses in Salzburgerland and the Salzkammergut and an online timetable, see www.svv.at.

Car & Motorcycle

Three motorways converge on Salzburg to form a loop around the city: the A1/E60 from Linz, Vienna and the east; the A8/E52 from Munich and the west; and the A10/E55 from Villach and the south. The quickest way to Tirol is to take the road to Bad Reichenhall in Germany and continue to Lofer (B178) and St Johann in Tirol.

Train

Salzburg's Hauptbahnhof was undergoing extensive renovation at the time of research.

Fast trains leave hourly for Vienna (€47.50, three hours) via Linz (€22, 1¼ hours). The express service to Klagenfurt (€35.50, three hours) goes via Villach. The quickest way to Innsbruck (€37.80, two hours) is by the 'corridor' train through Germany via Kufstein; trains depart at least every two hours. There are trains every hour or so to Munich (€34).

ⓘ Getting Around

TO/FROM THE AIRPORT Salzburg airport (www.salzburg-airport.com) is located 4km west of the city centre. Bus 2 goes there from the Hauptbahnhof (€2.10, 19 minutes). A taxi costs about €15.

BICYCLE Top Bike (www.topbike.at; 2hr/4hr/ day €6/10/15, 20% discount with all train tickets) rents bikes from just outside the train station.

BUS Bus drivers sell singles for €2.10. Other tickets, including day (€5) and week (€12.80) passes, must be bought from the automatic machines at stops or *Tabak* shops.

CAR & MOTORCYCLE The majority of the Old Town is pedestrianised. The nearest central parking area is the Altstadt Garage under the Mönchsberg. Attended car parks cost €1.40 to €2.40 per hour. On streets with automatic ticket machines (blue zones), a three-hour maximum applies (€0.50 for 30 minutes) between 9am and 7pm Monday to Friday and 9am and 4pm Saturday.

Schloss Hellbrunn

A prince-archbishop with a wicked sense of humour, Markus Sittikus built Italianate **Schloss Hellbrunn** (www.hellbrunn.at; Fürstenweg 37; adult/child €9.50/4.50; ⊙9am-5.30pm, to 9pm Jul & Aug) as a 17th-century summer palace and an escape from his Residenz functions.

The ingenious trick fountains and waterpowered figures are the big draw. When the tour guides set them off, expect to get wet! Admission includes entry to the baroque palace. The rest of the sculpture-dotted gardens are free to visit. Look out for the *Sound of Music* pavilion of 'Sixteen Going on Seventeen' fame.

Bus 25 runs to Hellbrunn, 4.5km south of Salzburg, every 20 minutes from Rudolfskai in the Altstadt.

Werfen

⧉06468 / POP 3020

The world's largest accessible ice caves, the soaring limestone turrets of the Tennengebirge mountains and a formidable medieval fortress are but the tip of the superlative iceberg in Werfen. Such salacious natural beauty hasn't escaped Hollywood producers – Werfen stars in WWII action film *Where Eagles Dare* (1968) and makes a cameo appearance in the picnic scene of *The Sound of Music*.

Both the ice caves and fortress can be visited as a day trip from Salzburg if you start early (tour the caves first and be at the fortress by 3pm for the falconry show), otherwise consult the **tourist office** (⧉53 88; www.werfen.at; Markt 24; ⊙9am-noon & 2-5pm Mon-Fri) for accommodation options.

◉ Sights & Activities

Eisriesenwelt　　　　　　　　ICE CAVES
(www.eisriesenwelt.at; adult/child €8.50/4.50, with cable car €19/9.50; ⊙9am-3.30pm May-Oct) Billed as the world's largest accessible ice caves, more than 1000m above Werfen in the Tennengebirge mountains, this glittering ice empire is a once seen, never forgotten experience. The 1¼-hour tour takes you through twinkling passageways and chambers, the carbide lamps picking out other-worldly ice sculptures. Dress for subzero temperatures.

Burg Hohenwerfen　　　　　　　FORTRESS
(adult/child €14/7.50; ⊙9am-5pm Apr-Oct) High on a wooded cliff top, Burg Hohenwerfen has kept watch over the Salzach Valley since 1077, although its current appearance dates from the 16th century. Highlights include far-reaching views over Werfen from the belfry, dungeons containing some pretty nasty torture instruments, and a dramatic falconry show (11am and 3pm). The walk up from the village takes 20 minutes.

❶ Getting There & Around

Werfen can be reached from Salzburg on the A10/E55 motorway or by train (€9.20, 40 minutes). In summer, minibuses (single/return €2.90/5.80) run every 25 minutes between Eisriesenstrasse in Werfen and the car park, a 20-minute walk from the cable car to Eisriesenwelt.

SALZKAMMERGUT

A picture-perfect wonderland of glassy blue lakes and tall craggy peaks, Austria's Lake District is a long-time favourite holiday destination, attracting visitors in droves from Salzburg and beyond.

Whether you're looking for a way to entertain the kids or hoping to commune with nature, the area is big on variety. The peaceful lakes offer limitless opportunities for boating, fishing, swimming or just lazing on the shore. Favourite waterside beauty spots include the picturesque villages of Hallstatt and St Wolfgang, and the Riviera-style port of Gmunden. You can also tour the salt mines that made the region wealthy or plunge into the depths of the fantastic Dachstein caves, where glittering towers of ice are masterfully illuminated in the depths of a mountain.

❶ Getting There & Around

BOAT Passenger boats ply the waters of the Attersee, Traunsee, Mondsee, Hallstätter See and Wolfgangsee.

BUS Regular buses connect the region's towns and villages, though less frequently on weekends. Timetables are displayed at stops, and tickets can be bought from the driver.

CAR & MOTORCYCLE To reach Salzkammergut from Salzburg by car or motorcycle, take the A1 or Hwy 158.

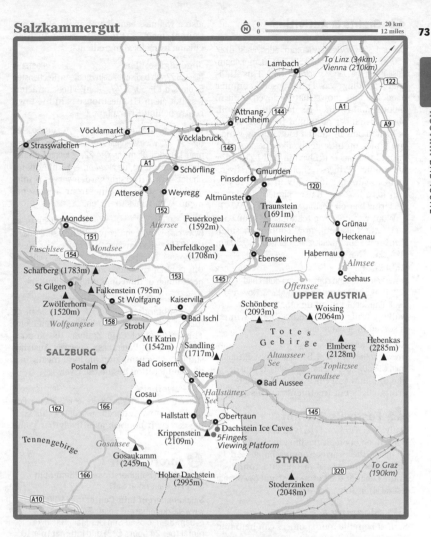

TRAIN The country's major rail routes bypass the heart of Salzkammergut, but regional trains cross through the area from north to south. This route begins at Attnang-Puchheim on the Salzburg–Linz line. The track from here connects to Bad Ischl, Hallstatt and Obertraun in one direction and to Gmunden in another. At the smaller, unattended stations *(unbesetzter Bahnhof)* you'll have to buy tickets from a machine on the platform or else purchase them from staff on the train (no surcharge applies).

After leaving Obertraun, the railway continues eastwards via Bad Aussee before connecting with the main Bischofshofen–Graz line at Stainach-Irdning.

Bad Ischl

📞 06132 / POP 14,050

During the last century of the Habsburg reign, Bad Ischl became the favourite summertime retreat for the imperial family and their entourage. Today the town and many of its dignified buildings still have a stately aura, and a perhaps surprisingly high proportion of the local women still go about their daily business in *Dirndl* (Austria's traditional full pleated skirt). It makes a good base for exploring the entire Salzkammergut region.

◎ Sights & Activities

Kaiservilla PALACE
(Jainzen 38; www.kaiservilla.com; adult/child €12/ 7.50, grounds only €4.50/3.50; ⊙9.30am-4.45pm, closed Thu-Tue Jan-Mar, closed Nov) This Italianate building was Franz Josef's summer residence and shows that he loved huntin', shootin' and fishin' – it's decorated with an obscene number of animal trophies. It can be visited only by guided tour, during which you'll pick up little gems, like the fact that Franz Josef was conceived in Bad Ischl after his mother, Princess Sophie, took a treatment to cure her infertility in 1828. It was also here that the Kaiser signed the letter declaring war on Serbia, which led to WWI.

What was once the teahouse of Franz Josef's wife, Elisabeth, now contains a small **Photomuseum** (adult/child €2/1.50; ⊙9.30am-5pm, closed Nov-Mar).

Cable Car CABLE CAR
(www.katrinseilbahn.com; return adult/child €17.50/11.50, ⊙closed Apr–mid-May & Nov–mid-Dec) The local mountain (1542m) with walking trails and limited skiing in winter is served by a cable car.

Kaiser Therme SPA
(www.eurothermen.co.at; Bahnhofstrasse 1; adult/ child €13.50/9.50; ⊙9am-midnight) If you'd like to follow in Princess Sophie's footprints, check out treatments at this spa.

✯ Festivals & Events

Daily free *Kurkonzerte* (spa concerts) take place in an open-air pavilion in the Kurpark or inside the nearby Congresshaus. Bad Ischl stages the works of operetta composer Franz Lehár at the **Lehár Festival** (www.lehar festival.at) in July and August.

🛏 Sleeping & Eating

Staff at both the tourist offices can help find rooms.

Hotel Garni Sonnhof HOTEL €€
(✆230 78; www.sonnhof.at; Bahnhofstrasse 4; s €65-95, d €90-150; 🅿🛜) Nestled in a leafy glade of maple trees next to the station, this hotel has cosy, traditional decor, a beautiful garden, chickens that deliver breakfast eggs, and a sunny conservatory. There's a sauna and a steam bath on-site.

Goldenes Schiff HOTEL €€
(✆242 41; www.goldenes-schiff.at; Adalbert Stifter-kai 3; s €98-109, d €144-176, apt €192; 🅿@🛜) The best rooms at this comfortable pick have large windows overlooking the river. There's

also a wellness centre and an excellent restaurant (mains €14 to €18) serving Austrian cuisine using local ingredients.

Jugendgästehaus HOSTEL €
(✆265 77; jgh.badischl@oejhv.or.at; Am Rechensteg 5; dm/s/d €16.50/31/47; ⊙🛜@) The characterless but clean HI guesthouse is in the town centre behind Kreuzplatz.

Weinhaus Attwenger AUSTRIAN €€
(✆233 27; www.weinhaus-attwenger.com, in German; Lehárkai 12; mains €14-22; ⊙lunch & dinner, closed Mon, closed Tue Nov-Apr; ⊙) This quaint chalet with a riverside garden serves prime-quality Austrian cuisine from a seasonal menu, with wines to match.

Café Sissy AUSTRIAN €€
(www.cafe-sissy.at, in German; Pfarrgasse 2; mains €11-18.50; ⊙8am-midnight) Pictures of Sissy (Empress Elisabeth) hang on the walls of this popular riverside cafe. You can breakfast here, lunch or dine on a Wiener schnitzel.

🏆 Grand Café & Restaurant Zauner Esplanade AUSTRIAN €€
(Hasner Allee 2; mains €10-18.50; ⊙10am-10pm) This offshoot of Café Zauner, the famous pastry shop at Pfarrgasse 7, serves Austrian staples, some using organic local meats, in a pleasant location beside the river.

K.u.K. Hofbeisl BEISL €
(Wirerstrasse 4; mains €8-20; ⊙8-3.30am) For quality grub at a decent price, try this simple eatery. It doubles as a lively bar come sundown.

ℹ Information

Post office (Bahnhofstrasse; ⊙8am-6pm Mon-Fri, 9am-noon Sat)

Salzkammergut Info-Center (✆240 00-0; www.salzkammergut.co.at; Götzstrasse 12; ⊙9am-8pm, closed Sun Oct-Mar) Has bike rental (per 24 hours €13) and internet (per 10 minutes €1.10).

Tourist office (✆277 57-0; www.badischl.at; Auböckplatz 5; ⊙8am-6pm Mon-Fri, 9am-6pm Sat, 10am-1pm Sun) Has a telephone service (8am to 10pm) for rooms and information.

ℹ Getting There & Around

BUS Buses depart from outside the train station, with hourly buses to Salzburg (€9.10, 1½ hours) via St Gilgen (€4.80, 40 minutes). Buses to St Wolfgang (€3.60, 30 minutes) go via Strobl.

CAR & MOTORCYCLE Most major roads in the Salzkammergut go to or near Bad Ischl; Hwy 158 from Salzburg and the north–south Hwy 145 intersect just north of the town centre.

TRAIN Hourly trains to Hallstatt (€3.60, 25 minutes) go via Steeg/Hallstätter See, at the northern end of the lake, and continue on the eastern side via Hallstatt station to Obertraun (€4.30, 30 minutes). A boat from Hallstatt station (€2.20) takes you to the township. There are also frequent trains to Gmunden (€7.20, 40 minutes) and Salzburg (€21, two hours) via Attnang-Puchheim.

Hallstatt

📞 06134 / POP 840

With pastel-hued homes, swans and towering mountains on either side of a glassy green lake, Hallstatt looks like some kind of greeting card for tranquillity. Boats chug lazily across the water from the train station to the village itself, which clings precariously to a tiny bit of land between mountain and shore. So small is the patch of land occupied by the village that its annual Corpus Christi procession takes place largely in small boats on the lake.

🔘 Sights & Activities

Hallstatt has been classified a Unesco World Heritage site for its natural beauty and for evidence of human settlement dating back 4500 years. Over 2000 graves have been discovered in and around the village, most dating from 1000 to 500 BC.

Salzbergwerk   SALT MINE

(funicular return plus tour adult/child €24/12, tour only €12/6; ⊙9.30am-4.30pm, closed mid-Oct–Apr) The region's major cultural attraction is situated high above Hallstatt on Salzberg (Salt Mountain). In 1734 the fully preserved body of a prehistoric miner was found and today he is known as the 'Man in Salt'. The standard tour revolves around his fate, with visitors travelling down an underground railway and miner's slides (a photo is taken of you while sliding) to an illuminated subterranean salt lake.

The mine can be reached on foot or with the **funicular railway** (one way adult/child €7/3.50).

Beinhaus   CHURCH

(Bone House; Kirchenweg 40; admission €1; ⊙10am-6pm, closed Nov-Apr) Don't miss the macabre yet beautiful Beinhaus behind Hallstatt's parish church. It contains rows of stacked skulls painted with flowery designs and the names of the deceased. The old

---

WORTH A TRIP

OBERTRAUN

At nearby Obertraun you'll find the intriguing **Dachstein Rieseneishöhle** (www.dachsteinwelterbe.at; cable car return plus one cave adult/child €27/15, one cave only adult/child €10.80/6). The caves are millions of years old and extend into the mountain for almost 80km in places. The ice itself is around 500 years old, but is increasing in thickness each year – the 'ice mountain' is 8m high, twice as high now as it was when the caves were first explored in 1910.

From Obertraun it's also possible to catch a cable car to **Krippenstein** (return adult/child €23/14; ⊙closed mid-Oct–Nov & Easter–mid-May), where you'll find the freaky **5Fingers viewing platform**, which protrudes over a sheer cliff face. Not for sufferers of vertigo.

Celtic pagan custom of mass burial has been practised here since 1600 (mainly due to the lack of graveyard space), and the last skull in the collection was added in 1995.

Hallstätter See   LAKE

You can hire boats and kayaks (per hour from €11) on the lake, or scuba dive with the **Tauchclub Dachstein** (📞0676/644 99 89; www.zauner-online.at; 2-3-hr course from €35).

🛏 Sleeping & Eating

Rooms fill quickly in summer, so book ahead, arrive early, or go straight for the tourist office and they'll help you find something, either in Hallstatt or Lahn (the southern part of the village).

Seehotel Grüner Baum   HOTEL **€€**

(📞8263; Marktplatz 104; s €80, d without view €140, d or ste with lake view €170-210; P@🛜) This hotel has its own pontoon and tastefully furnished rooms (most with balconies). Breakfast delivered to your bedside and sparkling lake views make this ideal for romantic sojourns.

**Bräugasthof am
Hallstätter See**   GUESTHOUSE **€€**

(📞8221; www.brauhaus-lobisser.com; Seestrasse 120; s €49-55, d €98, tr €130-135) A central, friendly guesthouse with a lakeside restaurant (mains €14 to €19) serving trout and other local specialities.

Gasthaus Mühle HOSTEL €
(☑8318; www.hallstatturlaub.at, in German; Kirchenweg 36; dm €23; ⊘closed Tue & Nov) This hostel with decent (if basic) dorms is handily situated on the way up to the church.

Balthazar im Rudolfsturm CAFE €
(Rudolfsturm; mains €10-13.50; ⊘9am-6pm, closed Nov–Apr; ⊜) With the most spectacular terrace in the region, Balthazar is situated 855m above Hallstatt. Both the views over the lake and the food are excellent.

ℹ️ Information

Tourist office (☑8208; www.dachstein-salzkammergut.at; Seestrasse 169; ⊘9am-6pm Mon-Fri, to 4pm Sat, to noon Sun, closed Sat & Sun Sep-Jun) Turn left from the ferry to reach the office. It stocks the free leisure map of lakeside towns, and hiking and cycling trails.

ℹ️ Getting There & Away

BOAT The last ferry connection leaves Hallstatt train station at 6.55pm (€2.20, 10 minutes). Ferry excursions do the circuit Hallstatt Lahn via Hallstatt Markt, Obersee, Untersee and Steeg return (€9.50, 90 minutes) three times daily from mid-July to August.

BUS Eight to 10 buses connect Hallstatt (Lahn) town with Obertraun (€1.90, eight minutes) daily.

CAR Access into the village is restricted by electronic gates from early May to late October. Staying overnight in town gives free parking and a pass to open the gates.

TRAIN Hallstatt train station is across the lake. The boat service from there to the village coincides with train arrivals. About a dozen trains daily connect Hallstatt and Bad Ischl (€3.60, 22 minutes) and Hallstatt with Bad Aussee (€3.60, 15 minutes).

Wolfgangsee

Wolfgangsee is a hugely popular place to spend the summer swimming, boating, walking or simply lazing by its soothing waters. Its two main resorts are St Wolfgang and St Gilgen, the first of which takes first prize in the beauty stakes.

Coming from Salzburg, the first town you come across is **St Gilgen**. It's a fine point from which to explore the surrounding region, and its **tourist office** (☑2348; www.wolfgangsee.at; Mondsee Bundesstrasse 1a; ⊘9am-8pm Mon-Fri, to 6pm Sat, 10am-5pm Sun) can help with accommodation and activities.

St Wolfgang, towards the southern end of Wolfgangsee, is squeezed between the

northern shoreline of the lake and the towering peak of Schafberg (1783m). Its **tourist office** (☑8003; www.wolfgangsee.at; Au 140; ⊘9am-8pm Mon-Fri, to 6pm Sat, 10am-5pm Sun) has plenty of information for travellers.

In the heart of the village you'll find the 14th-century **Pilgrimage Church** (donation €1; ⊘9am-6pm), a highly ornate example that still attracts pilgrims. Reaching the top of **Scharfberg** is an easy exercise – from May to October, a cogwheel railway climbs to its summit in 40 minutes (one way/return €19.60/28.60). Otherwise it's a three- to four-hour walk.

Both St Wolfgang and St Gilgen have numerous pensions, starting from about €25 per person; the local tourist offices have details.

On the lakefront, 1km east of St Wolfgang, **Camping Appesbach** (☑2206; www.appesbach.at; Au 99; campsite per adult/child/tent €7/4/7; ⊘closed Oct-Easter; P🚗) is a favourite with Austrian holidaymakers. A plusher option with lake views, a wellness area and two pools is **Im Weissen Rössl** (☑2306-0; www.weissesroessl.at; Im Stöckl 74; s €130-160, d €190-280; P@🛜🏊) the setting for Ralph Benatzky's operetta *The White Horse*.

A ferry operates May to October between Strobl and St Gilgen (one way €8.80, 75 minutes), stopping at points en route. Services are most frequent from June to early September. Boats run from St Wolfgang to St Gilgen almost hourly during the day (one way €6.50, 50 minutes); the free *Eintauchen & Aufsteigen* timetable from local tourist offices gives exact times.

A Postbus service from St Wolfgang via Strobl to St Gilgen (€3.90, 50 minutes) is frequent out of season, but tails off somewhat in summer when the ships run. For Salzburg (€6.40, 1¾ hours) you need to connect in St Gilgen or Strobl (€2.10, 12 minutes).

Northern Salzkammergut

Mondsee is popular for two reasons – its close proximity to Salzburg (only 30km) and its warm water. The main village on the lake, also called Mondsee, is home to an attractive 15th-century church that was used in the wedding scene of *The Sound of Music* and a small and helpful **tourist office** (☑2270; www.mondsee.at; Dr Franz Müller Strasse 3; ⊘8am-6pm Mon-Fri, 9am-6pm Sat & Sun, closed Sat & Sun Oct-May).

Lying to the east of Mondsee is **Attersee**, Salzkammergut's largest lake and a favourite with sailors. East again from Attersee you'll find **Traunsee** and its three main resorts: Gmunden, Traunkirchen and Ebensee. **Gmunden** is famous for its twin castles, linked by a causeway on the lake, and its green and white ceramics. Contact the local **tourist office** (📞643 05; www.traunsee.at; Toscanapark 1; ⊗8am-8pm Mon-Fri, 10am-7pm Sat & Sun) for information on accommodation and activities on and around the lake.

Buses run every hour to Mondsee from Salzburg (€5.70, 55 minutes). Gmunden is connected to Salzburg by train (€15.70, 1¼ hours), via Attnang-Puchheim.

TIROL

With converging mountain ranges behind lofty pastures and tranquil meadows, Tirol (also Tyrol) captures a quintessential Alpine panoramic view. Occupying a central position is Innsbruck, the region's jewel, while in the northeast and southwest are superb ski resorts. In the southeast, separated somewhat from the main state since part of South Tirol was ceded to Italy at the end of WWI, lies the protected natural landscape of the Hohe Tauern National Park, an Alpine wonderland of 3000m peaks, including the country's highest, the Grossglockner (3798m).

Innsbruck

📞0512 / POP 118,000

Tirol's capital is a sight to behold. The mountains are so close that within 25 minutes it's possible to travel from the heart of the city to over 2000m above sea level. Summer and winter outdoor activities abound, and it's understandable why some visitors only take a peek at Innsbruck proper before heading for the hills. But to do so is a shame, for Innsbruck has its own share of gems, including an authentic medieval Altstadt (Old Town), inventive architecture and vibrant student-driven nightlife.

⊙ Sights

Innsbruck's atmospheric, medieval Altstadt is ideal for a lazy stroll. Many of the sights listed below close an hour or two earlier in winter.

TOP CHOICE **Goldenes Dachl & Museum**   MUSEUM
(Golden Roof; Herzog-Friedrich-Strasse 15; adult/child €4/2; ⊗10am-5pm, closed Mon Oct-

ⓘ **CITY SAVERS**   **77**

The **Innsbruck Card** gives one visit to Innsbruck's main sights and attractions, a return journey on all cable cars and unlimited use of public transport including the Sightseer bus, which makes getting to some of the more remote sights easier. It's available at the tourist office and costs €29/34/39 for 24/48/72 hours (half-price for children).

Stay overnight in Innsbruck and you'll receive a **Club Innsbruck Card**, giving discounts on transport and activities, and allows you to join the tourist office's free guided hikes in summer.

Apr) Innsbruck's golden wonder is this Gothic oriel, built for Emperor Maximilian I and glittering with 2657 fire-gilt copper tiles. An audioguide whizzes you through the history in the museum; look for the grotesque tournament helmets designed to resemble the slit-eyed Turks of the rival Ottoman Empire.

Hofkirche   CHURCH
(www.tiroler-landesmuseum.at; Universitätstrasse; combined Volkskunstmuseum ticket adult/child €8/4; ⊗10am-6pm Mon-Sat, 12.30am-6pm Sun) The 16th-century Hofkirche is one of Europe's finest royal court churches. Top billing goes to the empty **sarcophagus** of Emperor Maximilian I (1459–1519), a masterpiece of German Renaissance sculpture, guarded by 28 giant bronze figures including Dürer's legendary King Arthur. You're now forbidden to touch the statues, but numerous inquisitive hands have already polished parts of the dull bronze, including Kaiser Rudolf's codpiece!

Volkskunstmuseum   MUSEUM
(Folk Art Museum; www.tiroler-landesmuseum.at; Universitätstrasse; combined Hofkirche ticket adult/child €8/4; ⊗10am-6pm Mon-Sat, 12.30am-6pm Sun) Next door to the Hofkirche, the Volkskunstmuseum houses Tyrolean folk art from handcarved sleighs and Christmas cribs to carnival masks and cow bells.

Hofburg   PALACE
(Imperial Palace; www.hofburg-innsbruck.at; Rennweg 1; adult/child €8/free; ⊗9am-5pm) Empress Maria Theresia gave this Habsburg palace a total baroque makeover in the 16th century. The highlight of the state apartments is the Riesensaal (Giant's Hall), lavishly adorned with frescos and paintings of

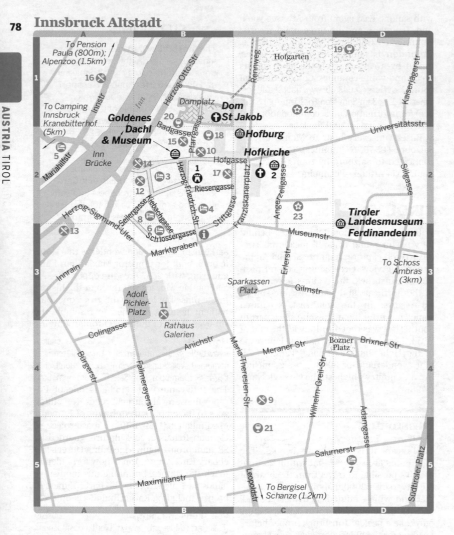

Maria Theresia and her 16 children, including Marie Antoinette.

Tucked behind the palace is the **Hofgarten** (admission free; ⊙daylight hr), an attractive garden for a botanical stroll.

Bergisel
SKI JUMP

(www.bergisel.info; adult/child €8.50/4; ⊙10am-6pm) Rising above Innsbruck like a celestial staircase, this glass-and-steel ski jump was designed by much-lauded Iraqi architect Zaha Hadid. From May to July, fans pile in to see athletes train, while preparations step up a gear in January for the World Cup Four Hills Tournament.

It's 455 steps or a two-minute funicular ride to the 50m-high **viewing platform**. Here, the panorama of the Nordkette range, Inn Valley and Innsbruck is breathtaking, though the cemetery at the bottom has undoubtedly made a few ski jumping pros quiver in their boots.

Bus 4143 and line TS run from the Hauptbahnhof to Bergisel.

Tiroler Landesmuseum
Ferdinandeum
ART MUSEUM

(www.tiroler-landesmuseum.at; Museumstrasse 15; adult/child €8/4; ⊙10am-6pm Tue-Sun) This treasure-trove of Tyrolean history and art contains the original reliefs used to design the Goldenes Dachl. In the gallery you'll find old master paintings, Gothic altarpieces, a handful of Kokoschka and Klimt originals, and Viennese actionism works with shock factor.

Schloss Ambras   CASTLE
(www.khm.at/ambras; Schlossstrasse 20; adult/child €10/free; ☺10am-5pm) Archduke Ferdinand II transformed Schloss Ambras from a fortress into a Renaissance palace in 1564. A visit takes in the ever-so-grand banquet hall, shining armour (look out for the 2.60m suit created for giant Bartlmä Bon) and room upon room of Habsburg portraits, with Titian, Velázquez and van Dyck originals. It's free to stroll or picnic in the expansive **gardens** (☺6am-8pm).

Schloss Ambras is 4.5km southeast of the centre. Take bus 4134 from the Hauptbahnhof to the castle for discounted entry and a free return journey.

FREE **Dom St Jakob**   CHURCH
(St James' Cathedral; Domplatz; ☺7.30am-9.30pm Mon-Sat, 8am-7.30pm Sun) Innsbruck's 18th-century cathedral is a feast of over-the-top baroque. The Madonna above the high altar is by the German Renaissance painter Lukas Cranach the Elder.

Alpenzoo   ZOO
(Weiherburggasse 37; adult/child €8/4; ☺9am-6pm) Home to Alpine wildlife like golden eagles, chamois and ibex. To get there, walk up the hill from Rennweg or take bus W from Marktplatz.

Stadtturm   TOWER
(city tower; Herzog-Friedrich-Strasse 21; adult/child €3/1.50; ☺10am-8pm) Climb this tower's 148 steps for 360-degree views of the city's rooftops, spires and surrounding mountains.

🏃 Activities

Anyone who loves playing in the great outdoors will be itching to head up into the Alps in Innsbruck.

Nordketten Bahnen   FUNICULAR
(www.nordkette.com; ☺8.30am-5.30pm) Zaha Hadid's space-age funicular runs every 15 minutes, whizzing you from the Congress Centre to the slopes in just 25 minutes. Tickets cost €14.10/23.40 one way/return to Seegrube and €15.60/26 to Hafelekar. Both afford superb views of Innsbruck and the Alps, and appeal to walkers and mountain bikers.

Guided Hikes   WALKING
(Innsbruck Information; ☏535 60; www.innsbruck.info; Burggraben 3; ☺9am-6pm) From late May

AROUND INNSBRUCK

Just 9km east of Innsbruck is the town of Hall in Tirol. The labyrinth of pretty cobbled streets at its medieval heart pays testament to the massive wealth it accumulated from silver mines over the centuries. You can learn more about this legacy at **Burg Hasegg** (Burg Hasegg 6; adult/child €8/6; ☉10am-5pm Tue-Sun), a 14th-century castle that had a 300-year career as a mint for silver *Thalers* (coins, the root of the modern word 'dollar').

Another 9km east along the valley in Wattens is **Swarovski Kristallwelten** (Swarovski Crystal Worlds; http://kristallwelten.swarovski.com; Kristallweltenstrasse 1; adult/child €9.50/ free; ☉9am-6.30pm), one of Austria's most-visited attractions. A crystal winterscape by Alexander McQueen, a kaleidoscopic crystal dome and a striking Terence Conran–designed shop are part of the fabulously glittering experience.

From Innsbruck, trains run frequently to Hall in Tirol (€2, eight minutes) and Fritzens-Wattens (€3.60, 16 minutes), 3km north of Swarovski Kristallwelten.

to October, Innsbruck Information arranges daily guided hikes from sunrise walks to lantern-lit strolls, free to those with a Club Innsbruck Card (see the boxed text, p77). Pop into the tourist office to register and browse the program.

Inntour ADVENTURE SPORTS
(www.inntour.com; Leopoldstrasse 4; ☉9am-6.30pm Mon-Fri, to 5pm Sat) A one-stop adrenalin shop, taking you canyoning (€75), tandem paragliding (€95), white-water rafting (€45) and bungee jumping from the 192m Europabrücke (Europe Bridge).

Olympia SkiWorld Innsbruck SKIING
(www.ski-innsbruck.at) Innsbruck is the gateway to this massive ski arena, covering nine surrounding resorts and 282km of slopes to test all abilities. The most central place to pound powder is the **Nordpark**, accessed by **cable car** (☉8am-7pm) running every 15 minutes. A three-/seven-day Innsbruck Glacier Ski Pass covering all areas costs €105/200; ski buses are free to anyone with an Innsbruck Card.

🛏 Sleeping

The tourist office has lists of private rooms costing between €20 and €40 per person.

TOP CHOICE Nepomuks HOSTEL €
(☏584 118; www.nepomuks.at; Kiebachgasse 16; dm/d €22/54; ☎) Could this be backpacker heaven? Nepomuks sure comes close, with its Altstadt location, well-stocked kitchen and high-ceilinged dorms with homely touches like CD players. The delicious breakfast in attached Café Munding, with homemade pastries, jam and fresh-roasted coffee, gets your day off to a grand start.

Hotel Weisses Kreuz HISTORIC HOTEL €€
(☏594 79; www.weisseskreuz.at; Herzog-Friedrich-Strasse 31; s €36-72, d €100-132; P@☎) Beneath the Altstadt's arcades, this atmospheric 500-year-old hotel has played host to famous guests including a 13-year-old Mozart. It remains comfortable to this day.

Pension Paula GUESTHOUSE €
(☏292 262; www.pensionpaula.at; Weiherburggasse 15; s/d €39/62; P) Nestled in the hills above Innsbruck and with great city views, this family-run pension has super-clean, homely rooms (most with balcony). It's 1km north of the Altstadt, near the Alpenzoo.

Romantik Hotel Schwarzer Adler HOTEL €€€
(☏587 109; www.deradler.com; Kaiserjägerstrasse 2; s €110-159, d €150-211, ste €295-480; P@☎) This boutique hotel's fabulously over-the-top suites glitter with Swarovski crystals; one features the solid marble bed Gianni Versace once slept in. Asian-inspired treatments pamper in the spa. It's about a five-minute walk west of the Hofburg along Universitätsstrasse.

Goldener Adler HISTORIC HOTEL €€
(☏571 111; www.goldeneradler.com; Herzog-Friedrich-Strasse 6; s/d €92/135; P✳☎) Since opening in 1390, the grand Goldener Adler has welcomed kings, queens and Salzburg's two biggest exports: Mozart and Mrs von Trapp. Rooms are elegant with gold drapes and squeaky-clean marble bathrooms.

Weisses Rössl GUESTHOUSE €€
(☏583 057; www.roessl.at; Kiebachgasse 8; s/d/ tr/q €80/120/135/160; P❀@☎) An antique rocking horse greets you at this 600-year-old guesthouse, with vaulted interiors and bright, spacious rooms. Host Mr Plank is a keen

hunter and the restaurant (mains €7 to €18) has a meaty menu.

Pension Stoi GUESTHOUSE €
(☑585 434; www.pensionstoi.at, in German; Salurnerstrasse 7; s/d/tr/q €44/69/85/98; P🖥) This central, family-run guesthouse occupies a rambling art nouveau villa. You'll need to schlep your bags (there's no lift) and buy your own breakfast.

Mondschein HOTEL €€
(☑227 84; www.mondschein.at; Mariahilfstrasse 6; s €87-105, d €105-180; P❄🖥) Like its name, the moon lights the way to this riverside hotel, set in a 15th-century fisherman's house. The cheery rooms sport Swarovski crystal-studded bathrooms.

Camping Innsbruck Kranebitterhof
CAMPING GROUND €
(Herzog-Friedrich-Strasse 21; adult/child €3/1.50; ⊙10am-8pm) Modern camping ground west of town, with Alpine views, a pizzeria and playground. Bus line O stops nearby or you can cycle along the River Inn.

✕ Eating

Bistros, cafes and traditional taverns line Altstadt lanes like Herzog-Friedrich-Strasse, Hofgasse and Kiebachgasse; most have alfresco seating in summer. Maria-Theresien-Strasse, the Rathaus Galerien mall and Universitätsstrasse are other good picks; the latter attracts students. Self-caterers will find **supermarkets** like Hofer and Billa on Museumstrasse.

TOP CHOICE **Chez Nico** VEGETARIAN €€
(☑586 398; www.chez-nico.at; Maria-Theresien-Strasse 49; lunch €12.50, 7-course menu €45; ⊙lunch & dinner Tue-Fri, dinner Sat; ✎) Take a creative Parisian chef with an artistic eye and a passion for herbs, et voilà, you get Chez Nico. Nicolas Curtil (Nico) cooks seasonal vegetarian delights like chanterelle-apricot goulash and porcini-sage ravioli at this intimate bistro.

Lichtblick FUSION €€€
(☑566 550; Rathaus Galerien; www.restaurant-lichtblick.at; lunch €8-13, set menus €35-46; ⊙10am-1am Mon-Sat) On the 7th floor of the Rathaus Galerien, this glass-walled restaurant is a glamorous setting for fusion cuisine and sweeping Innsbruck views.

Gasthaus Goldenes Dachl TYROLEAN €€
(☑589 370; www.gasthaus-goldenesdachl.at; Hofgasse 1; mains €10-18) Portions are generous

PICNIC GOODIES

s'Speckladele MEAT €
(Stiftgasse 4; ⊙9am-1pm & 2-6pm Tue-Fri, 9am-3pm Sat) This hole-in-the-wall shop has been doing a brisk trade in regional sausages, hams and speck made from 'happy pigs' for the past 60 years. Mini *Teufel* sausages with a chilli kick are the must-try.

s'Culinarium WINE €
(Pfarrgasse 1; ⊙10am-6pm Mon-Fri, 3-6pm Sat) Herby Signor will help you pick an excellent bottle of Austrian wine at his shop-cum-bar.

Markthalle MARKET €
(www.markthalle-innsbruck.at; Innrain; ⊙7am-6.30pm Mon-Fri, to 1pm Sat) Freshly baked bread, Tyrolean cheese, organic fruit, smoked ham and salami – it's all under one roof at this riverside covered market.

and the menu typically Tyrolean at this tavern, a cosy spot to try *Gröstl* (potatoes and bacon topped with a fried egg).

Ottoburg AUSTRIAN €€
(☑584 338; www.ottoburg.at; Herzog-Friedrich-Strasse 1; lunch €6-9, mains €17-26; ⊙Tue-Sun; 😊) This 12th-century castle hides a warren of wood-panelled *Stuben* (parlours). Dig into tournedos of venison, *Topfenknödel* (cottage cheese dumplings) and other hearty fare.

Cafe Munding CAFE €
(☑584 118; Kiebachgasse 16; cake €2-4; ⊙8am-8pm) Divine cakes, pastries and home-roasted coffee.

Mamma Mia PIZZERIA €
(☑562 902; Kiebachgasse 2; mains €5-8) No-frills Italian bistro with a great buzz, huge pizzas and a shady terrace.

Shere Punjab INDIAN €€
(☑282 755; www.sherepunjab.eu; Innstrasse 19; mains €9-12) Authentic Indian. Word has it even Bollywood stars come here for flavoursome biryanis and kormas.

🍷 Drinking

Besides a glut of bars in the Altstadt, a string of bars huddle under the railway arches on Ingenieur-Etzel-Strasse, otherwise known as the Viaduktbögen.

Moustache
BAR

(www.cafe-moustache.at, in German; Herzog-Otto-Strasse 8; ⊘11am-2am Tue-Sun) You too can try your hand at playing Spot-the-Moustache (Einstein, Charlie Chaplin and others), the preferred pastime at this retro newcomer. It has a terrace overlooking pretty Domplatz, as well as Club Aftershave in the basement.

Hofgarten Café
BAR

(Rennweg 6a; ⊘11am-2am Tue-Thu, to 4am Fri-Sun) DJs spin at this tree-shaded beer garden and star-studded pavilion. The happening events line-up skips from summer festivals to weekend house parties.

360°
BAR

(Rathaus Galerien; ⊘10am-1am Mon-Sat) There's no better place to see Innsbruck start to twinkle. Grab a cushion and drink in 360-degree views of the city and Alps from the balcony skirting the circular bar.

Theresienbräu
PUB

(Maria-Theresien-Strasse 53; ⊘10am-1am Mon-Wed, to 2am Thu-Sat, to midnight Sun) A lively microbrewery with a big beer garden for quaffing a cold one.

Elferhaus
PUB

(Herzog-Friedrich-Strasse 11; ⊘10am-2am) Nurse a beer beside gothic gargoyles at the bar or take a church-like pew to hear live rock bands play.

☆ Entertainment

For more entertainment options, pick up a copy of *Innsider*, found in cafes across town, or visit www.innsider.at (in German).

Tiroler Landestheater
THEATRE

(Maria-Theresien-Strasse 53; ⊘10am-1am Mon-Wed, to 2am Thu-Sat, to midnight Sun) This neoclassical theatre is the city's main stage for opera, dance and drama.

Weekender Club
CLUB

(www.weekenderclub.net, in German; Tschamlerstrasse 3; ⊘9pm-4am Mon, Fri & Sat) Happening warehouse club, with top DJs and concerts. It's a 10-minute walk south of Maria-Theresien-Strasse along Leopoldstrasse.

Treibhaus
CULTURAL CENTRE

(www.treibhaus.at, in German; Angerzellgasse 8; ⊘10am-1am) Young Innsbruckers flock to this cultural complex to enjoy the big garden terrace, the chilled atmosphere and regular DJs. There's free live music on Friday evenings.

ⓘ Information

Innsbruck Information (✆535 60; www.innsbruck.info; Burggraben 3; ⊘9am-6pm) Main tourist office with truckloads of info on the city and surrounds, including skiing and walking. Sells ski passes, public-transport tickets and city maps (€1); will book accommodation (€3 commission) and has an attached ticketing service.

International Telephone Discount (Südtirolerplatz 1; internet access per hour €2.50; ⊘9am-9pm Mon-Sat, 10am-9pm Sun) Cheap phone calls as well.

Landeskrankenhaus (✆50 40; Anichstrasse 35) The *Universitätklinik* (University Clinic) at the city's main hospital has emergency services.

Main post office (Maximilianstrasse 2)

ⓘ Getting There & Away

AIR Innsbruck Airport (www.innsbruck-airport.com), 4km to the west of the city centre, caters to national and international flights, handled mostly by Austrian Airlines, BA, easyJet and Welcome Air.

CAR & MOTORCYCLE The A12 and the parallel Hwy 171 are the main roads heading west and east. The B177, to the west of Innsbruck, continues north to Munich (Germany). The A13 is a toll road (€8) running south through the Brenner Pass to Italy and crossing the 192m Europabrücke, spanning the Sill River. Toll-free Hwy 182 follows the same route, passing under the bridge.

TRAIN Fast trains depart every two hours for Bregenz (€31.30, 2¾ hours), Salzburg (€37.80, two hours), Kitzbühel (€17.60, 1¾ hours) and Munich (€37, two hours). Six daily trains head for Lienz (€31.20, three to five hours); some pass through Italy while others take the long way round via Salzburgerland.

ⓘ Getting Around

TO/FROM THE AIRPORT The airport is 4km west of the centre and served by bus F. Buses depart every 15 or 20 minutes from Maria-Theresien-Strasse (€1.80); taxis charge about €8 to €10 for the same trip.

CAR & BICYCLE Street parking is very limited in the city centre. Parking garages (eg under the Altstadt) cost around €17 per day. **Inntour** (Leopoldstrasse 4; ⊘9am-6.30pm Mon-Fri, 9am-5pm Sat) rents city, mountain, freeride and children's bikes for €19/24/35/12 per day respectively.

PUBLIC TRANSPORT Single tickets on buses and trams cost €1.80 (from the driver; valid upon issue). A 24-hour ticket is €4.10.

Mayrhofen

📞 05285 / POP 3850

Tirol is ribbed by beautiful valleys, but the Zillertal is among the best, its soaring peaks begging outdoor escapades. A central place to base yourself is Mayrhofen, a mecca to skiers and après-skiers in winter, and mountain bikers, hikers and *Lederhosen*-clad *Volksmusik* (folk music) fans in summer.

Snow-sure Mayrhofen has varied skiing on 166km of slopes, one of Europe's best terrain parks for snowboarders and the infamous Harakiri, Austria's steepest piste with a 78% gradient. A ski pass, valid for all cable cars and lifts, costs €41.50 for one day.

The ultramodern **tourist office** (📞676 00; www.mayrhofen.at; Europahaus; ⏱8am-6pm Mon-Fri, 9am-6pm Sat, 9am-noon Sun) should be your first port of call for free *Info von A-Z* booklets in English.

To work your taste buds instead of your legs, pay a visit to **Sennerei Zillertal** (www.sennerei-zillertal.at; Hollenzen 116; admission with/without tasting €11.20/5.80; ⏱10am-3pm, closed Nov–mid-Dec), a grass-roots dairy. See how local cheeses are made on the production facility tour and then enjoy the chance to taste them.

DON'T MISS

SUMMER IN THE ZILLERTAL

The Zillertal is one of Austria's greatest outdoor playgrounds. Come summer the valley buzzes with cyclists, with 800km of well-marked trails reaching from easygoing valley jaunts to gruelling mountain passes. Bicycles are available for hire at train stations throughout the Zillertal for €8/12 per half-/full day; www.zillertal.at has maps, route descriptions and GPS downloads.

Hikers head for the pristine Alpine landscapes of **Naturpark Zillertaler Alpen** (www.naturpark-zillertal. at, in German). From May to October, the nature reserve runs guided walks, most costing around €5, from llama trekking to sunrise photo excursions. For adrenalin-fuelled pursuits like rock climbing, rafting and paragliding, try **Action Club Zillertal** (📞629 77; www.actionclub-zillertal.com; Hauptstrasse 458; ⏱9am-noon & 3-6pm) in Mayrhofen.

Pick up a handy accommodation booklet at the tourist office. Right in the centre, 500-year-old **Hotel Kramerwirt** (📞67 00; www.kramerwirt.at; Am Marienbrunnen 346; s/d €89/154, mains €8-21; P🐾) has spacious rooms, a whirlpool for relaxing moments and a traditional restaurant.

To gorge on *Schlutzkropf'n* (fresh pasta filled with cheese) and the like in the cosiest of surrounds, head to woodsy chalet **Wirtshaus zum Griena** (📞67 67; Dorfhaus 768; mains €7-15). Or assemble your own meaty snack at **Metzgerei Kröll** (Scheulingstrasse 382; snacks €3-8; ⏱7.30am-12.30pm & 2.30-6pm Mon-Fri, 7am-noon Sat), famous for its aromatic *Schlegeis-Speck* ham cured at 1800m. Pizza and pasta dominate the menu at **Mamma Mia** (📞67 68; Einfahrt Mitte 432; mains €7-9; ⏱11am-midnight).

Trains run regularly to Jenbach (55 minutes, €6.30), where they connect with services to Innsbruck (20 minutes; €7.20).

Kitzbühel

📞 05356 / POP 8450

Kitzbühel began life in the 16th century as a silver- and copper-mining town, and today preserves a charming medieval centre despite its other persona – as a fashionable and prosperous winter resort. It's renowned for the white-knuckled Hahnenkamm downhill ski race in January and the excellence of its slopes.

🏃 Activities

There's an Alpine **flower garden** (free) on Kitzbüheler Horn (note there's a toll road for drivers). The forest-fringed Schwarzsee, 3km to the northwest, is a fine location for summer **swimming**.

Skiing   SKIING

In winter there's first-rate intermediate skiing and freeriding on Kitzbüheler Horn to the north and Hahnenkamm to the south of town. A one-day ski pass costs €41.50, though some pensions and hotels offer reductions before mid-December or after mid-March.

Hiking   HIKING

Dozens of summer hiking trails thread through the Kitzbühel Alps; the tourist office gives walking maps and runs free guided hikes for guests staying in town. The Flex-Ticket covering all cable cars costs €33.50 (€42.50 with bus) for three out of seven days.

🛏 Sleeping & Eating

The tourist office can help with accommodation, but it's best to book well ahead. Rates leap up to 50% in the high winter season.

For self-caterers, there's a **Spar supermarket** (Bichlstrasse 22) and **Metzgerei Huber** (Bichlstrasse 14; snacks €3.50-7; Mon-Fri, 8am-12.30pm Sat) for carnivorous snacks.

Villa Licht   HOTEL €€
(📞622 93; www.villa-licht.at; Franz-Reich-Strasse 8; s/d €85/150; P 🛜 🏊) Pretty gardens, warm-hued rooms with pine trappings, mountain views – this charming Tyrolean chalet has the lot. Kids love the tree house and outdoor pool.

Snowbunny's Hostel   HOSTEL €
(📞067-6794 0233; www.snowbunnys.co.uk; Bichlstrasse 30; dm/d €25/60; @🛜) Friendly, laid-back hostel, a bunny-hop from the slopes. Dorms are fine, if a tad dark; breakfast is DIY-style in the kitchen. There's a TV lounge, ski storage room and a shop for backpacker staples (Vegemite, Jägermeister etc).

Pension Kometer   PENSION €€
(📞622 89; Gerbergasse 7; www.pension-kometer.com; s/d €57/94; P) Make yourself at home in the bright, sparklingly clean rooms at this family-run guesthouse. There's a relaxed lounge with games and DVDs. Breakfast is a treat with fresh breads, fruit and eggs.

Hosteria   ITALIAN €€
(📞753 02; Alf Petzoldweg 2; mains €8-16) Authentic antipasti and wood-fired pizzas are matched with fine wines and genuine smiles at this stylish little Italian.

Lois Stern   ASIAN €€
(📞748 82; www.loisstern.com, in German; Josef-Pirchl-Strasse 3; mains €17-25; ⏰Tue-Sat) Lois works his wok in the show kitchen of this intimate bistro. On the menu: Asian fusion cuisine from fiery tom-yam soup to stir-fried gambas.

ℹ Information

The **tourist office** (📞666 60; www.kitzbuehel.com; Hinterstadt 18; ⏰8.30am-6pm Mon-Wed, to 7.30pm Thu-Fri, 9am-6pm Sat, 10am-noon & 4-6pm Sun, closed Sun btwn seasons) has loads of info in English and a 24-hour accommodation board.

ℹ Getting There & Away

BUS It's quicker and cheaper to get from Kitzbühel to Lienz by bus (€13.80, two hours, twice daily) than by train.

CAR & MOTORCYCLE Kitzbühel is on the B170, 30km east of Wörgl and the A12/E45 motorway. Heading south to Lienz, you pass through some marvellous scenery. Hwy 108 (Felber Tauern Tunnel) and Hwy 107 (Grossglockner Rd; closed in winter) both have toll sections.

TRAIN The main train station is 1km north of central Vorderstadt. Trains run frequently from Kitzbühel to Innsbruck (€17.60, 1½ hours) and Salzburg (€25.60, 2½ hours). For Kufstein (€9.20, one hour), change at Wörgl.

Lienz

📞04852 / POP 11,950

The Dolomites rise like an amphitheatre around Lienz, straddling the Isel and Drau Rivers, and just 40km north of Italy. Those same arresting river and mountain views welcomed the Romans, who settled here some 2000 years ago. Lienz is also a stop-over for skiers and hikers passing through or on the way to the Hohe Tauern National Park.

⦿ Sights & Activities

Schloss Bruck   FORTRESS
(Schlossberg 1; adult/child €7.50/2.50; ⏰10am-6pm mid-May–late Oct) Lienz' biggest crowd-puller is its medieval fortress. The museum displays everything from Tyrolean costumes to emotive paintings by famous local son Albin Egger-Lienz.

Stadtpfarrkirche St Andrä   CHURCH
(Pfarrgasse 4; ⏰daylight hr) More of Albin Egger-Lienz' sombre works can be seen at the Gothic St Andrew's Church.

Aguntum   ANCIENT SITE
(www.aguntum.info; Stribach 97; adult/child €5/3; ⏰9.30am-6pm, closed Nov–mid-Apr) For an insight into Lienz' Roman past, visit the Aguntum archaeological site.

Skiing   SKIING
A €36 day pass covers skiing on the nearby **Zettersfeld** and **Hochstein** peaks. However, the area is more renowned for its 100km of cross-country trails; the town fills up for the annual **Dolomitenlauf** cross-country skiing race in mid-January.

Dolomiten Lamatrekking   LLAMA TREKKING
(📞680 87; www.dolomitenlama.at, in German) The Dolomites make for highly scenic hiking, with cable cars rising to Hochstein (return €13) and Zettersfeld (€10). From this outfitter you can enlist a gentle-natured llama to accompany you.

🛏 Sleeping & Eating

The tourist office can point you in the direction of good-value guesthouses and camping grounds.

Hotel Haidenhof HOTEL €€
(📞624 40; www.haidenhof.at, in German; Grafendorferstrasse 12; s/d €86/142; 🅿🛜) High above Lienz, this country retreat has a dress-circle view of the Dolomites. The spacious rooms and roof terrace maximise those views. Home-grown produce features in the restaurant (mains €7 to €20).

Romantik Hotel Traube HOTEL €€
(📞644 44; www.hoteltraube.at; Hauptplatz 14; s €68, d €128-152; 🅿@🏊) Right on the main square, Traube races you back to the Biedermeier era with its high ceilings and antique-meets-boutique rooms. The 6th-floor pool affords views over Lienz to the Dolomites.

Kirchenwirt AUSTRIAN €€
(📞625 00; Pfarrgasse 7; mains €8.50-16; ⏰9am-1am) Up on a hill opposite Stadtpfarrkirche St Andrä, this is Lienz' most atmospheric restaurant. Dine under the vaults or on the streamside terrace on local dishes like East Tyrolean milk-fed lamb.

ℹ Information

The **tourist office** (📞050-212 400; www.stadt-lienz.at; Europaplatz 1; ⏰8am-6pm Mon-Fri, 9am-noon & 5-7pm Sat) will find rooms free of charge, or you can use the hotel board (free telephone) outside. Free internet access is available at the local **library** (Muchargasse 4; ⏰9am-noon & 3-6pm Tue-Fri, 9am-noon Sat).

ℹ Getting There & Away

Except for the 'corridor' route through Italy to Innsbruck (€31.20, four hours), trains to the rest of Austria connect via Spittal Millstättersee to the east, including hourly trains to Salzburg (€33.70, 3½ hours). To head south by car, you must first divert west or east along Hwy 100.

Hohe Tauern National Park

If you thought Mother Nature pulled out all the stops in the Austrian Alps, Hohe Tauern National Park was her magnum opus. Straddling Tirol, Salzburg and Carinthia, this national park is the largest in the Alps; a 1786-sq-km wilderness of 3000m peaks, Alpine meadows and waterfalls. At its heart lies **Grossglockner** (3798m), Austria's highest mountain, which towers over the 8km-long **Pasterze Glacier**, best seen from the outlook at **Kaiser-Franz-Josefs-Höhe** (2369m).

The 48km **Grossglockner Road** (Hwy 107; www.grossglockner.at, in German) from Bruck in Salzburgerland to Heiligenblut in Carinthia is one of Europe's greatest Alpine drives. A feat of 1930s engineering, the road swings giddily around 36 switchbacks, passing jewel-coloured lakes, forested slopes and wondrous glaciers.

If you have wheels, you'll have more flexibility, although the road is open only between May and October, and you must pay tolls (per car/motorcycle €28/18).

The major village on the Grossglockner Road is **Heiligenblut**, dominated by mountain peaks and the needle-thin spire of its 15th-century pilgrimage church. Here you'll find a **tourist office** (📞20 01; www.heiligenblut.at, in German; Hof 4; ⏰9am-noon Mon-Fri, 9am-noon & 4-6pm Sat), which can advise on guided ranger hikes, mountain hiking and skiing. The village also has a campsite, a scattering of restaurants and a spick-and-span **Jugendherberge** (📞22 59; www.oejhv.or.at; Hof 36; dm/s/d €20/28/48; 🅿).

Bus 5002 runs frequently between Lienz and Heiligenblut on weekdays (€7.40, one hour); less frequently at weekends. From late June to late September, four buses run from Monday to Friday, three at weekends

---

WORTH A TRIP

KRIMML FALLS

The thunderous, three-tier **Krimml Falls** (www.wasserfaelle-krimml.at; adult/child €2/0.50, free Dec-Apr; ⏰ticket office 8am-6pm mid-Apr–late Oct) is Europe's highest waterfall at 380m, and one of Austria's most unforgettable sights. The pretty Alpine village of Krimml has a handful of places to sleep and eat; contact the **tourist office** (📞72 39; www.krimml.at; Oberkrimml 37; ⏰8am-noon, 2.30-6pm Mon-Fri, 8.30-10.30am & 4.30-6pm Sat) for more information.

Krimml is on Hwy 168 (which becomes Hwy 165). Buses run year-round from Krimml to Zell am See (€8.40, 1¼ hours, hourly).

between Heiligenblut and Kaiser-Franz-Josefs-Höhe (€4.10, 30 minutes). Timetables change regularly here though, so it's best to check with the tourist office in Lienz before setting off.

VORARLBERG

Vorarlberg has always been a little different. Cut off from the rest of Austria by the snow-capped Arlberg massif, this westerly region has often associated itself more with Switzerland than Vienna far to the east, and its citizens have developed a strong dialect Tyroleans even find hard to decipher.

Alluringly beautiful, this region is an aesthetic mix of mountains, hills and valleys. Trickling down from the Alps to the shores of Bodensee (Lake Constance), Vorarlberg is a destination in its own right, attracting everyone from classical-music buffs to skiers. It's also a gateway, by rail or water, to Germany, Liechtenstein and Switzerland.

Bregenz

☑05574 / POP 27,000

Bregenz has been a ritzy address for generations, which is not surprising considering its pretty location on the shores of Bodensee. Boating, cycling, and lounging on the lake's shores are the general activities here, and many visitors time a stay in Vorarlberg's capital to catch the annual Bregenzer Festspiele in summer.

◎ Sights

Kunsthaus ART MUSEUM
(www.kunsthaus-bregenz.at; Karl-Tizian-Platz; adult/child €8/free; ◎10am-6pm Tue-Sun, to 9pm Thu) The architecturally eye-catching Kunsthaus, by award-winning Swiss architect Peter Zumthor, hosts first-rate contemporary art exhibitions.

Oberstadt HISTORIC AREA
Set high above the modern centre is the Oberstadt, the storybook old town; look for the enormous onion dome of the **Martinsturm** (St Martin's Tower; www.martinsturm.at; Martinsgasse; adult/child €1/0.50; ◎10am-5pm Tue-Sun Apr-Oct), reputedly the largest in central Europe.

Pfänder Cable Car CABLE CAR
(Steinbruchgasse 4; one-way adult/child €6.30/3.10, return €10.80/5.40; ◎8am-7pm) For spectacular views of the lake, town and

not-so-distant Alps, catch the cable car which rises to 1064m.

☀ Activities

Bregenz' shimmering centrepiece is the **Bodensee**, Europe's third-largest lake, straddling Austria, Switzerland and Germany. Lakeside activities include **sailing** and **diving** at Lochau, 5km north of town, and **swimming**. The most central place for a quick dip or a barbecue is the **Pipeline**, a stretch of pebbly beach north of Bregenz, so-named for the large pipeline running parallel to the lake.

Bodensee Radweg CYCLING
(www.bodensee-radweg.com) In summer, the well-marked Bodensee Radweg that circumnavigates the Bodensee becomes an autobahn for lycra-clad *Radfahrer* (cyclists). Hire your own set of wheels at **Fahrradverleih Bregenz** (Bregenz Harbour; ◎9am-7pm May-Sep) for €16.50 per day.

✯ Festivals & Events

The **Bregenzer Festspiele** (Bregenz Festival; ☑407-6; www.bregenzerfestspiele.com), running from late July to late August, is the city's premier cultural festival. World-class operas and orchestral works are staged on the Seebühne, a floating stage on the lake, in the Festspielhaus and at the Vorarlberger Landestheater. Information and tickets are up for grabs about nine months before the festival.

⌂ Sleeping & Eating

Stop by the tourist office for a list of private rooms (around €30 per person). Prices soar and beds are at a premium during the Bregenzer Festspiele – book ahead.

Restaurants and cafes huddle along the lakefront and the streets of the Unterstadt. In summer, little beats a picnic on the banks of the Bodensee.

TOP CHOICE **Deuring-Schlössle** HISTORIC HOTEL €€€
(☑478 00; www.deuring-schloessle.at; Ehre-Guta-Platz 4; s/d/ste €111/222/386; ℙ@🛜) Bregenz' best rooms are found in this fabulously renovated old castle. Each one is decorated differently, but all have loads of medieval charm and grace. Its restaurant (mains around €30) is also Bregenz' best, with a sophisticated look and a market-fresh menu.

JUFA Gästehaus Bregenz HOSTEL €
(☑05708-35 40; www.jufa.at/bregenz; Mehrerauerstrasse 5; dm €27; ℙ@) Housed in a former

needle factory near the lake, this HI hostel now reels backpackers in with its super-clean dorms and excellent facilities including a common room and restaurant.

Hotel Weisses Kreuz HOTEL €€
(☏498 80; www.hotelweisseskreuz.at; Römerstrasse 5; s/d €119/146, mains €14-29; P✳@☎) Service is attentive at this central pick, with a restaurant rolling out seasonal Austrian fare. The smart rooms sport cherry wood furnishings, flat-screen TVs and organic bedding.

Cafesito CAFE €
(Maurachgasse 6; bagels €3-4; ☉7.45am-6.30pm Mon-Fri, 9am-4.30pm Sat) Tiny Cafesito does the best create-your-own bagels and smoothies in town. Lilac-yellow walls and modern art create a funky backdrop for a light lunch or cup of fair-trade coffee.

Wirtshaus am See AUSTRIAN €€
(☏422 10; www.wirtshausamsee.at; Seepromenade 2; mains €11-18) Snag a table on the lakefront terrace at this mock half-timbered villa, dishing up local specialities like buttery Bodensee whitefish and venison ragout. It's also a relaxed spot for quaffing a cold one.

❶ Information

Bregenz' **tourist office** (☏49 59-0; www.bregenz.ws; Rathausstrasse 35a; ☉9am-6pm Mon-Fri, to noon Sat) has information on the city and the surrounding area, and can help with accommodation.

❶ Getting There & Away

BOAT From April to mid-October, there's a frequent boat service between Bregenz and a number of towns and cities on the Bodensee, including Konstanz (one way €15, 4¼ hours) and Friedrichshafen (€12.40, two hours) in Germany. For information, consult www.bodenseeschiff fahrt.at (in German).

TRAIN Four daily trains go to Munich (€43.50, three hours) via Lindau, and Zürich (€33, 2¼ hours) via St Gallen (€12, 50 minutes). Nine trains daily depart for Innsbruck (€31, 2½ hours). Trains to Konstanz (€11.40, 1¾ hours) may be frequent, but require between one and four changes.

St Anton am Arlberg

☏05446 / POP 2270
At the heart of the wild and austerely beautiful Arlberg region lies St Anton am Arlberg. In 1901 the first ski club in the Alps

was founded here, downhill skiing was born and the village never looked back. Today the resort has legendary slopes and is Austria's unrivalled king of après ski.

🏃 Activities

Skiing SKIING
St Anton attracts both intermediate and advanced skiers and boarders, with 280km of slopes, fantastic backcountry opportunities and a freestyle park on Rendl. A ski pass covering the whole Arlberg region and valid for all 84 ski lifts costs €44.50/239 for one/seven days in high season.

Hiking HIKING
Naturally, hiking is the number-one summer pastime: the Wanderpass (€28/33 for three/seven days) gives you a head start with access to all lifts.

H2O Adventures ADVENTURE SPORTS
(☏05446-39 37; Arlrock, Bahnhofstrasse 1; ☉May–mid-Oct) H2O Adventures gets adrenalin pumping, with activities from rafting to canyoning and mountain biking.

🛏 Sleeping & Eating

Rates can be almost double those quoted below in high winter season, when you'll need to book well ahead. Hit Dorfstrasse for

BREGENZERWALD

Only a few kilometres southeast of Bregenz, the forest-cloaked slopes, velvet-green pastures and limestone peaks of the Bregenzerwald unfold. In summer it's a glorious place to spend a few days hiking the hills and filling up on all manner of home-made cheeses in Alpine dairies. Winter brings plenty of snow, and the area is noted for its downhill and cross-country skiing.

The **Bregenzerwald tourist office** (☏05512-23 65; www.bregenzerwald. at; Impulszentrum 1135, Egg; ☉9am-5pm Mon-Fri, 8am-1pm Sat & Sun) has information on the region, and cheese-lovers can consult www.kaesestrasse. at (in German) for the low-down on the **Cheese Road**. From Bregenz, buses travel to Bezau (€4.40, one hour), one of the region's main villages, at least every two hours; however, this offbeat region is easier to explore by car.

snack bars and restaurants serving everything from tapas to Tex-Mex with a side order of après-ski. Most restaurants and bars close in summer.

TOP CHOICE **Altes Thönihaus** GUESTHOUSE €
(☑28 10; www.altes-thoenihaus.at; Im Gries 1; s/d/q €28/52/80; 🛜) Dating to 1465, this listed wooden chalet oozes Alpine charm from every last beam. Fleecy rugs and pine keep the mood cosy in rooms with mountain-facing balconies. Downstairs there's a superb little spa and restored *Stube* (parlour).

Himmlhof GUESTHOUSE €€
(☑232 20; www.himmlhof.com; Im Gries 9; d €94-126; P) This *himmlisch* (heavenly) Tyrolean chalet has wood-clad rooms brimming with original features (tiled ovens, four-poster beds and the like). An open fire and spa beckon after a day's skiing.

Museum Restaurant AUSTRIAN €€
(☑24 75; Rudi-Matt-Weg 10; mains €10-16; ⊘dinner) Arlberger hay soup, succulent Tyrolean beef and fresh-from-the-pond trout land on your plate at this wood-panelled restaurant, picturesquely housed in the village museum.

ℹ Information

The **tourist office** (☑226 90; www.stanton amarlberg.com; Arlberg Haus; ⊘8.30am-7pm Mon-Fri, 9am-6pm Sat, 9am-noon & 3-5pm Sun) has information on accommodation, activities, maps and an accommodation board with free telephone outside.

ℹ Getting There & Away

St Anton is on the main railway route between Bregenz (€16.90, 1½ hours) and Innsbruck (€20, 1¼ hours). The town is close to the eastern entrance of the Arlberg Tunnel, the toll road connecting Vorarlberg and Tirol. The tunnel toll is €8.50 one way. You can avoid the toll by taking the B197, but no vehicles with trailers are allowed on this winding road.

UNDERSTAND AUSTRIA

History

Austria has been a galvanic force in shaping Europe's history. This landlocked little country was once the epicentre of the mighty Habsburg empire and, in the 20th century, a pivotal player in the outbreak of WWI.

Civilisation & Empire

Like so many European countries, Austria has experienced invasions and struggles since time immemorial. There are traces of human occupation since the ice age, but it was the Celts who made the first substantial mark on Austria around 450 BC. The Romans followed 400 years later, and in turn were followed by Bavarians and, in 1278, the House of Habsburg, who took control of the country by defeating the head of the Bavarian royalty.

The Habsburg Monarchy

For six centuries the Habsburgs used strategic marriages to maintain their hold over a territory that encompassed much of central and Eastern Europe and, for a period, even Germany. But defeat in WWI brought that to an end, when the Republic of Austria was formed in 1918.

The 16th and 17th centuries saw the Ottoman threat reach the gates of Vienna, and in 1805 Napoleon defeated Austria at Austerlitz. Austrian Chancellor Metternich cleverly reconsolidated Austria's power in 1815 after Waterloo, but the loss of the 1866 Austro-Prussian War, and creation of the Austro-Hungarian empire in 1867, diminished the Habsburg's influence in Europe.

However, these setbacks pale beside Archduke Franz Ferdinand's assassination by Slavic separatists in Sarajevo on 28 June 1914. When his uncle, the Austro-Hungarian emperor Franz Josef, declared war on Serbia in response, the ensuing 'Great War' (WWI) would prove the Habsburgs' downfall.

WWII & Postwar Austria

During the 1930s the Nazis began to influence Austrian politics, and by 1938 the recession-hit country was ripe for picking. Invading German troops met little resistance and Hitler was greeted on Heldenplatz as a hero by 200,000 Viennese.

Austria was heavily bombed during WWII, but the country recovered well, largely through the Marshall Plan and sound political and economic decisions (excluding its foray with the far-right Freedom Party and its controversial leader, Jörg Haider, in the 1990s). Austria has maintained a neutral stance since 1955, been home to a number of international organisations, including the UN, since 1979, and joined the EU in 1995.

Austria today enjoys the kind of economic, social and political stability that many other nations would dream of. Cities forging ahead include Linz, which seized the reins as European Capital of Culture in 2009, and Innsbruck, which is gearing up to host the first Winter Youth Olympics in 2012. Vienna, too, has plenty to look pleased about, topping the Mercer Quality of Living List in 2010 and with a shiny new Hauptbahnhof in the making. Meanwhile, up in the mountains, sustainability is the watchword, with an increasing number of resorts polishing their eco-credentials and using clean energy.

Arts & Architecture

Classical Music

What other country can match the musical heritage of Austria? Great composers were drawn to Vienna by the Habsburgs' generous patronage during the 18th and 19th centuries. The era most strongly associated with Austrian music is *Wiener Klassik* (Vienna Classic), which dates back to the mid- and late 18th century and has defined the way we perceive classical music today. It began life as a step down from the celestial baroque music of the royal court and church, and shifted the focus of performance onto the salons and theatres of upper middle-class society.

Joseph Haydn (1732–1809) is considered to be the first of the great composers of the *Wiener Klassik* era, followed by Salzburg wunderkind Wolfgang Amadeus Mozart (1756–91). Beethoven's musical genius reached its zenith in Vienna. *Lieder* (song) master Franz Schubert (1797–1828) was the last of the heavyweight *Wiener Klassik* composers.

Vienna Secession & Expressionism

In 1897, 19 progressive artists broke away from the conservative artistic establishment and formed the Vienna Secession (*Sezession*) movement, synonymous with art nouveau. Vienna turned out such talents as the painter Gustav Klimt (1862–1918); Schloss Belvedere showcases one of his finest works, *The Kiss*. Vienna-born architect Otto Wagner (1841–1918) ushered in a new, functional direction around the turn of the 20th century and gave the capital a metro system replete with attractive art nouveau stations.

Gustav Klimt strongly influenced the work of well-known Austrian expressionists like Egon Schiele (1890–1918), who was obsessed with capturing the erotic on canvas, and Oskar Kokoschka (1886–1980). The paintings of these three Austrian greats hang out in the Leopold Museum in Vienna's MuseumsQuartier.

Baroque Heyday

Thanks to the Habsburg monarchy and its obsession with pomp and splendour, Austria is packed with high-calibre architecture, which reached giddy heights of opulence during the baroque era of the late 17th and early 18th century. It took the graceful column and symmetry of the Renaissance and added elements of the grotesque, burlesque and the saccharin.

Johann Bernhard Fischer von Erlach (1656–1723), the mastermind behind Schloss Schönbrunn, was the country's greatest baroque architect. Like Fischer von Erlach, Austria's second architect of the era, Johann Lukas von Hildebrandt (1668–1745), was famous for his interior decorative work of palaces for the aristocracy such as Schloss Belvedere. Paul Troger (1698–1762) is Austria's master of the baroque fresco and his work is best appreciated at Stift Melk. Other baroque highlights include Karlskirche in Vienna, Salzburg's Dom and the Hofburg in Innsbruck.

Food & Drink

Staples & Specialities

Austria is famous for its Wiener schnitzel, for its tender goulash and for desserts like *Sacher Torte* (Sacher cake) and *Kaiserschmarrn* (sweet pancake with raisins). Certainly, these legendary classics are not to be missed, but the Austrian table offers a host of other regional and seasonal delights. Throw in excellent red wines from Burgenland and quality whites and reds from Lower Austria, Styria and elsewhere, and you have the makings of an exciting and unexpected culinary experience.

In Lower Austria try Waldviertel game, beef and poppy dishes, tangy cider from the Mostviertel, and pike and carp from Burgenland. The Wachau goes mad for *Marillen* (apricots) around mid-July. Styria is renowned for its *Almochsen* (meadow beef) and healthy, nutty pumpkin oil. Upper Austria is *Knödel* (dumpling) country, while the must-eat in neighbouring Salzburgerland is *Salzburger Nockerln,* a sweet soufflé. Freshwater fish in Carinthia, *Heumilchkäse* (hay

ⓘ PRACTICALITIES

» **Opening Hours** Most sights and tourist offices operate on reduced hours from November to March. Opening hours we provide are for the high season, so outside those months it can be useful to check ahead.

» **Seasonal Closures** In the Alps, many hotels, restaurants and sometimes tourist offices close between seasons, from around May to mid-June and mid-September to early December.

» **Concessions** Museums and sights have concessions for families, children (generally under-16-year-olds), students and senior citizens; you may need to show proof of age. Children under 12 years usually receive a substantial discount on rooms they share with parents.

» **Smoking** Unless a separate room has been set aside, smoking is not allowed in restaurants. It's legal to smoke anywhere on outdoor terraces. Whenever a hotel has designated nonsmoking rooms, we've included an icon to show this.

milk cheese) from Vorarlberg and Tirol's hearty *Gröstl* (a fry-up from leftover potatoes, pork and onions) are other regional specialities.

Where to Eat & Drink

Beyond the traditional restaurant, *Gasthaus* or *Gasthof,* you'll find coffee houses serving a handful of light or classic dishes like goulash, ethnic eat-in and take-away joints, and often corner Italian pizzerias. Solid Austrian fare is on the menu in Vienna's homely, good-value inns called *Beisl* (small taverns; from the Yiddish word for 'little houses'). In the winegrowing regions, rustic *Heurigen* (wine taverns) sell their wine directly from their own premises and food is available buffet-style. They open on a roster so pick up the local *Heurigenkalender* (*Heurigen* calendar) from the tourist offices.

For cheap food, try *Mensen* (university canteens). Another money-saving trick is to make lunch the main meal of the day, as many Austrians do; many restaurants provide a good-value *Tagesteller* or *Tagesmenü* (set meal) at this time. You can assemble your own picnic at local farmers' markets, where the freshest produce is sold.

SURVIVAL GUIDE

Directory A–Z

Accommodation

From simple mountain huts to five-star hotels fit for kings – you'll find the lot in Austria. Tourist offices invariably keep lists and details, and some arrange bookings for free or for a nominal fee. Some useful points:

» It's wise to book ahead at all times, particularly during the high seasons: July and August and December to April (in ski resorts).

» Some places require email confirmation but many are bookable online. Be aware that confirmed reservations in writing are considered binding, and cancellations within several days of arrival often involve a fee or full payment.

» Most hotel rooms in Austria have their own shower, although hostels and some rock-bottom digs have an *Etagendusche* (corridor shower).

» Very often a hotel won't have lifts; if this is important, always check ahead.

» In mountain resorts, high-season prices can be up to double the prices charged in the low season (May to June and October to November). In other towns, the difference may be 10% or less.

» In some resorts (not often in cities), a *Gästekarte* (guest card) is issued if you stay overnight, which offers discounts on things such as cable cars and admission.

» Locally, always check the city or region website, as many (such as in Vienna, Salzburg and Graz) have an excellent booking function.

Some useful websites:

Austrian Hotelreservation (www.austrian-hotelreservation.at)

Austrian National Tourist Office (www.austria.info)

Booking.com (www.booking.com)

Hostelling International (www.hihost els.com)

Hostelworld (www.hostelworld.com)

PRICE RANGES

Our reviews refer to double rooms with a private bathroom, except in hostels or where otherwise specified. Listings are arranged in order of preference, and quoted rates are for high season, which is April to October.

€€€ more than €200

€€ €80 to €200

€ less than €80

Activities

Austria is a wonderland for outdoorsy types, with much of the west given over to towering Alpine peaks. Opportunities for hiking and mountaineering are boundless in Tirol, Salzburgerland and the Hohe Tauern National Park, all of which have extensive Alpine hut networks (see www.alpenverein. at). Names like St Anton, Kitzbühel and Mayrhofen fire the imagination of serious skiers, but you may find cheaper accommodation and lift passes in little-known resorts; visit www.austria.info for the lowdown.

Business Hours

Banks 9am-3pm Mon-Fri, to 5.30pm Thu

Clubs 10pm to late

Cafes 7.30am-8pm; hours vary widely

Pubs till midnight or later

Restaurants noon-3pm, 7-11pm

Shops 9am-6.30pm Mon-Fri, 9am-5pm Sat

Supermarkets 9am to 7pm or 8pm Mon-Sat

Discount Cards

Regional Various discount cards are available, many of them covering a whole region or province. Some are free with an overnight stay. See destinations for details.

Student & Youth Cards International Student Identity Cards (ISIC) and European Youth Card (Euro<26; check www. euro26.org for discounts) will get you discounts at most museums, galleries and theatres. Admission is generally a little higher than the price for children.

Discount Rail Cards See p96.

WHERE TO STAY

Hotels & Pensions Hotels and pensions (B&Bs) are rated by the same criteria from one to five stars. Hotels offer more services, including bars, restaurants and parking, whereas pensions tend to be smaller and less standardised.

Hostels In Austria over 100 hostels (*Jugendherberge*) are affiliated with Hostelling International (HI). Facilities are often excellent. Four- to six-bed dorms with shower/toilet are the norm, though some places also have doubles and family rooms. See www.oejhv.or.at or www.oejhw.at for details.

Private Rooms *Privatzimmer* (private rooms) are cheap (often about €40 per double). On top of this, you will find *Bauernhof* (farmhouses) in rural areas, and some *Öko-Bauernhöfe* (organic farms).

Alpine Huts There are over 530 of these huts in the Austrian Alps; most are maintained by the Österreichischer Alpenverein (ÖAV; Austrian Alpine Club; www.alpenverein.at, in German). Meals are often available. Bed prices for nonmembers are around €26 to €44 in a dorm; ÖAV members pay half-price. Contact the ÖAV for lists of huts and to make bookings.

Rental Accommodation *Ferienwohnungen* (self-catering apartments) are ubiquitous in Austrian mountain resorts; advance booking is recommended. Contact a local tourist office for lists and prices.

Camping Austria has over 490 camping grounds, many well equipped and scenically located. Prices can be as low as €4 per person or small tent and as high as €10. Many close in winter, so phone ahead to check. Search for camping grounds by region at www.camping-club.at (in German).

Eco-Hotels To search *Bio-* or *Öko-* ('eco') hotels by region, see www.biohotels.info.

Embassies & Consulates

All of the embassies and consulates listed below are located in Vienna (telephone prefix ☏01). For a complete listing of other embassies and consulates, look in the Austrian telephone book under *Botschaften* (embassies) or *Konsulate* (consulates).

Australia (☏506 74-0; www.australian-embassy. at; Mattiellistrasse 2-4)

Canada (☏531 38-3000; www.kanada.at; Laurenzerberg 2)

New Zealand (consulate-general; ☏318 85 05; www.nzc.at; Salesianergasse 15/3)

UK (☏716 13-0; www.britishembassy.at; Jaurèsgasse 12)

USA (☏313 39-0; http://austria.usembassy.gov; Boltzmanngasse 16)

Food

Price ranges for restaurants listed in this book are indicated by the following:

€€€ more than €30

€€ €15 to €30

€ below €15

Gay & Lesbian Travellers

Austria is close to the Western European par on attitudes towards homosexuality. Vienna is more tolerant towards gays and lesbians than the rest of the country.

The *Spartacus International Gay Guide*, published by Bruno Gmünder (Berlin), is a good directory of gay entertainment venues worldwide (mainly for men). Online resources:

Gay.de (www.gay.at)

Gayboy (www.gayboy.at)

Gaynet (www.gayguide.at)

Rainbow (www.rainbow.or.at)

Language Courses

Many places, including some of Austria's universities, offer German courses, usually with the option of accommodation. Well-known course providers:

Berlitz (www.berlitz.at) Offers private, intensive day and evening courses in Vienna, Wiener Neustadt, Klagenfurt, Linz and Graz.

Inlingua Sprachschule (www.inlingua. at) Courses run for a minimum of two weeks and can either be taken in the morning or some evenings. Classes are limited to seven students and individual tuition is also available. Offices in Linz, Graz, Salzburg, Innsbruck, Klagenfurt and Vorarlberg.

Money

ATMs Some *Bankomaten* (ATMs) are 24 hours. Most accept at the very least Maestro debit cards and Visa and MasterCard credit cards.

Credit Cards Visa and MasterCard (Eurocard) are accepted a little more widely than American Express (Amex) and Diners Club.

Currency Austria's currency is the euro. Major train stations have currency offices, and there are also plenty of banks and *bureaux de changes*.

Taxes *Mehrwertsteuer* (MWST; value-added tax) is set at 20% for most goods. Prices are always displayed inclusive of all taxes. Shops with a 'Global Refund Tax Free Shopping' sticker have the paperwork to reclaim about 13% of this tax on single purchases over €75 by non-EU citizens or residents. See www.globalrefund.com for more information. Vienna and Salzburg airports have refund desks. It's easiest to claim this before leaving the country, rather than at home.

Tipping It's customary to tip about 10% in restaurants, bars and cafes, and in taxis; hand over the bill and the tip together. It also doesn't hurt to tip hairdressers, hotel porters, cloak-room attendants, cleaning staff and tour guides €1 or €2.

Transfers For emergency transfers, Western Union (www.westernunion.com) money offices are available in larger towns.

Public Holidays

New Year's Day (Neujahr) 1 January

Epiphany (Heilige Drei Könige) 6 January

Easter Monday (Ostermontag) March/April

Labour Day (Tag der Arbeit) 1 May

Whit Monday (Pfingstmontag) Sixth Monday after Easter

Ascension Day (Christi Himmelfahrt) Sixth Thursday after Easter

Corpus Christi (Fronleichnam) Second Thursday after Whitsunday

Assumption (Maria Himmelfahrt)
15 August

National Day (Nationalfeiertag)
26 October

All Saints' Day (Allerheiligen) 1 November

Immaculate Conception (Mariä Empfängnis) 8 December

Christmas Day (Christfest) 25 December

St Stephen's Day (Stephanitag)
26 December

Telephone

Area Codes Area codes begin with '0' (eg '01' for Vienna). Drop this when calling from outside Austria; use it for all landline calls inside Austria except for local calls or to special toll and toll-free numbers.

Directory Enquiries Call ✆0900 11 88 77 for international directory assistance.

Free & Toll Numbers 0800 numbers are free, 0810 and 0820 cost 0.10c and 0.20c respectively per minute, and 0900 numbers are exorbitant and best avoided.

Mobile Numbers Austrian mobile (*Handy*) telephone numbers begin with 0650 or higher up to 0683.

Public Telephones These take phonecards or coins; €0.20 is the minimum for a local call. Call centres are also widespread, and many internet cafes are geared for Skype calls.

Roaming The network works on GSM 1800 and is compatible with GSM 900 phones; it is not compatible with systems from the USA unless the mobile phone is at least a tri-band model. Roaming can get very expensive if your provider is outside the EU.

SIM Cards Phone shops sell prepaid SIM cards for about €10 (calls for about 0.10c per minute) that can be refilled at kiosks anywhere.

Tourist Information

Tourist offices, which are dispersed far and wide in Austria, tend to adjust their hours from one year to the next, so the hours listed in this chapter are a guide only and may have changed slightly by the time you arrive.

The **Austrian National Tourist Office** (ANTO; www.austria.info) has a number of overseas offices. There is a comprehensive listing on the ANTO website.

Visas

Visas for stays of up to three months are not required for citizens of the EU, much of Eastern Europe, Israel, USA, Canada, the majority of Central and South American nations, Japan, Korea, Malaysia, Singapore, Australia or New Zealand. All other nationalities require a visa; the Ministry of Foreign Affairs website at www.bmaa.gv.at has a list of Austrian embassies where you can apply for one.

Getting There & Away
Entering the Country

Paperwork A valid passport is required. The only exception to this rule is when entering from another Schengen country (all EU states minus Britain and Ireland); in this case, only a national identity card is required.

Border Procedures Formal border controls have been abolished if entering from another EU country and Switzerland, but spot checks may be carried out at the border or inside Austria itself.

Air

Vienna is the main transport hub for Austria, but Graz, Linz, Klagenfurt, Salzburg and Innsbruck all receive international flights. Flights to these cities are often a cheaper option than those to the capital, as are flights to Airport Letisko (Bratislava Airport), 60km east of Vienna in Slovakia.

Among the low-cost airlines, Ryanair and Air Berlin fly to Graz, Innsbruck, Klagenfurt, Linz, Salzburg and Vienna (Ryanair to Bratislava for Vienna).

Following are the key international airports in Austria:

Airport Letisko Bratislava (BTS; ✆421 2 3303 33 53; www.airportbratislava.sk) Serves Bratislava and has good transport connections to Vienna. Used by Ryanair.

Graz (GRZ; ✆0316-29 02-0; www.flughafen-graz.at)

Innsbruck (INN; ✆0512-225 25-0; www.innsbruck-airport.com)

Klagenfurt (KLU; ✆0463-41 5 00-0; www.klagenfurt-airport.com)

Linz (LNZ; ✆07221-600-0; www.flughafen-linz.at)

Salzburg (SZG; ✆0662-85800; www.salzburg-airport.com)

Vienna (VIE; ✆01-7007 22233; www.viennaairport.com)

Land

BUS

Buses depart from Austria for as far afield as England, the Baltic countries, the Netherlands, Germany and Switzerland. But most significantly, they provide access to Eastern European cities small and large – from the likes of Sofia and Warsaw, to Banja Luka, Mostar and Sarajevo.

Services operated by **Eurolines** (www.euro lines.at) leave from Vienna and from several regional cities.

CAR & MOTORCYCLE

There are numerous entry points into Austria by road from Germany, the Czech Republic, Slovakia, Hungary, Slovenia, Italy and Switzerland. All border-crossing points are open 24 hours.

Insurance Third-party insurance is a minimum requirement in Europe and you'll need to carry proof of this in the form of a Green Card. The car must also display a sticker indicating the country of origin.

Paperwork Proof of ownership of a private vehicle and a driver's licence should always be carried while driving. EU licences are accepted in Austria while all other nationalities require a German translation or an International Driving Permit (IDP).

Safety Requirements Carrying a warning triangle and first-aid kit in your vehicle is compulsory.

TRAIN

Austria has excellent rail connections. The main services in and out of the country from the west normally pass through Bregenz, Innsbruck or Salzburg en route to Vienna. Trains to Eastern Europe invariably leave from Südbahnhof in Vienna (closed for reconstruction 2011–12; see p96). Express services to Italy go via Innsbruck or Villach; trains to Slovenia are routed through Graz.

Express & High-Speed Trains Express trains are identified by the symbols EC (EuroCity; serving international routes) or IC (InterCity; serving national routes). The French TGV and the German InterCityExpress (ICE) trains are high-speed trains. Surcharges are levied for these.

London The fastest connection between London and Vienna by rail is on **Eurostar**

MOVING ON?

For tips, recommendations and reviews, head to shop.lonelyplanet.com to purchase downloadable PDFs of the Bulgaria, Romania and Ukraine chapters from Lonely Planet's *Eastern Europe* guide.

(www.eurostar.com) via Brussels and Frankfurt am Main. It takes a total of 14 hours.

Online Timetables ÖBB (www.oebb.at) Austrian National Railways, with national and international connections. Only national connections have prices online.

Reservations Extra charges can apply on fast trains and international trains, and it is a good idea (sometimes obligatory) to make seat reservations for peak times.

River & Lake

Hydrofoils run to Bratislava and Budapest from Vienna; slower boats cruise the Danube between the capital and Passau. The **Danube Tourist Commission** (www.danube -river.org) has a country-by-country list of operators and agents who can book tours. Germany and Switzerland can be reached from Bregenz.

Getting Around

Transport systems in Austria are highly developed and efficient. Individual bus and train *Fahrplan* (timetables) are readily available, as are helpful annual timetables.

Air

Flying within a country the size of Austria is not usually necessary. A couple of airlines serving longer routes:

Austrian Airlines (www.austrian.com) The national carrier and its subsidiaries Tyrolean Airways and Austrian Arrows offer several flights daily between Vienna and Graz, Innsbruck, Klagenfurt, Linz and Salzburg.

Welcome Air (www.welcomeair.at) Flights from Innsbruck to Graz.

Bicycle

Austria is an efficiently run paradise for cyclists, criss-crossed by plenty of designated cycling paths.

Bike Hire All cities have at least one bike shop that doubles as a rental centre; expect to pay around €10 to €15 per day.

Bike Touring Most tourist boards have brochures on cycling facilities and routes within their region. Separate bike tracks are common in cities, and long-distance tracks and routes also run along major rivers such as the Danube and lakes such as Wörthersee in Carinthia.

Bike Transport You can take bicycles on any train with a bicycle symbol at the top of its timetable. A day ticket costs €5 for regional, €10 for national (InterCity) and €12 for international trains. You can't take bicycles on buses.

Boat

The Danube serves as a thoroughfare between Vienna and Lower and Upper Austria. Services are generally slow, scenic excursions rather than functional means of transport.

Bus

Rail routes are often complemented by Postbus services, which usually depart from outside train stations. In remote regions, there are fewer services on Saturday and often none on Sunday. Generally, you can only buy tickets from the drivers. For information inside Austria, call ☑0810 222 333 (6am to 8pm); from outside Austria, call ☑+43 1 71101; or visit the website, www.postbus.at.

Car & Motorcycle

Autobahns ('A') and *Bundesstrassen* ('B') are major roads, while *Landstrassen* ('L') let you enjoy the ride and are usually good for cyclists. A daily motorail service links Vienna to Innsbruck, Salzburg and Villach.

AUTOMOBILE ASSOCIATIONS

Annual membership for Austria's two automobile associations costs €66 and includes a free 24-hour breakdown service. Nonmembers incur a fee for call-outs which varies, depending on the time of day. The two associations:

ARBÖ (☑24hr emergency assistance 123, office 050/123 123; www.arboe.at)

ÖAMTC (☑24hr emergency assistance 120, office 01-711 99-0; www.oeamtc.at)

HIRE

Multinational car-hire firms **Avis** (www.avis.at), **Budget** (www.budget.at), **Europcar** (www.

europcar.co.at) and **Hertz** (www.hertz.at) all have offices in major cities; ask at tourist offices for details. The minimum age for hiring small cars is 19 years, or 25 years for larger, 'prestige' cars. Customers must have held a driving licence for at least a year. Many contracts forbid customers to take cars outside Austria, particularly into Eastern Europe.

MOTORWAY & TUNNEL TOLLS

A *vignette* (motorway tax) is imposed on all autobahn; charges for cars/motorbikes are €7.90/4.50 for 10 days and €22.90/11.50 for two months. *Vignette* can be purchased at border crossings, petrol stations and *Tabak* shops. There are additional tolls (usually €2.50 to €10) for some mountain tunnels.

ROAD RULES

Children Under the age of 14 who are shorter than 1.5m must have a special seat or restraint.

Crash Helmet Compulsory for motorcyclists and their passengers, not for cyclists.

Drinking & Driving The penalty for drink-driving – over 0.05% – is a hefty on-the-spot fine and confiscation of your driving licence.

Driving Licence A licence should always be carried. If it's not in German, you need to carry a translation or International Driving Permit (IDP) as well.

Fines Can be paid on the spot, but ask for a receipt.

Give Way Rules Give way to the right at all times except when a priority road sign indicates otherwise. Trams always have priority.

Hitchhiking It's illegal to hitchhike on Austrian motorways.

Minimum Driving Age 18.

Parking Most town centres have *Kurzparkzone* (short-term parking zones) during office hours. *Parkschein* (parking vouchers) for such zones can be purchased from *Tabak* shops or pavement dispensers. Parking is unrestricted on unmarked streets.

Seat Belts Compulsory.

Snow Chains Carrying snow chains in winter is recommended (compulsory in some areas).

Speed Limits The speed limit is 50km/h in built-up areas, 130km/h on motorways and 100km/h on other roads. Except for the A1 (Vienna–Salzburg) and the A2 (Vienna–Villach), the speed limit is 110km/h on the autobahn from 10pm to 5am.

Which Side of the Road Drive on the right-hand side.

Train

Austria has a clean, efficient rail system, and if you use a discount card it's very inexpensive.

Disabled Passengers Use the ☎05-1717 number from 7am to 10pm for special travel assistance; do this at least 24 hours ahead of travel (72 hours ahead for international services). Staff at stations will help with boarding and alighting.

Fares The fares quoted in this chapter are for 2nd-class tickets.

Information ÖBB (☎05 17 17; www.oebb.at) is the main operator, supplemented with a handful of private lines. Tickets and timetables are available online.

RailJet It's worth seeking out RailJet train services connecting Vienna, Graz, Villach, Salzburg and Innsbruck, as they travel up to 200km/h.

Reservations In 2nd class within Austria this costs €3.50 for most express services; recommended for travel on weekends.

RAIL PASSES

Depending on the amount of travelling you intend to do in Austria, and your residency status, rail passes can be a good deal.

Eurail Austria Pass This handy pass is available to non-EU residents; prices start at €112 for three days' unlimited 1st-class travel within one month, and youths under 26 receive substantial discounts. See the website at www.eurail.com for all options (eg Austria–Germany Pass).

Interrail Passes are for European citizens and include One Country Pass Austria (three/four/six/eight days €172/191/252/290). Youths under 26 receive substantial discounts. See www.interrailnet.com for all options.

Vorteilscard Reduces fares by at least 45% and is valid for a year, but not on buses. Bring a photo and your passport or ID. It costs adult/under 26 years/senior €100/20/27).

Czech Republic

Best Places to Eat

» U malé velryby (p116)

» Pivovarský Klub (p116)

» Literární Kavárna Řetězová (p117)

» Laibon (p142)

» Rebio (p148)

Best Places to Stay

» Dahlia Inn

» Residence u černé věž (p137)

» Hotel Templ (p155)

» Hotel Rous (p135)

» Poet's Corner (p151)

Why Go?

More than two decades after the fall of the Berlin Wall, a host of European cities and countries have been touted as the 'new Prague' or the 'next Czech Republic'. The 'Where to next?' focus may have shifted to other destinations, but the original Prague and Czech Republic remain essential stops on any European journey.

Prague's inevitable transition from communist capital to modern metropolis is now complete, as centuries of history and glorious architecture compete with thoroughly 21st-century energy and impetus.

Elsewhere, castles and palaces abound – including the audacious cliff-top chateau at Český Krumlov – which illuminate the stories of powerful families and individuals whose influence was felt throughout Europe. Beautifully preserved Renaissance towns that withstood ravages of the communist era link the centuries, and idiosyncratic landscapes provide a stage for active adventures.

When to Go

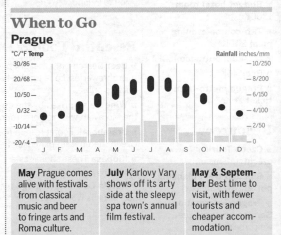

Prague

May Prague comes alive with festivals from classical music and beer to fringe arts and Roma culture.

July Karlovy Vary shows off its arty side at the sleepy spa town's annual film festival.

May & September Best time to visit, with fewer tourists and cheaper accommodation.

Fast Facts

» **Area** 78,864 sq km

» **Capital** Prague

» **Telephone country code** 420

» **Emergency** 112

Exchange Rates

Australia	A$1	17.64Kč
Canada	C$1	17.51Kč
euro	€1	24.41Kč
Japan	¥100	21.86Kč
New Zealand	NZ$1	13.26Kč
UK	UK£1	27.38Kč
USA	US$1	16.82Kč

Set Your Budget

» **Budget hotel room** 1300Kč

» **Two-course evening meal** 200Kč

» **Museum entrance** 150Kč

» **Beer** 40Kč

» **Prague metro-tram ticket** 26Kč

Resources

» **Czech Tourism** (www.czechtourism.com)

» **Bus and train planning portal** (www.idos.cz)

» **Prague Information Service** (www.praguewelcome.cz)

Connections

The Czech Republic is a convenient hub for exploring neighbouring countries. Prague is well connected to Berlin, Dresden, Nuremberg and Hamburg, and Plzeň is on the main train line from Nuremberg to Munich, via Prague. From Český Krumlov it's a short distance to Linz or Salzburg in Austria, with connections to Vienna and to Budapest in Hungary. For travel to Poland, Olomouc is a key transit point for trains to Warsaw and Kraków, and the eastern Czech city of Brno has regular bus and train services to Vienna and the Slovakian capital, Bratislava.

ITINERARIES

One Week

Experience Prague's exciting combination of its tumultuous past and energetic present. Top experiences include the grandeur of Prague Castle, Josefov's Jewish heritage, and getting pleasantly lost amidst the bewildering labyrinth of the Old Town. Take an essential day trip to Terezín, and then head south to Český Krumlov for a few days of riverside R&R.

Two Weeks

Begin in Prague before heading west for the spa scenes at Mariánské Lázně or Karlovy Vary. Balance the virtue and vice ledger with a few Bohemian brews in Plzeň before heading south for relaxation and rigour around Český Krumlov. Head east through České Budějovice en route to the Renaissance grandeur of Telč and Brno's cosmopolitan galleries and museums. Use the Moravian capital as a base for exploring the Moravian Karst caves and Mikulov's wine country, before continuing to under-rated Olomouc to admire the Holy Trinity Column. From Olomouc it's an easy trip back to Prague, or on to Poland.

Essential Food & Drink

» **Beer** Search out excellent *pivo* (beer) from smaller, local, microbreweries. Look for the hand-drawn blackboards outside pubs.

» **Wine** Be surprised by the up-and-coming vintages from the Moravian wine region around Mikulov.

» **Bramborák** Forget french fries – always order authentic Czech fried potato pancakes as a side dish.

» **Klobása** These sausages are a boozy late-night option in Wenceslas Square.

» **Kofola** Cola meets cough medicine: the uniquely Czech soft drink is worth sampling. You may even grow to like it.

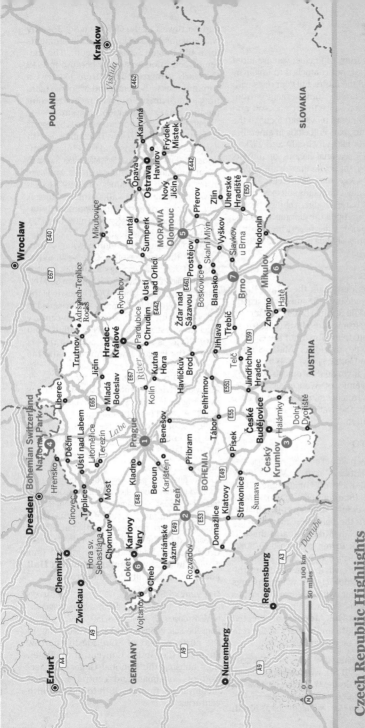

Czech Republic Highlights

1 Experience the glorious old-world heritage of **Prague** (p100), but also hip neighbourhoods like Vinohrady and Žižkov

2 Savour Czech beer at the best of the country's **microbreweries** (p160)

3 Spend a lazy day on the Vltava River around **Český Krumlov** (p139)

4 Explore the spectacular rock formations of the **Bohemian Switzerland National Park** (p127)

5 Admire the audacious Holy Trinity Column in underrated **Olomouc** (p150)

6 Take it easy in sleepy **Loket** (p132) or **Mikulov** (p155)

7 Boost your cultural firepower in the galleries and museums of **Brno** (p145)

PRAGUE

POP 1.22 MILLION

It's the perfect irony of Prague: you are lured there by the past, but compelled to linger by the present and the future. Fill your days with its artistic and architectural heritage – from Gothic and Renaissance to art nouveau and cubist – but after dark move your focus to the lively restaurants, bars and clubs in emerging neighbourhoods like Vinohrady and Žižkov. And if Prague's seasonal legions of tourists wear you down, that's OK. Just drink a glass of the country's legendary lager, relax and be reassured that quiet moments still exist: a private dawn on Charles Bridge, a chilled beer in Letná as you gaze upon the glorious cityscape of Staré Město or getting reassuringly lost in the intimate lanes of Malá Strana or Josefov.

◉ Sights

Central Prague nestles on the Vltava River, separating Hradčany (the medieval castle district) and Malá Strana (Little Quarter) on the west bank, from Staré Město (Old Town) and Nové Město (New Town) on the east.

Prague Castle overlooks Malá Strana, while the twin Gothic spires of Týn Church dominate Old Town Sq (Staroměstské nám). The broad avenue of Wenceslas Sq (Václavské nám) stretches southeast from Staré Město towards the National Museum and main train station.

STARÉ MĚSTO

TOP CHOICE **Old Town Square** HISTORIC AREA
(Staroměstské nám; Map p106; Ⓜ Staroměstská) Kick off in Prague's Old Town Square (Staroměstské nám), dominated by the twin Gothic steeples of **Týn Church** (1365), the baroque **Church of St Nicholas** (Kostel sv Mikuláše) and the **Old Town Hall clock tower** (adult/child 70/50Kč; ◷11am-6pm Mon, 9am-6pm Tue-Sun). From the top spy on the crowds below watching the **astronomical clock** (1410), which springs to life every hour with assorted apostles and a bell-ringing skeleton. In the square's centre is the **Jan Hus Monument**, erected in 1915 on the 500th anniversary of the religious reformer's execution (see p158).

Prague Jewish Museum MUSEUM
(Map p106; ☏221 711 511; www.jewishmuseum.cz; Ticket Reservation Centre, U Starého hřbitova 3a; adult/child 300/200Kč; ◷9am-6pm Sun-Fri Apr-Oct, to 4.30pm Nov-Mar; Ⓜ Staroměstská) North

and northwest of the Old Town Sq, **Josefov** was Prague's Jewish Quarter. Six monuments form the Prague Jewish Museum. The museum's collection exists only because in 1942 the Nazis gathered objects from 153 Jewish communities in Bohemia and Moravia, planning a 'museum of an extinct race' after completing their extermination program.

The **Klaus Synagogue** (Klauzová Synagóga; Map p106; U Starého hřbitova 1) exhibits Jewish customs and traditions, and the **Pinkas Synagogue** (Pinkasova Synagóga; Map p106; Široká 3) is a memorial to the Holocaust. Its walls are inscribed with the names of 77,297 Czech Jews, including Franz Kafka's three sisters. A few blocks northeast is the **Spanish Synagogue** (Španélská Synagóga; Map p106; Dušní 12), built in a Moorish style in 1868.

The oldest still-functioning synagogue in Europe, the early Gothic **Old-New Synagogue** (Staronová Synagóga; Map p106; Červená 1; adult/child 200/140Kč; ◷9.30am-5pm Sun-Thu, 9am-4pm Fri), dates from 1270. Opposite is the **Jewish town hall** (Židovská radnice; closed to the public) with its picturesque 16th-century clock tower. A combined ticket (adult/child 480/320Kč) is available for entry to the six sites of the Prague Jewish Museum and the Old-New Synagogue.

The **Old Jewish Cemetery** (Starý Židovský Hřbitov), entered from the Pinkas Synagogue, is Josefov's most evocative corner. The oldest of its 12,000 graves date from 1439. Use of the cemetery ceased in 1787 as it was becoming so crowded that burials were up to 12 layers deep.

Municipal House HISTORIC BUILDING
(Obecní dům; Map p106; www.obecni-dum.cz; nám Republiky 5; day tours adult/child 270/220Kč, night tours 310/260Kč; ◷10am-9.30pm; Ⓜ nám Republiky) The shopping street of Celetná leads east to the art nouveau Municipal House, decorated by the early 20th century's finest Czech artists. Included in the guided tour are the impressive **Smetana Concert Hall** and other beautifully decorated rooms.

Convent of St Agnes ART GALLERY
(Klášter sv Anežky; Map p106; www.ngprague.cz; U Milosrdných 17; adult/child 150/80Kč; ◷10am-6pm Tue-Sun; Ⓜ Staroměstská) Tucked away in the northern part of Staré Město's narrow streets is the Gothic Convent of St Agnes, now housing the National Gallery's collection of Bohemian and central European medieval art, from the 13th to the mid-16th centuries.

Two Days

Beat the tourist hordes with an early-morning stroll across **Charles Bridge**, and continue uphill on Nerudova to Hradčany and the glories of **Prague Castle**. Don't miss also seeing the superb 'Princely Collections' at the **Lobkowicz Palace**. Head back down to the **Franz Kafka Museum**, and cross the river again to the **Charles Bridge Museum**.

On day two, explore **Josefov**, Prague's original Jewish quarter, and then pack a hilltop picnic for the view-friendly fortress at **Vyšehrad**. Make time for a few Czech brews, either at the relaxed beer garden at **Letna Beer Garden** or the excellent **Pivovarský Klub**, before kicking on for robust Czech food at **U Ferdinanda**, or tapas and seafood at **U malé velryby**. For a nightcap head to a cool late-night spot like **Čili Bar** or **Duende**.

Museum of Czech Cubism   MUSEUM
(Muzeum Českého Kubismu; Map p106; www.ng prague.cz; Ovocný trh 19; adult/child 100/50Kč; ⊙10am-6pm Tue-Sun; Ⓜnám Republiky) Located in Josef Gočár's House of the Black Madonna, the angular collection of art and furniture is yet another branch of Prague's National Gallery. On the ground floor is the excellent Grand Cafe Orient.

Estates Theatre   HISTORIC BUILDING
(Stavovské Divadlo; Map p106; Ovocný trh 1; ⓂMůstek) To the south of the Old Town Sq is the neoclassical Estates Theatre, where Mozart's *Don Giovanni* premiered on 29 October 1787, with the maestro himself conducting. It's still used for performances.

NOVÉ MĚSTO & VYŠVHRAD

Wenceslas Square   HISTORIC AREA
(Václavské nám; Map p106; ⓂMůstek) Dating from 1348, Nové Město (New Town) is only 'new' when compared with the even older Staré Město. The sloping avenue of Wenceslas Sq, lined with shops, banks and restaurants, is dominated by a **statue of St Wenceslas** on horseback. Wenceslas Sq has always been a focus for demonstrations and public gatherings. Beneath the statue is a shrine to the victims of communism, including students Jan Palach and Jan Zajíc, who burned themselves alive in 1969 protesting against the Soviet invasion.

National Museum   MUSEUM
(Map p106; www.nm.cz; Václavské nám 68; adult/child 150/50Kč; free admission 1st Thu of month; ⊙10am-6pm, closed 1st Tue of month; ⓂMuzeum) The imposing National Museum has ho-hum collections covering prehistory, mineralogy and stuffed animals, but the grand interior is worth seeing for the pantheon of Czech historical luminaries. In 2010, a new annex showcasing special exhibitions opened across the street in a building that has been used – at different times – as the Prague Stock Exchange, the Czechoslovak Parliament and the studios of Radio Free Europe. Guided tours of this building run at 10am and 1pm on Wednesdays. In 2011 the main building of the museum is scheduled to close for five years for major renovations. Ask at the Prague Information Service for the latest news.

Charles Bridge Museum   MUSEUM
(Muzeum Karlova mostu; Map p106; www.muzeum karlovamostu.cz; Křížovnické nám; adult/child 150/70Kč; ⊙10am-8pm, to 6pm Oct-Apr; 🚊17, 18 to Karlovy lázě) Before or after strolling across Charles Bridge, examine the history of the Vltava's most famous crossing with displays on ancient bridge-building techniques, masonry and carpentry.

FREE Vyšehrad   Historic Area
(Map p102; www.praha-vysehrad.cz; ⊙9.30am-6pm Apr-Oct, to 5pm Nov-Mar; ⓂVyšehrad) Pack a picnic and head to the ancient clifftop fortress Vyšehrad, perched above the Vltava. Dominated by the towers of **Church of SS Peter & Paul** (Kostel sv Petra a Pavla) and founded in the 11th century, Vyšehrad was rebuilt in the neo-Gothic style between 1885 and 1903. Don't miss the art nouveau murals inside. The adjacent **Slavín Cemetery** contains the graves of many Czechs, including the composers Smetana and Dvořák. The view from the citadel's southern battlements is superb.

Mucha Museum   MUSEUM
(Muchovo Muzeum; Map p106; www.mucha.cz; Panská 7; adult/child 180/90Kč; ⊙10am-6pm; ⓂMůstek) Fans of artist Alfons Mucha, renowned for his art nouveau posters of garlanded Slavic maidens, can admire his work at the Mucha Museum, including an interesting video on his life and art.

Greater Prague

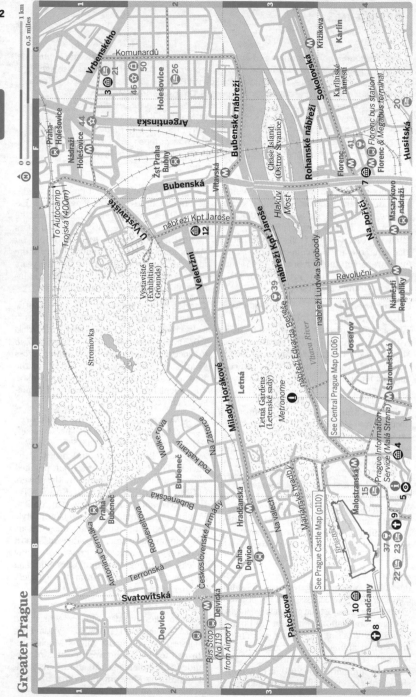

0 0.5 miles
0 1 km
N

G
Vrtbenského
Komunardů
Holešovice
3 21
46 50 26
Argentinská
Praha-Holešovice
Nádraží 44
Holešovice
Žst Praha Bubny
Bubenské nábřeží
Bubenská
Vltavská
Chase Island
(Ostrov Štvanice)
Rohanské nábřeží
Sokolovská
Křižíkova
Karlín
Karlínské náměstí
Husitská
20
Florenc bus station
Florenc & Megabus terminal
Florenc 41
7
Na poříčí
Masarykovo nádraží
Náměstí Republiky
Revoluční
Josefov
Staroměstská

F **E** **D**
To Autocamp
Trojská (400m)
U Výstaviště
nábřeží Kpt Jaroše
12
Výstaviště
(Exhibition Grounds)
Veletržní
Stromovka
nábřeží Kpt Jaroše
Hlávkův Most
nábřeží Ludvíka Svobody
39
nábřeží Edvarda Beneše
Vltava River

C **B** **A**
Milady Horákové
Letná
Letná Gardens
(Letenské sady)
Metronome
1
See Central Prague Map (p106)
Na Zátorce
Wolkerova
Wolkerova
Pod kaštany
Bubeneč
Bubenečská
Bubeneč
Praha-Bubeneč
Antonína Čermáka
Roosveltova
Československé Armády
Hradčanská
Na valech
Mariánské hradby
Brusnice
See Prague Castle Map (p110)
Prague Information
Service (Malá Strana)
Malostranská
15
4
5
9
37
22 23
10
Hradčany
8
Terronská
Praha-Dejvice
Svatovítská
Dejvická
Dejvice
Patočkova
Bus Stop
(No 119
from Airport)

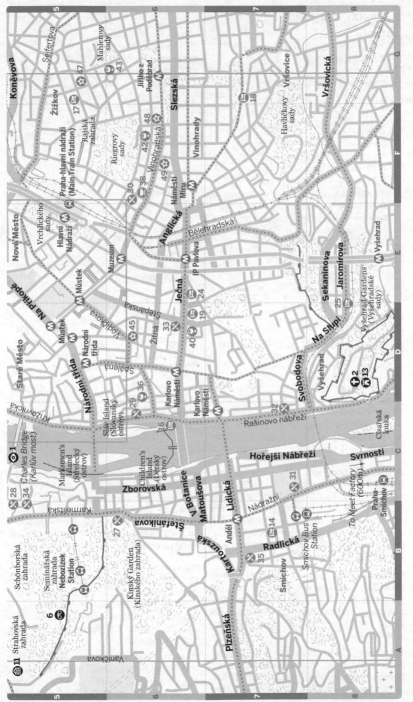

Prague City Museum   MUSEUM
(Hlavního Města Prahy Muzeum; Map p102; www.muzeumprahy.cz; Na Poříčí 52, Karlín; adult/child 120/50Kč; ⊙9am-6pm Tue-Sun; ⛔Florenc) This museum, housed in a grand, neo-Renaissance building near Florenc metro station, charts Prague's evolution from prehistory to the 19th century.

Lucerna pasáž   HISTORIC BUILDING
(Map p106; Lucerna Passage; ⛔Můstek) Just off Wenceslas Sq, the Lucerna pasáž is an art-nouveau shopping arcade now graced with David Černý's (see the box, p109) *Horse* sculpture.

Museum of Communism   MUSEUM
(Muzeum Komunismu; Map p106; www.muzeumkomunismu.cz; Na příkopě 10; adult/child 180/140Kč; ⊙9am-9pm; ⛔Můstek) The Museum of Com-

munism is tucked (ironically) behind McDonald's. The exhibition is fascinating through its use of simple everyday objects to illuminate the restrictions of life under communism. Be sure to watch the video about protests leading up to the Velvet Revolution. You'll never think of it as a pushover again.

HRADČANY

The Hradčany area west from Prague Castle is mainly residential, with shops and restaurants on Loretánská and Pohořelec. In 1598 Hradčany was almost levelled by Hussites and fire, and the 17th-century palaces were built on the ruins.

TOP CHOICE **Prague Castle**   CASTLE
(Pražský hrad; Map p110; www.hrad.cz; ⊙castle 9am-6pm Apr-Oct, 9am-4pm Nov-Mar, grounds 5am-midnight Apr-Oct, 9am-11pm Nov-Mar,

gardens closed Nov-Mar; 🚊22, 23 to Pražský hrad). The biggest castle complex in the world, Prague Castle is the seat of Czech power, housing the president's office and the ancient Bohemian crown jewels.

The **long tour** (adult/child 350/175Kč) includes the Old Royal Palace, the Story of Prague Castle exhibit, the Basilica of St George, St Vitus Cathedral, the Convent of St George, the Prague Castle Picture Gallery, and Golden Lane with Daliborka Tower. The **short tour** (adult/child 250/125Kč) focuses only on the Old Royal Palace, St Vitus Cathedral, the Basilica of St George, Golden Lane and the Story of Prague Castle exhibit. Buy tickets at the **Castle Information Centre** in the Second Courtyard. Most areas are wheelchair accessible. Count on about three hours for the long tour and two hours for the short tour. Tickets are valid for two days, but you can only visit each attraction once. DIY audio guides can also be rented. Entry to the castle courtyards and the gardens is free.

The main entrance is at the western end. The **changing of the guard**, with stylish uniforms created by Theodor Pistek (costume designer for the film *Amadeus*), takes place every hour, on the hour. At noon a band plays from the windows above.

The **Matthias Gate** (Matyášova Brána) leads to the Second Courtyard and the **Chapel of the Holy Cross** (Kaple sv Kříže). On the north side is the **Prague Castle Picture Gallery** (adult/child 150/80Kč, admission free 4-6pm Mon; ☉9am-5pm Apr-Oct, to 4pm Nov-Mar), with a collection of European baroque art.

The Third Courtyard is dominated by **St Vitus Cathedral** (Katedrala sv Víta; included on long and short tours), a French Gothic structure begun in 1344 by Emperor Charles IV, but not completed until 1929. Stained-glass windows created by early 20th-century Czech artists illuminate the interior, including one by Alfons Mucha (third chapel on the left as you enter the cathedral) featuring SS Cyril and Methodius. In the apse is the **tomb of St John of Nepomuk** – two tons of baroque silver watched over by hovering cherubs.

The 14th-century chapel on the cathedral's southern side with the black imperial eagle on the door contains the **tomb of St Wenceslas**, the Czechs' patron saint and the Good King Wenceslas of Christmas carol fame. Wenceslas' zeal in spreading Christianity and his submission to the German King Henry I saw him murdered by his brother, Boleslav I. According to legend he

was stabbed to death clinging to the Romanesque lion's-head handle that graces the chapel door. The smaller door on the far side, beside the windows, leads to the Bohemian crown jewels (not open to the public).

On the southern side of the cathedral's exterior is the **Golden Gate** (Zlatá brána), a triple-arched doorway topped by a 14th-century mosaic of the Last Judgment.

Also on the southern side is the **Story of Prague Castle** (www.story-castle.cz; adult/child 140/70Kč, free with tour tickets) exhibition. This multimedia take on history includes a 40-minute **documentary** (☉in English 9.45am, 11.14am, 12.45pm, 2.15pm & 3.45pm).

Opposite is the entrance to the **Old Royal Palace** (Starý Královský Palác) with its elegantly vaulted **Vladislav Hall** (1486–1502). Horsemen used to ride into the hall up the ramp at the far end for indoor jousts. Two Catholic councillors were thrown out the window of the adjacent **Chancellery** by irate Protestant nobles on 23 May 1618. This infamous Second Defenestration of Prague ignited the Thirty Years' War.

Leaving the palace, the Romanesque **St George's Basilica** (Bazilika sv Jiří) dates from 1142, and the nearby **St George's Convent** (Klášter sv Jiří; www.ngprague.cz; adult/child 150/80Kč, free with long tour; ☉10am-6pm Tue-Sun) was Bohemia's first convent, established in 973 by Boleslav II. It now showcases 19th-century Bohemian art.

Beyond, the crowds surge into the **Golden Lane**, a 16th-century tradesmen's quarter of tiny houses in the castle walls. Kafka lived and wrote at his sister's place at No 22 in 1916 and 1917.

On the right, before the castle's exit, is the **Lobkowicz Palace** (www.lobkowiczevents.cz/palace; Jiřská 3; adult/concession 275/175Kč; ☉10.30am-6pm). Built in the 1570s, this palace was home to the aristocratic Lobkowicz family until WWII when it was co-opted by the Nazis. The communists confiscated it in 1948, and it was returned to the family only in 2002. Now it is a private museum focused on the **Princely Collections**, with highlights including paintings by Canaletto and original sheet music by Mozart, Beethoven and Hadyn.

From the castle's eastern end, the Old Castle Steps lead to Malostranská metro station, or turn sharp right to wind through the **Gardens on the Ramparts**.

There are two main routes to the castle. You can catch the metro to Malostranská or tram 12, 20, 22 or 23 to Malostranská nám

CZECH REPUBLIC PRAGUE

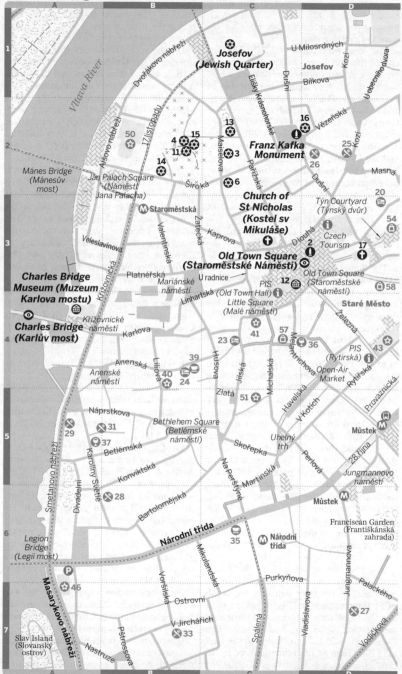

Josefov
(Jewish Quarter)

Josefov

Franz Kafka
Monument

Máneš Bridge
(Mánesův
most)

Jan Palach Square
(Náměstí
Jana Palacha)

Staroměstská

Church of
St Nicholas
(Kostel sv
Mikuláše)

Týn Courtyard
(Týnský dvůr)

Czech
Tourism

Old Town Square
(Staroměstské Náměstí)

Old Town Square
(Staroměstské
náměstí)

Charles Bridge
Museum (Muzeum
Karlova mostu)

Charles Bridge
(Karlův most)

Křížovnické
náměstí

Mariánské
náměstí

U radnice

PIS
(Old Town Hall)

Little Square
(Malé náměstí)

Staré Město

Anenské
náměstí

PIS
(Rytířská)

Open-Air
Market

Bethlehem Square
(Betlémské
náměstí)

Můstek

Můstek

Legion
Bridge
(Legií most)

Franciscan Garden
(Františkánská
zahrada)

Národní
třída

Národní třída

Slav Island
(Slovanský
ostrov)

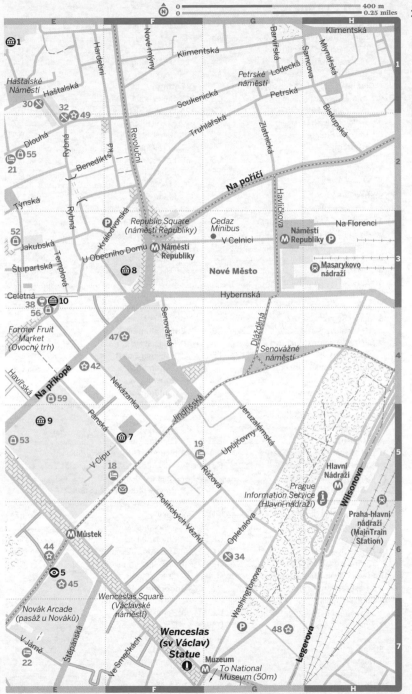

0 400 m
0 0.25 miles

Klimentská

E **F** **G** **H**

1

Nové mlýny

Klimentská

Barvířská

Samcova

Mlynářská

Petrské náměstí

Lodecká

Biskupská

Haštalské Náměstí

30

32 49

Haštalská

Hradební

Soukenická

Petrská

Dlouhá

55

21

Rybná

Dušní

Benediktská

Revoluční

Truhlářská

Zlatnická

Na poříčí

Havlíčkova

Týnská

Rybná

Králodvorská

Republic Square
(náměstí Republiky)

Cedaz
Minibus

V Celnici

Na Florenci

52

Jakubská

Templová

U Obecního Domu

Náměstí
Republiky

Náměstí
Republiky

Štupartská

8

Nové Město

Masarykovo
nádraží

Celetná

38

56

10

Hybernská

Former Fruit
Market
(Ovocný trh)

47

Senovážná

Dlážděná

Senovážné
náměstí

Havířská

Na příkopě

42

Nekázanka

59

9

Panská

Jindřišská

Jeruzalémská

53

7

Upujčovny

Hlavní
Nádraží

Wilsonova

V Cípu

18

Růžová

19

Prague
Information Service
(Hlavní nádraží)

Praha-hlavní
nádraží
(Main Train
Station)

Můstek

Politických Vězňů

44

5

45

34

Novák Arcade
(pasáž u Nováků)

Wenceslas Square
(Václavské
náměstí)

Opletalova

Washingtonova

48

Legerova

V Jámě

22

Štěpánská

Ve Smečkách

**Wenceslas
(sv Václav)
Statue**

Muzeum

To National
Museum (50m)

E **F** **G** **H**

Central Prague

THE CHALLENGING MR CĚRNÝ

David Cěrný's work polarises people. In Prague's Lucerna pasáž, he's hung St Wenceslas and his horse upside down, and across the river outside the Kafka Museum, Cěrný's *Piss* sculpture invites contributions by SMS. Rising above the city, like a faded relic from *Star Wars*, is the Žižkov Tower with Cěrný's giant babies crawling up the exterior.

Cěrný's other recent project is Meet-Factory (www.meetfactory.cz), a multi purpose gallery, artists' collective and performance space in a former railways workshop across the river in Smíchov.

and look forward to a brisk walk up Neru-dova. Alternatively take tram 22 or 23 to the Pražský hrad stop, where you can enter at the Second Courtyard.

Šternberg Palace ART GALLERY
(Map p102; www.ngprague.cz; adult/child 150/80Kč; ⊗10am-6pm Tue-Sun; ☒22, 23 to Pražský hrad) The 18th-century Šternberg Palace outside the castle entrance houses the National Gallery with the country's principal collection of 14th- to 18th-century European art.

Strahov Library MONASTERY
(Strahovská Knihovna; Map p102; ☒233 107 718; www.strahovskyklaster.cz; adult/child 80/50Kč; ⊗9am-noon & 1-5pm; ☒22, 23 to Pohořelec) A passage at Pohořelec 8 leads to the Strahov Library, the country's largest monastic library, built in 1679. The Philosophy and Theological Halls feature gorgeous frescoed ceilings.

Sanctuary of Our Lady of Loreta CHURCH
(Map p102; www.loreta.cz; Loretánské nám 7; adult/child 110/90Kč; ⊗9am-4.30pm Tue-Sun; ☒22, 23 to Pohořelec) The baroque Sanctuary of Our Lady of Loreta showcases precious religious artefacts, and the cloister houses a 17th-century replica of the Santa Casa from the Italian town of Loreta, reputedly the Virgin Mary's house in Nazareth, transported to Italy by angels in the 13th century.

MALÁ STRANA
Downhill from the castle are the baroque backstreets of Malá Strana (Little Quarter), built in the 17th and 18th centuries by victorious Catholic clerics and nobles on the foundations of their Protestant predecessors' Renaissance palaces.

Charles Bridge BRIDGE
(Karlův most; Map p102;☒17, 18 to Karlovy lázně) Malá Strana is linked to Staré Město by Charles Bridge. Built in 1357, and graced by 30 18th-century statues, until 1841 it was the city's only bridge. Climb the **Malá Strana bridge tower** (adult/child 50/30Kč; ⊗10am-6pm Apr-Nov) for excellent views. In the middle of the bridge is a bronze statue (1683) of St John of Nepomuk, a priest thrown to his death from the bridge in 1393 for refusing to reveal the queen's confessions to King Wenceslas IV. Visit the bridge at dawn before the tourist hordes arrive. The bridge has been undergoing painstaking restoration for several years, a process that should (hopefully!) be completed when you visit. Gangs of pickpockets work the bridge day and night, so watch your valuables.

St Nicholas Church CHURCH
(Kostel sv Mikuláše; Map p102; www.psalterium.cz; adult/child 70/35Kč; ⊗9am-5pm Mar-Oct, to 4pm Nov-Feb; ☒12, 20, 22, 23 to Malostranské nam) Near the cafe-crowded main square of Malostranské nám is the beautiful baroque St Nicholas Church. Take the stairs to the gallery to see the 17th-century *Passion Cycle* paintings. From April to October the church is used for **classical music concerts** (adult/child 490/300Kč; ⊗6pm Wed-Mon).

Wallenstein Palace HISTORIC BUILDING
FREE (Valdštejnský palác; Map p110; ⊗10am-4pm Sat & Sun; ☒12, 20, 22, 23 to Malostranské nam) East along Tomášská is the Wallenstein Palace, built in 1630 and now home to the Czech Republic's Senate. Albrecht von Wallenstein, a notorious general in the Thirty Years' War, defected from the Protestants to the Catholics and built this palace with his former comrades' expropriated wealth. In 1634 the Habsburg Emperor Ferdinand II learned that Wallenstein was about to switch sides again and had him assassinated. The adjacent **Wallenstein Gardens** boast a Renaissance loggia and bronze (replica) sculptures.

Franz Kafka Museum MUSEUM
(Map p102; www.kafkamuseum.cz; Cihelná 2b; adult/child 120/60Kč; ⊗10am-6pm; ⓜMalostranská) North of Charles Bridge is the innovative and arty Franz Kafka Museum. Kafka's diaries, letters and first editions provide a poignant balance to the T-shirt cliché the writer has become in tourist shops. In front is the **Piss sculpture** by Czech artist David Cěrný with two animatronic figures piddling in a puddle shaped like the Czech Republic.

Prague Castle

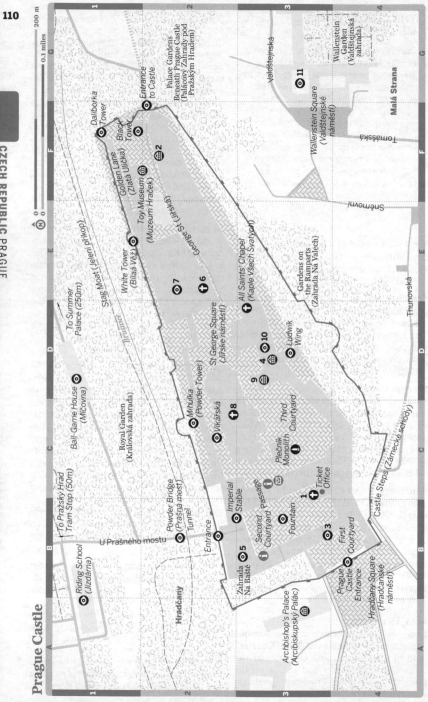

200 m
0.1 miles

Dalibořka Tower

Entrance to Castle

Black Tower

Golden Lane (Zlatá Ulička)

Toy Museum (Muzeum Hraček) 2

Palace Gardens Beneath Prague Castle (Palácovy Zahrady pod Pražským Hradem)

Wallenstein Garden (Valdštejnská zahrada)

11

Valdštejnská

Malá Strana

Tomášská

Stag Moat (Jelení příkop)

White Tower (Bílá Věž)

George St (Jiřská)

Šnemovní

To Summer Palace (250m)

Brusnice

7

6

All Saints' Chapel (Kaple Všech Svatých)

Gardens on the Ramparts (Zahrada Na Valech)

Thunská

Ball-Game House (Míčovna)

Royal Garden (Královská zahrada)

St George Square (Jiřské náměstí)

10

4

Ludwik Wing

9

Mihulka (Powder Tower)

Vikářská 8

Plečnik Monolith

Third Courtyard

Castle Steps (Zámecké schody)

To Pražský Hrad Tram Stop (50m)

Powder Bridge (Prašná most)

Tunnel

Entrance

Imperial Stable

Second Passage

Courtyard

Fountain

Ticket Office

1

3

First Courtyard

U Prašného mostu

Hradčany

5

Zahrada Na Baště

Archbishop's Palace (Arcibiskupský Palác)

Prague Castle Entrance

Hradčany Square (Hradčanské náměstí)

Riding School (Jízdárna)

ART FOR ART'S SAKE

Head to Holešovice for two stunning buildings showcasing contemporary art.

Start your arty day at the functionalist **Veletržní Palace** (Veletržní Palác; Map p102; www.ngprague.cz; Dukelských hrdinů 47; adult/child 250/120Kč; ⊙10am-6pm Tue-Sun; 🚊5, 12, 14, 15, 17 to Veletržni), originally built in 1928 to house trade exhibitions and now home to the National Gallery's superb collection of 20th- and 21st-century Czech and European art. Catch the all-glass lift from the Small Hall to the 5th floor to get a quick overview of the atrium displays. Work your way down to the 3rd floor for Czech cubist masterpieces and French impressionist works, and the 2nd floor for kinetic art and communist-era social realism. If you're not wonderfully overwhelmed after all that, it's foreign art from Klimt, Schiele and Picasso on the 1st floor. Wow.

Allow at least half a day at the Veletržni Palace, and then catch tram 5, 12 or 15 to the nearby **DOX Centre for Contemporary Art** (Map p102; www.doxprague.org; Poupětova 1; adult/child 180/90Kč; ⊙10am-6pm Sat-Mon, 11am-7pm Wed-Fri, closed Tues; 🚊5, 12, 15 to Ortenovo nám), stunning proof of Holešovice's growing confidence. The minimalist multilevel building occupies an entire corner block, providing Prague's most capacious gallery space, and is studded with a diverse range of thought-provoking contemporary art and photography.

Funicular Railway   LANDMARK
(Map p102; tram ticket 26Kč; ⊙every 10-20 min 9.15am-8.45pm; 🚊12, 20, 22, 23 to Újezd) Escape the tourist throngs on the cable car from Újezd to the rose gardens on **Petřín Hill**. Ascend 299 steps to the top of the view-friendly iron-framed **Petřín Lookout Tower** (Map p102; adult/child 100/50Kč; lift 50Kč extra; ⊙10am-10pm May-Sep, to 7pm Apr & Oct, to 5pm Sat & Sun Nov-Mar), built in 1891 in imitation of the Eiffel Tower. Behind the tower, a staircase leads to lanes winding back to Malostranské nám.

Prague Castle

◎ **Sights**
1 Chapel of the Holy Cross
   (Kaple sv Kríže).................................C3
2 Lobkowicz Palace..............................F2
3 Matthias Gate (Matyášova
   Brána)..B3
4 Old Royal Palace (Starý
   Královský Palác).............................D3
5 Prague Castle Picture Gallery...........B3
6 St George's Basilica (Bazilika
   sv Jiří)...E2
7 St George's Convent (Kláster
   sv Jiří)...E2
8 St Vitus Cathedral (Katedrala
   sv Víta)..C2
9 Story of Prague Castle.....................D3
10 Vladislav Hall...................................D3
11 Wallenstein Palace
   (Valdštejnský palác)........................G3

☞ **Tours**

Prague Tours   WALKING
(☑775 369 121; www.praguer.com; per person 400-1200Kč) Includes a Ghost Tour and specialist Kafka and architecture tours.

Prague Walks   WALKING
(☑608 339 099; www.praguewalks.com; per person 300-800Kč) From communism to Old Town pubs.

Wittmann Tours   JEWISH
(☑222 252 472; www.wittmann-tours.com; per person from 750Kč) Specialises in tours of Jewish interest, including day trips (1250Kč) to the Museum of the Ghetto at Terezín and visits to the Moravian town of Třebíč.

🎇 **Festivals & Events**

Prague Spring   CLASSICAL MUSIC
(www.festival.cz) From 12 May to 4 June, classical music kicks off summer.

Prague Fringe Festival   ARTS
(www.praguefringe.com) Eclectic action in late May and early June.

Czech Beer Festival   BEER
(www.ceskypivnifestival.cz) Lots of food, music and about 70 beers from around the country. Mid- to late May.

Khamoro   MUSIC & CULTURE
(www.khamoro.cz) Late May's annual celebration of Roma culture.

United Islands   MUSIC
(www.unitedislands.cz) World music in mid-June.

CHEAP THRILLS

Prague's great for walking, and some of the city's best sights seen on two legs are also free of charge:

» Stroll through the gardens and courtyards at **Prague Castle.**

» Visit **Charles Bridge** at dawn.

» Wander through the **Wallenstein Gardens**.

» Explore the fortress at **Vyšehrad**.

» Get free entry to the **National Museum** on the first Thursday of every month.

» Enjoy reduced admission charges at the various locations of the **National Gallery** (www.ngprague.cz) from 4pm to 6pm Tuesday to Sunday. It's free on the first Wednesday of the month from 3pm to 8pm.

» Catch tram 22 or 23 from Peace Square in Vinohrady all the way to Prague Castle for a DIY city tour. It might be the best 26Kč you ever spend.

» Make lunch your main meal of the day to save money on eating out, taking advantage of restaurants' daily menus (*denní menu* in Czech). You'll usually find the *denní menu* listed on a chalkboard out the front. Count on around 35Kč for soup and 100Kč for a main.

» Combine people-watching and great river views while grabbing a cheap-as-chips sunset beer and grilled sausage at the raffish Letna Beer Garden.

Prague International Jazz Festival JAZZ (www.jazzfestivalpraha.cz) Late November.

Christmas Market SEASONAL FESTIVAL 1 to 24 December in the Old Town Square.

🛏 Sleeping

At New Year, Christmas or Easter, and from May to September, book in advance. Prices quoted are for the high season: generally April to October. Rates can increase up to 15% at peak times. Rates normally decrease by 20% to 40% from November to March. Consider an apartment for stays longer than a couple of nights.

For better value stay outside of the Old Town (Staré Město) and take advantage of Prague's excellent public transport network.

Accommodation agencies include the following:

Ave Hotels (☑800 046 385; www.avehotels.cz) Online and telephone booking service.

Hostel.cz (☑415 658 580; www.hostel.cz) Around 60 hostels with online booking.

Mary's Travel & Tourist Service (☑222 254 007; www.marys.cz) Private rooms, hostels, apartments and hotels.

Prague City Apartments (☑800 800 722; www.prague-city-apartments.cz) Specialists in holiday apartments near the city centre.

STARÉ MĚSTO

U Zeleného Věnce PENSION €€ (Map p106; ☑222 220 178; www.uzv.cz; Řetězová 10; s/d/tr 1700/2200/2800Kč; 🅿@🛜; Ⓜ Staroměstská) Just a few minutes' amble from Old Town Square, the Green Garland is central yet very peaceful. The simply furnished bedrooms vary in size but all are spotlessly clean, and the attic rooms have exposed medieval roof beams.

Hotel Antik HOTEL €€ (Map p106; ☑222 322 288; www.antikhotels.com; Dlouhá 22; s/d 2590/2990Kč; 🅿@🛜; Ⓜ nám Republiky) The popular Antik has a modern tinge with flash bathrooms and flat screen TVs, but heritage fans can still celebrate its 15th-century building (no lift) beside an antique shop. It's a great area for bars and restaurants, so ask for a quieter back room.

Savic Hotel LUXURY HOTEL €€€ (Map p106; ☑233 920 118; www.hotelsavic.cz; Jilská 7; d/ste €169/239; 🅿@🛜; Ⓜ Staroměstská) Looking for somewhere romantic and central? Originally a Dominican convent, the Savic's combination of 14th-century heritage and 21st-century amenities avoids the chintzy overkill of other top-end places.

Hostel Týn HOSTEL € (Map p106; ☑224 808 333; www.tyn.prague-hostels. cz; Týnská 19; dm/s/d/tr 420/1300/1300/1440Kč; @; Ⓜ Staroměstská) In a quiet lane metres from Old Town Sq, you'll struggle to find better-value central accommodation. Downstairs is a good-value vegetarian Indian restaurant. Cash only.

NOVÉ MĚSTO

TOP CHOICE **Dahlia Inn** PENSION €
(Map p102; ☑222 517 518; www.dahlia inn.com; Lípová 1444/20 16; s/d €49/59; ❀@☎; MKarlovo nám) From the outside the building is nondescript, but a few floors up is a relaxed and friendly B&B with spacious rooms decorated in designer style, flat screen TVs and cool, classy bathrooms. The well-travelled British–Czech owner is a mine of information on local restaurants, bars and clubs.

Miss Sophie's HOSTEL/BOUTIQUE HOTEL €€
(Map p102; ☑296 303 530; www.miss-sophies. com; Melounova 3; dm 450Kč, s/d/apt from 1750/2050/3000Kč; @☎; MIP Pavlova) 'Boutique hostel' sums up this converted apartment building. Polished concrete blends with oak flooring, and the basement lounge is all bricks and black leather. Good restaurants await outside.

Botel Matylda HOTEL €€
(Map p102; ☑724 800 100; www.botelmatylda. cz; Masarykovo nábřeží-Manes 16; s/d/ste from €79/89/149; ❀☎; ☐17, 21 to Národní divadlo) Botel Matylda offers an absolute riverfront location with compact rooms/cabins decked out in polished wood. You're paying a little more for sleeping on a boat, but how many times can you say *ahoj* to ducks every morning? On the top deck is a romantic restaurant with good Italian food. The owners have recently added a second 'botel', the *Klotylda*, moored nearby.

Icon Hotel BOUTIQUE HOTEL €€€
(Map p106; ☑221 634 100; www.iconhotel.eu; V Jámě 6; d & ste €180-240; @☎; ☐3, 9, 14, 24 to Vodičkova) Here's design-savvy cool concealed down a quiet laneway. The handmade beds are extra-wide, and the crew at reception is unpretentious and hip. Linger in the downstairs bar before exploring Prague's nightlife.

Prague's Heaven HOSTEL €
(Map p102; ☑603 153 617; www.hostelpraha.eu; Jaromírova 20, Vyšehrad; dm 320-350Kč, s/d/tr/q from 850/1300/1500/1980; @☎; ☐17,18,24 to Svatoplukova) This quieter spot in Vyšehrad is ideal for travellers not interested in Prague's party town reputation. Apartment-style rooms and shiny new bathrooms huddle around a central lounge.

It's a 15-minute tram journey to central Prague.

Hostel Rosemary HOSTEL €
(Map p106; ☑222 211 124; www.praguecity hostel.cz; Růžová 5; dm 400-500Kč, s/tw/tr from 900/1300/1650Kč; @☎; MMůstek) Hostel Rosemary enjoys a quiet location near Wenceslas Sq and Prague's main train station. Rooms are light and airy with high ceilings; some include a private bathroom and kitchen.

Hostel AZ HOSTEL €
(Map p106; ☑246 052 409; www.hostel-az. com; Jindřišská 5; dm 320-350Kč, s/d/tr/q 950/1000/1450/1600Kč; @☎; MMůstek) This smaller, homely hostel enjoys a central location near Wenceslas Sq, an in-house laundromat and seven-bed dorms. It's down a shopping arcade so is relatively quiet after dark.

VINOHRADY & ŽIŽKOV

Czech Inn HOSTEL/BOUTIQUE HOTEL €€
(Map p102; ☑267 267 600; www.czech-inn.com; Francouzská 76, Vinohrady; dm 300-400Kč, d/tw/tr from 1400/1400/2100Kč; @☎; ☐5, 9, 26 to Husinecká) From dorms to private apartments, everything's covered at this designer hostel/hotel with good transport links. There are no kitchen facilities, but Vinohrady's restaurants and cheap eats are minutes away. A cool on-site bar lingers downstairs.

Clown & Bard Hostel HOSTEL €
(Map p102; ☑222 716 453; www.clownandbard. com; Bořivojova 102, Žižkov; dm 300-380Kč, d/tw/tr 1000/1400/2100Kč; @☎; ☐5, 9, 26 to Husinecka) The party crowd gravitates towards the thumping basement bar that stays open till midnight. Recharge at the all-veggie, all-you-can-eat breakfast any time until 2pm. Double rooms offer (slightly) more seclusion.

Hostel Elf HOSTEL €
(Map p102; ☑222 540 963; www.hostelelf.com; Husitská 11, Žižkov; dm 340-420Kč, s/d/tr from 980/1260/1440Kč; @☎; MFlorenc) Have the best of both worlds at this hip hostel a short-ish walk downhill from Žižkov's bars. Swap tales in the beer garden or grab quiet time in the hidden nooks and crannies. More expensive rooms have private bathrooms.

HOLEŠOVICE

Sir Toby's Hostel HOSTEL €
(Map p102; ☑283 870 635; www.sirtobys. com; Dělnická 24; dm 350-500Kč, s/d/tw/tr 1150/1400/1600/1800Kč; @☎; ☐1, 3, 5, 25 to

MIND YOUR MANNERS

It's customary to say *dobrý den* (good day) when entering a shop, cafe or quiet bar, and *na shledanou* (goodbye) when leaving.

Dělnická) In an up-and-coming suburb a 10-minute tram ride from the city centre, Sir Toby's is in a refurbished apartment building on a quiet street. Staff are friendly and knowledgeable, and there is a shared kitchen and lounge.

Hotel Leon   HOTEL €

(Map p102; ☑220 941 351; www.leonhotel.eu; Ortenovo nám 26; s/d/tr/q from 810/1380/1770/2000; @📶; Ⓜ️Nádraží Holešovice; 🚊5, 12 to Ortenovo nám) Bridging the gap between small hotel and hostel, the Leon has simply furnished compact rooms, some with private bathrooms, and a super-convenient tram stop just outside. The Nádraží Holešovice metro station is also just a short walk away. If you're travelling in a group of three or four, consider this spot rather than a crowded hostel dorm.

Autocamp Trojská   CAMPING GROUND €

(off Map p102; ☑283 850 487; www.autocamp -trojska.cz; Trojská 157; site per person 100Kč, plus per tent/car 150/90Kč; ⊘year-round; Ⓜ️Nádraží Holešovice then bus 112 to Kazanka) The most comfortable and secure of half a dozen camping grounds in this quiet northern suburb, Trojská offers a garden bar and restaurant, a laundry and an on-site shop.

MALÁ STRANA & SMÍCHOV

Little Town Budget Hotel   HOSTEL/HOTEL €

(Map p102; ☑242 406 965; www.littletownhotel. cz; Malostranské nám 11/260; dm 500-600Kč, s/d/ tr from 1000/1400/1650; @📶; 🚊12, 20, 22, 23 to Malostranské nám) A brilliant location in Malá Strana reveals excellent-value rooms arrayed around a quiet, central courtyard. Rooms are simply furnished with whitewashed walls and have a relaxed ambience verging on monastic. The more expensive three- and four-person self-contained rooms/apartments (1850Kč to 2400Kč) with kitchen and bathroom are excellent value for groups.

Augustine   LUXURY HOTEL €€€

(Map p102; ☑266 112 233; www.theaugustine.com; Letenská 12/33; d/ste from €340/800; 🅿️🌸@📶; 🚊12, 20, 22, 23 to Malostranské nám). Occupying a rambling former Augustinian monastery in Malá Strana, the Augustine has elegant

and spacious rooms, beautiful gardens and a premium spa with relax-at-all-costs services. The hotel's own specially brewed beer is served in a spectacular cellar bar.

Aparthotel Angel   APARTMENT €€

(Map p102; ☑242 211; www.aparthotelangel.com; Karla Engliše 2/3221, Smíchov; d/q from €69/79; 🅿️📶; Ⓜ️Anděl) These spacious and modern self-contained apartments in the midst of Smíchov's 21st-century regeneration are excellent value for travelling families. The Old Town and Prague Castle are a short tram ride away, and nearby are good local restaurants.

Hotel Sax   BOUTIQUE HOTEL €€

(Map p102; ☑257 531 268; www.hotelsax.cz; Jánský Vršek 328/3; d from €120; 🅿️@📶; 🚊12, 20, 22, 23 to Malostranské nám) In a quiet, atmospheric corner of Malá Strana, the eclectically furnished Hotel Sax has huge baths, big flat-screen TVs, primary-coloured leather couches and striking abstract photography; all tinged with a thoroughly 1960s design aesthetic.

🍴 Eating

Choose from good-value beer halls with no-nonsense fare, or enjoy a chic riverside restaurant with a high-flying clientele and prices to match.

Eating in Prague's tourist areas is pricey, but cheaper eats are available just a block or two away. Regular lunch specials (look for *denní menu* in Czech) will stretch your travel budget.

Most restaurants open from 11am to 11pm. Phone numbers are included for restaurants where bookings are recommended for dinner.

STARÉ MĚSTO

Céleste Bistro   MEDITERRANEAN €€

(Map p106; ☑773 222 422; www.celestebistro.cz; V Kolkovně 7; mains 275-415Kč; ⊘11.30am-2.30pm & 6pm-midnight Mon-Sat; Ⓜ️Staroměstská) Tucked away on one of the Old Town's loveliest streets, Céleste presents French and Mediterranean flavours in an expansive and modern space. Seafood incorporates Greek, Italian and Spanish touches, and the vegetarian and meat dishes are also excellent. Lunch (two/three courses 290/390Kč) is a good-value option.

La Degustation   CZECH €€€

(Map p106; ☑222 311 234; www.ladegustation.cz; Haštalská 18; degustation menus 1000-2250Kč; ⊘noon-2.30pm Tue-Thu, 6pm-midnight Mon-Sat; Ⓜ️nám Republiky) Traditional Bohemian flavours, some inspired by 19th-century cookbooks, are delivered across a variety of multicourse tasting menus. Allow three hours for the seven-course menu (2250Kč), or if you're pushed for time, try the shorter 'post-theatre' menu (1000Kč). Lunch specials at 120Kč per small plate are a good way to sample the degustation experience.

Lehká Hlava
VEGETARIAN €€

(Map p106; ☑222 220 665; www.lehkahlava.cz; Boršov 2; mains 120-210Kč; ☑; ☐17, 18 to Karlovy lázně) Lehká Hlava means 'clear head' and that's the normal outcome after a meal at this hip little cafe. In the kitchen the emphasis is on healthy, freshly prepared vegetarian and vegan dishes, ranging from hummus and roast vegetables to spinach burritos and a spicy oriental stir-fry. The cleansing flavours are matched by a soothing, slightly New Age ambience. Lehká Hlava is very popular, so it's worth booking ahead, even for lunch.

Lokal
CZECH €

(Map p106; Dlouhá 33; mains 130-240Kč; ☺; Ⓜnám Republiky) Welcome to a slick reinvention of a traditional Czech pub for the 21st century. Lokal specialises in traditional Czech recipes, usually prepared with a lighter, less fatty touch, and is very good value given its Old Town location. It's all robust and tasty, especially the three different types of freshly made sausage.

Kabul
AFGHANI €€

(Map p106; Karolíny Světlé 14; mains 160-310Kč; ☑; ⓂNárodní třída) On funky Karolíny Světlé, Kabul serves up authentic Afghan flavours in a kilim-bedecked space with a hidden courtyard. Menu highlights include *mantu* (Afghan ravioli with mint and spices), good kebabs, *kofte* (minced lamb meatballs) and excellent aubergine salad. Pop in for cheaper lunch specials (90Kč).

Bakeshop Praha
CAFE €

(Map p106; Kozí 1; snacks 60-180Kč; ☺7am-7pm; Ⓜnám Republiky) Bakeshop's corner spot offers innovative salads, superior pies and almost healthy quiche. It's a tad expensive and service can be hit or miss, but it's worth grabbing a coffee and watching Prague's cinematic scroll outside.

NOVÉ MĚSTO, SMÍCHOV & VINOHRADY

Oliva
MEDITERRANEAN €€

(Map p102; ☑222 520 288; Plavecká 4, Nové Město; mains 265-485Kč; ☺11.30am-3pm & 6pm-midnight Mon-Fri, from 6pm Sat; ☐3, 7, 16, 17, 21 to Výtoň)

Oliva's Mediterranean-influenced menu includes seafood risotto with fennel, chilli and anchovy, and monkfish stew with red capsicum, almonds and saffron. Tuna, duck and freshly made pasta also make an appearance.

Masala
INDIAN €€

(Map p102; ☑222 251 601; Mánesova 13, Vinohrady; mains 160-260Kč; ☑; ☐11 to Vinohradská tržnice) Prague's array of Indian restaurants has traditionally been an inconsistent bunch, but the relaxed and home-style Masala is now changing that. It's very popular with expats, and Masala's owners have quickly adapted to adding enough spicy heat to cater to their well-travelled clientele.

Karavanseráj
MIDDLE EASTERN €

(Map p102; Masarykovo nábřeží 22, Nové Město; mains 130-250Kč; ☑; ☐6, 9, 17, 18, 21 to Národní divadlo) Lebanese flavours dominate at this relaxed spot that's part ethnic eatery and part travellers' cafe, but the menu also touches down in India and Morocco. There's an ever-changing array of large format travel photography on the walls.

Restaurace u Šumavy
CZECH €

(Map p102; Štěpánská 3, Nové Město; mains 100-150Kč; ⓂIP Pavlova) Ensconced in a country-cottage decor, here's emphatic and tasty proof that good-value Bohemian food still exists in central Prague. Canny locals crowd in for lunch specials that remind them of their grandmother's cooking. The roast duck is good, and it's always worth taking a chance on the daily soup (*polévka*) special.

U Ferdinanda
CZECH €

(Map p106; cnr ulice Opletalova & Politických Vězňů, Nové Město; mains 100-180Kč; ⓂMuzeum) Welcome to a thoroughly modern spin on a classic Czech pub with beer courtesy of the Ferdinand brewery from nearby Benešov. Quirky gardening implements in corrugated iron decorate the raucous interior, and a younger local clientele crowds in for well-priced Czech food.

Home Kitchen
CAFE €

(Map p106; Jungmannova 8, Nové Město; mains 65-120Kč; ☺7.30am-7pm Mon-Fri, 8.30am-3pm Sat; ☑; ☐3, 9, 14, 24 to Lazarská) Organic soups, salads and home-style daily specials provide the perfect escape for lunch at this cosy brick-lined spot away from the tourist sprawl of Old Town Square. The daily soup special (65Kč including bread) may well have you returning the following day.

Na Verandách
CZECH €€
(Map p102; Nádražní 84, Smíchov; meals 150-300Kč; ⊞6, 12, 14 to Na Knížeci) Across the river in Smíchov, the Staropramen brewery's restaurant is a modern spot crowded with locals enjoying superior versions of favourite Czech dishes, and an 'it could be a long night' selection of different brews.

Zlatý klas
CZECH €€
(Map p102; Plzeňská 9, Smíchov; mains 120-230Kč; MAnděl) Easily the best of the traditional Czech pubs in the immediate Anděl area, Zlatý klas offers super-fresh 'tank beer' (tankové pivo), meaning the beer is served from large tanks and is free of the carbon dioxide used to pump the beer through the taps. It also offers well-done Czech grub, such as roast pork, goulash and fried breast of chicken. From the Anděl metro walk west on Plzeňská for 100m.

Modrý Zub
ASIAN €€
(Map p106; Jindřišská 5, Nové Město; mains 140-280Kč; ⟋; MMůstek) Sometimes all you want is healthy Asian food. The 'Blue Tooth' turns out authentic versions of pad Thai and satay you'll recall from your favourite Asian food hall back home.

Pizzeria Kmotra
PIZZA €
(Map p106; V Jirchářích 12to, Nové Město; pizza 100-180Kč; ⊞6, 9, 17, 18, 21 to Národní divadlo) More than 30 varieties feature at this cellar pizzeria that gets superbusy after 8pm.

HRADČANY & MALÁ STRANA

TOP CHOICE U malé velryby
SEAFOOD €€
(Map p102; ⟋257 214 703; www.umale velryby.cz; Maltézské nám 15, Malá Strana; tapas 55-65Kč, mains 365-375Kč; ⊙noon-3pm & 6-11pm; ⊞12, 20, 22, 23 to Malostranské nám) You'll need to book at this cosy backstreets eatery with only eight tables, where the friendly chef–owner from Ireland creates tasty miracles with (mainly) seafood. Try the seafood tagliatelle or the Basque chicken with saffron risotto, or settle in with a few tapas and a good bottle of wine.

Cukrkávalimonáda
CAFE €
(Map p102; ⟋257 530 628; Lázeňská 7, Malá Strana; mains 100-180Kč; ⊙9am-11pm; ⊞12, 20, 22, 23 to Malostranské nám) By day, homemade pastas, frittatas, ciabattas and salads are delicious diversions at this lovely courtyard cafe combining a modern look with beautiful Renaissance painted timber beams. After dark a more sophisticated bistro menu kicks in. Mid-afternoon pick-me-up drinks include elderflower flavoured with mint and lemon. The name translates as 'sugar, coffee, lemonade' – the Czech equivalent of 'eeny-meeny-miny-moe'.

Artisan Restaurant & Cafe
INTERNATIONAL €€
(Map p102; ⟋257 218 277; Rosickych 4, Malá Strana; mains 170-380Kč; ⊜; ⊞6, 9, 12, 20, 23 to Újezd) Good steaks, gourmet burgers and robust seafood dishes are the standouts at this well-priced and unpretentious bistro on the quieter edge of Malá Strana. The hickory-smoked 'Artisan Burger' with bacon and sweet potato fries is perfect comfort food. Two- or three-course lunches from 95Kč are great value.

▼ Drinking

Czech beers are among the world's best. The most famous brands are Budvar, Plzeňský Prazdroj (Pilsner Urquell) and Prague's own Staropramen. Independent microbreweries and regional Czech beers are also becoming more popular in Prague. Look out for blackboards advertising weekly specials.

Avoid the tourist areas, and you'll find local bars selling half-litres for 35Kč or less. Traditional pubs open from 11am to 11pm. More stylish modern bars open from noon to 1am, and often stay open till 3am or 4am on Friday and Saturday.

Bars & Pubs

TOP CHOICE Pivovarský Klub
BEER HALL
(Map p102; Křižíkova 17, Karlín; ⊜; MFlorenc) Submit to your inner hophead at this pub–restaurant–beer shop with interesting limited-volume draught beers and bottled brews from around the Czech Republic. Come for lunch, as it gets full of loyal regulars later on.

Pivovarský Dům
BEER HALL
(Map p102; cnr Ječná & Lipová, Nové Město; ⊞4, 6, 22, 23 to Štěpánská) The 'Brewery House' microbrewery conjures everything from a refreshing wheat beer to coffee and banana-flavoured styles – even a beer 'champagne'.

TOP CHOICE Duende
BAR
(Map p106; Karoliny Světlé 30, Nové Město; ⊙1pm-midnight Mon-Fri, 3pm-midnight Sat, 4pm-midnight Sun; MNárodní třída) Barely five minutes' walk from the tourist hubbub of Charles Bridge, this bohemian drinking den pulls in an arty, mixed-age crowd of locals. Peruse the quirky art on the walls, or listen to occasional live music.

U Sadu PUB

(Map p102; Škroupovo nám, Žižkov; M Jiřího z Poděbrad) Escape the overpriced tyranny of central Prague at this neighbourhood pub in grungy Žižkov. With its ragtag collection of memorabilia, including communist-era posters of forgotten politicians, nothing's really changed here in a few decades.

Čili Bar BAR

(Map p106; Kozná 10, Staré Město; ⊙from 5pm; M Můstek) This raffish bar is more Žižkov than Staré Město, with cool cocktails and a grungy tinge in welcome contrast to the crystal shops and Russian dolls around the corner.

Hostinec U Kocoura PUB

(Map p102; Nerudova 2, Malá Strana; ⊟12, 20, 22, 23 to Malostranské nám) The 'Tomcat' is a long-established traditional pub, still enjoying its reputation as a favourite of ex-president Havel, and still managing to pull in a mostly Czech crowd. Old-school authenticity and citrusy *kvasnicové* ('yeast beer') from the Bernard brewery make it an essential post-Castle stop. It's also a handy refuge from the souvenir shop overkill of Nerudova St.

Bokovka WINE BAR

(Map p102; Pštrossova 8, Nové Město; ⊙4pm-1am Sun-Thu, 4pm-3am Fri & Sat; M Karlovo nám) This compact wine bar is named after the movie *Sideways* (*bokovka* in Czech), and is owned by film-making wine lovers. Wines include a great selection of excellent Moravian vintages, and good-value food platters are perfect for two or more.

Letna Beer Garden BEER GARDEN

(Map p102; Letna Gardens, Bubeneč; ⊟12, 17 to Čechův most) This garden bar has views across the river of the Old Town and southwest to the castle. In summer it's packed with a young crowd enjoying cheap beer and grilled sausages. Sometimes the simple things in life are the best.

Cafes

TOP CHOICE **Literární Kavárna Řetězová** CAFE

(Map p106; Řetězová, Staré Město; ⊙noon-11pm Mon-Fri, 5-11pm Sat-Sun; ⊟17, 21 to Karlovy lázně) This is where you would have headed post-1989 to become the next great expat novelist. Two decades on, leave your laptop and notebook at home, take in the vintage black-and-white pics of famous Czech writers, and treat yourself to a coffee or a beer. When someone asks you, 'So what was the best cafe you went to Prague?' this is the correct answer.

Grand Cafe Orient CAFE

(Map p106; Ovocný trh 19, Nové Město; M nám Republiky) In the 'House of the Black Madonna', Josef Gočár's cubist gem, the reborn Grand Cafe Orient also features Gočár-designed lampshades and furnishings. He had nothing to do with the coffee and cake, but it's also pretty good.

Cafe Louvre CAFE

(Map p106; 1st fl, Národní třída 2; ⊜; M Národní Třída) Others are more famous, but the French-style Louvre is arguably Prague's most amenable grand cafe. The atmosphere is wonderfully olde worlde, but there's a proper nonsmoking section among its warren of rooms and it serves good coffee (a Prague rarity), as well as food. Pop in for breakfast before 11am, play a little billiards and check out the associated art gallery downstairs when leaving.

Kaaba CAFE

(Map p102; Mánesova 20, Vinohrady; ⊙8am-10pm Mon-Sat, 10am-10pm Sun; ⊟11 to Vino-hradská tržnice) Vinohrady's hipsters park themselves on 1950s-style furniture and recharge with snappy espresso, beer, wine and tasty snacks.

☆ **Entertainment**

From clubbing to classical music, puppetry to performance art, Prague offers plenty of entertainment. It's an established centre of classical music and jazz. For current listings see www.prague.tv or www.praguewelcome.cz.

Try the following ticket agencies:

Bohemia Ticket International (☎224 227 832; www.ticketsbti.cz) Nové Město (Map p106; Na příkopě 16, ⊙10am-7pm Mon-Fri, to 5pm Sat, to 3pm Sun; M nám Republiky); Staré Město (Map p106; Malé nám 13; ⊙9am-5pm Mon-Fri, to 1pm Sat; M Staroměstská)

Ticketpro (Map p106; ☎296 333 333; www.ticketpro.cz; Lucerna pasáž, Šéťépánská 61, Nové Město; ⊙noon-8.30pm Mon-Fri; M Můstek) Also has branches of the Prague Information Service.

Ticketstream (www.ticketstream.cz) Online bookings for events in Prague and the Czech Republic.

Performing Arts

Rudolfinum LIVE MUSIC

(Map p106; ☎227 059 227; www.ceskafilharmonie.cz; nám Jana Palacha, Staré Město; ⊙box office

10am-6pm Mon-Fri, plus 1hr before performances; MStaromětska) One of Prague's main concert venues is the Dvořák Hall in the neo-Renaissance Ruldolfinum, home to the Czech Philharmonic Orchestra.

Smetana Hall
LIVE MUSIC

(Obecní dům; Map p106; ☎222 002 101; www. obecni-dum.cz; nám Republiky 5, Staré Město; ⊙box office 10am-6pm Mon-Fri; Mnám Republiky) Another main concert venue is Smetana Hall in the art nouveau Municipal House. A highlight is the opening of the Prague Spring festival.

Prague State Opera
OPERA

(Státní opera Praha; Map p106; ☎224 227 266; www.opera.cz; Legerova 75, Nové Město; ⊙box office 10am-5.30pm Mon-Fri, 10am-noon & 1-5pm Sat & Sun; MMuzeum) Opera, ballet and classical drama (in Czech) are performed at this neo-Renaissance theatre. The box office is round the corner at Wilsonova 4.

National Theatre
THEATRE

(Národní divadlo; Map p106; ☎224 913 437; www. narodni-divadlo.cz; Národní třída 2, Nové Město; ⊙box office 10am-6pm; MNárodní třída) Classical drama, opera and ballet feature at this venue.

Estates Theatre
OPERA

(Stavovské divadlo; Map p106; ☎224 902 322; www.narodni-divadlo.cz; Ovocný trh 1, Staré Město; ⊙box office 10am-6pm; MStaromětska) Every night from mid-July to the end of August, **Opera Mozart** (☎271 741 403; www.mozart -praha.cz) performs *Don Giovanni*, which premiered here in 1787.

Divadlo Minor
CHILDREN'S THEATRE

(Map p102; ☎222 231 351; www.minor.cz; Vodičkova 6, Nové Město; ⊙box office 9am-1.30pm & 2.30-8pm Mon-Fri, 11am-6pm Sat & Sun; 🚋3, 9, 14, 24, Vodičkova) Kid-friendly shows including puppets and pantomime.

Nightclubs

Cross Club
ALTERNATIVE

(Map p102; www.crossclub.cz; Plynární 23, Holešovice; cover 50-120Kč; ⊙4pm-late; MNádraží Holešovice) It's worth visiting this place for the ever-changing sci-fi industrial decor alone, but the late night/early morning programme of eclectic dub, techno, reggae and live music is another essential reason to jump on the metro to the grungier, northern side of the river.

Roxy
ALTERNATIVE

(Map p106; www.roxy.cz; Dlouhá 33, Staré Město; admission 150-300Kč; ⊙10pm-6am; 🚋5, 8, 14 to Dlouhá třída) In a resurrected old cinema, the Roxy presents innovative DJs and the occasional global act. 'Free Mondays' will give you more money for beer.

Mecca
CLUB

(Map p102; www.mecca.cz; U Průhonu 3, Holešovice; cover varies; ⊙10pm-6am Wed-Sat; 🚋1, 3, 5, 25 to Dělnická) Prague's most fashionable dance club attracts film stars, fashionistas and fab types, plus occasional gigs by name DJs.

Live Music

MeetFactory
CLUB

(off Map p102; www.meetfactory.cz; Ke Sklárně 3213/15, Smíchov; ⊙varies by event; 🚋12, 14, 20 to Lihovar) A multifaceted workspace for visiting artists, and a gallery and entertainment venue, it's very much a fluid work in progress. It hosts everything from film screenings to concerts and DJ events. Get off at the Lihovar stop, look for the two giant red cars, and be careful crossing the five sets of train tracks. One last scramble up the muddy embankment and you're there.

Palác Akropolis
CLUB

(Map p102; www.palacakropolis.cz; Kubelikova 27, Žižkov; ⊙club 7pm-5am; 🚋5, 9, 26 to Lipanska) Get lost in the labyrinth of theatre, live music, clubbing, drinking and eating that makes up Prague's coolest venue. Hip hop, house, reggae or rocking Roma bands from Romania – anything goes. Kick your night off nearby at the quirky U Sadu pub.

Lucerna Music Bar
CLUB

(Map p106; www.musicbar.cz; Lucerna pasaž, Vodičkova 36, Nové Město; ⊙8pm-3am; MMůstek) Lucerna features local bands and almost-famous international acts. Jettison your musical snobbery at the wildly popular '80s and '90s nights on Friday and Saturday.

USP Jazz Lounge
JAZZ

(Map p106; www.jazzlounge.cz; Michalská 9, Staré Město; ⊙8pm-3am; MMůstek) A less traditional venue with modern jazz from 10pm. DJs kick on from midnight.

Blues Sklep
ROCK & BLUES

(Map p106; www.bluessklep.cz; Liliová 10, Staré Město; admission 100Kč; ⊙bar 7pm-230m, music 9pm-midnight; MStaromětská) Jazz, bebop, blues, funk and soul all feature at this Old Town cellar bar. They also serve the excellent and hard-to-find Ferdinand beer.

Gay & Lesbian Venues

The inner suburb of Vinohrady is developing as a gay quarter, and the city enjoys a relaxed scene.

Prague Saints   BAR

(Map p102; ☎222 250 326; www.praguesaints.cz; Polska 32; Vinohrady; 🚋11 to Vinohradská tržnice) This bar is a good intro to what's happening on the Prague gay scene. The vibe is low-key, friendly and inclusive; an ideal first stop in town.

Termix   DANCE CLUB

(Map p102; www.club-termix.cz; Trebízckého 4A, Vinohrady; ⊙8pm-5am Wed-Sun; 🚋11 to Vinohradská tržnice) A friendly mixed gay-and-lesbian scene with an industrial/high-tech vibe. Wednesdays are good fun with retro Czech pop.

Valentino   DANCE CLUB

(Map p102; www.club-valentino.cz; Vinohradská 40, Vinohrady; ⊙from 11am; 🚋11 to Vinohradská tržnice) Welcome to Prague's gay superclub, with three floors concealing two dance areas, four bars and rooms with exceedingly low lighting.

Cinemas

Most films are screened in their original language with Czech subtitles (*české titulky*), but Hollywood blockbusters are often dubbed into Czech (*dabing*); look for the labels 'tit.' or 'dab.' on listings. Tickets are around 180/140Kč for adult/child.

Kino Světozor   ART HOUSE

(Map p106; ☎224 946 824; www.kinosvetozor.cz; Vodičkova 41, Nové Město; Ⓜ Můstek) Your best bet for Czech films with English subtitles; under the same management as Kino Aero but more central. Plus it includes a cool DVD and movie poster shop.

Kino Aero   ART HOUSE

(off Map p102; ☎271 771 349; www.kinoaero.cz; Biskupcova 31, Žižkov; 🚋1, 9, 16 to Ohrada) This art-house cinema has themed weeks and retrospectives; often screens films with English subtitles.

Palace Cinemas   MAINSTREAM

(Map p106; www.palacecinemas.cz; Slovanský dům, Na příkopě 22, Nové Město; Ⓜ nám Republiky) A 10-screen multiplex showing current Hollywood films.

🔒 Shopping

Near the Old Town Sq, explore the antique shops of Týnská and Týnská ulička.

Pivní Galerie   BEER

(Map p102; www.pivnigalerie.cz; U Průhonu 9, ⊙noon-8pm Tue-Fri; 🚋1, 3, 5, 25 to U Průhonu) Just a quick tram ride from central Prague, you can purchase beers from across the Czech Republic – we counted around 170

from more than 30 breweries. Note the limited opening hours, so head to the Pivovarský Klub bar/restaurant/beer shop (p116) if you're in town from Saturday to Monday.

Kubista   DESIGN

(Map p106; www.kubista.cz; Ovocný trh 19, Staré Město; Ⓜ nám Republiky) Kubista specialises in limited-edition reproductions of distinctive cubist furniture and ceramics, and designs by masters of the form such as Josef Gočár and Pavel Janák. It also has a few original pieces for serious collectors with serious cash to spend.

Modernista   DESIGN

(Map p106; www.modernista.cz; Celetná 12, Staré Město; ⊙11am-7pm; Ⓜ nám Republiky) This classy showcase of Czech cubism, art deco and similar design features covetable but reasonably affordable ceramics, jewellery, posters and books. Downstairs a renovated vaulted Gothic space provides the ultimate showcase for larger, but equally desirable, examples of home and office furniture and lighting.

Botanicus   COSMETICS

(Map p106; Týn 3, Staré Město; Ⓜ nám Republiky) Prepare for sensory overload in this popular old apothecary, which sells natural health and beauty products in slightly nostalgic packaging. The scented soaps, herbal bath oils and shampoos, fruit cordials and handmade paper products are made from herbs and plants grown on an organic farm east of Prague.

Big Ben Bookshop   BOOKS

(Map p106; www.bigbenbookshop.com; Malá Štupartská 5, Staré Město; Ⓜ nám Republiky) English-language books about Prague and the Czech Republic.

Bontonland   MUSIC

(Map p106; Václavské nám 1, Nové Město; Ⓜ Můstek) Contemporary and traditional Czech music.

Granát Turnov   JEWELLERY

(Map p106; www.granat.eu; Dlouhá 28-30, Staré Město; Ⓜ nám Republiky). Has gold and garnet pieces plus more affordable gold-plated silver and *vltavín* (a dark-green semiprecious stone).

Manufaktura   HANDICRAFTS

(Map p106; www.manufaktura.biz; Melantrichova 17, Staré Město; Ⓜ Staroměstska) Sells traditional Czech handicrafts, wooden toys and handmade cosmetics.

Moser   CRYSTAL

(Map p106; www.moser-glass.com; Na příkopě 12, Nové Město; ⊙10am-8pm Mon-Fri, to 7pm Sat &

Sun; Mnám Republiky) Top-quality Bohemian crystal.

ℹ Information

Dangers & Annoyances

Pickpockets work the crowds at the astronomical clock, Prague Castle and Charles Bridge, and on the central metro and tramlines, especially crowded trams 9, 22 and 23.

Most taxi drivers are honest, but some operating from tourist areas overcharge their customers (even Czechs). Phone a reputable taxi company or look for the red and yellow signs for the 'Taxi Fair Place' scheme, indicating authorised taxi stands.

The park outside the main train station is a hang-out for dodgy types and worth avoiding late at night.

Emergency

If your passport or valuables are stolen, obtain a police report and crime number from the **Prague 1 Police Station** (☑224 222 558; Jungmannovo nám 9, Nové Mesto; ☺24hr; MMůstek). You'll need this for an insurance claim. There's usually an English-speaker on hand. The emergency phone number for the police is ☑158.

Internet Access

Many hotels, bars, fast-food restaurants and internet cafes provide wi-fi hotspots.

Globe Cafe & Bookstore (www.globebook store.cz; Pštrossova 6, Nové Město; per min 1.50Kč; ☺9.30am-midnight; MKarlovo nám)

Mobilarium (Rathova Pasaž, Na příkopě 23, Nové Město; per min 1.50Kč; ☺10am-7pm Mon-Fri, 11am-6pm Sat; Mnám Republiky)

Medical Services

Canadian Medical Care (☑235 360 133, after hours 724 300 301; www.cmcpraha. cz; Veleslavínská 1, Veleslavín; ☺8am-6pm Mon, Wed & Fri, to 8pm Tue & Thu; ☐20, 26 to Veleslavínská from MDejvická) Expat centre with English-speaking doctors, 24-hour medical aid and a pharmacy.

Na Homolce Hospital (☑257 271 111, after hours 257 272 527; www.homolka.cz; 5th fl, Foreign Pavilion, Roentgenova 2, Motol; ☐167 from MAnděl) Prague's main casualty department.

Polyclinic at Národní (☑222 075 120; 24hr emergencies 720 427 634; www.poliklinika. narodni.cz; Národní třída 9, Nové Město; ☺8.30am-5pm Mon-Fri; ☐Národní Třída) English-, French- and German-speaking staff.

Praha lékárna (☑224 946 982; Palackého 5, Nové Město; MMůstek) A 24-hour pharmacy; for emergency service after business hours, ring the bell.

Money

The major banks are best for changing cash, but using a debit card in an ATM gives a better rate of exchange. Avoid *směnárna* (private exchange booths), which advertise misleading rates and have exorbitant charges.

Post

Main post office (Jindřišská 14, Nové Město; ☺2am-midnight; MMůstek) Collect a ticket from the automated machines outside the main hall (press 1 for stamps and parcels, 4 for Express Mail Service – EMS).

Tourist Information

The **Prague Information Service** (Pražská informační služba, PIS; ☑12 444, in English and German; www.praguewelcome.cz) provides free tourist information with good maps at the following locations:

PIS Malá Strana Bridge Tower (Map p102; Charles Bridge; ☺10am-6pm Apr-Oct; ☐12, 20, 22, 23 to Malostranské nám)

PIS Old Town Hall (Map p106; Staroměstské nám 5, Staré Město; ☺9am-7pm Mon-Fri, to 6pm Sat & Sun Apr-Oct, to 6pm Mon-Fri, to 5pm Sat & Sun Nov-Mar; MStaroměstská) The main branch.

PIS Rytirská (Map p106; Rytirská 31; ☺9am-7pm Apr-Oct, 9am-6pm Nov-Mar; MMůstek)

PIS Train station (Praha hlavní nádraží; Map p106; Wilsonova 2, Nové Město; ☺9am-7pm Mon-Fri, to 6pm Sat & Sun; MHlavní nádraží)

If you're venturing beyond Prague, **Czech Tourism** (Map p106; www.czechtourism.com; Staroměstské nám, Staré Město; ☺9am-5pm Mon-Fri; MStaroměstská) has an office in Prague's Old Town Square.

ℹ Getting There & Away

Bus

The main terminal for international and domestic buses is **Florenc bus station** (ÚAN Florenc; Map p102; Křižíkova 4, Karlín; MFlorenc), 600m northeast of the main train station. Short-haul tickets are sold on the bus, and long-distance domestic tickets are sold in the newly renovated central hall.

Some regional buses depart from near metro stations Anděl, Dejvická, Černý Most, Nádraží Holešovice, Smíchovské Nádraží or Želivského, and some departures to České Budějovice or Český Krumlov depart from the Ná Knížecí or outside the outside Roztyly metro station. Check timetables and departure points at www.idos.cz.

Main bus companies:

Eurolines (☑245 005 245; www.elines.cz; Florenc bus station) Buses to all over Europe.

Megabus (☑775666 140; www.megabus.cz; Můstek metro station, Florenc bus station)

Links Prague with Karlovy Vary, Plzeň and Brno; also services throughout Europe.

Student Agency (☑800 100 1300; www.student agency.cz) Central Prague (Ječná 37; Nove Město); Florenc (Florenc bus station) Links major Czech cities; also services throughout Europe.

Key services from Florenc:

Brno 200Kč, 2½ hours, hourly

České Budějovice 213Kč, 2¾ hours, four daily

Český Krumlov 160Kč, three hours, seven daily

Karlovy Vary 140Kč, 2¼ hours, eight daily

Kutná Hora 120Kč, 1¼ hours, six daily

Plzeň 90Kč, 1½ hours, hourly

Train

Prague's main train station is **Praha-hlavní nádraží** (Map p106; ☑221 111 122; Wilsonova, Nové Město; Ⓜ Hlavní nádraží). At the time of research Praha-hlavní nádraží was undergoing major redevelopment. Check signage for the current locations of domestic and international ticket counters. Also buy train tickets and get timetable information from **ČD Centrum** (⊙6am-7.30pm) at the southern end of level 2 in Praha-hlavní nádraží.

Some international trains stop at Praha-Holešovice station on the northern side of the city, while some domestic services terminate at Praha-Smíchov south of Malá Strana. Check timetables and departure points at www.idos.cz.

Key services from Praha-hlavní nádraží:

Brno 316Kč, three hours, frequent

České Budějovice 213Kč, 2¾ hours, four daily

Karlovy Vary 294Kč, 3½ hours, four daily

Kutná Hora 100Kč, one hours, six daily

Plzeň 90Kč, 1½ hours, hourly

❶ Getting Around

To/From the Airport

Prague's Ruzyně airport is 17km west of the city centre. There are several options for travel to/from central Prague.

The **Airport Express** (50Kč; ⊙5am-10pm) bus service goes directly to the upper level of Prague's main train station (Praha-hlavní nádraží) from where you can access the metro system. Luggage is free on this service; buy your ticket from the driver. Another option is to catch it only as far as the Dejvická metro station (30Kč).

Cedaz Minibus (☑220 111 111; www.cedaz.cz; ⊙every 30min 7.30am-7pm) leaves from outside arrivals; buy your ticket from the driver. The minibus stops at the **Czech Airlines** (V Celnici 5; Ⓜ nám Republiky) office near the Hilton around nám Republiky (120Kč) or further out at the Dejvická metro station (90Kč). You can also get a Cedaz minibus from your hotel or any other

address (480Kč for one to four people, 960Kč for five to eight).

Otherwise, see the Dopravní podnik (DPP) desk in arrivals and take bus 119 (26Kč, 20 minutes, every 15 minutes) to the end of the line (Dejvická), then continue by metro into the city centre (another 10 minutes; no extra ticket needed). You'll also need a half-fare (13Kč) ticket for your backpack or suitcase if it's larger than 25cm x 45cm x 70cm.

AAA Taxis (☑14 014; www.aaataxi.cz; around 650Kč) are reputable and the drivers speak good English. To the airport should be around 600Kč.

Bicycle

City Bike (☑776 180 284; www.citybike-prague. com; Králodvorská 5, Staré Město; per day 500Kč; ⊙9am-7pm May-Sep; Ⓜ Staroměstská)

Car & Motorcycle

Challenges to driving in Prague include cobblestones, trams and one-way streets. Try not to arrive or leave on a Friday or Sunday afternoon or evening, when Prague folk are travelling to and from their weekend houses.

Central Prague has many pedestrian-only streets, marked with Pěší Zoná (Pedestrian Zone) signs, where only service vehicles and taxis are allowed; parking can be a nightmare. Meter time limits range from two to six hours at around 50Kč per hour. Parking in one-way streets is normally only allowed on the right-hand side.

Public Transport

All public transport is operated by **Dopravní podnik hl. m. Prahy** (DPP; ☑800 191 817; www. dpp.cz), with information desks at **Ruzyně airport** (⊙7am to 7pm) and in four metro stations – **Muzeum** (⊙7am to 9pm), **Můstek** (⊙7am to 6pm), **Anděl** (⊙7am to 6pm) and **Nádraží Holešovice** (⊙7am to 6pm) – where you can get tickets, directions, a multilingual system map, a map of Noční provoz (night services) and a detailed English-language guide to the whole system.

Buy a ticket before boarding a bus, tram or metro. Tickets are sold from machines at metro stations and major tram stops, at news-stands, Trafiky snack shops, PNS and other tobacco kiosks, hotels, all metro station ticket offices and DPP information offices.

A jízdenka (transfer ticket) is valid on tram, metro, bus and the Petřín funicular and costs 26Kč (half-price for six- to 15-year-olds); large suitcases and backpacks (anything larger than 25cm x 45cm x 70cm) also need a 13Kč ticket. Kids under six ride free. Validate (punch) your ticket by sticking it in the little yellow machine in the metro station lobby or on the bus or tram the first time you board; this stamps the time and date on it. Once validated, tickets remain valid for 75 minutes from the time of stamping, if validated between 5am and 10pm on weekdays, and for 90 minutes at other times. Within this period, you can make unlimited transfers between all types of public transport (you don't need to punch the ticket again).

There's also a short-hop 18/9Kč adult/child ticket, valid for 20 minutes on buses and trams, or for up to five metro stations. Being caught without a valid ticket entails a 400Kč on-the-spot fine (100Kč for not having a luggage ticket).

Tickets for 24 hours (100Kč) and three/five days (330/500Kč) are also available. If you're staying for longer and will be travelling a lot, consider a monthly pass (550Kč). All passes must be validated on first use only. Before shelling out on a pass, note that much of central Prague can be explored on foot.

The metro operates from 5am to midnight daily. Line A runs from northwest Prague at Dejvická to the east at Depo Hostivař; line B runs from the southwest at Zličín to the northeast at Černý Most; and line C runs from the north at Letňany to the southeast at Háje. Line A intersects line C at Muzeum, line B intersects line C at Florenc and line A intersects line B at Můstek.

After the metro closes, night trams (51 to 59) and buses (501 to 512) travel about every 40 minutes. Check if one of these services passes near where you're staying.

Taxi

Try to avoid getting a taxi in tourist areas such as Wenceslas Sq and outside the main train station. To avoid being ripped off, phone a reliable company such as **AAA** (☑14 014; www.aaaradiotaxi.cz) or **City Taxi** (☑257 257 257; www.citytaxi.cz). Both companies also offer online bookings.

Prague runs the 'Taxi Fair Place' scheme, with authorised taxis in 49 locations around key tourist areas. Look for the yellow and red signs. Drivers can charge a maximum of 40Kč flagfall plus 28Kč per kilometre and 6Kč while waiting, and must announce the estimated price in advance. On this basis any trip within the city centre should be around 170Kč.

AROUND PRAGUE

You can visit the following places on day trips using public transport.

Karlštejn

Erected by the Emperor Charles IV in the mid-14th century, **Karlštejn Castle** (☑274 008 154; www.hradkarlstejn.cz; Karlštejn; ☺9am-6pm Tue-Sun Jul & Aug, to 5pm May, Jun & Sep, to 4pm Apr & Oct) crowns a ridge above Karlštejn village. It's a 20-minute walk from the train station.

The highlight is the **Chapel of the Holy Rood**, where the Bohemian crown jewels were kept until 1420. The 55-minute guided tours (in English) on **Route I** costs 250/150Kč per adult/child. **Route II**, which includes the chapel (June to October only), are 300/200Kč adult/child and must be pre-booked. See online for details.

Trains from Praha-hlavní nádraží station to Beroun stop at Karlštejn (49Kč, 45 minutes, hourly).

Konopiště

The assassination of the heir to the Austro-Hungarian throne, Archduke Franz Ferdinand d'Este, sparked off WWI. For the last 20 years of his life he hid away southeast of Prague in his country retreat at **Konopiště Chateau** (www.zamek-konopiste.cz; Benešov; ☺9am-5pm Tue-Sun May-Aug; to 9am-4pm Tue-Fri, to 5pm Sat & Sun Sep; 9am-3pm Tue-Fri, to 4pm Sat & Sun Apr & Oct).

Three guided tours are available. **Tour III** (adult/child 300/200Kč) is the most interesting, visiting the archduke's private apartments, unchanged since the state took over the chateau in 1921. **Tour II** (adult/child 200/130Kč) takes in the **Great Armoury**, one of Europe's most impressive collections.

The castle is a testament to the archduke's twin obsessions of hunting and St George. Having renovated the massive Gothic and Renaissance building in the 1890s, Franz Ferdinand decorated his home with some of his 300,000 hunting kills. About 100,000 of them adorn the walls, marked with when and where it was slain. The **Trophy Corridor** and **Chamois Room** (both on Tour III) are truly bizarre.

His collection of St George–related artefacts includes 3750 items, many displayed in the Muzeum sv Jiří (adult/child 30/15Kč) at the front of the castle. From June to September weekend concerts are sometimes held in the castle's grounds.

Konopiště is 2.5km west of Benešov. There are direct trains from Prague's Hlavní nádraží (main train station) to Benešov u Prahy (68Kč, 1¼ hours, hourly). Buses depart from Florenc or the Roztyly metro station to Benešov on a regular basis (42Kč, 1¼ hours).

Local bus 2 (11Kč, six minutes, hourly) runs from a stop on Dukelská, 400m north of the train station (turn left out of the station, then first right on Tyršova and first left) to the castle car park. Or it's a 30-minute walk. Turn left out of the train station, go left across the bridge over the railway, and follow Konopištská street west for 2km.

Kutná Hora

In the 14th century, the silver-rich ore under Kutná Hora gave the now-sleepy town an importance in Bohemia second only to Prague. The local mines and mint turned out silver *groschen* for use as the hard currency of central Europe. The silver ore ran out in 1726, leaving the medieval townscape largely unaltered. Now with several fascinating and unusual historical attractions, the Unesco World Heritage–listed town is a popular day trip from Prague.

In early June, the town hosts an **International Music Festival** (www.mfkh.cz), with chamber-music recitals in venues including the soaring Cathedral of St Barbara.

◉ Sights

TOP CHOICE Sedlec Ossuary CHURCH
(www.kostnice.cz; Zamecka 127; adult/child 50/30Kč; ⊘8am-6pm Apr-Sep, 9am-noon & 1-5pm Oct & Mar, 9am-noon & 1-4pm Nov-Mar) From Kutná Hora hlavní nádraží, walk south for 10 minutes to the remarkable Sedlec Ossuary. When the Schwarzenberg family purchased Sedlec monastery in 1870, a local woodcarver got creative with the bones of 40,000 people from the centuries-old crypt. Skulls and femurs are strung from the vaulted ceiling, and the central chandelier contains at least one of each bone in the human body.

From the Kutná Hora bus station catch bus 1B and get off at the 'Tabak' stop. A tourist minibus also shuttles between the Ossuary and the Cathedral of St Barbara.

Cathedral of St Barbara CHURCH
(www.chramsvatebarbory.cz; Jakubská ulice; adult/child 50/30Kč; ⊘9am-6pm Apr-Oct, 10am-4pm Nov-Mar) The Gothic cathedral of St Barbara rivals Prague's St Vitus in magnificence, its soaring nave culminating in elegant, six-petalled ribbed vaulting. The ambulatory chapels preserve original 15th-century frescos, some showing miners at work.

Old Town HISTORIC AREA
The Old Town lies south of **Palackého nám**, the main square. From the square's western end, Jakubská leads to **Church of St James** (1330). Further east is the **Italian Court** (Vlašský dvůr; Havlíčkovo nám 552; adult/child 100/80Kč; ⊘9am-6pm Apr-Sep, 10am-4pm Oct-Mar), the former Royal Mint. Florentine craftsmen began stamping silver coins here in 1300. It houses a mint museum and a 15th-century **Audience Hall** with 19th-century murals depicting the election of Vladislav Jagiello as King of Bohemia in 1471 and the Decree of Kutná Hora being proclaimed by Wenceslas IV and Jan Hus in 1409.

Czech Silver Museum MUSEUM
(www.cms-kh.cz; adult/child 70/40Kč, English-speaking guide 400Kč; ⊘10am-6pm Jul & Aug, 9am-5pm Apr-May & Sep-Oct, closed Mon year-round) From the southern side of St James Church, Ruthardská leads to the **Hrádek** (Little Castle), a 15th-century palace housing the Czech Silver Museum. Don a miner's helmet to join the 1½-hour **Way of Silver tour** (adult/child 120/80Kč) through 500m of medieval mine shafts beneath the town. Kids need to be at least seven for this tour. A combination ticket for the museum and the mine tour (adult/child 140/90Kč) is also available.

Jesuit College HISTORIC BUILDING
Beyond the Hrádek is a 17th-century former Jesuit college, with a terrace featuring 13 **baroque statues** of saints, inspired by those on Prague's Charles Bridge. The second one along of a woman holding a chalice is St Barbara, the patron saint of miners and Kutná Hora.

⊨ Sleeping

Penzión u Kata PENSION €
(☑327 515 096; www.ukata.cz; Uhelná 596; s/d/tr 500/760/1140Kč; ℗@⊛) You won't lose your head over the rates at this good-value family hotel called the 'Executioner'. Bikes can be hired for 200Kč per hour and it's a short stroll from the bus station. Downstairs is a welcoming Czech beer hall and restaurant.

Hotel u Vlašského dvora HOTEL €€
(☑327 514 618; www.vlasskydvur.cz; 28 Řijna 511; s/d 1190/1500Kč; @⊛) Brightly coloured rooms linger just off Kutná Hora's main square, and a cooked breakfast downstairs in the almost-hip cafe makes a nice change from the usual cheese and sliced meat buffet.

✗ Eating & Drinking

Pivnice Dačický BEER HALL €
(Rakova 8; mains 100-250Kč) Try Kutná Hora's dark beer at this traditional beer hall. Rustle up three drinking buddies and order the Gamekeepers Reserve, a huge platter that demands at least a second beer. There are six different brews available, so try not to miss the bus back to Prague.

Kutná Hora

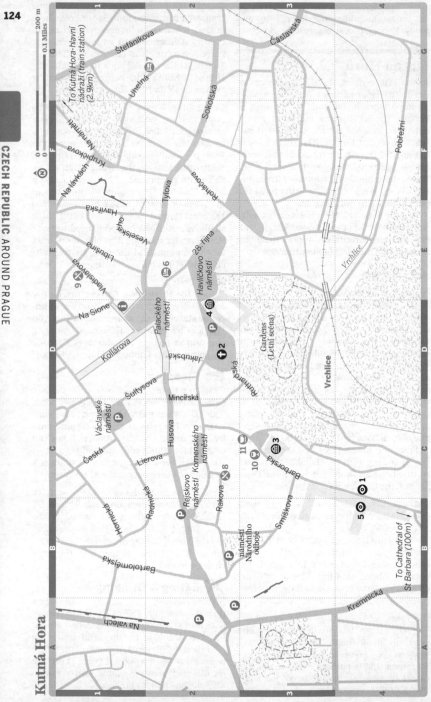

0   200 m
0   0.1 Miles

To Kutná Hora-hlavní
nádraží (train station)
(2.9km)

Na náměti

Krupičkova

Na lávkách

Štefánikova

Uhelná

Veselského Havířská

Libušína

Vladislavova

Na Sioně

Sokolská

Rohačova

Tylova

Palackého
náměstí

Kollárova

Šultysova

Mincířská

Václavské
náměstí

Česká

Lierova

Husova

Radnická

Hornická

Bartolomějská

Na valech

Rejskovo
náměstí

Komenského
náměstí

Rakova

náměstí
Národního
odboje

Kremnická

Smíškova

Barborská

Ruthardská

Jakubská

28. října

Havlíčkovo
náměstí

Čáslavská

Pobřežní

Vrchlice

Gardens
(Letní scéna)

Vrchlice

To Cathedral of
St Barbara (100m)

Kutná Hora

U Sňeka Pohodáře PIZZA €
(Vladislavova 11; pizza 100-130Kč) Kutná Hora's best Italian flavours are at this cosy local favourite that's very popular for takeout or dine-in pizza and pasta. And no, we don't know why it's called the 'Happy Snail'.

Kavárna Mokate CAFE €
(Baborská 7; coffee & cake 70-80Kč; ◎8.30am-9.30pm Mon-Thu, 9am-midnight Fri & Sat, noon-7pm Sun) It's not just good coffee at this place with rustic tiled floors, and mismatched furniture from your last student flat – a global array of teas complements yummy cakes.

Baborska BAR
(Baborská 35; ◎4pm-1am Mon-Thu, 4pm-3am Fri-Sat, 4-10pm Sun) Cosy, cosmopolitan and crafting very good cocktails, Baborska is a lively spot if you do decide to miss that last bus back to Prague.

❶ Information

The **information centre** (☑327 512 378; www.kutnahora.cz; Palackého nám 377; ◎9am-6pm Apr-Sep, 9am-5pm Mon-Fri, 10am-4pm Sat & Sun Oct-Mar) books accommodation, provides internet access (1Kč per minute) and rents bicycles (220Kč per day).

❶ Getting There & Away

Kutná Hora hlavní nádraží (the main train station) is 3km northeast of the Old Town centre. The bus station is more conveniently located on the Old Town's northeastern edge.

BUS There are about six direct buses a day, on weekdays only, from Prague's Florenc bus station to Kutná Hora (62Kč, 1¼ hours). A few also travel from Prague Černý Most metro station. A bus leaves Prague Florenc at 8.10am for an early start.

TRAIN There are direct trains from Prague's Hlavní nádraží (main train station) to Kutná Hora-hlavní nádraží (98Kč, 55 minutes, seven daily). Each has a good connection by local train (10Kč, eight minutes) to Kutná Hora-město station, adjacent to the old town.

❶ Getting Around

On weekdays local bus 1 runs between the bus station and the main train station (Kutná Hora-hlavní nádraží) every 30 minutes; get off at the Sedlec-Tabak stop (beside a big church) for Sedlec Ossuary. Look for the 'Kostnice' sign.

On weekends, the route is served by bus 7 (every one to two hours). Buy your ticket (9Kč) from the driver. A taxi from the station into town costs around 100Kč.

During summer a special tourist minibus (40Kč per person) travels a loop including the train station, the Sedlec Ossuary, and the Cathedral of St Barbara.

BOHEMIA

The ancient land of Bohemia makes up the western two-thirds of the Czech Republic. The modern term 'bohemian' comes to us via the French, who thought that Roma came from Bohemia; the word *bohémien* was later applied to people living an unconventional lifestyle. The term gained currency in the wake of Puccini's opera *La Bohème* about poverty-stricken artists in Paris.

Terezín

The massive fortress at Terezín (Theresenstadt in German) was built by the Habsburgs in the 18th century to repel the Prussian army, but the place is better known as a notorious WWII prison and concentration camp. Around 150,000 men, women and children, mostly Jews, passed through en route to the Auschwitz-Birkenau extermination camps: 35,000 of them died here of hunger, disease or suicide, and only 4000 ultimately survived. From 1945 to 1948 the fortress served as an internment camp for the Sudeten Germans, who were expelled from Czechoslovakia after the war.

Terezín also played a tragic role in deceiving the world about the ultimate goals of the

Nazi's 'Final Solution'. Official visitors were immersed in a charade, with Terezín being presented as a Jewish 'refuge', complete with shops, schools and cultural organisations – even an autonomous Jewish 'government'. As late as April 1945, Red Cross visitors delivered positive reports.

The **Terezín Memorial** (www.pamatnik -terezin.cz) consists of the Museum of the Ghetto in the Main Fortress, and the Lesser Fortress, a 10-minute walk east across the Ohře River. Admission to one part costs 160/130Kč per adult/child; a combined ticket is 200/150Kč. Ask at the ticket office about historical films in the museum's cinema.

The **Museum of the Ghetto** (☺9am-5.30pm) records daily life in the camp during WWII, through moving displays of paintings, letters and personal possessions. Entry to the Museum of the Ghetto includes entry to the Magdeburg Barracks and vice versa.

Around 32,000 prisoners, many of them Czech partisans, were incarcerated in the **Lesser Fortress** (☺8am-6pm Apr-Oct, to 4.30pm Nov-Mar). Take the grimly fascinating self-guided tour through the prison barracks, workshops, morgues and mass graves, before arriving at the bleak execution grounds where more than 250 prisoners were shot.

At the **Magdeburg Barracks** (cnr Tyršova & Vodárenská; ☺9am-6pm Apr-Oct, to 5.30pm Nov-Mar), the former base of the Jewish 'government', are exhibits on the rich cultural life – including music, theatre, fine arts and literature – that flourished against this backdrop of fear. Most poignant are the copies of *Vedem* ('In the Lead') magazine, published by 100 boys from 1942 to 1944. Only 15 of the boys survived the war.

❶ Getting There & Away

Buses (80Kč, one hour) leave hourly from outside Prague's Holešovice metro station. Most continue on to Litoměřice, the nearest town. The last bus back to Prague from Terezín usually leaves at 6.20pm. Frequent buses (9Kč, 10 minutes) link Litoměřice to Terezín.

Litoměřice

POP 25,100

Founded by German colonists in the 13th century, Litoměřice prospered in the 18th century as a royal seat and bishopric. The town centre features picturesque buildings and churches, some designed by the locally born baroque architect Ottavio Broggio.

The Old Town lies across the road to the west of the train and bus stations, guarded by the remnants of the 14th-century town walls. Walk along Dlouhá to the central square, Mírové nám.

◉ Sights

The main square is lined with Gothic arcades and facades dominated by the tower of **All Saints Church**, the step-gabled **Old Town Hall** and the distinctive **House at the Chalice** (Dům U Kalicha), housing the present town hall. Sprouting from the roof is a copper chalice, the traditional symbol of the Hussite church. The slim baroque facade at the square's elevated end is the **House of Ottavio Broggio**.

Along Michalská on the square's southwest corner is another Broggio design, the **North Bohemia Fine Arts Gallery** (Michalská 7; adult/child 32/18Kč; ☺9am-noon & 1-5pm Tue-Sun) with the priceless Renaissance panels of the Litoměřice altarpiece.

Turn left on Michalská and follow Domská to Domské nám on Cathedral Hill, passing the baroque **St Wenceslas Church**, on a side street to the right. Atop the hill is the town's oldest church, the 11th-century **St Stephen Cathedral**.

Follow the arch on the cathedral's left and descend down steep and cobbled Máchova. At the foot of the hill turn left then first right, up the zigzag steps to the **Old Town walls**. Follow the walls right to the next street, Jezuitská, then turn left back to the square.

🏃 Activities

The **Porta Bohemica 1** (www.osobni-lod.cz; adult 60-160Kč, child 30-80Kč; ☺daily July-Aug, Thu-Sun Jun & Sep, Fri-Sun May) operates cruises on the Labe River. **Cruise One** (7 hours; ☺Mon, Wed, Fri & Sat) runs north to Lovosice, Velké Žernoseky, Píštany and Ústí nad Labem, while **Cruise Two** (7 hours, ☺Tue, Thu, Sun) cruises south to Roudnice nad Labem and Šětí. Costs vary depending on the destination from Litoměřice, and there is full restaurant and bar service on board.

🛏 Sleeping

U Svatého Václava   PENSION €
(☎416 737 500; www.upfront.cz/penzion; Svatovaclavská 12; s/d 750/1300Kč) Beside St Wenceslas Church, this popular haven has well-equipped rooms, hearty cooked breakfasts and owners whose English is better than they think.

Pension Prislin   PENSION €

(☎416 735 833; www.prislin.cz; Na Kocandě 12; s/d/tr/q 800/1100/1500/1800Kč) Pension Prislin has a friendly dog called Baltimore and a switched-on owner who's decorated his pension in bright colours. The spacious apartments take up to five travellers.

✖ Eating & Drinking

Radniční sklípek   CZECH €€

(Mírové nám 21; mains 150-280Kč) Keep your head down in this underground labyrinth that does great grills accompanied by a mainly local wine list. In summer, the meaty action spills onto the main square.

U Štěpána Pizzeria   PIZZA €

(Dlouhá 43; pizza 45-145Kč) Around 300m from the downhill end of the square, this spot has a monk as a logo, but there's definitely nothing frugal about the pizza toppings.

Gurmănie   CAFE €

(Novobranská 14; snacks 70-1000Kč; ⊙9am-5pm Mon-Fri, 9am-3pm Sat; 🛜) At the top end of the square, Gurmănie has tasty ciabatta sandwiches and tortilla wraps, plus salads and pasta. Say *ahoj* to Litoměřice's best coffee.

ℹ Information

The **information centre** (☎416 732 440; www.litomerice.cz; Mírové nám 15/7; ⊙9am-6pm May-Sep, 8am-4pm Mon-Fri & 8-11am Sat Oct-Apr) in the town hall books accommodation and runs walking tours. Internet is available; for wi-fi grab a coffee at the Gurmănie cafe.

ℹ Getting There & Away

Buses (80Kč, one hour) leave approximately hourly from outside Prague's Holešovice train station. Most stop first in Terezín. There are also frequent bus connections between Litoměřice and Terezín (9Kč, 10 minutes).

Bohemian Switzerland National Park

The main road and rail route between Prague and Dresden follows the fast-flowing Labe (Elbe) River, gouging a sinuous, steep-sided valley through a sandstone plateau on the border between the Czech Republic and Germany. The landscape of sandstone pinnacles, giddy gorges, dark forests and high meadows is the Bohemian Switzerland National Park (Národní park České Švýcarsko),

named after two 19th-century Swiss artists who settled here.

⊙ Sights & Activities

Just south of the German border, **Hřensko** is a cute village of half-timbered houses crammed into a sandstone gorge where the Kamenice River joins the Labe. It's overrun with German day trippers at summer weekends, but upstream, peaceful hiking trails begin.

A signposted 16km (five to six hours) circular hike explores the main sights. From Hřensko's eastern end a trail leads via ledges, walkways and tunnels through the mossy chasms of the **Kamenice River Gorge**.

Two sections – **Edmundova Soutěska** (Edmund's Gorge; ⊙9am-6pm May-Aug, Sat & Sun only Apr, Sep & Oct) and **Divoká Soutěska** (Savage Gorge; ⊙9am-5pm May-Aug, Sat & Sun only Apr, Sep & Oct) – have been dammed. Continue by punt and a ferryman through a canyon 5m wide and 50m to 150m deep. Each ferry trip costs 60/30Kč per adult/child.

A kilometre beyond the end of the second boat trip, a blue-marked trail leads uphill to the Hotel Mezní Louka. Across the road, a red-marked trail continues through the forest to the spectacular rock formation **Pravčická Brána** (www.pbrana.cz; adult/child 75/25Kč; ⊙10am-6pm Apr-Oct), the largest natural arch in Europe. Crouched beneath is the **Falcon's Nest**, a 19th-century chateau housing a national park museum and restaurant. From here the red trail descends westward back to Hřensko.

The area is also popular with climbers. Ask at the Hřensko information office about climbing day trips, and hire gear from **Hudy Sport** around 400m up the Kamenice River Gorge road.

🛏 Sleeping & Eating

Pension Lugano   PENSION €

(☎412 554 146; www.hrensko-lugano.cz; Hřensko; s/d 500/1000Kč) A cheerful place in the centre of Hřensko serving terrific breakfasts at a riverside restaurant.

Hotel Mezní Louka   HOTEL €

(☎412 554 220; www.mezni-louka.cz; Mezní Louka 71; s/d 900/1450Kč) In the hills, this is a 19th-century hiking lodge with a decent restaurant (mains 90Kč to 170Kč).

Camp Mezní Louka   CAMPING GROUND €

(☎412 554 084; r.kolarova@npcs.cz; campsites per tent/bungalow 110/510Kč) Across the road from Hotel Mezní Louka.

If you have a car, base yourself in either Janov or Jetřichovice. In Janov **Pension Pastis** (☑142 554 037; www.pastis.cz; Janov 22; s/d 540/1080Kč; 🐾) has an excellent restaurant; in Jetřichovice try **Pension Dřevák** (☑412 555 015; s/d incl breakfast 700/1050Kč), housed in a 19th-century wooden building. Bookings can be made at www.ceskosaske-svycarsko.cz.

ℹ️ Information

The **Hřensko information office** (☑414 554 286; www.ceskosaske-svycarsko.cz; ⊘9am-6pm Apr-Oct) is on the corner of the road from Děčín.

ℹ️ Getting There & Away

Boat

From May to September, the **Poseidon** (www. labskaplavebni.cz) travels along the Labe River from Děčín to **Hřensko** (adult/child 100/50Kč; ⊘9.30am Mon-Fri, 9am & 1pm Sat-Sun) and back to **Děčín** (adult/child 120/60Kč; ⊘10.30am Mon-Fri, 10am & 2pm Sat-Sun). **Return tickets** (adult/concession 180/80Kč) are also available. From mid-April to September it's also possible to travel by river from Hřensko to Bad Schandau and Königstein in Germany on MS *Sächsische Schweiz*.

Bus

From Prague, take a bus from Florenc (120Kč, 1¾ hours, five daily) to Děčín. Buses run every two hours from Děčín to Hřensko (22Kč, 30 minutes) and from Děčín via Česká Kamenice or Hřensko to Jetřichovice, Vysoká Lípa or Mezná.

Train

Catch a Dresden-bound train and get off at Bad Schandau (280Kč, two hours, eight daily), in Germany, and then a local train back to Schöna on the German bank of the river opposite Hřensko. From the station, a ferry (20Kč, three minutes, 6am to 10pm April to September, 8am to 6pm October to March) crosses to Hřensko on demand.

ℹ️ Getting Around

In summer, keep an eye out for the big red **Nationalpark Express**, a heritage double-decker bus that crosses over from Germany and provides regular transport to Pravčická Brána and Mezní Louka.

Karlovy Vary

POP 60,000

Karlovy Vary is the closest the Czech Republic has to a glam resort, but it's still glam with a small 'g', and it's popular with the Zimmer frame set. Well-heeled hypochondriacs, increasingly from Russia and the Middle East, make the pilgrimage to try to enjoy courses of 'lymphatic drainage' and 'hydrocolonotherapy' – all activities that should be outlawed under several international agreements. And every spa season sees more and more signage in Russia's Cyrillic alphabet. Maybe the town should be called Karlovy Varygrad instead.

If you're really keen to discover the dubious pleasures of a steam inhalation session or a sulphur bath, you'll need to make a prior appointment. If not, there's good hiking in the surrounding hills, and a busy arts and entertainment programme.

The **Karlovy Vary International Film Festival** in early July is well worth attending. More than 200 films are shown, tickets are easy to get, and a funky array of concurrent events (including buskers and world music concerts) give this genteel town a much-needed annual energy transfusion.

⊙ Sights

Mill Colonnade   HISTORIC BUILDING

At the central spa district is the neoclassical Mill Colonnade (Mlýnská Kolonáda), with occasional summer concerts. Other elegant colonnades and 19th-century spa buildings are scattered along the Teplá River, with the 1970s concrete Hotel Thermal spoiling the effect slightly.

FREE **Hot Springs**   SPRINGS

Purchase a *lázeňský pohárek* (spa cup) and some *oplátky* (spa wafers) and sample the various hot springs. Infocentrum has a leaflet describing the 12 springs in the 'drinking cure', ranging from the **Rock Spring** (Skalní Pramen), which dribbles just 1.3L per minute, to the robust **Geyser Vřídlo**, which spurts 2000L per minute in a 14m-high jet. The latter is housed in the 1970s **Geyser Colonnade** (Vřídelní Kolonáda; ⊘10am-6pm Mon-Fri, to 4pm Sat & Sun).

To look inside the old spa buildings without enduring the dubious rigours of *proktologie* and *endoskopie*, nip into **Spa No 3** (Lázně III) just north of the Mill Colonnade.

The most splendid spa building is the restored **Spa No 1** (Lázně I) at the south end of town, dating from 1895 and once housing Emperor Franz Josef's private baths. Across the river is the baroque **Grandhotel Pupp**, a former meeting place of European aristocrats.

Diana Funicular Railway   CABLE CAR

(one way/return adult 40/70Kč, child 20/35Kč; ⊘9am-6pm) North of the Grandhotel Pupp, a narrow alley leads to the bottom station of the Diana Funicular Railway, which climbs 166m to great views from the **Diana Look-**

OPLÁTKY

As Monty Python asked: 'Do you get wafers with it?' In Karlovy Vary the answer is a resounding 'yes', with locals prescribing the following method of taking your spring water: have a sip from your *lázeňský pohárek* (spa cup), then dull the sulphurous taste with a big, round sweet wafer called *oplátky;* these are sold for 12Kč each at spa hotels, speciality shops and at a stall in front of the Hotel Thermal. Steer clear of the fancy chocolate or hazelnut flavours, though; they're never as crunchily fresh and warm as the standard flavour. *Oplátky* are also a big hit in Mariánské Lázně.

out **Tower**. It's a pleasant walk back down through the forest.

Moser Glass Museum   MUSEUM
(Sklářské Muzeum Moser; www.moser-glass.com; Kpt Jaroše 19; adult/child 80/50Kč; ⊙9am-5pm) Just out of town, Moser Glass Museum has more than 2000 items on display. Afterwards get hot under the collar at the adjacent **glassworks** (adult/child 120/70Kč; ⊙9am-2.30pm). Combined tickets (adult/child 180/100Kč) are also available.

🏃 Activities

Castle Spa (Zámecké Lázně; ☑353 222 649; www.edengroup.cz; Zámechý vrch; treatments from €30; ⊙7.30am-7.30pm Mon-Fri, from 8.30am Sat & Sun) is a modernised spa centre, complete with a subterranean thermal pool. It still retains a heritage ambience.

For a cheaper paddle head to the **open-air thermal pool** (per hr 80Kč; ⊙8am-8pm). Follow the 'Bazén' signs up the hill behind Hotel Thermal.

✨ Festivals & Events

Karlovy Vary International Film Festival (www.kviff.com) is held in early July, **Karlovy Vary Folklore Festival** in early September, and the classical music festival, **Dvořák Autumn**, in September.

🛏 Sleeping

Accommodation is pricey, and can be tight during weekends and festivals; definitely book ahead. Infocentrum can find hostel, pension and hotel rooms. Consider staying in Loket and visiting Karlovy Vary as a day trip.

Hotel Maltézsy Kříž   HOTEL €€
(☑353 169 011; www.maltezskykriz.cz; Stará Louka 50; s/d/apt €69/117/133; @🗟🗟) Oriental rugs and wooden floors combine at this spiffy recent opening with cosy rooms and a more spacious double-storeyed apartment. Bathrooms are decked out in warm earth tones.

Hotel Boston   HOTEL €€
(☑353 362 711; www.boston.cz; Luční vrch 9; s/d 1850/1950Kč; ⊝🗟) Tucked away down a quiet lane, this family-owned hotel has relatively spacious rooms decorated in bright colours with new bathrooms. The flash cafes of Stará Louka are just around the corner.

Hotel Ontario   HOTEL €€
(☑353 222 091; www.hotelontario.cz; Zámecký vrch; s/d 2450/2850Kč; 🅿@🗟) Look forward to great views and just maybe Karlovy Vary's friendliest team on reception. They call the stylishly appointed lodgings 'rooms', but they're actually compact apartments. The hotel is a stiff five-minute walk uphill.

Hotel Kavalerie   HOTEL €
(☑353 229 613; www.kavalerie.cz; TG Masaryka 43; s/d from 950/1225Kč; 🅿) Friendly staff abound in this cosy spot above a cafe. It's located near the bus and train stations, and nearby eateries can help you avoid the spa district's high restaurant prices. Rooms are starting to look a bit worn, but it's still OK value in an expensive destination.

Chebský dvůr   PENSION €
(☑353 229 332; www.volny.cz/egerlaender; Tržíště 39; s/d 950/1300Kč) Simple and clean rooms above a Czech–German restaurant.

🍴 Eating & Drinking

La Scala   ITALIAN €
(Jaltská 12; mains 120-190Kč) Karlovy Vary's best Italian flavours are hidden downstairs under an office building. Kick off your night with a drink in their stylish bar. Good-value lunch specials are 90Kč.

Tandoor   INDIAN €
(IP Pavlova 25; mains 120-180Kč; 🖋) Located under a block of flats, Tandoor turns out the winning combo of authentic Indian flavours, smooth, creamy lassis and Gambrinus beer for just 28Kč. Vegetarian options abound, and if you're after a serious chilli hit, order the chicken phall (140Kč).

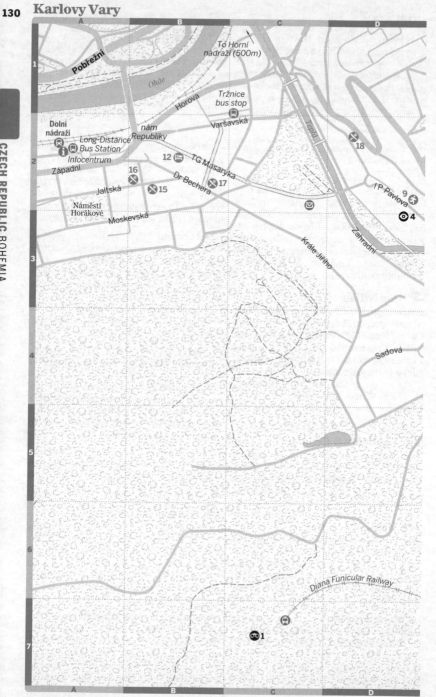

Pobřežní

Ohře

To Horní
nádraží (500m)

Horova

Tržnice
bus stop

Dolní
nádraží

Long-Distance
Bus Station

Infocentrum

Západní

nám
Republiky

Varšavská

TG Masaryka

12

Dr Bechera

17

Jaltská

16

15

Náměstí
Horákové

Moskevská

18

I P Pavlova

9

4

Krále Jiřího

Zahradní

Sadová

Diana Funicular Railway

1

◎ Sights

⊕ Activities, Courses & Tours

🛏 Sleeping

✖ Eating

🍷 Drinking

CZECH REPUBLIC KARLOVY VARY

Kus   CAFE €
(Bělehradská 8; snacks 50-70Kč; ⊙7am-5pm Mon-Fri) This cosy cafe and bakery serves salads, pasta and homemade desserts with an organic and vegetarian tinge.

Rad's Baguettes   BAKERY €
(cnr Zeyerova & Dr Bechera; baguettes 30-40Kč; ⊙7am-6pm Mon-Fri, 8am-noon Sat) Just say no to the high prices of local restaurants with tasty salads and filled baguettes at Rad's.

Cafe Elefant   CAFE €
(Stará Louka 30; coffee 50Kč) Classy old-school spot for coffee and cake. A tad touristy, but still elegant and refined.

Bernard   PUB
(Ondřejská 120/14) Live jazz occasionally features at this cosy pub with a backstreets location. If not, there's always the sunny terrace to look forward to.

ℹ Information

Infocentrum (www.karlovyvary.cz) Dolní nádraží (☏353 232 838; Západni; ⊙9am-6pm Mon-Fri,

10am-5pm Sat & Sun); Spa No 3 (☑353 321 176; ☺10am-5pm) Loads of information on the town, plus maps, accommodation help and internet (2Kč per minute).

Moonstorm Internet (TG Masaryka 31; per min 2Kč; ☺9am-9pm)

ℹ Getting There & Away

BUS Student Agency (www.studentagency.cz) and **Megabus** (www.megabus.cz) run frequent buses to/from Prague Florenc (from 100Kč, 2¼ hours, eight daily) departing from the main bus station beside Dolní nádraží train station. There are direct buses to Plzeň (92Kč, 1½ hours, hourly). Buses to/from Loket, a recommended base for visiting Karlovy Vary, run throughout the day (28Kč, 20 minutes).

TRAIN Karlovy Vary has two train stations: Dolní nádraží (Lower Station), beside the main bus station, and Horní nádraží (Upper Station), across the Ohře River to the north. There are direct (but slow) trains from Karlovy Vary to Prague Holešovice (294Kč, 3½ hours). The train journey to Mariánské Lázně (60Kč, 1¾ hours) is slow but scenic.

ℹ Getting Around

Prague trains arrive at Horní nádraží. Take bus 11, 12 or 13 (12Kč) from across the road to the Tržnice bus stop; bus 11 continues to Divadelní nám in the spa district. Alternatively it's 10 minutes on foot.

The Tržnice bus stop is three blocks east of Dolní nádraží and the main bus station, in the middle of the town's modern commercial district. Pedestrianised TG Masaryka leads east to the Teplá River; from here the old spa district stretches upstream for 2km along a steep-sided valley.

Loket
POP 3200

Nestled in a bend of the Ohře River, Loket is a gorgeous little place that's attracted many famous visitors from nearby Karlovy Vary. A plaque on the facade of the Hostinec Bílý Kůň on the chocolate-box town square commemorates Goethe's seven visits.

Most people visit Loket as a day trip from Karlovy Vary, but it's also a sleepy place to ease off the travel accelerator for a few days, especially when the day trippers have all departed. Loket also makes a good base for visiting Karlovy Vary.

In the second half of July, the annual **Loket Summer Cultural Festival** (www. loketfestival.info) features classical music and opera on an outdoor stage near the river, with the castle as a dramatic backdrop.

◉ Sights

TOP CHOICE **Loket Castle** CASTLE
(adult/child with English-speaking guide 90/60Kč, with English text 80/45Kč; ☺9am-4.30pm Apr-Oct, to 3.30pm Nov-Mar) Highlights include two rooms of the town's lustrous porcelain and the views from the castle's tower. During summer the castle courtyard is also used for occasional live gigs with everything from local bands to visiting reggae DJs. Ask at Infocentrum or the local musos at the Lazy River Hostel.

Black Gate Tower LOOKOUT
(Černá Věž; TG Masaryka; admission 20Kč; ☺10am-5pm Jul & Aug, Fri-Sun only May, Jun & Sep) Loket's striking tower houses a small art gallery and wine shop, and offers some tip-top photo opportunities.

⫟ Activities
HIKING & RAFTING
Ask at Infocentrum about short walks in the surrounding forests. You can also walk from Karlovy Vary to Loket along a 17km (three-hour) blue-marked trail, starting at the Diana lookout.

Karlovy Vary is also the destination for one-day rafting trips along the Ohře River with **Dronte** (☑274 779 828; www.dronte. cz). Rafting on the Ohře is a quieter alternative to Český Krumlov and the Vltava River. Costs are from 1100Kč to 1600Kč per person, including transport. Ask at Infocentrum.

🛏 Sleeping & Eating

Lazy River Hostel HOSTEL €
(☑776 235 417; www.hostelloket.com; Kostelní 61; dm/d/tr 300/800/1200/Kč; @🛜) The welcoming Lazy River Hostel has a heritage ambience with ancient wooden floors and Old Town views. The friendly owners have a castle-full of ideas for day trips, so look forward to staying longer than planned.

Penzion Ve Skalé PENSION €
(☑352 624 936; www.penzionveskale.cz; Nádražní 232, 61; s/d 650/1200Kč; ℗🛜) Spacious and romantic rooms feature at this pension up the hill from the train station. You're forgoing an Old Town location, but the excellent-value rooms compensate.

Pizzeria na Růžka PIZZA €
(cnr TG Masaryka & Kostelní; pizza 100-140Kč) Has a Mediterranean ambience and excellent thin-crust wood-fired pizzas. The sunny terrace is popular with cyclists.

Hrnčírna Galerie Café
CAFE €

(TG Masaryka 32; ⊙2-6pm Fri-Sun; @) This funky main-square cafe conceals an art space for local artists and a cosy garden. Loket's best coffee and internet access comes as standard.

Pivovar Sv Florian
BEER HALL €

(TG Masaryka 81) In the basement of the restored Hotel Císař Ferdinand, enthusiastic locals brew one of Bohemia's best beers. Ask about their nightly terrace barbecues during summer.

❶ Information

Infocentrum (☎352 684 123; www.loket. cz; TG Masaryka 12; ⊙10.30am-5pm) can book accommodation and has internet access.

❶ Getting There & Away

Frequent bus departures link Karlovy Vary to Loket (28Kč, 20 minutes). The bus arriving from Karlovy Vary stops across the bridge from the Old Town. Walk across the bridge to reach the castle, accommodation and tourist information.

Plzeň

POP 175,000

Plzeň (Pilsen in German) is the hometown of Pilsner Urquell (Plzeňský prazdroj), the world's original lager beer. 'Urquell' (in German; *prazdroj* in Czech) means 'original source' or 'fountainhead', and the local style is now imitated across the world.

Pilsner Urquell is now owned by international conglomerate SAB-Miller, and some beer buffs claim the brew's not as good as before. One taste of the town's tasty *nefiltrované pivo* (unfiltered beer) will have you disputing that claim, and the original brewery is still an essential stop for beer aficionados.

The capital of West Bohemia is a sprawling industrial city, but has an attractive Old Town wrapped in tree-lined gardens. Plzeň's industrial heritage includes the massive Škoda Engineering Works. These armament factories were bombed heavily during WWII and now make machinery and locomotives.

Plzeň is an easy day trip from Prague, but the buzzing pubs and smaller microbreweries of this university town also reward an overnight stay.

◉ Sights

Brewery Museum
MUSEUM

(www.prazdroj.cz; Veleslavínova 6; guided tour adult/child 120/90Kč, with English text 90/60Kč; ⊙10am-5pm) The Brewery Museum is in a medieval malt house. A **combined entry** (adult/child 250/130Kč) that includes the Pilsner Urquell Brewery is also available.

Pilsner Urquell Brewery
BREWERY

(www.prazdroj.cz; guided tour adult/child 150/80Kč; ⊙10am-5pm) Beer fans should make the pilgrimage east across the river to the famous Pilsner Urquell Brewery. Visiting the hallowed brewery involves travelling deep into a series of tunnels, with the ultimate reward of a superior, just-tapped glass on Pilsner Urquell.

WORTH A TRIP

MARIÁNSKÉ LÁZNĚ & CHODOVÁ PLANÁ

For a more relaxed Bohemian spa experience than bustling Karlovy Vary, consider Mariánské Lázně. Perched at the southern edge of the Slavkov Forest (Slavkovský Les), the spa town formerly known as Marienbad drew such luminaries as Goethe, Thomas Edison and King Edward VII. Even old misery-guts Franz Kafka was a regular visitor, enjoying the pure waters and getting active on the walking trails that criss-cross the rolling forest. In contemporary times the appeal of spa services, heritage hotels and gentle exercise is complemented by a busy summertime cultural program, including mid-August's **Chopin Music Festival** (www.chopinfestival.cz). You can also catch a local bus (18Kč, 20 minutes) to nearby Chodová Planá and bath in giant hoppy tubs of lager in the Czech Republic's first (and still the best) **beer spa** (www.chodovar.cz).

From Prague, Mariánské Lázně can be reached by train (238Kč, five hours) on trains to Cheb from Prague's main train station (Praha-hlavní nádraží). Buses (170Kč, three hours) run from Prague's Florenc bus station. There are also trains (101Kč, 1½ hours, eight per day) and buses (80Kč, one hour, four daily) to/from Plzeň. From the adjacent bus and train stations at the southern end of Mariánské Lázně, catch trolleybus 5 to the spa area's main bus stop. The **information office** (www.marianskelazne.cz) is 200m uphill on the left.

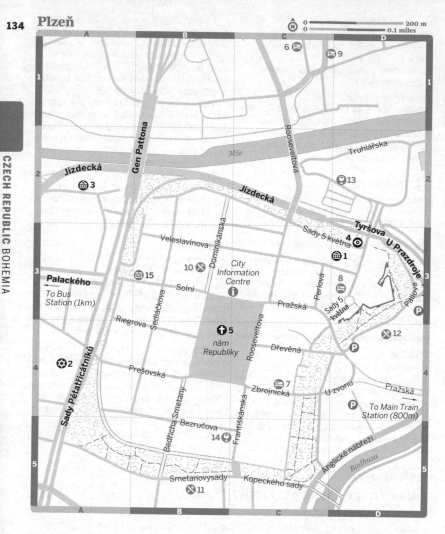

Plzeň Historical Underground HISTORIC AREA
(www.plzenskepodzemi.cz; adult/child 90/60Kč;
⊙10am-5pm) In previous centuries beer was
brewed, stored and served in the tunnels
beneath the Old Town. Take a 30-minute
guided tour through 500m of tunnels at the
Plzeň Historical Underground. The temperature is a chilly 10°C, so wrap up and bring
a torch (flashlight). Tours begin at the Brewery Museum.

Great Synagogue SYNAGOGUE
(Sady Pětatřicátníků 11; adult/child 55/35Kč;
⊙10am-6pm Sun-Fri Apr-Oct) The Great Synagogue, west of the Old Town, is the third-
largest in the world – only those in Jerusa-
lem and Budapest are bigger. It was built in
the Moorish style in 1892 by the 2000 Jews
who lived in Plzeň at the time. An English
guide costs 500Kč extra. The building is often used for concerts and art and photography exhibitions.

Patton Memorial Pilsen MUSEUM
(Podřežni 10; adult/child 60/40Kč; ⊙9am-1pm &
2-5pm Tue-Sun) North of the Great Synagogue
is the Patton Memorial Pilsen, with an interesting and poignant display on the liberation of Plzeň in 1945 by the American army
under General George Patton.

Plzeň

Sights

1 Brewery Museum D3
2 Great Synagogue A4
3 Patton Memorial Pilsen A2
4 Plzeň Historical Underground D3
5 St Bartholomew Church & Tower B4

Sleeping

6 Euro Hostel C1
7 Hotel Rous C4
8 Pension City D3
9 Pension Stará Plzeň C1

Eating

10 Dominik Rock Cafe B3
11 Mêšťanská beseda B5
12 Restaurant Gondola D4

Drinking

Caffe Emily .... (see 7)
13 Groll Pivovar D2
14 Music Bar Andêl B5
Na Parkánu .... (see 1)
Na Parkánu .... (see 4)

Information

15 Main Post Office B3

St Bartholomew Church CHURCH
(adult/child 20/10Kč; ⏲10am-4pm Mon-Fri) In summer people congregate at the outdoor beer bar in nám Republiky, the sunny Old Town square, beneath the Gothic Church of St Bartholomew. Inside the 13th-century structure there's a Gothic *Madonna* (1390) on the high altar and fine stained-glass windows. Climb the 102m church **tower** (adult/child 30/10Kč; ⏲10am-6pm, weather dependent), the highest in Bohemia, for great views of Plzeň's rugged sprawl.

Sleeping

Hotel Rous BOUTIQUE HOTEL €€
(☎602 320 294; www.hotelrous.cz; Zbrojnicka 113/7; s/d from 1690/2290Kč; P@wi-fi) This 600-year-old building incorporates the warmth of the original stone walls with modern furnishings. Bathrooms are art deco cool in black and white. Breakfast is taken in a garden cafe concealed amid remnants of Plzeň's defensive walls. Downstairs, the Caffe Emily serves the hotel's very own microbrewed beer.

Pension Stará Plzeň PENSION €
(☎377 259 901; www.pension-sp.cz; Na Roudné 12; s/d from 875/1250Kč; P@wi-fi) Rooms are light and sunny with skylights, wooden floors and huge beds. A newly completed addition has transformed old stables into spacious accommodation with high ceilings. Cross the river north on Rooseveltova, veer right into Luční and turn left into Na Roudné.

Pension City PENSION €
(☎377 326 069; www.pensioncityplzen.cz; Sady 5 května 52; s/d 1050/1400Kč; Pwi-fi) On a quiet, central street near the river, the City is popular with both local and overseas guests. Welcoming English-speaking staff are a good source of local information. Rooms are showing a bit of wear and the wi-fi is patchy, but the buffet breakfast continues to be one of Bohemia's best.

Euro Hostel HOSTEL €
(☎377 259 926; www.eurohostel.cz; Na Roudne 13; dm 350-400Kč; wi-fi) In newly renovated rooms in the associated Hotel Roudna, the Euro Hostel is Plzeň's best budget accommodation. The location is around five minutes' walk from the main square. The hostel has a quiet vibe – save your partying for Prague or Česky Krumlov. Cross the river north on Rooseveltova, veer right into Luční and turn left into Na Roudné.

Eating & Drinking

Dominik Rock Cafe CAFE €
(Dominikánská 3; mains 130Kč; ⏲10am-11pm Mon-Wed, to 2am Thu, to 4am Fri, 1pm-2am Sat, 1pm-10pm Sun) Get lost in the nooks and crannies of this vast student hang-out. There's cool beats all day every day, and excellent beer, pizza and sandwiches are served in the nicely grungy beer garden.

Mêšťanská Beseda CAFE
(Kopeckého sady 13) Cool heritage cafe, sunny beer garden, expansive exhibition space and occasional arthouse cinema – Mêšťanská Beseda is hands-down Plzeň's most versatile venue. The beautifully restored Viennese-style coffee house is perfect for a leisurely coffee and cake. Check out who's performing at the attached theatre.

Slunečnice VEGETARIAN €
(Jungmanova 10; baguettes 70Kč; ⏲11am-10pm; vegetarian) Fresh sandwiches, self-service salads and vegetarian dishes are available here. For around 120Kč you can buy a heaped plate. The fresh juice and smoothie bar is another tasty distraction.

PLZEŇ'S OTHER BEERS

Pilsner Urquell may enjoy the international reputation, but beer fans should also seek out these other examples of West Bohemian hoppy goodness.

» **Groll Pivovar** (Truhlářska 10; mains 100-200Kč) Enjoy a beer garden lunch at this recently opened microbrewery. Their own beers are complemented by well-priced steaks and salads. From Sady 5 května, cross over busy Tyršova to Truhlářska.

» **Caffe Emily** (Hotel Rous, Zbrojnicka 113/7; mains 120-200Kč) Another beer garden – this time tucked into the old city walls – and another couple of local brews to try.

» **Restaurace Gondola** (Hotel Gondola, Pallova 12; mains 115-220Kč) Plzeň's Purkmistr brewery (www.purkmistr.cz) has a suburban location, so the best bet for visitors is to try their beers at the centrally located restaurant at the Hotel Gondola. Ask about their regular seasonal brews.

Na Parkanu   PUB €
(Veleslavínova 4; mains 100-150Kč) Attached to the Brewery Museum, Na Parkanu lures a mix of tourists and locals with good-value meals and a summer garden. Don't leave without trying the *nefiltrované pivo* (unfiltered beer). It's not our fault if you stay for another.

Music Bar Anděl   LIVE MUSIC
(Bezručova 7; 🎵) By day a coolly hip cafe, the Anděl is transformed after dark into a rocking live-music venue featuring the best of touring Czech bands and occasional international acts. It also has a good vegetarian menu.

ℹ Information

American Center Plzeň (Dominikánská 9; per hr 60Kč; ⊙10am-10pm) Internet access.

City Information Centre (www.plzen.eu) nám Republiky (městské informační středisko; 📞378 035 330; nám Republiky 41; ⊙9am-6pm); train station (📞972 524 313; ⊙9am-7pm Apr-Sep, to 6pm Oct-Mar)

ℹ Getting There & Away

Express buses run to/from Prague Florence (90Kč, 1½ hours, hourly). Buses also link Plzeň to Karlovy Vary (84Kč, 1¾ hours, five daily) and Mariánské Lázně (80Kč, 1¼ hours, four daily).

Fast trains link Plzeň and Prague hlavní nádraží (147Kč, 1½ hours, eight daily), České Budějovice (174Kč, two hours, five daily) and Mariánské Lázně (101Kč, 1½ hours, eight per day)

ℹ Getting Around

The main bus station is west of the centre on Husova. Plzeň-hlavní nádraží, the main train station, is on the eastern side of town, 10 minutes' walk from nám Republiky, the Old Town square. Tram 2 (12Kč) goes from the train station through the centre of town and on to the bus station.

České Budějovice

POP 100,000

After Plzeň, conduct the ultimate Bohemian beer taste test at České Budějovice (Budweis in German), the home of Budvar lager. The regional capital of South Bohemia is also a picturesque medieval city. Arcing from the town square are 18th-century arcades leading to bars that get raffishly rowdy at weekends.

◉ Sights

Nám Přemysla Otakara II   HISTORIC AREA
The broad expanse of Nám Přemysla Otakara II, centred on the **Samson Fountain** (1727) and surrounded by 18th-century arcades, is one of the largest town squares in Europe. On the western side stands the baroque **town hall** (1731), topped with figures of the cardinal virtues: Justice, Wisdom, Courage and Prudence. On the square's opposite corner is the 72m-tall **Black Tower** (adult/child 25/15Kč; ⊙10am-6pm daily Jul & Aug, closed Mon Apr-Jun, Sep & Oct), dating from 1553.

The streets around the square, especially Česká, are lined with old burgher houses. West near the river is the former **Dominican monastery** (1265) with a tall tower and a splendid pulpit. Adjacent is the **Motorcycle Museum** (Piaristické nám; adult/child 50/20Kč; ⊙10am-6pm Apr-Oct), with a fine collection of Czech Jawas and WWII Harley-Davidsons. The **Museum of South Bohemia** (Jihočeské Muzeum; adult/child 60/30Kč; ⊙9am-5.30pm Tue-Sun) showcases history, books, coins, weapons and wildlife.

Budweiser Budvar Brewery   BREWERY
(www.budvar.cz; cnr Pražská & K Světlé; adult/child 100/50Kč; ⊙9am-5pm Mar-Dec, closed Sun & Mon Jan-Feb) The Budweiser Budvar Brewery is

3km north of the main square. Group tours run every day and the 2pm tour (Monday to Friday only) is open to individual travellers. The highlight is a glass of real-deal Budvar deep in the brewery's chilly cellars. Catch bus 2 to the Budvar stop (12Kč).

In 1876 the founders of American brewer Anheuser-Busch chose the brand name Budweiser because it was synonymous with good beer. Since the late 19th century, both breweries have used the name, but in mid-2010 the European Union ruled that Anheuser-Busch were unable to register the brand name 'Budweiser' in the EU.

🛏 Sleeping

TOP CHOICE **Residence u černé věž** APARTMENTS €€
(☎725 178 584; www.residenceucerne veze.cz; U Černé věž 13; apt from 2300Kč; ⊜ P ⬤) Four centrally located townhouses have been given a thoroughly 21st-century makeover to create 18 furnished, self-contained apartments. The decor is crisply modern with high ceilings, spotless bathrooms and fully equipped kitchens. Rates exclude breakfast.

Hotel Savoy HOTEL €€
(☎387 201 719; www.hotel-savoy-cb.cz; B Smetany; s/d/tr 1350/1850/2350Kč; P @ ⬤) The new-ish Savoy has a quiet location just outside the Old Town and spacious, modern rooms with art deco furniture – trust us, the combination works. The younger English-speaking crew at reception can recommend CB's best pubs and restaurants.

Hotel Budweis BOUTIQUE HOTEL €€
(☎389 822 111; www.hotelbudweis.cz; Biskupská 130/3; s/d 2490/2990Kč; ⊜ P ⬤) A restored heritage building and an absolute riverside location make the newly opened Budweis the flashest place to stay in town. All areas are nonsmoking, and the city's interesting historical precinct is just metres away.

Penzión Centrum PENSION €
(☎387 311 801; www.penzioncentrum.cz; Biskupská 130/3; s/d 1000/1400Kč; P ⬤) Huge rooms with queen-size beds and crisp linen make this an excellent reader-recommended spot near the main square. Right next door there's a good vegetarian restaurant.

Cafe Hostel HOSTEL €
(☎387 204 203; Panská 13; www.cafehostel.cz; dm 350Kč; ⬤) Simple and central dorm accommodation above a buzzy cafe and bar. Look forward to lots of local knowledge and regular live music in the evenings.

Ubytovna u nádraží HOTEL €
(☎972 544 648; www.ubytovna.vors.cz; Dvořákova 161/14; s 420-460Kč, d 640-690Kč; ⊜ ⬤) A renovated tower block a few hundred metres from the bus and train stations has simple accommodation with shared bathrooms. Rates exclude breakfast but shared kitchens are available.

🍴 Eating

Greenhouse VEGETARIAN €
(Biskupská 130/3; meals 120Kč; ⊙8am-5pm Mon-Fri; ☑) České Budějovice's best vegetarian flavours are at this modern self-service cafe. The healthy array of soups, salads and casseroles changes daily, with wraps and baguettes for smaller appetites. Here's your best chance to try organic beer as well.

Fresh Salad & Pizza PIZZA €
(Hroznová 21; salads 70-90Kč, pizza 100-140Kč) This lunch spot with outdoor tables does exactly what it says on the tin: healthy salads and (slightly) less healthy pizza dished up by a fresh and funky youthful crew.

Indická (Gateway of India) INDIAN €
(Piaristická 28; mains 110-170Kč; ⊙closed Sun) From Chennai to České comes respite for travellers wanting something different. Request spicy because they're used to dealing with slightly timid Czech palates. Daily lunch specials (80Kč to 100Kč) are good value.

Pekarna Rolo BAKERY €
(Dr Stejskala 7; ⊙7.30am-6pm Mon-Fri, 7am-noon Sat) Excellent baked goods, open sandwiches and fresh fruit cover all the bases for an on-the-go combination of eating and strolling.

🍺 Drinking

TOP CHOICE **Masné kramý** BEER HALL €€
(Krajinská 13; mains 140-240Kč) The best place in town for a cold Budvar is this beer hall in České Budějovice's 16th-century meat markets. Try the hard-to-find Budvar Super Strong, or the superb unfiltered yeast beer, *kroužkovaný ležák*. Tuck yourself away in one of the cosy booths and enjoy all this hoppy goodness with lashings of hearty Czech food.

CK Solnice CAFE €
(www.bazilika.cz; Česká 141/66) This cafe and versatile performance space could be the most bohemian venue in all of South Bohemia. It's got an arty, student vibe, České Budejovice's best espresso and cold beer, and an eclectic programme of art, music

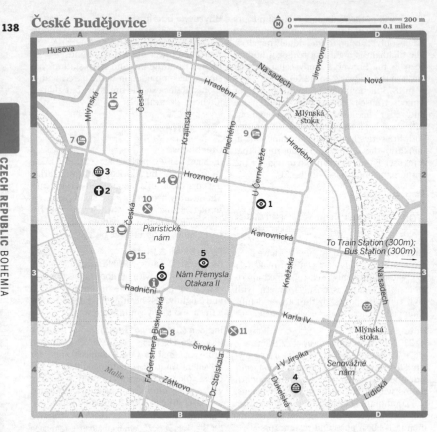

and dance throughout the year. Check the website for what's on.

Cafe Hostel CAFE €
(Panská 13; 🛜) This cosy cafe and bar features occasional DJ sets and live music. The scruffy rear garden could charitably be described as a work in progress. Upstairs are a couple of simple, but spotless, dorm rooms.

Singer Pub BAR
(Česká 55) With Czech and Irish beers, plus good cocktails, don't be surprised if you get the urge to rustle up something on the Singer sewing machines on every table. If not, challenge the regulars to a game of *foosball* with a soundtrack of noisy rock.

ℹ️ Information

There's free access at the Municipal Information Centre and wi-fi at Cafe Hostel.

Municipal Information Centre (Městské Informarční Centrum; ☎386 801 413; www.c-budejovice.cz; nám Přemysla Otakara II 2; ⏰8.30am-6pm Mon-Fri, 8.30am-5pm Sat, 10am-4pm Sun May-Sep, 9am-5pm Mon-Fri, to 1pm Sat Oct-Apr; @) books tickets, tours and accommodation.

ℹ️ Getting There & Away

BUS České Budějovice's bus station is 300m southeast of the train station above the Mercury Central shopping centre on Dvořákova.

The bus to Brno (220Kč, 3½ hours) travels via Telč (92Kč, two hours). Buses regularly shuttle south to Český Krumlov (32Kč, 45 minutes) and north to Prague's Na Knížecí Metro station (152Kč, 2¼ hours).

TRAIN From the train station it's a 10-minute walk west down Lannova třída, then Kanovnická, to nám Přemysla Otakara II, the main square. There are trains from České Budějovice to Prague (213Kč, 2½ hours, hourly) and Plzeň (174Kč, two hours, five daily). Frequent trains trundle to Český Krumlov (46Kč, 45 minutes).

České Budějovice

Heading for Vienna (620Kč, four hours, two daily) you'll have to change at České Velenice, or take a direct train to Linz (420Kč, 2¼ hours, one daily).

Hluboká nad Vltavou

Hluboká nad Vltavou's neo-Gothic **chateau** (www.zamek-hluboka.eu; ⊙9am-5pm Jul & Aug, closed Mon Apr-Jun & Sep-Oct), was rebuilt by the Schwarzenberg family in 1841–71 with turrets and crenellations inspired by England's Windsor Castle. The palace's 144 rooms remained in use up to WWII.

There are three English-language tours available. **Tour 1** (adult/child 220/150Kč) focuses on the castle's public areas, while **Tour 2** (adult/child 230/150Kč) goes behind the scenes in the castle apartments. **Tour 3** (adult/child170/80Kč) explores the kitchens. The park is open throughout the year (no admission charge).

The **information centre** (✆387 966 164; www.visithluboka.cz; Masarykova 35) can assist with finding accommodation, but Hluboká is an easy day trip from České Budějovice by local bus (18Kč, 20 minutes, two hourly).

Český Krumlov

POP 14,600

Crowned by a stunning castle, Český Krumlov's glorious Renaissance and baroque buildings enclosed by a meandering arc of the Vltava River, producing a captivating Old Town of narrow lanes and footbridges.

The town's original Gothic fortress was rebuilt as an imposing Renaissance chateau in the 16th century. Since the 18th century the town's appearance has been largely unchanged, and careful renovation and restoration has replaced the architectural neglect of the communist era. In 1992 Český Krumlov was granted Unesco World Heritage status.

For too many travellers, Český Krumlov is just a hurried day trip, but its combination of dazzling architecture and watery fun on the Vltava deserve more attention. After dark in the Old Town is a magical time, and you can easily fill three days by adding a day trip to the nearby Newcastle mountains area.

During summer, busloads of day-tripping tourists pour in, but either side of July and August, the town is (slightly) more subdued and secluded. Come in winter to experience the castle blanketed in snow.

⊙ Sights

TOP CHOICE **Český Krumlov Castle** CASTLE (✆380 704 721; www.castle.ckrumlov.cz; ⊙9am-6pm Tue-Sun Jun-Aug, to 5pm Apr, May, Sep & Oct) The Old Town, almost encircled by the Vltava River, is watched over by Český Krumlov Castle and its ornately decorated **Round Tower** (50/30Kč). Three different guided tours are on offer: **Tour I** (adult/child 240/140Kč) takes in the Renaissance and baroque apartments that the aristocratic Rožmberk and Schwarzenberg families called home; **Tour II** (adult/child 180/110Kč) visits the Schwarzenberg apartments used in the 19th century; and the **Theatre Tour** (adult/child 380/220Kč; ⊙10am-4pm Tue-Sun May-Oct) explores the chateau's remarkable rococo theatre, complete with original stage machinery. Wandering through the courtyards and gardens is free.

The path beyond the fourth courtyard leads across the spectacular **Most ná Plášti** to the castle gardens. A ramp to the right leads to the **former riding school**, now a restaurant. The relief above the door shows cherubs offering the head and boots of a vanquished Turk – a reference to Adolf von Schwarzenberg, who conquered the Turkish

Český Krumlov

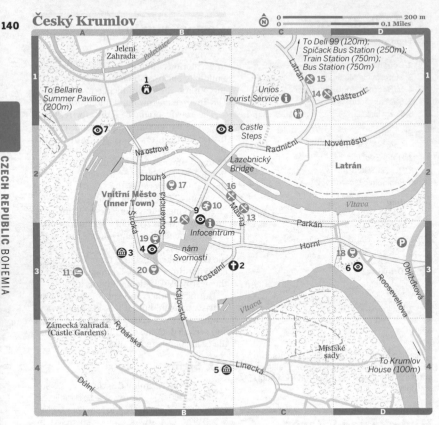

fortress of Raab in the 16th century. From here the Italian-style **Zámecká zahrada** (castle gardens) stretch away towards the **Bellarie summer pavilion**.

Nám Svornosti   SQUARE
Across the river is nám Svornosti, the Old Town square, overlooked by the Gothic **Town Hall**. Above the square is the striking Gothic **Church of St Vitus** (1439).

Egon Schiele Art Centrum   ART GALLERY
(www.schieleartcentrum.cz; Široká 70-72; adult/child 120/700Kč; ☺10am-6pm) The Egon Schiele Art Centrum is an excellent gallery showcasing the Viennese painter Egon Schiele (1890–1918). The attached **cafe** (☺10am-7pm) is appropriately arty and has a good selection of Moravian wines.

Fotoateliér Seidel   MUSEUM
(www.seidel.cz; Linecká 272; admission 130K; ☺9am-4pm) The Fotoateliér Seidel presents a retrospective of the work of local photog-raphers Josef Seidel and his son František. Especially poignant are the images record-ing early 20th-century life in nearby moun-tain villages.

Eggenberg Brewery   BREWERY
(www.eggenberg.cz; Latrán 27; tours with/without tasting 130/100Kč; ☺tours 11am) The Eggen-berg Brewery is also where most canoeing and rafting trips end. Relive your experi-ences on the Vltava's gentle rapids in the brewery's beer garden. Book brewery tours at Infocentrum.

🏃 Activities & Tours

Maleček   RIVER RAFTING
(☎380 712 508; http://en.malecek.cz; Roosevel-tova 28; ☺9am-5pm) Rents out canoes, rafts and rubber rings. A one-hour splash in a two-person canoe costs 400Kč, or you can rent a canoe for a full day trip down the river from Rožmberk (850Kč, six to eight hours).

Český Krumlov

Sebastian Tours SIGHTSEEING
(☏607 100 234; www.sebastianck-tours.com; 5 Května Ul, Plešivec; per person 599Kč) Offers southern Bohemia on guided tours, including stops at Hluboká nad Vltavou and České Budějovice.

Expedicion ADVENTURE
(☏607 963 868; www.expedicion.cz; Soukenická 33; ⊘9am-6.30pm) Offers bike rental (280Kč a day), horse riding (300Kč an hour) and action-packed day trips (1680Kč, including lunch) incorporating horse-riding, fishing, mountain biking and rafting in the Newcastle mountains.

Krumlov Tours WALKING TOUR
(☏723 069 561; www.krumlovtours.com; nám Svornosti; per person 200-250Kč) Has walking tours with regular departure times; good for solo travellers.

Oldřiška Baloušková WALKING TOUR
(oldriskab@gmail.com) Offers tailored walking tours for 450Kč per hour. It's recommended you contact her by email a few days before you arrive in town.

✿ Festivals & Events

Infocentrum sells tickets to most festivals.

Five-Petalled Rose Festival FOLK CULTURE
In mid-June; features two days of street performers, medieval games.

Chamber Music Festival CLASSICAL MUSIC
Late June to early July.

Český Krumlov International Music Festival CLASSICAL MUSIC
(www.festivalkrumlov.cz) July to August.

Jazz at Summer's End Festival JAZZ
(www.jazz-krumlov.cz) Mid-September.

⎙ Sleeping

Pension Sebastian PENSION €
(☏608 357 581; www.sebastianck.com; 5 Května Ul, Plešivec; s/d/tr incl breakfast 1090/1250/1590Kč; ⊘Apr-Oct; 🅿🛜) An excellent option just 10 minutes' walk from the Old Town, and therefore slightly cheaper. Larger four-bed rooms (1780Kč) are good for families and there's a pretty garden for end-of-day drinks and diary writing. The well-travelled owners also run tours of the surrounding region.

Krumlov House HOSTEL €
(☏380 711 935; www.krumlovhostel.com; Rooseveltova 68; dm/d/tr 300/750/1350Kč; ❋🛜) Perched above the river, Krumlov House is friendly and comfortable and has plenty of books, DVDs and local info to feed your inner backpacker. Lots of suggestions for day trips, too.

Hostel Skippy HOSTEL €
(☏380 728 380; www.skippy.wz.cz; Plesivecka 123; dm/d 300/650Kč) Smaller and less boisterous than some other CK hostels, Skippy is more like staying at a friend's place. The creative owner, 'Skippy', is an arty muso type, so you might be surprised with an impromptu jam session in the front room.

Pension Rožmberk Royale PENSION €
(☏380 727 858; www.pensionroyale.cz; Rožmberk nad Vltavou; s/d 800/1300Kč; 🅿🛜) This pension has an absolute riverfront location in the sleepy village of Rožmberk nad Vltavou. A castle looms above the village, and it's a short, scenic bus ride (28Kč, 35 minutes, seven daily) from Český Krumlov. A pleasant stroll just around the river reveals a good fish restaurant.

Dilettante's Hangout PENSION €
(☏728 280 033; www.dilettanteshangout.com; Plesivecke nám 93; r 890-990Kč; ⊜) Don't be fooled by the bland exterior: inside this intimate

WORTH A TRIP

BOHEMIAN ROOTS – TÁBOR

The Old Town of Tábor was a formidable natural defence against invasion. Six centuries ago, the Hussite religious sect founded Tábor as a military bastion in defiance of Catholic Europe. Based on the biblical concept that 'nothing is mine and nothing is yours, because everyone owns the community equally', all Hussites participated in communal work, and possessions were allocated equally in the town's main square. This exceptional nonconformism gave the word 'bohemian' the connotations we associate with it today. Religious structures dating from the 15th century line the town square, and it's possible to visit the 650m stretch of underground tunnels the Hussites used for refuge in times of war.

Today Tábor is an ideal overnight refuge from Prague if the tourist throngs of the Czech capital are wearing you down. The annual **Tabor Meetings Festival** is held on the second weekend in September. Expect medieval merriment with lots of food, drink and colourfully dressed locals celebrating their Hussite heritage. See www.tabor.cz for more information.

Penzión Alfa (☑381 256 165; www.pensionalfa.cz; Klokotská; s/d/tr 570/900/1300Kč; ☎) occupies a cosy corner just metres from the main square. Downstairs get your Geronimojo back at the funky Native American–themed cafe. Right on the main square, the **Hotel Nautilus** (☑380 900 900; www.hotelnautilus.cz; Žižkovo nám 20; s/d from €96/116; P☎) is a splurgeworthy and very cool boutique hotel.

Travel to Tábor by bus, either from Prague Florenc (92Kč, 1½ hours, eight daily) or České Budějovice (62Kč, one hour, 15 daily).

homestay are two romantic and arty rooms decorated with mementos of the artistic owner's global wanderings. Both rooms are unique, but each is equally cosy and eclectic. Owner Matya and her kids are great hosts.

Pension Kapr PENSION €
(☑602 409 360; www.penzionkapr.cz; Rybářská 28; s 1000Kč, d 1220-1600Kč; P@☎) OK, it may be named after a fish (carp), but this riverside pension with exposed bricks and 500 years of history has a quiet location and wonderful views of the Old Town. The lovely rooms with whitewashed walls and wooden floors are all named after the owners' children.

Castle View Apartments APARTMENTS €€
(☑731 108 677; http://accommodation-cesky -krumlov.castleview.cz; Satlavska 140; d 2000-3500Kč) Furnished apartments are better value than top-end hotels in Český Krumlov. Castle View has seven apartments with spacious bathrooms and decor combining sophistication and romance in equal measure. Five of the apartments can sleep up to five people. Infocentrum can also recommend other furnished apartments.

Kemp Nové Spolí CAMPING GROUND €
(☑380 728 305; www.kempkrumlov.cz; campsites per person 50Kč; ☉Jun-Aug; ☎) Located on the Vltava River about 2km south of town, it has basic facilities but an idyllic location. Take bus 3 from the train or bus station to the

Spolí mat. šk. stop; otherwise it's a half-hour walk from the Old Town.

✖ Eating

TOP CHOICE **Laibon** VEGETARIAN €
(☑728 676 654; Parkán 105; mains 100-180Kč) Candles and vaulted ceilings create a great boho ambience in the best little vegetarian teahouse in Bohemia. The riverside setting's pretty fine as well. Order the blueberry dumplings for dessert and don't miss the special 'yeast beer' from the Bernard brewery. Ask David, the well-travelled owner, where he's headed next.

Láb CZECH €
(nám Svornosti; mains 110-160Kč) CK's best pub is hidden away on the edge of the main square. The kitchen also serves other more touristy eateries, but you're guaranteed a cheaper, and more local, experience here. Apparently the local mayor is a big fan of the good-value 80Kč lunch menu.

U Dwau Maryí CZECH €
(☑380 717 228; Parkán 104; mains 110-220Kč) The 'Two Marys' medieval tavern recreates old recipes and is your best chance to try dishes made with buckwheat and millet: all tastier than they sound. Wash the food down with a goblet of mead (a drink made with honey) or a 21st-century pilsner. In summer it's a tad touristy, but the stunning riverside castle views easily compensate.

Nonna Gina
PIZZA €
(☎380 717 187; Klášterní ul 52; pizza & pasta 90-170Kč) Authentic Italian flavours from the authentic Italian Massaro family feature in this pizzeria down a quiet lane. Grab an outdoor table and pretend you're in Naples.

Deli 99
CAFE €
(Latrán 106; snacks 50-80Kč; ⊙7am-7pm Mon-Sat, 8am-5pm Sun; 🛜) Bagels, sandwiches, organic juices and wi-fi all tick the box marked 'Slightly Homesick Traveller'.

Potraviny
SUPERMARKET €
(Latrán 55) Self-catering central, especially if you're going rafting.

🍺 Drinking

Na louži
PUB
(Kájovská 66) Nothing's changed in this wood-panelled *pivo* parlour for almost a century. Locals and tourists pack Na louži for huge meals and tasty dark beer from the Eggenberg brewery.

Divadelní Klub Ántré
CAFE
(☎602 336 320; Horní Braná 2; ⊜🛜) This non-smoking arty cafe–bar in the town theatre has a sprawling terrace overlooking the river. There's free wi-fi, and it's always worth dropping by to see if any music gigs are scheduled.

Cikánská jizba
CZECH €€
(☎380 717 585; Dlouhá 31; mains 140-230Kč; ⊙3pm-midnight Mon-Sat) At the 'Gypsy Room' there's live Roma music at the weekends to go with the menu of meaty Czech favourites.

La Bohème
BAR
(Soukenická; ⊙from 5pm) With art deco styling, La Bohème is your best bet for a quieter spot with good cocktails. From 5pm to 8pm, there's a 30% 'Happy Hour' discount.

❶ Information

Infocentrum (☎380 704 622; www.ckrumlov.cz; nám Svornosti 1; ⊙9am-6pm) Transport and accommodation info, maps, internet access (5Kč per five minutes) and audio guides (100Kč per hour). A guide for disabled visitors is available.

Unios Tourist Service (☎380 725 110; www.visitceskykrumlov.cz; Zámek 57; ⊙9am-6pm) Accommodation bookings and an internet cafe.

❶ Getting There & Away

Student Agency (www.studentagency.cz) buses depart frequently from Prague Ná Knížecí (180Kč, three hours) via České Budějovice. In

July and August this route is very popular and booking a couple of days ahead is recommended.

The main bus station is east of the town centre, but if you're arriving from České Budějovice or Prague get off at the Špičák bus stop (the first in the town centre, just after you pass beneath a road bridge). Local buses (32Kč, 50 minutes, seven daily) run to České Budějovice, for onward travel to Brno or Plzeň (see www.idos.cz).

Direct shuttle buses to Austria are offered by several companies. For a train, you'll need to first head to České Budějovice.

Šumava

The Šumava region's forested hills stretch for 125km along the border with Austria and Germany. Before 1989 the range was divided by the Iron Curtain, a line of fences, watchtowers, armed guards and dog patrols between Western Europe and the communist East. In a different era, the hills are now popular for hiking, cycling and cross-country skiing. The best English-language websites are www.sumava.com and www.czech-mountains.eu/sumava-en, especially for hiking and cycling.

The **Povydří trail** along the Vydra (Otter) River in the northern Šumava is one of the national park's most popular walks. It's an easy 7km hike along a deep, forested river valley between Čeňkova Pila and Antýgl. Buses run between Sušice and Modrava, stopping at Čeňkova Pila and Antýgl.

Around the peak of **Boubín** (1362m), the 46-hectare *prales* (virgin forest) is the only part of the Šumava forest that is largely untouched by human activity. The trailhead is 2km northeast of the zastávka Zátoň train stop (not Zátoň town train station) at Kaplice, where there is car parking as well as basic camping facilities. From here it's an easy 2.5km to U pralesa Lake on a blue and green marked trail. Remain on the blue trail for a further 7.5km to reach the summit of Boubín. Return by following the trail southwest. The complete loop takes about five hours.

If you'd rather use wheels, the **Šumava Trail** is a weeklong bike ride through dense forests and past mountain streams from Český Krumlov to Domažlice.

Trains runs from České Budějovice (123Kč, three hours) and Český Krumlov (85Kč, 1¾ hours) to Volary. From May to August, buses cover a similar route (88Kč, two hours).

From Volary, trains continue north to Strakonice via Zátoň (30Kč, 30 minutes, four daily) and Kubova Huť (37Kč, 35 minutes, four daily).

WORTH A TRIP

SLAVONICE

Barely hanging onto the Czech Republic's coat-tails (the border with Austria is just 1km away), Slavonice is a little town any country would be proud to own. Slavonice's initial prosperity during the Thirty Years' War produced two squares dotted with stunning Renaissance architecture. Economic isolation followed when the main road linking Prague and Vienna was diverted in the 18th century, and in the 20th century Slavonice's proximity to the Cold War border with Austria maintained its isolation. The town's architectural treasures were spared the socialist makeover other parts of the country endured, and now (once the Austrian day trippers have left) Slavonice resurrects its compellingly moody atmosphere like nowhere else.

Slavonice is on a little-used train line from Telč (45Kč, one hour). The sleepy **tourist office** (☎384 493 320; www.mesto-slavonice.cz) is on the main square, nám Miru. Just off nám Miru, **Besidka** (☎606 212 070; www.besidka.cz; d 1490Kč; 🖥) has spacious loft-style rooms and a cosmopolitan downstairs cafe that might just serve the Czech Republic's best wood-fired pizzas. Try to visit on a weekday as it's often booked by in-the-know Prague expats at weekends.

The Povydří trail is best approached from Sušice, which can be reached by direct bus from Prague Ná Knížecí (123Kč, 2½ hours, two daily). Another bus links Sušice with Čeňkova Pila and Antýgl (50Kč, one hour, two or three daily).

Adršpach-Teplice Rocks

The Czech Republic's most extraordinary scenery lies near Poland, in a protected landscape region known as the Adršpach-Teplice Rocks (Adršpašsko-Teplické skály). Thick layers of stratified sandstone have been eroded and fissured by water and frost to form giant towers and deep, narrow chasms. Discovered by mountaineers in the 19th century, the region is popular with rock climbers and hikers. Sandy trails lead through pine-scented forests and loop through the pinnacles, assisted occasionally by ladders and stairs.

In summer the trails are busy; book accommodation at least a week ahead. In winter (snow lingers to mid-April) you'll have the area mainly to yourself, but some trails may be closed. Try to avoid weekends, when Polish busloads visit en masse.

There's a small **information office** (☎491 586 012; www.skalyadrspach.cz; 🕒8am-12.30pm & 1-5pm Apr-Oct) near the Adršpach train station.

👁 Sights & Activities

Two main formations – **Adršpach Rock Town** (Adršpašské skalní město) and **Teplice Rock Town** (Teplické skalní město) – comprise a single nature reserve. At each entrance there's a **ticket booth** (adult/child 60/30Kč; 🕒8am-6pm Apr-Nov) with handy 1:25,000 trail maps on offer. Outside the official opening hours, entry is free. It's an additional 25Kč for a boat trip on a compact lake secreted in the rocks. Buy tickets on the boat.

If you're pushed for time, walk the **green loop trail** (1½ hours), starting at Adršpach and progressing through deep mossy ravines and soaring rock towers to the Great Lookout (Velké panorama). Admire the view of pinnacles escalating above the pines, before threading through the Mouse Hole (Myší dírá), a vast vertical fissure barely a shoulder-width wide.

The **blue loop trail** (2½ hours), starting at Teplice, passes a metal staircase leading strenuously to Střmen, a rock tower once occupied by an outlaw's timber castle, before continuing through the area's most spectacular pinnacles to the chilly ravine of Siberia (Sibiř).

An excellent **day hike** (four to five hours), taking in the region's highlights, links the head of the Teplice trail, beyond Sibiř, to Adršpach via the Wolf Gorge (Vlčí rokle). Return from Adršpach to Teplice by walking along the road (one hour) or by train (10 minutes).

To experience the rock towns more closely, contact Tomas Pycha at **Tomadventure** (☎775 158 538; www.tomadventure.org, climbing instruction per hr 300Kč). Climbing tuition for beginners to advanced is available, and Tomas also rents out bicycles for 250Kč per day.

🛏 Sleeping & Eating

Pension Dita   PENSION €
(☎606 611 640; www.pensiondita.cz; per person 250-400Kč; 🅿🖥) This just may be the most

welcoming pension in East Bohemia, with spacious attic rooms including small kitchenettes. Their snazzy new garden bungalows are especially comfortable. Dita is a 10-minute walk from the Teplice rock town, and one minute from a good restaurant.

Hotel Javor
HOTEL €€

(☎491 586 182; www.hotel-adrspach.cz; s/d 1400/1800Kč; P@🖤) Located just out of Adršpach, the Javor has 41 smart rooms decked out in modern furniture with skylights galore. Downstairs the restaurant also achieves a lighter touch with good mixed grills, salads and pasta.

Skalní Mlýn
PENSION €

(☎491 586 961; www.skalni-mlyn.cz; s/d/tr 600/1200/1800Kč) In a quiet setting between Teplice and Adršpach, this restored river mill has rustic rooms, a good restaurant and friendly dogs who like to be fed furtively under the table. Four-person log cabins (2400Kč) are available from July to September.

❶ Getting There & Away

There are direct buses from Prague's Černý Most metro station to Trutnov (160Kč, 2¾ hours, hourly). From Trutnov catch a train to Teplice nad Metují-Skály (46kč, 1¼ hours) via Adršpach (40Kč, one hour). Note that some express trains do not stop at Teplice nad Metují-Skály, so change to a local train at Teplice nad Metují or walk. Buses also run from Trutnov to Teplice nad Metují-Skály (46kč, one hour) and Adršpach (36Kč, 50 minutes). Check www.idos.cz for timetables.

MORAVIA

Away from the tourist commotion of Prague and Bohemia, Moravia provides a quietly authentic experience. Olomouc and Telč are two of the country's prettiest towns, and bustling Brno serves up Czech urban ambience without the tourists. Mildly active travellers can explore the stunning landscapes of the Moravian Karst region, and everyone can celebrate with a good vintage from the Moravian wine country.

Brno

POP 387,200

Brno's attractions may not seem obvious after the showy buzz of Prague, but after a short stay you'll see the traditional Moravian reserve melting away in the Old Town's bars and restaurants. Leave the touristy commotion back in Prague, and you'll have Brno's stellar array of museums and galleries almost to yourself. Despite having a population of less than 400,000, Brno behaves just like the confident, cosmopolitan capital (ie of Moravia) that it is.

◉ Sights & Activities

Ask at the tourist information office about Brno's many other excellent museums and art galleries.

Špilberk Castle
CASTLE

(www.spilberk.cz; ⊙9am-5pm Tue-Sun). Founded in the early 1200s, Brno's castle was lived in by the Czech kings before being transformed into a military fortress in the 18th century. In this form the castle became 'home' to enemies of the Austro-Hungarian Empire, with a multinational band of rebels was incarcerated in the so-called Prison of Nations. The prison closed in 1853, but was reopened by the occupying Nazis in WWII.

The castle is now home to **Brno City Museum** (exhibitions adult/child 70/50Kč). The two most popular exhibitions are **From Castle to Fortress**, on the castle's history, and **Prison of Nations**, on the role Špilberk played in the 18th and 19th centuries. Other exhibitions of the focus on the history, art and architecture of Brno. A combined ticket (adult/child 120/60Kč) gives access to all displays.

Špilberk's **casemates** (kasematy; adult/child 70/35Kč), the dark corridors beneath the bastions, also can be visited. In Špilberk's time as the 'Prison of Nations', the casemates were reserved for the toughest and most dangerous of prisoners.

After the gloom of the casemates, lighten up in the exquisite **baroque pharmacy** (adult/child 30/15Kč; ⊙9am-6pm Tue-Sun May-Sep) dating from the mid-18th century, or climb the **lookout tower** (adult/child 30/15Kč).

The castle is approachable only on foot, up a steepish hill through the quiet gardens.

Capuchin Monastery
MONASTERY

(Kapucínské nám 5; adult/child 60/30Kč, English text 40Kč extra; ⊙9am-noon & 1pm-4.30pm May-Sep, closed Mon mid-Feb–Apr & Oct–mid-Dec) The Capuchin Monastery's well-ventilated crypt allows the natural mummification of dead bodies. On display are the desiccated corpses of 18th-century monks, abbots and local notables, including chimney-sweeper Barnabas Orelli, who is still wearing his boots. In the glass-topped coffin in a separate room is Baron von Trenck – soldier, adventurer, gambler and womaniser.

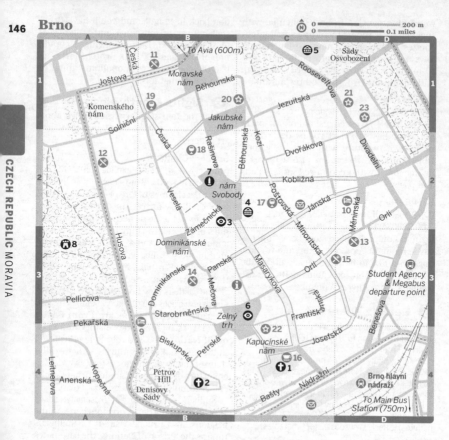

Museum of Romany Culture MUSEUM
(Muzeum romské kultury; www.rommuz.cz;
Bratislavská 67; adult/child 40/20Kč; ⊙10am-5pm
Tue-Fri, closed Mon & Sat) This excellent museum provides an overdue positive showcase of Romany culture. Highlights include music-packed videos, and period photographs from across Europe. There's a good cafe and musical concerts are held occasionally. This part of town can be dangerous after dark, but it's a safe area to walk in during the day.

Parnassus Fountain MONUMENT
The sloping **Zelný trh** (Cabbage Market) is the heart of the Old Town, and where live carp were sold from the baroque Parnassus Fountain (1695) at Christmas. The fountain is a symbolic cave encrusted with allegorical figures. Hercules restrains three-headed Cerberus, watchdog of the underworld, and the three female figures represent the ancient empires of Babylon (crown), Persia (cornucopia) and Greece (quiver of arrows).

Cathedral of SS Peter & Paul CHURCH
From the top of the Cabbage Market take Petrská to Petrov Hill. Climb the **tower** (adult/child 35/30Kč; ⊙11am-6pm Mon-Sat, from 11.45am Sun) or descend into the **crypt** (adult/child 20/10Kč; ⊙as per tower). At the foot of the cathedral is a charming courtyard cafe.

Nám Svobody SQUARE
The city's main square combines mainly 19th-century buildings with a few older monuments. The **plague column** dates from 1680, and the **Dům Pánů z Lipé** (House of the Lords of Lipé) at No 17 is a Renaissance palace (1589–96) with a 19th-century *sgraffito* facade and arcaded courtyard (now filled with shops). On the square's eastern side is the quirky **House of the Four Mamlases**, dating from 1928 and with four moronic 'Atlas' figures struggling to hold the building and their loincloths up at the same time.

Brno

Mendel Museum MUSEUM
(www.mendel-museum.com; Mendlovo nám 1; adult/
child 60/30Kč; ☺10am-5pm Tue-Sun) Gregor
Mendel (1822–84), the Augustinian monk
whose studies of peas and bees at Brno's
Abbey of St Thomas established modern ge-
netics, is commemorated in the Mendel Museum, housed in the abbey itself. Catch tram
1 from the train station to Mendlovo nám.

Vila Tugendhat NOTABLE BUILDING
(☎545 212 118; www.tugendhat.eu; Černopolní 45)
Brno is dotted with cubist, functionalist and
internationalist buildings, and one of the
finest is the functionalist Vila Tugendhat designed by Mies van der Rohe in 1930. At the
time of research, this amazing Unesco World
Heritage–listed family home was closed for
significant restoration work. Check the website, phone ahead or ask at the Brno tourist information office for the latest status.

When it does reopen, booking ahead will be
mandatory.

🎉 Festivals & Events

Festival of Sacred Music CLASSICAL MUSIC
(www.mhf-brno.cz) Held around Easter in
Brno's old churches.

Ignis Brunensis Fireworks Festival
FIREWORKS
(www.ignisbrunensis.cz) International pyro-
technics action in late May.

Moto Grand Prix MOTORSPORT
(www.motogp.com) World-renowned motorcycle race in mid-August. Accommodation
is regularly booked out.

🛏 Sleeping

Accommodation increases in cost and demand when major trade fairs are on, especially in mid-April and mid-September (see
www.bvv.cz for a calendar of trade fairs).
Most hotel websites also list the specific
dates when their rates increase.

Hotel Europa HOTEL €€
(☎545 421 400; www.hoteleuropa.cz; trída kpt
Jaroše 27; s/d from 1360/1600Kč; [P][@][⎙]) Art
nouveau touches and excellent service in reception give way upstairs to spacious rooms
with modern bathrooms. The breakfast
spread is one of Brno's best. Look forward to
a quiet tree-lined location a 15-minute stroll
from central Brno.

Comsa Brno Palace LUXURY HOTEL €€€
(☎532 156 777; www.comsabrnopalace.com;
Šilingrovo nám 2; r from €149; [P][@][⎙]) Five-star
heritage luxury comes to Brno at the recently opened Comsa Brno Palace. The lobby
blends glorious 19th-century architecture
with thoroughly modern touches, and the
spacious rooms are both contemporary and
romantic. The location on the edge of Brno's
old town is excellent.

Hotel Omega HOTEL €
(☎543 213 876; www.hotelomega.eu; Křídlovická
19b; s/d 950/1450Kč; [P][⎙]) In a quiet neighbourhood, 1km from the centre, this tourist
information favourite has spacious rooms
with modern pine furniture. A couple of
three- and four-bed rooms cater to travelling
families, and breakfast comes complete with
castle views. Catch tram 1 from the train station to the Václavská stop.

Penzion Na Starém Brně PENSION €
(☎543 247 872; www.pension-brno.com; Mendlovo nám 1a; s/d incl breakfast 960/1290Kč; [P]) An

atmospheric Augustinian monastery conceals five compact rooms that come reader-recommended. Just metres away there's a Moravian wine bar. Catch tram 1 from the train station to Mendlovo nám.

Hostel Fléda
HOSTEL €
(✆533 433 638; www.hostelfleda.com; Štefánikova 24; dm/tw from €12/32; @🛜) One of Brno's best music clubs also offers funky and colourful rooms a quick tram ride from the centre. A nonsmoking cafe and good bar reinforce a social vibe. Catch tram 1 or 6 to the Hrnčirská stop. It's not recommended if you're looking for a quiet night, though.

Travellers' Hostel
HOSTEL €
(✆542 213 573; www.travellers.cz; Jánská 22; dm 290Kč; ⊘Jul & Aug) Set in the heart of the Old Town, this place provides the most central cheap beds in the city – for July and August anyway.

✖ Eating

Rebio
TOP CHOICE
VEGETARIAN €
(Orli 16; mains 80-120Kč; ⊘8am-7pm Mon-Fri, 10am-3pm Sat; ✍) Healthy risottos and veggie pies stand out in this self-service spot that changes its tasty menu every day. Organic beer and wine is available, and there's another **branch** (Mečova 2; ⊘9am-9pm Mon-Fri, 11am-8pm Sat-Sun) on the 1st floor of the Velký Spalicek shopping centre.

Avia
MEDITERRANEAN €
(Botanická 1; mains 90-140Kč) Avia's buzzy but elegant dining room is tucked underneath a striking functionalist Hussite church in a leafy suburb. The oft-changing menu presents robust Mediterranean flavours including risotto, grilled eggplant with feta cheese, and Tuscanstyle soup. Wines from the nearby Moravian vineyard region regularly feature. Catch tram 1 or 6 to the Antonínská stop, turn left into Smetanova and then right into Botanická.

Hansen
CZECH €€
(Besední dům, Komenského nám 8; mains 160-300Kč) Modern interpretations of classic Czech cuisine feature at the gloriously elegant restaurant in the headquarters of the Brno Philharmonic. The spacious alfresco terrace is the city's most romantic place for a meal, all at prices a fraction of far-off, touristy Prague.

Brabander
INTERNATIONAL €€
(Joštova 4; mains 150-340Kč) This cellar restaurant serves up innovative food – on a Brno scale anyway – with a lighter Mediterranean and Asian touch. A good wine list adds to the appeal of one of Brno's best.

Spolek
CAFE €
(Orli 22; mains 70-100Kč; ⊘closed Sun) The service is unpretentious at this cool, studenty haven with interesting salads, soups, pasta and wine.

🍷 Drinking

Pivnice Pegas
PUB
(Jakubská 4) *Pivo* melts any Moravian reserve as the locals become pleasantly noisy. Don't miss the *Pšeničné pivo* (unfiltered wheat beer) with a slice of lemon. Good luck finding a table, or grab a spot at Brno's longest bar.

Cafe Tungsram
CAFE
(Kapucínské nám 7/531; ⊘8am-10pm Mon-Sat, 10am-9pm Sun) This arty cafe mixes minimalist style and a heritage ambience; check out the restored floor tiles. Brno's best coffee is provided by a guy who really knows his stuff, and beer and wine is available for later in the day.

Zelená Kočka
PUB
(Solniční 1; ☻) Tasty beers from the tiny Dalešice brewery are the main drawcard at this relaxed spot in central Brno, but the food is damn good too and it's all nonsmoking. And no, we don't know why it's called the 'Green Cat'.

Starobrno Brewery
PUB
(Hlinky 160/12) Brno's longest-established brewery is at its best in the beer garden on a warm summer's evening – especially if there is a band playing live music. Catch tram 1 from the train station to Mendlovo náměstí.

Minach
CAFE
(Poštovská 6; per chocolate 13Kč; ⊘10am-7pm Mon-Sat, from 2pm Sun) More than 50 kinds of handmade chocolates and bracing coffee make this an essential mid-morning or mid-afternoon detour.

☆ Entertainment

Brno offers excellent theatre and classical music. Find entertainment listings in the free monthly *Metropolis,* ask at the tourist information office or see the website of the **Národní Divadlo Brno** (National Theatre Brno; www.ndb.cz). Tickets for performances at the Reduta and Janáček Theatres can be obtained through the **Theatre Booking Office** (✆542 321 285; www.ndb.cz; Dvořákova 11; ⊘8am-5.30pm Mon-Fri, 9am-noon Sat). For tickets to rock, folk and classical concerts, visit the **Central Booking Office** (☎542 210 863; Běhounská 17; ☺10am-6pm Mon-Fri).

Fléda
CLUB

(www.fleda.cz; Štefánikova 24; ☺to 2am) DJs, Brno's up-and-coming bands and occasional touring performers all rock the stage at Brno's best music club. Catch tram 1 or 6 to the Hrnčirská stop.

Klub Desert
CLUB

(www.dodesertu.com; Rooseveltova 24; ☺5pm-3am Mon-Thu, 10am-3am Fri, 5pm-2am Sat-Sun) Part cool bar and cafe and part intimate performance venue, Klub Desert features Brno's most eclectic live late-night line-up. Gypsy bands, neo-folk – anything goes.

Janáček Theatre
THEATRE

(Janáčkovo divadlo; Sady Osvobození) Opera and ballet are performed at this modern theatre.

Reduta Theatre
CLASSICAL MUSIC

(Reduta divadlo; Zelný trh 4) The restored Reduta showcases Mozart's work (he played there in 1767).

❶ Information

Cyber Cafe (Velký Spalicek shopping centre, Mečova 2; per hr 60Kč; ☺9am-11pm) There's a wi-fi hotspot throughout the surrounding shopping centre.

Lékárna Koliště (☎545 424 811; Koliště 47) A 24-hour pharmacy.

Tourist information office (Kulturní a Informační Centrum; KIC; ☎542 211 090; www.ticbrno.cz; Radnická 8; ☺8am-6pm Mon-Fri, 9am-5.30pm Sat & Sun Apr-Sep, 9am-5pm Sat, 9am-5pm Sun Nov-Mar) Sells maps and books accommodation. Free internet up to 15 minutes.

Úrazová nemocnice (☎545 538 111; Ponávka 6) Brno's main hospital.

❶ Getting There & Away

AIR ČSA (www.csa.cz) flies from Prague daily, **Ryan Air** (www.ryanair.com) four times a week from London and **Wizz Air** (www.wizzair.com) three times a week from London. Brno's **Tuřany Airport** (☎545 521 302; www.airport-brno.cz) is 7.5km southeast of the train station.

BUS There are frequent buses from Brno to Prague (200Kč, 2½ hours, hourly), Bratislava (135Kč, 2¼ hours, hourly) and Vienna (180Kč, two hours, five per day). The departure point is either the main bus station or near the train station opposite the Grand Hotel. Check your ticket. Private companies **Student Agency** (☎841 101 101; www.studentagency.cz) and **Megabus** (☎234 704 977; www.megabus.cz) both leave from their ticket booths north of the train station.

TRAIN Run to Prague (316Kč, three hours) every two hours. Direct Eurocity trains from Brno to Vienna (1¾ hours, five daily) arrive at Vienna's Südbahnhof. There are frequent trains to Bratislava in Slovakia (two hours), and direct trains to Berlin (7½ hours), Dresden (five hours) and Hamburg (10 hours) in Germany.

See www.idos.cz for bus and train information.

❶ Getting Around

Bus 76 runs from the train station and bus station to the airport (22Kč). A taxi will cost around 300Kč.

Buy public transport tickets from vending machines, news-stands or at the **DPMB Information Office** (☎543 174 317; www.dpmb.cz; Novobranská 18; ☺6am-6pm Mon-Fri, 8am-3.30pm Sat). Tickets valid for 15/60/90 minutes cost 18/22/24Kč, and allow unlimited transfers; 24-hour tickets are 68Kč. A 10-minute, no-transfer ticket is 14Kč. For taxis, try **City Taxis** (☎542 321 321).

Around Brno

SLAVKOV U BRNA

Slavkov u Brna is better known in history by its Austrian name, Austerlitz. On 2 December 1805 the Battle of the Three Emperors was fought here, when Napoleon Bonaparte's Grande Armée defeated the combined forces of Emperor Franz I (Austria) and Tsar Alexander I (Russia). During lulls in the fighting, Napoleon stayed at **Slavkov Chateau** (zámek Slavkov; www.zamek-slavkov.cz; chateau tours adult/child 60/40Kč, in English 105/85Kč; ☺9am-4pm Jun-Aug, Tue-Sun only May & Sep-Nov). As well as tours of the chateau's luxuriant interiors, visitors can experience the multimedia **Virtual Battle exposition** (adult/child 70/50Kč). Promising '3-D virtual reality' but delivering a slightly enhanced PowerPoint presentation, it does illuminate the surrounding terrain on which the battle was fought.

The battle was decided at **Pracký kopec**, 12km west of Slavkov, now marked by the **Cairn of Peace** (Mohyla míru; adult/child 75/35Kč; ☺9am-6pm Jul & Aug, 9am-5pm May, Jun & Sep, 9am-5pm Tue-Sun Apr, 9am-3.30pm Tue-Sun Oct-Mar) with a museum on the conflict that claimed 20,000 lives. Annual re-enactments take place around 2 December.

Slavkov is 21km east of Brno and reached by bus (36Kč, 25 minutes) or train (42Kč, 35 minutes). Pracký kopec is awkward to reach by public transport. Take a local train from Brno to Ponětovice (28Kč, 20 minutes) and walk 3.5km southeast through Prace.

CZECH REPUBLIC AROUND BRNO

MORAVIAN KARST

A good day trip from Brno, the limestone plateau of the Moravian Karst (Moravský kras) is riddled with caves and canyons carved by the subterranean Punkva River. There's a car park at **Skalní Mlýn** with an information desk and ticket office. A **mini-train** (adult/child return 70/60Kč; ☺Apr-Sep) travels along the 1.5km between the car park and the caves. Otherwise it's a 20-minute stroll through forest.

The **Punkva Caves tour** (Punkevní jeskyně; www.smk.cz; adult/child 160/80Kč; ☺8.20am-3.50pm Apr-Sep, 8.40am-2pm Mon-Fri & 8.40am-3.40pm Sat & Sun Oct, 8.40am-2pm Tue-Sun Nov-Mar) involves a 1km walk through limestone caverns to the bottom of the **Macocha Abyss**, a 140m-deep sinkhole. Small, electric-powered boats then cruise along the underground river back to the entrance. At weekends and in July and August tickets for cave tours can sell out in advance, so book ahead online.

Beyond the Punkva Caves entrance, a **cable car** (adult/child return 80/70Kč, combined tourist train & cable-car ticket 120/100Kč) travels to the upper rim of the Macocha Abyss. Afterwards, wander down on the blue-marked trail (2km).

Kateřinská Cave (Kateřinská eskyně; adult/child 70/50Kč; ☺8.20am-4pm Apr-Sep, to 2pm Oct, 10am, noon & 2pm Feb-Mar) is 300m from the Skalní Mlýn car park. Usually less crowded, the 40-minute tour explores two massive chambers.

From Brno trains run to Blansko (35Kč, 30 minutes, hourly). Buses depart from Blansko bus station (across the bridge from the train station) to Skalní Mlýn (16Kč, 15 minutes, five daily April to September). You can also hike an 8km trail from Blansko to Skalní Mlýn (two hours).

Olomouc

POP 105,000

While show-offs Prague, Karlovy Vary and Český Krumlov are constantly praised, Olomouc goes quietly about its authentically Moravian business, and emerges as the Czech Republic's most underrated destination.

An Old Town rivalling Prague's Old Town Sq combines with the graceful campus of the country's second-oldest university. Moravia's most impressive religious structures play host to a thrilling history and one of the Czech Republic's best museums. And, with tourist numbers at a relative trickle, Olomouc is a great-value destination.

☉ Sights & Activities

HORNÍ NÁM & AROUND

TOP CHOICE Holy Trinity Column   MONUMENT

The Unesco World Heritage–listed Holy Trinity Column (Sousoší Nejsvětější trojice), built between 1716 and 1754, is a baroque structure reminiscent of a Buddhist stupa. The square is ringed by historic facades and features two of the city's six baroque fountains.

Town Hall   HISTORIC BUILDING

The splendid Town Hall was built in 1378, though its present appearance dates from 1607. Don't miss the **astronomical clock** on the north side, remodelled in communist style so that each hour is announced by ideologically pure workers instead of pious saints. The best display is at noon. In front of the town hall, a brass model of Olomouc will help you get your bearings.

St Moritz Cathedral   CHURCH

Down Opletalova is the immense, Gothic St Moritz Cathedral (chrám sv Mořice), built slowly from 1412 to 1530. The cathedral's peace is shattered every September with an International Organ Festival; the cathedral's own organ is Moravia's mightiest.

DOLNÍ NÁM & AROUND

Church of the Annunciation of St Mary
    CHURCH

The 1661 Church of the Annunciation of St Mary (kostel Zvěstování Panny Marie) has a beautifully sober interior, in contrast to the square's other two attractions: the opulent 16th-century Renaissance **Hauenschild Palace** (not open to the public), and the **Marian Plague Column** (Mariánský morový sloup).

St Michael Church   CHURCH

Picturesque lanes thread northeast to the green-domed St Michael Church (kostel sv Michala). The baroque interior includes a rare painting of a pregnant Virgin Mary. Draped around the entire block is an active **Dominican seminary** (Dominikánský klášter).

NÁM REPUBLIKY & AROUND

Nám Republiky   HISTORIC AREA

The original Jesuit college complex, founded in 1573, stretches along Universitní and into nám Republiky, and includes the **Church of St Mary of the Snows** (kostel Panny Marie Sněžné), with many fine frescos.

Olomouc Museum of Art ART GALLERY
(Olomoucký muzeum umění; www.olmuart.cz; Denisova 47; adult/child 50/25Kč; ☺10am-6pm Tue-Sun) This gallery has an excellent collection of 20th-century Czech painting and sculpture. Admission includes entry to the Archdiocesan Museum.

Bomb Shelter HISTORIC STRUCTURE
(admission 20Kč; ☺2pm Thu, 10am, 1pm & 4pm Sat mid-May–mid-Sep) Olomouc is all about centuries-old history, but this more recent relic of the Cold War is also worth exploring on a guided tour. The shelter was built between 1953 and 1956 and was designed to shelter a lucky few from the ravages of a chemical or nuclear strike. Book at the tourist information office.

Regional History Museum MUSEUM
(Vlastivědné muzeum; www.vmo.cz; nám Republiky 5; adult/child 40/20Kč; ☺9am-6pm Tue-Sun Apr-Sep, 10am-5pm Wed-Sun Oct-Mar) The Regional History Museum has historical, geographical and zoological displays.

VÁCLAVSKÉ NÁM & AROUND
To the northeast, the pocket-sized Václavské nám has Olomouc's most venerable buildings, with one converted into perhaps the Czech Republic's finest religious museum.

Archdiocesan Museum MUSEUM
(www.olmuart.cz; Václavské nám 3; adult/child 50/25Kč; ☺10am-6pm Tue-Sun) The early 12th-century **Přemysl Palace** (Přemyslovský palác) is now the Archdiocesan Museum with treasures from the 12th to the 18th centuries, when Olomouc was the Moravian capital. A thoughtful makeover showcases the site's diverse architecture from several centuries, and many of the ecclesiastical treasures are superb. Admission includes entry to the Olomouc Museum of Art.

St Wenceslas Cathedral CHURCH
(Václavské nám; ☺9am-2pm Tue, Thu & Sat, 9am-4pm Wed & 11am-5pm Sun) Originally a Romanesque basilica first consecrated in 1131, the adjacent St Wenceslas Cathedral (dóm sv Václava) was rebuilt several times before having a 'neo-Gothic' makeover in the 1880s.

☞ Tours

Olomouc Tours (☏775 345 570; www.olomouctours.com; by donation Jul & Aug, rest of year 200Kč) offers two-hour walking tours led by the guys from Poet's Corner Hostel. They leave from the astronomical clock daily at 10am in July

and August. During other months you'll need to book. Cycling tours (350Kč, two hours) are also available.

🎉 Festivals & Events

The **Olomouc Beer Festival** (www.beerfest.cz) is one of the Czech Republic's biggest. Held in June, with around 20 different breweries and loads of live folk, blues and rock, it's pretty well Beervana for curious hopheads.

Much more sedate is **Flora Olomouc** (www.flora-ol.cz), a world-renowned horticultural exhibition and fair in August.

🛏 Sleeping

Poet's Corner HOSTEL €
(☏777 570 730; www.hostelolomouc.com; 3rd fl, Sokolská 1; dm/s/tw/tr/q 350/650/900/1200/1600Kč; ☺🏠) Aussie owners Greg and Francie are a wealth of local information at this friendly and well-run hostel. Bicycles can be hired for 100Kč per day. In summer there's a two-night minimum stay, but Olomouc's definitely worth it.

Penzion Na Hradě PENSION €€
(☏585 203 231; www.penzionnahrade.cz; Michalská 4; s/d 1590/1790; ☺🏠) Tucked away in the robust silhouette of St Michael church, this designer pension has sleek, cool rooms and professional service creating a contemporary ambience in the heart of the old town.

Pension Křivá PENSION €€
(☏585 209 204; www.pension-kriva.cz; Křivá 8; s/d 1450/1950Kč; 🏠) This new opening gets a lot of things right: spacious rooms with cherrywood furniture, flash bathrooms with even flasher toiletries, plus a cosy cafe downstairs. The quiet laneway location doesn't hurt either.

Ubytovna Marie HOSTEL €€
(☏585 220 220; www.ubytovnamarie.cz; třída Svobody 41 5; r per person 500Kč; ☺🏠) Spick-and-span (if spartan) double and triple rooms with shared bathrooms and kitchens make this new spot popular with long-stay overseas students. Significant discounts kick in after five nights.

🍴 Eating & Drinking

U kašny CZECH €
TOP CHOICE (Dolní nám 43; mains 120-250Kč) Your first choice – cosy cellar bar or breezy garden bar – is easy. After that, indecisive travellers may take some time selecting one of the rotating mix of excellent beers from smaller

Olomouc

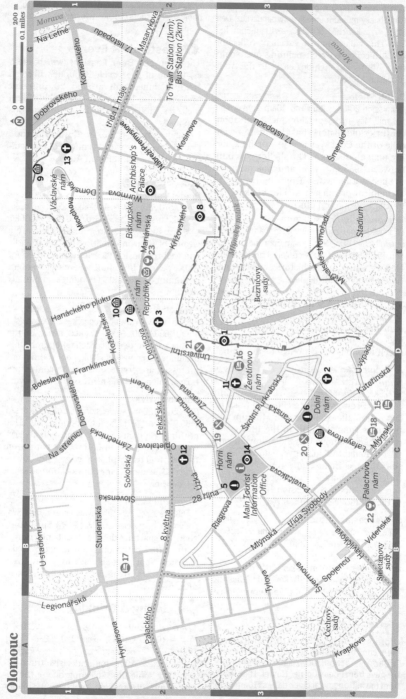

200 m
0.1 miles

Morava

Na Letné
Komenského
Dobrovského
17 listopadu
Masarykova
To Train Station (1km);
Bus Station (2km)

třída 1. máje
Nábřeží Přemyslovců
Kosinova
17 listopadu
Šmeralova

Václavské nám
9
13
Wurmova
Domská
Biskupské nám
Archbishop's Palace
Mariánská
23
Mlčochova
8
Křížkovského
Michalské stromořadí
Stadium

Hanáckého pluku
Koželužská
Denisova
nám Republiky
7
10
3
Univerzitní
21
1
Bezručovy sady
Mlýnský potok

Boleslavova
Franklinova
Kačení
Pekařská
Zámečnická
Ostružnická
Žerotínovo nám
16
11
Panská
Školní
Purkrabská
6
Dolní nám
2
U výpadu
Kateřinská

Na střelnici
Dobrovského
Opletalova
12
Uzká
19
20
4
Lafayettova
Mlýnská
18
15

Studentská
Sokolská
Slovenská
8 května
Riegrova
28 října
5
14
Horní nám
Main Tourist Information Office
Pavelčákova
třída Svobody
Palachovo nám
22
Vídeňská

U stadiónu
17
Legionářská
Hynaisova
Palackého
Mlýnská
Týlova
Švermova
Spojenců
Havlíčkova
Krapkova
Čechovy sady
Smetanovy sady

Olomouc

regional breweries. U kašny's meals are deliciously meaty, and don't miss Moravia's best *bramboráčky* (potato pancakes).

Cafe 87 CAFE
(Denisova 87; chocolate pie 40Kč, coffee 40Kč; ⊙8am-9pm) Locals flock to this funky cafe beside the Museum of Art for coffee and the famous chocolate pie. Some locals still prefer the dark chocolate to the white chocolate. Maybe one day we'll be convinced. It's a top spot for breakfast too.

Hanácacká Hospoda CZECH €
(Dolní nám 38; mains 100-180Kč) In the same building as the Hauenschild Palace, the menu lists everything in the local Haná dialect. It's worth persevering because the huge Moravian meals are tasty and supreme

value. Don't worry – they have an English menu if you're still coming up to speed with Haná.

Vila Primavesi INTERNATIONAL €€
(☑777 749 288; Universtiní 7; mains 180-250Kč; ⊜) In an art nouveau villa that played host to Austrian artist Gustav Klimt in the early 20th century, Vila Primavesi is Olomouc's newest eatery. On summer evenings enjoy meals like tuna steak and risotto in the lovely gardens. Lunch specials are good value. Phone ahead for dinner.

Green Bar VEGETARIAN €
(Ztacená 3; meals 100Kč; ⊙10am-5pm Mon-Fri, to 2pm Sat; ⊜⍟) Around 100Kč will get you a feast of salads, couscous and vegie lasagna at this self-service vegetarian cafe. It's popular with overseas students.

Moritz BEER HALL €
(Nešverova 2; mains 100-180Kč; ⊜) This microbrewery and restaurant is a firm local favourite. We reckon it's a combination of the terrific beers, good-value food and a praiseworthy 'No smoking' policy. In summer, the beer garden's the only place to be.

Svatováclavský Pivovar BEER HALL €
(Mariánská 4; meals 100-200Kč; ⊜) Relocated to spacious digs in Olomouc's university precinct, the city's 'other' microbrewery also has a praise-worthy nonsmoking policy. Try the zingy *hefeweizen* (wheat beer) with the gloriously pungent Olomouc cheese and potato fritters. Occasionally the brewmasters have a crack at conjuring up seasonal beers, including a very interesting *višňové pivo* (cherry beer).

❶ Information

Slam.cz (Slovesnská 12; per min 1Kč; ⊙9am-9pm) Includes wi-fi for laptop travellers.

Tourist information office (Olomoucká informační služba; ☑585 513 385; www.olomouc -tourism.cz; Horní nám; ⊙9am-7pm) Sells maps and makes accommodation bookings. Audio guides (150Kč for three hours) include a map detailing 28 points of interest.

❶ Getting There & Away

Frequent buses link Olomouc with Brno (92Kč, 1¼ hours) and Prague's Florenc bus station (220Kč, 3¾ hours).

Five direct fast trains (130Kč, 1½ hours) link Brno and Olomouc daily. Trains from Prague (3210Kč, 3¼ hours) leave from Praha-hlavní nádraží. Faster SC Pendolino trains (510Kč, 2¼ hours) stop at Olomouc en route to Ostrava.

From Olomouc to Poland there are two direct trains to Warsaw at 12.37am and 12.54pm daily (six hours), and one to Kraków at 12.37am (4½ hours).

Direct trains link Olomouc to Košice at 1.54pm (5½ hours) in Slovakia, but for Bratislava you'll need to change at Břeclav.

ℹ Getting Around

The main train station (hlavní nádraží) is 2km east of the old town, over the Morava River and its tributary the Bystřice (catch tram 2, 4 or 6 for the town centre). The bus station is 1km further east (catch tram 4 to town).

Telč

POP 6000

Telč is a quiet town, with a gorgeous old centre ringed by medieval fish ponds and unspoilt by modern buildings. Unwind with a good book and a glass of Moravian wine at one of the local cafes.

The bus and train stations are a few hundred metres apart on the eastern side of town. A 10-minute walk along Masarykova leads to nám Zachariáše z Hradce, the Old Town square.

Telč's **tourist information office** (☎567 243 145; www.telc-etc.cz; nám Zachariáše z Hradce 10; ☺8am-5pm Mon-Fri, 10am-5pm Sat & Sun; @) books accommodation in private homes (around 300Kč to 400Kč per person). Internet access is 1Kč per minute.

◉ Sights

Nám Zachariáše z Hradce   TOWN SQUARE
In a country full of gorgeous Old Town squares, Telč's Unesco World Heritage–listed and cobblestoned nám Zachariáše z Hradce may outshine the lot. When the day trippers have departed, the Gothic arcades and elegant Renaissance facades are a magical setting.

Water Chateau   CASTLE
(www.zamek-telc.cz; ☺9am-5pm Tue-Sun May-Sep, to 4pm Apr & Oct) At the square's northwestern end is the Water Chateau. The one-hour **Tour A** (adult/child 110/70Kč, in English 210Kč) visits the Renaissance halls, while 45-minute **Tour B** (adult/child 80/50Kč; ☺9am-5pm Tue-Sun May-Sep only) visits the private apartments, inhabited by the aristocratic owners until 1945. At the castle's entrance is the **Chapel of All Saints**, where trumpeting angels guard the tombs of Zacharias of Hradec, the castle's founder, and his wife.

⊨ Sleeping

Accommodation can be hard to get and expensive during the annual **Prázdniny v Telči folk music festival** in late July and early August. Book ahead.

Penzion Kamenné Slunce   PENSION €
(☎732 193 510; www.kamenne-slunce.cz; Palackého 2; s/d/apt 600/900/2000Kč; ☻) Lots of brick, exposed beams and warm wooden floors make this a very welcoming spot just off the main square. Hip bathrooms with colourful tiles are further proof of Telč's coolest place to stay.

Hotel Pangea   HOTEL €
(☎567 213 122; www.pangea.cz; Na Baště 450; s/d 1200/1400Kč; Ⓟ☀@☎☎) Huge buffet breakfasts and loads of facilities make the functional Pangea good value. Outside July and August, rates fall by up to 30%. Ask for a room down the lane away from the occasional road noise.

Penzión Danuše   PENSION €
(☎567 213 945; www.telc-etc.cz/cz/privat/danuse; Hradebni 25; s/d 500/1000Kč, 4-bed apt 2000Kč) Discreet wrought-iron balconies and wooden window boxes provide a touch of class just off the main square.

✖ Eating & Drinking

Šenk Pod Věži   CZECH €
(Palackého 116; mains 110-200Kč) Sizzling grills and tasty pizza are the big drawcards at this cosy and traditional restaurant tucked under the tower. The outdoor terrace has views of a couple of domesticated deer.

Kavárna Antoniana   CAFE €
(nám Zachariáše z Hradce; coffee & cake 70Kč) Documentary photography from around Moravia will get you planning your next destination at this modern refuge from the Renaissance glories outside. Have a coffee or something stronger.

Pizzerie   PIZZA €
(☎567 223 246; nám Zachariáše z Hradce 32; pizza 80-140Kč) Top-notch pizzas and to-die-for town square views.

U Marušky   BAR
(☎605 870 854; Palackého) Telč's hipper younger citizens crowd this buzzy bar for cool jazz and tasty eats.

ℹ Getting There & Around

Five buses daily travel from Prague Florenc to Telč (150Kč, three hours). Buses between České

Budějovice and Brno also stop at Telč (100Kč, two hours, two daily).

Trains (43Kč, one hour) rumble south to the beautiful village of Slavonice on a little-used branch line. It's a great way to connect two of the Czech Republic's loveliest villages.

Hračky Cyklo Sport (nám Zachariáše z Hradce 23; per day 100Kč; ⌚8am-5pm Mon-Fri, 9am-noon Sat) rents out bicycles, and you can hire **rowboats** (per 30min 20Kč; ⌚10am-6pm Jul & Aug) from outside the East gate.

Moravian Wine Country

Heading south from Brno to Vienna is the Moravian wine country. Czech wine has improved greatly since the fall of communism in 1989, with small producers concentrating on the high-quality end of the market. Czech red wines, such as the local speciality Svatovavřinecké (St Lawrence), are mediocre, but dry and fruity whites can be good, especially the Riesling *(Vlašský Ryzlink)* and Müller-Thurgau varietals.

There are lots of *vinné sklepy* (wine cellars), *vinoteky* (wine shops) and *vinárny* (wine bars) to explore, as well as spectacular chateaux. The terrain is relatively flat, so cycling is a leisurely way to get around. See www.wineofczechrepublic.cz for touring routes and more information.

MIKULOV

POP 7600

Described by Czech poet Jan Skácel as a 'piece of Italy moved to Moravia by God's hand', Mikulov is an excellent base for exploring the neighbouring Lednice-Valtice Cultural Landscape. The nearby Palavá Hills are a mecca for hiking and cycling.

Topped with an imposing chateau and studded with a legacy of baroque and Renaissance façades, Mikulov deserves its growing popularity amid the burgeoning Moravian wine country. And once you've experienced enough pretty Renaissance architecture, the legacy of Mikulov's once-thriving Jewish community is a compelling alternative. See the box, p157, for more opportunities to explore Moravia's Jewish heritage.

If you're travelling from Brno to Vienna, Mikulov is a good stopping-off point.

Sights & Activities

A pleasant way to visit smaller, local vineyards across the rolling countryside is by bicycle on the **Mikulov Wine Trail**. The Mikulov tourist office can recommend a one-day ride that also takes in the nearby chateaux at Valtice and Lednice. Bicycles and additional cycle touring information are available from **Top Bicycle** (☎519 513 745; www.topbicycle.com; Náměstí 24/27). Ask at the travel agency opposite the tourist office.

Mikulov Chateau CASTLE
(☎519 309 019; www.rmm.cz; adult/concession 70/35Kč; ⌚9am-5pm Tue-Sun May-Sep, to 4pm Apr & Oct) Torched by the retreating German army in February 1945, Mikulov's spectacular castle has now been painstakingly restored. Three separate tour routes detail the history of the aristocratic Dietrichstein family (40Kč), the archaeology of Roman and German civilisation in the nearby Palavá Hills (30Kč), and the history of viticulture in the area (30Kč). In the cellar is the largest wine barrel in central Europe, made by Kryštof Secht of Brno in 1643.

Jewish Quarter HISTORIC AREA
The hub of Mikulov's historical Jewish quarter is the former **synagogue** (synagóga; ⌚519 510 255; Husova 11; adult/concession 20/10Kč; ⌚1-5pm Tue-Sun mid-May–Oct), now used as an exhibition space. The **Jewish Cemetery** (Židovský hřbitov; adult/concession 20/10Kč; ⌚9am-5pm Mon-Fri Jul-Aug), founded in the 15th century, is off Brněnská. There are tours every half-hour. An 'instructive trail' now runs through the Jewish quarter, with information plaques in English. You can pick it up at the end of Husova near Alfonse Muchy. Above the Jewish quarter is **Goat Hill** (Kozí hrádek) topped with a 15th-century **lookout tower** (admission 20Kč; ⌚9am-6pm Apr-Oct).

Holy Hill LANDMARK
(Svatý kopeček). The 1km path to this 363m peak is through a nature reserve and past grottos depicting the Stations of the Cross to the compact **Church of St Sebastian**. The blue-marked trail begins at the bottom of the main square on Svobody. The whitewashed church and the white limestone on the hill almost give it a Mediterranean ambience. Ask at the tourist information about other walking trails in the nearby Pavlovské hills.

Sleeping

TOP CHOICE **Hotel Templ** BOUTIQUE HOTEL €€
(☎519 323 095; www.templ.cz; Husova 50; s/d from 1390/1650Kč, apt 2490Kč; 📶) Here you'll find discreetly furnished rooms and a selection of stylish restaurants in a restored Renaissance mansion. It's also an excellent

place to learn about the local wines. Each room is named after flowers or birds found in the nearby Palavá Hills.

Penzion Fontána Mikulov   PENSION €
(✆519 510 241; www.fontana.euweb.cz; Piaristů 6; s/d/tr 500/650/950Kč) By day this friendly couple run the local stationery shop. After hours the focus is on the clean and colourful rooms attached to their house. Buy a bottle of local wine and fire up the garden barbecue for dinner.

Fajká Penzion   PENSION €
(✆732 833 147; www.fajka-mikulov.cz; Alfonse Muchy 18; s/d 400/800Kč) Bright, newly decorated rooms sit above a cosy wine bar. Out back is a garden restaurant if you really, really like the local wine.

✗ Eating & Drinking

Petit Café   CAFE €
(Náměstí 27; crepes 40-70Kč; 🕸) Tasty crepes and coffee are dished up in a hidden courtyard meets herb garden. Later at night have a beer or a glass of wine.

Restaurace Templ   CZECH €€
(✆519 323 095; Husova; mains 130-240Kč; 🕸) The best restaurant in town is matched by a fine wine list specialising in local varietals. Choose from the either the more formal (nonsmoking) restaurant or the more relaxed wine garden.

Vinařské Centrum   WINE BAR
(Náměstí 11; 🕘9am-6pm Mon-Sat, 10am-5pm Sun) This winebar and retail shop has an excellent range of local wines available in small tasting glasses (15Kč to 50Kč), plus whole bottles when you've made up your mind.

❶ Information

Tourist office (✆519 510 855; www.mikulov. cz; Nám 30; 🕘8am-6pm Mon-Fri, 9am-6pm Sat & Sun Jun-Sep; 8am-noon & 12.30-5pm Mon-Fri, 9am-4pm Sat-Sun Apr, May & Oct; 8am-noon & 1-4pm Mon-Fri Nov-Mar) Organises tours (including specialist outings for wine buffs) and accommodation, and has internet access (1Kč per minute).

❶ Getting There & Away

There are five buses daily from Mikulov to Lednice (35Kč, one hour), and five daily from Brno (62Kč, 1¾ hours). From Brno, Tourbus travel through Mikulov en route to Vienna.

There are eight daily trains from Znojmo (62Kč, one hour) and Břeclav (43Kč, 30 minutes), some which have direct connections with Brno and Bratislava. Some trains also link from Břeclav to Vienna. See www.idos.cz.

LEDNICE & VALTICE

A few kilometres east of Mikulov, the **Lednice-Valtice Cultural Landscape** consists of 200 sq km of woodland, artificial lakes and avenues dotted with baroque, neoclassical and neo-Gothic chateaux. Effectively Europe's biggest landscaped garden, it was created over several centuries by the dukes of Liechtenstein and is now a Unesco World Heritage site.

The massive neo-Gothic **Lednice Chateau** (✆519 340 128; www.zamek-lednice.com; 🕘9am-6pm Tue-Sun May-Aug, to 5pm Tue-Sun Sep, to 4pm Sat & Sun only Apr & Oct) was the Liechtensteins' summer palace. Studded with battlements, pinnacles and gargoyles, it gazes across an island-dotted artificial lake. **Tour 1** (adult/child 120/70Kč, 45 min) visits the major rooms, while **Tour 2** (adult/child 120/70Kč, 45 min) concentrates on the Liechtenstein apartments. Both tours last 45 minutes. Alternatively visit the gardens for free, or cruise on a **pleasure boat** (🕘9.30am-5pm Jul & Aug, Tue-Sun May, Jun & Sep, Sat & Sun Apr & Oct). Routes take you from the chateau to an incongruous minaret (adult/child 80/40Kč) or from the minaret to nearby Janův castle (adult/child 120/60Kč).

During summer the **Birds of Prey show** (www.zayferus.cz; adult/child 90/45Kč) presents birds soaring and hunting above Lednice's meadows.

Valtice's huge baroque chateau houses the **National Wine Salon** (Národní salon vín; ✆519 352 072; www.salonvin.cz; Zámek 1; 🕘9.30am-5pm Tue-Thu, 10.30am-6pm Fri, 10.30am-5pm Sat-Sun Jun-Sep). The cellars of the chateau are the place to buy and try local wines. Tasting programs cost from 120Kč to 250Kč or, if 'stickies' are your thing, for 399Kč you can sample nine equally luscious dessert wines. Unfortunately you'll need at least five thirsty and likeminded travellers.

❶ Getting There & Away

There's around five buses per day from Mikulov to Lednice, and regular buses shuttle the short distance between Lednice and Valtice (14Kč, 15 minutes). If you get an earlyish start from Mikulov, it's a good day trip to catch the bus to Lednice, another bus to Valtice and then catch the train back to Mikulov.

Regular trains link Mikulov to Valtice (22Kč, 15 minutes) and Břeclav (38Kč, 30 minutes) with connections to Brno, Bratislava and Vienna.

Moravia, the eastern part of the modern Czech Republic, has a rich Jewish heritage dating back to 13th century. According to a 1930 census, 356,830 people in the Czechoslovak region identified themselves as Jewish by religion. However, by the end of WWII, it's estimated that the Nazi regime had killed around 263,000 of these people.

More than seven decades later, awareness of Moravia's centuries-old Jewish history is increasing, and several towns and villages are essential stops for heritage travellers.

Mikulov's former Jewish precinct stands in melancholy contrast to the beautiful scenery surrounding the town, while the Moravian villages of Boskovice and Třebíč feature two of Central Europe's best-preserved Jewish ghettos.

The undoubted highlight of **Boskovice** is the beautifully restored **Maoir Synagogue** (admission 30Kč; ⊘9am-5pm Tue-Fri & 1-5pm Sat-Sun May-Sep, 1-5pm Sat-Sun Apr & Oct), originally built in 1698 and decorated with exquisite baroque frescoes in the 18th century. Download the 'Jewish Town' PDF from www.boskovice.cz for more information.

Boskovice is best reached by regular buses from either Brno (48Kč, 50 minutes) or Olomouc (63Kč, 1½ hours).

Southwest of Boskovice, **Třebíč** (www.trebic.cz) was another historical centre of Judaism in Moravia, but the Jewish population was annihilated during WWII, with only 10 of Třebíč's 281 Jews surviving the war. The Jewish quarter is now a Unesco World Heritage site, and the riverside district's winding alleys are studded with historical structures, including the restored **Rear Synagogue** (adult/concession 40/20Kč; ⊘10am-noon & 1-5pm) with an excellent historical model of the ghetto. Around 600m north of the ghetto, the 17th-century **Jewish cemetery** (⊘8am-8pm Sun-Fri May-Sep, 8am-6pm Mar, Apr & Oct, 9am-4pm Nov-Feb) is the largest in the country with more than 11,000 graves, the oldest dating from 1641.

Třebíč is easily reached by bus from Brno (70Kč, 1½ hours) or Telč (40Kč, 45 minutes). The town is also visited on tours operated by Prague-based **Wittman Tours** (www.wittman-tours.com).

UNDERSTAND CZECH REPUBLIC

History

Over the centuries, the Czechs have been invaded by the Habsburgs, the Nazis and the Soviets, and the country's location has meant domestic upheavals have not stayed local for long. Their rejection of Catholicism in 1418 resulted in the Hussite Wars. The 1618 revolt against Habsburg rule ignited the Thirty Years' War, and the German annexation of the Sudetenland in 1938 helped fuel WWII. The liberal reforms of 1968's Prague Spring led to tanks rolling in from across the Eastern Bloc, and the peaceful ousting of the government during 1989's Velvet Revolution was a model for freedom-seekers everywhere.

Bohemian Beginnings

Ringed by hills, the ancient Czech lands of Bohemia and Moravia have formed natural territories since earliest times. Slavic tribes from the east settled and were united from 830 to 907 in the Great Moravian Empire.

Christianity was adopted after the arrival in 863 of the Thessalonian missionaries Cyril and Methodius, who created the first Slavic (Cyrillic) alphabet.

In the 9th century, the first home-grown dynasty, the Přemysls, erected some huts in what was to become Prague. This dysfunctional clan gave the Czechs their first martyred saints – Ludmila, killed by her daughter-in-law in 874, and her grandson, the pious Prince Václav (or Good 'King' Wenceslas; r 921–29), murdered by his brother Boleslav the Cruel.

The Přemysls' rule ended in 1306, and in 1310 John of Luxembourg came to the Bohemian throne through marriage, and annexed the kingdom to the German empire. The reign of his son, Charles IV (1346–78), who became Holy Roman Emperor, saw the first of Bohemia's two 'Golden Ages'. Charles founded Prague's St Vitus Cathedral, built Charles Bridge and established Charles University. The second was the reign of Rudolf II (1576–1612), who made Prague the capital of the Habsburg Empire and attracted artists, scholars and scientists to his court. Bohemia and Moravia remained under Habsburg dominion for almost four centuries.

Under the Habsburg Thumb

In 1415 the Protestant religious reformer Jan Hus, rector of Charles University, was burnt at the stake for heresy. He inspired the nationalist Hussite movement that plunged Bohemia into civil war (1419–34).

When the Austrian and Catholic Habsburg dynasty ascended the Bohemian throne in 1526, the fury of the Counter-Reformation was unleashed after Protestants threw two Habsburg councillors from a Prague Castle window. This escalated into the Catholic -Protestant Thirty Years' War (1618–48), which devastated much of Central Europe.

The defeat of the Protestants at the Battle of White Mountain in 1620 marked the start of a long period of forced re-Catholicisation, Germanisation and oppression of Czech language and culture.

National Reawakening

The Czechs started to rediscover their linguistic and cultural roots at the start of the 19th century, during the so-called *Národní obrození* (National Revival). Overt political activity was banned, so the revival was culturally based. Important figures included historian Josef Palacký and composer Bedřich Smetana.

An independent Czech and Slovak state was realised after WWI, when the Habsburg empire's demise saw the creation of the Czechoslovak Republic in October 1918. Three-quarters of the Austro-Hungarian empire's industrial power was inherited by Czechoslovakia, as were three million Germans, mostly in the border areas of Bohemia (the *pohraniči*, known in German as the Sudetenland).

The Czechs' elation was to be short-lived. Under the Munich Pact of September 1938, Britain and France accepted the annexation of the Sudetenland by Nazi Germany, and in March 1939 the Germans occupied the rest of the country (calling it the Protectorate of Bohemia and Moravia).

Most of the Czech intelligentsia and 80,000 Jews died at the hands of the Nazis. When Czech paratroopers assassinated the Nazi governor Reinhardt Heydrich in 1942, the entire town of Lidice was wiped out in revenge.

Communist Coup

After the war, the Czechoslovak government expelled 2.5 million Sudeten Germans – including antifascists who had fought the Nazis – from the Czech borderlands and confiscated their property. During the forced marches from Czechoslovakia many were interned in concentration camps and tens of thousands died.

In 1947 a power struggle began between the communist and democratic forces, and in early 1948 the Social Democrats withdrew from the postwar coalition. The result was the Soviet-backed coup d'état of 25 February 1948, known as *Vítězný únor* (Victorious February). The new communist-led government established a dictatorship, which resulted in years of oppression. In the 1950s thousands of noncommunists fled the country. Others were captured and imprisoned, and hundreds were executed or died in labour camps.

Prague Spring & Velvet Revolution

In April 1968 the new first secretary of the Communist Party, Alexander Dubček, introduced liberalising reforms to create 'socialism with a human face' – known as the 'Prague Spring'. Censorship ended, political prisoners were released and economic decentralisation began. Moscow was not happy, but Dubček refused to buckle and Soviet tanks entered Prague on 20 August 1968, closely followed by 200,000 Soviet and Warsaw Pact soldiers.

Many Communist Party functionaries were expelled and 500,000 party members lost their jobs after the dictatorship was re-established. Dissidents were summarily imprisoned and educated professionals were made manual labourers.

The 1977 trial of the underground rock group the Plastic People of the Universe (for disturbing the peace at an unauthorised music festival) inspired the formation of the human-rights group Charter 77. The communists saw the musicians as threatening the status quo, but others viewed the trial as an assault on human rights. Charter 77's group of Prague intellectuals, including the playwright–philosopher Václav Havel, continued their underground opposition throughout the 1980s.

By 1989 Gorbachev's perestroika and the fall of the Berlin Wall on 9 November raised expectations of change. On 17 November an official student march in Prague was smashed by police. Daily demonstrations followed, culminating in a general strike on 27 November. Dissidents led by Havel formed the Anti-Communist Civic Forum

The films of Jan Hrebejk (b 1967) – *Musíme si pomáhat* (Divided We Fall, 2000), *Pupendo* (2003) and *Horem pádem* (Up and Down, 2004) – all cover different times in the country's tumultuous 20th-century history.

Jiří Menzel's take on writer Bohumil Hrabal's *I Served the King of England* (2006) enjoyed art-house success, and *Občan Havel* (Citizen Havel, 2008) is a fascinating documentary about Václav Havel. A recent critical and box office hit was *Kajínek* (2010), a thriller about the Czech Republic's most notorious hit man.

Buy Czech films on DVD at Kino Světozor in Prague (p119).

and negotiated the resignation of the Communist government on 3 December, less than a month after the fall of the Berlin Wall.

A 'Government of National Understanding' was formed, with Havel elected president on 29 December. With no casualties, the days after 17 November became known as *Sametová revoluce* (the Velvet Revolution).

Velvet Divorce

Following the end of communist central authority, antagonisms between Slovakia and Prague re-emerged. The federal parliament granted both the Czech and Slovak Republics full federal status within a Czech and Slovak Federated Republic (ČSFR), but this failed to satisfy Slovak nationalists.

Elections in June 1992 sealed Czechoslovakia's fate. Václav Klaus' ODS took 48 seats in the 150-seat federal parliament, while 24 went to the Movement for a Democratic Slovakia (HZDS), a left-leaning Slovak nationalist party led by Vladimír Mečiar.

In July the Slovak parliament declared sovereignty, and on 1 January 1993 Czechoslovakia ceased to exist for the second time. Prague became capital of the new Czech Republic, and Havel was elected its first president.

A New Country

Thanks to booming tourism and a solid industrial base, the Czech Republic enjoyed negligible unemployment and by 2003 Prague enjoyed Eastern Europe's highest standard of living. However, capitalism also meant a lack of affordable housing, rising crime and a deteriorating health system.

The Czech Republic became a member of NATO in 1999, and joined the EU on 1 May 2004. With EU membership, greater numbers of younger Czechs are now working and studying abroad, seizing opportunities their parents didn't have. The Czech Republic is scheduled to adopt the euro in 2012.

People & Religion

The population of the Czech Republic is 10.2 million; 95% of the population are Czech and 3% are Slovak. Only 150,000 of the three million Sudeten Germans evicted after WWII remain. A significant Roma population (0.3%) is subject to hostility and racism, suffering from poverty and unemployment.

Most Czechs are atheist (39.8%) or nominally Roman Catholic (39.2%), but church attendance is low. There are small Protestant (4.6%) and Orthodox (3%) congregations. The Jewish community (1% in 1918) today numbers only a few thousand.

Czech Literature

Franz Kafka and other German-speaking Jewish writers strongly influenced Prague's literary scene in the early 20th century.

After WWI Jaroslav Hašek devoted himself to lampooning the Habsburg empire. His folk masterpiece *The Good Soldier Švejk* is a riotous story of a Czech soldier during WWI.

Bohumil Hrabal (1914–97), one of the finest Czech novelists of the 20th century, wrote *The Little Town Where Time Stood Still*, a gentle portrayal of the machinations of small-town life.

Milan Kundera (b 1929) is the most renowned Czech writer internationally, with his novel *The Unbearable Lightness of Being* being adapted as a film. His first work, *The Joke*, explores the communist era's paranoia.

Art & Music

Though he is associated with the French art nouveau movement, Alfons Mucha's (1860–1939) heart remained at home in Bohemia. Much of his work reflects themes of Slavic suffering, courage and cross-nation brotherhood.

TOP PLACES TO TRY CZECH BEER

There is an increasing number of excellent Czech regional beers also worth investigating. Buy the *Good Beer Guide to Prague & the Czech Republic* by long-time Prague resident Evan Rail. In Prague it's available at Shakespeare & Sons (www.shakes.cz) or the Globe Bookstore & Cafe (www.globebookstore.cz).

Keep up to date with Evan's ongoing investigation of the Czech beer scene at www.beerculture.org. Here's our pick to get you started on your hoppy way.

» Pivovarský Klub (p116), Prague

» Groll Pivovar (p136), Plzeň

» Pivovar Sv Florian (p133), Loket

» Pivnice Pegas (p148), Brno

» Moritz (p153) & Svatováclavský Pivovar (p153), Olomouc

David Černý (b 1967) is a contemporary Czech sculptor. For more on his confrontational work, see the box, p109.

Bedřich Smetana (1824–84), an icon of Czech pride, incorporated folk songs and dances into his classical compositions. Antonín Dvořák's (1841–1904) most popular works include the symphony *From the New World,* his *Slavonic Dances* of 1878 and 1881, the operas *The Devil & Kate* and *Rusalka,* and his religious masterpiece *Stabat Mater.*

More recently, the Plastic People of the Universe played a role in the Velvet Revolution, and still stage the occasional live gig. Newer bands to watch for include Please the Trees and Sunshine Caravan. Gipsy.cz are a successful hip-hop group drawn from the Czech Republic's Roma community.

Czech Cuisine

The classic Bohemian dish is *knedlo-zelo-vepřo* – bread dumplings, sauerkraut and roast pork. Also look out for *cesneková* (garlic soup), *svíčková na smetaně* (roast beef with sour-cream sauce and cranberries) and *kapr na kmíní* (fried or baked carp with caraway seed).

A *bufet* or *samoobsluha* is a self-service cafeteria with *chlebíčky* (open sandwiches), salads, *klobásy* (spicy sausages), *špekačky* (mild pork sausages), *párky* (frankfurters), *guláš* (goulash) and of course *knedlíky.*

A *pivnice* is a pub without food, while a *hospoda* or *hostinec* is a pub or beer hall serving basic meals. A *vinárna* (wine bar) has anything from snacks to a full-blown menu. The occasional *kavárna* (cafe) has a full menu, but most only serve snacks and desserts. A *restaurace* is any restaurant.

In Prague and other main cities, you'll find an increasing number of excellent vegetarian restaurants, but smaller towns remain limited. There are a few standard *bezmasá jídla* (meatless dishes) served by most restaurants. The most common are *smažený sýr* (fried cheese) and vegetables cooked with cheese sauce.

For non-smoking premises, look out for signs saying *Kouření zakázano.*

Beer & Wine

One of the first words of Czech you'll learn is *pivo* (beer). Most famous are Budvar and Pilsner Urquell, but there are many other local brews to be discovered.

Most beer halls have a system of marking everything you eat or drink on a small piece of paper that is left on your table, then totted up when you pay (say *zaplatím, prosím* – I'd like to pay, please).

The South Moravian vineyards around the town of Mikulov produce improving *bílé víno* (white wines).

The Landscape

The landlocked Czech Republic is bordered by Germany, Austria, Slovakia and Poland. The land is made up of two river bsins: Bohemia in the west, drained by the Labe (Elbe) River flowing north into Germany; and Moravia in the east, drained by the Morava River flowing southeast into the Danube. Each basin is ringed by low, forest-clad hills, notably the Šumava range along the Bavarian–Austrian border in the southwest, the Krušné hory (Ore Mountains) along the northwestern border with Germany, and the Krkonoše mountains along the Polish border east of Liberec. The country's highest peak, Sněžka (1602m), is in the Krkonoše.

South Bohemia has hundreds of linked fishponds and artificial lakes, and East Bohemia is home to the striking 'rock towns' of the Adršpach-Teplice Rocks.

Environment

Single-minded industrial development policies during successive communist governments caused environmental havoc for decades. Since the Velvet Revolution, policies have changed significantly, and standards have increased to meet EU regulations. Private involvement in environmental projects is adding to progress. Groups include the **Friends of Nature Society** (www.novyprales.cz), which is active in returning forested areas to indigenous vegetation.

SURVIVAL GUIDE

Directory A–Z

Accommodation

Outside the peak summer season, hotel rates can fall by up to 40%. Booking ahead – especially in Prague – is recommended for summer and around Christmas and Easter. There is no law banning smoking in rooms, but a growing number of midrange and top-end options can provide nonsmoking accommodation.

PRICE RANGES

In this chapter prices quoted are for rooms with a private bathroom and a simple breakfast, unless otherwise stated. The following price indicators apply (for a high-season double room):

€€€ more than 3700Kč

€€ 1600Kč to 3700Kč

€ less than 1600Kč

CAMPING

Most campsites are open from May to September only and charge around 80Kč to 100Kč per person. Camping on public land is prohibited. See **Czech Camping** (www.czechcamping.com) and **Do Kempu** (www.czech-camping.com) for information and online booking.

HOSTELS

Prague and Český Krumlov are the only places with a choice of backpacker-oriented hostels. Dorm beds costs around 450Kč in Prague and 350Kč to 450Kč elsewhere. Booking ahead is recommended. **Czech Youth Hostel Association** (www.czechhostels.com) offers information and booking for Hostelling International (HI) hostels.

PRIVATE ROOMS & PENSIONS

Look for signs advertising private rooms (*privát* or *Zimmer frei*). Most tourist information offices can book for you. Expect to pay from 450Kč to 550Kč per person outside Prague. Bathrooms are usually shared.

Pensions (*penzióny*) are small, often family-run, accommodation offering rooms with private bathroom and breakfast. Rates range from 1000Kč to 1500Kč for a double room (1900Kč to 2500Kč in Prague). See **Czech Pensions** (www.czechpension.cz).

HOTELS

Hotels in central Prague, Český Krumlov and Brno can be expensive, but smaller towns are usually significantly cheaper. Two-star hotels offer reasonable comfort for 1000Kč to 1200Kč for a double, or 1200Kč to 1500Kč with private bathroom (around 50% higher in Prague). It's always worth asking for a weekend discount in provincial Czech cities and towns. See **Czech Hotels** (www.czechhotels.net), **Czech Hotels.cz** (ww.czechhotels.cz), **Discover Czech** (www.discoverczech.com) and **Sleep in Czech** (www.sleepinczech.com)

Business Hours

Banks 8.30am-4.30pm Mon-Fri

Bars 11am-midnight

Museums & Castles Usually closed Mon year-round

Restaurants 11am-11pm

Shops 8.30am-6pm Mon–Fri, 8.30am-noon Sat

Embassies & Consulates

Most embassies and consulates are open at least 9am to noon Monday to Friday. All of the following are in Prague.

Australia (☑221 729 260; www.australia.pl/wsaw/Pragueaddres.html; 6th fl, Klimentská 10, Nové Město) Honorary consulate for emergency assistance only. The Australian Embassy in Warsaw covers the Czech Republic.

Austria (✆257 090 511; www.aussenminister
ium.at/prag; in German & Czech; Viktora Huga 10,
Smíchov)

Bulgaria (✆222 211 258; bulvelv@mbox.vol.cz;
Krakovská 6, Nové Město)

Canada (✆272 101 800; www.canada.cz;
Muchova 6, Bubeneč)

France (✆251 171 711; www.france.cz, in French
& Czech; Velkopřerovské nám 2, Malá Strana)

Germany (✆257 113 111; www.deutschland.cz, in
German & Czech; Vlašská 19, Malá Strana)

Hungary (✆233 324 454; huembprg@vol.cz;
Českomalínská 20, Bubeneč)

Ireland (✆257 530 061; www.embassyofireland.
cz; Tržiště 13, Malá Strana)

Netherlands (✆224 312 190; www.netherlands
embassy.cz; Gotthardská 6/27, Bubeneč)

New Zealand (✆222 514 672; egermayer@
nzconsul.cz; Dykova 19, Vinohrady) Honorary
consulate providing emergency assistance
only; the nearest NZ embassy is in Berlin.
Visits only by appointment.

Poland (www.ambpol.cz) consulate (✆224
228 722; konspol@mbox.vol.cz; Vúžlabině
14, Strašnice); embassy (✆257 099 500;
Valdštejnská 8, Malá Strana) Go to the consulate for visas.

Russia (✆233 374 100; embrus@tiscali.cz; Pod
Kaštany 1, Bubeneč)

Slovakia (✆233 113 051; www.slovakemb.cz, in
Slovak; Pelléova 87/12, Bubeneč)

South Africa (✆267 311 114; www.saprague.cz;
Ruská 65, Vršovice)

UK (✆257 402 111; www.britain.cz; Thunovská 14,
Malá Strana)

Ukraine (; ✆233 342 000; emb_cz@mfa.gov.ua;
Charlese de Gaulla 29, Bubeneč)

USA (✆257 022 000; www.usembassy.cz; Tržiště
15, Malá Strana)

Food

Restaurants open as early as 11am and carry
on till midnight; some take a break between
lunch and dinner. In this chapter, the following price indicators apply (for a main meal):

€€€ more than 500Kč
€€ 200Kč to 500Kč
€ less than 200Kč

For information on Czech cuisine, see p160.

Gay & Lesbian Travellers

Homosexuality is legal in the Czech Republic,
but Czechs are not yet used to seeing public
displays of affection; it's best to be discreet.
For online information including links to accommodation and bars see the following:

Prague Saints (www.prague saints.cz) Information on Prague's gay scene; they also
run a popular bar (p119).

Prague Gay Guide (www.prague.gayguide.net)

Holidays

New Year's Day 1 January; also anniversary of the founding of the Czech Republic.

Easter Monday March/April

Labour Day 1 May

Liberation Day 8 May

SS Cyril and Methodius Day 5 July

Jan Hus Day 6 July

Czech Statehood Day 28 September

Republic Day 28 October

**Struggle for Freedom and Democracy
Day** 17 November

Christmas 24 to 26 December

Internet Access

Accommodation, bars and restaurants with
shared internet terminals (🖳) or wi-fi (🛜)
are indicated throughout the chapter. Most
Czech accommodation now offers wi-fi access, and internet cafes remain common
throughout the country. An increasing number of Infocentrum (tourist information) offices also offer internet access. Data transfer
speeds are generally good; rates are around
1Kč per minute.

Money
ATMS
ATMS linked to the most common global
banking networks can be easily located in all
major cities, and smaller towns and villages.

CASH & CREDIT CARDS
The Czech crown (Koruna česká; Kč) has
appreciated against other currencies in recent years and Prague is no longer a budget
destination. Keep small change handy for
use in public toilets, telephones and tram-
ticket machines, and try to keep some small
denomination notes for shops, cafes and restaurants. Changing larger notes from ATMs
can be a problem.

Credit cards are widely accepted in petrol stations, midrange and top-end hotels, restaurants and shops.

EXCHANGING MONEY

Use ATMs or to change cash and get a cash advance on credit cards at the main banks. Beware of *směnárna* (private exchange offices), especially in Prague – they advertise misleading rates, and often charge exorbitant commissions or 'handling fees'. There is no black market for currency exchange, and anyone who offers to change money in the street is dodgy.

TIPPING

» **Bars** Leave small change as a tip
» **Restaurants** Optional, but increasingly expected in Prague; round the bill up the next 20Kč or 30Kč (5% to 10%)
» **Taxi drivers** As per restaurants

Post

The Czech Republic has a reliable postal service. Mail can be held at Prague Poste Restante, Jindřišská 14, 11000 Praha 1, Czech Republic.

Telephone

All Czech phone numbers have nine digits; dial all nine for any call, local or long distance. Buy phonecards from post offices and news-stands from 1000Kč.

Mobile-phone coverage (GSM 900) is excellent. If you're from Europe, Australia or New Zealand, your own mobile phone should be compatible. Purchase a Czech SIM card from any mobile-phone shop for around 500Kč (including 300Kč of calling credit). Local mobile phone numbers start with the following; 601 to 608 and 720 to 779. The Czech Republic's country code is ☑420.

Tourist Information

ABC Prague (www.abcprague.com) English-language news.

Czech Tourism (www.czechtourism.com) Official tourist information.

Czech.cz (www.czech.cz) Informative government site on travel and tourism, including visa requirements.

IDOS (www.idos.cz) Train and bus timetables.

Mapy (www.mapy.cz) Online maps.

Prague Information Service (www.praguewelcome.cz) Official tourist site for Prague.

Travellers with Disabilities

Ramps for wheelchair users are becoming more common, but cobbled streets, steep hills and stairways often make getting around difficult. Public transport is still problematic, but a growing number of trains and trams have wheelchair access. Major tourist attractions such as Prague Castle also offer wheelchair access. Anything described as *bezbarierová* is 'barrier free'.

Prague Integrated Public Transport (www.dpp.cz) See the 'Barrier Free' information online.

Prague Wheelchair Users Organisation (Pražská organizace vozíčkářů; ☑224 827 210; www.pov.cz, in Czech; Benediktská 6, Staré Město)

Visas

The Czech Republic is part of the Schengen Agreement, and citizens of most countries can spend up to 90 days in the country in a six-month period without a visa. For travellers from some other countries, a Schengen Visa is required; you can only do this from your country of residence. Check www.czech.cz for the latest information.

Getting There & Away

Located in the geographic heart of Europe, the Czech Republic is easily reached by air from key European hubs or overland by road or train from neighbouring countries.

Flights, tours and rail tickets can be booked online at www.lonelyplanet.com/travel_services.

Entering the Czech Republic

With an economy that depends heavily on tourism, the Czech Republic has wisely kept red tape to a minimum for foreign visitors. If you're travelling overland into the Czech Republic, or have already flown into a European hub like Frankfurt or Amsterdam, note that under the Schengen Agreement there's no border control between the Czech Republic and other member countries.

Air

Most international flights arrive in Prague, with Frankfurt, Amsterdam or Munich being the most relevant major European hubs if flying from Asia, Oceania or North America.

The Czech Republic's second city, Brno, receives flights regular flights from London. **Czech Airlines** (www.czechairlines.com) has a good safety record and is a member of the Skyteam airline alliance. International airports:

Prague-Ruzyně Airport (www.prg.aero)

Brno-Tuřany Airport (www.airport-brno.cz)

Land

The Czech Republic has border crossings with Germany, Poland, Slovakia and Austria.

BUS

Prague's main international bus terminal is Florenc bus station. The peak season for bus travel is mid-June to the end of September, with daily buses to major European cities. Outside this season, frequency falls to two or three a week. Neighbouring international destinations are listed below.

Between them, **Student Agency** (www.studentagency.eu), **Tourbus** (www.tourbus.cz) and **Eurolines** (www.elines.cz) cover services across Europe. Private shuttle buses also link Český Krumlov with Vienna, Linz and Salzburg. Bus services to/from Prague:

Berlin €29, 4½ hours, daily

Bratislava €14, 4¼ hours, several daily

Dresden €23, 2¼ hours, daily

Frankfurt €60, 7½ hours, daily

Košice €19.50, 10 hours, four daily

Munich €35, 5¼ hours, two daily

Vienna €24, 4½ hours, several daily

Warsaw 890Kč, 12 hours, three per week

Bus services to/from Brno:

Bratislava €10, two hours, several daily

Košice €15.50, seven hours, four daily

Krakow 702Kč, five hours, weekly

Vienna €8, two hours, several daily

Warsaw 1026Kč, 10 hours, weekly

CAR & MOTORCYCLE

In order to use Czech motorways, motorists need to buy a *nálepka* (motorway tax coupon), which are on sale at border crossings and petrol stations. See www.ceskedalnice. cz for more information. Drivers must also have their passport, vehicle registration papers and the 'green card' that shows they carry at least third-party liability insurance (see your domestic insurer about this).

TRAIN

International train tickets can be purchased online with **České Dráhy** (Czech Railways; www. cd.cz). International trains arrive at Prague's main train station (Praha-hlavní nádraží, or Praha hl. n.), or the outlying Holešovice (Praha Hol.) and Smíchov (Praha Smv.) stations, as well as Brno's main train station.

Inter-Rail (Zone D) passes are valid in the Czech Republic, and in 2009 the country became part of the Eurail network.

As well as those listed below, there are also services between České Budějovice and Linz, and from Olomouc to Warsaw and to Krakow. Train services to/from Prague:

Berlin 737Kč, five hours, daily

Bratislava 500Kč, 4¼ hours, several daily

Dresden 483Kč, 2¼ hours, several daily

Frankfurt 1245Kč, seven hours, two daily

Munich €35, six hours, two daily

Vienna 483Kč, five hours, several daily

Warsaw 477Kč, 8½ hours, two daily

Train services to/from Brno:

Bratislava 210Kč, 1½ hours, several daily

Vienna 229Kč, two hours, several daily

Getting Around

Air

The Czech Republic is compact and internal flights are limited. **Czech Airlines** (☎800 310 310; www.czechairlines.com) links Prague with Brno, Karlovy Vary, Ostrava and Brno.

Bicycle

The Czech Republic offers excellent opportunities for cycle touring and has many dedicated trails. See http://www.czech.cz/en/67105-cycling for information.

Cyclists should be careful as minor roads are often narrow and potholed. In towns, cobblestones and tram tracks can be a dangerous combination, especially after rain. Theft can be a problem so always lock up your bike.

It's easy to transport your bike on Czech trains. Purchase your train ticket and then take it with your bicycle to the train luggage office.

Bus

Within the Czech Republic, buses are often faster, cheaper and more convenient than trains. Many bus routes have reduced frequency (or none) at weekends. Buses occasionally leave early so get to the station at least 15 minutes before the official departure time. Check bus timetables and prices at www.idos.cz. Main bus companies:

CŠAD (☑information line 900 144 444) The national bus company links cities and smaller towns.

Megabus (www.megabus.cz) Links Prague with Karlovy Vary, Brno and Plzeň.

Student Agency (www.studentagency.cz) Has destinations including Prague, Brno, České Budějovice, Český Krumlov, Karlovy Vary and Plzeň.

DECIPHERING THE TIMETABLES
» Crossed hammers means the bus runs on *pracovní dny* (working days; ie Monday to Friday only).
» A Christian cross means the bus runs on Sundays and public holidays.
» Numbers in circles refer to particular days of the week (1 is Monday, 2 Tuesday etc).
» *Jede* means 'runs'.
» *Nejede* means 'doesn't run'.
» *Jede denne* means 'runs daily'.
» *V* is 'on', *od* is 'from' and *do* is 'to' or 'until'.

Car & Motorcycle
DRIVING LICENCE
Foreign driving licences are valid for up to 90 days. Strictly speaking, licences that do not include photo identification need an International Driving Permit as well, although this rule is rarely enforced.

FUEL
Leaded petrol is available as *special* (91 octane) and *super* (96 octane), and unleaded as *natural* (95 octane) or *natural plus* (98 octane). The Czech for diesel is *nafta* or just *diesel*. *Autoplyn* (LPG gas) is available in every major town but at very few outlets.

HIRE
Small local companies offer better prices, but are less likely to have fluent, English-speaking staff. It's often easier to book by email than by phone. Typical rates for a Škoda Fabia are around 700Kč a day, including unlimited kilometres, collision-damage waiver and value-added tax (VAT). Bring your credit card as a deposit. A motorway tax coupon is included with most rental cars. Local operators in Prague:

Secco Car (☑220 802 361; www.seccocar.cz; Přístavní 39, Holešovice)

Vecar (☑224 314 361; www.vecar.org; Svatovítská 7, Dejvice)

ROAD RULES
Driving is on the right hand side of the road, and road rules reflect the rest of Europe.
» A vehicle must be equipped with a first-aid kit and a red and white warning triangle.
» Using seat belts is compulsory.
» Drinking and driving is forbidden (the blood alcohol level is zero).
» Speed limits are 30km/h or 50km/h in built-up areas, 90km/h on open roads and 130km/h on motorways.
» Motorbikes are limited to 80km/h.

Police can hit you with on-the-spot fines of up to 2000Kč for speeding and other traffic offences (be sure to insist on a receipt).

Local Transport
Local transport is very affordable, well organised and runs from around 4.30am to midnight daily. Purchase tickets in advance from news-stands and vending machines. Validate tickets in time-stamping machines on buses and trams and at the entrance to metro stations.

Tours
Ave Bicycle Tours (www.bicycle-tours.cz) Cycle touring specialists.

E-Tours (www.etours.cz) Nature, wildlife and photography tours.

Greenways Travel Club (www.visitgreenways.com) From cycling and walking to beer and wine, Czech glass and Czech music tours.

Top Bicycle (www.topbicycle.com) Biking and multisport tours.

Train
Czech Railways provides efficient train services to almost every part of the country. See www.idos.cz and www.cd.cz for fares and timetables.

TICKETS
The sales clerks at ticket counters outside of Prague may not speak English, so write down your destination with the date and time you wish to travel. If you're paying by credit card, let them know *before* they issue the ticket. Ticket categories:

EC (EuroCity) Fast, comfortable international trains, stopping at main stations only, with 1st- and 2nd-class coaches; supplementary charge of 60Kč; reservations recommended. Includes 1st-class only SC Pendolino trains that run from Prague to Olomouc, Brno and Ostrava, with links to Vienna and Bratislava.

Ex (express) As for IC, but no supplementary charge.

IC (InterCity) Long-distance and international trains with 1st- and 2nd-class coaches; supplement of 40Kč; reservations recommended.

Os *(osobní)* Slow trains using older rolling stock that stop in every one-horse town; 2nd-class only.

R *(rychlík)* The main domestic network of fast trains with 1st- and 2nd-class coaches and sleeper services; no supplement except for sleepers; express and *rychlík* trains are usually marked in red on timetables.

Sp *(spěšný)* Slower and cheaper than *rychlík* trains; 2nd class only.

Germany

Why Go?

Beer or wine? That sums up the German conundrum. One is at the heart of a pilsner-swilling culture, is the very reason for one of the world's great parties (Oktoberfest) and is consumed with pleasure across the land. The other is responsible for gorgeous vine-covered valleys, comes in myriad forms and is enjoyed everywhere, often from cute little green-stemmed glasses.

And the questions about Germany continue. Berlin or Munich? Castle or club? Ski or hike? East or west? BMW or Mercedes? In fact, the answers are simple: both. Why decide? The beauty of Germany is that rather than choosing, you can revel in the contrasts.

Berlin, edgy and vibrant, is a grand capital in a constant state of reinvention. Munich rules Bavaria, the centre of national traditions. Half-timbered villages bring smiles as you wander their cobblestoned and castle-shadowed lanes. Exploring this country and all its facets keeps visitors happy for weeks.

Best Places to Eat

» Cafe Jacques (p186)
» Wolfshöhle (p253)
» Bratwursthäusle (p233)
» Feynsinn (p270)
» Wurstküche (p235)

Best Places to Stay

» Michelberger Hotel (p184)
» Hotel Blauer Bock (p222)
» Kogge (p287)
» Hotel Sankt Nepomuk (p229)
» Hotel Elch (p233)

When to Go

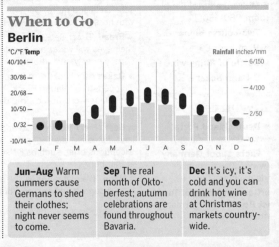

Berlin

Jun–Aug Warm summers cause Germans to shed their clothes; night never seems to come.

Sep The real month of Oktoberfest; autumn celebrations are found throughout Bavaria.

Dec It's icy, it's cold and you can drink hot wine at Christmas markets country-wide.

Fast Facts

» **Area** 356,866 sq km

» **Population** 85 million

» **Capital** Berlin

» **Telephone** country code ☏49; international access code ☏00

» **Emergency** ☏112

Exchange Rates

Australia	A$1	€0.74
Canada	C$1	€0.74
Japan	¥100	€0.87
New Zealand	NZ$1	€0.56
UK	UK£1	€1.16
USA	US$1	€0.67

Set Your Budget

» **Midrange hotel double room** €80–150

» **Two-course dinner** €12

» **1L of beer** €9

» **Bottle of Rhine wine** €6

» **U-Bahn ticket** €2

Resources

» **Deutschland Portal** (www.deutschland.de)

» **Facts about Germany** (www.tatsachen-ueber -deutschland.de)

» **German National Tourist Board** (www.germany -tourism.de)

Connections

At the heart of Europe, Germany has a superb railway that's well linked to surrounding countries. Freiburg and Stuttgart have services south to Switzerland and Italy, Munich is close to the Czech Republic and Austria (including Salzburg and Innsbruck), Berlin is close to Poland, Hamburg has frequent services to Denmark, Cologne is good for fast trains to the Netherlands and Belgium (including Brussels for Eurostar to London), and Frankfurt is the base for high-speed trains to Paris, Strasbourg and other parts of France.

ITINERARIES

One week

Starting in Berlin, spend three days in and around the city, then head south through the wonderful little Thuringian town of Weimar and the tiny Bavarian town of Bamberg before ending up in Munich.

Two weeks

Start in Munich for some Bavarian joy, then head up to the goofy castles in Füssen. Take in some of the Bavarian Alps and the fun of Freiburg. Explore the Black Forest, soak up Baden-Baden and settle in for a boat voyage down the Rhine in Mainz. Pop up to Hamburg then south to the old East and Dresden. Finish it all in Berlin.

Essential Food & Drink

» **Sausage** (*Wurst*) More than 1500 types are made countrywide. From sweet, smoky and tiny Nurnbergers to imposing Thüringers to that fast-food remedy for the munchies, the sliced and drowned currywurst.

» **Mustard** (*Senf*) The perfect accompaniment to sausages, schnitzels and more, German mustards can be hot, laced with horseradish or rich with seeds. Or all three.

» **Bread** (*Brot*) Get Germans talking about bread and often their eyes will water as they describe their favourite type – usually hearty and whole-grained in infinite variations.

» **Cakes** (*Kuchen*) From the confectionery fantasy of the whipped-cream-laden Black Forest cake to all manner of apple-laden, crumb-covered delights, sweet tooths never feel ignored.

» **Beer** (*Bier*) Mostly crisp and clear, the many lagers of the land are easily quaffed, preferably from huge steins. But exceptions exist, such as Kölsch in Cologne and Rauchbier in Bamberg.

» **Wine** (*Wein*) It's not all sweet and it's not all white; the best is superb and comes from 13 distinct regions.

BERLIN

♫030 / POP 3.41 MILLION

You live history in Berlin. You might be distracted by the trendy, edgy, gentrified streets, by the bars bleeding a laid-back cool factor, by the galleries sprouting talent and pushing the envelope, but make no mistake – reminders of its once-divided past assault you while modernity sits around the corner. Norman Foster's Reichstag dome, Peter Eisenman's Holocaust Memorial and the iconic Brandenburg Gate are all contained within a few neighbouring blocks. Potsdamer Platz and its shiny Sony Center hosts Berlin's star-studded film festival each year, a stone's throw from where only 20 years ago you could climb up a viewing platform in the West and peer over the wall to glimpse the alternate reality of the East. Casually strolling along Bernauerstrasse near trendy Prenzlauer Berg, you suddenly place your foot on a brick-marked line in the pavement marking where the wall once stood.

Renowned for its diversity and its tolerance, its alternative culture and its night-owl stamina, the best thing about the German capital is the way it reinvents itself and isn't shackled by its mind-numbing history. And the world knows this – expatriates and a steady increase of out-of-towners are flocking to see what all the fuss is about.

Meanwhile, creative types flock here to write that book, paint their hearts out or simply live the ultimate bohemian life (though the low price tag that often inspires these romantic lifestyle choices is steadily climbing). Still, in Berlin nobody questions artistic intentions, experimental philosophies or lofty ideas, and it's perfectly fine to try, fail and try again. Some arrive seeking (and finding) Hemingway's Paris or Warhol's New York, but everyone unearths something extraordinary that often makes home seem, well, banal and conservative.

In the midst of it all, students rub shoulders with Russian émigrés, fashion boutiques inhabit monumental German Democratic Republic (GDR) buildings, Turkish residents live next door to famous DJs and the nightlife has long left the American sector as edgy clubbers watch the sun rise over the neon-lit Universal Music headquarters in the city's east.

In short, all human life is here, and don't expect to get much sleep.

History

United, divided, united again, Berlin has a roller-coaster past. The merging of two medieval trading posts, it enjoyed its first stint as a capital in 1701, when it became the leading city of the state of Brandenburg-Prussia. Under Prussian King Friedrich I and his son, Friedrich II, Berlin flourished culturally and politically.

The Industrial Revolution, when commercial giants such as Siemens emerged, also boosted the city. As workers flooded to Berlin's factories, its population doubled between 1850 and 1870. 'Deutschland' was a latecomer to the table of nationhood, but in 1871 Berlin was again proclaimed a capital, this time of the newly unified Germany.

By 1900 the city was home to almost two million people, but after WWI it fell into decline and, like the rest of Germany, suffered an economic crisis and hyperinflation. There was a brief, early communist uprising in the capital in 1918, led by Karl Liebknecht and Rosa Luxemburg (whose names now adorn Berlin streets). However, that was quickly squashed, and during the following Weimar Republic (1919–33) Berlin

BERLIN IN TWO DAYS

Investigate the **Brandenburg Gate** area, including the **Reichstag** and the **Holocaust Memorial**. Walk east along Unter den Linden, stopping at the **Bebelplatz book-burning memorial**. Veer through the **Museumsinsel** for window-shopping and cafe-hopping through **Hackescher Markt**. In the evening, explore the bars of Prenzlauer Berg, along Kastanieanallee and Pappelallee, stopping for a drink in **Fleischmöbel**.

Start the next day at the **East Side Gallery** remnant of the Berlin Wall, before heading to **Checkpoint Charlie** and the nearby **Jewish Museum**. Take the U-Bahn to **Kurfürstendamm** and catch scenic bus 100 back to the **Fernsehturm**. Later, explore Kreuzberg nightlife around Kottbusser Tor and go clubbing – **Berghain/Panoramabar** is best if you are short on time. Alternatively, head for the **Berliner Ensemble**.

Germany Highlights

1 Party day and night in **Berlin** (p169); save sleep for somewhere else as there's no time here with the clubs, museums, bars and ever-changing zeitgeist

2 Time your journey for **Oktoberfest** (p222), Munich's orgy of suds, or just hang out in a beer garden

3 Go slow in Germany's alluring small towns like **Bamberg** (p229), with winding lanes, smoked beer (!) and a lack of cliché

4 Compare the soaring peaks of the Dom in **Cologne** (p267) with the towering glasses of the city's famous beer

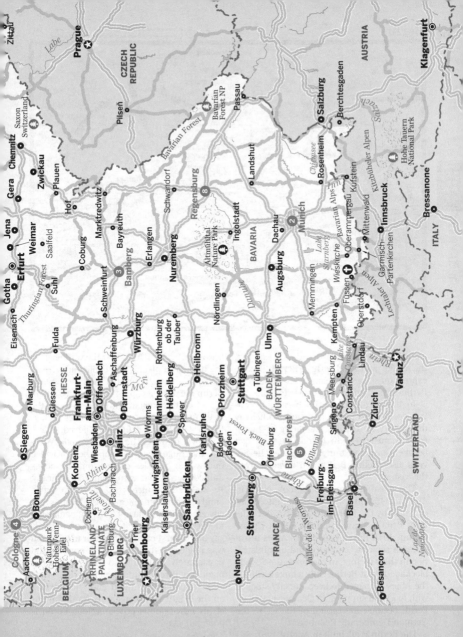

5 Go cuckoo in the **Black Forest** (p248), discovering its chilly crags, misty peaks and endless trails

6 Get into the swing of **Dresden** (p192), with a creative culture beyond the restorations

7 Cycle around one of the world's great harbours in **Hamburg** (p282), then follow the trail of the Beatles

8 Discover **Regensburg** (p234), Germany's Unesco-recognised ancient gem, with traces of Rome and Tuscany (and great sausages!) around every corner

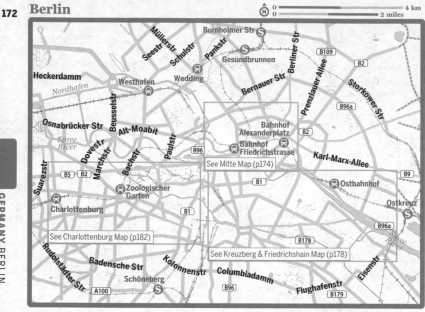

gained a reputation for decadence. Cabaret, the savage political theatre of Bertolt Brecht, expressionist art and jazz all flourished as Berliners partied to forget their troubles.

In the mid-1930s Berlin became a centrepiece of Nazi power and suffered heavily during WWII. During the Battle of Berlin from August 1943 to March 1944, British bombers targeted the city nightly. The Soviets also shelled Berlin and invaded from the east.

The Potsdam Conference took place in August 1945 and split the capital into zones occupied by the four victorious powers – the USA, Britain, France and the Soviet Union. In June 1948 the three Western Allies introduced a separate currency and administration in their sectors. In response, the Soviets blockaded West Berlin. Only a huge airlift by the Allies managed to keep the city stocked with food and supplies. In October 1949 East Berlin became the capital of the GDR, the German Democratic Republic.

The Berlin Wall, built in August 1961, was originally intended to prevent the drain of skilled labour from the East, but soon became a Cold War symbol. For decades East Berlin and West Berlin developed separately, until Hungary breached the Iron Curtain in May 1989; the Berlin Wall followed on

9 November. By 1 July 1990 the wall was being hacked to pieces. The Unification Treaty signed on 3 October that year designated Berlin the official capital of Germany, and in June 1991 the parliament voted to move the seat of government from Bonn back to Berlin. In 1999 that was finally achieved.

Times, however, have been tough. Without the huge national subsidies provided during the decades of division, the newly unified Berlin has struggled economically. In 2001 the centre-right mayor resigned amid corruption allegations, leaving the city effectively bankrupt. Current centre-left mayor Klaus Wowereit, Berlin's first openly gay mayor, first came into power in 2001 and was re-elected in 2006 – he is popular and passionately dedicated to his city, but has made few inroads into the crisis. But Wowereit remains undaunted and tries to look on the bright side, constantly reminding us of his now-famous proclamation, 'Berlin is poor, but sexy'.

Orientation

Standing at Berlin's Brandenburg Gate, on the former East-West divide, you can see many major sights. Looking east, your eye follows Unter den Linden past the Museumsinsel (Museum Island) in the Spree River, to the needle-shaped Fernsehturm (TV tower) at Alexanderplatz.

If you turn west, you face the golden Siegessäule (Victory Column) along the equally huge thoroughfare of Strasse des 17 Juni, which cuts through the middle of Berlin's central park, the Tiergarten. To your right, just near the Brandenburg Gate, is the glass-domed Reichstag and beyond that the new government district and the snazzy Hauptbahnhof (main train station). The cluster of skyscrapers diagonally off to the left, with the unusual circus-tent roof, is Potsdamer Platz.

On the other, far west side of the Tiergarten, out of sight near Zoo station, sits the one-time centre of West Berlin, including the shopping street of the Kurfürstendamm (or 'Ku'damm').

Although wealthier, more mature Berliners still happily frequent the west, the eastern districts are the most happening. Even Mitte, or the centre, now lies east of the former wall. As Mitte heads northeast, it merges into the trendy district of Prenzlauer Berg. Friedrichshain, another popular neighbourhood, is found several kilometres east of the centre, around Ostbahnhof.

Kreuzberg, south of Mitte, has two sides: western Kreuzberg was the alternative hub of West Berlin and is still hanging in there, with some interesting restaurants and bars; eastern Kreuzberg is grungier, hopping and definitely where the 'kool kids' – and adults – hang out. Further east and south is the rapidly gentrifying Kreuzkölln, which is loosely defined as the area where Kreuzberg and neighbouring Neukölln overlap. The upscale southwestern districts of Charlottenburg, Schöneberg and Wilmersdorf offer nice restaurants and a calm atmosphere, though some may find them a tad sterile in comparison with places further east.

◉ Sights

Brandenburg Gate LANDMARK
(Brandenburger Tor; Map p174; Pariser Platz; Ⓜ S-Bahn Unter den Linden) Finished in 1791 as one of 18 city gates, the neoclassical Brandenburg Gate became an East-West crossing point after the Berlin Wall was built in 1961. A symbol of Berlin's division, it was a place US presidents loved to grandstand. John F Kennedy passed by in 1963. Ronald Reagan appeared in 1987 to appeal to the Russian leader, 'Mr Gorbachev, tear down this wall!'. In 1989 more than 100,000 Germans poured

through it as the wall fell. Five years later, Bill Clinton somewhat belatedly noted: 'Berlin is free'. The crowning Quadriga statue, a winged goddess in a horse-drawn chariot (once kidnapped by Napoleon and briefly taken to Paris), was cleaned in 2000 along with the rest of the structure.

Reichstag HISTORIC BUILDING
(Parliament; Map p174; ✆ 2273 2152; www.bundestag.de; Platz der Republik 1; admission free; ◷ 8am-midnight, last admission 10pm; Ⓜ S-Bahn Unter den Linden) Just northwest of the Brandenburg Gate stands the glass-domed landmark with four national flags fluttering. A fire here in 1933 allowed Hitler to blame the communists and grab power, while the Soviets raised their flag here in 1945 to signal Nazi Germany's defeat. Today the building is once again the German seat of power, but it's the glass cupola added during the 1999 refurbishment that 10,000-plus people a day flock to see. Walking along the internal spiral walkway by British star architect Lord Norman Foster feels like being in a postmodern beehive. To beat the queues, book a table at the upmarket rooftop restaurant **Käfer** (✆ 2262 9935; www.feinkost-kaefer.de), which uses a separate entrance. With young children in tow, you're allowed to bypass the queue, too.

Holocaust Memorial MEMORIAL
(Denkmal für die ermordeten Juden Europas; Map p174; ✆ 2639 4336; www.stiftung-denkmal.de; Cora-Berliner-Strasse 1; admission free; ◷ field 24hr, information centre 10am-8pm Tue-Sun, last entry 7.15pm Apr-Sep, 10am-7pm Tue-Sun, last entry 6.15pm Oct-Mar; Ⓜ S-Bahn Unter den Linden) Just south of the Reichstag, this grid of 2711 'stelae', or differently shaped concrete columns, is set over 19,000 sq metres of gently undulating ground. The slate-grey expanse of walkways and pillars can be

WANT MORE?

For in-depth information, reviews and recommendations at your fingertips, head to the Apple App Store to purchase Lonely Planet's *Berlin City Guide* iPhone app.

Alternatively, head to **Lonely Planet** (www.lonelyplanet.com/germany/berlin) for planning advice, author recommendations, traveller reviews and insider tips.

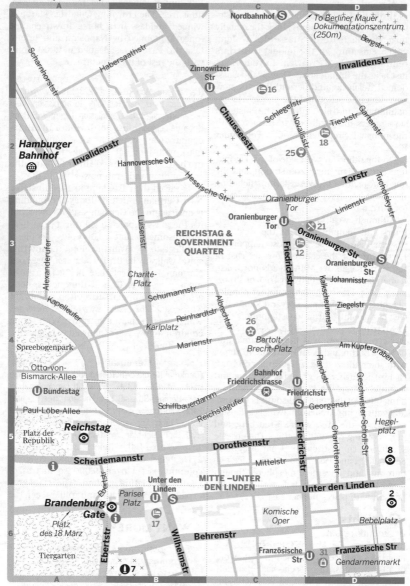

Nordbahnhof

To Berliner Mauer
Dokumentationszentrum
(250m)
Bergstr

Invalidenstr

Zinnowitzer
Str

16

Chausseestr

Schlegelstr

Novalisstr

Tieckstr

Gartenstr

18

**Hamburger
Bahnhof**

Invalidenstr

Hannoversche Str

25

Torstr

Tucholskystr

Hessische Str

Oranienburger
Tor

Linienstr

Oranienburger
Tor

21

Luisenstr

**REICHSTAG &
GOVERNMENT
QUARTER**

Friedrichstr

12

Oranienburger
Str

Alexanderufer

Charité-
Platz

Schumannstr

Reinhardtstr

Albrechtstr

Kalkscheunenstr

Johannisstr

Ziegelstr

Kapelleufer

Karlplatz

Marienstr

26

Bertolt-
Brecht-Platz

Am Kupfergraben

Spreebogenpark

Planckstr

Geschwister-Scholl-Str

Otto-von-
Bismarck-Allee

Bahnhof
Friedrichstrasse

Friedrichstr

U Bundestag

Paul-Löbe-Allee

Schiffbauerdamm

Reichstagufer

Georgenstr

Hegel-
platz

Reichstag

Platz der
Republik

Dorotheenstr

Friedrichstr

Charlottenstr

8

Scheidemannstr

Mittelstr

Unter den
Linden

**MITTE –UNTER
DEN LINDEN**

Unter den Linden

2

**Brandenburg
Gate**

Pariser
Platz

17

Komische
Oper

Bebelplatz

Platz
des 18 März

Behrenstr

Tiergarten

Ebertstr

Wilhelmstr

Französische
Str

31

Französische Str

Gendarmenmarkt

7

entered from any side, but presents varied sombre perspectives as you move through it. For historical background, designer Peter Eisenman has created an underground information centre in the southeast corner of the site.

Unter den Linden   HISTORIC AVENUE

Celebrated in literature and lined with lime (or linden) trees, the renowned street Unter den Linden (Map p174) was the fashionable avenue of old Berlin. Today, after decades of communist neglect, it's been rebuilt and has

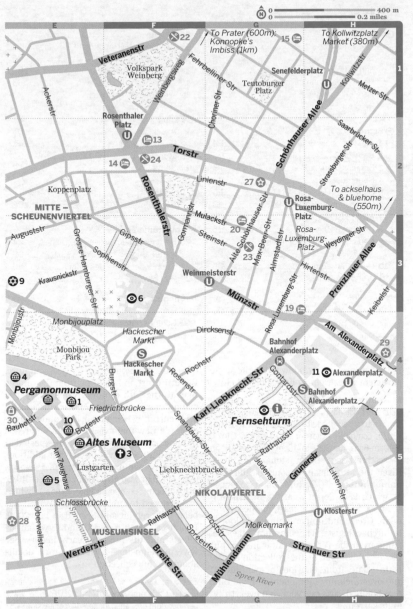

0 400 m
0 0.2 miles

To Prater (600m);
Konnopke's
Imbiss (1km)

To Kollwitzplatz
Market (380m)

Veteranenstr

Volkspark
Weinberg

Senefelderplatz

Teutoburger
Platz

Rosenthaler
Platz

Torstr

14 ⊟ 24

Koppenplatz

Linienstr

27 ✪

MITTE –
SCHEUNENVIERTEL

Rosa-
Luxemburg-
Platz

Augustatr

Mulackstr

Gipsstr

Steinstr

20

Rosa-
Luxemburg-
Platz

To ackselhaus
& bluehome
(550m)

23

Krausnickstr

Weinmeisterstr

Münzstr

Hirtenstr

Prenzlauer Allee

Am Alexanderplatz

Monbijouplatz

Hackescher
Markt

Dircksenstr

19 ⊟

Bahnhof
Alexanderplatz

29 ✪

Monbijou
Park

Hackescher
Markt

Rochstr

11 ◉ Alexanderplatz

Pergamonmuseum

Friedrichbrücke

Karl-Liebknecht-Str

Bahnhof
Alexanderplatz

10

Altes Museum

Fernsehturm

Lustgarten

Liebknechtbrucke

NIKOLAIVIERTEL

Rathausstr

Grunerstr

28

Schlossbrücke

Klosterstr

MUSEUMSINSEL

Molkenmarkt

Werderstr

Breite Str

Stralauer Str

Mühlendamm

Spree River

finally regained its former status. The thoroughfare stretches east from the Brandenburg Gate down to the Museumsinsel area, passing by shops, embassies, opera houses, museums and Berlin's revered **Humboldt University**.

Bebelplatz   MEMORIAL
(Bebl Square; Map p174; Ⓜ Französische Strasse)
Set on the Unter den Linden opposite the Humboldt University, this **book-burning memorial** is a reminder of the first major Nazi book-burning, which occurred in May

Mitte (Berlin)

GERMANY BERLIN

1933. A transparent window tile in the stone pavement reveals empty bookshelves below.

Museumsinsel   MUSEUM
(Museums Island; ☑all museums 2090 5577; www.smb.museum; adult/concession per museum €10/5, combined ticket for all museums €14/7; ◔10am-6pm Tue-Sun, to 10pm Thu; MS-Bahn Hackescher Markt) Lying along the Spree River, the Museumsinsel contains the **Pergamonmuseum** (Map p174; Am Kupfergraben 5), which is to Berlin what the British Museum is to London: a feast of Mesopotamian, Greek and Roman antiquities looted by archaeologists. The museum takes its name from the Pergamon Altar inside, but the real highlight of the collection is the Ishtar Gate from Babylon, a magnificent and overwhelming monument of royal blue that boldly dwarfs everyone and everything in its surrounds.

The **Alte Nationalgalerie** (Old National Gallery; Map p174; Bodestrasse 1-3) houses 19th-century European sculpture and painting; the **Altes Museum** (Map p174; Am Lustgarten) features classical antiquities but is scheduled for restoration and may be closed in the coming years; and the **Bodemuseum** (Map p174; Monbijoubrücke) houses sculpture, Byzantine art and painting from the Middle Ages to the 19th century. Watch for special exhibitions at each. The entire Museumsinsel is currently being renovated and redeveloped – a new main visitor reception area is in the works and construction is expected to last until 2015. One of the newest additions was the reopening of the **Neues Museum** (New Museum; Map p174; adult/concession €10/5; ◔10am-6pm Sun-Wed, to 8pm Thu-Sat), which was reduced to rubble during WWII. It has been fully rebuilt and opened in late 2009. It houses Queen Nefertiti and Egyptian artefacts and the pre- and early history. See www.museumsinsel-berlin.de for details about the full collection.

Berliner Dom   CHURCH
(Berlin Cathedral; Map p174; ☑2026 9136 www.berliner-dom.de; adult/under 14/concession €5/free/3; ◔9am-8pm Mon-Sat, from noon Sun Apr-Sep, to 7pm Oct-Mar; MS-Bahn Hackescher Markt) Overlooking the 'island' is this stately former royal court church – come here mainly for the exceptional view of the city from its top gallery, glass mosaics of the dome and to glimpse the Sauer organ (over 7000 pipes).

Deutsches Historisches Museum MUSEUM
(German History Museum; Map p174; ☑203 040;
www.dhm.de; Unter den Linden 2; admission €6;
⊙10am-6pm; Ⓜ S-Bahn Hackescher Markt) Some
come for the permanent exhibition on German
history, but the museum is still arguably
most notable for the glass-walled spiral
staircase by modernist architect IM Pei (creator
of the Louvre's glass pyramid).

Hackescher Markt HISTORIC AREA
(Ⓜ S-Bahn Hackescher Markt) A complex of
shops and apartments around eight courtyards,
the **Hackesche Höfe** (Map p174) is
commercial and touristy, but it's definitely
good fun to wander around the big-name
brand shops and smaller boutiques or simply
people watch in the cafes and restaurants
– the atmosphere is always lively.

Neue Synagogue & Centrum Judaicum
SYNAGOGUE
(Map p174; ☑8802 8300; www.cjudaicum.de; Oranienburger
Strasse 28-30; adult/concession €3/2;
⊙10am-8pm Sun & Mon, to 6pm Tue-Thu, to 5pm
Fri, reduced hr Nov-Apr; Ⓜ S-Bahn Hackescher
Markt) The original New Synagogue, finished
in 1866 in what was then predominantly
Jewish part of the city, was Germany's largest
synagogue at that time. It was destroyed
in World War II and rebuilt after the Berlin
Wall fell. Now this space doubles as a museum
and cultural centre illustrating its history
of local Jewish life.

Hamburger Bahnhof MUSEUM
(Map p174; ☑3978 3439; www.hamburgerbahnhof.
de; Invalidenstrasse 50; adult/concession €12/6;
⊙10am-6pm Tue-Fri, 11am-8pm Sat, 11am-6pm
Sun; Ⓜ Hauptbahnhof/Lehrter Stadtbahnhof) This
contemporary-art museum is housed in a
former neoclassical train station and showcases
works by Warhol, Lichtenstein, Cy
Twombly and Keith Haring.

Fernsehturm LANDMARK
(Map p174; ☑242 3333; www.berlinerfernsehturm.
de; adult/concession €10/6.50; ⊙9am-midnight
Mar-Oct, from 10am Nov-Feb; Ⓜ Alexanderplatz)
Call it Freudian or call it *Ostalgie* (nostalgia

IF WALLS COULD TALK

Remnants of the 155km Berlin Wall are scattered across the city, but you can follow all
or sections of its former path along the 160km-long **Berliner Mauerweg** (Berlin Wall
Trail; www.berlin.de/mauer), a signposted walking and cycling path that follows the former
border fortifications, either along customs-patrol roads in West Berlin or border-control
roads used by GDR guards. Along the route, 40 multilingual information stations provide
historical context, highlight dramatic events and relate stories about daily life in the divided
city.

The longest surviving stretch of the wall is the **East Side Gallery** (Map p178; www.
eastsidegallery.com; Mühlenstrasse; Ⓜ S-Bahn Warschauer Strasse) in Friedrichshain. Panels
along this 1.3km section of graffiti and art include the famous portrait of Soviet leader
Brezhnev kissing GDR leader Erich Hönecker and a Trabant car seemingly bursting
through the (now crumbling) concrete.

The sombre **Berliner Mauer Dokumentationszentrum** (Berlin Wall Documentation
Centre; off Map p174; ☑464 1030; www.berliner-mauer-dokumentationszentrum.de; Bernauer
Strasse 111; admission free; ⊙10am-6pm Tue-Sun Apr-Oct, to 5pm Nov-Mar; Ⓜ U-Bahn Bernau-
ersrasse) is a memorial containing a section of the original wall, photos of the surrounding
area (before and during the lifespan of the wall), newspaper clippings and listening stations featuring old West and East Berlin radio programs as well as eyewitness testimonies.
Be sure to climb the tower for a view of an artistic re-creation of no-man's land as well as
the **Kapelle der Versöhnung** (Chapel of Reconciliation), a modern round structure of
pressed earth and slim wooden planks built on the site of an 1894 red-brick church blown
up in 1985 in order to widen the border strip. A 15-minute remembrance service for those
killed while attempting to flee from east to west is held at noon Tuesday to Friday.

In Kreuzberg, the famous sign at **Checkpoint Charlie** (Map p178) still boasts 'You are
now leaving the American sector'. But it and the reconstructed US guardhouse are just
tourist attractions now. For a less light-hearted view of the past, visit **Haus am Checkpoint Charlie** (Map p178; ☑253 7250; www.mauer-museum.com; Friedrichstrasse 43-45;
adult/concession €12.50/9.50; ⊙9am-10pm; Ⓜ Kochstrasse/Stadtmitte). Tales of spectacular
escape attempts include through tunnels, in hot-air balloons and even using a one-man
submarine.

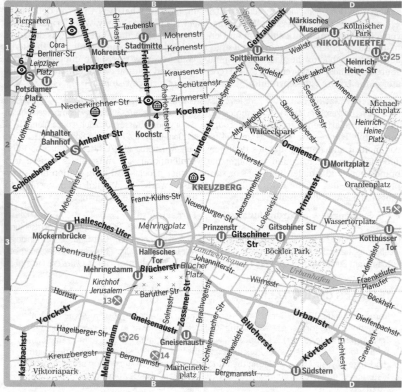

GERMANY BERLIN

for the communist East or *Ost*), but Berlin's once-mocked socialist Fernsehturm TV tower is fast becoming its most-loved symbol. Originally erected in 1969 and the city's tallest structure, its central bauble was decorated as a giant football for the 2006 FIFA World Cup, while its 368m outline still pops up in numerous souvenirs. That said, ascending 207m to the revolving (but musty) Telecafe is a less singular experience than visiting the Reichstag dome.

The Turm dominates **Alexanderplatz**, a former livestock and wool market that became the low-life district chronicled by Alfred Döblin's 1929 novel *Berlin Alexanderplatz* and then developed as a 1960s communist showpiece. Even in a city so often described as one big building site, today's Alexanderplatz is an unusual hive of construction activity as it is transformed into the next Potsdamer Platz–style development. However, its communist past still

echoes through the retro **World Time Clock** (Map p174) and along the portentous **Karl-Marx-Allee**, which leads several kilometres east from the square to Friedrichshain.

Bauhaus Archiv
MUSEUM

(Map p182; ☎ 254 0020; www.bauhaus.de; Klingelhöferstrasse 14; adult/concession Sat-Mon €7/4, Wed-Fri €6/3; ☉10am-5pm Wed-Mon; Ⓜ Nollendorfplatz) This avant-garde museum includes drawings, chairs and other Modernist objects from the famous Bauhaus school of design – as well as a very tempting shop. The school itself survives in Dessau (see p209).

Neue Nationalgalerie
MUSEUM

(Map p182; ☎ 266 2951; www.neue-nationalgalerie. de; Potsdamer Strasse 50; adult/concession €10/5; ☉10am-6pm Tue, Wed & Fri, to 10pm Thu, 11am-6pm Sat & Sun; Ⓜ S-Bahn Potsdamer Platz) Berlin's best collection of 20th-century works by Picasso, Klee, Munch, Dalí, Kandinsky and many German expressionists are housed in

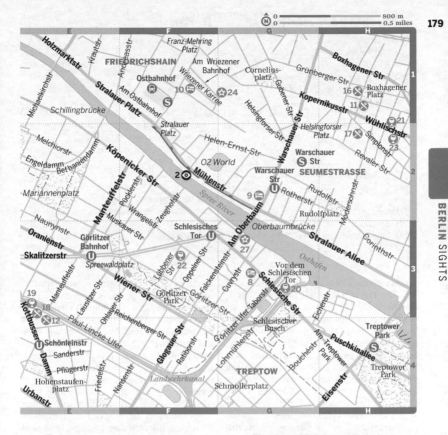

an exquisite 'temple of light and glass' built by Bauhaus-director Ludwig Mies van der Rohe.

Potsdamer Platz
HISTORIC AREA

(Map p178; M S-Bahn Potsdamer Platz)The lid was symbolically sealed on capitalism's victory over socialism in Berlin when this postmodern temple to Mammon was erected in 2000 over the former death strip. Under the big-top, glass-tent roof of the **Sony Center** and along the malls of the Legolike **Daimler City**, people swarm in and around shops, restaurants, offices, loft apartments, clubs, a cinema, a luxury hotel and a casino – all revitalising what was the busiest square in prewar Europe.

During the International Film Festival Berlin (see p181), Potsdamer Platz welcomes Hollywood A-listers. In between you can rub shoulders with German cinematic heroes – particularly Marlene Dietrich – at the **Filmmuseum** (300 9030; www.filmmuseum-berlin.de; Potsdamer Strasse 2; adult/conces-

sion €6/4.50; 10am-6pm Tue, Wed & Fri-Sun, to 8pm Thu). There's also 'Europe's fastest lift' to the 100m-high **Panorama Observation Deck** (www.panoramapunkt.de; adult/concession €4.50/3; 11am-8pm, last entry 7.30pm).

But, as ever in Berlin, the past refuses to go quietly. Just north of Potsdamer Platz lies the **former site of Hitler's Bunker**.

Topographie des Terrors
MEMORIAL

(Map p178; 2548 6703; www.topographie.de; Niederkirchner Strasse 8; admission free; 10am-8pm May-Sep, to dusk Oct-Apr; M S-Bahn Potsdamer Platz) This is an eye-opening and graphic collection of text and images surrounding WWII, mounted on the ruins of the Gestapo and SS headquarters. Note: this memorial may not be suitable for children.

TOP CHOICE Jewish Museum
MUSEUM

(Map p178; 2599 3300; www.juedisches-museum-berlin.de; Lindenstrasse 9-14; adult/concession €5/2.50; 10am-10pm Mon, to 8pm

Tue-Sun, last entry 1hr before closing; MHallesches Tor) The Daniel Libeskind building that is the Jüdisches Museum is as much the attraction as the Jewish-German history collection within. Designed to disorientate and unbalance with its 'voids', cul-de-sacs, barbed metal fittings, slit windows and uneven floors, this still-somehow-beautiful structure swiftly conveys the uncertainty and sometime-terror of past Jewish life in Germany. It's a visceral experience, after which the huge collection itself demands your concentration. The building's footprint is a ripped-apart Star of David.

Kaiser-Wilhelm-Gedächtniskirche & Kurfürstendamm CHURCH
(Map p182; ☑218 5023; www.gedaechtniskirche -berlin.de; Breitscheidplatz; ⊘memorial hall 10am-4pm Mon-Sat, hall of worship 9am-7pm; MHallesches Tor) West Berlin's legendary shopping thoroughfare and avenue, the Ku'damm (the nickname for its full name Kurfürstendamm), has lost some of its cachet since the wall fell, but is worth visiting for its landmark church, which remains in ruins – just as British bombers left it on 22 November 1943 – as an antiwar memorial. Only the broken west tower still stands. In 1961 the modern hall of worship was built adjacent to the church.

Stasi Museum MUSEUM
(☑553 6854; www.stasimuseum.de; House 22, Ruschestrasse 103; adult/concession €5/4; ⊘11am-6pm Tue-Fri, 2-6pm Sat & Sun; MMagda-

lenenstrasse) This imposing compound, formerly the secret police headquarters, now contains the Stasi Museum. It's largely in German, but well worth it to get a sense of the impact the Stasi had on the daily lives of GDR citizens through the museum's extensive photos and displays of the astounding range of surveillance devices, as well as exhibits of the tightly sealed jars used to retain cloths containing body-odour samples. The museum is currently undergoing renovation and items have been temporarily relocated in another building (still part of the Stasi complex) – the temporary site is equally engaging – though former Stasi head Mielke's office can only be seen in photos. At the time of writing it was schedule to be reopened in its original space towards late 2011.

☞ Tours
Guided tours in Berlin are phenomenally popular; you can choose Third Reich, Wall, bunker, communist, boat or bicycle tours, as well as guided pub crawls. Expect to pay around €15 and up.

New Berlin WALKING TOURS
(☑017-9973 0397; www.newberlintours.com) Free (yup, free) 3½-hour introductory walking tours. These leave at 10.30am and 12.30pm from Dunkin' Donuts opposite the Zoologisher Garten train station, and 11am and 1pm outside Starbucks at Pariser Platz near the Brandenburg Gate. Guides are enthusiastic, knowledgeable...and accept tips.

Trabi Safari
CAR TOURS

(℡275 2273; www.trabi-safari.de; €30-80) Tool around Berlin in a Trabant car; operates from the Berlin Hi-Flyer near Checkpoint Charlie.

Fat Tire Bike Tours
BIKE TOURS

(http://fattirebiketours.com/berlin) Offers a huge range of tours, from standard city tours to themed tours along the former course of the Berlin Wall and/or a Cold War tour, historical tours and more.

✿ Festivals & Events

International Film Festival Berlin
FILM FESTIVAL

(℡259 200; www.berlinale.de) The Berlinale, held in February, is Germany's answer to the Cannes and Venice film festivals.

Christopher Street Day
GAY EVENT

(℡2362 8632; www.csd-berlin.de) Held on the last weekend in June, Germany's largest gay event has been running for more than 30 years.

Fuckparade
DANCE EVENT

(www.fuckparade.org) Each August this anti-establishment, antigentrification demonstration dances to its own noncommercial techno beat.

🛏 Sleeping

Berlin's independent hostels are far superior to the standard DJH (www.jugendherberge.de) locations in town.

ℹ NIGHT AT THE MUSEUMS

All museums listed on www.smb.museum are free on Thursday for four hours before closing time – this includes the **Pergamonmuseum** and the **Altes Museum** (see p176). Alternatively, museumophiles will love the **Schau-Lust Museen Berlin Pass** (℡250 025). A mere €19 gives you admission to more than 70 museums (not including Checkpoint Charlie) over three days.

MITTE & PRENZLAUER BERG

Lette'm Sleep
HOSTEL €

(℡4473 3623; www.backpackers.de; Lettestrasse 7; dm from €11, tw without bathroom from €49, apt from €69; ⊛@⊚; ⓂEberswalder Strasse) Located within stumbling distance of the Prenzlauer Berg nightlife action, this colourful and convenient party hostel is simply groovy, baby, groovy.

Roof
APARTMENT €€

(℡6951 8833; www.roof-berlin.com; studio/1-bed apt €85/115, reduced rates after 3 nights; ⊚) Proprietor Ariane has two studios and a one-bedroom apartment – all tastefully decorated in soothing colours with comfy, contemporary touches – peppered around central Prenslauer Berg. She'll even stock the fridge for you with breakfast or snacks like wine and cheese (€25 for either) on request.

DON'T MISS

BERLIN'S TIERGARTEN, A SWATH OF GREEN

Lolling about in the grass on a sunny afternoon is the quintessential Berlin pastime. Germans adore the outdoors and flock to urban green spaces whenever the weather is fine. They also dislike tan lines, so don't be surprised if you stumble upon locals sunbathing in the nude.

The Tiergarten is criss-crossed by a series of major roads and anchored by the Brandenburg Gate and the Reichstag on its northwestern edge. It's a tangle of curved walking and cycling paths, tiny ponds, open fields and thick woods. You'll probably get lost, but there are dozens of maps scattered about to help you find your way.

From the Reichstag, the Tiergarten's **carillon** (John-Foster-Dulles-Allee; 🚌100 or 200) and the **Haus der Kulturen der Welt** (House of World Cultures; John-Foster-Dulles-Allee) are clearly visible. The latter was the US contribution to the 1957 International Building Exposition and it's easy to see why locals call it the 'pregnant oyster'.

Further west, the wings of the **Siegessäule** (Victory Column; 🚌100 or 200) were the *Wings of Desire* in that famous Wim Wenders film. This golden angel was built to commemorate Prussian military victories in the 19th century. Today, as the end point of the annual Christopher Street Parade, she's also a gay icon. However, there are better views than those at the column's peak.

Charlottenburg (Berlin)

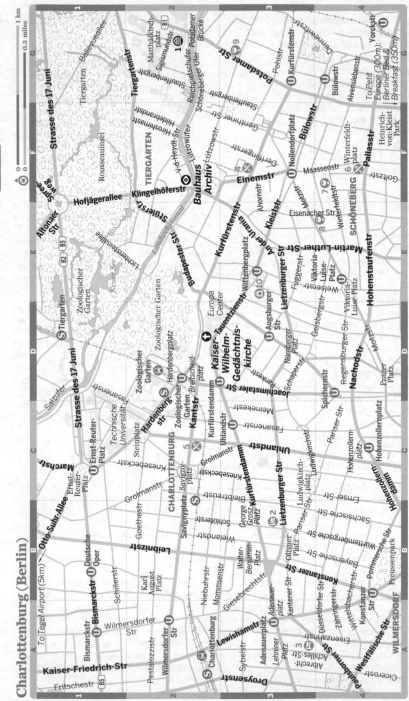

0 0.5 miles
0 1 km

To Tegel Airport (5km);

Bismarckstr

Deutsche Oper

Otto-Suhr-Allee

Ernst-Reuter-Platz

Marchstr

Kaiser-Friedrich-Str

Fritschestr

Schillerstr

Karl-August-Platz

Wilmersdorfer Str

Leibnizstr

Pestalozzistr

Lewishamstr

Charlottenburg

Droysenstr

Sybelstr

Gieselbrechtstr

Mommsenstr

Niebuhrstr

Walter-Benjamin-Platz

Schillerstr

Wielandstr

Schlüterstr

Bleibtreustr

Krumme Str

Grolmanstr

Goethestr

Savignyplatz

Savignyplatz

CHARLOTTENBURG

Hardenberg-str

Knesebeckstr

Steinplatz

Technische Universität

Zoologischer Garten

Zoologischer Garten

Hardenbergplatz

Hardenbergstr

Zoologischer Garten

Fasanenstr

Kantstr

Kurfürstendamm

Uhlandstr

Meinekestr

Fasanenstr

Joachimstaler Str

Kaiser-Wilhelm-Gedächtnis-Kirche

Tauentzienstr

Breitscheid-platz

Europa Center

Wittenbergplatz

Budapester Str

Nürnberger Platz

Augsburger Str

Schaperstr

Spichernstr

Nachodstr

Ansbacher Str

An der Urania

Kurfürstenstr

Kleiststr

Martin-Luther-Str

Einemstr

Bauhaus Archiv

Klingelhöferstr

Stülerstr

Von-der-Heydt-Str

Lützowufer

Landwehrkanal

Lützowstr

Derfflingerstr

Genthiner Str

Schöneberger Ufer

Reichpietschufer

Schöneberger Str

Potsdamer Str

Potsdamer Brücke

Sigismundstr

Matthäikirch-platz

Stauffenbergstr

Hildebrandstr

Tiergartenstr

Tiergartenstr

TIERGARTEN

Hofjägerallee

Hiroshimastr

Tiergarten

Rousseauinsel

Neuer See

Rousseauallee

Bellevueallee

Strasse des 17 Juni

Strasse des 17 Juni

Spree

Spreeweg

Altonaer Str

Salzufer

Ernst-Reuter-Platz

Fasanenstr

Strasse des 17 Juni

Lichtensteinallee

Zoologischer Garten

Nollendorfplatz

Maassenstr

Einemstr

Eisenacher Str

Winterfeldtstr

Winterfeldtplatz

Goltzstr

Nostitzstr

SCHÖNEBERG

Motzstr

Fuggerstr

Welserstr

Gelbergstr

Regensburger Str

Lietzenburger Str

Viktoria-Luise-Platz

Hohenstaufenstr

Bülowstr

BÜLOWSTR

Frobenstr

Gleditschstr

Pallasstr

Pohlstr

Kurfürstenstr

Yorckstr

Dennewitzstr

Bülowstr

Alvenslebenstr

Heinrich-von-Kleist-Park

Prager Platz

Pariser Str

Konstanzer Str

Ludwigkirch-platz

Ludwigkirchstr

Emser Str

Sächsische Str

Hohenzollern-platz

Hohenzollerndamm

Hohenzollernplatz

Pommersche Str

Württembergische Str

Bayerische Str

Ludwigkirch-str

Uhlandstr

Lietzenburger Str

George-Grosz-Platz

Kurfürstendamm

Olivaer Platz

Adenauerplatz

Adenauerplatz

Lehniner Platz

Xantener Str

Düsseldorfer Str

Zähringerstr

Albrecht-Achilles-Str

Eisenzahnstr

Paulsborner Str

Wittelsbacherstr

Cicerostr

Westfälische Str

WILMERSDORF

B1

B2

B5

G

F

E

D

C

B

1

2

3

4

1

2

3

4

5

6

7

8

9

10

N

Charlottenburg (Berlin)

ackselhaus & bluehome HOTEL €€
(off Map p174; ☎4433 7633; www.ackselhaus. de; Belforter Strasse 21; ste from €105, apt from €150; @ 🛜; Ⓜ Senefelder Platz) This Zen oasis, spread across two buildings, offers exquisitely designed suites or apartments (most with kitchenettes). Each has a different theme, from Italian to Hollywood; all exude an element of exquisite class, calm and humour – the African suite, for example, has stuffed animal heads mounted on the wall.

Hotel Honigmond HOTEL €€
(Map p174; ☎284 4550; www.honigmond-berlin.de; Tieckstrasse 12; s/d from €105/115; 🌐@🛜; Ⓜ Oranienburger Tor) A perfect choice for a romantic weekend (or simply those seeing a touch of elegance and class). This tasteful hotel is all creaky wooden floors and four-poster beds. Sister property **Garden Hotel Honigmond** (Map p174; ☎2844 5577; www.honigmond-berlin. de; Invalidenstrasse 122; s/d from €103/113; 🌐@🛜; Ⓜ Zinnowitzer Strasse) offers similar rooms but includes a tranquil back garden.

EastSeven HOSTEL €
(Map p174; ☎9362 2240; www.eastseven.de; Schwedter Strasse 7; dm from €18, s/d from €38/52; @🛜; Ⓜ Senefelder Platz) Retro and homey, with spotless rooms and sturdy pine furniture, there is a youthful elegance here rarely present in hostels. The lovely garden is perfect for summer barbecues.

Hotel Greifswald HOTEL €
(☎4442 7888; www.hotel-greifswald.de; Greifswalderstrasse 211; s/d/tr/apt from €57.50/69/90/75; @🛜; Ⓜ Senefelder Platz) You'd never guess this informal, quiet hotel set back from the street around a sweet courtyard is regularly home to bands and even rock stars – until you see their photos in the lobby. We love the sumptuous breakfast buffet (€7.50) served until noon.

Circus Hotel HOTEL €€
(Map p174; ☎2000 3939; www.circus-berlin.de; Rosenthalerstrasse 1; s €70, d from €80, ste €100, apt €115-170; 🌐@🛜; Ⓜ U-Bahn Rosenthaler Platz) The fancier younger sister to the Circus Hostel across the intersection, this hotel has given careful attention to every detail – the result is a retro twist on minimalism, airy rooms, bold-coloured walls and super-shiny wood flooring.

Malzcafe HOTEL €€
(☎702 21357; www.malzcafe.de; Veteranenstrasse 10; s/d/q €80/110/150, apt from €109; 🌐@🛜; Ⓜ Rosenthaler Platz) A small hotel above an adjoining cafe, you'll be made to feel right at home in minimalist rooms with soft, soothing tones, high ceilings and plenty of space. A pleasant terrace is divine in warm weather, and you're a short hop to both the heart of Mitte and Prenzlauer Berg.

Arcotel Velvet HOTEL €€
(Map p174; ☎278 7530; www.arcotelhotels.com; Oranienburger Strasse 52; d/ste from €140/150; 🌐🛜; Ⓜ Oranienburger Tor) Floor-to-ceiling windows give front rooms a bird's-eye view of the bustling street and, combined with bathrooms separated only by gauze curtains, create a feeling of loft living. If you plan to retire before 2am, request a room facing the back – the main road gets quite loud and rowdy at weekends.

Lux 11 HOTEL €€€
(Map p174; ☎936 2800; www.lux-eleven.com; Rosa-Luxemburg-Strasse 9-13; r/ste from €165/205; 🌐@🛜; Ⓜ Weinmeisterstrasse/Alexanderplatz) A liberal use of white makes this slick, streamlined hotel a haven of unpretentious minimalism. All rooms feature a tiny kitchenette (kettle, coffee makers, two-pot stove and a handful of cookware).

ℹ FREE PICKS

Welcome news for budget travellers: in comparison to other European capitals, Berlin is generally quite inexpensive, and several key sights and experiences are completely free:

» **Brandenburg Gate** (p173) The symbol of Berlin and of reunified Germany is a must-see on any Berlin itinerary.

» **Kaiser-Wilhelm-Gedächtniskirche** (p180) This left-as-it-was-bombed church on the Ku'damm is a vivid reminder of WWII.

» **Tiergarten** (p181) Let yourself get lost in this oasis of green.

» **New Berlin walking tours** (p180) They're free, and guides are chock-full of information about their beloved city.

» **Holocaust Memorial** (p173) An experiential monument to the victims of the Holocaust.

» **East Side Gallery** (p177) The longest remaining section of the wall is a memorial to freedom.

Hotel Adlon Kempinski
HOTEL €€€
(Map p174; ☎226 10; www.kempinski.com, Am Pariser Platz, Unter den Linden 77; r from €450; ❄✳@🅿📶✉; ⓂS-Bahn Unter den Linden) Still remembered mostly for being the hotel where Michael Jackson had his baby-dangling episode, this luxurious hotel is situated just on the doorstep of the Brandenburg Gate. It's also known for its Schochu cocktail bar, a swanky spot featuring elegant, gold Asian touches.

Wombat's City Hostel
HOSTEL €
(Map p174; ☎8471 0820; www.wombats-hostels. com; Alte Schönhauser Strasse 2; dm/d €24/65, apt with kitchen €80; @📶; ⓂRosa-Luxemburg-Platz) A popular member of the Mitte hostel scene, rooms and dorms (all en suite) are decorated with modern touches, and doubles offer long balconies. A hopping lounge and all-you-can-eat breakfast buffet (€3.70) round out the package. Discounts are available from November to February.

Circus Hostel
HOSTEL €
(Map p174; ☎2839 1433; www.circus-hostel.de; Weinbergsweg 1a; dm from €21, s/d without bathroom €42/58, with bathroom €52/72, 2-/4-person apt €95/150; @📶; ⓂU-Bahn Rosenthaler Platz) This stalwart is one of the most popular hostels in town, with a great central location and friendly staff. Rooms feature splashes of vibrant colour and modern, Ikea-like furnishings. There's a two-night minimum stay for apartments. It's quite the party hostel with free beer on Mondays and Thursdays and a kickin' on-site bar that holds regular karaoke nights.

KREUZBERG & FRIEDRICHSHAIN

Die Fabrik
HOTEL €
(Map p178; ☎611 7716; www.diefabrik.com; Schlesische Strasse 18; dm €20, s/d/tr/q from €40/54/70/85; ❄@; ⓂSchlesisches Tor) A cross between a hostel and a hotel (it feels more like the latter), these tidy and simple rooms are a steal. Plenty of spotless shower and toilet facilities are located on each floor; the larger doubles come with washbasins and tiny sitting areas. Solar power heats 100% of your hot water in the sunny months (and a smaller percentage in other seasons). Wi-fi is available in the lobby only.

Michelberger Hotel
HOSTEL €
(Map p178; ☎2977 8590; www.michelberger hotel.com; Warschauer Strasse 39; s/d/tr from €60/70/150; 📶; ⓂPrinzenstrasse, Hallesches Tor) This trendy design hotel is funky and fun and offers downmarket rates in stylish digs – think loft beds and sleek furniture. Minimalism dominates but the clean lines mean small spaces still feel roomy.

Ostel
HOSTEL €
(Map p172; ☎2576 8660; www.ostel.eu; Wriezener Karree 5; dm/d/apt €15/56/120; ❄@📶; ⓂOstbahnhof) *Ostalgie* – nostalgia for the communist East – is taken to a whole new level at this hostel/hotel with original socialist GDR furnishings and portraits of Honecker and other former socialist leaders. You can even stay in a 'bugged' Stasi Suite. You might think you've entered a surreal time machine – until you access the free wi-fi that is. At the time of writing the hotel was due to open a DDR restaurant, mimicking the old-school

Interhotels, the socialist hotel chain that dominated before the wall fell.

Eastern Comfort Hostelboot HOSTEL €
(✆6676 3806; www.eastern-comfort.com; Mühlenstrasse 73-77; dm €18, s/d from €55/78, bedding €5; @🛜; ⓂS-Bahn Warschauer Strasse) This moored boat-turned-hostel is close to the East Side Gallery, is convenient for both Kreuzberg and Friedrichshain and features cosy rooms and dorms (all en suite). If it's full ask about the 18 units in the Western Comfort boat across the river (check in at Eastern Comfort).

CHARLOTTENBURG & SCHÖNEBERG

Hotel Bogota HOTEL €€
(Map p182; ✆881 5001; www.bogota.de; Schülterstrasse 45; d without bathroom from €65, with bathroom €90-150; ⊖🛜; ⓂUhlandstrasse) With oodles of charm and character at affordable prices, this is a must for vintage-furniture lovers. Ask about the landmark building's fascinating fashion history (which will explain the snazzy photos adorning the walls).

Berliner Bed & Breakfast HOTEL €
(off Map p182; ✆2437 3962; www.berliner-bed-and-breakfast.de; Langenscheidtstrasse 5; s/d/tr/q without bathroom €35/55/68/78; ⓂKleistpark) Lofty ceilings and gorgeous wood floors dominate in this small, unique space with themed rooms (Asia, retro, fashionable). Excellent breakfast provisions are left for guests each day, which you prepare yourself in the communal kitchen.

Propeller Island City Lodge HOTEL €€€
(Map p182; ✆891 9016; www.propeller-island.de; Albrecht-Achilles-Strasse 58; r per person from €75; ⊖@🛜; ⓂAdenauerplatz) Keen to sleep in a bed suspended by ropes, or in a coffin, or on a pile of chopped logs? If you've dreamed it you can probably find it in one of the themed rooms (oh, and slightly more standard spaces are available too).

✕ Eating

Berliners love to eat out – it's relaxed and affordable and patrons often linger long after finishing their meals. Many of the best finds are in the budget category. Restaurants usually open from 11am to midnight, with varying *Ruhetage* or rest days. Cafes often close around 8pm, though just as many stay open until 2am or later.

Berlin is a snacker's paradise, with Turkish (your best bet), wurst (sausage), Greek, Italian and Chinese *Imbiss* stalls throughout the city. Meat eaters should not leave the city without trying Berlin's famous currywurst.

For self-caterers, there's the excellent organic **Kollwitzplatz market** (off Map p174; ⊙9am-4pm Sat & Sun; ⓂSenefelderplatz), the relaxed **Winterfeldtplatz farmers market** (Map p182; ⊙Wed & Sat) and the bustling, ultracheap **Türkenmarkt** (Turkish market; Map p178; ⊙noon-6:30pm Tue & Fri).

MITTE & PRENZLAUER BERG

Oderquelle GERMAN €€
(✆4400 8080; Oderberger Strasse 27; mains €8-16; ⊙dinner; ⓂEberswalder Strasse) Modern German food in such mellow, convivial digs is rare, almost as rare as snagging a table here after 7pm, so be sure to reserve. This is one of the best places in Berlin for consistently excellent service, exceptional wine and typical German dishes – think elegant, modern comfort food.

La Focacceria PIZZA €
(Map p174; Fehrbelliner Strasse 24; slices €1.75; ⊙11am-11pm; ⓂRosenthaler Platz) A character-filled focaccia and pizza joint with an intense local following – perfect for an afternoon snack after a hard day's shopping or sightseeing.

Konnopke's Imbiss WURST STAND €
(off Map p174; Schönhauser Allee 44a; snack €2; ⊙6am-8pm Mon-Fri, noon-7pm Sat; ⓂEberswalder Strasse) The quintessential wurst stand under the elevated U-Bahn tracks. We think Konnopke's serves the best currywurst in town.

Assel GERMAN €€
(Map p174; ✆281 2056; Oranienburger Strasse 21; mains €5-16; ⓂOranienburger Strasse or Hackescher Markt) One of the few exceptional picks on a particularly touristy and busy stretch of Mitte. Come for coffee, a bite or a full meal and stretch out in the wooden booths made from old S-Bahn seats. Plus, the toilets are entertaining (you'll see).

Sankt Oberholz INTERNATIONAL €
(Map p174; Rosenthaler Strasse 72a; dishes €5-8; 🛜; ⓂRosenthaler Platz) Berlin's '*Urbanen Pennern*' (officeless, self-employed creative types) have been flocking here for years with their laptops for the free wi-fi access, but we like it for the people watching – especially from the lofty lifeguard chairs out front. Soups, sandwiches and salads are always satisfying.

Monsieur Vuong ASIAN €€
(Map p174; Alte Schönhauser Strasse 46; mains €7 Ⓜ Weinmeisterstrasse, Rosa-Luxemburg-Platz or Alexanderplatz) Berlin's original designer Asian soup den is trendy, packed and consistently serves amazing Vietnamese fare. Arrive early to avoid queuing.

KREUZBERG & FRIEDRICHSHAIN

Hasir TURKISH €
(Map p178; Adalbertstrasse 10; mains €5-10; ⏱24hr; Ⓜ Kottbusser Tor) Local lore says this is the birthplace of Berlin's doner kebab – we haven't seen proof but we do know it tastes fantastic and we can indulge on proper chairs. It's also a fab spot to try simple Turkish fare.

Bürgeramt Früstücksklub BURGERS €
(Map p178; Krossenerstrasse 22; burgers €2-4; ⏱from 11am Mon-Fri, from 10am Sat & Sun; Ⓜ Samariterstrasse; 🖉) A mere 13 types of burgers, including chicken and veggie versions, are cooked up with love and a smile in this wee space – if you can't snag a seat, head to the tree-filled square opposite. Hearty breakfast fare is also available.

TOP CHOICE **Cafe Jacques** INTERNATIONAL €€
(Map p178; 🖉694 1048; Maybachufer 8; mains €12-20; Ⓜ Schönleinstrasse) Dishes hover around French and North African mainstays but Italian fare features too – frankly, it's all so lovingly and exceptionally prepared, you can't go wrong with anything you order. No surprise then that the devoted clientele flock here and linger over top-quality wine, flickering candlelight and the relaxed vibe. Reserve or be disappointed – one peek inside and you'll want to hop in and get a piece of this unfussy space and inviting atmosphere.

Nansen INTERNATIONAL €€
(🖉301 1438; Maybachufer 39; mains €10-19; ⏱dinner; Ⓜ Schönleinstrasse) At this local favourite in this gentrified part of town, you can dine on seasonal modern German cuisine in a romantic, candlelit space – most menu items are sourced locally.

Papaya THAI €
(Map p178; Krossener Strasse 11; mains €5-11; Ⓜ Frankfurter Tor) Don't come here for the decor (it's bland) but do come for homemade Thai specialities. It's a prime spot to fill up on quick, satisfying, budget fare before hitting the plethora of bars and clubs on its doorstep.

🌿 **Foodorama** INTERNATIONAL €€
(Map p178; Bergmannstrasse 94; mains €7-14; Ⓜ Mehringdamm) Germany's first climate-neutral restaurant has cafeteria-style digs but features the unlikely (organic currywurst and Wiener schnitzel) plus Asian stir-fries and German cucumber salad.

Curry 36 SAUSAGES €
(Map p178; Mehringdamm 36; snacks €2-6; ⏱9am-4pm Mon-Sat, to 3pm Sun; Ⓜ Mehringdamm) This is Kreuzberg's most popular sausage stand, as evidenced by the daily queues (yes, it really is worth the wait).

Schneeweiss GERMAN €
(Map p178; 🖉2904 9704; Simplonstrasse 16; day menu €7-10, Ⓜ S-Bahn Warschauer Strasse) Subtly embossed vanilla wallpaper, a long, central table and parquet flooring keep neutral 'Snow White' feeling more après-ski than icy. The vaguely German 'Alpine' food is excellent.

CHARLOTTENBURG & SCHÖNEBERG

Café Einstein Stammhaus AUSTRIAN €€
(Map p182; 🖉261 5096; www.cafeeinstein.com, in German; Kurfürstenstrasse 58; mains €15-23; ⏱9am-1am; Ⓜ Nollendorfplatz) You'll think you've hopped to another capital at this Viennese coffee house. Choose from schnitzel, strudel and other Austrian fare in the polished, palatial digs.

Schwarzes Café INTERNATIONAL €
(Map p182; Kantstrasse 148; dishes €5-10; Ⓜ S-Bahn Zoo or Savignyplatz) Founded in 1978, this 24-hour food 'n' booze institution must have seen half of Berlin pass through it (or pass out in it) at some point. Don't leave without checking out the toilets.

Engelbecken BAVARIAN €€
(🖉615 2810; Witzleben Strasse 31; mains €8-20; ⏱dinner daily, lunch Sun; Ⓜ Sophie Charlotte Platz) Come here for what many rate as Berlin's best Bavarian food, with *Schweinbraten* (pork sausages), schnitzels, dumplings and sauerkraut. All meats are organic.

Petite Europe ITALIAN €€
(off Map p182; 🖉781 2964; Langenscheidtstrasse 1; mains €5-12; ⏱dinner; Ⓜ Kleistpark) Pizzas, pastas and other straightforward Italian dishes are still going strong at this 40-year-old institution.

🍷 **Drinking**

Gemütlichkeit, which roughly translates as 'cosy, warm and friendly, with a decided lack of anything hectic', dominates the upscale bars of the west as well as the hipper, more underground venues in the east. Prenzlauer Berg, the first GDR sector to develop a happening nightlife, still attracts visitors, creative types and gay customers, but as its residents have aged (and produced many, many babies) its nightlife has become more subdued. Clubs and bars in Mitte around Hackescher Markt cater to a cool, slightly older and wealthier crowd. Friedrichshain boasts a young, hipster feel and Kreuzberg remains the alternative hub, becoming grungier as you move east. Charlottenburg and Winterfeldtplatz are fairly upmarket and mature, but liberal.

Bars without food open between 5pm and 8pm and may close as late as 5am (if at all).

Madame Claude BAR
(Map p178; Lübbener Strasse 19; MSchlesiches Tor) Kick back with a beer and pretend you've stepped into the pages of Alice in Wonderland. Run by a threesome (of course), tables and chairs live on the ceiling, coat hooks are upside down and the shoes dangling above made us grin like the Cheshire cat. True to Berlin it's shabby and slightly gritty, with secondhand furniture and a DJ doling out tracks from a hip Mac.

Hops & Barley PUB
(Map p178; ☑2936 7534; Wühlisch Strasse 40; MS-Bahn Warschauer Strasse) Excellent ciders and beers – brewed on site at this convivial microbrewery – pack them in every night. It's set inside a former butcher shop littered with aged-but-refurbished wood tables and school desks.

Kumpelnest 3000 BAR
(Map p182; Lützowstrasse 23; MKurfürstenstrasse) Once a brothel, always an experience: the Kumpelnest has been famed since the '80s for its wild, inhibition-free nights. Much of the original whorehouse decor remains intact.

Fleischmöbel BAR
(Oderberger Strasse 2; ⊘from noon; MEberswalder Strasse) Despite its odd name, which means Meat Furniture, the furniture is merely secondhand at this loungey cafe. It morphs into a convivial drinking den after dark, with serious locals engaging in intense conversations.

Ankerklause BAR
(Map p178; ☑693 5649; Kottbusser Damm 104; MKottbusser Tor) Slightly kitsch but always a winner, this nautical-themed bar in an old harbour master's house is worthy of a brew or two. Thursdays it turns into a casual dance floor with music suiting most tastes.

Reingold COCKTAIL BAR
(Map p174; Novalisstrasse 11; MOranienburger Tor) Gold walls and sleek furnishings manage to be both glam and retro in this recently revamped Mitte bar. Pricey (but exceptional) cocktails contain freshly squeezed juices and house-made fruit syrups.

Süss War Gestern BAR
(Map p178; Wülischstrasse 43; MS-Bahn Ostkreuz). Street art–covered walls, 1970s decorations and comfortable sofas make this outpost worth the trek. Most nights feature a DJ spinning anything from funk to soul to electric music.

Rote Lotte COCKTAIL BAR
(☑017 7345 3693; Oderbergerstrasse 38; MEberswalder Strasse) Plush sofas and booths have an old-world feel in this stylish crowd pleaser – perfect for a quiet, civilised drink.

Prater BEER GARDEN
(off Map p174; Kastanienallee 7-9; MEberswalder Strasse) A summer institution, Berlin's oldest beer garden (since 1837) invites you in for a tall chilled draft under the canopy of chestnut trees.

Green Door COCKTAIL BAR
(Map p182; Winterfeldtstrasse 50; MNollendorfplatz) Ring the doorbell to get them to open the namesake green door and let you into this tiny neighbourhood bar. Cocktails are on offer.

Wohnzimmer BAR
(☑445 5458; Lettestrasse 6; ⊘10am-4am; MEberswalder Strasse) The vintage furnishings often match up well with the style of its patrons in this laid-back Prenlauer Berg stalwart.

Freischwimmer BAR
(Map p178; Vor dem Schlesischen Tor 2a; ⊘from 2pm Mon-Fri, from 11am Sat & Sun, reduced hr in winter; MSchlesisches Tor). It was a boathouse, now it's a bar that entices with its chill vibe and a view of the tranquil canal.

☆ Entertainment
Berlin's legendary nightlife needs little introduction. Whether alternative, underground, cutting edge, saucy, flamboyant or even highbrow, it all crops up here.

Berlin also has a thriving scene of no-holds-barred sex clubs. The notorious **Kit Kat Club** (Map p178; ☑7889 9704; Bessemerstrasse 14; MAlt-Tempelhof) is the original and best.

Berlin boasts a liberal – no, wild is more like it – gay scene where anything goes. Still going strong since the 1920s, Schöneberg is the original gay area, but these days Prenzlauer Berg is the trendiest. Friedrichshain also has a small student-y gay scene. Skim through **Berlin Gay Web** (http://berlin.gay-web.de, in German) for all things gay in Berlin, or **Girl Ports** (www.girlports.com/lesbiantravel/destinations/berlin), a lesbian travel magazine.

SchwuZ (Map p178; ✆693 7025; www.schwuz.de; Mehringdamm 61; ☉from 11pm Fri & Sat; ⓜMehringdamm) is one of the longest-running mixed nightclubs; there's a cafe here all week too.

Hafen (Map p182; ✆211 4118; Motzstrasse 19; ⓜNollendorfplatz) is a Schöneberg staple with a consistent party scene. There's also an eclectic quiz night on Mondays (in English first Monday of the month).

Nightclubs

Few clubs open before 11pm (and if you arrive before midnight you may be dancing solo) but they stay open well into the early hours – usually sunrise at least. As the scene changes so rapidly, it's always wise to double-check listings magazines or ask locals. Admission charges, when they apply, range from €5 to €20.

Berghain/Panoramabar CLUB
(Map p178; www.berghain.de; Wrienzer Bahnhof; ☉from midnight Thu-Sat; ⓜOstbahnhof) If you only make it to one club in Berlin, this is where you need to go. The upper floor (Panoramabar, aka 'Pannebar') is all about house; the big factory hall below (Berghain) goes hard-core techno. Expect cutting-edge sounds in industrial surrounds.

Kaffee Burger CLUB
(Map p174; ✆2804 6495; www.kaffeeburger.de; Torstrasse 60; ⓜRosa-Luxemburg-Platz) The original GDR '60s wallpaper is part of the decor at this arty bar, club and music venue in Mitte. Burger hosts popular monthly readings by local (mainly expat) writers in English, but many come here for indie, rock, punk and cult author Wladimir Kaminer's twice-monthly *Russendisko* (Russian disco; www.russendisko.de).

Watergate CLUB
(Map p178; ✆6128 0394; www.water-gate.de; Falckensteinstrasse 49a; ☉from 11pm Fri & Sat; ⓜSchlesisches Tor) Watch the sun rise over the Spree River through the floor-to-ceiling windows of this fantastic lounge. The music is mainly electro, drum'n'bass and hip hop.

Weekend CLUB
(Map p174; www.week-end-berlin.de; Am Alexanderplatz 5; ☉from 11pm Thu-Sat; ⓜAlexanderplatz) Tear your eyes from the beautiful people and gaze through the 12th-floor windows, across the *Blade Runner* landscape of dug-up Alexanderplatz and over Berlin. (Alexanderplatz 5 is the one with the Sanyo logo.) Thursdays are best, while Saturdays see an invasion of suburban weekend warriors. Its rooftop deck is sublime on a summer night.

Music & Theatre

Staastsoper Unter den Linden OPERA HOUSE
(Map p174; ✆information 203 540, tickets 2035 4555; www.staatsoper-berlin.de; Unter den Linden 5-7; ⓜS-Bahn Unter den Linden) This is the handiest and most prestigious of Berlin's three opera houses, where unsold seats go on sale cheap an hour before curtains-up.

Berliner Ensemble THEATRE
(Map p174; ✆information 284 080, tickets 2840 8155; www.berliner-ensemble.de; Bertolt-Brecht-Platz 1; ⓜFriedrichstrasse) 'Mack the Knife' had its first public airing here, during the *Threepenny Opera's* premiere in 1928. Bertolt Brecht's former theatrical home continues to present his plays.

🔒 Shopping

While Hackescher Markt (p177) is increasingly commercial, plenty of cutting-edge boutiques are found in Prenzlauer Berg (especially along Kastanienallee and Stargarder Strasse) and in the side streets of Kreuzberg.

Flea market–hopping is a popular local pastime on the weekend, particularly Sundays. The **Berlin Art & Nostalgia Market** (Map p174; Georgenstrasse, Mitte; ☉8am-5pm Sat & Sun; ⓜS-Bahn Friedrichstrasse) is heavy on collectables, books, ethnic crafts and GDR memorabilia; the **Flohmarkt am Mauerpark** (Bernauer Strasse 63, Mauerpark; ☉10am-5pm Sun;

Ⓜ Eberwalder Strasse) is known for its vintage wear and young-designer retro fashions; and the **Flohmarkt am Arkonaplatz** (Arkonaplatz; ⊙10am-5pm Sun; Ⓜ Bernauerstrasse) is the best spot to hit if you're looking for retro 1960s and 1970s furniture and accessories.

KaDeWe   DEPARTMENT STORE
(Map p182; www.kadewe.de; Tauentzienstrasse 21-24; ⊙10am-8pm Mon-Thu, to 9pm Fri, 9.30am-8pm Sat; Ⓜ U-Bahn Wittenbergplatz) Germany's most renowned retail emporium, equivalent to Harrods. The 6th-floor gourmet food halls are extraordinary, and the store is near the principal western shopping thoroughfare of Kurfürstendamm.

Galeries Lafayette   DEPARTMENT STORE
(Map p174; www.galeries-lafayette.de; Friedrichstrasse 76-78; ⊙10am-8pm Mon-Sat; Ⓜ U-Bahn Französiche Strasse) The famous Parisian department store also has a branch in Mitte, including a floor of fancy French food and swanky spots to grab a tipple after a hard day's shop.

ℹ Information

Internet access is a breeze to find in Berlin – and the entire Sony Center at Potsdamer Platz is a free public hot spot.

Berlin Tourismus (☑250 025; http://visit berlin.de/de) Alexanderplatz (Map p174; Alexa Shopping Centre; ⊙10am-6pm); Brandenburg Gate (Map p174; ⊙10am-6pm); Hauptbahnhof (Ground floor, Europa Platz entrance; ⊙8am-10pm); Reichstag (Map p174; ⊙10am-6pm); Zoologisher Garten station (Kurfürstendamm 21; ⊙10am-8pm Mon-Sat, to 6pm Sun)

Berlin Welcome Card (www.berlin-welcome card.de; 48/72hr €16.90/22.90, incl Potsdam & up to 3 children €18.90/25.90) Free public transport, plus museum and entertainment discounts.

Kassenärztliche Bereitschaftsdienst (Public Physicians' Emergency Service; ☑310 031; www.kvberlin.de, in German) Medical phone referral service.

Post office (Map p174; Rathausstrasse 5; ⊙8am-7pm Mon-Fri, to 4pm Sat; Ⓜ Alexanderplatz)

ℹ Getting There & Away

Air

Berlin has two international airports, reflecting the legacy of the divided city. The larger one is in the northwestern suburb of **Tegel** (TXL), about 8km from the city centre; the other is in **Schönefeld** (SXF), about 22km southeast of town. Tegel is due to be decommissioned, with Schönefeld

being expanded into **Berlin Brandenburg International** (BBI). It has an estimated completion date of mid-2012. For information about either, go to www.berlin-airport.de or call ☑0180-500 0186.

Bus

Berlin is well connected to the rest of Europe by a network of long-distance buses. Most buses arrive at and depart from the **Zentraler Omnibusbahnhof** (ZOB; ☑302 5361; Masurenallee 4-6; Ⓜ Kaiserdamm/Witzleben), opposite the Funkturm radio tower. Tickets are available from travel agencies or at the bus station.

Car

Lifts can be organised by ride-share agency **ADM Mitfahrzentrale** (www.mf24.de, in German) Hardenbergplatz (☑194 420; Hardenbergplatz 14; ⊙9am-8pm Mon-Fri, 10am-2pm Sat, 10am-4pm Sun); Bahnhof Zoo (☑194 240; ⊙9am-8pm Mon-Fri, 10am-6pm Sat & Sun).

Train

Regular long-distance services arrive at the architecturally spectacular **Hauptbahnhof** (www. berlin-hauptbahnhof.de), with many continuing east to Ostbahnhof. ICE and IC trains leave hourly to every major city in Germany and there are also connections to central Europe. Sample fares include Leipzig (€36, 1¼ hours), Hamburg (€68, 1½ to two hours), Stralsund (€38 to €46, 2¾ to 3¼ hours) and Prague (€62, 4½ to five hours).

Unfortunately the few lockers available are hidden in the parking garage.

ℹ Getting Around

Berlin's public transport system is excellent – leave your car at home. The comprehensive network of U-Bahn and S-Bahn trains, buses, trams and ferries covers most corners.

To/From the Airport

SCHÖNEFELD The S9 train travels through all the major downtown stations, taking 40 minutes to Alexanderplatz.

The faster 'Airport Express' trains travel the same route half-hourly to Bahnhof Zoo (30 minutes), Friedrichstrasse (23 minutes), Alexanderplatz (20 minutes) and Ostbahnhof (15 minutes). Note that these are regular regional RE or RB trains designated as Airport Express in the timetable. Trains stop about 400m from the terminals, which are served by a free shuttle bus every 10 minutes. Walking takes five to 10 minutes.

Buses 171 and X7 link the terminals directly with the U-Bahn station Rudow (U7), with onward connections to central Berlin.

PUBLIC TRANSPORT TICKETS

Three tariff zones exist – A, B and C. Unless venturing to Potsdam, the outer suburbs or Schönefeld Airport, you'll only need an AB ticket.

TICKET	AB (€)	BC (€)	ABC (€)
Single	2.10	2.50	2.80
Day pass	6.10	6.30	6.50
Group day pass (up to 5 people)	15.40	15.90	16.10
7-day pass	26.20	27.00	32.30

The fare for any of these trips is €2.80. A taxi to central Berlin costs about €35.

TEGEL Tegel (TXL) is connected to Mitte by the JetExpressBus TXL (30 minutes) and to Bahnhof Zoo (Zoo Station) in Charlottenburg by express bus X9 (20 minutes). Bus 109 serves the western city – it's slower but useful if you're headed somewhere along Kurfürstendamm (30 minutes). Tegel is not directly served by the U-Bahn, but both bus 109 and X9 stop at Jakob-Kaiser-Platz (U7), the station closest to the airport.

Any of these trips costs €2.10. Taxi rides cost about €20 to Bahnhof Zoo and €23 to Alexanderplatz.

Bicycle

Flat and bike-friendly, with special bike lanes, abundant green spaces and peaceful waterways, Berlin is best explored by tooling around on two wheels. For details on following the course of the former Berlin Wall by bike along the marked Berliner Mauerweg, see p177. Bicycles (Fahrräder) may be taken aboard designated U-Bahn and S-Bahn cars (though not on buses) for the price of a reduced single ticket.

Many hostels and hotels rent bicycles to their guests, or can refer you to an agency. Expect to pay from €10 per day and €50 per week. A minimum cash deposit and/or ID is required. One reliable outfit with English-speaking staff and six branches throughout central Berlin is **Fahrradstation** (☏0180-510 8000; www.fahrrad station.de).

Car & Motorcycle

Garage parking is expensive (about €2 per hour) and vehicles entering the environmental zone (within the S-Bahn rail ring) must display a special sticker (Umweltplakette; €5 to €15). Order it online at www.berlin.de/sen/umwelt/luftquali-taet/de/luftreinhalteplan/doku_umweltzone. shtml. The fine for getting caught without the sticker is €40.

Public Transport

One type of ticket is valid on all public transport, including the U-Bahn, buses, trams and ferries run by **Berliner Verkehrsbetriebe** (☏194 49; www.bvg.de), as well as the S-Bahn and regional RE, SE and RB trains operated by **Deutsche Bahn** (www.bahn.de).

For ticket prices and zones see the boxed text this page.

Most tickets are available from vending machines located in the stations, but must be validated before use. If you're caught without a validated ticket, there's a €40 on-the-spot fine.

Services operate from 4am until just after midnight on weekdays, with many Nachtbus (night bus) services in between. At weekends, they run all night long (except the U4).

Taxi

Taxi stands are located at all main train stations and throughout the city. Order a taxi on ☏0800-222 2255.

BRANDENBURG

Although it surrounds bustling Berlin, the Brandenburg state of mind is quiet, rural and gentle, with vast expanses of unspoilt scenery, much of it in protected nature reserves. Its landscape is quilted in myriad shades, from emerald beech forest to golden fields of rapeseed and sunflowers, but it's also rather flat, windswept and perhaps even a bit melancholic.

Potsdam

☏0331 / POP 150,000

Featuring ornate palaces and manicured gardens dotted around a huge riverside park, the Prussian royal seat of Potsdam is the most popular day trip from Berlin. Elector Friedrich Wilhelm of Brandenburg laid the ground for the town's success when he made it his second residence in the 17th century. But Friedrich II (Frederick the Great) commissioned most of the palaces in the mid-18th century.

In August 1945 the victorious WWII Allies chose nearby Schloss Cecilienhof for the Potsdam Conference, which set the stage for the division of Berlin and Germany into occupation zones.

◉ Sights

Park Sanssouci   HISTORIC SITE
(admission free; ☉dawn to dusk) At the heart of Park Sanssouci lies a celebrated rococo palace, **Schloss Sanssouci** (☏969 4190; adult/concession Apr-Oct €12/8, Nov-Mar €8/5; ☉10am-6pm Tue-Sun Apr-Oct, to 5pm Nov-Mar). Built in 1747, it has some glorious interiors. Only 2000 visitors are allowed entry each day (a Unesco rule), so tickets are usually sold by 2.30pm, even in quiet seasons. Tours run by the tourist office guarantee entry.

The late-baroque **Neues Palais** (New Palace; ☏969 4255; adult/concession €6/5; ☉10am-6pm Wed-Mon Apr-Oct, to 5pm Nov-Mar) was built

in 1769 as the royal family's summer residence. It's one of the most imposing buildings in the park and the one to see if your time is limited.

The **Bildergalerie** (Picture Gallery; ☏969 4181; adult/concession €2/1.50; ☉10am-6pm Tue-Sun mid-May–Oct) contains a rich collection of 17th-century paintings by Rubens, Caravaggio and other big names.

Many consider the **Chinesisches Haus** (Chinese House; ☏969 4222; admission €2; ☉10am-6pm Tue-Sun mid-May–Oct) to be the pearl of the park. It's a circular pavilion of gilded columns, palm trees and figures of Chinese musicians and animals, built in 1757.

Schloss Cecilienhof   PALACE
(☏969 4244; tours adult/concession €6/5; ☉9am-6pm Tue-Sun Apr-Oct, to 5pm Nov-Mar) When outgoing British Prime Minister Winston Churchill and his accompanying successor Clement Attlee arrived at this palace in 1945 for the Potsdam Conference they must have immediately felt at home. Located in the separate New Garden, northeast of the centre on the bank of the Heiliger See, this is an incongruously English-style country manor in rococo-heavy Potsdam.

WORTH A TRIP

SACHSENHAUSEN CONCENTRATION CAMP

In 1936 the Nazis opened a *Konzentrationslager* (concentration camp) for men in a disused brewery in Sachsenhausen, 35km north of Berlin. By 1945 about 220,000 prisoners had passed through the gates – labelled, as at Auschwitz in Poland, *Arbeit Macht Frei* (Work Sets You Free). About 100,000 were murdered here.

After the war the Soviets and the communist leaders of the new GDR set up Spezi-allager No 7 (Special Camp No 7) for political prisoners, ex-Nazis, monarchists and others, jailing 60,000 and killing up to 12,000.

The **Sachsenhausen Memorial and Museum** (☏03301-200 200; www.stiftung-bg.de; admission free; ☉8.30am-6pm mid-Mar–mid-Oct, to 4pm mid-Oct–mid-Mar) consists of several parts. The **Neues Museum** (New Museum) includes a history of anti-Semitism and audiovisual material. East of it are **Barracks 38 and 39**, reconstructions of two typical huts housing most of the 6000 Jewish prisoners brought to Sachsenhausen after Kristallnacht (9–10 November 1938). Number 38 was rebuilt after being torched by neo-Nazis in September 1992. North of here is the prison and prison yard, where you'll find a **memorial** to the homosexuals who died here. The recently revamped **Lagermuseum** (Camp Museum), situated in what was once the camp kitchen, houses exhibits illustrating the everyday life in the camp during its various phases, including some artwork produced by the inmates. Left of the tall **monument** (1961), erected by the GDR in memory of political prisoners interned here, is the **crematorium** and **Station Z extermination site**, a pit for shooting prisoners in the neck with a wooden 'catch' where bullets could be retrieved and recycled.

The easiest way to get to Sachsenhausen from Berlin is to take the frequent S1 train to Oranienburg (€2.80, 50 minutes). The walled camp is a signposted 20-minute walk from Oranienburg station.

Filmpark Babelsberg MUSEUM
(☑721 2755; www.filmpark.de; Grossbeerenstrasse; adult/child/concession €19/13/16; ☺10am-6pm Apr-Oct) Germany's **UFA Film Studios** was where Fritz Lang's *Metropolis* was shot and FW Murnau filmed the first Dracula movie, *Nosferatu*. Since a relaunch in 1999, it's helped Berlin regain its film-making crown, with Roman Polanski's *The Pianist* and Quentin Tarantino's *Inglorious Bastards* both made here. The visitor experience includes theme-park rides and a studio tour – the daily stunt show (2pm) is worth catching. The studios are east of the city centre.

Altstadt HISTORIC AREA
The **Brandenburger Tor** (Brandenburg Gate) at the western end of the Old Town on Luisenplatz isn't a patch on the one in Berlin but it is older, dating from 1770. From here, pedestrian Brandenburger Strasse runs due east, providing the town's main eating strip.

Standing out from its surrounds is the pretty **Holländisches Viertel** (Dutch Quarter). Towards the northern end of Friedrich-Ebert-Strasse, it has 134 gabled red-brick houses, built for Dutch workers who came to Potsdam in the 1730s at the invitation of Friedrich Wilhelm I. The homes have been well restored and now house all kinds of interesting galleries, cafes and restaurants.

Tours

Weisse Flotte BOAT
(☑275 9210; www.schiffahrt-in-potsdam.de; Lange Brücke 6; ☺9.45am-7pm Apr-Oct) Boats cruise the Havel and the lakes around Potsdam, departing from the dock near Lange Brücke, with frequent trips to Wannsee (one way/return €9/12) and around the castles (€10).

Information

Potsdam tourist office (☑275 580; www. potsdamtourismus.de; Brandenburger Strasse 3; ☺9.30am-6pm Mon-Fri, 9.30am-4pm Sat & Sun Apr-Oct, 10am-6pm Mon-Fri, 9.30am-2pm Sat & Sun Nov-Mar) Near the Hauptbahnhof.

Park Sanssouci Besucherzentrum (Park Sanssouci Visitor Centre; ☑969 4202; www. spsg.de; An der Orangerie 1; ☺8.30am-5pm Mar-Oct, 9am-4pm Nov-Feb) Near the windmill and Schloss Sanssouci.

Getting There & Away

S-Bahn line S7 links central Berlin with Potsdam Hauptbahnhof about every 10 minutes. Some regional (RB/RE) trains from Berlin stop at all three stations in Potsdam. Your ticket must cover Berlin Zones A, B and C (€2.80) to travel here.

Potsdam Hauptbahnhof is just southeast of the city centre, across the Havel River. As this is still quite a way – 2km – from Park Sansoucci, you might like to change here for a train going one or two stops to Charlottenhof (for Schloss Sanssouci) or Sanssouci (for Neues Palais).

SAXONY

With its restored 'old German' roots, Saxony has emerged as one of the biggest draws for visitors to Germany. Restored and revitalised Dresden combines classicism with creativity. Just up the fabled Elbe River, Meissen is a gem of a medieval town with a palace and cathedral high on a hill.

Its history dating back to the Germanic tribes of over 1000 years ago, Saxony embodies many of the classic qualities associated with Germany. Dresden and Leipzig have a long tradition in the arts and are today centres of culture. And even though the local dialect can be impenetrable to those with mere schoolbook German, that same classic German traces its roots right back to here.

The state is fairly compact and high-speed rail links make the region easily accessible from all corners of Germany.

Dresden

☑0351 / POP 484,000
Proof that there is life after death, Dresden has become one of Germany's most popular attractions, and for good reason. Restorations have returned the city to the glory days when it was famous throughout Europe as 'Florence on the Elbe', owing to the efforts of Italian artists, musicians, actors and master craftsmen who flocked to the court of Augustus the Strong, bestowing countless masterpieces upon the city. Death came suddenly when, shortly before the end of WWII, Allied bombers blasted and incinerated much of the baroque centre, a beautiful jewel-like area dating from the 18th century. More than 25,000 people died, and in bookstores throughout town you can peruse texts showing the destruction (or read about it in Kurt Vonnegut's classic *Slaughterhouse Five*).

Rebuilding began under the communist regime in the 1950s and accelerated greatly after reunification. The city celebrated its 800th anniversary in 2006 and, while much focus is on the restored centre, you should cross the River Elbe to the Neustadt, where edgy new clubs and cafes open every week, joining the scores already there.

◎ Sights

Dresden is best explored on foot, where one monument after another reveals itself and you're free to amble down alleys to make your own discoveries.

Frauenkirche　　　　　　　CATHEDRAL
(Church of Our Lady; www.frauenkirche-dresden.org; Neumarkt; ◎10am-6pm) One of Dresden's most beloved icons, the Frauenkirche was rebuilt in time for the city's 800th anniversary celebrations in 2006. Initially constructed between 1726 and 1743 under the direction of baroque architect George Bähr, it was Germany's greatest Protestant church until February 1945, when bombing raids flattened it. The communists decided to leave the rubble as a war memorial; after reunification, calls for reconstruction prevailed, although the paucity of charcoal-tinged original stones shows just how much is new.

Look for the very few blackened stones on the exterior, these were salvaged from the rubble of the original. Otherwise – not surprisingly – the church feels brand new, especially inside. Most moving is the melted cross from the original. You can also climb to the top for good views. The surrounding Neumarkt is part of a massive redevelopment designed to evoke prewar Dresden, although at this point it feels all too bland and reconstituted.

Semperoper　　　　　　HISTORIC BUILDING
(www.semperoper-erleben.de; Theaterplatz; tour adult/child €8/4; ◎varies) Designed by Gustav Semper, this neo-Renaissance opera house *is* Dresden. The original building opened in 1841 but burned down less than three decades later. Rebuilt in 1878, it was pummelled in WWII and reopened in 1985 after the communists invested a fortune restoring it. The best way to appreciate it is through one of the many performances (see p197).

Residenzschloss　　　　　　PALACE
(www.skd.museum; Schlossplatz) The Residenzschloss, a massive neo-Renaissance palace, has ongoing restoration projects. Its many features include the **Hausmannsturm** (Servants' Tower; adult/child €3/2; ◎10am-6pm Wed-Mon), which has sobering pictures of the complete WWII destruction.

TOP CHOICE *Grünes Gewölbe*
(Green Vault; adult/child €10/5; ◎10am-7pm Wed-Mon) This is one of the world's fin-

ⓘ NAVIGATING DRESDEN 193

The Elbe River splits Dresden in a rough V-shape, with the **Neustadt** (new city) to the north and the **Altstadt** (old city) to the south.

There are two main train stations: the restored **Hauptbahnhof** on the southern side of town, and **Dresden-Neustadt** north of the river. Most trains stop at both.

From the Hauptbahnhof, pedestrian-only **Prager Strasse** leads north into the Altstadt. Here there's a mix of communist-era triumphalism and modern-day commercialism. The lovely **Brühlsche Terrasse** runs along the Elbe between the Albertinum and the Zwinger, with boat docks below.

In the Neustadt, home to much of the city's nightlife, the main attractions for visitors are the **Albertplatz** and **Louisenstrasse** quarters. Here you'll find all manner of shops, galleries, funky boutiques and dozens of cafes, bars and clubs.

est collections of precious objects. Treasures include the world's biggest green diamond, tiny pearl sculptures and a stunning group of 137 gem-studded figures by Johann Melchior Dinglinger, court jeweller of Augustus the Strong. Even cynics will marvel at the wafer-thin creations in amber. Buy timed tickets in advance from the office or online.

Hofkirche
(◎9am-5pm) This baroque Catholic church contains the heart of Augustus the Strong. Free **concerts** (◎11.30am Wed &Sat) are extraordinary.

Fürstenzug
(Procession of Princes; Augustusstrasse) Outside, you'd need a really wide-angle lens to get a shot of Wulhelm Walther's amazing 102m-long tiled mural on the wall of the former Stendehaus (Royal Stables). The scene, a long row of royalty on horses, was painted in 1876 and then transferred to some 24,000 Meissen porcelain tiles in 1906.

Verkehrsmuseum
(Transport Museum; Augustusstrasse 1; adult/child €4.50/2.50; ◎10am-5pm Tue-Sun) This transport museum is fittingly located in the Johanneum, the old stables. Motoring back towards the 20th century, this is a fascinating

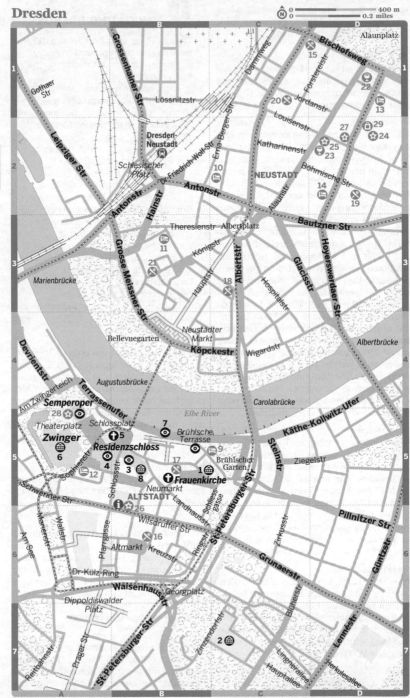

collection, including penny farthings, trams, dirigibles and carriages. Visitors can watch a melancholy 40-minute film with original black-and-white footage of 1930s Dresden.

Zwinger MUSEUMS
(www.skd.museum; Theaterplatz 1; ⊙10am-6pm Tue-Sun) Dresden's elaborate 1728 fortress, an attraction in its own right with a popular ornamental courtyard, also houses six major museums. The most important is the **Galerie Alte Meister** (adult/child €10/7.50), which features masterpieces including Raphael's *Sistine Madonna*. The **Rüstkammer** (Armoury; adult/child €3/2) has a superb collection of ceremonial weapons. The dazzling **Porzelansammlung** (Porcelain Collection; adult/child €6/3.50) is filled with flamboyant breakables.

Albertinum MUSEUM
(www.skd.museum; Brühlsche Terrasse; adult/child €8/6; ⊙10am-6pm) Massive renovations ended in 2010 and the results are stunning. A light-filled enclosed courtyard welcomes you into this treasure trove of art. Highlights include the **Münzkabinett** collection of antique coins and medals, and the **Skulpturensammlung**, which includes classical

and Egyptian works. The **Galerie Neue Meister** has renowned 19th- and 20th-century paintings from leading French and German Impressionists.

Deutsches Hygiene-Museum MUSEUM
(www.dhmd.de; Lingnerplatz 1; adult/child €7/3; ⊙10am-6pm Tue-Sun) Awash in displays relating to the ravages of venereal disease, the theory of eugenics and reasons to bathe.

☞ Tours

Sächsische Dampfschiffahrt RIVER TOUR
(www.saechsische-dampfschiffahrt.de; adult/child from €16/8) Ninety-minute Elbe tours leave from the Terrassenufer dock several times daily in summer aboard the world's oldest fleet of paddle-wheel steamers. There's also service to villages along the river such as Meissen.

Stadtrundfahrt Dresden BUS TOUR
(www.stadtrundfahrt.com; adult/child €20/10) This narrated hop-on, hop-off tour has 22 stops in the centre and the elegant outer villa districts along the Elbe. It includes short tours of the Zwinger, Fürstenzug, Frauenkirche and Pfunds Molkerei.

🛏 Sleeping

Accommodation in Dresden can be very expensive in the high season. Luckily, several good-value budget places can be found in the lively Neustadt. Although rising property prices in the area are taking a toll, some quirky places soldier on.

Lollis Homestay   HOSTEL €

(☎810 8458; www.lollishome.de; Görlitzer Strasse 34; dm €13-19, s €30-38, d €40-42, linen €2, breakfast €3; @🛜) Dresden's quirkiest hostel has two contenders for Germany's most outlandish dorms: one containing a real Trabant you can bed down in for the night; the other a Giant's Room with oversize furniture that makes guests feel like Tom Thumb. In addition there's free bike rental.

Kempinski Hotel Taschenbergpalais

HOTEL €€€

(☎491 20; www.kempinski-dresden.de; Taschenberg 3; r €200-400; ❄@🛜🏊) This restored 18th-century mansion is Dresden's heavyweight, with views over the Zwinger, incredibly quiet corridors, and doors that seem impervious to anything outside, protecting the 214 rooms and suites. In winter the courtyard turns into an ice rink.

Hotel Martha Hospiz   HOTEL €€

(☎817 60; www.hotel-martha-hospiz.de; Nieritzstrasse 11; r €80-140; 🛜) Fifty rooms decked out in Biedermeier style, an attractive winter garden and a sound on-site restaurant with Saxon cooking and local wine make this a very pleasant place to lay your hat. It's all very slick.

Rothenburger Hof   HOTEL €€

(☎812 60; www.rothenburger-hof.de; Rothenburger Strasse 15-17; r €75-160, apt €140-180; ❄🛜🏊) This quiet launch pad for Neustadt explorations counts among its assets apartments with kitchenette and balcony, a Moorish-style steam room and a great pool. The included breakfast is lavish.

Hotel Kipping   HOTEL €€

(☎478 500; www.hotel-kipping.de; Winckelmannstrasse 6; s/d from €70/80; @🛜) Just south of the Hauptbahnhof, this is a family-run, family-friendly hotel that comes with 20 comfortable rooms in a house right out of the *Addams Family*. The bar and cafe are especially appealing.

EV-Ref Gemeinde zu Dresden   PENSION €

(☎438 230; www.ev-ref-gem-dresden.de; Brühlscher Garten 4; s/d from €60/75) The name is not a marketer's dream, but this pension is amazing value in a great location – on the river and overlooking the Albertinum. This historic retirement home makes rooms available for travellers whenever a resident has permanently 'checked out'. Rooms have showers and TV and often great views; breakfast is included.

Hostel & Backpacker Kangaroo-Stop

HOSTEL €

(☎314 3455; www.kangaroo-stop.de; Erna-Berger-Strasse 8-10; dm/s/d from €13/29/40; @🛜) Welcoming and low-key, with rooms spread over two buildings: one for backpackers and the other for families. So which will see more immature behaviour? The big breakfast buffet costs €5. Dresden-Neustadt station is nearby.

Ibis Dresden Lilienstein   HOTEL €€

(☎4856 6663; www.ibishotel.com; Prager Strasse 13; r €60-120; ❄🛜) Together with the adjoining Ibis Dresden Bastei and the Ibis Dresden Königstein, this enormous complex dating from the communist era has more than 900 rooms, meaning vacancies in summer. The decor is 'cheap and cheerful'. It's a three-minute walk from the Hauptbahnhof.

Campingplatz Mockritz   CAMPING GROUND €

(☎471 5250; www.camping-dresden.de; Boderitzerstrasse 30; per adult/tent/car €6/3/6) Friendly little campsite 3km south of the Hauptbahnhof. Take bus 76 from the Hauptbahnhof and get off at the stop 'Campingplatz Mockritz'.

🍴 Eating

The Neustadt has oodles of cafes and restaurants, many found along Königstrasse and the streets north of Albertplatz. This is the most interesting part of town at night. South of the river, look near the Altmarkt, and Münzgasse/Terrassengasse, between Brühlsche Terrasse and the Frauenkirche.

Off Albertstrasse, the **Neustädter Markthalle** is a gorgeously restored old market hall (enter on Metzer Strasse) with food stalls good for picnics and amazingly cheap wurst lunches.

TOP CHOICE **Wenzel Prager Bierstuben** CZECH €€
(Königstrasse 1; mains €7-20; ⏰11am-midnight) This busy beer hall serves up oceans of Czech lager under arched brick ceilings. Always crowded, the menu leans towards traditional meaty mains. The garlic soup is sublime, and the cured pork with horseradish a delight.

Villandry

MEDITERRANEAN €€

(Jordanstrasse 8; mains €8-20; ☉6.30-11.30pm Mon-Sat) The folks in the kitchen here sure know how to coax maximum flavour out of even the simplest, often organic, ingredients, and to turn them into super-tasty Mediterranean treats for eyes and palate. Meals are best enjoyed in the lovely courtyard.

Raskolnikoff

CAFE €

(www.raskolnikoff.de; Böhmische Strasse 34; mains €5-14) This bohemian cafe in a former artists' squat was one of the Neustadt's first post-Wende pubs. The menu is sorted by compass direction (borscht to quiche Lorraine to smoked fish) and there's a sweet little ivy-lined beer garden out back, plus a gallery and pension (rooms €40 to €55) upstairs.

Gänsedieb

GERMAN €€

(Weisse Gasse 1; mains €8-18) One of nearly a dozen choices on Weisse Gasse, the 'Goose Thief' serves hearty schnitzels, goulash and steaks alongside a full range of Bavarian Paulaner beers. The name was inspired by the iconic 1880 fountain outside.

Café Europa

CAFE €€

(Königsbrücker Strasse 68; mains €6-15; ☉24hr; 🛜) Smart open-all-hours cafe with newspapers and free internet. Come here to regroup during the early hours.

Grand Café

CAFE €€

(An der Frauenkirche 12; mains €10-20; ☉10am-1am) Yummy cakes and more ambitious mains in the gold-trimmed Coselpalais, plus tables on a large patio and good views of Frauenkirche.

🍸 Drinking & Entertainment

Dresden's nightlife is ever changing and the Neustadt still has plenty of that proletariat/GDR vibe: grunge beats swank every time. Many of the places listed under Eating are also good just for a drink.

Dresden is synonymous with opera, and performances at the spectacular **Semperoper** (www.semperoper.de; Theaterplatz) are brilliant. Tickets cost from €10, but they're usually booked out well in advance. Check for returns. Some performances by the renowned philharmonic are also held here, but most are in the GDR-era **Kulturpalast** (www.kulturpalast-dresden.de; Schlossstrasse 2), which hosts a wide range of events.

TOP CHOICE Café 100

WINE BAR

(Alaunstrasse 100) Off a courtyard, you'll pass hundreds of empty bottles on the way in, a foreshadowing of the lengthy wine list and delights that follow. Candles give the underground space a romantic yet edgy glow. The place to take that someone you met on the train.

Scheunecafé

CAFE

(Alaunstrasse 36-40) Set back from the street, this place combines Indian food (mains €7 to €12), a vast beer garden, live music and DJs into a fun and funky stew.

Blue Note

JAZZ

(www.jazzdepartment.com; Görlitzer Strasse 2b; ☉until 5am) Small, smoky and smooth, this converted smithy has live jazz almost nightly until 11pm, then turns into a night-owl magnet until the wee hours. The talent is mostly regional.

Strasse E

CLUB

(www.strasse-e.de; Werner-Hartmann-Strasse 2) Dresden's most high-octane party zone is in an industrial area between Neustadt and the airport. Half a dozen venues here cover the entire spectrum of danceable sound, from disco to dark wave, electro to pop. Take tram 7 to Industriegelände.

Katy's Garage

LIVE MUSIC

(Alaunstrasse 48) This rockin' shanty town, a key venue for live gigs and club nights throughout the week, is centred around a former tyre shop.

Queens

GAY BAR

(Görlitzer Strasse 3) The kitsch decor is the perfect backdrop for this pulsating hot spot, famous for its *Schlager* (schmaltzy German pop songs) parties.

🛍 Shopping

Altmarkt-Gallerie anchors a vast shopping area that extends along Prager Strasse and Pfarrgasse, but the most interesting oddball shops are found in the Neustadt. With one exception: **Fem2Glam** (www.fem2glam.com; Prager Strasse 8/8a) has made waves with its popular line of dildos made from polished (fear not: they're sealed!) Elbe River sandstone.

If a good book is more your style, **Thalia** (Dr-Külz-Ring 12) has loads of Dresden-related texts.

ℹ Information

Dresden City-Card (per 48hr €21) Provides admission to museums, discounted city tours and boat tours and free public transport. Buy it at the tourist office.

Dresden Regio-Card (per 72hr €32) Everything offered by the City-Card plus free transport on the entire regional transport network. Valid as far as the Czech border and Meissen.

Tourist office (www.dresden-tourist.de; Kulturpalast, Schlossstrasse; ⊙10am-7pm Mon-Fri, 10am-6pm Sat, 10am-3pm Sun) Also houses the central ticket office.

ℹ Getting There & Around

Dresden's **airport** (DRS; www.dresden-airport. de), served by Lufthansa and Air Berlin among others, is 9km north of the city centre, on S-Bahn line 2 (€1.90, 20 minutes).

Dresden is well linked with regular train services through the day to Leipzig (€29, 70 minutes), Berlin-Hauptbahnhof by IC/EC train (€36, 2¼ hours) and Frankfurt-am-Main by ICE (€89, 4½ hours).

Dresden's **public transport network** (www. dvbag.de) charges €1.90 for a single-trip ticket; day tickets cost €5 and can be bought on trams. Trams 3, 7, 8 and 9 provide good links between the Hauptbahnhof, Altstadt and Neustadt.

Around Dresden

MEISSEN
☑03521 / POP 29,000

Straddling the Elbe around 25km upstream from Dresden, Meissen is a compact, perfectly preserved Saxon town, popular with day trippers. Crowning a rocky ridge above it is the Albrechtsburg palace, which in 1710 became the cradle of European porcelain manufacture. The world-famous Meissen china, easily recognised by its trademark insignia, is still the main draw for coach parties. Fortunately, the cobbled lanes, dreamy nooks and idyllic courtyards of the Altstadt (old town) make escaping from the shuffling crowds a snap.

◎ Sights

The **Markt** is framed by the **Rathaus** (town hall; 1472) and the Gothic **Frauenkirche**, which – fittingly – has a porcelain carillon.

Meissen's medieval fortress, the 15th-century **Albrechtsburg** (www.albrechtsburg -meissen.de; Domplatz 1; adult/child €8/4; ⊙10am-6pm Mar-Oct, to 5pm Nov-Feb), crowns a ridge high above the Elbe River and is reached by steep lanes. It contains the former **ducal palace** and **Meissen Cathedral**, a magnificent Gothic structure. It is widely seen as the birthplace of Schloss architecture, with its ingenious system of internal arches. Augustus the Strong of Saxony created Europe's first porcelain factory here in 1710.

Next door, the towering 13th-century **Albrechtsburg Cathedral** (☑452 490; Domplatz 7; adult/child €4/2; ⊙10am-6pm Mar-Oct, to 4pm Nov-Feb) contains an altarpiece by Lucas Cranach the Elder.

Meissen has long been renowned for its chinaware, with its trademark insignia of blue crossed swords. Meissen's porcelain factory is now 1km southwest of the Altstadt in an appropriately beautiful building, the **Porzellan-Museum** (www.meissen. com; Talstrasse 9; adult/child €9/4.50; ⊙9am-6pm May-Oct, to 5pm Nov-Apr), which dates to 1916. There are often long queues for the workshop demonstrations, but you can view the porcelain collection upstairs at your leisure.

ℹ Information

Tourist office (www.touristinfo-meissen.de; Markt 3; ⊙10am-6pm Mon-Fri, to 4pm Sat & Sun Apr-Oct, 10am-5pm Mon-Fri, to 3pm Sat Nov-Mar)

ℹ Getting There & Away

Half-hourly S-Bahn trains run from Dresden's Hauptbahnhof and Neustadt train stations (€5.50, 40 minutes). To visit the porcelain factory, get off at Meissen-Triebischtal (one stop after Meissen).

A more pleasant way to get here is by steamer (between May and September). Boats leave from the **Sächsische Dampfschiffahrt** (☑866 090; www.saechsische-dampfschiffahrt.de) dock in Dresden once daily (€17 return, two hours).

SAXON SWITZERLAND

Sächsische Schweiz (Saxon Switzerland; www. saechsische-schweiz.de) is a 275-sq-km national park 50km south of Dresden, near the Czech border. Its wonderfully wild, craggy country is dotted with castles and tiny towns along the mighty Elbe River. The landscape varies unexpectedly and radically: its forests can look deceptively tropical, while the worn cliffs and plateaux recall the parched expanses of New Mexico or central Spain (generally without the searing heat).

The highlight of the park is the **Bastei lookout**, on the Elbe River some 28km southeast of Dresden. One of the most breathtaking spots in the whole of Germany, it features fluted pinnacles 305m high and unparalleled views of the surrounding forests, cliffs and mountains, as well as a sweeping view along the river itself.

There are myriad routes for hiking (and cycling). Get here on the S1 train to Königstein, which makes a good base.

Leipzig

📞 0341 / POP 515,000

In Goethe's *Faust*, a character named Frosch calls Leipzig 'a little Paris'. He was wrong – Leipzig is more fun and infinitely less self-important than the Gallic capital. It's an important business and transport centre, a trade-fair mecca and arguably the most dynamic city in eastern Germany.

Leipzig also has some of the finest classical music and opera in the country, and its fine art and literary scenes are flourishing. Once home to Bach, Wagner and Mendelssohn, and to Goethe, it more recently earned the sobriquet *Stadt der Helden* (City of Heroes) for its leading role in the 1989 democratic revolution.

You can easily fill a day or more wandering the centre of town.

⊙ Sights

Leipzig's compact centre lies within a ring road that outlines the town's medieval fortifications. To reach the city centre from the Hauptbahnhof, cross Willy-Brandt-Platz and continue south along Nikolaistrasse for five minutes. The **Markt** is the city focus and has been revamped with the installation of a new underground S-Bahn station for a cross-city line set to open in 2013.

Don't rush from sight to sight – wandering around Leipzig is a pleasure in itself, with many of the blocks around the central Markt criss-crossed by old internal shopping passages. Four good ones: **Steibs Hof** (100-year-old blue tiles and classic cafes), **Specks Hof** (soaring atrium, bookshops, cafes), **Jägerhofpassage** (galleries, theatre, antiques) and the classic **Mädlerpassage** (grand design, the famous Auerbachs Keller).

TOP CHOICE Stasi Museum   MUSEUM
(www.runde-ecke-leipzig.de; Dittrichring 24; admission free; ⊙10am-6pm) Former headquarters of the East German secret police, the Stasi Museum has exhibits on propaganda, amazingly hokey disguises, surveillance photos and other forms of 'intelligence', all part of the chilling machinations of the GDR's all-out zeal for controlling, manipulating and repressing its own people.

Museum der Bildenden Künste   MUSEUM
(Museum of Fine Arts; www.mdbk.de; Katharinenstrasse 10; adult/child €5/free; ⊙10am-6pm Tue & Thu-Sun, noon-8pm Wed) Leipzig's liveliest museum, the Museum der Bildenden Künste, is housed in a stunning glass cube of a building that provides both a dramatic – and echoey – backdrop to its collection, which spans old masters and the latest efforts of local artists.

Zeitgeschichtliches Forum   MUSEUM
(Forum of Contemporary History; 📞222 20; Grimmaische Strasse 6; admission free; ⊙9am-6pm Tue-Fri, 10am-6pm Sat & Sun) Haunting and uplifting by turns, the Zeitgeschichtliches Forum tells the story of the GDR from division and dictatorship to resistance and reform. It does a good job of chronicling the 1989 revolution, which started here, and it captures the tragic drama of the original Iron Curtain division.

Bach Museum   MUSEUM
(www.bach-leipzig.de; Thomaskirchhof 16; adult/child €6/free; ⊙10am-6pm Tue-Sun) Johann Sebastian Bach worked here from 1723 until his death in 1750. The newly revamped collection focuses on the composer's busy life in Leipzig. Multimedia displays allow you to get inside his head as he was composing music. Just across is **Thomaskirche** (Thomaskirchhof 18), where he lead the choir (and was only hired after three others turned the job down).

Other Music Sites   HISTORIC BUILDINGS
Other stars of the real, real, real oldies beat in Leipzig include Felix Mendelssohn-Bartholdy, who lived (and died) in the **Mendelssohn-Haus** (www.mendelssohn-stiftung.de; Goldschmidtstrasse 12; admission €4.50; ⊙10am-6pm); and Robert Schumann, who spent the first four years of his marriage to Leipzig pianist Clara Wieck in the **Schumann-Haus** (www.schumann-verein.de; Inselstrasse 18; admission €3; ⊙2-5pm Wed-Fri, 10am-5pm Sat & Sun).

Neues Rathaus   HISTORIC BUILDING
(New Town Hall; 📞1230; Martin-Luther-Ring; ⊙7am-4.30pm Mon-Fri) Off the southern ring road is the 108m-high tower of the baroque Neues Rathaus. Though the origins date to the 16th century, its current manifestation was completed in 1905. The interior makes it one of the finest municipal buildings in Germany; the lobby houses rotating exhibitions, mostly on historical themes.

Völkerschlachtdenkmal   MONUMENT
(Battle of Nations Monument; Prager Strasse; adult/child €5/3; ⊙10am-6pm Apr-Oct, to 4pm Nov-Mar) Some 100,000 soldiers died in the epic 1813 battle that led to the decisive victory of

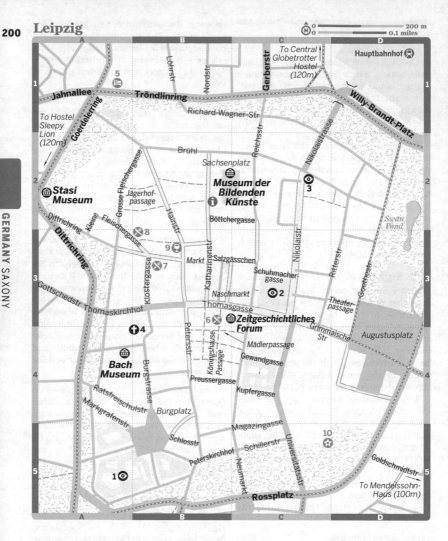

Prussian, Austrian and Russian forces over Napoleon's army. Built a century later, the Völkerschlachtdenkmal is a sombre and imposing 91m colossus that towers above southeastern Leipzig, not far from the actual killing fields. Climb the 500 steps for a view of the region. Take tram 15 from the station (direction: Meusdorf).

Alte Spinnerei ARTIST STUDIOS
(www.spinnerei.de; Spinnereistrasse 7; ⊙11am-6pm Tue-Sat) 'Cotton to culture' is the motto of this 19th-century cotton-spinning factory–turned–artist colony. Around 80 New Leipzig School artists, including Neo

Rauch, have their studios in this huge pile of red-brick buildings, alongside designers, architects, goldsmiths and other creative types. Their work is displayed in about 10 galleries, including **Galerie Eigen+Art** (☑960 7886; www.eigen-art.com), internationally renowned for championing young artists. Take the S-1 to Plagwitz.

🛏 Sleeping

Midrange accommodation in the centre is fairly unexciting and usually the preserve of the big chains (particularly the many Accor brands).

Hotel Fürstenhof HOTEL €€€
(📞1400; www.starwood.de; Tröndlinring 8; r from €200; ❄️@🛜🏊) This intimate but grand hotel, with a 200-year pedigree, is part of the luxury branch of the Starwood chain. It has updated old-world flair, impeccable service, a gourmet restaurant and an oh-so-soothing grotto-style pool and spa.

Central Globetrotter Hostel HOSTEL €
(📞149 8960; www.globetrotter-leipzig.de; Kurt-Schumacher-Strasse 41; dm €14-18, s/d €28/40; @🛜) In a busy location just north of the train station, this 80-room hostel offers bare-bones accommodation. Some rooms boast murals, albeit ones that won't win any scholarships to the Art Academy of Leipzig. Breakfast is €4 extra.

Hotel Markgraf HOTEL €€
(📞303 030; www.markgraf-leipzig.de; Körnerstrasse 36; r €85-100; 🛜) This smartly run hotel puts you within staggering distance of the Karl-Liebknecht-Strasse nightlife. Many rooms overlook a pretty little park and there's a sauna for relaxing. Take tram 10 or 11 south to Südplatz.

Hotel Kosmos HOTEL €€
(📞233 4422; www.hotel-kosmos.de; Gottsched-strasse 1; s/d from €50/80) Right on a street with burgeoning nightlife, this low-key place in a grand building combines GDR-era furniture with murals in themed rooms. The murals next to the bed in the Marilyn Monroe room may fool the foolhardy.

Hotel Vier Jahreszeiten HOTEL €€
(📞985 10; www.guennewig.de; Kurt-Schumacher-Strasse 23-29; s €73-114, d €92-150; @🛜) Close to the train station, this anonymous but well-run place has 67 comfortable rooms and serves up a good buffet breakfast in the atrium.

Hostel Sleepy Lion HOSTEL €
(📞993 9480; www.hostel-leipzig.de; Käthe-Kollwitz-Strasse 3; dm from €15, s/d €30/45; @🛜) Budget-minded nomads will feel welcome at this low-key hostel, with 60 clean and comfy beds in cheerfully painted rooms with private facilities. The major sights – and bars – are just steps away.

Camping Am Auensee CAMPING GROUND €
(📞465 1600; www.motel-auensee.de; Gustav-Esche-Strasse 5; campsites per person from €6, cabins €40-60) This camping ground is in a pleasant wooded spot on the city's northwestern outskirts (take tram 10 or 11 to Anna Berger Strasse). The cabins are A-frame bungalows.

🍴 Eating

TOP CHOICE Auerbachs Keller GERMAN €€
(📞216 100; www.auerbachs-keller-leipzig.de; Mädlerpassage; mains €14-22) Founded in 1525, Auerbachs Keller is one of Germany's classic restaurants, serving typically hearty fare. Goethe's *Faust – Part I* includes a scene here, in which Mephistopheles and Faust carouse with some students before they ride off on a barrel. The historic section of the restaurant includes the Goethe room and the *Fasskeller;* note the carved tree trunk in the latter, depicting the whole barrel-riding adventure. There's excellent traditional chow, too.

Gosenschenke 'Ohne Bedenken'
BEER GARDEN €€
(Menckestrasse 5; mains €6-16) This historic Leipzig institution, backed by the city's prettiest beer garden, is *the* place to sample Gose, a local top-fermented beer often

served with a shot of liqueur. The menu has a distinctly carnivorous bent. Take tram 12 to Fritz-Seger-Strasse.

Zill's Tunnel
GERMAN €€

(Barfussgässchen 9; mains €9-15) Empty tables are a rare sight at this outstanding restaurant offering a classic menu of robust Saxon dishes. Sit on the outside terrace, in the rustic cellar, or in the covered 'tunnel' courtyard.

Zum Arabischen Coffe Baum
CAFE €€

(Kleine Fleischergasse 4; mains €8-15) Leipzig's oldest coffee bar has a staid old restaurant and cafe offering excellent meals over three floors, plus a free coffee museum at the top. Composer Robert Schumann met friends here, and if you ask nicely you can sit at his regular table.

Drinking & Entertainment

Barfussgässchen and Kleine Flieschergasse, west of the Markt, form one of Leipzig's two 'pub miles', packed with outdoor tables that fill up the second the weather turns warm. The other is on Gottschedstrasse, a wider nightlife strip just west of the Altstadt.

Leipzig has a famously raw music scene. In late May, the world's largest **Goth Festival** (www.wave-gotik-treffen.de) attracts over 20,000 leather-clad, dark-side partiers.

To hear the more sedate works of native-born Bach, the Thomaskirche has frequent free recitals and performances by the boy's choir he once led. Mendelssohn-Haus has concerts on Sundays (adult/child €12/8).

TOP CHOICE Conne Island
LIVE MUSIC

(www.conne-island.de; Koburger Strasse 3) This former squatter's haunt has morphed into the city's top venue for punk, indie, ska, rock and hip-hop concerts. It's in the southern suburb of Connewitz; take tram 9 to Koburger Brücke.

Werk II
VENUE

(www.werk-2.de; Kochstrasse 132) This large cultural centre in an old factory is great for catching up-and-coming bands, alternative film and theatre, or even circus acts. It's in Connewitz; take tram 9 to Connewitzer Kreuz.

Moritz-Bastei
CLUB

(www.moritzbastei.de; Universitätsstrasse 9) One of the best student clubs in Germany, in a spacious cellar below the old city walls. It has live music or DJs most nights and runs films outside in summer.

Spizz
BAR

(Markt 9) Classic brass instruments dangle above the stage at this city slicker, where you might catch some cool jazz. It has three levels, a good range of wines and beers, and a fine sidewalk cafe that's good day or night.

ℹ Information

The Hauptbahnhof contains a modern mall with over 140 shops and (radically for Germany) it is open from 6am to 10pm daily. You'll find good bookshops, a post office, banks and much more.

Leipzig Card (1/3 days €9/19) Free or discounted admission to attractions, plus free travel on public transport. Available from the tourist office and most hotels.

Tourist office (www.leipzig.de; Katharinenstrasse 8; ◔9.30am-6pm Mon-Fri, to 4pm Sat, to 3pm Sun)

ℹ Getting There & Away

Leipzig-Halle airport (LEJ; www.leipzig-halle-airport.de) has regional flights. Ryanair serves tiny **Altenburg airport** (ADC; www.flughafen-altenburg.de), some 53km from Leipzig. There's a shuttle bus (€12, 1¾ hours) timed to coincide with flights.

Leipzig is an important rail hub and fittingly has a monumental Hauptbahnhof. Regular services include Dresden (€29, 70 minutes), Munich (€87, five hours), Berlin-Hauptbahnhof by ICE (€42, 70 minutes) and Frankfurt (€70, 3½ hours).

ℹ Getting Around

Trams (www.lvb.de) are the main public-transport option, with most lines running via the Hauptbahnhof. The S-Bahn circles the city's outer suburbs. A single ticket costs €2 and a day card €5. The vast project of building an S-Bahn line under the city centre is due for completion late in 2013.

THURINGIA

Thuringia likes to trade on its reputation as the 'green heart' of Germany, an honour helped by the former GDR's dodgy economy, which limited development. These days its main towns of Erfurt and Weimar are popular for their historic centres and long histories. In fact the latter is a microcosm of German history – high and low – over the last 500 years.

While the communist era may have been relatively benign, the previous decades were not. The Nazis had numerous concentration camps here, including the notorious Buchenwald and the nightmare of Mittelbau Dora. But yet again, in contrast, Weimar was the place where Germany tried a liberal democracy in the 1920s and in previous centuries it was home to notables such as Bach, Schiller, Goethe and Thomas Mann.

Erfurt

☎ 0361 / POP 201,000

Thuringia's capital is a scene-stealing combo of sweeping squares, time-worn alleyways, perky church towers, idyllic river scenery, and vintage inns and taverns. On the little Gera River, Erfurt was founded by the indefatigable missionary St Boniface as a bishopric in 742. Rich merchants founded the university in 1392, allowing students to study common law, rather than religious law. Its most famous graduate was Martin Luther, who studied philosophy here before becoming a monk at the local Augustinian monastery in 1505.

This is a city to stroll. It's a five-minute walk north along Bahnhofstrasse to Anger, the main shopping and business artery. The Gera River bisects the Altstadt, spilling off into numerous creeks.

◉ Sights

Krämerbrücke

(Merchants' Bridge) Unique in this part of Europe, this medieval bridge is an 18m-wide, 120m-long curiosity spanning the Gera River. Quaint houses and shops line both sides of the narrow road. It has a powerful magnetism for tourists.

Dom St Marien   CATHEDRAL

(Domplatz; ⊙9am-5pm Mon-Fri, to 4.30pm Sat, 2-4pm Sun, shorter hr in winter) It's hard to miss Erfurt's cathedral casting its massive shadow over Domplatz from an artificial hill built specially for it. Ironically, it was originally only planned as a simple chapel in 752; by the time it was completed it was the rather strange, huge amalgam you see today. In July the stone steps leading up to the cathedral are the site of the opera festival Domstufenfestspiele.

Severikirche   CHURCH HALL

(⊙9am-6pm Mon-Fri, shorter hr in winter) Next to the cathedral, this impressive 1280 five-aisled church hall boasts a stone Madonna (1345), a 15m-high baptismal font (1467) and

the sarcophagus of St Severus, whose remains were brought to Erfurt in 836.

Augustinerkloster   HISTORIC BUILDING

(www.augustinerkloster.de; Augustinerstrasse; tours adult/child €5/3; ⊙tours 10am-5pm Mon-Sat, 11am-3pm Sun) Augustinerkloster, now a nunnery, has a strong pedigree: Martin Luther was a monk here from 1505 to 1511 and, after being ordained in the chapel, read his first Mass here. You can view Luther's cell and an exhibit on the Reformation. The grounds and church are free.

Zitadelle Petersberg   HISTORIC BUILDING

North of the Dom complex and west of Andreasstrasse, many of the city's lesser churches were demolished to erect this impressively tough-looking fortress – hence the reason why Erfurt has so many steeples without churches attached. There is a fascinating series of subterranean tunnels within the thick walls, which can only be seen on a guided tour from the tourist office (enquire there for times and prices).

Alte Synagoge   HISTORIC BUILDING

(Old Synagogue; www.alte-synagoge.erfurt.de; Waagegasse 8; adult/child €5/1.50; ⊙10am-6pm Tue-Sun) One of the oldest Jewish houses of worship in Europe, with roots in the 12th century. After the pogrom of 1349, it was converted into a storehouse and, after later standing empty for decades, has now been restored as a museum.

🛏 Sleeping

Hotel Zumnorde   HOTEL €€

(☎568 00; www.hotel-zumnorde.de; Anger 50/51; r €100-170; ✴🐾) The 50 rooms and suites are modern, quite large and avoid decoration-overload in this fine hotel in the centre. There's a pretty garden hiding behind the noble facade. Enter from Weitergasse. The included breakfast buffet is vast.

Opera Hostel   HOSTEL €

(☎6013 1366; www.opera-hostel.de; Walkmühlstrasse 13; dm €14-18, r €40-80; @🐾) Run with smiles and aplomb, this upmarket hostel in a historic building scores big with wallet-watching global nomads. You'll sleep like a log in bright, spacious rooms, many with an extra sofa for chilling, and make friends in the communal kitchen and on-site lounge-bar.

Hotel am Kaisersaal   HOTEL €€

(☎658 560; www.hotel-am-kaisersaal.de; Futterstrasse 8; r €80-100) The 36 rooms are tip-top and appointed with all expected mod cons in this highly rated hotel. Request a room facing the yard, though, if street noise disturbs. It's close to the Krämerbrücke.

✖ Eating

You'll find interesting and trendy restaurants and cafes along Michaelisstrasse and Marbacher Gasse. Look for *Puffbohnenpfanne* (fried broad beans with roast bacon), an Erfurt speciality. For a quick treat, have a classic Thuringer bratwurst hot off the grill from a **food stand** (Schlösserstrasse; meal €1.80) near a small waterfall.

Zum Güldenen Rade   GERMAN €€
(Marktstrasse 50; mains €10-16) For the best potato dumplings in town, report to this gorgeous patrician town house, which centuries ago housed a tobacco factory. Aside from the classic version with gravy, you can also order them with more esoteric stuffings, such as spinach and salmon, or with black pudding and liver pâté.

Zum Goldenen Schwann   GERMAN €
(Michaelisstrasse 9; mains €5-14) It's not so much the unpretentious traditional food that makes this place popular locally, rather the highly rated unfiltered boutique beer. Good for Thuringian cuisine.

Steinhaus   GASTROPUB €
(Allerheiligenstrasse 20-21; mains €5-10) The ceiling beams may be ancient, but the crowd is intergenerational at this rambling gastro pub/beer garden in the historic Engelsburg. Dips, baguettes, pasta and gratins should keep your tummy filled and your brain balanced.

❶ Information

Tourist office (www.erfurt-tourismus.de)
Benediktsplatz (Benediktsplatz 1; ⊘10am-7pm Mon-Fri, 10am-6pm Sat, 10am-4pm Sun Apr-Dec, 10am-6pm Mon-Sat, 10am-4pm Sun Jan-Mar) Petersberg (⊘11am-6.30pm Apr-Oct, 11am-4pm Nov & Dec)

❶ Getting There & Around

Erfurt's flashy Hauptbahnhof is on a line with frequent services linking Leipzig (€27, one hour) and Weimar (€8, 15 minutes). Hourly ICE/IC services go to Frankfurt (€51, 2¼ hours) and Berlin-Hauptbahnhof (€56, 2½ hours).

Eisenach

Eisenach is home to the Wartburg, the only German castle to be named a Unesco World Heritage site. Composer Johann Sebastian Bach was born here but he plays second fiddle to the awe-inspiring edifice in stone and half-timber high on the hill.

The **tourist office** (www.eisenach.info; Markt 24; ⊘10am-6pm Mon-Fri, 10am-5pm Sat & Sun) can help you find accommodation if your day trip gets extended.

The **Wartburg** (www.wartburg-eisenach. de; tour adult/child €8/5; ⊘tours 8.30am-5pm Mar-Oct, 9am-3.30pm Nov-Feb), parts of which date from the 11th century, is perched high above the town on a wooded hill. It is said to go back to Count Ludwig der Springer (the Jumper); you'll hear the story of how the castle got its name many times, but listen out for how Ludwig got his peculiar moniker as well.

The castle owes its huge popularity to **Martin Luther**, who went into hiding here from 1521 to 1522 after being excommunicated; during this time he translated the entire New Testament from Greek into German, contributing enormously to the development of the written German language. His modest, wood-panelled **study** is part of the guided tour (available in English), which is the only way to view the interior. The **museum** houses the famous Cranach paintings of Luther, and important Christian artefacts from all over Germany. Most of the rooms you'll see are extravagant 19th-century impressions of medieval life rather than original fittings; the re-imagined Great Hall inspired Richard Wagner's opera *Tannhäuser*. Between Easter and October crowds can be horrendous; arrive before 11am.

Frequent trains run to Erfurt (€12 to €15, 30 to 45 minutes) and most continue the short distance to Weimar.

Weimar

🖉03643 / POP 65,000
Neither a monumental town nor a medieval one, Weimar appeals to those whose tastes run to cultural and intellectual pleasures. After all, this is the epicentre of the German Enlightenment, a symbol for all that is good and great in German culture. An entire pantheon of intellectual and creative giants lived and worked here: Goethe, Schiller, Bach, Cranach, Liszt, Nietzsche, Gropius, Herder, Feininger, Kandinsky, Klee...the list goes on.

You'll see reminders of them wherever you go – here, a statue; there, a commemorative plaque decorating a house facade –

plus scores of museums and historic sites. In summer, Weimar's many parks and gardens lend themselves to taking a break from the intellectual onslaught.

Internationally, of course, Weimar is better known as the place where the constitution of the Weimar Republic was drafted after WWI, though there are few reminders of this historical moment. The ghostly ruins of the Buchenwald concentration camp, on the other hand, provide haunting evidence of the terrors of the Nazi regime. The Bauhaus and classical Weimar locations are protected as Unesco World Heritage sites.

◉ Sights

A good place to begin a tour is in front of the neo-Gothic 1841 **Rathaus** on the Markt. Directly east is the **Cranachhaus**, where painter Lucas Cranach the Elder lived for two years before his death in 1553. Just south is the other extreme of local history, the Nazi-era Hotel Elephant.

TOP CHOICE Goethe Sites   HISTORIC SITES

The **Goethe Nationalmuseum** (Frauenplan 1; adult/child €8.50/2.50; ⊙9am-6pm Tue-Sun) focuses not so much on the man but his movement, offering a broad overview of German classicism, from its proponents to its patrons. Admission is included to the adjoining **Goethe Haus**, where such works as *Faust* were written, and which focuses much more on the man himself. He lived here from 1775 until his death in 1832. Goethe's original 1st-floor living quarters are reached via an expansive Italian Renaissance staircase decorated with sculpture and paintings brought back from his travels to Italy. You'll see his dining room, study and the bedroom with his deathbed. Because demand often exceeds capacity, you'll be given a time slot to enter. Once inside, you can stay as long as you want.

Goethes Gartenhaus (adult/child €4.50/2; ⊙10am-6pm Apr-Oct, to 4pm Nov-Mar) was his beloved retreat and stands in the alluring **Park an der Ilm**.

Bauhaus Museum   MUSEUM

(Theaterplatz; adult/child €5/1; ⊙10am-6pm) The Bauhaus School and movement were founded here in 1919 by Walter Gropius, who managed to draw artists such as Kandinsky, Klee, Feininger and Schlemmer as teachers. The exhibition at the museum chronicles the evolution of the group and explains its design innovations, which continue to shape our lives. In 1925 the Bauhaus moved to Des-

sau and in 1932 to Berlin, where it was dissolved by the Nazis the following year. Once the form is in line with its function, a much grander museum is planned for 2013.

Schlossmuseum   MUSEUM

(Burgplatz 4; adult/child €6/2.50; ⊙10am-6pm Tue-Sun Apr-Oct, 10am-4pm Nov-Mar) Housed in the **Stadtschloss**, the former residence of the ducal family of Saxe-Weimar, the museum boasts the **Cranach Gallery**, several portraits by **Albrecht Dürer** and collections of Dutch masters and German romanticists. A €90-million project for a full restoration is now in the works. Note that the courtyard was used by both the Nazis and the communists for interrogating political prisoners.

Other Historic Sites   HISTORIC SITES

Goethe's fellow dramatist Friedrich von Schiller lived in Weimar from 1799 until his early death in 1805; his house is now the **Schiller Museum** (Schillerstrasse 12; adult/child €5/2; ⊙9am-6pm Wed-Mon). The study at the end of the 2nd floor contains the desk where he penned *Wilhelm Tell* and other works.

Liszt Haus (Marienstrasse 17; adult/child €4/1; ⊙10am-6pm Tue-Sun Apr-Oct) is on the western edge of Park an der Ilm. Composer and pianist Franz Liszt lived here in 1848 and again from 1869 to 1886, when he wrote *Hungarian Rhapsody* and *Faust Symphony*. It reopened in 2011 (the official year of Liszt!) after a major rehab.

🛌 Sleeping

The tourist office can help find accommodation, especially at busy times. There are many pensions scattered about the centre, which is where you should stay.

Hotel Anna Amalia   HOTEL €

(⌨495 60; www.hotel-anna-amalia.de; Geleitstrasse 8-12; r €60-90, apt €130-180; 🛜) The Mediterranean look, with its nice, fresh colour scheme, exudes feel-good cheer in this family-run hotel near Goetheplatz. For more panache and elbow room, book one of the apartments, which sleep up to four. Good breakfast buffet.

Hotel Elephant   HOTEL €€€

(⌨8020; www.starwood.de; Markt 19; r from €120-250; @🛜) A true classic, the 1937 marble Bauhaus-Deco splendour of the 99-room, five-star Elephant has seen most of Weimar's great and good come and go. Just to make the point, a golden Thomas Mann looks out over the Markt from a balcony in front.

Weimar

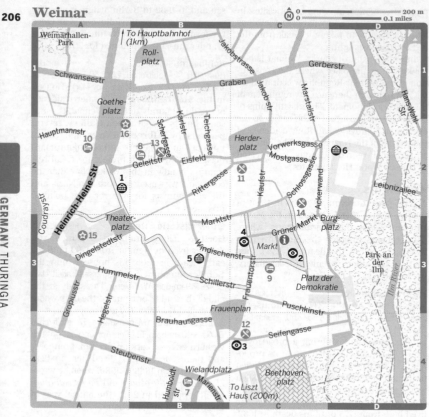

Labyrinth Hostel
HOSTEL €

(☎811 822; www.weimar-hostel.com; Goetheplatz 6; dm €13-21, r €30-50; @🛜) Loads of imagination has gone into this professionally run hostel with artist-designed rooms. In one double, for example, the bed perches on stacks of books, while another comes with a wooden high-platform bed. Bathrooms are shared and so are the kitchen and the lovely rooftop terrace. Dorm 8 has a balcony.

Hotel Amalienhof
HOTEL €€

(☎5490; www.amalienhof-weimar.de; Amalienstrasse 2; r €90-110) This charming 35-room church-affiliated hotel has classy antique furnishings, richly styled rooms that subtly point to history, and a late breakfast buffet for those who take their holidays seriously.

✖ Eating

Jo Hanns
BISTRO €€

(Scherfgasse 1; mains €10-20) The food is satisfying but it's the 130 wines from the Saale-Unstrut region – many served by the glass – that draw people inside the cosy maroon walls or outside on the terrace. Food is inventive, with many specials.

Gasthaus zum Weissen Schwan
GERMAN €€

(Frauentorstrasse 23; mains €11-20; ⏰noon-midnight Wed-Sun) At this venerable inn, you can fill your tummy with Goethe's favourite dish (boiled beef with herb sauce, red beet salad and potatoes), which actually hails from his home town of Frankfurt. The rest of the menu, though, is upmarket Thuringian.

Estragon
CAFE €

(Herderplatz 3; meals €4-8; ⏰lunch) There are days when a bowl of steamy soup feels as warm and embracing as a hug from a good friend. This little soup kitchen turns mostly organic ingredients into delicious flavour combos served in three sizes. It shares digs with a small organic supermarket.

Residenz-Café   CAFE **€€**
(Grüner Markt 4; mains €6-16; ☑) The 'Resi', an enduring Weimar favourites, has something for everyone's taste. The Lovers' Breakfast is €20 for two; the inspired meat and vegetarian dishes may well have you swooning, too.

☆ Entertainment

Studentenclub Kasseturm   VENUE
(www.kasseturm.de; Goetheplatz 10; ☑6pm-late) A classic student club, the Kasseturm is a historic round tower with three floors of live music, DJs, cabaret and €2 beers.

Deutsches Nationaltheater   THEATRE
(German National Theatre; www.nationaltheater -weimar.de; Theaterplatz; ☑closed Jul & Aug) This historic venue shows classic and contemporary plays, plus ballet, opera and classical music.

❶ Information

Stiftung Weimarer Klassik (www.klassik -stiftung.de) The organisation responsible for Weimar's Unesco monuments and museums has an info-filled website.

Tourist information (www.weimar.de; Markt 10; ☑9.30am-7pm Mon-Fri, to 4pm Sat & Sun) Discount cards start at €10.

❶ Getting There & Away

Weimar's Hauptbahnhof is a 20-minute walk from the centre. It's on a line with frequent services linking Leipzig (€24, one hour) and Erfurt (€8, 15 minutes). Two-hourly ICE/IC services go to Berlin-Hauptbahnhof (€53, 2¼ hours).

Most buses serve Goetheplatz, on the northwestern edge of the Altstadt. Don't have time for the 20-minute walk before the next train departs? A cab costs €6.

Buchenwald

This **concentration-camp museum** (www. buchenwald.de; ☑9am-6pm Apr-Oct, 9am-4pm Nov-Mar) and memorial are located just 10km north of Weimar. The contrast between the brutality of the former and the liberal humanism of the latter is hard to comprehend.

Between 1937 and 1945, more than onefifth of the 250,000 people incarcerated here died. The location on the side of a hill only added to the torture of the inmates, as there are sweeping views of the region – an area where people were free while those here died. Various parts of the camp have been restored and there is an essential museum with excellent exhibits. There's also a heart-breaking display of art created by the prisoners. Murals of flowers speak volumes about what was lost. A visit can occupy several hours.

After the war, the Soviets turned the tables but continued the brutality by establishing Special Camp No 2, in which 7000 so-called anticommunists and ex-Nazis were literally worked to death. Their bodies were found after the reunification in mass graves north of the camp, near the Hauptbahnhof.

In Weimar, **Buchenwald Information** (Markt 10; ☑9.30am-6pm Mon-Fri, to 3pm Sat & Sun) is an excellent resource.

To reach the camp, take bus 6 (€1.80, 15 minutes, hourly) from Weimar.

SAXONY-ANHALT

Once the smog-filled heart of GDR industry, Saxony-Anhalt (Sachsen-Anhalt) isn't on everyone's must-visit list. In fact, while the landscape is looking much greener these days, the flow of human traffic is mainly in an outbound direction, as many young people head west in search of jobs.

Still, the state has some strong drawcards: this is the home of the Bauhaus legacy and the wonderful bordering landscape of the Harz region.

Magdeburg

📞 0391 / POP 230,000

Something old, something new: Magdeburg is constantly characterised by the juxtaposition of those two. Home to Germany's most ancient cathedral, the city also boasts the last of Austrian architect Friedensreich Hundertwasser's bonkers buildings and is a model of GDR-style wide boulevards and enormous *Plattenbauten* (concrete tower blocks) apartments. A small enclave of early-20th-century terraces and cobbled streets around Hasselbachplatz also stands out so remarkably that entering and leaving this historic district is like being transported in a time machine.

◉ Sights

Magdeburg is most famous for its 13th-century **Dom** (📞 543 2414; Domplatz; admission free; ⊙10am-4pm Mon-Sat, 11.30am-4pm Sun), which is apparently the oldest on German soil. However, the town also has a 21st-century attraction in Friedensreich Hundertwasser's **Green Citadel** (Grüne Zitadelle; 📞 400 9650; www.gruene-zitadelle.de; Breiter Weg 8-10; German tours €6; ⊙information office 10am-6pm, tours 11am, 3pm & 5pm Mon-Fri, hourly 10am-5pm Sat & Sun). The last design by the famous Austrian architect, this apartment and shopping complex was completed in 2005, five years after his death. It evinces all his signature features – irregular windows, free-form walls and golden domes. The building is pink, but derives its name from its natural architecture and grass-covered roof.

The historic area surrounding **Hasselbachplatz** is an attraction in its own right and full of bars, clubs and restaurants.

🛏 Sleeping & Eating

Green Citadel HOTEL €€
(📞 620 780; www.hotel-zitadelle.de; Breiter Weg 9; s €105-135, d €125-145, breakfast €11; @🖥) Fans of Hundertwasser can ponder the architect's penchant for uneven, organic forms in these elegant rooms. The attached cafe (dishes €4 to €5, open 7am to 7pm) is open to the public, serving breakfast and light meals.

DJH Magdeburg HOSTEL €
(📞 532 101; www.jugendherberge.de; Leiterstrasse 10; dm/s/tw €20/30/45, over 27yr extra €3; @) The smart, modern premises, generous space, good facilities and quiet but central location make this a winner.

Liebig INTERNATIONAL €
(📞 555 6754; Liebigstrasse 1-3; ⊙10am-late) Private alcoves and pleated curtains lining the walls create a feeling of warmth and privacy amid this trendy bar-cafe-restaurant. Mediterranean fare, curries and steaks are all served.

Amsterdam ITALIAN €
(📞 662 8680; Olvenstedter Strasse 9; mains €5-13; ⊙10am-1am Sun-Thu, 10am-2am Fri, 3pm-2am Sat; 🖥) There's nothing Dutch about this welcoming bistro, with food ranging from bruschetta and panini to tuna steaks, a dedicated vegetarian selection and sumptuous breakfasts served until 5pm on weekdays and 6pm on Sundays.

ℹ Information

Tourist Information Magdeburg (📞 194 33; www.magdeburg-tourist.de; Ernst-Reuter-Allee 12; ⊙10am-6.30pm Mon-Fri, to 4pm Sat Apr-Oct, 10am-6pm Mon-Fri, to 3pm Sat Nov-Mar)

ℹ Getting There & Away

There are trains to/from Berlin (€24.70, one hour and 40 minutes, hourly), while regular IC and RE trains run to Leipzig (€20.30, 1¼ hours, around every two hours).

Dessau-Rosslau

📞 0340 / POP 89,000

'Less is more' and 'form follows function' – both these dictums were taught in Dessau, home of the influential Bauhaus School. Between 1925 and 1932, some of the century's greatest artists and architects breathed life into the ground-breaking principles of modernism here, among them Walter Gropius, Paul Klee, Wassily Kandinsky and Ludwig Mies Van der Rohe. Their legacy still stands proud, in the immaculate Bauhaus School building, the lecturers' purpose-built homes and other pioneering constructions.

The Bauhaus was born in Weimar in 1919, and it sought brief respite in Berlin (see p178) before being disbanded by the Nazis in 1933. But as the site of the movement's heyday and the 'built manifesto of Bauhaus ideas', Dessau is the true keeper of the flame.

⊙ Sights

Bauhaus founder Walter Gropius considered architecture the ultimate creative expression. So his first realised project, the **Bauhaus Gebäude** (Bauhaus Building; ☑650 8251; www.bauhaus-dessau.de; Gropiusallee 38; exhibition hall adult/concession €5/4, with Meisterhäuser €12/8, tours €4/3; ⊙10am-6pm, German tours 11am & 2pm, extra tours Sat & Sun), is extremely significant. Once home to the Hochschule für Gestaltung (Institute for Design), where the architect and his colleagues taught, today it houses a postgraduate college. You can visit the changing exhibitions and

---

DON'T MISS

BEWITCHING HARZ

The **Harz Mountains** constitute a mini-Alpine region straddling Saxony-Anhalt and Lower Saxony. Here, medieval castles overlook fairy-tale historic towns, while there are caves, mines and numerous hiking trails to explore.

The region's highest – and most famous – mountain is the Brocken, where one-time visitor Johann Wolfgang von Goethe set the 'Walpurgisnacht' chapter of his play *Faust*. His inspiration in turn came from folk tales depicting *Walpurgisnacht*, or *Hexennacht* (witches' night), as an annual witches' coven. Every 30 April to 1 May it's celebrated enthusiastically across the Harz region.

Goslar

Goslar is a truly stunning 1000-year-old city with beautifully preserved half-timbered buildings and an impressive **Markt**. The town's **Kaiserpfalz** is a reconstructed Romanesque 11th-century palace. Just below there's the restored **Domvorhalle**, which displays the 11th-century 'Kaiserstuhl' throne, used by German emperors.

Brocken's summit is an easy day trip from Goslar. Take a bus (810) or train (faster) from Goslar to Bad Harzburg and then a bus (820) to Torfhaus, where the 8km Goetheweg trail begins.

If climbing a mountain is not your thing, a mere wander around town and a stroll along the circumference of town, a green space dotted with bucolic lakes and bits of the old city wall, makes for a fine day.

The **tourist office** (☑05321-780 60; www.goslar.de; Markt 7; ⊙9.15am-6pm Mon-Fri, 9.30am-4pm Sat, to 2pm Sun Apr-Oct, 9.15am-5pm Mon-Fri, 9.30am-2pm Sat Nov-Mar) can help with accommodation, which includes a **DJH Hostel** (☑05321-222 40; www.jugendherberge.de; Rammelsbergerstrasse 25; dm €20.50-23.50) and hotels **Die Tanne** (☑05321-343 90; www.die-tanne.de; Bäringerstrasse 10; s €40-65, d €65-100) and the fancier **Kaiserworth** (☑05321-7090; www.kaiserworth.de; Markt 3; s €80-101, d €122-207, apt €182-252; @). For a special experience, don't miss **Fortezza** (☑05321-4803; Thomasstrasse 2; mains €8-17), a Spanish restaurant ensconced in a 16th-century tower attached to the old city wall.

As well as being serviced by **buses** (www.rbb-bus.de), Goslar is connected by train to Hanover (€15.20, one hour and 10 minutes).

Quedlinburg

The Unesco World Heritage town of Quedlinburg is best known for its spectacular castle district, perched on a 25m-high plateau above its historic half-timbered buildings. Originally established during the reign of Heinrich I (919–36), the present-day Renaissance **Schloss** (palace) dates from the 16th century. Its centrepiece is the restored baroque **Blauer Saal** (Blue Hall).

Contact **Quedlinburg-Tourismus** (☑03946-905 625; www.quedlinburg.de; Markt 2; ⊙9.30am-6.30pm Mon-Fri, to 3pm Sat, to 2pm Sun Apr–mid-Oct, 9.30am-5pm Mon-Fri, to 1pm Sat mid-Oct–Mar) for more information. Lodgings include a **DJH hostel** (☑03946-811 703; www.jugendherberge.de; Neuendorf 28; dm €16.50-19.50, bedding €3) and the hotels **Pension Zum Altstadtwinkel** (☑03946-91 9975; Hohe Strasse 15; s/d/apt €35/66/120; ☎) and **Romantik Hotel Theophano** (☑03946-963 00; www.hoteltheophano.de; Markt 13-14; s/d from €69/79).

There are hourly trains to Magdeburg (from €13.80, one hour and 10 minutes).

wander through a small section. However, taking a tour is best; it gets you into otherwise closed rooms, even if you don't understand German.

Since a key Bauhaus aim was to 'design for living', the three white, concrete **Meisterhäuser** (Master Craftsmen's Houses; www.meisterhaeuser.de; Ebertallee 63-71; admission to all 3 houses adult/concession €5/4, combination ticket with Bauhaus Gebäude €12/8; ⊙10am-6pm Tue-Sun mid-Feb–Oct, to 5pm Nov–mid-Feb) are a fascinating insight into this philosophy and style of living.

🛏 Sleeping & Eating

In Dessau-Rosslau, you really can eat, drink and sleep Bauhaus. For a different diet, investigate the main thoroughfare of Zerbster Strasse.

Bauhaus dorms   HOSTEL €
(☏650 8318; kaatz@bauhaus-dessau.de; Gropiusallee 38; s/d €25/40) Since the Bauhaus school was renovated in 2006, you can really live the modernist dream by hiring the former students' dorms inside.

Hotel-Pension An den 7 Säulen   HOTEL €
(☏619 620; Ebertallee 66; s €47-52, d €65-72) This relaxed pension (with an Ayurvedic spa) has a glass-fronted breakfast room overlooking the Meisterhäuser across the leafy street.

Kornhaus   INTERNATIONAL €€
(☏640 4141; Kornhausstrasse 146; mains €8-15) This is Bauhaus gone a touch upscale on the edge of the Elbe River, where you can lounge on the wide balcony and contemplate the curve of the river and the building all at once.

Bauhaus Klub   BAR
(Gropiusallee 38' mains €3-7) Starting to see a pattern here? The occasional cool dude in black polo-neck jumper and horn-rimmed glasses can be seen among the broad mix of people in this basement bar of the Bauhaus school. In the same building as the Klub, student favourite **Bauhaus Mensa** (☏650 8421; Gropiusallee 38; mains €3-10; ⊙8am-2pm Mon-Fri) offers cheap cafeteria-style meals.

ⓘ Information

Bauhaus Foundation (☏650 8251; www.bauhaus-dessau.de; Gropiusallee 38; ⊙10am-6pm) Offers educational info on, and tours of, Bauhaus buildings, sometimes in English.

Tourist office (☏204 1442, accommodation reservations 220 3003; www.dessau-tourismus.de; Zerbster Strasse 2c; ⊙9am-6pm Mon-Fri, 9am-1pm Sat Apr-Oct, 9am-5pm Mon-Fri, 10am-1pm Sat Nov-Mar)

ⓘ Getting There & Away

RE trains run to Berlin every one to two hours (€21, 1¾ hours). Dessau is equidistant from Leipzig and Magdeburg (both €10.50, 45 minutes to one hour), with frequent services to each.

MECKLENBURG-WESTERN POMERANIA

Mecklenburg-Vorpommern combines historic Hanseatic-era towns like Schwerin, Wismar and Stralsund with holiday areas such as Warnemünde and Rügen Island. It is off the path for many travellers, but in summer it seems like half the country is here, lolling on the sands in some state of undress. Outside of these somewhat mild times (this is a region where the beaches are dotted with large, wicker beach baskets to provide shelter) the intrepid visitor is rewarded with journeys far from the maddening crowds.

Schwerin
☏0385 / POP 95,860
State capital Schwerin has a modest dignity befitting its status. The oldest city in Mecklenburg-Western Pomerania, it has numerous lakes, including one that is the town's centrepiece. Buildings are an interesting mix of 16th- to 19th-century architecture. It's small enough to explore on foot and, if you're on the move, you can see it as part of a half-day break on a train journey. But Schwerin's beauty and charm are invariably infectious, and few people regret spending extra time here.

◉ Sights

Southeast of the Alter Garten, over the causeway on the Burginsel (Burg Island), the striking neo-Gothic **Schloss Schwerin** (☏525 2920; www.schloss-schwerin.de; adult/child €4/2.50; ⊙10am-6pm mid-Apr–mid-Oct, 10am-5pm Tue-Sun mid-Oct–mid-Apr) was built in the mid-1800s around the chapel of a 16th-century ducal castle and is quite rightly the first attraction visitors head to upon arrival. The causeway is overlooked by a statue of **Niklot**, an early Slavic prince, who was defeated by Heinrich der Löwe (Henry the Lion) in 1160. The huge, graphic picture of his death is a highlight of the castle's interior.

You don't get better examples of north German red-brick architecture than the 14th-century Gothic **Dom** (☑565 014; Am Dom 4; ☺11am-2pm Mon-Fri, 11am-4pm Sat, noon-3pm Sun), towering above the Markt. You can climb up to the platform in the 19th-century tower (adult/child €1.50/0.50).

The enormous neoclassical building in the Alter Garten, the **Staatliches Museum** (☑595 80; www.museum-schwerin.de; Alter Garten 3; adult/concession €6/4; ☺10am-6pm Tue-Sun Apr-Oct, 10am-5pm Tue-Sun Nov-Mar), permanently displays old Dutch masters including Rembrandt, Rubens and Brueghel, as well as oils by Lucas Cranach the Elder and collections of more modern works by Marcel Duchamp and Ernst Barlach.

🛏 Sleeping & Eating

Hotel Nordlicht   HOTEL €€
(☑558 150; www.hotel-nordlicht.de; Apothekerstrasse 2; s/d/apt from €54/82/86; ⊛☎) Simple furnishings, helpful staff, spotless rooms (some with balconies) and walls covered with interesting old photos of Schwerin round out this excellent budget choice in a quiet part of town.

Hotel Niederländischer Hof   HOTEL €€
(☑591 100; www.niederlaendischer-hof.de; Karl-Marx-Strasse 12-13; s €87-124, d €125-170 incl breakfast; ☎) You can't beat the Pfaffenteich location or the elegant rooms and marble bathrooms at this exceedingly classy hotel. There's even a library with an open fire for those contemplative German winters.

DJH Hostel   HOSTEL €
(☑326 0006; www.jugendherberge.de; Waldschulweg 3; dm under/over 26yr incl breakfast €17.50/20.50) This basic hostel is about 4km south of the city centre, just opposite the zoo. Take tram 1 to Marienplatz, then bus 14 to the last stop, Jugendherberge.

Friedrich's   FRENCH €
(☑555 473; Friedrichstrasse 2; mains €8-15; ☑) Overlooking the Pfaffenteich, this Parisian-style cafe has a casual atmosphere, a classy, friendly bar area and an uncomplicated selection of salads, fish, grills and vegetarian dishes. The waterfront terrace is divine in warm weather.

Historisches Weinhaus Wöhler   GERMAN €€
(☑555 830; www.weinhaus-woehler.com; Puschkinstrasse 26; mains €9-21) Stained-glass windows tell you that this place is indeed historic. Open since 1895, the building dates to the 18th century. The restaurant offers classic

Mecklenburg specialities and there's even a fun tapas bar for a quick non-Germanic bite. The beer garden is alluring and you can sleep it off in the comfortable rooms (€85 to €160) upstairs.

ℹ Information

Schwerin-Information (☑592 5212; www.schwerin.de; Markt 14; ☺9am-7pm Mon-Fri, 10am-6pm Sat & Sun Apr-Oct, 9am-6pm Mon-Fri, 10am-4pm Sat & Sun Nov-Mar)

ℹ Getting There & Away

Schwerin is on the line linking Hamburg (€21.70 to €25, 50 minutes to 1¼ hours) with Stralsund (€31.70, two hours). Services to Rostock (€14.90 to €18.80, one hour) are frequent, as are those to Wismar (€6.90, 30 minutes). There are RE trains to Berlin-Hauptbahnhof (€31.70, 2¼ hours).

Wismar

☑03841 / POP 45,200

Wismar, a Hanseatic gem that's fast being discovered, joined the powerful trading league in the 13th century – the first town east of Lübeck to do so. For centuries it was in and out of Swedish control – hence the 'Swedish heads' dotted across town. Quieter than Rostock or Stralsund, Wismar can fill up with visitors quickly in high season; it's definitely worth an overnight stay, and is also the gateway to **Poel Island**, a lovely little piece of green to the north.

◉ Sights & Activities

The old harbour, **Alter Hafen**, with old boats swaying in the breeze, evokes trading days from centuries ago. Featured in the 1922 film *Nosferatu*, it is still a focal point of activity in Wismar. **Clermont Reederei** (☑224 646; www.reederei-clermont.de; adult/child €8/4) operates hour-long harbour cruises five times daily from May to September, four times daily in April and four times on Saturday and Sunday in March, leaving from Alter Hafen. Daily boats also go to Poel Island (adult return €14, May to September). Various other companies run tours on historic ships during summer; contact the **harbour** (☑389 082; www.alterhafenwismar.de, in German) for details.

Running through town, the **Grube** (channel) is the last artificial medieval waterway in the north and should be a part of any stroll through the historic quarter. The **Wasserkunst** is a 12-sided well from

1602 that anchors a corner of the attractive Markt.

The town's historical museum, **Schab-bellhaus** (⌨282 350; www.schabbellhaus. de; Schweinsbrücke 8; adult/child €2/1, free Fri; ☺10am-8pm Tue-Sun May-Oct, to 5pm Nov-Apr), has taken over a former Renaissance brewery (1571), just south of the St-Nikolai-Kirche across the canal. The museum's pride and joy is the large 16th-century tapestry *Die Königin von Saba vor König Salomon* (The Queen of Sheba before King Solomon).

Wismar was a target for British and American bombers just weeks before the end of WWII. Of the three great red-brick churches that once rose above the rooftops, only **St-Nikolai-Kirche** (St-Nikolai-Kirchhof; admission €1; ☺8am-8pm May-Sep, 10am-6pm Apr & Oct, 11am-4pm Nov-Mar), built from 1381 to 1487, remains intact. Massive **St-Georgen-Kirche** (admission by donation; ☺10am-8pm Jul & Aug, 10am-6pm Mar-Jun & Sep-Dec, 10am-6pm Mon-Sat, 10am-4pm Sun Jan & Feb) has been extensively renovated for combined use as a church, concert hall and exhibition space. In 1945 a freezing populace was driven to burn what was left of the church's beautiful wooden statue of St George and the dragon. The great brick **steeple** (☺10am-8pm Apr-Oct), built in 1339, of the 13th-century **St-Marien-Kirche**, towers above the city.

🛏 Sleeping & Eating

Along the Alter Hafen, seafood (including delicious fish sandwiches from as little as €2) is sold directly from a handful of bobbing boats. Most are open 9am to 6pm daily, and from 6am on Saturday during Wismar's weekly fish market.

Bio Hotel Reingard   HOTEL €€
(⌨284 972; www.reingard.de; Weberstrasse 18; s €58-62, d €86-88 incl breakfast) Wismar's most charming place to stay is this boutique hotel with its handful of artistic rooms, leafy little garden and gourmet *bio* (organic) restaurant (menus from €30 for two people; by arrangement). There's even a small adjoining **museum** containing the owner's 300,000-strong collection of buttons and vintage belt buckles.

Pension Chez Fasan   HOTEL €
(⌨213 425; www.unterkunft-pension-wismar.de; Bademutterstrasse 20a; s without bathroom €21, s/d with bathroom €24/45, breakfast €5) This is the best budget deal in town. Rooms in the three-building complex come with satellite TV and a great central location.

DJH Hostel Wismar   HOSTEL €
(⌨32 680; www.jugendherberge.de; Juri Gagarin Ring 30a; dm incl breakfast & linen under/over 26yr €20.50/25.10) Popular with large groups, this hostel is simple and clean. It's a 15-minute walk from the train station; alternatively take bus D to Philip Müller Strasse.

Zur Reblaus Wein- und Kaffeestube   CAFE €
(www.zur-reblaus.de; Neustadt 9; snacks €4-9; ☺2-10pm May-Sep, closed Sun Oct-Apr) A snug wine bar and cafe where locals come for a drink or a *Kaffeeklatsch* (chat over coffee); try the house speciality pie, the *Trummertorte*. Rooms are also available upstairs for the attached pension (single/double from €38/55).

Brauhaus am Lohberg   SEAFOOD €€
(Kleine Hohe Strasse 15; mains €7-15) Spread over a series of warehouses dating back to the 16th century, this popular spot is honouring Wismar's long tradition of brewing by once again making its own beer. There's a good seafood menu.

ℹ Information

In the Altstadt you'll find **tourist information** (⌨251 3025; www.wismar.de; Am Markt 11; ☺9am-6pm Mar-Dec, 9am-6pm Mon-Sat, 10am-4pm Sun Jan & Feb).

ℹ Getting There & Away

Trains travel the coastal branch lines to Rostock (€10, 70 minutes, hourly) and Schwerin (€6.80, 30 minutes, hourly).

Rostock & Warnemünde

⌨0381 / POP 200,400
Rostock, the largest city in sparsely populated northeastern Germany, is a major Baltic port and shipbuilding centre. Its chief suburb – and chief attraction – is Warnemünde, 12km north of the centre. Counted among eastern Germany's most popular beach resorts, it's hard to see it as a small fishing village these days, but the boats still bring in their catches, and some charming streets and buildings persist amid the tourist clutter.

First mentioned in 1161 as a Danish settlement, Rostock began taking shape as a German fishing village around 1200. In the 14th and 15th centuries, it was an important Hanseatic trading city; parts of the city centre, especially along Kröpeliner Strasse, retain the flavour of this period.

◉ Sights

Lined with 15th- and 16th-century burghers' houses, Kröpeliner Strasse is a lively, cobbled pedestrian street that runs west from Neuer Markt to the **Kröpeliner Tor** (📷454 177; adult/child €2/1; ⊙10am-6pm), a 55m-high tower you can climb.

The **Kloster Zum Heiligen Kreuz** (Holy Cross Convent; Klosterhof 18) was established in 1270 by Queen Margrethe I of Denmark; today it houses the **Cultural History Museum** (📷203 590; admission free; ⊙10am-6pm Tue-Sun), with an excellent and varied collection, including large numbers of everyday items used by locals over the centuries.

Rostock's pride and joy, the **Marienkirche** (📷453 325; Am Ziegenmarkt; admission by donation; ⊙10am-6pm Mon-Sat, 11.15am-5pm Sun May-Sep, 10am-noon & 2-4pm Mon-Sat, 11.15am-noon Sun Oct-Apr), built in 1290, was the only one of Rostock's four main churches to survive WWII unscathed. The long north–south transept was added after the ceiling collapsed in 1398. Notable features include the 12m-high astrological clock (1470–72) and the Gothic bronze baptismal font (1290).

Warnemünde, the lively seafront to the north lined with hotels and restaurants, is where the tourists congregate. Its broad, sandy beach stretches west from the **lighthouse** (1898) and the **Teepott** exhibition centre, and is chock-a-block with bathers on hot summer days.

🛏 Sleeping

Jellyfish Hostel   HOSTEL €
(📷444 3858; www.jellyfish-hostel.com; Beginenberg 25, Rostock; dm/s/d per person from €15/31/25; @📶) Set in a landmark building, this palatial place features rooms with moulded ceilings and lots of space. The buffet breakfast is €4.

Pension Zum Steuermann   HOTEL €
(📷511 68; www.pension-zum-steuermann.de; Alexandrinenstrasse 57, Warnemünde; apt €45-120) These cheerful blue-and-white former fishermen's houses are tucked away down a side street. They have a relaxed, beachy feel and are popular with families.

Hotel Kleine Sonne   HOTEL €€
(📷497 3153; www.die-kleine-sonne.de; Steinstrasse 7; s €52-82, d €104-164, breakfast €11; @) This lovely place lives up to its name with sunny yellow and red detailing, and semaphore prints by Berlin artist Nils Ausländer. If you're cycling, you can get two nights' accommodation, a packed lunch, three-course dinner, cycling itineraries and bike storage for €159/238 per single/double. All guests have free use of the wellness centre at the Steigenberger Hotel Sonne.

DJH hostel Warnemünde   HOSTEL €
(📷548 170; www.jugendherbergen-mv.de; Parkstrasse 47; dm under/over 26yr €25.20/30.80; @📶) This fantastic hostel is in a converted weather station just minutes from the western end of the Warnemünde beach, near Diedrichshagen. The tower rooms are particularly popular with families, who tend to dominate in the July and August holiday period.

Hotel Verdi   HOTEL €
(📷252 240; www.hotel-verdi.de; Wollenweberstrasse 28; s/d/studio/apt incl breakfast from €59/79/84/119; 📶) Opening to an umbrella-shaded, timber-decked terrace is this sparkling little hotel just near the Petrikirche and Alter Markt, with a handful of attractively decorated rooms, larger studios with kitchenettes, and a ground-floor holiday apartment sleeping up to four people. All are great value.

Steigenberger Hotel Sonne   HOTEL €€€
(📷497 30; www.hotel-sonne-rostock.de; Neuer Markt 2; s/d from €79/158, breakfast €17; @📶) It's hard for the interior to compete with the ornate facade at this hotel – a confection of stepped gables and iron lacework topped with a golden 'sun'. However, the rooms do their best in tones of brown, red and yellow, and there's a clutch of classy restaurants.

🍴 Eating

Excellent fish and wurst stalls set up shop on Rostock's Neuer Markt and Warnemünde's harbour most mornings.

Weineckeck Krahnstöver   PUB FARE €€
(Grosse Wasser Strasse 30; mains €10-18; ⊙closed Sun) One side is a wine bar with a pub feel, the other side a proper restaurant: both sides have a loyal local following and offer a lengthy list of wines that you sip in the warm, old-fashioned atmosphere between dark wood walls.

Café Kloster   INTERNATIONAL €€
(📷375 7950; Klosterhof 6; mains €9-15; ⊙closed Sun; 🍴) This sweet bistro offers soups, salads and plenty of veggie fare, with seating available in its art-filled interior or under a massive pear tree in its hidden garden.

Krahnstöver Likörfabrik WINE BAR €

(Grosse Wasserstrasse 30/Grubenstrasse 1; mains €6-12) This late-15th-century former liquor factory is an excellent example of late Gothic architecture. The wine bar has an inventive menu; around the corner, the Kneipe seems as old as the building and dishes up hearty fare.

Zur Kogge GERMAN €

(☑493 4493; Wokrenterstrasse 27; mains €9-17) Touristy but still unmissable, this is Rostock's oldest restaurant. Cosy wooden booths are lined with stained-glass decorations of Hanseatic coats of arms and monster fish threatening sailing ships, while life preservers hang from the walls. The menu is dominated by fish, but you can enjoy coffee and cake between meal times if you want to avoid the crowds.

ℹ Information

Tourist information (☑381 2222; www.rostock.de; Neuer Markt 3; ⊙10am-7pm Mon-Fri, 10am-4pm Sat & Sun Jun-Aug, 10am-6pm Mon-Fri, 10am-4pm Sat & Sun May & Sep, 10am-6pm Mon-Fri, 10am-3pm Sat Oct-Apr)

Warnemünde-Information (☑548 000; www.warnemuende.de; Am Strom 59; ⊙9am-6pm Mon-Fri, 10am-4pm Sat & Sun Mar-Oct, 10am-5pm Mon-Fri, 10am-3pm Sat Nov-Feb)

ℹ Getting There & Around

Rostock is on the busy **train** line that links Hamburg (€29.90 to €38, 1¾ to 2½ hours) to Stralsund (€12.80, one hour). Services to/from Schwerin (€14.70 to €18.50, one hour) are frequent, as is the branch line to Wismar (€10, 70 minutes, hourly). There are RE trains to Berlin-Hauptbahnhof (€34.80, 2½ to 2¾ hours, every two hours).

Ferries sail to/from Denmark, Sweden, Latvia and Finland. Boats depart from the **Übersee-hafen** (overseas seaport; www.rostock-port.de), which is on the east side of the Warnow. Take tram 1, 2, 3 or 4 to Dierkower Kreuz (tram 3 or 4 from the Hauptbahnhof), then change for bus 49 to Seehafen. There is an S-Bahn to Seehafen, but it's a 20-minute walk from the station to the piers (not fun if you're dragging heavy bags).

There are frequent **S-Bahn** services linking Rostock to Warnemünde (€1.70, 20 minutes). In Rostock, tram lines 3, 4 and 6 link the train station with the centre. The area lends itself to bike touring. **Radstation** (☑240 1153; www.radstation-rostock.de; Hauptbahnhof; per day from €7; ⊙10am-6pm Mon-Fri, to 1pm Sat) is convenient for rentals.

Stralsund

☑03831 / POP 57,600

You instantly know you're next to the sea here. Possessing an unmistakable medieval profile, Stralsund was the second-most powerful member of the medieval Hanseatic League, after Lübeck. In 1648 Stralsund, Rügen Island and Pomerania came under the control of the Swedes – who had helped in their defence. The city remained Swedish until 1815, when it was incorporated into Prussia.

An attractive town of imposing churches and elegant town houses, Stralsund boasts more examples of classic red-brick Gothic gabled architecture than almost anywhere else in northern Germany. It has some excellent sights, including the fantastic new aquarium Ozeaneum. Stralsund is a great place to visit if you want to get a feel for Baltic culture.

⦿ Sights

Alter Markt HISTORIC AREA

One of the two structures dominating the Alter Markt is the gorgeous 14th-century **Rathaus**, with its late-Gothic decorative facade. The upper portion has slender copper turrets and gables that have openings to prevent strong winds from knocking over the facade. This ornate design was Stralsund's answer to its rival city, Lübeck, which has a similar town hall. The sky-lit gallery overhanging the vaulted walkway is held aloft by shiny black pillars on carved and painted bases.

Exit through the eastern walkway to the main portal of the other dominant presence in the Alter Markt, the 1270 **Nikolaikirche** (☑299 799; ⊙10am-4pm Mon-Sat, 2-4pm Sun). Modelled after the Marienkirche in Lübeck (p291) and bearing a fleeting resemblance to Notre Dame, it's filled with art treasures. Also worth a closer look are the **high altar** (1470), 6.7m wide and 4.2m tall, showing Jesus' entire life, and the mostly inaccurate **astronomical clock** (1394), allegedly the oldest in the world.

Neuer Markt HISTORIC AREA

The Neuer Markt is dominated by the massive 14th-century **Marienkirche** (☑298 965; ⊙10am-5pm), another superb example of north German red-brick construction. Check out the huge **F Stellwagen organ** (1659), festooned with music-making cherubs. You can climb the steep wooden steps up the

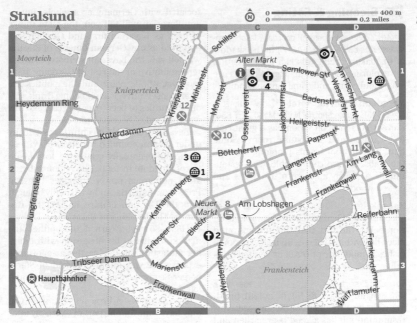

tower (adult/concession €4/2) for a sweeping view of the town and Rügen Island.

Meeresmuseum   MUSEUM
(Oceanographic Museum; ☎265 010; www.meeres museum.de; Katharinenberg 14-20; adult/child €7.50/5, combination ticket incl Ozeaneum adult/child €18/11; ⏰10am-6pm Jun-Sep, 10am-5pm Oct-May) North of Neuer Markt, a 13th-century convent church is now a museum that showcases displays on local sea life and the people who catch it.

Ozeaneum   AQUARIUM
(☎265 0610; www.ozeaneum.de; Hafeninsel Stralsund; adult/child €14/8, combination ticket incl Meeresmuseum adult/child €18/11; ⏰9.30am-9pm Jun-Sep, 9.30am-7pm Oct-May) The massive white structure on the harbour is an aquarium that takes you on a spectacular journey through the ecosystems of the Baltic, the North Sea and the North Atlantic.

Kulturhistorisches Museum   MUSEUM
(☎287 90; Mönchstrasse 25-27; adult/child €4/2; ⏰10am-5pm Tue-Sun) Stralsund's cultural history museum has a large historical collection, paintings by Caspar David Friedrich and Philipp Otto Runge, faience (tin-glazed earthenware), playing cards and Gothic altars, as well as various outlying exhibitions in restored houses.

👉 Tours

Weisse Flotte (☎0180-321 2120; www.weisse -flotte.com; Fährstrasse 16; one way adult/child €2.50/1.30; ⏰May-Oct) runs seven ferries daily to the scenic fishing village of Altefähr, on Rügen Island. One-hour **harbour cruises** (adult/child €7/4) also depart four times daily during summer months.

🍴 Sleeping & Eating

Pension Cobi   PENSION €
(☎278 288; www.pension-cobi.de; Jakobiturmstrasse 15; s €35-45, d €50-70; ☎) In the shadow of the Jakobikirche, this is a great location for exploring the Altstadt. The 14 rooms are smart and clean, and some have balconies.

Norddeutscher Hof Hotel   HOTEL €
(☎293 161; www.nd-hof.de; Neuer Markt 22; r €50-100; ☎) This maroon vision has a great central location and 13 historic rooms. Some have ancient roof beams plunging through the walls. All are comfortable. The restaurant is a stylish melange of tin walls and carved wood.

Hansekeller   GERMAN €€
(Mönchstrasse 48; mains €8-14) A simple exterior belies the fact that this underground place lies within. It serves up hearty regional dishes at moderate prices in its vaulted brick cellar.

Torschliesserhaus   PUB FARE €
(Am Kütertor 1; mains €8-16) In a 1281 building right by a fragment of the city wall, this restaurant-pub has a good beer garden and tasty local fare heavy on seafood.

Tiffany   INTERNATIONAL €
(Am Langenwall; buffet €7; ⊙9am-6pm Tue-Sun) This loosely themed breakfast bar is simply fantastic, darling.

Finally, there's a great stand (sausages €1.80) with grilled sausages at the **morning farmers market** (8am to 1pm Monday to Saturday) on Neuer Markt, and boats in the harbour sell just-out-of-the-ocean seafood sandwiches (€3 to €5).

ℹ️ Information

Tourismuszentrale (☎246 90; www.stralsund tourismus.de; Alter Markt 9; ⊙10am-6pm Mon-Fri, to 4pm Sat & Sun May-Oct, 10am-5pm Mon-Fri, to 4pm Sat Nov-Apr)

ℹ️ Getting There & Away

Stralsund is on the line to Hamburg (€48, three hours) via Rostock (€12.80, one hour) and Schwerin (€32, two hours). Direct trains go to Berlin (from €36, 2¾ to 3¼ hours).

BAVARIA

Bavaria (Bayern) can seem like every German stereotype rolled into one. Lederhosen, beer halls, oompah bands and romantic castles are just some Bavarian clichés associated with Germany as a whole. But as any Bavarian will tell you, the state thinks of itself as Bavarian first and German second. And as any German outside of Bavaria will tell you, the Bavarian stereotypes aren't representative of the rest of Germany. It's a mostly Catholic place and the politics are often conservative, even if people drink serious quantities of beer (over 90 years ago this was the land of beer-hall putsches).

Bavaria was ruled for centuries as a duchy under the line founded by Otto I of Wittelsbach, and eventually graduated to the status of kingdom in 1806. The region suffered amid numerous power struggles between Prussia and Austria, and was finally brought into the German empire in 1871 by Bismarck. The last king of Bavaria was Ludwig II (1845–86), who earned the epithet 'the mad king' due to his obsession with building fantastic fairy-tale castles at enormous expense. He was found drowned in Starnberger See in suspicious circumstances and left no heirs.

Bavaria draws visitors year-round. If you only have time for one part of Germany after Berlin, this is it. Munich, the capital, is the heart and soul. The Bavarian Alps, Nuremberg and the medieval towns on the Romantic Road are other important attractions.

Munich

☎089 / POP 1.35 MILLION

Pulsing with prosperity and *Gemütlichkeit* (cosiness), Munich (München) revels in its own contradictions. Folklore and age-old traditions exist side by side with sleek BMWs, designer boutiques and high-powered industry. Its museums include world-class collections of artistic masterpieces, and its music and cultural scenes rival Berlin.

Despite all its sophistication, Munich retains a touch of provincialism that visitors find charming. The people's attitude is one of live-and-let-live, and Müncheners will be the first to admit that their 'metropolis' is little more than a *Weltdorf*, a world village. During Oktoberfest visitors descend on the Bavarian capital in their zillions to raise a glass to this fascinating city.

History

Originally settled by monks from the Benedictine monastery at Tegernsee in the 7th and 8th century, the city itself wasn't founded until 1158 by Heinrich der Löwe. In 1255 Munich became the home for the Wittelsbach dukes,

RÜGEN ISLAND

Germany's largest island, Rügen is at times hectic, relaxed, windblown and naked – fitting, perhaps, since the resort tradition here reflects all aspects of Germany's recent past. In the 19th century, luminaries such as Einstein, Bismarck and Thomas Mann came to unwind in the fashionable coastal resorts. Later both Nazi and GDR regimes made Rügen the holiday choice for dedicated comrades.

The island's highest point is the 117m **Königsstuhl** (king's throne), the chalk cliffs of which tower above the sea. Much of Rügen and its surrounding waters are either national park or protected nature reserves, and the **Bodden** inlet area is a bird refuge popular with birdwatchers.

Other popular tourist destinations are **Jagdschloss Granitz** (1834), a castle surrounded by lush forest, and **Prora**, the location of a 2km-long workers' retreat built by Hitler before the war. It is a surreal sight and is home to several museums, including the **Dokumentationszentrum Prora** (☎03839-313 991; www.proradok.de; Objektstrasse 1; adult/concession €5/4; ⊗9.30am-7.30pm Jun-Aug, 10am-6pm Mar-May, Sep & Oct, 11am-4pm Nov-Feb), which looks at the huge construction's history.

Tourismus Rügen (☎03838-807 70; www.ruegen.de; Am Markt 4, Bergen; ⊗8am-6pm Mon-Fri) and **Tourismusgesellschaft Binz** (☎03838-134 60; www.binz.de; Zeppelinstrasse 7, Binz; ⊗10am-6pm Mon-Fri) are your best bets for information.

The main resort town is Binz in eastern Rügen. Trains from Stralsund arrive here (€12, 45 minutes, every two hours), but to get around the island and really appreciate it, a car is vital.

princes and kings who ruled for the next 700 years. The city suffered through the Black Plague, first in 1348 and again in 1623, when two-thirds of the population died.

Munich has been the capital of Bavaria since 1503, but didn't really achieve prominence until the 19th century under the guiding hand of Ludwig I. Ludwig became more conservative and repressive, and carried on an affair with the actress and dancer Lola Montez. He was forced to abdicate in favour of his son, Maximilian II, who started a building renaissance, promoting science, industry and education.

At the turn of the last century there were 500,000 residents, but in the aftermath of WWI Munich became a hotbed of right-wing political ferment. Hitler staged a failed coup attempt in Munich in 1923, but the National Socialists seized power only a decade later. WWII brought bombing and more than 6000 civilian deaths until American forces entered the city in 1945. Then, in 1972, the Munich Olympics turned disastrous when 11 Israeli athletes were murdered.

Today it is the centre of major German industries such as Siemens and BMW.

⊙ Sights

Munich is a sprawling metropolis. Wandering the centre is rewarding but you'll need public transport to get out to some of the key sights like the palaces.

Palaces

Residenz   PALACE

(Max-Joseph-Platz 3) Bavarian rulers lived in this vast pile from 1385 to 1918. Apart from the palace itself, the **Residenzmuseum** (www.residenz-muenchen.de; adult/child €6/free; ⊗9am-6pm Apr–mid-Oct, 10am-5pm mid-Oct–Mar) has an extraordinary array of 100 rooms containing no end of treasures and artworks. The entrance is on Max-Joseph-Platz. In the same building, the **Schatzkammer** (Treasure Chamber; adult/child €6/free) exhibits jewels, crowns and ornate gold.

Schloss Nymphenburg   PALACE

(www.schloesser.bayern.de; adult/child €5/4; ⊗9am-6pm Apr–mid-Oct, 10am-4pm mid-Oct–Mar) This was the royal family's very impressive summer home. Parts date from 17th century. The surrounding park deserves a long, regal stroll. All this splendour is northwest of the city centre, via tram 17 from the Hauptbahnhof.

Art Museums

Alte Pinakothek   ART MUSEUM

(www.pinakothek.de; Barer Strasse 27; adult/child €7/5, Sun €1; ⊗10am-8pm Tue, to 6pm Wed-Sun) A stroll northeast of the centre, this treasure

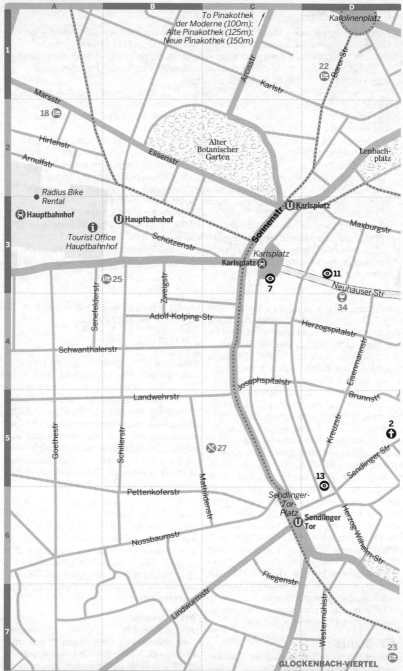

GERMANY BAVARIA

To Pinakothek
der Moderne (100m);
Alte Pinakothek (125m);
Neue Pinakothek (150m)

Karolinenplatz

Marsstr

18

Hirtenstr

Arnulfstr

Elisenstr

Alter
Botanischer
Garten

Arcisstr

Karlstr

Beren-Str

22

Lenbach-
platz

Radius Bike
Rental

Hauptbahnhof

Hauptbahnhof

Tourist Office
Hauptbahnhof

Schützenstr

Sonnenstr

Karlsplatz

Maxburgstr

Karlsplatz

Karlsplatz

Senefelderstr

25

Zweigstr

Adolf-Kolping-Str

7

11

Neuhauser Str

34

Herzogspitalstr

Schwanthalerstr

Josephspitalstr

Eisenmannstr

Brunnstr

Goethestr

Schillerstr

Landwehrstr

27

2

Pettenkoferstr

Mathildenstr

13

Kreuzstr

Sendlinger Str

Nussbaumstr

Sendlinger-
Tor-
Platz

Sendlinger
Tor

Herzog-Wilhelm-Str

Fliegenstr

Lindwurmstr

Westermühlstr

23

GLOCKENBACH-VIERTEL

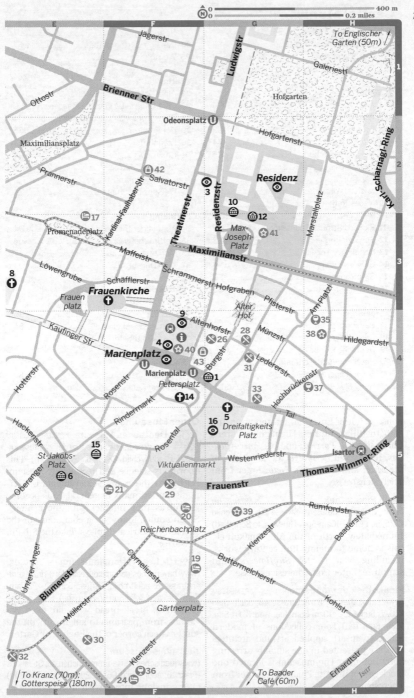

400 m
0.2 miles

To Englischer
Garten (50m)

Jägerstr

Galeriestr

Brienner Str

Ottostr

Hofgarten

Maximiliansplatz

Odeonsplatz U

Hofgartenstr

Prannerstr

Residenz

42

Salvatorstr

3

17

10

12

Promenadeplatz

Maffeistr

Max-
Joseph-
Platz

41

Löwengrube

Maximilianstr

8

Schäfflerstr

Schrammerstr Hofgraben

Frauen
platz

Frauenkirche

Alter
Hof

Pfisterstr

Am Platzl

Kaufinger Str

9

Altenhofstr

28

35

4

26

38

40

Marienplatz

43

31

Marienplatz U
Marienplatz U

Petersplatz

1

33

14

37

5

16

Dreifaltigkeits
Platz

15

St-Jakobs-
Platz

Viktualienmarkt

Westenriederstr

Isartor

6

Thomas-Wimmer-Ring

21

29

Frauenstr

Rumfordstr

20

39

Reichenbachplatz

Klenzestr

Baaderstr

19

Buttermelcherstr

Gärtnerplatz

Kohlstr

Blumenstr

30

32

36

24

To Kranz (70m);
Götterspeise (180m)

To Baader
Café (60m)

Erhardtstr

Isar

GERMANY MUNICH

Central Munich

house is full of European masters from the 14th to 18th centuries. Highlights: Dürer's Christ-like *Self Portrait* and his *Four Apostles,* Rogier van der Weyden's *Adoration of the Magi* and Botticelli's *Pietà.* Enter from Theresienstrasse.

Neue Pinakothek
ART MUSEUM

(www.pinakothek.de; Barer Strasse 29; adult/child €7/5, Sun €1; ☉10am-5pm Thu-Mon, to 8pm Wed) Immediately north of the Alte Pinakothek, this is home to mainly 19th-century works, including Van Gogh's *Sunflowers,* and sculpture. Enter from Theresienstrasse.

Pinakothek der Moderne
ART MUSEUM

(www.pinakothek.de; Barer Strasse 40; adult/child €10/7, Sun €1; ☉10am-6pm Tue, Wed & Fri-Sun, 10am-8pm Thu) Four collections of modern art, graphic art, applied art and architecture are presented in one suitably arresting 2002 building. The museum is located one block east of the Alte Pinakothek; enter from Theresienstrasse.

Other Museums

⟨TOP CHOICE⟩ Deutsches Museum
SCIENCE MUSEUM

(www.deutsches-museum.de; Museuminsel 1; adult/child €8.50/3; ☉9am-5pm) This enormous science and technology museum celebrates the many achievements of Germans, and humans in general. Kids become gleeful as they interact with the exhibits. So do adults. Many get a charge out of the shocking electrical displays. Take the S-Bahn to Isartor.

Bayerisches Nationalmuseum
MUSEUM

(www.bayerisches-nationalmuseum.de; Prinzregentenstrasse 3; adult/child €5/free, Sun €1; ☉10am-5pm Tue, Wed & Fri-Sun, to 8pm Thu) East of the Hofgarten, break bread with old, dead Bavarians, from peasants to knights. It's off the southeastern corner of the Englischer Garten.

Jüdisches Museum
MUSEUM

(www.juedisches-museum-muenchen.de; St-Jakobs-Platz 16; adult/child €6/3; ☉10am-6pm Tue-Sun) Offers insight into Jewish history, life and culture in Munich. The Nazi era is dealt with, but the accent of this modern museum is clearly on contemporary Jewish culture.

Stadtmuseum
MUSEUM
(www.stadtmuseum-online.de; St-Jakobs-Platz 1; adult/child €4/2, Sun free; ⏰10am-6pm Tue-Sun) You went in for an hour and spent two; this superbly redone city museum puts the foam on the stein of Munich history – good and bad. Multimedia displays bring Munich's many characters to life.

BMW Museum
CAR MUSEUM
(www.bmw-welt.de; adult/child €12/6; ⏰10am-6pm Tue-Sun) North of the city, auto-fetishists get stoked at this bowl-shaped temple adjacent to BMW's headquarters and factory. Exhibits are extensive and on weekdays you can tour the factory. Take the U3 to Olympiazentrum.

Parks & Gardens

TOP CHOICE **Englischer Garten**
PARK
One of the largest city parks in Europe, this grand park is a great place for strolling, especially along the Schwabinger Bach. In summer nude sunbathing is the rule rather than the exception. It's not unusual for hundreds of naked people to be in the park during a normal business day, with their clothing stacked primly on the grass. If they're not doing this, they're probably drinking merrily at one of the park's three beer gardens (see the boxed text, p225).

Botanical Gardens
GARDEN
(www.botmuc.de; Menzinger Strasse 65; adult/child €4/free; ⏰varies with season, generally 9am-6pm) The gorgeous municipal gardens are two stops past Schloss Nymphenburg on tram 17.

Olympia Park Complex
PARK
The glorious grounds of the 1972 Olympics continue to thrill today. If you like heights, take a ride up the lift of the 290m **Olympiaturm** (Olympic Tower; adult/child €4.50/3; ⏰9am-midnight). And if you fancy a swim, the **Olympic Pool Complex** (admission €4; ⏰7am-11pm) will have you feeling like Mark Spitz while you imagine seven gold medals around your neck – or just work on your breaststroke. Take the U3 to Olympia Zentrum.

A MUNICH STROLL

The pivotal **Marienplatz** is a good starting point for a tour of Munich's heart. Dominating the square is the towering neo-Gothic **Neues Rathaus** (new town hall), with its ever-dancing **Glockenspiel** (carillon), which performs at 11am and noon (also at 5pm from March to October), bringing the square to an expectant standstill (note the fate of the Austrian knight...). Two important churches are on this square: the baroque star **St Peterskirche** (Rindermarkt 1; church free, tower adult/child €1.50/1; ⏰9am-7pm Apr-Oct, to 6pm Nov-Mar) and, behind the **Altes Rathaus**, the often-forgotten **Heiliggeistkirche** (Tal 77; ⏰7am-6pm).

Walk north along the genteel Theatinerstrasse, a staid street today with a notorious past. On November 9, 1923, Hitler and his followers marched up the street during their 'beer hall putsch' to seize control of Bavaria. A hail of gunfire at the **Feldherrnhalle** in front of Odeonsplatz ended the revolution – but not for long.

Return south on Theatinerstrasse, and cut west to the landmark of Munich, the late-Gothic **Frauenkirche** (Church of Our Lady; Frauenplatz 1; ⏰7am-7pm Sat-Wed, 7am-8.30pm Thu, 7am-6pm Fri) with its then-trendy 16th-century twin onion domes. Go inside and join the hordes gazing at the grandeur of the place, or scale the 98m **tower** (adult/child €3/1.50; ⏰10am-5pm Mon-Sat Apr-Oct) for some Alps spotting. Continue west to the large, grey 16th-century **Michaelskirche** (Neuhauserstrasse 52; ⏰8am-7pm), Germany's earliest and grandest Renaissance church.

Further west is the **Richard Strauss Fountain** and the medieval **Karlstor**, an old city gate. Double back towards Marienplatz and turn right onto Eisenmannstrasse, which becomes Kreuzstrasse and converges with Herzog-Wilhelm-Strasse at the medieval gate of **Sendlinger Tor**. Go down the shopping street Sendlinger Strasse to the **Asamkirche** (Sendlinger Strasse 34), a flamboyant 17th-century church designed by brothers Cosmas Damian and Egid Quirin Asam. The ornate marble facade won't prepare you for the opulence inside, where scarcely an inch is left unembellished.

Walk east through St-Jakobs-Platz to buy some well-earned refreshments at the **Viktualienmarkt**.

DON'T MISS

OKTOBERFEST

Hordes come to Munich for **Oktoberfest** (www.oktoberfest.de; ⊙10am-11.30pm, from 9am Sat & Sun), running the 15 days before the first Sunday in October. Reserve accommodation well ahead and go early in the day so you can grab a seat in one of the hangar-sized beer 'tents'. The action takes place at the Theresienwiese grounds, about a 10-minute walk southwest of the Hauptbahnhof. While there is no entrance fee, those €9 1L steins of beer (called *Mass*) add up fast. Although its origins are in the marriage celebrations of Crown Prince Ludwig in 1810, there's nothing regal about this beery bacchanalia now: expect mobs, expect to meet new and drunken friends, expect decorum to vanish as night sets in and you'll have a blast.

A few tips:

» Locals call it *Weisn* (meadow)

» The Hofbräu Festhalle tent is big with tourists

» The Augustiner tent draws traditionalists

» Traditional Oktoberfest beer should be a rich copper colour; order it instead of the tourist-satisfying pale lager

☞ Tours

Mike's Bike Tours　　　BIKE TOURS
(www.mikesbiketours.com; tours from €24) Enjoyable (and leisurely) city cycling tours in English. Tours depart from the archway at the Altes Rathaus on Marienplatz.

Munich Walk Tours　　　WALKING TOURS
(www.munichwalktours.de; tours from €12) Walking tours of the city on topics from Nazis to beer. Meet under the Glockenspiel on Marienplatz.

City Bus 100　　　BUS
Ordinary city bus that runs from the Hauptbahnhof to the Ostbahnhof via 21 of the city's museums and galleries. This includes all three Pinakothek, the Residenz and the Bayerisches Nationalmuseum.

🛏 Sleeping

Munich has no shortage of places to stay – except during Oktoberfest or some busy summer periods, when the wise (meaning those with a room) will have booked. Many budget and midrange places can be found in the cheerless streets around the train station. If you can, avoid it as you'll find hotels with more charm and atmosphere elsewhere.

Munich's youth hostels that are DJH- and HI-affiliated do not accept guests over age 26, except group leaders or parents accompanying a child.

TOP CHOICE Hotel Blauer Bock　　　HOTEL €€
(☏231 780; www.hotelblauerbock.de; Sebastiansplatz 9; r €60-150; 🛜) A whiff of roasted almonds away from the Viktualienmarkt, this tidy hotel once provided shelter for Benedictine monks and has an ideal location that's the envy of more prestigious abodes. It's comfy, familiar and spacious. Cheaper rooms share bathrooms. The included breakfast buffet offers creative options beyond the norm.

Bayerischer Hof　　　HOTEL €€€
(☏212 00; www.bayerischerhof.de; Promenadeplatz 2-6; r €180-400; ❄@🛜🏊) Room doors fold away into the stucco mouldings at the Hof, one of the grande dames of the Munich hotel trade. It boasts a super-central location, a pool and a jazz club. Marble, antiques and oil paintings abound, and you can dine till you drop at any one of the three fabulous restaurants. Rates include a champagne breakfast.

Pension Gärtnerplatz　　　HOTEL €€
(☏202 5170; www.pension-gaertnerplatztheater.de; Klenzestrasse 45; r €80-130; 🛜) Escape the tourist rabble, or reality altogether, in this eccentric establishment where rooms are a stylish interpretation of Alpine pomp. The room named 'Sisi' will have you sleeping in a canopy bed guarded by a giant porcelain mastiff. The hotel is well located near trendy cafes and shops.

Deutsche Eiche　　　HOTEL €€
(☏231 1660; www.deutsche-eiche.com; Reichenbachstrasse 13; r incl breakfast €80-160, apt from €200; 🛜) Traditionally it's been a gay outpost, but style junkies of all sexual persuasions should enjoy the plushly designed

rooms. Cheaper rooms are more utilitarian; near the trendy Gärtnerplatz. Also on the premises is a bathhouse.

Hotel am Viktualienmarkt
HOTEL €€

(☎231 1090; www.hotel-am-viktualienmarkt.de; Utzschneiderstrasse 14; r €50-120; ☎) Owner Elke and her daughter Stephanie run this perfectly located property with panache and a sunny attitude. A steep staircase (no lift) leads to rooms, the nicest of which have wooden floors and framed poster art. Book far ahead.

Hotel Olympic
HOTEL €€

(☎231 890; www.hotel-olympic.de; Hans-Sachs-Strasse 4; r €95-200; ❄@☎) If you're into designer decor, Frette linens and chocolates on your pillow, go elsewhere. But if you like a hip location (the buzzing Glockenbach-Viertel), public areas doubling as an art gallery, and 38 spacious rooms, give this one a try. Rooms facing the inner courtyard are quieter.

Meininger City Hostel & Hotel
HOSTEL, HOTEL €

(☎420 956 053; www.meininger-hostels.de; Landsbergerstrasse 20; dm/r from €18/45; @☎) This hotel-hostel combo scores big points for three reasons: rooftop bar, amenities and service. About 600m west of the Hauptbahnhof, it has 380 beds in 95 cheerful rooms ranging in size from singles to 12-bed dorms. The Augustiner brewery is within stumbling distance.

Wombat's
HOSTEL, HOTEL €

(☎5998 9180; www.wombats-hostels.com; Senefelderstrasse 1; dm €12-24, r from €70; @☎) Style, comfort and location are hallmarks of this hotel-cum-hostel. You'll sleep well in pine beds with real mattresses (free linen), reading lamps in doubles, and dorms with en suite bathrooms. Breakfast is an extra €4.

Leonardo Boutique Hotel Savoy
HOTEL €€

(☎287 870; www.leonardo-hotels.com; Amalienstrasse 25; r €80-180; ☎) In a Maxvorstadt area thick with modest hotels and cafes, the Savoy stands out after a stylish refit that has given it trappings of luxury. Big windows look across to other inns so you can compare rooms. The frolic of Schwabing is just north.

Hotel Uhland
HOTEL €€

(☎543 350; www.hotel-uhland.de; Uhlandstrasse 1; r €70-200; ☎) The Uhland is an enduring favourite with regulars who expect their hotel to feel like a home away from home. Three generations of family members organise amenities like bike rentals or mix-your-own breakfast muesli. Make a splash in the waterbed suite after a day at the nearby Oktoberfest grounds.

Hotel Marienbad
HOTEL €€

(☎595 585; www.hotelmarienbad.de; Barer Strasse 11, Maxvorstadt; r €50-150; ☎) Back in the 19th century, Wagner, Puccini and Rilke shacked up in what once ranked among Munich's finest hotels. Still friendly and well maintained, it now flaunts an endearing alchemy of styles, from playful art nouveau to campy 1960s utilitarian.

Creatif Hotel Elephant
HOTEL €€

(☎555 785; www.creatif-hotel-elephant.com; Lämmerstrasse 6; r €60-150; ☎) The Creatif is a polychromatic and friendly place bursting with flowers. Its 44 rooms are stylish and comfortable, in an Ikea sort of way.

Campingplatz Thalkirchen
CAMPING GROUND €

(☎7243 0808; www.camping-muenchen.de; Zentralländstrasse 49; campsites per person/tent €5/4; ☺mid-Mar–end Oct) To get to this camping ground, southwest of the city centre, take the U3 to Thalkirchen and catch bus 135 (about 15 minutes).

Tent
CAMPING GROUND €

(☎141 4300; www.the-tent.com; In den Kirschen 30; campsites €5.50 plus per person €5.50, bed in main tent €11; ☺Jun-Sep) Pads and blankets provided for the bagless; bring your own lock for the lockers. Take tram 17 to the Botanic Gardens then follow the signs to a legendary international party.

✖ Eating

Clusters of restaurants can be found anywhere there's pedestrian life. The streets in and around Gärtnerplatz and Glockenbach-Viertel are the flavour of the moment. You can always do well in and around Marienplatz and the wonderful Viktualienmarkt.

WANT MORE?

For in-depth information, reviews and recommendations at your fingertips, head to the Apple App Store to purchase Lonely Planet's *Munich City Guide* iPhone app.

Alternatively, head to **Lonely Planet** (www.lonelyplanet.com/germany /munich) for planning advice, author recommendations, traveller reviews and insider tips.

Restaurants

TOP CHOICE **Der Pschorr** GERMAN €€
(Viktualienmarkt 15; mains €10-18) Shining like a jewel box across a square, this modern high-ceilinged restaurant, operated by one of the main local brewers, is the 21st-century version of a beer hall. Creative dishes, including new takes on old German classics, stream out from the open kitchen. There's even a bit of Med-flair to the long list of daily specials.

Daylesford ORGANIC €€
(Ledererstrasse 3; mains from €9-17; ⊙9am-8pm Mon-Sat; ✐) Right in the middle of pure-pork land, you can eat your veggies again and again with glee (and sneak an organic cheeseburger while you're at it). Food couldn't be fresher: luscious bakery items share space with deli salads and more.

Weisses Brauhaus BAVARIAN €€
(Tal 7; mains €9-20) The place for classic Bavarian fare in an ancient beer-hall setting. Everything from *Weissewurst* (beloved local white sausage) to hearty traditional fare such as boiled ox cheeks is on offer. The menu has changed little in decades.

Café Osteria La Vecchia Masseria
ITALIAN €€
(Mathildenstrasse 3; mains €7-15) This is one of the best Italian places in Munich, loud but unquestionably romantic. Earthy wood tables, antique tin buckets, baskets and clothing irons conjure up the ambience of an Italian farmhouse. The chef comes out to greet customers in his trademark straw hat.

Haxnbauer GERMAN €€
(Sparkassenstrasse; mains €10-22) Meats of all kinds roast in the windows of this modern take on a trad restaurant. The wood is dark, as are the crispy bits on the much-favoured roast goose. Always popular; excellent quality.

Fraunhofer GERMAN €€
(Fraunhoferstrasse 9; mains €6-16; ⊙4.30pm-1am) This classic brewpub contrasts 'ye olde worlde' atmosphere (mounted animal heads and a portrait of Ludwig II) with a menu that offers progressive takes on classical fare. Big with hipsters *and* their parents.

Cafes

Götterspeise CAFE €
(Jahnstrasse 30; snacks from €3) If the Aztecs thought of chocolate as the elixir of the gods, then this shop-cum-cafe must be heaven. Cocoa addicts satisfy their cravings with rave-worthy French chocolate cake, thick, hot drinking chocolate and chocolate-flavoured 'body paint' for those wishing to double their sins.

Uni Lounge CAFE €
(Geschwister-Scholl-Platz 1; meals €4-8) Enjoy a cheap breakfast, lazy lunch or cocktails to a soundtrack of high-minded conversation beneath the whitewashed vaulting of this student hang-out. The outdoor seating is ringed by grand university buildings.

Nil CAFE €€
(Hans-Sachs-Strasse 2; meals €8-14; ⊙8am-4am) Right in trendy Glockenbach-Viertel, this hip place draws a straight and gay crowd in the know. Tables outside are packed when the sun shines; inside it's packed all night long.

Kranz CAFE €€
(Hans-Sachs-Strasse 12; mains €8-16) A luxe cafe in the heart of the edgy and trendy streets of the Glockenbach-Viertel. Posh desserts beg you go easy on the organic burgers. Excellent sidewalk tables.

Baader Café CAFE €
(Baaderstrasse 47; meals €6-14) This literary think-and-drink place gets everyone from short skirts to tweed jackets to mingle beneath the conversation-fuelling map of the world. Lines form early for Sunday brunch.

Markets

TOP CHOICE **Viktualienmarkt** OUTDOOR MARKET
(⊙Mon-Fri & Sat morning) Just south of Marienplatz is a large open-air market, where you can put together a picnic feast to take to the Englischer Garten. The fresh produce, cheese and baked goods are hard to resist. Or relax here under the trees, at tables provided by one of the many beer and sausage vendors. This is the place to see the German's love of all things organic.

Alois Dallmayr FOOD HALL
(Dienerstrasse 14) You'll find one of the world's great delicatessens behind the mustard-yellow awnings, its sparkling cases filled with fine foods. This is the place to come if you want a pet crayfish (see their fountain home).

🍷 Drinking

Apart from the beer halls and gardens, Munich has no shortage of lively pubs. Schwabing and Glockenback-Viertel are good places to follow your ears. Many places

BEER HALLS & BEER GARDENS

Beer drinking is not just an integral part of Munich's entertainment scene, it's a reason to visit. Germans drink an average of 130L of the amber liquid each per year, while Munich residents manage much more. Locals will be happy to help ensure that you don't bring down the average.

Beer halls can be vast boozy affairs seating thousands, or much more modest neighbourhood hang-outs. The same goes for beer gardens. Both come in all shapes and sizes. What's common is a certain camaraderie among strangers, huge 1L glasses of beer (try putting one of those in your carry-on) and lots of cheap food – the saltier the better. Note that in beer gardens, tradition allows you to bring your own food, a boon if you want an alternative to pretzels, sausages and the huge white radishes served with, you guessed it, salt.

On a warm day there's nothing better than sitting and sipping among the greenery at one of the Englischer Garten's classic beer gardens. **Chinesischer Turm** is justifiably popular while the nearby **Hirschau** on the banks of Kleinhesseloher See is less crowded. Other top choices:

Augustiner Bräustuben (Landsberger Strasse 19) Depending on the wind, an aroma of hops envelops you as you approach this ultra-authentic beer hall inside the actual Augustiner brewery. The Bavarian grub here is superb, especially the *Schweinshaxe* (pork knuckles). Giant black draught horses are stabled behind glass on your way to the loo. It's about 700m west of the Hauptbahnhof.

Hofbräuhaus (Am Platzl 9) The ultimate cliché of Munich beer halls. Tourists arrive by the busload but no one seems to mind that this could be Disneyland (although the theme park wasn't once home to Hitler's early speeches, like this place was). Wander upstairs for echoes of the past, a small museum and possibly a seat.

Zum Dürnbrau (Tal 21) Tucked into a corner off Tal, this is a great and authentic little alternative to the Hofbräuhaus. There's a small beer garden, and drinkers of dark draughts enjoy pewter-topped mugs.

Augustiner Bierhalle (Neuhauser Strasse 27) What you probably imagine an old-style Munich beer hall looks like, filled with laughter, smoke and clinking glasses.

serve food; most are open until 1am or later on weekends.

Alter Simpl
PUB

(Türkenstrasse 57, Maxvorstadt; meals from €8) Thomas Mann and Hermann Hesse used to knock 'em back at this legendary thirst parlour. Alter Simpl is also a good place to satisfy midnight munchies as bar bites are available until one hour before closing time.

Morizz
BAR

(Klenzestrasse 43) This mod art deco–style lounge with red leather armchairs and mirrors for posing and preening goes for a more moneyed clientele and even gets the occasional local celebrity drop-in. Packed on weekends.

Trachtenvogl
LOUNGE

(Reichenbachstrasse 47, Gärtnerplatzviertel; ☺10am-1am) At night you'll have to shoehorn your way into this buzzy lair favoured by a chatty, boozy crowd of scenesters, artists and students. Daytimes are mellower at this former folkloric garment shop.

☆ Entertainment

Munich is one of the cultural capitals of Germany; the publications and websites listed on p226 can guide you to the best events. For tickets, try **München Ticket** (www.muenchen ticket.de; Neues Rathaus, Marienplatz).

Nightclubs & Live Music

Kultfabrik
CLUBS

(www.kultfabrik.de; Grafingerstrasse 6; ☺8pm-6am) There are more than 25 clubs for you to sample in this old potato factory before you end up either mashed or fried (or both). Electro and house beats charge up the crowd at the loungey **apartment 11**, the Asian-themed **Koi** and **Drei Türme** (www.dreituerme.de), a chic living-room club disguised as a Hollywood castle and lit by a forest of glass-fibre tubes. It's close to the Ostbahnhof station.

GAY & LESBIAN MUNICH

Much of Munich's gay and lesbian nightlife is around **Gärtnerplatz** and the **Glockenback-Viertel**. Any of the nightspots in this area listed earlier (such as Nil and Morizz) will have a mixed crowd.

Our Munich and *Sergej* are monthly guides easily found in this neighbourhood. Another good resource is **Max&Milian** (Ickstattstrasse 2), Munich's best gay bookstore.

Deutsche Eiche (p222) caters to gay and lesbian guests.

Jazzbar Vogler JAZZ
(Rumfordstrasse 17, Gärtnerplatzviertel) This intimate watering hole brings some of Munich's baddest cats to the stage. You never know who might show up for Monday's blues-jazz-Latin jam session.

Atomic Café CLUB
(www.atomic.de; Neuturmstrasse 5; ⊘10pm-4am, 9pm on concert nights Tue-Sun) This bastion of indie sounds with funky '60s decor is known for bookers with a knack for catching upwardly hopeful bands before their big break.

Theatre
Residenztheater (Max-Joseph-Platz 2) is the home of the **Bavarian State Opera** (www.staatsoper.de) and also the site of many cultural events (particularly during the opera festival in July).

🛍 Shopping

All shoppers converge on the Marienplatz to buy designer shoes or kitschy souvenirs. The stylish department store **Ludwig Beck** (236 910; Marienplatz 11) has something for everyone. Bypass Calvin et al for more unusual European choices. Nearby Maximilianstrasse is a fashionable street that is ideal for simply strolling and window shopping. Close by, **Hugendubel** (Salvatorplatz 2) is crammed with English-language titles.

To truly 'unchain' yourself, though, you should hit the Gärtnerplatzviertel and Glockenbach-Viertel, bastions of well-edited indie stores and local-designer boutiques. Hans-Sachs-Strasse and Reichenbachstrasse are especially promising. Maxvorstadt, especially Türkenstrasse, also has an interesting line-up of stores with stuff you won't find on the high street back home.

Munich has eight **Christmas markets** from late November, including a big one on Marienplatz. For more on these popular events, see p234.

ℹ Information

For late-night shopping and services such as pharmacies and currency exchange, the Hauptbahnhof's multilevel shopping arcades cannot be beaten.

Discount Cards
City Tour Card (www.citytourcard.com; 1/3 days €9.80/18.80) Includes transport and discounts of between 10% and 50% for about 30 attractions. Available at some hotels, MVV (Munich public transport authority) offices and U-Bahn and S-Bahn vending machines.

Medical Services
Ärztlicher Bereitschaftsdienst (☑01805-191 212; ⊘24hr) Emergency medical service.

Bahnhof-Apotheke (☑598 119; Bahnhofplatz 2, Ludwigsvorstadt) Pharmacy.

Tourist Information
EurAide (☑593 889; www.euraide.de; Hauptbahnhof; ⊘9am-noon & 1-5pm, longer hr in summer) Dispenses savvy travel advice in English, sells and validates rail passes, explains train-ticket savings and discounts many tours; staff work in the DB Travel Centre at counter 1.

Tourist office (www.muenchen.de) Hauptbahnhof (Bahnhofplatz 2; ⊘9.30am-6.30pm Mon-Sat, 10am-6pm Sun, longer hr in summer & during holidays); Marienplatz (Neues Rathaus, Marienplatz 8; ⊘10am-8pm Mon-Fri, to 4pm Sat) Be sure to ask for the excellent and free guides *Young and About in Munich, National Socialism in Munich* and various neighbourhood guides.

Websites
www.muenchen-tourist.de Munich's official website.

www.munichfound.com Munich's expat magazine.

www.toytowngermany.com English-language community website with specialised Munich pages; partnered with Berlin's excellent The Local.

ℹ Getting There & Away
Air
Munich's sparkling white **airport** (MUC; www.munich-airport.de) is second in importance only to Frankfurt for international and national connections. Flights will take you to all major destinations worldwide.

Bus

Munich has a new **bus station** (ZOB; www.zob-muenchen.de; Arnulfstrasse) that already looks typical of the daggy genre. Ticket windows and small waiting areas are on the top floor. It's 500m west of the Hauptbahnhof, at the S-Bahn stop Hackerbrücke. Among the operators here are **Touring** (www.touring.de), which also runs **Europabus** services.

Munich is a stop for the **Romantic Road bus** (www.romanticroadcoach.de); see p302.

Car & Motorcycle

The main hire companies have counters together on the second level of the Hauptbahnhof. For arranged rides, the **Mitfahrzentrale** (🖉194 40; www.mitfahrzentrale.de; Lämmerstrasse 6; ☺8am-8pm) is near the Hauptbahnhof. The cost is split with the driver and you can reach most parts of Germany for well under €40.

Train

Train services to/from Munich are excellent. There are rapid connections at least every two hours to all major cities in Germany, as well as daily trains to other European cities, including the following:

DESTINATION	PRICE	DURATION (HR)
Paris	€140	6
Vienna	€75	4
Zürich	€65	4¼

Hourly ICE services include the following:

DESTINATION	PRICE	DURATION (HR)
Berlin	€113	5¾
Frankfurt	€89	3
Hamburg	€115	5½

ⓘ Getting Around

To/From the Airport

Munich's international airport is connected by the S8 and the S1 to Marienplatz and the Hauptbahnhof (€9.60). Service takes about 40 minutes; there's a train every 10 minutes from 4am until 12.30am or so. The S8 route is slightly faster. A ticket that's good all day costs €10.40.

Taxis make the long haul for at least €60.

Bicycle

Pedal power is popular in relatively flat Munich. **Radius Bike Rental** (www.radiustours.com; Hauptbahnhof, near track 32; ☺10am-6pm May-Sep) rents out two-wheelers from €15 per day. Other tour companies have similar rates.

Car & Motorcycle

It's not worth driving in the city centre – many streets are pedestrian-only. The tourist office has a map that shows city parking places (€2 or more per hour).

Public Transport

Munich's excellent **public transport network** (MVV; www.mvv-muenchen.de) is zone-based, and most places of interest to tourists (except Dachau and the airport) are within the 'blue' inner zone (*Innenraum;* €2.40). MVV tickets are valid for the S-Bahn, U-Bahn, trams and buses, but they must be validated before use. The U-Bahn ceases operating around 12.30am Monday to Friday and 1.30am on Saturday and Sunday, but there are some later buses and S-Bahns. Rail passes are valid exclusively on the S-Bahn.

Kurzstrecke (short rides) cost €1.20 and are good for no more than four stops on buses and trams, and two stops on the U- and S-Bahns. *Tageskarte* (day passes) for the inner zone cost €5.20, while three-day tickets cost €12.80.

Taxi

Taxis (🖉216 10) are expensive and not much more convenient than public transport.

Dachau

The first Nazi concentration camp was **Dachau** (www.kz-gedenkstaette-dachau.de; Alte-Roemerstrasse 75; admission free; ☺9am-5pm Tue-Sun), built in March 1933. Jews, political prisoners, homosexuals and others deemed 'undesirable' by the Third Reich were imprisoned in the camp. More than 200,000 people were sent here; more than 30,000 died at Dachau, and countless others died after being transferred to other death camps. An English-language documentary is shown at 11.30am and 3.30pm. A visit includes camp relics, memorials and a very sobering museum.

Take the S2 (direction: Petershausen) to Dachau and then bus 726 to the camp. A Munich XXL day ticket (€7) will cover the trip.

Romantic Road

The popular and schmaltzily named Romantic Road (Romantische Strasse) links a series of picturesque Bavarian towns and cities. It's not actually one road per se, but rather a 353km route chosen to highlight as many quaint towns and cities as possible in western Bavaria.

From north to south it includes the following major stops:

» **Würzburg** The starting point, featuring 18th-century artistic splendour among the vineyards.

» **Rothenburg ob der Tauber** The medieval walled hub of cutesy, picturesque Bavarian touring.

» **Dinkelsbühl** Another medieval walled town replete with moat and watchtowers; a smaller Rothenburg. The town is best reached by bus or car.

» **Augsburg** A medieval and Renaissance city with many good places for a beer.

» **Wieskirche** Stunning Unesco-recognised church.

» **Füssen** The southern end of the route, and the cute and over-run home of mad King Ludwig's castles.

In addition to these principal stops, more than a dozen little towns clamour for attention – and your money. A good first stop is the info-packed website www.romanticroad. de. Also look for the excellent and free large map and route description at tourist offices.

ⓘ Getting There & Around

The principal cities and towns listed above are all easily reached by train – see the individual listings for details. But to really explore the route, you are best off with your own transport. The entire length is copiously marked with brown signs in German, English and Japanese. With a car, you can blow through places of little interest and linger at those that appeal.

Bus

A popular way to tour the Romantic Road is the **Romantic Road bus** (☑069 719126-268; www.romanticroadcoach.de; ◷phone line 9am-6pm Mon-Fri).

Starting in Frankfurt in the north and Füssen in the south, a bus runs in each direction each day covering the entire route. However, seeing the entire whack in one day is only for those with unusual fortitude and a love of buses. Stops are brief (17 minutes for Wieskirche, *Schnell!* 35 minutes for Rothenburg, *Schnell!* etc) so you'll want to choose places where you can break the trip for a day (stopovers are allowed). But of course this leads you to decide between a 30-minute visit and a 24-hour one.

The buses depart mid-April to mid-October, south from Frankfurt Hauptbahnhof at 8am and north from Füssen at 8am, and take about 12 hours. The total fare (tickets are bought on board) is a pricey €105. Rail-pass holders get a paltry 20% discount. You can also just ride individual segments (eg Rothenburg to Augsburg costs €26), which may be the best use.

Würzburg

☑0931 / POP 135,000

Nestled among river valleys lined with vineyards, Würzburg beguiles even before you reach the city centre. Three of the four largest wine-growing estates in all of Germany are here and most of the delicate whites produced locally never leave the region – the locals will always reach for a wine glass first. Over 1300 years old, Würzburg was rebuilt after being bombed late in WWII (it took only 17 minutes to almost completely destroy the city). The grand buildings are amazing, even if the town itself is a tad drab.

⊙ Sights

The magnificent, sprawling Unesco-listed **Residenz** (www.residenz-wuerzburg.de; Balthasar-Neumann-Promenade; adult/child €7/6; ◷9am-6pm Apr-Oct, 10am-4pm Nov-Mar), a baroque masterpiece by Neumann, took a generation to build and boasts the world's largest ceiling fresco (graphic artists take note: he didn't need Photoshop); the **Hofgarten** at the back is a beautiful spot.

The interior of the **Dom St Kilian** (museum €5; ◷10am-7pm Tue-Sun Apr-Oct, to 5pm Tue-Sun Nov-Mar) and the adjacent **Neumünster**, an 11th-century church in the old town housing the bones of St Kilian, the patron saint of Würzburg, continue the baroque themes of the Residenz.

Neumann's fortified **Alter Kranen** (old crane), which serviced a dock on the riverbank south of Friedensbrücke, is now the **Haus des Frankenweins** (Kranenkai 1), where you can taste Franconian wines (for around €3 per glass).

The medieval fortress **Marienberg**, across the river on the hill, is reached by crossing the 15th-century stone **Alte Mainbrücke** (old bridge) from the city and walking up Tellstiege, a small alley. It encloses the **Fürstenbau Museum** (adult/child €4/3; ◷9am-6pm Tue-Sun Apr-Oct), featuring the Episcopal apartments, and the regional **Mainfränkisches Museum** (Festung Marienberg; adult/child €4/3; ◷10am-5pm Tue-Sun Apr-Oct, to 4pm Tue-Sun Nov-Mar). For a simple thrill, wander the walls enjoying the panoramic views.

🛏️ Sleeping & Eating

Würzburg's many *Weinstuben* (cosy places to enjoy wine in a traditional setting) are excellent places for sampling the local vintages. Look for crests of gilded grapes over entrances. Sanderstrasse has a good strip of lively bars.

Babelfish Hostel
HOSTEL €

(☏304 0430; www.babelfish-hostel.de; Haugerring 2; dm €17-23, r €45-70; @🛜) This green-powered, independent hostel has moved to new digs in a bank building across from the Hauptbahnhof. Facilities include spotless dorms, rooftop terrace and bike rental (€5 per day).

Hotel Rebstock
HOTEL €€

(☏309 30; www.rebstock.com; Neubaustrasse 7; r €85-170; ❄️🛜) Class, hospitality and a touch of nostalgia are the characteristics of this elegant hotel, one of Würzburg's best. Meticulously restored, this rococo mansion has 70 superbly furnished rooms.

Hotel Till Eulenspiegel
HOTEL €€

(☏355 840; www.hotel-till-eulenspiegel.de; Sanderstrasse 1a; r €70-120; 🛜) Run by the gregarious Johannes, the 18 rooms are comfortable and some have sunny balconies. There's also a small but good *Weinstube* (wine bar) and a pub serving unusual Bavarian microbrews.

Zum Stachel
GERMAN €€

(☏527 70; www.weinhaus-stachel.de; Gressengasse 1; mains €12-22; ⊘closed Sun) There's a restaurant at this 15th-century watering hole, but better yet is to just enjoy a drink on one of its stone balconies overlooking the *Romeo and Juliet*–like Renaissance courtyard.

Weinstuben Juliusspital
WEINSTUBE €€

(☏540 80; Juliuspromenade 19; mains €8-20) This rambling place serves up a long list of wines (especially local whites). You can have a meal or just a drink at one of the many old wooden tables.

ℹ️ Information

The **tourist office** (www.wuerzburg.de; Marktplatz; ⊘10am-6pm Mon-Fri, 10am-2pm Sat & Sun May-Oct, reduced hr & closed Sun other times), in the rococo masterpiece Falkenhaus, runs 90-minute English-language **city walks** (€6; ⊘1pm Fri & Sat May-Oct).

ℹ️ Getting There & Away

Würzburg is served by frequent ICE trains from Frankfurt (€33, 70 minutes) and Nuremberg (€33, 69 minutes). It's a major stop for the ICE trains on the Hamburg–Munich line. It is also on the Romantic Road bus route (€19, 1½ hours to/from Rothenburg). The stop is in front of the train station.

Bamberg

☏0951 / POP 71,000

Off the major tourist routes, Bamberg is revered by those in the know. It boasts a beautifully preserved collection of 17th- and 18th-century merchants' houses, palaces and churches. It is bisected by a large canal and fast-flowing river that are spanned by cute little bridges, and it even has its own local style of beer. No wonder it has been recognised by Unesco as a World Heritage site. Could it be the best small town in Germany?

◉ Sights

Bamberg's main appeal is its fine buildings – the sheer number, their jumble of styles and the ambience this creates. Most attractions are spread on either side of the Regnitz River, but the **Altes Rathaus** (Obere Brücke) is actually solidly perched on its own islet. Its lavish murals are among many around town.

The princely and ecclesiastical district is centred on **Domplatz**, where the Romanesque and Gothic **cathedral** (⊘8am-6pm Apr-Sep, to 5pm Oct-Mar), housing the statue of the chivalric king-knight, the *Bamberger Reiter*, is the biggest attraction. Look for the enigmatic statue, the *Lächelnde Engel* (Smiling Angel).

Across the square, the imposing 17th-century **Neue Residenz** (www.schloesser.bay ern.de; Domplatz 8; adult/child €4/3; ⊘9am-6pm Apr-Sep, 10am-4pm Oct-Mar) has 40 rooms filled with treasures and opulent decor.

Above Domplatz is the former Benedictine **monastery of St Michael**, at the top of Michaelsberg. The **Kirche St Michael** (Franziskanergasse 2; ⊘9am-6pm) is a must-see for its baroque art and the herbal compendium painted on its ceiling. The garden terraces afford another marvellous overview of the city's splendour.

🛏️ Sleeping

Some of the breweries also rent rooms – a major convenience.

TOP CHOICE **Hotel Sankt Nepomuk**
HOTEL €€

(☏984 20; www.hotel-nepomuk.de; Obere Mühlbrücke 9; r €95-145; 🛜) Named aptly after the patron saint of bridges, this is a classy establishment in a half-timbered former mill right on the Regnitz. It has a superb restaurant (mains €15 to €30) with a terrace, 24 comfy rustic rooms and bikes for rent.

Backpackers Bamberg HOSTEL €
(☏2221 718; www.backpackersbamberg.de; Heiliggrabstrasse 4; dm €15-18, r €40-60; ☞) Newly relocated to a large and accommodating half-timbered building, this hostel is a fine budget choice. It's a five-minute walk from the train station towards the old town. Furnishings are new and the decor has a freeform flair.

Hotel Europa HOTEL €€
(☏309 3020; www.hotel-europa-bamberg.de; Untere Königstrasse 6-8; r €75-120) Smell the spaghetti from one of the 46 rooms above Bamberg's best Italian restaurant. Ask for a room at the front with views of the Dom and the red-tiled roofs of the Altstadt. Breakfast is in the restaurant or out in the sunny courtyard.

✗ Eating & Drinking

Bamberg's unique style of beer is called *Rauchbier,* which literally means smoked beer. With a bacon flavour at first, it is a smooth brew that goes down easily.

TOP **Schlenkerla** GERMAN €€
CHOICE (Dominikanerstrasse 6; mains €8-15; ☺Wed-Mon) Featuring a warren of rooms decked out with lamps fashioned from antlers, this 16th-century restaurant is famous for tasty Franconian specialities and *Rauchbier,* served directly from oak barrels. This should be your one stop if you only have time for one (stop, not beers...).

Klosterbräu GERMAN €
(Obere Mühlbrücke 1-3; mains €6-12) This beautiful half-timbered brewery is Bamberg's oldest. It draws *Stammgäste* (regular local drinkers) and tourists alike, who wash down filling slabs of meat and dumplings with its excellent range of ales.

Brauereigasthof Fässla GERMAN €
(☏265 16; www.faessla.de; Obere Königstrasse 19-21; mains €7-10) Chairs at the on-site restaurant are embossed with Fässla's cute coat of arms – a gnome rolling a giant beer barrel. Enjoy the light pilsner here, then head upstairs for a snooze (rooms €40 to €70).

ℹ Information

The **tourist office** (www.bamberg.info; Geyerswörthstrasse 3; ☺9.30am-6pm Mon-Fri, 9.30am-2.30pm Sat & Sun) is in the old town.

ℹ Getting There & Away

Two trains per hour go to/from both Würzburg (€17, one hour) and Nuremberg (€20, one hour). Bamberg is also served by ICE trains running between Munich (€58, two hours) and Berlin (€74, 3¾ hours) every two hours.

Rothenburg ob der Tauber

☏09861 / POP 12,000

In the Middle Ages, Rothenburg's town fathers built strong walls to protect the town from siege; today they are the reason the town is under siege from tourists. The most stereotypical of all German walled towns, Rothenburg can't help being so cute.

Granted 'free imperial city' status in 1274, it's a confection of twisting cobbled lanes and pretty architecture enclosed by towered stone walls. Swarmed during the day, the underlying charm oozes out after the last bus leaves.

Note that the gaggle of Christmas shops and 'museums' are quite wily – once in, you have to walk the entire labyrinth in order to escape.

◉ Sights

The **Rathaus on Markt** was commenced in Gothic style in the 14th century but completed in Renaissance style. The **tower** (admission €2) gives a majestic view over the town and the Tauber Valley.

According to legend, the town was saved during the Thirty Years War when the mayor won a challenge by the Imperial General Tilly and downed more than 3L of wine at a gulp. This **Meistertrunk** scene is re-enacted by the clock figures on the tourist office building (eight times daily in summer). Actors re-enact other famous scenes from the past (but not the mythical assault on the tour bus by fudge vendors) at 6.30pm Friday, May to September.

Totally uncommercial, **Jakobskirche** (Klingengasse 1; adult/child €2/1; ☺9am-5pm) is sober and Gothic. Marvel at the carved *Heilige Blut Altar* (Holy Blood Altar).

The **Reichsstadt Museum** (www.reichsstadtmuseum.rothenburg.de; Klosterhof 5; adult/under 18yr €3/2; ☺10am-5pm Apr-Oct, 1-4pm Nov-Mar), in the grandiose former convent, features the superb 1494 *Rothenburger Passion* in 12 panels.

🛏 Sleeping & Eating

Resist the temptation to try a *Schneeball,* a crumbly ball of bland dough with the taste and consistency of chalk – surely one of Europe's worst 'local specialities'.

Altfränkische Weinstube HOTEL €
(☎6404; www.altfraenkische-weinstube-rothen burg.de; Am Klosterhof 7; r €60-80; 🛜) Hiding in a quiet side street near the Reichsstadtmuseum, this enchantingly characterful inn has six atmosphere-laden rooms, all with bathtubs and most with four-poster or canopied beds. The restaurant (open for dinner only) serves up sound regional fare with a dollop of medieval cheer.

Pension Raidel HOTEL €
(☎3115; www.romanticroad.com/raidel; Wenggasse 3; r €25-60) This half-timbered inn has 500-year-old exposed beams studded with wooden nails, and musical instruments for guests to play. Some rooms share bathrooms.

Zur Höll GERMAN €€
(Burggasse 8; dishes €6-18) This medieval wine tavern, with an appreciation for slow food and a name that means hell, is in the town's oldest original building, dating back to the year 900. The menu of regional specialities is limited but refined, though it's the wine that people really come for.

❶ Getting There & Away

There are hourly trains to/from Steinach, a transfer point for service to Würzburg (total journey €13, 70 minutes). Rothenburg is a crossroads for tourist buses. Romantic Road buses pause here for 35 minutes.

Nuremberg
☎0911 / POP 498,000

Nuremberg (Nürnberg) woos visitors with its wonderfully restored medieval Altstadt, its grand castle and its magical *Christkindlmarkt* (Christmas market). Thriving traditions also include sizzling *Nürnberger Bratwürste* (finger-sized sausages) and *Lebkuchen* – large, soft gingerbread cookies, traditionally eaten at Christmas time but available here year-round. Both within and beyond the high stone wall encircling the Altstadt is a wealth of major museums that shed light on Nuremberg's significant history.

Nuremberg played a major role during the Nazi years, as documented in Leni Riefenstahl's film *Triumph of the Will*, and during the war-crimes trials afterwards. It has done an admirable job of confronting this ugly past with museums and exhibits.

And it has recaptured much of the charm lost when bombing raids flattened the centre; it is still the heart of the German toy industry.

◉ Sights

The scenic **Altstadt** is easily covered on foot. On Lorenzer Platz there's the **St Lorenzkirche**, noted for the 15th-century tabernacle that climbs like a vine up a pillar to the vaulted ceiling.

To the north is the bustling **Hauptmarkt**, where the most famous **Christkindlmarkt** in Germany is held from the Friday before Advent to Christmas Eve. The church here is the ornate **Pfarrkirche Unsere Liebe Frau**; the clock's figures go strolling at noon. Near the Rathaus is **St Sebalduskirche** (⊙9.30am-6pm), Nuremberg's oldest church (dating from the 13th century), with the shrine of St Sebaldus.

Kaiserburg CASTLE
(www.schloesser.bayern.de; adult/child incl museum €6/5; ⊙9am-6pm Apr-Sep, 10am-4pm Oct-Mar) Climb up Burgstrasse to this enormous 15th-century fortress for good views of the city. The walls spread west to the tunnelgate of **Tiergärtnertor**, where you can stroll behind the castle to the gardens.

Germanisches Nationalmuseum MUSEUM
(www.gnm.de; Kartäusergasse 1; adult/child €8/5; ⊙10am-6pm Tue & Thu-Sun, to 9pm Wed) The most important general museum of German culture in the country, this stunner displays works by German painters and sculptors, an archaeological collection, arms and armour, musical and scientific instruments and, of course, toys.

⟨TOP CHOICE⟩ Nuremberg Trials Memorial
HISTORICAL SITE
(www.memorium-nuremberg.de; Bärenschanzstrasse 72; adult/child €5/3; ⊙10am-6pm Wed-Mon) From 1945 to 1949 suspected Nazis were tried for war crimes in Nuremberg, which was chosen because it had been the spiritual home of the Third Reich. The top leaders, such as von Ribbentrop and Streicher, received death sentences; others, such as Göring, committed suicide ahead of the noose. The transcripts are still studied today and show that the rule of law can contend with evil. The courthouse where the trials were held is still in use and is now home to a compelling and comprehensive **exhibit** about the world's first efforts to prosecute genocide. **Courtroom 600**, where

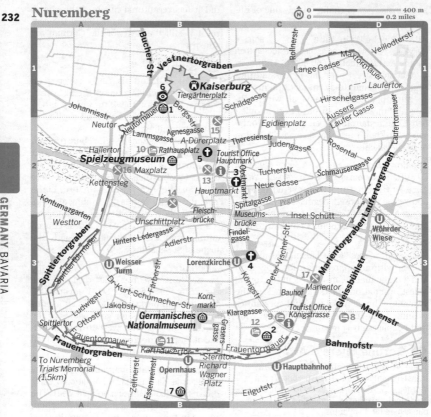

the trials were held, can be toured when it is not in use.

Other Museums MUSEUMS
Nuremberg has a lot of toy companies and the **Spielzeugmuseum** (Toy Museum; Karlstrasse 13-15; adult/child €5/3; ⊙10am-5pm Tue-Fri, to 6pm Sat & Sun) presents their products in their infinite variety.

The **Verkehrsmuseum** (Transportation Museum; www.dbmuseum.de; Lessingstrasse 6; adult/child €4/2; ⊙9am-5pm Tue-Sun) has a trainload of exhibits on the German railways.

Albrecht-Dürer-Haus (Albrecht-Dürer-Strasse 39; adult/child €5/2.50; ⊙10am-5pm Fri-Wed, to 8pm Thu) is where Dürer, Germany's renowned Renaissance draughtsman, lived from 1509 to 1528. A digital version of wife Agnes leads tours.

The sleekly curving **Neues Museum** (www.nmn.de; Luitpoldstrasse 5; adult/child €4/3; ⊙10am-8pm Tue-Fri, to 6pm Sat & Sun) contains a superb collection of contemporary art and design.

Luitpoldhain HISTORICAL SITE
Nuremberg's role during the Third Reich is well known. The Nazis chose this city as their propaganda centre and for mass rallies, which were held at Luitpoldhain, a (never completed) sports complex of megalomaniac proportions.

Don't miss the **Dokumentationzentrum** (www.museen.nuernberg.de; Bayernstrasse 110; adult/child €5/3; ⊙9am-6pm Mon-Fri, 10am-6pm Sat & Sun) in the north wing of the massive unfinished Congress Hall, which would have held 50,000 people for Hitler's spectacles. The museum's absorbing exhibits trace the rise of Hitler and the Nazis, and the important role Nuremberg played in the mythology. Take tram 9 or 6 to Doku-Zentrum.

🛏 Sleeping

Nuremberg hosts many a trade show through the year (including a huge toy fair in February). During these times – and

Christmas market weekends – rates soar like a model rocket.

TOP CHOICE Hotel Elch
HOTEL €€

(☑249 2980; www.hotel-elch.com; Irrerstrasse 9; r €65-110; 🌐) This dramatically historic hotel, with a logo of the namesake elk, occupies a 14th-century half-timbered house that wears every one of its years on its skew facade. The spotless and petite rooms are up a narrow medieval staircase. Breakfast is served in the quaint woody restaurant, the Schnitzelria, which does a good line in Franconian beers and, yes, schnitzel.

Lette 'm Sleep
HOSTEL €

(☑992 8128; www.backpackers.de; Frauentormauer 42; dm €16-20, r from €50; @🌐) A backpacker favourite, this independent hostel is just five minutes' walk from the Hauptbahnhof. Private rooms share bathrooms, however you can read to your heart's content in the private facilities of several apartments (from €65), which also have kitchens.

Art & Business Hotel
HOTEL €€

(☑232 10; www.art-business-hotel.com; Gleissbühlstrasse 15; r €60-150; 🌐) You don't have to be an artist or a business person to stay at this stylish, up-to-the-minute place, a retro sport shoe's throw from the Hauptbahnhof. Rooms are a study in diligently composed minimalism, while technicolour art and design brings cheer to the communal spaces.

Hotel Drei Raben
HOTEL €€

(☑274 380; www.hotel3raben.de; Königstrasse 63; r €100-185; 🌐) This designer theme hotel builds upon the legend of three ravens perched on the building's chimney stack, who tell each other stories from Nuremberg lore. Each of the 21 rooms uses its style and

humour to tell a particular tale – from the life of Dürer to the history of the locomotive.

Probst-Garni Hotel
HOTEL, PENSION €€

(☑203 433; www.hotel-garni-probst.de; Luitpoldstrasse 9; r €60-100) Nuremberg's most reasonably priced pension is squeezed on the 3rd floor of a vintage building. Recent renovations have given the rooms furnishings that are prim and proper. The letters from happy guests are sweet.

✕ Eating

Don't leave Nuremberg without trying its famous *Nürnberger Bratwürste*. Order 'em by the dozen with *meerrettich* (horseradish) on the side. Restaurants line the hilly lanes above the Burgstrasse.

TOP CHOICE Bratwursthäusle
GERMAN €€

(http://die-nuernberger-bratwurst.de; Rathausplatz 2; meals €6-14; ⊘closed Sun) A local legend and *the* place for flame-grilled and scrumptious local sausages. Get them with *Kartoffelsalat* (potato salad). There are also nice tree-shaded tables outside.

Marientorzwinger
GERMAN €€

(Lorenzer-strasse 33; mains €8-17) This is the last remaining *Zwinger* eatery (taverns built between the inner and outer walls when they relinquished their military use) in Nuremberg. Chomp on sturdy Franconian staples or a veggie dish in the simple wood-panelled dining room or the leafy beer garden, and swab the decks with a yard of Fürth-brewed Tucher.

Hütt'n
GERMAN €€

(Burgstrasse 19; mains €8-15; ⊘dinner Wed-Mon) Be prepared to queue for a table at this local haunt. The special here is the *Ofenfrische*

DON'T MISS

CHRISTMAS MARKETS

Beginning in late November every year, central squares across Germany – especially those in Bavaria – are transformed into Christmas markets or *Christkindlmarkts* (also known as *Weihnachtsmärkte*). Folks stamp about between the wooden stalls, perusing seasonal trinkets (from treasures to schlock) while warming themselves with tasty *glühwein* (mulled, spiced red wine) and treats such as sausages and potato pancakes. The markets are popular with tourists but locals love 'em too, and bundle themselves up and carouse for hours. Nuremberg's **market** (www.christkindlesmarkt.de) fills much of the centre and attracts two million people.

Krustenbraten: roast pork with crackling, dumplings and sauerkraut salad. There's also a near-endless variety of schnapps and beers.

Café am Trödelmarkt CAFE €
(Trödelmarkt 42; dishes €3-5; ⊙9am-6pm) A gorgeous place on a sunny day, this multilevel waterfront cafe overlooks the covered Henkersteg bridge. It's popular for its fresh and tasty continental breakfasts.

Kettensteg BEER GARDEN €
(Maxplatz 35; mains €6-14) Right by the river and with its own suspension bridge to the other side, this beer garden and restaurant is fine on a summer day and cosy in winter. The basic fare is tasty and absorbs lots of beer.

❶ Information

Nürnberg + Fürth Card (€21) Good for two days of unlimited public transport and admissions.

Tourist office (www.tourismus.nuernberg.de) Künstlerhaus (Königstrasse 93; ⊙9am-7pm Mon-Sat, 10am-4pm Sun); Hauptmarkt (Hauptmarkt 18; ⊙9am-6pm Mon-Sat, 10am-4pm Sun)

❶ Getting There & Around

Nuremberg's **airport** (NUE; www.airport-nuernberg.de) is a hub for budget carrier Air Berlin, which has services throughout Germany, as well as flights to London. There's frequent service to the airport on the S-2 line (€2, 12 minutes).

The city is also a hub for train services. Sample fares:

DESTINATION	PRICE	DURATION (HR)
Berlin-Hauptbahnhof	€89	4½
Frankfurt	€48	2
Munich	€49	1
Stuttgart	€38	2¼

Tickets on the bus, tram and U-Bahn system cost €2 each. Day passes are €4.

Regensburg

📞0941 / POP 129,000

On the wide Danube River, Regensburg has relics of all periods as far back as the Romans, yet doesn't have the tourist mobs you'll find in other equally attractive German cities. Oh well, their loss. At least Unesco noticed. It recognised that Regensburg has the only intact medieval centre in Germany. Amid the half-timbers, Renaissance towers that could be in Tuscany mix with Roman ruins. Meanwhile, some 25,000 students keep things lively.

From the main train station, walk up Maximilianstrasse for 10 minutes to reach the centre.

◉ Sights

A veritable miracle of engineering in its time, the **Steinerne Brücke** (Stone Bridge) was cobbled together between 1135 and 1146. For centuries it remained the only solid crossing along the entire Danube.

Lording over Regensburg, **Dom St Peter** (Domplatz; ⊙6.30am-6pm Apr-Oct, to 5pm Nov-Mar) ranks among Bavaria's grandest Gothic cathedrals. Construction of this green-hued twin-spired landmark began in the late 13th century, mostly to flaunt the city's prosperity. The cavernous interior's prized possessions include kaleidoscopic stained-glass windows.

The **Altes Rathaus** (adult/child incl museum €6/3; ⊙tours in English 3pm Apr-Oct, 2pm Nov, Dec & Mar) was progressively extended from medieval to baroque times and was the seat of the Reichstag for almost 150 years.

The **Roman wall**, with its **Porta Praetoria** arch, follows Unter den Schwibbögen onto Dr-Martin-Luther-Strasse.

Lavish **Schloss Thurn und Taxis** (www. thurnundtaxis.de; Emmeramsplatz 5; tours adult/ child €11.50/9; ⊙11am-5pm Mon-Fri, 10am-5pm Sat & Sun) includes the castle proper (*Schloss*) and the royal stables (*Marstall*). The adjoining **Basilika St Emmeram** is a riot of rococo and has a perfect cloister. You need to join a **tour** (⊙in German hourly, in English 1.30pm Jun–mid-Sep) to see the sights.

🛏 Sleeping & Eating

Atmospheric hotels with modern style can be found scattered through the medieval centre. Hidden around corners you'll find cafes with good wine and boisterous beer gardens.

TOP CHOICE **Altstadthotel am Pach**   HOTEL €€
(⊙298 610; www.regensburghotel.de; Untere Bachgasse 9; r €80-150; 📶) Those who have shaped Regensburg history, from Marcus Aurelius to Emperor Karl V, are commemorated in the 21 rooms of this high-concept hotel. Rooms vary in size but all are warmly furnished with thick carpets, comfy mattresses and a minifridge.

Hotel Goldenes Kreuz   HOTEL €€
(⊙558 12; www.hotel-goldeneskreuz.de; Haidplatz 7; r €80-140; 📶) Surely the best deal in town, the nine fairy-tale rooms here each bear the name of a crowned head and are fit for a kaiser. Huge mirrors, dark antique and Bauhaus furnishings, four-poster beds, chubby exposed beams and parquet flooring produce a stylish opus in leather, wood, crystal and fabric.

Brook Lane Hostel   HOSTEL €
(⊙690 0966; www.hostel-regensburg.de; Obere Bachgasse 21; dm €15-20, s/d/apt from €35/45/140; 📶) Regensburg's only backpacker hostel has spanking-new dorms and bathrooms, and its very own food store.

TOP CHOICE **Wurstküche**   SAUSAGES €
(⊙466 210; Thundorferstrasse 3; meals €7-10; ⊙8am-7pm) The Danube rushes past this little house that's been cooking up the addictive local version of Nuremberg sausages since 1135. Which is better? These or the northern version? (Better try both.)

Dicker Mann   GERMAN €€
(Krebsgasse 6; mains €6-15) One of the oldest restaurants in town, this stylish, very traditional restaurant has dependable Bavarian food, swift service and a lively flair thanks to its young and upbeat staff. On a balmy

evening, grab a table in the lovely beer garden out back.

Spitalgarten   BEER GARDEN €
(St Katharinenplatz 1; meals €5-10) A veritable thicket of folding chairs and slatted tables by the Danube, this is one of the best places in town for some al fresco quaffing. It claims to have brewed beer (today's Spital) here since 1350, so it probably knows what it's doing by now.

ℹ Information

There's internet access at coin-operated terminals (€1 per 15 minutes) on the top level of the train station.

Tourist office (www.regensburg.de; Altes Rathaus; ⊙9am-6pm Mon-Fri, to 4pm Sat & Sun)

ℹ Getting There & Away

Regensburg is on the busy train line between Nuremberg (€24, one hour) and Vienna, Austria (€75, four hours). There are hourly trains to Munich (€25, 1½ hours).

Augsburg

✆ 0821 / POP 270,000

Originally established by the Romans in 15 BC, Augsburg later became a centre of Luther's Reformation. Today it's a lively provincial city, criss-crossed by little streams, that has an appealing ambience and vitality. It makes a good day trip from Munich or as part of a Romantic Road foray.

◉ Sights

Look for the very impressive onion-shaped towers on the 17th-century **Rathaus** (Rathausplatz; admission to Golden Hall €2; ⊙10am-6pm) and the adjacent **Perlachturm**, a former guard tower. North of here is the 10th-century **Dom Maria Heimsuchung** (Hoher Weg; ⊙10am-6pm Mon-Sat), which has more 'modern' additions, such as the 14th-century doors showing scenes from the Old Testament.

The Fuggers – a 16th-century banking family and *not* a Renaissance version of the Fockers – left their mark everywhere. They have lavish tombs inside **St Anna Kirche** (Im Annahof 2, off Annastrasse; ⊙10am-noon Tue-Sat, 3-5pm Tue-Sun), a place also known for being a Martin Luther bolt-hole (massive renovations are ongoing so it may be closed periodically). The amazingly named 16th-century **Fuggerei** (adult/child €4/2; ⊙9am-8pm Apr-Oct,

9am-6pm Nov-Mar) was built with banking riches to house the poor, which, remarkably, it still does. The excellent **museum** (Mittlere Gasse 14; free with Fuggerei admission) shows how they've lived.

🛏 Sleeping & Eating

Hotel am Rathaus   HOTEL €€
(☑346 490; www.hotel-am-rathaus-augsburg. de; Am Hinteren Perlachberg 1; r €70-125; 🖭) As central as it gets, and moments away from Rathausplatz, this boutique hotel has fresh neutral decor and a sunny little breakfast room. The trendy Italian restaurant is surprisingly good.

Ratskeller   GERMAN €€
(Rathausplatz 2; mains €8-15) Avoid cliché with ambiently lit corners and anterooms and mezzanines strewn with comfy lounges. There's a wide terrace out back for serious quaffing. Ratskeller's kitchen is renowned for its *Schweinebraten* – roast pork with dumplings and red-cabbage sauerkraut.

Bauerntanz   GERMAN €€
(Bauerntanzgässchen 1; mains €8-16) Framed by lace curtains, this dark-timber place with copper lamps serves big portions of creative Swabian and Bavarian food. There's outdoor seating.

ℹ Information

Tourist office (☑502 0724; www.augsburg -tourismus.de; Maximilian Strasse 57; ⊙9am-6pm Mon-Fri, 10am-5pm Sat, 10am-2pm Sun Apr-Oct, 9am-5pm Mon-Fri, 10am-2pm Sat Nov-Mar)

ℹ Getting There & Away

Trains between Munich and Augsburg are frequent (€12 to €20, 40 minutes); it's on the main line to Frankfurt. The Romantic Road bus stops at the train station and the Rathaus.

Füssen
☑08362 / POP 18,000

Never have so many come to a place with so few inhabitants by comparison. Close to the Austrian border and the foothills of the Alps, Füssen is often overlooked by the mobs swarming the two castles associated with King Ludwig II in nearby Schwangau, which fulfil everyone's fantasy image of a castle.

If Füssen anchors a fairy-tale vision of Germany through King Ludwig's castles, the town itself is not quite the ugly stepsister but rather the practical-accountant stepsister. It has some baroque architecture and you can actually sense a certain Alpine serenity after dark while locals count the change from the day's day-tripper invasion.

⊙ Sights

Neuschwanstein and **Hohenschwangau** castles provide a fascinating glimpse into the romantic king's state of mind (or lack thereof) and well-developed ego. Hohenschwangau is where Ludwig lived as a child. It's not as cute, even though both castles are 19th-century constructions, but it draws less crowds and visits are more relaxed. The adjacent Neuschwanstein is Ludwig's own creation (albeit with the help of a theatrical designer). Although it was unfinished when he died in 1886, there is plenty of evidence of Ludwig's twin obsessions: swans and Wagnerian operas. The sugary pastiche of architectural styles, alternatively overwhelmingly beautiful and just a little too much, reputedly inspired Disney's Fantasyland castle.

Tickets may only be bought from the **ticket centre** (www.ticket-center-hohenschwangau. de; Alpenseestrasse 12, Hohenschwangau; adult/ child €9/free, incl Schloss Hohenschwangau €17/ free; ⊙tickets 8am-5.30pm Apr-Sep, 9am-3.30pm Oct-Mar). In summer it's worth the €1.80 surcharge each to reserve ahead. To walk to Hohenschwangau from there takes about 20 minutes, while Neuschwanstein is a 45-minute steep hike. Horse-drawn carriages (€6) and shuttle buses (€2) shorten but don't eliminate the hike. The walk between the castles is a piney 45-minute stroll.

Take the bus from Füssen train station (€2, 15 minutes, hourly) or share a **taxi** (☑7700; up to 4 people €10). Go early to avoid the worst of the rush.

And remember, as soon as you leave the main trails, you're in beautiful and untrammelled Alpine wilderness.

🛏 Sleeping & Eating

A pavilion near the tourist office has a computerised list of vacant rooms in town; most of the cheapest rooms, at around €20 per person, are in private homes just a few minutes from the Altstadt.

Altstadt Hotel zum Hechten   HOTEL €
(☑916 00; www.hotel-hechten.com; Ritterstrasse 6; r €50-100; 🖭) Set around a quiet inner courtyard, this child-friendly place is one of Füssen's oldest Altstadt hotels, with rustic public areas and bright, modern guest rooms in a sizes small to XL. The restaurant

is a rollicking place for a drink; skip the schnitzel.

Drinking

Giovanni's Weinladen   WINE
(Lechhalde 2) Bottles line the walls of this wine store, which also sells by the glass. A few tables out front on a terrace take in some tree-clad hills and you can move on from the genteel charms of the grape to something with more of a kick like grappa.

ℹ Information

Tourist office (☑938 50; www.fuessen.de; Kaiser-Maximillian-Platz 1; ⊘9am-5pm Mon-Fri, 10am-2pm Sat, 10am-noon Sun)

ℹ Getting There & Away

Train connections to Munich and Augsburg (€23, two hours) run every hour. Füssen is the start of the Romantic Road and the **Romantic Road bus** (www.romanticroadcoach.de; ⊘8am daily mid-Apr–mid-Oct) service. Day trips from Munich are widely promoted.

RVO bus 9606 (www.rvo-bus.de) connects Füssen, via Wieskirche and Oberammergau, with Garmisch-Partenkirchen (€3, 2¼ hours, five to six daily).

BAVARIAN ALPS

While not quite as high as their sister summits further south in Austria and Switzerland, the Bavarian Alps (Bayerische Alpen) still are standouts, owing to their abrupt rise from the rolling Bavarian foothills. Stretching westward from Germany's southeastern corner to the Allgäu region near Lake Constance, the Alps take in most of the mountainous country fringing the southern border with Austria.

Berchtesgaden

☑08652 / POP 7900
Steeped in myth and legend, the Berchtesgadener Land enjoys a natural beauty so abundant that it's almost preternatural. Framed by six formidable mountain ranges and home to Germany's second-highest mountain, the Watzmann (2713m), the dreamy, fir-lined valleys are filled with gurgling streams and peaceful Alpine villages.

Much of the terrain is protected by law as the Nationalpark Berchtesgaden, which embraces the pristine Königssee, one of Germany's most photogenic lakes. Yet, Berchtes-

WIESKIRCHE

This Unesco World Heritage–listed **church** (www.wieskirche.de; ⊘8am-7pm May-Oct, to 5pm Nov-Apr) is a jaw-dropping spectacle of 18th-century rococo excess. Its white pillars tower over a tiny village 25km northeast of Füssen. The church can be reached by the **Romantic Road bus** (www.romanticroadcoach.de) or **RVO bus 9606** (www.rvo-bus.de), which runs between Füssen and Garmisch-Partenkirchen via Wieskirche and Oberammergau (five to six daily).

gaden's history is also indelibly entwined with the Nazi period, as chronicled at the disturbing Dokumentation Obersalzberg. The Eagle's Nest, a mountaintop lodge built for Hitler, is now a major tourist attraction.

⊙ Sights & Activities

Dokumentation Obersalzberg   MUSEUM
(www.obersalzberg.de; Salzbergstrasse 41, Obersalzberg; adult/child & student €3/free; ⊘9am-5pm daily Apr-Oct, 10am-3pm Tue-Sun Nov-Mar) In 1933 quiet Obersalzberg (some 3km from Berchtesgaden) became the southern headquarters of Hitler's government, a dark period that's given the full historical treatment at this at-times heartbreaking and compelling museum. You can visit tunnels that were dug for a fortunately unfulfilled Nazi last stand, but the exhibits – including the erudite English audio guide (€2) – are the real draw. It shows how Hitler gained the support of the masses through his demonization of 'elites' while cigarette companies increased sales by including a picture of the dictator in every pack.

To get there take bus 838 from the 1938-vintage Hauptbahnhof in Berchtesgaden. It's hourly weekdays but infrequent at weekends. A cab costs about €20.

Eagle's Nest   HISTORIC SITE
Berchtesgaden's creepiest – yet impressive – draw is the Eagle's Nest atop Mt Kehlstein, a sheer-sided peak at Obersalzberg. Perched at 1834m, the innocent-looking lodge (called Kehlsteinhaus in German) has sweeping views across the mountains and down into the valley where the Königssee shimmers. Ironically, though it was built for him, Hitler is said to have suffered from vertigo and rarely visited.

ℹ ALP-HOPPING

While the public transport network is good, the mountain geography means there are few direct routes between the top Alpine draws; sometimes a shortcut via Austria is quicker (such as by road between Füssen and Garmisch-Partenkirchen). Bus rather than rail routes are often more practical. For those who are driving, the **German Alpine Road** (Deutsche Alpenstrasse) is a scenic way to go.

Drive or take bus 849 from Dokumentation Obersalzberg to Kehlstein, where you board a special **bus** (www.kehlsteinhaus.de; adult/child €16/9) that drives you up the mountain. It runs between 9am and 4pm, and takes 35 minutes.

Eagle's Nest Tours (☑649 71; www.eagles-nest-tours.com; Königsseer Strasse 2; adult/6-12yr €48/30; ⊙1.30pm mid-May–Oct) has four-hour tours in English that cover the war years; they leave from near the train station.

Salzbergwerk SALT MINE
(www.salzzeitreise.de; adult/child €15/10; ⊙9am-5pm May-Oct, 11am-3pm Nov-Apr) The 1½-hour tours of this salt mine combine history with a carnival.

Alpine Beauty NATURAL ATTRACTIONS
Crossing the beautiful, emerald-green **Königssee**, an alpine lake situated 5km south of Berchtesgaden (and linked by hourly buses in summer) is sublime. There are frequent boat tours (€13) across the lake to the pixel-perfect chapel at **St Bartholomä**.

The wilds of **Berchtesgaden National Park** offer some of the best **hiking** in Germany. A good introduction to the area is a 2km path up from St Bartholomä beside the Königssee to the Watzmann-Ostwand, a massive 2000m-high rock face where scores of overly ambitious mountaineers have died.

🛏 Sleeping & Eating

Berchtesgaden town proper is just up the hill from the train station and is rather staid. You might want to make your visit a day trip from Salzburg. There's no need to linger here when there's so much nearby.

Hotel Bavaria HOTEL €€
(☑660 11; www.hotelbavaria.net; Sunklergässchen 11; r €50-130) A short hop from the station, this guest house, run by the same family for a century, has romantically beamed rooms with four-poster beds and modern bathrooms. Looking at the views from some of the pricier quarters with balconies, you'd think the hotel had been lined up specially to catch the vistas.

ℹ Information

The **tourist office** (www.berchtesgaden.de; Königsseer Strasse 2; ⊙8.30am-6pm Mon-Fri, to 5pm Sat, 9am-3pm Sun Apr–mid-Oct, reduced hr other times) is just across the river from the train station.

ℹ Getting There & Away

There is hourly train service to Berchtesgaden from Munich (€30, 2½ hours), which usually requires a change in Frilassing. There are hourly connections to nearby Salzburg in Austria (€10, one hour); bus 840 from the station takes 45 minutes.

Garmisch-Partenkirchen
☑08821 / POP 27,000
The Alpine towns of Garmisch and Partenkirchen were merged for the 1936 Winter Olympics (it's making another bid for the 2020 Games). Munich residents' favourite getaway spot, this year-round resort is also a big draw for skiers, snowboarders, hikers and mountaineers. On sunny days, an ascent of Zugspitze will astound.

⊙ Sights & Activities

The huge **ski stadium** outside town hosted the Olympics. From the pedestrian Am Kurpark, walk up Klammstrasse, cross the tracks and veer left on the first path to reach the stadium and enjoy the spectacular views.

An excellent short hike from Garmisch is to the **Partnachklamm gorge**, via a winding path above a stream and underneath the waterfalls. You take the Graseck cable car and follow the signs.

An excursion to the **Zugspitze** (www.zugspitze.de) summit, Germany's highest peak (2962m), is a spectacular outing from Garmisch. There are various ways up, including the **Bayerische Zugspitzbahn rack-railway**, just west of the main train station, summit cable car or Eibsee cable car. You can use any combination of these modes for adult/child €47/9 round trip. Or you can scale it in two days. The summit is a winter playground year-round, with glaciers, snow and on clear days (the only times you should do this), extraordinary views of the Alps.

Garmisch is bounded by three separate ski areas – **Zugspitze plateau** (the highest), **Alpspitze/Hausberg** (the largest) and **Eckbauer** (the cheapest). Day ski passes range from €19 for Eckbauer to €37 for Zugspitze. The optimistically named Happy Ski Card is a pass for the entire region (from €69 for two days). A web of cross-country ski trails runs along the main valleys.

For ski hire and courses try the following:

Skischule (☑4931; www.skischule-gap.de; Am Hausberg 8)

Sport Total (☑1425; www.agentursporttotal.de; Marienplatz 18) Also organises paragliding, mountain biking, rafting and ballooning.

🛏 Sleeping & Eating

The tourist office has a 24-hour, outdoor room-reservation board. Choices are many.

Hotel Garmischer Hof HOTEL €€
(☑9110; www.garmischer-hof.de; Chamonixstrasse 10; s €59-94, d €94-136; 🐾🅿) Generations of athletes, artists and outdoor enthusiasts have stayed at this refined chateau, property of the Seiwald family since 1928. Tasteful and cosy are the rooms, many with incredible Alpine views. Breakfast is served in the vaulted cafe-restaurant with a garden terrace.

Hostel 2962 HOSTEL €
(☑957 50; www.hostel2962.com; Partnachauenstrasse 3; dm/d from €20/60; 🐾) An old converted hotel, this is still essentially a typical Garmisch lodge. Rooms have some rather arch detailing that has some fun with Alpine clichés.

Bräustüberl GERMAN €€
(☑2312; Fürstenstrasse 23, Garmisch; mains €6-17) Conversation flows as freely as the beer at this quintessential Bavarian brew-pub, complete with enormous enamel coal-burning stove and dirndl-clad waitresses. Opt for the beer hall in winter and the beer garden in summer.

ℹ Information

Tourist office (☑180 700; www.gapa.de; Richard-Strauss-Platz 1, Garmisch; ⊙8am-6pm Mon-Sat, 10am-noon Sun) Near the station.

Zugspitzcard (www.zugspitzcard.com; adult/child from €44/25) Includes cable-car and railway rides and discounts, admission to museums and activities.

ℹ Getting There & Away

From Garmisch there is train service to Munich (€19, 80 minutes, hourly) and to Innsbruck, Austria (€15, 80 minutes, every two hours)via Mittenwald. **RVO bus 9606** (www.rvo-bus.de), from in front of the train station, runs to Füssen (€3, 2¼ hours, five to six daily), via Oberammergau and Wieskirche.

Oberammergau
☑08822 / POP 5500

A blend of genuine piety, religious kitsch and monumental commercial greed, Oberammergau sometimes seems to sink under the weight of day trippers. Sadly, the crowds may distract from the town's triple charms: its gorgeous valley setting below the jagged Kofel peak, a 500-year-old woodcarving tradition and a wealth of houses painted with *Lüftlmalerei* (idealised external murals).

Oberammergau, about 20km north of Garmisch-Partenkirchen, is known worldwide for hosting the famous **Passion Play** (www.passionplay-oberammergau.com), acted out by much of the townfolk roughly every 10 years since 1634 to give thanks for being spared from the plague. The next one is in 2020.

Hourly trains connect Munich with Oberammergau (€18, 1¾ hours) with a change at Murnau. **RVO bus 9606** (www.rvo-bus.de) links Oberammergau with Füssen and the Wieskirche as well as Garmisch-Partenkirchen five to six times daily.

BADEN-WÜRTTEMBERG

With the exception of cuckoo clocks in the Black Forest, Baden-Württemberg runs a distant second in the cliché race to Bavaria. But that's really all the better, as it leaves more for you to discover on your own.

It's a pretty land of misty hills, shadowy conifers and cute villages that rewards exploration. If you want a big and quaint German village with lots of history, there's Heidelberg. Baden-Baden is the sybaritic playground for spa-goers, and Freiburg has youthful vibrancy in an intriguing package. Finally, Lake Constance is a misty redoubt bordering Switzerland and has all the pleasures a large body of water can offer.

The prosperous modern state of Baden-Württemberg was created in 1951 out of three smaller regions: Baden, Württemberg and Hohenzollern (thank goodness the names stopped at two).

Stuttgart

☎ 0711 / POP 592,000

Hemmed in by vine-covered hills, comfortable Stuttgart enjoys a quality of life funded by its fabled car companies: Porsche and Mercedes. It's also Baden-Württemberg's state capital and the hub of its industries. At the forefront of Germany's economic recovery from the ravages of WWII, Stuttgart started life less auspiciously in 950 as a horse stud farm. About 80% of the city centre was destroyed in WWII, but there are a few historical buildings left and – no surprise – car museums.

◉ Sights

Stretching southwest from the Neckar River to the city centre is the **Schlossgarten**, an extensive strip of parkland divided into three sections (Unterer, Mittlerer and Oberer), complete with ponds, swans, street entertainers and modern sculptures. At the gardens' southern end they encompass the sprawling baroque **Neues Schloss** (Schlossplatz).

Next to the turreted, Renaissance-esque **Altes Schloss** is the city's oldest square, Schillerplatz, with its **Friedrich Schiller statue** in honour of the poet, and the 12th-

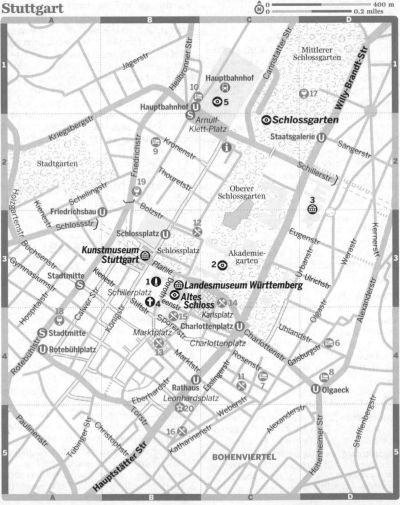

Stuttgart

century **Stiftskirche** (Stiftstrasse 12) with its twin 61m-high late-Gothic towers.

The **tower** at the daggy main train station sports a revolving three-pointed star of the Mercedes-Benz. Get up close and personal and enjoy great views as part of the **TurmForum** (Hauptbahnhof; admission free; ⊙10am-9pm Apr-Sep, to 6pm Oct-Mar), an exhibition promoting the now notorious **Stuttgart 21 scheme** (www.bahnprojekt-stuttgart-ulm.de) to radically transform the station and surrounding tracks. When construction began in 2010, huge street protests shut down the city and the political ramifications are ongoing.

Museums & Galleries MUSEUMS

The Altes Schloss houses the **Landesmuseum Württemberg** (www.landesmuseum-stuttgart.de; Schillerplatz 6; adult/child €4.50/free; ⊙10am-5pm Tue-Sun), where exhibits include Roman-era discoveries.

Possibly more beautiful than the works within, the **Kunstmuseum Stuttgart** (www.kunstmuseum-stuttgart.de; Kleiner Schlossplatz 1; adult/child €5/3.50; ⊙10am-6pm Tue, Thu, Sat & Sun, to 9pm Wed & Fri) glows like a radioactive sugar cube at night. Highlights include works by Otto Dix, Dieter Roth and Willi Baumeister.

Adjoining the Schlossgarten you'll find the thriving **Staatsgalerie** (www.staatsgalerie.de; Konrad-Adenauer-Strasse 30; adult/child €5.50/4; ⊙10am-6pm Wed & Fri-Sun, to 8pm Tue & Thu), which houses an excellent collection from the Middle Ages to the present. It's especially rich in old German masters from the surrounding Swabia region.

TOP CHOICE Car Museums MUSEUMS

An arms race has broken out between the local auto giants, with both building vast and costly monuments to themselves.

The motor car was first developed by Gottlieb Daimler and Carl Benz at the end of the 19th century. The impressive **Mercedes-Benz Museum** (www.museum-mercedes-benz.com; Mercedesstrasse 100; adult/child €8/4; ⊙9am-6pm Tue-Sun) is in the suburb of Bad-Cannstatt; take S-Bahn 1 to Neckarpark. Don't mention Chrysler.

For even faster cars, cruise over to the striking **Porsche Museum** (www.porsche.com; Porscheplatz 1; adult/child €8/4; ⊙9am-6pm Tue-Sun); take S-Bahn 6 to Neuwirtshaus, north of the city. No word yet on whether they'll be adding a VW wing.

Pick up the excellent free booklet *Automotive Heritage* from the tourist office.

🛌 Sleeping

Der Zauberlehrling HOTEL €€€

(📞237 7770; www.zauberlehrling.de; Rosenstrasse 38; r €120-280; ❋🐾🛜) This consciously chic 'design hotel' in the Bohnenviertel has 17 named rooms, each unique and each a design sensation. Make a splash – or go down – in the Titanic-themed room with its waterbed. Amenities abound, including a breakfast garden.

City Hotel HOTEL €€

(📞210 810; www.cityhotel-stuttgart.de; Uhlandstrasse 18; r €80-120; 🛜) Eschew the anonymity of Stuttgart's cookie-cutter chains for this intimate hotel just off Charlottenplatz.

Stuttgart

The 31 rooms are light, clean and modern, if slightly lacklustre. Breakfast on the terrace in summer is a bonus.

Hotel Unger HOTEL €€

(209 90; www.hotel-unger.de; Kronenstrasse 17; r €90-200;) Right near the Hauptbahnhof, this hotel's corporate feel is offset by its snappy attention to detail and comfort. Guests rave about the generous breakfast with smoked fish, fresh fruit and pastries. Floors six and seven have good views.

InterCity Hotel HOTEL €€

(222 8233; www.intercityhotel.com; Hauptbahnhof; r €60-180;) Right in the train station, the large rooms are utilitarian but a mere crawl from trains and a few steps from the centre. This is the perfect location if you plan a quick getaway or late arrival, plus you can watch any Stuttgart 21 protests.

Hostel Alex 30 HOSTEL €

(838 8950; www.alex30-hostel.de; Alexanderstrasse 30; dm €22, r €35-100; @) Tidy and orderly, near the Bohnenviertel. Take U-Bahn lines 5, 6 or 7 to Olgaeck.

✖ Eating

Stuttgart is a great place to sample Swabian specialities such as *Spätzle* (home-made noodles) and *Maultaschen* (a hearty ravioli in broth). Local wines edge out beer in popularity.

The **food market** (Marktplatz; ⊙7.30am-1pm Tue, Thu & Sat) and the **Markthalle** (market hall; Dorotheenstrasse 4; ⊙7am-6.30pm Mon-Fri, 7am-4pm Sat), with their bounty of local produce and gourmet items, are the best features of the otherwise humdrum Marktplatz.

TOP CHOICE Weinstube Fröhlich SWABIAN €€

(Leonhardstrasse 5; mains €8-15) Hard in the midst of Stuttgart's paltry red-light district, this restaurant is traditional but not a period piece. Creative takes on local standards include superb *Maultaschen* and plate-covering schnitzel. The hardwood floors allow the food to shine. As the name implies, the local wine list is long.

Basta SWABIAN €€

(Wagnerstrasse 39; mains €10-18) The hum of chatter and herby smells fill this snug Bohnenviertel bistro, which has an intensely loyal following. Each flavour shines through in dishes like wild-garlic *Maultaschen*. Wine lovers have plenty of choice, and the bar is a classy place for a drink even if not dining.

BOHEMIAN BEANS

Stuttgart's most interesting neighbourhood is a short stroll from the centre. The **Bohnenviertel** (Bean District) takes its name from the diet of the poor tanners, dyers and craftsmen who lived here. Today the district's cobbled lanes and gabled houses harbour idiosyncratic galleries, workshops, bookstores, wine taverns, cafes and a red-light district.

Grand Café Planie CAFE €€

(Charlottenplatz 17; mains €5-15) Fully luxe, like a loaded E-class sedan, this fin de siècle cafe features a print of the *Grossstadt* triptych by the realist Otto Dix. You may wish the realism didn't extend to the lavish array of tortes in a long case, but have one anyway.

Café Künstlerbund CAFE €

(Schlossplatz 2; mains €7-10) Shelter under the arches facing the park or out in the sunshine at this funky cafe that's part of a large gallery. The drinks menu is huge, as are the choices for breakfast. When the weather gets nasty, duck into the groovy upstairs room.

♟ Drinking & Entertainment

Hans-im-Glück Platz, centred on a namesake fountain depicting the caged Grimm's fairy-tale character Lucky Hans, is a hub of bars. Club- and lounge-lined Theodor-Heuss-Strasse is thronged with sashaying hipsters. A **beer garden** (Cannstatter Strasse 18) in the Mittlerer Schlossgarten, northeast of the main train station, has beautiful views over the city.

Palast der Republik BAR

(Friedrichstrasse 27) A legendary and tiny pillbox of a bar that pulls a huge crowd of laid-back, genial drinkers. Statuary and stickers abound.

Kiste JAZZ CLUB

(Hauptstätter Strasse 35; ⊙4pm-2am Mon-Thu, to 3am Fri & Sat) This hole-in-the-wall bar, often jam-packed, is the city's leading jazz venue, with concerts nightly except Sunday, starting at 9.30pm or 10pm.

Muttermilch LOUNGE

(www.muttermilch-stuttgart.de; Theodor-Heuss-Strasse 23) Good-looking Stuttgarters dance to soul and funk in nouveau Alpine chic before hopping off to other nearby clubs.

ℹ Information

Königstrasse is the spine of central Stuttgart, with most of the major stores and malls.

Stuttcard (from €18) Free museum entry and transport, plus discounts on events, activities and guided tours. Sold at the tourist office and some hotels.

Tourist office (www.stuttgart-tourist.de; Königstrasse 1a; ⊙9am-8pm Mon-Fri, 9am-6pm Sat, 11am-6pm Sun)

ℹ Getting There & Around

Stuttgart's **airport** (SGT; www.stuttgart-airport.com) is south of the city and includes service from Air Berlin, Germanwings and Lufthansa. It's served by S2 and S3 trains (€3.30, 30 minutes from the Hauptbahnhof).

There are frequent train departures for all major German cities, and many international ones, such as Zürich and Paris.

DESTINATION	PRICE	DURATION (HR)
Frankfurt	€57	1¼
Munich	€53	2¼
Nuremberg	€38	2¼

One-way fares on Stuttgart's **public transport network** (www.vvs.de) are €2 in the central zone; a central-zone day pass is €6.

Tübingen

☏07071 / POP 84,000

Forty kilometres south of Stuttgart, Tübingen mixes all the charms of a late-medieval city – a hilltop fortress, cobbled alleys and half-timbered houses – with the erudition and mischief of a university town. Wander the winding alleys of old stone walls, then take a boat ride down the Neckar River.

On **Marktplatz**, the centre of town, is the 1435 **Rathaus**, with its baroque facade and astronomical clock. The nearby late-Gothic **Stiftkirche** (Am Holz-markt; ⊙9am-5pm) houses the tombs of the Württemberg dukes and has excellent medieval stained-glass windows. The Renaissance **Schloss Hohentübingen** (Burgsteig 11), now part of the university, has fine views over the steep, red-tiled rooftops of the old town, and a museum.

🛏 Sleeping & Eating

Hotel am Schloss   HOTEL €€

(☏929 40; www.hotelamschloss.de; Burgsteige 18; r €65-135; 🛜) Some come for the restaurant's legendary *Maultaschen* (mains €9 to €15), some for peerless castle views, and others for the dapper rooms ensconced in a 16th-century building.

Wurstküche   GERMAN €€

(Am Lustnauer Tor 8; mains €10-16) Stroll up a hill for fine local foods sourced from organic farmers.

Weinhaus Beck   WINE TAVERN

(Am Markt 1) Rarely an empty table at this convivial wine tavern beside the Rathaus.

ℹ Getting There & Away

The definition of a day trip: trains between Tübingen and Stuttgart run every 30 minutes (€12, one hour).

Heidelberg

☏06221 / POP 146,000

Heidelberg's baroque old town built from rose-hued sandstone, lively university atmosphere, excellent pubs and evocative half-ruined castle make it hugely popular with visitors, 3.5 million of whom flock here each year. They are following in the footsteps of the 19th-century romantics, most notably the poet Goethe. Britain's William Turner also loved the city, which inspired him to paint some of his greatest landscapes.

Less starry-eyed was Mark Twain (www.mark-twain-in-heidelberg.de), who in 1878 began his European travels with a three-month stay in Heidelberg, recounting his bemused observations in *A Tramp Abroad*.

◉ Sights

TOP CHOICE   **Schloss**   CASTLE

(www.schloss-heidelberg.de; adult/child €5/3, tours €4; ⊙8am-5.30pm) Heidelberg's imposing icon is one of Germany's finest

ℹ HEIDELBERG FAST TRACK

Heidelberg's captivating **old town** starts to reveal itself only after a charm-free 15-minute walk east from the main train station. Cut to the chase and go direct to the heart of town with bus 32 to Universitätsplatz or bus 33 to Bergbahn, whichever leaves first. Later, stroll west the length of Hauptstrasse (the town's shopping spine) to Bismarckplatz and catch a tram to the station.

Heidelberg

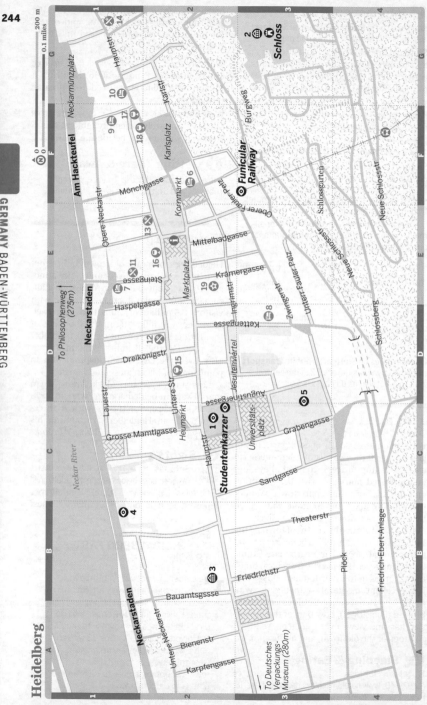

Schloss

Neckarstaden

To Philosophenweg (275m)

Neckar River

Am Hackteufel

Neckarmünzplatz

Hauptstr

Karlstr

Karlplatz

Mönchgasse

Obere Neckarstr

Kornmarkt

Mittelbadgasse

Marktplatz

Steingasse

Kramergasse

Haspelgasse

Ingrimstr

Kettengasse

Dreikönigstr

Untere Str

Heumarkt

Augustinergasse

Jesuitenviertel

Studentenkarzer

Universitäts-platz

Grosse Mamtlgasse

Grabengasse

Sandgasse

Theaterstr

Plöck

Friedrichstr

Bauamtsgsse

Friedrich-Ebert-Anlage

Bienenstr

Karpfengasse

Untere Neckarstr

Neckarstaden

Funicular Railway

Burgweg

Schlossgarten

Neue Schlossstr

Neue Schlossstr

Unter Fauler Pelz

Zwingerstr

Oberer Fauler Pelz

Schlossberg

To Deutsches Verpackungs-Museum (280m)

GERMANY HEIDELBERG

examples of grand Gothic-Renaissance architecture. The building's half-ruined state only enhances its romantic appeal (Twain called it 'the Lear of inanimate nature'). Seen from anywhere in the Altstadt, this striking red-sandstone castle dominates the hillside. The entry fee covers the castle, the **Grosses Fass** (Great Vat), an enormous 18th-century keg capable of holding 221,726L; and the **Deutsches Apothekenmuseum** (German Pharmaceutical Museum; Schlosshof 1).

Ride the **Funicular Railway** (one way €4; ◷9am-8pm summer, to 5pm other times) to the castle from lower Kornmarkt station, or enjoy an invigorating 15-minute walk up steep, stone-laid lanes. Either way be sure to walk down, especially through the less-crowded paths to the east. The funicular continues up to the **Königstuhl**, where there are good views (additional fare €9).

Old Town   HISTORIC QUARTER
Dominating Universitätsplatz are the 18th-century **Alte Universität** and the **Neue Universität**. On the back side, find the **Studentenkarzer** (student jail; Augustinergasse 2; adult/child €3/2.50; ◷10am-6pm Tue-Sun Apr-Sep, 10am-4pm Tue-Sat Oct-Mar). From 1778 to 1914 this jail was used for misbehaved students (crimes included drinking, singing and womanising). The **Marstall** is the former arsenal, now a student Mensa (cafeteria).

The **Kurpfälzisches Museum** (Palatinate Museum; ☑583 402; Hauptstrasse 97; adult/child €3/2; ◷10am-6pm Tue-Sun) contains paintings, sculptures and the jawbone of the 600,000-year-old Heidelberg Man.

The Heidelberg region has been a major global supplier of printing equipment, much of it used to create packaging for products. The **Deutsches Verpackungs-Museum** (German Museum of Packaging; Hauptstrasse 22; adult/child €3.50/2.50; ◷1-6pm Wed-Sun) celebrates classic packages such as the Nivea jar as well as less successful items such as Titanic-brand cigarettes.

A stroll along the **Philosophenweg**, north of the Neckar River, gives a welcome respite from Heidelberg's tourist hordes.

The tourist office runs English-language **guided tours** (adult/student €7/5; ◷tours 10.30am Fri & Sat Apr-Oct) that depart from the Löwenbrunnen (Lions Fountain) at Universtätsplatz.

⊟ Sleeping

Finding any accommodation during Heidelberg's high season can be difficult. Arrive early in the day or book ahead.

Hotel Goldener Hecht   HOTEL €€
(☑536 80; www.hotel-goldener-hecht.de; Steingasse 2; r €65-110; ☏) Goethe almost slept here: the hotel would have kept the famous author had the clerk on duty not been so uppity. Ever since, guests at this family-run place have received a warm welcome. Some of the 13 sparkling rooms, each unique, have views of the Neckar River.

Kulturbrauerei Hotel   HOTEL €€
(☑502 980; www.heidelberger-kulturbrauerei.de; Leyergasse 6; r €110-180; ☏) Great beer comes second at this swank microbrewery hotel.

The stylish rooms are decked out in soft creams with shiny parquet floors and large windows. Some rooms on the top floor have soaring A-frame ceilings.

Hotel Zum Pfalzgrafen
HOTEL €€

(☎204 89; www.hotel-zum-pfalzgrafen.de; Kettengasse 21; r €70-110) Polished pine floors are a nice touch at this family-run place, which has 24 clean-lined rooms that belie the hotel's classic 18th-century facade. The breakfast buffet is included.

Hotel Am Kornmarkt
HOTEL €€

(☎905 830; www.hotelamkornmarkt.de; Kornmarkt 7; r €40-110) Discreet and understated, this Altstadt favourite has 20 pleasant, well-kept rooms. The pricier rooms have great views of the Kornmarkt, while cheaper ones share spotless hall showers.

Steffi's Hostel
HOSTEL €

(☎0176-2016 2200; www.hostelheidelberg.de; Alte Eppelheimer Strasse 50; dm €20-24, r €45-60; @ 🛜) Backpackers sing the praises of this hostel, housed in a one-time brick factory near the Hauptbahnhof. Steffi greets guests warmly with bounteous perks.

Sudpfanne
HOSTEL €

(☎163 636; www.heidelberger-sudpfanne.de; Hauptstrasse 223; dm €16; 🛜) Right in the centre of things, the mood is set by the wine-barrel entrance (it's also a cafe).

✖ Eating

Try heading down the small streets leading away from Marktplatz to increase your ratio of locals.

Zur Herrenmühle
GERMAN €€

(Hauptstrasse 239; mains €9-24; ☺dinner Mon-Sat) Serves traditional, classic south-German food that veers so far south that Italian flavours drift in. Dine under the ancient wood beams of a 17th-century mill or outside in a serene garden. Rustically elegant, with geraniums hanging over the windows.

Schiller's Café
CAFE €

(Heiliggeiststrasse 5; snacks €2-4) Whisper quietly about this half-timbered cafe, housed in one of Heidelberg's oldest buildings, where the movie *Schille* was filmed. Hot chocolates with cinnamon, home-made cakes, quiches, and wines are mostly organic.

Brauhaus Vetter
GERMAN €€

(Steingasse 9; mains €7-14) A popular brewery that serves up lots of hearty fare to absorb the suds. The copper kettles gleam. Groups of six or more can order the Brewer's feast, a sausage, pretzel, radish, meat and cheese smorgasbord.

Café Burkardt
CAFE €

(Untere Strasse 27; cake & snacks €3-8) Full of doily-draped nooks and dark-wood crannies, this nostalgic cafe tempts with Heidelberg's tastiest tarts and cheesecakes. Opt for a table in the courtyard, where Weimar Republic president Friedrich Ebert was born.

🍷 Drinking & Entertainment

'German university life is a very free life; it seems to have no restraints.' So observed Mark Twain, and two centuries later little has changed; you won't have to go far to find a happening backstreet bar. Lots of the action centres on Untere Strasse.

Two ancient pubs, **Zum Roten Ochsen** (☎209 77; Hauptstrasse 213) and **Zum Sepp'l** (☎230 85; Hauptstrasse 217), are now filled with tourists reliving the uni days they never had.

Cave54
LIVE MUSIC

(www.cave54.de; Krämergasse 2; ☺Thu-Sun) For live jazz and blues, head to this stone cellar that oozes character. Some nights there's a DJ.

MaxBar
CAFE

(Marktplatz 5) A French-style cafe with classic views of the Marktplatz. Perfect for a beer or a pastis, it's especially popular on weekend nights. Wave to the Napoleon bust above the bar.

Destille
BAR

(Untere Strasse 16) Known for the tree trunk behind the bar, this mellow and hugely popular pub pours stiff drinks that inspire the chess players here to make rather unorthodox moves.

ℹ Information

Heidelberg Card (from €13) Discounts and free admission to many sights.

Tourist office (☎194 33; www.heidelberg-marketing.de) Hauptbahnhof (Willy-Brandt-Platz 1; ☺9am-7pm Mon-Sat year-round, 10am-6pm Sun Apr-Nov); Marktplatz (☺8am-5pm Mon-Fri, 10am-5pm Sat)

ℹ Getting There & Around

There are hourly IC trains to/from Frankfurt (€19, one hour) and Stuttgart (€24, 40 minutes). The frequent service to Mannheim (€5, 15 minutes) has connections to cities throughout Germany.

Bismarckplatz is the main public-transport hub. One-way tickets for the excellent bus and tram system (www.vrn.de) are €2.20.

Baden-Baden

☏07221 / POP 55,000

Who would want to bathe naked with a bunch of strangers? That's the question at the heart of the matter in Baden-Baden, the storied and ritzy spa town. The answer, of course, should be, anyone who wants to enjoy a truly self-indulgent experience.

And let's see, shall we call them, well, prudes can still get a bit of the pleasure while staying suited and segregated. The natural hot springs have attracted visitors since Roman times, but this small city only really became fashionable in the 19th century, when it became a destination of royalty. It is stately, closely cropped and salubrious. Take the 69°C plunge.

◉ Sights & Activities

Baths
BATHS

The 19th-century **Friedrichsbad** (www.roem isch-irisches-bad.de; Römerplatz 1; bathing program €21-31; ☉9am-10pm) is the reason for your journey. It's decadently Roman in style and provides a muscle-melting 16-step bathing program. No clothing is allowed inside; several sections are mixed on most days.

The more modern **Caracalla-Therme** (www.caracalla.de; Römerplatz 1; entrance from €14; ☉8am-10pm) is a vast, modern complex of outdoor and indoor pools, and hot- and cold-water grottoes. You must wear a bathing suit and bring your own towel.

Historic Town
HISTORIC BUILDINGS

The 2000-year-old **Römische Badruinen** (Roman Bath Ruins; Römerplatz 1; adult/child €2.50/1; ☉11am-noon & 3-6pm mid-Mar–mid-Nov) are worth a quick look, but for a real taste of Baden-Baden head to the **Kurhaus**, built in the 1820s, which houses the ornate **casino** (www.casino-baden-baden.de; Kaiserallee 1; admission €3, guided tours adult/child €4/2; ☉tours 9.30am-noon, gambling after 2pm), which improves greatly after the entryway that looks like a meeting hall. Wear what you want for tours; for gambling men must wear a coat and tie (rentals €11).

Enjoy a taste of the warm and salty water that made Baden-Baden famous at the stolid, porticoed **Trinkhalle** (Pump Room; Kaiserallee 3). The water's free but a flimsy plastic cup (an eco nightmare!) will cost you €0.20.

🛏 Sleeping & Eating

Most restaurants huddle in the pedestrianised stretch around Leopoldsplatz. Nightlife is suited for people who've had the life boiled out of them.

Steigenberger Europäischer Hof
HOTEL €€€

(☏93 30; www.badischer-hof.steigenberger.com; Kaiserallee 2; r €160-300; @🛜🖢) Suitably grand to go with the climes locally, this 120-bed dowager stays dolled up morning to night. Rooms span the gamut, from 'economy' with views of the courtyard to rather grand luxe options with balconies and views of the park and passing swells.

Hotel am Markt
HOTEL €

(☏270 40; www.hotel-am-markt-baden.de; Marktplatz 18; r €43-80; @) This peach-fronted hotel next to the Stiftskirche is a real find. Its 23 rooms are homey, bathrooms squeaky-clean and the silence is broken only by church bells.

Rizzi
ITALIAN €€€

(Augustaplatz 1; mains €16-24) A summertime Italian favourite, this stout pink villa's tree-shaded patio faces Lichtentaler Allee. Fresh seafood, saffron-infused risotto and enticing pastas pair nicely with local rieslings.

Jensens
CAFE €

(Sophienstrasse 45; meals €5-9; 🛜) Opposite Caracalla-Therme, this bistro with a patio has a hip feel with its pepper-red walls, wood floors and jazzy tunes. Honour nearby Strasbourg with a *Flammkuchen* on the patio.

ℹ Information

The **tourist office** (www.baden-baden.com; Kaiserallee 3; ☉10am-5pm Mon-Sat, 2-5pm Sun) is in the Trinkhalle.

ℹ Getting There & Around

Baden-Airpark (FKB; www.badenairpark.de) has daily Ryanair service but, like many tiny airports served by the budget carrier, getting to/from the airport can be a challenge. Consult the airport website for details on the sketchy service.

Baden-Baden is on the busy Mannheim-Basel train line. Frequent local trains serve Karlsruhe (€8, 15 minutes) and Offenburg (€9, 20 minutes), from where you can make connections to much of Germany.

Buses 201, 216 and 245 traverse the 7km to Leopoldsplatz (€2).

BLACK FOREST

The Black Forest (Schwarzwald) gets its name from its dark canopy of evergreens, which evoke mystery and allure in many. Although some parts heave with visitors, a 20-minute walk from even the most crowded spots will put you in quiet countryside interspersed with enormous traditional farmhouses and patrolled by amiable dairy cows. It's not nature wild and remote, but bucolic and picturesque.

The Black Forest is east of the Rhine between Karlsruhe and Basel. It's shaped like

Black Forest (Schwarzwald)

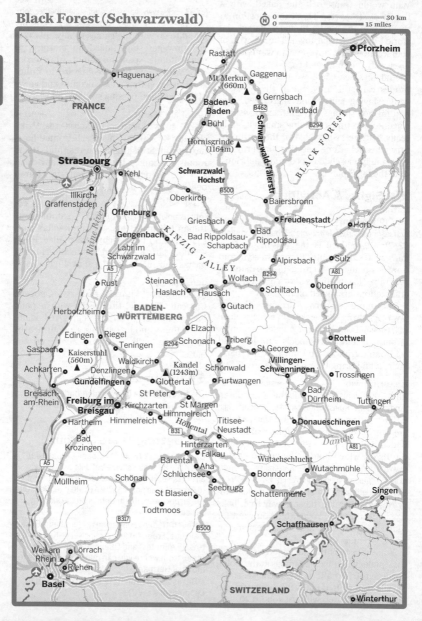

0 — 30 km
0 — 15 miles

a bean, about 160km long and 50km wide. From north to south there are four good bases for your visit: Freudenstadt, Schiltach, Triberg and Titisee. Each has good train links.

With a car you'll find a visit especially rewarding, as you can wander the rolling hills and deep valleys at will. One of the main tourist roads is the Schwarzwald-Hochstrasse (B500), which runs from Baden-Baden to Freudenstadt and from Triberg to Waldshut. Other thematic roads with maps provided by tourist offices include Schwarzwald Bäderstrasse (spa town route), Schwarzwald Panoramastrasse (panoramic view route) and Badische Weinstrasse (wine route). Make certain you have an excellent commercial regional road map with you, too.

And, yes, there are many, many places to buy cuckoo clocks (you pay at least €150 for a good one).

Freudenstadt

📞07441 / POP 24,000

Freudenstadt is a good base for exploring the northern Black Forest and hikes into the surrounding countryside. It's most notable feature is a vast cafe- and shop-lined **market square** that is the largest in the country. The **tourist office** (www.freudenstadt.de; Marktplatz 64; ⊙9am-6pm Mon-Fri, 10am-2pm Sat & Sun May-Oct, shorter hr other times) is good for local hiking ideas.

The Gaiser family extend a warm welcome at **Hotel Adler** (📞915 20; www.adler-fds.de; Forststrasse 15-17; r €45-95, mains €8-18; 🛜), a guesthouse with comfy, fusty rooms and a terrace. The bistro serves Swabian faves like *Spätzle* (egg noodles).

Don't judge **Hotel Schwanen** (📞915 50; www.schwanen-freudenstadt.de; Forststrasse 6; r €40-110, mains €9-16; 🛜) by its 1970s-style reception, as the rooms have a mod patina (dig the stripes behind the bed). The restaurant is famous for its *Riesenpfannkuchen* (giant pancakes).

From Freudenstadt, hourly trains run south to Schiltach (€7, 30 minutes) and north to the important transfer point of Karlsruhe (€16, 1½ hours). Stuttgart has hourly trains (€16, 1½ hours).

Alpirsbach

A small town, Alpirsbach, 10km north of Schiltach, is worth a trip for its 12th-century Benedictine abbey, **Kloster Alpirsbach**

(admission €4; ⊙10am-5.30pm Mon-Sat, 11am-4.30pm Sun, shorter hr in winter). It's often uncrowded and if you find yourself alone in the large Romanesque complex it can be quite eerie. The cloisters are impressive, as is the small museum that documents the lives of those who lived here.

Just across the old complex you'll find what's kept the monks busy all these years: the **Alpirsbacher Klosterbräu** (Marktplatz 1; tours €6.50; ⊙tours 2.30pm) brewery. Tours include a couple of glasses of the brew. To sample them all, head to nearby **Löwen-Post** (📞07444-955 95; www.loewen-post.de; Markplatz 12; r €40-70, mains €6-12), where you can get a sampling flight of six of the monks' finest. The food is top-notch Swabian and the rooms in the old inn have an unfussy, modern vibe.

Alpirsbach is a stop for the hourly trains linking Schiltach and Freudenstadt.

Schiltach

📞07836 / POP 4000

A contender for the prettiest town in the Black Forest is Schiltach, where there is the always-underlying roar of the intersecting Kinzig and Schiltach Rivers. Half-timbered buildings lean at varying angles along the criss-crossing hillside lanes.

The **tourist office** (www.schiltach.de; Hauptstrasse 5; ⊙10am-5pm Mon-Fri, to 2pm Sat Apr-Oct) can help with accommodation and has a lot of English-language information. Be sure not to miss the **Schüttesäge-museum** (Hauptstrasse 1; ⊙11am-5pm Tue-Sun Apr-Oct), which is part of an old mill built on the river. It shows what water power could do. The **Markt** has several tiny museums that cover local history and culture. Most are open in the afternoons during the tourist season.

There are numerous hotels and restaurants in the compact centre. Choosing a room is an adventure at **Gasthof Sonne** (☑957 570; www.sonneschiltach.de; Marktplatz 3; r €43-80; 🛜). Shall it be a romantic rose-tinged nest or an armour-filled knight's chamber? The restaurant is excellent.

Nineteen generations of the same family have run the 16th-century inn **Weysses Rössle** (☑387; www.weysses-roessle.de; Schenkenzeller Strasse 42; r €50-70; 🛜), where countrified rooms feature snazzy bathrooms. The woodsy tavern uses locally sourced, organic fare.

Schiltach is on the train line linking Offenburg (€8, 45 minutes) via Hausach to Freudenstadt (€5, 30 minutes), with hourly services. Change at Hausach for Triberg (€7, 50 minutes).

Triberg

☑07722 / POP 5400

Heir to the Black Forest cake recipe, nesting ground of the world's biggest cuckoos and spring of Germany's highest waterfall – Triberg is a torrent of Schwarzwald superlatives and attracts gushers of guests.

Start with a troll, er, we mean stroll (but trolls of the garden kind are sold in all the many gift shops). There's a one-hour walk to the stair-stepped **waterfalls**; it starts near the **tourist office** (www.triberg.de; Wallfahrtstrasse 4; ◷10am-5pm), which also has a small museum. The duelling oversized cuckoos are at opposite ends of town (we prefer the one in Schonach).

Above the shop of master woodcarver Gerald Burger is **Kukucksnest** (☑869 487;

ⓘ BLACK FOREST SAVINGS

Most Black Forest hotels will give you a **Schwarzwald-Gästekarte** (Black Forest Guest Card) for discounts or freebies on museums, ski lifts, events and attractions. Some versions entitle you to free use of public transport.

Tourist offices in the Black Forest sell the three-day **SchwarzwaldCard** (www.blackforest-tourism.com; adult/child €32/21) for admission to around 150 attractions and activities.

Wallfahrtstrasse 15; r €50-60), a beautiful nest he has carved for guests.

The kirsch-scented Black Forest cake at **Café Schäfer** (www.cafe-schaefer-triberg. de; Hauptstrasse 33; ◷9am-6pm, from 11am Sun, closed Wed) is the real deal; it has the original recipe to prove it.

Triberg is midway on the spectacular Karlsruhe (€22, 1½ hours) to Konstanz (€22, 1½ hours) train line. There are hourly services and good connections. Change at Hausach for Schiltach and Freudenstadt. The station is 1.7km from the centre; take any bus to the Markt.

Furtwangen

In Furtwangen, 17km south of Triberg, visit the **Deutsches Uhrenmuseum** (German Clock Museum; www.deutsches-uhrenmuseum.de; Gerwigstrasse 11; adult/child €4/3; ◷9am-6pm Apr-Oct, 10am-5pm Nov-Mar) for a look at the traditional Black Forest skill of clock-making. A fun demo shows what puts the 'cuc' and the 'koo' in the namesake clock. Buses from Triberg stop here.

Titisee-Neustadt

☑07651 / POP 12,000

The iconic glacial **lake** here draws no shortage of visitors to the busy village of Titisee-Neustadt. Walking around Titisee or paddle-boating across it are major activities. If you have wheels, ride or drive into the surrounding rolling meadows to see some of the truly enormous traditional house-barn combos.

The **tourist office** (www.titisee-neustadt.de; Strandbadstrasse 4; ◷9am-6pm Mon-Fri, 10am-1pm Sat & Sun) can help you arrange a farm stay. The short streets radiating off the lakefront are lined with clock and schlock shops. But fanciers will be in hog heaven for all the **Black Forest ham outlets**. It's time to picnic!

Titisee is linked to Freiburg by frequent train services (€10, 40 minutes). To reach Triberg to the north, there are scenic hourly connections via Neustadt and Donaueschingen (€16, two hours).

Feldberg

The Black Forest **ski season** runs from late December to March. While there is good downhill skiing, the area is more suited to cross-country skiing. The centre for winter

HELL TO HEAVEN

Just south of Furtwangen, look for a tiny road off to the west evocatively called the **Hexenloch** (Witch's Hole). This narrow road penetrates deep into a narrow valley of rushing white water and tall trees. It alone is worth the cost of a car hire – which is the only way to enjoy the hole. Even on warm days it's cold as a witch's you-know-what down here (one family in the valley actually installed a mirror on a mountain to shine a beam of reflected sunshine). The road follows the bends in the river and you'll see shaded banks of snow months after it has melted elsewhere. Look for small roadhouses with little spinning water wheels.

West of the south end of the Hexenloch road, **St Peter** is a tiny town that offers a start at redemption with a twin-towered, onion-domed namesake abbey. It's an 18th-century vision in gold, glitter and gilt that would do any Las Vegas designer proud.

Finish your quest with a baptism. Going northwest of Furtwangen on the Katzensteigstrasse, follow signs for the 7km drive to **Donauquelle**, a spring that is a source of the Danube. High on a knoll, a short path leads down to the water burbling forth from the ground, beginning an adventure that ends 2900km later in the Black Sea. Hikes here fan out in all directions. You can bed down amid the beauty and tranquillity at **Kolmenhof** (☑07723-931 025; www.kolmenhof.de; r from €85), a mountain chalet with a cafe with organic food and slow-food principles. Heaven indeed.

sports is around Titisee (the ski jumps are a prominent landmark), with uncrowded downhill ski runs at **Feldberg** (www.liftverbund-feldberg.de; day pass adult/child €27/15) and numerous graded cross-country trails.

In summer you can use the lifts to reach the summit of the sallow-sloped Feldberg (1493m) for a wondrous panorama that stretches to the Alps.

Feldberg is 15km south of Titisee. It can be reachcd by bus 7300 from Titisee (€4, 12 minutes, hourly) or in season by free ski shuttles.

Freiburg im Breisgau

☑0761 / POP 214,000

Nestled between hills and vineyards, Freiburg im Breisgau has a medieval Altstadt made timeless by a thriving university community. There's a sense of fun here exemplified by the *bächle* (tiny medieval canals) running down the middle of streets. Perhaps being Germany's sunniest city contributes to the mood.

Founded in 1120 and ruled for centuries by the Austrian Habsburgs, Freiburg has retained many traditional features, although major reconstruction was necessary following WWII. The monumental 13th-century cathedral is the city's key landmark but the real attractions are the vibrant cafes, bars and street life, plus the local wines. The best

times for tasting are July, for the four days of *Weinfest* (Wine Festival), or August, for the nine days of *Weinkost* (wine tasting).

◉ Sights

Medieval Freiburg　　　　HISTORIC QUARTER

The major sight in Freiburg is the 700-year-old **Münster** (Cathedral; Münsterplatz; tower adult/child €1.50/1; ⊙9.30am-5pm Mon-Sat, 1-5pm Sun), a classic example of both high-and late-Gothic architecture that looms over Münsterplatz, Freiburg's market square. Ascend the **west tower** to the stunning pierced spire for great views of Freiburg and, on a clear day, the Kaiserstuhl wine region and the Vosages Mountains to the west. Spend time in contemplation of the art-filled **chapels** and **choirs**, then search out the **gargoyle** outside that once spouted water from his butt.

South of the Münster stands the solid red **Kaufhaus**, the 16th-century merchants' hall. You can sense the Middle Ages – but not the smell – along **Fischerau** and **Gerberau**.

The bustling **university quarter** is northwest of the **Martinstor** (one of the old city gates). On the walk in from the station, note the field of **grape vines** from around the world.

Augustinermuseum　　　　MUSEUM

(☑201 2531; Salzstrasse 32; adult/child €6/4; ⊙10am-5pm Tue-Sun) A fine collection of

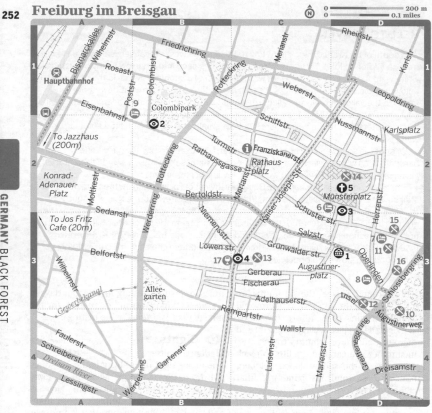

medieval art, including works by Matthias Grünewald and Cranach plus lavish stained-glass windows, is the highlight of this museum, which has reopened after a massive refit.

Schauinslandbahn CABLE CAR
(www.bergwelt-schauinsland.de; one way/return adult €8/12, child €5/7; ⏰9am-5pm Jan-Jun, to 6pm Jul-Sep, 9.30am-5pm Oct-Dec) Ride high to the **Schauinsland peak** (1284m). From these Black Forest highlands numerous easy and well-marked trails make the Schauinsland area ideal for day walks. From Freiburg take tram 4 south to Günterstal and then bus 21 to Talstation.

🛏 Sleeping

Hotel zum Roten Bären HOTEL €€
(☎387 870; www.roter-baeren.de; Oberlinden 12; r €100-180; 🖥) Billed as Germany's oldest guest house, this blush-wine-pink hotel near Schwabentor dates to 1120. Though

the vaulted cellar is medieval, rooms are modern, creak-free and have sleek wood furnishings.

Hotel Schwarzwälder Hof HOTEL €€
(☎380 30; www.schwarzwaelder-hof.eu; Herren-strasse 43; r €65-110; 🖥) This bijou hotel has an unrivalled style-for-euro ratio. Some of the 42 rooms have postcard views of the Alt-stadt. A wrought-iron staircase has such a dramatic sweep that you may be tempted to make your entrance twice. Bargain singles share bathrooms.

Hotel Oberkirch HOTEL €€
(☎202 6868; www.hotel-oberkirch.de; Münster-platz 22; r €95-175; 🖥) Our readers sing the praises of this green-shuttered, 250-year-old hotel, with the Münster views of a million postcards. The 26 countrified rooms reveal a Laura Ashley love of florals. Enjoy a floral bouquet from the excellent wine selection on offer in the garden.

Freiburg im Breisgau

GERMANY FREIBURG IM BREISGAU

Black Forest Hostel
HOSTEL €

(☑881 7870; www.blackforest-hostel.de; Kartäuser-strasse 33; dm €14-23, s/d €30/50; @) Freiburg's funkiest budget digs are five minutes' stroll from the centre. Overlooking vineyards, this former factory has been lovingly revamped as an industrial-themed hostel. Bike hire costs €5 per day.

Park Hotel Post
HOTEL €€€

(☑385 480; www.park-hotel-post.de; Am Colombi-park 63; r €110-200; ☎) Slip back to the more graceful age of art nouveau at this refined pile overlooking Colombipark, with 45 summery rooms decorated in pastel blues and yellows. Attentive service and generous breakfasts sweeten the deal.

✗ Eating & Drinking

The fragrant smoke around the Münster at lunch isn't incense, it's the smoke from dozens of grills loaded with sausages. Get one on a bun and pile it with grilled onions (€2). On Saturday you can have veggies (and fruit and cheese and...) with your wurst when the weekly **produce market** operates. It's one of Germany's best.

Otherwise, your choices are myriad. Freiburg likes a good meal out – and a drink. Or two.

TOP CHOICE **Wolfshöhle**
FUSION €€€

(☑790 98; www.wolfshoehle-freiburg.de; Konvikstrasse 8; mains €18-30; ◐lunch & dinner Thu-Tue) Fresh fare from the region – that simple philosophy guides the ever-changing menu here at one of Freiburg's best. The classic old exterior hides a thoroughly modern dining room, with sleek wood surfaces and black leather seating. Swabian favourites and dishes from neighbouring regions transcend the everyday. Book.

Markthalle
MARKET HALL €

(Grünwälderstrasse 2; meals €3-8; ◐7am-8pm) Just when you think you've seen all the stalls here that sell food from around the world, you round a corner and there's more. Each has a speciality, whether it's South Asian, Italian or simply a bevy of the heartiest soups you could hope to warm by. Find a communal table, get a glass of local wine or beer and enjoy.

Hausbrauerei Feierling
BREWERY €€

(Gerberau 46; mains €6-12; ☑) Starring one of Freiburg's best beer gardens, this brewpub serves great vegetarian options and humungous schnitzels with *Brägele* (chipped potatoes). If you drink one too many, take care not to fall in the stream or you may become dinner for the open-jawed *Krokodil*. Huge, fun beer gardens.

Schlappen
PUB €

(☑334 94; Löwenstrasse 2; ◐11am-1am Mon-Thu, to 3am Fri & Sat, 3pm-1am Sun) With its jazz-themed back room and poster-plastered walls, this student watering hole is a perennial fave. Try a *Flammkuche* (tasty, crispy Alsatian pizza), then forget about it with absinthe.

Englers Weinkrügle
GERMAN €€

(Konvikstrasse 12; mains €8-15; ◐Tue-Sun) A warm, woody *Weinstube* with wisteria growing out front and regional flavours on the menu. The trout in various guises is delicious. If you were wondering what's the deal with local wine, answers abound.

Zylinder Feinkost
ITALIAN DELI €

(Konviktstrasse 51; snacks €5-8; ◐lunch) Opera plays in this little Italian deli, where Matteo's passion for the minutiae of Chianti and antipasti is contagious. Pull up a stack of crates for a glass of *prosecco* and home-made focaccia with wafer-thin prosciutto.

Biergarten Greiffenegg-Schlössle

BEER GARDEN €

(Schlossbergring 3; mains €5) Perched above Freiburg, this terrace beer garden is great for watching the sun set over the city's red rooftops. Save your strength for drinking and ride the elevator up and stumble down. The restaurant inside the villa is upmarket.

☆ Entertainment

Jazzhaus

JAZZ

(www.jazzhaus.de; Schnewlinstrasse 1) Under the brick arches of a wine cellar, this venue hosts first-rate jazz, rock and hip-hop concerts (€10 to €30) at 8pm at least three nights a week. It morphs into a club on weekends.

Jos Fritz Cafe

LOUNGE

(www.josfritzcafe.de; Wilhelmstrasse 15) Down a little alley past the recycling bins, this cafe hosts concerts of alternative bands and events such as political discussions (stir things up with 'Is Merkel too liberal?').

❶ Information

The **tourist office** (www.freiburg.de; Rathausplatz 2-4; ⊙8am-8pm Mon-Fri, 9.30am-5pm Sat, 10am-noon Sun Jun-Sep, 8am-6pm Mon-Fri, 9.30am-2.30pm Sat, 10am-noon Sun Oct-May) is well stocked with hiking and cycling maps to the region.

❶ Getting There & Around

Freiburg shares **EuroAirport** (www.euroairport.com) with Basel (Switzerland) and Mulhouse (France). It buzzes with low-cost carriers. The **Airport Bus** (www.freiburger-reisedienst.de) runs almost every hour (adult/child €20/10, 55 minutes).

Fast trains connect Freiburg to Basel (€23, 45 minutes, hourly) and north to Frankfurt (€61, two hours, hourly) and beyond.

Cut across the Rhine to France's cute Colmar. Bus 1076 makes the run two to three times daily (€8, 1¼ hours).

Single rides on the efficient local bus and tram system cost €2.20. A 24-hour pass is €5. Trams depart from the bridge over the train tracks.

LAKE CONSTANCE

Lake Constance (Bodensee) is an oasis in landlocked southern Germany. Even if you never make contact with the water, this giant bulge in the sinewy course of the Rhine offers a splash of refreshment. Historic towns line its vineyard-dappled periphery, which can be explored by boat or bicycle or on foot. While sun is nice, the lake is best on one of the many misty days, when it is shrouded in mystery.

Constance's southern side belongs to Switzerland and Austria, where the snow-capped Alps provide backdrops across the lake so ideal that you may decide to unwisely chuck it all and start a postcard business. The German side of Lake Constance features three often-crowded tourist centres in Constance, Meersburg and the island of Lindau. It's essentially a summer area, when it abounds with aquatic joy.

❶ Getting There & Around

Trains link Lindau and Constance, and buses fill in the gaps to places like Meersburg. By car, the B31 hugs the northern shore of Lake Constance, but it can get rather busy. The Constance–Meersburg car ferry run by BSB ferries (p255) provides a vital link for those who don't want to circumnavigate the entire lake and a chance for some watery vistas.

The most enjoyable, albeit slowest, way to get around is on the **Bodensee-Schiffsbetriebe** (BSB; www.bsb-online.com) boats, which, from Easter to late October, call several times a day at the larger towns along the lake; there are discounts for rail-pass holders.

Numerous schemes exist for discounted travel and admissions spanning the three countries surrounding the lake; ask at tourist offices.

Constance

♪ 07531 / POP 81,000

Constance (Konstanz) nudges the Swiss border. It's a lake town where the allure of the waters sometimes drowns the rather remarkable old town. The main attraction is fittingly named Mainau Island.

It achieved historical significance in 1414, when the Council of Constance convened to try to heal huge rifts in the Catholic Church. The consequent burning at the stake of the religious reformer Jan Hus as a heretic, and the scattering of his ashes over the lake, did nothing to block the Reformation.

◉ Sights & Activities

TOP CHOICE **Old Town**

HISTORIC QUARTER

The city's most visible feature is the Gothic spire of the **Münster** (⊙9am-6pm Mon-Sat, 10am-6pm Sun), added in 1856 to a church that was started in 1052. You'll feel like a treasure hunter as you make one find after another within. Get the brilliant walking tour brochure from the tourist office and explore the **Altstadt** (Old Town), which seems to have a medieval surprise around every corner.

Lakefront NATURAL FEATURE
Head across to **Mainau Island** (www.mainau.de; adult/child €16/free; ☺sunrise to sunset), with its baroque castle set in vast and gorgeous gardens with seasonal displays. Take bus 4 (€2, 20 minutes) or a BSB ferry from the harbour behind the station (€6, one hour, hourly).

Five rocky shore areas optimistically called **beaches** are open from May to September, including the **Strandbad Horn** (the best and most crowded), with bush-shrouded nude bathing. Take bus 5 or walk for 20 minutes north around the shore.

Directly in front of town, the **Stadtgarten** is ideal for an idyll; paths lead past yachts, monuments, gardens and cafes.

🍴 Sleeping & Eating
The following are in the Altstadt.

Hotel Barbarossa HOTEL €€
(☎128 990; www.barbarossa-hotel.com; Obermarkt 8-12; r €50-130; 🅟) Charming old place, carefully restored (although the floors still creak). White walls set off beautiful wooden antiques. The art deco restaurant (mains €8 to €20) has fine local specialities.

Hotel Augustiner Tor HOTEL €€
(☎282 450; www.hotel-augustiner-tor.de; Bodanstrasse 18; r €80-150; 🅟) This cleverly restored turn-of-the-century hotel offers unrivalled value for money. Streamlined rooms exude Scandinavian simplicity with clean lines, creamy beige leather and wood floors.

Hafenmeisterei CAFE €€
(Hafenstrasse 8; mains €11-20) Hafenmeisterei blends beach-shack breeziness with a cool lounge vibe. Reggae grooves play as chefs sizzle up wok and fish dishes in the open kitchen. One of many bodacious outdoor terraces on the harbour.

Brauhaus Johann Albrecht BEER HALL €€
(Konradigasse 2; mains €8-16) A rambling beer hall with a rustic menu featuring daily specials. The food here offers good value and the beer, brewed on the premises in copper vats, goes down fine, especially on the terrace in summer.

DJH Hostel HOSTEL €
(☎322 60; www.jugendherberge-konstanz.de; Zur Allmannshöhe 18; dm €22) Occupying a

water tower, with neat dorms, a bistro and gardens. It's 4km northeast of the Altstadt, served by buses 1 and 4.

ℹ Information
The **tourist office** (www.konstanz.de/tourismus; Bahnhofplatz 43; ☺9am-6.30pm Mon-Fri, to 4pm Sat, 10am-1pm Sun Apr-Oct, 9.30am-12.30pm & 2-6pm Mon-Fri Nov-Mar) is in the train station.

ℹ Getting There & Away
Constance has trains to Offenburg (€29, 2¼ hours, hourly) via Triberg in the Black Forest, and Stuttgart (€38, 2¼ hours, every two hours). There are good connections into Switzerland (which is 200m south!), including Zürich (€18, 1¼ hours, hourly). All services depart from the restored landmark Gothic station. Bike-hire shops are nearby.

BSB Ferries (www.bsb-online.com) on various schedules serve numerous destinations including Meersburg (€5, 30 minutes) and Lindau (€15, three to four hours).

Meersburg
☑07532 / POP 5300
Constance is the big city compared to Meersburg across the lake. The winding, hilly, cobblestone streets, vine-patterned hills and a sunny lakeside promenade make it a good stop if travelling by ferry or car.

The **tourist office** (www.meersburg.de; Kirchstrasse 4; ☺9am-6pm Mon-Fri, 10am-2pm Sat, reduced hr in winter) is in the Altstadt and can help find accommodation if you decide to stay.

Steigstrasse is lined with delightful half-timbered houses, each boasting a gift shop. The modest 11th-century **Altes Schloss** (adult/child €8.50/4.50; ☺9am-6.30pm Mar-Oct) is the oldest structurally intact castle in Germany.

The Constance to Meersburg **car ferry** (www.bsb-online.com) runs from the northeastern Constance suburb of Staadand. BSB ferries stop on their shore-hopping voyages between Constance (€5, 30 minutes) and Lindau (€14, 2½ to three hours).

Lindau
☑08382 / POP 26,500
A forgotten corner of Bavaria. Most people assume this medieval little island-city is part of Baden-Württemberg but it's not. Here

you'll see the blue-and-white Bavarian state colours, and sudsy brews trump the wines found elsewhere along the lake.

Connected to the nearby lakeshore by bridges, this is a charming, nearly car-free town. Key sights (often adorned with murals) include the **Altes Rathaus** (Reichsplatz), the **city theatre** (Barfüsser-platz) and the little harbour's **Seepromenade**, with its Bavarian Lion monument and **lighthouse**. When the haze clears, the Alps provide a stunning backdrop for watersports that include windsurfing and rowing.

Alte Post (🖋934 60; www.alte-post-lindau.de; Fischergasse 3; r €60-140; ⊘closed late Dec–late Mar; 🛜) is a 300-year-old coaching inn that was once a stop on the Frankfurt–Milan mail run. Sitting pretty on cobbled Fischergasse, it's well-kept, light and spacious, and the rooms have chunky pine furnishings and wicker chairs.

The 18th-century **Hotel Garni Brugger** (🖋934 10; www.hotel-garni-brugger.de; Bei der Heidenmauer 11; r €55-100; ⊘closed Dec; 🛜), with 23 bright rooms decked out in floral fabrics and pine, is run by a family that bends over to please. Guests can thaw out in the sauna in winter.

Carving through the centre of the island, Lindau's cobbled main street, **Maximilianstrasse**, is lined with elegant cafes, restaurants and ice-cream shops.

ⓘ Information

The **tourist office** (🖋260 030; www.lindau.de; Ludwigstrasse 68; ⊘9am-6pm Mon-Fri, 2-6pm Sat & Sun May-Sep, 9am-5pm Mon-Fri Oct-Apr) is opposite the train station.

ⓘ Getting There & Away

Lindau has trains to Ulm (€22, 1¾ hours, hourly) on the Munich–Stuttgart line, Munich (€38, 2¼ hours, every two hours) and direct to Zürich (€25, four times daily). Trains to nearby Bregenz (€5, nine minutes, two hourly) let you connect to the rest of Austria and Switzerland.

BSB Ferries (www.bsb-online.com) on various schedules serve destinations including Meersburg (€14, 2½ to three hours) and Constance (€15, three to four hours).

RHINELAND-PALATINATE

Rhineland-Palatinate (Rheinland-Pfalz) is deeply riven by rivers, and the names of two – Rhine and Moselle – are synonymous with the wines made from the grapes growing on their hillsides. Created after WWII from parts of the former Rhineland and Rhenish Palatinate regions, its turbulent history goes all the way back to the Romans, as seen in Trier. In recent centuries it was hotly contested by the French and a variety of German states, which produced many of its now-crumbling fortresses.

This land of wine and great natural beauty reaches its apex in the verdant Moselle Valley towns, such as Cochem, and along the heavily touristed Rhine, where rich hillside vineyards provide a backdrop for noble castles and looming medieval fortresses. For this part of Germany, focus your attention on the water, the land it courses through and the fruit of the vines on its hillsides.

Moselle Valley

Exploring the vineyards and wineries of the Moselle (Mosel) Valley is an ideal way to get a taste of German culture and people – and, of course, the crisp, light wines. Take the time to slow down and savour a glass or two.

Like a vine right before harvest, the Moselle hangs heavy with visitor fruit. Castles and half-timbered towns are built along the sinuous river below steep, rocky cliffs planted with vineyards (they say locals are born with one leg shorter than the other so that they can easily work the vines). It's one of the country's most scenic regions, with a constant succession of views rewarding the intrepid hikers who brave the hilly trails.

Many winemakers have their own small pensions but accommodation is hard to find in May when people enjoy a spring awakening, on summer weekends and during the local wine harvest (mid-September to mid-October). Note also that much of the region – like the vines themselves – goes into a deep slumber from November to March, albeit after an autumn explosion of colour.

ⓘ Getting There & Around

The most scenic part of the Moselle Valley runs 195km from Trier to Koblenz; it's most practical to begin your Moselle Valley trip from either of these two.

It is not possible to travel the entire length of the banks of the Moselle River via rail. Local and fast trains run every hour between Trier and Koblenz, but the only riverside stretch of this line is between Cochem and Koblenz (however, it's a scenic dandy). Apart from this run – and the scenic Moselweinbahn line taking tourists between Bullay and Traben-Trarbach – travellers use buses, ferries, bicycles or cars to travel between most of the upper Moselle towns.

Moselbahn (www.moselbahn.de) runs eight buses on weekdays (fewer at weekends) between Trier and Bullay (three hours each way), a pretty route following the river's winding course and passing through numerous quaint villages. Buses leave from outside the train stations in Trier and Bullay.

The relaxed way to explore the Moselle in the high season is by boat. From May to early October, **Köln-Düsseldorfer (KD) Line** (www.k-d.com) ferries sail daily between Koblenz and Cochem (€25 one way, 5¼ hours upstream, 4¼ hours downstream). Other smaller ferry companies also operate on the Moselle from various towns. Eurail and German Rail passes are valid for all normal KD Line services, and travel on your birthday is free.

The Moselle is a popular area among cyclists, and for much of the river's course there's a separate 'Moselroute' bike track. Most towns have a rental shop or two; ask at the tourist offices. Many of the Moselbahn buses also carry bikes.

KOBLENZ
☎0261 / POP 110,000

Koblenz is an important ferry and train junction at the confluence of the Rhine and Moselle Rivers. The **tourist office** (www.touristik-koblenz.de; Bahnhofsplatz 7; ⊙9am-6pm Mon-Sat year-round, plus 10am-6pm Sun Apr-Oct) is in a modern building in front of the Hauptbahnhof.

The **Deutsches Eck** is a park at the dramatic meeting point of the rivers. It's dedicated to German unity and is a good reason for a riverside stroll.

South of Koblenz, at the head of the beautiful Eltz Valley, **Burg Eltz** (www.burg-eltz.de; adult/child €8/5.50; ⊙9.30am-5.30pm Apr-Oct) is not to be missed. Towering over the surrounding hills, this superb medieval castle has frescoes, paintings, furniture and ornately decorated rooms. Burg Eltz is best reached by train to Moselkern on the Trier line, from where it's a 50-minute walk up through the forest. Alternatively, a shuttle bus runs in peak season.

In town, many of Koblenz' restaurants and pubs are in the Altstadt, around Münzplatz and Burgstrasse, and along the Rhine. The small towns in either river valley offer more atmospheric accommodation than those in town.

The busy KD Line ferry dock is a 10-minute walk from the train station. Trains fan out in all directions: up the Moselle to Trier (€20, 1½ hours, hourly) via Cochem and Bullay; north along the Rhine to Cologne (€20, one hour, two hourly) and south on the Rhine to Mainz (€20, one hour, two hourly).

COCHEM
☎02671 / POP 5400

This often-crowded German town has narrow alleyways and one of the most beautiful castles in the region. It's also a good base for hikes into the hills. The **tourist office** (www.cochem.de; Endertplatz; ⊙9am-5pm Mon-Sat, 10am-noon Sun, reduced hr in winter) is next to the Moselbrücke bridge.

For a great view, head up to the **Pinnerkreuz** with the chairlift on Endertstrasse (€5). The perfect crown on the 100m-high hill, **Reichsburg Castle** (www.reichsburg-cochem.de; adult/6-17yr €5/3; ⊙9am-5pm) is a 15-minute walk from town. Its idealised form can be credited to its 1877 construction (it was never needed to actually *function* as a castle).

Many local vineyards offer tours that include a chance to wander the vines, enjoy the views, have a picnic, sample some cheese, visit the gift shop and, oh, try the wine.

Hotel-Pension Garni Villa Tummelchen (☎910 520; www.villa-tummelchen.com; Schlossstrasse 22; r from €55-80; ☎) is a bit up the hill from town and thus has sweeping Moselle vistas. It's worth an extra couple of euros to get a room with a balcony and a view.

Tucked away uphill from the Markt and its fountain, **Zom Stüffje** (www.zom-stueffje.de; Oberbachstrasse 14; mains €8-18; ⊙Wed-Mon) is richly decorated with dark timber and murals, and serves classic German fare and some of the better local vintages.

This is the terminus for KD Line boats from Koblenz. Trains on the Trier–Koblenz line run twice hourly to Bullay (€5, 10 minutes), where you can pick up the Moselbahn bus.

COCHEM TO TRIER
To explore the little villages along the Moselle upstream from often-oversubscribed Cochem, take the train from there to **Bullay**, from where you can catch the Moselbahn bus and town-hop the rest of the way to Trier.

TRABEN-TRARBACH
Full of fanciful art-nouveau villas, the double town of Traben-Trarbach is a welcome relief from the 'romantic half-timbered town' circuit. Pick up a map of the town at

the **tourist office** (www.traben-trarbach.de; Bahnstrasse 22). The ruined medieval **Grevenburg**, which, unlike its Cochem cousin, survived the 19th century without being 'restored', sits high in the craggy hills above Trarbach and is reached from the Markt via a steep footpath.

Weingut Caspari (www.weingut-caspari. de; Weiherstrasse 18, Trarbach; mains €5-15) is a rustic, old-time *Strausswirtschaft* (winerycum-eatery) that serves hearty local specialities, such as *Feiner Grillschinken Moselart* (boiled ham with potato puree and sauerkraut). It's six short blocks inland from the bridge.

BERNKASTEL-KUES

The twin town of Bernkastel-Kues is at the heart of the middle Moselle region. On the right bank, Bernkastel has a charming **Markt**, a romantic ensemble of half-timbered houses with beautifully decorated gables.

On Karlstrasse, the alley to the right as you face the Rathaus, the tiny **Spitzhäuschen** resembles a giant bird's house, its narrow base topped by a much larger, precariously leaning, upper floor.

Get your heart pumping by hoofing it from the Spitzhäuschen up to **Burg Landshut**, a ruined 13th-century castle – framed by vineyards and forests – on a bluff above town; allow 30 to 60 minutes. You'll be rewarded with glorious valley views and a cold drink at the **beer garden** (◷10am-6pm mid-Feb–Nov).

Trier

⏲0651 / POP 101,000

Trier is touted as Germany's oldest town and you'll find more Roman ruins here than anywhere else north of the Alps. Although settlement of the site dates back to 400 BC, Trier itself was founded around 16 BC as Augusta Treverorum, the capital of Gaul, and was second in importance only to Rome in the Western Roman Empire. Its proximity to France can be tasted in its cuisine, while its large student population injects life among the ruins.

◉ Sights

Like a high-school history class in a day, only now with wine at the end, Trier's sights span at least 23 centuries. A **Combi-Ticket** (adult/child €6/5) is good for most of the historical sites.

Roman Ruins   HISTORICAL BUILDINGS

The town's chief landmark is the **Porta Nigra** (adult/child €3/1.50; ◷9am-6pm Apr-Sep, to 5pm Mar & Oct, to 4pm Nov-Feb), the imposing city gate on the northern edge of the town centre. Its construction dates back to the 2nd century AD.

Additional Roman sites include the **Amphitheatre** (Olewigerstrasse; adult/child €3/1.50; ◷9am-6pm Apr-Sep, to 5pm Mar & Oct, to 4pm Nov-Feb) and the gloomy underground caverns of the **Kaiserthermen** (Im Palastgarten).

Middle Ages Buildings   HISTORICAL BUILDINGS

Trier's massive (and massively restored) Romanesque **Dom** (www.dominformation.de; Liebfrauenstrasse 12; ◷6.30am-6pm Apr-Oct, to 5.30pm Nov-Mar) shares a 1600-year history with the nearby and equally impressive **Konstantin Basilika** (⏲724 68; Konstantinplatz; ◷10am-6pm Mon-Fri, noon-6pm Sun Apr-Oct).

The early-Gothic **Dreikönigenhaus** (Simeonstrasse 19) was built around 1230 as a protective tower. The original entrance was on the second level, accessible only by way of a retractable rope ladder.

Museums   MUSEUMS

The **Karl Marx Haus** (www.fes.de/marx; Brückenstrasse 10; adult/child €3/2; ◷10am-6pm daily Apr-Oct, 2-5pm Tue-Sun Nov-Mar) is the suitably modest birthplace of the man. It is a major pilgrimage stop for the growing numbers of mainland Chinese tourists to Europe. The walls are lined with manifestos.

Near Porta Nigra, **Städtisches Museum** (www.museum-trier.de; Simeonstrasse 60; adult/child €5/free; ◷9.30am-6pm Tue-Sun) fills a renovated 11th-century Trier monastery with two millennia of Trier history.

🛏 Sleeping

Hotel Römischer Kaiser
HOTEL €€

(☎977 00; www.friedrich-hotels.de; Am Porta-Nigra-Platz 6; r €75-150; 🛜) The Kaiser is in an elegant, old corner building. The 43 rooms are comfortable, decorated in soft colours and have parquet floors; some have balconies. Ceilings are regally high. Unwind after a long day tracking Romans on the sunny terrace.

Hille's Hostel
HOSTEL €

(☎710 2785; www.hilles-hostel-trier.de; Gartenfeldstrasse 7; dm €15-19, s/d €41/52; @) The rooms here are furnished with Ikea bunk beds and are set back from the road amid some hardy palms. There's a big kitchen and the chance to ponder the mugs of previous guests that line the walls.

Hotel Paulin
HOTEL €€

(☎147 4010; www.hotel-paulin-trier.de; Paulinstrasse 13; r €60-120; 🛜) In a low-key, modern building right across from the old centre, this tidy 24-room hotel offers something even a weary Roman can appreciate: a comfy night's sleep at a good price. As for the bacchanalia, that's up to you…

Hotel Pieper
HOTEL €€

(☎230 08; www.hotel-pieper-trier.de; Thebäerstrasse 39; r €50-120; 🛜) An excellent family-run hotel on a residential street with a few neighbourhood cafes, just five minutes from the station. Rooms are comfy and have free wi-fi. Best of all is the bounteous breakfast buffet that includes treats like fresh pineapple.

🍴 Eating

The narrow and historic Judengasse, near the Markt, has several small bars and clubs. There's a cluster of stylish places on Viehmarktplatz and another bunch in front of the Dom. In summer getting a seat at a cafe can feel like battling a lion.

Walderdorff's
CAFE €€

(www.walderdorffs.de; Domfreihof 1a; mains €8-16) A high-concept wine bar and cafe across from the Dom. Score one of the dozens of tables out front or inside in the stylish surrounds. The food is fresh and light; look for salads, sandwiches and many seasonal specials.

Zum Domstein
BISTRO €€

(www.domstein.de; Am Hauptmarkt 5; mains €10-20, Roman dinner €15-33) A touristy but fun German-style bistro where you can either feast like the ancient Romans (fried zucchini? Not bad.) or dine on more conventional German and international fare. Avoid indecision and have a wine flight (sampler).

Kartoffel Kiste
SPUD CAFE €€

(www.kiste-trier.de; Fahrstrasse 13-14; mains €8-16) A local favourite, this place specialises in baked, breaded, soupified and sauce-engulfed potatoes, as well as steaks. There is an extraordinary bronze fountain fronting its many outdoor tables.

ℹ Information

Tourist office (www.trier.de; An der Porta Nigra; ⊙9am-6pm Mon-Sat, 10am-5pm Sun May-Oct, reduced hr in winter). Offers good two-hour guided city walking tours (adult/child €7/3.50, 1.30pm Saturday May to October) in English; located at the Porta Nigra, a 10-minute walk from the train station along the Theodor-Heuss-Allee.

Trier-Card (from €9) Discounts and free public transport.

ℹ Getting There & Away

Trier has a train service to Koblenz (€20, 1½ hours, hourly) via Bullay and Cochem, as well as to Luxembourg (€16, 50 minutes, hourly).

Rhine Valley – Koblenz to Mainz

A trip along the mighty Rhine is a highlight for most travellers, as it should be. The section between Koblenz and Mainz provides vistas of steep vineyard-covered mountains punctuated by brooding castles. It really is rather magical. Spring and autumn are the best times to visit the Rhine Valley; in summer it's overrun and in winter most towns go into hibernation.

Though the trails here may be a bit more crowded with day trippers than those along the Moselle, hiking along the Rhine is excellent. The slopes and trails around Bacharach are justly famous.

Every town along the route offers cute little places to stay or camp and atmospheric places to eat and drink.

ℹ Getting There & Around

Although Koblenz and Mainz are the best starting points, the Rhine Valley is also easily accessible from Frankfurt on a very long day trip, but it could drive you to drink, as it were.

Each mode of transport on the Rhine has its own advantages and all are equally enjoyable.

Try combining several. The **Köln-Düsseldorfer (KD) Line** (www.k-d.com) runs slow and fast boats daily between Koblenz and Mainz (as well as the less-interesting stretch between Cologne and Koblenz). The journey takes about four hours downstream and about 5½ hours upstream (€47, free with rail pass). Boats stop at riverside towns along the way.

Frequent train services through the area operate on both sides of the Rhine River, but are more convenient on the left bank. You can travel non-stop on IC/EC trains or by slower regional RB or RE services. The ride is amazing; sit on the right heading north and on the left heading south. Note that most stations don't have lockers.

ST GOAR & ST GOARSHAUSEN
☎06741 / POP 3100

These two towns are on opposite sides of the Rhine; St Goar is on the left bank. One of the most impressive castles on the river is **Burg Rheinfels** (www.st-goar.de; adult/child €5/2.50; ⊙9am-6pm Apr-Oct, 11am-5pm Sat & Sun in good weather Nov-Mar) in St Goar. An absolute must-see, the labyrinthine ruins reflect the greed and ambition of Count Dieter V of Katzenelnbogen, who built the castle in 1245 to help levy tolls on passing ships ('African or European?'). Across the river, just south of St Goarshausen, is the Rhine's most famous sight, the **Loreley Cliff**. Legend has it that a maiden sang sailors to their deaths against its base. It's worth the trek to the top of the Loreley for the view.

St Goar's **Jugendherberge** (☎388; www.djh.de; Bismarckweg 17; dm/s/d €18/30/50) is right below the castle. **Hotel Hauser** (☎333; www.hotelhauser.de; Heerstrasse 77; r €50-80) is relaxed like an old easy chair. Large restau-

rant windows and all 13 rooms overlook the Rhine. Have a drink on the patio.

BACHARACH
☎06743 / POP 2400

Walk beneath one of the thick-arched gateways in Bacharach's medieval walls and you'll find yourself in a beautifully preserved medieval village. The **tourist office** (☎919 303; www.bacharach.de; Oberstrasse 45; ⊙9am-5pm Mon-Fri, 10am-4pm Sat Apr-Oct) will mind day trippers' bags.

Bacharach's **Jugendherberge** (☎1266; www.djh.de; dm from €20) is a legendary facility housed in the Burg Stahleck castle. The **Hotel Kranenturm** (☎1308; www.kranenturm.com; Langstrasse 30; r €50-100; @) is a turreted fantasy of stone, and also offers filling meals.

Part of the old ramparts, the **Rhein Hotel** (☎1243; www.rhein-hotel-bacharach.de; Langstrasse 50; r €60-130, mains €9-18; ✴🛜) has 14 well-lit, soundproofed rooms with compact bathrooms and original artwork. The restaurant serves regional dishes.

MAINZ
☎06131 / POP 185,000

A short train ride from Frankfurt, Mainz has an attractive old town that's a good day trip. It can't compare to the compact beauty of the nearby towns along the Rhine, but impresses with its massive **Dom** (Domstrasse 3; ⊙9am-6pm Tue-Fri, to 4pm Sat, 1-3pm Sun), which has a blend of Romanesque, Gothic and baroque architecture. **St Stephanskirche** (Weisspetrolse 12; ⊙10am-noon & 2-5pm) has stained-glass windows by Marc Chagall.

Mainz's museums include the standout **Gutenberg Museum** (www.gutenberg-museum.de; Liebfrauenplatz 5; adult/child €5/3; ⊙9am-5pm Tue-Sat, 11am-3pm Sun), which contains two namesake copies of the first printed Bible. For more information on attractions in Mainz, visit the **tourist office** (www.touristik-mainz.de; Brückenturm am Rathaus; ⊙9am-6pm Mon-Fri, 10am-4pm Sat, 11am-3pm Sun).

Trains along the Rhine to Koblenz (€20, one hour) run twice hourly. Heidelberg (€20, one hour, hourly) is an easy trip, as is Frankfurt via the Frankfurt airport (€10, 40 minutes, several per hour).

RHINE TOWNS

Besides those listed in this section, here's the low-down on some other towns along the Rhine route. All have train and boat service.

» **Boppard** Roman walls and ruins (left bank).

» **Oberwesel** Numerous towers and walkable walls of a ruined castle (left bank).

» **Assmannshausen** Small, relatively untouristed village with nice hotels, sweeping views and good hikes (right bank).

» **Rüdesheim** Overrated and overvisited town of trinkets and hype (right bank).

HESSE

The Hessians, a Frankish tribe, were among the first to convert to Lutheranism in the early 16th century. Apart from a brief period of unity in that same century under Philip the Magnanimous, Hesse (Hessen) remained a motley collection of principalities and, later, of Prussian administrative districts until proclaimed a state in 1945. Its main cities are Frankfurt-am-Main, Kassel and the capital, Wiesbaden.

Besides being a transport hub, Frankfurt-am-Main offers its own diversions, although you'll find that the rest of Germany will soon beckon.

Frankfurt-am-Main

♪069 / POP 645,000

Variously called 'Mainhattan' and 'Bankfurt', Frankfurt is indeed on the Main (pronounced 'mine') River and, after London, is Europe's centre of finance. Both sobriquets also refer to the city's soaring skyline of bank-owned skyscrapers.

But while all seems cosmopolitan, it is often just a small town at heart. Streets get quiet in the evenings, the long list of museums has no really outstanding stars, and it has cute old pubs you would only ever think to find in country towns. But when a major convention is in town, such as the Frankfurt Book Fair, it feels as bustling and jammed as any metropolis.

Frankfurt-am-Main is Germany's most important transport hub for air, train and road connections, so you will probably end up here at some point, though truthfully it will probably be best enjoyed as a gateway to someplace else rather than a focus of your trip. Note that Frankfurt is often officially referred to as Frankfurt-am-Main, or Frankfurt/Main, since there is another, smaller town named Frankfurt (Frankfurt-an-der-Oder) located near the Polish border.

◉ Sights

Frankfurt has the most skyscraper-filled skyline in Europe. Banks and related firms have erected a phalanx of egotistical edifices along Mainzer Landstrasse and the Taunusanlange. Tallest (not just locally but within all the EU) at 259m is the pudgy yet pinnacled **Commerzbank Building** on Kaiserplatz. It was designed by Sir Norman Foster.

Get your head in the clouds atop the **Main Tower** (www.maintower-restaurant.de; Neue Mainzer Strasse 52-58; adult/child €5/3.50; ☺10am-9pm Apr-Oct, 10am-7pm Nov-Mar, weather permitting), with its open-air viewing platform 200m up. There is also a **cocktail bar** (☺5.30pm-1am, to 2am Fri & Sat) and restaurant.

Altstadt   HISTORIC QUARTER

Frankfurt has room for all its high-rises because about 80% of the old city was wiped off the map by two Allied bombing raids in March 1944. Although postwar reconstruction was subject to the hurried demands of the new age, rebuilding efforts were more thoughtful in the **Römerberg**, the old central area of Frankfurt west of the cathedral, where ersatz 14th- and 15th-century buildings provide a glimpse of the beautiful city that once was. The old town hall, or **Römer**, is in the northwestern corner of Römerberg and consists of three 15th-century houses topped with Frankfurt's trademark stepped gables.

East of Römerberg, behind the Historischer Garten (which has the remains of

---

ⓘ **NAVIGATING FRANKFURT**

The **airport** is 11 minutes by train southwest of the city centre. The **Hauptbahnhof** is on the western side of the city, but it's still within walking distance of the centre.

The best route to the centre through the sleazy train-station area is along **Kaiserstrasse**. This leads to **Kaiserplatz** and on to a large square called **An der Hauptwache**. This is the retail hub, with stores stretching along in all directions, principally along the **Zeil**.

The area between the former prison/police station (Hauptwache) and the **Römerberg**, in the tiny vestige of Frankfurt's original old city, is the centre of Frankfurt. The **Main River** flows just south of the Altstadt, with several bridges leading to one of the city's most charming areas, **Sachsenhausen**. Its northeastern corner, known as **Alt-Sachsenhausen**, has quaint old houses and narrow alleyways.

Just northeast of the centre, Frankfurt's village roots are most strongly felt in **Bornheim**. The neighbourhood's spine, **Berger Strasse**, is lined with funky small shops, cafes and pubs.

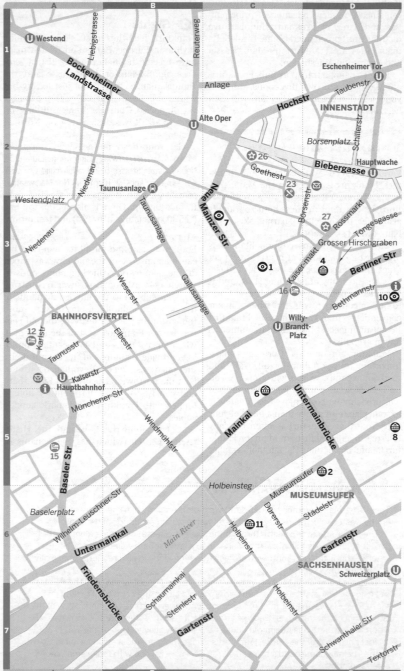

GERMANY HESSE

Westend

Liebigstrasse

Reuterweg

Bockenheimer Landstrasse

Anlage

Eschenheimer Tor

Hochstr

Taubenstr

INNENSTADT

Schillerstr

Alte Oper

Börsenplatz

26

Hauptwache

Biebergasse

Goethestr

Taunusanlage

Westendplatz

Niedenau

23

Börsenstr

27 Rossmarkt

Töngesgasse

Niedenau

Taunusanlage

Neue Mainzer Str

7

Grosser Hirschgraben

Weserstr

Gallusanlage

1

4

Berliner Str

Kaiser-makt

16

Bethmannstr

10

BAHNHOFSVIERTEL

Elbestr

Willy-Brandt-Platz

12

Karlstr

Taunusstr

Kaiserstr

Hauptbahnhof

Münchener Str

Windmühlstr

6

Mainkai

Untermainbrücke

8

Baseler Str

15

Baselerplatz

Wilhelm-Leuschner-Str

Holbeinsteg

Museumsufer

2

Dürerstr

Städelstr

MUSEUMSUFER

Untermainkai

Main River

Holbeinstr

11

Gartenstr

SACHSENHAUSEN

Schweizerplatz

Holbeinstr

Friedensbrücke

Schaumainkai

Steinlestr

Gartenstr

Schwanthaler Str

Textorstr

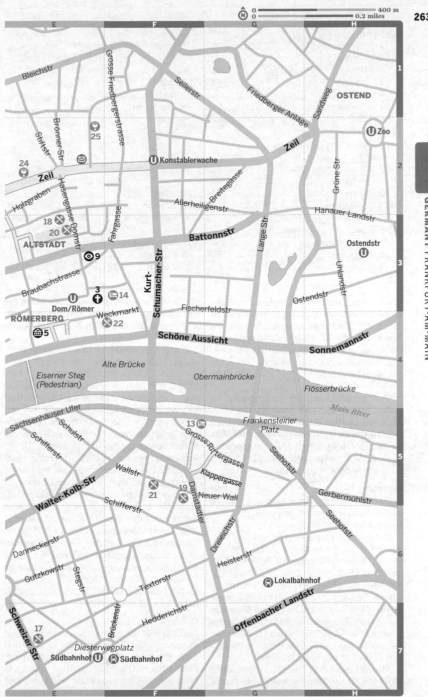

400 m
0.2 miles

OSTEND

Zoo

Bleichstr

Grosse Friedbergerstrasse

Seilerstr

Friedberger Anlage

Sandweg

Brönner Str

Stiftstr

25

Konstablerwache

Zeil

Grüne Str

24

Zeil

Hasengasse

Fahrgasse

Holzgraben

Allerheiligenstr

Breitegasse

Hanauer Landstr

18

20

ALTSTADT

Dornstr

Battonnstr

Lange Str

Ostendstr

9

Kurt-Schumacher-Str

Braubachstrasse

3

14

RÖMERBERG

Dom/Römer

Weckmarkt

Fischerfeldstr

Ostendstr

Uhlandstr

5

22

Schöne Aussicht

Sonnemannstr

Alte Brücke

Eiserner Steg
(Pedestrian)

Obermainbrücke

Flösserbrücke

Main River

Sachsenhäuser Ufer

Schulstr

13

Frankensteiner
Platz

Schifferstr

Grosse Rittergasse

Seehofstr

Wallstr

Klappergasse

WALTER-KOLB-Str

Schifferstr

21

19

Neuer Wall

Gerbermühlstr

Damstädter

Seehofstr

Danneckerstr

Dreieichstr

Gutzkowstr

Stegstr

Heisterstr

Lokalbahnhof

Textorstr

Brückenstr

Hedderichstr

Offenbacher Landstr

Schweizer Str

17

Diesterwegplatz

Südbahnhof

Südbahnhof

Roman and Carolingian foundations), is the **Frankfurter Dom** (Domplatz 14; museum adult/child €3/2; ☉church 9am-noon & 2.30-8pm), the coronation site of Holy Roman emperors from 1562 to 1792. It's dominated by the elegant 15th-century Gothic **tower** – one of the few structures left standing after the 1944 raids (see the pictures inside).

'Few people have the imagination for reality' uttered the ever-pithy Johann Wolfgang von Goethe. Read more quotes at the **Goethe-Haus** (www.goethehaus-frankfurt.de; Grosser Hirschgraben 23-25; adult/student €5/2.50; ☑10am-6pm Mon-Sat, 10am-5.30pm Sun), where he was born in 1749.

Museums   MUSEUMS

Frankfurt's museum list is long and a mixed bag. To sample them all, buy a 48-hour **Museumsufer ticket** (€15).

North of the cathedral, the excellent **Museum für Moderne Kunst** (Museum of Modern Art; www.mmk-frankfurt.de; Domstrasse 10; adult/child €8/4; ☉10am-6pm Tue & Thu-Sun, to 8pm Wed) features works of modern art by Joseph Beuys, Claes Oldenburg and many others. Nearby, the **Historisches Museum** (www.historisches-museum.frankfurt.de; Saalgasse 19; adult/child €4/2; ☉10am-6pm Tue & Thu-Sun, to 8pm Wed) has a model showing the vast extent of prewar medieval Frankfurt.

Also on the north bank, the **Jüdisches Museum** (Jewish Museum; www.jewishmuseum.de; Untermainkai 14-15; adult/child €4/2; ☉10am-5pm Tue & Thu-Sun, to 8pm Wed) is housed in the former mansion of the Rothschild family and details the city's rich Jewish life before WWII.

Numerous museums line the south bank of the Main River along the so-called Museumsufer (Museum Embankment). Pick of the crop is the **Städel Museum** (www.staedelmuseum.de; Schaumainkai 63; adult/child €10/free; ☉10am-5pm Tue & Fri-Sun, to 9pm Wed & Thu), with a world-class collection of paintings by artists from the Renaissance to the 20th century, including Botticelli, Dürer, Van Eyck, Rubens, Rembrandt, Vermeer, Cézanne and Renoir. An expansion may mean that collections shift during construction.

Other museums among the gaggle include the interesting, design-oriented **Museum für Angewandte Kunst** (Museum of Applied Arts; www.angewandtekunst-frankfurt.de; Schaumainkai 17; adult/child €8/4; ☉10am-5pm Tue & Thu-Sun, to 8pm Wed) and the **Deutsches Architekturmuseum** (www.dam-online.de; Schaumainkai 43; adult/child €6/3; ☉11am-6pm Tue & Thu-Sun, to 8pm Wed), which takes an academic look at architecture.

Outdoor Frankfurt   PARKS

Northwest of the centre, there's the botanical **Palmengarten** (Siesmayerstrasse 63; adult/child €5/2; ☉9am-6pm), next door to **Grüneburg Park**. Walk the banks of the Main, which has been much-beautified of late, and you'll find plenty of benches popular for BYO frivolity.

🛏 Sleeping

Frankfurt's good public transport means nothing is very distant no matter where you stay.

Predictably, much of Frankfurt's budget accommodation is in the grotty Bahnhofsviertel, which surrounds the station; be sure to check out the room first. The streets north to the Messe (convention centre) are a bit better and convenient for early departures. During large trade fairs the town is booked out months in advance and rates soar.

TOP CHOICE **Villa Orange** HOTEL €€
(📞405 840; www.villa-orange.de; Hebelstrasse 1, Nordend; r €80-180; ❇@🛜) Offering tranquillity, modern German design and small-hotel comforts (eg a quiet corner library), this century-old villa has 38 spacious rooms. The lavish breakfast buffet is organic. On weekends, rates fall.

Hotel am Dom HOTEL €€
(📞138 1030; www.hotelamdom.de; Kannengiessergasse 3; r €90-130; 🛜) This unprepossessing, 30-room hotel has immaculate rooms, apartments with kitchenettes and four-person suites just a few paces from the cathedral. A large breakfast buffet is included.

Steigenberger Frankfurter Hof HOTEL €€€
(📞215 02; www.steigenberger.de; Am Kaiserplatz; r from €160; ❇@🛜) Schopenhauer used to lunch here but his pessimism is unlikely to dampen your enthusiasm for this cosmopolitan and elegant 19th-century neo-Renaissance institution, Frankfurt's most gracious and traditionally luxurious grand hotel.

Hotel Am Berg HOTEL €€
(📞660 5370; www.hotel-am-berg-ffm.de; Grethenweg 23; r €50-110) Located in a sandstone building in the quiet backstreets of Sachsenhausen, this hotel close to the Südbahnhof has large rooms (some sharing bathrooms) that could have been sets for a '70s porn movie. Seek refuge out back.

Hotel Excelsior HOTEL €
(📞256 080; www.hotelexcelsior-frankfurt.de; Mannheimer Strasse 7-9, Bahnhofsviertel; r €60-100; @) Behind a newish, light-green facade, this 197-room place offers excellent value, with a free business centre; free coffee, tea, veggies and cakes in the lobby; and free landline phone calls throughout Germany.

Concorde Hotel HOTEL €€
(📞242 4220; www.hotelconcorde.de; Karlstrasse 9; r €60-120; ❇🛜) Understated yet well-run,

this establishment in a restored art deco building near the Hauptbahnhof is a good choice any time, but especially on weekends. Multicoloured mood lights are a feature of the rooms – the red-light setting goes with the neighbourhood.

DJH Hostel HOSTEL
(📞610 0150; www.jugendherberge-frankfurt.de; Deutschherrnufer 12, Sachsenhausen; dm €17-25, r €35-75; @) Advance bookings are advisable; within easy walking distance of the city centre and nightspots.

🍴 Eating

Known to the locals as Fressgasse (Munch-Alley), the Kalbächer Petrolse and Grosse Bockenheimer Strasse area, between Opernplatz and Börsenstrasse, has some mediumpriced restaurants and fast-food places with outdoor tables in summer.

Wallstrasse and the surrounding streets in Alt-Sachsenhausen also have lots of lively midpriced restaurants. Bornheim, along strollable Berger Strasse, is another excellent choice.

Look for a bounty of outdoor stands serving food and drinks to gregarious crowds from April to October in the streets south of the Zeil.

Restaurants

Eckhaus GERMAN €€
(Bornheimer Landstrasse 45; mains €8-15) The smoke-stained walls, the iron fan above the door and those ancient floorboards all suggest an inelegant, long-toothed past. The hallmark rösti have been served in this restaurant-bar for over 100 years. Take the U-4 to Merianplatz.

Lobster CONTINENTAL €€
(Wallstrasse 21; mains €15-20; ⊙6pm-1am Mon-Sat, hot dishes until 10.30pm) This cosy, friendly *Weinbistrot* (wine bistro) serves up mouthwatering meat and fish dishes that are 'a little bit French'. Offerings are listed on chalkboards. On a quiet Sachsenhausen street.

Mutter Ernst GERMAN €€
(Alte Rothofstrasse 12; mains €9-18; ⊙closed Sun) The ancient amber-coloured glass windows look into a timeless dining room. Grab a wooden table among the panelled walls for some excellent trad German fare.

Metropol BISTRO €€
(Weckmarkt 13-15; mains €8-16) Serves dishes from a changing menu that fluctuates between inspired and bistro staples. Has a

lovely courtyard out the back where children can chill out. A good place to pause and refresh while touring.

Cafes

Café Mozart
CAKES €

(Töngesgasse 23; cakes from €2) Sample Frankfurt's traditional torte scene by joining the grannies and other trad-lovers who beat a path to this popular cafe to linger over coffee for hours on end.

Café Kante
CAFE €

(Kantstrasse 13; breakfast €3-7; ☺7am-7pm) Walk into this classic Bornheim cafe and you'll be overwhelmed by the delicious aroma of fantastic coffee, breads, cakes and croissants. It's half a block east of Merianplatz U-bahn station.

Apple-Wine Taverns

Apple-wine taverns are Frankfurt's great local tradition. They serve *Ebbelwoi* (Frankfurt dialect for *Apfelwein*), an alcoholic apple cider, along with local specialities like *Handkäse mit Musik* (literally, 'handcheese with music'). This is a round cheese soaked in oil and vinegar and topped with onions; your bowel supplies the music. Anything with the sensational local sauce made from herbs, *Grünesauce,* is a winner. Some good *Ebbelwoi* taverns are situated in Alt-Sachsenhausen.

TOP CHOICE Fichte Kränzi
APPLE WINE €€

(Wallstrasse 5; mains €7-15) Just superb. A smallish place down an alley with a large, shady tree outside. The schnitzels are tops, as is the patter from the waiters.

Adolf Wagner
APPLE WINE €€

(Schweizer Strasse 71; meals €8-15) This old place has one of the most atmospheric interiors in Sachsenhausen. The garden is appealing as well.

Apfelwein Solzer
APPLE WINE €€

(www.solzer-frankfurt.de; Berger Strasse 260, Bornheim; mains €7-15) With wood-panelled walls and a covered courtyard.

Markets

Off Hasenpetrolse, **Kleinmarkthalle** (Hasengasse 5-7; ☺7.30am-6pm Mon-Fri, to 3pm Sat) is a great produce market with loads of fruit, vegetables, meats and hot food.

🍷 Drinking

Many of the places listed under Eating are good for a drink, especially the apple-wine joints. Wander down the streets of Alt-Sachsenhausen to hear the echoes of the millions of American military personnel who drank at the gaudy bars here during the Cold War.

Weidenhof
BAR

(Zeil 104) Drinking games here can revolve around 'spot the shopping bag' – and you'll need plenty of fortitude for this as bags abound at this high-concept bar and terrace right in the middle of Frankfurt's thronged main shopping street.

Wein-Dünker
WINE BAR

(Berger Strasse 265) This musty little wine cellar, down to the right as you enter the courtyard, is not retro, it's real. Descend, rub your eyes and try some of Germany's finest. A good place to meet real Frankfurters.

Zum Schwejk
GAY BAR

(Schafergasse 20) This is a popular gay bar and one of several on this street. Nice tables out front.

☆ Entertainment

Ballet, opera and theatre are strong features of Frankfurt's entertainment scene. Free *Frizz* has good listings (in German) of what's on in town.

Forsythe Company
DANCE

(www.theforsythecompany.de; Bockenheimer Depot, Carlo-Schmid-Platz 1) Easily the world's most-talked-about dance company; the work of William Forsythe is often on tour.

U60311
CLUB

(Rossmarkt 6) A top club for techno, U60311 draws the best talent from around Europe. It's underground, literally, and often still going at noon from the night before.

Jazzkeller
JAZZ

(www.jazzkeller.com; Kleine Bockenheimer Strasse 18a, Innenstadt) Look hard to find this place – a great jazz venue with mood – hidden in a cellar under an alley that obliquely intersects Goethestrasse. Live jazz except on Friday, when there's dancing to Latin and funk.

ℹ Information

Frankfurt Card (1/2 days €9/13) Gives 50% off admission to important attractions and unlimited travel on public transport.

Tourist office (www.frankfurt-tourismus.de) Hauptbahnhof (☺8am-9pm Mon-Fri, 9am-6pm Sat & Sun) Römer (Römerberg 27; ☺9.30am-5.30pm Mon-Fri, 10am-4pm Sat & Sun) The latter is at the northwest corner of the Römerberg square.

Post office airport (departure lounge B; ⊙7am-9pm); Hauptbahnhof (⊙7am-7.30pm Mon-Fri, 8am-4pm Sat); Innenstadt (Zeil 90, ground fl, Karstadt department store; ⊙9.30am-8pm)

Reisebank airport (Terminal 1, arrival hall B; ⊙6am-11pm); Hauptbahnhof (⊙7am-9pm) The train-station branch is at the head of platform 1.

⊙ Getting There & Away

Air

Germany's largest airport is **Frankfurt airport** (FRA; www.frankfurt-airport.com), a vast labyrinth with connections throughout the world. It's served by most major airlines, although not many budget ones.

Only cynics like Ryanair would say that Frankfurt has another airport. **Frankfurt-Hahn airport** (HHN; www.hahn-airport.de) is 70km west of Frankfurt. Buses from Frankfurt's Hauptbahnhof take about two hours – longer than the flight from London. Given the journey time it's fitting the bus company is called **Bohr** (☑06543-501 90; www.bohr-omnibusse.de; adult/child €12/6; ⊙hourly).

Bus

Long-distance buses leave from the south side of the Hauptbahnhof, where you'll find **Eurolines** (www.eurolines.eu; Mannheimer Strasse 15), with services to most European destinations.

The **Romantic Road bus** (www.romanticro adcoach.de) leaves from the south side of the Hauptbahnhof.

Car

Frankfurt-am-Main features the famed Frankfurter Kreuz, the biggest autobahn intersection in the country. All the main car-hire companies have offices in the main hall of the Hauptbahnhof and at the airport.

Train

The Hauptbahnhof handles more departures and arrivals than any station in Germany. Among the myriad services:

DESTINATION	PRICE	DURATION (HR)
Berlin	€111	4
Hamburg	€106	3½
Munich	€89	3¼

For Cologne take the fast (€63, 1¼ hours) ICE line or the slower and more scenic line along the Rhine (€41, 2½ hours, hourly).

Many long-distance trains also serve the airport. This station, Fernbahnhof, is 300m beyond the S-Bahn station, which is under Terminal 1.

⊙ Getting Around

To/From the Airport

S-Bahn lines S8 and S9 run every 15 minutes between the airport and Frankfurt Hauptbahnhof (€3.80, 11 minutes, 4.15am to 1am), usually continuing via Hauptwache and Konstablerwache. Taxis (about €40) take 30 minutes without traffic jams.

The airport train station has two sections: platforms 1 to 3 (below Terminal 1, hall B) handle S-Bahn connections, while IC and ICE connections are in the long-distance train station (Fernbahnhof), 300m distant.

Public Transport

Both single and day tickets for Frankfurt's excellent **transport network** (RMV; www.traffiq.de) can be purchased from automatic machines at almost any train station or stop. Single tickets cost €2.40 and a *Tageskarte* (24-hour ticket) costs €6 (€9.35 with the airport).

Taxi

Taxis are slow compared to public transport and expensive at €2.75 flag fall plus a minimum of €1.65 per km (more at night). There are numerous taxi ranks throughout the city, or you can book a cab (☑230 001).

NORTH RHINE-WESTPHALIA

From vibrant Cologne to elegant Düsseldorf to stately Bonn, the heavily populated Rhine-Ruhr region goes far beyond its coal and steels industries and offers historic towns and cities, each with a distinct life and atmosphere.

Cologne

☑0221 / POP 1 MILLION

Cologne (Köln) seems almost ridiculously proud to be the home of Germany's largest cathedral. The twin-tower shape of its weather-beaten Gothic hulk adorns the strangest souvenirs – from trifles like egg cosies and slippers to fancier fare like glassware and expensive jewellery. However, this bustling Rhine-side metropolis has much more to offer than its most recognisable and ubiquitous symbol. As early as the 1st century AD, Colonia Agrippinensis was an important Roman trading settlement. Today it's one of Germany's most multicultural spots, with a vibrant nightlife only partly fuelled by the local *Kölsch* beer.

◎ Sights

Dom   CATHEDRAL

(www.koelner-dom.de; admission free; ⊙6am-7.30pm, no visitors during services) As easy as it is to get church fatigue in Germany, the huge Kölner Dom is one you shouldn't miss. Blackened with age, this gargoyle-festooned Gothic cathedral has a footprint of 12,470 sq metres, with twin spires soaring to 157m. Although its ground stone was laid in 1248, stop-start construction meant it wasn't finished until 1880, as a symbol of Prussia's drive for unification. Just over 60 years later it escaped WWII's heavy night bombing largely intact.

Sunshine filtering softly through stained-glass windows and the weak glow of candles are the only illumination in the moody, high-ceilinged interior.

Behind the altar lies the cathedral's most precious reliquary, the **Shrine of the Three Magi** (c 1150–1210), which reputedly contains the bones of the Three Wise Men. Brought to Cologne from Milan in the 12th century, it can just be glimpsed through the gates to the inner choir.

To see the shrine properly, you need to take a **guided tour** (adult/concession €6/4; ⊙in English 10.30am & 2.30pm Mon-Sat, 2.30pm Sun). Alternatively, you can embark on the

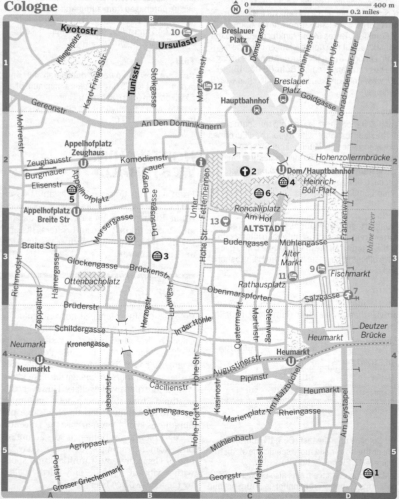

Cologne

seriously strenuous endeavour of climbing the 509 steps of the Dom's **south tower** (adult/concession €2.50/1.50; ⏱9am-6pm May-Sep, to 5pm Mar, Apr & Oct, to 4pm Nov-Feb). You pass the 24-tonne **Peter Bell**, the world's largest working clanger, before emerging at 98.25m to magnificent views.

Two prominent museums sit right next to the cathedral. The **Römisch-Germanisches Museum** (Roman Germanic Museum; ☎2212 2304; www.museenkoeln.de; Roncalliplatz 4; adult/concession €8/4; ⏱10am-5pm Tue-Sun) displays artefacts from the Roman settlement in the Rhine Valley. The **Museum Ludwig** (☎2212 6165; www.museenkoeln.de; Bischofsgartenstrasse 1; adult/concession €9/6, 50% off first Thu evening of each month; ⏱10am-6pm Tue-Sun, to 10pm first Thu of each month) has an astoundingly good collection of 1960s pop art, German expressionism and Russian avant-garde painting, as well as photography.

Kolumba   MUSEUM
(☎933 1930; www.kolumba.de; Kolumbastrasse 4; adult/under 18yr/concession €5/free/3; ⏱noon-5pm Wed-Mon) Encased in the ruins of the late-Gothic church St Kolumba, with layers of foundations going back to Roman times, this is a magnificent design by Swiss architect Peter Zumthor, 2009 winner of the Pritzker Prize, the 'architectural Oscar'. Exhibits span the arc of religious artistry from the early days of Christianity to the present. Coptic textiles, Gothic reliquary and medieval painting are juxtaposed with works by Bauhaus legend Andor Weiniger and edgy room installations.

NS Dokumentationszentrum   MUSEUM
(☎2212 6332; www.museenkoeln.de/nsdok; Appellhofplatz 23-25; adult/concession €3.60/1.50; ⏱10am-4pm Tue, Wed & Fri, 10am-6pm Thu, 11am-4pm Sat & Sun) Cologne's Third Reich history is poignantly documented here. The basement of the building was the local Gestapo prison, where scores of people were interrogated, tortured and killed. Inscriptions on the basement cell walls offer a gut-wrenching record of the emotional and physical pain endured by inmates.

Chocolate Museum   MUSEUM
(☎931 8880; www.schokoladenmuseum.de; Am Schokoladenmuseum 1a; adult/concession €7.50/7; ⏱10am-6pm Tue-Fri, 11am-7pm Sat & Sun, last entry 1hr before closing) South along the riverbank is this glass-walled museum where you nibble on samples while learning the history and process of chocolate-making. Don't miss the 'Cult chocolate' floor.

☞ Tours

Day cruises and Rhine journeys can be organised through **KD River Cruises** (☎208 8318; www.k-d.com; Frankenwerft 35). Day trips (10.30am, noon, 2pm and 6pm) cost €7.20. Sample one-way fare to Bonn is €12.50.

✦ Festivals & Events

Held just before Lent in late February or early March, Cologne's **Carnival** (Karneval) rivals Munich's Oktoberfest for exuberance, as people dress in creative costumes and party in the streets. Things kick off the Thursday before the seventh Sunday before Easter and last until Monday *(Rosenmontag)*, when there are formal and informal parades.

⬛ Sleeping

Accommodation prices in Cologne increase by at least 20% when fairs are on. For more options, see the tourist office, which offers a room-finding service (€3).

Hotel Hopper et cetera   HOTEL €€
(☎924 400; www.hopper.de; Brüsseler Strasse 26; s €80-270, d €120-295; ◉) Parquet flooring, white linen and red chairs lend an elegant simplicity to this former monastery's rooms. The package is rounded off with a bar and sauna in separate parts of the vaulted cellar.

Pension Jansen   HOTEL €
(☎251 85; www.pensionjansen.de; 2nd fl, Richard Wagner Strasse 18; s €31-45, d €62-65) This cute, well-cared-for pension has six individually decorated rooms with cheerful colours

and motifs. Details like handmade wreaths hanging on aqua walls – or a big red rose screen-printed on the bed linen – convey a homey atmosphere. Book early.

Hotel Cristall
HOTEL €€

(☎163 00; www.hotelcristall.de; Ursulaplatz 9-11; s €72-184, d €90-235; @🛜) Angular red, orange and purple sofas greet you in the lobby of this recently expanded boutique hotel. Rooms in the newest wing feature luxuriously minimalist spaces with slate showers and black carpeting; the main building has simpler rooms with a stylish but less-modern look.

Das Kleine Stapelhäuschen
HOTEL €

(☎272 7777; www.koeln-altstadt.de/stapelhaeuschen; Fischmarkt 1-3; s/d from €45/68; @🛜) A small, friendly hotel housed in a 12th-century building in the centre of the old town, just off the riverbank. Exposed beams, antique furnishings and simple but cosy touches give rooms a homey feel.

Lint Hotel
HOTEL €€

(☎920 550; www.lint-hotel.de; Lintgasse 7; s/d €85/129; 🛜) Modern, clean rooms with parquet flooring and light, white bedspreads fill this ecofriendly hotel in the heart of the old town. The staff will be happy to tell you all about the solar panels and how they keep waste to a minimum.

Station Hostel for Backpackers
HOSTEL €

(☎912 5301; www.hostel-cologne.de; Marzellenstrasse 44-56; dm €17-20, s/d/tr €39/55/75; @🛜) You can't get more convenient than this friendly six-floor hostel around the corner from the train station. The rooms could use some sprucing up but they're perfectly simple and clean. Breakfast costs €3, or you can use the guest kitchen.

Meininger City Hostel & Hotel
HOSTEL €

(☎355 332 014; www.meininger-hostels.com; Engelbertstrasse 33-35; dm €17-24, s/d/tr from €43/68/84, breakfast €3.50; @🛜) Located in a former hotel, this charming hostel in the cool Zülpicher Viertel district is loaded with retro appeal coupled with modern rooms featuring lockers, reading lamps, a small TV and bathrooms.

✖ Eating

While Cologne's beer halls serve excellent meals, the city overflows with restaurants – for the largest variety and the most happening atmosphere, head to the Zülpicher and Belgisches Viertel neighbourhoods.

Alcazar
PUB FARE €

(Bismarckstrasse 39; snacks €4-9, mains €10-16; ✍) The food and atmosphere are both hearty and warming at this old-school, slightly hippie pub. The changing menu always has one veggie option.

Metzgerei & Salon Schmitz
INTERNATIONAL €

(Aachener Strasse 28; snacks €4-8) Whether you prefer sidling up to the long bar or grabbing an ultracomfy sofa in the retro lounge, Schmitz is a perfect pit stop for relaxed chats over coffee or cocktails. If hunger strikes, pop next door to **Metzgerei Schmitz**, a deli in a former butcher's shop.

MoschMosch
ASIAN €

(Pfeilstrasse 25-27; dishes €7-11; ⊙11am-11pm) This sleek Japanese noodle bar offers flavourful ramen noodle soups and teppanyaki dishes in a candlelit space in the heart of the trendy Belgisches Viertel.

Feynsinn
TOP CHOICE
INTERNATIONAL €€

(☎240 9210; Rathenauplatz 7; mains €7-18) The glint of artfully arranged glasses behind the mirrored bar will catch your eye from the street, as will the broken-glass chandeliers. Inside, under murals, students, creative types and tourists tuck into seasonal cuisine (menu changes weekly) as well as traditional Cologne fare such as *Himmel and Aad* (literally Heaven and Earth, which is mashed potatoes and apple sauce). The owners have even started to raise their own pigs and cattle.

Weinstube Bacchus
INTERNATIONAL €€

(☎217 986; Rathenauplatz 17; mains €9-20; ⊙dinner) Dark-wood tables, yellow walls that are lined with paintings by local artists (all pieces are for sale), a seasonal international menu and an almost exclusively German wine list make this casual wine bar–restaurant popular among the locals.

🍺 Drinking & Entertainment

As in Munich, beer in Cologne reigns supreme. More than 20 local breweries turn out a variety called *Kölsch*, which is relatively light and slightly bitter. The breweries run their own beer halls and serve their wares in skinny 200mL glasses. For more options, take a tram to Zülpicherplatz and explore.

Früh am Dom
BEER HALL

(☎258 0394; Am Hof 12-14) This three-storey beer hall and restaurant (including cellar bar) is the most central, with black-and-white flooring, copper pans and tiled ovens keeping it real, despite the souvenir shop. It's open for breakfast.

Fiffi Bar
COCKTAIL BAR

(Rolandstrasse 99) Look for the pink lei–wearing bull-terrier statue mounted above the entrance of this hilarious retro, red-vinyl, dog-themed joint. We personally recommend ordering the Frozen Setter (Cuervo, pineapple and lemon) but perhaps you'd prefer the Sweet Lassie (rum, banana and cream)?

Katt-Winkel
COCKTAIL BAR

(Greesbergstrasse 2) Housed in a cool, triangular space, this gay cafe-bar welcomes everyone. It's a relaxing spot to unwind to mellow music with an expertly mixed cocktail.

Päffgen
BEER HALL

(Friesenstrasse 64-66) Another favourite, this thrumming wood-lined room has its own beer garden. It's not far from the bars of the Belgisches Viertel.

Hotelux
VODKA BAR

(Rathenauplatz 22) Red walls, red booths and red lights; Hotelux serves cocktails and over 30 types of 'Soviet water' (ie vodka) to students and intellectual types.

Gebäude 9
CLUB

(☑814 637; Deutz-Mülheimer Strasse 127-129) Once a factory, this is now a Cologne nightlife stalwart spinning drum'n'bass, indie pop, gypsy music and '60s trash to film noir and puppets.

Underground
LIVE MUSIC

(☑542 326; Vogelsanger Strasse 200; ⊘Mon & Wed-Sat) This complex combines a pub and two concert halls where indie and alt-rock bands play several times a week. Otherwise it's party time with different music nightly (no cover). There's a beer garden in summer.

ⓘ Information

Köln Welcome Card (24/48/72hr €9/14/19) Discount card that includes free public transport (including Bonn) and discounted museum admission. Available from the tourist office.

Main post office (☑01802-3333; WDR Centre, Breite Strasse 6-26; ⊘9am-7pm Mon-Fri, to 2pm Sat)

Tourist office (☑2213 0400; www.koelntourismus.de; Unter Fettenhennen 19; ⊘9am-8pm Mon-Sat, 10am-5pm Sun)

ⓘ Getting There & Away
Air
Cologne-Bonn airport (CGN; www.airport-cgn.de) is growing in importance. There are now direct flights to New York, while budget airlines German Wings and easyJet, among others, fly here.

Car
The city is on a main north–south autobahn route and is easily accessible for drivers. The popular German ride-share agency **ADM-Mitfahrzentrale** (☑194 40; www.citynetz-mitfahrzentrale.de; Maximinen Strasse 2) is near the train station.

Train
There are frequent RE services operating to Düsseldorf (€11 to €16, 25 to 30 minutes) and Aachen (€13.90, 50 minutes to one hour). Frequent EC, IC, or ICE trains go to Hanover (from €55, 2¾ to three hours), Frankfurt (from €39, one to 2¼ hours, three hourly) and Berlin (€104, 4¼ hours, hourly). Frequent Thalys high-speed services connect Cologne to Paris (from €95, four hours) via Brussels, and ICE trains go to Amsterdam (from €59, 2½ hours).

ⓘ Getting Around
Cologne's mix of buses, trams and U-Bahn and S-Bahn trains is operated by **VRS** (☑01803-504 030; www.vrsinfo.de) in cooperation with Bonn's system.

Short trips (up to four stops) cost €1.60, longer ones €2.40. Day passes are €6.90 for one person and €10.10 for up to five people travelling together. Buy your tickets from the orange ticket machines at stations and aboard trams; be sure to validate them.

Cologne is flat and cycle-friendly. Bicycle hire is available next to the main train station at **Radstation** (☑139 7190; www.radstationkoeln.de; Am Hauptbahnhof/Breslauerplatz; per 3hr/1/3/7 days €5/10/20/40; ⊘5.30am-10.30pm Mon-Fri, 6.30am-8pm Sat, 8am-8pm Sun).

Bonn
☑0228 / POP 312,000

South of Cologne on the Rhine's banks, Beethoven's birthplace became West Germany's temporary capital in 1949. But exactly 50 years later it was demoted when most (but not all) government departments returned to Berlin. These days several large company headquarters reside here, including telecommunications giant Deutsche Telekom, Deutsche Post World Net (German postal service plus international express mail service DHL) and renowned German TV broadcaster Deutsche Welle.

An excellent collection of museums and a quiet, compact old town filled with

18th-century baroque architecture make Bonn a worthwhile day trip.

The **tourist office** (☏775 000; www.bonn-regio.de; Windeckstrasse 1; ☉9am-6.30pm Mon-Fri, 9am-4pm Sat, 10am-2pm Sun) is a three-minute walk along Poststrasse from the Hauptbahnhof, and can fill you in with any extra details.

Ludwig van Beethoven fans will head straight to the **Beethoven-Haus** (☏981 7525; www.beethoven-haus-bonn.de; Bonngasse 24-26; adult/concession €4/3; ☉10am-6pm Mon-Sat, 11am-6pm Sun Apr-Oct, to 5pm Nov-Mar), where the composer was born in 1770. The house contains memorabilia concerning his life and music, including his last piano, with an amplified sounding board to accommodate his deafness. The annual Beethoven Festival takes place August to September.

The **Haus der Geschichte der Bundesrepublik Deutschland** (FRG History Museum; ☏916 50; www.hdg.de; Willy-Brandt-Allee 14; admission free; ☉9am-7pm Tue-Sun) presents Germany's postwar history. It is part of the Museumsmeile, four museums that also include the **Kunstmuseum Bonn** (☏776 260; www.kunstmuseum-bonn.de; Friedrich-Ebert-Allee 2; adult/concession €5/2.50; ☉10am-6pm Tue & Thu-Sun, to 9pm Wed) and the **Kunst-und Ausstellungshalle der Bundesrepublik Deutschland** (☏917 1200; www.bundeskunsthalle.de; Friedrich-Ebert-Allee 2; adult/concession €8/5; ☉10am-9pm Tue & Wed, to 7pm Thu-Sun).

The unfiltered ale is a must at **Brauhaus Bönnsch** (☏650 610; Sterntorbrücke 4; mains €7-15; ☉11am-1am), a congenial brew-pub adorned with photographs of famous politicians: Willy Brandt to, yes, Arnold Schwarzenegger. Schnitzel, spare ribs and sausage dominate the menu, but the *Flammkuchen* (Alsatian pizza) is still a perennial bestseller.

From Cologne, it's quicker to take an RE train to Bonn (€6.50, 30 minutes) than a tram (€8.50 day pass, 55 minutes). For river trips, see p269.

Düsseldorf

☏0211 / POP 585,000

'D-Town' or 'the City D', as local magazine editors like to call Düsseldorf, is Germany's fashion capital. But that means Jil Sander and Wolfgang Joop rather than cutting-edge street wear, as you'll soon discover observing fur-clad *Mesdames* with tiny dogs along the ritzy shopping boulevard of the Königsallee.

Indeed, this elegant and wealthy town could feel stiflingly bourgeois if it weren't for its lively old-town pubs, its position on the Rhine, its excellent art galleries and the postmodern architecture of its Mediahafen.

◉ Sights

Düsseldorf has a lively **Altstadt**, which is filled with enough restaurants, beer halls and pubs to have earned it the slightly exaggerated title of the 'longest bar in the world'. In the central Marktplatz you'll find a **statue** of the former ruler, or elector, Jan Wellem.

What really sets the city apart, however, is the contemporary architecture of its **Mediahafen**. Here, in the city's south, docks have been transformed into an interesting commercial park, most notably including the **Neuer Zollhof**, three typically curved and twisting buildings by Bilbao Guggenheim architect Frank Gehry. You'll find a map of the park on a billboard located behind (ie on the street side of) the red-brick Gehry building.

For a bird's-eye view of the Mediahafen, and indeed all of Düsseldorf, catch the express elevator to the 168m viewing platform of the neighbouring **Rheinturm** (adult/child €3.50/1.90; ☉10am-11.30pm). There's also a revolving restaurant and cocktail bar a level above, at 172.5m.

It's a pleasant stroll between the Mediahafen and the Altstadt along the riverside **Rheinuferpromenade**. Alternatively, you can join the city's elite window-shopping along the **Königsallee**, or 'Kö' – Düsseldorf's answer to Rodeo Drive.

Three excellent galleries, two sharing the same collection, form the backbone of Düsseldorf's reputation as a city of art.

Reopened in 2010, the **K20** (☏838 10; www.kunstsammlung.de; Grabbeplatz 5; adult/concession €10/5, combination ticket K20 & K21 €17/8.50; ☉10am-6pm Tue-Fri, 11am-6pm Sat & Sun) museum features a brand-new wing and early-20th-century masters, including an extensive Paul Klee collection.

K21 (☏838 1600; www.kunstsammlung.de; Ständehausstrasse 1; adult/concession €10/5, combination ticket K20 & K21 €17/8.50; ☉10am-6pm Tue-Fri, 11am-6pm Sat & Sun) concentrates on art from 1990 onwards. Highlights include Nam June Paik's *TV Garden*, local artist Katarina Fritsch's giant black mouse sitting on a sleeping man, the psychedelically decorated bar and the glassed-in roof.

KIT – Kunst im Tunnel (☏892 0769; www.kunst-im-tunnel.de; Mannesmannufer 1b; adult/

Düsseldorf

Düsseldorf

concession €4/3) literally translates as 'Art in the Tunnel', which is exactly what you get in the former road tunnel. Revolving exhib-

its – often by local students from the Düsseldorfer Art Academy – line the concrete curved walls of this surreal, subterranean space. The riverside cafe upstairs is a popular drinking spot during clement weather.

⌂ Sleeping

Hotel Berial　　　　　　　　　　HOTEL €
(☏ 490 0490; www.hotelberial.de; Gartenstrasse 30; s/d from €40/60; @☏) An inviting ambience reigns here, thanks to the friendly staff and the contemporary furnishings. Decor features lots of blue, blond wood, glass bathroom doors and some bright prints. The breakfast buffet is truly gargantuan.

Stage 47　　　　　　BOUTIQUE HOTEL €€€
(☏ 388 030; www.stage47.de; Graf-Adolf-Strasse 47; s/d from €160/180; @☏) Behind the drab exterior, movie glamour meets design chic at this urban boutique hotel. Rooms are named for famous people, some of whom have actually stayed in the environs dominated by

black, white and grey tones. Nice touches: an iHome and a Nespresso coffee maker.

Sir & Lady Astor
HOTEL €€

(☎173 370; www.sir-astor.de; Kurfürstenstrasse 18 & 23; s €83-170, d €95-240; @🖘) The twin-hotel features two parts across the street from each other: Sir Astor features only African and Scottish motifs, while Lady Astor is more international and themed rooms evoke Asia, the Middle East and beyond.

Backpackers-Düsseldorf
HOSTEL €

(☎302 0848; www.backpackers-duesseldorf.de; Fürstenwall 180; dm €22, incl linen, towel & breakfast; @🖘) This modern hostel adds bright colours, table football and soft beds to come out a real winner. Near the Mediahafen, it's reached from the train station by bus 725 to Kirchplatz, from where there are several trams into town.

Jugendgästehaus
HOSTEL €

(☎557 310; www.jugendherberge.de; Düsseldorfer Strasse 1; dm/s/tw €25/42/62; @🖘) Situated in upscale Oberkassel, recent renovations turned this 368-room hostel into a snazzy, modern place that feels more like a boutique hotel. All rooms are en suite and breakfast is served in a large, airy space overlooking the Rhine.

✖ Eating & Drinking

Ohme Jupp
BISTRO €

(☎326 406; Ratinger Strasse 19; ⊗8am-1am) Casual, artsy cafe serving breakfast and seasonal blackboard specials; also a popular after-work drinking den.

Libanon Express
MIDDLE EASTERN €

(Berger Strasse 19-21; cafe €3-14, restaurant €10-19) Crammed with mirrors and tiles – and with recommendations stickered on the window – this cafe serves great kebabs, falafel and other Middle Eastern specialities.

Zum Uerige
BREWPUB

(☎866 990; Berger Strasse 1) In this noisy, cavernous place, the trademark Uerige Alt beer (a dark and semisweet brew typical of Düsseldorf) flows so quickly that the waiters just carry around trays and give you a glass whenever they spy one empty. It also serves hearty German fare, so it doubles as an excellent place for a bite.

Galapagoz
BAR

(☎355 8983; www.galapagoz.de; Klosterstrasse 68a) Tuck into this tiny cafe-bar for fantastic cocktails, wines and snacks (the menu is written on the slate tiles that wrap their

way around) in a laid-back South American space. It's primarily a gay hangout, but everyone is welcome.

Lido
BAR

(☎1576 8730; www.lido1960.de; Am Handelshafen 15) This bar in a glass-and-steel cube extending out over the water in the Mediahafen, and its smooth outdoor lounge-deck, is *the* place to see and be seen on a hot summer night.

ℹ Information

Düsseldorf Welcome Card (24/48/72hr €9/14/19) Discount card offering free public transport and discounted museum admission. Available from the tourist office.

Tourist office (www.duesseldorf-tourismus.de) main office (☎172 0222; Immermannstrasse 65b; ⊗9.30am-6.30pm Mon-Sat); old town (☎1720 2840; Marktstrasse/Ecke Rhein-strasse; ⊗10am-6pm)

ℹ Getting There & Away

From **Düsseldorf International Airport** (DUS; www.duesseldorf-international.de), trains go directly to other German cities, while frequent S-Bahn services (1 and 7) head to Düsseldorf train station.

Low-cost carrier Ryanair flies to **Niederrhein (Weeze) airport** (NRN; www.flughafen-nie-derrhein.de). A **shuttle bus** (☎06543-501 90; www.bohr-omnibusse.de) to Düsseldorf (€15, 1¼ hours) leaves soon after the planes' scheduled arrivals.

The many **train** services from Düsseldorf include to Cologne (€10.50 to €16, 25 to 30 minutes), Frankfurt-am-Main (€70, 1½ to 1¾ hours), Hanover (€53, 2½ hours) and Berlin (€97, 4¼ hours).

ℹ Getting Around

The metro, trams and buses are useful to cover Düsseldorf's distances. Most trips within the city cost €2.30; longer trips to the suburbs are €4.50. Day passes are €5.30.

Aachen

☎0241 / POP 247,000

A spa town with a hopping student population and tremendous amounts of character, Aachen has narrow cobbled streets, quirky fountains, shops full of delectable *Printen* (local biscuit, a bit like gingerbread), and a pretty cathedral, which make for an excellent day trip from Cologne or Düsseldorf or a worthy overnight stop.

◎ Sights

Next to the tourist office is the **Elisenbrunnen** (Elisa Fountain); despite its sulphuric, rotten-egg smell, you *can* drink the water – it's supposedly good for the digestion.

In the far left-hand corner of the park, behind the Elisenbrunnen, you'll find the **Geldbrunnen** (Gold Fountain), which represents the circulation of money. The comical figures around the pool clutch their coins or purses while the water is sucked down the central plughole (jokingly known as 'the taxman').

Head east along the top of the park here, towards Forum M, and turn left into Buchkremerstrasse. Soon you'll reach a fountain with a scary-looking creature. This is the mythological **Bahkauv**, which was rumoured to jump on the backs of those returning late from the pub and demand a lift all the way home.

Buchkremerstrasse becomes Buchel. Turn left just past Leo van den Daele, then right again, and you'll come to Hühnermarkt, with its **Hühnerdiebbrunnen** (Chicken-thief fountain). The hasty thief hasn't noticed one of his stolen chickens is a rooster that's about to unmask him by crowing.

From here, Aachen's main **Markt** is visible just to the northeast. The 14th-century **Rathaus** (adult/concession €2/1; ⊙10am-5pm Mon-Fri, 10am-1pm & 2-5pm Sat & Sun) overlooks the Markt, while a fountain statue of **Charlemagne** is in the middle.

Head back down the hill along Krämerstrasse until you come to the **Puppenbrunnen** (Puppet fountain), where you're allowed to play with the movable bronze figures.

Continuing in the same direction for 50m, you'll arrive at Aachen's famous Dom.

Dom CATHEDRAL
(Kaiserdom or Münster; www.aachendom.de; ⊙7am-7pm Apr-Oct, 7am-6pm Nov-Mar) While Cologne's cathedral wows you with its size and atmosphere, Aachen's similarly Unesco-listed Dom impresses with its shiny neatness. The small, Byzantine-inspired **octagon** at the building's heart dates from 805 but its ceiling mosaics still glitter and its marble columns still gleam.

The building's historical significance is twofold: not only did Charlemagne order it built, but 30 Holy Roman emperors were crowned here from 936 to 1531.

The brass **chandelier** hanging in the centre was donated by Emperor Friedrich Barbarossa in 1165. Standing at the main altar and looking back towards the door, it's just possible to glimpse Charlemagne's simple marble throne. The man himself lies in the golden **shrine** behind the altar. The cathedral became a site of pilgrimage after his death.

Carolus Thermal Baths BATHS
(⊘182 740; www.carolus-thermen.de; Stadtgarten/Passstrasse 79; admission with/without sauna from €22/11; ⊙9am-11pm) The 8th-century Franks were first lured to Aachen for its thermal springs. And just over 1200 years later, the state-of-the-art Carolus Thermen are still reeling them in.

That's hardly surprising, for the complex is part therapeutic spa – good for rheumatism etc – and part swimming centre. Quirky currents whiz you around one pool, water jets bubble up in another and taps pour out cold water in yet another. Only diehard fans should pay for the sauna, as there's – bizarrely – a steam room accessible to all.

The baths are in the city garden, northeast of the centre.

🛏 Sleeping

Hotel Drei Könige HOTEL €€
(⊘483 93; www.h3k-aachen.de, in German; Büchel 5; s €90-130, d €120-160, apt €130-240; 🛜) The radiant Mediterranean decor is an instant mood enhancer at this family-run favourite with its doesn't-get-more-central location. Some rooms are a tad small but the two-room apartment sleeps up to four. Breakfast on the 4th floor comes with heavenly views over the rooftops and the cathedral.

Hotel Benelux HOTEL €€
(⊘400 030; www.hotel-benelux.de; Franzstrasse 21-23; s €94-109, d €120-154; 🛜) This well-run hotel is clean and uncluttered, with tasteful art in all its rooms. The rooftop garden with the enclosed gazebo is a bonus.

Jugendgästehaus HOSTEL €
(⊘711 010; www.jugendherberge.de; Maria-Theresia-Allee 260; dm/s/tw €23/37/57; @) This modern DJH outpost sits on a hill overlooking the city, and gets lots of school groups. Take bus 2 to Ronheide.

✕ Eating & Drinking

Aachen's students have their own 'Latin Quarter' along Pontstrasse, with dozens of bars and cheap eats. The street heads northeast off the Markt and runs for nearly 1km.

Leo van den Daele INTERNATIONAL €
(Büchel 18) A warren of 17th-century rooms all linked by crooked stairs across four

merchants' homes, this nationally renowned cafe specialises in gingerbread, or *Printen*. You can also enjoy light meals – soups, sandwiches, quiches and *pastetchen* (vol-au-vents) – among its tiled stoves and antique knick-knacks.

Kaiser Wetter ITALIAN €€
(☏9437 9950; www.kaiserwetter-ac.de; Hof 5) Stop by for a drink, a snack or a light meal of salads and pizzas at this restaurant-lounge in the centre of town. Relax at the outdoor tables under the shadow of giant Roman pillars or step inside the modern interior.

Anna's Tafel FRENCH €€
(☏5593 5537; Pontstrasse 62; mains €10-14) This tiny, quiet wine bar–restaurant with unfinished wood tables and romantic candelabras serves seasonal French specialities, cheese and charcuterie plates and decadent desserts. A great escape from the student crowds just up the road.

Apollo Kino & Bar BAR/CLUB
(☏900 8484; Pontstrasse 141-149) This cavernous basement joint does double duty as an art-house cinema and a sweaty dance club for the student brigade. Alt sounds rule on Mondays and salsa on Tuesdays, but on other nights it could be anything from dancehall to disco, house to power pop.

ℹ Information

Tourist office (☏180 2960/1; www.aachen. de; Atrium Elisenbrunnen, Kapuzinergraben; ⊙9am-6pm Mon-Fri, 9am-2pm Sat, also 10am-2pm Sun Easter-Dec)

ℹ Getting There & Around

There are frequent trains to Cologne (€13.90 to €19.50, 30 minutes to one hour) and twice-hourly service to Düsseldorf (from €17.20, 70 minutes to 1½ hours). The high-speed Thalys train passes through regularly on its way to Brussels and Paris (from €87, three hours).

Buses cost €1.50 (trip of a few stops only), €2.20 (regular single) or €6.10 (day pass).

LOWER SAXONY

Lower Saxony (Niedersachsen) likes to make much of its half-timbered towns. Hamelin is certainly a true fairy-tale beauty, and leaning Lüneberg is quite unlike any other town you'll see. The state is also home to the global headquarters of Volkswagen and the business-minded capital, Hanover, as well as the pretty Harz mountains (see the boxed text, p209).

Hanover

☏0511 / POP 518.000

German comedians – yes, they do exist – like to dismiss Hanover as 'the autobahn exit between Göttingen and Walsrode'. However, the capital of Lower Saxony is far livelier than its reputation assumes, and its residents are remarkably friendly and proud of their small city. While it's famous for hosting trade fairs, particularly the huge CEBIT computer show in March, it also boasts acres of greenery in the Versailles-like gardens, Herrenhäuser Gärten.

Parts of the central Altstadt look medieval, but few of them are. They're mostly clever fakes built after intense WWII bombing.

⊙ Sights & Activities

The enormous **Grosser Garten** (Large Garden; admission €3, free in winter) is the highlight of the **Herrenhäuser Gärten** (☏1684 7576; www.herrenhaeuser-gaerten.de; ⊙9am-sunset). It has a small maze and Europe's tallest fountain. Check the website in summer for **Wasserspiele**, when all fountains are synchronised, and the night-time **Illuminations**. The **Niki de Saint Phalle Grotto** is a magical showcase of the artist's work. She was French – her colourful figures adorn the famous Stravinsky fountain outside the Centre Pompidou in Paris – but developed a special relationship with Hanover. There's a popular beer garden in the Grosser Garten. Alternatively, the flora of the **Berggarten** (Mountain Garden; admission €2, combined entry with Grosser Garten €4) is interesting. Adjacent lies the **Sea Life Hannover** (☏56 669 0101; adult/child €14.95/10.95, incl Grosser Garten & Berggarten adult/child €15.50/11.95; ⊙10am-5pm), a 3500-sq-metre educational aquarium with friendly staff and clever displays.

The **Neues Rathaus** (new town hall) was built between 1901 and 1913. Town models in the foyer reveal the extent of WWII devastation. Further east lies the Leine River and, since 1974, **Die Nanas** – three fluorescent-coloured, earth-mama sculptures by de Saint Phalle – have lived here. They're best seen on Saturday, when there's a flea market at their feet.

In summer, the **Machsee** (lake) has ferries (crossing €3, tour €6) and numerous boats for hire. There's a free public **swimming beach** on the southeast shore.

🛏 Sleeping

The tourist office only finds private rooms during trade fairs but can arrange hotel bookings year-round for €7.

City Hotel Flamme
HOTEL €€

(☑388 8004; www.cityhotelflamme.de; Lammstrasse 3; s/d €69/99; @🛜) This art hotel features endearing touches such as goodnight stories on bedside tables. Rooms are arranged around a tropical-feeling atrium that has an inviting bar. Accommodation is spotless and the staff are friendly.

City Hotel am Thielenplatz
HOTEL €€

(☑327 691; www.smartcityhotel.de; Thielenplatz 2; s €58.50-68.50, d €77-87; @🛜) Crisp, white, retro furnishings and high ceilings dominate in the airy space here. Some bathrooms are miniscule but overall this place is excellent value and only a short walk from the train station. The reception desk is located in the popular downstairs bar.

Jugendherberge
HOSTEL €

(☑131 7674; www.jugendherberge.de; Ferdinand-Wilhelm-Fricke-Weg 1; dm under/over 27yr from €23.90/26.90; @) This large, space lab–like structure houses a modern hostel with breakfast room and terrace bar overlooking the river in an area that feels more country than city. Take U3 or U7 to Fischerhof, cross the mini red suspension bridge and turn right.

GästeResidenz PelikanViertel
HOTEL €€

(☑399 90; Pelikanstrasse 11; s €46-69, d €66-89, tr €92-109; @) Upmarket student residence meets budget hotel, this huge complex (located in the former Pelikan fountain-pen factory) has a wide range of Ikea-style rooms, all with kitchenettes. Prices skyrocket during trade-fair periods. Take U3, U7 or U9 to Pelikanstrasse.

🍴 Eating & Drinking

Markthalle
INTERNATIONAL €

(Karmarschstrasse 49; dishes €4-10; ☉7am-8pm Mon-Wed, to 10pm Thu & Fri, to 4pm Sat) This huge covered market of food stalls (sausages, sushi, tapas and more), gourmet delis and standing-only 'bars' is a no-nonsense, atmospheric place for a quick bite. It's also heaving each Friday evening with people proclaiming *Prost!* (Cheers!) to the start of the weekend.

Spandau
INTERNATIONAL €€

(Engelbosteler Damm 30; mains €6-14; ☉10am-1am Sun-Wed, 10am-2am Thu-Sat) Retro-'70s Spandau in Hanover's Nordstadt is more like Berlin's Kreuzberg – a place where students from the nearby university and the local Turkish community rub shoulders.

Café-Bar Celona
CAFE, BAR €€

(☑353 8576; Knochenhauerstrasse 42; mains €7-16) Latin-themed and plant-filled, this cafe-bar is fine any time of day (or night) for a bite, a drink, or both. Book ahead for its massive (and massively popular) all-you-can-eat Sunday brunch (€8.95).

Mr Phung Kabuki
JAPANESE €€

(Friedrichswall 10) Boats bob by on the water-based sushi chain, and you can order all manner of pan-Asian and wok dishes in this airy, trendy restaurant with an enormous range of spirits.

ℹ Information

Hannover Tourismus (☑information 1234 5111, room reservations 1234 555; www.hannover.de; Ernst- August-Platz 8; ☉9am-6pm Mon-Fri, 9am-2pm Sat, also 9am-2pm Sun Apr-Sep)

ℹ Getting There & Around

Hanover's **airport** (HAJ; www.hannover-airport. de) has many connections, including on low-cost carrier Air Berlin.

There are frequent IC/ICE train services running to/from Hamburg (€34 to €39, 1¼ to 1½ hours), Berlin (€53 to €58, 1½ to two hours), Cologne (€54 to €61, 2¾ to 3¼ hours) and Munich (€112, 4¼ to 4¾ hours), among other destinations.

U-Bahn lines from the Hauptbahnhof are boarded in the station's north (follow the signs towards Raschplatz), except the U10 and U17, which are overground trams leaving from near the tourist office.

Most visitors only travel in the central 'Hanover' zone. Single tickets are €2.10 and day passes €4.10.

The S-Bahn (S5) takes 17 minutes to the airport (€2.80).

Around Hanover

CELLE

☑05141 / POP 70,800

With row upon row of ornate half-timbered houses, all decorated with scrolls and allegorical figures, Celle is a pleasant place for a leisurely day trip. Even the tourist office,

Tourismus Region Celle (☎1212; www.region -celle.com; Markt 14; ☺9am-6pm Mon-Fri, 10am-4pm Sat, 11am-2pm Sun May-Sep, 9am-5pm Mon-Fri, 10am-1pm Sat Oct-Apr), is located in a striking building, the **Altes Rathaus** (1561–79), which boasts a wonderful Weser Renaissance stepped gable, topped with the ducal coat of arms and a golden weather vane.

Lying just west of the Rathaus is the 13th-century **Stadtkirche** (☎7735; An der Stadtkirche 8; tower adult/concession €1/0.50; ☺10am-6pm Tue-Sat Apr-Dec, to 5pm Jan-Mar, tower 10-11.45am & 2-4.45pm Tue-Sat). You can climb up the 235 steps to the top of the church steeple for a view of the city, or just watch as the city trumpeter climbs the 220 steps to the white tower below the steeple for a trumpet fanfare in all four directions. The spectacle is most entertaining and takes place daily at 9.30am and 5.30pm (sometimes more frequently during the summer months – enquire at the tourist office).

Further west lies the magnificently proportioned wedding-cake **Schloss** (Ducal Palace; ☎123 73; Schlossplatz; tours adult/concession €5/3; ☺tours hourly 11am-3pm Tue-Sun Apr-Oct, 11am & 3pm Tue-Sun, plus 1pm Sat & Sun Nov-Mar). Built in 1292 by Otto Der Strenge (Otto the Strict) as a town fortification, the building was expanded and turned into a residence in 1378. The last duke to live here was Georg Wilhelm (1624–1705), and the last royal was Queen Caroline-Mathilde of Denmark, who died here in 1775.

The Schloss can only be visited on guided tours (in German), but there are explanatory brochures in English for sale. Highlights include the magnificent baroque theatre, the private apartment of Caroline-Mathilde and, above all, the chapel. Its original Gothic form is evident in the high windows and vaulted ceiling, but the rest of the intricate interior is pure Renaissance. The duke's pew was above; the shutters were added later so His Highness could snooze during the three-hour services.

Across from the palace stands Celle's **Kunstmuseum** (Art Museum; ☎123 55; www.

WORTH A TRIP

VOLKSWAGEN CITY

Volkswagen *is* the Lower Saxon town of **Wolfsburg** – and the huge VW emblem adorning the company's global headquarters (and a factory the size of a small country) won't let you forget it. 'Golfsburg', as it's nicknamed after one of VW's most successful models, does a nice sideline in modern architecture. But really, the top reason people come here is to experience the theme park called Autostadt, which tells you everything you ever wanted to know about VW.

Spread across 25 hectares, **Autostadt** (Car City; ☎0800-2886 782 38; www.autostadt. de; Stadtbrücke; adult/child/concession/family €15/6/12/38, entry after 4pm €7; ☺9am-6pm) is a celebration of all things Volkswagen. Exhibitions run the gamut of automotive design and engineering, the history of the Beetle and the marketing of individual marques, including VW itself, Audi, Bentley, Lamborghini, Seat and Skoda.

Included in the admission price is the **CarTower Discovery**, a fun glass lift that whisks you up to the 20th floor as if you were an actual car (vehicles are stored inside the towers). At the top you have a sweeping view of the city and complex. Most exciting for wannabe race-car drivers, there are obstacle courses and safety training (€25 to €28) where you can take an adrenalin-fuelled spin.

The space-age building beside the train station is **Phaeno** (☎0180-106 0600; www. phaeno.de; Willy Brandt-Platz 1; adult/child/concession/family €12/7.50/9/26.50; ☺9am-5pm Mon-Fri, 10am-6pm Sat & Sun), a science centre designed by British-based Iraqi architect Zaha Hadid. Some 250 hands-on exhibits and experiments – wind up your own rocket, watch thermal images of your body – provide hours of fun. It's very physical, but also requires concentration. Instructions and explanations come in German and English.

Wolfsburg's centre lies just southeast of the Hauptbahnhof. Autostadt is north across the train tracks. Head through the 'tunnel' under the Phaeno science centre and you'll see the footbridge. **Wolfsburg tourist office** (☎05361 899 930; www.wolfsburg.de; Willy Brandt-Platz 3; ☺9am-6pm Mon-Fri, 10am-3pm Sat & Sun) is in the train station.

Frequent RE/IC/ICE train services arrive from Hanover (from €12.90, 30 minutes to one hour) and Berlin (from €34.40, one to 1¼ hours).

kunst.celle.de; Schlossplatz 7; adult/concession incl Bomann Museum €5/3, free Fri; ⊘10am-5pm Tue-Fri, to 6pm Sat & Sun), which bills itself as 'the world's first 24-hour museum'. It's claiming this after a €4-million refurbishment created a transparent glass facade that showcases electric-light installations right through the evening – the exterior colour changes from red, orange, purple, gold and blue during the last few hours of darkness. During the day, you can visit the contemporary German paintings, sculptures and objects of collector Robert Simon.

In the older building adjacent, you'll still find the regional-history **Bomann Museum** (⌨125 44; www.bomann-museum.de; Schlossplatz 7; adult/concession incl Kunstmuseum €5/3; ⊘10am-5pm Tue-Sun, last entry 4.15pm). Here, among other things, you can wander through rooms furnished in 19th-century style.

Various train services run to Celle from Hanover (€8.40 to €10.50, 20 to 35 minutes) and Hamburg (€23.80 to €28, one to 1½ hours). The Altstadt is about a 15-minute walk east of the Hauptbahnhof.

HAMELIN

⌨05151 / POP 58,700

If you were to believe the 'Pied Piper of Hamelin' fairy tale, this quaint, ornate town on the Weser River ought to be devoid of both rats and children. According to legend, the Pied Piper *(Der Rattenfänger)* was employed by Hamelin's townsfolk to lure their pesky rodents into the river in the 13th century. When they refused to pay him, however, he picked up his flute again and led their kids away.

However, it is a bedtime story, after all. International tourism means the reality is very different. Everywhere you look along Hamelin's cobbled streets are – you guessed it – fake rats and happy young children.

The train station is about 800m east of the centre. To get to **Hameln Tourist Information** (⌨957 823; www.hameln.com; Diesterallee 1; ⊘9am-6.30pm Mon-Fri, 9.30am-4pm Sat, 9.30am-1pm Sun May-Sep, 9am-6pm Mon-Fri, 9.30am-1pm Sat & Sun Oct & Apr) take bus 2, 3, 4, 21, or 33.

The best way to explore is to follow the **Pied Piper trail** – the line of white rats drawn on the pavements. There are information posts at various points. They're in German, but at least you know when to stop to admire the various restored 16th- to 18th-century half-timbered houses.

The detailed Weser Renaissance style dominates the Altstadt – the **Rattenfänger-haus** (Rat Catcher's House; Osterstrasse 28), from 1602, is perhaps the finest example, with its steep and richly decorated gable. Also not to be missed is the **Hochzeitshaus** (Wedding House; 1610–17) at the Markt end of Oster-strasse. The **Rattenfänger Glockenspiel** at the far end chimes daily at 9.35am and 11.35am, while a **carousel of Pied Piper figures** twirls at 1.05pm, 3.35pm and 5.35pm.

Between May and September you can watch the **Pied Piper open-air play** at noon on Sunday and the comic musical *Rats* on Wednesday at 4.30pm; both are free and are performed at the Hochzeitshausplatz in the centre of town – contact the tourist office for details.

Frequent S-Bahn trains (S5) head from Hanover to Hamelin (€10.30, 45 minutes). By car, take the B217 to/from Hanover.

BREMEN

⌨0421 / POP 550,000

It's a shame the donkey, dog, cat and rooster in Grimm's *Die Bremerstadmusikanten* (Town Musicians of Bremen) never actually made it here – they would have fallen in love with the place. This little city is big on charm, from the statues of the famous fairy-tale characters to the jaw-dropping art-nouveau laneway to the impressive Markt. On top of that, the waterfront promenade along the Weser River is a relaxing refuge filled with outdoor cafes, and the student district along Ostertorsteinweg knows it's got a good thing going and leaves little to be desired.

◉ Sights & Activities

Bremen's **Markt** is striking, particularly its ornate, gabled **Rathaus**. In front stands a 13m-tall medieval statue of the knight **Roland**, Bremen's protector. On the building's western side, you'll find a sculpture of the **Town Musicians of Bremen** (1951). Local artist Gerhard Marcks has cast them in their most famous pose, scaring the robbers who invaded their house, with the rooster atop the cat, perched on the dog, on the shoulders of the donkey.

Also on the Markt is the twin-towered **Dom St Petri**, the most interesting – and slightly macabre – feature of which is its **Bleikeller** (Lead Cellar; ⌨365 0441; adult/concession €1.40/1; ⊘10am-5pm Mon-Fri, 10am-2pm Sat, noon-5pm Sun Easter-Oct) Here, open coffins

GERMANY BREMEN

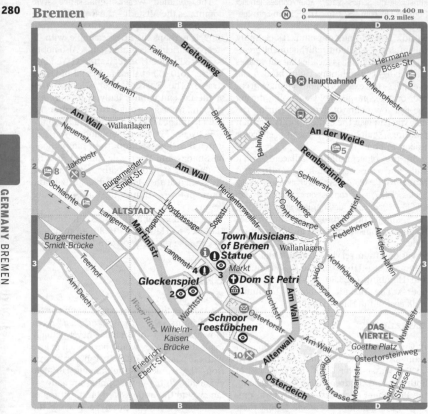

reveal eight corpses that have mummified in the dry underground air. The Bleikeller has its own entrance, south of the main cathedral door.

If the Markt is memorable, then nearby **Böttcherstrasse** is unique. It's an opulent art deco street commissioned by Ludwig Roselius, the inventor of decaffeinated coffee and founder of the company Hag. He later managed to save it from the Nazis, who thought it 'degenerate'. Under the golden relief you enter a world of tall brick houses, shops, galleries, restaurants, a **Glockenspiel** and several museums (which can easily be skipped). If you can, peek in the back door of 'Haus Atlantis' (aka the Hilton hotel), for its phantasmagorical, multicoloured, glasswalled **spiral staircase**.

The maze of narrow, winding alleys known as the **Schnoorviertel** was once the fishermen's quarter and then the red-light district. Now its doll's house–sized cottages

are souvenir shops and restaurants. The cute **Schnoor Teestübchen** (Wüste Stätte 1) serves Frisian tea and cakes.

With more time, make a visit to **Beck's Brewery** (☏5094 5555; Am Deich 18-19; tours in German & English €9.50; ☺2pm & 3.30pm Thu & Fri, 12.30pm, 2pm, 3.30pm & 5pm Sat Jan-Apr, additionally 11am & 12.30pm Thu & Fri, 9.30am & 11am Sat May-Dec) or the oyster-shaped **Universum Science Center** (☏334 60; www.usc-bremen.de; Wiener Strasse 2; adult/concession & child €18.50/12.50; ☺9am-6pm Mon-Fri, 10am-7pm Sat & Sun, last entry 90min before closing).

🛌 Sleeping

Bremer Backpacker Hostel HOSTEL €
(☏223 8057; www.bremer-backpacker-hostel.de; Emil-Waldmannstrasse 5-6; dm/s/d €17/28/46, bedding €3; @ 🛜) A friendly place five minutes from the train station, here you'll find simply furnished but spotless rooms spread out over several levels (each floor is named after

Bremen

a continent), a full kitchen, a living room and a cheerful courtyard.

Hotel Bölts am Park   HOTEL €€
(☑346 110; www.hotel-boelts.de; Slevogtstrasse 23; s/d €70/90; @�) This family-run hotel in a leafy neighbourhood has real character, from the old-fashioned breakfast hall to its well-proportioned rooms. A few singles with hall showers and toilets cost €48.

Hotel Überfluss   HOTEL €€€
(☑322 860; www.hotel-ueberfluss.com; Langenstrasse 72/Schlachte; s €139-154, d €184-199, ste €359; ��@�) Dragging quaint Bremen into the 21st century is this jaw-dropping design hotel. It's all green-tinted windows overlooking the Weser River, and shiny black bathrooms. The friendly staff and the lobby, which displays bits of the old city wall found when constructing the hotel, make this place feel unique and more than worth the splurge.

DJH Hostel Bremen   HOSTEL €
(☑163 820; www.jugendherberge.de; Kalkstrasse 6; dm under/over 27yr €23.50/26.50, s/d €36.50/63; @�) Looking like a work of art from outside, with a yellow-and-orange Plexiglas facade and slit rectangular windows, this refurbished building more resembles a museum than a hostel. Comfortable dorms are all en suite, there's a bar-breakfast room with huge glass windows overlooking the Weser River, and a rooftop terrace. Take tram 3 or 5 to Am Brill.

✕ Eating & Drinking

The student quarter in and around Ostertorsteinweg, Das Viertel, is full of restaurants and cafes and has a vaguely bohemian atmosphere. The waterfront promenade, Schlachte, is more expensive and mainstream. The Marktplatz is home to oodles of cheap snack stands.

Piano   CAFE/BAR
(Fehrfeld 64; mains €6-13) One of the most enduringly popular cafes in the student quarter, excellent for an evening tipple or a snack from its pizza, pasta, steaks and veggie casserole menu. Breakfast is served until 4pm.

Apadana   PERSIAN €
(cnr Heinkenstrasse & Faulenstrasse; mains €6-13) This family-run, hospitable Persian restaurant serves lovingly prepared, traditional fare in a simple, quiet space. It's excellent for solo diners, with a large stack of magazines on hand to read.

Restaurant Flett   GERMAN €€
(☑320 995; Böttcherstrasse 3-5) Despite all the tourists, this is the best place in Bremen to try local specialities such as *Labskaus* (a hash of beef or pork with potatoes, onion and herring) or *Knipp* (fried hash and oats).

Katzen Café   INTERNATIONAL €€
(☑326 621; Schnoor 38) This Moulin Rouge–style restaurant opens out into a rear sunken terrace bedecked with flowers. The menu runs the gamut from Alsatian to Norwegian, with seafood a strong theme.

Wohnzimmer   BAR
(☑163 2064; Ostertorsteinweg 99) This bar and lounge mostly gets a relaxed 20s and 30s crowd, who hang out on the sofas – which explains the name 'Living Room' – or lounge around on the mezzanine levels in non-smoker and smoker areas.

ℹ Information

Tourist office (☑01805-101030; www.bremen-tourism.de) Hauptbahnhof (⊙9am-7pm Mon-Fri, 9.30am-6pm Sat & Sun); branch office (Obernstrasse/Liebfrauenkirchhof; ⊙10am-6.30pm Mon-Fri, 10am-4pm Sat & Sun)

ℹ Getting There & Around

Flights from **Bremen airport** (BRE; www.airport-bremen.de) include low-cost carriers Air Berlin and Ryanair.

WORTH A TRIP

LÜNEBURG, THE WOBBLY TOWN

With an off-kilter church steeple, buildings leaning on each other and houses with swollen 'beer-belly' facades, it's as if charming Lüneburg has drunk too much of the Pilsener lager it used to brew.

Of course, the city's wobbly angles and uneven pavements have a more prosaic cause. For centuries until 1980, Lüneburg was a salt-mining town, and as this 'white gold' was extracted from the earth, ground shifts and subsidence knocked many buildings sideways. Inadequate drying of the plaster in the now-swollen facades merely added to this asymmetry.

But knowing the scientific explanation never detracts from the pleasure of being on Lüneburg's comic-book crooked streets.

Between Hanover (€26, one hour by train) and Hamburg (€13.20, 30 minutes), the city's an undemanding day trip from either. From the train station, head west into town towards the highly visible, 14th-century **St Johanniskirche**, the 106m-high spire of which leans 2.2m off true. Local legend has it that the architect tried to kill himself by jumping off it. (He fell into a hay cart and was saved, but celebrating his escape later in the pub he drank himself into a stupor, fell over, hit his head and died after all.)

The church stands at the eastern end of the city's oldest square, **Am Sande**, full of typically Hanseatic stepped gables. At the western end stands the beautiful black-and-white **Industrie und Handelskammer** (Trade and Industry Chamber).

Continue one block past the Handelskammer and turn right into restaurant-lined Schröderstrasse, which leads to the Markt, where the ornate **Rathaus** (town hall) contains the **tourist office** (☑04131 207 6620; www.lueneburg.de; ⊙9am-6pm Mon-Fri, to 4pm Sat, 10am-4pm Sun May-Sep, 9am-5pm Mon-Fri, to 2pm Sat Oct-Apr).

Admire the square before continuing west along Waagestrasse and down our favourite Lüneburg street, **Auf dem Meere**, en route to the **St Michaeliskirche**. Here the wonky facades and wavy pavements are like something from a Tim Burton film.

It's too late now to regain your equilibrium, so head back along Am Flock for the pubs on **Am Stintmarkt** on the bank of the Ilmenau River.

Frequent trains go to Hamburg (€20.80 to €28, one hour to 1¼ hours), Hanover (€21 to €30, one hour to 80 minutes) and Cologne (€60, three hours).

Tram 6 leaves the airport frequently, heading to the centre (€2.20, 16 minutes). Other trams cover most of the city. Single bus and tram tickets cost €2.20; a day pass (€5.90 for one adult and two children) is excellent value.

HAMBURG

☑040 / POP 1.77 MILLION

It comes as no surprise that Hamburg is stylishly expanding itself by 40% without batting an eye – this is a city where ambition flows through the ubiquitous waterways and designer-clad residents cycle to their media jobs with a self-assurance unmatched by any other German city. The site of Europe's largest urban-renewal project is a never-ending forest of cranes that are efficiently transforming old city docks into

an extension of the city – it all makes you wonder: what *can't* this city achieve? Decent weather; that's one thing it can't buy, build or create. But residents are passionately dedicated to their beloved city and will rarely fret about drizzly skies – they just open up their designer umbrellas and get on with it.

Germany's leading port city has always been forward-thinking and liberal. Its dynamism, multiculturalism and hedonistic red-light district, the Reeperbahn, all arise from its maritime history. Joining the Hanseatic League trading bloc in the Middle Ages, Hamburg has been enthusiastically doing business with the rest of the world ever since. In the 1960s it nurtured the musical talent of the Beatles. Nowadays it's also a media capital and the wealthiest city in Germany.

◉ Sights & Activities

Old Town   HISTORIC AREA

Hamburg's medieval **Rathaus** (☑4283 120 10; tours adult/child €3/0.50, ⊙English-language tours hourly 10.15am-3.15pm Mon-Thu, to 1.15pm Fri, to 5.15pm Sat, to 4.15pm Sun; Ⓜ Rathausmarkt or Jungfernstieg) is one of Europe's most opulent. North of here, you can wander through the **Alsterarkaden**, the Renaissance-style arcades sheltering shops and cafes alongside a canal or 'fleet'.

For many visitors, however, the city's most memorable building is south in the Merchants' District. The 1920s, brown-brick **Chile Haus** (cnr Burchardstrasse & Johanniswall; Ⓜ Mönckebergstrasse/Messberg) is shaped like an ocean liner, with remarkable curved walls meeting in the shape of a ship's bow and staggered balconies that look like decks.

Alster Lakes   LAKES

A cruise on the Binnenalster and Aussenalster is one of the best ways to appreciate the elegant side of the city. **ATG Alster-Touristik** (☑3574 2419; www.alstertouristik.de; 2hr trip adult/child €9.50/4.25; ☺Apr-Oct; Ⓜ Jungfernstieg) is a good bet. The company also offers 'fleet' tours and winter tours through the icy waters.

Better yet, hire your own rowboat or canoe. Opposite the Atlantic Hotel you'll find **Segelschule Pieper** (☑247 578; www.segelschule-pieper.de; An der Alster; per hr from €15; ☺Apr-Oct; Ⓜ Hauptbahnhof).

Speicherstadt & Harbour   HISTORIC AREA

The beautiful red-brick, neo-Gothic warehouses lining the Elbe archipelago south of the Altstadt once stored exotic goods from around the world. Now the so-called **Speicherstadt** (Ⓜ Messberg/Baumwall) is a popular sightseeing attraction. It's best appreciated by simply wandering through its streets or taking a Barkassen boat up its canals. **Kapitän Prüsse** (☑313 130; www.kapitaen-pruesse.de; Landungsbrücke No 3; adult/child from €12.50/5.50) offers regular Speicherstadt tours, leaving from the port. Other Barkassen operators simply tout for business opposite the archipelago.

Another way to see the Speicherstadt is from the **High-Flyer Hot Air Balloon** (☑3008 6968; www.highflyer-hamburg.de; per 15min €15; ☺10am-midnight, to 10pm winter, weather permitting) tethered nearby.

The Speicherstadt merges into the **HafenCity**, an area where the old docks are being transformed into a 155-hectare extension of the city – what looks like a never-ending construction zone is actually Europe's largest inner-city development project. When finished, the area will house a university, approximately 6000

apartments and more. It's estimated that in the next 20 years, it will extend the centre city of Hamburg by about 40%. Some 40,000 people will work here, and 12,000 will live here. The squat brown-brick former warehouse at the far west of the zone is being transformed into the new **Elbphilharmonie** (Elbe Philharmonic Hall; http://elbphilharmonie-bau.de), due for completion by 2012. Pritzker Prize–winning Swiss architects Herzog & de Meuron are responsible for the design, which, like their Tate Modern building in London, boasts a glass top. This time, however, they're being far more ambitious, as the glass facade should be taller than its brick base and the roof line will rise in wavelike peaks to reflect the waterfront location. Get details and ponder models detailing the magnitude of the project at the **HafenCity InfoCenter** (☑3690 1799; Am Sandtorkai 30; ☺10am-6pm Tue, Wed & Fri-Sun, to 8pm Thu May-Sep). HafenCity will be connected to the Hauptbahnhof and several other central transport hubs when the new U-Bahn line (U4) opens in late 2011.

Port and Elbe River cruises start in summer at the St Pauli Landungsbrücken. **Hadag** (☑311 7070; www.hadag.de; Brücke 2; 1hr harbour trip adult/child from €10/5.50) offers some of the best deals and cruises.

Reeperbahn   RED LIGHT DISTRICT

(Ⓜ Reeperbahn) No discussion of Hamburg is complete without mentioning St Pauli, home of the Reeperbahn, Europe's biggest red-light district. Sex shops, peep shows, dim bars and strip clubs line the streets, which generally start getting crowded with the masses after 8pm or 9pm. This is also where the notorious **Herbertstrasse** (a block-long street lined with brothels that's off-limits to men under 18 and to female visitors of all ages) is located as well as the **Erotic Art Museum** (☑317 4757; www.eroticartmuseum.de; Bernhard-Nocht-Strasse 69; adult €5; ☺noon-10pm, to midnight Fri & Sat) and the **Condomerie** (☑319 3100; www.condomerie.de; Spielbudenplatz 18; ☺noon-midnight), with its extensive collection of prophylactics and sex toys.

WANT MORE?

Head to **Lonely Planet** (www.lonelyplanet.com/germany/hamburg) for planning advice, author recommendations, traveller reviews and insider tips.

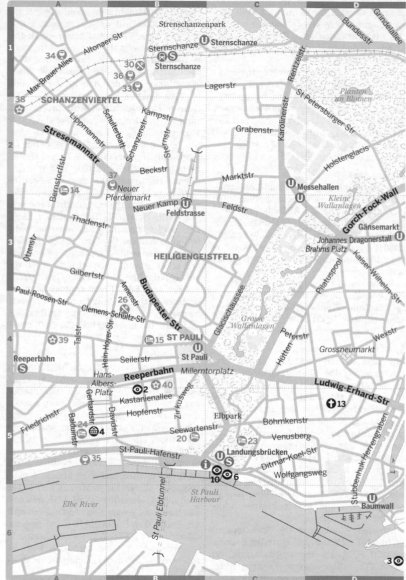

Fischmarkt

MARKET

Here's the perfect excuse to stay up all Saturday night. Every Sunday between 5am and 10am, curious tourists join locals of every age and walk of life at the famous Fischmarkt in St Pauli. The market has been running since 1703, and its undisputed stars are the boisterous *Marktschreier* (market criers) who hawk their wares at full volume. Live bands also entertainingly crank out cover versions of ancient German pop songs in the adjoining *Fischauktion-*

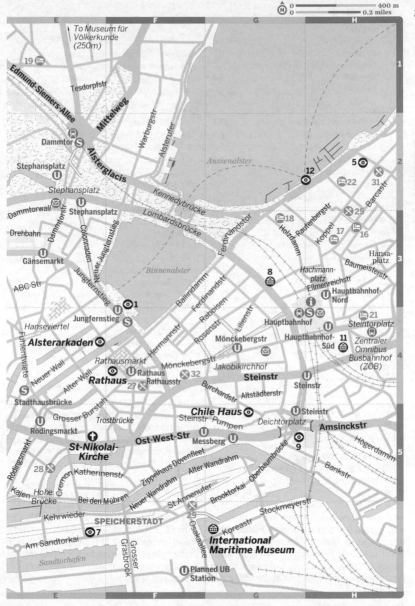

shalle (Fish Auction Hall). Take bus 112 to Hafentreppe.

International Maritime Museum MUSEUM
(☎300 93 300; www.internationales-maritimes
-museum.de; Koreastrasse 1; adult/concession
€10/7; ☻10am-6pm Tue, Wed & Fri-Sun, 10am-

8pm Thu; Ⓜ︎Messberg) Ensconced within HafenCity (p283), this nine-floor, enormous space examines 3000 years of maritime history through displays of model ships, naval paintings, navigation tools and educational exhibits explaining the seas and its tides and currents. Added bonus: sweeping views of the HafenCity development project greet you at every window.

Museum für Völkerkunde   MUSEUM
(☎01805-308 888; www.voelkerkundemuseum.com; Rothenbaumchaussee 64; admission €5, after 4pm Fri free; ⊙10am-6pm Tue, Wed & Fri-Sun, to 9pm Thu; ⓜHallerstrasse or Dammtor) The Museum of Ethnology demonstrates sea-going Hamburg's acute awareness of multiculturalism and its aims to promote respect of the world and its cultures. You'll be awestruck by the giant statues from Papua New Guinea, placed prominently at the top of the stairs.

Hamburger Kunsthalle   MUSEUM
(☎428 131 200; www.hamburger-kunsthalle.de; Glockengiesserwall; adult/concession €8.50/5; ⊙10am-6pm Tue, Wed & Fri-Sun, to 9pm Thu); ⓜHauptbahnhof) Consists of two buildings, the old one housing old masters and 19th-century art, and a white concrete cube –

the Galerie der Gegenwart – showcasing contemporary German artists, including Rebecca Horn, Georg Baselitz and Gerhard Richter, alongside international stars such as David Hockney, Jeff Koons and Barbara Kruger.

Museum für Kunst und Gewerbe   MUSEUM
(☎428 542 732; www.mkg-hamburg.de; Steintorplatz 1; adult/concession €8/5, from 5pm Tue, Wed & Thu €5; ⊙11am-6pm Tue & Fri-Sun, to 9pm Wed & Thu; ⓜHauptbahnhof) This Museum of Arts & Crafts offers something for everyone with its period rooms, photography, posters, graphic design and textiles.

St Michaeliskirche   CHURCH
(tower adult/concession €3/2; ⊙10am-6pm Apr-Oct, to 5pm Nov-Mar; ⓜStadthausbrücke) This is one of Hamburg's most recognisable landmarks and northern Germany's largest Protestant baroque church. From the tower of 'Der Michel', as it's commonly called, you have panoramic views.

St-Nikolai-Kirche

CHURCH

(Ost-West-Strasse; adult/child €3.70/3; ⊙10.30am-5.30pm; ⓜRödingsmarkt) This WWII-damaged church is now an antiwar memorial, with some chilling photos of the then-bombed-out city.

🛏 Sleeping

Fritz Hotel

BOUTIQUE HOTEL €€

(☏8222 2830; www.fritzhotel.com; Schanzenstrasse 101-103; s/d €60/90; 🛜; ⓜSternshanze) Run by fun, friendly staff, this stylish town-house hotel is as cool as a cucumber in shades of white and grey and splashes of red. It's great for urbanistas who'll be happy finding their own breakfast at neighbourhood cafes (though the hotel offers fresh fruit and coffee) and who aren't perturbed by a bit of street noise (some rooms have balconies overlooking the action; ask for one of the quieter rooms out the back).

Backpackers St Pauli

HOSTEL €

(☏2351 7043; www.backpackers-stpauli.de; Bernstorffstrasse 98; dm €19.50-24, d/tr from €60/75, linen €2, breakfast & snacks €2-4.30; @🛜; ⓜFeldstrasse) Entered via a bright cafe, this is a great new addition to Hamburg's hostel scene, with a cool, subterranean, maritime-themed lounge containing a small kitchenette, a sunny outdoor terrace, table football and light-filled rooms (some with bathrooms) with good-sized lockers.

Superbude Hotel, Hostel & Lounge

HOSTEL €

(☏380 8780; www.superbude.de; Spaldingstrasse 152; dm €16-22, d €59-89; @🛜; ⓜBerliner Tor) This hostel-hotelnear St Georg is just about the snazziest hotel-hostel we've ever seen. Housed in a former printing factory, the modern, spacious dorms and rooms feel like trendy loft spaces. Quirky touches include plungers used as wall 'hooks', a metallic polka-dot entrance, slate stone flooring, cow-hide rugs and two entertainment rooms (one with Nintendo, Wii and table football; the other is a mini cinema). Breakfast is €7, laundry facilities are free and bike rental costs €4 per day.

Jugendherberge-Auf dem Stintfang

HOSTEL €

(☏313 488; www.jugendherberge.de; Alfred-Wegener-Weg 5; dm from €22.90; @🛜; ⓜLandungsbrücken) Modern, clean and convenient (head out of the U-Bahn station, up the steps to the massive modern complex at the top of the hill), this DJH hostel overlooks the Elbe River and the harbour. With lots of large, noisy school groups, however, it's very keen on rules, and you're locked out part of the day.

Kogge

HOTEL €

(☏312 872; www.kogge-hamburg.de; Bernhard-Nocht-Strasse 59; s €29.50-33, d €48.40-55;@🛜; ⓜLandungsbrücken or Reeperbahn) We wanna rock 'n' roll all night at this friendly, fun rock 'n' roll bar and hotel sitting on a quite street around the corner from the noisy Reeperbahn territory. Themed rooms include those named 'Bollywood', 'Punk Royal', 'Disco Dream' and all share shower and toilet facilities. Popular with musicians and perfect for travellers planning to party all night and sleep until late (standard check out is 2pm).

Hotel Annenhof

HOTEL €

(☏243 426; www.hotelannenhof.de; Lange Reihe 23; s €40-50, d €70-80; ⓜHauptbahnhof) The Annenhof's attractive, cheerful rooms have polished wooden floorboards and clean, simple furnishings. There's no breakfast but plenty of cafes nearby.

Hotel Village

HOTEL €€

(☏480 6490; www.hotel-village.de; Steindamm 4; s/d from €72/95, without bathroom from €52/68; @🛜; ⓜHauptbahnhof) A former bordello going straight, it has boudoirs that feature various mixes of red velvet, gold flock wallpaper and leopard prints, and sometimes even blue neon–lit bathrooms or mirrors above the bed – don't be surprised if you stumble upon a photo shoot during your stay. It's a fun, functional space a stone's throw from the main train station. Breakfast is included.

Hotel Fresena

HOTEL €€

(☏410 4892; www.hotelfresena.de; Moorweidenstrasse 34; s €75-99, d €88-130; @; ⓜDammtor) Palatial, clean, modern rooms; high ceilings; African statues; and cool theatre photographs give this place character without clutter. If it's full the building houses four other pensions and the friendly staff will help you find a room elsewhere. Breakfast is €9.

Hotel Wedina

HOTEL €€

(☏280 8900; www.wedina.de; Gurlittstrasse 23; s/d main bldg incl breakfast from €98/118, other bldg incl breakfast from €108/138; 🛜; ⓜHauptbahnhof) You might find a novel instead of a chocolate on your pillow at Wedina, a hotel that's a must for bookworms and literary groupies. Jonathan Franzen, Vladimir Nabokov and JK Rowling are just some of the authors who've stayed and left behind signed books.

The hotel is spread over four buildings, offering a choice of traditional decor in the main red building or modern, urban living in its green, blue and yellow houses. The hotel also offers bike hire (€8 per day).

Hotel Hafen
HOTEL €€

(☏311 1370; www.hotel-hafen-hamburg.de; Seewartenstrasse 9; r from €120, breakfast €16; @🛜; ⓂLandungsbrücken) Location, location, location. This privately owned behemoth of a hotel (353 rooms) looms over the heart of Hamburg's harbour from a small hill. If you're lucky enough to score a harbour-facing room (no guarantees, but it's worth asking), the views are extraordinary. In addition to the refurbished, historic main building – a former seamen's home – there are newer modern wings.

Galerie-Hotel Sarah Petersen
PENSION €€

(☏249 826, 0173 200 0746; www.galerie-hotel-sarah-petersen.de; Lange Reihe 50; s €88-155, d €98-165; ❄@; ⓂHauptbahnhof) This delightful *pensione* (guest house) inside a historic 1790 town house is an extension of its welcoming artist-owner's personality, whose paintings decorate the walls of his 'gallery of dreams'. Furnishings include a mix of contemporary, antique and art-deco styles. Our pick of its five rooms is the top-floor terrace studio, with a romantic rooftop terrace, kitchenette and separate living area. Breakfast costs €9.50.

Schlaflounge
B&B €€

(☏3868 5387; www.schlaflounge.de, in German; Vereinsstrasse 54b; s/d €65/89, breakfast €10; ⓂChristuskirche) Live like a local in this stylish, streamlined B&B in an appealing residential quarter with relaxed neighbourhood bars and excellent restaurants nearby. Attractive rooms incorporate blond wood and either brown and ochre or dark-red and aqua colour schemes. Breakfast includes organic fruit and home-made jam.

East
HOTEL €€€

(☏309 933; www.east-hamburg.de; Simon-von-Utrecht-Strasse 31; d/apt/ste from €165/175/275; 🛜; ⓂSt Pauli) Pillars, walls and lamps emulate organic forms in the public areas of this warm, richly decorated design hotel. Floors are themed by plants and spices.

Hotel Atlantic
HOTEL €€€

(☏288 80; www.kempinski.atlantic.de; An der Alster 72-79; s €270-370, d €300-500, ste from €500, breakfast €33; 🛜🏊; ⓂHauptbahnhof Nord) Imagine yourself aboard a luxury ocean liner in this grand 252-room hotel, which opens onto Holzdamm. Built for cruise passengers, it has ornate stairwells, wide hallways and subtle maritime touches. Suites – including BMW and James Bond suites – are a big leap up from the standard accommodation. Significantly cheaper rates are often available online.

✗ Eating

The **Schanzenviertel** (ⓂFeldstrasse/Schanzenstern) swarms with cheap eateries; try Schulterblatt for Portuguese outlets or Susanenstrasse for Asian and Turkish. Many fish restaurants around the Landungsbrücken are overrated and touristy. St Georg's **Lange Reihe** (ⓂHauptbahnhof) offers many characterful eating spots to suit every budget, and there is a seemingly endless selection of simple but quality, high-value sushi joints all over town.

Fleetschlösschen
INTERNATIONAL €€

(Brooktorkai 17; snacks €7-10; ⊘8am-8pm Mon-Fri, 11am-6pm Sat & Sun; ⓂMessberg) This former customs post overlooks a Speicherstadt canal and the HafenCity development and has a narrow, steel spiral staircase to the toilets. There's barely room for 20 inside, but its several outdoor seating areas are brilliant in sunny weather. The owner's collection of *Kleinods* (small treasures) includes centuries-old Dutch pottery unearthed during the construction of HafenCity.

Café Paris
FRENCH €€

(Rathausstrasse 4; mains €10-19; ⊘from 9am Mon-Fri, from 10am Sat & Sun; ⓂRathaus) At this stalwart in the city centre, be sure to admire the spectacular maritime- and industry-themed ceiling murals and tiles. On weekends breakfast is served until 4pm in this bustling French brasserie.

Geel Haus
GERMAN €€

(Koppel 76; dishes €5-10; ⊘from 6pm; ☏; ⓂHauptbahnhof) A casual, homey neighbourhood favourite tucked away on a quiet street in St Georg with an emphasis on Austrian and German fare, plus plenty of veggie options.

frank und frei
PUB FAR €

(Schanzenstrasse 93; mains €5-16; ⓂSternschanze) Big, bustling and laid-back restaurant-pub, with brick walls, wooden booths, shiny pillars and a stylish curved wooden bar, offering simple German fare, salads and pastas. It's a great place to unwind with a beer, a bite or a full meal.

DON'T MISS

SOUPY EEL

Tired of wurst and dumplings? Well, you're in a port city now so specialities generally involve seafood, veering away from stereotypical German fare. *Labskaus* is a dish of boiled, marinated beef put through the grinder with mashed potatoes and herring and served with a fried egg, red beets and pickles. Or perhaps you'd prefer *Aalsuppe* (eel soup) spiced with dried fruit, ham, vegetables and herbs? **Deichgraf** (☑364 208; www.deichgraf-hamburg.de; Deichstrasse 23; mains €18-29; ⊘lunch Mon-Sat, dinner Sat; Ⓜ Rödingsmarkt) is one leading local restaurant that can acquaint you with these and other local dishes.

Café Koppel   INTERNATIONAL €
(Lange Reihe 66; dishes €4.50-9; ☑; Ⓜ Hauptbahnhof) Set back from busy Lange Reihe, with a garden in summer, this largely veggie cafe is a refined oasis in an airy space housing galleries and artists' workshops. The menu includes great breakfasts, lots of salads, stews, jacket potatoes, curries and pasta.

Café Mimosa   INTERNATIONAL €
(Clemens-Schultz-Strasse 87; dishes €5-12; Ⓜ St Pauli) A welcome change from the greasy fast-food joints in the nearby Reeperbahn, this gem of a neighbourhood cafe serves delicious pastas, healthy salads, proper coffee and home-made cakes in a theatrical space of stripped floors, bare wooden tables with brass candlesticks and red-and-cream-painted walls. There's a smattering of pavement tables.

Mr Cherng   ASIAN €€
(Speersort 1; mains €6-11; Ⓜ Rathaus) A favourite with city office workers, high-quality Chinese, Thai and Japanese cuisine is served at impressively low prices, especially at the all-you-can-eat sushi buffet.

🍸 Drinking & Entertainment

Südhang   WINE BAR
(☑4309 9099; www.suedhang-hamburg.de; Susannenstrasse 29; ⊘from noon Mon-Sat, from 4pm Sun; Ⓜ Sternschanze) Walk through the shoe store, head up the stairs and enter this friendly wine bar, with polished mahogany tables and low lighting, perched right above the hustle of the neighbourhood.

Zoë 2   BAR
(Neuer Pferdemarkt 17; ⊘from noon; Ⓜ Feldstrasse) The sister living room to the original Zoë in Berlin (which, sadly, closed years ago) is alive and kicking with battered sofas, rough-hewn walls and old lampshades.

Tower Bar   COCKTAIL BAR
(www.hotel-hafen-hamburg.de; Seewartenstrasse 9; ⊘6pm-1am Mon-Thu, 6pm-2.30am Fri-Sun; Ⓜ Landungsbrücken) For an elegant, mature evening, repair to this 14th-floor eyrie at the Hotel Hafen for unbeatable harbour views.

Nouar   BAR
(Max-Brauer-Allee 275; ⊘from 7pm; Ⓜ Sternschanze) A popular late-night bar with students and other denizens of the nearby Schanzenviertel, this place has that relaxed secondhand look going on and a fondness for football during the week.

Fritz Bauch   BAR
(☑430 0194; Bartelstrasse 6; ⊘from 5pm; Ⓜ Sternschanze) A down-to-earth neighbourhood bar in the middle of the Schanzenviertel with yellow and pale-pink walls; wooden arched ceilings; basic, no-nonsense drinks and hopping music.

Meanie Bar/Molotow Club   CLUB
(☑310 845; www.molotowclub.com; Spielbudenplatz 5; ⊘from 6pm; Ⓜ Reeperbahn) One of the few venues along the Reeperbahn with real local cred, retro Meanie Bar sits above the Molotow Club, where an independent-music scene thrives.

Grosse Freiheit 36/Kaiserkeller   LIVE MUSIC
(☑3177 7811; Grosse Freiheit 36; ⊘from 10pm Tue-Sat; Ⓜ Reeperbahn) Wedged between live-sex theatres and peep shows, this is popular for live rock and pop, particularly as the Beatles played in the basement Kaiserkeller.

Astra Stube   CLUB
(www.astra-stube.de; Max-Brauer-Allee 200; ⊘from 9.30pm Mon-Sat Ⓜ St Pauli) This graffiti-covered red building underneath the railway tracks looks totally unpromising, but it's actually a pioneer of Hamburg's underground scene, with DJs playing experimental electro, techno and drum 'n' bass.

ℹ Information

Dangers & Annoyances

Although safe, Hamburg contains several red-light districts around the train station and Reeperbahn. The Hansaplatz in St Georg can feel a bit dicey after dark. Fortunately, there's a strong police presence in these areas.

LIFE'S A BEACH BAR

Following the trend in Paris, Zürich and Berlin, river-beach bars in Hamburg are *the* place to be in the summer. The city beach season kicks off around April and lasts until at least September, as patrons come to drink, listen to music, dance and generally hang out on the waterfront. Leading venues, open daily, include **Lago Bay** (www.lago.cc, in German; Grosse Elbstrasse 150; Ⓜ Königstrasse), a stylish retreat where you can actually swim, while free exercise classes will help you keep fit, er, between cocktails. **StrandPauli** (www. strandpauli.de, in German; St-Pauli-Hafenstrasse 84; 🚊 112) is a more laid-back stretch of sand with a youthful feel, and **Strandperle** (www.strandperle-hamburg.de, in German; Övelgönne 1; 🚊 112) is the original Hamburg beach bar. It's little more than a kiosk but the people-watching is tops, as patrons linger over the newspaper with a drink or a coffee – think of it as a sandy, al fresco cafe-lounge.

Emergency
Police station Hauptbahnhof (Kirchenallee exit); St Pauli (Davidwache, Spielbudenplatz 31; Ⓜ Reeperbahn)

Post
Main post office (🖉 01802-3333; Dammtorstrasse 14; ⊙ 8.30am-6pm Mon-Fri, 9am-noon Sat; Ⓜ Jungfernstieg)

Post office (🖉 01802-3333; Mönckebergstrasse 7; ⊙ 9am-7pm Mon-Fri, to 3pm Sat; Ⓜ Hauptbahnhof)

Tourist Information
Hamburg Tourismus (🖉 information 3005 1200, hotel bookings 3005 1300; www. hamburg-tourismus.de) Hauptbahnhof (Kirchenallee exit; ⊙ 8am-9pm Mon-Sat, 10am-6pm Sun); Landungsbrücken (btwn piers 4 & 5; ⊙ 8am-6pm Apr-Oct, 10am-6pm Nov-Mar; Ⓜ Landungsbrücken); airport (🖉 5075 1010; ⊙ 6am-11pm) Sells the Hamburg Card (one/three/five days €8.50/19.90/34.90), which offers free public transport and museum discounts.

ⓘ Getting There & Away
Air
Hamburg's **airport** (HAM; www.flughafen-hamburg.de) has frequent flights to domestic and European cities, including on low-cost carrier Air Berlin.

For flights to/from Ryanair's so-called 'Hamburg-Lübeck' (actually an hour away) see p292.

Bus
The **Zentral Omnibus Busbahnhof** (ZOB, central bus station; 🖉 247 5765; www.zob-hamburg. de; Adenauer Allee 78) is most popular for services to Central and Eastern Europe. **Eurolines** (🖉 4024 7106; www.eurolines.com) has buses to Prague (€65) and Vilnius (€85).

Car & Motorcycle
The A1 (Bremen–Lübeck) and A7 (Hanover–Kiel) cross south of the Elbe River.

Train
When reading train timetables, remember that there are two main train stations: Hamburg Hauptbahnhof and Hamburg-Altona. There are frequent RE/RB trains to Lübeck (€11.50, 45 minutes), as well as various services to Hanover (from €35, 1¼ to 1½ hours) and Bremen (from €20.90, one to 1¼ hours). In addition there are EC/ICE trains to Berlin (from €65, 1½ to two hours), Cologne (from €78, four hours) and Munich (from €125, 5½ to six hours) as well as EC trains to Copenhagen (from €81, 4¾ hours).

ⓘ Getting Around
To/From the Airport
The S1 S-Bahn connects the airport directly with the city centre, including the Hauptbahnhof. The journey takes 24 minutes and costs €2.70.

Bicycle
Hamburg is a fantastic place to explore by bike, with extensive cycle lanes (many along the water). For bike hire, try **Fahrradladen St Georg** (🖉 243 908; Schmilinskystrasse 6; per day €10).

Public Transport
There is an integrated system of buses and U-Bahn and S-Bahn trains. A single journey costs €2.70; day tickets, bought from machines before boarding, cost €6.30, or €5.30 after 9am. From midnight to dawn the night-bus network takes over from the trains, converging on the main metropolitan bus station at Rathausmarkt.

SCHLESWIG-HOLSTEIN

Sandwiched between the North and Baltic Seas, Schleswig-Holstein is Germany's answer to the Côte d'Azur. Of course, the weather here often makes it a pretty funny sort of answer, as dark clouds and strong winds whip in across the flat peninsula. Still, people flock to the beaches on the coasts, and the countryside in between has a stark beauty.

Lübeck

📞 0451 / POP 220,900

Two pointed cylindrical towers of Lübeck's Holstentor (gate) greet you upon arrival – if you think they're a tad crooked, you're not seeing things: they lean towards each other across the stepped gable that joins them. Right behind them, the streets are lined with medieval merchants' homes and spired churches forming the city's so-called 'crown'. It's hardly surprising that this 12th-century gem is on Unesco's World Heritage list.

◉ Sights

The impossibly cute city gate or **Holstentor** (📞122 4129; adult/concession €5/2.50; ⊙10am-6pm Apr-Dec, 11am-5pm Tue-Sun Jan-Mar) serves as Lübeck's museum as well as its symbol. The six gabled brick buildings east of the Holstentor are the **Salzspeicher**, once used to store the salt from Lüneburg that was pivotal to Lübeck's Hanseatic trade.

Behind these warehouses, the Trave River forms a moat around the old town, and if you do one thing in Lübeck in summer, it should be a boat tour. From April to September, **Maak-Linie** (📞706 3859; www.maak-linie.de) and **Quandt-Linie** (📞777 99; www.quandt-linie.de) depart regularly from either side of the Holstentorbrücke. Prices are €9/4/6.50 per adult/child/student.

Each of Lübeck's churches offers something different. The shattered bells of the **Marienkirche** (Schüsselbuden 13; admission €1; ⊙10am-6pm Apr-Sep, to 5pm Oct, to 4pm Tue-Sun Nov-Mar) still lie on the floor where they fell after a bombing raid. There's also a little devil sculpture outside, with an amusing fairy tale (in English). The tower lift in the **Petrikirche** (📞397 730; www.st-petri-luebeck.de, in German; Schüsselbuden 13; adult/concession €3/2; ⊙9am-9pm Apr-Sep, 10am-7pm Oct-Mar) affords superb views.

The **Rathaus** (📞122 1005; Breite Strasse 64; adult/concession €3/1.50; ⊙tours 11am, noon & 3pm Mon-Fri) is ornate, but all the tours are in German. If you have a sweet tooth, head across the street to **JG Niederegger shop and cafe** (Breite Strasse 89) and pick up a

chocolate-coated marzipan treat, a gift, or both.

In the Middle Ages, Lübeck was home to numerous craftspeople and artisans. Their presence caused demand for housing to outgrow the available space, so tiny single-storey homes were built in courtyards behind existing rows of houses. These were then made accessible via little walkways from the street.

Almost 90 such *Gänge* (walkways) and *Höfe* (courtyards) still exist, among them charitable housing estates built for the poor, the *Stiftsgänge* and *Stiftshöfe*. The most famous of the latter are the beautiful **Füchtingshof** (Glockengiesserstrasse 25; ⊙9am-noon & 3-6pm) and the **Glandorps Gang** (Glockengiesserstrasse 41-51), which you can peer into.

If you head south along An der Obertrave southwest of the Altstadt, you'll pass one of Lübeck's loveliest corners, the **Malerwinkel** (Painters' Quarter), where you can take a break on garden benches among blooming flowers, gazing out at the houses and white picket fences across the water.

A few steps further, fans of *The Tin Drum* shouldn't miss the **Günter Grass-Haus** (📞122 4192; www.guenter-grass-haus.de; Glockengiesserstrasse 21; adult/concession €5/2.50, 'Kombi' card with Buddenbrookhaus €7/4; ⊙10am-5pm Apr-Dec, 11am-5pm Jan-Mar), which includes a fine collection of manuscripts and sculptures. Fellow Nobel Prize–winning author Thomas Mann *(Death in Venice)* was born in Lübeck and he's commemorated in the award-winning **Buddenbrookhaus** (📞122 4190; www.buddenbrookhaus.de; Mengstrasse 4; adult/concession €5/2.50; 'Kombi' card with Günter Grass-Haus €7/4; ⊙11am-6pm Apr-Dec, 11am-5pm Jan-Mar).

For children, there's a fantastic **Theater Figuren Museum** (📞786 26; www.tfm-luebeck.com; Am Kolk 14; adult/child/concession €5/2.50/3; ⊙10am-6pm Apr-Oct, 11am-5pm Tue-Sun Nov-Mar). It's a private collection of some 1200 puppets, props, posters and more, from Europe, Asia and Africa. The adjoining cafe is also a good place to refuel.

Alternatively, ask the tourist office about the nearby seaside resort of **Travemünde**.

🛏 Sleeping

Hotel zur Alten Stadtmauer   HOTEL €
(📞737 02; www.hotelstadtmauer.de; An der Mauer 57; s/d from €55/65, without bathroom from €37/55; 📶) With pine furniture and splashes of red or yellow, this simple, 25-room hotel

is bright and cheerful. The wooden flooring means sound carries, but customers here tend not to be quieter types. Back rooms overlook the river.

Hotel Lindenhof　　　　　HOTEL €€
(☎872 100; www.lindenhof-luebeck.de; Lindenstrasse 1a; s €65-95, d €85-135 incl breakfast; @) Its rooms are businesslike and small, but a healthy breakfast buffet, friendly service and little extras (free biscuits, newspapers and a 6am-to-midnight snack service) propel the Lindenhof into a superior league.

Hotel Jensen　　　　　HOTEL €€
(☎702 490; www.hotel-jensen.de; An der Obertrave 4-5; s €75-85, d €93-115 incl breakfast; @) Classic and romantic, this old *Patrizierhaus* (mansion house) is conveniently located facing the Salzspeicher across the Trave River. Its seafood restaurant, Yachtzimmer, is also excellent.

Klassik Altstadt Hotel　　BOUTIQUE HOTEL €€
(☎702 980; www.klassik-altstadt-hotel.de; Fischergrube 52; s/d €76/138, ste from €135; 🛜) Each room at this elegantly furnished boutique hotel is dedicated to a different German writer or artist, such as Thomas Mann and Johann Sebastian Bach, as well as international luminaries like Denmark's Hans Christian Andersen. It's close to many of the city's best dining options, but it also has a solid in-house restaurant (mains €11.50 to €14.50).

Rucksackhotel　　　　　HOSTEL €
(☎706 892; www.rucksackhotel-luebeck.de; Kanalstrasse 70; dm €13-15, s €28, d €34-40, linen €3, breakfast €3-5; @🛜) None of the rooms at this 30-bed hostel are en suite, but it has a relaxed atmosphere and good facilities, including a well-equipped kitchen, as well as round-the-clock access.

DJH Hostel Altstadt　　　HOSTEL €
(☎702 0399; www.jugendherberge.de; Mengstrasse 33; dm from €19) Standard hostel in the old town – it isn't particularly new, but it's cosy and central.

Two very cheap and basic places are Sleep-Inn (☎719 20; www.cvjm-luebeck.de; Grosse Petersgrube 11; dm from €14) and the Hotel Am Dom (☎399 9430; www.cvjm-luebeck.de; Dankwartsgrube 43; s & d from €37).

✖ Eating

Markgraf　　　　INTERNATIONAL €€€
(☎706 0343; www.markgraf-luebeck.de, in German; Fischergrube 18; mains €13-21; ☺dinner Tue-Sun) This historic restaurant is the epitome of elegance, with white tablecloths and silverware laid out under the chandeliers and black ceiling beams of a 14th-century house. The cuisine displays Mediterranean and Asian influences.

Schiffergesellschaft　　　FRISIAN €€
(☎767 76; www.schiffergesellschaft.de; Breite Strasse 2; mains €11-25) The fact it's a tourist magnet can't detract from the thrilling atmosphere of this 500-year-old guildhall. Seafood-heavy Frisian specialities and local beer are the way to go.

Nui　　　　　　　　ASIAN €€
(Beckergrube 72; mains €6-13; ☺lunch & dinner Mon-Fri, 3-10pm Sat) Tempting aromas waft from artfully arranged plates in this trendy but relaxed Thai/Japanese restaurant.

Suppentopf　　　　INTERNATIONAL €
(Fleischerstrasse 36; soups €3.50; ☺11am-4pm Mon-Fri) It's always bustling here, so join Lübeck's office workers for a stand-up lunch of delicious, often spicy, soup.

❶ Information

Staff at the **Lübeck Travemünde Tourismus** (☎01805 882 233; www.lubeck-tourism.de; Holstentorplatz 1; ☺9.30am-7pm Mon-Fri, 10am-3pm Sat, 10am-2pm Sun Jun-Sep, 9.30am-6pm Mon-Fri, 10am-3pm Sat Oct-May) can organise city tours and sell discount cards.

❶ Getting There & Away

Lübeck's **airport** (LBC; www.flughafen-luebeck. de) is linked to several cities in Germany and to London by budget carriers Ryanair and easyJet.

Synchronised shuttle buses take passengers straight to Hamburg (one way €9, 55 minutes), while scheduled bus 6 (€2.50) serves Lübeck's Hauptbahnhof and central bus station. Frequent trains run from the airport train station (300m from the terminal) north to Lübeck's Hauptbahnhof, and south as far as Büchen, from where there are connections to Hamburg.

NORTH FRISIAN ISLANDS

Part playground of the rich and famous, part nature-lovers' utopia, the grass-covered dunes, ochre cliffs, traditional reed-thatched cottages and just-off-the-boat seafood of Germany's North Frisian Islands provide a restorative escape from the everyday. Pondering the sunset on a beach, the wind gusts blow away every inch of whatever may plague you on the mainland. Sylt, the largest island of the Frisian archipelago, is the northernmost point in the country and sees the most action. Quieter and more remote, Amrum and Föhr lie just to the south and east.

Sylt

☑04651 / POP 21,100

Sylt can't be labelled without scratching your head. Downtown **Westerland**, the largest town, is largely filled with high-rises that obscure views of the beach, although some pretty thatched houses and simple brick homes dot the outskirts. Some of the world's best **windsurfing** can also be found off this shore.

Further north, pretty **Kampen** is largely where the wealth is most obvious, with ritzy restaurants and celebrity guests. But it's also home to the 52.5m-tall, ochre-coloured **Uwe Dune**. Climb the wooden steps to the top for a stunning 360-degree view.

Towards **List**, on the island's northern tip, is the popular **Wanderdünengebiet**, where people hike between grass-covered dunes. Or try List's beach-side **sauna**.

Inside the Westerland train station, there's an **information pavilion** (☑846 1029; ☺9am-4pm, reduced hr in winter) or try **Westerland Tourism** (☑9980, 0180 550 9980; www. westerland.de; Strandstrasse 35; ☺9am-6pm Mon-Fri May-Oct, 9am-5pm Mon-Fri Nov-Apr).

⌖ Sleeping

Accommodation is at a premium in summer, but ask the tourist office about cheaper private rooms. Significant discounts can be found outside the summer months. Beware that credit cards are not always accepted – even in some midrange hotels. A small *Kurtaxe*, or resort tax, will be added to your bill.

Romantik Hotel Jörg Müller

BOUTIQUE HOTEL €€€

(☑277 88; www.hotel-joerg-mueller.de, in German; Südermarkt Strasse 8, Westerland; r incl breakfast €160-260) Gourmands are in for a treat at this boutique establishment run by one of Germany's best-known foodie families. Its pastel-hued rooms are romantic hideaways, but the real lure is the gourmet breakfast and three restaurants, including Jörg Müller's signature gastronomic restaurant (menus from €32 up to €118 for a six-course blowout). If you're inspired, Müller also offers cooking classes (six-hour class €240, including five-course meal and paired wines).

MUDDY WATERS

It's a tad messy but a tonne of fun. The best *Wattwandern* – walking on tidal flats from one point to another (the same as Dutch *wadlopen*) – is between the islands of Amrum and Föhr. Full-day excursions (from €26) can be combined with various boat trips. Contact Westerland Tourism.

Long Island House Sylt B&B €€

(☑04651-995 9550; www.sylthotel.de; Eidumweg 13, Westerland; s €88-116, d €126-196 incl breakfast; @☏) Mirrors like portholes, unpolished wood and painted cane chairs exude simple but elegant, beachy comfort. There's a spacious garden and breakfast includes local specialities and traditional Frisian tea.

DJH Hostel HOSTEL €

(☑835 7825; www.jugendherberge.de; Fischerweg 36-40, Westerland; dm under/over 26yr incl breakfast €20.10/23.10; ☺closed mid-late Dec) Westerland's new hostel is set amid the dunes, a 45-minute walk from the Bahnhof. Alternatively, take bus 2 in the direction of Rantum/Hörnum to the Dikjen Deel stop. If you're after something even further away from it all, there are also DJH hostels at **List-Mövenberg** (www.jugendherberge.de/jh /list) and **Hörnum** (www.jugendherberge.de/jh /hoernum).

✖ Eating

Alte Friesenstube RESTAURANT €€€

(☑1228; Gaadt 4, Westerland; mains €19-25; ☺from 6pm Tue-Sun) You won't find sojourning celebs at this charmingly old-fashioned, family-run restaurant. Set inside Sylt's oldest reed-thatched cottage (1648), lined with decorative wall tiles and tiled ovens, what you will find are homely regional specials listed on a largely incomprehensible handwritten menu in *Plattdütsch* dialect (helpfully translated by staff).

Kupferkanne CAFE €€

(☑410 10; Stapelhooger Wai, Kampen; meals €6-15) Giant mugs of coffee or Frisian tea and enormous, home-made slices of cake are de rigueur at this WWII bunker–turned-cafe. Dine outdoors on wooden tables surrounded by a maze of low bramble hedges overlooking the Wadden Sea, or inside where it's easy (and fun) to get lost in its cavernous nooks and crannies.

GERMANY SYLT

AMRUM & FÖHR

Tiny Amrum is renowned for its fine white *Kniepsand* (sand bank). There's a 10km stroll from the tall **lighthouse** at Wittdün to the village of Norddorf, and an 8km return hike along the beach. The **tourist office** (☏04682-94 030; www.amrum.de; ferry landing, Wittdün; ☉hours vary) can provide accommodation.

The 'green isle' of Föhr is interesting for its Frisian culture. Its main village, **Wyk**, boasts plenty of windmills, there are 16 northern hamlets tucked behind dikes up to 7m tall, and there's the large 12th-century church of **St Johannis** in Nieblum. The **Föhr information service** (☏04681-300; www.foehr.de) can help with more details. There is no camping here.

WDR (☏800; www.wdr-wyk.de) has ferries to Föhr (€7, 45 minutes) and Amrum (€9, two hours) from Dagebüll Hafen.

Gosch　　　　　　　SEAFOOD €€
(Friedrichstrasse 15b; fish sandwiches €4-7, meals €8-13) This fast-fish chain has colonised mainland Germany, but it originated in Sylt and remains here in force.

Sansibar　　　　　INTERNATIONAL €€€
(☏964 646; Hörnumer Strasse 80; Rantum; mains €14-35) Reservations are a must at this airy grass-roof pavilion on the beach north of Hörnum, ideal for a sunset drink or dinner.

ⓘ Getting There & Around

Sylt is connected to the mainland by a narrow causeway exclusively for trains. Regular services travel from Hamburg (Altona and Hauptbahnhof) to Westerland (from €32.50 return, three to 3¼ hours).

If driving, you must load your vehicle onto a **car train** (☏995 0565; www.syltshuttle.de; return €80) in Niebüll near the Danish border. There are constant crossings (usually at least once an hour) in both directions, and no reservations can be made.

There's also a **car ferry** (☏0180-310 3030; www.sylt-faehre.de; return from €61) from Havneby, Denmark to List at the north of the island.

Air Berlin has several services a week from Berlin, Düsseldorf and others to **Sylt/Westerland airport** (GWT; www.flughafen-sylt.de); Lufthansa arrives from Frankfurt, Hamburg and Munich.

Sylt's two north–south bus lines run every 20 to 30 minutes, and three other frequent lines cover the rest of the island.

UNDERSTAND GERMANY

History

Events in Germany have often dominated the European stage, but the country itself is a relatively recent invention: for most of its history Germany has been a patchwork of semi-independent principalities and city-states, occupied first by the Roman Empire, then the Holy Roman Empire and finally the Austrian Habsburgs. Perhaps because of this, many Germans retain a strong regional identity, despite the momentous events that have occurred since.

The most significant medieval events in Germany were pan-European in nature – Martin Luther brought on the Protestant Reformation with his criticism of the Catholic Church in Wittenberg in 1517, a movement that sparked the Thirty Years War. Germany became the battlefield of Europe, only regaining stability after the Napoleonic Wars with increasing industrialisation and the rise of the Kingdom of Prussia. In 1866 legendary Prussian 'Iron Chancellor' Otto von Bismarck brought the German states together, largely by force, and a united Germany emerged for the first time in 1871, under Kaiser Wilhelm I.

WWI & the Rise of Hitler

With the advent of the 20th century, Germany's rapid growth soon overtaxed the political talents of Kaiser Wilhelm II and led to mounting tensions with England, Russia and France. When war broke out in 1914, Germany's only ally was a weakened Austria-Hungary. Gruelling trench warfare on two fronts sapped the nation's resources, and by late 1918 Germany sued for peace. The kaiser abdicated and escaped to the Netherlands. Amid widespread public anger and unrest, a new republic, which became known as the Weimar Republic, was proclaimed.

The Treaty of Versailles in 1919 chopped huge areas off Germany and imposed heavy reparation payments. These were impossible to meet, and when France and Belgium occupied the Rhineland to ensure continued payments, the subsequent hyperinflation and miserable economic conditions provided fertile ground for political extremists. One of these was Adolf Hitler, an Austrian drifter, would-be artist and German army veteran.

Led by Hitler, the National Socialist German Workers' Party (or Nazi Party) staged an abortive coup in Munich in 1923. This landed Hitler in prison for nine months, during which time he wrote *Mein Kampf*.

In 1929 the worldwide economic Depression hit Germany hard, which led to unemployment, strikes and demonstrations. The Communist Party, headed by Ernst Thälmann, gained strength, but wealthy industrialists began to support the Nazi Party and police turned a blind eye to Nazi street thugs.

The Nazis increased their strength in general elections, and in 1933 replaced the Social Democrats as the largest party in the Reichstag (parliament), with about one-third of the seats. Hitler was appointed chancellor and one year later assumed absolute control as führer (leader).

WWII & the Division of Germany

From 1935 Germany began to re-arm and build its way out of the economic depression with strategic public works such as the autobahns (freeways). Hitler reoccupied the Rhineland in 1936, and in 1938 annexed Austria and, following a compromise agreement with Britain and France, parts of Czechoslovakia.

All of this took place against a backdrop of growing racism at home. The Nuremberg Laws of 1935 deprived non-Aryans – mostly Jews and Roma (sometimes called Gypsies) – of their German citizenship and many other rights. On 9 November 1938 the horror escalated into *Kristallnacht* (night of broken glass), in which synagogues and Jewish cemeteries, property and businesses across Germany were desecrated, burned or demolished.

In September 1939, after signing a pact that allowed both Stalin and himself a free hand in the east of Europe, Hitler attacked Poland, which led to war with Britain and France. Germany quickly occupied large parts of Europe, but after 1942 began to suffer increasingly heavy losses. Massive bombing reduced Germany's cities to rubble, and the country lost 10% of its population. Germany surrendered unconditionally in May 1945, soon after Hitler's suicide.

At the end of the war, the full scale of Nazi racism was exposed. 'Concentration camps', intended to rid Europe of people considered undesirable according to Nazi doctrine, had exterminated some six million Jews and one million more Roma, communists, homosexuals and others in what has come to be known as the Holocaust, history's first 'assembly line' genocide.

At conferences in Yalta and Potsdam, the Allies (the Soviet Union, the USA, the UK and France) redrew the borders of Germany, making it around 25% smaller than it had become after the Treaty of Versailles 26 years earlier. Germany was divided into four occupation zones.

In the Soviet zone of the country, the communist Socialist Unity Party (SED) won the 1946 elections and began a rapid nationalisation of industry. In September 1949 the Federal Republic of Germany (FRG) was created out of the three western zones; in response the German Democratic Republic (GDR) was founded in the Soviet zone the following month, with (East) Berlin as its capital.

From Division to Unity

As the West's bulwark against communism, the FRG received massive injections of US capital, and experienced rapid economic development (the *Wirschaftswunder* or 'economic miracle') under the leadership of Konrad Adenauer. The GDR, on the other hand, had to pay US$10 billion in war reparations to the Soviet Union and rebuild itself from scratch.

A better life in the west increasingly attracted skilled workers away from the miserable economic conditions in the East. As these were people the GDR could ill afford to lose, it built a wall around West Berlin in 1961 and sealed its border with the FRG.

In 1971 a change to the more flexible leadership of Erich Honecker in the East, combined with the *Ostpolitik* (East Politics) of FRG chancellor Willy Brandt, allowed an easier political relationship between the two Germanys. In the same year the four occupying powers formally accepted the division of Berlin.

Honecker's policies produced higher living standards in the GDR, yet East Germany barely managed to achieve a level of prosperity half that of the FRG. After Mikhail

Gorbachev came to power in the Soviet Union in March 1985, the East German communists gradually lost Soviet backing.

Events in 1989 rapidly overtook the GDR government, which resisted pressure to introduce reforms. When Hungary relaxed its border controls in May 1989, East Germans began crossing to the West. Tighter travel controls resulted in would-be defectors taking refuge in the FRG's embassy in Prague. Meanwhile, mass demonstrations in Leipzig spread to other cities and Honecker was replaced by his security chief, Egon Krenz, who introduced cosmetic reforms. Then suddenly on 9 November 1989, a decision to allow direct travel to the West was mistakenly interpreted as the immediate opening of all GDR borders with West Germany. That same night thousands of people streamed into the West past stunned border guards. Millions more followed in the next few days, and the dismantling of the Berlin Wall began soon thereafter.

The trend at first was to reform the GDR but, in East German elections held in early 1990, citizens voted clearly in favour of the pro-reunification Christian Democratic Union (CDU). A Unification Treaty was drawn up to integrate East Germany into the Federal Republic of Germany, enacted on 3 October 1990. All-German elections were held on 2 December that year and, in the midst of national euphoria, the CDU-led coalition, which strongly favoured reunification, soundly defeated the Social Democrat opposition. The CDU's leader, Helmut Kohl, earned the enviable position of 'unification chancellor'.

Two Decades Somewhat Whole

In 1998 a coalition of Social Democrats (SPD), led by Gerhard Schröder, and Bündnis 90/die Grünen (the Greens party) took political office from Kohl and the CDU amid allegations of widespread financial corruption in the unification-era government.

Schröder and the SDP-Greens only narrowly managed to retain office in the 2002 general election. In 2004 things looked even worse. The slashing of university funding brought students out in protest for several weeks, and a botched reform of the public health-insurance system was one of the most unpopular pieces of legislation ever, resulting in massive gains for the supposedly discredited CDU at subsequent local elections.

These advances paid off in 2005 as Schröder went down in national elections, although just barely. The winner by a very narrow margin was Angela Merkel and the CDU. Not only is Merkel the first woman chancellor in German history but she is also the first one who grew up in the old GDR.

During her first term in office, Merkel proved to be a cautious leader, forming a coalition with the SPD. Her style, devoid of even a trace of drama-queen, struck a chord with many Germans and her popularity remained at over 50% even as the CDU's popularity fell somewhat on increasingly harsh economic times. She was reelected in 2009 but her popularity has waned since as Germany's export-based economy has been battered by global recession. The national mood is glum, especially as German funds are a major part of EU bailouts for Greece and others.

Over two decades after reunification, the overall stereotypes of the West and the old East – that the *Wessis* are arrogant while the *Ossis* simply bitch – had become ingrained in German culture. But now both agree on one thing: times used to be better.

Arts

Germany's meticulously creative population has made major contributions to international culture, particularly during the 18th century when the Saxon courts at Weimar and Dresden attracted some of the greatest minds of Europe. With such rich traditions to fall back on, inspiration has seldom been in short supply for the new generations of German artists, despite the upheavals of the country's recent history.

Literature

The undisputed colossus of the German arts was Johann Wolfgang von Goethe: poet, dramatist, painter, politician, scientist, philosopher, landscape gardener and perhaps the last European to achieve the Renaissance ideal of excellence in many fields. His greatest work, the drama *Faust,* is the definitive version of the legend, showing the archetypal human search for meaning and knowledge.

Goethe's close friend Friedrich Schiller was a poet, dramatist and novelist. His most famous work is the dramatic cycle *Wallenstein,* based on the life of a treacherous general of the Thirty Years War who plotted to make himself arbiter of the empire. Schiller's other great play, *Wilhelm Tell*, dealt with the right of the oppressed to rise against tyranny.

On the scientific side, Alexander von Humboldt contributed much to environmentalism through his studies of the relationship of plants and animals to their physical surroundings. His contemporary, the philosopher Georg Wilhelm Friedrich Hegel, created an all-embracing classical philosophy that is still influential today.

Postwar literature was influenced by the politically focused Gruppe 47. It included writers such as Günter Grass, winner of the 1999 Nobel Prize for Literature, whose modern classic *Die Blechtrommel* (The Tin Drum) humorously follows German history through the eyes of a young boy who refuses to grow up. Christa Wolf, an East German novelist and Gruppe 47 writer, won high esteem throughout Germany. Her 1963 story *Der geteilte Himmel* (Divided Heaven) tells of a young woman whose fiancé abandons her for life in the West.

A wave of recent novelists has addressed modern history in a lighter fashion. *Helden wie wir* (Heroes Like Us) by Thomas Brussig, an eastern German, tells the story of a man whose penis brings about the collapse of the Berlin Wall, while the GDR's demise is almost incidental to the eponymous barfly in Sven Regener's *Herr Lehmann* (Mr Lehmann). Also from Berlin is Russian-born Wladimir Kaminer (a possible mayoral candidate in 2011), whose books document stranger-than-fiction lives in the capital. His *Russian Disco* has been translated into English.

Bitterness in the East over the reunification is given a full airing in the darkly satirical *New Lives* by Ingo Schulze. The same subject matter is given a more entertaining take in Christoph Hein's *Settlement*, which follows the rise of Germany's richest man.

Music
CLASSICAL
Forget brass bands and oompah music – few countries can claim the impressive musical heritage of Germany. Even a partial list of household names would have to include Johann Sebastian Bach, Georg Friedrich Handel, Ludwig van Beethoven, Richard Strauss, Robert Schumann, Johannes Brahms, Felix Mendelssohn-Bartholdy, Richard Wagner and Gustav Mahler, all of whom are cele-

brated in museums, exhibitions and festivals around the country.

These musical traditions continue to thrive: the Berlin Philharmonic, Dresden Opera and Leipzig Orchestra are known around the world, and musical performances are hosted almost daily in every major theatre in the country.

POP
Germany has also made significant contributions to the contemporary-music scene. Internationally renowned artists include punk icon Nina Hagen, '80s balloon girl Nena and rock bands from the Scorpions to Die Toten Hosen and current darlings Wir sind Helden. Gothic and hard rock have a disproportionately large following in Germany, largely thanks to the success of death-obsessed growlers Rammstein.

For real innovation, though, the German dance-music scene is second to none, particularly in Frankfurt and Berlin. Kraftwerk pioneered the original electronic sounds, which were then popularised in raves and clubs such as Berlin's Tresor in the early '90s. Paul van Dyk was among the first proponents of euphoric trance, which pushed club music firmly into the commercial mainstream. DJs such as Ian Pooley, Westbam and Ellen Allien now play all over the world. Germany has the largest electronic-music scene in the world and it is on full display (in every way) at Berlin's B-Parade (www.b-parade.de).

The German pop scene is led by the goth/punk/boy-band fusion Tokio Hotel. Their chart-topping songs are led by the big-haired and androgynous Bill Kaulitz. Their appeal crosses borders: they won MTV's music award for Best Group in 2009.

Architecture
The scope of German architecture is such that it could easily be the focus of an entire visit. The first great wave of buildings came with the Romanesque period (800–1200), examples of which can be found at Trier cathedral, the churches of Cologne and the chapel of Charlemagne's palace in Aachen.

The Gothic style (1200–1500) is best viewed at Freiburg's Münster cathedral, Cologne's cathedral and the Marienkirche in Lübeck. Red-brick Gothic structures are common in the north of Germany, with buildings such as Schwerin's Dom and Stralsund's Nikoliakirche.

For classic baroque, Balthasar Neumann's superb Residenz in Würzburg, the magnificent cathedral in Passau and the many classics of Dresden's old centre are must-sees. The neoclassical period of the 19th century was led by Karl Friedrich Schinkel, whose name crops up all over Germany.

In 1919 Walter Gropius founded the Bauhaus movement in an attempt to meld theoretical concerns of architecture with the practical problems faced by artists and craftspeople. The Bauhaus flourished in Dessau, but with the arrival of the Nazis, Gropius left for Harvard University.

Albert Speer was Hitler's favourite architect, known for his pompous neoclassical buildings and grand plans to change the face of Berlin. Most of his epic works ended up unbuilt or flattened by WWII.

Frankfurt shows Germany's take on the modern high-rise. For a glimpse of the future of German architecture, head to Potsdamer Platz, Leipziger Platz and the new government area north of the Reichstag in Berlin, which are glitzy swathes of glass, concrete and chrome.

Visual Arts

The Renaissance came late to Germany but flourished once it took hold, replacing the predominant Gothic style. The draughtsman Albrecht Dürer of Nuremberg was one of the world's finest portraitists, as was the prolific Lucas Cranach the Elder, who worked in Wittenberg for more than 45 years. The baroque period brought great sculpture, including works by Andreas Schlüter in Berlin, while romanticism produced some of Germany's most famous paintings, best exemplified by Caspar David Friedrich and Otto Runge.

At the turn of the 20th century, expressionism established itself with great names like Swiss-born Paul Klee and the Russian-born painter Wassily Kandinsky, who were also associated with the Bauhaus design school. By the 1920s, art had become more radical and political, with artists like George Grosz, Otto Dix and Max Ernst exploring the new concepts of Dada and surrealism. Käthe Kollwitz is one of the era's few major female artists, known for her social-realist drawings.

The only works encouraged by the Nazis were of the epic style of propaganda artists like Mjölnir; nonconforming artists such as sculptor Ernst Barlach and painter Emil Nolde were declared 'degenerate' and their pieces destroyed or appropriated for secret private collections.

Since 1945 abstract art has been a mainstay of the German scene, with key figures like Joseph Beuys, Monica Bonviciniand and Anselm Kiefer achieving worldwide reputations. Leipzig is a hot spot for art; figurative painters like Neo Rauch are generating much acclaim.

Sport

Football (soccer) is the number-one spectator sport in Germany, as in most other European countries. Germany hosted the cup in 2006 in new or rebuilt stadiums all over the country. Although Germany finished third (Italy beat France in the final in Berlin), it was widely praised for hosting a fantastic series of matches, and many Germans took great pride in their time on the world stage.

Germany did one better at Euro 2008, although it lost to Spain in the final in Vienna. Spain again proved troublesome in the 2010 World Cup, beating Germany in the semifinals.

The Bundesliga is the top national league, with seasons running from September to June. Notable top-flight teams include Bayern München, Borussia Dortmund and VfB Stuttgart. The Deutscher Fussball-Bund (DFB; www.dfb.de) is the national body responsible for all levels of the game.

International sports are also very well attended, especially when the relevant national teams are in form. Major tennis, athletics, Grand Prix, swimming, cycling and water-polo events are all features of the German sporting calendar.

Environment

Germans are wholly on board with various green schemes. Households and businesses participate enthusiastically in waste-recycling programs. A refund system applies to a wide range of glass bottles and jars, while containers for waste paper and glass can be found in each neighbourhood. The government is a signatory of the major international treaties on climate change and runs its own campaigns to save energy and reduce CO_2 emissions domestically. Despite a somewhat hostile climate for such schemes, requirements for solar power in residential and commercial buildings are proliferating.

Food & Drink

German Specialities

Wurst (sausage), in its hundreds of forms, is by far the most universal main dish. Regional favourites include bratwurst (spiced sausage), *Weisswurst* (veal sausage) and *Blutwurst* (blood sausage). Other popular main dishes include *Rippenspeer* (spare ribs), *Rotwurst* (black pudding), *Rostbrätl* (grilled meat), *Putenbrust* (turkey breast) and many forms of schnitzel (breaded pork or veal cutlet).

Potatoes feature prominently in German meals, as *Bratkartoffeln* (fried), *Kartoffelpüree* (mashed), Swiss-style rösti (grated then fried) or *Pommes Frites* (French fries). A Thuringian speciality is *Klösse*, a ball of mashed and raw potato that is then cooked into a dumpling. A similar Bavarian version is the *Knödel*. *Spätzle,* a noodle variety from Baden-Württemberg, is a common alternative.

Germans are keen on rich desserts. Popular choices are the *Schwarzwälder Kirschtorte* (Black Forest cherry cake) – one worthwhile tourist trap – as well as endless varieties of *Apfeltasche* (apple pastry). In the north you're likely to find berry *Mus*, a sort of compote. Desserts and pastries are often enjoyed during another German tradition, the 4pm coffee break.

Drinks

Beer is the national beverage and it's both excellent and relatively cheap. Each region and brewery has its own distinctive taste and body.

Some types:

Pils The crisp pilsener Germany is famous for, often refreshingly and slightly bitter.

Alt Dark and full-bodied.

Weizenbier Made with wheat instead of barley malt, served in a tall, 500mL glass. Light in colour, it's lovely on a hot day.

Export Tastes like bland lagers anywhere.

Bockbier Often dark and the best is seasonal.

Helles Bier Light beer.

Dunkles Bier Dark (the best is richly flavoured).

Kölsch The light, sweet beer of Cologne, served in tiny glasses.

Berliner Weisse A low-alcohol wheat beer mixed with woodruff or raspberry syrup.

Rauchbier A Bamberg speciality; smoked to a dark-red colour, it tastes like bacon. (Really.)

German wines are exported around the world, and for good reason. They are inexpensive and typically white, light and intensely fruity. A *Weinschorle* or *Spritzer* is white wine mixed with mineral water. The Rhine and Moselle Valleys are the classic wine-growing regions.

The most popular nonalcoholic choices are mineral water and soft drinks, coffee and fruit or black tea. Bottled water almost always comes bubbly *(mit Kohlensäure)* – order *ohne Kohlensäure* if you're bothered by bubbles.

Where to Eat & Drink

Besides German food in restaurants, pubs beer halls and more, you'll enjoy huge variety. Italian, Turkish, Greek and Chinese are all popular. Stand-up food stalls *(Schnellimbiss* or *Imbiss)* offer doner kebabs to traditional German sausages to the ubiquitous and wildly popular currywurst (sausage served sliced, swimming in ketchup and sprinkled with curry powder) with beer.

Eating venues are supposed to be non-smoking, though this is not always followed in small, family-run places.

Vegetarians

Most German restaurants will have at least a couple of vegetarian dishes on the menu, although it is advisable to check anything that doesn't specifically say it's meat-free, as bacon and chicken stock are undeclared ingredients in German cuisine. Asian and Indian restaurants will generally be quite happy to make vegetarian dishes on demand. Vegans may find themselves having to explain exactly what they do and don't eat to get something suitable.

Habits & Customs

Restaurants always display their menus outside with prices, but watch for daily or lunch specials chalked onto blackboards. Lunch is the main meal of the day; getting a main meal in the evening is never a problem, but you may find that the dish or menu of the day only applies to lunch.

Rather than leaving money on the table, tip when you pay by stating a rounded-up figure or saying *'es stimmt so'* (that's the right amount). A tip of 10% is generally about right.

SURVIVAL GUIDE

Directory A–Z

Accommodation

Germany has all types of places to unpack your suitcase, from hostels, camping grounds and family hotels to chains, business hotels and luxury resorts. Reservations are a good idea, especially if you're travelling in the busy summer season (June to September). Local tourist offices will often go out of their way to find something in your price range.

Germany has more than 2000 organised camping grounds, several hundred of which stay open throughout the year. Prices are around €3 to €5 for an adult, plus €3 to €7 for a car and/or tent. Look out for ecologically responsible camping grounds sporting the Green Leaf award from the ADAC motoring association.

Deutsches Jugendherbergswerk (DJH; www.jugendherberge.de) coordinates the official Hostelling International (HI) hostels in Germany. Rates in gender-segregated dorms, or in family rooms, range from €13 to €25 per person, including linen and breakfast. People over 27 are charged an extra €3 or €4.

Indie hostels are more relaxed and can be found in most large cities.

PRICE RANGES

Prices we list include private bathroom unless otherwise stated and are quoted at high-season rates. Breakfast is not included unless specified. Most rooms are non-smoking.

€€€   more than €150

€€   €80 to €150

€   less than €80

Business Hours

Banks & government offices 9.30am to 4pm Monday to Friday

Bars & cafes 11am to 1am

Clubs Mostly 10pm to 4am

Post offices 9am to 6pm Monday to Friday

Restaurants 10am or 11am to 10pm, with a 3pm to 6pm break

Shops 9am to 6pm Monday to Saturday (also Sunday in large cities); many more are staying open to 8pm or later on days other than Thursday

Discount Cards

Many cities offer discount cards. These cards will usually combine up to three days' free use of public transport with free or reduced admission to major local museums and attractions. They're generally a good deal if you want to fit a lot in; see the Information section under the relevant destination and ask at tourist offices for full details.

Embassies & Consulates

The following embassies are all in Berlin. Many countries also have consulates in cities such as Frankfurt and Munich.

Australia (☑030-880 0880; www.australian -embassy.de; Wallstrasse 76-79)

ℹ **SMOKE & MIRRORS**

Germany was one of the last countries in Europe to legislate smoking, which it did in 2007–08, and, by all accounts, it hasn't done a very effective job. Each of the 16 states was allowed to introduce its own antismoking laws, creating a rather confusing patchwork. In most states, smoking is a no-no in schools, hospitals, airports, train stations and other public facilities. But when it comes to bars, pubs, cafes and restaurants, every state does it just a little differently. Bavaria has the toughest laws, which ban smoking practically everywhere, although an exception was made for Oktoberfest tents; so-called 'smoking clubs' are also permitted.

In most states, lighting up is allowed in designated smoking rooms. However, in July 2008 Germany's highest court ruled this scheme unconstitutional because it discriminates against one-room establishments. These may now allow smoking, provided they serve no food and only admit patrons over 18. So far enforcement has been sporadic, to say the least, despite the threat of fines.

Canada (☎030-203 120; www.kanada-info.de; Leipziger Platz 17)

New Zealand (☎030-206 210; www.nzem bassy.com; Friedrichstrasse 60)

UK (☎030-204 570; http://ukingermany.fco.gov. uk; Wilhelmstrasse 70)

USA (☎030-830 50; http://germany.usembassy. gov/; Pariser Platz 2)

Food

The following price categories for the cost of a main course are used in the listings in this chapter.

€€€ more than €20

€€ €10 to €20

€ less than €10

Gay & Lesbian Travellers

Overall, Germans are tolerant of gays (*Schwule*) and lesbians (*Lesben*) although, as elsewhere in the world, cities (Berlin!) are more liberal than rural areas, and younger people tend to be more open-minded than older generations. Discrimination is more likely in eastern Germany and in the conservative south, where gays and lesbians tend to keep a lower profile.

Legal Matters

By law you must carry some form of photographic identification, such as your passport, national identity card or driving licence. Reporting theft to the police is usually a simple, if occasionally time-consuming, matter. Remember that the first thing to do is show some form of identification.

If driving in Germany, you should carry your driving licence and obey road rules carefully (see p304). The permissible blood-alcohol limit is 0.05%; drivers caught exceeding this amount are subject to stiff fines, a confiscated licence and even jail time. Drinking in public is not illegal, but be discreet about it.

Illegal drugs are widely available, especially in clubs. Cannabis possession is a criminal offence and punishment may range from a warning to a court appearance. Dealers face far stiffer penalties, as do people caught with any other 'recreational' drugs.

Money

ATMS

Automatic teller machines can be found outside banks and at train stations.

ⓘ TIPPING

Restaurant bills always include a service charge *(Bedienung)* but most people add 5% or 10% unless the service was truly abhorrent.

» **Bellhops** €1 per bag
» **Maids** €1 per night
» **Bartenders** 5%
» **Taxi drivers** around 10%

CREDIT CARDS

All major international cards are recognised, and you will find that most hotels, restaurants and major stores accept them (although *not* all railway ticket offices). Always check first to avoid disappointment. Shops may levy a 5% surcharge (or more) on credit cards to offset the commissions charged by card providers.

EXCHANGE

The easiest places to change cash in Germany are the banks or foreign-exchange counters at airports and train stations, particularly those of the Reisebank. The main banks in larger cities generally have money-changing machines for after-hours use, although they don't often offer reasonable rates.

Public Holidays

Germany observes eight religious and three secular holidays nationwide. Shops, banks, government offices and post offices are closed on these days. States with predominantly Catholic populations, such as Bavaria and Baden-Württemberg, also celebrate Epiphany (6 January), Corpus Christi (10 days after Pentecost), Assumption Day (15 August) and All Saints' Day (1 November). Reformation Day (31 October) is only observed in eastern Germany.

The following are *gesetzliche Feiertage* (public holidays):

Neujahrstag (New Year's Day) 1 January

Ostern (Easter) Good Friday, Easter Sunday and Easter Monday

Christi Himmelfahrt (Ascension Day) Forty days after Easter

Maifeiertag/Tag der Arbeit (Labour Day) 1 May

Pfingsten (Whit/Pentecost Sunday & Monday) Fifty days after Easter.

Tag der Deutschen Einheit (Day of German Unity) 3 October

Weihnachtstag (Christmas Day)
25 December

Zweite Weihnachtstag (Boxing Day)
26 December

Safe Travel

Although the usual cautions should be taken, theft and other crimes against travellers are relatively rare in Germany. Africans, Asians and southern Europeans may encounter racial prejudice, especially in eastern Germany, where they can be singled out as convenient scapegoats for economic hardship. However, the animosity is usually directed against immigrants, not tourists.

Telephone

German phone numbers consist of an area code followed by the local number, which can be between three and nine digits long.

Country code ☏49

International access code ☏00

International directory inquiries ☏118 34 for an English-speaking operator

National directory inquiries ☏118 37 for an English-speaking operator, or www.dastelefonbuch.de

Operator assistance ☏0180-200 1033

Travellers With Disabilities

Germany is fair at best (but better than much of Europe) for the needs of travellers with disabilities, with access ramps for wheelchairs and/or lifts in some public buildings. Resources include the following:

Deutsche Bahn Mobility Service Centre (☏01805-996 633, ext 9 for English operator; www.bahn.de; ◷8am-8pm Mon-Fri, 8am-4pm Sat) Train access and route-planning information. Useful English site content.

German National Tourism Office (www.deutschland-tourismus.de) Has an entire section (under Travel Tips) about barrier-free travel in Germany.

Natko (www.natko.de) Central clearing house for inquiries about 'tourism without barriers' in Germany.

Getting There & Away

Air

Budget carriers, Lufthansa and international airlines serve numerous German airports from across Europe and the rest of the world. Frankfurt and Munich are the hubs.

Berlin Schönefeld (SXF; www.berlin-airport.de)

Berlin Tegel (TXL; www.berlin-airport.de)

Cologne/Bonn (CGN; www.airport-cgn.de)

Düsseldorf (DUS; www.duesseldorf-international.de)

Frankfurt (FRA; www.frankfurt-airport.de)

Frankfurt-Hahn (HHN; www.hahn-airport.de)

Hamburg (HAM; www.flughafen-hamburg.de)

Munich (MUC; www.munich-airport.de)

Stuttgart (STR; www.flughafen-stuttgart.de)

For information about individual German airports, see listings within the chapter.

Land

BUS

Travelling by bus between Germany and the rest of Europe is cheaper than by train or plane, but journeys will take a lot longer.

Eurolines (www.eurolines.com) is a consortium of national bus companies operating routes throughout the continent. The German affiliate is **Touring** (www.touring.de). Sample one-way fares and travel times:

ROUTE	PRICE	DURATION (HR)
Budapest–Frankfurt	€98	13–18
Florence–Munich	€76	9
London–Cologne	€60	13
Paris–Munich	€61	13
Warsaw–Berlin	€58	11

Eurolines has a discounted youth fare for those under 26 that saves you around 10%. Tickets can be purchased throughout Germany at most train stations.

CAR & MOTORCYCLE

Germany is served by an excellent highway system. If coming from the UK, the quickest option is the Channel Tunnel. Ferries take longer but are cheaper. You can be in Germany three hours after the ferry docks.

Autobahns and highways become jammed on weekends in summer and before and after holidays.

TRAIN

A favourite way to get to Germany from elsewhere in Europe is by train. See p630 for details on trains in Central Europe.

Conventional long-distance trains between major German cities and other countries are often called EuroCity (EC) trains. High-speed trains now also link Germany to some other parts of Europe. Often, longer international routes are served by at least one day train and sometimes a night train as well. The main German hubs with the best connections for major European cities include the following:

Cologne High-speed Thalys trains to France and Belgium (with Eurostar connections from Brussels to London), InterCity Express (ICE) trains to the Netherlands.

Frankfurt ICE trains to Paris.

Hamburg Scandinavia.

Munich High-speed trains to Paris and Vienna; regular trains to southern and southeastern Europe.

Stuttgart High-speed trains to Italy and Switzerland.

Sea

Germany's main ferry ports are Kiel, Lübeck and Travemünde in Schleswig-Holstein, and Rostock and Sassnitz (on Rügen Island) in Mecklenburg-Western Pomerania. All have services to Scandinavia and the Baltic states.

Getting Around

Air

There are lots of domestic flights, many with budget carriers such as **Air Berlin** (www.air berlin.com) and **Germanwings** (www.german wings.com), as well as **Lufthansa** (www.luf thansa.com). But with check-in and transit times, flying is less efficient than a fast train.

Bicycle

Radwandern (bicycle touring) is very popular in Germany. Pavements are often divided into separate sections for pedestrians and cyclists – be warned that these divisions are taken very seriously. Favoured routes include the Rhine, Moselle, Elbe and Danube Rivers and the Lake Constance area.

Simple three-gear bicycles can be hired from around €15/40 per day/week, and more robust mountain bikes from €20/50.

Cycling is allowed on all roads and highways but not on the autobahns. Cyclists must follow the same rules of the road as ve-

MOVING ON? 303

For tips, recommendations and reviews, head to shop.lonelyplanet.com to purchase a downloadable PDF of the Denmark chapter from Lonely Planet's *Scandinavia* guide, or the Belgium, France and Netherlands chapters from *Western Europe*..

hicles. Helmets are not compulsory, even for children, but wearing one is still a good idea.

Bicycles may be taken on most trains but you must buy a separate *Fahrradkarte* (bicycle ticket). These cost €9 on long-distance trains and €4.50 on regional trains (RB, RE and S-Bahn, valid all day). Bicycles are not allowed on high-speed ICE trains. There is no charge at all on some trains; for specifics enquire at a local station or call Deutsche Bahn on the **DB Radfahrer-Hotline** (bicycle hotline; ☎01805-151 415). Free lines are also listed in DB's complimentary *Bahn & Bike* brochure, as are the almost 250 stations throughout the country where you can hire bikes for between €3 and €13.

Germany's main cycling organisation is the **Allgemeiner Deutscher Fahrrad Club** (ADFC; www.adfc.de).

Boat

Boats are most likely to be used for basic transport when travelling to or between the Frisian Islands, though tours along the Rhine, Elbe and Moselle Rivers are also popular. During summer there are frequent services on Lake Constance but, with the exception of the Constance–Meersburg and the Friedrichshafen–Romanshorn car ferries, these boats are really more tourist crafts than transport options. From April to October, excursion boats ply lakes and rivers in Germany and can be a lovely way to see the country.

Bus

The bus network in Germany functions primarily in support of the train network. Bus stations or stops are usually located near the train station in any town. Consider using buses when you want to cut across two train lines and avoid long train rides to and from a transfer point. A good example of where to do this is in the Alps, where the best way to follow the peaks is by bus.

However a few buslines are vying to lure train passengers with cheap fares – even if comfort and travel times are inferior. These include the following:

Berlin Linien Bus (www.berlinlinienbus.de) Connects major cities (primarily Berlin, but also Munich, Düsseldorf and Frankfurt) with each other as well as holiday regions such as the Harz and the Bavarian Alps. Express service between Berlin and Hamburg is popular (€9 to €22, 3¼ hours, 12 daily).

Touring (www.touring.de) The German affiliate of **Eurolines** (www.eurolines.com) has services that include the popular Romantic Road bus in Bavaria and overnight buses between major cities.

Car & Motorcycle

Cars are impractical in urban areas. Vending machines on many streets sell parking vouchers that must be displayed clearly behind the windscreen. Leaving your car in a central *Parkhaus* (car park) can cost a fortune, as much as €20 per day or more.

AUTOMOBILE ASSOCIATIONS

ADAC (Allgemeiner Deutscher Automobil-Club; ☎roadside assistance 0180-222 2222, if calling from mobile phone 222 222; www.adac.de) offers roadside assistance to members of its affiliates, including British AA, American AAA and Canadian CAA.

DRIVING LICENCES

Visitors do not need an international driving licence to drive in Germany; bring your licence from home.

HIRE

You usually must be at least 21 years of age to hire a car in Germany. You'll need to show your licence and passport, and make sure you keep the insurance certificate for the vehicle with you at all times.

Rental companies are not always convenient to train stations, so check if you plan to pick up a car when you hop off. Agencies include the following:

Avis (☎0180-555 77; www.avis.de)

Europcar (☎0180-580 00; www.europcar.de)

Hertz (☎0180-533 3535; www.hertz.de)

Sixt (☎0180-526 0250; www.sixt.de)

INSURANCE

You must have third-party insurance to enter Germany with a vehicle.

ROAD CONDITIONS

The autobahn system of motorways runs throughout Germany. Road signs (and most motoring maps) indicate national autobahn routes in blue with an 'A' number, while international routes have green signs with an 'E'. Though efficient, the autobahns are often busy, and visitors frequently have trouble coping with the high speeds. Secondary roads (usually designated with a 'B' number) are easier on the nerves and much more scenic, but can be slow going.

ROAD RULES

Road rules are easy to understand, and standard international signs are in use. You drive on the right, and cars are right-hand drive. Right of way is usually signed, with major roads given priority, but at unmarked intersections traffic coming from the right always has right of way.

The blood-alcohol limit for drivers is 0.05%. Obey the road rules carefully: the German police are very efficient and issue heavy on-the-spot fines. Germany also has one of the highest concentrations of speed cameras in Europe.

Speed limits:

Towns & cities 50km/h

Open road/country 100km/h

Autobahn Unlimited but many exceptions as posted

Public Transport

Public transport is excellent within big cities and small towns, and is generally based on buses, *Strassenbahn* (trams) and the S-Bahn and/or U-Bahn (underground trains). Tickets cover all forms of transit, and fares are determined by zones or time travelled, sometimes both. Multiticket strips and day passes are generally available, offering better value than single-ride tickets.

Make certain that you have a ticket when boarding – only buses and some trams let you buy tickets from the driver. In some cases you will have to validate the ticket on the platform or once aboard. Ticket inspections are frequent (especially at night and on holidays) and the fine is a non-negotiable €50 or more.

Train

Operated almost entirely by **Deutsche Bahn** (DB; www.bahn.de), the German train system is the finest in Europe and is generally the best way to get around the country. There are independent operators, such as ALX, which runs between Munich and Regensburg.

Trains run on an interval system, so wherever you're heading, you can count on a service at least every two hours. Schedules are integrated throughout the country so that connections between trains are time-saving and tight, often only five minutes. Of course this means that when a train is late, connections are missed and you can find yourself stuck waiting for the next train.

CLASSES
It's rarely worth buying a 1st-class ticket on German trains; 2nd class is usually quite comfortable. There's more difference between the train classifications – basically the faster a train travels, the plusher (and more expensive) it is.

Train types include the following:

CNL, EN, D These are night trains, although an occasional D may be an extra daytime train.

ICE Sleek InterCityExpress services run at speeds up to 300km/h. The trains are very comfortable and feature cafe cars.

IC/EC Called InterCity or EuroCity, these are the premier conventional trains of DB. When trains are crowded, the open-seating coaches are much more comfortable than the older carriages with compartments.

RE RegionalExpress trains are local trains that make limited stops. They are fairly fast and run at one- or two-hourly intervals.

RB RegionalBahn are the slowest DB trains, not missing a single cow or town.

S-Bahn These suburban trains run frequent services in larger urban areas and rail passes are usually valid. Not to be confused with U-Bahns, which are run by local authorities that don't honour rail passes.

COSTS
Standard DB ticket prices are distance-based. You will usually be sold a ticket for the shortest distance to your destination.

Sample fares for one-way, 2nd-class ICE travel include Frankfurt–Berlin (€113), Frankfurt–Hamburg (€109) and Frankfurt–Munich (€91).

Regular full-fare tickets are good for four days from the day you tell the agent your journey will begin, and you can make unlimited stopovers along your route during that time. In this chapter train fares given between towns are all undiscounted 2nd class.

Discounts
DB sells Savings Fares that discount the high cost of regular tickets and are sold like airline tickets (ie trains with light loads may have tickets available at a discount, others none). Ask at the ticket counters, use the vending machines or book through www.bahn.de. For web purchases, the tickets arrive as email, which you then print out. It's easy.

The following are among the most popular discounts offered by DB (2nd class):

BahnCard 25/50/100 Only worthwhile for extended visits to Germany, these discount cards entitle holders to 25/50/100% off regular fares and cost €57/230/3800.

Dauer-Spezial 'Saver fare' tickets sold at a huge discount on the web.

Savings Fare 25 Round-trip tickets bought three or more days in advance and restricted to specific trains save 25%.

Savings Fare 50 Same conditions as the fare above but also including a Saturday-night stay.

Schönes Wochenende 'Happy Weekend' tickets allow unlimited use of RE, RB and S-Bahn trains on a Saturday or Sunday between midnight and 3am the next day, for up to five people travelling together, or one or both parents and all their children/grandchildren for €37. They are best suited to weekend day trips from urban areas.

RESERVATIONS
During peak periods, a seat reservation (€3.50) on a long-distance train can mean the difference between squatting near the toilet or relaxing in your own seat. Reservations can be made using vending machines or the web.

SCHEDULE INFORMATION
The DB website is excellent. There is extensive info in English and you can use it to sort out all the discount offers and schemes. In addition it has an excellent schedule feature that works not just for Germany but the rest of Europe.

Telephone information is also available: reservations ☏118 61; toll-free automated timetable ☏0800-150 7090.

TICKETS

Many train stations have a *Reisezentrum* (travel centre), where staff sell tickets and can help you plan an itinerary (ask for an English-speaking agent). Smaller stations may only have a few ticket windows and the smallest ones aren't staffed at all. In this case, you must buy tickets from multilingual vending machines. These are also plentiful at staffed stations and convenient if you don't want to queue at a ticket counter. Both agents and machines accept major credit cards.

Buying your ticket on the train carries a surcharge (€3 to €8). Not having a ticket carries a stiff penalty.

TRAIN PASSES

Agencies outside Germany sell German Rail Passes for unlimited travel on all DB trains for a number of days in a 30-day period. Sample 2nd-class prices for adults/under 26 are €188/150 for four days. With web discounts available, passes may not be good value. Try the DB website to compare.

Most Eurail and Inter-Rail passes are valid in Germany.

Central Europe Revealed

Natural Attractions »
Regal Residences »
Pivo & Vino »

Church of Assumption on Bled Island, Lake Bled, Slovenia

Natural Attractions

With the mountain rooftop of Europe, the Alps, stretching across four Central European countries, it should come as no surprise that nature is a strong drawcard here. Wide river valleys, age-old forests and interesting rock formations add to the attraction.

Black Forest

1 Large stands of evergreens interspersed with farmhouses and wandering cows make for a bucolic scene in Germany's Black Forest (p248). Though the villages can get quite busy, venture down the path and you'll find solitude among the trees.

Danube Valley

2 Austria's Danube Valley (p56) is arguably the most picturesque section of Central Europe's central river. Terraced vineyards line river banks, castle ruins sit high above and medieval cities dot the landscape.

Adršpach-Teplice Rocks

3 Fantastic sandstone formations draw rock climbers and hikers galore to eastern Czech Republic's Adršpach-Teplice Rocks (p144). Eroded chasms and soaring pinnacles make following the sandy, pine-studded trails an other-worldly experience.

Swiss Alps

4 The Swiss Alps (p577) have the tallest peaks of Europe's tallest mountains. So whether you don your boots and go hiking, ride the world's highest train or enjoy the view from a glacial lakeside cafe, it's superlative.

Clockwise from top left

1. Triberg waterfall (p250), Black Forest, Germany **2.** Wachau, Danube Valley, Austria **3.** Adršpach-Teplice Rocks, Czech Republic **4.** Glacier hiking at Jungfrau (p589), Switzerland

Regal Residences

Kings, queens and the nobles of old sure knew how to live. They've left behind an impressive legacy of ornate palaces, romantic castles and stony fortresses for modern-day travellers to wonder at all across Central Europe.

JOHN ELK III/LONELY PLANET IMAGES ©

Spiš Castle

1 The sprawling hilltop remains of this Slovakian fortress (p505) are impressive enough – just imagine the daunting sight the castle once posed. A Romanesque palace and small chapel are intact, but walking among the ruined rooms is almost more evocative.

Schloss Mirabell

2 At this Austrian palace (p65) it's not just the Marble Hall, open for concerts, that attracts. People are also drawn to the meticulous, fountain-filled garden surrounds. You may recognise them as where the von Trapp children sang 'Do-Re-Mi' in the *Sound of Music*.

Neuschwanstein Castle

3 A sugary pastiche of architectural styles, Germany's Neuschwanstein (p236) is the crenulated castle of fairy tale and legend. 'Mad' King Ludwig II's obsession with swans, Wagnerian opera and theatrical design are evident in the flights of fancy throughout.

Bellinzona

4 A trio of medieval castles sits lakefront where three Swiss valleys converge. With such a setting, it's surprising the crowds aren't larger. All the better for you to enjoy Castelgrande, Castello di Montebello and Castello di Sasso Corbaro (p604).

JOSEF BECK/IMAGEBROKER

Clockwise from top left
1. Spiš Castle, Spišské Podhradie, Slovakia **2.** Schloss Mirabell gardens, Salzburg, Austria **3.** Neuschwanstein Castle, Füssen, Germany

Pivo & Vino

Whether you call it *bier* or *pivo*, *wein* or *vino*, the region's beer and wine are worth talking about. Germany and the Czech Republic are known worldwide for their hoppy brews and beer halls, and the wine cellars of Austria and Hungary provide an excellent alternative for imbibing.

Czech Brews

1 Beer gardens and halls are the establishments of choice for enjoying a good Czech brew. And you can always go straight to the factory – for Pilsner Urquell in Plzeň (p133) and Budvar in České Budějovice (p136).

Hungarian Wine

2 Hungary's Tokaj (p368) dessert wines have been famous for centuries; sample them from a 600-year-old cellar. Even more fun are the outdoor tasting tables in Eger's wine valley (p365), which produces a full-bodied red called Bikavér (Bull's Blood).

1. Pilsner Urquell billboard, Czech Republic
2. Wine-tasting in Tokaj, Hungary

Hungary

Includes »

Best Places to Stay

- » Lánchíd 19 (p323)
- » Fábián Panzió (p359)
- » Hotel Korona (p363)
- » Mala Garden (p349)
- » Hotel Senator Ház (p366)

Best Places to Eat

- » Köleves (p329)
- » Csalogány 26 (p328)
- » Váci Remete (p339)
- » Matróz (p345)
- » Ferenc Pince (p352)

Why Go?

Where else but Hungary can you laze about in an open-air thermal spa while snow patches glisten around you, then head to a local bar where a Romani band yelps while a crazed crowd whacks its boot heels? Or follow that spa visit with a trip to a wine cellar to taste the local vintage alongside arguably the region's best, and spiciest, cooking?

If these pursuits don't appeal, there are always Roman ruins, ancient castles and even the occasional Turkish minaret, holdovers from centuries of Ottoman rule, in cities like Pécs and Eger. In the countryside, you can see 'cowboys' riding astride five horses, storks nesting on streetlamps and a sea of apricot trees blooming.

Cosmopolitan Budapest is filled with world-class opera, great clubs, monumental buildings, and the mighty Danube River flowing through its centre.

When to Go

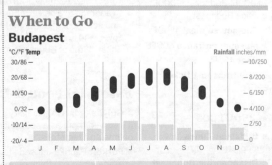

May Spring is in full swing, which means reliable weather, cool temperatures and flowers.

July-August Sunny, but can be unbearably hot, so decamp to the countryside or Lake Balaton.

September Sunshine, mild temps and grape-harvest festivals; this may be the best time to visit.

» **Currency** Hungarian forint (Ft)

» **Language** Hungarian

» **Money** ATMs abundant

» **Visas** None for EU, USA, Canada, Australia, and New Zealand

Fast Facts

» Area: 93,000 sq km

» Capital: Budapest

» Telephone area code: 36

» Emergency: 112

Exchange Rates

Australia	A$1	194Ft
Canada	C$1	187Ft
euro	€1	264Ft
Japan	¥100	218Ft
New Zealand	NZ$1	143Ft
UK	UK£1	296Ft
USA	US$1	178Ft

Set Your Budget

» **Budget hotel room** 14,000Ft Budapest, 9000Ft outside Budapest

» **Two-course meal** 4500Ft

» **Museum entrance** 800Ft

» **Beer** 450Ft

» **City transport ticket** 320Ft

Resources

» **Budapest Times** (www.budapesttimes.hu)

» **Disappearing Budapest** (http://disappearingbudapest.blogspot.com)

» **Hungarian National Tourism** (www.hungary.com)

Connections

Hungary lies at the centre of Central Europe and is easy to get to by rail, road or even boat. Rail connections are particularly good to and from Vienna. The Austrian Federal Railway's high-speed Railjet covers the distance between Vienna and Budapest in under three hours and includes a stop in Győr. Rail connections are also good to Bratislava and Prague, with continuing service to popular travel destinations like Berlin and Kraków. Rail connections to other neighbouring states, including Croatia, Serbia and Romania, are less frequent, though they're also reliable with some advance planning. Buses fan out in all directions from Budapest and nearly all corners of the Europe can be reached within 24 hours. Regular hydrofoil service links Budapest to Bratislava and Vienna. Budapest is the country's only practical destination by air but is well served by commercial and budget carriers.

ITINERARIES

One week

Spend at least four days in Budapest, checking out the sights, museums and cafes. On your fifth day take a day trip to a Danube Bend town: see the open-air museum in Szentendre or the cathedral at Esztergom. Day six can be spent getting a morning train to Pécs to see the lovely Turkish remains and check out the many galleries in town. If you've still got the travel bug, on day seven try some local wine in Eger, a baroque town set in red-wine country.

Two weeks

If you're here in summer, make sure you spend some time exploring the towns around Lake Balaton, or just chill out on the beach by the side of this popular lake. Tihany is a rambling hillside village filled with craftsmen's houses set on a peninsula that is a protected nature zone. Keszthely is an old town with a great palace in addition to a beach. Alternatively, head south to Pécs and see more of the Great Plain. Szeged is on the Tisza River, and Kecskemét is further north. Finish your trip in Tokaj, home of Hungary's most famous wine.

Essential Food & Drink

» **Gulyás** (goulash) Hungary's signature dish, though here it's served more as a soup than a stew and made with beef, onions and tomatoes.

» **Pörkölt** Paprika-infused stew; closer to what you might imagine when you think of goulash.

» **Galuska** Small, gnocchi-like dumplings that make a good accompaniment to soak up the sauce in a pörkölt.

» **Halászlé** Highly recommended fish soup made from poached freshwater fish, tomatoes, green peppers and paprika.

BUDAPEST

🎵 1 POP 1.7 MILLION

There's no other Hungarian city like Budapest in terms of size and importance. Home to almost 20% of the national population, Hungary's capital (*főváros*, or main city) is the nation's administrative, business and cultural centre; everything of importance starts or finishes here.

But it's the beauty of Budapest – both natural and constructed – that makes it stand apart. Straddling a gentle curve in the Danube, the city is flanked by the Buda Hills on the west bank and the beginnings of the Great

Hungary Highlights

1 Ease your aching muscles in the warm waters of Budapest's **thermal baths** (p317), and try a spa treatment for good measure

2 Learn about the defiance showed by **Eger** (p365) to Turkish invaders, and how the city's Bull's Blood wine got its name

3 Watch the cowboys ride at Bugac in **Kiskunsági**

Nemzeti Park (p361), in the heart of the Hungarian *puszta* (plain)

4 Absorb the Mediterranean climate and historic architecture of the southern city of **Pécs** (p355), including its intriguing Mosque Church

5 Take a pleasure cruise across (or a dip in) Central Europe's largest body of

fresh water, **Lake Balaton** (p348)

6 Get lost in Hungary's best nightlife, especially the bars and pubs in **Pest** (p330)

7 Mill about with artists, free thinkers, and daytrippers at the too-cute-for-words artists' colony **Szentendre** (p335)

Plain to the east. Architecturally, it is a gem, with enough baroque, neoclassical, eclectic and art nouveau elements to satisfy anyone.

In recent years, Budapest has taken on the role of the region's party town. In the warmer months outdoor beer gardens called *kertek* are heaving with partygoers, and the world-class Sziget Music Festival in August is a cultural magnet. And you need not venture out for fun; the city's scores of new hostels offer some of the best facilities and most convivial company in Europe.

History

Strictly speaking, the story of Budapest begins only in 1873 with the administrative union of three cities that had grown together: Buda, west of the Danube; Óbuda (Buda's oldest neighbourhood) to the north; and Pest on the eastern side of the river. But the area had already been occupied for thousands of years.

The Romans built a settlement at Aquincum (Óbuda) during the first centuries of the Common Era. In the 1500s, the Turks arrived uninvited and stayed for almost 150 years. The Habsburg Austrians helped kick the invaders out, but then made themselves at home for 200 more years.

In the late 19th century, under the dual Austro-Hungarian monarchy, the population of Budapest soared. Many notable buildings date from that boom period. The 20th century was less kind. Brutal fighting toward the end of WWII, with Hungary on the losing side, brought widespread destruction and new overlords, this time the Soviets. The futile 1956 revolution left thousands dead and buildings that to this day remain pockmarked with bullet holes. Thankfully, those times feel long gone. With Hungary a member of the European Union, Budapest is once again a sophisticated capital of a proud nation with a distinctive heritage.

◉ Sights & Activities

Budapest is an excellent city for sightseeing, especially on foot. The Castle District in Buda contains a number of museums, both major and minor, but the lion's share is in Pest. Think of Margaret Island as a green buffer between the two – short on things to see, but a great place for a breather.

BUDA

CASTLE HILL

Castle Hill (Várhegy) is arguably Budapest's biggest tourist draw and a first port of call for any visit to the city. Here, you'll find most of Budapest's remaining medieval buildings, the Royal Palace, some sweeping views over Pest across the river and a festive mood year round.

Magdalene Tower   RUIN
(Magdolona toronye; Map p322; Kapisztrán tér) Magdalene Tower is all that's left of a Gothic church destroyed here during WWII.

Buda Hills Viewpoint   SCENIC VIEW
For a peek into the life of the Budapest bourgeoisie, walk along the ramparts promenade to check out the mansions of the Buda Hills in the distance. At the third alleyway as you are walking along, turn left to reach Szentháromság tér and the Holy Trinity statue (Szentháromság szobor; Map p322) at its centre.

Matthias Church   CHURCH
(Mátyás Templom; Map p322; www.matyas-templom.hu; Szentháromság tér 2; adult/concession 950/500Ft; ⊘9am-5pm Mon-Sat, 1-5pm Sun) The gorgeous, neo-Gothic Matthias Church has a colourful tiled roof and lovely murals inside. Franz Liszt's *Hungarian Coronation Mass* was played here for the first time at the coronation of Franz Joseph and Elizabeth in 1867. Buy tickets to enter the church and the Fishermen's Bastion at ticket counters across from the entrance to the church.

Fishermen's Bastion   MONUMENT
(Halászbástya; Map p322; Szentháromság tér; adult/concession 500/200Ft; ⊘8.30am-11pm) This fanciful, neo-Gothic arcade built on the fortification wall is prime picture-taking territory, with views of the river and the parliament beyond. Across the square is Hungary's first king, immortalised in the equestrian St Stephen statue (Szent István szobor).

Sikló   FUNICULAR RAILWAY
(Map p322; I Szent György tér; one way/return adult 840/1450Ft, child 520/940Ft; ⊘7.30am-10pm, closed 1st & 3rd Mon of month) The Sikló is a funicular railway that takes you down the hill to Clark Ádám tér. The views from the little capsule, across the Danube and over to Pest, are glorious.

Royal Palace   PALACE
(Királyi Palota; Map p322) The massive Royal Palace occupies the far end of Castle Hill; inside are the Hungarian National Gallery (Nemzeti Galéria; www.mng.hu; I Szent György tér 6; adult/concession 900/450Ft; ⊘10am-6pm Tue-Sun) and the Budapest History Museum (Budapesti Történeti Múzeum; www.btm.hu; I Szent György tér 2; adult/concession 1300/650Ft;

10am-6pm daily mid-Mar–mid-Sep, 10am-4pm Wed-Mon mid-Sep–mid-Mar).

Royal Wine House & Wine Cellar Museum
WINE MUSEUM

(Borház és Pincemúzeum; Map p322; www.kiralyi borok.com; I Szent György tér, Nyugati sétány; adult/concession 900/500Ft; noon-8pm) The Royal Wine House & Wine Cellar Museum is situated in what were once the royal cellars, dating back to the 13th century. Tastings cost around 1500/2000/3000Ft for three/four/six wines. You can also elect to try various types of Hungarian champagne and *pálinka* (fruit brandy).

GELLÉRT HILL

The 'other peak' overlooking the Danube, south of Castle Hill, is Gellért Hill. The Liberty Monument sits at its top.

Liberty Monument
MONUMENT

(Szabadság szobor; Map p322) The Liberty Monument, a gigantic statue of a lady with a palm frond proclaiming freedom throughout the city, is visible from almost anywhere in town. The monument was erected as a tribute to the Soviet soldiers who died liberating Hungary in 1945, but the victims' names in Cyrillic letters that used to adorn the plinth, as well as the memorial statues of Soviet soldiers, were removed in 1992.

FREE **Citadella**
FORTRESS

(Map p322; www.citadella.hu; admission free; 24hr) Built by the Habsburgs after the 1848 revolution to 'defend' the city from further Hungarian insurrection, the Citadella was never used as a fortress. Excellent views, exhibits, a restaurant and a hotel can be enjoyed here. Take tram 19 along the riverfront from Clark Ádám tér and climb the stairs behind the waterfall and St Gellért statue (Szent Gellért szobor), then follow the path through the park opposite the entrance to the Danubius Hotel Gellért.

Gellért Baths
BATHHOUSE

(Gellért Fürdő; Map p324; 466 6166; Danubius Hotel Gellért, XI Kelenhegyi út; admission 3900/3600Ft with/without private changing room; 6am-7pm daily May-Sep, 6am-7pm Mon-Fri & 6am-5pm Sat & Sun Oct-Apr) Below Gellért Hill is the city's most famous thermal spa, the Gellért Baths, where majestic domes hang above healing waters. This art nouveau palace has dreamy spas where you can soak for hours while enjoying its elegant and historic architecture.

Memento Park
STATUE PARK

(www.mementopark.hu; XXII Balatoni út 16; adult/concession 1500/1000Ft; 10am-dusk) In Buda's southwest is Memento Park, a kind of historical dumping ground for socialist statues deemed unsuitable since the early '90s. It's a major tourist attraction and there's a direct bus from Deák tér in Pest at 11am daily, with a second bus at 3pm July and August (adult/concession return 4500/3500Ft, including admission). To go independently, take tram 19 from Clark Ádám tér to the XI Etele tér Terminus, then catch bus 150 to the park.

Aquincum Museum
RUINS

(Aquincumi Múzeum; Map p318; www.aquincum.hu; III Szentendre út 139; adult/concession 1000/500Ft; 10am-6pm daily May-Sep, 10am-5pm Tue-Sun Oct-Apr) Seven kilometres north of Buda's centre is the Aquincum Museum, containing the most complete ruins of a 2nd-century Roman civilian town left in Hungary. Take the HÉV from the Batthyány tér metro stop.

BUDA HILLA

Buda Hills
LANDSCAPE

(Map p318) With 'peaks' up to 500m, a comprehensive system of trails and no lack of unusual conveyances to get you around, the Buda Hills are the city's playground and are a welcome respite from hot, dusty Pest in summer.

Heading for the hills is more than half the fun. From Moszkva tér metro station on the M2 line in Buda, walk westward along Szilágyi Erzsébet fasor for 10 minutes (or take tram 18 or 56 for two stops) to the circular Hotel Budapest at Szilágyi Erzsébet fasor 47. Directly opposite is the terminus of the 1874 Cog Railway (Fogaskerekű vasút; Map p318; www.bkv.hu; Szilágyi Erzsébet fasor 14-16; admission 320Ft; 5am-11pm). The cog climbs for 3.6km in 14 minutes three or four times an hour to Széchenyi-hegy (427m), one of the prettiest residential areas in Buda.

At Széchenyi-hegy, you can stop for a picnic in the attractive park south of the old-time station or board the narrow-gauge Children's Railway (Gyermekvasút; www.gyermekvasut.hu; adult/child 1 section 500/300Ft, entire line 700/350Ft; closed Mon Sep-Apr), two minutes to the south on Hegyhát út. The railway, with eight stops, was built in 1951 by Pioneers (socialist Scouts) and is now staffed entirely by schoolchildren aged 10 to 14 – the engineer excepted. The little train chugs along for 12km, terminating at Hűvösvölgy.

Budapest

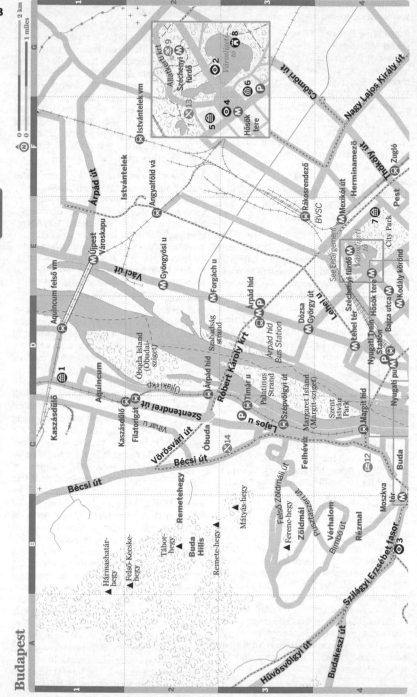

Állatkerti krt 🗒 9
Széchenyi
fürdő Ⓜ

Ⓚ Istvántelek vm

Ⓧ 13
🏛 5   🏛 6
Ⓞ 4   Ⓜ
Hősök
tere

Ⓚ 8

◎ 2

*Városligeti
to*

Ⓟ

Csömöri út

Nagy Lajos Király út

Istvántelep

Ⓚ Angyalföld vá

Árpád út

Újpest
Ⓜ Városkapu

Ⓜ Aquincum felső vm

Váci út

Ⓜ Gyöngyösi u

Ⓜ Forgách u

Ⓚ Rákosrendező

BVSC

Ⓜ Mexikói út

Herminamező út

Thököly út

Zugló

Pest

🏛 7

City Park

Ⓜ Kodály körönd

Bajza utca Ⓜ

*Károlyliget
to*

Ⓜ Széchenyi fürdő

See Enlargement

Árpád híd Ⓜ
Ⓟ

Dózsa
György út Ⓜ

Lehel u

Ⓜ Lehel tér

Nyugati Train
Ⓟ Station

Ⓚ Nyugati pu

Nyugati híd

Ⓚ

Ⓓ Aquincum

🏛 1

Kaszásdűlő

Kaszásdűlő Ⓚ
Filatorigát Ⓚ

Szentendrei út

Óbuda
Ⓟ Lajos u Ⓚ

Vörösvári út

Bécsi út

Ⓧ 14

Vihar u

Óbuda Island
(*Óbudai-
sziget*)

Újlaki rkp

Szabadság
strand

Róbert Károly krt

Tímár u Ⓚ

Szépvölgyi út Ⓚ

Árpád híd Ⓚ

Palatinus
Strand

Margaret Island
(*Margit-sziget*)

Szent
István
Park

Árpád híd
Bus Station

Felhévíz

Ⓜ Margit híd

Buda

🏛 12

Felső Zöldmáli út

Zöldmáli
Pusztaszeri út

Felső-
Ferenc-hegy

Vérhalom

Bimbó út

Rézmal

Ⓜ Moszkva
tér

Szilágyi Erzsébet fasor

◎ 3

Budakeszi út

Hűvösvölgyi út

▲ Hármashatár-
hegy

▲ Felső-Kecske-
hegy

Tábor-
hegy ▲

▲ Remete-hegy

Remetehegy

**Buda
Hills**

▲ Mátyás-hegy

Bécsi út

Bécsi út

🗒 0   0   2 km
0   1 miles

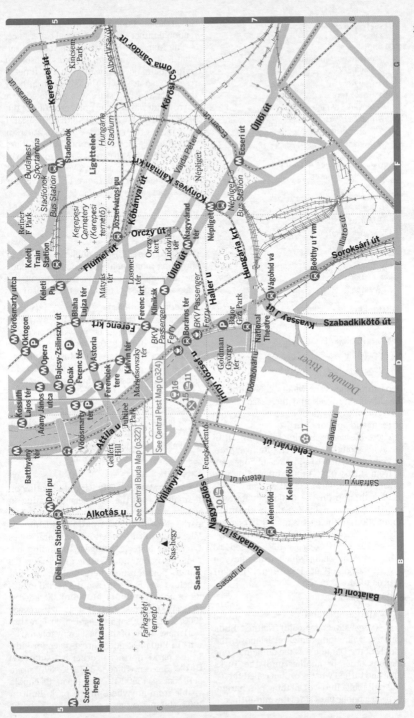

Departure times vary widely depending on the day or the week and the season – but count on one every hour or so between 9am or 10am and 5pm or 6pm.

There are walks fanning out from all of the stops along the Children's Railway line, or you can return to Moszkva tér on tram 56 from Hűvösvölgy. A more interesting way down, however, is to get off at János-hegy, the fourth stop on the Children's Railway and the highest point (527m) in the hills. About 700m to the east is a **chairlift** (libegő; adult/child 750/450Ft; ⊙9.30am-5pm mid-May–mid-Sep, 10am-4pm mid-Sep–mid-May, closed 2nd & 4th Mon each month), which will take you down to Zugligeti út. From here, bus 291 returns to Moszkva tér.

MARGARET ISLAND

FREE **Margaret Island** ISLAND
(Margit-sziget; Map p318) Neither Buda nor Pest, 2.5km-long Margaret Island in the middle of the Danube was the domain of one religious order or another until the Turks came and turned what was then called the Island of Rabbits into – of all things – a harem. It's been a public park since the mid-19th cen-

tury. Like the Buda Hills, the island is a recreational rather than educational experience.

The Margaret Bridge, which touches the island at its southern tip, was closed to traffic for major renovation at the time of research, so access to the island from both the Buda and Pest sides was restricted to a narrow sidewalk on the northern edge of the bridge. Bus 26 covers the length of the island as it makes the run between Nyugati train station and Árpád Bridge bus station. Cars are allowed on Margaret Island from Árpád Bridge only as far as the two big hotels at the northeastern end; the rest is reserved for pedestrians and cyclists.

PEST

HŐSÖK TERE & AROUND

Hősök tere PUBLIC SQUARE
(Heroes' Sq; Map p318) This public space holds a sprawling monument constructed to honour the millennial anniversary (in 1896) of the Magyar conquest of the Carpathian Basin.

Museum of Fine Arts MUSEUM
(Szépművészeti Múzeum; Map p318; www.mfab. hu; XIV Dózsa György út 41; adult/concession 1600/800Ft; ⊙10am-5.30pm Tue-Sun) Across the street from Hősök tere, the Museum of Fine Arts houses a collection of foreign art, including an impressive number of El Grecos.

Palace of Art MUSEUM
(Műcsarnok; Map p318; www.mucsarnok.hu; XIV Hősök tere; adult/concession 1400/700Ft; ⊙10am-6pm Tue, Wed & Fri-Sun, to 8pm Thu) Don't miss the Palace of Art, a large contemporary-art gallery, opposite the museum.

City Park PARK
(Városliget; Map p318) City Park has boating on a small lake in the summer, ice-skating in winter and duck-feeding year round. The park's **Vájdahunyad Castle** (Vájdahunyad Vár) was built in varied architectural styles typical of historic Hungary, including baroque, Romanesque, Gothic and Tudor. It's fun to poke around here, but there's not much to see. Further east, the varied exhibits of the **Transport Museum** (Közlekedési Múzeum; XIV Városligeti körút 11; adult/concession 1000/500Ft; ⊙10am-5pm Apr-Oct, to 4pm Jan-Mar) make it one of the most enjoyable museums in Budapest and a great place for kids. In the park's northern corner is **Széchenyi Baths** (Széchenyi Fürdő; ☑363 3210; XIV Állatkerti út 11; admission 3500Ft; ⊙6am-10pm), its cupola visible from anywhere in the park. Built in 1908, this place has a dozen thermal baths

and five swimming pools. The peaceful atmosphere of the indoor thermal baths, saunas and massage area contrasts with the buzzing atmosphere of the main pool.

Terror House   MUSEUM
(Terror Háza; Map p324; www.terrorhaza.hu; Andrássy út 60; adult/concession 1800/900Ft; ⊙10am-6pm Tue-Fri, to 7.30pm Sat & Sun) The headquarters of the dreaded secret police have now been turned into the Terror House. The museum focuses on the crimes and atrocities committed by Hungary's fascist and Stalinist regimes. The years leading up to the 1956 uprising get the lion's share of the exhibition space.

Hungarian State Opera House   THEATRE
(Magyar Állami Operaház; Map p324; ☑332 8197; www.operavisit.hu; Andrássy út 22; tours adult/concession 2800/1400Ft, mini concert after tour 500Ft; ⊙3pm & 4pm) The opulence of the 1884 neo-Renaissance Hungarian State Opera House is a real treat; try to make it to an evening performance here.

PARLIAMENT & AROUND

TOP CHOICE **Parliament**   HISTORIC BUILDING
(Parlament; Map p324; ☑441 4904; www. parlament.hu; V Kossuth Lajos tér 1-3; admission free EU citizens, or adult/concession 3200/1600Ft; ⊙8am-6pm Mon-Fri, 8am-4pm Sat, 8am-2pm Sun) The huge, riverfront Parliament dominates Kossuth Lajos tér. English-language tours are given at 10am, noon and 2pm; email tourist. office@parlament.hu for tour information.

Ethnography Museum   MUSEUM
(Néprajzi Múzeum; Map p324; www.neprajz.hu; V Kossuth Lajos tér 12; adult/concession 100/500Ft; ⊙10am-6pm Tue-Sun) Across the park is the Ethnography Museum, which has an extensive collection of national costumes among the permanent displays on folk life and art.

St Stephen's Basilica   CHURCH
(Szent István Bazilika; Map p324; V Szent István tér; adult/concession 500/300Ft; ⊙9am-5pm Apr-Sep, 10am-4pm Oct-Mar) Look for the mummified right hand of St Stephen in the chapel of the colossal St Stephen's Basilica near Bajcsy-Zsilinszky út.

JEWISH QUARTER

TOP CHOICE **Great Synagogue (Dohány Synagogue)**   SYNAGOGUE
(Nagy Zsinagóga; Map p324; VII Dohány utca 2; ⊙10am-6.30pm Mon-Thu, to 2pm Fri, to 5.30pm Sun) Northeast of the Astoria metro stop is what remains of the Jewish quarter. The twin-towered, 1859 Great Synagogue has a museum with a harrowing exhibit on the Holocaust, and behind the synagogue is the Memorial of the Hungarian Jewish Martyrs (p324) in the shape of a weeping willow. The ticket office sells three tours: Tour 1 (adult/concession 3400/2750Ft) includes the Great Synagogue, the memorial, the nearby Rumbach synagogue and the Jewish museum; Tour 2 (2750/2050Ft) omits the Rumbach synagogue; Tour 3 (2400/1650Ft) omits the Rumbach synagogue and the museum. Get there early because queues get long. Hours are short in winter.

Hungarian National Museum   MUSEUM
(Magyar Nemzeti Múzeum; Map p324; www.hnm. hu; VIII Múzeum körút 14-16; adult/concession 1100/550Ft; ⊙10am-6pm Tue-Sun) The Hungarian National Museum has historic relics from archaeological finds to coronation regalia. To find the museum from the Great Synagogue, duck under the Astoria metro underpass to cross busy Rákóczi út and walk about 100m further.

⚲ Tours

Mahart PassNave   CRUISE OPERATOR
(Map p324; ☑484 4013; www.mahartpassnave.hu; Vigadó tér Pier; ⊙Apr-Oct) Mahart PassNave operates cruises on the Danube. There are regular two-hour sightseeing cruises (adult/concession 2990/1490Ft), and lunch and dinner buffet cruises (adult/concession 5990/2990Ft), and a number of specialty tours. Tickets can be purchased at the pier before departure.

Discover Budapest   CYCLING & WALKING
(Map p324; ☑269 3843; www.discoverbudapest. com; VI Lázár utca 16; ⊙9am-7pm Apr-Oct, 10am-6pm Nov-Mar) Discover Budapest books cycling tours (adult/concession 5500/5000Ft) of the city, a fun way to tour Budapest. The same company also books **Absolute Walking Tours** (☑269 3843; www.absolutetours.com), whose repertoire includes an entertaining 3½-hour city walking tour (adult/concession 4500/4000Ft), the communism-themed Hammer & Sickle Tour (adult/concession 7000/6500 Ft) and the Gastro Food & Wine Tour (7000Ft, no concession).

✪ Festivals & Events

Many festivals and events are held in and around Budapest. Look out for the tourist board's annual *Events Calendar* for a complete listing.

Budapest Spring Festival   CLASSICAL MUSIC
(www.springfestival.hu) In March to April.

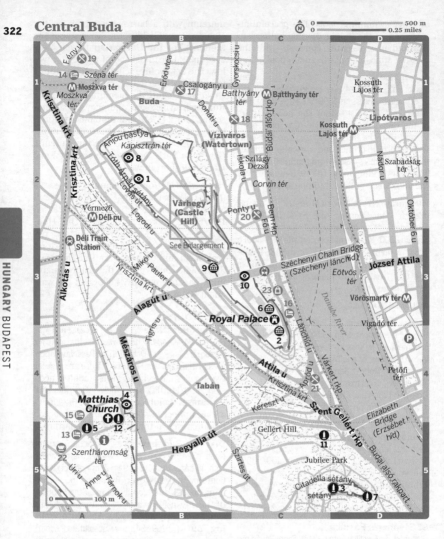

Sziget Music Festival INDIE MUSIC
(www.sziget.hu) On Óbudai sziget (Óbuda Island), arguably Central Europe's premiere indie music fest, from late July to early August.

Hungarian Formula One Grand Prix AUTO RACE
(www.hungaroring.hu) At Mogyoród, 24km northeast of Budapest, usually held in late July or early August.

Budapest International Wine Festival WINE
(www.winefestival.hu) Held in September.

Budapest International Marathon MARATHON
(www.budapestmarathon.com) In early October.

🛏 Sleeping

Accommodation prices and standards remain reasonable in Budapest. Many year-round hostels occupy middle floors of old apartment buildings (with or without a lift) in central Pest. Come summer (July to late August), student dormitories at colleges and universities open to travellers.

Private rooms in Budapest homes generally cost 6000Ft to 7500Ft for a single,

7000Ft to 8500Ft for a double, and 10,000Ft to 13,000Ft for a small apartment. Two brokers are **Best Hotel Service** (Map p324; 318 4848; www.besthotelservice.hu; V Sütő utca 2; 8am-8pm) and **To-Ma Travel Agency** (Map p324; 353 0819; www.tomatour.hu; V Október 6 utca 22; 9am-noon & 1-8pm Mon-Fri, 9am-5pm Sat & Sun).

BUDA

Lánchíd 19   BOUTIQUE HOTEL €€€
(Map p322; 419 1900; www.lanchid19hotel.hu; I Lánchíd utca 19; s/d/ste from €120/140/300;) This boutique number facing the Danube won a design award in 2008. Its facade features images created by special sensors that reflect the movement of the Danube, and its rooms are equally impressive, containing distinctive artwork and unique chairs designed by art students. Seasonal discounts on the hotel website can bring the price of a double down to €75 a night.

Back Pack Guesthouse   HOSTEL €
(Map p318; 385 8946; www.backpackbudapest.hu; XI Takács Menyhért utca 33; beds in yurt 3000Ft, dm large/small 3800/4500Ft, d 11,000Ft;) A hippyish, friendly place, though relatively small, with around 40 beds. There's a lush garden in the back with a hammock stretched invitingly between trees. Take bus 7 to Tétényi út (from Keleti train station) or tram 18 to Móricz Zsigmond Kő'rtér to catch bus 7 to Tétényi út (from Déli train station).

Danubius Hotel Gellért   LUXURY HOTEL €€
(Map p324; 889 5500; www.danubiusgroup.com/gellert; XI Szent Gellért tér 1; s/d/ste from €80/145/240;) Peek through the doors of this turn-of-the-20th-century grand dame, even if you don't choose to stay here. The 234-room, four-star hotel has loads of character, and its famous thermal baths (p317) are free for guests. Prices depend on your room's view and the quality of its bathroom.

Papillon Hotel   HOTEL €
(Map p318; 212 4750; www.hotelpapillon.hu; II Rózsahegy utca 3/b; s/d/tr/apt from €44/54/69/78;) This small 20-room hotel in Rózsa-domb has a delightful back garden with a small swimming pool, and some rooms have balconies. There are also four apartments available in the same building, one of which has a lovely roof terrace.

Burg Hotel   HOTEL €€
(Map p322; 212 0269; www.burghotelbudapest.com; I Szentháromság tér 7-8; s/d/ste from €105/115/134;) Prices have crept up here at the Burg, located at the centre of Castle Hill, just opposite Matthias Church. Ask for a room overlooking Matthias Church for a truly historic wake-up view. The 26 partly

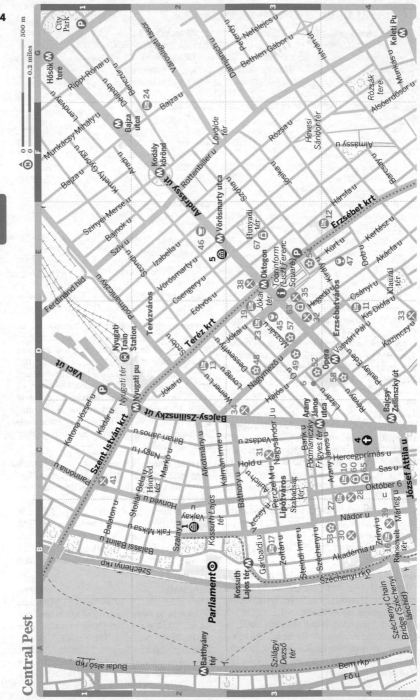

Central Pest

HUNGARY BUDAPEST

500 m
0.2 miles

City Park

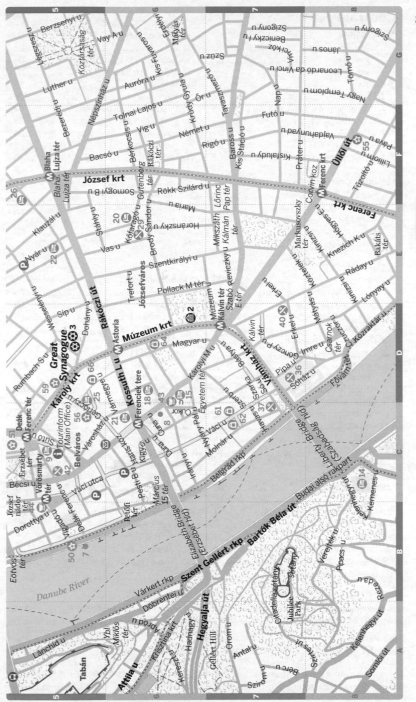

Berzsenyi u

Légszesz u

Vay A u

Közraktárság tér

Luther u

Bezerédi u

Népszínház u

Aurora u

Tolnai Lajos u

Vig u

Bacsó u

Berkocsis u

Blaha Lujza tér

József krt

Blaha Lujza tér

Klauzál u

Nyár u

Somogyi B u

Gutenberg tér

Rökk Szilárd u

Kőfaragó u

Bródy Sándor u

Stáhly u

Vas u

Horánszky u

Szentkirályi u

Józsefváros

Trefort u

Pollack M tér

Rákóczi út

Dohány u

Wesselényi u

Síp u

Great Synagogue

Károly krt

Rumbach S u

Deák Ferenc tér

Vármegye u

Kossuth L u

Gerlóczy u

Városháza u

Tourinform (Main Office)

Belváros

Erzsébet tér

Vörösmarty tér

Bécsi u

József nádor tér

Dorottya u

Deák Ferenc u

Petőfi tér

Váci utca

Március 15 tér

Eötvös tér

Danube River

Tabán

Attila u

Ybl Miklós tér

Lánchíd u

Krisztina krt

Apród u

Döbrentei u

Várkert rkp

Szent Gellért rkp

Hegyalja út

Gellért Hill

Jubilee Park

Citadella sétány

Szirom u

Bérc u

Antal u

Orom u

Oromi út

Keszte

Kemenes u

Bartók Béla út

Budai alsó rakpart

Liberty Bridge (Szabadság híd)

Fővám tér

Közraktár u

Csarnok tér

Kálvin tér

Múzeum krt

Magyar u

Astoria

Ferenc krt

József krt

Ferenciek tere

Egyetem tér

Cukor u

Szerb u

Molnár u

Váci u

Belgrád rkp

Erzsébet Bridge (Erzsébet híd)

Szigony u

Benitzky I u

Leonárdó da Vinci u

Nagy Templom u

Futó u

Vajdahunyad u

Práter u

Ferenc krt

Tűzoltó u

Liliom u

Páva u

Üllői út

Corvin köz

Krs Stáció u

Baross u

Rigó u

Német u

Kis Fuvaros u

Őr u

Krúdy Gyula u

Mátyás tér

Szüz u

Szabó Ervin tér

Kálmán tér

Lőrinc Pap tér

Mikszáth Kálmán tér

Markusovszky tér

Baláty tér

Bakáts tér

Ráday u

Erkel u

Knezich u

Kinizsi u

Lónyay u

Csepel

Várkert rkp

Central Pest

refurbished rooms are fairly ordinary, but location is everything here.

Büro Panzió PENSION €
(Map p322; ☎212 2929; www.buropanzio.hu; II Dékán utca 3; s/d/tr/q from €34/43/59/72; ❄@) This pension looks basic from the outside, but its 10 compact rooms are comfortable and have TV and telephone. The central Moszkva tér transportation hub – metro stop, tram stations – is seconds away.

Hotel Kulturinnov HOTEL €€
(Map p322; ☎224 8102; www.mka.hu; I Szentháromság tér 6; s/d/tr €64/80/96;❄) A small hotel sitting in the belly of the grandiose

Hungarian Culture Foundation, a neo-Gothic structure dating back to 1904. The rooms are unimpressive, but you can't beat the scenic locale, on top of Castle Hill.

Martos Hostel HOSTEL €
(Map p318; ☑209 4883; http://hotel.martos.bme. hu; XI Sztoczek utca 5-7; s/d/tr/q/apt from 4000/6000/9000/12,000/15,000Ft;@) Primarily student accommodation, Martos is open year-round to all. It's a few minutes' walk from Petőfi Bridge (or take tram 4 or 6).

Zugligeti Niche Camping CAMPING GROUND €
(☑200 8346; www.campingniche.hu; XII Zugligeti út 101; camp sites per person 1800Ft, tents/camp-ervans 1700/3200Ft) An excellent option for mixing a city break with a hiking holiday: the camp is in the Buda Hills at the bottom station of a chairlift. Take bus 158 from Moszkva tér to the terminus.

PEST
Soho Hotel BOUTIQUE HOTEL €€
(Map p324; ☑872 8216; www.sohohotel.hu; VII Dohány utca 64; s/d/ste from €125/135/199; ✳@) This delightfully stylish boutique hotel sports a foyer bar in eye-popping reds, blues and lime greens. The non-allergenic rooms have bamboo matting on the walls, parquet floors and a music/film theme throughout.

Four Seasons Gresham Palace Hotel
LUXURY HOTEL €€€
(Map p324; ☑268 6000; www.fourseasons.com; V Roosevelt tér 5-6; s/d/ste from €300/340/1000; ✳✳) Restored to its bygone elegance, with mushroom-shaped windows, whimsical ironwork and glittering gold decorative tiles on the exterior, the Four Seasons inhabits the art nouveau Gresham Palace (1907) and provides superb views of the Danube through Roosevelt Park.

Cotton House PENSION €€
(Map p324; ☑354 2600; www.cottonhouse.hu; Jókai utca 26; r €60-99;@) This 23-room guesthouse has a Jazz Age/speakeasy theme, complete with old radios and vintage telephones. Prices vary, depending on the season and whether there's a shower, tub or spa in the bathroom.

Garibaldi Guesthouse B&B €
(Map p324; ☑302 3457; www.garibaldiguesthouse. hu; V Garibaldi utca 5; r from €44, apt per person €25-45) This old building belongs to a gregarious owner who has many apartments available over several floors, as well as private rooms in apartments with shared bathroom and kitchen.

Home-Made Hostel HOSTEL €
(Map p324; ☑302 2103; www.homemadehostel.com; VI Teréz körút 22; dm/d/q from 3500/12,000/20,000Ft;@) This cosy, extremely welcoming hostel has unique decor, with recycled tables hanging upside down from the ceiling and old valises serving as lockers. The old-style kitchen is also a blast from the past.

Gingko Hostel HOSTEL €
(Map p324; ☑266 6107; www.gingko.hu; V Szép utca 5; dm/d/tr 3500/11,000/15,000Ft;@) This very green hostel is one of the best kept in town and the fount-of-all-knowledge manager keeps it so clean you could eat off the floor. There are books to share and a positively enormous double giving on to Reáltanoda utca.

Connection Guest House PENSION €
(Map p324; ☑267 7104; www.connectionguesthouse.com; VII Király utca 41; s/d from €35/50;@) This central gay-friendly pension above a leafy courtyard attracts a young crowd due to its proximity to nightlife venues. Three of the seven rooms share bathroom facilities. Excellent, user-friendly hotel website.

Corinthia Grand Hotel Royal LUXURY HOTEL €€€
(Map p324; ☑479 4000; www.corinthia.hu; VII Erzsébet körút 43-49; r/ste from €179/310; ✳@✳) Decades in the remaking, this five-star beauty has been carefully reconstructed in the Austro-Hungarian style of heavy drapes, sparkling chandeliers and large, luxurious ballrooms. Its restored Royal Spa, dating from 1886 but now as modern as tomorrow, is a legend reborn.

Erzsébet Hotel HOTEL €€
(Map p324; ☑889 3700; www.danubiusgroup. com/erzsebet; V Károlyi Mihály utca 11-15; s/d from €72/84; ✳@) The Erzsébet is in a very good location in the centre of the university district, within easy walking distance of the pubs and bars of Ráday utca. The 123 rooms, mostly twins, are spread across eight floors. They tend to be small and somewhat dark, but they're comfortable enough.

Leo Panzió PENSION €€
(Map p324; ☑266 9041; www.leopanzio.hu; V Kossuth Lajos utca 2/a; s/d from €79/99;✳) Just steps from Váci utca, this B&B with a lion motif is in the middle of everything. A dozen of its 14 immaculate rooms look down on busy Kossuth Lajos utca, but they all have

double glazing and are quiet. Rates drop considerably in low season.

Radio Inn
APARTMENT €€
(Map p324; ☑342 8347; www.radioinn.hu; VI Benczúr utca 19; r from €64) Spacious apartments with full kitchens, sitting areas and one or two bedrooms are the drawcard here, perfect for a longer stay. Embassies are your neighbours on the quiet, tree-lined street near Bajza utca metro stop (M1 yellow line).

Red Bus Hostel
HOSTEL €
(Map p324; ☑266 0136; www.redbusbudapest.hu; V Semmelweiss utca 14; dm/s/d/tr 3000/9000/9000/12,500Ft;@) Red Bus is a central and well-managed place, with large and airy dorms as well as five private rooms. It's a quiet spot with a fair number of rules – the full 16 are listed in reception – so don't expect to party here.

Marco Polo Hostel
HOSTEL €
(Map p324; ☑413 2555; www.marcopolohostel.com; VII Nyár utca 6; dm/s/d/tr/q from 3500/12,000/15,000/19,000/24,000;@) Very central flagship hostel. All rooms other than dorms have telephones and TVs, and there's a lovely courtyard.

Medosz Hotel
HOTEL €
(Map p324; ☑374 3001; www.medoszhotel.hu; VI Jókai tér 9; s/d/tr/ste from €49/59/69/89) Well priced for its central location, the Medosz is opposite the restaurants and bars of Liszt Ferenc tér. The rooms are spare but comfortable.

Hotel Anna
HOTEL €€
(Map p324; ☑327 2000; www.annahotel.hu; VIII Gyulai Pál utca; s/d/ste from €66/82/88) Anna has 30 fairly basic rooms scattered over three floors of two 18th-century buildings that surround an enormous courtyard and garden. It's not the greatest value for money in town, but the rooms are quiet and the location is great.

Central Backpack King Hostel
HOSTEL €
(Map p324; ☑06 30 200 7184; centralbpk@freemail.hu; V Október 6 utca 15; dm/d/tr/q from €12/50/70/80;@) This upbeat place has dorm rooms with between seven and nine beds on one floor, and doubles, triples and quads on another.

✕ Eating

Very roughly, a cheap two-course sit-down meal for one person with a glass of wine or beer in Budapest costs 3500Ft, while the same meal in a midrange eatery would be 7000Ft. An expensive meal ranges up to 10,000Ft. Unless otherwise stated, restaurants listed below are open from 10am or 11am to 11pm or midnight. It's always best to arrive by 9pm or 10pm, though, to ensure being served. It is advisable to book tables at medium-priced to expensive restaurants, especially at the weekend.

Ráday utca and Liszt Ferenc tér are the two most popular traffic-free streets. The moment the weather warms up, tables and umbrellas spring up on the pavements and the people of Budapest crowd the streets.

BUDA

For self-catering in Buda, visit the **Fény utca market** (Map p322; II Fény utca; ◷6am-6pm Mon-Fri, 6am-2pm Sat), just next to the Mammut shopping mall.

Csalogány 26
HUNGARIAN €€€
(Map p322; ☑201 7892; I Csalogány utca 26; mains 4000-6000Ft; ◷noon-3pm & 7-10pm Tue-Sat) One of the best restaurants in Budapest turns out superb Hungarian and international dishes at prices that, while no bargain, are considered good value for the quality of what's on offer. Reserve for the evenings.

Tabáni Terasz
HUNGARIAN €€
(Map p322; ☑201 1086; I Apród utca 10; mains 2600-4900Ft) This delightful terrace and cellar restaurant at the foot of Castle Hill has a modern take on Hungarian cuisine, with lighter dishes and an excellent wine selection.

Kisbuda Gyöngye
HUNGARIAN €€
(Map p318; ☑368 6402; III Kenyeres utca 34; mains 2100-4800Ft; ◷noon-midnight Mon-Sat) A traditional and very elegant Hungarian restaurant in Óbuda, with an antique-cluttered dining room evoking a fin de siècle atmosphere.

Pavillon de Paris
FRENCH €€€
(Map p322; ☑225 0174; II Fő utca 20; mains 4700-5400Ft; ◷noon-midnight Tue-Sat) A change in management in 2010 saw the replacement of the popular Jardin de Paris with this more upscale, and more serious, version of French and Continental cooking. The back garden is a delight in the warmer months.

Szent Jupát
HUNGARIAN €
(Map p322; II Dékán utca 3; mains 1700-3600Ft; ◷noon-2am Sun-Thu, to 4am Fri & Sat) This is the classic late-night choice for solid, even stodgy, Hungarian fare, and there's half a dozen vegetarian choices too. It's just north of Moszkva tér and opposite the Fény utca market – enter from II Retek utca 16.

Marcello

ITALIAN €

(Map p318; XI Bartók Béla út 40; mains 2200Ft; ☺noon-10pm Mon-Sat) Popular with students from the nearby university, this family-owned eatery has good Italian fare at affordable prices.

Édeni Vegan

VEGETARIAN €

(Map p322; I Iskola utca 31; mains 900-1200Ft; ☺8am-9pm Mon-Thu, 8am-6pm Fri, 11am-7pm Sun) Located in a town house just below Castle Hill, this self-service place offers solid but healthy vegan and vegetarian fare.

PEST

A self-catering option is the **Hold utca market** (Map p324; V Hold utca 13; ☺10am-6pm Mon-Fri, 10am-1pm Sat) near Szabadság tér. The **Nagycsarnok** (Great Market; Map p324; IX Vámház körút 1-3; ☺9am-6pm Mon-Sat) is a vast historic market built of steel and glass. Head here for fruit, vegetables, deli items, fish and meat.

The **Rothschild Supermarket** (Map p324; VI Teréz körút 19; ☺24hr), near Oktogon, is an around-the-clock supermarket.

Köleves

HUNGARIAN/JEWISH €€

(Map p324; ☑322 1011; Kazinczy utca 35 & Dob utca 26; mains 1600-3200Ft) Always buzzing, 'Stone Soup' attracts a young crowd with its delicious Hungarian- and Jewish-inspired dishes like catfish stew and noodles. The lively decor and reasonable prices draws a nice mix of visitors and local hipsters.

Bagolyvár

HUNGARIAN €€

(Map p318; ☑468 3110; XIV Állatkerti út 2; mains 2850-4250Ft) Serving imaginatively reworked Hungarian classics, the 'Owl's Castle' attracts the Budapest foodie cognoscenti. It's staffed entirely by women – in the kitchen, at table and front of house.

Klassz

FINE DINING €€

(Map p324; ☑413 1545; www.klassz.eu; VI Andrássy út 41; mains 2400-4200Ft; ☺11.30am-11pm Mon-Sat, 11.30am-6pm Sun) Klassz is focused on wine, but the food is also of a high standard. Varieties of foie gras and native *mangalica* pork are permanent stars on the menu, with dishes such as Burgundy-style leg of rabbit and lamb trotters with vegetable ragout playing cameo roles.

Menza

HUNGARIAN €€

(Map p324; ☑413 1482; VI Liszt Ferenc tér 2; mains 1990-3690Ft) This stylish restaurant on Budapest's most lively square takes its name from the Hungarian for a school canteen – something it is anything but. It's always packed

with diners who come for its simply but perfectly cooked Hungarian classics with a modern twist. Reservations necessary.

Első Pesti Rétesház

BAKERY €

(Map p324; ☑428 0135; V Október 6 utca 22; strudels 360Ft; ☺9am-11pm) The decor may resemble a Magyar Disneyland, with olde-worlde counters, painted plates on the walls and curios embedded in plexiglass washbasins. However, the First Strudel House of Pest is just the place to taste this Hungarian pastry filled with apple, cheese, poppy seeds or sour cherries.

Soul Café

INTERNATIONAL €

(Map p324; ☑217 6986; IX Ráday utca 11-13; mains 2100-4500Ft) One of the better choices along a street heaving with so-so restaurants and iffy cafes, the Soul has inventive European cuisine and decor and a great terrace on both sides of the street.

Fülemüle

HUNGARIAN €€

(Map p324; ☑266 7947; VIII Kőfaragó utca 5; mains 2300-4900Ft; ☺noon-10pm Sun-Thu, noon-11pm Fri & Sat) Quaint Hungarian restaurant that seems frozen in time in the interwar period. Dishes mingle Hungarian and international tastes with some old-style Jewish favourites.

Salaam Bombay

INDIAN €€

(Map p324; ☑411 1252; V Mérleg utca 6; mains 2400-4200Ft; ☺noon-3pm & 6-11pm) If you hanker after a fix of authentic curry or tandoori in a bright, upbeat environment, look no further than this attractive eatery just east of Roosevelt tér. As would be expected, there's a wide choice of vegetarian dishes.

Pireus Rembetiko Taverna

GREEK €€

(Map p324; ☑266 0292; V Fóvám tér 2-3; mains 2490-4990Ft) Overlooking the Nagycsarnok (Great Market) at the foot of Liberty Bridge, this place serves reasonably priced and pretty authentic Greek fare.

Marquis de Salade

CAUCASIAN €

(Map p324; ☑302 4086; VI Hajós utca 43; mains 2400-3400Ft) Taking its cue from its odd name, this basement restaurant is a strange hybrid of a place, with dishes from Russia and Azerbaijan as well as Hungary. There are lots of quality vegetarian choices on the menu.

Vapiano

ITALIAN €

(Map p324; V Bécsi utca 5; mains 1400-2200Ft) A very welcome addition is this self-serve pizza and pasta bar where everything is prepared on site. You'll be in and out in no time, but the taste will pleasantly linger.

Govinda
VEGETARIAN €

(Map p324; V Vigyázó Ferenc utca 4; set menu 1250-1450Ft; ⊙11.30am-8pm Mon-Fri, noon-8pm Sat & Sun) Basement restaurant northeast of the Széchenyi Chain Bridge serves wholesome salads, soups and desserts as well as daily set menus.

Szeráj
KEBABS €

(Map p324; XIII Szent István körút 13; mains 600-1600Ft, ⊙9am-4am Mon-Thu, to 5am Fri & Sat, to 2am Sun) Inexpensive self-service Turkish place for *lahmacun* (or 'Turkish pizza'), falafel and kebabs.

🍸 Drinking

One of Budapest's ceaseless wonders is the number of bars, cellars, cafes, clubs and general places to drink.

Budapest in the 19th century rivalled Vienna in its cafe culture, though cafe numbers waned under communism. The majority of the surviving traditional cafes are in Pest, but Buda can still lay claim to a handful.

Budapest is also loaded with pubs and bars, and there's enough variation to satisfy all tastes. In summer, the preferred drinking venues are the *kerteks*, outdoor spaces that double as beer gardens and music clubs.

The best places to drink are in Pest (Buda's too sleepy to stay up all night), especially along Liszt Ferenc tér and Radáy utca, which have a positively festive feel during the summer.

BUDA

Kisrabló
PUB

(Map p318; XI Zenta utca 3) Attractive and well-run pub that's very popular with students. Take tram 19 or 49 one stop past Danubius Hotel Gellért.

Ruszwurm
CAFE

(Map p322; I Szentháromság utca 7; ⊙10am-7pm) This is the perfect place for coffee and cake in the Castle District, though it can get pretty crowded.

PEST

For coffee in exquisite art nouveau surroundings, two places are particularly noteworthy. **Gerbeaud** (Map p324; V Vörösmarty tér 7; ⊙9am-9pm;❋), Budapest's cake-and-coffee-culture king, has been serving since 1870. Or station yourself where Hungary's dreaded ÁVH secret police once had its HQ, at **Lukács** (Map p324; VI Andrássy út 70; ⊙8.30am-8pm Mon-Fri, 9am-8pm Sat, 9.30am-8pm Sun).

Szimpla
BAR

(Map p324; VII Kertész utca 48) This distressed-looking, very unflashy place remains one of the most popular drinking venues south of Liszt Ferenc tér. There's live music in the evenings from Tuesday to Thursday.

Centrál Kávéház
COFFEE HOUSE

(Map p324; V Károlyi Mihály utca 9; ⊙8am-midnight) One of the finest coffee houses in the city, with high, decorated ceilings, lace curtains, pot plants, elegant coffee cups and professional service. You can have an omelette breakfast here, eat a full-on meal, or just sit down with a coffee or beer and enjoy the atmosphere.

Kiadó Kocsma
PUB

(Map p324; VI Jókai tér 3) The 'Pub for Rent' is a great place for a swift pint and a quick bite (salads and pasta), and is just a stone's throw away from Liszt Ferenc tér.

☆ Entertainment

Budapest has a nightlife that can keep you up for days on end – and not just because the techno beat from the club next to your hotel is keeping you awake. There are nightclubs, bars, live concerts (classical and folk), Hungarian traditional dancing nights, opera treats, ballet, DJ bars and random **Cinetrip** (www.cinetrip.hu) club nights at the thermal spas. It's usually not difficult to get tickets or get in; the hard part is deciding what to do.

To find out what's on, check out the free *Budapest Funzine* (www.funzine.hu) published every second Thursday and available at hotels, bars, cinemas and various tourist spots. More comprehensive is the freebie *PestiEst* (www.est.hu, in Hungarian) and the ultrathorough *Pesti Műsor* (Budapest Program; www.pestimusor.hu, in Hungarian), with everything from clubs and films to art exhibitions and classical music.

The free *Koncert Kalendárium,* published monthly (bimonthly in summer), covers the performing arts, including classical concerts, opera and dance. A hip little publication with all sorts of insider's tips is the *Budapest City Spy Map*. It's available free at pubs and bars.

Gay & Lesbian Venues

Alter Ego
GAY & LESBIAN

(Map p324; www.alteregoclub.hu; VI Dessewffy utca 33; ⊙10pm-5am Fri & Sat) One of the city's leading gay clubs, with a cool crowd (think attitude) and arguably the best dance music.

Café Eklektika
GAY & LESBIAN

(Map p324; VI Nagymező utca 30) This lesbian-owned cafe and restaurant in attractive new digs is a great place for a meal and a little LGBT information gathering. Attracts a youthful, arty crowd.

Performing Arts

Classical concerts are held regularly in the city's churches, including Matthias Church (p316) on Castle Hill in Buda.

A useful ticket broker, with outlets across town, is **Ticket Express** (Map p324; ☑030 303 0999; www.tex.hu; VI Andrássy út 18; ⊙10am-6.30pm Mon-Fri, to 3pm Sat). **Ticket Pro** (Map p324; ☑555 5155; www.ticketpro.hu; VII Károly körút 9; ⊙9am-9pm Mon-Fri, 10am-2pm Sat) also sells tickets to plays, concerts and sporting events, while the **Symphony Ticket Office** (Szimfonikus Jegyiroda; Map p324; ☑302 3841; VI Nagymező utca 19; ⊙10am-6pm Mon-Fri, 10am-2pm Sat) specialises in classical music events.

Hungarian State Opera House
OPERA

(Magyar Állami Operaház; Map p324; ☑353 0170; www.opera.hu; VI Andrássy út 22) Take in a performance while admiring the incredibly rich interior decoration. The ballet company performs here as well.

Liszt Ferenc Zeneakadémia
CONCERT HALL

(Liszt Academy of Music; Map p324; ☑342 0179; VI Liszt Ferenc tér 8) You can hear the musicians practising from outside this magnificent concert hall, which hosts classical music performances.

Live Music

Fonó Budai Zeneház
LIVE MUSIC

(Map p318; www.fono.hu; XI Sztregova utca 3; ⊙2-10pm Wed-Fri, 7-10pm Sat) The best place in Budapest for folk music of any kind, including the diverse sounds of Hungarian, Transylvanian, Balkan, Romani, klezmer and tango.

Kalamajka Táncház
LIVE MUSIC

(Map p324; V Arany János utca 10; ⊙8.30pm-midnight Sat) The Kalamajka is an excellent place to hear authentic Hungarian music, especially on its dance nights, when everyone gets up and takes part.

Columbus Jazzklub
JAZZ

(Map p324; www.majazz.hu; V Pesti alsó rakpart at Lánchíd bridgehead) Jazz on a boat moored in the Danube, just off the northern end of V Vigadó tér, hosting big-name local and international performers. Music starts at 8pm nightly.

Nightclubs

Not all clubs and music bars in Budapest levy a cover charge, but those that do will ask for between 1000Ft and 2500Ft at the door. Nightclubs usually open from 4pm to 2am Sunday to Thursday and until 4am on Friday and Saturday; some open only at weekends.

Mappa Club
CLUB

(Map p324; IX Lilliom utca 41) An arty crowd makes the scene beneath this cultural house and exhibition space, enjoying some of the best DJs in town. Formerly the popular Trafó Bár Tangó.

Merlin
CLUB

(Map p324; www.merlinbudapest.org; V Gerlóczy utca 4) One of those something-for-everyone places, with everything from jazz and breakbeat to techno and house.

Gödör Klub
CLUB

(Map p324; V Erzsébet tér) This large underground club is a real mixed bag, offering a mix of folk, world, rock and pop, played to an audience of all ages.

🛍 Shopping

As well as the usual folk arts, wines, spirits, food and music, Budapest has more distinctive items such as hand-blown glassware and antique books. But there are those who consider the city's flea markets their shopping highlight – and they certainly are a distinctive Budapest experience. Shops are generally open from 9am or 10am to 6pm during the week, and till 1pm on Saturday.

There's an excellent selection of Hungarian wines at **Bortársaság Lánchíd** (Map p322; I Lánchíd utca 5; ⊙noon-9pm Mon-Fri, 10am-7pm Sat) in Buda, and you can pick up the Hungarian fruit-flavoured brandy *pálinka* at **Mester Pálinka** (Map p324; ☑374 0388; V Zrínyi utca 18).

Two major flea markets take place in Budapest during the week. The closest to the city centre is **Városligeti Bolhapiac** (Map p318; ⊙7am-2pm Sat & Sun) in City Park. There's junk and antiques, and the best things are to be found early in the morning. The real market mamma, though, is the **Ecseri Piac** (XIX Nagykőrösi út 156; ⊙8am-4pm Mon-Fri, 6am-3pm Sat, 8am-1pm Sun), on the southeast edge of town. International antiques dealers come to scout on Saturdays, so things can get pricey. Take bus 54 from Boráros tér in Pest or, for a quicker journey, the red-numbered express bus 84E, 89E or 94E from the Határ utca stop on the M3 metro line and get off at the Fiume utca stop. Then follow the crowds over the pedestrian bridge.

Handicrafts

Folkart Centrum HANDICRAFTS
(Map p324; V Váci utca 58) Everything Magyar, whether made here or in China, is available here, from embroidered waistcoats and tablecloths to painted eggs and plates.

Intuita HANDICRAFTS
(Map p324; V Váci utca 67) Purveyor of modern Hungarian crafted items such as hand-blown glass, jewellery, ceramics and bound books.

Books

Központi Antikvárium BOOKS
(Map p324; V Múzeum körút 13-15) For antique and second-hand books, try the Central Antiquarian, which was established in 1885. This stretch of Múzeum Körút is a treasure trove of second-hand book and map shops.

Bestsellers BOOKS
(Map p324; V Október 6 utca 11; ⊗9am-6.30pm Mon-Fri, 10am-5pm Sat, 10am-4pm Sun) The best English-language bookshop in town.

Irók Boltja BOOKS
(Map p324; VI Andrássy út 45; ⊗10am-7pm Mon-Fri, to 1pm Sat) Good selection of Hungarian writers in translation.

Red Bus Second-hand Bookstore BOOKS
(Map p324; V Semmelweiss utca 14; ⊗11am-6pm Mon-Fri, 10am-2pm Sat) Used English-language books.

Treehugger Dan's Bookstore BOOKS
(Map p324; VI Csengery utca 48; ⊗10am-7pm Mon-Fri, 10am-5pm Sat) Tiny shop sells mostly second-hand English-language books; also does trade-ins and serves organic fairtrade coffee.

❶ Information

Dangers & Annoyances

Overall, Hungary is a safe country with little violent crime, but scams can be a problem in the capital. Those involving attractive young women, gullible guys, expensive drinks in nightclubs and a frogmarch to the nearest ATM accompanied by inhouse security have been all the rage in Budapest for well over a decade now, so be aware. Overcharging in taxis is also not unknown.

Watch out for pickpockets: the usual method is for someone to distract you while an accomplice makes off with your goods. Pickpocketing is most common in markets, the Castle District, Váci utca and Hősök tere, near major hotels and on certain popular buses (eg 7) and trams (2, 4, 6, 47 and 49). Watch out too for occasional fake ticket controllers on trams and metros who show a badge and then take your money.

As for personal security, some locals avoid Margaret Island after dark during the low season, and both residents and visitors give the dodgier parts of the VIII and IX districts (areas of prostitution activity) a wide berth.

Discount Cards

See p376 for details on the Hungary Card.

Budapest Card (www.budapestinfo.hu; 48/72hr card 6300/7500Ft) Offers access to many museums, unlimited public transport and discounts on tours and other services. Buy it at hotels, travel agencies, large metro station kiosks and tourist offices.

Emergency

The national phone number for emergencies is ☎112.

District V Police Station (☎373 1000; V Szalay utca 11-13) Pest's most central police station.

Internet Access

Most hostels offer internet access, often free of charge. These following are among the most accessible internet cafes in Budapest.

Electric Café (VII Dohány utca 37; per hr 200Ft; ⊗9am-midnight) Huge place, very popular with travellers.

Vist@ Netcafe (XIII Váci utca 6; per hr 400Ft; ⊗24h) In Pest. One of the few internet cafes open 24 hours.

Medical Services

FirstMed Centers (☎224 9090; I Hattyú utca 14, 5th fl; ⊗8am-8pm Mon-Fri, 9am-2pm Sat) On call 24/7 for emergencies.

SOS Dent (☎269 6010; VI Király utca 14; ⊗24hr) Dentist.

Teréz Patika (☎311 4439; VI Teréz körút 41; ⊗8am-8pm Mon-Fri, 8am-2pm Sat) Extended-hours pharmacy.

Money

You'll find ATMs everywhere.

K&H Bank (V Váci utca 40) Central.

OTP Bank (V Deák Ferenc utca 7-9) Favourable rates.

Post

Main post office (Map p324; V Petőfi Sándor utca 13-15; ⊗8am-8pm Mon-Fri, to 2pm Sat) Just minutes from Deák Ferenc tér.

Tourist Information

Tourinform main office (Map p324; ☎438 8080; V Sütő utca 2; ⊗8am-8pm); Castle Hill (Map p322; ☎488 0475; I Szentháromság tér; ⊗9am-7pm May-Oct, 10am-6pm Nov-Apr); Liszt Ferenc

Sq (Map p324; ☑322 4098; VI Liszt Ferenc tér 11; ⊙10am-6pm Mon-Fri)

Travel Agencies

Discover Budapest (Map p324; ☑269 3843; www.discoverbudapest.com; VI Lázár utca 16; ⊙9.30am-6.30pm Mon-Fri, 10am-4pm Sat & Sun) Visit this one-stop shop for helpful tips and advice, accommodation bookings, internet access, and cycling and walking tours.

Vista (☑429 9760; www.vista.hu; VI Andrássy utca 1; ⊙9.30am-6pm Mon-Fri, to 2.30pm Sat) Good choice for all travel needs, both for inbound travellers (room bookings, sightseeing tours) and outbound (travel tickets, package tours).

❶ Getting There & Away

Air

The main international carriers fly in and out of Terminal 2 at Budapest's **Ferihegy International Airport** (☑1-296 7000; www.bud.hu), 24km southeast of the centre on Hwy 4; low-cost airlines use the older Terminal 1 next door. For carriers flying to Hungary, see p378.

Boat

Mahart PassNave (www.mahartpassnave.hu; Belgrád rakpart ☑484 4013; Vigadó tér Pier ☑484 4005), with two docks, runs ferries and hydrofoils from Budapest. A hydrofoil service on the Danube River between Budapest and Vienna (5½ to 6½ hours) operates daily from late April to early October; passengers can disembark at Bratislava with advance notice (four hours). Adult one-way/return fares for Vienna are €89/109 and for Bratislava €79/99. Students with ISIC cards receive about a €20 discount, and children between two and 14 years of age travel for half price. Boats leave from the Nemzetközi hajóállomás (International Ferry Pier).

There are ferries departing at 10.30am daily for Szentendre (one way/return 1490/2235Ft, 1½ hours) from May to September, decreasing to 9am departures on weekends only in April and October.

Vác (one way/return 1990/2990Ft, 40 minutes), Visegrád (one way/return 2690/3990Ft, one hour) and Esztergom (one way/return 3290/4990Ft, 1½ hours) can be reached by fast hydrofoil from Budapest at 9.30am at weekends between May and September (and also on Friday from June to August). There are also slower daily ferries at 8am from Budapest to Vác (one way/return 1490/2235Ft, 2½ hours), Visegrád (one way/return 1590/2385Ft, 3½ hours) and Esztergom (one way/return 1990/2985Ft, 5½ hours) between June and August. Services run on Friday and weekends in May, and weekends only in September.

When day-tripping to the Danube Bend by ferry, remember to check the return departure time when you arrive at your destination. Most sail to Budapest between 4.30pm and 6.45pm.

Bus

Volánbusz (☑382 0888; www.volanbusz.hu), the national bus line, has an extensive list of destinations from Budapest. All international buses and some buses to/from southern Hungary use **Népliget bus station** (Map p318; IX Üllői út 131). **Stadionok bus station** (Map p318; XIV Hungária körút 48-52) generally serves places to the east of Budapest. Most buses to the northern Danube Bend arrive at and leave from the **Árpád híd bus station** (Map p318; off XIII Róbert Károly körút). All stations are on metro lines, and all are in Pest. If the ticket office is closed, you can buy your ticket on the bus.

HUNGARY BUDAPEST

INTERNATIONAL BUSES FROM BUDAPEST

DESTINATION	PRICE (FT)	DURATION (HR)	FREQUENCY
Bratislava, Slovakia	3700	4	1 daily
Florence, Italy	22,900	14	3 weekly
Frankfurt, Germany	14,900	14	1 daily
London, UK	29,900	25	6 weekly
Munich, Germany	15,900	10	4 weekly
Paris, France	24,900	22	3 weekly
Prague, Czech Republic	10,900	7½	3 weekly
Rijeka, Croatia	12,900	8¼	1 weekly
Rome, Italy via Florence	26,900	19	3 weekly
Sofia, Bulgaria	12,500	12	3 weekly
Subotica, Serbia	3900	4½	2 daily
Vienna, Austria	5900	3½	5 daily

INTERNATIONAL TRAINS FROM BUDAPEST

DESTINATION	PRICE (€)	DURATION (HR)
Berlin, Germany	45	12
Bratislava, Slovakia	17	2½
Bucharest, Romania	75	13-15
Frankfurt, Germany	75	15
Kyiv, Ukraine, via Csop & continuing to Moscow	96	24
Ljubljana, Slovenia	40	8½
Munich, Germany	60	7-9
Prague, Czech Republic	40	7
Sofia, Bulgaria	78	18
Thessaloniki, Greece	90	23
Venice, Italy	54	14
Vienna, Austria	25	3
Warsaw, Poland	60	12
Zürich, Switzerland	80	12

Car & Motorcycle

Car rental is not recommended if you are staying in Budapest. The public transport network is extensive and cheap, whereas parking is scarce and road congestion is high.

If you want to venture into the countryside, travelling by car is an option. Daily rates start at around €60 per day with unlimited kilometres. If the company does not have an office at the airport, it will usually provide free pick-up and delivery within Budapest or at the airport. All the major international chains have branches in Terminal 2 at Ferihegy airport.

Two good local options:

Recent (☑453 0003; www.recentcar.hu; ◷9am-6pm) Reliable outfit.

Fox Autorent (☑382 9000; www.foxautorent. com; ◷8am-6pm) Another good bet.

Train

The Hungarian State Railways, MÁV, administers the country's extensive rail network. Contact the **MÁV-Start passenger service centre** (☑06 40 494949; www.mav-start.hu) for 24-hour information on domestic train departures and arrivals. The website has a useful timetable (in English) for planning routes. Fares are usually noted for destinations within Hungary.

Buy tickets at one of Budapest's three main train stations. Always confirm your departure station when you buy your tickets, since stations can vary depending on the train.

Keleti train station (Eastern; Map p318; VIII Kerepesi út 2-4) handles international trains from Vienna, including the express Railjet trains, and most other points west, plus domestic trains to/from the north and northeast. For some international destinations, as well as domestic ones to/from the northwest and the Danube Bend, head for **Nyugati train station** (Western; Map p324; VI Nyugati tér). For trains bound for Lake Balaton and the south, go to **Déli train station** (Southern; Map p322; I Krisztina körút 37). All train stations are on metro lines.

❶ Getting Around
To/From the Airport

The simplest way to get to town is to take the **Airport Minibus** (☑296 8555; www.airport shuttle.hu; one way/return 2990/4990Ft) directly to the place you're staying. Buy tickets at clearly marked stands in the arrivals halls.

An alternative is travelling with **Zóna Taxi** (☑365 5555), which has a monopoly on airport taxis. Fares to most central locations range from 5200Ft to 6000Ft. Of course, you can take any taxi to the airport, and several companies offer a flat fare (between 4800Ft and 5400Ft) to/from Ferihegy.

The cheapest (and slowest) way to get into the city centre from Terminal 2A and 2B is to take city bus 200 (320Ft, or 400Ft on the bus), which terminates at the Kőbánya-Kispest metro station. Look for the stop on the footpath between terminals 2A and 2B. From its final stop, take the M3 metro into the city centre. The total cost is 640Ft to 800Ft. Bus 93 runs from Terminal 1 to Kőbánya-Kispest metro station.

Trains also link Terminal 1 with Nyugati station. They run between one and six times an hour between 4am and 11pm and cost 365Ft (or around 600Ft if you board the hourly IC train). The journey takes 20 minutes.

Boat

From May to August, the **BKV passenger ferry** (Map p318; ☑258 4636; www.bkv.hu) departs from Boráros tér Terminus beside Petőfi Bridge, south of the centre, and heads for III Pünkösdfürdő in Óbuda, a 2¼-hour trip with 14 stops along the way. Tickets (adult/concession 900/450Ft from end to end) are sold on board. The ferry stop closest to the Castle District is Batthyány tér, and Petőfi tér is not far from Vörösmarty tér, a convenient place to pick up the boat on the Pest side.

Public Transport

Public transport is run by **BKV** (☑258 4636; www.bkv.hu). The three underground metro lines (M1 yellow, M2 red, M3 blue) meet at Deák tér in Pest. The HÉV suburban railway runs north from Batthyány tér in Buda. A *turista* transport pass is only good on the HÉV within the city limits (south of the Békásmegyer stop). There's also an extensive network of buses, trams and trolleybuses. Public transport operates from 4.30am until 11.30pm, and 35 night buses run along main roads.

A single ticket for all forms of transport is 320Ft (60 minutes of uninterrupted travel on the same metro, bus, trolleybus or tram line *without* transferring/changing). A transfer ticket (490Ft) is valid for one trip with one validated transfer within 90 minutes. The three-day *turista* pass (3850Ft) or the seven-day pass (4600Ft) make things easier, allowing unlimited travel inside the city limits. Keep your ticket or pass handy; the fine for 'riding black' is 6000Ft on the spot, or 12,000Ft if you pay later at the **BKV Office** (☑258 4636; VII Akácfa utca 18; ☺6am-8pm Mon-Fri, 8am-1.45pm Sat).

Taxi

Taxi drivers overcharging foreigners in Budapest has been a problem for some time. Never get into a taxi that lacks an official yellow licence plate, the logo of the taxi firm and a visible table of fares. If you have to take a taxi, it's best to call one; this costs less than if you flag one down. Make sure you know the number of the landline phone you're calling from, as that's how the dispatcher establishes your address (though you can call from a mobile as well). Dispatchers usually speak English. **City Taxi** (☑211 1111), **Főtaxi** (☑222 2222) and **Rádió Taxi** (☑377 7777) are reliable companies. Note that rates are slightly higher at night. Tip about 10% of the fare to reward good service.

North of Budapest, the Danube breaks through the Pilis and Börzsöny Hills in a sharp bend before continuing along the Slovak border. The Roman Empire had its northern border here, and medieval kings ruled Hungary from majestic palaces overlooking the river at Esztergom and Visegrád. East of Visegrád the river divides, with Szentendre and Vác on different branches. Today the easy access to historic monuments, rolling green scenery – and vast numbers of souvenir craft shops – lure many day-trippers from Budapest.

Szentendre

☑26 / POP 23,500

Once an artists' colony, now a popular day trip 19km north of Budapest, pretty little Szentendre (*sen*-ten-dreh) has narrow, winding streets and is a favourite with souvenir-shoppers. The charming old centre has plentiful cafes and art-and-craft galleries, and there are a few Serbian Orthodox churches, dating from the time when Christian worshippers fled here centuries ago to escape the Turkish invaders, that are worth checking out. Expect things to get crowded in summer and at weekends. Outside town is the largest open-air village museum in the country.

◉ Sights

Fő tér   PUBLIC SQUARE

Begin your sightseeing at the colourful Fő tér, the town's main square. Here you'll find many structures from the 18th century, including the 1763 **Memorial Cross** (Emlékkereszt) and the 1752 Serbian Orthodox **Blagoveštenska Church** (Blagoveštenska Templom; admission 300Ft; ☺10am-5pm Tue-Sun), which is small but stunning.

All the pedestrian lanes surrounding the square burst with shops, the merchandise spilling out into displays on the streets.

Margit Kovács Ceramic Collection   MUSEUM

(Kovács Margit Kerámiagyüjtemény; Vastagh György utca 1; adult/concession 1000/500Ft; ☺10am-6pm) Downhill to the east of the square, off a side street on the way to the Danube, is the Margit Kovács Ceramic Collection. Kovács (1902–77) was a ceramicist who combined Hungarian folk, religious and modern themes with a hint of Gothic to create her figures.

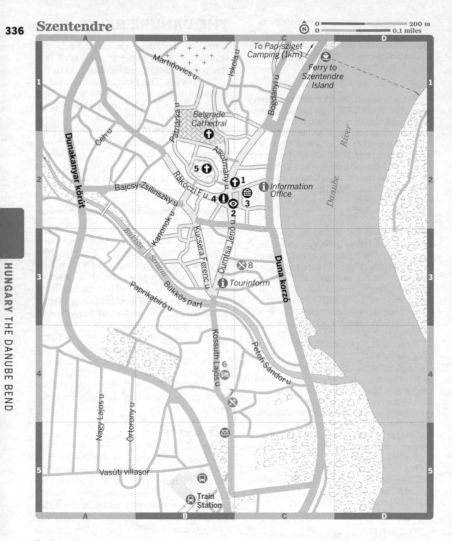

Parish Church of St John   CHURCH
(Szent Janos Plébánia Templom; Várhegy) Uphill to the northwest from the square, a narrow passageway leads up from between Fő tér 8 and 9 to Castle Hill (Vár-domb) and the Parish Church of St John, rebuilt in 1710, from where you get great views of the town and the Danube.

Open-Air Ethnographic Museum
      OPEN-AIR MUSEUM
(Szabadtéri Néprajzi Múzeum; www.skanzen.hu; Sztaravodai út; adult/concession 1400/700Ft; ⊙9am-5pm Tue-Sun late Mar-Oct) Don't miss the extensive Open-Air Ethnographic Mu-

seum, 3km outside town. Walking through the fully furnished ancient wooden and stone homes, churches and working buildings brought here from around the country, you can get a real sense of what rural life was – and sometimes still is – like in different regions of Hungary. In the centre of the park stand Roman-era ruins. Frequent weekend festivals offer you a chance to see folk costumes, music and dance, as well as home crafts. To get here, take the hourly buses marked 'Skansen' from stop 7 at the town's bus station.

Szentendre

🛏 Sleeping & Eating

Seeing Szentendre on a day trip from Budapest is probably your best bet. The town can be easily covered in a day, even if you spend a couple of hours at the open-air museum. For private rooms in town, visit the Tourinform office. Being a tourist town, there are plenty of places to grab a bite to eat.

Mathias Rex   PENSION €€
(☑505 570; www.mathiasrexhotel.hu; Kossuth Lajos utca 16; s/d 10,000/15,000Ft) Attractive, family-run pension about 10 minutes' walk from Fő tér. The spotless rooms are done out in high-quality dark woods and crisp linens. Guests have use of the backyard garden, and the cellar restaurant is one of the best in this part of town.

Pap-sziget Camping   CAMPING GROUND €
(☑310 697; www.pap-sziget.hu; camp sites per adult/concession 1200/700Ft, tents 3000Ft, bungalows from 11,000Ft; ⊙May–mid-Oct;🏊) Large shady trees, a sandy beach and numerous tent and caravan sites. Bungalows are basic. Take bus 11 from Szentendre.

Erm's   HUNGARIAN €
(Kossuth Lajos utca 22; mains around 2000Ft) This unpretentious spot a bit away from the day-tripper throng serves very good Hungarian specialities like fish stew, and even some vegetarian choices. The simple wooden tables dressed in lacy cloth are reminiscent of yesteryear.

Palapa   HUNGARIAN €
(☑302 418; Batthyány utca 4; mains 1500-3000Ft; ⊙5pm-midnight Mon-Fri, noon-midnight Sat & Sun) For a change from Hungarian cuisine, try the Mexican-inspired cooking here.

ℹ Information

There are no left-luggage offices at the HÉV train or bus stations.

Main post office (Kossuth Lajos utca 23-25) Across from the bus and train stations.

OTP Bank (Dumtsa Jenő utca 6) Just off Fő tér.

Silver Blue (Dunakanyar Körút 14; per hr 400Ft; ⊙10am-8pm Mon-Sat) Internet cafe near the train and bus terminals.

HUNGARY SZENTENDRE

THE AQUATIC HIGHWAY

No other river in Europe is as evocative as the Danube. It has been immortalised in legends, tales, songs, paintings and movies, and has played an essential role in the cultural and economic life of millions of people since the earliest human cultures settled along its banks.

Originating in Germany's Black Forest, the river cuts an unrelenting path through – or along the border of – 10 countries, and after 2800km empties itself into the Black Sea in Romania. It is second only in length to the Volga in Europe (although, at 6400km, the Amazon dwarfs both) and, contrary to popular belief, is green-brown rather than blue. Around 2400km of its length is navigable, making it a major transport route across the continent.

Even though only 12% of the river's length is located in its territory, Hungary is greatly influenced by the Danube. The entire country lies within the Danube river basin, and being so flat, it is highly prone to flooding. As early as the 16th century, massive dyke systems were built for flood protection. However, it's hard to stop water running where it wants to – as recently as 2006 the river burst its banks, threatening to fill Budapest's metro system and putting the homes of 32,000 people in danger.

Despite the potential danger the river is much loved, and has even been awarded its own day. On 29 June every year cities along the Danube host festivals, family events and conferences in honour of the mighty waterway. If you'd like to join in, visit www.danube day.org for more information.

THE MUMMIES OF VÁC

Between 1731 and 1801 the original crypt of Vác's Dominican church functioned as a place of burial for the general public, but it was later bricked up and forgotten. The microclimatic conditions underground were perfect for mummification – a cool temperature and minimal ventilation allowed the bodies of the deceased to remain in exceptional condition for centuries. When renovation work on the church began in 1994, the crypt was rediscovered. Of the 262 bodies exhumed over the ensuing months, 166 were easily identified through church records. It was a goldmine for historians; the clothing, jewellery and general appearance of the corpses helped to shed light on the burial practices and the local way of life in the 18th century.

The majority of mummies now reside in the vaults of the Hungarian National Museum (p321) in Budapest but three are on display in the **Memento Mori exhibition** in Vác, near the Dominican church. It also showcases some colourfully painted coffins, clothes and jewellery of the deceased, a registry of those buried and a brief history of the church and its crypt.

Tourinform (☑317 965; szentendre@tourinform.hu; Bercsényi utca 4; ☺9.30am-4.30pm Mon-Fri year-round, 10am-2pm Sat & Sun mid-Mar–Oct) Hands out maps and can make recommendations on shopping, dining and hotel rooms. In 2010 the office moved to this temporary location on a side street just along the Duna korzó. It wasn't clear at the time of research if the office would still be here or would move back to its former location (Dumtsa Jenő utca 22).

❶ Getting There & Away

The most convenient way to get to Szentendre is to take the commuter HÉV train from Buda's Batthyány tér metro station to the end of the line (one way about 450Ft, 45 minutes, every 10 to 15 minutes).

For ferry services from Budapest, see p379.

Vác

☑27 / POP 33,300

Lying on the eastern bank of the river, Vác (*vahts*) is an unpretentious town with interesting historic relics, from its collection of baroque town houses to its vault of 18th-century mummies. It's also the place to view glorious sunsets over the Börzsöny Hills reflected in the Danube.

Vác is an old town. Uvcenum – the town's Latin name – is mentioned in Ptolemy's 2nd-century *Geographia* as a river crossing on an important road. The town's medieval centre and Gothic cathedral were destroyed during the Turkish occupation; reconstruction under several bishops in the 18th century gave Vác its present baroque appearance.

❂ Sights

Március 15 tér   PUBLIC SQUARE

Március 15 tér, the main square, has the most colourful buildings in Vác. At the centre of the square, you'll find a **crypt** (Március 15 tér; adult/concession 500/250Ft; ☺9am-5pm Tue-Sun May-Sep), the only remnant of the medieval St Michael's Church. It contains a brief history of the church and town in the Middle Ages.

Dominating the square is the **Dominican church** (Fehérek temploma; Március 15 tér 19). The church is best known for holding a cache of fascinating mummies (see boxed text, above), a small collection of which remain on view at the nearby **Memento Mori** (Március 15 tér 19; adult/concession 1000/500Ft; ☺10-5pm Tue-Sun) exhibition. Also worth seeking out is the 1764 **Town Hall** (Március 15 tér 11), considered a baroque masterpiece. Opposite is the former **Bishop's Palace** (Március 15 tér 6). Next door, the **Vác Diocesan Museum** (Március 15 tér 4; adult/concession 500/200Ft; ☺2-6pm Wed-Fri, 10am-6pm Sat & Sun) displays a tiny portion of the treasures the Catholic Church amassed in Vác over the centuries.

Triumphal Arch   MONUMENT

North of the main square is the Triumphal Arch (Diadalív-kapu), the only such structure in Hungary. It was built by Bishop Migazzi in honour of a visit by Empress Maria Theresa and her husband Francis of Lorraine in 1764. From here, dip down one of the narrow side streets (such as Molnár utca) to the west for a stroll along the Danube. The **old city walls** and Gothic **Pointed Tower** (now a private home) are near Liszt Ferenc sétány 12.

FREE **Vác Cathedral** CHURCH
(Váci székesegyház; ⊙10am-noon & 1.30-5pm Mon-Sat, 7.30am-7pm Sun) Tree-lined Konstantin tér to the southeast is dominated by colossal Vác Cathedral, which dates from 1775 and was one of the first examples of neoclassical architecture in Hungary.

⌣ Sleeping & Eating

Vác is an easy day trip from Budapest, but there are some accommodation and dining options if you want to stay over.

Fónagy & Walter PENSION €
(☎310 682; www.fonagy.hu; Budapesti főút 36; r 9000Ft) Fónagy & Walter is a pension of the 'homely' variety – rooms are lovingly prepared, and the wine selection from the private cellar is outstanding.

Vörössipka BOUTIQUE HOTEL €€
(☎501 055; okktart@netelek.hu; Honvéd utca 14; s/d 9000/14,000Ft) If Fónagy & Walter is full, consider this plain hotel located away from the centre. Rooms lack character, but they're clean and definitely adequate for a night.

Váci Remete HUNGARIAN €€
(☎302 199; Fürdő utca; mains 2100-3600Ft) Worth seeking out for lunch or dinner. This eatery impresses with views of the Danube from its handsome terrace, a top-notch wine selection and a fine choice of Hungarian specialities.

Duna Presszó CAFE €
(Március 15 tér 13) Duna is the quintessential cafe: dark-wood furniture, chandeliers and the occasional resident drunk. If you are looking for cakes and arguably even better coffee, head to **Chococafe** (Március 15 tér 20) in a far corner of the square, next to the carillon.

☆ Entertainment

Imre Madách Cultural Centre THEATRE
(☎316 411; Dr Csányi László körút 63) This circular centre can help you with what's on in Vác, such as theatre, concerts and kids' shows.

ℹ Information

Main post office (Posta Park 2) Off Görgey Artúr utca.

Matrix (Rév köz; per hr 280Ft; ⊙9am-1pm Mon-Fri) Small internet cafe.

OTP Bank (Dunakanyar shopping centre, Széchenyi utca)

Tourinform (☎316 160; www.tourinformvac.hu; Március 15 tér 17; ⊙10am-7pm Mon-Fri, 10am-2pm Sat mid-Jun–Aug, 9am-5pm Mon-Fri, 10am-noon Sat Sep–mid-Jun) Helpful English-speaking staff. Located on the main square.

ℹ Getting There & Away

Car ferries (1460/420/420/350Ft per car/bicycle/adult/concession, every 15 to 30 minutes 6am to 8pm) cross over to Szentendre Island; a bridge connects the island's west bank with the mainland at Tahitótfalu. From there hourly buses run to Szentendre. You can also catch half-hourly buses (500Ft, 50 minutes) and trains (600Ft, 40 minutes) from Vác to Budapest.

Visegrád

☑26 / POP 1700

The spectacular vista from the ruins of Visegrád's (*vish*-eh-grahd) 13th-century citadel, high on a hill above a curve in the Danube, is what pulls visitors to this sleepy town. The first fortress here was built by the Romans as a border defence in the 4th century. Hungarian kings constructed a mighty citadel on the hilltop, and a lower castle near the river, after the 13th-century Mongol invasions. In the 14th century a royal palace was built on the flood plain at the foot of the hills, and in 1323 King Charles Robert of Anjou, whose claim to the local throne was being fiercely contested in Buda, moved the royal household here. For nearly two centuries Hungarian royalty alternated between Visegrád and Buda.

The destruction of Visegrád came first at the hands of the occupying Turks and then at the hands of the Habsburgs, who destroyed the citadel to prevent Hungarian independence fighters from using it. All trace of the royal palace, situated close to the town centre not far from the riverbank, was lost until 1934 when archaeologists, by following descriptions in literary sources, uncovered the ruins that you can visit today.

The small town has two distinct areas: one to the north around the Mahart ferry pier and another, the main town, about 1km to the south, near the Nagymaros ferry.

◉ Sights & Activities

Royal Palace RUIN
(Királyi Palota; Fő utca 29; adult/concession 1100/550Ft; ⊙9am-5pm Tue-Sun) The partial reconstruction of the royal palace, near the main town, only hints at the structure's former magnificence. Inside, a small museum is devoted to the history of the palace and its excavation and reconstruction. To find the palace from the Mahart ferry, walk south in the direction of the Nagymaros ferry about

400m and turn in toward town to find Fő utca. The entrance is across from a children's playground.

Solomon's Tower
MUSEUM

(Salamon Torony; adult/concession 700/350Ft; ☺9am-5pm Tue-Sun May-Sep) North of the main town and just a short walk from the Mahart ferry port, the ruin of Solomon's Tower was once part of a lower castle used to control river traffic. These days, the tower houses the royal palace's original Gothic fountain along with some town-history exhibits. To find the tower from the Mahart ferry, cross the road and then turn left onto a paved path, walking uphill.

Visegrád Citadel
RUIN

(Visegrád Cittadella; adult/concession 1400/700Ft; ☺9.30am-5.30pm daily mid-Mar–mid-Oct, 9.30am-5.30pm Sat & Sun mid-Oct–mid-Mar) From just beyond Solomon's Tower, you can climb a very steep path uphill to the Visegrád Citadel directly above. While the citadel (1259) ruins themselves are not as spectacular as their history, the view of the Danube Bend from the walls is well worth the climb. An alternative, less steep path leads to the citadel from the town centre area. Find the trail behind the Catholic church on Fő tér.

🛏 Sleeping & Eating

As with the other towns in the Danube Bend, Visegrád is an easy day trip from Budapest, so it's not necessary to stay over. **Visegrád Tours** (☏398 160; Rév utca 15; ☺8am-5.30pm), a travel agency in the town centre, provides information and books private rooms for around 5000Ft per person per night.

Hotel Honti
PENSION €

(☏398 120; www.hotelhonti.hu; Fő utca 66; s/d from €40/55;@) Honti is a friendly pension filled with homey rooms. Its large garden and table tennis are available for guest use, and bicycles can be hired for 2000Ft per day.

Reneszánsz
HUNGARIAN €€

(☏398 081; Fő utca 11; mains 2000-4000Ft) Step through this restaurant's doors to be greeted by a medieval banquet and men in tights with silly hats. If you're in the right mood, it can be quite a hoot. The convenient location is right across the street from the Mahart ferry port.

Don Vito Pizzeria
ITALIAN €

(Fő utca 83; mains 1300-2200Ft) This handsome pizza and pasta joint in the town centre offers a relaxing terrace out back or a more formal – and air-conditioned – main dining room inside.

ⓘ Getting There & Away

Frequent buses go to Visegrád from Budapest's Árpád híd bus station (600Ft, 1¼ hours, hourly), the Szentendre HÉV station (400Ft, 45 minutes, every 45 minutes) and Esztergom (400Ft, 40 minutes, hourly).

For ferry services from Budapest, see p379.

Esztergom

📱33 / POP 31,000

It's easy to see the attraction of Esztergom, even (or especially) from a distance. The city's massive basilica, sitting high above the town and Danube River, is an incredible sight, rising magnificently from its rural setting.

The significance of this town is even greater than its architectural appeal. The 2nd-century Roman emperor-to-be Marcus Aurelius wrote his famous *Meditations* while he camped here. In the 10th century, Stephen I, founder of the Hungarian state, was born and crowned at the cathedral. From the late 10th to the mid-13th centuries Esztergom served as the Hungarian royal seat. In 1543 the Turks ravaged the town and much of it was destroyed, only to be rebuilt in the 18th and 19th centuries.

◉ Sights & Activities

FREE **Esztergom Basilica**
CHURCH

(Esztergomi Bazilika; www.bazilika-esztergom.hu; Szent István tér 1; ☺6am-6pm) Hungary's largest church is the Esztergom Basilica. Perched on Castle Hill, its 72m-high central dome can be seen for many kilometres around. Reconstructed in the neoclassical style, much of the building dates from the 19th century; the oldest section is the red-marble 1510 **Bakócz Chapel** (Bakócz Kápolna). The **treasury** (kincsház; adult/concession 800/400Ft; ☺9am-4.30pm Mar-Oct, 11am-3.30pm Sat & Sun Nov & Dec) contains priceless objects, including ornate vestments and the 13th-century Hungarian coronation cross. If you're fit and up for a challenge, climb up to the massive **cupola** (admission 500Ft; ☺9am-4.45pm) for some amazing views of the river and town below. Among those buried in the **crypt** (altemplom; admission 200Ft; ☺9am-4.45pm) under the cathedral is Cardinal Mindszenty, who was imprisoned by the communists for refusing to allow Hungary's Catholic schools to be secularised.

Castle Museum
MUSEUM

(Vár Múzeum; adult/concession 840/420Ft; ☺10am-6pm Tue-Sun Apr-Oct, 10am-4pm Tue-Sun Nov-Mar) At the southern end of the hill is the Castle Museum, inside the reconstructed remnants of the medieval royal palace (1215), which was built upon previous castles. The earliest excavated sections on the hill date from the 2nd to 3rd centuries.

Watertown
HISTORICAL DISTRICT

Southwest of the cathedral along the banks of the Little Danube, narrow streets wind through the Víziváros (Watertown) district, home to the 1738 **Watertown Parish Church** (Víziváros Plébánia Templom) at the start of Berényi Zsigmond utca. The **Christian Museum** (Keresztény Múzeum; www.christianmuseum.hu; Berényi Zsigmond utca 2; adult/concession 800/400Ft; ☺10am-6pm Wed-Sun May-Oct, 11am-3pm Tue-Sun Nov, Dec, Mar & Apr) is in the adjacent Primate's Palace (1882). The stunning collection of medieval religious art includes a statue of the Virgin Mary from the 11th century.

Szent István strandfürdő'
SWIMMING POOL

(Kis-Duna sétány 1; adult/concession 1100/800Ft; ☺9am-7pm May-Sep) Just east of the Little Danube are outdoor thermal pools and stretches of grass 'beach'.

Aquasziget Esztergom
WATER PARK

(Táncsics Mihály utca 5; admission 2950Ft, after 4pm 2100Ft; ☺9am-8pm May-Sep) This modern water park, with pools and water slides, is a bit livelier than the Szent István pool and great for kids. You'll find it on the opposite side of the Little Danube canal from the main town, just across the Bottyán Bridge.

🛏 Sleeping & Eating

Although frequent transportation connections make Esztergom an easy day trip from Budapest, you might want to stop a night if you are going on to Slovakia. Contact Gran Tours (p341) about private rooms (3000Ft to 4000Ft per person) or apartments (from 9000Ft).

Self-caterers can shop at the **Match** (Bajcsy-Zsilinszky utca; ☺6.30am-8pm Mon-Fri, 6.30am-6pm Sat, 8am-noon Sun), next to the OTP Bank, or the small town **market** on Simor János utca.

Ria Panzió
PENSION €€

(☎313 115; www.riapanzio.com; Batthyány Lajos utca 11; s/d 9000/12,000Ft;@) This is a family-run place in a converted town house just down from the basilica. Relax on the terrace or arrange an adventure through the own-

ers: you can rent a bicycle or take a water-skiing trip on the Danube in summer. The owners are friendly; our only gripe was the lacklustre breakfast.

Alabárdos Panzió
PENSION €€

(☎312 640; www.alabardospanzio.hu; Bajcsy-Zsilinszky utca 49; s/d 8500/11,000Ft) Alabárdos isn't flashy but it does provide neat, tidy and sizeable accommodation. Offers unexpected extras like a laundry room and a small beauty parlour on the premises. The location is great if you want to be close to the cathedral: the hotel is at the base of Castle Hill.

Gran Camping
CAMPING GROUND €

(☎411 953; www.grancamping-fortanex.hu; Nagy-Duna sétány 3; camp sites per adult/concession/tent/tent & car 1300/700/1100/1400Ft, bungalows 16,000-22,000Ft, dm/d/tr 2900/13,000/14,000Ft; ☺May-Sep;⛵) Small but centrally located, this camping ground has space for 500 souls in various forms of accommodation, as well as a good-size swimming pool. It's a 10-minute walk along the Danube from the cathedral.

Padlisán
HUNGARIAN €

(☎311 212; Pázmány Péter utca 21; mains 1500-3000Ft) With a sheer rock face topped by a castle bastion as its backdrop, Padlisán has a dramatic setting. Thankfully its menu doesn't let the show down, featuring modern Hungarian dishes and imaginative salads.

Múzeumkert
HUNGARIAN €

(Batthyány Lajos utca 1; mains 1800-3600Ft) A combination restaurant and cocktail bar, just down from the Csú'ló'k Csárda, serves very good Hungarian dishes by day (try the tender veal stew in paprika sauce); by night it morphs into one of the few places near the basilica where you can relax over a beer or cocktail till late.

Csülök Csárda
HUNGARIAN €

(Batthyány Lajos utca 9; mains 1800-3600Ft) The Pork Knuckle Inn – guess the speciality here – is a charming eatery popular with visitors and locals alike. It serves up good home cooking (try the bean soup), in huge portions.

ⓘ Information

OTP Bank (Rákóczi tér 2-4) Does foreign-exchange transactions.

Post office (Arany János utca 2) Just off Széchenyi tér.

Gran Tours (☎502 001; Széchenyi tér 25; ☺8am-5pm Mon-Fri, 9am-noon Sat Jun-Aug, 8am-4pm Mon-Fri Sep-May) The best source of information in town.

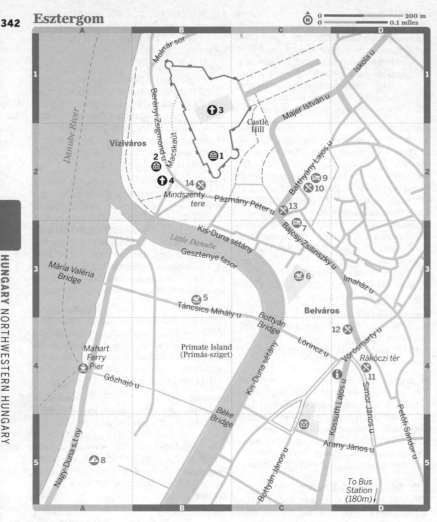

ℹ️ Getting There & Away

Buses run to/from Budapest's Árpád híd bus station (700Ft, 1½ hours) and to/from Visegrád (400Ft, 45 minutes) at least hourly. Hourly buses also link Esztergom to Szentendre (800Ft, 1½ hours).

The most comfortable way to get to Esztergom from Budapest is by rail. Trains depart from Budapest's Nyugati train station (1100Ft, 1½ hours) at least hourly. Cross the Mária Valéria Bridge into Štúrovo, Slovakia, and you can catch a train to Bratislava, which is 1½ hours away.

For ferry services from Budapest, see p379.

NORTHWESTERN HUNGARY

A visit to this region is a boon for anyone wishing to see remnants of Hungary's Roman legacy, medieval heritage and baroque splendour. This swath of land was fortunate in largely avoiding the Ottoman destruction wrought on the country in the 16th and 17th centuries. Its seminal towns – Sopron and Győr – managed to save their medieval centres from total devastation, and exploring their cobbled streets and hidden courtyards is a magical experience. They also house a

Esztergom

cornucopia of baroque architecture, something rare in Hungary. Equally rewarding are reminders of Roman settlement, and the region's natural beauty.

Győr

📱96 / POP 130,000

Not many tourists make the effort to stop at Győr (German: Raab), which is all the more reason to visit. This large city with the tricky name (pronounced *jyeur*) is a surprisingly splendid place, with a medieval heart hidden behind a commercial facade.

Midway between Budapest and Vienna, Győr sits at the point where the Mosoni-Danube, Rábca and Rába Rivers meet. This was the site of a Roman town named Arrabona. In the 11th century, Stephen I established a bishopric here, and in the 16th century a fortress was erected to hold back the Turks. The Ottomans captured Győr in

1594 but were able to hold on to it for only four years. For that reason Győr is known as the 'dear guard', watching over the nation through the centuries.

◉ Sights & Activities

Bécsí kapu tér   PUBLIC SQUARE
The enchanting 1725 **Carmelite Church** (Karmelita Templom; Bécsí kapu tér) and many fine baroque palaces line riverfront Bécsí kapu tér. On the northwestern side of the square are the fortifications built in the 16th century to stop the Turks. A short distance to the east is **Napoleon House** (Napoleon-ház; Király utca 4), named after the French military leader (see boxed text below). Walk the old streets and stop in at a pavement cafe or two.

FREE **Basilica**   CATHEDRAL
(Bazilika; Apor Vilmos püspök tere; ⊗8am-noon & 2-6pm) North up Káptalan-domb (Chapter Hill), in the oldest part of Győr, is the solid baroque Basilica. Situated on the hill, it was originally Romanesque, but most of what you see inside dates from the 17th and 18th centuries. Don't miss the Gothic **Héderváry Chapel** (Héderváry-kápolna) at the back of the cathedral, which contains a glittering 15th-century gold bust of King (and St) Ladislas.

Diocesan Treasury & Library   MUSEUM
(Egyházmegyei Kincstár és Könyvtár; adult/concession 700/400Ft; ⊗10am-4pm Tue-Sun Mar-Oct) East of the Basilica is the Diocesan Treasury & Library. Of particular value in its collection are the Gothic chalices and Renaissance mitre embroidered with pearls, but stealing the show is the precious library, containing almost 70,000 volumes printed before 1850. At the bottom of the hill on Jedlik Ányos utca is the **Ark of the Covenant** (Frigyláda), a statue dating from 1731. From here you can head north to a bridge overlooking the junction of the city's three rivers.

NAPOLEONIC PAUSE

France's Napoleon Bonaparte once spent a night in Hungary – in Győr to be precise. The vertically challenged military commander slept over at Király utca 4, due east of Bécsí kapu tér, on 31 August 1809. The building is now called Napoleon-ház (Napoleon House), appropriately enough. And why did Bonaparte choose Győr to make his grand entrée into Hungary? The city was near the site of the Battle of Raab, which had taken place just 11 weeks earlier between Franco-Italian and Austrian–Hungarian armies. Bonaparte's side won, and an inscription on the Arc de Triomphe in Paris still recalls 'la bataille de Raab'.

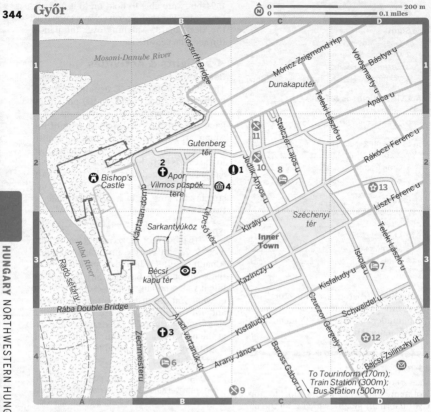

0   200 m
0   0.1 miles

Mosoni-Danube River

Kossuth Bridge

Gutenberg tér

Bishop's Castle

Apor Vilmos püspök tere

Sarkantyúköz

Bécsi kapu tér

Rába River

Radó sétány

Rába Double Bridge

Móricz Zsigmond rkp

Dunakaputér

Vörösmarty u

Bástya u

Apáca u

Rákóczi Ferenc u

Steidzer Lajos u

Teleki László u

Jedlik Ányos u

Liszt Ferenc u

Széchenyi tér

Inner Town

Király u

Lépcső köz

Kazinczy u

Kisfaludy u

Iskola u

Teleki László u

Czuczor Gergely u

Schweidel u

Arany János u

Kisfaludy u

Barross Gábor u

Bajcsy-Zsilinszky út

To Tourinform (170m);
Train Station (300m);
Bus Station (500m)

Győr

◎ Sights

1 Ark of the Covenant	C2
2 Basilica	B2
3 Carmelite Church	B4
4 Diocesan Treasury & Library	B2
5 Napoleon House	B3

🛏 Sleeping

6 Hotel Klastrom	B4
7 Kertész Pension	D3
8 Soho Café & Pension	C2

🍴 Eating

9 Kaiser Supermarket	C4
10 La Máreda	C2
11 Matróz	C2

✪ Entertainment

12 Győr National Theatre	D4
13 Rómer Ház	D2

Rába Quelle   SWIMMING POOL
(☑514 900; Fürdő tér 1; adult/concession per day 2400/1800Ft, per 3hr 1950/1550Ft; ⏱thermal baths 9am-8.30pm, pool 8am-8pm Mon-Sat) The water temperature in the pools at thermal bath Rába Quelle ranges from 29°C to 38°C. You can also take advantage of its fitness and wellness centres.

🎊 Festivals & Events

Győr has a couple of festivals held every summer that are worth catching. The **Hungarian Dance Festival** (www.magyartanc fesztival.hu) is held in late June, and the **Győr Summer Cultural Festival** runs from late June to late July.

🛏 Sleeping & Eating

The **Kaiser supermarket** (Arany János utca 16; ⏱7am-7pm Mon-Fri, 6.30am-3pm Sat, 8am-1pm Sun) is the place to head for self-catering purposes. Széchenyi tér, the town's outsized

PANNONHALMA ABBEY

Take half a day and make the short trip from Győr to the ancient and impressive **Pannonhalma Abbey** (Pannonhalmi Főapátság; ☎570 191; www.bences.hu; Vár utca 1; foreign-language tours adult/student/family 2500/1500/6000Ft; ☺9am-4pm Tue-Sun Apr & Oct–mid-Nov, 9am-5pm daily Jun-Sep, 10am-3pm Tue-Sun mid-Nov–Mar), now a Unesco World Heritage site. Most buildings in the complex date from the 13th to the 18th centuries; highlights include the Romanesque basilica (1225), the Gothic cloister (1486) and the impressive collection of ancient texts in the library. Because it's an active monastery, the abbey must be visited with a guide. English and German tours leave at 11.20am and 1.20pm from April to September, with an extra tour at 3.20pm from June to September. Between October and March, foreign-language tours must be booked in advance.

There are buses to the abbey from Győr at 8am, 10am and noon (around 400Ft, 30 minutes, 21km).

central square, is the perfect place to people-watch over a coffee or ice-cream cone.

Hotel Klastrom BOUTIQUE HOTEL €€€
(☎516 910; www.klastrom.hu; Zechmeister utca 1; s/d/tr 12,500/17,500/20,000Ft; ⏸) This delightful three-star hotel occupies a 300-year-old Carmelite convent south of Bécsi kapu tér. Rooms are charming and bright, and extras include a sauna, a solarium, a pub with a vaulted ceiling, and a restaurant with seating in a leafy and peaceful garden.

Kertész Pension PENSION €€
(☎317 461; www.kerteszpanzio.com; Iskola utca 11; s/d/tr/q 8000/12,000/14,100/16,000Ft) The 'Gardener' has very simple rooms on offer, but it's well located in downtown Győr and staff couldn't be friendlier.

Soho Café & Pension PENSION €
(☎550 465; www.sohocafe.hu; Kenyér köz 7; s/d/tr 7000/10,000/13,000Ft) Győr's cheapest in-town pension has simple no-frills rooms and two big pluses: it's just a block from Széchenyi tér and has a ground-floor cafe with free wi-fi, friendly staff, and good coffee and beer.

TOP CHOICE Matróz HUNGARIAN €
(☎336 208; Dunakapu tér 3; mains 1100-2200Ft) Matróz makes the best damn fish dishes around, from warming carp soup to delicate pike-perch fillets. The handsome vaulted brick cellar, complete with dark-blue tiled oven and nautical memorabilia, completes this wonderful little eatery.

La Maréda INTERNATIONAL €€
(☎510 982; Apáca utca 4; mains 1600-3500Ft) If the wait for a table is too long over at Matróz, try this upmarket bistro that serves Hungarian specialties like duck and turkey

breast but adds a gourmet touch (such as topping the turkey breast with baked apple and smoked cheese).

☆ Entertainment

A good source of information for what's on in Győr is the free magazine *Győri Est*.

Győr National Theatre THEATRE
(Győri Nemzeti Színház; ☎520 600; Czuczor Gergely utca 7) The celebrated Győr Ballet and the city's opera company and philharmonic orchestra all perform at this modern venue. Tourinform can help with performance schedules.

Rómer Ház BAR & CINEMA
(☎550 850; www.romerhaz.eu; Teleki László utca 21) One-stop shop for entertainment, featuring an independent cinema upstairs, and regular live concerts and club nights down in the dungeon.

ℹ Information

Darius Café (Czuczor Gergely utca 6; per hr 210Ft; ☺1-9pm Mon-Fri, 3-10pm Sat) Internet access on several computers in a convivial atmosphere and decent coffee to boot.

Main post office (Bajcsy-Zsilinszky út 46; ☺8am-6pm Mon-Fri) There's a branch office at the main train station.

OTP Bank (Baross Gábor 16)

Tourinform (☎311 771; www.gyortourism.hu; Árpad út 32; ☺9am-6pm Jun-Aug, 9am-5pm Mon-Fri, 9am-1pm Sat Sep-May) Small but helpful tourist office located in a small kiosk astride Baross Gábor utca.

ℹ Getting There & Away

Buses travel to Budapest (2480Ft, two hours, hourly), Pannonhalma (460Ft, 30 minutes, half-hourly), Esztergom (1830Ft, 2½ hours, one daily) and Balatonfüred (1800Ft, 2½ hours, six daily).

Győr is well connected by express train to Budapest's Keleti and Déli train stations (2480Ft, 1½ hours, half-hourly), and 10 daily trains connect Győr with Vienna's Westbahnhof (6000Ft, 1½ hours).

Sopron

📱99 / POP 59,000

Sopron (*shop*-ron) is an attractive border town with a history that stretches back to Roman times and beyond. It boasts some well-preserved Roman ruins and a fetching medieval square, bounded by the original town walls, that invites an hour or two of aimless meandering. That said, in summer, it's teeming with day-trippers from Austria (Vienna is only 70km away) who come here for inexpensive dental work and the inevitable *kaffee und kuchen* before and after. This is one place in Hungary where any scrap of high-school German you can pull out will be amply rewarded. On our visit, even the tourist office couldn't muster any English.

The Mongols and Turks never got this far so, unlike many Hungarian cities, numerous medieval buildings remain in use. The town's close history with Austria goes

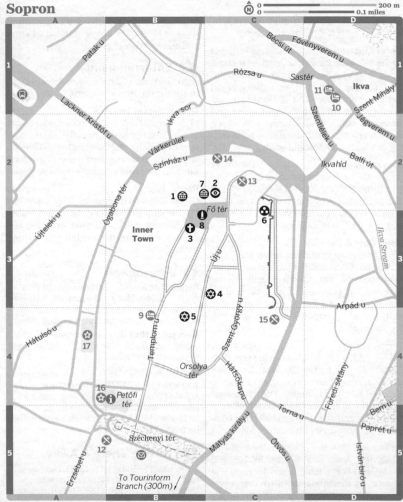

Sopron

back centuries and Sopron could easily have landed on the other side of the border if it weren't for a referendum in 1921 in which town residents voted to remain part of Hungary. The rest of Bürgenland (the region to which Sopron used to belong) went to Austria. The area is known for its good red wines, such as Kékfrancos, and once you've strolled through the quiet backstreets, you can opt for a glass or two at a local cafe or restaurant.

Sopron Festival Weeks (www.prokultura. hu) runs from late June to mid-July.

◉ Sights & Activities

Fő tér   PUBLIC SQUARE
Fő tér is the main square in Sopron; there are several museums, monuments and churches scattered around it. At the time of research much of the square was fenced off as workers were repairing the cobblestones; several attractions, including the massive **Firewatch Tower** (Tűztorony), were closed. It wasn't clear if the tower would reopen by 2011, but be prepared for some minor inconveniences. The 60m-high tower rises above the Old Town's northern gate and is visible from all around. The building is a true architectural hybrid: the 2m-thick square base, built on a Roman gate, dates from the 12th

century, the middle cylindrical and arcaded balcony was built in the 16th century and the baroque spire was added in 1680. If it's open, you can climb to the top for views of the Alps. In the centre of Fő tér is the 1701 **Trinity Column** (Szentháromság Ozlop). Just off the square, along the town wall, are the small **open-air ruins** (admission free; ◷24hr), with reconstructed Roman walls and 2nd-century houses dating from the time when Sopron was a tiny Roman outpost known as Scarbantia. On the north side of the square are Storno House and Fabricus House, each holding a pair of museums.

Storno House   MUSEUM
(Storno Ház; Fő tér 8) This house has a so-so exhibit on Sopron's more recent history on the 1st floor, but the floor above holds the more worthy **Storno Collection** (adult/concession 1000/500Ft; ◷10am-6pm Tue-Sun Apr-Sep, 2-6pm Tue-Sun Oct-Mar), displaying the interiors of a successful 19th-century family who furnished their apartment with priceless found objects from the Romanesque and Gothic periods.

Fabricius House   MUSEUM
(Fabricius Ház; Fő tér 6) Fabricius is home to a fascinating **archaeological exhibition** (adult/concession 700/350Ft; ◷10am-6pm Tue-Sun Apr-Sep, 10am-2pm Tue-Sun Oct-Mar), with stone sculptures and other remains recovered from Roman times. Upstairs, there is an exhibition dedicated to **urban apartments** (adult/concession 800/400Ft; ◷10am-6pm Tue-Sun Apr-Sep, 10am-2pm Tue-Sun Oct-Mar), where you can see how Sopron's residents lived in the 17th and 18th centuries.

Goat Church   CHURCH
(Kecske Templom; Templom utca 1; admission free; ◷8am-9pm mid-Apr–Sep, 8am-6pm Oct–mid-Apr) Near the centre of Fő tér is the 13th-century Goat Church, whose name comes from the heraldic animal of its chief benefactor. Just off the main nave is the **Chapter Hall** (Káptalan Terem), part of a 14th-century Franciscan monastery, with frescos and stone carvings.

Synagogues   SYNAGOGUES
The **New Synagogue** (Új Zsinagóga; Új utca 11) and **Old Synagogue** (Ó Zsinagóga; Új utca 22; adult/concession 600/300Ft; ◷10am-6pm Tue-Sun May-Oct), both built in the 14th century, are reminders of the town's once substantial Jewish population. The latter contains a museum of Jewish life.

🛏 Sleeping & Eating

For self-catering supplies, head for Match (Várkerület 100; ⊗6.30am-7pm Mon-Fri, 6.30am-3pm Sat) supermarket.

TOP CHOICE Wieden Pension PENSION €
(☑523 222; www.wieden.hu; Sas tér 13; s/d/tr/apt from 7700/10,900/12,900/11,900Ft;@) Sopron's cosiest pension is located in an attractive old town house within easy walking distance of the Inner Town. The rooms are sparsely furnished but comfortable; the friendly reception desk will go out of its way to make you feel at home.

Hotel Wollner BOUTIQUE HOTEL €€
(☑524 400; www.wollner.hu; Templom utca 20; s/d/apt from €75/90/110;@) A worthy splurge option in the heart of the Old Town, with elegant period doubles hidden away in a 300-year-old baroque town palace. The courtyard restaurant is one of the best in town.

Jégverem Pension PENSION €
(☑510 113; www.jegverem.hu; Jégverem utca 1; s/d 6900/8900Ft) An excellent and central bet, with five suitelike rooms in an 18th-century ice cellar in the Ikva district. Even if you're not staying here, try the terrace restaurant for enormous portions of pork, chicken and fish dishes.

Vákació Vendégház HOSTEL €
(☑338 502; www.vakacio-vendeghazak.hu; Ady Endre út 31; dm 2800Ft) Cheap lodgings not far west of the town centre. Rooms are clean and furnished with two to 10 beds; bus 10 will drop you off not far from the front door. Phone in advance for reservations; note the reception opens only at 4pm.

Graben HUNGARIAN €
(Várkerület 8; mains 1000-1800Ft) The secluded garden terrace is a welcoming lunch or dinner spot for well-prepared Hungarian dishes, including fresh lightly baked pike-perch. In winter dine below in a Gothic cellar.

Generális-Corvinus INTERNATIONAL €
(Fő tér 7-8; mains 1100-2100Ft) This large restaurant is in reality two eateries – one serving decent Hungarian cuisine, the other acceptable pizzas. The tables on the main square are a welcome respite for refreshment and people-watching.

Dömöröi CAFE €
(Széchenyi tér 13) In a city that takes its cultural cues from Vienna, what could be more natural than a Viennese-style coffeehouse? Arguably the best ice cream in town.

☆ Entertainment

Ferenc Liszt Conference & Cultural Centre CONCERT HALL
(Liszt Ferenc Kulturális Központ; ☑517 517; Liszt Ferenc tér) A concert hall, cafe and exhibition space all rolled into one. The information desk has the latest on classical music and other cultural events in town.

Petőfi Theatre THEATRE
(☑517 517; www.prokultura.hu; Petőfi tér 1) This beautiful building with mosaics on its facade is Sopron's leading theatre.

ℹ Information

Main post office (Széchenyi tér 7-10)

OTP Bank (Várkerület 96a)

Tourinform main branch (☑517 560; sopron@tourinform.hu; Liszt Ferenc utca 1; ⊗9am-6pm daily mid-Jun–Aug, 9am-5pm Mon-Fri & 9am-noon Sat Sep–mid-Jun); southern branch (☑505 438; Deák tér 45; ⊗9am-5pm Mon-Fri, 9am-noon Apr-Oct) Both branches offer free internet access and a plethora of tourist information.

ℹ Getting There & Away

There are two buses a day to Budapest (3300Ft, 3¾ hours), and seven to Győr (1500Ft, two hours). The bus station is northwest of the Old Town on Lackner Kristóf utca.

Trains run to Budapest's Keleti train station (3500Ft, 2¾ hours, eight daily) via Győr. You can also travel to Vienna's Meidling station (4200Ft, three hours, up to 15 daily), pending reconstruction of Vienna's Südbahnhof sometime in 2012.

LAKE BALATON

Central Europe's largest expanse of fresh water is Lake Balaton, covering 600 sq km. The main activities include swimming, sailing and sunbathing, but the lake is also popular with cyclists lured here by the more than 200km of marked bike paths that encircle the lake.

The southern shore is mostly a forgettable jumble of tacky resorts, with the exception of party town Siófok. The northern shore, however, is yin to the southern's yang. Here the pace of life is more refined, and the forested hills of the Balaton Uplands National Park create a wonderful backdrop. Historical towns such as Keszthely and Balatonfüred dot the landscape, while Tihany, a peninsula cutting the lake almost in half, is home to an important historical church.

Siófok

📞 84 / POP 23,900

Siófok (*shee*-a-folk) is officially known as 'Hungary's summer capital' – unofficially it's called 'Hungary's Ibiza'. In July and August, nowhere in the country parties as hard or stays up as late as this lakeside resort, which attracts an ever-increasing number of international DJs and their avid followers. Outside the summer months Siófok returns to relative normality.

Greater Siófok stretches for some 17km, as far as the resort of Balatonvilágos (once reserved exclusively for communist honchos) to the east and Balatonszéplak to the west.

◉ Sights & Activities

There are rowing boats and sailing boats for hire at various locations along the lake, including Nagy Strand. Lake cruises run from late May to mid-September, generally daily at 10am, 11.30am, 1pm, 2.30pm, 4pm and 5.30pm. There are additional cruises at 11am, 2pm and 4pm daily from late April to late May.

Water Tower MONUMENT
(víztorny; Szabadság tér) The town's wooden water tower, built in 1912, affords an impressive view out over the town and lake beyond. As we were researching this guide the tower was closed for renovation. It was expected to reopen by 2012.

Nagy Strand BEACH
(adult/concession 1000/500Ft) Nagy Strand, 'Big Beach', is centre stage on Petőfi sétány; free concerts are often held here on summer evenings. There are many more managed swimming areas along the lakeshore, which cost around the same as Nagy Strand.

Galerius SWIMMING POOL
(📞506 580; www.galerius-furdo.hu, in Hungarian; Szent László utca 183; pools adult/concession 2900/2500Ft, sauna & pools 3400Ft; ⏰9am-9pm) Galerius is 4km west of downtown Siófok. It offers a plethora of indoor thermal pools, saunas and massages.

🛏 Sleeping & Eating

Prices quoted are for the high season in July and August. Tourinform can help find you a private room (prices starting around €15 per person), or an apartment for slightly more.

Mala Garden BOUTIQUE HOTEL €€€
TOP CHOICE (📞506 687; www.malagarden.hu; Petőfi sétány 15a; r 21,900-36,900Ft;❋) Most of Siófok's accommodation options pale in comparison with this gorgeous boutique hotel. It's reminiscent of Bali, with Indonesian art lining the walls, a small manicured flower garden at the rear of the hotel and an excellent restaurant serving Asian cuisine.

Hotel Yacht Club BOUTIQUE HOTEL €€
(📞311 161; www.hotel-yachtclub.hu; Vitorlás utca 14; s/d €52/112; ❋@❋) Overlooking the harbour is this excellent little hotel with cosy rooms, some of which have balconies overlooking the lake, and a modern wellness centre. Bicycles can be hired.

Siófok Város College HOSTEL €
(📞312 244; www.siofokvaroskollegiuma.sulinet.hu; Petőfi sétány 1; dm 2700Ft) Close to the action in central Siófok, it's hard to beat this basic college accommodation for price and location.

Roxy INTERNATIONAL €
(Szabadság tér; mains 1200-3000Ft) Pseudo-rustic restaurant–pub in the commercial centre at Szabadság tér attracts diners with a wide range of international dishes and surprisingly imaginative Hungarian mains.

☆ Entertainment

South Balaton Cultural Centre (📞311 855; Fő tér 2), Siófok's main cultural venue stages concerts, dance performances and plays. However, most visitors to Siófok are interested in more energetic entertainment. Turnover of bars and clubs is high, but the following manage to attract punters year after year:

Flőrt CLUB
(www.flort.hu; Sió utca 4) Well-established club with visiting DJs and light shows.

Palace CLUB
(www.palace.hu; Deák Ferenc utca 2) Hugely popular club. Accessible by free bus that leaves from the Palace cafe along the beach promenade (Petőfi sétány).

Renegade BAR
(Petőfi sétány 9) Wild pub near the beach; table dancing and live music are common.

❶ Information

Main post office (Fő utca 186)

OTP Bank (Szabadság tér 10a)

Tourinform (📞310 117; tourinform@siofokportal. hu; Fő utca 174-176; ⏰8am-7pm Mon-Fri, 10am-7pm Sat & Sun mid-Jun–mid-Sep, 8am-4pm

Mon-Fri, 9am-noon Sat mid-Sep–mid-Jun). Hands out city maps and can advise on and book rooms in season starting at about 3500Ft per person. Note the office is normally based in an old *víztorony* (water tower), but was temporarily relocated inside the Atrium shopping centre (until late 2011) while the water tower undergoes repair work.

❶ Getting There & Away

From April to October, at least four daily passenger ferries run between Siófok and Balatonfüred (1360Ft, 50 minutes), some of which carry on to Tihany. Up to eight ferries follow the same route in July and August.

The bus and train stations are in Millennium Park just off Fő utca. Buses serve a lot of destinations from Siófok, but you'll find the more frequent train connections of more use. Trains to Nagykanizsa pass through all the resorts on the southern edge of the lake, and there are several daily train connections to and from Budapest (2160Ft, two hours).

Balatonfüred

☑87 / POP 13,000

Walking the hillside streets, you'll catch glimpses of the easy grace that 18th- and 19th-century Balatonfüred (*bal*-ah-tahn fuhr-ed) enjoyed. In those days the wealthy and famous built large villas on its tree-lined streets, hoping to take advantage of the health benefits of the town's thermal waters. In more recent times, the lake frontage has received a massive makeover and now sports the most stylish marina on the lake. The hotels here are a bit cheaper than those on the neighbouring Tihany peninsula, making this a good base for exploring. Most of the action, including the beaches, hotels and restaurants, are clustered along the shoreline.

◉ Sights & Activities

Cruises
BOAT RIDES

The park along the central shore, near the ferry pier, is worth a promenade. You can take a one-hour **pleasure cruise** (☑342 230; www.balatonihajozas.hu; ferry pier; adult/concession 1400/600Ft) four times a day, from late May to mid-September. The **retro disco boat** (disco hajo; ☑342 230; www.balatonihajozas. hu; ferry pier; cruise 1800Ft), a two-hour cruise with music and drinks, leaves at 9pm Tuesday, Thursday and Friday.

Kisfaludy Strand
BEACH

(Aranyhíd sétány; adult/concession 550/350Ft; ⊙8am-6pm mid-May–mid-Sep) Along the foot-path 800m northeast of the pier, Kisfaludy Strand is a relatively sandy beach. You can explore the waterfront by bike (see p351).

Kossuth Forrásvíz
SPA

The heart of the old spa town is Gyógy tér, where Kossuth Forrásvíz (Kossuth Spring, 1853) dispenses slightly sulphurous water that people actually drink for health. Don't stray far from a bathroom afterwards.

⌂ Sleeping

Prices fluctuate throughout the year and usually peak between early July and late August; high-season prices are quoted here. **SunCity Tours** (☑06 30 947 2679; Csokonai utca 1) can help with finding you a place, as can **Fontaine Room Service** (☑343 673; Honvéd utca 11). There are lots of houses with rooms for rent on the streets north of Kisfaludy Beach.

Hotel Blaha Lujza
BOUTIQUE HOTEL €€

(☑581 219; www.hotelblaha.hu; Blaha Lujza utca 4; s/d €40/60) This was once the holiday home of the much-loved 19th-century Hungarian actress–singer Blaha Lujza. Its rooms are a little compact but very comfy.

Villa Balaton
BOUTIQUE HOTEL €

(☑788 290; www.balatonvilla.hu; Deák Ferenc utca 38; s/d 6250/12,500Ft) The large, bright rooms of this pastel-yellow villa uphill from the lake are available for rent. Each has its own balcony overlooking a sunny garden and grapevines, and guests can make use of the well-equipped kitchen.

Füred Camping
CAMPING GROUND €

(☑580 241; fured@balatontourist.hu; Széchenyi utca 24; camp sites per adult/concession/tent 1600/1200/5500Ft, bungalows/caravans from 17,000/23,000Ft; ⊙mid-Apr–early Oct) Sprawling beachfront complex 1km west of the centre, with water-sport rentals, swimming pools, tennis courts, a restaurant and a convenience store.

✗ Eating & Drinking

La Riva
FINE DINING €€

(Zákonyi Ferenc sétány 4; mains 1500-4000Ft) Taking pride of place on the modern marina's waterfront is La Riva, a restaurant that combines imaginative cooking and the prospect of a relaxed table over the water. Pasta and pizza are the mainstays of the menu, but don't overlook the daily blackboard specials.

Balaton
HUNGARIAN €

(Kisfaludy utca 5; mains 1000-3000Ft) This cool, leafy oasis amid all the hubbub is set back

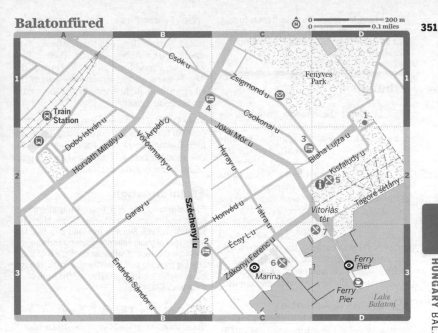

Balatonfüred

from the lake in a shaded park area. It serves generous portions and, like so many restaurants in town, has an extensive fish selection.

Stefánia Vitorlás   HUNGARIAN €
(Tagore sétány 1; mains 1500-3000Ft) Enormous wooden eatery sitting right on the lake's edge at the foot of the pier. Watch the yachts sail in and out of the harbour while enjoying Hungarian cuisine and local wine.

Karolina   CAFE €
(Zákonyi Ferenc sétány 4) Karolina, just to the left of La Riva, is a sophisticated cafe-bar

that serves excellent coffee, teas and local wines.

ℹ Information

OTP Bank (Petőfi Sándor utca 8)

Post office (Zsigmond utca 14; ☉8am-4pm Mon-Fri)

Tourinform (✆580 480; balatonfured@tourin form.hu; Kisfaludy utca 1; ☉9am-7pm Mon-Fri, to 6pm Sat, to 1pm Sun Jul & Aug, 9am-5pm Mon-Fri, to 1pm Sat Jun & Sep, 9am-4pm Mon-Fri Oct-May) Helpful tourist office.

ℹ Getting There & Around

The adjacent bus and train stations are on Dobó István utca, about 1km uphill from the lake. Buses to Tihany (250Ft, 30 minutes) leave every 30 minutes or so throughout the day. Several buses daily head to the northwestern lakeshore towns including Keszthely (1200Ft, 1½ hours).

Budapest-bound buses (2400Ft) depart from Balatonfüred four times daily and take between two and three hours to get there. Trains (2480Ft, three daily) take about as long. There are a number of towns on the train line with 'Balaton' or 'Füred' somewhere in their name, so double-check which station you're getting off at.

From April to September, half a dozen daily ferries ply the water from Balatonfüred to Tihany (1040Ft, 30 minutes) and Siófok (1360Ft, 50 minutes).

A good way to explore the waterfront is to rent a bike from **Tempo 21** (☑480 671; Deák Ferenc utca 56; per hr/day 350/2400Ft; ☺9am-6pm mid-May–mid-Sep).

Tihany

☑87 / POP 1500

The place with the greatest historical significance on Lake Balaton is Tihany (*tee-hah-nee*), a hilly peninsula jutting 5km into the lake. Activity here is centred on the tiny town of the same name, which is home to the celebrated Abbey Church. Contrasting with this are the hills and marshy meadows of the peninsula's nature reserve, which has an isolated, almost wild feel to it.

The peninsula has beaches on both its eastern and western coasts and a big resort complex on its southern tip. However, you can easily shake off the tourist hordes by going hiking. Bird-watchers, bring your binoculars: the trails have abundant avian life.

⊙ Sights & Activities

Abbey Church   CHURCH
(Apátság Templom; adult/concession 800/400Ft; ☺9am-6pm May-Sep, 10am-5pm Apr & Oct, 10am-3pm Nov-Mar) You can spot twin-towered Abbey Church, dating from 1754, from a long way off. Entombed in the crypt is the abbey's founder, King Andrew I. The admission fee includes entry to the attached **Abbey Museum** (Apátsági Múzeum). Behind the church a path leads to outstanding views.

Open-air Folk Museum   MUSEUM
(Szabadtéri Néprajzi Múzeum; Pisky sétány 10; adult/concession 400/300Ft; ☺10am-6pm May-Sep) Follow the pathway along the ridge north from the church in the village to reach the tiny Open-air Folk Museum.

⫚ Sleeping & Eating

Tihany is an easy day trip (by bus or boat) from Balatonfüred, so there's no reason to stay over unless you're hiking. If you are looking for lodgings, one option is to look for a '*zimmer frei*' (German for 'room for rent') sign on the small streets north of the church.

Adler   BOUTIQUE HOTEL €€
(☑538 000; www.adler-tihany.hu; Felsőkopaszhegyi utca 1a; r €45-56, apt €72-99; ❋☒) Features large, whitewashed rooms with balconies, and there's a spa bath, sauna and restaurant on the premises.

TOP CHOICE **Ferenc Pince**   HUNGARIAN €€
(☑448 575; Cserhegy 9; mains from 1500Ft; ☺noon-11pm Wed-Mon) About 2km south of the Abbey Church, Ferenc is a wine- and food-lover's dream. During the day, its terrace offers expansive views of the lake, while at night the lights of the southern shore are visible.

Rege Café   CAFE €
(Kossuth Lajos utca 22; ☺10am-6pm) From its high vantage point near the Abbey Church, this modern cafe has an unsurpassed panoramic view of Lake Balaton.

ⓘ Information

Tourinform (☑448 804; tihany@tourinform.hu; Kossuth Lajos utca 20; ☺9am-7pm Mon-Fri, 10am-6pm Sat & Sun mid-Jun–mid-Sep, shorter hours rest of year) sells hiking maps and film, and provides tourist information. Note that the office is tricky to find from the main road, though it's easily visible from just beyond the front of the Abbey Church.

ⓘ Getting There & Away

Buses travel along the 14km of mostly lakeside road between Tihany village and Balatonfüred's train and bus stations (280Ft, 30 minutes) at least 13 times a day.

The harbour where ferries heading to and from Balatonfüred dock is a couple of kilometres downhill from the village of Tihany, which occupies a bluff on the eastern edge of the peninsula. Passenger ferries sail between Tihany and Balatonfüred from April to September (1040Ft, 30 minutes, six daily). You can follow a steep path up to the village from the pier to reach the Abbey Church.

Keszthely

☑83 / POP 21,800

At the very western end of the Balaton sits Keszthely (*kest*-hey), a place of grand townhouses and a gentle ambience far removed from the lake's tourist hot spots. Its small, shallow beaches are well suited to families, and there are enough accommodation options to suit most holidaymakers. Of its handful of museums and historical buildings, nothing tops the Festetics Palace, a lavish baroque residence. The town lies just over 1km northwest of the lake and with the exception of a few guesthouses, almost everything stays open year-round. If you visit in May, you might catch the town's annual Balaton Festival.

The bus and train stations, side by side at the end of Mártírok útja, are fairly close to

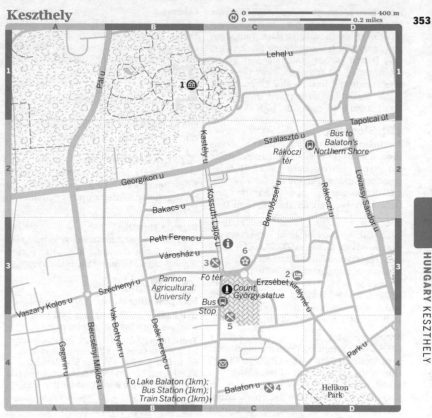

Keszthely

⊙ Sights
1 Festetics Palace B1

🛏 Sleeping
2 Bacchus C3

🍴 Eating
3 CBA C3
4 Lakoma C4
5 Pelso Café C4

⊛ Entertainment
6 Balaton Theatre C3

the water. The beaches and the ferry pier lie to the southeast through a small park. The main commercial centre, where everything happens, is about 500m north of the bus and trains stations uphill, along the main street, Kossuth Lajos utca.

⊙ Sights & Activities

Festetics Palace   PALACE
(Festetics Kastély; ☎312 190; Kastély utca 1; adult/concession 2000/1000Ft; ⊗9am-6pm Jul & Aug, 10am-4pm Sep-Jun) The glimmering white, 100-room Festetics Palace was first built in 1745; the wings were extended out from the original building 150 years later. About a dozen rooms in the one-time residence have been turned into a museum. Many of the decorative arts in the gilt salons were imported from England in the mid-1800s. The **Helikon Library** (Helikon Könyvtár), in the baroque south wing, is known for its 100,000 volumes and its hand-carved furniture, crafted by a local artisan. To reach the palace, follow Kossuth Lajos utca, the long pedestrian street in the centre of the Old Town.

Lakeside Area   BEACH
The lakeside area centres on the long ferry pier. From March to October you can take

a one-hour **pleasure cruise** (☑312 093; www.
balatonihajozas.hu; ferry pier; adult/concession
1400/600Ft) on the lake at 11am, 1pm, 3pm
and 5pm daily. If you're feeling like a swim,
City Beach (Városi Strand) is just to the
southwest of the ferry pier, near plenty of
beer stands and food booths. **Libás Beach**
(Libás Strand) is smaller and quieter. It's
about 200m northeast of the pier.

🛏 Sleeping

Tourinform can help find private rooms
(from 3500Ft per person). Otherwise, strike
out on your own (particularly along Móra Ferenc utca) and keep an eye out for '*szoba kiadó*' or '*zimmer frei*' signs (Hungarian and
German, respectively, for 'room for rent').

Bacchus HOTEL €€
(☑510 450; www.bacchushotel.hu; Erzsébet királyné
utca 18; s/d/apt 12,300/16,500/24,800Ft) Bacchus' central position and immaculate rooms
make it a popular choice with travellers.
Equally pleasing is its atmospheric cellar,
which is divided between a fine restaurant
and a wine museum (admission free, open
11am to 11pm) where tastings are available.

Ambient Hostel HOSTEL €
(☑06 30 460 3536; http://hostel-accommodation.
fw.hu; Sopron utca 10; dm/d from 3500/7800Ft; @)
Only a short walk north of the palace is a
hostel with basic, cheap dorms, each of
which comes with its own bathroom. Laundry service is available 3pm to 5pm, from
Monday to Friday. Note that reception closes
by 9.30pm, so be sure to call ahead if your
train or bus gets you in later than that.

Tokajer B&B €
(☑319 875; www.pensiontokajer.hu; Apát utca 21;
s/d/apt from €33/50/70; ❄@🏊) Spread over
four buildings in a quiet area of town, Tokajer has slightly dated rooms, but they're
still in good condition. Extras include a
mini-wellness centre and free use of bicycles.

Castrum Camping CAMPING GROUND €
(☑312 120; www.castrum.eu; Móra Ferenc
utca 48; camp sites per adult/concession/tent
1400/1000/2000Ft; ☉Apr-Oct;🏊) North of the
stations, this large camping ground is green
and spacious and has a big pool.

🍴 Eating

If you need groceries, shop while admiring
the beautiful stained-glass windows of the
CBA (Kossuth Lajos utca 35) supermarket, just at
the intersection Kossuth Lajos utca and Fő ter.

Lakoma HUNGARIAN €
(☑313 129; Balaton utca 9; mains 1000-2600Ft)
With a good fish selection, grill/roast specialities and a back garden that transforms
itself into a leafy dining area in the summer
months, it's hard to go wrong.

Pelso Café CAFE €
(Fő tér; coffee & cake from 300Ft; ☉9am-9pm; 🛜)
This modern two-level cafe at the southern
end of the main square does decent coffee,
cake and cocktails. Has free wi-fi.

☆ Entertainment

The biweekly *ZalaEst* booklet, available
from Tourinform, is a good source of
information on entertainment activities in
Keszthely.

Balaton Theatre THEATRE
(☑515 230; www.balatonszinhaz.hu, in Hungarian;
Fő tér 3) Catch the latest in theatre performances at this venue on the main square.

ℹ Information

Main post office (Kossuth Lajos utca 48)
OTP Bank (Kossuth Lajos utca 38) Facing a
small park near the centre of town.
Tourinform (☑314 144; keszthely@tourinform.
hu; Kossuth Lajos utca 28; ☉9am-8pm Mon-
Fri, to 6pm Sat mid-Jun–mid-Sep, 9am-5pm
Mon-Fri, to 12.30pm Sat mid-Sep–mid-Jun) Has
information on the whole Lake Balaton area.

ℹ Getting There & Away

The future of **Balaton airport** (☑554 060; www.
flybalaton.com), 15km southwest of Keszthely at
Sármellék, was unclear as this book was being
researched. The airport has served as a convenient hub for incoming budget flights from Germany and the UK but has recently experienced
financial problems.

Back on the ground, buses from Keszthely to
Hévíz (220Ft, 15 minutes) leave at least every 30
minutes during the day. Other places served by
buses include Balatonfüred (1200Ft, 1½ hours,
seven daily) and Budapest (3300Ft, three hours,
seven daily). The bus is faster than the train for
reaching Budapest.

Keszthely is on a railway branch line linking
the lake's southeastern shore with Budapest
(3500Ft, four hours, six daily). To reach towns
along Lake Balaton's northern shore by train,
you have to change at Tapolca (380Ft, 30 minutes, hourly).

From April to September, **Balaton Shipping
ferries** (www.balatonihajozas.hu) link Keszthely
with Badacsonytomaj (1560Ft, two hours, four
daily) and other, smaller lake towns.

SOUTH CENTRAL HUNGARY

Southern Hungary is a region of calm, a place to savour life at a slower pace. It's only marginally touched by tourism, and touring through the countryside is like travelling back in time. Passing through the region, you'll spot whitewashed farmhouses whose thatched roofs and long colonnaded porticoes decorated with floral patterns seem unchanged over the centuries.

Historically, the area bordering Croatia and Serbia has often been 'shared' between Hungary and these countries, and it's here that the remnants of the 150-year Turkish occupation can be most strongly felt.

The region is bounded by the Danube River to the east, the Dráva River to the south and west, and Lake Balaton to the north. It's generally flat, with the Mecsek and Villány Hills rising in isolation from the plain. The weather always seems to be a few degrees warmer here than in other parts of the country; the sunny clime is great for grape-growing, and oak-aged Villány reds are well regarded.

Pécs

🕽72 / POP 156,000

Blessed with a mild climate, an illustrious past and a number of fine museums and monuments, Pécs (pronounced *paich*) is one of the most pleasant and interesting cities to visit in Hungary. For those reasons and more – a handful of universities, the nearby Mecsek Hills, a lively nightlife – many travellers put it second only to Budapest on their Hungary must-see list.

Lying equidistant from the Danube to the east and the Dráva to the south, Pécs enjoys a microclimate that lengthens the summer and is ideal for viticulture and fruit production. An especially fine time to visit is during a warm *indián nyár* (Indian summer), when the light seems to take on a special quality.

Pécs' history stretches back nearly 2000 years and the city remains marked by the dynasties that have come and gone. The Roman settlement of Sopianae on this site was the capital of the province of Lower Pannonia for 400 years. Christianity flourished here as early as the 4th century, and in 1009 Stephen I made Pécs a bishopric. The Mongols swept through here in 1241, prompting the authorities to build massive city walls, parts of which are still standing.

The Turkish occupation began in 1543 and lasted nearly a century and a half, lending Pécs an Ottoman patina that's immediately visible at the Mosque Church that stands at the heart of the city's main square.

In recognition of Pécs' remarkable past, as well as its cultural and geographic proximity to the Balkans, the city was named a European Cultural Capital in 2010. That designation helped to bring millions of euros of investment into the historic core and helped the city to rejuvenate its impressive coterie of museums.

⊙ Sights & Activities

The main sights are clustered in three areas: Széchenyi tér, Dóm tér (dominated by the Basilica of St Peter) and Káptalan utca, Pécs' 'museum street'.

FREE **Mosque Church**　　　　　　CHURCH
(Mecset Templom; Széchenyi tér; ⊙10am-4pm mid-Apr–mid-Oct, shorter hours rest of year) The curiously named Mosque Church dominates the city's central square. It has no minaret and has been a Christian place of worship for a long time, but the Islamic elements inside, such as the mihrab on the southeastern wall, reveal its original identity. Constructed in the mid-16th century from the stones of an earlier church, the mosque underwent several changes of appearance over the years – including the addition of a steeple. In the late 1930s the building was restored to its medieval form.

Hassan Jakovali Mosque　　　　MOSQUE
(Hassan Jakovali Mecset; adult/concession 500/250Ft; ⊙9.30am-6pm Wed-Sun late Mar-Oct) West along Ferencesek utcája, you'll pass the ruins of the 16th-century Turkish **Pasa Memi Baths** (Memi Pasa Fürdője) before you turn south on Rákóczi utca to get to the 16th-century Hassan Jakovali Mosque. Though wedged between two modern buildings, this smaller mosque is more intact than its larger cousin, the Mosque Church, and comes complete with a minaret. There's a small museum of Ottoman history inside.

Zsolnay Porcelain Museum　　MUSEUM
(Zsolnay Porcélan Múzeum; Káptalan utca 2; adult/concession 700/350Ft; ⊙10am-5pm Tue-Sun) From the northern end of Széchenyi tér, climb Szepessy Ignéc utca and turn left (west) on Káptalan utca, a street lined with museums and galleries. The Zsolnay Porcelain Museum is on the eastern end of this strip. English translations provide a good history of

Pécs

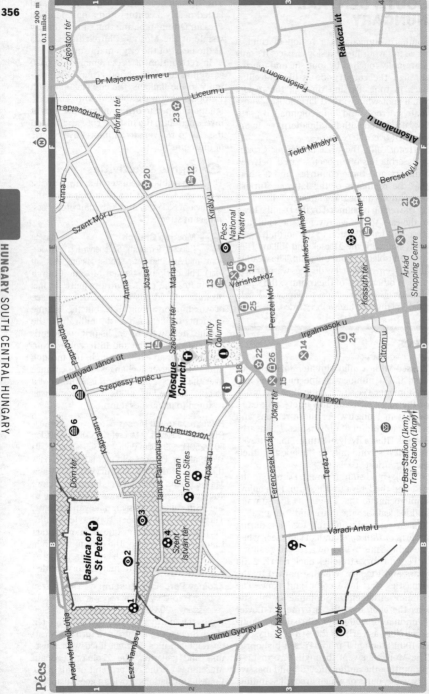

200 m
0.1 miles

Basilica of St Peter

Mosque Church

Trinity Column

Pécs National Theatre

Ágoston tér

Dr Majorossy Imre u

Liceum u

Felsőmalom u

Rákóczi út

Alsómalom u

Toldi Mihály u

Bercsényi u

Papnövelde u

Flórián tér

Anna u

Szent Mór u

Anna u

József u

Mária u

Király u

Munkácsy Mihály u

Tímár u

Arkád Shopping Centre

Kossuth tér

Perczel Mór u

Várisházköz

Hunyadi János út

Széchenyi tér

Szepessy Ignéc u

Pannónia u

Irgalmasok u

Citrom u

Káptalan u

Dóm tér

Janus Pannonius u

Roman Tomb Sites

Szent István tér

Apáca u

Vörösmarty u

Ferencesek utcája

Jókai tér

Jókai Mór u

Teréz u

Váradi Antal u

Kórház tér

Klimó György u

Aradi vértanúk útja

Esze Tamás u

To Bus Station (1km);
Train Station (1km)

Pécs

the artistic and functional ceramics produced from this local factory's illustrious early days in the mid-19th century to the present.

TOP CHOICE Modern Hungarian Art Gallery
ART GALLERY
(Modern Magyar Képtár; Káptalan utca 4; adult/concession 700/350Ft; ⊙noon-6pm Tue-Sun Apr-Oct, 10am-4pm Tue-Sun Nov-Mar) At the excellent Modern Hungarian Art Gallery you can get a comprehensive overview of Hungarian art from 1850 till today. In 2010 the museum hosted a groundbreaking exhibition on 1920s and early '30s Bauhaus architecture, and Pécs' contribution to it.

Basilica of St Peter CHURCH
(Szent Péter Bazilika; Dóm tér; adult/concession 800/500Ft; ⊙9am-5pm Mon-Sat, 1-5pm Sun) At Dóm tér the walled bishopric complex contains the four-towered Basilica of St Peter. The oldest part of the building is the 11th-century crypt. The 1770 **Bishop's Palace** (Püspöki Palota; adult/concession 1500/700Ft; ⊙tours 2pm, 3pm & 4pm Thu late Jun–mid-Sep) stands in front of the cathedral. Also near the square is a nearby 15th-century **barbican** (barbakán), the only stone bastion to survive from the old city walls.

Cella Septichora Visitors Centre RUINS
(Janus Pannonius utca; adult/concession 1200/600Ft; ⊙10am-6pm Tue-Sun) On the southern side of Dom tér is the Cella Septichora

Visitors Centre, which illuminates a series of early Christian burial sites that have been on Unesco's World Heritage list since 2000. The highlight is the so-called **Jug Mausoleum** (Korsós Sírkamra), a 4th-century Roman tomb whose name comes from a painting of a large drinking vessel with vines.

Early Christian Tomb Chapel RUINS
(Ókeresztény sírkápolna; Szent István tér 12; adult/concession 400/200Ft; ⊙10am-6pm Tue-Sun) Across Janus Pannonius utca from the Cella Septichora Visitors Centre, the early Christian tomb chapel dates from about AD 350 and has frescos of Adam and Eve, and Daniel in the lion's den.

Synagogue SYNAGOGUE
(zsinagóga; Kossuth tér; adult/concession 500/300Ft; ⊙10am-noon & 12.45-5pm Sun-Fri May-Oct) Pécs' beautifully preserved 1869 synagogue is south of Széchenyi tér.

🛏 Sleeping

Tourinform can help book private rooms, which start at around 4000Ft per person.

Hotel Főnix BOUTIQUE HOTEL €€
(☑311 680; www.fonixhotel.hu; Hunyadi János út 2; s/d 7100/11,300Ft; ❄@) Odd angles and sloping eaves characterise the asymmetrical Hotel Főnix. Rooms are plain and those on the top floor have skylights.

Palatinus City Center
HOTEL €€

(☎889 400; www.danubiushotels.com; Király utca 5; s/d from €75/104; ✺@) For art nouveau glamour, Palatinus is *the* place in Pécs. An amazing marble reception has a soaring Moorish-detailed ceiling. It's a shame that the rooms are not as luxurious, but still, in Pécs, it's as plush as it gets.

Hotel Diána
PENSION €€

(☎328 594; www.hoteldiana.hu; Tímár utca 4a; s/d/tr from 11,350/16,350/20,350Ft; ✺@) This very central pension offers 20 spotless rooms, comfortable kick-off-your-shoes decor and a warm welcome.

Nap Hostel
HOSTEL €

(☎950 684; www.naphostel.com; Király utca 23-25; dm/d from 2500/11,000Ft;@) Clean, friendly hostel has dorms and a double room on the 1st floor of a former bank. There's also a large kitchen. Enter from Szent Mór utca.

🍴 Eating & Drinking
Pubs, cafes and fast-food eateries line pedestrian-only Király utca. Another good bet is tiny and more intimate Jókai tér. Get self-catering supplies at the **Interspar** (Bajcsy-Zsilinszky utca 11; ☉7am-9pm Mon-Thu & Sat, 7am-10pm Fri, 8am-7pm Sun) supermarket in the basement of the Árkád shopping centre.

[TOP CHOICE] Az Elefánthoz
ITALIAN €

(☎216 055; Jókai tér 6; mains 1600-2100Ft) With its welcoming terrace overlooking Jókai tér and quality Italian cuisine, this place is a sure bet for first-rate food in the centre. Has a wood-fired stove for pizzas, though the pasta dishes are also worth a look.

Corso
FINE DINING €€€

(☎525 198; Király utca 14; mains 2400-4600Ft) One of Hungary's top restaurants and arguably the most prestigious meal in town. Dining is on two levels, with the top featuring refined Hungarian cooking with Italian and French influences. The ground floor is slightly less expensive, but equally good. Here the focus is on traditional Hungarian dishes.

Áfium
BALKAN €

(☎511 434; Irgalmasok utca 2; mains 1400-1900Ft; ☉11am-1am) With Croatia and Serbia so close, it's a wonder that more restaurants don't offer cuisine from south of the border. Don't miss the bean soup served covered with a top of freshly baked bread. Decently priced set lunches during the week.

Korhely
INTERNATIONAL €

(Boltív köz 2) This popular *csapszék* (tavern) has peanuts on the table, shells on the floor, a half-dozen beers on tap and a sort of 'retro socialist meets Latin American' decor.

Coffein Café
CAFE €

(Széchenyi tér 9) For the best views across Széchenyi tér to the Mosque Church and Király utca, find a perch at this cool cafe done up in the warmest of colours.

☆ Entertainment
Pécs has well-established opera and ballet companies as well as a symphony orchestra. Tourinform has schedule information. The free biweekly *Pécsi Est* also lists what's on around town.

House of Artists
EXHIBITION SPACE

(Művészetek Háza; ☎522 834; www.pmh.hu, in Hungarian only; Széchenyi tér 7-8) This is a cultural venue that hosts classical-music performances. A schedule is posted outside.

Bóbita Puppet Theatre
THEATRE

(Bóbita Bábszínház; ☎210 301; www.bobita.hu; Mária utca 18) Lively puppet theatre with a varied program aimed at audiences of all ages. At the time of research there were plans afoot to move the theatre to a new location a bit further from the centre.

Cyrano Lounge
CLUB

(Czindery utca 6; ☉8pm-5am Fri & Sat) A popular nightclub next to the big Árkád shopping centre.

Varázskert
OUTDOOR CLUB

(Király utca 65-67; ☉6pm-3am summer) Big open-air beer garden and late-hours music club at the far end of Király utca.

🛍 Shopping
Pécs has been known for its leatherwork since Turkish times, and you can pick up a few bargains around the city. Try **Blázek** (☎332 460; Teréz utca 1), which deals mainly in handbags and wallets. **Zsolnay** (☎310 220; Jókai tér 2) has a porcelain outlet south of Széchenyi tér. **La Gourmet** (Király utca 8) specialises in wines from Pécs and nearby Villány.

ℹ Information
There are plenty of banks and ATMs scattered around town.

Main post office (Jókai Mór utca 10) In a beautiful art nouveau building (1904) with a colourful Zsolnay porcelain roof.

Tourinform (📞213 315; pecs@tourinform.hu; Széchenyi tér 1; ☉8am-6pm Mon-Fri, 10am-8pm Sat & Sun Jun-Aug, 8am-5.30pm Mon-Fri, 10am-2pm Sat May, Sep & Oct, 8am-4pm Mon-Fri Nov-Apr) Tons of local info, including lists of hotels and museums. The office can help book private rooms, advise on transport and rent bikes. Note that Tourinform was planning to move in 2011, but did not know where.

Webforrás (Boltív köz 2; per hr 420Ft) Just off Király utca is an internet cafe.

ℹ Getting There & Away

Buses for Harkány (500Ft, 40 minutes) leave regularly throughout the day. At least five buses a day connect Pécs with Budapest (3600Ft, 4½ hours), three with Siófok (2480Ft, three hours) and eight with Szeged (3400Ft, 4½ hours).

Pécs is on a main rail line with Budapest's Déli train station (4400Ft, three hours, nine daily). One daily train runs from Pécs to Osijek (two hours) in Croatia, with continuing service to the Bosnian capital, Sarajevo (nine hours).

SOUTHEASTERN HUNGARY

Like the Outback for Australians or the Old West for Americans, the Nagyalföld (Great Plain) holds a romantic appeal for Hungarians. Images of shepherds guiding their flocks with moplike *puli* dogs and cowboys riding across the *puszta* (plain) are scattered throughout the nation's poetry and painting. The Great Plain covers some 45,000 sq km east and southeast of Budapest. Beyond its big-sky-country appeal, the Great Plain is also home to cities of graceful architecture, winding rivers and easygoing afternoons.

Kecskemét

📞76 / POP 107,000

Located about halfway between Budapest and Szeged, Kecskemét (*kech*-kah-mate) is a green, pedestrian-friendly city with interesting art nouveau architecture. Colourful buildings, fine small museums and the region's excellent *barackpálinka* (apricot brandy) beckon. And Kiskunsági Nemzeti Park, the *puszta* of the Southern Plain, is right at the back door. Day-trip opportunities include hiking in the sandy, juniper-covered hills, a horse show at Bugac or a visit to one of the area's many horse farms. Note that central Kecskemét is made up of

squares that run into one another, and consequently it's hard to tell them apart.

☉ Sights

Szabadság tér   PUBLIC SQUARE
The square's eclectic buildings include the Technicolor art nouveau style of the 1902 **Ornamental Palace** (Cifrapalota; Rákóczi út 1), recently refurbished and covered in multicoloured majolica tiles. The palace houses the **Kecskemét Gallery** (Kecskeméti Képtár; adult/concession 320/160Ft; ☉10am-5pm Tue-Sun), with its fine interiors and a small collection of modern Hungarian paintings.

Kossuth tér   PUBLIC SQUARE
Kossuth tér is dominated by the massive 1897 art nouveau **Town Hall** (Városháza), which is flanked by the baroque **Great Church** (Nagytemplom; Kossuth tér 2; ☉9am-noon & 3-6pm Tue-Sun, mornings only Oct-Apr) and the earlier **Franciscan Church of St Nicholas** (Szent Miklós Templom), parts of which date from the 13th century. Nearby is the magnificent 1896 **József Katona Theatre** (Katona József Színház; Katona József tér 5), a neo-baroque performance venue with a statue of the Trinity (1742) in front of it.

Hungarian Folk Craft Museum   MUSEUM
(Népi Iparmüvészeti Múzeum; Serfőző utca 19a; adult/concession 400/200Ft; ☉10am-5pm Tue-Sat Feb-Nov) The Hungarian Folk Craft Museum has a definitive collection of regional embroidery, weaving and textiles, as well as some furniture, woodcarving and agricultural tools. A few handicrafts are for sale at the entrance.

🛏 Sleeping

Tourinform can help you locate the numerous colleges that offer dormitory accommodation in July and August.

Fábián Panzió   PENSION €
(📞477 677; www.panziofabian.hu; Kápolna utca 14; s/d from 9000/12,000Ft; ✻@🖸) The world-travelling family that owns this small guesthouse know how to treat a visitor well. The exceptionally friendly staff help their guests plan each day's excursions, teapots are available for in-room use, wireless internet is free and bikes are available for hire.

Hotel Három Gúnár   BOUTIQUE HOTEL €€
(📞483 611; Batthyány utca 1; s/d 10,500/14,900Ft;✻) Four multihued town houses – flowerboxes and all – have been transformed to contain 49 smallish rooms (the best are Nos 306 to 308). Simple veneer

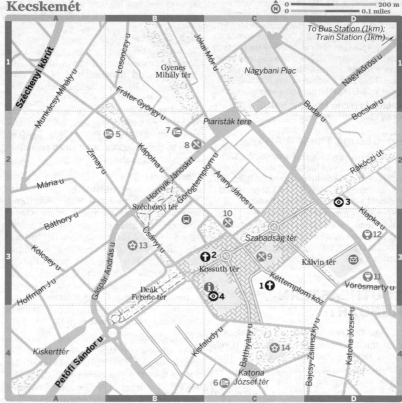

furnishings in the rooms are less cheery than the exterior facade. There's an onsite restaurant.

Teachers' College HOSTEL €
(Tanítóképző Kollégium; ☑486 977; loveikollegium@ tfk.kefo.hu; Piaristák tere 4; s/d 2500/5000Ft; ⊙mid-Jun–Aug) A good choice among the academic accommodation options, with a central location.

✕ Eating

Liberté Étterem HUNGARIAN €€
(☑509 175; Szabadság tér 2; mains 1200-3200Ft) Artistic presentations come with your order, whether it's the traditional stuffed cabbage or the mixed sautéed chicken with aubergine. This is modern Hungarian done well. Its outside tables have some of the best seats in town for people-watching. Our only gripe is the 10% service charge automatically added to the tab, so there's no need to leave a tip.

Lordok HUNGARIAN €
(Kossuth tér 6-7; mains 400-700Ft; ⊙7am-11pm) This popular self-service canteen and adjoining trendier coffeeshop does triple duty as a cheap and tasty lunch option, a place for a midafternoon caffeine break and comfortable spot for an after-dinner beer or cocktail.

Italia ITALIAN €
(☑484 627; Hornyik János körút 4; mains 1200-1400Ft) More fast food than restaurant, so a better choice for something quick and cheap than a meal to remember.

☗ Drinking

For drinks the Western-themed pub **Wanted Söröző** (Csányi János körút 4; ⊙10am-midnight Mon-Sat, from 4pm Sun) sits handily across from the more alternative **Black Cat Pub** (Csányi János körút 6; ⊙11am-midnight Sun-Thu, to 2am Fri & Sat), making for quite the convivial corner.

Kecskemét

☆ Entertainment

Tourinform has a list of what concerts and performances are on, or check out the free weekly magazine *Kecskeméti Est*.

József Katona Theatre   THEATRE
(Katona József Színház; ☎483 283; Katona József tér 5) Experience operettas and symphony performances in this grand 19th-century building. Tourinform can let you know if something's happening during your trip.

Bling Bling Nights   CLUB
(www.blingblingnights.hu; Malom, Korona tér 2) Hip-hop, house, R&B – the nightclub atop Malom Shopping Centre is definitely eclectic. Most of the action occurs on weekend nights, but occasional parties happen throughout the week as well.

❶ Information

Lordok Internetpont (Kossuth tér 6-7; per hr 720Ft; ⊙9am-10pm) Internet access. Find the entrance in a shopping passage behind the Lordok canteen and coffeeshop.

Main post office (Kálvin tér 10)

OTP Bank (Malom Centre, Korona utca 2)

Tourinform (☎481 065; kecskemet@tour inform.hu; Kossuth tér 1; ⊙8am-7pm Mon-Fri, 10am-8pm Sat & Sun Jul-Aug, 8am-6pm

Mon-Fri Sep-Jun) In the northeastern corner of the large Town Hall. Rents bikes and can advise on outings to the nearby Kiskunsági National Park.

❶ Getting There & Away

The main bus and train stations are opposite each other in József Katona Park. Frequent buses depart for Budapest (1700Ft, 1½ hours, hourly) and for Szeged (1700Ft, 1¾ hours, hourly). A direct rail line links Kecskemét to Budapest's Nyugati train station (1900Ft, 1½ hours, hourly) and Szeged (1650Ft, one hour, hourly).

Kiskunsági Nemzeti Park

Totalling 76,000 hectares, **Kiskunsági Nemzeti Park** (Kiskunság National Park; www. knp.hu) consists of half a dozen 'islands' of protected land. Much of the park's alkaline ponds and sand dunes are off limits. Bugac (*boo*-gats) village, about 30km southwest of Kecskemét, is the most accessible part of the park.

The highlight of a trip here is a chance to see a popular **horse show** (admission 1400Ft; ⊙12.15pm May-Oct), where the horse herders race one another bareback and ride 'five-in-hand'. It's a breathtaking performance in which one *csikós* (cowboy) gallops five horses at full speed while standing on the backs of the rear two.

There are also several nature and educational hiking trails in the vicinity, with explanatory sign-posting in English, where you can get out and see this amazing ecosystem of dunes and bluffs and swamps.

The only problem, and it's a formidable one if you don't have your own wheels, is trying to get here. There's a morning bus to Bugac from Kecskemét (600Ft, 50 minutes) that goes daily at 11am, but it won't get you there in time for the 12.15pm show. Alternatively, you could plan to spend the night in Bugac, leaving on the bus the first day, hiking in the afternoon, and then returning to Kecskemét the second day after the horse show on the 3.50pm bus.

If you've got your own transportation, follow route 54 out of Kecskemét in the direction of Soltvadkert. Turn off the road at the 21km marker and follow a dirt track a couple of kilometres toward Bugacpuszta and then follow signs to the **Karikás Csárda** (☎575 112; Nagybugac 135; mains 1600-2100Ft; ⊙8am-8pm May-Oct), a kitschy but decent restaurant that also doubles as a ticket and information booth to the horse show and small **herder museum** (admission free; ☉10am-5pm May-Oct). You can get to the show by foot or ride a **horse-drawn carriage** (adult/concession incl horse show 3000/1800Ft; ☉11.15pm May-Oct). The Tourinform office in Kecskemét can help plan an outing to the national park; the owners of the Fábián Panzió in Kecskemét are another good source of information on how best to access the park and the horse show.

One overnight option in the park, though it's not very close to the horse show, is **Somodi Tanya** (☏377 095; www.samoditanya.hu; Fúló'pháza; r per person about 2000Ft), a lovely dude ranch with crisp, clean rooms where you can ride horses or just laze around and look at the sky.

Szeged

☑62 / POP 170,000

Szeged (*seh*-ged) is a bustling border town with a handful of historic sights that line the embankment along the Tisza River and a clutch of sumptuous art nouveau town palaces that are in varying states of repair and disrepair. It's also a big university town, which means lots of culture, lots of partying and an active festival scene that lasts throughout the year.

For centuries, the city's perch at the confluence of the Maros and Tisza Rivers brought prosperity and growth. That happy relationship turned sour in 1879, when the Tisza overflowed its banks, wiping out much of the central city. Most of the historic architecture you see today dates from the late 19th and early 20th centuries.

The **Szeged Open-Air Festival** (☏541 205; www.szegediszabadteri.hu) is held in Dom tér from mid-July to late August.

◉ Sights & Activities

TOP CHOICE **New Synagogue** SYNAGOGUE
(Új Zsinagóga; www.zsinagoga.szeged.hu; Gutenberg utca 13; adult/concession 400/300Ft; ☉10am-noon & 1-5pm Sun-Fri Apr-Sep, 10am-2pm Sun-Fri Oct-Mar) To the west of the centre, the New Synagogue is the most beautiful Jewish house of worship in Hungary and is still in use. An ornate blue-and-gold painted interior graces the 1903 art nouveau building.

Ferenc Móra Museum MUSEUM
(Móra Ferenc Múzeum; www.mfm.u-szeged.hu; Roosevelt tér 1; adult/concession 700/350Ft; ☉10am-5pm Tue-Sun) The huge, neoclassical Ferenc Móra Museum overlooks the Tisza River. It contains a colourful collection of folk art from Csongrád County with descriptions in several languages and an exhibit of 7th-century gold work by the Avar, a mysterious people who are thought to have originated somewhere in Central Asia. The best exhibit showcases an even more obscure group, the Sarmatians, who originated in present-day Iran.

FREE **Dom tér** PUBLIC SQUARE
The city's ecclesiastical heart is dominated by the twin-spired **Votive Church** (Dom tér; admission free; ☉9am-5pm Mon-Sat, 1-5pm Sun), which was pledged following the 1879 flood but not finished until 1930. While the exterior is something of an architectural monstrosity, the interior is impressive, with a gigantic nave and an organ that boasts more than 11,000 pipes. Next door is the tiny, Romanesque **Demetrius Tower** (admission free; ☉by appointment), the city's oldest structure, and the last remnants of a church built here in the 11th century. For appointments, inquire at the local Tourinform office (p364). There's also a small **Church Museum** (Dom tér 5; adult/concession 100/50Ft; ☉10am-6pm Tue-Sat), where you can see religious artefacts through the ages from around the plains. Running along three sides of the square is the **National Pantheon** (Nemzeti Emlékcsarnok; admission free;

⌚24hr), with statues and reliefs of 80 Hungarian notables.

Pick Salami & Szeged Paprika Museum
MUSEUM

(Pick Szalámi és Szegedi Paprika Múzeum; Felső Tisza-part 10; www.pickmuseum.hu; adult/concession incl salami tasting & paprika sample 880/660Ft; ⌚3-6pm Tue-Sat) Just north of the Old Town ring road is the Pick Salami & Szeged Paprika Museum. Two floors of exhibits show traditional methods of salami production. There's a small gift stand in the museum and a butcher shop around the corner in this factory building.

🛏 Sleeping

TOP CHOICE **Hotel Korona** BOUTIQUE HOTEL €€
(☎555 787; www.hotelkoronaszeged.hu; Petőfi Sándor sgt 4; s/d 14,000/18,000Ft;❄) This modern, clean, well-run hotel comes as a pleasant surprise after seeing so many other family-owned hotels in converted villas that simply don't hold up. Firm mattresses, thick cotton sheets, sparkling baths and the big buffet breakfast all justify the premium room rate. Ask for a quiet room facing the courtyard. Free parking at the back.

Szeged

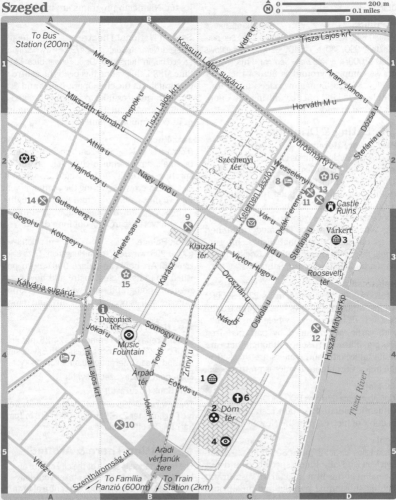

Tisza Hotel　　　　　　BOUTIQUE HOTEL **€€€**
(☑478 278; www.tiszahotel.hu; Széchenyi tér 3; s/d classic 14,500/19,000Ft, superior 18,200/23,000Ft;✳) Top-notch hotel with an old-world feel off central Széchenyi tér. Superior rooms have air-conditioners and mini-bars, as well as antique throw rugs, wooden floors and big wooden beds. Splurge option.

Família Panzió　　　　　　PENSION **€€**
(☑441 122; www.familiapanzio.hu; Szentháromság utca 71; s/d/tr 8400/11,200/14,000Ft;✳) This family-run guesthouse with contemporary furnishings in a great Old Town building is often booked up. The reception area may be dim, but rooms have high ceilings and loads of light.

Partfürdő　　　　　　CAMPING GROUND **€**
(☑430 843; Közép-kikötő sor; camp sites per person/tent 990/380Ft, r 5400-6900Ft, bungalows 8000-12,000Ft; ⊙mid-May–Sep;✳) This green, grassy camping ground is across the river in New Szeged. Bungalows sleep up to four people. Gets kind of crazy during the open-air festival in midsummer.

✕ Eating & Drinking

Port Royal Étterem　　　　　　INTERNATIONAL **€**
(☑547 988; Stefánia 4; mains 1500-2300Ft; ⊙11am-midnight Mon-Thu, to 2am Fri & Sat, to 11pm Sun) There's an unmistakeable nautical theme running through this popular restaurant and cocktail bar. Maybe it's the suspended boat above the bar or the wooden planks for flooring. Whatever, it works. The modern kitchen turns out tasty traditional dishes, international faves and veggie options. Cocktails are served till 2am Friday and Saturday.

Halászcsárda　　　　　　HUNGARIAN **€€**
(☑555 980; Roosevelt tér 14; mains 2200-3600Ft) An institution that knows how to prepare the best fish dish in town – whole roasted pike with garlic, accompanied by pan-fried frog legs and fillet of carp soup. Although there are white tablecloths and waiters are dressed to the nines, the outdoor terrace is pretty casual.

Taj Mahal　　　　　　INDIAN **€**
(Gutenberg utca 12; mains 1700-2300Ft) Pleasantly authentic Indian–Pakistani restaurant, just a couple of metres from the New Synagogue.

Agni　　　　　　VEGETARIAN **€**
(Tisza Lajos körút 76; mains 800-1100Ft; ⊙11am-7pm Mon-Fri) Daily lunch specials round out the menu at this little vegetarian restaurant. Try the substantial paprika-and-mushroom stew with millet. Closed weekends.

A Cappella　　　　　　CAFE **€**
(Kárász 6, cnr Kárász utca & Klauzál tér) Giant sidewalk cafe with a full range of cakes, ice creams and frothy coffee concoctions.

Grand Café　　　　　　CAFE **€**
(Deák Ferenc utca 18; ⊙2pm-midnight Mon-Fri, 5pm-2am Sat & Sun) Climb up to the 2nd floor to find this small but trendy cafe–bar with a decidedly '60s feel. They also hold regular screenings of classic films.

☆ Entertainment

Szeged's status as a university town means that there's a vast array of bars, clubs and other nightspots, especially around Dugonics tér. Nightclub programs are listed in the free *Szegedi Est* magazine.

Szeged National Theatre　　　　　　THEATRE
(Szegedi Nemzeti Színház; ☑479 279; www.szinhaz.szeged.hu, in Hungarian; Deák Ferenc utca 12-14) Since 1886, this venue has been the centre of cultural life in the city. Opera, ballet and drama performances take to its stage. Szeged is known throughout Hungary for the quality of its contemporary dance.

Jazz Kocsma　　　　　　LIVE MUSIC
(Kálmány Lajos 14; ⊙4pm-2am Mon-Sat) The kind of small, smoky music club that no self-respecting university town would be without. Gets pretty crowded during the academic year for live music on Friday and Saturday nights. Things slow down considerably in summer, but still worth searching out for a drink.

Reök Palace　　　　　　EXHIBITION SPACE
(☑541 205; www.reok.hu, in Hungarian; Tisza Lajos körút 56) Art nouveau palace that's been polished up to its original lustre and now hosts regular photography and visual arts exhibitions as well as occasional theatre and dance.

❶ Information

Cyber Arena (Deák Ferenc utca 24-26; per hr 500Ft; ⊙24hr) Internet access with Skype setups and cheap international phonecards.

Main post office (Széchenyi tér 1)

OTP Bank (Klauzál tér 4)

Tourinform (☑488 699; http://tip.szegedvaros.hu; Dugonics tér 2; ⊙9am-5pm Mon-Fri, to 1pm Sat) Tourist office hidden in a courtyard.

❶ Getting There & Around

The train station is south of the city centre on Indóház tér; from here, tram 1 takes you along Boldogasszony sugárút into the centre of town. The bus station, on Mars tér, is west of the centre within easy walking distance via pedestrian-only Mikszáth Kálmán utca.

Buses run to Pécs (3360Ft, 4¼ hours, seven daily) and Debrecen (3890Ft, five hours, two daily). Buses run to the Serbian city of Subotica up to four times daily.

Szeged is on the main rail line to Budapest's Nyugati train station (3000Ft, 2¾ hours, hourly); trains also stop halfway along in Kecskemét (2100Ft, 1¼ hours, hourly). You have to change in Békéscsaba (1600Ft, two hours, half-hourly) to get to Arad in Romania.

NORTHEASTERN HUNGARY

If ever a Hungarian wine were world-famous, it would be tokay (occasionally spelled *tokaj*). And this is where it comes from, a region of Hungary containing microclimates conducive to wine production. The chain of wooded hills in the northeast constitutes the foothills of the Carpathian Mountains, which stretch along the Hungarian border with Slovakia. Though you'll definitely notice the rise in elevation, Hungary's highest peak of Kékes is still only a proverbial bump in the road at 1014m. The highlights here are wine towns Eger and Tokaj, and Szilvásvárad – the Hungarian home of the snow-white Lipizzaner horse.

Eger

♪36 / POP 58,300

Filled with wonderfully preserved baroque architecture, Eger (*egg*-air) is a jewelbox of a town containing gems aplenty. Explore the bloody history of Turkish conquest and defeat at its hilltop castle, climb a Turkish minaret, hear an organ performance at the ornate basilica...but best of all, go from cellar to cellar in the Valley of Beautiful Women (yes, it's really called that), tasting the celebrated Bull's Blood wine from the region where it's made.

It was here in 1552 that Hungarian defenders, led by local hero Captain István Dobó, temporarily stopped the Turkish advance into Western Europe and helped preserve Hungary's identity (see boxed text, p368). However, the persistent Ottomans returned in 1596 and finally captured Eger Castle. They were evicted nearly 100 years later, in 1687.

In the 18th century, Eger played a central role in Ferenc Rákóczi II's attempt to overthrow the Habsburgs, and it was then that a large part of the castle was razed by the Austrians. Eger has some of Hungary's finest architecture, especially examples of Copf (Zopf in Hungarian), a transitional style between late baroque and neoclassicism found only in central Europe.

◎ Sights & Activities

Eger Castle
FORTRESS

(Egri Vár; www.egrivar.hu; Vár 1; adult/concession incl museum 1300/650Ft; ⊙9am-6pm Tue-Sun Apr-Oct, 10am-4pm Tue-Sun Nov-Mar) The most striking attraction, with the best views of town, is Eger Castle, a huge walled complex at the top of the hill off Dósza tér. It was first fortified after an early Mongol invasion in the 13th century; the earliest ruins on site are the foundations of St John's Cathedral, built in the 12th century and destroyed by the Turks. The excellent **István Dobó Castle Museum** (Dobó István Vármuzeum), inside the Bishop's Palace (1470) within the castle grounds, explores the history and development of the castle and the town. Other onsite exhibits such as the **Waxworks** (Panoptikum; adult/concession 450/300Ft) and the **Minting Exhibit** (Éremverde; adult/concession 400/250Ft) cost extra. Even on days when the museums are closed, you can walk around the grounds and battlements and enjoy the views if you buy a *sétaljegy* (strolling ticket, adult/concession 700/350Ft).

Minaret
MINARET

(Knézich Károly utca; admission 200Ft; ⊙10am-6pm Apr-Oct) A 40m-high minaret, minus the mosque, is allegedly Europe's northernmost remains of the Ottoman invasion in the 16th century. You can climb to the top with a great view of the castle, though the 97 steep steps provide a pretty good workout.

FREE Minorite Church
CHURCH

(Minorita Templom; Dobó István tér; admission free; ⊙9am-5pm Tue-Sun) The Minorite Church, built in 1771, is a glorious baroque building. In the town's main square, in front of the church, are statues of national hero István Dobó and his comrades-in-arms routing the Turks in 1552.

Eger Basilica
CHURCH

(Egri Bazilika; Pyrker János tér 1) The first thing you see as you come into town from the bus or train station is the mustard-coloured, neoclassical basilica, with its gigantic pillars. It was built in 1836 and is free to enter. You can tour the caverns below the basilica to see the archbishop's enormous former wine cellar at the **Town Under the Town** (Pyrker János tér; adult/concession 950/500Ft; ⊙10am-8pm Apr-Sep,

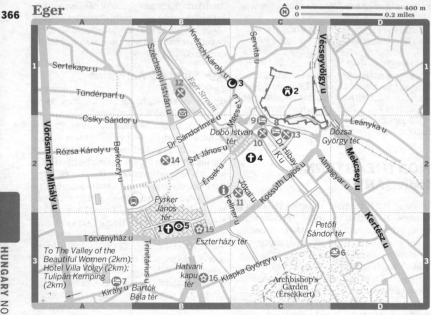

10am-5pm Oct-Mar) exhibition. Most tours are given only in Hungarian, though it might be worth it on a hot day, anyway, since the cellar remains chilly year-round. Bring a sweater.

City Thermal Baths BATHHOUSE
(Városi Térmalfürdő; ✆413 356; Fürdő utca 1-3; adult/ concession 1600/1400Ft; ⏲6am-8pm Apr-Oct, 9am-7pm Nov-Mar) The Archbishop's Garden was once the private reserve of papal princes, but today it is open to the public. Inside the park, the City Thermal Baths has open-air and covered pools with different temperatures and mineral contents. From June to August you can pay 1000Ft extra to get into the modern 'adventure' complex with bubbling massage pools and a castle-themed kids' pool.

FREE **Szépasszony völgy** WINE CELLARS
(Valley of the Beautiful Women; off Király utca) To sample Eger's wines, visit the extravagantly named 'Valley of the Beautiful Women', home to dozens of small wine cellars that truck in, store and sell Bull's Blood and other regional red and white wines. It's about 1km southwest of the town centre. Walk the horseshoe-shaped street through the valley and stop in front of one that strikes your fancy and ask 'megkosztólhatok?' to taste their wares (around 220Ft per decilitre). If you want wine to go, you can bring an empty bottle and have

it filled for about 500Ft per litre. The cellar's outdoor tables fill up on a late summer afternoon as locals cook *gulyás* in the park and strains from a gypsy violinist float up from the restaurants at the valley's entrance. A taxi back to the centre costs about 1200Ft.

🛏 Sleeping

Tourinform has a glossy booklet of accommodation, including private rooms, for the city and the surrounding area.

Hotel Senator Ház BOUTIQUE HOTEL €€€
(✆411 711; www.senatorhaz.hu; Dobó István tér 11; s/d 17,900/23,000Ft; ❄) Warm and cosy rooms with traditional 19th-century period furnishings fill the upper floors of this delightful 18th-century inn on Eger's main square. The ground-floor reception area could easily moonlight as a history museum. The hotel's terrace restaurant is *the* place in town for dinner alfresco, usually accompanied by live music.

Dobó Vendégház BOUTIQUE HOTEL €€
(✆421 407; www.vendeghaz.hu; Dobó utca 19; s/d 9000/13,000Ft) A pleasant and affordable guest house, just a few steps from Eger's main square. The rooms are large and airy, with big wooden beds and fresh white-cotton linens. Some rooms open onto shared balconies off the back with pretty views towards

Eger

town. Take a look at 3a. The friendly reception speaks only halting English at best, but a little sign language goes a long way.

Hotel Villa Völgy　　　BOUTIQUE HOTEL €€€
(☎321 664; www.hotelvillavolgy.hu; Tulipánkert utca 5; s/d 3-star 14,900/20,900Ft, 4-star 20,900/24,900Ft; ☀) A classy, modern villa with a big outdoor swimming pool that's a welcome splurge, especially if you're travelling with children in the hot summer. Adults will appreciate the close proximity to the 'Valley of the Beautiful Women' wine cellars. Rooms come in three- and four-star options, with the latter offering in-room safes, minibars and air-conditioning. Enclosed parking costs 1000Ft per night.

Barók Tér Panzió　　　PENSION €
(☎515 556; www.bartokpanzio.com; Bartók Béla tér 8; s/d 6000/9000Ft) Big, cool rooms in summer, and the location is convenient to both the in-town sights and the wine cellars of the Valley of Beautiful Women. Rates include breakfast.

Tulipán Kemping　　　CAMPING GROUND €
(☎311 542; Szépasszony völgy utca 71; camp sites per person/tent 1940Ft, bungalows 6000Ft;☀) Many of the camping sites here are in an open, shadeless field, but you're surrounded

by vineyards and are stumbling distance from the valley wine cellars.

✘ Eating & Drinking

At the base of the 'Valley of Beautiful Women' (Szépasszony völgy utca), outside town, you'll find several small terrace büfé (snack bars) that have all the Hungarian favourites and plenty of wine (or beer) to wash it all down with. In the centre, there are lots of cafes along pedestrianised Széchenyi István utca. A good strip for dining is along Dobó István tér, heading up toward the castle. The area is known for its pistrang (trout) dishes.

Head to the covered **market** (piac; Katona István tér; ⊙6am-6pm Mon-Fri, to 1pm Sat, to 10am Sun) to buy fruit, vegetables, meat and bread.

TOP/**CHOICE** **Palacsintavár**　　　CREPERIE €
(Dobó István utca 9; mains 1600-1800Ft) Pop art lines the walls, and groovy music provides the soundtrack to this eclectic eatery. Palacsintak (crêpelike pancakes) are served with an abundance of fresh vegetables and range in flavour from Asian to Italian, and even local versions that feature hot peppers and chicken livers. Try to time your arrival for off-meal times, as the wait at the lunch and dinner rush hours can stretch to an hour or more.

Szántófer Vendéglő　　　HUNGARIAN €€
(☎517 298; Bródy utca 3; mains 1500-2400Ft) One of the better choices in town for hearty, homestyle Hungarian food. Farming equipment and cooking utensils hang on the walls, and the covered courtyard out back is perfect for escaping the heat.

Capri Pizza　　　ITALIAN €
(☎410 877; Bajcsy-Zsilinszky utca 4; mains 900-1400Ft) An ordinary pizzeria that will do in a pinch if you're looking for something quick, cheap and central.

Bikavér Borház　　　BAR €
(Dobó István tér 10) After dinner, head to this tastings bar just across from the Senator Ház hotel for a nightcap or two of some of the region's best wines, served by the glass or the bottle. The waiters can guide you with the right selection, and bring along a plate of cheese or grapes to help you cleanse your palate. They also sell bottles to take home.

☆ Entertainment

The Tourinform office can tell you what concerts and musicals are on. The free Egri Est magazine has nightlife listings.

AS STRONG AS A BULL

The story of the Turkish attempt to take Eger Castle is the stuff of legend. Under the command of István Dobó, a mixed bag of 2000 soldiers held out against more than 100,000 Turks for a month in 1552. As every Hungarian kid in short trousers can tell you, the women of Eger played a crucial role in the battle, pouring boiling oil and pitch on the invaders from the ramparts.

If we're to believe the tale, it seems that Dobó sustained his weary troops with a ruby-red vintage of the town's wine. When they fought on with increased vigour – and stained beards – rumours began to circulate among the Turks that the defenders were gaining strength by drinking the blood of bulls. The invaders departed, and the legend of Bikavér (Bull's Blood) was born.

Géza Gárdonyi Theatre   THEATRE
(Gárdonyi Géza Színház; ☑310 026; Hatvani kapu tér 4) Dance, opera and drama are staged at this theatre.

Broadway Studio   CLUB
(Pyrker János tér 3; ☺10pm-6am Tue & Sat) This bizarre, cavernous dance club beneath the cathedral's steps parties hard weekends. Check kiosks around town for events. Expect to pay a cover of 800Ft to 1000Ft.

ℹ Information

Egri Est Café (Széchenyi István utca 16; per hr 300Ft; ☺11am-midnight Sun-Thu, to 2am Fri & Sat) Cafe-bar with internet access.

OTP Bank (Széchenyi István utca 2)

Post office (Széchenyi István utca 22; ☺8am-8pm Mon-Fri, to 1pm Sat)

Tourinform (☑517 715; eger@tourinform.hu; Bajcsy-Zsilinszky utca 9; ☺9am-5pm Mon-Fri, to 1pm Sat & Sun, closed Sun mid-Sep–mid-Jun) Offers guided historical tours at weekends (300Ft per person). Good source for information on nearby Szilvásvárad.

ℹ Getting There & Away

The main train station is a 15-minute walk south of town, on Vasút utca, just east of Deák Ferenc utca. Egervár train station, which serves Szilvásvárad and other points north, is a five-minute walk north of the castle along Vécseyvölgy utca. The bus station is west of Széchenyi István utca, Eger's main drag.

Hourly buses make the trip from Eger to Szilvásvárad (500Ft, 45 minutes). Other destinations include Kecskemét (2200Ft, 4½ hours, three daily) and Szeged (3500Ft, 5¾ hours, two daily). To get to Tokaj by bus, you have to go past it to Nyíregyháza and get another bus back.

Up to seven direct trains a day head to Budapest's Keleti train station (2300Ft, 2½ hours). Otherwise, Eger is on a minor train line linking Putnok and Füzesabony, so you have to change

at the latter for Debrecen (2160Ft, three hours). You can also catch a local train to Szilvásvárad (640Ft, one hour, six daily).

Tokaj

☑47 / POP 5100

The sweet and sultry wines produced here have been around for centuries, thanks to the area's volcanic soil and unique microclimate, which promotes the growth of *Botrytis cinerea* (noble rot) on the grapes. The result is Tokaji Aszú, a world-class dessert wine.

Today Tokaj (*toke*-eye) is a picturesque little town of old buildings, wine cellars and nesting storks. The 66-sq-km Tokaj-Hegyalja wine-producing region, a microclimate along the southern and eastern edges of the Zemplén Hills, was declared a World Heritage site in 2002.

Tokaj is divided into two areas: a larger commercial area near the Millennium Hotel, and a smaller, more pedestrian-friendly part further beyond. It's here where you'll find the Tourinform office, several pensions, the museum and the best wine cellars.

◉ Sights & Activities

TOP CHOICE **Rákóczi Cellar**   WINE CELLAR
(Rákóczi Pince; Kossuth tér 15; ☺11am-8pm) Head to the 600-year-old Rákóczi Cellar for a tasting and a tour. Bottles of wine mature underground in the long cavelike corridors (one measures 28m by 10m). A flight of six Tokaj wines costs about 3000Ft. The correct order of sampling Tokaj wines is: Furmint, dry Szamorodni, sweet Szamorodni and then the Aszú wines, moving from three to six *puttony*, the measurement used for sweetness. Six, by the way, is the sweetest.

Tokaj Museum MUSEUM
(Tokaji Múzeum; Bethlen Gábor utca 13; adult/concession 600/300Ft; ☺10am-5pm Tue-Sun) The Tokaj Museum leaves nothing unsaid about the history of Tokaj, the region and its wines.

Great Synagogue SYNAGOGUE
(Nagy Zsinagóga; Serház utca 55; admission 200Ft) The eclectic 19th-century Great Synagogue was used as a German barracks during WWII, but it's once again gleaming after a thorough renovation.

🛏 Sleeping & Eating

Private rooms on offer along Hegyalja utca are convenient to the train station and are surrounded by vineyards. There are several camping grounds spread out along the banks of the Tisza River across from the town centre.

Millennium Hotel BOUTIQUE HOTEL €€
(☑352 247; www.tokajmillennium.hu; Bajcsy-Zsilinszky utca 34; s/d 12,900/14,900Ft; 🅰@) Equidistant from the train station and town centre; the only drawback to this hotel's location is the busy road out front. Pleasant beer garden, though.

Huli Panzió PENSION €
(☑352 791; www.hulipanzio.hu; Rákóczi út 16; s/d 4000/8000Ft;🅰) Bright and simple pension with 12 down-to-earth rooms. Enjoy breakfast (800Ft) at the ground-floor restaurant.

Vaskó Panzió PENSION €
(☑352 689; http://vaskopanzio.fw.hu; Rákóczi út 12; r 8000Ft) The supremely central Vaskó has eight cute rooms, and windowsills bedecked with flowerpots. It's above a private wine cellar and the proprietor can organise tastings. Breakfast costs an additional 700Ft per person.

Tisza Camping CAMPING GROUND €
(☑06 30 432 8242; Strand 1; per person tent sites/bungalows 1000/1700Ft; ☺Apr-Oct) Nothing special, but you'll find shady tent sites and basic bungalows adjacent to the river.

Degenfeld HUNGARIAN €€
(☑552 006; Kossuth tér 1; mains 1950-3650Ft) Expert wine pairings accompany each exquisite dish, such as duck leg in honey-mustard sauce or pork medallions in pepper sauce. Also sells Degenfeld's own wines, including local favourite 'Fortissimo 2008' for 3200Ft per bottle.

Fakapu HUNGARIAN €
(Rákóczi út 27; mains 1000-1650Ft) Just what you'd expect in Tokaj: a cute terrace–wine cellar that offers simple Hungarian soups, stews and plates of smoked meats to accompany wine tastings. Great choice for a light (and mostly liquid) lunch.

🛍 Shopping

You can buy wine at any of the places mentioned for tasting, or stop at the **Furmint Vinotéka** (☑353 340; Bethlen Gábor utca 12; ☺9am-6pm) wine shop for a large local selection.

ⓘ Information

Tourinform (☑552 070; www.tokaj-turizmus.hu; Serház utca 1; ☺9am-6pm Mon-Fri, 10am-7pm Sat & Sun Jun-Aug, 9am-5pm Mon-Fri Sep-May) Just off Rákóczi út. Hands out a handy booklet of wine cellars in the area and organizes weekend 'wine bus' tours (from 3200Ft per person) with visits to two or three wineries, depending on the day.

ⓘ Getting There & Away

Trains arrive 1200m south of the town centre; walk north on Baross Gábor utca and turn left on Bajcsy-Zsilinszky út, which turns into Rákóczi út, the main thoroughfare. The bus station is more convenient, in town on Seráz utca.

No direct buses connect Tokaj with Budapest or Eger; train travel is your best option here. Up to 10 trains a day head west to Budapest Keleti (3840Ft; 2½ hours), and at least one train daily goes east to Debrecen (1650Ft, two hours).

Debrecen

☑52 / POP 215,000

Flanked by the golden Great Church and historic Aranybika Hotel, the main square of Hungary's second city is quite pretty; a surprise given the unattractive industrial zones and apartment blocks you pass when arriving by bus or train. During summer, street festivals fill the pedestrian core with revellers, and the city's array of museums and its town thermal baths will keep you busy for a day or two. The Debrecen Flower Carnival happens in late August; Debrecen Jazz Days is in September.

The area around Debrecen (*deb*-re-tsen) has been settled since the earliest times. Debrecen's wealth, based on salt, the fur trade and cattle-raising, grew steadily through the Middle Ages and increased during the Turkish occupation. Debrecen played a pivotal role in the 1848 nationalist revolt, and it experienced a major building boom in the late 19th and early 20th centuries.

A ring road, built on the city's original earthen walls, encloses the Belváros, or Inner Town. This is bisected by Piac utca, which runs northward from the train station (Petőfi tér) to Kálvin tér, site of the Great Church and Debrecen's centre. The bus station (Külső-Vásártér) is on the 'outer marketplace' at the western end of Széchenyi utca.

◉ Sights & Activities

Great Church
CHURCH

(Kálvin tér; adult/concession 350/250Ft; ⏱9am-4pm Mon-Fri, 9am-1pm Sat, noon-4pm Sun Apr-Oct, 10am-1pm Mon-Sat, 11.30am-1pm Sun Nov-Mar) Many of the town's big sights are at the northern end of Piac utca, including the yellow neoclassical Great Church. Built in 1821, it has become so synonymous with Debrecen that mirages of its twin clock towers were reportedly seen on the Great Plain early last century. Climb the 210 steps to the top of the west clock tower for grand views over the city.

Reformed College
MUSEUM

(Református Kollégium; Kálvin tér 16; adult/concession 700/350Ft, English-language tours 3500Ft; ⏱10am-4pm Tue-Sat, to 1pm Sun) North of the church stands the 1816 Reformed College, the site of a prestigious secondary school and theological college since the Middle Ages. It houses exhibits on religious art and sacred objects (including a 17th-century chalice made from a coconut) and on the school's history.

Aquaticum
BATHHOUSE

(www.aquaticum.hu; adult/concession 2100/1600Ft; ⏱10am-10pm) You can wander along leafy trails and rent a **paddle boat** (per hr 1000Ft; ⏱9am-8pm Jun-Aug) in Nagyerdei Park, north of the centre. But the main attraction here is Aquaticum, a complex of 'Mediterranean Enjoyment Baths' offering all manner of slides and waterfalls, spouts and grottoes within its pools.

🛏 Sleeping

Loads of dormitory accommodation is available in July and August; ask at Tourinform for details.

Aquaticum Wellness Hotel
BOUTIQUE HOTEL €€

(☎514 111; www.aquaticum.hu; Nagyerdei park 1; s/d €105/140; ✳@🐾) Kids' programs, babysitting, bike rental, spa services, a swimming pool, and loads of other amenities make Aquaticum attractive to both adults and children. Room rates include breakfast and dinner, as well as access to all of the spas and pools.

Aranybika
HOTEL €€

(☎508 600; www.civishotels.hu; Piac utca 11-15; s/d from €40/60; ✳🐾) Try as we might, we just can't give this landmark art nouveau hotel on the central square an enthusiastic thumbs up. The historic exterior has been spruced up by the Civis hotel chain, which owns the property, but the rooms remain stubbornly stuck in the communist 1970s, with drab carpets and plain, proletarian furnishings. On the plus side, the location is unbeatable, the reception desk is helpful, and the property admittedly does have a faded retro charm. Plump for the 'superior' rooms, which are larger and cooler than standard.

Szí Panzió
PENSION €

(☎322 200; www.szivpanzio.hu; Szív utca 11; r 7800Ft) The chief advantage at this out-of-the way guesthouse is its proximity to both the rail and bus stations (about 300m from both). The area is a little depressing, but the rooms themselves are clean and quiet, and some even have air-conditioning.

Maróthi György College
HOSTEL €

(☎502 780; Blaháné utca 15; s/d 3500/7000Ft) Right across from a large church, this is a central place to stay. Rooms are fairly basic (containing just a bed and a desk), and facilities are shared. There are simple kitchens available, along with a courtyard and a basketball court for guest use.

🍴 Eating & Drinking

There's a **grocery shop** (Piac utca 75; ⏱24hr) within walking distance of the train station and a small covered **fruit and vegetable market** (Csapó utca; ⏱5am-3pm Mon-Sat, to 11am Sun) right in the centre.

Trinacria da Tano e Pippo
ITALIAN €€

(☎416 988; Batthyány utca 4; mains 1500-3500Ft) Upscale trattoria that serves well-prepared pasta dishes, including homemade raviolis, as well as very good wood-fired pizzas. Call ahead to reserve a table on the terrace in summer.

Eve's Café and Lounge
CAFE €

(☎322 222; Simonffy utca 1b; sandwiches 800-1000Ft) Pleasantly upscale cafe serves breakfasts as well as very good sandwiches and salads throughout the day. Pedestrianised Simonffy utca is the nicest spot in the centre to sit back with a coffee and people-watch.

Csokonai Söröző
HUNGARIAN €€

(☎410 802; Kossuth utca 21; mains 1800-3200Ft) Medieval decor, sharp service and excellent

Hungarian specialities all help to create one of Debrecen's best eating experiences. This cellar pub–restaurant also serves the odd international dish, like turkey enchiladas with beans.

Klári Salátabár VEGETARIAN €
(2412 203; Bajcsy-Zsilinszky utca 3; per 100g 150-350Ft; 9am-7pm Mon-Fri) Tiny, canteen-like salad bar serves salad greens and vegetables by weight as well as a range of fried foods, like mushrooms, cheese and fish.

☆ Entertainment

Pick up a copy of the biweekly entertainment freebie *Debreceni Est* (www.est.hu) for music listings. For bars and late-night cafes, check out Simonffy utca. For clubs, most of the action is along Bajcy-Zsilinszky.

Csokonai Theatre THEATRE
(2455 075; www.csokonaiszinhaz.hu; Kossuth utca 10) Three-tiered gilt balconies, ornate ceiling frescos, and elaborate chandeliers: the Csokonai is everything a 19th-century theatre should be. Musicals and operas are staged here.

Jazz Klub BAR
(Bajcsy-Zsilinszky utca 4) This subterranean music bar has a big open-air terrace out back in summer. It's a good place to relax over an evening beer.

Cool Music and Dance Club CLUB
(Bajcsy-Zsilinszky utca 1-3; cover charge 500-800Ft) DJs spin house and techno tunes here most weekends; Fridays see frequent theme parties.

ℹ Information

Data Net Cafe (Kossuth utca 8; per hr 480Ft; 9am-midnight) Internet and cheap international calls.

Ibusz (2415 555; Révész tér 2; 8am-5pm Mon-Fri, 9am-1pm Sat) Travel agency renting private apartments.

Main post office (Hatvan utca 5-9)

OTP Bank (Piac utca 16 & 45) Both have ATMs.

Tourinform (2412 250; http://portal.debrecen.hu) town hall office (Piac utca 20; 9am-8pm Mon-Fri, 9am-5pm Sun Jun-Aug, 9am-5pm Mon-Fri Sep-May); summer booth (Kossuth tér; 10am-6pm Jun-Sep)

ℹ Getting There & Away

Buses are quickest if you're going directly to Eger (2300Ft, 2½ hours) or Szeged (3400Ft, five hours, three daily).

Frequently departing trains will get you to Budapest (4000Ft, 3¼ hours) and Tokaj (1650Ft,

1½ hours). The night train from Budapest to Moscow stops here at 9.36pm.

UNDERSTAND HUNGARY

History

Pre-Hungarian Hungary

The plains of the Carpathian Basin attracted waves of migration, from both east and west, long before the Magyar tribes decided to settle there. The Celts occupied the area in the 3rd century BC, but the Romans conquered and expelled them just before the Christian era. The lands west of the Danube (Transdanubia) in today's Hungary became part of the Roman province of Pannonia, where a Roman legion was stationed at the town of Aquincum (now called Óbuda). The Romans brought writing, planted the first vineyards and built baths near some of the region's many thermal springs.

A new surge of nomadic tribespeople, the Huns, who lent Hungary its present-day name, arrived on the scene with a leader who would become legendary in Hungarian history. By AD 441, Attila and his brother Bleda had conquered the Romans and acquired a reputation as great warriors. This reputation still runs strong and you will notice that many Hungarians carry the name Attila, even though the Huns have no connection with present-day Hungarians and the Huns' short-lived empire did not outlast Attila's death (453), when remaining tribespeople fled back from whence they came. Many tribes filled the vacuum left by the Huns and settled in the area, such as the Goths, Longobards and the Avars, a powerful Turkic people who controlled parts of the area from the 5th to the 8th centuries. The Avars were subdued by Charlemagne in 796, leaving space for the Franks and Slavs to move in.

The Conquest

Magyar (Hungarian) tribes are said to have moved in around 896, when Árpád led the alliance of seven tribes into the region. The Magyars, a fierce warrior tribe, terrorised much of Europe with raids reaching as far as Spain. They were stopped at the Battle of Augsburg in 955 and subsequently converted to Christianity. Hungary's first king and its patron saint, István (Stephen), was crowned on Christmas Day in 1000, marking the foundation of the Hungarian state.

Medieval Hungary was a powerful kingdom that included Transylvania (now in Romania), Transcarpathia (now in Ukraine), modern-day Slovakia and Croatia. Under King Matthias Corvinus (1458–90), Hungary experienced a brief flowering of Renaissance culture. However, in 1526 the Ottomans defeated the Hungarian army at Mohács and by 1541 Buda Castle had been seized and Hungary sliced in three. The central part, including Buda, was controlled by the Ottomans, while Transdanubia, present-day Slovakia and parts of Transcarpathia were ruled by Hungarian nobility based in Pozsony (Bratislava) under the auspices of the Austrian House of Habsburg. The principality of Transylvania, east of the Tisza, prospered as a vassal state of the Ottoman Empire.

Habsburg Hegemony & the Wars

After the Ottomans were evicted from Buda in 1686, the Habsburg domination of Hungary began. The 'enlightened absolutism' of the Habsburg monarchs Maria Theresa (r 1740–80) and her son Joseph II (r 1780–90) helped the country leap forward economically and culturally. Rumblings of Hungarian independence surfaced off and on, but it was the unsuccessful 1848 Hungarian revolution that really started to shake the Habsburg oligarchy. After Austria was defeated in war by Prussia in 1866, a weakened empire struck a compromise with Hungary in 1867, creating a dual monarchy. The two states would be self-governing in domestic affairs, but act jointly in matters of common interest, such as foreign relations. The Austro-Hungarian monarchy lasted until WWI.

After WWI and the collapse of the Habsburg Empire in November 1918, Hungary was proclaimed a republic. But she had been on the losing side of the war. The 1920 Treaty of Trianon stripped the country of more than two-thirds of its territory – a hot topic of conversation to this day.

In 1941 Hungary's attempts to recover lost territories saw the nation go to war on the side of Nazi Germany. When leftists tried to negotiate a separate peace in 1944, the Germans occupied Hungary and brought the fascist Arrow Cross Party to power. The Arrow Cross immediately began deporting hundreds of thousands of Jews to Auschwitz. By early April 1945 Hungary was defeated and occupied by the Soviet army.

Communism

By 1947 the communists assumed complete control of the government and began nationalising industry and dividing up large estates among the peasantry. On 23 October 1956, student demonstrators demanding the withdrawal of Soviet troops were fired upon. The next day Imre Nagy, the reformist minister of agriculture, was named prime minister. On 28 October Nagy's government offered an amnesty to all those involved in the violence and promised to abolish the hated secret police, the ÁVH (known as ÁVO until 1949). On 4 November Soviet tanks moved into Budapest, crushing the uprising. By the time the fighting ended on 11 November, thousands had been killed. Then the reprisals began: an estimated 20,000 people were arrested; 2000 were executed, including Nagy; another 250,000 fled to Austria.

By the 1970s Hungary had abandoned strict central economic control in favour of a limited market system, often referred to as 'Goulash Communism'. In June 1987 Károly Grósz took over as premier and Hungary began moving towards full democracy. The huge numbers of East Germans who were able to slip through the Iron Curtain by leaving via Hungary contributed to the eventual crumbling of the Berlin Wall.

The Republic

At their party congress in February 1989 the Hungarian communists agreed to surrender their monopoly on power. The Republic of Hungary was proclaimed in October, and democratic elections were scheduled for March 1990. Hungary changed its political system with scarcely a murmur, and the last Soviet troops left the country in June 1991.

The painful transition to a full market economy resulted in declining living standards for most people and a recession in the early 1990s, but the early years of the 21st century saw astonishing growth. Hungary became a member of NATO in 1999 and the European Union (EU) in 2004.

In December 2007 Hungary joined the Schengen zone of European countries, abandoning border controls with its EU neighbours Austria, Slovakia and Slovenia. Late in 2008, reeling from the fallout of the global financial crisis, Hungary was forced to approach the International Monetary Fund for economic assistance, though the economy began a modest recovery in 2010. Hungary originally aimed to adopt the euro by

2010, but the effects of the crisis have since obliged the government to delay adoption for several more years.

People

Some 10.2 million people live within the national borders, and another five million Hungarians and their descendants are abroad. The estimated 1.45 million Hungarians in Transylvania constitute the largest ethnic minority in Europe, and there are another 530,000 in Slovakia, 293,000 in Serbia, 156,000 in Ukraine and 40,500 in Austria.

Ethnic Magyars make up approximately 93% of the population. Many minority groups estimate their numbers to be significantly higher than official counts. There are 13 recognised minorities in the country, including Germans (2.6%), Serbs and other South Slavs (2%), Slovaks (0.8%) and Romanians (0.7%). The number of Roma is officially put at 1.9% of the population, though some sources place the figure as high as 4%.

Of those Hungarians declaring religious affiliation, about 52% are Roman Catholic, 16% Reformed (Calvinist) Protestant, 3% Evangelical (Lutheran) Protestant, and 2.6% Greek Catholic and Orthodox. Hungary's Jews number around 100,000, down from a pre-WWII population of nearly eight times that amount.

Literature & the Arts

The history of Hungarian highbrow culture includes world-renowned composers such as Béla Bartók and Franz Liszt, and the Nobel Prize-winning writer Imre Kértesz and his innovative contemporary Peter Esterházy. Hungary's proximity to classical-music hub Vienna, as well as the legacy of the Soviet regard for the 'proper arts', means that opera, symphony and ballet are high on the entertainment agenda, and even provincial towns have decent companies.

For the more contemporary branches of artistic life, Budapest is the focus, containing many art galleries and theatre and dance companies. The capital is also a centre for folk music and crafts that have grown out of village life or minority culture.

Literature

Hungary has some excellent writers, both of poetry and prose. Sándor Petőfi (1823–49) is Hungary's most celebrated poet. A line from his work *National Song* became the rallying cry for the War of Independence between 1848 and 1849, in which he fought and is commonly thought to have died.

Contemporary Hungarian writers whose work has been translated into English and are worth a read include Tibor Fischer, Péter Esterházy and Sándor Márai. The most celebrated Hungarian writer is the 2002 Nobel Prize winner Imre Kertész. Among his novels available in English are *Fateless* (1975), *Detective Story* (1977), *Kaddish for an Unborn Child* (1990) and *Liquidation* (2003). Another prominent contemporary writer, who died in 2007 at age 90, was Magda Szabó (*Katalin Street,* 1969; *The Door,* 1975).

Classical & Traditional Music

As you will no doubt see from the street names in every Hungarian town and city, the country celebrates and reveres its most influential musician, composer and pianist Franz (or Ferenc) Liszt (1811–86). The eccentric Liszt described himself as 'part Gypsy', and in his *Hungarian Rhapsodies,* as well as in other works, he does indeed weave Romani motifs into his compositions.

Ferenc Erkel (1810–93) is the father of Hungarian opera, and his stirringly nationalist *Bánk Bán* is a standard at the Hungarian State Opera House in Budapest. Béla Bartók (1881–1945) and Zoltán Kodály (1882–1967) made the first systematic study of Hungarian folk music; both integrated some of their findings into their compositions.

Hungarian folk musicians play violins, zithers, hurdy-gurdies, bagpipes and lutes on a five-tone diatonic scale. Look out for Muzsikás, Marta Sebestyén, Ghymes (Hungarian folk band from Slovakia) and the Hungarian group Vujicsics, which mixes in elements of southern Slav music. Another folk musician with eclectic tastes is the Paris-trained Bea Pálya, who combines such sounds as traditional Bulgarian and Indian music with Hungarian folk.

Romani music, found in restaurants in its schmaltzy form (best avoided), has become a fashionable thing among the young, with Romani bands playing 'the real thing' in trendy bars till the wee hours: it's a dynamic, hopping mix of fiddles, bass and cymbalom (a stringed instrument played with sticks). A Romani band would never be seen without the tin milk bottle used as a drum, which gives Hungarian Roma music its characteristic sound. It's reminiscent of traditional Indian music, an influence that perhaps harks back to the Roma's Asian roots. Some modern Romani music groups – Kalyi Jag (Black Fire) from northeastern Hungary, Romano Drom (Gypsy Road) and Romani Rota (Gypsy Wheels) – have added guitars, percussion and even electronics to create a whole new sound.

Klezmer music (traditional Eastern European Jewish music) has also made a comeback in the playlists of the young and trendy.

Pop music is as popular here as anywhere. Indeed, Hungary has one of Europe's biggest pop spectacles, the annual Sziget Music Festival (p321). It has more than 1000 performances over a week and attracts an audience of up to 385,000 people. Popular Hungarian musical artists to look out for include pop singers Magdi Rúzsa and Laci Gáspár and pop/folk band Nox.

Visual Arts

Favourite painters from the 19th century include realist Mihály Munkácsy (1844–1900), the so-called painter of the plains, and Tivadar Kosztka Csontváry (1853–1919). Győző Vásárhelyi (1908–97), who changed his name to Victor Vasarely when he emigrated to Paris, is considered the 'father of op art'. Contemporary painters to keep an eye out for include Árpád Müller and the late Endre Szász (1926–2003).

In the 19th and early 20th centuries, the Zsolnay family created world-renowned decorative art in porcelain. Ceramic artist Margit Kovac (1902–77) produced a large number of statues and ceramic objects during her career. The traditional embroidery, weavings and ceramics of the nation's *népművészet* (folk art) endure, and there is at least one handicraft store in every town.

Environment

The Landscape

Hungary occupies the Carpathian Basin to the southwest of the Carpathian Mountains. Water dominates much of the country's geography. The Duna (Danube River) divides the Nagyalföld (Great Plain) in the east from the Dunántúl (Transdanubia) in the west. The Tisza (597km in Hungary) is the country's longest river, and historically has been prone to flooding. Hungary has hundreds of small lakes and is riddled with thermal springs. Lake Balaton (596 sq km, 77km long), in the west, is the largest freshwater lake in Europe outside Scandinavia. Hunga-

ry's 'mountains' to the north are merely hills, with the country's highest peak being Kékes (1014m) in the Mátra Range.

Wildlife

There are a lot of common European animals in Hungary (deer, hares, wild boar and foxes), as well as some rare species (wild cat, lake bat and Pannonian lizard), but most of the country's wildlife comes from the avian family. Hungary is a premier European spot for bird-watching. Around 75% of the country's 480 known vertebrates are birds, for the most part waterfowl attracted by the rivers, lakes and wetlands. The rare black stork, a smaller, darker version of its common cousin, also spends time in Hungary on its migration from Africa to Europe.

National Parks

There are 10 national parks in Hungary. Bükk Nemzeti Park, north of Eger, is a mountainous limestone area of forest and caves. Kiskunsági Nemzeti Park and Bugac, near Kecskemét, and Hortobágy Nemzeti Park (www.hnp.hu) in the Hortobágy Puszta (a World Heritage site), outside Debrecen, protect the unique grassland environment of the plains.

Environmental Issues

Environmental disaster struck Hungary in 2010, when toxic industrial sludge from an aluminium factory in Ajka, in western Hungary, broke through barriers and leeched into local rivers. Initial fears that the sludge would contaminate the Danube proved unfounded and the sludge should pose no hazard to visitors. In spite of the spill, there's been a marked improvement in both the public's awareness of environmental issues and the government's dedication to environmental safety.

Food & Drink

Hungarian Cuisine

The omnipresent seasoning in Hungarian cooking is paprika, a mild red pepper that appears on restaurant tables as a condiment beside the salt and black pepper, as well as in many recipes. *Pörkölt,* a paprika-infused stew, can be made from different meats, including *borju* (veal), and usually it has no vegetables. *Galuska* (small, gnocchi-like dumplings) are a good accompaniment to soak up the sauce. The well-known *paprikas csirke* (chicken paprikash) is stewed chicken in a tomato, cream and paprika sauce; it's

THE GRAND PRIX

The Hungarian Formula One Grand Prix, held in late July or early August, is the year's biggest sporting event. The **Hungaroring** (www.hungaroring.hu) track is 19km north of Budapest, in Mogyórod, but hotels in the capital fill up and prices skyrocket during the event.

not as common here as in Hungarian restaurants abroad. *Töltött káposzta* (cabbage rolls stuffed with meat and rice) is cooked in a roux made with paprika, and topped with sour cream, as is *székelygulyás* (stewed pork and sour cabbage). Another local favourite is *halászlé* (fisher's soup), a rich mix of several kinds of poached freshwater fish, tomatoes, green peppers and (you guessed it) paprika.

Leves (soup) is the start to any main meal in a Hungarian home; some claim that you will develop stomach disorders if you don't eat a hot, daily helping. *Gulyás* (goulash), although served as a stew outside Hungary, is a soup here, cooked with beef, onions and tomatoes. Traditional cooking methods are far from health-conscious, but they are tasty. Frying is a nationwide obsession, and you'll often find fried turkey, pork and veal schnitzels on the menu.

For dessert you might try the cold *gyümölcs leves* (fruit soup) made with sour cherries and other berries, or *palincsinta* (crêpes) filled with jam, sweet cheese or chocolate sauce. A good food-stand snack is *lángos*, fried dough that can be topped with cheese and/or *tejföl* (sour cream).

Where to Eat & Drink

An *étterem* is a restaurant with a large selection, formal service and formal prices. A *vendéglő* is smaller and more casual, and serves home-style regional dishes. The overused term *csárda*, which originally meant a rustic country inn with Romani music, can now mean anything – including 'tourist trap'. To keep prices down, look for *étkezde* (a tiny eating place that may have a counter or sit-down service), *önkiszolgáló* (a self-service canteen), *kinai gyorsbüfé* (Chinese fast food), *grill* (which generally serves gyros or kebabs and other grilled meats from the counter) or a *szendvicsbar* (which has open-faced sandwiches to go).

For this guide, budget eating is defined as establishments charging up to around 2500Ft per main course. Midrange are places where most mains cost between 2500Ft and 4000Ft. Top end is anything above that.

Wine has been produced in Hungary for hundreds of years, and you'll find it available by the glass or bottle everywhere. There are plenty of pseudo-British/Irish/Belgian pubs, smoky *sörözők* (Hungarian pubs, often in a cellar, where drinking is taken very seriously), *borozók* (wine bars, usually a dive) and nightclubs, but the most pleasant place to imbibe a cocktail or coffee may be in a cafe. A *kávéház* may primarily be an old-world dessert shop, or it may be a bar with an extensive drinks menu; either way they sell alcoholic beverages in addition to coffee. In spring, pavement tables sprout up alongside the new flowers.

Vegetarians & Vegans

Traditional Hungarian cuisine and vegetarianism are definitely not a match made in heaven. However, things are changing and there are places even in the provinces that serve good vegetarian meals. Where there are no vegetarian restaurants, you'll have to make do with what's on the regular menu or shop for ingredients in the markets.

Some not very light but widely available dishes for vegetarians to look for are *rántott sajt* (fried cheese), *gombafejek rántva* (fried mushroom caps), *gomba leves* (mushroom soup) and *túrós* or *káposzta csusza* (short, wide pasta with cheese or cabbage). *Bableves* (bean soup) usually contains meat.

SURVIVAL GUIDE

Directory A–Z

Accommodation

Hungary has a wide variety of lodging options, ranging from youth hostels and camping grounds at the low end, to private rooms, pensions (*panziók*), hotels and luxury boutiques at the high. Prices are highest in Budapest, and the high season for lodging typically runs from April to October and the Christmas and New Year holidays. For this guide, budget accommodation is defined as under 10,000Ft per double per night in the provinces (under 15,000Ft in Budapest). Midrange is between 10,000Ft and 15,000Ft in the countryside (15,000Ft and 30,000Ft in Budapest). Top end is anything above that.

Hungary's camping grounds are listed in Tourinform's *Camping Hungary* map and

The Magyar are a polite people and their language is filled with courtesies. To toast someone's health before drinking, say *egéségére* (egg-eh-shaig-eh-ray), and to wish them a good appetite before eating, *jo étvágat* (yo ate-vad-yaht). If you're invited to someone's home, always bring a bunch of flowers and/or a bottle of good local wine.

brochure (www.camping.hu). Facilities are generally open May to October and can be difficult to reach without a car.

The **Hungarian Youth Hostels Association** (MISZSZ; www.miszsz.hu) keeps a list of year-round hostels throughout Hungary. In general, year-round hostels have a communal kitchen, laundry and internet service, and sometimes a lounge; a basic bread-and-jam breakfast may be included. Having an HI card is not required, but it may get you a 10% discount. A useful hostel website with online booking (only in Hungarian) is www.hihostels.hu.

From July to August, students vacate college and university dorms, and administration opens them to travellers. Facilities are usually – but not always – basic and shared. Local Tourinform offices can help you locate such places.

Renting a private room in a Hungarian home is a good budget option and can be a great opportunity to get up close and personal with the culture. Prices outside Budapest run from 3500Ft to 6000Ft per person per night. Tourinform offices can usually help with finding these; otherwise look for houses with signs reading *'szoba kiadó'* or *'Zimmer frei'*.

An engaging alternative is to stay in a rural village or farmhouse, but only if you have wheels: most of these places are truly remote. Contact Tourinform, the **National Federation of Rural & Agrotourism** (FA TOSZ; ☑1-352 9804; VII Király utca 93) or the **Centre of Rural Tourism** (☑1-321 2426; www.falutur.hu; VII Dohány utca 86) in Budapest.

Activities

Canoeing For canoeists, **Ecotours** (☑030-606-1651; www.ecotours.hu) leads seven-day Danube River canoe-camping trips (tent rental and food extra) for about €600, as well as shorter Danube Bend and Tisza River trips.

Cycling Hungary's flat terrain makes it ideal for cycling. **Velo-Touring** (☑1-319 0571; www.velo-touring.hu) has a great selection of seven-night trips in all regions, from a senior-friendly Danube Bend tour (€689) to a bike ride between spas on the Great Plain (€847). Lake Balaton is circled by a long cycling track that takes four to five days to complete at a leisurely pace.

Hiking/Birdwatching Hiking enthusiasts may enjoy the trails around Tihany at Lake Balaton, the Bükk Hills north of Eger or the plains at Bugac Puszta south of Kecskemét. Birdwatchers could explore these same paths or take a tour with **Birding Hungary** (www.birdinghungary.com).

Horseback Riding There's a helpful HNTO *Riding in Hungary* booklet on equestrian tourism, or you could contact the **Hungarian Equestrian Tourism Association** (MLTSZ; ☑1-456 0444; IX Ráday utca 8, Budapest). **Pegazus Tours** (☑1-317 1644; www.pegazus.hu; V Ferenciek tere 5, Budapest) organises horse-riding tours.

Spas Hungary has more than 100 thermal baths open to the public. For locations, ask Tourinform for the *Spa & Wellness* booklet. For more about Budapest spas, check out www.spasbudapest.com.

Business Hours

Banks 9am-5pm Mon-Fri, 9am-noon Sat

Museums 9am or 10am-5pm or 6pm Tue-Sun

Restaurants roughly 11am-midnight

Courses

Debreceni Nyári Egyetem (Debrecen Summer University; ☑52-532 595; www.nyariegyetem.hu; Egyetem tér 1, Debrecen) is the best-known school for studying Hungarian. It organises intensive two- and four-week courses during July and August and 80-hour, two-week advanced courses during winter. The **Debrecen Summer University Branch** (☑1-320 5751; www.nyariegyetem.hu/bp; V Báthory utca 4) in Budapest also offers courses.

Discount Cards

The **Hungary Card** (☑1-266 3741; www.hungarycard.hu; 7900Ft) gives 50% discounts on six return train fares and some bus and boat travel, free entry to many museums, up to 20% off selected accommodation, and 50%

off the price of the Budapest Card (p332). It's available at Tourinform offices.

Embassies & Consulates

Embassies in Budapest (phone code ☎1) include the following.

Australia (☎457 9777; XII Királyhágó tér 8-9)

Austria (☎479 7010; VI Benczúr utca 16)

Canada (☎392 3360; II Ganz utca 12-14)

Croatia (☎354 1315; VI Munkácsy Mihály utca 15)

France (☎374 1100; VI Lendvay utca 27)

Germany (☎488 3500; I Úri utca 64-66)

Ireland (☎301 4960; V Szabadság tér 7-9)

Netherlands (☎336 6300; II Füge utca 5-7)

Romania (☎384 0271; XIV Thököly út 72)

Serbia (☎322 9838; VI Dózsa György út 92/a)

Slovakia (☎460 9010; XIV Stefánia utca 22-24)

Slovenia (☎438 5600; II Cseppkő utca 68)

South Africa (☎392 0999; II Gárdonyi Géza út 17)

UK (☎266 2888; V Harmincad utca 6)

Ukraine (☎422 4122; XII Nógrádi út 8)

USA (☎475 4400; V Szabadság tér 12)

Food

Price ranges are budget (€; under 2500Ft), midrange (€€; 2500Ft to 5000Ft) and top end (€€€; over 5000Ft).

Gay & Lesbian Travellers

Budapest has a large and active gay population, and Pécs and Szeged also have sizeable gay scenes. Check the **Budapest GayGuide. net** (www.gayguide.net) for up-to-date information on gay-friendly clubs and accommodation, as well as a small list of venues in the countryside. **Labrisz** (www.labrisz.hu) is a lesbian association with a good website with a small English-language section.

Media

Budapest has two English-language newspapers: the weekly *Budapest Times* (www. budapesttimes.hu), with interesting reviews and opinion pieces, and the business-oriented bi-weekly *Budapest Business Journal* (http:// bbj.hu). Both are available on newsstands.

Money

The unit of currency is the Hungarian forint (Ft). Coins come in denominations of five, 10, 20, 50, 100 and 200Ft, and notes are denominated in 500, 1000, 2000, 5000, 10,000

and 20,000Ft. ATMs are everywhere, even in small villages, though some UK readers have reported problems using UK credit and debit cards. It's always best to check with your home bank before leaving to avoid disappointment. Tip waiters, hairdressers and taxi drivers approximately 10% of the bill.

Post

Postcards and small letters mailed within Europe cost 210Ft. To addresses outside Europe, expect to pay 240Ft. Mail addressed to poste restante in any town or city will go to the main post office *(főposta)*. When collecting poste-restante mail, look for the sign *'postán maradó küldemények'*.

Public Holidays

New Year's Day 1 January

1848 Revolution Day 15 March

Easter Monday March/April

International Labour Day 1 May

Whit Monday May/June

St Stephen's Day 20 August

1956 Remembrance Day 23 October

All Saints' Day 1 November

Christmas Holidays 25 and 26 December

Telephone

Hungary's country code is ☎36. To make an outgoing international call, dial ☎00 first. To dial city-to-city (and all mobile phones) within the country, first dial ☎06, wait for the second dial tone and then dial the city code and phone number. All localities in Hungary have a two-digit city code, except for Budapest, where the code is ☎1.

In Hungary you must always dial ☎06 when ringing mobile telephones, which have specific area codes depending on the telecom company: **Pannon GSM** (☎06 20; www. pgsm.hu), **T-Mobile** (☎06 30; www.t-mobile.hu) or **Vodafone** (☎06 70; www.vodafone.hu).

Consider buying a rechargeable SIM card. All of the major telephone companies offer some kind of prepaid SIM plan for around 4000Ft where you get a local number and calls, texts and data downloads are charged at local rates. These often include credit built into the card. Once the credit is exhausted, you can buy recharge cards at mobile-phone stores and supermarkets.

There's also a plethora of phonecards for public phones on offer, including T-Com's **Barangoló**, which comes in denominations of 1000Ft and 5000Ft; **NeoPhone** (www.neophone.hu), with cards also valued at 1000Ft, 2000Ft and 5000F; and **Pannon**, offering cards for 1000Ft, 3000Ft and 5000Ft. It can cost as little as 8Ft per minute to call the USA, Australia and New Zealand using such cards. Telephone boxes with a black-and-white arrow and red target on the door and the word '*Visszahívható*' display a telephone number, so you can be phoned back.

Tourist Information

The **Hungarian National Tourist Office** (HNTO; www.hungarytourism.hu) has a chain of over 140 **Tourinform** (☎hotline 1-438 8080; www.tourinform.hu) information offices across the country. These are the best places to ask general questions and pick up brochures.

Travellers with Disabilities

Hungary's record in this regard is so-so. Wheelchair ramps and toilets fitted for people with disabilities do exist, though not as commonly as in Western Europe. Audible traffic signals are becoming more common in big cities. For more information, contact the **Hungarian Federation of Disabled Persons' Associations** (MEOSZ; ☎1-388 5529; www.meoszinfo.hu, in Hungarian; III San Marco utca 76) in Budapest.

Visas

EU citizens do not need visas to visit Hungary and can stay indefinitely. Citizens of the USA, Canada, Israel, Japan, New Zealand and Australia do not require visas to visit Hungary for stays of up to 90 days.

Check with the **Ministry for Foreign Affairs** (www.mfa.gov.hu) for an up-to-date list of which country nationals require visas.

Getting There & Away

Air

Airports & Airlines

The vast majority of international flights land at **Ferihegy International Airport** (☎1-296 7000; www.bud.hu) on the outskirts of Budapest. **Balaton airport** (www.flybalaton.com) is another possible arrival destination, though as we were researching this guide, the airport's future was in doubt. It is located 15km southwest of Keszthely near Lake Balaton. Hungary's national carrier is **Malév Hungarian Airlines** (MA; ☎06 40 212121; www.malev.hu).

Major airlines, aside from Malév, servicing Hungary:

Aeroflot (SU; www.aeroflot.com)

Air Berlin (AB; www.airberlin.com)

Air France (AF; www.airfrance.com)

Alitalia (AZ; www.alitalia.com)

Austrian Airlines (OS; www.aua.com)

British Airways (BA; www.ba.com)

CSA (OK; www.csa.cz)

easyJet (EZY; www.easyjet.com)

El Al (LY; www.elal.co.il)

EgyptAir (MS; www.egyptair.com)

Finnair (AY; www.finnair.com)

germanwings (4U; www.germanwings.com)

LOT Polish Airlines (LO; www.lot.com)

Lufthansa (LH; www.lufthansa.com)

Ryanair (FR; www.ryanair.com)

SAS (SK; www.flysas.com)

Tarom (RO; www.tarom.ro)

Turkish Airlines (TK; www.thy.com)

Wizz Air (W6; www.wizzair.com)

Land

Hungary's entry into the Schengen zone means that there are no border controls with Austria, Slovakia and Slovenia. Standard border procedures exist with Ukraine, Romania, Serbia and Croatia.

There are excellent land transport connections with Hungary's neighbours. Most of the departures listed are from Budapest, though other cities and towns closer to the various borders can also be used as springboards.

Bus

Most international buses arrive at the Népliget bus station in Budapest. **Eurolines** (www.eurolines.com), in conjunction with its Hungarian affiliate, **Volánbusz** (☎1-382 0888; www.volanbusz.hu), is the international bus company of Hungary. Useful international buses include those from Budapest to Vienna, Bratislava in Slovakia, Subotica in Serbia, Rijeka in Croatia, Prague in the Czech Republic and Sofia in Bulgaria. For more details, see p379.

Car & Motorcycle

Foreign driving licences are valid for one year after entering Hungary. Drivers of cars and riders of motorbikes also need the vehicle's registration papers. Third-party insurance is compulsory for driving in Hungary; if your car is registered in the EU, it's assumed you have it. Other motorists must show a Green Card or buy insurance at the border.

Travel on Hungarian motorways requires pre-purchase of a highway pass (E-vignette). Unlike many other countries, this is not a sticker, but rather your licence-plate number is entered into a computer database where it can be screened by highway-mounted surveillance cameras. Passes are available at border stops. Prices are 1530Ft for four days, 2550Ft for 10 days and 4200Ft for one month.

Train

The Hungarian State Railways, MÁV (☑1-444 4499; www.mav-start.hu) links up with international rail networks in all directions, and its schedule is available online.

Eurail passes are valid, but not sold, in Hungary. EuroCity (EC) and Intercity (IC) trains require a seat reservation and payment of a supplement. Most larger train stations in Hungary have left-luggage rooms open from at least 9am to 5pm. There are three main train stations in Budapest, so always note the station when checking a schedule online.

Some direct train connections from Budapest include Austria, Slovakia, Romania, Ukraine (continuing to Russia), Croatia, Serbia, Germany, Slovenia, Czech Republic, Poland, Switzerland, Italy, Bulgaria and Greece. See p380 for details.

Ticket and information offices are located at rail stations.

River

A hydrofoil service on the Danube River between Budapest and Vienna operates daily from late April to early October; passengers can disembark at Bratislava with advance notice. See p379 for more details.

Getting Around

Note that Hungary does not have any scheduled internal flights.

Boat

In summer there are regular passenger ferries on Lake Balaton and on the Danube from Budapest to Szentendre, Vác, Visegrád and Esztergom. Details of the schedules are given in the relevant destination sections.

Bus

Domestic buses, run by the Volán (www.volan. eu) association of coach operators, cover an extensive nationwide network.

Timetables are posted at stations and stops. Some footnotes you could come across include *naponta* (daily), *hétköznap* (weekdays), *munkanapokon* (on work days), *munkaszüneti napok kivételével naponta* (daily except holidays) and *szabad és munkaszüneti napokon* (on Saturday and holidays). A few large bus stations have luggage rooms, but these generally close by 6pm.

Car & Motorcycle

Most cities and towns require that you pay for street parking (usually 9am to 6pm workdays) by buying temporary parking passes from machines. Most machines take only coins (so keep a lot handy); place the time-stamped parking permit on the dashboard. The cost averages about 200Ft an hour in the countryside and up to 400Ft on central Budapest streets. Parking fines average about 3500Ft.

Automobile Associations

The so-called 'Yellow Angels' of the Hungarian Automobile Club do basic breakdown repairs for free if you belong to an affiliated organisation such as AAA in the USA or AA in the UK. You can telephone 24 hours a day on ☑188 nationwide.

Fuel & Spare Parts

Ólommentes benzin (unleaded petrol 95/98 octane) is available everywhere. Most stations also have *gázolaj* (diesel).

Hire

In general, you must be at least 21 years old and have had your licence for at least a year to rent a car. Drivers under 25 sometimes have to pay a surcharge. Rental agencies are common in large cities and at Budapest airport. Local rental rates are relatively high, and if you plan on renting a car during your stay, you're best advised booking online before you travel.

Road Rules

The most important rule to remember is that there's a 100% ban on alcohol when you are driving, and this rule is strictly enforced.

Using a mobile phone while driving is prohibited in Hungary. *All* vehicles must have their headlights switched on throughout the day outside built-up areas. Motorcyclists must have their headlights on at all times.

Hitching

In Hungary, hitchhiking is legal except on motorways. Hitchhiking is never an entirely safe way to travel and we don't recommend it, but if you're willing, **Kenguru** (www.ken guru.hu) is an agency that matches riders with drivers.

Local Transport

Public transport is efficient and extensive, with bus and, in many towns, trolleybus services. Budapest and Szeged also have trams, and there's an extensive metro and a suburban commuter railway in Budapest. Purchase tickets at newsstands before travelling and validate them once aboard. Inspectors do check tickets, especially on the metro lines in Budapest.

Train

MÁV (☑06 40 494 949; www.mav-start.hu) operates reliable train services on its 8000km of tracks. Schedules are available online, and computer information kiosks are popping up at rail stations around the country. Second-class domestic train fares range from 150Ft for a journey of less than 5km to about 4000Ft for a 300km trip. First-class fares are usually 25% more. IC trains are express trains, the most comfortable and modern. *Gyorsvonat* (fast trains) take longer and use older cars; *személyvonat* (passenger trains) stop at every village along the way. Seat reservations *(helyjegy)* cost extra and are required on IC and some fast trains; these are indicated on the timetable by an 'R' in a box or a circle (a plain 'R' means seat reservations are available but not required).

In all stations a yellow board indicates departures *(indul)* and a white board arrivals *(érkezik)*. Express and fast trains are indicated in red, local trains in black. In some stations, large black-and-white schedules are plastered all over the walls.

Most train stations have left-luggage offices that are open at least from 9am to 5pm.

If you're travelling with a bicycle, many trains now transport bikes in cars marked with a bicycle symbol. When buying tickets, let the ticket seller know you are bringing a bike. Bike fare is normally half the regular passenger fare.

Consider purchasing the Hungary pass from Eurail, available to non-European residents only, before entering the country. It costs US$99/139 for five/10 days of 1st-class travel in a 15-day period, and US$75/89 for youths in 2nd class. Children aged five to 11 pay half price. You would, however, need to use it a lot to get your money's worth.

Liechtenstein

Best Places to Eat

» Torkel (p383)

» Bergrestaurant
Sareiserjoch (p385)

Best Places to Stay

» Gasthof Löwen (p383)

» Kulm (p385)

Why Go?

Liechtenstein makes a fabulous trivia subject – *Did you know it is the sixth smallest country in the world?... It's still governed by an iron-willed monarch who lives in a gothic castle on a hill... Yes, it really is the world's largest producer of false teeth.* It's worth visiting this pocket-sized principality solely for the cocktail-party bragging rights, but keep the operation covert. This theme-park micronation takes its independence seriously and would shudder at the thought of being visited for novelty value alone.

Liechtenstein wows with its stunning natural beauty. Measuring just 25km by 6km, it's barely larger than Manhattan, doesn't have an international airport and is reached by public bus from Switzerland and Austria. Vaduz is not the most soulful place on earth, but if you've come this far – coachloads of day trippers do simply for the souvenir passport stamp – venture away from the capital. A riot of hiking and cycling trails offering spectacular views of craggy cliffs, quaint villages and lush green forests awaits you.

When to Go
Vaduz

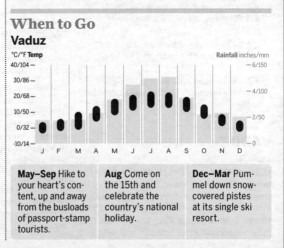

May–Sep Hike to your heart's content, up and away from the busloads of passport-stamp tourists.

Aug Come on the 15th and celebrate the country's national holiday.

Dec–Mar Pummel down snow-covered pistes at its single ski resort.

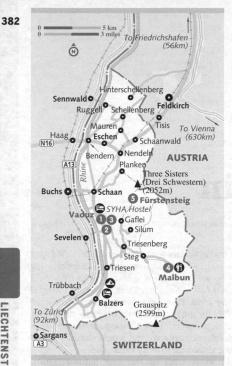

Liechtenstein Highlights

1 Snap a picture of the **Schloss Vaduz** with its stunning mountain backdrop (p382)

2 Get a souvenir **passport stamp** and send a postcard home (p384)

3 Taste royal wine at the **Hofkellerei des Fürstens**, the prince's own winery (p382)

4 Hit the slopes at **Malbun**, so you can say you've skied the Liechtenstein Alps (p385)

5 Test yourself with extreme hiking along the legendary **Fürstensteig trail** (p384)

VADUZ

POP 5160

Vaduz is the kind of capital city where the butcher knows the baker. With its tidy, quiet streets, lively patio cafes and big Gothic-looking castle on a hill, it feels more like a village than anything else. It's also all that most visitors to Liechtenstein will see, and at times it can feel like its soul has been sold to cater to the whims of the tourist hordes. Souvenir shops, tax-free luxury goods stores and cube-shaped concrete buildings dominate the small, somewhat bland town centre enclosed by Äulestrasse and the pedestrian-only Städtle.

◉ Sights & Activities

Schloss Vaduz CASTLE
(Fürst-Franz-Josef Strasse 150) Although Vaduz Castle is not open to the public, its exterior graces many a photograph and it is worth climbing up the hill for. At the top, there's a magnificent vista of Vaduz with a spectacular mountain backdrop. There's also a network of walking trails along the ridge. For a peek inside the castle grounds, arrive on 15 August (Liechtenstein's national day), when there are magnificent fireworks and the prince invites the entire country over to his place for a glass.

Liechtensteinisches Landesmuseum MUSEUM
(National Museum; ☎239 68 20; www.landes museum.li; Städtle 43; adult/concession Sfr8/5, incl Kunstmuseum Sfr15/5; ◉10am-5pm Tue-Sun, to 8pm Wed) This well-designed museum provides an interesting romp through the principality's history.

Kunstmuseum Liechtenstein MUSEUM
(☎235 03 00; www.kunstmuseum.li; Städtle 32; adult/concession Sfr12/8, incl Landesmuseum Sfr15/5; ◉10am-5pm Tue-Sun, to 8pm Thu) The mainstay of this museum is contemporary art, not the prince's collection of old masters, which has been relocated to the Palais Liechtenstein museum (p43) in Vienna.

Postmuseum MUSEUM
(☎236 61 05; 1st fl, Städtle 37; admission free; ◉10am-noon & 1-5pm) On the first floor, above the post office, this museum showcases all national stamps issued since 1912.

Hofkellerei des Fürstens VINEYARD
(☎232 10 18; www.hofkellerei.li; ◉shop open 8am-noon & 1.30-6.30pm Mon-Fri, 9am-1pm Sat) You must be in a group for a tour at the prince's vineyard, 1km north of the centre of Vaduz. Independent travellers can visit and indulge in a taste at the shop.

Mitteldorf HISTORIC AREA
To see how Vaduz once looked, head northeast from the pedestrian zone to this charming quarter of traditional houses and verdant gardens.

Sleeping

Gasthof Löwen HOTEL $$
(☎238 11 41; www.hotel-loewen.li; Herrengasse 35; s/d Sfr199/299; P☎) Historic and creakily elegant, this six-centuries-old inn has eight spacious rooms with antique furniture and modern bathrooms. There's a cosy bar, fine-dining restaurant and a rear outdoor terrace overlooking grapevines.

Landgasthof Au HOTEL $$
(☎232 11 17; Austrasse 2; s/d Sfr90/140, with shared bathroom Sfr68/110; P) A couple of bus stops south of Vaduz town centre (about a 10-minute walk), this simple, family-run place is a reasonable budget option. A couple of the bigger doubles have terraces.

Camping Mittagspitze CAMPING GROUND $
(☎392 36 77, 392 23 11; www.campingtriesen.li; per adult/child/car Sfr9/4/5, per tent Sfr6-8; ⊙year-round; ☒) A well-equipped camping ground in a leafy spot with a restaurant, TV lounge, playground and kiosk, and a swimming pool in summer. Find it 3.5km outside Vaduz, south of Triesen.

SYHA Hostel HOSTEL $
(☎232 50 22; www.youthhostel.ch/schaan; Untere Rütigasse 6; dm/s/d Sfr33/57/84; ⊙Mar-Oct) This hostel caters particularly to cyclists and families. Halfway between Schaan and Vaduz, it's within easy walking distance of both towns. Reception is open from 10am to 5pm.

Landhaus am Giessen HOTEL $$
(☎235 00 35; www.giessen.li; Zollstrasse 16; s/d Sfr100/150; P☒☎) A fairly modern affair with comfortable and good-sized, if comparatively charmless, rooms. It has a sauna and offers massages.

Hotel Falknis HOTEL $
(☎232 63 77; Landstrasse 92; s/d with shared bathroom Sfr55/110; P) Basic rooms located north of the centre – 15 minutes on foot or take the bus.

Eating

Pedestrian-only Städtle has a clutch of footpath restaurants and cafes.

TOP CHOICE **Torkel** SWISS $$$
(☎232 44 10; Hintergasse 9; mains Sfr42-60; ⊙lunch & dinner Mon-Fri, dinner Sat) Just above the prince's vineyards sits His Majesty's ivy-clad restaurant. The garden terrace enjoys a wonderful perspective of the castle above, while the ancient, wood-lined interior is cosy in winter. Food mixes classic with modern.

Adler Vaduz INTERNATIONAL $$
(☎232 21 31; www.adler.li; Herrengasse 2; mains Sfr18-50; ⊙lunch & dinner Mon-Fri) A pleasant restaurant in the Hotel Adler, offering a broad selection of cuisine, from pasta to *rindsfilet vom grill auf steinpilzrisotto mit trüffel-rotweinsauce nappiert* (beef steak

NUTS & BOLTS

- **Capital** Vaduz
- **Currency** Swiss franc (Sfr)
- **Area** 155 sq km
- **Telephone codes** country code ☎423; international access code ☎00
- **Emergency** ☎112; ambulance ☎144; fire ☎118; police ☎117
- **Official language** German, although – as in Switzerland – the Swiss-German dialect is the de facto spoken language
- **Visas** Schengen rules apply
- **Exchange rates** A$1 = Sfr0.95; C$1 = 0.93Sfr; €1 = Sfr1.29; ¥100 = Sfr1.12; NZ$1 = Sfr0.68; UK£1 = Sfr1.46; US$1 = Sfr0.87
- **Famous for** dentures, postcards stamped by the country's postal service
- **Phrases** *gruezi* (hello; good day); *merci vielmal* (thank you very much); *adieu* (goodbye); *sprechen sie Englisch?* (do you speak English?)
- **Hostel bed** Sfr40 to Sfr60
- **One-day/week ski pass** Sfr45/205
- **Connections** Austria and Switzerland are the two obvious places to move on to from this tiny nation: to cross the border, hop on a local bus at the Swiss border towns of Buchs or Sargans, or at Austrian next-door-neighbour Feldkirch.

Vaduz

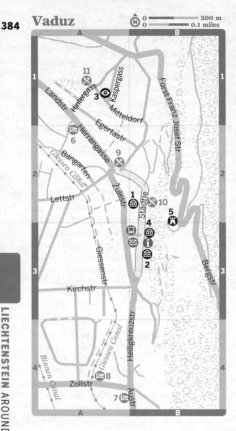

N 0 ———— 200 m
0 ———— 0.1 miles

full of information, can recommend excellent day hikes nearby and sells souvenir passport stamps for Sfr3.

Post office (Äulestrasse 38; 7.45am-6pm Mon-Fri, 8-11am Sat)

AROUND VADUZ

Outside Vaduz the air is crisp and clear with a pungent, sweet aroma of cow dung and flowers. The countryside, dotted with tranquil villages and enticing churches set to a craggy alps backdrop, is about as idyllic and relaxing as it gets.

Triesenberg, on a terrace above Vaduz, commands excellent views over the Rhine valley. It has a pretty, onion-domed church and the **Walsermuseum** (262 19 26; www. triesenberg.li; Jonaboda 2; adult/concession Sfr2/1; 7.45-11.45am & 1.30-5.45pm Mon-Fri, 7.45-11am & 1.30-5pm Sat), devoted to the Walser community, whose members came from Switzerland's Valais to settle in the 13th century. Take bus 21 from Vaduz.

There are loads of well-marked **cycling routes** through Liechtenstein (look for signs with a cycle symbol; distances and directions will also be included), as well as 400km of **hiking trails** (see www.wander wege-llv.li). The most famous is the **Fürstensteig trail**, a rite of passage for nearly every Liechtensteiner. You must be fit and not suffer from vertigo, as the path is narrow in places, reinforced with rope handholds and/or falls away to a sheer drop. The hike,

fillet with mushroom risotto and a truffle and red-wine sauce).

Café Wolf   INTERNATIONAL $$

(232 23 21; Städte 29; mains Sfr18-50; lunch & dinner) This relaxed cafe and restaurant has pavement tables in summer and a menu that mixes Swiss and international cuisine – anything from pizza to pseudo-Asian dishes.

Landgasthof Au   INTERNATIONAL $$

(232 11 17; Austrasse 2; mains Sfr18-36; lunch & dinner Wed-Sun) The Landgasthof Au garden restaurant has a good name for its local grub, which ranges from ham omelettes to a couple of vegetarian dishes and a kids' menu.

Information

Liechtenstein Center (239 63 00; www.tourismus.li; Städte 37; 9am-5pm) This snazzy, modern timber structure is chock-

which takes up to four hours, begins at the **Berggasthaus Gaflei** (take bus 22 from Triesenberg). Travel light and wear good shoes.

Malbun

POP 32

Welcome to Liechtenstein's one and only ski resort: found at the end of the road from Vaduz, the 1600m-high resort of Malbun feels like – in the nicest possible sense – the edge of the earth.

The road from Vaduz terminates at Malbun. There is an ATM by the lower bus stop. The **tourist office** (☑263 65 77; www.malbun.li; ⊙9am-noon & 1.30-5pm Mon-Sat, closed mid-Apr–May & Nov–mid-Dec) is on the main street.

Although rather limited in scope – the runs are mostly novice with a few intermediate and cross-country ones thrown in – the skiing is inexpensive for this part of the world and it does offer some bragging rights. Indeed, older British royals such as Prince Charles learned to ski here.

A general ski pass (including the Sareis chair lift) costs Sfr45/205 per day/week for adults and Sfr29/127 for children. One day's equipment rental from **Malbun Sport** (☑263 37 55; www.malbunsport.li; ⊙8am-6pm Mon-Fri, plus Sat & Sun Dec-Mar) costs Sfr60 including skis, shoes and poles.

Hotel Walserhof (☑264 43 23; Sfr140) is a simple mountain house with four doubles and cheerful outdoor dining. **Kulm** (☑237 27 79; www.hotelkulm.com; Sfr180) is a solid chalet with modern double rooms inside the timber house. For gob-smacking mountain views over dinner, it's hard to beat **Bergrestaurant Sareiserjoch** (☑268 21 01; www.sareis.li; mains Sfr20-35; ⊙Jun–mid-Oct & mid-Dec–Apr), at the end of the Sareis chair lift. Go for *käsknöpfli* (cheese-filled dumplings).

History

Liechtenstein was created by the merger of the domain of Schellenberg and the county of Vaduz in 1712 by the powerful Liechtenstein family. A principality under the Holy Roman Empire from 1719 to 1806, Liechtenstein finally achieved its full sovereign independence in 1866. A modern constitution was drawn up in 1921, but even today the prince retains the power to dissolve parliament and must approve every act before it becomes law. Prince Franz Josef II was the first ruler to live in the castle above the capital city of Vaduz. He died in 1989 and was succeeded by his son, Prince Hans-Adam II.

Liechtenstein has no military service and its minuscule army was disbanded in 1868. It is known for wine production, postage stamps, dentures and its status as a tax haven. In 2000 Liechtenstein's financial and political institutions were rocked by allegations that money laundering was rife in the country. In response to international outrage, banks agreed to stop allowing customers to bank money anonymously. But the principality remains under pressure to introduce more reforms.

In 2003 Hans-Adam won sweeping powers to dismiss the elected government, appoint judges and reject proposed laws. The following year he handed the day-to-day running of the country to his son Alois.

Scandal rocked the principality again in 2008 when it was discovered that more than 1000 high-flying Germans had evaded tax by depositing large sums of money in trusts run by a Liechtenstein bank partly owned

LIECHTENSTEIN TRIVIA

» Liechtenstein is the only country in the world named after the people who purchased it.

» In its last military engagement in 1866, none of its 80 soldiers was killed. In fact, 81 returned, including a new Italian 'friend'. The army was disbanded soon afterwards.

» Low business taxes means around 75,000 firms, many of them so-called 'letter box companies' with nominal head offices, are registered here – about twice the number of the principality's inhabitants.

» Liechtenstein is Europe's fourth-smallest nation (only the Vatican, Monaco and San Marino are smaller).

» If you ever meet the prince in the pub, make sure he buys a round. The royal family is estimated to be worth UK£3.3 billion.

by the royal family. Liechtenstein didn't dispute that such money could have wound up in its banks (tax evasion is not considered a crime). It was, at that time, considered an uncooperative country by the OECD (that is, a tax haven), but it accused Germany of spying. The country bowed to pressure in 2009 and began exchanging information with the British government. It was removed from the list of uncooperative countries that same year.

Food & Drink

Liechtenstein's cuisine borrows from its larger neighbours, and it is generally good quality but expensive. Basic restaurants provide simple but well-cooked food. Soups are popular and filling, and cheeses form an important part of the diet, as do rösti and wurst.

As in neighbouring Switzerland, restaurants are generally open five or six days a week for lunch and dinner (usually closed between 3pm and 6pm or 7pm). Cafes usually stay open all day, and bars tend to open from lunchtime until around midnight.

SURVIVAL GUIDE

Directory A–Z

Liechtenstein and Switzerland share almost everything, so for more information about Liechtenstein basics, see p612.

Unlike much of the rest of Europe, smoking in public places has yet to be banned in Liechtenstein, meaning you can freely smoke in hotels, restaurants and so on.

Unlike much of the rest of Europe, smoking in public places has yet to be banned in Liechtenstein, meaning you can freely smoke in hotels, restaurants and so on.

Business Hours

Offices 8am to 5pm, Monday to Friday

Restaurants 11:30am to 2:30pm for lunch, 5pm to 10pm for dinner

Shops 10am to 6 or 7pm Monday to Friday, to 4 or 5pm Saturday, closed on Sunday. Food stores open at 7 or 8am. Smaller shops close for an hour at lunch and tend to shut down around 5pm Monday through Friday.

> **WANT MORE?**
>
> Head to **Lonely Planet** (www.lonely planet.com/liechtenstein) for planning advice, author recommendations, traveller reviews and insider tips.

PRICE RANGES

Accommodation prices listed in this chapter are for double rooms with bathrooms during high season. We have used the following symbols to indicate price:

$$$	more than Sfr380
$$	Sfr125 to Sfr380
$	less than Sfr125

The following price indicators for the cost of a main course are used in the listings:

$$$	more than Sfr40
$$	Sfr20 to Sfr40
$	less than Sfr20

Getting There & Away

The nearest airports are Friedrichshafen (Germany) and Zürich (Switzerland), with train connections to the Swiss border towns of Buchs and Sargans. From there, there are usually buses to Vaduz (from Buchs Sfr2.50, Sargans Sfr3.75). Buses also run every 30 minutes from the Austrian border town of Feldkirch; you sometimes have to change at Schaan to reach Vaduz. The Vaduz bus station is on Städtle 38, next to the post office.

A few trains from Buchs to Feldkirch stop at Schaan (bus tickets are valid).

If you're travelling by road, the N16 from Switzerland passes through Liechtenstein via Schaan and ends at Feldkirch. The A13 follows the Rhine along the border. Minor roads cross into Liechtenstein at each motorway exit.

Getting Around

Bus travel is cheap and reliable; all fares cost Sfr2.40, or Sfr3.60 for journeys exceeding 13km (such as Vaduz to Malbun). Grab a timetable from the Vaduz tourist office.

Poland

Includes »

Why Go?

If they were handing out prizes for 'most eventful history', Poland would be sure to get a medal. The nation has spent centuries at the pointy end of history, grappling with war and invasion. Nothing, however, has succeeded in suppressing the Poles' strong sense of nationhood and cultural identity. As a result, centres such as bustling Warsaw and cultured Kraków exude a sophisticated energy that's a heady mix of old and new.

Away from the cities, Poland is a diverse land, from its northern beaches to its magnificent southern mountains. In between are towns and cities dotted with ruined castles, picturesque squares and historic churches.

Although prices are rising as its post-communist economy gathers momentum, Poland is still good value for travellers. As the Polish people work on combining their distinctive national identity with their place in the heart of Europe, it's a fascinating time to visit this beautiful country.

Best Places to Stay

» Castle Inn (p397)
» Hotel Żubrówka (p404)
» Grand Hotel Lublinianka (p419)
» Hotel Sabała (p426)
» Dom Zachariasza Zappio (p445)

Best Places to Eat

» Sketch (p398)
» Momo (p413)
» Restauracja JaDka (p435)
» Restauracja Pod Łososiem (p446)

When to Go

Warsaw

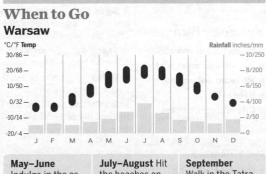

May–June
Indulge in the asparagus season, when Poland's restaurants serve this vegetable.

July–August Hit the beaches on Poland's long, sandy Baltic coast.

September
Walk in the Tatra Mountains, bedding down in a cosy hikers' refuge.

Fast Facts

» **Area** 312, 685 sq km

» **Capital** Warsaw

» **Telephone country code** 48

» **Emergency**: 999 (ambulance), 998 (fire), 997 (police), 112 (from mobile phones)

Exchange rates

Australia	A$1	2.90zł
Canada	C$1	2.86zł
euro	€1	3.95zł
Japan	¥100	3.31zł
New Zealand	NZ$1	2.18zł
UK	UK£1	4.48zł
USA	US$1	2.75zł

Set Your Budget

» **Budget hotel room** 150zł

» **Two-course meal** 50zł

» **Museum entrance** 10zł

» **Beer** 6-9zł

» **City transport ticket** 2.50zł

Resources

» **Official travel site** (www.poland.travel)

» **News and website directory** (www.poland.pl)

Connections

Due to its central position, Poland offers plenty of possibilities for onward travel. The country is well connected by train: there are direct connections to Berlin from both Warsaw (via Poznań) and Kraków; to Prague from Warsaw and Kraków; and to Kyiv from Warsaw and Kraków (via Przemyśl and Lviv). Trains also link Warsaw to Minsk and Moscow, and Gdańsk to Kaliningrad. International buses head in all directions, including eastward to the Baltic States. From southern Zakopane, it's easy to hop to Slovakia via bus, or even minibus. And from the Baltic coast ports of Gdańsk, Gydnia and Świnoujscie, ferries head to various ports in Denmark and Sweden.

ITINERARIES

One Week

Spend a day exploring Warsaw with a stroll round the Old Town and a stop at the Warsaw Rising Museum. The next day, head to Kraków for three days, visiting the Old Town, Wawel Castle, the former Jewish district of Kazimierz, and Wieliczka. Take a day trip to Oświęcim, then head on to Zakopane for two days.

Two Weeks

Follow the above itinerary, then on the eighth day travel to Wrocław for two days. Progress north to Toruń for a day, then onward to Gdańsk for two days, exploring the Old Town and visiting Westerplatte. Wind down with a couple of days at the seaside in Sopot.

Essential Food & Drink

» **Żurek** This hearty sour soup comes with sausage and hard-boiled egg, or try *barszcz* (red beetroot soup).

» **Bigos** Extinguish hunger pangs with this thick sauerkraut and meat stew, or *placki ziemniaczane* (potato pancakes often topped with a meaty sauce).

» **Beer** It's good, cold and inexpensive, and often served in colourful beer gardens.

» **Vodka** Try it plain, or ask for *myśliwska* (flavoured with juniper berries).

» **Szarlotka** Sweets include this apple cake with cream and the weighty *sernik* (baked cheesecake).

Poland Highlights

① Experience the beauty and history of Kraków's **Wawel Castle** (p405)

② Meet European bison and other magnificent fauna at **Białowieża National Park** (p403)

③ Hunt for **gnome statues** in the Old Town of Wrocław (p431)

④ Remember the victims of Nazi genocide at former extermination camp **Auschwitz-Birkenau** (p416)

⑤ Soak up the cosmopolitan vibe of **Gdańsk** (p442) and take a dip in the Baltic at nearby **Sopot** (p448)

⑥ Enjoy the skiing or hiking life of the **Tatra Mountains** (p427)

⑦ Discover Warsaw's tragic wartime history at the **Warsaw Rising Museum** (p396)

WARSAW

POP 1.7 MILLION

Warsaw (Warszawa in Polish, var-*shah*-va) may not be the prettiest of Poland's cities, but there's no mistaking its dynamism. As the bustling capital and business centre of the nation, Warsaw is home to an array of dining and nightlife that's the equal of any European city its size.

It's true, however, that Warsaw can be hard work. The city centre sprawls across a wide area, quite separate from the attractive but tourist-heavy Old Town, and its traffic-choked streets lined with massive concrete buildings can be less than enthralling.

However, look at Warsaw with a historic perspective and you'll see the capital in an entirely new light. As a city that's survived everything fate could throw at it – including the complete destruction of its historic heart in WWII – Warsaw is a place with an extraordinary backstory.

When you factor in its entertainment options; the beauty of its reconstructed Old Town, Royal Way and former Royal Parks; and the history represented by the Stalinist-era Palace of Culture and the Warsaw Rising Museum, what emerges is a complex city that well repays a visit.

History

The Mazovian dukes were the first rulers of Warsaw, establishing it as their stronghold in the 14th century. The city's strategic central location led to the capital being transferred from Kraków to Warsaw in 1596, following the earlier union of Poland and Lithuania.

Although the 18th century was a period of catastrophic decline for the Polish state, Warsaw underwent a period of prosperity during this period. Many magnificent churches, palaces and parks were built, and cultural and artistic life blossomed. The first (short-lived) constitution in Europe was instituted in Warsaw in 1791.

In the 19th century Warsaw declined in status to become a mere provincial city of the Russian Empire. Following WWI, the city was reinstated as the capital of a newly independent Poland and once more began to thrive. Following the Warsaw Rising of 1944, the city centre was devastated and the entire surviving population forcibly evacuated. Upon war's end, the people of Warsaw returned to the capital, and set about rebuilding its historic heart.

Since the fall of communism, and particularly since Poland's entry into the EU, Warsaw has been undergoing an economic boom, which has reshaped its commercial heart.

◉ Sights

The Vistula River divides the city. The western left-bank sector features the city centre, including the Old Town, the historic nucleus of Warsaw. Almost all tourist attractions, as well as most tourist facilities, are on this side of the river.

If arriving by train, Warszawa Centralna station is, as the name suggests, within walking distance of the city centre and major attractions. If you arrive by bus at either major PKS bus station, you can take a train from an adjoining station into the centre.

OLD TOWN

Castle Square HISTORIC SQUARE

(Map p392) Known as Plac Zamkowy in Polish, this square is the main gateway to the Old Town. All the buildings here were superbly rebuilt from their foundations after WWII, earning the Old Town a place on Unesco's World Heritage List. Within the square stands the **Monument to Sigismund III Vasa**, who moved the capital from Kraków to Warsaw in 1596.

Royal Castle CASTLE

(Map p392; Plac Zamkowy 4; adult/concession 22/14zł; ☉10am-4pm Mon-Sat, 11am-4pm Sun, closed Mon Oct-Apr) The dominant feature of the square is this massive 13th-century castle, also reconstructed after the war. The highlight of the sumptuously decorated rooms is the Senators' Antechamber, where landscapes of 18th-century Warsaw by Bernardo Bellotto (Canaletto's nephew) are on show.

Historical Museum of Warsaw MUSEUM

(Map p392; www.mhw.pl; Rynek Starego Miasta 42; adult/concession 8/4zł, free Sun; ☉11am-6pm Tue & Thu, 10am-3.30pm Wed & Fri, 10.30am-4.30pm Sat & Sun) Off the magnificent **Old Town Market Sq** (Rynek Starego Miasta) is the Warsaw Historical Museum. At noon it shows an English-language film depicting the wartime destruction of the city (admission 6zł).

Barbican FORTIFICATION

(Map p392; ul Nowomiejska) Northwest of the Old Town Market Sq along ul Nowomiejska is the Barbican, an imposing fortified section of the medieval city walls. You can clamber onto the city walls via walkways

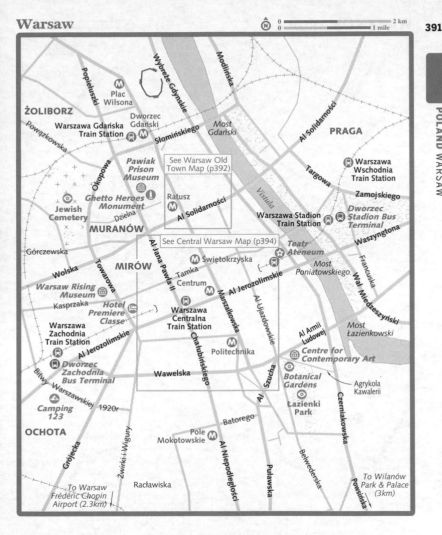

ŻOLIBORZ

Popiełuszki

Plac
Wilsona

Dworzec
Gdański

Warszawa Gdańska
Train Station

Powązkowska

Słomińskiego

Wybrzeże Gdyńskie

Modlińska

Most
Gdański

Al Solidarności

PRAGA

Warszawa
Wschodnia
Train Station

Targowa

Zamojskiego

Okopowa

Pawiak
Prison
Museum

See Warsaw Old
Town Map (p392)

Ratusz

Al Solidarności

Vistula

Dworzec
Stadion Bus
Terminal

Jewish
Cemetery

Ghetto Heroes
Monument

Dzielna

MURANÓW

Warszawa Stadion
Train Station

Waszyngtona

Górczewska

See Central Warsaw Map (p394)

Teatr
Ateneum

Francuska

Wolska

Towarowa

MIRÓW

Al Jana Pawła II

Świętokrzyska

Tamka

Centrum

Al Jerozolimskie

Most
Poniatowskiego

Wał Miedzeszyński

Warsaw Rising
Museum

Kasprzaka

Hotel
Premiere
Classe

Warszawa
Centralna
Train Station

Marszałkowska

Al Ujazdowskie

Al Armii
Ludowej

Most
Łazienkowski

Warszawa
Zachodnia
Train Station

Al Jerozolimskie

Chałubińskiego

Politechnika

Szucha

Centre for
Contemporary Art

Bitwy

Dworzec
Zachodnia
Bus Terminal

Wawelska

Botanical
Gardens

Agrykola
Kawalerii

Warszawskiej

1920r

Al

Łazienki
Park

Czerniakowska

Camping
123

OCHOTA

Żwirki i Wigury

Pole
Mokotowskie

Batorego

Al Niepodległości

Puławska

Belwederska

To Warsaw
Frédéric Chopin
Airport (2.3km)

Racławiska

Grójecka

To Wilanów
Park & Palace
(3km)

Powsińska

here and get a feel for the height of the Old Town above the Vistula.

Marie Skłodowska-Curie Museum MUSEUM
(Map p392; ul Freta 16; adult/concession 10/5zł; ⊙10am-4pm Tue-Sat, 10am-3pm Sun) North along ul Freta is the Marie Skłodowska-Curie Museum, which features unexciting displays about the great lady, who, along with husband Pierre, discovered radium and polonium, and laid the foundations for radiography, nuclear physics and cancer therapy.

St John's Cathedral CHURCH
(Map p392; ul Świętojańska 8; crypt 2zł; ⊙10am-1pm & 3-5.30pm Mon-Sat) Near the castle is Warsaw's oldest church, the 15th-century Gothic St John's Cathedral.

Adam Mickiewicz Museum of Literature
MUSEUM
(Map p392; Rynek Starego Miasta 20; adult/concession 6/5zł, free Sun; ⊙10am-4pm Mon, Tue & Fri, 11am-6pm Wed & Thu, 11am-5pm Sun) This literary museum features exhibits on Poland's most revered literary figure and other leading writers.

Monument to the Warsaw Rising
MONUMENT
(Map p392; cnr ul Długa & ul Miodowa) West of the Old Town, this striking set of statuary

Warsaw Old Town

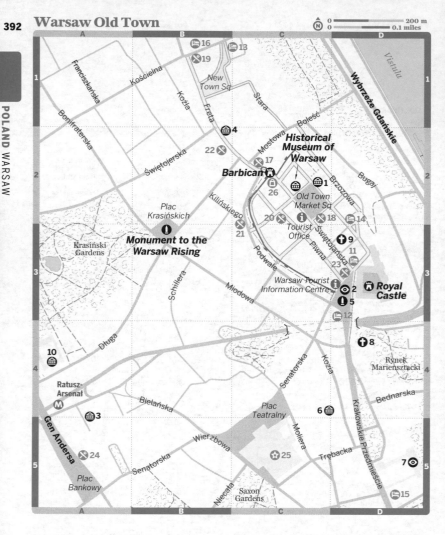

honours the heroic Polish revolt against German rule in 1944.

State Archaeological Museum MUSEUM (Map p392; ul Długa 52; adult/concession 8/4zł, free Sun; ⊙9am-4pm Mon-Thu & Sat, 10am-4pm Sun) Near the Ratusz-Arsenał metro station the State Archaeological Museum is located in a 17th-century former arsenal.

ROYAL WAY (SZLAK KRÓLEWSKI)

This 4km route links the Royal Castle with Łazienki Park (see p393) via ul Krakowskie Przedmieście, ul Nowy Świat and Al Ujazdowskie. Bus 180 runs along or near this route and continues south to Wilanów Park (see p395). Bus 100 also runs on Saturday and Sunday from May to September, between Plac Zamkowy and Łazienki Park.

Saxon Gardens GARDENS (Map p394; ⊙24hr) West of the Royal Way are these attractive gardens, at whose entrance stands the small but poignant **Tomb of the Unknown Soldier**. It's housed within the only surviving remnant of the Saxon Palace that once stood here and was destroyed by the Nazis. The ceremonial **changing of the guard** takes place at noon on Sunday.

POLAND WARSAW

Church of the Holy Cross CHURCH
(Map p394; ul Krakowskie Przedmieście 3; ☺erratic)
Further south along the Royal Way is this prominent 17th-century church. Chopin's heart is preserved in the second pillar on the left-hand side of the main nave. It was brought from Paris, where he died of tuberculosis aged only 39.

Chopin Museum MUSEUM
(Map p394; ul Okólnik 1; adult/concession 22/13zł, free Tue; ☺noon-8pm Tue-Sun) To learn more about Poland's most renowned composer, head along ul Tamka to this institution devoted to his life and work. On show are letters, handwritten musical scores and the great man's last piano.

National Museum MUSEUM
(Map p394; www.mnw.art.pl; Al Jerozolimskie 3; adult/concession 12/7zł, incl temporary exhibitions 17/10zł, free Sat; ☺10am-4pm Tue-Thu, noon-9pm Fri, noon-6pm Sat & Sun) East of the junction of ul Nowy Świat and Al Jerozolimskie is the National Museum, with an impressive collection of Greek and Egyptian antiquities, Coptic frescos, medieval woodcarvings and Polish paintings. Look out for the surrealistic fantasies of Jacek Malczewski.

Łazienki Park GARDENS
(Map p391; ☺daylight hr) This large, shady and popular park is best known for the 18th-century **Palace upon the Water** (adult/concession 12/9zł; ☺9am-4pm Tue-Sun). It was the summer residence of Stanisław August Poniatowski, the last king of Poland, who was deposed by the Russian army and confederation of Polish magnates in 1792. The park was once a royal hunting ground attached to Ujazdów Castle.

Also within the boundary of the park is the **Old Orangery** (adult/concession 6/4zł), which contains a sculpture gallery and an 18th-century theatre. Between noon and 4pm every Sunday from May to September, **piano recitals** are held among the nearby rose gardens.

St Anne's Church CHURCH
(Map p392; ul Krakowskie Przedmieście 68; ☺11am-8pm) Just south of the Royal Castle, this ornate 15th-century church has impressive views from its **tower** (adult/concession 3/2zł; ☺11am-8pm May-Oct).

Museum of Caricature MUSEUM
(Map p392; www.muzeumkarykatury.pl; ul Kozia 11; adult/concession 5/3zł, free Sat; ☺11am-6pm Tue-Sun) Along a side street off ul Krakowskie Przedmieście is this quirky museum, exhibiting numerous original works by Polish and foreign caricaturists, created from the 18th century onwards.

Radziwiłł Palace PALACE
(Map p392) Further south along ul Krakowskie Przedmieście you'll see the Radziwiłł Palace, the residence of the Polish president. Not open to the public.

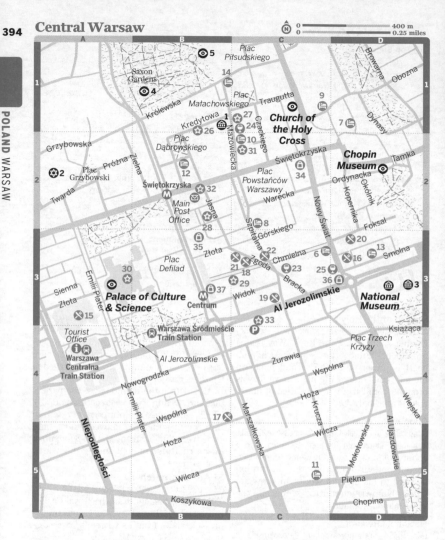

Ethnographic Museum   MUSEUM
(Map p394; ul Kredytowa 1; adult/concession
10/5zł, Wed free; ⊙10am-4pm Tue-Sat, noon-5pm
Wed, 10am-5pm Sat & Sun) South of the Tomb
of the Unknown Soldier, in the Saxon
Gardens, is the Ethnographic Museum. It
displays Polish folk costumes, and regional
arts and crafts.

Polish Army Museum   MUSEUM
(Map p394; Al Jerozolimskie 3; adult/concession
10/5zł, free Wed; ⊙10am-4pm Wed-Sun) Next
door to the National Museum is this museum recording the history of the Polish

army, with military vehicles outside and
miscellaneous militaria within.

Centre for Contemporary Art   ART GALLERY
(Map p391; www.csw.art.pl; Al Ujazdowskie 6;
adult/concession 12/6zł, free Thu; ⊙noon-7pm
Tue-Sun) This cutting-edge gallery is housed
in the reconstructed Ujazdów Castle, originally built during the 1620s.

Botanical Gardens   GARDENS
(Map p391; adult/concession 5/2.50zł; ⊙10am-
8pm Apr-Aug, 10am-6pm Sep-Oct) Further
south from the Centre for Contemporary

Art are these small but pleasant gardens, suitable for whiling away an idle hour on a sunny day.

WILANÓW

Wilanów Park GARDENS
(ul Wisłostrada; adult/concession 5/3zł, free Tue; ☉9am-dusk) Another magnificent park lies 6km southeast of Łazienki Park. Its centrepiece is the splendid **Wilanów Palace** (www.wilanow-palac.art.pl; adult/concession 20/15zł, free Sat; ☉9.30am-4.30pm Mon-Sat, 10.30am-6.30pm Sun), the summer residence of King Jan III Sobieski, who ended the Turkish threat to Central Europe by defeating the Turks at Vienna in 1683. In summer, be prepared to wait. The last tickets are sold one hour before closing time.

In the well-kept park behind the palace is the **Orangery** (admission fee varies with exhibitions; ☉10am-6.30pm), which houses an art gallery. The **Poster Museum** (adult/concession 10/6zł, free Mon; ☉noon-4pm Mon, 10am-6pm Tue-Sun) in the former royal stables is a repository of Poland's world-renowned poster art.

To reach Wilanów, take bus 116 or 180 from ul Nowy Świat or Al Ujazdowskie.

CITY CENTRE

Palace of Culture & Science LANDMARK
(Map p394; www.pkin.pl; Plac Defilad 1; ☉9am-6pm) Massive, brooding and inescapable, this towering structure has become an emblem of the city, as it's slowly rehabilitated from its Stalinist past. It has a particularly sinister aspect at dusk, though it's also a handy landmark. The palace was built in the early 1950s as a 'gift of friendship' from the Soviet Union (the kind of unwanted gift that's hard to hide away), and is still one of Europe's tallest buildings (over 230m). The clock faces were added to the building in the post-communist period.

The **observation terrace** (adult/concession 20/15zł) on the 30th floor provides a panoramic view, though it can be very cold and windy.

WARSAW IN TWO DAYS

Wander through the **Old Town** and tour the **Royal Castle**. Head along the **Royal Way**, dropping into the **Museum of Caricature** en route, then have lunch at ever-so-cool **Sketch**. Take the lift to the top of the **Palace of Culture & Science** for views of the city, before promenading through the nearby **Saxon Gardens**.

The next day, visit the **Warsaw Rising Museum** in the morning, followed by lunch at one of the many restaurants along ul Nowy Œwiat. Spend the afternoon exploring **Łazienki Park**, before sipping a cocktail at **Sense**. Finish off the day with a visit to the nightclub district around **ul Mazowiecka**, or take in a concert at **Filharmonia Narodowa**.

WEST OF THE CITY CENTRE

TOP CHOICE Warsaw Rising Museum MUSEUM
(Map p391; ul Grzybowska 79; adult/concession 7/5zł, free Sun; ⊙8am-6pm Mon, Wed & Fri, 8am-8pm Thu, 10am-6pm Sat & Sun) This impressive museum commemorates Warsaw's insurrection against its Nazi occupiers in 1944, which was destined to end in defeat and the destruction of much of the city and its population. The Rising was viciously suppressed by the Germans (while the Red Army stood by on the opposite bank of the Vistula), with more than 200,000 Poles dying by its conclusion.

The moving story of the Rising is retold here via photographs, exhibits and audiovisual displays. The centrepiece is a massive memorial wall emitting a heartbeat and selected audio recordings. At the end of the journey there's a replica 1944 cafe, underlining the fact that life went on, even in the worst days of the struggle. Captions are in Polish and English. Catch trams 22 or 24 from Al Jerozolimskie, heading west.

FORMER JEWISH DISTRICT

The suburbs northwest of the Palace of Culture & Science were once predominantly inhabited by Jewish Poles. During WWII the Nazis established a Jewish ghetto in the area, but razed it to the ground after crushing the Warsaw Ghetto Uprising in April 1943.

Jewish Cemetery CEMETERY
(Map p391; ul Okopowa 49/51; admission 4zł; ⊙10am-5pm Mon-Thu, 9am-1pm Fri, 11am-4pm Sun) The most poignant remainder of the wartime tragedy is Europe's largest Jewish resting place. Founded in 1806, it has more than 100,000 gravestones. Visitors must wear a head covering to enter, and it's accessible from the Old Town on bus 180, heading north from ul Nowy Świat.

Ghetto Heroes Monument MONUMENT
(Map p391; cnr ul Anielewicza & ul Zamenhofa) This monument to the Jewish ghetto established here by the Nazis remembers its victims via pictorial plaques.

FREE Pawiak Prison Museum MUSEUM
(Map p391; ul Dzielna 24/26; ⊙10am-4pm Wed-Sun) Once a Gestapo prison during the Nazi occupation, this institution now contains moving exhibits, including letters and other personal items.

Jewish Historical Institute MUSEUM
(Map p392; ☑22 827 9221; www.jewishinstitute. org.pl; ul Tłomackie 3/5; adult/concession 10/5zł; ⊙9am-4pm Mon-Wed & Fri, 11am-6pm Thu) Houses permanent exhibits about the Warsaw Ghetto, as well as local Jewish artworks.

Nożyk Synagogue SYNAGOGUE
(Map p394; ul Twarda 6; admission 6zł; ⊙9am-8pm Mon-Fri, 11am-8pm Sun) Further south is this neo-Romanesque place of worship, Warsaw's only synagogue to survive WWII.

✦ Festivals & Events

International Book Fair BOOKS
(www.bookfair.pl) May

Mozart Festival MUSIC
(www.operakameralna.pl) June/July

Warsaw Summer Jazz Days MUSIC
(www.adamiakjazz.pl) July

Street Art Festival THEATRE
(www.sztukaulicy.pl) July

Warsaw Autumn International Festival of Contemporary Music MUSIC
(www.warsaw-autumn.art.pl) September

Warsaw Film Festival FILM
(www.wff.pl) October

🛏 Sleeping

Not surprisingly, Warsaw is the most expensive Polish city for accommodation, though there's a number of reasonably priced hostels around town. The tourist offices (p401) can help find a room.

Castle Inn
HOTEL €€

(Map p392; ☑22 425 0100; www.castleinn.eu; ul Świętojańska 2; s/d from 235/265zł) Progress up the stairs to the striking purple decor and shiny tiles of this Old Town accommodation, situated in a 17th-century tenement house. All rooms overlook either Castle Sq or St John's Cathedral, and come in a range of playful styles.

Oki Doki Hostel
HOSTEL €

(Map p394; ☑22 828 0122; www.okidoki.pl; Plac Dąbrowskiego 3; dm 37-73zł, s/d 132/220zł) There are no drab dorms here. Each is decorated thematically using the brightest paints available; try the communist (red with a big image of Lenin). Lower bunks have good headroom, and the shared bathrooms are clean and bright. The hostel also has a bar, free washing machine and a kitchen, and hires out bikes (27zł per day).

Nathan's Villa Hostel
HOSTEL €

(Map p394; ☑22 622 2946; www.nathansvilla.com; ul Piękna 24/26; dm 45-70zł, r 170-200zł) Nathan's sunlit courtyard leads to well-organised dorms, while private rooms are comfortable and decorated with monochrome photographs of Polish attractions. The kitchen is well set up, and there's a laundry, a book exchange and games to while away rainy days.

Hotel Le Regina
HOTEL €€€

(Map p392; ☑22 531 6000; www.mamaison.com/ leregina; ul Kościelna 12; d/ste from €160/700; ✳☀) It's not cheap, but Le Regina is a jaw-dropping combination of traditional architecture and contemporary design. The enormous rooms feature king-size beds with headboards of dark, polished wood. Deluxe rooms also have timber floors, and terraces with courtyard views. All rooms sport spectacular bathrooms with marble benchtops.

Apartments Apart
APARTMENTS €€

(Map p394; ☑22 351 2250; www.apartmentsapart. com; ul Nowy Świat 29/3; apt from €75) Company offering a range of apartments dotted through the Old Town and the city centre. Most include a washing machine in addition to a kitchen. Check online first, as last-minute web specials can be great value.

Hotel Bristol
HOTEL €€€

(Map p392; ☑22 551 1000; www.lemeridien.pl; ul Krakowskie Przedmieście 42/44; r from 750zł; ☀) Established in 1899 and restored to its former glory after a massive renovation, the Bristol is touted as Poland's most luxurious hotel. Its neoclassical exterior houses a feast of original art nouveau features, and huge, traditionally decorated rooms. Attentive staff cater to your every whim.

Hotel Premiere Classe
HOTEL €€

(Map p391; ☑22 624 0800; www.premiere-classe -warszawa.pl, in Polish; ul Towarowa 2; r 189zł) If you're not bothered too much by room size, this modern hotel makes a good base. Rooms are small but bright, and neatly set up with modern furnishings. Friendly staff is a plus. Guests can use the restaurants, bars and fitness centre in the neighbouring sister hotels.

Sofitel Victoria
HOTEL €€€

(Map p394; ☑22 657 8011; www.sofitel.com; ul Królewska 11; r from 490zł; ☀) The very model of a modern business hotel, with a spacious marble foyer, and a lounge area housing a small library of books on Polish culture and history. The rooms are conservatively decorated, with gleaming bathrooms.

Hostel Helvetia
HOSTEL €

(Map p394; ☑22 826 7108; www.hostel-helvetia. pl; ul Kopernika 36/40; dm 45-57zł, r 160-220zł) Bright hostel with an attractive combined lounge and kitchen. Dorms have lockers available, and there's one small women-only dorm. Bike hire is 25zł per day. Enter from the street behind, ul Sewerynów.

Hostel Kanonia
HOSTEL €

(Map p392; ☑22 635 0676; www.kanonia.pl; ul Jezuicka 2; dm/s/d 45/190/220zł) Housed in a historic building in the heart of the Old Town, accommodation is mostly in dorms, with only one double and one triple. Some rooms have picturesque views onto the cobblestone streets, and there's a dining room with basic kitchen facilities.

Dom Literatury
HOTEL €€€

(Map p392; ☑22 635 0404; www.fundacjadl.com/ hotele.html, in Polish; ul Krakowskie Przedmieście 87/89; s/d 220/370zł) Within a grand historic building, this accommodation features rambling halls and staircases bedecked with pot plants and sizeable paintings. There is a maze of comfortable rooms, many of which have excellent views of the Old Town and the Vistula. You're paying for the location, however, rather than the standard, and you can't expect too much English from the friendly staff.

Hotel Harenda
HOTEL €€

(Map p394; ☑22 826 0071; www.hotelharenda. com.pl; ul Krakowskie Przedmieście 4/6; s/d from 310/340zł) Boasting a great location just off the Royal Way, the Harenda's rooms are neat and clean, with solid timber furniture and an old-fashioned vibe. Breakfast is an additional 25zł.

Hotel Gromada Centrum
HOTEL €€

(Map p394; ☑22 582 9900; www.gromada.pl; Plac Powstańców Warszawy 2; s/d from 250/300zł) Centrally located, the Gromada is a big concrete box but also a great launching pad for exploring the central city. Upstairs from the funky green foyer, the featureless brown-carpeted corridors stretch out into the distance like an optical illusion. The rooms are plain, but clean and spacious.

Smolna Youth Hostel
HOSTEL €

(Map p394; ☑22 827 8952; www.hostelsmolna30.pl; ul Smolna 30; dm/s/d 40/70/130zł) Very central and very popular, though there's a midnight curfew (2am in July and August) and reception is closed between 10am and 4pm. It's simple but clean, and there's a lounge and kitchen area. Note that guests are separated into dorms according to gender, and reception is up four flights of stairs.

Dom Przy Rynku Hostel
HOSTEL €

(Map p392; ☑22 831 5033; www.cityhostel.net; Rynek Nowego Miasto 4; dm 55zł; ☺Jul-Sep) Only open in summer and located in a quiet corner of the busy New Town, Przy Rynku is a neat, clean and friendly hostel occupying a 19th-century house. Its rooms accommodate two to five people, and there's a kitchen and laundry for guest use.

Camping 123
CAMPING GROUND €

(Map p391; ☑22 823 3748; www.astur.waw.pl; ul Bitwy Warszawskiej 1920r 15/17; per person/tent 14/14zł, s/d 41/70zł; ▨) Set in extensive grounds near the Dworzec Zachodnia bus station. The cabins are available from mid-April to mid-October, and there's a tennis court nearby.

Hotel Mazowiecki
HOTEL €

(Map p394; ☑22 827 2365; www.hotelewam.pl; ul Mazowiecka 10; s/d from 112/140zł) Basic budget accommodation in a handy location on one of the city centre's nightlife strips. Most rooms have access only to shared bathrooms, but a few have en suites.

✘ Eating

The most recent revolution to conquer the Polish capital has been a gastronomic one. A good selection of restaurants can be found in the Old Town and New Town, and in the area between ul Nowy Świat and the Palace of Culture & Science.

Self-caterers can buy groceries at the **Albert Supermarket** (Map p394; ul Złota 59) in the Złote Tarasy shopping centre behind Warszawa Centralna train station; and **ML Delikatesy** (Map p392; ul Piwna 47) in the Old Town.

Sketch
TOP CHOICE
INTERNATIONAL €€

(Map p394; ☑60 276 2764; ul Foksal 19; mains 16-48zł; ☺noon-1am) Shiny bright restaurant and bar with orange furniture and cool wait staff. Mains include baguettes, salads, pasta and grilled dishes. At weekends the joint throws a 'before party' with DJs in its upstairs room from 10pm.

Bar Mleczny Pod Barbakanem
CAFETERIA €

(Map p392; ul Mostowa 27/29; mains 4-9zł; ☺8am-5pm Mon-Fri, 9am-5pm Sat & Sun) Near the Barbican, this popular former milk bar that survived the fall of the Iron Curtain continues to serve cheap, unpretentious food in an interior dominated by tiles. Fill up while peering out through the lace curtains at the passing tourist hordes.

Podwale Piwna Kompania
GRILL €€

(Map p392; ☑22 635 6314; ul Podwale 25; mains 22-50zł; ☺11am-1am Mon-Sat, noon-1am Sun) The restaurant's name (The Company of Beer) gives you an idea of the lively atmosphere in this eatery just outside the Old Town's moat. The menu features lots of grilled items and dishes such as roast duck, Wiener schnitzel, pork ribs and steak. There's a courtyard for outdoor dining.

Cô tú
ASIAN €

(Map p394; Hadlowo-Usługowe 21; mains 13-19zł; ☺10am-9pm Mon-Fri, 11am-7pm Sat & Sun) The wok at this simple Asian diner never rests, as hungry Poles can't get enough of the excellent dishes coming from the kitchen. The menu is enormous, covering seafood, vegetables, beef, chicken and pork, and you'll never have to wait more than 10 minutes for your food despite the queues. Duck through the archway at Nowy Świat 26 to find it.

Restauracja Pod Samsonem
JEWISH €€

(Map p392; ☑22 831 1788; ul Freta 3/5; mains 12-33zł) Situated in the New Town, and frequented by locals looking for inexpensive and tasty meals with a Jewish flavour. Interesting appetisers include Russian pancakes with salmon, and 'Jewish caviar'. Spot the bas relief of Samson and the lion above the next door along from the entrance.

Tukan Salad Bar VEGETARIAN €
(Map p392; ☎22 531 2520; Plac Bankowy 2; mains 9-18zł; ⊖8am-8pm Mon-Fri, 10am-6pm Sat) Vegetarian-friendly outlet offering a wide choice of salads. As the name suggests, look for the toucan on the door. It's hidden from the street in the arcade running parallel.

Restauracja Przy Zamku POLISH €€€
(Map p392; ☎22 831 0259; Plac Zamkowy 15; mains 39-85zł) An attractive, old-world kind of place with hunting trophies on the walls and attentive, apron-wearing waiters. The top-notch Polish menu includes fish and game and a bewildering array of entrées – try the excellent hare pâté served with cranberry sauce.

Dżonka ASIAN €€
(Map p394; ☎22 621 5015; ul Hoża 54; mains 16-30zł; ⊖11am-7pm Mon-Fri, noon-6pm Sat & Sun) This hidden gem serves a range of Asian dishes, covering Chinese, Japanese, Korean and Thai cuisine. Though small (just six tables), it has loads of personality, with dark timber surfaces, bamboo place mats and Japanese newspapers plastering the walls. There's some spicy food on the menu, including Sichuan cuisine, though it's been toned down a little for Polish palates.

London Steakhouse BRITISH €€
(Map p394; ☎22 827 0020; Al Jerozolimskie 42; mains 22-85zł) You'll find it hard to convince yourself you're in London, but it's fun to spot the UK memorabilia among the cluttered decor, while being served by waitresses wearing Union Jack neckties and miniskirts. Steaks dominate the menu, which also includes fish and chips. A full English breakfast is served daily from 11am to 2pm.

Bazyliszek Restauracja POLISH €€
(Map p392; ☎22 831 1841; Rynek Starego Miasta 1/3; mains 21-45zł) Step beneath the basilisk into this restaurant in a prime spot on Old Town Market Sq. It serves mainly Polish-style dishes, with forays into foreign cuisine like Argentinian steak.

Green Way VEGETARIAN €
(Map p394; ☎22 696 9321; ul Hoża 54; mains 8-15zł; ⊖10am-8pm Mon-Fri, 11am-7pm Sat & Sun) Slicker than the usual outlets of this chain, with a cafe ambience and a good outdoor dining zone. Take your pick of the international menu, which includes goulash, curry, samosas and enchiladas. Portions are hefty, and there's no table service.

Taqueria Mexicana MEXICAN €€
(Map p394; ☎22 556 4720; ul Zgoda 5; mains 24-54zł) Brightly hued place festooned with Mexican rugs, and featuring a central bar. Varieties of tacos, enchiladas and fajitas adorn the menu, and there's a 15zł set lunch from Monday to Friday.

Gospoda Pod Kogutem POLISH €€
(Map p392; ☎22 635 8282; ul Freta 50; mains 17-40zł) Cosy eatery at the top of the New Town, presenting quality versions of Polish classics in a soothing dark green interior. Eat outside in summer. If you're game, try pig's trotters 'the Polish way'.

Krokiecik CAFETERIA €
(Map p394; ul Zgoda 1; mains 10-20zł) Attractive cafeteria serving a range of inexpensive and tasty dishes, including good soups. The house speciality is *krokiety* (filled savoury pancakes).

Zgoda Grill Bar POLISH €€€
(Map p394; ☎22 827 9934; ul Zgoda 4; mains 28-45zł) A bright, informal place serving up a range of tasty Polish standards. There's also a decent salad bar available.

🍷 Drinking

TOP CHOICE **Sense** BAR
(Map p394; ul Nowy Świat 19; ⊖noon-late) A very modern venue with a mellow atmosphere. Comfortable banquettes sit beneath strings of cube-shaped lights, and there's an extensive wine and cocktail list. Try the house speciality, ginger rose vodka. There's also an impressive food menu if you're hungry.

Paparazzi BAR
(Map p394; ul Mazowiecka 12) This is one of Warsaw's flashest venues, where you can sip a bewildering array of cocktails under blown-up photos of Hollywood stars. It's big and roomy, with comfortable seating around the central bar.

Między Nami CAFE-BAR
(Map p394; ul Bracka 20) A mix of bar, restaurant and cafe, 'Between You & Me' attracts a trendy set with its designer furniture, whitewashed walls, and excellent vegetarian menu. There's no sign over the door; look for the white awnings and chilled crowd.

☆ Entertainment
Nightclubs
There's no shortage of good clubs in Warsaw. Explore ul Mazowiecka, ul Sienkiewicza and the area around ul Nowy Świat for nightclub

action. **Free jazz concerts** also take place in the Old Town Market Sq on Saturdays at 7pm in July and August.

Enklawa CLUB
(Map p394; www.enklawa.com, in Polish; ul Mazowiecka 12; ⊙9pm-4am Tue-Sat) Funky space with comfy plush seating, two bars and plenty of room to dance. Check out the long drinks list, hit the dance floor or observe the action from a stool on the upper balcony. Wednesday night is 'old school' night, with music from the '70s to '90s.

Tygmont JAZZ CLUB
(Map p394; ☑22 828 3409; www.tygmont.com.pl; ul Mazowiecka 6/8; ⊙7pm-late) Hosting both local and international acts, the live jazz here is both varied and plentiful. Concerts start around 8pm but the place fills up early, so either reserve a table or turn up at opening time. Dinner is also available.

Underground Music Café CLUB
(Map p394; www.under.pl, in Polish; ul Marszałkowska 126/134) A swarm of students and backpackers pour into this basement club for its cheap beer, dark lighting and selection of music that varies from '70s and '80s to house, R&B and hip-hop. Enter via the below-ground staircase facing McDonald's.

El Presidente CLUB
(Map p394; www.elpresidente.pl; ul Kredytowa 9; ⊙8pm-10pm Mon-Thu, 8pm-late Fri-Sat, noon-10pm Sun) Slickly decorated dance space with an illuminated gold bar contrasting with the black interior. Patrons are dressed to impress, and dance to dawn on Saturday and Sunday mornings.

Performing Arts
Advance tickets for most theatrical events can be bought at **ZASP Kasy Teatralne** (Map p394; ☑22 621 9454; Al Jerozolimskie 25; ⊙9am-7pm Mon-Fri) or from **EMPiK** Wars & Sawa shopping mall (Map p394; ul Marszałkowska 116/122); Royal Way (Map p394; ul Nowy Świat 15/17).

Teatr Ateneum THEATRE
(Map p391; ☑22 625 2421; www.teatrateneum.pl, in Polish; ul Jaracza 2) This place leans towards contemporary Polish-language productions.

Teatr Wielki OPERA
(Map p392; ☑22 692 0200; www.teatrwielki.pl; Plac Teatralny 1) The Grand Theatre hosts opera and ballet in its aptly grand premises.

Filharmonia Narodowa CLASSICAL MUSIC
(Map p394; ☑22 551 7111; www.filharmonia.pl; ul Jasna 5) Classical-music concerts are held here.

Cinemas
To avoid watching Polish TV in your hotel room, catch a film at the central **Kino Atlantic** (Map p394; ul Chmielna 33) or enjoy a flick in socialist-era glory at **Kinoteka** (Map p394; Plac Defilad 1) within the Palace of Culture & Science.

🔒 Shopping
There are also plentiful antique, arts and crafts shops around the Old Town Market Sq, so brandish your credit card and explore.

Wars & Sawa MALL
(Map p394; ul Marszałkowska 104/122) A sprawling modern shopping mall in the city centre.

Lapidarium JEWELLERY
(Map p392; ☑22 635 6828; www.lapidarium.pl; ul Nowomiejska 15/7) One of the most interesting shops on Old Town Market Sq; offers jewellery and communist-era collectibles.

American Bookstore BOOKS
(Map p394; ☑22 827 4852; ul Nowy Świat 61) For guidebooks and maps.

EMPiK BOOKS
Wars & Sawa shopping mall (Map p394; ul Marszałkowska 116/122); Royal Way (Map p394; ul Nowy Świat 15/17) A good source of English-language books, newspapers and magazines.

ℹ Information
Discount Cards
Warsaw Tourist Card (www.warsawcard.com; 1/3 days 35/65zł) Free or discounted access to museums, public transport and some theatres, sports centres and restaurants. Available from tourist offices and some accommodation.

Internet Access
Expect to pay around 5zł per hour for internet access in Warsaw. Several convenient but dingy internet cafes are also located within Warszawa Centralna train station.

Verso Internet (ul Freta 17; ⊙8am-8pm Mon-Fri, 9am-5pm Sat, 10am-4pm Sun) Enter from the rear, off ul Świętojerska.

Warsaw Point Gallery (Złote Tarasy, ul Złota 59; ⊙9am-10pm) Pay at the information desk of this shopping mall.

Medical Services
Apteka Grabowskiego (Warszawa Centralna; ⊙24hr) Nonstop pharmacy at the train station.

Centrum Medyczne LIM (☏22 458 7000; www.cm-lim.com.pl; 3rd fl, Marriott Hotel, Al Jerozolimskie 65/79) Offers specialist doctors, laboratory tests and house calls.

Dental-Med (☏22 629 5938; ul Hoża 27) A central dental practice.

Hospital of the Ministry of Internal Affairs & Administration (☏22 508 2000; ul Wołoska 137) A hospital preferred by government officials and diplomats.

Money

Banks, foreign-exchange offices (*kantors*) and ATMs are easy to find around the city centre. *Kantors* open 24 hours can be found at Warszawa Centralna train station and the airport, but exchange rates at these places are about 10% lower than in the city centre. Avoid changing money in the Old Town, where the rates can be even lower.

American Express (Marriott Hotel, Al Jerozolimskie 65/79; ☉7am-11pm)

Post

Main post office (Map p394; ul Świętokrzyska 31/33; ☉24hr)

Tourist Information

Each tourist office provides free city maps and free booklets, such as the handy *Warsaw in Short* and the *Visitor*, and sells maps of other Polish cities; offices also help with booking hotel rooms.

Free monthly tourist magazines worth seeking out include *Faces* and *Welcome to Warsaw*. The comprehensive *Warsaw Insider* (9.90zł) and *Warsaw in Your Pocket* (5zł) are also useful.

Tourist office (☏22 19431; www.warsawtour.pl) Old Town (Map p392; Rynek Starego Miasta 19; ☉9am-9pm May-Sep, 9am-7pm Oct-Apr); Okęcie airport (☉8am-8pm May-Sep, 8am-7pm Oct-Apr); main hall of Warszawa Centralna train station (Map p394; ☉8am-8pm May-Sep, 8am-7pm Oct-Apr).

Warsaw Tourist Information Centre (Map p392; ☏22 635 1881; www.wcit.waw.pl; pl Zamkowy 1/13; ☉9am-6pm Mon-Fri, 10am-6pm Sat & Sun) Helpful privately run tourist office in the Old Town.

Travel Agencies

Orbis Travel (☏22 827 7140; ul Bracka 16)

Our Roots (☏22 620 0556; ul Twarda 6) Offers Jewish heritage tours.

Trakt (☏22 827 8068; www.trakt.com.pl; ul Kredytowa 6) Guided tours of Warsaw and beyond.

ℹ Getting There & Away

Air

The **Warsaw Frédéric Chopin airport** (www.lotnisko-chopina.pl) is more commonly called Okęcie airport.

The useful tourist office is on the arrivals level of Terminal 2.

At the arrivals level there are ATMs and several *kantors*. There are also car-rental companies, a left-luggage room and a newsagent where you can buy public transport tickets.

Domestic and international flights can be booked at the **LOT office** (☏0801 703 703; Al Jerozolimskie 65/79), or at any travel agency. Other airlines are listed on p469.

Bus

Warsaw has two major bus stations for PKS buses. **Dworzec Zachodnia** (Western Bus Station; Map p391; www.pksbilety.pl; Al Jerozolimskie 144) handles domestic buses heading south, north and west of the capital, including up to 11 daily to Częstochowa (41zł, 3½ hours), 13 to Gdańsk (53zł, six hours), seven to Kraków (48zł, six hours), 11 to Olsztyn (35zł, 4½ hours), 15 to Toruń (42zł, four hours), five to Wrocław (54zł, seven hours) and five to Zakopane (60zł, eight hours). This complex is southwest of the city centre and adjoins the Warszawa Zachodnia train station. Take the commuter train that leaves from Warszawa Śródmieście station.

Dworzec Stadion (Stadium Bus Station; Map p391; www.pksbilety.pl; ul Sokola 1) adjoins the Warszawa Stadion train station. It is also easily accessible by commuter train from Warszawa Śródmieście. Dworzec Stadion handles some domestic buses to the east and southeast, including 16 daily to Lublin (23zł, three hours), four to Białystok (33zł, 3½ hours) and three to Zamość (35zł, 4¾ hours).

International buses depart from and arrive at Dworzec Zachodnia or, occasionally, outside Warszawa Centralna. Tickets are available from the bus offices at Dworzec Zachodnia, from agencies at Warszawa Centralna or from any of the major travel agencies in the city. **Eurolines Polska** (www.eurolinespolska.pl) operates a huge number of buses to destinations throughout Eastern and Western Europe; some sample routes include Amsterdam (225zł, 22 hours, four weekly), Cologne (200zł, 20½ hours, daily), London (300zł, 27 hours, four weekly), Paris (260zł, 26½ hours, four weekly), Rome (370zł, 28 hours, three weekly) and Vienna (175zł, 13 hours, four weekly).

Train

Warsaw has several train stations, but the one that most travellers will use is **Warszawa Centralna** (Warsaw Central; Map p394; Al Jerozolimskie 54). Refer to the relevant destination sections in this chapter for information about services to/from Warsaw.

Warszawa Centralna is not always where trains start or finish, so make sure you get on or off promptly; and guard your belongings against pickpocketing and theft at all times.

The station's main hall houses ticket counters, ATMs and snack bars, as well as a post office, newsagents and a tourist office. Along the underground mezzanine level leading to the platforms are several *kantors* (one of which is open 24 hours), a **left-luggage office** (⊘7am-midnight), lockers, eateries, outlets for local public transport tickets, internet cafes and bookshops.

Tickets for domestic and international trains are available from counters at the station (but allow at least an hour for possible queuing). Tickets for immediate departures on domestic and international trains are also available from numerous, well-signed booths in the underpasses leading to Warszawa Centralna.

Some domestic trains also stop at Warszawa Śródmieście station, 300m east of Warszawa Centralna, and Warszawa Zachodnia, next to Dworzec Zachodnia bus station.

❶ Getting Around
To/From the Airport
The cheapest way of getting from the airport to the city centre is bus 175, which leaves every 10 to 15 minutes and travels via Warszawa Centralna train station and ul Nowy Świat, terminating at Plac Piłsudskiego, about a 500m walk from Castle Sq in the Old Town. If you arrive in the wee hours, night bus N32 links the airport with Warszawa Centralna every 30 minutes.

The taxi fare between the airport and city centre is from 40zł to 45zł. Official taxis displaying a name, telephone number and fares can be arranged at the official taxi counters at the international arrivals level.

Car
Warsaw traffic isn't fun, but there are good reasons to hire a car for jaunts into the countryside. Major car-rental companies are listed in the local English-language publications, and include **Avis** (☑22 650 4872; www.avis.pl), **Hertz** (☑22 500 1620; www.hertz.com.pl) and **Sixt** (☑22 511 1550; www.sixt.pl). For more details about car hire, see p470.

Public Transport
Warsaw's public transport operates from 5am to 11pm daily. The fare (2.80zł) is valid for one ride only on a bus, tram, trolleybus or metro train travelling anywhere in the city.

Warsaw is the only place in Poland where ISIC cards get a public-transport discount (of 48%).

Tickets are available for 60/90 minutes (4/6zł), one day (9zł), three days (16zł), one week (32zł) and one month (78zł). Buy tickets from kiosks (including those marked 'RUCH') before boarding, and validate them on board.

A metro line operates from the suburb of Ursynów (Kabaty station) at the southern city limits to Młociny in the north, via the city centre (Centrum), but is of limited use to visitors. Local commuter trains head out to the suburbs from the Warszawa Śródmieście station.

Taxi
Taxis are a quick and easy way to get around – as long as you use official taxis and drivers use their meters. Beware of unauthorised 'Mafia' taxis parked in front of top-end hotels, at the airport, outside Warszawa Centralna train station and in the vicinity of most tourist sights.

MAZOVIA & PODLASIE

After being ruled as an independent state by a succession of dukes, Mazovia shot to prominence during the 16th century, when Warsaw became the national capital. The region has long been a base for industry, the traditional mainstay of Poland's second-largest city, Łódź. To the east of Mazovia, toward the Belarus border, lies Podlasie, which means 'land close to the forest'. The main attraction of this region is the impressive Białowieża National Park.

Łódź
POP 745,000

Little damaged in WWII, Łódź (pronounced woodge) is a lively, likeable place with a wealth of attractive art nouveau architecture, and the added bonus of being off the usual tourist track. It's also an easy day trip from Warsaw. Łódź became a major industrial centre in the 19th century, attracting immigrants from across Europe. Though its textile industry slumped in the post-communist years, the centrally located city had some success in attracting new investment in more diverse commercial fields.

Many of the attractions are along ul Piotrkowska, the main thoroughfare. You'll find banks and *kantors* here, and on ul Kopernika, one street west. You can't miss the bronze statues of local celebrities along ul Piotrkowska, including pianist Artur Rubenstein, seated at a baby grand. The helpful **tourist office** (⊘8am-7pm Mon-Fri, 10am-4pm Sat & Sun May-Oct, 8am-6pm Mon-Fri, 10am-2pm Sat Nov-Apr) hands out free tourist brochures.

◉ Sights
As Łódź is famous for being the centre of Poland's cinema industry (giving rise to the nickname 'Holly-Woodge'), film buffs will find some attractions of interest here. Along

ul Piotrkowska near the Grand Hotel, you can follow the **Walk of Fame**, a series of star-shaped plaques honouring Polish stars and directors such as Roman Polański.

Cinematography Museum
MUSEUM

(www.kinomuzeum.pl; Plac Zwycięstwa 1; adult/concession 8/5zł; ⊙10am-4pm Tue, Wed & Fri, 11am-6pm Thu, Sat & Sun) Three blocks east of ul Piotrkowska's southern pedestrian zone. Worth a look both for its collection of old cinema gear and its mansion setting.

Historical Museum of Łódź
MUSEUM

(ul Ogrodowa 15; adult/concession 8/5zł, free Sun; ⊙10am-2pm Mon, 2-6pm Wed, 11am-4pm Tue, Thu, Sat & Sun) Northwest of Plac Wolności, at the north end of the main drag.

Manufaktura
MALL

(www.manufaktura.com; ul Karskiego 5) Close by the Historical Museum is this fascinating shopping mall and entertainment centre constructed within a massive complex of historic red-brick factory buildings.

Dętka
TOUR

(Plac Wolności 2; adult/concession 5/3zł; ⊙noon-7pm Thu-Sun Jun-Sep) Guided tours every half-hour through the old brick sewer system beneath the city's streets, with exhibits en route. Operated by the Historical Museum.

Herbst Palace
MUSEUM

(ul Przędzalniana 72; adult/concession 7/4.50zł, free Thu; ⊙noon-5pm Wed, Thu & Fri, 11am-4pm Tue, Sat & Sun) Stately home, which has been converted into an appealing 19th-century art museum. It's accessible by bus 55 heading east from the cathedral at the southern end of ul Piotrkowska.

Jewish Cemetery
CEMETERY

(www.jewishlodzcemetery.org; ul Bracka 40; admission 4zł, free first Sun of month; ⊙9am-5pm Sun-Thu & 9am-3pm Fri Apr-Oct, 9am-3pm Sun-Fri Nov-Mar) One of the largest in Europe. It's 3km northeast of the city centre and accessible by tram 6 from a stop one block north of Plac Wolności to its terminus at Strykowska. Enter from ul Zmienna.

🛏 Sleeping & Eating

The tourist office can provide information about all kinds of accommodation.

Youth Hostel
HOSTEL €

(☑42 630 6680; www.yhlodz.pl; ul Legionów 27; dm 18-30zł, s/d from 45/70zł) This place is excellent, so book ahead. It features nicely decorated rooms in a spacious old build-ing, with free laundry and a kitchen. It's 250m west of Plac Wolności.

Hotel Savoy
HOTEL €€

(☑42 632 9360; www.hotelsavoy.com.pl; ul Traugutta 6; s/d from 130/272zł) Well positioned just off central ul Piotrkowska, with simple but spacious, light-filled rooms with clean bathrooms.

Hotel Centrum
HOTEL €€

(☑42 632 8640; www.centrumhotele.pl; ul Kilińskiego 59; s/d from 207/308zł) A little further east, offers neatly renovated rooms in a communist-era behemoth, handy for the Łódź Fabryczna train station.

Chłopska Izba
POLISH €€

(☑42 630 8087; ul Piotrkowska 65; mains 11-37zł; ⊙noon-11pm) On ul Piotrkowska is this restaurant with folksy decor, serving up tasty versions of all the Polish standards.

Esplanada
EUROPEAN €€

(☑42 630 5989; ul Piotrkowska 100; mains 19-45zł) A vibrant eatery serving quality Polish and German cuisine in an attractive historic venue.

❶ Getting There & Away

From the **airport** (www.airport.lodz.pl), which can be reached by city buses 55, 65 and L (2.40zł, 20 minutes), there are flights via Ryanair to several British and Irish destinations, including London (at least daily) and Dublin (twice weekly). There are no domestic flights.

From the convenient Łódź Fabryczna train station, 400m east of the city centre, you can travel to Warsaw (33zł, 1½ hours, hourly), Częstochowa (25zł, two hours, four daily) and Kraków (40zł, 4½ hours, two daily). From the Łódź Kaliska train station, 1.2km southwest of central Łódź and accessible by tram 12 from the city centre, trains go to Warsaw (35zł, 1¾ hours, four daily), Częstochowa (35zł, two hours, seven daily), Kraków (51zl, five hours, four daily), Wrocław (46zł, four hours, five daily), Poznań (31zł, 4½ hours, five daily), Toruń (37zł, 2½ hours, 12 daily) and Gdańsk (56zł, seven hours, five daily). Buses head in all directions from the bus terminal, next to the Łódź Fabryczna train station.

Białowieża National Park

Once a centre for hunting and timber-felling, Białowieża (Byah-wo-*vyeh*-zhah) is now Poland's oldest national park. Its significance is underlined by Unesco's unusual recognition of the reserve as both a Biosphere Reserve *and* a World Heritage Site. The forest contains over 100 species of birds, along with elk, wild boars and wolves. Its major drawcard is the magnificent European bison, which was once extinct outside zoos, but has been successfully reintroduced to its ancient home.

◉ Sights & Activities

The logical visitor base is the charming village of **Białowieża**. The main road to Białowieża from Hajnówka leads to the southern end of Palace Park (the former location of the Russian tsar's hunting lodge), then skirts around the park to become the village's main street, ul Waszkiewicza.

European Bison Reserve   ZOO
(Rezerwat Żubrów; adult/concession 6/3zł; ⊙9am-5pm May-Sep, 8am-4pm Tue-Sun Oct-Apr) An open-plan zoo containing many mighty bison, as well as wolves, strange horse-like tarpans and mammoth żubrońs (hybrids of bison and cows). Entrance to the reserve is just north of the Hajnówka–Białowieża road, about 4.5km west of the PTTK office – look for the signs along the żebra żubra (bison's rib) trail, or follow the green or yellow marked trails. Alternatively, catch a local bus to the stop at the main road turn-off (3zł) and walk a kilometre to the entrance, but ask the driver first if the bus is taking a route past the reserve.

Strict Nature Reserve   FOREST
(adult/concession 6/3zł; ⊙9am-5pm) The main attraction is the Strict Nature Reserve, whose boundaires begin about 1km north of Palace Park. It can only be visited on a three-hour tour with a licensed guide along an 8km trail (165zł for an English-speaking guide). Guides (in many languages) can be arranged at the PTTK office or any travel agency in the village. Note that the reserve does close sometimes due to inclement weather.

Although this is the only chance to encounter bison in their natural habitat, the creatures can be shy of visitors and you may not see them at all; visit the European Bison Reserve if you want a guarantee of spotting żubry. Even without bison for company, however, being immersed in one of Europe's last remnants of primeval forest is a special experience.

A comfortable way to visit the nature reserve is by horse-drawn cart (three hours), which costs 150zł in addition to guide and entry fees and holds four people. Otherwise, it may be possible (with permission from the PTTK office) to visit the reserve by bicycle (with a guide). A shop near the PTTK office hires out bikes (35zł per day), as do several hotels and pensions.

Palace Park   PARK
(⊙daylight hr) The elegant Palace Park is only accessible on foot, bicycle or horse-drawn cart across the bridge from the PTTK office. English-language signage explains its natural and historic features of interest.

Natural History Museum   MUSEUM
(adult/concession 12/6zł; ⊙9am-4.30pm) Within Palace Park is this excellent museum, with displays on local flora and fauna. There's a viewing tower (6zł), which you can climb for leafy vistas.

🛏 Sleeping & Eating

There are plenty of homes along the road from Hajnówka to Białowieża offering private rooms for about 40/70zł for singles/doubles.

TOP CHOICE Pokoje Gościnne BPN   HOTEL €
(☑85 682 9729; hotel@bpn.com.pl; s/d 120/130zł) Sparkling three-star option slap bang in the middle of Palace Park, with a good restaurant next door. Even the tsar would have been happy to lay his head here as an alternative to his old hunting lodge. Breakfast is 20zł extra.

Hotel Żubrówka   HOTEL €€€
(☑85 681 2303; www.hotel-zubrowka.pl; ul Olgi Gabiec 6; s/d from 380/420zł; ✉) Just across the way from the PTTK office, this is the town's best hotel. It's eccentrically decorated with animal hides, a working miniature water wheel, and pseudo cave drawings along the corridors. Rooms are predictably clean and comfortable, and there's a cafe, restaurant and nightclub on the premises, along with a sumptuous new swimming pool and wellness centre.

Paprotka Youth Hostel   HOSTEL €
(☑85 681 2560; www.paprotka.com.pl; ul Waszkiewicza 6; dm from 30zł, s/d 50/102zł) One of the best in the region. The rooms are light and spruce, with high ceilings and potted plants; the bathrooms are clean, and the kitchen is excellent. There's a washing machine as well.

Pension Gawra   HOTEL €
(☑85 681 2804; www.gawra.bialowieza.com; ul Polecha 2; d/tr from 130/150zł) A quiet, homey place with large rooms lined with timber in a hunting lodge-style, overlooking a pretty garden just behind the Hotel Żubrówka. The doubles with bathrooms are much more spacious than those without.

Pensjonacik Unikat   HOTEL €
(☑85 681 2774; www.unikat.bialowieza.com; ul Waszkiewicza 39; s/d 110/140zł) A bit too fond

of dead creatures' hides as decor, but good value with its tidy wood-panelled rooms, one of which is designed for disabled access. The restaurant offers specialities such as Belarus-style potato pancakes, and has a menu in both German and English.

ℹ Information

Money can be changed at the Hotel Żubrówka; the hotel also has an ATM by the entrance and offers public internet access in its foyer.

Serious hikers should contact the **National Park office** (☑85 682 9700; www.bpn.com.pl; ☺7.30am-3.30pm Mon-Fri) inside Palace Park. Most maps of the national park (especially the one published by Północnopodlaskie Towarzystwo Ochrony Ptaków (PTOP), North Podlasian Bird Protection Society) detail several enticing hiking trails.

Post office (☺7am-5pm Mon-Fri) At the western end of ul Waszkiewicza.

PTTK (Polskie Towarzystwo Turystyczno-Krajoznawcze, Polish Tourist Country Lovers Society; ☑85 681 2295; www.pttk.bialowieza. pl; ul Kolejowa 17; ☺8am-4pm) At the southern end of Palace Park.

ℹ Getting There & Away

Białowieża is a notoriously tricky place to reach by public transport. From Warsaw, the only direct option is the single daily bus to the village, departing at 2.50pm from Dworzec Stadion (39zł, 4½ hours).

Alternatively, head first from Warsaw to Białystok by train (39zł, 2½ hours, 13 daily) or bus (33zł, 3½ hours, four daily), from where two buses a day travel to Białowieża, at 6.30am and 3.20pm (11zł, 2½ hours). If you arrive in Białystok by train, cross the walkbridge to the bus station.

If you miss the direct Białowieża bus from Białystok, catch a bus to Hajnówka instead (10zł, two hours, twice hourly). From here you can switch to one of nine daily PKS bus services to Białowieża (5zł, one hour). A number of private companies also run fairly squeezy minibuses between Hajnówka and Białowieża (5zł, one hour, at least hourly).

MAŁOPOLSKA

Małopolska (literally 'lesser Poland') is a stunning area within which the visitor can spot plentiful remnants of traditional life amid green farmland and historic cities. The region covers a large swathe of southeastern Poland, from the former royal capital, Kraków, to the eastern Lublin Uplands.

Kraków
POP 755,000

While many Polish cities are centred on an attractive Old Town, none can compare with Kraków for sheer, effortless beauty. With a charming origin involving the legendary defeat of a dragon by either Prince Krakus or a cobbler's apprentice (depending on which story you believe), and with a miraculous escape from destruction in WWII, the city seems to have led a lucky existence.

As a result, Kraków is blessed with magnificent buildings and streets dating back to medieval times, and a stunning historic centrepiece, Wawel Castle.

Just south of the castle lies Kazimierz, the former Jewish quarter, reflecting both new and old. Its silent synagogues are a reminder of the tragedy of WWII, while the district's tiny streets and low-rise architecture have become home in recent years to a lively nightlife scene.

Not that you'll have trouble finding nightlife anywhere in Kraków, or a place to sleep. As the nation's biggest tourist drawcard, the city has hundreds of restaurants, bars and other venues tucked away in its laneways and cellars. Though hotel prices are above the national average, and visitor numbers high in summer, this vibrant, cosmopolitan city is an essential part of any tour of Poland.

◉ Sights & Activities
WAWEL HILL

Kraków's main draw for tourists is Wawel Hill. South of the Old Town, this prominent mount is crowned with a castle containing a cathedral, both of which are enduring symbols of Poland.

FREE **Wawel Castle** CASTLE
(Map p406; ☑12 422 5155; www.wawel. krakow.pl; grounds; ☺6am-dusk) You can choose from several attractions within this magnificent structure, each requiring a separate ticket, valid for a specific time. There's a limited daily quota of tickets for some parts, so arrive early if you want to see everything.

Most popular are the splendid **State Rooms** (adult/concession 17/10zł, free Sun Nov-Mar; ☺9.30am-5pm Tue-Fri, 11am-6pm Sat & Sun Apr-Oct, 10am-4pm Tue-Sun Nov-Mar) and the **Royal Private Apartments** (adult/concession 24/18zł; ☺9.30am-5pm Tue-Fri & 11am-6pm Sat & Sun Apr-Oct, 9.30am-4pm Tue-Sat Nov-Mar). Entry to the latter is only allowed on a guided tour; you may have to accompany a Polish

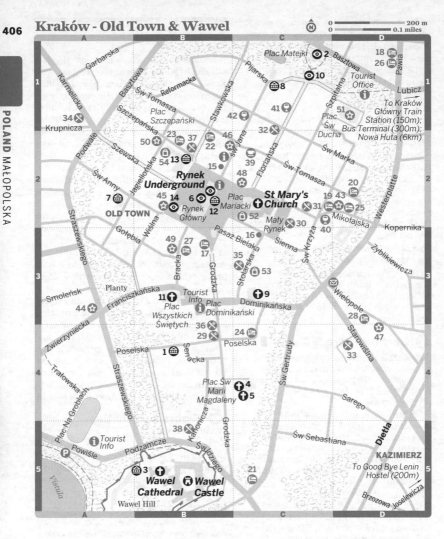

language tour if it's the only one remaining for the day. If you want to hire a guide who speaks English or other languages, contact the on-site **guides office** (☎12 422 1697).

The 14th-century **Wawel Cathedral** (Map p406; www.katedra-wawelska.pl; ◷9am-5pm Mon-Sat, 12.30-5pm Sun) was the coronation and burial place of Polish royalty for four centuries. Ecclesiastical artefacts are displayed in its small **Cathedral Museum** (Map p406; adult/concession 12/7zł; ◷10am-3pm Tue-Sun). Admission includes access to the **Royal Tombs**, including that of King Kazimierz Wielki; and the **bell tower** of the golden-domed **Sigismund Chapel** (1539), which contains the country's largest bell (11 tonnes).

Other attractions within the castle grounds include the **Museum of Oriental Art** (adult/concession 8/5zł; ◷9.30am-5pm Tue-Fri & 11am-6pm Sat & Sun Apr-Oct, 9.30am-4pm Tue-Sat Nov-Mar); the **Crown Treasury & Armoury** (adult/concession 15/8zł; free Mon; ◷9.30am-5pm Tue-Fri & 11am-6pm Sat & Sun Apr-Oct, 9.30am-4pm Tue-Sun Nov-Mar); the **Lost Wawel** (adult/concession 8/5zł; free Mon Apr-Oct, free Sun Nov-Mar; ◷9.30am-1pm Mon, 9.30am-5pm Tue-Fri & 11am-6pm Sat & Sun Apr-Oct, 9.30am-4pm Tue-Sat & 10am-4pm Sun Nov-Mar), a well-displayed set of intriguing archaeological exhibits; and the atmospheric **Dragon's Den** (admission 3zł; ☺10am-5pm Apr-Oct). Go here last, as the exit leads out onto the riverbank.

OLD TOWN

Kraków's Old Town is a harmonious collection of historic buildings dating back centuries, ringed by a linear park known as the Planty which replaced the old city walls in the 19th century. It's an eminently walkable area.

Main Market Square HISTORIC SQUARE

This vast square (Rynek Główny in Polish) is the focus of the Old Town, and is Europe's largest medieval town square (200m by 200m). Its most prominent feature is the 15th-century **town hall tower** (Map p406; adult/concession 7/5zł; ☺10.30am-6pm May-Oct), which you can climb.

Cloth Hall HISTORIC BUILDING

(Sukiennice; Map p406; Rynek Główny 1) At the centre of the square is this 16th-century Renaissance building, housing a large souvenir market. Here you can enter **Rynek Underground** (www.podziemiarynku.com; adult/concession 13/10zł; free Mon; ☺10am-8pm Wed-Mon, 10am-4pm Tue), a fascinating new attraction beneath the market square, consisting of an underground route through medieval market stalls and other long-forgotten chambers. The experience is enhanced by holograms and other audiovisual wizardry. The recently renovated upstairs **Gallery of 19th-Century Polish Painting** (muzeum.krakow.pl; adult/concession 12/6zł; ◉10am-8pm Tue-Sun) exhibits art from a range of genres, including Polish Impressionism.

St Mary's Church   CHURCH
(Map p406; Rynek Główny 4; adult/concession 6/4zł; ◉11.30am-6pm Mon-Sat, 2-6pm Sun) This 14th-century place of worship fills the northeastern corner of the square. The huge main altarpiece by Wit Stwosz (Veit Stoss in German) of Nuremberg is the finest Gothic sculpture in Poland, and is opened ceremoniously each day at 11.50am.

Every hour a *hejnał* (bugle call) is played from the highest tower of the church. The melody, played in medieval times as a warning call, breaks off abruptly to symbolise the moment when, according to legend, the throat of a 13th-century trumpeter was pierced by a Tatar arrow. Between May and August you can climb the **tower** (adult/concession 5/3zł).

English Language Club   SOCIAL GROUP
(Map p406; ul Sienna 5; admission 2zł; ◉6-8pm Wed) Just south of St Mary's, this social group has met weekly since the dying days of communism, when local students wanted to make contact with foreign visitors. Its meetings are a fun way to meet a mixed bunch of Poles, expats and tourists in a relaxed setting.

Collegium Maius   HISTORIC BUILDING
(Map p406; ul Jagiellońska 15; adult/concession 12/6zł; ◉10am-2.20pm Mon-Fri, 10am-1.20pm Sat) West of the square is the oldest surviving university building in Poland. Guided tours of its fascinating academic collection run half-hourly and there's usually a couple in English, at 11am and 1pm. Even if you don't go on a tour, step into the magnificent arcaded courtyard for a glimpse of the beautiful architecture.

Florian Gate   FORTIFICATION
From St Mary's Church, walk up ul Floriańska to this 14th-century gate. It's a tourism hotspot, with crowds, buskers, and artists selling their work along the remnant section of the old city walls. Beyond it is the **Barbican** (Map p406; adult/concession 6/4zł; ◉10.30am-6pm Apr-Oct), a defensive bastion built in 1498.

Czartoryski Museum   MUSEUM
(Map p406; ul Św Jana 19) Near the Florian Gate, this museum features an impressive collection of European art, including Leonardo da Vinci's *Lady with an Ermine*. Also on display are Turkish weapons and artefacts, including a campaign tent from the 1683 Battle of Vienna. At the time of research it was undergoing a major renovation, expected to take until 2012.

Historic Churches   CHURCH
South of the Main Market Sq, Plac Wszystkich Świętych is dominated by two 13th-century monastic churches: the **Dominican Church** (Map p406; ul Stolarska 12; ◉9am-6pm) to the east and the **Franciscan Church** (Map p406; Plac Wszystkich Świętych 5; ◉9am-5pm) to the west. The latter is noted for its stained-glass windows.

Further south along ul Grodzka is the early 17th-century Jesuit **Church of SS Peter & Paul** (Map p406; ul Grodzka 64; ◉dawn-dusk), Poland's first baroque church. The Romanesque 11th-century **Church of St Andrew** (Map p406; ul Grodzka 56; ◉9am-6pm Mon-Fri) was the only building in Kraków to withstand the Tatars' attack of 1241.

Archaeological Museum   MUSEUM
(Map p406; ul Poselska 3; adult/concession 7/5zł, free Sun; ◉9am-2pm Mon-Wed, 2-6pm Thu, 10am-2pm Fri & Sun) Between the churches in the southern section of the Old Town you'll find this small but interesting museum, with displays on local prehistory and ancient Egyptian artefacts, including animal mummies.

Historical Museum of Kraków   MUSEUM
(Map p406; www.mhk.pl; Rynek Główny 35; adult/concession 8/6zł, free Sat; ◉10am-5pm Tue-Sun) On the northwest corner of the Rynek, this institution contains paintings, documents and oddments relating to the city.

KAZIMIERZ

Founded by King Kazimierz the Great in 1335, Kazimierz was originally an independent town. In the 15th century, Jews were expelled from Kraków and forced to resettle in a small prescribed area in Kazimierz, separated by a wall. The Jewish quarter later became home to Jews fleeing persecution from throughout Europe.

By the outbreak of WWII there were 65,000 Jewish Poles in Kraków (around 30% of the city's population), and most lived in Kazimierz. Tragically, this thriving community was devastated in the Holocaust.

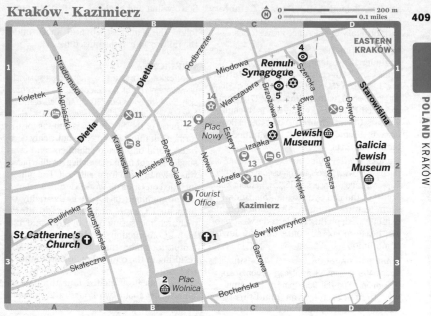

It's easy to take a self-guided walking tour around Kazimierz with the *Jewish Kazimierz Short Guide* booklet, available from the Jarden Jewish Bookshop (see p415).

Jewish Museum   MUSEUM
(Map p409; ul Szeroka 24; adult/concession 8/6zł, free Mon; ☺10am-2pm Mon & 10am-5pm Tue-Sun Apr-Oct, 10am-2pm Mon & 9am-4pm Wed-Sun Nov-Mar) The eastern Jewish quarter is dotted with synagogues. The most significant, the 15th-century Old Synagogue, is the oldest in Poland. It now houses a museum with exhibitions on Jewish traditions.

Remuh Synagogue   SYNAGOGUE
(Map p409; ul Szeroka 40; adult/concession 5/2zł; ☺9am-4pm Sun-Fri) A short walk north from the Old Synagogue is this small 16th-century place of worship, still used for religious

services. Behind it, the **Remuh Cemetery** (admission free; ☺9am-6pm Mon-Fri) boasts some extraordinary Renaissance gravestones.

Historic Churches   CHURCH
Kazimierz's western Catholic quarter includes the 14th-century Gothic **St Catherine's Church** (Map p409; ul Augustian 7; ☺only during services), with an imposing 17th-century gilded high altar, while the 14th-century **Corpus Christi Church** (Map p409; ul Bożego Ciała 26; ☺9am-7pm Mon-Sat) is crammed with baroque fittings.

Galicia Jewish Museum   MUSEUM
(Map p409; www.galiciajewishmuseum.org; ul Dajwór 18; adult/concession 15/8zł; ☺10am-6pm) South of the Old Synagogue, this fine museum features an impressive photographic exhibition, depicting modern-day traces of southeastern Poland's once thriving Jewish community.

Izaak's Synagogue   SYNAGOGUE
(Map p409; ul Kupa 18; adult/concession 5/3zł; ☺9am-5pm Sun-Thu, 9am-1pm Fri) Heading west from ul Szeroka, you'll find this restored synagogue, decorated with impressive frescos from the 17th century.

Ethnographic Museum   MUSEUM
(Map p409; Plac Wolnica 1; adult/concession 9/5zł, free Sun; ☺11am-7pm Tue-Sat & 11am-3pm Sun May-Sep, 10am-6pm Mon, 10am-3pm Wed-Fri & 10am-2pm Sat & Sun Oct-Apr) Kazimierz's Old Town Hall contains this museum, displaying a collection of regional crafts and costumes.

PODGÓRZE
During the war the Nazis relocated Jews to a walled ghetto in this district, just south of Kazimierz across the Vistula River. They were exterminated in the nearby Płaszów Concentration Camp, as portrayed in Steven Spielberg's haunting film, *Schindler's List*.

TOP CHOICE **Schindler's Factory**   MUSEUM
(www.mhk.pl; ul Lipowa 4; adult/concession 15/13zł; ☺10am-2pm Mon, 10am-6pm Tue-Sun) This impressive new museum covering the Nazi occupation of Kraków in WWII is housed in the former enamel factory of Oskar Schindler that was immortalised in *Schindler's List*. Well-organised, innovative exhibits tell the moving story of the city from 1939 to 1945, recreating urban elements such as a tram carriage, a train station underpass and a crowded ghetto apartment within the factory's walls. It's an experience that shouldn't be missed. From the main post office in the Old Town, catch any tram down ul

Starowiślna and alight at the first stop over the river at Plac Bohaterów Getta. From here, follow the signs east along ul Kącik, under the railway line to the museum.

WIELICZKA
Wieliczka Salt Mine   UNDERGROUND MUSEUM
(www.kopalnia.pl; ul Daniłowicza 10; adult/concession 64/49zł; ☺7.30am-7.30pm Apr-Oct, 8am-5pm Nov-Mar) Wieliczka (vyeh-*leech*-kah), 15km southeast of the city centre, is famous for this former salt mine. It's an eerie but richly decorated world of pits and chambers, and every single element from chandeliers to altarpieces was hewn by hand from solid salt. The mine is included on Unesco's World Heritage list.

The highlight of a visit is the richly ornamented **Chapel of the Blessed Kinga**, a church measuring 54m by 17m, and 12m high. Construction of this underground temple took more than 30 years (1895–1927), resulting in the removal of 20,000 tonnes of rock salt.

The obligatory guided tour through the mine takes about two hours (a 2km walk). Tours in English operate approximately hourly between 10am and 5pm, increasing to half-hourly from 8.30am to 6pm in July and August. If you're visiting independently, you must wait for a tour to start. Last admission to the mine is shortly before closing time.

The best way to get to Wieliczka is by minibus (2.50zł; look for the 'Salt Mine' sign on the windscreen), departing frequently between 6am and 8pm from ul Pawia near the Galeria Krakowska shopping mall next to Kraków Główny train station. Alternatively, bus 304 travels from the same area to the salt mine and requires a suburban ticket (3zł), which you can obtain from ticket vending machines. Get off at the 'Wieliczka Kopalnia Soli' stop.

☞ Tours

These companies operate tours of Kraków and surrounding areas.

Jarden Tourist Agency   JEWISH HERITAGE
(Map p409; ☎12 421 7166; www.jarden.pl; ul Szeroka 2) The best agency for tours of Polish Jewish heritage. Its showpiece, 'Retracing Schindler's List' (two hours by car), costs 60zł per person. All tours require a minimum of three and must be booked in advance. Tours are in English, but other languages can be arranged.

Cracow Tours   TOURS
(Map p406; ☎66 221 5931; www.cracowtours.pl; Rynek Główny 41) Inside the E Wedel choco-

There's another side to Kraków that few tourists see. Catch tram 4 or 15 from Kraków Główny train station, or tram 22 from Kazimierz, east to Plac Centralny in Nowa Huta. This suburb was a 'workers' paradise' district built by the communist regime in the 1950s to counter the influence of the city's religious and intellectual traditions. Its immense, blocky concrete buildings stretch out along broad, straight streets, a fascinating contrast to the Old Town's delicate beauty.

late shop, offering city tours, and tours of Auschwitz-Birkenau and the salt mines.

Crazy Guides   COMMUNIST HERITAGE
(☑50 009 1200; www.crazyguides.com) Offers entertaining tours of the city's communist-era suburbs, in restored cars of the time.

★★ Festivals & Events

Organ Music Festival   MUSIC
March

Krakow International Film Festival   FILM
(www.kff.com.pl) May/June

Lajkonik Pageant   HISTORIC
In May/June, seven days after Corpus Christi.

Jewish Culture Festival   JEWISH
(www.jewishfestival.pl) June/July

**International Festival of
Street Theatre**   THEATRE
July

Summer Jazz Festival   MUSIC
(www.cracjazz.com) July/August

Kraków Christmas Crib Competition
                                                CHRISTMAS
December

🛏 Sleeping

Kraków is unquestionably Poland's major tourist destination, with prices to match. Booking ahead in the busy summer months is recommended.

An agency offering decent rooms around town is **Jordan Tourist Information & Accommodation Centre** (Map p406; ☑12 422 6091; www.jordan.pl; ul Pawia 8; s/d around 130/150zł); ☺8am-6pm Mon-Fri, 9am-2pm Sat.

TOP CHOICE Wielopole   HOTEL €€€
(Map p406; ☑12 422 1475; www.wielopole.pl; ul Wielopole 3; s/d 318/438zł; ❋) Smart and simple modern rooms in a renovated block on the eastern edge of the Old Town, with narrow beds but spotless bathrooms. The tariff includes an impressive buffet breakfast.

Mama's Hostel   HOSTEL €
(Map p406; ☑12 429 5940; www.mamashostel. com.pl; ul Bracka 4; dm 50-60zł, d 180zł) Centrally located red-and-orange lodgings with a beautiful sunlit lounge overlooking a courtyard and with the aroma of freshly roasted coffee drifting up from a cafe below in the mornings. There's a washing machine on-site.

Nathan's Villa Hostel   HOSTEL €
(Map p409; ☑12 422 3545; www.nathansvilla.com; ul Św Agnieszki 1; dm from 45zł, d 180zł) Comfy rooms, sparkling bathrooms, a laundry and a friendly atmosphere make this place a big hit with backpackers, and its cellar bar, mini-cinema, beer garden and pool table add to the appeal. Conveniently located between the Old Town and Kazimierz.

AAA Kraków Apartments   APARTMENTS €€
(☑12 346 4670; www.krakow-apartments.biz; apt from 290zł) Company renting out renovated apartments in the vicinity of the Old Town, with a smaller selection in Kazimierz. Cheaper rates are available for longer stays.

Hotel Amadeus   HOTEL €€€
(Map p406; ☑12 429 6070; www.hotel-amadeus. pl; ul Mikołajska 20; s/d €130/150) Everything about this hotel says 'class'. The rooms are tastefully furnished, though singles are rather small given the price. One room has wheelchair access, and there's a sauna, a fitness centre and a well-regarded restaurant. While hanging around the Amadeus' foyer, you can check out photos of famous guests.

Hotel Stary   HOTEL €€€
(Map p406; ☑12 384 0808; www.stary.hotel.com. pl; ul Szczepańska 5; s/d 800/900zł; ❋❋) Setting new standards for accommodation in Poland, the Stary is housed in an 18th-century aristocratic residence that exudes charm. The fabrics are all natural, the bathroom surfaces Italian marble, and there's a fitness centre, swimming pool and rooftop terrace to enjoy.

FREE THRILLS

If you're short of a złoty, take advantage of these *gratis* Kraków attractions:

» Visit the beautiful courtyard of the **Collegium Maius** (p408).

» Soak up the heady historical atmosphere of the grounds of **Wawel Castle** (p405).

» Examine the intriguing collection of the **Jewish Museum** (p409) in Kazimierz for free on Mondays.

» Catch the historic *hejnał* (bugle call) being played from the tower of **St Mary's Church** (p408) each hour.

» Observe the crowds watching the artists displaying their work on the wall next to the 14th-century **Florian Gate** (p408)

Hotel Abel
HOTEL €€

(Map p409; ☎12 411 8736; www.hotel abel.pl; ul Józefa 30; s/d 170/200zł) Reflecting the character of Kazimierz, this hotel has a distinctive personality, evident in its polished wooden staircase, arched brickwork and age-worn tiles. The comfortable rooms make a good base for exploring the historic Jewish neighbourhood.

Greg & Tom Hostel
HOSTEL €

(Map p406; ☎12 422 4100; www.gregtomhostel. com; ul Pawia 12; dm 50zł, d from 130zł) This well-run hostel is spread over two locations; the private rooms are a 10-minute walk away on ul Warszawska. The staff are friendly, the rooms are clean and laundry facilities are included.

Cracow Hostel
HOSTEL €

(Map p406; ☎12 429 1106; www.cracowhostel.com; Rynek Główny 18; dm 40-85zł, d 170zł) This place is perched high above the Main Market Sq, with an amazing view of St Mary's Church from the roomy but comfortable lounge. There's also a kitchen and washing machine.

Good Bye Lenin Hostel
HOSTEL €

(☎12 421 2030; www.goodbyelenin.com; ul Joselewicza 23; dm 35zł, d 140zł) Comically decorated communist-themed hostel, with numerous common spaces including a basement bar with a pool table and a small garden. There's a washing machine, and one female-only dorm with six beds. It's hidden away down a grungy back street.

Hotel Royal
HOTEL €€

(Map p406; ☎12 421 3500; www.hotelewam.pl; ul Św Gertrudy 26-29; s/d from 220/320zł) Impressive art nouveau edifice with loads of old-world charm, just below Wawel Castle. It's split into two sections: the higher-priced rooms are cosy, and far preferable to the fairly basic rooms at the back.

Camping Smok
CAMPING €

(☎12 429 8300; www.smok.krakow.pl; ul Kamedulska 18; per person/tent 22/15zł, r 120-200zł) It's small, quiet and pleasantly located 4km west of the Old Town. To get here from outside the Kraków Główny train station building, take tram 1, 2 or 6 to the end of the line in Zwierzyniec (destination marked 'Salwator') and change for any westbound bus (except bus 100).

Tournet Pokoje Gościnne
HOTEL €€

(Map p409; ☎12 292 0088; www.accommoda tion.krakow.pl; ul Miodowa 7; s/d from 150/200zł) This is a neat pension in Kazimierz, offering simple but comfortable and quiet rooms with compact bathrooms. At the time of research, the owners were adding a restaurant.

Hotel Wit Stwosz
HOTEL €€€

(Map p406; ☎12 429 6026; www.wit-stwosz. com.pl; ul Mikołajska 28; s/d 295/390zł) In a historic town house belonging to St Mary's Church, and decorated in a suitably religious theme. Rooms are compact and simply furnished, but tasteful and attractive.

Hotel Wawel
HOTEL €€€

(Map p406; ☎12 424 1300; www.hotelwawel.pl; ul Poselska 22; s/d 330/460zł; ✿) Ideally located just off busy ul Grodzka, this is a pleasant place offering tastefully decorated rooms with timber highlights. It's far enough from the main drag to minimise noise.

Hotel Saski
HOTEL €€€

(Map p406; ☎12 421 4222; www.hotelsaski.com. pl; ul Sławkowska 3; s/d 290/390zł) The Saski occupies a historic mansion, complete with a uniformed doorman, rattling old lift and ornate furnishings. The rooms themselves are comparatively plain.

Hotel Campanile HOTEL €€€
(Map p406; ☑12 424 2600; www.campanile.com; ul Św Tomasza 34; r 359zł) Straightforward chain hotel whose biggest asset is its location within the Old Town, in a quiet back street on the edge of the Planty. Breakfast is 32zł extra.

✖ Eating

Kraków is a food paradise, tightly packed with restaurants serving a wide range of international cuisines.

One local speciality is *obwarzanki* (ring-shaped pretzels powdered with poppy seeds, sesame seeds or salt) available from street vendors dozing next to their barrows throughout the city.

Self-caterers can stock up at the **supermarket** within the Galeria Krakowska shopping mall, next to the main train station.

TOP CHOICE Momo VEGETARIAN €
(Map p409; ☑60 968 5775; ul Dietla 49; mains 8-17zł; ☺11am-8pm) Vegans will cross the doorstep of this Kazimierz restaurant with relief – the majority of the menu is completely animal free. The space is decorated with Indian craft pieces, and serves up subcontinental soups, stuffed pancakes and rice dishes, with a great range of cakes. The Tibetan dumplings are a treat worth ordering.

Restauracja Pod Gruszką POLISH €€
(Map p406; ☑12 346 5704; ul Szczepańska 1; mains 12-59zł; ☺noon-midnight) A favourite haunt of writers and artists, this upstairs establishment is the eatery that time forgot, with its elaborate old-fashioned decor featuring chandeliers, lace tablecloths, age-worn carpets and sepia portraits. The menu covers a range of Polish dishes, the most distinctive being the soups served within small bread loaves.

Il Calzone ITALIAN €€
(Map p406; ☑12 429 5141; ul Starowiślna 15a; mains 15-44zł; ☺noon-11pm Mon-Thu) This pleasant slice of Italy is a well-kept secret, tucked away in a quiet nook set back from the street. Considering its pleasant whitewashed decor and charming outdoor terrace, the food is excellent value.

Ariel JEWISH €€
(Map p409; ☑12 421 7920; ul Szeroka 18; mains 11-51zł) Atmospheric Jewish restaurant packed with old-fashioned timber furniture and portraits, serving a range of kosher dishes. Try the Berdytchov soup (beef, honey and

cinnamon) for a tasty starter. There's often live music here at night.

Nostalgia POLISH €€
(Map p406; ☑12 425 4260; ul Karmelicka 10; mains 19-76zł; ☺noon-11pm) A refined version of the traditional Polish eatery, Nostalgia features a fireplace, overhead timber beams, uncrowded tables and courteous service. Wrap yourself around Russian dumplings, a 'Hunter's Stew' of cabbage, meat and mushrooms, or vegie options such as potato pancakes. In warm weather there's an outdoor dining area.

Pimiento ARGENTINIAN €€€
(Map p406; ☑12 422 6672; ul Stolarska 13; mains 25-130zł) This upmarket grill serves a dizzying array of steaks to suit both appetite and budget, and offers some reasonable vegetarian alternatives for the meat averse. Factor the South American wine list into your calculations, and you have a classy night out.

Metropolitan INTERNATIONAL €€
(Map p406; ☑12 421 9803; ul Sławkowska 3; mains 16-69zł; ☺7.30am-midnight Mon-Sat, 7.30am-10pm Sun) Attached to Hotel Saski, this place has nostalgic B&W photos plastering the walls, and is a great place for breakfast. It also serves pasta, grills and steaks, including luxurious items such as beef tenderloin in a truffle sauce.

Casa della Pizza PIZZA €€
(Map p406; ☑12 421 6498; Mały Rynek 2; mains 21-48zł; ☺noon-late) This unpretentious place is away from the bulk of the tourist traffic, with a menu of pizzas and pasta. The downstairs bar section is the Arabian-styled **Shisha Club**, serving Middle Eastern food.

Gruzińskie Chaczapuri GEORGIAN €€
(Map p406; ☑50 954 2802; ul Floriańska 26; mains 15-29zł) Cheap and cheerful place serving up tasty Georgian dishes. Grills, salads and steaks fill out the menu, and there's a separate vegetarian selection with items such as the traditional Georgian cheese pie with stewed vegetables.

Pod Aniołami POLISH €€€
(Map p406; ☑12 421 3999; ul Grodzka 35; mains 26-62zł; ☺1pm-midnight) This eatery 'under the angels' offers high-quality Polish food in a pleasant cellar atmosphere, though it can get a little smoky. Specialities include the huntsman's smoked wild boar steak.

Kuchnia i Wino MEDITERRANEAN €€
(Map p409; ☑12 430 6710; ul Józefa 13; mains 12-52zł; ☺noon-10pm) The name – 'Cuisine and Wine' – may not suggest this bistro has a

lot of imagination, but just try one of its delightfully inspired Mediterranean dishes and you'll be impressed.

Balaton
HUNGARIAN €€
(Map p406; ☎12 422 0469; ul Grodzka 37; mains 16-36zł; ⏰noon-10pm) Balaton's shabby decor may not seem inviting, but it's a very popular place for simple Hungarian food and seems to fill up quickly every night.

Smak Ukraiński
UKRAINIAN €€
(Map p406; ☎12 421 9294; ul Kanonicza 15; mains 18-22zł; ⏰noon-10pm) This Ukrainian restaurant presents authentic dishes in a cosy little cellar decorated with provincial flair. Expect lots of dumplings, *borscht* and waiters in waistcoats.

Green Way
VEGETARIAN €
(Map p406; ☎12 431 1027; ul Mikołajska 14; mains 7-16zł; ⏰10am-10pm Mon-Fri, 11am-9pm Sat & Sun) The Green Way offers good value vegetarian fare such as vegie curry, enchiladas and salads.

Drinking

There are hundreds of pubs and bars in Kraków's Old Town, many housed in ancient vaulted cellars, which get very smoky. Kazimierz also has a lively bar scene, centred on Plac Nowy and its surrounding streets.

Paparazzi
BAR
(Map p406; ul Mikołajska 9; ⏰11am-1am Mon-Fri, 4pm-4am Sat & Sun) Bright, modern place, with B&W press photos of celebrities covering the walls. The drinks menu includes cocktails such as the Polish martini, built around bison grass vodka. There's also inexpensive bar food.

Singer
CAFE-BAR
(Map p409; ul Estery 20; ⏰9am-4am Sun-Thu, 9am-5am Fri & Sat) Laidback hang-out of the Kazimierz cognoscenti, this relaxed cafebar's moody candlelit interior is full of character. Alternatively, sit outside and converse over a sewing machine affixed to the table.

Le Scandale
BAR
(Map p409; Plac Nowy 9; ⏰8am-3am) Smooth Kazimierz drinking hole with low blackleather couches, ambient lighting and a gleaming well-stocked bar. Full of mellow drinkers sampling the extensive cocktail list.

Cafe Camelot
CAFE
(Map p406; ul Św Tomasza 17; ⏰9am-midnight) For coffee and cake, try this genteel haven hidden around an obscure street corner in the Old Town. Its cosy rooms are cluttered with lace-covered candlelit tables and a quirky collection of wooden figurines featuring spiritual or folkloric scenes.

Pod Papugami
PUB
(Map p406; ul Św Jana 18; ⏰noon-2am) This is a vaguely Irish cellar pub decorated with old motorcycles and other assorted odds and ends. A good place to hide from inclement weather, with its pool table and tunnel-like maze of rooms.

Piwnica Pod Złotą Pipą
PUB
(Map p406; ul Floriańska 30; ⏰noon-midnight) Less claustrophobic than other cellar bars, with lots of tables for eating or drinking. Decent bar food and international beers on tap.

☆ Entertainment

The comprehensive Polish-English booklet *Karnet* (4zł), published by the city authorities' tourist office (see p415), lists almost every event in the city. In addition, the tourist office located at ul Św Jana 2 specialises in cultural events, and can book tickets to many of them.

Nightclubs

TOP CHOICE
Alchemia
BAR/CLUB
(Map p409; ul Estery 5; ⏰9am-3am) This Kazimierz venue exudes a shabby-is-the-new-cool look with rough-hewn wooden benches, candlelit tables and a companionable gloom. It hosts regular live music gigs and theatrical events through the week.

Piano Rouge
JAZZ CLUB
(Map p406; ☎12 431 0333; www.thepianorouge.com; Rynek Główny 46; ⏰11am-2am) A sumptuous cellar venue decked out with classic sofas, ornate lampshades and billowing lengths of colourful silk. There's a dizzying array of nightly live jazz, and a restaurant.

Łubu-Dubu
CLUB
(Map p406; ul Wielopole 15; ⏰7pm-late) The name of this place (*woo*boo-*doo*boo) is as funky as its decor. It's a grungy upstairs joint that's an echo of the past, from the garish colours to the collection of objects from 1970s Poland. DJs spin 'old school' tracks, and a series of rooms creates spaces for talking or dancing as the mood strikes.

Black Gallery
PUB/CLUB
(Map p406; ul Mikołajska 24; ⏰5pm-late) Underground pub-cum-nightclub with a modern aspect: split levels, exposed steel frame lighting and a metallic bar. It really gets going

after midnight. It also has a more civilised courtyard, open from 2pm.

Rdza CLUB
(Map p406; www.rdza.pl; ul Bracka 3/5; ⊙7pm-late) This basement club attracts some of Kraków's more sophisticated clubbers, with its Polish house music bouncing off exposed brick walls and comfy sofas. Guest DJs start spinning at 9pm.

Performing Arts

Stary Teatr THEATRE
(Map p406; ☑12 422 4040; www.stary-teatr.pl, in Polish; ul Jagiellońska 5) This accomplished theatre company offers quality productions. To overcome the language barrier, pick a Shakespeare play you know well from the repertoire, and take in the distinctive Polish interpretation.

Teatr im Słowackiego OPERA/THEATRE
(Map p406; ☑12 422 4022; www.slowacki.krakow. pl, in Polish; Plac Św Ducha 1) This grand place, built in 1893, focuses on Polish classics, large theatrical productions and opera.

Filharmonia Krakowska CLASSICAL MUSIC
(Map p406; ☑12 422 9477; www.filharmonia. krakow.pl; ul Zwierzyniecka 1) Hosts one of the best orchestras in the country; concerts are usually held on Friday and Saturday.

Cinemas

Two convenient cinemas are **Kino Sztuka** (Map p406; cnr ul Św Tomasza & ul Św Jana) and **Kino Pod Baranami** (Map p406; Rynek Główny 27), the latter located within a courtyard off the Main Market Sq.

🔒 Shopping

The place to start (or perhaps end) your Kraków shopping is at the large **souvenir market** within the Cloth Hall, selling everything from fine amber jewellery to tacky plush dragons.

Galeria Plakatu ART
(Map p406; ⊙012 421 2640; www.cracowposter gallery.com; ul Stolarska 8; ⊙11am-6pm Mon-Fri, 11am-2pm Sat) Fascinating examples of Polish poster art can be purchased here.

EMPiK BOOKS
(Map p406; Rynek Główny 5; ⊙9am-10pm) For foreign newspapers, magazines, novels and maps.

Sklep Podróżnika BOOKS
(Map p406; ul Jagiellońska 6; ⊙11am-7pm Mon-Fri, 10am-3pm Sat) For regional and city maps, as well as Lonely Planet titles.

Jarden Jewish Bookshop BOOKS
(Map p409; ul Szeroka 2) Located in Kazimierz; is well stocked with titles on Poland's Jewish heritage.

ℹ️ Information

Discount Cards

Kraków Tourist Card (www.krakowcard. com; 2/3 days 50/65zł) Available from tourist offices, the card includes travel on public transport and entry to many museums.

Internet Access

Greenland Internet Cafe (ul Floriańska 30; per hr 4zł; ⊙9am-midnight)

Klub Garinet (ul Floriańska 18; per hr 4zł; ⊙9am-10pm)

Money

Kantors and ATMs can be found all over the city centre. It's worth noting, however, that many *kantors* close on Sunday, and some located near Rynek Główny and the main train station offer terrible exchange rates – check around before proffering your cash. There are also exchange facilities at the airport, with even less attractive rates.

Post

Main post office (Map p406; ul Westerplatte 20; ⊙8am-8pm Mon-Fri, 8am-2pm Sat)

Tourist Information

Two free magazines, *Welcome to Cracow & Małopolska* and *Visitor: Kraków & Zakopane* are available at upmarket hotels. The *Kraków in Your Pocket* booklet (5zł) is also very useful, packed with entertaining reviews of local sights and eateries.

Tourist office ul Św Jana (Map p406; ☑12 421 7787; www.karnet.krakow.pl; ul Św Jana 2; ⊙10am-6pm); Cloth Hall (Map p406; ☑12 433 7310; Rynek Główny 1; ⊙9am-7pm May-Sep, 9am-5pm Oct-Apr); northeastern Old Town (Map p406; ☑12 432 0110; ul Szpitalna 25; ⊙9am-7pm May-Sep, 9am-5pm Oct-Apr); southern Old Town (Map p409; ☑12 616 1886; Plac Wszystkich Świętych 2; ⊙9am-7pm May-Sep, 9am-5pm Oct-Apr); Wawel Hill (Map p409; ul Powiśle 11; ⊙9am-7pm); Kazimierz (Map p409; ☑12 422 0471; ul Józefa 7; ⊙9am-5pm); Nowa Huta (☑12 643 0303; Os Sloneczne 16; ⊙10am-2pm Tue-Sat); airport (☑12 285 5431; John Paul II International airport, Balice; ⊙9am-7pm) Helpful city-run service; the office at ul Św Jana 2 specialises in cultural events.

ℹ️ Getting There & Away

For information on travelling from Kraków to Zakopane or Oświęcim (for Auschwitz-Birkenau), refer to the relevant destination sections.

Air

The **John Paul II International airport** (www. lotnisko-balice.pl) is more often called Balice airport, after the suburb in which it's located, about 15km west of the Old Town. The airport terminal hosts several car-hire desks, along with currency exchanges offering unappealing rates. To get to the Old Town by public transport, step aboard the free shuttle bus to the nearby train station, from the sign marked 'PKP' outside the airport. Buy tickets on board the train from a vending machine (7zł) or the conductor (8zł) for the 17-minute train journey to Kraków Główny station.

LOT flies between Kraków and Warsaw several times a day, and offers direct connections from Kraków to Frankfurt, Munich, Paris and Vienna, with flights to New York and Chicago during the summer months. Bookings for all flights can be made at the **LOT office** (☑0801 703 703; ul Basztowa 15). There are also domestic flights via Jet Air to Poznań (three weekly) and Gdańsk (twice weekly).

A range of other airlines, including several budget operators, connect Kraków to cities in Europe, including an array of destinations across Britain and Ireland. There are direct flights daily to and from London via easyJet and Ryanair. Dublin is serviced daily by Ryanair and Aer Lingus.

Bus

If you've been travelling by bus elsewhere in Poland, Kraków's modern main **bus terminal** (ul Bosacka 18) will seem like a palace compared to the usual facility. It's located on the other side of the main train station from the Old Town. Taking the train will generally be quicker, but buses of interest to visitors run to Lublin (40zł, five hours, six daily), Zamość (44zł, seven hours, four daily) and Cieszyn on the Czech border (18zł, three hours, seven daily).

Train

The lovely old **Kraków Główny train station** (Plac Dworcowy), on the northeastern outskirts of the Old Town, handles all international trains and most domestic rail services. The railway platforms are about 150m north of the station building, and you can also reach them from the adjacent Galeria Krakowska shopping mall.

Each day from Kraków, 20 trains head to Warsaw, most of them fast Express InterCity services (110zł, 2½ hours). There are also 17 trains daily to Wrocław (48zł, 4¾ hours), 10 to Częstochowa (33zł, 2¼ hours), six to Łódź (40zł, 4½ hours), 14 to Poznań (56zł, 7½ hours), eight to Toruń (58zł, eight hours), nine to Zakopane (35zł, 3½ hours), 14 to Przemyśl (46zł, four hours) and two to Lublin (53zł, 4¾ hours). The 10 services to Gdynia via Gdańsk are evenly split between five TLK trains (68zł, 13 hours) and five much faster Express InterCity services (129zł, nine hours).

Oświęcim

POP 40,800

Few place names have more impact than Auschwitz, which is seared into public consciousness as the location of history's most extensive experiment in genocide. Every year hundreds of thousands visit Oświęcim (osh-*fyen*-cheem), the Polish town that give its German name to the infamous Nazi death camp, to learn about its history and to pay respect to the dead.

Established in disused army barracks in 1940, Auschwitz was initially designed to hold Polish prisoners, but was expanded into the largest centre for the extermination of European Jews. Two more camps were subsequently established: Birkenau (Brzezinka, also known as Auschwitz II), 3km west of Auschwitz; and Monowitz (Monowice), several kilometres west of Oświęcim. In the course of their operation, between one and 1.5 million people were murdered in these death factories – about 90% of these were Jews.

Auschwitz   MEMORIAL

Auschwitz was only partially destroyed by the fleeing Nazis, so many of the original buildings remain as a bleak document of the camp's history. A dozen of the 30 surviving prison blocks house sections of the **State Museum Auschwitz-Birkenau** (☑33 844 8100; www.auschwitz.org.pl; admission free; ☺8am-7pm Jun-Aug, 8am-6pm May & Sep, 8am-5pm Apr & Oct, 8am-4pm Mar & Nov, 8am-3pm Dec-Feb). In 2007, Unesco decided to adopt the wordy title Auschwitz Birkenau – German Nazi Concentration and Extermination Camp (1940–45) for its World Heritage listing of the site, in order to make it clear that conquered Poland had taken no part in Auschwitz's establishment or operation.

About every half-hour, the cinema in the visitors centre at the entrance shows a 15-minute documentary film (adult/concession 3.50/2.50zł) about the liberation of the camp by Soviet troops on 27 January 1945. It's shown in several languages throughout the day; check the schedule at the information desk as soon as you arrive. The film is not recommended for children under 14 years old. The visitors centre also has a cafeteria, bookshops, a *kantor* and a left-luggage room.

Some basic explanations in Polish, English and Hebrew are provided on-site, but you'll understand more if you buy the small *Auschwitz Birkenau Guide Book* (translated into about 15 languages) from the visitors centre.

Between May and October it's compulsory to join a tour if you arrive between 10am and 3pm. English-language **tours** (adult/concession 39/30zł, 3½ hours) of Auschwitz and Birkenau leave at 10am, 11am, 1pm and 3pm daily, and can also occur when a group of 10 people can be formed. Tours in a range of other languages can be arranged in advance.

Auschwitz is an easy day trip from Kraków. However, if you want to stay overnight, **Centre for Dialogue and Prayer** (☑33 843 1000; www.centrum-dialogu.oswiecim.pl; ul Kolbego 1; campsite per person 25zł, s/d 104/208zł) is 700m southwest of Auschwitz. It's comfortable and quiet, and the price includes breakfast. Most rooms have en suites, and full board is also offered.

FREE **Birkenau** MEMORIAL (⊙8am-7pm Jun-Aug, 8am-6pm May & Sep, 8am-5pm Apr & Oct, 8am-4pm Mar & Nov, 8am-3pm Dec-Feb) Birkenau, otherwise known as Auschwitz II, was where the murder of huge numbers of Jews took place. This vast (175 hectares), purpose-built and grimly efficient camp had more than 300 prison barracks and four huge gas chambers complete with crematoria. Each chamber held 2000 people and electric lifts raised the bodies to the ovens. The camp could hold 200,000 inmates.

Although much of the camp was destroyed by retreating Nazis, the size of the place, fenced off with barbed wire stretching almost as far as the eye can see, provides some idea of the scale of this heinous crime. The viewing platform above the entrance provides further perspective. In some ways, Birkenau is even more shocking than Auschwitz and there are fewer tourists. There is no compulsory tour requirement at Birkenau in the warmer months.

❶ Getting There & Away

Auschwitz-Birkenau is usually visited as a day trip from Kraków.

From Kraków Główny train station, 12 mostly slow trains go to Oświęcim (13zł, 1½ hours) each day, though more depart from Kraków Płaszów train station.

Far more convenient are the approximately hourly buses each day to Oświęcim (11zł, 1½ hours) departing from the bus station in Kraków, which either pass by or terminate at the museum. The return bus timetable to Kraków is displayed at the Birkenau visitors centre. There are also numerous minibuses to Oświęcim from the minibus stands off ul Pawia, next to Galeria Krakowska.

Every half-hour from 11.30am to 4.30pm between 15 April and 31 October, buses shuttle passengers between the visitor centres at Auschwitz and Birkenau (buses run to 5.30pm in May and September, and until 6.30pm June to August). Otherwise, follow the signs for an easy walk (3km) or take a taxi. Auschwitz is also linked to the town's train station by local buses every 30 to 40 minutes.

Most travel agencies in Kraków offer organised tours of Auschwitz (including Birkenau), from 90zł to 120zł per person. Check with the operator for exactly how much time the tour allows you at each site, as some run to a very tight schedule.

Lublin
POP 350,000

If the crowds are becoming too much in Kraków, you could do worse than jump on a train to Lublin. This attractive eastern city has many of the same attractions – a beautiful Old Town, a castle, and good bars and restaurants – but is less visited by international tourists.

Though today the city's beautifully preserved Old Town is a peaceful blend of Gothic, Renaissance and baroque architecture, Lublin has an eventful past. In 1569 the Lublin Union was signed here, uniting Poland and Lithuania; and at the end of WWII, the Soviet Union set up a communist government in Lublin, prior to the liberation of Warsaw.

◎ Sights & Activities
OLD TOWN
Lublin Castle CASTLE
This substantial fortification, standing on a hill at the northeastern edge of the Old Town, has a dark history. It was built in the 14th century, then rebuilt as a prison in the 1820s. During the Nazi occupation, more than 100,000 people passed through its doors before being deported to the death camps. Its major occupant is now the **Lublin Museum** (www.zamek-lublin.pl; ul Zamkowa 9; adult/concession 7.50/5.50zł; ⊙9am-4pm Wed-Sat, 9am-5pm Sun). On display are paintings, silverware, porcelain, woodcarvings and weaponry, mostly labelled in Polish. Check out the alleged 'devil's paw-print' on the 17th-century table in the foyer, linked to a local legend.

At the eastern end of the castle is the gorgeous 14th-century **Chapel of the Holy Trinity** (adult/concession 7.50/5.50zł; ⊙9am-4pm Tue-Sat, 9am-5pm Sun), accessible via the museum. Its interior is covered with polychrome Russo-Byzantine frescos painted in 1418 – possibly the finest medieval wall paintings in Poland.

Lublin

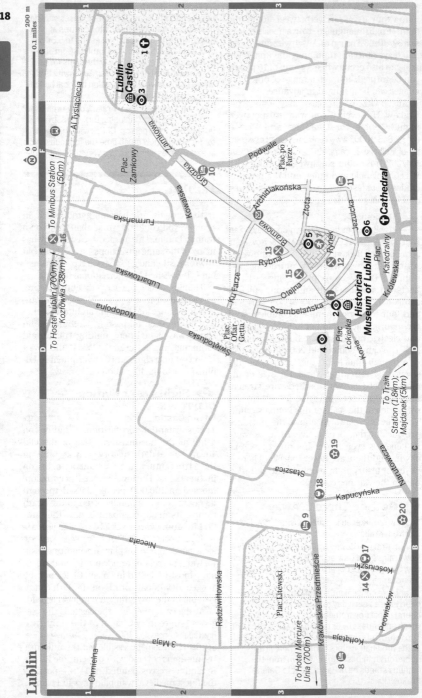

200 m
0.1 miles

To Minibus Station (50m)

To Hostel Lublin (700m); Kozłówka (38km)

Lublin Castle

1

3

Al Tysiąclecia

Plac Zamkowy

Zamkowa

Grodzka

Podwale

Plac po Farze

10

Archidiakońska

Złota

11

Cathedral

Furmańska

Kowalska

Bramowa

5

7

Jezuicka

6

Plac Katedralny

13

Rybna

Ku Farze

 Rynek

12

Plac Lublin

2

Historical Museum of Lublin

Lubartowska

15

Olejna

Szambelańska

Królewska

Wodopojna

Świętoduska

Plac Ofiar Getta

Kozia

4

Plac Łokietka

To Train Station (1.8km); Majdanek (5km)

Niecała

19

Staszica

18

Kapucyńska

Narutowicza

9

Plac Litewski

20

Radziwiłłowska

Kościuszki

17

14

Krakowskie Przedmieście

To Hotel Mercure Unia (700m)

3 Maja

Chmielna

Kołłątaja

Peowiaków

8

Lublin

Underground Route   WALKING TOUR
(Rynek 1; adult/concession 10/7zł; ☺10am-4pm)
This 280m trail winds its way through connected cellars beneath the Old Town, with historical exhibitions along the way. Entry is from the neoclassical **Old Town Hall** in the centre of the pleasant Market Sq (Rynek) at approximately two-hourly intervals; check with the tourist office for exact times.

Historical Museum of Lublin   MUSEUM
(Plac Łokietka 3; adult/concession 3.50/2.50zł; ☺9am-4pm Wed-Sat, 9am-5pm Sun) Situated within the 14th-century **Kraków Gate**, a remnant of medieval fortifications, this institution displays documents and photos relating to the city's history. Daily at noon, a bugler plays a special tune atop the **New Town Hall** opposite the gate (if you like bugling, don't miss the annual National Bugle Contest here on 15 August).

Cathedral   CHURCH
(Plac Katedralny; ☺dawn-dusk) Located near the Trinitarian Tower is this 16th-century place of worship and its impressive baroque frescos. The painting of the Virgin Mary is said to have shed tears in 1949, so it's a source of pride and reverence for local believers.

Archdiocesan Museum   MUSEUM
(Plac Katedralny; adult/concession 7/5zł; ☺10am-2.30pm Tue-Fri. 10am-5pm Sat & Sun) This museum of sacred art also offers expansive views of the Old Town, as it's housed within the lofty Trinitarian Tower (1819).

MAJDANEK

FREE **Majdanek State Museum**   MEMORIAL
(www.majdanek.pl; ☺9am-4pm) About 4km southeast of the Old Town is one of the largest Nazi death camps, where some 235,000 people, including more than 100,000 Jews, were massacred. Barracks, guard towers and barbed wire fences remain in place; even more chilling are the crematorium and gas chambers.

A short explanatory **film** (admission 3zł) can be seen in the visitors centre, from which a marked 'visiting route' (5km) passes the massive stone **Monument of Fight & Martyrdom** and finishes at the domed **mausoleum** holding the ashes of many victims.

Trolleybus 156 and bus 23 depart from a stop near the Bank Pekao on ul Królewska, and travel to the entrance of Majdanek.

🛏 Sleeping

TOP CHOICE **Grand Hotel Lublinianka**   HOTEL €€€
(☎81 446 6100; www.lublinianka.com; ul Krakowskie Przedmieście 56; s/d from 300/360zł; ❆) The swankiest place in town includes free use of a sauna and spa. The cheaper (3rd-floor) rooms have skylights but are relatively small, while 'standard' rooms are spacious and have glitzy marble bathrooms.

CZĘSTOCHOWA

This pilgrimage destination 114km northwest of Kraków is dominated by the graceful **Paulite Monastery of Jasna Góra** (☑34 365 3888; www.jasnagora.pl; admission free; ☺dawn-dusk), sited atop a hill in the centre of town. Founded in 1382, it's the home of the *Black Madonna*, a portrait claimed to be the source of miracles. In recognition of these feats, in 1717 the painting was crowned Queen of Poland. It's well worth a day trip to the monastery to check out its three museums, and of course to meet the *Black Madonna*.

Częstochowa has regular train connections with Kraków, Łódź, Warsaw, Zakopane and Wrocław. For more details, browse Lonely Planet's *Poland* country guide, visit www. info.czestochowa.pl, or step into the Częstochowa **tourist office** (☑34 368 2250; Al Najświętszej Marii Panny 65; ☺9am-5pm Mon-Sat).

One room is designed for wheelchair access, and there's a good restaurant on-site.

Hotel Waksman HOTEL €€
(☑81 532 5454; www.waksman.pl; ul Grodzka 19; s/d 200/220zł) This small gem is excellent value for its quality and location. Just within the Grodzka Gate in the Old Town, it offers elegantly appointed rooms with different colour schemes, and an attractive lounge with tapestries on the walls.

Hostel Lublin HOSTEL €
(☑79 288 8632; www.hostellublin.pl; ul Lubartowska 60; dm 40zł, r 95zł) The city's first modern hostel is situated within a former apartment building and contains neat, tidy dorms, a basic kitchenette and a cosy lounge. Take trolleybus 156 or 160 north from the Old Town.

Hotel Europa HOTEL €€€
(☑81 535 0303; www.hoteleuropa.pl; ul Krakowskie Przedmieście 29; s/d from 380/420zł, ste 1150zł; ❄) Central hotel offering smart, thoroughly modernised rooms with high ceilings and elegant furniture, in a restored 19th-century building. Two rooms are designed for wheelchair access, and there's a nightclub downstairs.

Hotel Mercure Unia HOTEL €€
(☑81 533 2061; www.orbis.pl; Al Racławickie 12; s/d from 275/315zł; ❄) This business hotel is big, central and convenient, and offers all modern conveniences, though it's lacking in atmosphere. There's a gym, bar and restaurant on the premises. Breakfast is 35zł extra per person.

Dom Nauczyciela HOTEL €€
(☑81 533 8285; www.lublin.oupis.pl/hotel; ul Akademicka 4; s/d from 134/162zł) Value-packed accommodation in the heart of the university quarter, west of the Old Town. Rooms have old-fashioned decor but are clean, with good

bathrooms. Some rooms have views over the city, and there are bars and eateries nearby.

Youth Hostel HOSTEL €
(☑81 533 0628; ul Długosza 6; dm 32zł, d 72zł) Modest but well run. Simple rooms are decorated with potted plants, and there's a kitchen and a pleasant courtyard area with seating. It's 100m up a poorly marked lane off ul Długosza; take the second left turning when walking down from ul Racławickie.

Camping Marina CAMPING €
(☑81 745 6910; www.graf-marina.pl, in Polish; ul Krężnicka 6; per tent 16zł, cabins from 70zł) Lublin's only camping ground is serenely located on a lake about 8km south of the Old Town. To get there, take bus 25 from the stop on the main road east of the train station.

Lubelskie Samorządowe Centrum Doskonalenia Nauczycieli HOSTEL €
(☑81 532 9241; www.lscdn.pl; ul Dominikańska 5; dm 52zł) This place is in an atmospheric Old Town building, and has rooms with between two and five beds. It's good value and often busy, so book ahead.

✖ Eating & Drinking

There's a supermarket located near the bus terminal.

TOP CHOICE Magia INTERNATIONAL €€
(☑81 532 3041; ul Grodzka 2; mains 20-65zł; ☺noon-midnight) Charming, relaxed restaurant with numerous vibes to choose from within its warren of dining rooms and large outdoor courtyard. Dishes range from tiger prawns and snails to deer and duck, with every sort of pizza, pasta and pancake between.

Oregano MEDITERRANEAN €€
(☑81 442 5530; ul Kościuszki 7; mains 19-50zł; ☺noon-11pm) This pleasant, upmarket restaurant specialises in Mediterranean cui-

sine, featuring pasta, paella and seafood. There's a well-organised English menu, and the chefs aren't scared of spice.

Biesy   POLISH **€€**
(☑81 532 1648; Rynek 18; mains 12-47zł) Atmospheric cellar eatery with multiple nooks and crannies. Its tasty speciality is large pizza-like baked tarts with a variety of toppings.

Pizzeria Acerna   PIZZA **€**
(☑81 532 4531; Rynek 2; mains 10-35zł) The Acerna is a popular eatery on the main square, serving cheap pizzas and pasta in dazzling variations.

Tamara Café   CAFE-BAR **€€**
(ul Krakówskie Przedmieście 36) This cafe-bar takes its *vino* very seriously. Whether you're a cultured wine connoisseur, a courtyard cocktail fancier, or a hungry tippler who wants some vodka with (or in) your meal, pull up a chair.

Caram'bola Pub   PUB **€**
(ul Kościuszki 8; ☉10am-late Mon-Fri, noon-late Sat & Sun) This pub is a pleasant place for a beer or two. It also serves inexpensive bar food, including Lublin's ubiquitous pizzas.

☆ Entertainment

Club Koyot   CLUB
(ul Krakowskie Przedmieście 26; ☉5pm-late Wed-Sun) This club is concealed in a courtyard and features live music or DJs most nights.

Kino Bajka   CINEMA
(ul Radziszewskiego 8) If you'd prefer a movie to music, this art house cinema is located in the university district.

Teatr im Osterwy   THEATRE
(☑81 532 4244; ul Narutowicza 17) Lublin's main theatrical venue, which features mostly classical plays.

❶ Information

Main post office (ul Krakowskie Przedmieście 50; ☉24hr)

Net Box (ul Krakowskie Przedmieście 52; per hr 5zł; ☉9am-9pm Mon-Fri, 10am-8pm Sat, 2-6pm Sun) Internet access in a courtyard off the street.

Tourist office (☑81 532 4412; www.loit.lublin. pl; ul Jezuicka 1/3; ☉9am-7pm Mon-Fri, 10am-5pm Sat & 10am-4pm Sun May-Sep, 9am-5pm Mon-Fri & 10am-4pm Sat Oct-Apr) Lots of free brochures, including the city walking-route guide *Tourist Routes of Lublin*, which includes a chapter outlining the *Heritage Trail of the Lublin Jews*.

❶ Getting There & Away

From the **bus terminal** (Al Tysiąclecia), opposite the castle, buses head to Białystok (43zł, 5½ hours, five daily), Kraków (42zł, 5½ hours, five daily), Olsztyn (48zł, 8¾ hours, three daily), Przemyśl (32zł, four hours, four daily), Zakopane (56zł, nine hours, four daily), Zamość (16zł, two hours, hourly) and various destinations within Warsaw (30zł, three hours, at least hourly). Private minibuses also head to various destinations, including Zamość (12zł, 1½ hours, half-hourly), from the **minibus station** north of the bus terminal.

The **train station** (Plac Dworcowy) is 1.2km south of the Old Town and accessible by bus 1 or 13. When leaving the station, look for the bus stop on ul Gazowa, to the left of the station entrance as you walk down the steps (not the trolleybus stop). Alternatively, trolleybus 150 from the station is handy for the university area and the youth hostel. Ten trains go daily to Warsaw (37zł, 2½ hours), two travel to Kraków (53zł, 4¾ hours) and one heads to Przemyśl (44zł, four hours).

Around Lublin

The hamlet of **Kozłówka** (koz-*woof*-kah), 38km north of Lublin, is famous for its sumptuous late-baroque **palace**, which houses the **Museum of the Zamoyski Family** (☉81 852 8310; www.muzeumzamoyskich.pl; adult/concession for entry to all sections 24/12zł; ☉10am-4pm Tue-Sun mid-Mar–Oct, 10am-3pm Nov–mid-Dec). The collection in the **main palace** (adult/concession 16/8zł) features original furnishings, ceramic stoves and a large collection of paintings. You must see this area on a Polish-language guided tour, whose starting time will be noted at the top of your ticket. An English-language tour (best organised in advance) costs an extra 52zł. The entrance fee to this section also includes entry to the 1907 **chapel**.

Even more interesting is the incongruous **Socialist-Realist Art Gallery** (adult/concession 6/3zł), decked out with numerous portraits and statues of communist-era leaders. It also features many idealised scenes of farmers and factory workers striving for socialism. These stirring works were originally tucked away here in embarrassment by the communist authorities, after Stalin's death led to the decline of this all-encompassing artistic style.

From Lublin, there's one morning bus that passes through Kozłówka on the way to Puławy, departing at 8.30am (8zł, 50 minutes). Alternatively, you can catch one of the frequent buses from Lublin to Lubartów, then take one of the regular minibuses that pass Kozłówka from there.

A bus heads back to Lublin from Kozłówka around 3.30pm, and another around 6.30pm. Double-check bus timetables before you visit the museum so you can plan your departure accordingly. If you get stuck, take a minibus to Lubartów, from where there is regular transport back to Lublin.

Zamość

POP 66,500

While most Polish cities' attractions centre on their medieval heart, Zamość (*zah-moshch*) is pure Renaissance. The streets of its attractive, compact Old Town are perfect for exploring, and its central market square is a symmetrical delight, reflecting the city's glorious 16th-century origins.

Zamość was founded in 1580 by Jan Zamoyski, the nation's chancellor and commander-in-chief. Designed by an Italian architect, the city was intended as a prosperous trading settlement between Western Europe and the region stretching east to the Black Sea.

In WWII, the Nazis earmarked the city for German resettlement, sending the Polish population into slave labour or concentration camps. Most of the Jewish population of the renamed 'Himmlerstadt' was exterminated.

The splendid architecture of Zamość's Old Town was added to Unesco's World Heritage list in 1992. Since 2004, EU funds have been gradually restoring Zamość to its former glory.

◉ Sights

Great Market Square   HISTORIC SQUARE
The Great Market Sq (Rynek Wielki) is the heart of Zamość's attractive Old Town. This impressive Italianate Renaissance square (exactly 100m by 100m) is dominated by the lofty, pink **town hall** and surrounded by colourful arcaded burghers' houses, many adorned with elegant designs. The **Museum of Zamość** (ul Ormiańska 30; adult/concession 6/3zł; ⊙9am-4pm Tue-Sun) is based in two of the loveliest buildings on the Rynek and houses interesting exhibits, including paintings, folk costumes, archaeological finds and a scale model of the 16th-century town.

Cathedral   CHURCH
(ul Kolegiacka; ⊙dawn-dusk) Southwest of the square, this mighty 16th-century holy place hosts the tomb of Jan Zamoyski in the chapel to the right of the high altar. The **bell tower** (admission 2zł; ⊙May-Sep) can be climbed for good views of the historic cathedral bells and the Old Town. In the grounds,

the **Sacral Museum** (admission 2zł; ⊙10am-4pm Mon-Fri & 10am-1pm Sat & Sun May-Sep, 10am-1pm Sun Oct-Apr) features various robes, paintings and sculptures.

Synagogue   SYNAGOGUE
(ul Pereca 14) Before WWII, Jewish citizens accounted for 45% of the town's population (of 12,000) and most lived in the area north and east of the palace. The most significant Jewish architectural relic is this Renaissance place of worship, built in the early 17th century. At the time of research it was under renovation, being converted into a cultural centre and Jewish museum that should be open by the time you read this.

Bastion   FORTIFICATION
(ul Łukasińskiego) On the eastern edge of the Old Town is the best surviving bastion from the original city walls. You can take a **tour** (adult/child 5/3zł; ⊙8am-6pm) through the renovated fortifications, checking out displays of military gear and views over the city. Tickets must be bought from the tourist office in Great Market Sq, and the tour only runs when a minimum of 10 people have gathered.

Zamoyski Palace   PALACE
This former palace (closed to the public) lost much of its character when it was converted into a military hospital in the 1830s. To the north of the palace stretches a beautifully landscaped **park**. To its south is the **Arsenal Museum** (ul Zamkowa 2; adult/concession 6/3zł; ⊙9am-4pm Tue-Sun), housing an unremarkable collection of cannons, swords and firearms.

🛏 Sleeping

Hotel Zamojski   HOTEL €€€
(☏84 639 2516; www.orbis.pl; ul Kołłątaja 2/4/6; s/d 237/355zł; ❋) The best joint in town is situated within three connected old houses, just off the square. The rooms are modern and tastefully furnished, and there's a good on-site restaurant and cocktail bar, along with a fitness centre.

Hotel Arkadia   HOTEL €€
(☏84 638 6507; www.arkadia.zamosc.pl; Rynek Wielki 9; s/d from 140/160zł) With just nine rooms, this compact place offers a pool table and restaurant in addition to lodgings. It's charming but shabby, though its location right on the market square is hard to beat.

Pokoje Gościnne OSiR   HOSTEL €
(☏84 677 5460; ul Królowej Jadwigi 8; dm 24zł, s/d/tr 90/125/150zł) Located in a sprawling sport-

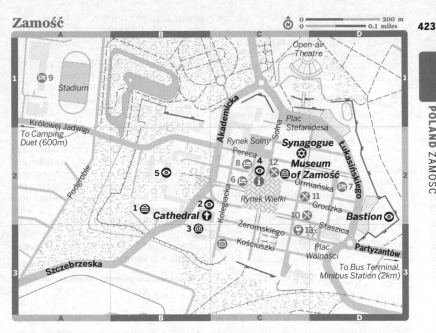

Zamość

◎ Top Sights

◎ Sights

🛏 Sleeping

⊗ Eating

☕ Drinking

ing complex, a 15-minute walk west of the Old Town, and packed with old trophies and students playing table tennis. Rooms are plainly furnished, clean and comfortable, although the bathrooms fall short of the ideal.

Hotel Jubilat   HOTEL **€€**
(☑84 638 6401; www.hoteljubilat.pl; ul Kardynała Wyszyńskiego 52; s/d from 136/177zł) An acceptable, if slightly drab, place to spend the night, right beside the bus station. It couldn't be handier for late arrivals or early departures, but it's a long way from anywhere else. It has a restaurant and fitness club.

Hotel Renesans   HOTEL **€€**
(☑84 639 2001; www.hotelrenesans.pl; ul Grecka 6; s/d from 156/222zł) It's ironic that a hotel named after the Renaissance is housed in the Old Town's ugliest building. However, it's central and the rooms are surprisingly modern and pleasant.

Camping Duet   CAMPING GROUND **€**
(☑84 639 2499; ul Królowej Jadwigi 14; s/d 75/90zł; ⊛) West of the Old Town, Camping Duet has neat bungalows, tennis courts, a restaurant, sauna and Jacuzzi. Larger bungalows sleep up to six.

Youth Hostel HOSTEL €
(✆84 638 9500; ul Zamoyskiego 4; dm 15zł;
☺Jul-Aug) You can find this hostel in a
school building 1.5km east of the Old
Town, not far from the bus terminal. It's
basic but functional and very cheap.

✖ Eating & Drinking

For self-caterers, there's the handy **Lux mini-supermarket** (ul Grodzka 16; ☺7am-8pm Mon-Sat, 8am-6pm Sun) near the Rynek.

Restauracja Muzealna POLISH €€
(✆84 638 7300; ul Ormiańska 30; mains 14-27zł;
☺11am-10pm Mon-Sat, 11am-9pm Sun) Subterranean restaurant in an atmospheric cellar
below the main square, bedecked with ornate timber furniture and portraits of nobles. It serves a better class of Polish cuisine
at reasonable prices, and has a well-stocked
bar.

Bar Asia POLISH €
(ul Staszica 10; mains 5-9zł; ☺8am-5pm Mon-Fri,
8am-4pm Sat) For hungry but broke travellers, this old-style *bar mleczny* is ideal. It
serves cheap and tasty Polish food, including
several variants of *pierogi* (dumplings), in a
minimally decorated space.

Corner Pub PUB
(ul Żeromskiego 6) This cosy Irish-style pub is
a good place to have a drink. It has comfy
booths and the walls are ornamented with
bric-a-brac such as antique clocks, swords
and model cars.

❶ Information

K@fejka Internetowa (Rynek Wielki 10; per
hr 3zł; ☺9am-5pm Mon-Fri, 10am-2pm Sat)
Internet access.

Main post office (ul Kościuszki)

Tourist office (✆84 639 2292; Rynek Wielki
13; ☺8am-6pm Mon-Fri & 10am-5pm Sat &
Sun May-Sep, 8am-5pm Mon-Fri & 9am-2pm
Sat Oct-Apr) Sells the glossy *Zamość – A Short
Guidebook* (9.50zł).

❶ Getting There & Away

The **bus terminal** (ul Hrubieszowska) is 2km
east of the Old Town and linked by frequent city
buses, primarily buses 0 and 3. Daily buses go to
Kraków (44zł, seven hours, four daily), Warsaw
(35zł, 4¾ hours, three daily) and Lublin (16zł,
two hours, hourly).

Quicker and cheaper are the minibuses that
travel every 30 minutes between Lublin and
Zamość (12zł, 1½ hours). They leave from the
minibus station opposite the bus terminal in
Zamość and from a corner north of the bus terminal in Lublin. Check the changeable timetable
for departures to other destinations, including
Warsaw and Kraków.

Ela Travel (✆84 639 3001; ul Grodzka 18)
sells international bus and air tickets.

CARPATHIAN MOUNTAINS

The Carpathians (Karpaty) stretch from the
southern border with Slovakia into Ukraine,
and their wooded hills and snowy mountains are a beacon for hikers, skiers and
cyclists. The most popular destination here
is the resort town of Zakopane in the heart
of the Tatra Mountains (Tatry). Elsewhere,
historic regional towns such as Przemyśl
and Sanok offer a relaxed pace and unique
insights into the past.

Zakopane

POP 27,300
Nestled at the foot of the Tatra Mountains,
Zakopane is Poland's major winter sports
centre, though it's a popular destination
year-round. It may resemble a tourist trap,
with its overcommercialised, overpriced
exterior, but it also has a relaxed, laid-back
vibe that makes it a great place to chill for
a few days, even if you're not planning on
skiing or hiking.

Zakopane played an important role in
sustaining Polish culture during the foreign
rule in the 19th century, thanks to the many
artistic types who settled during this period.

◉ Sights & Activities

Mt Gubałówka MOUNTAIN
Mt Gubałówka (1120m) offers excellent
views over the Tatras and is a popular destination for tourists who don't feel overly
energetic. The **funicular** (adult/concession
one way 10/8zł, return 15/12zł; ☺8am-10pm Jul &
Aug, 8.30am-6pm Apr-Jun & Sep, 8.30am-6pm Oct
& Nov) covers the 1388m-long route in less
than five minutes, climbing 300m from the
funicular station, which is just north of ul
Krupówki.

Tatra Museum MUSEUM
(ul Krupówki 10; adult/concession 7/5.50zł, free
Sun; ☺9am-5pm Tue-Sat, 9am-3pm Sun) Check
out exhibits about regional history, ethnography and geology here, along with
displays on local flora and fauna.

Zakopane

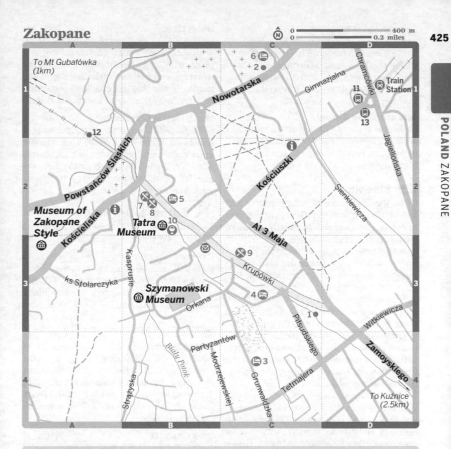

Zakopane

Museum of Zakopane Style MUSEUM
(ul Kościeliska 18; adult/concession 7/5.50zł;
⊙9am-5pm Wed-Sat, 9am-3pm Sun) Fittingly
housed in the 1892 Villa Koliba, the first
house to be designed by artist and architect Stanisław Witkiewicz in the distinctive architectural style which became the
trademark of Zakopane in the late 19th
century.

Szymanowksi Museum   MUSEUM

(ul Kasprusie 19; adult/concession 6/3zł, free Sun; ⊙10am-4pm Tue-Sun) This institution within the Villa Atma is dedicated to the great composer Karol Szymanowski, who once lived here. It hosts piano recitals in summer.

Jaszczurówka Chapel   CHURCH

(ul Balzera) Perhaps Witkiewicz's greatest design achievement is this attractive place of worship, located along the road to Morskie Oko.

🛏 Sleeping

Given the abundance of private rooms and decent hostels, few travellers actually stay in hotels. The tourist office usually knows of great bargains in guest houses.

Some travel agencies in Zakopane can arrange private rooms, but in the high season they may not want to offer anything for less than three nights. Expect a double room (singles are rarely offered) to cost about 80zł in the high season in the town centre, and about 60zł for somewhere further out.

Locals offering private rooms may approach you at the bus or train stations; alternatively, just look out for signs posted in the front of private homes – *noclegi* and *pokoje* both mean 'rooms available'.

Like all seasonal resorts, accommodation prices fluctuate considerably between low season and high season (December to February and July to August). Always book accommodation in advance at peak times, especially on weekends. The following rates are for high season.

⌂TOP CHOICE Hotel Sabała   HOTEL €€€

(⊉18 201 5092; www.sabala.zakopane.pl; ul Krupówki 11; s/d from 340/440zł; 🐾) Built in 1894 but thoroughly up-to-date, this striking timber building has a superb location overlooking the picturesque pedestrian thoroughfare. It offers cosy, attic-style rooms, and there's a sauna and solarium on the premises. A candlelit restaurant has views of street life.

Carlton   HOTEL €€

(⊉18 201 4415; www.carlton.pl; ul Grunwaldzka 11; s/d/tr 100/200/300zł) Good-value pension in a grand old house away from the main drag, featuring light-filled rooms with modern furniture. There's an impressive shared balcony overlooking the road, and a big comfy lounge lined with potted plants.

Hotel Litwor   HOTEL €€€

(⊉18 202 4200; www.litwor.pl; ul Krupówki 40; s/d 476/595zł; 🐾🌊) This sumptuous four-star place, with large, restful rooms, has all the usual top-end facilities, including a gym and sauna. It also has an excellent restaurant serving classy versions of traditional dishes.

Youth Hostel Szarotka   HOSTEL €

(⊉18 201 3618; www.szarotkaptsm.republika.pl; ul Nowotarska 45; dm 40zł, d 100zł) This friendly, homey place gets packed in the high season. There's a kitchen and washing machine on-site. It's on a noisy road about a 10-minute walk from the town centre.

🍴 Eating & Drinking

The main street, ul Krupówki, is lined with all sorts of eateries.

Czarny Staw   GRILL €€

(⊉18 201 3856; ul Krupówki 2; mains 12-46zł; ⊙10am-1am) Offers a tasty range of Polish dishes, including a variety of dumplings, and much of the menu is cooked before your very eyes on the central grill. There's a good salad bar, and live music most nights.

Pstrąg Górski   SEAFOOD €€

(⊉18 206 4613; ul Krupówki 6; mains 15-30zł; ⊙9am-10pm) This self-service fish restaurant, done up in traditional style and overlooking a narrow stream, serves some of the freshest trout, salmon and sea fish in town. It's excellent value.

Stek Chałupa   POLISH €€

(⊉18 201 5918; ul Krupówki 33; mains 12-32zł; ⊙8am-midnight) Big friendly barn of a place, with homey decor and waitresses in traditional garb. The menu features meat dishes, particularly steaks, though there are vegetarian choices among the salads and *pierogi*.

Appendix   CAFE-BAR

(ul Krupówki 6; ⊙11am-midnight) A mellow venue for an alcoholic or caffeine-laden drink, hidden away above the street with an ambient old-meets-new decor. It hosts live music most weekends.

ℹ Information

Centrum Przewodnictwa Tatrzańskiego (Tatra Guide Centre; ⊉18 206 37 99; ul Chałubińskiego 42a; ⊙9am-3pm) Arranges English- and German-speaking mountain guides.

Księgarnia Górska (ul Zaruskiego 5) Bookshop in the reception area of the Dom Turysty PTTK, sells regional hiking maps.

Main post office (ul Krupówki; ☉7am-8pm Mon-Fri, 8am-2pm Sat)

Tourist office (☏18 201 2211) Bus station (ul Kościuszki 17; ☉9am-5pm daily Jul & Aug, 9am-5pm Mon-Fri Sep-Jun); Town (ul Kościeliska 7; ☉9am-5pm daily Jul & Aug, 9am-5pm Mon-Fri Sep-Jun) These offices offer advice, sell hiking and city maps, and can also arrange rafting trips down the Dunajec River.

Widmo (ul Galicy 6; per hr 5zł; ☉7.30am-midnight Mon-Fri, 9am-midnight Sat & Sun) Internet access.

❶ Getting There & Away

From the **bus terminal** (ul Chramcówki), PKS buses run to Kraków every 45 to 60 minutes (18zł, two hours). Two private companies, **Trans Frej** (www.trans-frej.com.pl, in Polish) and **Szwagropol** (www.szwagropol.pl, in Polish), also run comfortable buses from here (18zł) at the same frequency. At peak times (especially weekends), you can buy your tickets for the private buses in advance from offices a short distance west of the bus station in Zakopane. Tickets are also available in Kraków from **Fogra Travel** (ul Pawia 12). The minibus station opposite the bus terminal is most useful for journeys to towns within the Tatra Mountains.

From Zakopane, PKS buses also head to Lublin (56zł, nine hours, four daily), Sanok (42zł, 6½ hours, one daily), Przemyśl (45zł, nine hours, one daily) and Warsaw (60zł, eight hours, five daily). Two daily buses head to Poprad in Slovakia (18zł). PKS buses – and minibuses from opposite the bus terminal – regularly travel to Lake Morskie Oko and on to Polana Palenica. To cross into Slovakia, get off this bus/minibus at Łysa Polana, cross the border on foot, and take another bus to Tatranská Lomnica and the other Slovak mountain towns.

From the **train station** (ul Chramcówki), nine trains a day go to Kraków (35zł, 3½ hours), two to Częstochowa (48zł, 5½ hours), four to Lublin (56zł, nine hours), two to Gdynia via Gdańsk (70zł, 16 hours), one to Łódź (56zł, 8¼ hours), one to Poznań (60zł, 11½ hours) and four to Warsaw (58zł, 8½ hours).

Tatra Mountains

The Tatras, 100km south of Kraków, are the highest range of the Carpathian Mountains, providing a dramatic range of rugged scenery that's a distinct contrast to the rest of Poland's flatness. Roughly 60km long and 15km wide, this mountain range stretches across the Polish–Slovak border. A quarter is in Poland and is mostly part of the Tatra National Park (about 212 sq km). The Polish Tatras contain more than 20 peaks over

2000m, the highest of which is Mt Rysy (2499m).

◉ Sights & Activities

Cable Car to Mt Kasprowy Wierch CABLE CAR (www.pkl.pl; adult/concession return 42/32zł; ☉7am-9pm Jul & Aug, 7.30am-5pm Apr-Jun, Sep & Oct, 8am-4pm Nov) The cable-car trip from Kuźnice (2km south of Zakopane) to the summit of Mt Kasprowy Wierch (1985m) is a classic tourist experience enjoyed by Poles and foreigners alike. At the end of the trip, you can get off and stand with one foot in Poland and the other in Slovakia. The one-way journey takes 20 minutes and climbs 936m. The cable car normally shuts down for two weeks in May, and won't operate if the snow and, particularly, the winds are dangerous.

The view from the top is spectacular (clouds permitting). Two chairlifts transport skiers to and from various slopes between December and April. A restaurant serves skiers and hikers alike. In summer, many people return to Zakopane on foot down the Gąsienicowa Valley, and the most intrepid walk the ridges all the way across to Lake Morskie Oko via Pięciu Stawów, a strenuous hike taking a full day in good weather.

If you buy a return ticket, your trip back is automatically reserved for two hours after your departure, so buy a one-way ticket to the top (32zł) and another one down (26zł), if you want to stay longer. Mt Kasprowy Wierch is popular; so in summer, arrive early and expect to wait. PKS buses and minibuses to Kuźnice frequently leave from Zakopane.

Lake Morskie Oko LAKE
The emerald-green Lake Morskie Oko (Eye of the Sea) is among the loveliest lakes in the Tatras. PKS buses and minibuses regularly depart from Zakopane for Polana Palenica (30 minutes), from where a road (9km) continues uphill to the lake. Cars, bikes and buses are not allowed up this road, so you'll have to walk, but it's not steep (allow about two hours one way). Alternatively, take a horse-drawn carriage (50/30zł uphill/downhill, but very negotiable) to within 2km of the lake. In winter, transport is by horse-drawn four-seater sledge, which is more expensive. The last minibus to Zakopane returns between 5pm and 6pm.

Hiking HIKING
If you're doing any hiking in the Tatras get a copy of the *Tatrzański Park Narodowy* map (1:25,000), which shows all hiking trails in the area. Better still, buy one or more of

the 14 sheets of *Tatry Polskie*, available at Księgarnia Górska (p426) in Zakopane. In July and August these trails can be overrun by tourists, so late spring and early autumn are the best times. Theoretically you can expect better weather in autumn, when rainfall is lower.

Like all alpine regions, the Tatras can be dangerous, particularly during the snow season (November to May). Remember the weather can be unpredictable. Bring proper hiking boots, warm clothing and waterproof rain gear – and be prepared to use occasional ropes and chains (provided along the trails) to get up and down some rocky slopes. Guides are not necessary because many of the trails are marked, but they can be arranged in Zakopane (see p426) for about 350zł per day.

There are several picturesque valleys south of Zakopane, including the **Dolina Strążyska**. You can continue from the Strążyska by the red trail up to **Mt Giewont** (1909m), 3½ hours from Zakopane, and then walk down the blue trail to Kuźnice in two hours.

Two long and beautiful forested valleys, the **Dolina Chochołowska** and the **Dolina Kościeliska**, are in the western part of the park, known as the Tatry Zachodnie (West Tatras). These valleys are ideal for cycling. Both are accessible by PKS buses and minibuses from Zakopane.

The Tatry Wysokie (High Tatras) to the east offer quite different scenery: bare granite peaks and glacial lakes. One way to get there is via cable car to **Mt Kasprowy Wierch**, then hike eastward along the red trail to Mt Świnica (2301m) and on to the Zawrat pass (2159m) – a tough three to four hours from Mt Kasprowy. From Zawrat, descend northwards to the Dolina Gąsienicowa along the blue trail and then back to Zakopane.

Alternatively, head south (also along the blue trail) to the wonderful **Dolina Pięciu Stawów** (Five Lakes Valley), where there is a mountain refuge 1¼ hours from Zawrat. The blue trail heading west from the refuge passes Lake Morskie Oko, 1½ hours from the refuge.

Skiing   SKIING
Zakopane boasts four major ski areas (and several smaller ones) with more than 50 ski lifts. Mt Kasprowy Wierch and **Mt Gubałówka** offer the best conditions and the most challenging slopes in the area, with the ski season extending until early May. Lift tickets cost 10zł for one ride at Mt Kasprowy Wierch, and 2zł on the smaller lift at Mt Gubałówka. Alternatively, you can buy a day

card (100zł) at Mt Kasprowy Wierch, which allows you to skip the queues. Purchase your lift tickets on the relevant mountain.

Another alternative is the **Harenda chairlift** (☎18 206 4029; www.harendazakopane. pl; ul Harenda 63; ◎9am-6pm) just outside Zakopane, in the direction of Kraków. A one-way/return ticket is 7/10zł.

Ski equipment rental is available at all facilities except Mt Kasprowy Wierch. Otherwise, stop off on your way to Kuźnice at the **ski rental** place near the Rondo in Zakopane. Other places in Zakopane, such as **Sukces Ski Rental** (☎18 206 4197; ul Nowotarska 39) and **Sport Shop & Service** (☎18 201 5871; ul Krupówki 52a), also rent ski gear.

🛏 Sleeping

Tourists are not allowed to take their own cars into the park; you must walk in, take the cable car or use an official vehicle owned by the park or a hotel or hostel.

Camping is also not allowed in the park, but eight PTTK mountain refuges/hostels provide simple accommodation. Most refuges are small and fill up fast; in midsummer and midwinter they're invariably packed beyond capacity. No one is ever turned away, however, though you may have to crash on the floor if all the beds are taken. Don't arrive too late in the day, and remember to bring along your own bed mat and sleeping bag. All refuges serve simple hot meals, but the kitchens and dining rooms close early (sometimes at 7pm).

The refuges listed here are open all year, but some may be temporarily closed for renovations or because of inclement weather. Check the current situation at the **PTTK office** (☎18 201 2429; ul Krupówki 12) in Zakopane.

Kalatówki Mountain Hotel   HOTEL **€€**
(☎18 206 3644; www.kalatowki.pl; s/d from 81/154zł) This large and decent accommodation is the easiest to reach from Zakopane. It's a 40-minute walk from the Kuźnice cable-car station.

Dolina Pięciu Stawów Hostel   HOSTEL **€**
(☎18 207 7607; www.piecstawow.pl; dm 30-35zł) This is the highest (1700m) and most scenically located refuge in the Polish Tatras.

Hala Kondratowa Hostel   HOSTEL **€**
(☎18 201 9114; dm 28zł) This place is about 30 minutes beyond Kalatówki on the trail to Giewont. It's in a terrific location and has a great atmosphere, but it is small.

Roztoka Hostel HOSTEL €
(☎18 207 7442; dm 28-30zł) Hikers wishing to traverse the park might want to begin here. It's accessible by the bus or minibus to Morskie Oko.

Morskie Oko Hostel HOSTEL €
(☎18 207 7609; www.schroniskomorskieoko.pl; dm 27-49zł) An early start from Zakopane would allow you to visit Morskie Oko in the morning and stay here at night.

Dunajec Gorge

An entertaining and leisurely way to explore the Pieniny Mountains is to go **rafting** (www.flisacy.com.pl) on the Dunajec River, which winds along the Polish–Slovak border through a spectacular and deep gorge.

The trip starts at the wharf (Przystan Flisacka) in Sromowce-Kąty, 46km northeast of Zakopane, and you can finish either at the spa town of Szczawnica (adult/concession 44/22zł, 2¼ hours, 18km), or further on at Krościenko (adult/concession 53/27zł, 2¾ hours, 23km). The raft trip operates between April and October, but only starts when there's a minimum of 10 passengers.

The gorge is an easy day trip from Zakopane. Catch a regular bus to Nowy Targ (5zł, 30 minutes, hourly) from Zakopane to connect with one of five daily buses (7zł, one hour) to Sromowce-Kąty. From Szczawnica or Krościenko, take the bus back to Nowy Targ (8zł, one hour, hourly) and change for Zakopane. Krościenko has frequent bus links with Szczawnica, and two buses travel daily between Szczawnica and Kraków (15zł, 2½ hours). You can also return to the Sromowce-Kąty car park by bus with the raftsmen.

To avoid waiting around in Sromowce-Kąty for a raft to fill up, organise a trip at any travel agency in Zakopane, or at the tourist office. The cost is around 90zł per person, and includes transport, equipment and guides.

Sanok

POP 39,400

Nestled in a picturesque valley in the foothills of the Bieszczady Mountains, Sanok has been subject to Ruthenian, Hungarian, Austrian, Russian, German and Polish rule in its eventful history. Although it contains an important industrial zone, it's also a popular base for exploring the mountains.

The helpful **tourist office** (☎13 464 4533; www.sanok.pl; Rynek 14; ◉9am-5pm Mon-Fri year-round, 9am-1pm Sat & Sun May-Oct) on the market square is the best place to find brochures on Sanok's attractions. You can check email at **Prox** (ul Kazimierz Wielkiego 6; per hr 3zł) further west.

Sanok is noted for its unique **Museum of Folk Architecture** (www.skansen.mblsanok.pl; ul Rybickiego 3; adult/concession 10/6zł; ◉8am-6pm May-Sep, 8am-2pm Oct-Apr), which features architecture from regional ethnic groups. Walk north from the town centre for 2km along ul Mickiewicza and ul Białogórska, then cross the bridge and turn right. Back in the centre of town, the **Historical Museum** (ul Zamkowa 2; adult/concession 10/7zł; ◉8am-noon Mon, 9am-3pm Tue-Sun) is housed in a 16th-century castle and contains an impressive collection of Ruthenian icons, along with a modern art gallery.

Sanok's surrounding villages are attractions in their own right, as many have lovely old churches. The marked **Icon Trail** takes hikers or cyclists along a 70km loop, passing by 10 village churches, as well as attractive mountain countryside. Trail leaflets and maps (in English, German and French) are available from the tourist office, as well as information on other themed trails, including a Jewish heritage route.

Find convenient budget accommodation at **Hotel Pod Trzema Różami** (☎13 463 0922; www.podtrzemarozami.pl; ul Jagiellońska 13; s/d 80/100zł), about 300m south of the market square. Further south (another 600m) and up the scale is **Hotel Jagielloński** (☎13 463 1208; www.hoteljagiellonski.bieszczady24.pl; ul Jagiellońska 49; s/d 120/160zł), with distinctive wooden furniture, parquetry floors and a good restaurant. Sanok's most comfortable option is **Hotel Sanvit** (☎13 465 5088; www.sanvit.sanok.pl; ul Łazienna 1; s/d 130/175zł), just west of the market square, with bright, modern rooms, shining bathrooms, spa treatments and a restaurant.

Karczma Jadło Karpackie (☎13 464 6700; Rynek 12; mains 8-25zł) is an amenable, down-to-earth bar and restaurant on the market square. A good place to have a drink, alcoholic or otherwise, is **Weranda Caffe** (ul 3 Maja 14; ◉10am-10pm), a cosy cafe-bar with a fireplace, and outdoor seating in summer.

The bus terminal and adjacent train station are about 1km southeast of the market square. Three buses go daily to Przemyśl (12zł, two hours), and one to Zakopane (42zł, 6½ hours). Buses also head regularly to

WORTH A TRIP

LAKE SOLINA

In the far southeastern corner of Poland, wedged between the Ukrainian and Slovak borders, lies **Lake Solina**. This sizeable reservoir (27km long and 60m deep) was created in 1968 when the San River was dammed. Today it's a popular centre for water sports and other recreational pursuits.

Polańczyk is the best place to base yourself. This pleasant town on the lake's western shore offers a range of attractions, including sailing, windsurfing, fishing and beaches. There are also numerous hotels and sanatoriums offering spa treatments.

There are regular buses from Sanok to Polańczyk each day. For more details, check out Lonely Planet's *Poland* country guide, visit www.karpaty.turystyka.pl or step into the local **tourist office** (☑13 470 3028; ul Wiejska 2, Polańczyk).

Kraków and Warsaw. Train journeys to these destinations, however, may require multiple changes.

Przemyśl

POP 66,400

Everything about Przemyśl (*psheh*-mishl) feels big: its sprawling market square, the massive churches surrounding it, and the broad San River flowing through the city.

Luckily the area of most interest to visitors – around the sloping **Market Sq** (Rynek) – is compact and easily explored. The **tourist office** (☑16 675 2164; www.przemysl.pl; ul Grodzka 1; ☺8am-6pm Mon-Fri & 9am-5pm Sat Apr-Sep, 9am-5pm Mon-Fri & 10am-2pm Sat Oct-Mar) is situated above the southwest corner of the square.

About 350m southwest of the square are the ruins of a 14th-century **castle** (ul Zamkowa), built by Kazimierz Wielki. In a modern building just northeast of Rynek, you can learn about the history of the surrounding region at the **National Museum of the Przemyśl Lands** (Plac Joselewicza; adult/concession 8/4zł; ☺10am-3pm Tue-Sat, 11am-3pm Sun).

For variety, visit the curious **Museum of Bells and Pipes** (ul Władycze 3; adult/concession 5/3zł; ☺10am-3pm Tue-Sat, 11am-3pm Sun) in the old Clock Tower, where you can inspect several floors worth of vintage bells, elaborately carved pipes and cigar cutters (the city has long been famous across Poland for manufacturing these items). From the top of the tower there's a great view.

Przemyśl has a selection of inexpensive accommodation, including the central **Dom Wycieczkowy Podzamcze** (☑16 678 5374; ul Waygarta 3; dm 25zł, s/d 47/68zł), on the western edge of the Old Town. Its rooms have seen

some wear, but it's pleasant enough for the price.

More comfort is available at **Hotel Europejski** (☑16 675 7100; www.hotel-europejski.pl; ul Sowińskiego 4; s/d/tr/ste 110/140/170/210zł) in a renovated old building facing the attractive facade of the train station. An impressive staircase leads to simple, light rooms with high ceilings. Another option is **Hotel Gromada** (☑16 676 1111; www.gromada.pl; ul Wybrzeże Piłsudskiego 4; s/d 186/249zł), a big, business-friendly chain hotel west of the Old Town.

A worthy place to eat is **Restauracja Piwnica Mieszczańska** (☑16 675 0459; Rynek 9; mains 7-30zł), on the Rynek. It must be Poland's only cellar restaurant with access to a skylight, and is decorated with mini-chandeliers and lace tablecloths. The bourgeoisie platter (three kinds of meat) will interest ardent carnivores, and there's a reasonable selection of soups and fish dishes.

Restauracja Dominikańska (☑16 678 2055; Plac Dominikański 3; mains 5-25zł; ☺10am-10pm) is an elegantly appointed eatery in the quieter northeastern corner of the Market Sq, serving affordable Polish classics.

If you fancy a drink, **Bistro Absynt** (Plac Dominikański 4), on the northwest corner of Rynek, is a relaxed space from which to sip and people-watch.

From Przemyśl, buses run to Lviv (95km) in Ukraine several times a day and regularly to all towns in southeastern Poland, including Sanok (12zl, two hours, three daily). Trains run to Lublin (44zł, four hours, one daily), Kraków (46zł, four hours, 14 daily) and Warsaw (56zł, 6¾ hours, three daily), and stop here on the way to/from Lviv. The bus terminal and adjacent train station in Przemyśl are about 1km northeast of the Rynek.

SILESIA

Silesia (Śląsk, *shlonsk*, in Polish) is a fascinating mix of landscapes. Though the industrial zone around Katowice has limited attraction for visitors, beautiful Wrocław is a historic city with lively nightlife, and the Sudeten Mountains draw hikers and other nature lovers.

The history of the region is similarly diverse, having been governed by Polish, Bohemian, Austrian and German rulers. After two centuries as part of Prussia and Germany, the territory was largely included within Poland's new borders after WWII.

Wrocław

POP 632,000

When citizens of beautiful Kraków enthusiastically encourage you to visit Wrocław (*vrotswahf*), you know you're onto something good. The city's delightful Old Town is a gracious mix of Gothic and baroque styles, and its large student population ensures a healthy number of restaurants, bars and nightclubs.

Wrocław has been traded back and forth between various rulers over the centuries, but began life in the year 1000 under the Polish Piast dynasty and developed into a prosperous trading and cultural centre. In the 1740s it passed to Prussia, under the German name of Breslau. Under Prussian rule, the city became a major textile manufacturing centre, greatly increasing its population.

Upon its return to Poland in 1945, Wrocław was a shell of its former self, having sustained massive damage in WWII. Though 70% of the city was destroyed, sensitive restoration has returned the historic centre to its former beauty.

◉ Sights

OLD TOWN

TOP CHOICE **Gnomes of Wrocław**   STATUES
See if you can spot the diminutive statue of a gnome at ground level, just to the west of the Jaś i Małgosia houses; he's one of over 150, which are scattered through the city. Whimsical as they are, they're attributed to the symbol of the Orange Alternative, a communist-era dissident group that used ridicule as a weapon, and often painted gnomes where graffiti had been removed by the authorities. You can buy a gnome map (5zł) from the tourist office and go gnome-spotting.

Market Square   HISTORIC SQUARE
In the centre of the Old Town is Poland's second-largest old market square (after Kraków), known in Polish as the Rynek. It's an attractive, rambling space, lined by beautifully painted facades and with a complex of old buildings in the middle. The southwestern corner of the square opens into **Salt Place** (Plac Solny), once the site of the town's salt trade and now home to a 24-hour flower market.

City Dwellers' Art Museum   MUSEUM
(adult/concession 7/5zł; ☉10am-5pm Tue-Sat, 10am-6pm Sun) The beautiful town hall (built 1327–1504) on the southern side of the square has stately rooms on show, with exhibits featuring the art of gold and the stories of famous Wrocław inhabitants.

Jaś i Małgosia   HISTORIC BUILDINGS
(ul Św. Mikołaja) In the northwestern corner of the market square are two attractive small houses linked by a baroque gate. They're a couple better known to English speakers as Hansel and Gretel.

Church of St Mary Magdalene   CHURCH
(ul Łaciarska; ☉9am-4pm Mon-Sat) One block east of the Rynek is this Gothic church with a Romanesque portal from 1280 incorporated into its southern external wall. Climb the 72m high tower and its connected **bridge** (adult/concession 4/3zł, ☉10am-8pm Apr-Oct) for a lofty view.

Church of St Elizabeth   CHURCH
(ul Elżbiety 1; admission 5zł; ☉9am-6pm Mon-Fri, 11am-5pm Sat, 1-5pm Sun) Behind houses and gnomes is this monumental 14th-century church with its 83m-high tower, which you can climb for city views.

EAST OF THE OLD TOWN

Panorama of Racławice   MONUMENTAL ARTWORK
(www.panoramaraclawicka.pl; ul Purkyniego 11; adult/concession 20/15zł; ☉9am-5pm Tue-Sun May-Oct, 9am-4pm Tue-Sun Nov-Apr) Wrocław's pride and joy (and major tourist attraction) is this giant 360-degree painting of the 1794 Battle of Racławice, in which the Polish peasant army, led by Tadeusz Kościuszko, defeated Russian forces intent on partitioning Poland. Created by Jan Styka and Wojciech Kossak for the centenary of the battle in 1894, the painting is an immense 114m long and 15m high, and was brought here by Polish immigrants displaced from Lviv after WWII. Due to the communist government's uneasiness about glorifying a famous Russian defeat, however,

Wrocław

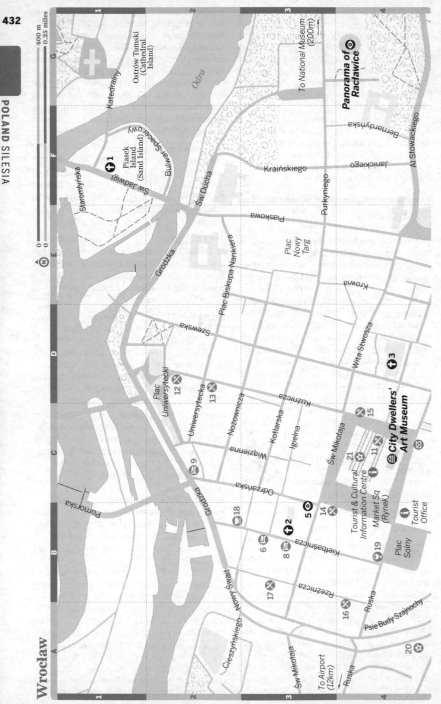

400 m
0.25 miles

Katedralny

Ostrów Tumski
(Cathedral
Island)

Odra

To National Museum
(200m)

Panorama of
Racławice

Bernardyńska

Staromłyńska

Piasek Island
(Sand Island)

Św Jadwigi

Bulwar Spacerowy

Św Ducha

Kraińskiego

Janickiego

Al Słowackiego

Purkyniego

Grodzka

Piaskowa

Plac Biskupa Nankiera

Plac Nowy
Targ

Szewska

Krowia

Wita Stwosza

Plac
Uniwersytecki

Uniwersytecka

Nożownicza

Kuźnicza

Kotlarska

Igielna

Wiązienna

Św Mikołaja

City Dwellers'
Art Museum

Pomorska

Grodzka

Odrzańska

Tourist & Cultural
Information Centre

Market Sq
(Rynek)

Tourist
Office

Cieszyńskiego Nowy Świat

Kiełbaśnicza

Rzeźnicza

Plac
Solny

Ruska

Psie Budy Szajnochy

To Airport
(12km)

Św Mikołaja

Ruska

the panorama wasn't re-erected until 1985, in a circular building east of the Old Town.

Obligatory tours (with audio in English, French, German, Spanish, Russian and other languages) run every 30 minutes between 9am and 4.30pm from April to November, and 10am and 3pm from December to March. The ticket also allows entry to the National Museum on the same day.

National Museum MUSEUM
(www.mnwr.art.pl; Plac Powstańców Warszawy 5; adult/concession 15/10zł, free Sat; ☉10am-4pm Wed-Fri & Sun, 10am-6pm Sat) Near the Panorama, this museum exhibits Silesian medieval art, and a fine collection of modern Polish painting. Entry is included with a ticket to the Panorama.

ECCLESIASTICAL DISTRICT

Cathedral of St John the Baptist CHURCH
(Plac Katedralny; ☉10am-6pm Mon-Sat, except during services) This Gothic cathedral has a unique lift to whisk you to the top of its **tower** (adult/concession 5/4zł) for superb views. Next door to the cathedral is the **Archdiocesan Museum** (Plac Katedralny 16; adult/concession 3/2zł; ☉9am-3pm Tue-Sun) of sacred art.

Church of Our Lady on the Sand CHURCH
(ul Św Jadwigi; ☉erratic) North of the river is Piasek Island (Sand Island), where you'll find this 14th-century place of worship with lofty Gothic vaults and a year-round nativity scene.

Church of the Holy Cross & St Bartholomew CHURCH
(Plac Kościelny; ☉9am-6pm) Cross the small bridge to Ostrów Tumski (Cathedral Island), a picturesque area full of churches, and walk to this two-storey Gothic structure, built between 1288 and 1350.

Botanical Gardens GARDENS
(ul Sienkiewicza 23; adult/concession 7/5zł; ☉8am-6pm Apr-Oct) North of the cathedral are these charming gardens, where you can chill out among the chestnut trees and tulips.

SOUTH OF THE OLD TOWN

Historical Museum MUSEUM
(www.mmw.pl; ul Kazimierza Wielkiego 35; adult/concession 15/10zł; ☉10am-5pm Tue, Wed, Fri & Sat, 1-8pm Thu, 10am-6pm Sun) Housed in a grand former palace, this institution highlights the main events in Wrocław's thousand-year history, and includes an art collection covering the past two centuries.

Wrocław

Passage   MONUMENT
(corner of ul Świdnicka & ul Piłsudskiego) This fascinating sculpture depicts a group of pedestrians being swallowed by the pavement, only to re-emerge on the other side of the street.

✹ Festivals & Events

Jazz on the Odra International Festival   MUSIC
(www.jnofestival.pl) February/March

Musica Polonica Nova Festival   MUSIC
(www.musicapolonica nova.pl, in Polish) May

Wratislavia Cantans   MUSIC
(www.wratislaviacantans.pl) September

Wrocław Marathon   SPORT
(www.wroclawmaraton.pl) September

🛏 Sleeping

Hotel Patio   HOTEL €€
(☎71 375 0400; www.hotelpatio.pl; ul Kiełbaśnicza 24; s/d from 249/279zł; ❄) Pleasant lodgings a short hop from the main square, housed within two buildings linked by a covered sunlit courtyard. Rooms are clean and light, sometimes small but with reasonably high ceilings. There's a restaurant, bar and hairdresser on-site.

Nathan's Villa Hostel   HOSTEL €
(☎71 344 1095; www.nathansvilla.com; ul Świdnicka 13; dm from 40zł, r from 150zł) This comfortable 96-bed place is conveniently placed about 150m south of the Rynek. It does accept noisy Polish school groups in addition to backpackers, so check before you check in.

Art Hotel   HOTEL €€
(☎71 787 7100; www.arthotel.pl; ul Kiełbaśnicza 20; s/d from 270/310zł; ❄) Elegant but affordable accommodation in a renovated apartment building. Rooms feature tastefully restrained decor, quality fittings and gleaming bathrooms. Within the hotel is a top-notch restaurant, and there's a fitness room to work off the resultant kilojoules.

Hostel Babel   HOSTEL €
(☎71 342 0250; www.babelhostel.pl; ul Kołłątaja 16; dm from 45zł, d 140zł) A tatty old staircase leads up to pleasant budget accommodation. Dorms are set in renovated apartment rooms with ornate lamps and decorative ceilings. Bathrooms are shiny clean, and guests have free access to a kitchen and washing machine. There's a DVD player for rainy days.

Hotel Tumski   HOTEL €€€
(☎71 322 6099; www.hotel-tumski.com.pl; Wyspa Słodowa 10; s/d from 260/380zł) This is a neat hotel in a peaceful setting overlooking the river, offering reasonable value for money. It's ideal for exploring the lovely ecclesiastical quarter, and there's a good restaurant attached.

Hotel Zaułek   HOTEL €€
(☎71 341 0046; www.hotelzaulek.pl; ul Garbary 11; s/d from 260/330zł) Run by the university, this guest house accommodates just 18 visitors in a dozen homey rooms. The 1pm checkout is a plus for heavy sleepers, and weekend

prices are a steal. Breakfast is an additional 12zł, and half and full board is available.

Hotel Europejski
HOTEL €€

(☑71 772 1000; www.silfor.pl; ul Piłsudskiego 88; s/d 179/219zł) Apparently a leopard can change its spots – the formerly drab Europejski is now a smart business hotel. Rooms are clean and bright, and very handy for the train station. Breakfast is an extra 25zł.

MDK Youth Hostel
HOSTEL €

(☑71 343 8856; www.mdk.kopernik.wroclaw.pl; ul Kołłątaja 20; dm from 27zł, d from 72zł) Not far from the train station, this is a basic place, located in a grand mustard-coloured building. Some dorms are huge and beds are packed close together. It's almost always full, so book ahead.

Hotel Europeum
HOTEL €€€

(☑71 371 4500; www.europeum.pl; ul Kazimierza Wielkiego 27a; s/d 320/350zł; ✷) Business-oriented hotel with stylish rooms in a great location near the Market Sq. Rates drop dramatically at weekends.

Old Town Apartments
APARTMENTS €€

(☑22 351 2260; www.warsawshotel.com; ul Nowy Świat 29/3, Warsaw; apt from €55) Warsaw-based agency with modern, fully furnished one-bedroom apartments around Wrocław's Market Sq. Weekly rates are available.

✗ Eating & Drinking

TOP CHOICE **Restauracja JaDka**
POLISH €€€

(☑71 343 6461; www.jadka.pl; ul Rzeźnicza 24/25; mains 46-82zł; ☉noon-10pm) Arguably the best restaurant in town, presenting impeccable modern versions of Polish classics amid elegant table settings in delightful Gothic surrounds. There's loads of character in the interior, with tables bearing lacy white tablecloths dotted beneath brick archways, illuminated by low-lit lamps.

Bazylia
CAFETERIA €

(Plac Uniwersytecki; mains 2.15zł per 100g; ☉8am-7pm) Inexpensive and bustling modern take on the classic *bar mleczny,* in a curved space with huge plate-glass windows overlooking the venerable university buildings. The menu has a lot of Polish standards such as *bigos* and *gołąbki,* and a decent range of salads and other vegetable dishes. Everything is priced by weight at the same rate; order and pay at the till before receiving your food.

Darea
KOREAN €€€

(☑71 343 5301; ul Kuźnicza 43/45; mains 26-60zł; ☉noon-11pm) With management at the LG Electronics factory in nearby Kobierzyce top-heavy with Koreans, it was inevitable that Wrocław would produce a place serving dishes like *bibimbab* and *bulgogi.* You won't find better Korean anywhere in Poland.

La Scala
ITALIAN €€

(☑71 372 5394; Rynek 38; mains 16-140zł) Offers authentic Italian food and particularly good desserts. Some dishes are pricey, but you're really paying for the location. The cheaper trattoria at ground level serves good pizza and pasta.

Mexico Bar
MEXICAN €€

(☑60 090 4577; ul Rzeźnicza 34; mains 16-35zł; ☉11am-midnight) Compact, warmly lit restaurant featuring sombreros, backlit masks and a chandelier made of beer bottles. There's a small bar to lean on while waiting for a table. All the Tex-Mex standards are on the menu, but book at least two days ahead for a table on weekends.

Karczma Lwowska
POLISH €€€

(☑71 343 9887; Rynek 4; mains 26-41zł; ☉11am-midnight) Has a great spot on Market Sq, with outdoor seating in summer, and offers the usual meaty Polish standards in a space with a rustic rural look. It's worth stopping by to try the beer, served in ceramic mugs.

Bar Wegetariański Vega
VEGETARIAN €

(☑71 344 3934; Rynek 1/2; mains 5-7zł; ☉8am-7pm Mon-Fri, 9am-5pm Sat & Sun) This is a cheap cafeteria in the centre of the Rynek, offering vegie dishes in a light green space. Good choice of soups and crepes. Upstairs there's a vegan section, open from noon.

Pub Guinness
PUB

(Plac Solny 5; ☉noon-2am) No prizes for guessing what this pub serves. A lively, fairly authentic Irish pub, spread over three levels on a busy corner. The ground-floor bar buzzes with student and traveller groups getting together, and there's a restaurant and beer cellar as well. A good place to wind down after a hard day's sightseeing.

Cafe Artzat
CAFE

(ul Malarska 30) This low-key cafe just north of the Church of St Elizabeth is one of the best places in town to recharge the batteries over coffee or tea and a good book.

☆ Entertainment

Check out the bimonthly *Visitor* (free and in English) for details of what's on in this important cultural centre. It's available from the tourist office and upmarket hotels.

TOP CHOICE **PRL** BAR/CLUB

(Rynek Ratusz 10; ⊙noon-late) The dictatorship of the proletariat is alive and well in this tongue-in-cheek venue inspired by communist nostalgia. Disco lights play over a bust of Lenin, propaganda posters line the walls, and red menace memorabilia is scattered through the maze of rooms. Descend to the basement – beneath the portraits of Stalin and Mao – if you'd like to hit the dance floor. Tuesday is karaoke night.

Teatr Polski THEATRE

(☑71 316 0777; www.teatrpolski.wroc.pl; ul Zapolskiej 3) Wrocław's main theatrical venue stages classic Polish and foreign drama.

Filharmonia CLASSICAL MUSIC

(☑71 342 2001; www.filharmonia.wroclaw.pl; ul Piłsudskiego 19) This place hosts concerts of classical music, mostly on Friday and Saturday nights.

Kino Helios CINEMA

(www.heliosnet.pl; ul Kazimierza Wielkiego 19a) If you're after a movie, head to this modern multiplex screening English-language films.

ℹ Information

Internet Netvigator (ul Igielna 14; per hr 3zł; ⊙9am-midnight)

Main post office (Rynek 28; ⊙6.30am-8.30pm Mon-Sat)

Tourist office (☑71 344 3111; www.wroclaw -info.pl; Rynek 14; ⊙9am-9pm Apr-Oct, 9am-7pm Nov-Mar)

Tourist & Cultural Information Centre (☑71 342 0185; www.wroclaw-info.pl; ul Sukiennice 12; ⊙10am-8pm) Handles cultural ticket sales and offers internet access.

W Sercu Miasta (ul Przejście Żelaźnicie 4; per hr 5zł; ⊙10am-11pm Mon-Fri, 10am-9pm Sat, noon-11pm Sun) Internet access down a laneway in the middle of Rynek.

ℹ Getting There & Away

Air

From **Copernicus airport** (www.airport.wro claw.pl), LOT flies frequently between Wrocław and Warsaw. It also heads daily to Brussels and Frankfurt, and twice daily to Munich. Tickets can be bought at the **LOT office** (☑0801 703 703; ul Piłsudskiego 36). Jet Air also links Wrocław to Gdańsk.

A range of budget carriers connect Wrocław with other European cities, including several British and Irish regional destinations. Ryanair and Wizz Air fly daily to London, while Ryanair heads five times a week to Dublin.

The airport is in Strachowice, about 12km west of the Old Town. The half-hourly bus 406 and infrequent night bus 249 link the airport with Wrocław Główny train station and the bus terminal.

Bus

The **bus terminal** (ul Sucha 11) is south of the main train station, and offers five daily buses to Warsaw (44zł, seven hours). For most other travel, however, the train is more convenient.

Train

The **Wrocław Główny train station** (ul Piłsudskiego 105) was built in 1856 and is a historical monument in itself. Every day, trains to Kraków (48zł, 4¾ hours) depart every one or two hours, with similarly frequent services to Warsaw (118zł, 5½ hours), usually via Łódź. Wrocław is also linked by train to Poznań (37zł, 2½ hours, at least hourly), Częstochowa (37zł, three hours, four daily), Toruń (51zł, five hours, two daily) and Szczecin (56zł, five hours, seven daily). Note that when travelling to/from Wrocław at the weekend, you'll be in competition with thousands of itinerant university students, so book your ticket as soon as possible.

Sudeten Mountains

The Sudeten Mountains (Sudety) run for more than 250km along the Czech–Polish border. The Sudetes feature dense forests, amazing rock formations and deposits of semiprecious stones, and can be explored along the extensive network of trails for **hiking** or **mountain biking**. The highest part of this old eroded chain is Mt Śnieżka (1602m).

Szklarska Poręba, at the northwestern end of the Sudetes, offers superior facilities for **hiking** and **skiing**. It's at the base of Mt Szrenica (1362m), and the town centre is at the upper end of ul Jedności Narodowej. The small **tourist office** (☑75 754 7740; www.sz klarskaporeba.pl; ul Jedności Narodowej 1a; ⊙8am-4pm Mon-Fri, 9am-5pm Sat & Sun) has accommodation info and maps. Nearby, several trails begin at the intersection of ul Jedności Narodowej and ul Wielki Sikorskiego. The red trail goes to **Mt Szrenica** (two hours) and offers a peek at **Wodospad Kamieńczyka**, a spectacular waterfall.

Karpacz to the southeast has more nightlife on offer, although it attracts fewer serious mountaineers. It's loosely clustered along a 3km road winding through Łomnica Valley at the base of Mt Śnieżka. The **tourist office** (☑75 761 8605; www.karpacz.pl; ul Konstytucji 3 Maja 25) should be your first port of call. To reach the peak of Mt Śnieżka on foot, take one of the trails (three to four hours) from Hotel Biały Jar. Some of the trails pass by one of two splendid postglacial lakes: **Mały Staw** and **Wielki Staw**.

The bus is the fastest way of getting around the region. Every day from Szklarska Poręba, about three buses head to Wrocław (29zł, 3½ hours) and one train plods along to Warsaw (60zł, 11½ hours). From Karpacz, get one of hourly buses to Jelenia Góra (8zł, 40 minutes), from where buses and trains go in all directions.

For the Czech Republic, take a bus from Szklarska Poręba to Jakuszyce (5zł, 15 minutes), cross the border on foot to Harrachov (on the Czech side) and take another bus from there.

WIELKOPOLSKA

Wielkopolska (Greater Poland) is the region where Poland came to life in the Middle Ages, and is referred to as the Cradle of the Polish State. As a result of this ancient eminence, its cities and towns are full of historic and cultural attractions.

The royal capital moved from Poznań to Kraków in 1038, though Wielkopolska remained an important province. Its historic significance didn't save it from international conflict, however, and the region became part of Prussia in 1793. Wielkopolska rose against German rule at the end of WWI and became part of the reborn Poland. The battles of WWII later caused widespread destruction in the area.

Poznań

POP 556,000

No one could accuse Poznań of being too sleepy. Between its regular trade fairs, student population and visiting travellers, it's a vibrant city with a wide choice of attractions. There's a beautiful Old Town at its centre, with a number of interesting museums, and a range of lively bars, clubs and restaurants. The surrounding countryside is also good for cycling and hiking.

Poznań grew from humble beginnings, when 9th-century Polanian tribes built a wooden fort on the island of Ostrów Tumski. From 968 to 1038 Poznań was the de facto capital of Poland. Its position between Berlin and Warsaw has always underlined its importance as a trading town, and in 1925 a modern version of its famous medieval trade fairs was instituted. The fairs, filling up the city's hotels for several days at a time, are the lynchpin of the city's economy.

As it's at the heart of Wielkopolska, Poznań makes a good transport hub from which to explore the region.

◉ Sights

OLD TOWN

Poznań's Old Town is centred on its attractive and ever-busy **Old Market Sq** (Stary Rynek), lined with restaurants and bars. There are several small museums of varying degrees of interest dotted around the square, in its central buildings and nearby; ask at the tourist office for the full list.

Historical Museum of Poznań   MUSEUM
(Stary Rynek 1; adult/concession 5.50/3.50zł, free Sat; ⊘9am-3pm Tue-Thu, noon-9pm Fri, 11am-6pm Sat & Sun) Located within the Renaissance **town hall** (built 1550–60), this museum displays splendid period interiors. If you're outside the building at noon, look up. Every midday two mechanical metal goats above its clock butt their horns together 12 times, echoing an improbable centuries-old legend of two animals escaping a cook and fighting each other in the town hall tower.

Wielkopolska Military Museum   MUSEUM
(Stary Rynek 9; adult/concession 5.50/3.50zł, free Sat; ⊘9am-3pm Tue-Thu, noon-9pm Fri, 11am-6pm Sat & Sun) Exhibits of arms from Poland's many conflicts over the centuries, dating from the 11th century to the present.

Museum of Musical Instruments   MUSEUM
(Stary Rynek 45; adult/concession 5.50/3.50zł, free Sat; ⊘9am-3pm Tue-Thu, noon-9pm Fri, 11am-6pm Sat & Sun) Large though unimaginative collection of music-making devices, displayed over multiple levels.

Franciscan Church   CHURCH
(ul Franciszkańska 2; ⊘8am-8pm) This 17th-century church, one block west of the square, has an ornate baroque interior,

Poznań

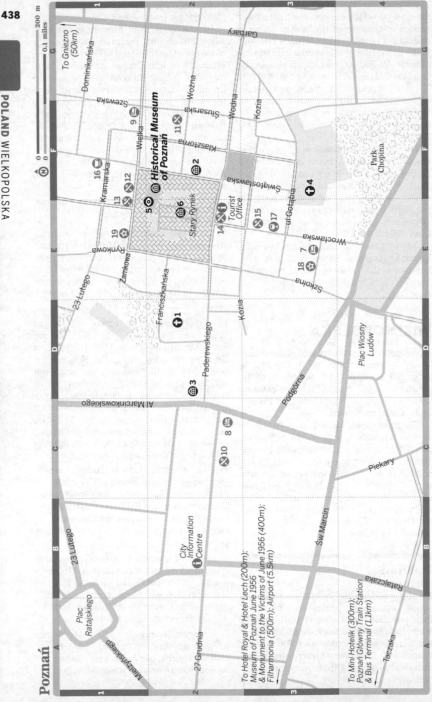

Historical Museum of Poznań

Stary Rynek

Tourist Office

City Information Centre

Park Chopina

Plac Wiosny Ludów

Plac Ratajskiego

To Gniezno (50km)

To Hotel Royal & Hotel Lech (200m);
Museum of Poznań June 1956
& Monument to the Victims of June 1956 (400m);
Filharmonia (500m); Airport (5.5km)

To Mini Hotelik (300m);
Poznań Główny Train Station
& Bus Terminal (1.1km)

0   200 m
0   0.1 miles

Poznań

complete with wall paintings and rich stucco work.

Parish Church of St Stanislaus CHURCH
(ul Gołębia 1; ⊘erratic) Two blocks south of the Old Market Sq is this large, pink, baroque place of worship with monumental altars dating from the mid-17th century.

WEST OF THE OLD TOWN
Monument to the Victims of June 1956 MONUMENT
(Plac Mickiewicza) Emotive memorial to the dead and injured of the massive 1956 strike by the city's industrial workers, which was crushed by tanks. It's in a park west of the prominent Kaiserhof building.

National Museum: Paintings & Sculpture Gallery MUSEUM
(Al Marcinkowskiego 9; adult/concession 10/6zł, free Sat; ◷9am-3pm Tue-Thu, noon-9pm Fri, 11am-6pm Sat & Sun) This museum branch displays mainly 19th- and 20th-century Polish paintings.

Museum of Poznań June 1956 MUSEUM
(ul Św Marcin 80/82; adult/concession 4/2zł, free Sat; ◷9am-5pm Tue-Fri, 10am-4pm Sat & Sun) In the Zamek Cultural Centre within the Kaiserhof, there's more detail to be uncovered of the 1956 strike.

Palm House GREENHOUSE
(ul Matejki 18; adult/concession 5.50/4zł; ◷9am-5pm Tue-Sat, 9am-6pm Sun) This huge greenhouse (built in 1910) contains 17,000 species of tropical and subtropical plants. It's located in Park Wilsona, 1km southwest of the train station.

NORTH OF THE OLD TOWN
Citadel Park HISTORIC PARK
This park, about 1.5km north of the Old Town, was once the site of a 19th-century Prussian citadel, where 20,000 German troops held out for a month in February 1945. The fortress was destroyed by artillery fire but the site now incorporates both the **Poznań Army Museum** (Al Armii Poznań; admission free; ◷9am-4pm Tue-Sat, 10am-4pm Sun) and the nearby **Poznań Citadel Museum** (Al Armii Poznań; adult/concession 4/2zł, free Fri; ◷9am-4pm Tue-Sat, 10am-4pm Sun).

EAST OF THE OLD TOWN
Ostrów Tumski HISTORIC AREA
This river island is dominated by the monumental, double-towered **Poznań Cathedral** (ul Ostrów Tumski), originally built in 968. The Byzantine-style **Golden Chapel** (1841) and the mausoleums of Mieszko I and Boleslaus the Brave are behind the high altar. Opposite the cathedral is the 15th-century Gothic **Church of the Virgin Mary** (ul Panny Marii 1/3). The island is 1km east of the Old Town (take any eastbound tram from Plac Wielkopolski).

Lake Malta RECREATIONAL ZONE
Some 1.6km east of the Old Town is this body of water, a favourite weekend destination for Poles. It holds sailing regattas, outdoor concerts and other events in summer, and in winter there's a ski slope in operation.

A fun way to visit the lake is to take tram 4, 8 or 17 from Plac Wielkopolski to the Rondo Śródka stop on the other side of Ostrów Tumski. From the nearby terminus, you can catch a miniature train along the **Malta**

Park Railway (ul Jana Pawła II; adult/concession 5/3.50zł; ⊙10am-6.30pm Apr-Oct), which follows the lake's shore to the **New Zoo** (ul Krańcowa 81; adult/concession 11/7zł; ⊙9am-7pm Apr-Sep, 9am-4pm Oct-Mar). This sprawling institution houses diverse species, including Baltic grey seals, in a pine forest environment.

🎭 Festivals & Events

The largest trade fairs take place in January, June, September and October.

Poznań Jazz Fair   MUSIC
March

St John's Fair   CULTURAL
Cultural festival in June.

**Malta International Theatre
Festival**   THEATRE
(www.malta-festival.pl) June

🛏 Sleeping

During trade fairs, the rates of Poznań's accommodation dramatically increases. A room may also be difficult to find, so it pays to book ahead. Prices given here are for outside trade fair periods.

Check out **Biuro Zakwaterowania Przemysław** (⌨61 866 3560; www.przemyslaw. com.pl; ul Głogowska 16; s/d from 60/90zł, apt from 180zł; ⊙8am-6pm Mon-Fri, 10am-2pm Sat), an accommodation agency not far from the train station. Rates for weekends and stays of more than three nights are cheaper than the prices quoted here.

TOP **Hotel Stare Miasto**   HOTEL €€
CHOICE (⌨61 663 62 42; www.hotelstaremiasto.pl; ul Rybaki 36; s/d 215/340zł; 🅿) Elegant, value-for-money hotel with a tasteful chandeliered foyer and a spacious breakfast room. Rooms can be small, but are clean and bright with lovely starched white sheets. Some upper rooms have skylights in place of windows.

Rezydencja Solei   HOTEL €€
(⌨61 855 7351; www.hotel-solei.pl; ul Szewska 2; s/d 199/299zł) Temptingly close to the Old Market Sq, this tiny hotel offers small but cosy rooms in an old-fashioned residential style, with wallpaper and timber furniture striking a homey note. The attic suite is amazingly large and can accommodate up to four people.

Frolic Goats Hostel   HOSTEL €
(⌨61 852 4411; www.frolicgoatshostel.com; ul Wrocławska 16/6; dm from 50zł, d 170zł) Named after the feisty goats who fight above the town hall clock, this hostel is aimed squarely at the international backpacker. There's a washing machine on the premises, bike hire is available for 30zł per day and room rates are unaffected by trade fairs. Enter from ul Jaskółcza.

Hotel Rzymski   HOTEL €€
(⌨61 852 8121; www.hotelrzymski.pl; Al Marcinkowskiego 22; s/d from 250/310zł) Offers the regular amenities of three-star comfort, and overlooks Plac Wolności. The decor has a lot of brown, and rooms aren't quite as grand as the elegant facade suggests, but they're a decent size.

Mini Hotelik   HOTEL €
(⌨61 633 1416; Al Niepodległości 8a; s/d from 65/129zł) Like it says on the label, this is a small place in an old building between the train station and the Old Town. It's basic but clean, with colourfully painted chambers. Some rooms share a bathroom. Enter from ul Taylora.

Youth Hostel No 3   HOSTEL €
(⌨61 866 4040; ul Berwińskiego 2/3; dm 35zł) Cheap lodgings about a 15-minute walk southwest of the train station along ul Głogowska, adjacent to Park Wilsona. It's a basic 'no frills' option, but fills up fast with students and school groups. There's a 10pm curfew.

Hotel Royal   HOTEL €€€
(⌨61 858 2300; www.hotel-royal.com.pl; ul Św Marcin 71; s/d 320/420zł) This is a gorgeous place set back from the main road. Rooms have huge beds and sparkling bathrooms.

Hotel Lech   HOTEL €€
(⌨61 853 0151; www.hotel-lech.poznan.pl; ul Św Marcin 74; s/d 200/295zł) Hotel Lech has standard three-star decor, but rooms are relatively spacious and the bathrooms are modern. Flash your ISIC card for a discount.

🍴 Eating & Drinking

Tapas Bar   SPANISH €€
(⌨61 852 8532; Stary Rynek 60; mains 18-72zł; ⊙noon-midnight) Atmospheric place dishing up authentic tapas and Spanish wine in a room lined with intriguing bric-a-brac including jars of stuffed olives, Mediterranean-themed artwork and bright red candles. Most tapas dishes cost 18zł to 22zł, so forget the mains and share with friends.

Cymes   JEWISH €€
(⌨61 851 6638; ul Woźna 2/3; mains 20-29zł; ⊙1-10pm) If you're tired of pork for dinner, this ambient Jewish restaurant is the logical place to go. The interior is warm and cosy, done out like a residential dining room with

WORTH A TRIP

GNIEZNO

If you're staying in Poznań, it's worth checking out historic Gniezno, one of Poland's oldest settlements. It was probably here that Poland's Duke Mieszko I was baptised in 966, the starting point of Catholicism's major role in the nation's story. In 1025, Bolesław Chrobry was crowned in the city's cathedral as the first Polish king. Gniezno probably also functioned as Poland's first capital before Poznań achieved that honour, though history is murky on this point.

Whatever the case, Gniezno makes a good day trip from Poznań, or a short stopover. Setting out from its attractive broad **market square**, you can investigate its historic **cathedral**, dating from the 14th century, and a **museum** dedicated to Poland's origins, situated on the nearby lakeside.

An hour north of Gniezno is the Iron Age village of **Biskupin**, unearthed in the 1930s and partly reconstructed. Passing by it is a **tourist train** that links the towns of Żnin and Gąsawa, both of which have regular bus transport to Gniezno. Gniezno itself is linked to Poznań by frequent trains and buses throughout the day.

For more details, check out Lonely Planet's *Poland* country guide, visit www.turysty-ka.powiat-gniezno.pl, or drop into Gniezno's **tourist office** (☑61 428 4100; ul Tumska 12).

---

ceramic plates on the walls. On the menu are various poultry and fish dishes, including a whole goose for eight people, to be ordered 24 hours beforehand.

Gospoda Pod Koziołkami   POLISH €€
(☑61 851 7868; Stary Rynek 95; mains 12-27zł; ☺11am-10pm) Homey bistro within Gothic arches on the ground floor, and a grill in the cellar. The menu is crammed with tasty Polish standards, including some distinctively Wielkopolska specialities.

Bar Caritas   CAFETERIA €
(☑61 852 5130; Plac Wolności 1; mains 6-12zł; ☺8am-7pm Mon-Fri, 10am-5pm Sat, noon-5pm Sun) You can point at what you want without resorting to your phrasebook at this cheap and convenient milk bar. There are many variants of *naleśniki* (crepes) on the menu. Lunchtimes get crowded, so be prepared to share a table.

Sioux   AMERICAN €€
(☑61 851 6286; Stary Rynek 93; mains 24-100zł; ☺noon-11pm) As you'd expect, this is a Western-themed place, complete with waiters dressed as cowboys. Bizarrely named dishes such as 'Scoundrels in Uniforms from Fort Knox' (chicken legs) are on the menu, along with lots of steaks, ribs, grills and enchiladas.

Proletaryat   BAR
(ul Wrocławska 9; ☺1pm-2am Mon-Sat, 3pm-2am Sun) Small, red communist nostalgia bar with an array of socialist-era gear on the walls, including the obligatory bust of Lenin

in the window, and various portraits of the great man and his comrades. Play 'spot the communist leader' while sipping a boutique beer from the Czarnków Brewery.

Bodega   CAFE-BAR
(ul Żydowska 4) On a street populated with cafes, Bodega's sleek modern lines stand out. The geometrically sharp interior is composed of mellow chocolate and gold tones, with candles on the tables. Good coffee is accompanied by sweet temptations.

Trattoria Valpolicella   ITALIAN €€
(☑61 855 7191; ul Wrocławska 7; mains 23-66zł; ☺1-11pm) Serves a wide variety of pasta and other Italian specialities, well suited to a glass of vino, in convincingly rustic Mediterranean surroundings.

Bar Wegetariański   VEGETARIAN €
(☑61 851 0410; ul Rybaki 10; mains 5-20zł; ☺11am-6pm Mon-Fri, 11am-3pm Sat) This cheap eatery offers tasty meat-free dishes, including its signature wholemeal crepes stuffed with mushrooms and cabbage.

☆ Entertainment

Lizard King   LIVE MUSIC
(Stary Rynek 86; ☺noon-2am) Simultaneously happening and laid-back, this venue is in prime position on the Old Market Sq. Friendly crowds sit drinking and eating in the split-level space, casting the occasional glance at the lizard over the bar. There's live music later in the week, mostly rock, jazz or blues, usually from 9pm.

Czarna Owca CLUB
(ul Jaskółcza 13; ☺noon-2am Mon-Fri, 5pm-2am Sat) Literally 'Black Sheep', this is a popular club with nightly DJs playing a mix of genres including R&B, house, rock, Latin, soul and funk. There's a disco night on Friday and a retro night on Tuesday.

Teatr Wielki THEATRE
(☑61 659 0280; www.opera.poznan.pl; ul Fredry 9) The main venue for opera and ballet.

Filharmonia CLASSICAL MUSIC
(☑61 853 6935; www.filharmonia.poznan.pl; ul Św Marcin 81) Offers classical concerts at least weekly.

ℹ Information

City Information Centre (☑61 851 9645; ul Ratajczaka 44; ☺10am-7pm Mon-Fri, 10am-5pm Sat) Handles bookings for cultural events.

Main post office (ul Kościuszki 77; ☺7am-8pm Mon-Fri, 8am-3pm Sat)

Tourist office (☑61 852 6156; Stary Rynek 59; ☺9am-8pm Mon-Sat, 10am-6pm Sun May-Sep, 10am-6pm Mon-Fri Oct-Apr)

Tunel (Poznań Główny train station; per hr 5zł; ☺24hr) Internet access beneath the train station concourse.

ℹ Getting There & Away

From **Poznań airport** (www.airport-poznan.com.pl), LOT flies at least three times a day to Warsaw, twice daily to Frankfurt and twice daily to Munich. Tickets are available from the **LOT office** (☑0801 703 703) at the airport or from **Orbis Travel** (☑61 851 2000; Al Marcinkowskiego 21).

There are also five domestic flights a week via Jet Air to each of Kraków and Gdańsk. A vast array of other European cities are serviced from Poznań, including London via Wizz Air and Ryanair (at least daily); Dublin via Ryanair (four times a week); and Copenhagen via SAS (five times a week). The airport is in the western suburb of Ławica, 7km from the Old Town and accessible by bus L from the main train station, or buses 48, 59 and night bus 242 from the 'Bałtyk' stop near Rondo Kaponiera.

The **bus terminal** (ul Towarowa 17) is a 10-minute walk east of the train station. However, most destinations can be reached more comfortably and frequently by train.

The busy **Poznań Główny train station** (ul Dworcowa 1) offers services to Kraków (56zł, 7½ hours, 14 daily), Szczecin (42zł, 2½ hours, at least hourly), Gdańsk and Gdynia (53zł, six hours, eight daily), Toruń (25zł, two hours, eight daily) and Wrocław (37zł, 2½ hours, at least hourly) and Warsaw (51zł, 3½ hours, at least hourly).

POMERANIA

Pomerania (Pomorze in Polish) is an attractive region with diverse drawcards, from beautiful beaches to architecturally pleasing cities. It covers a large swathe of territory along the Baltic coast, from the German border in the west, to the lower Vistula Valley in the east. A sandy coastline stretches from Gdańsk to western Szczecin, and Toruń lies inland. Pomerania was fought over by Germanic and Slavic peoples for a millennium, before being incorporated almost fully within Poland after WWII.

Gdańsk

POP 456,000

Port cities are usually lively places with distinctive personalities, and Gdańsk is no exception. From its busy riverside waterfront to the Renaissance splendour of its charming narrow streets, there's plenty to like about this coastal city.

And few Polish cities occupy such a pivotal position in history as Gdańsk. Founded more than a millennium ago, it became the focus of territorial tensions when the Teutonic Knights seized it from Poland in 1308. The city joined the Hanseatic League in 1361, and became one of the richest ports in the Baltic through its membership of the trading organisation. Finally, the Thirteen Years' War ended in 1466 with the Knights' defeat and Gdańsk's return to Polish rule.

This to-and-fro between Germanic and Polish control wasn't over, however – in 1793 Gdańsk was incorporated into Prussia, and after the German loss in WWI it became the autonomous Free City of Danzig. The city's environs are where WWII began, when the Nazis bombarded Polish troops stationed at Westerplatte. Gdańsk suffered immense damage during the war, but upon its return to Poland in 1945, its historic centre was faithfully reconstructed.

In the 1980s, Gdańsk achieved international fame as the home of the Solidarity trade union, whose rise paralleled the fall of communism in Europe. Today it's a vibrant city and a great base for exploring the Baltic coast.

◉ Sights
MAIN TOWN
Royal Way HISTORIC ROUTE
The historic parade route of Polish kings runs from the western **Upland Gate** (built

ŚWIEBODZIN

If you're a lover of the bizarre, you could do worse than take a day trip to the town of Świebodzin, 100km west of Poznań. In November 2010 a local priest and a group of enthusiastic followers managed to erect a 33m-high **statue of Jesus Christ** (taller than the one in Rio) on a hilltop overlooking the town. The project caused great controversy among Catholics across the nation, and media reports suggested the 400-tonne figure was built cheaply on insufficient foundations – so if you're interested in seeing it, it might be better to get there sooner rather than later.

Świebodzin is on the busy railway line between Poznań and Berlin, with three direct train connections from Poznań each day.

in the 1770s on a 15th-century gate), onward through the **Foregate** (which once housed a torture chamber) and **Golden Gate** (1614), and east to the Renaissance **Green Gate** (1568). Along the way it passes through beautiful **ul Długa** (Long Street) and **Długi Targ** (Long Market).

Amber Museum MUSEUM
(www.mhmg.gda.pl/bursztyn; adult/concession 10/5zł, free Tue; ⊙10am-2.30pm Tue, 10am-3.30pm Wed-Sat, 11am-3.30pm Sun) Following the royal lead and starting from the Upland Gate, walk east to the Foregate. Within this structure, you can visit this museum, wherein you can marvel at the history of so-called 'Baltic gold'.

State Archaeological Museum MUSEUM
(ul Mariacka 25/26; adult/concession 6/4zł, free Sat; ⊙8am-4pm Tue-Fri, 10am-4pm Sat & Sun) When you reach the Green Gate, step through and follow the riverside promenade north to the 14th-century **St Mary's Gate**, which houses an overly generous number of formerly diseased ancient human skulls, displays of amber, and river views from the adjacent **tower** (admission 3zł).

St Mary's Church CHURCH
(⊙8.30am-6pm, except during services) From St Mary's Gate, stroll west along picturesque ul Mariacka and admire the gracious 17th-century burgher houses and amber shops. At the western end of the street is this gigantic 14th-century place of worship. Watch little figures troop out at noon from its 14m-high astronomical clock, adorned with zodiacal signs. You can also climb the 405 steps of the **tower** (adult/concession 5/3zł) for a giddy view over the town.

Central Maritime Museum MUSEUM
(ul Ołowianka 9-13; one section adult/concession 8/5zł, all sections 18/10zł; ⊙10am-4pm) On the waterfront north of St Mary's Gate, you'll

find the 15th-century **Gdańsk Crane**, the largest of its kind in medieval Europe and capable of hoisting loads of up to 2000kg. It's part of a maritime history museum which has a presence on both sides of the Motława. Its branch on the east bank offers a fascinating insight into Gdańsk's seafaring past, including the **Sołdek Museum Ship**, built here just after WWII.

Dom Uphagena MUSEUM
(ul Długa; adult/concession 10/5zł, free Tue; ⊙10am-3pm Tue, 10am-4pm Wed-Sat, 11am-4pm Sun) This historic 18th-century residence features ornate furniture.

Historical Museum of Gdańsk MUSEUM
(ul Długa 47; adult/concession 10/5zł, free Tue; ⊙10am-3pm Tue, 10am-4pm Wed-Sat, 11am-4pm Sun) Inside the towering Gothic town hall is this institution depicting photos of old Gdańsk, and the damage caused to the city during WWII.

Neptune's Fountain FOUNTAIN
Near the town hall is this decorative fountain (1633), which legend says once gushed forth *goldwasser*, the iconic Gdańsk liqueur.

Artus Court Museum MUSEUM
(ul Długi Targ 43/44; adult/concession 10/5zł, free Tue; ⊙10am-3pm Tue, 10am-4pm Wed-Sat, 11am-4pm Sun) Merchants used to congregate in this building, which boasts lavish interior decoration. Also note the adjacent **Golden House** (1618), which has a strikingly rich facade.

Free City of Danzig Historical Zone MUSEUM
(ul Piwna 19/21; admission 5zł; ⊙11am-6pm) Small but intriguing display of items from the interwar era when Gdańsk operated as a 'free city', independent of both Poland and Germany.

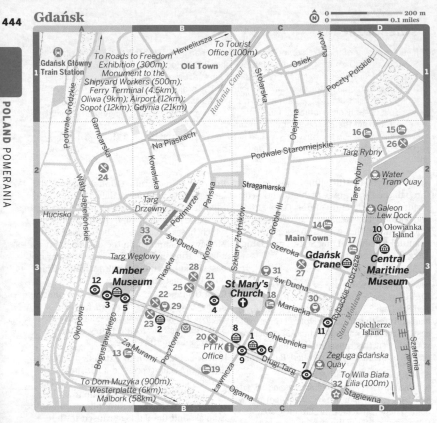

OLD TOWN
Almost totally destroyed in 1945, the Old Town has never been completely rebuilt, but contains some gems worth visiting.

TOP CHOICE Roads to Freedom Exhibition
MUSEUM
(ul Wały Piastowskie 24; adult/concession 6/4zł; ☉10am-4pm Tue-Sun) At the north end of the Old Town is this excellent museum. Its exhibits chart the decline and fall of Polish communism and the rise of the Solidarity trade union. It's a place that anyone interested in Gdańsk's history should visit.

Monument to the Shipyard Workers
MONUMENT
(Plac Solidarności) A short walk further north, this soaring structure stands at the entrance to the Gdańsk Shipyards. It was erected in late 1980 in memory of 44 workers killed during the riots of December 1970, and was

the first monument in a communist regime to commemorate the regime's victims.

OLIWA
Park Oliwski
GARDENS
(ul Cystersów; ☉8am-8pm) Some 9km northwest of the Main Town is the towering **Oliwa Cathedral**, located within this lovely set of gardens. It was built in the 13th century with a Gothic facade and a long, narrow central nave. The famous baroque organ is used for recitals each hour between 10am and 3pm Monday to Saturday in July and August. There's an **Ethnographic Museum** (ul Cystersów 19; adult/concession 8/5zł; ☉10am-5pm Tue-Sun) housed in the nearby Old Granary, and the **Modern Art Gallery** (adult/concession 9/6zł; ☉10am-5pm Tue-Sun) can be found in the former Abbots' Palace.

To reach the park, take the commuter train to the Gdańsk Oliwa station (3.10zł). From there, it's a 10-minute walk; head (west) up ul

Gdańsk

Poczty Gdańsk, turn right (north) along the highway and look for the signs (in English) to 'Ethnographic Museum' and 'Cathedral'.

WESTERPLATTE
World War II Memorial   MEMORIAL

WWII began at 4.45am on 1 September 1939, when the German battleship *Schleswig-Holstein* began shelling the Polish naval post at this location, 7km north of Gdańsk's Main Town. The 182-man Polish garrison held out against ferocious attacks for a week before surrendering.

The enormity of this event is marked by a hilltop **memorial** (admission free; ⊘24hr), a small **museum** (ul Sucharskiego 1; adult/concession 3/2zł; ⊘9am-4pm May-Sep) and **ruins** remaining from the Nazi bombardment.

Bus 106 (25 minutes) goes to the park every 15 minutes from a stop outside the main train station in Gdańsk. Alternatively, see p448 for details of excursion boats from the Main Town to Westerplatte.

✾ Festivals & Events

International Organ Music Festival   MUSIC
(www.gdanskie-organy.com, under Concerts) June to August

International Street & Open-Air Theatre Festival   THEATRE
(www.feta.pl) July

Sounds of the North Festival   MUSIC
(www.nck.org.pl) Folkloric music festival in July/August

St Dominic's Fair   SHOPPING
(www.mtgsa.pl, under Jarmark Św Dominika) Annual shopping fair in August.

International Shakespeare Festival THEATRE
(www.shakespearefestival.pl) July/August

🛏 Sleeping

Accommodation can be tight in the warmer months. If you're having trouble finding accommodation, check with the PTTK office. Also consider staying in nearby Sopot (p448) or Gdynia (p449).

Dom Zachariasza Zappio HOSTEL €
⁅TOP CHOICE⁆ (☑58 322 0174; www.zappio.pl; ul Świętojańska 49; dm 45zł, s/d 92/158zł) At long last there's a hostel in the Main Town, located in an atmospheric former convent building next to St John's Church. Rooms are brightly furnished with contemporary furniture, and there's a fantastic beer garden.

Kamienica Gotyk
HOTEL €€

(☏60 284 4535; www.gotykhouse.eu; ul Mariacka 1; s/d 280/310zł) This Gothic guest house claims to be Gdańsk's oldest residence. Inside, the rooms are compact but neat, with clean bathrooms. The location is impressive, with St Mary's Church and the cafes and shops of ul Mariacka just outside the door.

Happy Seven Hostel
HOSTEL €

(☏58 320 8601; www.happyseven.com; ul Grodzka 16; dm from 45zł, d 150zł) New hostel in which each dorm has a light-hearted theme, including the 'Travel' dorm plastered with maps and the soothing green 'Jungle' dorm. The cool retro lounge contains a games console.

Kamienica Zacisze
APARTMENT €€€

(☏69 627 4306; www.apartments.gdansk.pl; ul Ogarna 107; apt from 350zł) Set within a quiet courtyard off the street, this communist-era workers' dormitory building has been transformed into a set of light, airy apartments for up to six people. Each apartment has high ceilings, a fully equipped kitchen and loads of space. Excellent value for the location and quality.

Dom Muzyka
HOTEL €€

(☏58 326 0600; www.dommuzyka.pl; ul Łąkowa 1/2; s/d/ste 220/310/460zł; ❊) Gorgeous white rooms with arched ceilings and quality furniture, inside the Music Academy some 300m east of the city centre. From July to August, a second wing of the building offers cheaper student-style accommodation. It's hard to spot from the street; head for the door on the city end of the courtyard within the big yellow-brick building.

Apartments Poland
APARTMENT €€

(☏58 346 9864; www.apartmentpoland.com; apt €30-70) A company with renovated properties scattered through the Tri-City Area (Gdańsk/Sopot/Gdynia), including a number in central Gdańsk. Some are big enough for families or other groups. Be aware of the additional electricity charge, based on a meter reading, when checking out.

Dom Harcerza
HOTEL €

(☏58 301 3621; www.domharcerza.pl; ul Za Murami 2/10; dm 39zł, s/d from 75/140zł) The rooms are small but cosy at this place, which offers the best value and location for any budget-priced hotel. It's popular (so book ahead), and can get noisy when large groups are staying here. There's a charming old-fashioned restaurant on the ground floor.

Hostel Targ Rybny
HOSTEL €

(☏58 301 5627; www.gdanskhostel.com.pl; ul Grodzka 21; dm 55zł, d from 150zł) Hostel overlooking the quay on the Motława River. It's a little cramped and starting to show its age, but is sociable, with a comfy lounge area. It also offers bike rental (20zł per day).

Camping Nr 218 Stogi
CAMPING GROUND €

(☏58 307 3915; www.kemping-gdansk.pl; ul Wydmy 9; per person/tent 13/6zł, cabins 60-130zł; ❊May-Sep) This camping ground is only 200m from the beach in the seaside holiday centre of Stogi, about 5.5km northeast of the Main Town. Tidy cabins sleep between two and five people, and facilities include a volleyball court and children's playground. Take tram 8 or 13 from the main train station in Gdańsk.

Willa Biała Lilia
HOTEL €€

(☏58 301 7074; www.bialalilia.pl; ul Spichrzowa 16; s/d 250/320zł) The White Lily Villa is an attractive accommodation choice a short walk east of the Main Town on Spichlerze Island. Rooms are neat and clean, and the staff are helpful.

Hotel Hanza
HOTEL €€€

(☏58 305 3427; www.hanza-hotel.com.pl; ul Tokarska 6; s/d/ste from 695/745/985zł; ❊) The Hanza is attractively perched along the waterfront near the Gdańsk Crane, and offers elegant, tasteful rooms in a modern building. Some rooms have enviable views over the river.

✖ Eating

For self-catering, visit **Kos Delikatesy** (ul Piwna 9/10; ☻24hr) in the Main Town.

Restauracja Pod Łososiem
POLISH €€€

(☏58 301 7652; ul Szeroka 52/54; mains 40-70zł; ☻noon-10pm) This is one of Gdańsk's oldest and most highly regarded restaurants, and is particularly famous for its salmon dishes and the gold-flecked liqueur *goldwasser*, which was invented here. Red-leather seats, brass chandeliers and a gathering of gas lamps fill out the posh interior.

Euro
EUROPEAN €€

(☏58 305 2383; ul Długa 79/80; mains 12-110zł) This elegant eatery is an antidote to the tourist traps along ul Długa, with its fine timber furniture and tasteful decor. The menu ranges widely, from humble *pierogi* to sturgeon in a champagne sauce.

U Dzika
POLISH €€

(☏58 305 2676; ul Piwna 59/61; mains 15-39zł; ☻11am-10pm) Pleasant eatery with a nice outdoor terrace, specialising in *pierogi*. If you're feeling adventurous, try the Fantasy Dumplings, comprising cottage cheese, cinnamon, raisins and peach.

Czerwone Drzwi INTERNATIONAL €€
(☎58 301 5764; ul Piwna 52/53; mains 18-65zł; ☺noon-10pm) Step through the Red Door into a relaxed, refined cafe atmosphere, which helps you digest the small but interesting menu of *pierogi*, pasta and Polish classics.

Bar Mleczny Neptun CAFETERIA €
(ul Długa 33/34; mains 2-13zł; ☺7.30am-7pm Mon-Fri, 10am-6pm Sat & Sun) This joint is a cut above your run-of-the-mill milk bar, with potted plants, lace curtains, decorative tiling and old lamps for decor.

Green Way VEGETARIAN €
(☎58 301 4121; ul Garncarska 4/6; mains 4-12zł; ☺10am-8pm Mon-Fri, noon-7pm Sat & Sun) Popular with local vegetarians, this eatery serves everything from soy cutlets to Mexican goulash in an unfussy green-and-orange space. There's another, more central, branch at ul Długa 11.

Przystań Gdańska POLISH €€
(☎58 301 1922; ul Wartka 5; mains 15-32zł) An atmospheric place to enjoy outdoor dining, with a view along the river to the Gdańsk Crane. Serves Polish classics and a range of fish dishes.

🍺 Drinking

Spiritus Sanctus BAR
(ul Grobla I 13; ☺5-10pm) If you're tired of beer and vodka, head for this stylish wine bar opposite St Mary's Church. While you're enjoying your Slovenian white or Croatian red, you can marvel at the amazing decor, a jumble of abstract art and classic objets d'art.

Cafe Ferber CAFE-BAR
(ul Długa 77/78; ☺9.30am-late) It's startling to step straight from Gdańsk's historic main street into this very modern cafe-bar, dominated by bright red panels, a suspended ceiling and boxy lighting. Partake of breakfast, well-made coffee, international wines and cocktail creations, such as the *szary kot* (grey cat).

Kamienica CAFE-BAR
(ul Mariacka 37/39) The best of the bunch on ul Mariacka is this excellent two-level cafe with a calm, sophisticated atmosphere and the best patio on the block. It's as popular

for daytime coffee and cakes as it is for a sociable evening beverage.

☆ Entertainment

Miasto Aniołów CLUB
(www.miastoaniolow.com.pl, in Polish; ul Chmielna 26) The City of Angels covers all the bases – late-night revellers can hit the spacious dance floor, crash in the chill-out area, or hang around the atmospheric deck overlooking the Motława River. Nightly DJs play disco and other dance-oriented sounds.

State Baltic Opera Theatre OPERA
(☎58 763 4912; www.operabaltycka.pl; Al Zwycięstwa 15) This place is in the suburb of Wrzeszcz, not far from the train station at Gdańsk Politechnika.

Teatr Wybrzeże THEATRE
(☎58 301 1328; www.teatrwybrzeze.pl, in Polish; ul Św Ducha 2) Next to the Arsenal is the main city theatre. Both Polish and foreign classics (all in Polish) are part of the repertoire.

ℹ Information

Almatur (☎58 301 2424; Długi Targ 11) Travel agency.

Jazz 'n' Java (ul Tkacka 17/18; per hr 6zł; ☺10am-10pm) Internet access.

Kawiarnia Internetowa (Cinema City, ul Karmelicka 1; per hr 6zł; ☺9am-12.30am Mon-Sat, 9.30am-12.30am Sun) Free coffee over 30 minutes' access.

Main post office (ul Długa 22; ☺24hr)

Orbis Travel (☎58 301 4544; ul Podwale Staromiejskie 96/97) Travel agency.

PTTK office (☎58 301 1343; www.pttk-gdansk.pl; ul Długa 45; ☺10am-6pm Mon-Fri, 8.30am-4.30pm Sat & Sun)

Tourist office (☎58 301 4355; www.got.gdansk.pl; ul Heweliusza 29; ☺8am-4pm Mon-Fri) Well-concealed from the casual visitor, but helpful.

ℹ Getting There & Away

Air
From **Lech Wałęsa airport** (www.airport.gdansk.pl), LOT has at least five daily flights to Warsaw, and at least three daily to Frankfurt and Munich. Tickets can be bought at the **LOT office** (☎0801 703 703; ul Wały Jagiellońskie 2/4).

Gdańsk is also connected to a plethora of other European cities, including London via Ryanair and Wizz Air (at least daily); Dublin via Ryanair (daily); and Copenhagen via SAS (up to three daily).

The airport is accessible by bus 110 from the Gdańsk Wrzeszcz local commuter train station, or bus 210 or night bus N3 from outside the

Gdańsk Główny train station. Taxis cost 45zł to 55zł one way.

Boat

Polferries (www.polferries.pl) offers daily services between Gdańsk and Nynäshamn (19 hours) in Sweden in summer (less frequently in the low season). The company uses the **ferry terminal** (ul Przemysłowa 1) in Nowy Port, about 5km north of the Main Town and a short walk from the local commuter train station at Gdańsk Brzeźno. Orbis Travel and the PTTK office in Gdańsk provide information and sell tickets.

Between April and October, **Żegluga Gdańska excursion boats** (www.zegluga.pl) leave regularly from the dock near the Green Gate in Gdańsk for Westerplatte (adult/concession return 45/22zł). Further north along the dockside, you can board the Galeon Lew (adult/concession return 40/22zł), a replica 17th-century galleon, for hourly cruises to Westerplatte. Just north of the galleon is the Water Tram, a ferry which heads to Hel (18/9zł, three daily) each weekend during May, then daily from June to August. Bicycles cost an extra 3zł to transport.

Bus

The **bus terminal** (ul 3 Maja 12) is behind the main train station and connected to ul Podwale Grodzkie by an underground passageway. Useful bus destinations include Frombork (17zł, three hours, two daily), Warsaw (52zł, six hours, nine daily) and Świnoujście (63zł, 8½ hours, one daily).

Train

The city's main train station, **Gdańsk Główny** (ul Podwale Grodzkie 1), is conveniently located on the western outskirts of the Old Town. Most long-distance trains actually start or finish at Gdynia, so make sure you get on/off quickly here.

Each day 10 trains (mainly Express InterCity services) head to Warsaw, (114zł, 5½ hours). There are also trains to Malbork (16zł, 1¼ hours, at least hourly), Elbląg (20zł, 1½ hours, 10 daily), Olsztyn (37zł, three hours, six daily), Giżycko (51zł, five hours, two daily), Kraków (129zł, eight hours, 10 daily), Poznań (51zł, 4¾ hours, seven daily), Toruń (39zł, four hours, 11 daily) and Szczecin (56zł, 5½ hours, four daily). Trains also head to Białystok (58zł, 7¾ hours, two daily) and Lublin (63zł, nine hours, two daily).

❶ Getting Around

The local commuter train – the SKM – runs every 15 minutes between 6am and 7.30pm, and less frequently thereafter, between Gdańsk Główny and Gdynia Główna train stations, via Sopot and Gdańsk Oliwa train stations. (Note: the line to Gdańsk Nowy Port, via Gdańsk Brzeźno, is a separate line that leaves less regularly from Gdańsk Główny.) Buy tickets at any station and validate them in the yellow boxes at the platform entrance, or purchase them prevalidated from vending machines on the platform.

Around Gdańsk

Gdańsk is part of the so-called Tri-City Area including Gdynia and Sopot, which are easy day trips from Gdańsk.

SOPOT
POP 38,600

Since the 19th century, Sopot, 12km north of Gdańsk, has been one of the Baltic coast's most fashionable seaside resorts. It has an easy-going atmosphere, good nightlife and long stretches of sandy beach.

◉ Sights & Activities

From the tourist office, head down ul Bohaterów Monte Cassino, one of Poland's most attractive pedestrian streets, past the surreal **Crooked House** (Krzywy Domek; ul Bohaterów Monte Cassino 53) shopping centre to Poland's longest pier (515m), the famous **Molo** (www.molo.sopot.pl; adult/concession 4.30/2.20zł; ⊙8am-dusk Apr-Sep). Various attractions and cultural events can be found near and along the structure.

Opposite Pension Wanda, the **Sopot Museum** (ul Poniatowskiego 8; adult/concession 5/3zł, free Thu; ⊙10am-4pm Tue-Fri, 11am-6pm Sat & Sun) has displays recalling the town's 19th-century incarnation as the German resort of Zoppot.

⌂ Sleeping & Eating

There are no real budget options in Sopot, and prices increase during the busy summer season. Bistros and cafes serving a wide range of cuisines sprout up in summer along the promenades.

Zhong Hua Hotel   HOTEL €€€
(☑58 550 2020; www.hotelchinski.pl; Al Wojska Polskiego 1; s/d 310/350zł) Attractive accommodation in a striking wooden pavilion on the seafront. The foyer is decked out in Chinese design, with hanging lanterns and beautiful timber furniture. The theme extends to the small but pleasant rooms, with views of the water.

Hotel Eden   HOTEL €€
(☑58 551 1503; www.hotel-eden.com.pl; ul Kordeckiego 4/6; s/d 200/300zł) One of the less expensive places in town. It's a quiet, old-fashioned pension with high ceilings, classic furniture and recently renovated bathrooms, overlooking a park one street from the beach.

Willa Karat II
HOTEL €€

(☑58 550 0742; www.willakarat.pl; ul 3 Maja 31; s/d 150/250zł) Cosy budget lodgings a few blocks from the beach, with light, spacious rooms and clean bathrooms, and plants decorating the corridors. There's a kitchen and dining area for guest use. From the train station, walk right along ul Kościuszki, then left along ul 3 Maja towards the coast.

Mandarynka
BAR €€

(ul Bema 6; ⊘noon-10pm) One street south of the main drag, this is a very cool confection of timber tables, scarlet lampshades and huge orange cushions. There's a food menu, and a DJ in action upstairs most nights.

Pension Wanda
HOTEL €€€

(☑58 550 3038; ul Poniatowskiego 7; s/d 280/360zł) The Wanda is a homey place with light, airy rooms, in a handy location about 500m south of the pier. Some rooms have sea views.

Cafe del Arte
CAFE

(ul Bohaterów Monte Cassino 53) This classy cafe, within the Crooked House, is a great place to enjoy coffee, cake and ice cream surrounded by artistic objects in the combined cafe-gallery.

ℹ Information

Tourist office (☑58 550 3783; www.sopot. pl; ul Dworcowa 4; ⊘9am-7pm Jun-Aug, 10am-6pm Sep-May) About 50m from the Sopot train station.

ℹ Getting There & Away

From the **Sopot train station** (ul Dworcowa 7), local SKM commuter trains run every 15 minutes to Gdańsk Główny (4.50zł, 15 minutes) and Gdynia Główna (3.10zł, 10 minutes) train stations. Excursion boats leave several times a day (May to September) from the Sopot pier to Hel (adult/concession return 30/20zł). The Water Tram also links Sopot with Hel (16/8zł, three daily) each weekend during May, then daily from June to August.

GDYNIA
POP 249,000

As a young city with a busy port atmosphere, Gdynia, 9km north of Sopot, is less atmospheric than Gdańsk or Sopot. It was greatly expanded as a seaport after this coastal area (but not Gdańsk) became part of Poland following WWI. However, it's worth dropping into on a day trip.

◉ Sights & Activities

From the main Gdynia Główna train station on Plac Konstytucji, follow ul 10 Lutego east for about 1.5km to the **Southern Pier**.

Moored on the pier's northern side are two interesting museum ships. First up is the curiously sky-blue destroyer **Błyskawica** (adult/concession 8/4zł; ⊘10am-4.30pm Tue-Sun), which escaped capture in 1939 and went on to serve successfully with Allied naval forces throughout WWII.

Beyond it is the beautiful three-masted frigate **Dar Pomorza** (adult/concession 8/4zł; ⊘10am-6pm daily Jul-Sep, 10am-4pm Tue-Sun May, Jun & Oct), built in Hamburg in 1909 as a training ship for German sailors. There's information in English on the dockside.

A 20-minute walk uphill (follow the signs) from Teatr Muzyczny on Plac Grunwaldzki (about 300m southwest of the start of the pier) leads to **Kamienna Góra**, a hill offering wonderful views.

⛔ Sleeping & Eating

Gdynia is best visited as a day trip, but there are some reasonable accommodation options. There are several cheap eateries in the city centre, and upmarket fish restaurants along the pier.

Willa Lubicz
HOTEL €€€

(☑58 668 4740; www.willalubicz.pl; ul Orłowska 43; s/d from 340/380zł) If you're looking for style, you could try this quiet, upmarket place with a chic 1930s ambience at the southern end of town; Gdynia Orłowo is the nearest train station. Third-floor rooms have views of the sea.

Hotel Antracyt
HOTEL €€

(☑58 620 1239; www.hotel-antracyt.pl; ul Korzeniowskiego 19; s/d from 180/220zł) Located in the southern part of central Gdynia, on a hill in an exclusive residential area, with fine views over the water.

China Town Hotel
HOTEL €

(☑58 620 9221; ul Dworca 11a; s/d 100/140zł) Inexpensive lodgings can be found here, opposite the train station. The rooms are plain but serviceable for a night, though singles are very small.

Bistro Kwadrans
POLISH €€

(☑58 620 1592; Skwer Kościuszki 20; mains 12-18zł; ⊘9am-10pm Mon-Fri, 10am-10pm Sat, noon-10pm Sun) On the north side of the square between ul 10 Lutego and the pier, this is a great place for tasty Polish food. It also serves up pizzas, including an improbable variant involving banana and curry.

ℹ️ Information

Tourist office (☎58 622 3766; www.gdynia.pl; ul 10 Lutego 24; ☺9am-6pm Mon-Sat, 9am-4pm Sun May-Sep, 9am-5pm Oct-Apr) About 150m east of the main train station.

ℹ️ Getting There & Away

Local commuter trains link Gdynia Główna train station with Sopot (3.10zł) and Gdańsk (4.50zł) every 15 minutes. From the same station, trains run hourly to Hel (15zł, two hours) and half-hourly to Lębork (16zł, one hour), where you can change for Łeba. From the small bus terminal outside, minibuses also go to Hel (14zł, two hours, six daily).

Stena Line uses the **Terminal Promowy** (ul Kwiatkowskiego 60), about 5km northwest of Gdynia. It offers twice-daily services between Gdynia and Karlskrona (10½ hours) in Sweden. Take bus 150 from ul Władysława IV.

Between May and September, excursion boats leave Gdynia's Southern Pier to Hel (adult/concession one way 45/30zł, return 60/42zł), from a point beyond the Dar Pomorza.

HEL
POP 3900

Never was a town more entertainingly named – English speakers can spend hours creating amusing twists on 'to Hel and back', or 'a cold day in Hel'. In fact, this old fishing village at the tip of the Hel peninsula north of Gdańsk is an attractive place to visit, and a popular beach resort. The pristine, wind-swept **beach** on the Baltic side stretches the length of the peninsula. On the southern side, the sea is popular for **windsurfing**; equipment can be rented in the villages of **Władysławowo** and **Jastarnia**.

The **Fokarium** (ul Morska 2; admission 2zł; ☺8.30am-dusk), off the main road along the seafront, is home to endangered Baltic grey seals. It also has a good souvenir shop for those 'I'm in Hel' postcards to send to friends back home. The 15th-century **Gothic church**, further along the esplanade, houses the **Museum of Fishery** (ul Nadmorski 2; adult/concession 6/4zł; ☺10am-4pm Tue-Sun).

Visitors often stay in private rooms offered within local houses (mostly from May to September), at about 90zł per double. **Captain Morgan** (☎58 675 0091; www.captainmorgan. hel.org.pl; ul Wiejska 21; d 100zł) also offers plain, clean rooms, and good seafood in a quirky pub stuffed with maritime memorabilia.

To Hel, minibuses leave every hour or so from the main train station in Gdynia (14zł, two hours). Several trains depart from Gdynia (15zł, two hours, hourly), and from May to September from Gdańsk (23zł, three hours,

six daily). Hel is also accessible by excursion boat from Gdańsk, Sopot and Gdynia – see the Getting There & Away section for each of these destinations for details.

MALBORK
POP 38,300

The magnificent **Malbork Castle** (☎55 647 0800; www.zamek.malbork.pl; adult/concession 37/27zł; ☺9am-7pm Tue-Sun May-Aug, 10am-5pm Tue-Sun Apr & Sep, 10am-3pm Tue-Sun Oct-Mar) is the centrepiece of this town, 58km southeast of Gdańsk. It's the largest Gothic castle in Europe, and was once known as Marienburg, headquarters of the Teutonic Knights. It was constructed by the order in 1276 and became the seat of their Grand Master in 1309. Damage sustained in WWII has been repaired since the conflict's end, and it was placed on the Unesco World Heritage List in 1997. The entry fee includes a compulsory Polish-language tour, along with an audioguide offering a tour in English and other languages (you pick up this item from a separate booth next to the castle gate). Alternatively, an English-speaking guide can be obtained for 210zł. On Mondays there's a limited tour for a bargain basement 8zł.

Hotel Grot (☎55 646 9660; www.grothotel.pl; ul Kościuszki 22d; s/d 199/289zł) is classy accommodation for its price range, with contemporary furniture and an impressive restaurant. It's set back off the street in the town centre.

Hotel Zamek (☎55 246 0220; www.hotelpro dus.pl; ul Starościńska 14; s/d 200/300zł) is inside a restored medieval building in the Lower Castle. The rooms are a bit old-fashioned, but the bathrooms are up-to-date. The restaurant has character, but can be crowded with tour groups.

The **Youth Hostel** (☎55 272 2408; www.ssm malbork.webpark.pl, in Polish; ul Żeromskiego 45; dm 28zł, d 62zł) is a reasonable budget option in a local school about 500m south of the castle.

Restauracja Piwniczka (☎55 273 3668; ul Starościńska 1; mains 11-89zł; ☺10am-7pm) is an atmospheric cellar restaurant beneath the west wall of the castle.

The castle is 1km west of the train and bus stations. Leave the train station, turn right, cut across the highway, head down ul Kościuszki and follow the signs. Malbork is an easy day trip by train from Gdańsk (16zł, 1¼ hours, at least hourly). Malbork is also connected to Olsztyn (33zł, two hours, six daily), and eight trains head daily to Toruń (21zł, three hours), including three operated by private company Arriva.

Toruń

POP 206,000

The first thing to strike you about Toruń, south of Gdańsk, is its collection of massive red-brick churches, looking more like fortresses than places of worship. The city is defined by its striking Gothic architecture, which gives its Old Town a distinctive appearance and its promotional slogan: *gotyk na dotyk* (touch gothic). The city is a pleasant place to spend a few days, offering a nice balance between a relaxing slow pace and engaging entertainment diversions.

Toruń is also famous as the birthplace of Nicolaus Copernicus, a figure you cannot escape as you walk the streets of his home town – you can even buy gingerbread men in his likeness. The renowned astronomer spent his youth here, and the local university is named after him.

Historically, Toruń is intertwined with the Teutonic Knights, who established an outpost here in 1233. Following the Thirteen Years' War (1454–66), the Teutonic Order and Poland signed a peace treaty here, which returned to Poland a large area of land stretching from Toruń to Gdańsk.

Toruń was fortunate to escape major damage in WWII, and as a result is the best-preserved Gothic town in Poland. The Old Town was added to Unesco's World Heritage List in 1997.

⊙ Sights

Old Town Market Square   HISTORIC AREA
The starting point for any exploration of Toruń is the Old Town Market Sq (Rynek Staromiejski). It's the focal point of the Old Town, lined by elegant facades and dominated by the massive 14th-century **Old Town Hall**.

In front of the town hall is an elegant **statue of Copernicus**. Look for other interesting items of statuary around the square, including a dog and umbrella from a famous Polish comic strip, a donkey that once served as a punishment device, and a fabled violinist who saved Toruń from a plague of frogs.

Regional Museum   MUSEUM
(www.muzeum.torun.pl; Rynek Staromiejski 1; adult/concession 10/6zł; ⊙10am-6pm Tue-Sun May-Sep, 10am-4pm Tue-Sun Oct-Apr) Within the town hall, this institution features a fine collection of 19th- and 20th-century Polish art. Other displays recall the town's guilds, and there's an exhibition of medieval stained glass and religious paintings. Climb

the 40m-high **tower** (adult/concession 10/6zł; ⊙10am-4pm Tue-Sun Apr, 10am-8pm Tue-Sun May-Sep) for great views.

House of Copernicus   MUSEUM
(ul Kopernika 15/17; adult/concession 10/7zł; ⊙10am-6pm Tue-Sun May-Sep, 10am-4pm Tue-Sun Oct-Apr) In 1473, Copernicus was allegedly born in the brick Gothic house that now contains this fairly dull museum, presenting replicas of the great astronomer's instruments (though there's now some doubt he was really born here).

More engaging, if overpriced, is the museum's short **audiovisual presentation** (adult/concession 12/7zł) regarding Copernicus' life in Toruń; and the extravagantly titled **World of Toruń's Gingerbread** (adult/concession 10/6zł). Visitors are guided by a costumed medieval townswoman and given the chance to bake their own *pierniki* (gingerbread). A combined ticket to any two of the three attractions costs 18/11zł.

Cathedral of SS John the Baptist & John the Evangelist   CHURCH
(ul Żeglarska; adult/concession 3/2zł; ⊙9am-5.30pm Mon-Sat, 2-5.30pm Sun Apr-Oct) One block south of the Old Town Market Sq is this place of worship with its massive **tower** (adult/concession 6/4zł) and bell, founded in 1233 and completed more than 200 years later. No sightseeing allowed during services.

Teutonic Knights' Castle Ruins   RUINS
(ul Przedzamcze; adult/concession 6/4zł; free Mon; ⊙10am-6pm Mar-Oct, 10am-4pm Nov-Feb) East of the remnants of the Old Town walls are the ruins of the Teutonic Castle, destroyed in 1454 by angry townsfolk protesting against the knights' oppressive regime.

Far Eastern Art Museum   MUSEUM
(Rynek Staromiejski 35; adult/concession 7/4zł, free Wed; ⊙10am-6pm Tue-Sun May-Sep, 10am-4pm Tue-Sun Oct-Apr) The richly decorated, 15th-century **House Under the Star**, with its baroque facade and spiral wooden staircase, contains this collection of art from Asia.

Explorers' Museum   MUSEUM
(ul Franciszkańska 11; adult/concession 8/5zł, free Wed; ⊙11am-6pm Tue-Sun May-Sep, 10am-4pm Tue-Sun Oct-Apr) A street back from the Old Town Market Sq is this small but interesting display of artefacts from the collection of inveterate wanderer Antonio Halik.

Ethnographic Museum   MUSEUM
(ul Wały Sikorskiego 19; adult/concession 14/9zł; ⊙9am-4pm Wed & Fri, 10am-5pm Tue, Thu-Sun)

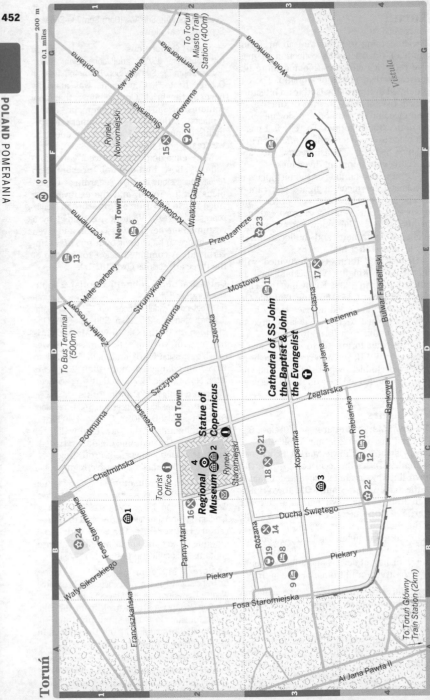

Toruń

Statue of Copernicus 1

Regional Museum 2

Cathedral of SS John the Baptist & John the Evangelist

Old Town

New Town

Rynek Nowomiejski

Rynek Staromiejski

Tourist Office

Vistula

To Toruń Miasto Train Station (400m)

To Bus Terminal (500m)

To Toruń Główny Train Station (2km)

Al Jana Pawła II

200 m
0.1 miles

Szpitalna
św Jakuba
Ślusarska
Browarna
Piernikarska
Wola Zamkowa
Jęczmienna
Królowej Jadwigi
Wielkie Garbary
Małe Garbary
Przedzamcze
Zaułek Prosowy
Prosta
Strumykowa
Podmurna
Mostowa
Ciasna
Łazienna
Szeroka
Bulwar Filadelfijski
Podmurna
Szczytna
Szewska
św Jana
Żeglarska
Kopernika
Bankowa
Rabiańska
Chełmińska
Panny Marii
Różana
Ducha Świętego
Piekary
Piekary
Fosa Staromiejska
Fosa Staromiejska
Wały Sikorskiego
Franciszkańska

Toruń

In a park just north of the Old Town is this showcase of traditional customs, costumes and weapons.

🛏 Sleeping

Toruń is blessed with a plentiful number of hotels within converted historic buildings in its Old Town; but as they're fairly small, it pays to book ahead.

Green Hostel　　　　　　　HOSTEL €
(☑56 561 4000; www.greenhostel.eu; ul Małe Garbary 10; s/d 50/100zł) It may be labelled as a hostel, but there are no dorms. Instead, this new budget accommodation boasts shiny inexpensive rooms, a kitchen and a pleasant lounge. Great option for the price.

Hotel Pod Czarną Różą　　　　HOTEL €€
(☑56 621 9637; www.hotel czarnaroza.pl; ul Rabiańska 11; s/d 170/210zł) 'Under the Black Rose' is spread between a historic inn and a newer wing facing the river, though its interiors present a uniformly clean up-to-date look. Some doubles come with small but functional kitchens.

Orange Hostel　　　　　　　HOSTEL €
(☑56 652 0033; www.hostelorange.pl; ul Prosta 19; dm 30zł, s/d 50/90zł) The wave of Polish hostels for the international backpacker has finally swept over sleepy Toruń. Orange is in a handy location, its decor is bright and cheer-

ful, and its kitchen is an impressive place to practise the gentle art of self-catering.

Hotel Petite Fleur　　　　　　HOTEL €€
(☑56 621 5100; www.petitefleur.pl; ul Piekary 25; s/d 210/270zł) Just opposite the Gotyk, the Petite Fleur offers fresh, airy rooms in a renovated old town house, some with exposed original brickwork and rafters. It also has a French cellar restaurant.

Hotel Pod Orłem　　　　　　HOTEL €€
(☑56 622 5024; www.hotel.torun.pl; ul Mostowa 17; s/d from 130/165zł) This hotel is great value, and although the rooms are smallish, have squeaky wooden floors and some contain poky bathrooms, the service is good and it's central. The foyer and corridors are fun with their jumble of framed pop-art images and old photos.

Camping Nr 33 Tramp　　CAMPING GROUND €
(☑56 654 7187; www.mosir.torun.pl; ul Kujawska 14; camping per person 9zł, tents 6-12zł, s/d from 50/65zł; ☉May-Sep) There's a choice of cabins or hotel-style rooms at this camping ground on the edge of the train line, along with an on-site snack bar. It's a five-minute walk west of the main train station.

Hotel Retman　　　　　　　HOTEL €€
(☑56 657 4460; www.hotelretman.pl; ul Rabiańska 15; s/d 190/250zł) Attractively decorated accommodation offering spacious, atmospheric rooms with red carpet

and solid timber furniture. Downstairs is a good pub and restaurant.

Hotel 1231 HOTEL €€€
(☎56 619 0910; www.hotelesolaris.pl; ul Przedzamcze 6; s/d 340/400zł) Elegant four-star accommodation in the shadow of the Old Town walls, with pleasantly appointed rooms and a cellar restaurant and bar.

Hotel Gotyk HOTEL €€
(☎56 658 4000; www.hotel-gotyk.com.pl; ul Piekary 20; s/d 190/270zł) Housed in a fully modernised 14th-century building just off the Old Town Market Sq, rooms are very neat, with ornate furniture and high ceilings, and all come with sparkling bathrooms.

✖ Eating & Drinking
Toruń is famous for its *pierniki*, which come in a variety of shapes, and can be bought at **Sklep Kopernik** (☎56 622 8832; Rynek Staromiejski 6).

TOP CHOICE **Gospoda Pod Modrym Fartuchem** POLISH, INDIAN €€
(☎56 622 2626; Rynek Nowomiejski 8; mains 16-30zł; ◷10am-10pm) This pleasant, unpretentious 15th-century pub on the New Town Sq has been visited by Polish kings and Napoleon. The usual meat-and-cabbage Polish dishes are joined by an array of Indian food, including a good vegetarian selection.

Bar Mleczny Pod Arkadami CAFETERIA €
(ul Różana 1; mains 1-9zł; ◷9am-7pm Mon-Fri, 11am-6pm Sat & Sun) This classic milk bar is just off the Old Town Market Sq, with a range of low-cost dishes. It also has a takeaway window serving a range of tasty *zapiekanki* (toasted rolls with cheese, mushrooms and tomato sauce) and sweet waffles.

Parmis MIDDLE EASTERN €
(☎56 621 0607; ul Mostowa 7; mains 8-23zł; ◷noon-midnight) A splash of Middle Eastern cuisine in northern Poland, in a cheerful venue decorated with colourful lanterns. The menu contains many variants of kebabs, along with soups, salads and pizzas.

Tantra BAR
(ul Ślusarska 5; ◷5pm-late) This astonishingly decorated bar is done out in an Indian and Tibetan theme and layered with cloth and other artefacts from the subcontinent. Sit on the cushion-strewn divans, order a drink from the long list and meditate on the infinite.

Manekin POLISH €
(☎56 621 0504; Rynek Staromiejski 16; mains 8-15zł) Vaguely Wild West decor adorns

this inexpensive central restaurant specialising in *naleśniki* (crepes). It offers a variety of filled pancakes, including vegetarian options.

Kona Coast Café CAFE
(ul Piekary 22; ◷7.30am-7pm Mon-Fri, 10am-9pm Sat, 10.30am-5pm Sun) Serves excellent freshly ground coffee, along with home-made lemonade, chai and various cold drinks. There's also a light meal menu.

☆ Entertainment
Piwnica Pod Aniołem LIVE MUSIC
(Rynek Staromiejski 1) Set in a splendid spacious cellar in the Old Town Hall, this bar offers live music some nights. Check the posters outside for the latest gigs.

Koci Ogon CLUB
(ul Rabiańska 17; ◷5pm-2am Sun-Thu, 5pm-4am Fri & Sat) This is a lively cellar club with rock DJs most nights from 9pm.

Teatr im Horzycy THEATRE
(☎56 622 5222; Plac Teatralny 1) The main stage for theatre performances.

Dwór Artusa CLASSICAL MUSIC
(☎56 655 4929; Rynek Staromiejski 6) This place often presents classical music.

Nasze Kino CINEMA
(www.naszekino.pl, in Polish; ul Podmurna 14) Cool little arthouse cinema embedded within part of the Old Town wall, its single screen showing a range of non-Hollywood films.

❶ Information
Ksero Uniwerek (ul Franciszkańska 5; per hr 3zł; ◷8am-7pm Mon-Fri, 9am-4pm Sat) Internet access.

Main post office (Rynek Staromiejski; ◷24hr)

Tourist office (☎56 621 0931; www.it.torun.pl; Rynek Staromiejski 25; ◷9am-4pm Mon & Sat, 9am-6pm Tue-Fri, 10am-2pm Sun) Offers useful advice and hires out handheld MP3 players with English-language audio tours of the city (10zł per four hours).

❶ Getting There & Away
The **bus terminal** (ul Dąbrowskiego) is a 10-minute walk north of the Old Town, but most places can be reached more efficiently by train.

The **Toruń Główny train station** (Al Podgórska) is on the opposite side of the Vistula River and linked to the Old Town by bus 22 or 27 (get off at the first stop over the bridge). Some trains stop at the more convenient **Toruń Miasto train station** (Plac 18 Stycznia), about 500m east of the New Town.

From the Toruń Główny train station, there are trains to Poznań (25zł, two hours, eight daily), Gdańsk and Gdynia (39zł, four hours, 11 daily), Kraków (58zł, eight hours, eight daily), Łódź (37zł, 2½ hours, 12 daily), Olsztyn (27zł, 2½ hours, eight daily), Wrocław (51zł, five hours, two daily) and Warsaw (48zł, three hours, 10 daily). There are also eight daily trains to Malbork (21zł, three hours), including three operated by private company Arriva. Trains travelling between Toruń and Gdańsk often change at Bydgoszcz, and between Toruń and Kraków you may need to get another connection at Inowrocław.

Szczecin

POP 406,000

Szczecin (*shcheh-*cheen) is the major city and port of northwestern Poland. Massive damage in WWII accounts for the unaesthetic mish-mash of new and old buildings in the city centre, but enough remains to give a sense of the pre-war days. The broad streets and massive historic buildings bear a strong resemblance to those of Berlin, for which Szczecin was once the main port as the German city of Stettin. Szczecin may not have the seamless charm of Toruń or Wrocław, but it's worth a visit if you're travelling to/from Germany.

◉ Sights

TOP CHOICE **Szczecin Underground**

HISTORIC SHELTER
(☎91 434 0801; www.schron.szczecin.pl; ul Kolumba 1/6; admission 15zł; ◷noon) At the train sta-

tion you can join a fascinating guided tour which takes you through a German-built bomb shelter that later became a Cold War fallout shelter. Pay at the Centrum Wynajmu i Turystyki office.

FREE **Castle of the Pomeranian Dukes**

CASTLE
(ul Korsazy 34; ◷dawn-dusk) This huge and austere castle was originally built in the mid-14th century, then was enlarged in 1577 and rebuilt after major damage from airborne bombing in WWII. Its **Castle Museum** (adult/concession 4/3zł, free Thu; ◷10am-6pm Tue-Sun) explains the building's convoluted history, with special exhibitions mounted from time to time.

Museum of the City of Szczecin MUSEUM
(ul Mściwoja 8; adult/concession 10/5zł, free Thu; ◷10am-6pm Tue-Fri, 10am-4pm Sat & Sun) A short walk south from the castle is the attractive 15th-century Old Town Hall, which contains a museum dedicated to the history of the city. Nearby is the charmingly rebuilt Old Town with its cafes, bars and clubs.

Kino Pionier 1909 HISTORIC BUILDING
(www.kino-pionier.com.pl, in Polish; ul Wojska Polskiego 2) Possibly the oldest continuously operating cinema in the world, having opened in 1909 – though there's a Danish rival that may be one year older. Either way, it's both a historic site and an atmospheric place to catch a film, about 400m west of the tourist office past Plac Zwycięstwa.

WORTH A TRIP

BALTIC BEACHES

Between Gdańsk and the western city of Szczecin, there are numerous seaside towns with unpolluted waters, offering fine sandy beaches during summer. Here are a few places for a sunbathing detour on your journey west along the Baltic coast towards the German border:

» **Łeba** Pleasant holiday town with wide sandy beaches, also the gateway to Słowiński National Park and its ever-shifting sand dunes.

» **Ustka** Once the summer hang-out of German Chancellor Otto von Bismarck, this fishing port is full of atmosphere.

» **Darłowo** A former medieval trading port with an impressive castle, and two beaches linked by a pedestrian bridge over a river.

» **Kołobrzeg** This coastal city offers historic attractions, spa treatments and Baltic cruises.

» **Międzyzdroje** A popular seaside resort and the gateway to Wolin National Park.

» **Świnoujście** On a Baltic island shared with Germany, this busy port town boasts a long sandy shore and pleasant parks.

For more details, check out Lonely Planet's *Poland* country guide, or www.poland.travel.

🛏 Sleeping & Eating

Hotel Campanile HOTEL €€
(📞91 481 7700; www.campanile.com; ul Wyszyńskiego 30; r 273zł) Neat and spacious rooms in a handy position for everything: the Old Town, the train and bus stations, and the central shopping zone.

Youth Hostel PTSM HOSTEL €
(📞91 422 4761; www.ptsm.home.pl; ul Monte Cassino 19a; dm 24zł, d from 54zł) This hostel has clean, spacious rooms and is 2km northwest of the tourist office. Catch tram 1 north to the stop marked 'Piotr Skargi', then walk right one block.

Hotelik Elka-Sen HOTEL €€
(📞91 433 5604; www.elkasen.szczecin.pl; Al 3 Maja 1a; s/d 120/180zł) Simple, light-filled rooms in a basement location in the centre of town. Just south of the tourist office, enter from the side street.

Camping PTTK Marina CAMPING GROUND €
(📞91 460 1165; www.campingmarina.pl; ul Przestrzenna 23; per person/tent 15/9zł, s/d 80/120zł) On the shore of Lake Dąbie – get off at the Szczecin Dąbie train station and ask for directions (2km).

Haga DUTCH €€
(📞91 812 1759; ul Sienna 10; mains 12-24zł) This informal place in the Old Town produces excellent Dutch-style filled pancakes from a menu listing more than 400 combinations.

Karczma Polska Pod Kogutem POLISH €€
(📞91 434 6873; Plac Lotników 3; mains 16-67zł) Northwest of Al Niepodległości, this restaurant serves top-notch traditional Polish food. Roast rabbit in hazelnut sauce, anyone?

ℹ Information

The **tourist office** (📞91 434 0440; Al Niepodległości 1; ⊙9am-5pm Mon-Fri, 10am-2pm Sat) is helpful, as is the **cultural & tourist information office** (📞91 489 1630; ul Korsazy 34; ⊙10am-6pm) in the castle. The **post office** (Al Niepodległości 41/42) and banks can be found along Al Niepodległości, the main street.

ℹ Getting There & Away

The **airport** (www.airport.com.pl) is in Goleniów, 45km northeast of the city. A shuttle bus (18zł) operated by **Interglobus** (📞91 485 0422; www.interglobus.pl) picks up from stops outside the LOT office and the train station before every flight, and meets all arrivals. Alternatively, a taxi should cost around 120zł.

LOT flies between Szczecin and Warsaw three times a day. Book at the **LOT office** (📞0801 703 703; ul Wyzwolenia 17), about 200m from the northern end of Al Niepodległości. International flights on Ryanair include London (four weekly), Liverpool (twice weekly) and Dublin (twice weekly). Oslo (twice weekly) is reached via Norwegian.

The **bus terminal** (Plac Grodnicki) and the nearby **Szczecin Główny train station** (ul Kolumba) are 600m southeast of the tourist office, though bus departures are of limited interest. Trains travel regularly to Poznań (42zł, 2½ hours, at least hourly), Gdańsk (56zł, 5½ hours, four daily) and Warsaw (58zł, six hours, six daily). Trains also head north to Świnoujście (19zł, two hours, hourly).

Another way to reach Świnoujście is via **ferry** (📞91 488 5564; www.wodolot-szczecin.pl; ul Jana z Kolna 7; adult/concession €14/7; ⊙Apr-Sep), which travels daily from a quay north of the castle across the waters of the Szczeciński Lagoon (1¼ hours).

Advance tickets for trains and ferries are available from **Orbis Travel** (📞91 434 2618; Plac Zwycięstwa 1), about 200m west of the main post office.

WARMIA & MASURIA

The most impressive feature of Warmia and Masuria is its beautiful postglacial landscape dominated by thousands of lakes, linked to rivers and canals, which host aquatic activities like yachting and canoeing. This picturesque lake district has little industry, and remains unpolluted and attractive, especially in summer. Like much of northern Poland, the region has changed hands between Germanic and Polish rulers over the centuries.

Elbląg-Ostróda Canal

The longest navigable canal still used in Poland stretches 82km between Elbląg and Ostróda. Constructed between 1848 and 1876, this waterway was used to transport timber from inland forests to the Baltic. To overcome the 99.5m difference in water levels, the canal utilises an unusual system of five water-powered slipways so that boats are sometimes carried across dry land on rail-mounted trolleys.

Usually, **excursion boats** (⊙May-Sep) depart from both Elbląg and Ostróda daily at 8am (adult/concession 90/70zł, 11 hours), but actual departures depend on available passengers. For information, call the **boat** operators (☑Elbląg 55 232 4307, Ostróda 89 646 3871; www.zegluga.com.pl).

Pensjonat Boss (☎55 239 3729; www.pens jonatboss.pl; ul Św Ducha 30; s/d 160/230zł) is one of several small hotels in Elbląg's Old Town, offering comfortable rooms above its own bar. **Camping Nr 61** (☑55 641 8666; www.camp ing61.com.pl; ul Panieńska 14; per person/tent 12/5zł, cabins d 60zł; ☺May-Sep), right at Elbląg's boat dock, is a pleasant budget option. In Ostróda, try **Hotel Promenada** (☑89 642 8100; www. hotelpromenada.pl; ul Mickiewicza 3; s/d 160/200zł), 500m east of the bus and train stations.

Elbląg is accessible by frequent trains from Gdańsk (20zł, 1½ hours, 10 daily), Malbork (7zł, 30 minutes, hourly) and Olsztyn (17zł, 1½ hours, 10 daily); and by bus from Frombork (9zł, 45 minutes, at least hourly). Ostróda is regularly connected by train to Olsztyn (9zł, 40 minutes, hourly) and Toruń (23zł, two hours, eight daily), and by bus to Elbląg (15zł, 1½ hours, at least hourly).

Frombork

POP 2500

It may look like the most uneventful town in history, but Frombork was once home to the famous astronomer Nicolaus Copernicus. It's where he wrote his ground-breaking *On the Revolutions of the Celestial Spheres*, which established the theory that the earth travelled around the sun. Beyond the memory of its famous resident, it's a charming, sleepy settlement that was founded on the shore of the Vistula Lagoon in the 13th century. It was later the site of a fortified ecclesiastical township, erected on Cathedral Hill.

The hill is now occupied by the extensive **Nicolaus Copernicus Museum** (ul Katedralna 8), with several sections requiring separate tickets. Most imposing is the red-brick Gothic **cathedral** (adult/concession 6/3zł; ☺9.30am-5pm Mon-Sat May-Sep, 9am-4pm Mon-Sat Oct-Apr), constructed in the 14th century. The nearby **Bishop's Palace** (adult/concession 5/3zł; ☺9am-4pm Tue-Sun) houses various exhibitions on local history, while the **belfry** (adult/concession 6/3zł; ☺9.30am-5pm May-Aug, 9am-4pm Sep-Apr) is home to an example of Foucault's pendulum. A short distance from the main museum, the **Hospital of the Holy Ghost** (adult/concession 5/3zł; ☺10am-4pm Tue-Sat) exhibits historical medical instruments and manuscripts.

Dom Familijny Rheticus (☑55 243 7800; www.domfamilijny.pl; ul Kopernika 10; s/d 88/120zł) is a small, quaint hotel with cosy rooms and good facilities, a short walk to the east of the bus stop. Breakfast is an extra 15zł.

Camping Nr 12 (☑55 243 7744; ul Braniewska 14; per person/tent 7/10zł, dm 25zł, d 58zł; ☺May-Sep) is a camping ground at the eastern end of town, on the Braniewo road. It has basic cabins and a snack bar on the grounds.

The bus station is on the riverfront about 300m northwest of the museum. Frombork can be directly reached by bus from Elbląg (9zł, 45 minutes, at least hourly) and Gdańsk (17zł, three hours, two daily). The best place to get on and off is the bus stop directly below the museum on ul Kopernika.

Olsztyn

POP 176,000

Olsztyn (*ol-shtin*) is a pleasant, relaxed city whose rebuilt Old Town is home to cobblestone streets, art galleries, cafes, bars and restaurants. As a busy transport hub, it's also the logical base from which to explore the region, including the Great Masurian Lakes district.

It's also another city on the Copernicus trail, as the great astronomer once served as administrator of Warmia, commanding Olsztyn Castle from 1516 to 1520. From 1466 to 1772 the town belonged to the kingdom of Poland. With the first partition of the nation, Olsztyn became Prussian then German Allenstein, until it returned to Polish hands in 1945.

⊙ Sights

Old Town HISTORIC DISTRICT
Olsztyn's attractive historic centre was rebuilt after WWII destruction, and centres on the **Market Sq** (Rynek). One of its most striking features is the **High Gate**, a surviving fragment of the 14th-century city walls.

Museum of Warmia & Masuria MUSEUM
(ul Zamkowa 2; adult/concession 9/7zł; ☺9am-5pm Tue-Sun May-Aug, 10am-4pm Tue-Sun Sep-Apr) West of the square, the 14th-century Castle of the Chapter of Warmia contains this historical museum. Its exhibits star Copernicus, who made some astronomical observations here in the early 16th century, along with collections of coins, art and armour.

Cathedral of St James the Elder CHURCH
(ul Długosza) The red-brick Gothic cathedral to the east dates from the 14th century, and its 60m tower was added in 1596. The interior is an appealing blend of old and new decoration, including the bronze main doors which depict Pope John Paul II's visit in 1991.

Olsztyn

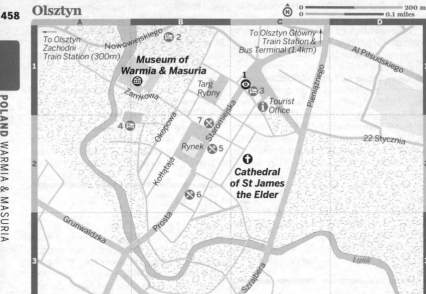

🛏 Sleeping

Polsko-Niemieckie Centrum Młodzieży

HOTEL €€

(☎89 534 0780; www.pncm.olsztyn.pl; ul Okopowa 25; s/d/ste from 195/250/350zł) This place is situated next to the castle. The rooms (some with views of the castle) are plain, but have gleaming bathrooms. There's a good sunlit restaurant off the foyer.

Hotel Pod Zamkiem

HOTEL €€

(☎89 535 1287; www.hotel-olsztyn.com.pl; ul Nowowiejskiego 10; s/d from 160/220zł) Charmingly old-fashioned pension, featuring an extravagant stairwell constructed of dark timber carved with German text; avoid the damp ground-floor rooms. It's near the castle.

Hotel Wysoka Brama

HOTEL €

(☎89 527 3675; www.hotelwysokabrama.olsztyn. pl; ul Staromiejska 1; s/d from 55/70zł) Offers cheap but basic rooms in a very central location next to the High Gate.

✖ Eating

Restauracja Staromiejska

POLISH €€

(☎89 527 5883; ul Stare Miasto 4/6; mains 15-45zł; ⊙10am-10pm) In classy premises on the Rynek, this restaurant serves quality Polish standards at reasonable prices. There's a range of *pierogi* and *naleśniki* on the menu.

Bar Dziupla

POLISH €

(☎89 527 5083; Rynek 9/10; mains 9-25zł; ⊙8.30am-9pm) This small place is renowned among locals for its tasty Polish food, such as *pierogi*. It also does a good line in soups.

Restauracja Hammurabi

MIDDLE EASTERN €

(☎89 534 0513; ul Prosta 3/4; mains 7-40zł; ⊙11am-11pm Fri & Sat, 11am-9pm Sun-Thu) The Hammurabi offers some inexpensive Middle Eastern choices in a cheerful Arabian setting, along with pizzas and steaks.

❶ Information

The **tourist office** (☑89 535 3565; ul Staromiejska 1; ☺8am-5pm Mon-Fri & 10am-3pm Sat & Sun May-Sep, 8am-4pm Mon-Fri Oct-Apr) is next to the High Gate, and can help with finding accommodation.

For snail mail, go to the **main post office** (ul Pieniężnego; ☺6am-7pm); for cybermail, visit the **library** (ul Stare Miasto 33; free; ☺9am-6.30pm Mon-Fri, 9am-2pm Sat) in the centre of the Market Sq.

❶ Getting There & Away

From the **bus terminal** (ul Partyzantów), useful buses travel to Białystok (46zł, five hours, six daily) and Warsaw (32zł, four hours, 11 daily).

Trains depart from **Olsztyn Główny train station** (ul Partyzantów) to Kętrzyn (16zł, 1½ hours, seven daily), Giżycko (19zł, two hours, seven daily), Białystok (48zł, 4½ hours, two daily), Warsaw (44zł, four hours, four daily), Gdańsk (37zł, three hours, six daily) and Toruń (27zł, 2½ hours, eight daily).

Note that a smaller train station, **Olsztyn Zachodni** (ul Konopnickiej), is located nearer to the Old Town, about 300m west of the castle along ul Nowowiejskiego and ul Konopnickiej; but you're unlikely to find services such as taxis here.

Great Masurian Lakes

The Great Masurian Lakes district east of Olsztyn has more than 2000 lakes, which are remnants of long-vanished glaciers, and surrounded by green hilly landscape. The largest lake is Lake Śniardwy (110 sq km). About 200km of canals connect these bodies of water, so the area is a prime destination for yachties and canoeists, as well as those who love to hike, fish and mountain-bike.

The detailed *Wielkie Jeziora Mazurskie* map (1:100,000) is essential for anyone exploring the region by water or hiking trails. The *Warmia i Mazury* map (1:300,000), available at regional tourist offices, is perfect for more general use.

✽ Activities

The larger lakes can be sailed from Węgorzewo to Ruciane-Nida, while canoeists might prefer the more intimate surroundings of rivers and smaller lakes. The most popular kayak route takes 10 days (106km) and follows rivers, canals and lakes from Sorkwity to Ruciane-Nida. Brochures explaining this route are available at regional tourist offices. There's also an extensive network of **hiking** and **mountain-biking** trails around the lakes.

Most travellers prefer to enjoy the lakes in comfort on **excursion boats**. Boats run daily (May to September) between Giżycko and Ruciane-Nida, via Mikołajki; and daily (June to August) between Węgorzewo and Ruciane-Nida, via Giżycko and Mikołajki. However, services are more reliable from late June to late August. Schedules and fares are posted at the lake ports.

ŚWIĘTA LIPKA

This village boasts a superb 17th-century church (☺7am-7pm), one of the purest examples of late-baroque architecture in Poland. Its lavishly decorated organ features angels adorning the 5000 pipes, and they dance to the organ's music. This mechanism is demonstrated several times daily, and recitals are held Friday nights from June to August.

Ask any of the regional tourist offices for a list of homes in Święta Lipka offering private rooms. There are several eateries and places to drink near the church.

Buses run to Kętrzyn every hour or so, but less often to Olsztyn.

WOLF'S LAIR

An eerie attraction at Gierłoż, 8km east of Kętrzyn, is the **Wolf's Lair** (Wilczy Szaniec; ☑89 752 4429; www.wolfsschanze.pl; adult/concession 12/6zł; ☺8am-dusk). This was Hitler's wartime headquarters for his invasion of the Soviet Union, and his main residence from 1941 to 1944.

In 1944 a group of high-ranking German officers tried to assassinate Hitler here. The leader of the plot, Claus von Stauffenberg, arrived from Berlin on 20 July for a regular military staff meeting. A frequent guest, he entered the meeting with a bomb in his briefcase. He placed it near Hitler and left to take a prearranged phone call, but the briefcase was then unwittingly moved by another officer. Though the explosion killed and wounded several people, Hitler suffered only minor injuries. Von Stauffenberg and some 5000 people allegedly involved in the plot were subsequently executed.

On 24 January 1945, as the Red Army approached, the Germans blew up Wolfsschanze (as it was known in German), and most bunkers were at least partly destroyed. However, huge concrete slabs – some 8.5m thick – and twisted metal remain. The **ruins**

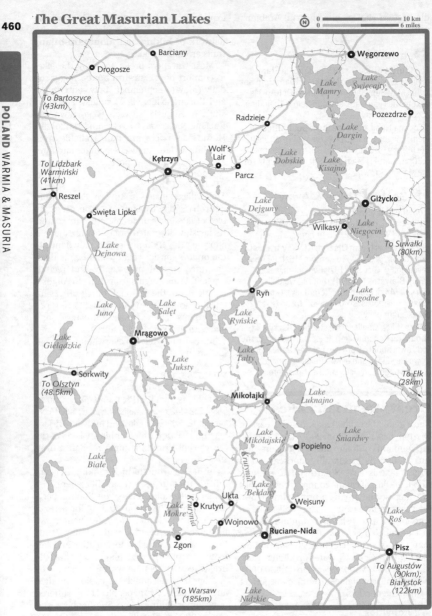

are at their most atmospheric in winter, with fewer visitors and a thick layer of snow.

A large map is posted at the entrance, with features of interest clearly labelled in English (Hitler's personal bunker, perhaps aptly, is unlucky number 13). Booklets outlining a self-guided walking tour are avail-able in English and German at the kiosk in the car park. The services of English-speaking guides are also available for 50zł.

Hotel Wilcze Gniazdo (☎89 752 4429; kontakt@wolfsschanze.pl; s/d 70/100zł), situated in original buildings within the complex, is fairly basic but adequate for one night. A restaurant is attached.

Catch one of several daily PKS buses (5zł, 15 minutes) from Kętrzyn to Węgorzewo (via Radzieje, not Srokowo) and get off at the entrance. Contact the Kętrzyn **tourist office** (☏89 751 4765; ul Mickiewicza 1; ☉8am-3.30pm Mon-Fri) for updated transport details.

GIŻYCKO
POP 29,600

Giżycko (ghee-*zhits*-ko) is the largest lakeside centre in the region, set on the northern shore of Lake Niegocin. Near the main square (Plac Grunwaldzki) is the very helpful **tourist office** (☏87 428 5265; www.gizycko. turystyka.pl; ul Wyzwolenia 2; ☉9am-5pm Mon-Fri, 10am-2pm Sat May-Sep, 9am-5pm Mon-Fri Oct-Apr).

A notable historic site is the 19th-century **Boyen Fortress** (ul Turystyczna 1; adult/concession 6/3zł; ☉9am-6pm), built by the Prussians to defend the border with Russia.

Sailing boats are available from **Almatur** (☏87 428 5971; ul Moniuszki 24), 700m west of the fortress, and at **Centrum Mazur** (☏87 428 3871; ul Moniuszki 1) at Camping Nr 1 Zamek.

Wama Tour (☏87 429 3079; ul Konarskiego 1) rents out bicycles (30zł per day), and Hotel Zamek has kayaks (8zł per hour). Żegluga **Mazurska** (☏87 428 2578; ul Kolejowa 8) operates excursion boats, and you can arrange car rental through **Fiat Autoserwis** (☏87 428 5986; ul 1 Maja 21).

🛏 Sleeping & Eating

Hotel Cesarski HOTEL €€
(☏87 732 7670; www.cesarski.eu; Plac Grunwaldzki 8; s/d 180/250zł) Formerly the favoured accommodation of Prussian royals and known as the Kaiserhof, this renovated hotel is great value for its quality and central location.

Hotel Zamek HOTEL, CAMPING GROUND €
(☏87 428 2419; www.cmazur.pl; campsite per person 15zł, dm 26zł, r from 180zł; ☉May-Oct) This combined hotel and camping ground provides a decent standard of accommodation for the price, and hires out bikes for 12zł per hour.

Boyen Fortress Youth Hostel HOSTEL €
(☏87 428 2959; dm 16-20zł; ☉Jul & Aug) Has a character-packed location within the battlements, and offers the usual basic but clean facilities.

Kuchnie Świata INTERNATIONAL €
(☏87 429 2255; Plac Grunwaldzki 1; mains 9-46zł) A good dining choice is this cheery red-and-orange space serving up an eclectic range of dishes, including pizza and pasta, along with *placki ziemniaczane* and other Polish favourites.

🛈 Getting There & Away

From the train station, on the southern edge of town near the lake, trains run to Kętrzyn (7zł, 30 minutes, eight daily), Olsztyn (19zł, two hours, seven daily) and Gdańsk (51zł, five hours, two daily).

From the adjacent bus terminal, buses travel regularly to Mikołajki (11zł, one hour, hourly), Olsztyn (20zł, 2¾ hours, eight daily) and Warsaw (39zł, five hours, eight daily).

MIKOŁAJKI
POP 3800

Mikołajki (mee-ko-*wahy*-kee), 86km east of Olsztyn, is a great base for exploring the lakes, and it's a picturesque little village in its own right. The **tourist office** (☏87 421 6850; www. mikolajki.pl; Plac Wolności 3; ☉10am-6pm Jun-Aug, 10am-6pm Mon-Sat May & Sep) is in the town centre. In the colder months you can source tourist information from the **town council offices** (ul Kolejowa 7; ☉7am-3pm Mon-Fri Oct-Apr).

Sailing boats and kayaks can be hired from **Cicha Zatoka** (☏87 421 6275; Al Spacerowa 1) at the waterfront on the other side of the bridge from the town centre, and also from the appropriately named **Fun** (☏87 421 6277; ul Kajki 82).

Lake Śniardwy and **Lake Łuknajno** are ideal for cycling. The tourist office can provide details and maps, and bikes can be rented from Pensionjat Mikołajki (30zł per day).

🛏 Sleeping & Eating

You'll find pensions and homes offering private rooms dotted along ul Kajki, the main street leading around Lake Mikołajskie; more pensions can be found along the roads to Ruciane-Nida and Ełk. There are plenty of eateries situated along the waterfront and around the town square to cater for high-season visitors.

Pensjonat Mikołajki HOTEL €€
(☏87 421 6437; www.pensjonatmikolajki.prv.pl; ul Kajki 18; s/d from 120/180zł) An attractive place to stay, with timber panelling and a prime lakefront location. Some rooms have balconies overlooking the water.

Camping Nr 2 Wagabunda CAMPING GROUND €
(☏87 421 6018; www.wagabunda-mikolajki.pl; ul Leśna 2; per person/tent 14/14zł, cabins from 110zł; ☉May-Oct) Across the bridge, this

camping ground is 1km southwest of the town centre.

Pizzeria Królewska PIZZA €
(✆87 421 6323; ul Kajki 5; mains 10-25zł; ⊙noon-10pm) A reasonable pizza restaurant open year-round, in cosy cellar premises.

❶ Getting There & Away

From the **bus terminal** (Plac Kościelny) next to the bridge, two buses go to Olsztyn (16zł, two hours) each day. Otherwise, get a bus (8zł, 40 minutes, hourly) to Mrągowo and change there for Olsztyn. Buses also go hourly to Giżycko (11zł, one hour), and two daily to Warsaw (41zł, five hours). A private company, **Agawa** (✆69 825 6928) runs an express service daily to Warsaw year-round, departing from the bus terminal.

UNDERSTAND POLAND

History

Poland's history started with the Polanians (People of the Plains). During the early Middle Ages, these Western Slavs moved into the flatlands between the Vistula and Odra Rivers. Mieszko I, Duke of the Polanians, adopted Christianity in 966 and embarked on a campaign of conquest. A papal edict in 1025 led to Mieszko's son Bolesław Chrobry (Boleslaus the Brave) being crowned Poland's first king.

Poland's early success proved fragile, and encroachment from Germanic peoples led to the relocation of the royal capital from Poznań to Kraków in 1038. More trouble loomed in 1226 when the Prince of Mazovia invited the Teutonic Knights to help convert the pagan tribes of the north. These Germanic crusaders used the opportunity to create their own state along the Baltic coast. The south had its own invaders to contend with, and Kraków was attacked by Tatars twice in the mid-13th century.

The kingdom prospered under Kazimierz III 'the Great' (1333–70). During this period, many new towns sprang up, while Kraków blossomed into one of Europe's leading cultural centres.

When the daughter of Kazimierz's nephew, Jadwiga, married the Grand Duke of Lithuania, Jagiełło, in 1386, Poland and Lithuania were united as the largest state in Europe, eventually stretching from the Baltic to the Black Sea.

The Renaissance was introduced to Poland by the enlightened King Zygmunt during the 16th century, as he lavishly patronised the arts and sciences. By asserting that the earth travelled around the sun, Nicolaus Copernicus revolutionised the field of astronomy in 1543.

The 17th and 18th centuries produced disaster and decline for Poland. First it was subject to Swedish and Russian invasions, and eventually it faced partition by surrounding empires. In 1773 Russia, Prussia and Austria seized Polish territory in the First Partition; by the time the Third Partition was completed in 1795, Poland had vanished from the map of Europe.

Although the country remained divided through the entire 19th century, Poles steadfastly maintained their culture. Finally, upon the end of WWI, the old imperial powers dissolved, and a sovereign Polish state was restored. Very soon, however, Poland was immersed in the Polish-Soviet War (1919–1921). Under the command of Marshal Jozef Piłsudski, Poland had to defend its newly gained eastern borders from longtime enemy Russia, now transformed into the Soviet Union and determined to spread its revolution westward. After two years of impressive fighting by the outnumbered Poles, an armistice was signed, retaining Vilnius and Lviv within Poland.

Though Polish institutions and national identity flourished during the interwar period, disaster soon struck again. On 1 September 1939, a Nazi blitzkrieg rained down from the west; soon after, the Soviets invaded Poland from the east, dividing the country with Germany. This agreement didn't last long, as Hitler soon transformed Poland into a staging ground for the Nazi invasion of the Soviet Union. Six million Polish inhabitants died during WWII (including the country's three million Jews), brutally annihilated in death camps. At the war's end, Poland's borders were redrawn yet again. The Soviet Union kept the eastern territories and extended the country's western boundary at the expense of Germany. These border changes were accompanied by the forced resettlement of more than a million Poles, Germans and Ukrainians.

Peacetime brought more repression. After WWII, Poland endured four decades of Soviet-dominated communist rule, punctuated by waves of protests, most notably the paralysing strikes of 1980–81, led by the Solidarity trade union. Finally, in the open elections of 1989, the communists fell from power and in 1990 Solidarity leader Lech Wałęsa became Poland's first democratically elected president.

The post-communist transition brought radical changes, which induced new social hardships and political crises. But within a decade Poland had built the foundations for a market economy, and reoriented its foreign relations towards the West. In March 1999, Poland was granted full NATO membership, and it joined the EU in May 2004.

In the 2007 parliamentary elections, Poles decisively rejected the Eurosceptic policies of the Law and Justice party's government, eccentrically headed by the twin Kaczyński brothers as president (Lech) and prime minister (Jarosław). The new centrist government of prime minister Donald Tusk's Civic Platform set a pro-business, pro-EU course, and Lech Kaczyński looked certain to lose the presidential election set for late 2010.

Fate intervened in a shocking manner, however, as Kaczyński was killed in an air crash in April 2010, during an attempted landing at Smolensk, Russia. He had been en route to a commemoration of the Soviet massacre of Polish officers in the nearby Katyń forest in 1940. Also killed in the crash were numerous senior military and government officials, along with relatives of the Katyń victims. The Polish public was stunned by the scale of the tragedy, and campaigning for the following election was subdued. Although the late president's twin brother Jarosław made a surprisingly good showing, in July 2010 Tusk's party ally Bronisław Komorowski was elected as president.

The Poles

For centuries Poland was a multicultural country, home to large Jewish, German and Ukrainian communities. Its Jewish population was particularly large, and once numbered more than three million. However, after Nazi genocide and the forced resettlements that followed WWII, the Jewish population declined to 10,000 and Poland became an ethnically homogeneous country, with some 98% of the population being ethnic Poles.

More than 60% of the citizens live in towns and cities. Warsaw is by far the largest urban settlement, followed by Kraków, Łódź, Wrocław, Poznań and Gdańsk. Upper Silesia (around Katowice) is the most densely inhabited area, while the northeastern border regions remain the least populated.

Between five and 10 million Poles live outside Poland. This émigré community, known as 'Polonia', is located mainly in the USA (particularly Chicago).

Poles are friendly and polite, but not overly formal. The way of life in large urban centres increasingly resembles Western styles and manners. However, Poles' sense of personal space may be a bit cosier than you are accustomed to – you may notice this trait when queuing for tickets or manoeuvring along city streets.

In the countryside, a more conservative culture dominates, evidenced by traditional gender roles and strong family ties. Both here and in urban settings, many Poles are devoutly religious. Roman Catholicism is the dominant Christian denomination, adhered to by more than 80% of Poles. The Orthodox church's followers constitute about 1% of the population, mostly living along a narrow strip on the eastern frontier.

The election of Karol Wojtyła, the archbishop of Kraków, as Pope John Paul II in 1978, and his triumphal visit to his homeland a year later, significantly enhanced the status of the church in Poland.

The overthrow of communism was as much a victory for the Church as it was for democracy. The fine line between the Church and the state is often blurred in Poland, and the Church is a powerful lobby on social issues. Some Poles have grown wary of the Church's influence in society and politics, but Poland remains one of Europe's most religious countries, and packed-out churches are not uncommon.

Arts

Literature

Poland has inherited a rich literary tradition dating from the 15th century, though its modern voice was shaped in the 19th century, during the long period of foreign occupation. It was a time for nationalist writers such as the poet Adam Mickiewicz (1798–1855), and Henryk Sienkiewicz (1846–1916), who won a Nobel Prize in 1905 for *Quo Vadis?* This nationalist tradition was revived in the communist era when Czesław Miłosz was awarded a Nobel Prize in 1980 for *The Captive Mind*.

At the turn of the 20th century, the avant-garde 'Young Poland' movement in art and literature developed in Kraków. The most notable representatives of this movement were writer Stanisław Wyspiański (1869–1907), also famous for his stained-glass work; playwright Stanisław Ignacy Witkiewicz

(1885–1939), commonly known as Witkacy; and Nobel laureate Władisław Reymont (1867–1925). In 1996 Wisława Szymborska (b 1923) also received a Nobel Prize for her poetry.

Music

The most famous Polish musician was undoubtedly Frédéric Chopin (1810–49), whose music displays the melancholy and nostalgia that became hallmarks of the national style. Stanisław Moniuszko (1819–72) injected a Polish flavour into 19th-century Italian opera music by introducing folk songs and dances to the stage. His *Halka* (1858), about a peasant girl abandoned by a young noble, is a staple of the national opera houses.

On a more contemporary note, popular Polish musicians you might catch live in concert include the controversial Doda (pop singer); Feel (pop-rock band); Łzy (pop-rock band); Indios Bravos (reggae band); and Kasia Cerekwicka (pop singer). Poland's equivalent of the Rolling Stones is Lady Pank, a rock band formed in 1982 and still going strong.

Visual Arts

Poland's most renowned painter was Jan Matejko (1838–93), whose monumental historical paintings hang in galleries throughout the country. Wojciech Kossak (1857–1942) is another artist who documented Polish history; he is best remembered for the colossal painting *Panorama of Racławice,* on display in Wrocław (p431).

A long-standing Polish craft is the fashioning of jewellery from amber. Amber is a fossil resin of vegetable origin that comes primarily from the Baltic region, and appears in a variety of colours from pale yellow to reddish brown. The best places to buy it are Gdańsk, Kraków and Warsaw.

Polish poster art has received international recognition; the best selection of poster galleries is in Warsaw and Kraków.

Cinema

Poland has produced several world-famous film directors. The most notable is Andrzej Wajda, who received an Honorary Award at the 1999 Academy Awards. *Katyń,* his moving story of the Katyń massacre in WWII, was nominated for Best Foreign Language Film at the 2008 Oscars. Western audiences are more familiar with the work of Roman Polański, who directed critically acclaimed films such as *Rosemary's Baby* and *Chinatown.* In 2002 Polański released the incredibly moving film *The Pianist,* which was filmed in Poland and set in the Warsaw Ghetto of WWII. The film went on to win three Oscars and the Cannes Palme d'Or. The late Krzysztof Kieślowski is best known for the *Three Colours* trilogy. The centre of Poland's movie industry, and home to its prestigious National Film School, is Łódź.

The Landscape

Geography

Poland covers an area of 312,685 sq km, approximately as large as the UK and Ireland put together, and is bordered by seven nations and one sea.

The northern edge of Poland meets the Baltic Sea. This broad, 524km-long coastline is spotted with sand dunes and seaside lakes. Also concentrated in the northeast are many postglacial lakes – more than any country in Europe, except Finland.

The southern border is defined by the mountain ranges of the Sudetes and Carpathians. Poland's highest mountains are the rocky Tatras, a section of the Carpathian Range it shares with Slovakia. The highest peak of the Polish Tatras is Mt Rysy (2499m).

The area in between is a vast plain, sectioned by wide north-flowing rivers. Poland's longest river is the Vistula (Wisła), which winds 1047km from the Tatras to the Baltic.

About a quarter of Poland is covered by forest. Some 60% of the forests are pine trees, but the share of deciduous species, such as oak, beech and birch, is increasing.

National Parks & Animals

Poland's fauna includes hare, red deer, wild boar and, less abundantly, elk, brown bear and wildcat. European bison, which once inhabited Europe in large numbers, were brought to the brink of extinction early in the 20th century and a few hundred now live in Białowieża National Park (p403). The Great Masurian Lakes district (p459) attracts a vast array of bird life, such as storks and cormorants. The eagle, though rarely seen today, is Poland's national bird and appears on the Polish emblem.

Poland has 23 national parks, but they cover less than 1% of the country. No permit is necessary to visit these parks, but most have small admission fees. Camping in the parks is sometimes allowed, but only at specified sites. Poland also has a network of less strictly preserved areas called 'landscape parks', scattered throughout the country.

The Cuisine

Staples & Specialities

Various cultures have influenced Polish cuisine, including Jewish, Ukrainian, Russian, Hungarian and German. Polish food is hearty and filling, abundant in potatoes and dumplings, and rich in meat.

Poland's most famous dishes are *bigos* (sauerkraut with a variety of meats), *pierogi* (ravioli-like dumplings stuffed with cottage cheese, minced meat, or cabbage and wild mushrooms) and *barszcz* (red beetroot soup, better known by the Russian word *borscht*).

Hearty soups such as *żurek* (sour soup with sausage and hard-boiled eggs) are a highlight of Polish cuisine. Main dishes are made with pork, including *golonka* (boiled pig's knuckle served with horseradish) and *schab pieczony* (roast loin of pork seasoned with prunes and herbs). *Gołąbki* (cabbage leaves stuffed with mince and rice) is a tasty alternative.

Placki ziemniaczane (potato pancakes) and *naleśniki* (crepes) are also popular dishes.

Poles claim the national drink, *wódka* (vodka), was invented in their country. It's usually drunk neat and comes in a number of flavours, including *myśliwska* (flavoured with juniper berries), *wiśniówka* (with cherries) and *jarzębiak* (with rowanberries). The most famous variety is *żubrówka* (bison vodka), flavoured with grass from the Białowieża Forest. Other notable spirits include *krupnik* (honey liqueur), *śliwowica* (plum brandy) and *goldwasser* (sweet liqueur containing flakes of gold leaf).

Poles also appreciate the taste of *zimne piwo* (cold beer); the top brands, found everywhere, include Żywiec, Tyskie, Lech and Okocim, while regional brands are available in every city.

Where to Eat & Drink

The cheapest place to eat Polish food is a *bar mleczny* (milk bar), a survivor from the communist era. These no-frills, self-service cafeterias are popular with budget-conscious locals and backpackers alike. Up the scale, the number and variety of *restauracja* (restaurants) has ballooned in recent years, especially in the big cities. Pizzerias have also become phenomenally popular with Poles. And though Polish cuisine features plenty of meat, there are vegetarian restaurants to be found in most cities.

Menus usually have several sections: *zupy* (soups), *dania drugie* (main courses) and *dodatki* (accompaniments). The price of the main course may not include a side dish – such as potatoes and salads – which you choose (and pay extra for) from the *dodatki* section. Also note that the price for some dishes (particularly fish and poultry) may be listed per 100g, so the price will depend on the total weight of the fish or meat. In this guide, budget (€) restaurant mains start below 10zł, midrange (€€) mains cost between 10zł and 25zł, and top-end (€€€) mains start above 25zł.

Poles start their day with *śniadanie* (breakfast); the most important and substantial meal of the day, *obiad,* is normally eaten between 2pm and 5pm. The third meal is *kolacja* (supper). Most restaurants, cafes and cafe-bars are open from 11am to 11pm. It's rare for Polish restaurants to serve breakfast, though milk bars and snack bars are open from early morning. In the Eating sections of this chapter, only nonstandard restaurant hours are listed.

Smoking is common in bars and restaurants, though there have been unsuccessful proposals to ban it from public spaces. However, many restaurants offer nonsmoking options.

SURVIVAL GUIDE

Directory A–Z

Accommodation

In Poland, budget (€) accommodation includes camping grounds, dorms, or doubles costing up to 150zł; midrange (€€) accommodation will cost between 150zł and 350zł a double; and top-end digs (€€€) will set you back upwards of 350zł per night. Unless otherwise noted, rooms have private bathrooms and the rate includes breakfast.

Camping

Poland has hundreds of camping grounds, and many offer good-value cabins and bungalows. Most open May to September, but some only open their gates between June and August.

Hostels

Schroniska młodzieżowe (youth hostels) in Poland are operated by Polskie Towarzystwo Schronisk Młodzieżowych (PTSM;

www.ptsm.org.pl), a member of Hostelling International. Most only open in July and August, and are often very busy with Polish students; the year-round hostels have more facilities. These youth hostels are open to all, with no age limit. Curfews are common, and many hostels close between 10am and 5pm.

A growing number of privately operated hostels operate in the main cities, and are geared towards international backpackers. They're open 24 hours and offer more modern facilities than the old youth hostels, though prices are higher. These hostels usually offer free use of washing machines, in response to the near-absence of laundromats in Poland.

A dorm bed can cost anything from 25zł to 75zł per person per night. Single and double rooms, if available, start at about 150zł a night.

Hotels

Hotel prices often vary according to season, especially along the Baltic coast, and discounted weekend rates are common.

If possible, check the room before accepting. Don't be fooled by hotel reception areas, which may look great in contrast to the rest of the establishment. On the other hand, dreary scuffed corridors can sometimes open into clean, pleasant rooms.

Accommodation (sometimes with substantial discounts) can be reliably arranged via the internet through www.poland4u.com and www.hotelspoland.com.

Mountain Refuges

Polskie Towarzystwo Turystyczno-Krajoznawcze (PTTK; www.pttk.pl) runs a chain of *schroniska górskie* (mountain refuges) for hikers. They're usually simple, with a welcoming atmosphere, and serve cheap, hot meals. The more isolated refuges are obliged to accept everyone, so can be crowded in the high season. Refuges are normally open all year, but confirm with the nearest PTTK office before setting off.

Private rooms & apartments

Some destinations have agencies (usually called *biuro zakwaterowania* or *biuro kwater prywatnych*), which arrange accommodation in private homes. Rooms cost about 100/130zł per single/double. The most important factor to consider is location; if the home is in the suburbs, find out how far it is from reliable public transport.

During the high season, home owners also directly approach tourists. Also, private homes in smaller resorts and villages often have signs outside their gates or doors offering a *pokoje* (room) or *noclegi* (lodging).

In Warsaw, Kraków, Wrocław and Gdańsk, some agencies offer self-contained apartments, which are an affordable alternative to hotels and allow for the washing of laundry.

Activities

Hikers can enjoy marked trails across the Tatra Mountains (p427), where one of the most popular climbs is up the steep slopes of Mt Giewont (1894m). The Sudeten Mountains (p436) and the Great Masurian Lakes district (p466) also offer good walking opportunities. National parks worth hiking through include Białowieża National Park (p403), Kampinos National Park just outside Warsaw, and Wielkopolska National Park outside Poznań. Trails are easy to follow and detailed maps are available at most larger bookshops.

As Poland is fairly flat, it's ideal for cyclists. Bicycle routes along the banks of the Vistula River are popular in Warsaw, Toruń and Kraków. Many of the national parks – including Tatra (near Zakopane) and Słowinski (near Łeba) – offer bicycle trails, as does the Great Masurian Lakes district. For more of a challenge, try cycling in the Bieszczady ranges around Sanok (p429). Bikes can be rented at most resort towns and larger cities.

Zakopane (p424) will delight skiers from December to March, and facilities are cheaper than the ski resorts of Western Europe. Other sports on offer here include hang-gliding and paragliding. Another place to hit the snow is Szklarska Poręba (p436) in Silesia.

Throngs of yachties, canoeists and kayakers enjoy the network of waterways in the Great Masurian Lakes district (p459) every summer; boats are available for rent from all lakeside towns, and there are even diving excursions. Windsurfers can head to the beaches of the Hel peninsula (p450).

Books

God's Playground: A History of Poland, by Norman Davies, offers an in-depth analysis of Polish history. The condensed version, *The Heart of Europe: A Short History of Poland,* also by Davies, has greater emphasis on the 20th century. *The Polish Way: A Thousand-Year History of the Poles and their Culture,* by Adam Zamoyski, is a superb cultural overview. The wartime Warsaw Rising is vividly brought to life in Norman Davies' *Rising '44,* and *The*

Polish Revolution: Solidarity 1980-82, by Timothy Garton Ash, is entertaining and thorough. *Jews in Poland* by Iwo Cyprian Pogonowski provides a comprehensive record of half a millennium of Jewish life. Evocative works about rural life in interwar Poland include Bruno Schultz's *Street of Crocodiles* and Philip Marsden's *The Bronski House.*

Business Hours

Banks 8am-5pm Mon-Fri, sometimes 8am-2pm Sat

Cafes & restaurants 11am-11pm

Shops 10am-6pm Mon-Fri, 10am-2pm Sat

Nightclubs 9pm-late

Dangers & Annoyances

Poland is a relatively safe country, and crime has decreased significantly since the immediate post-communism era. Be alert, however, for thieves and pickpockets around major train stations, such as Warszawa Centralna. Robberies have been a problem on night trains, especially on international routes. Try to share a compartment with other people if possible.

Theft from cars is a widespread problem, so keep your vehicle in a guarded car park whenever possible. Heavy drinking is common and drunks can be disturbing, though rarely dangerous.

As Poland is an ethnically homogeneous nation, travellers of a non-European appearance may attract curious glances from locals in outlying regions. Football (soccer) hooligans are not uncommon, so avoid travelling on public transport with them (especially if their team has lost!).

Embassies & Consulates

All diplomatic missions listed are located in Warsaw unless stated otherwise.

Australia (☎22 521 3444; www.australia.pl; ul Nowogrodzka 11)

Belarus (☎22 742 0710; www.belembassy.org/poland; ul Wiertnicza 58)

Canada (☎22 584 3100; www.canada.pl; ul Matejki 1/5)

Czech Republic (☎22 525 1850; www.mzv.cz/warsaw; ul Koszykowa 18)

France Warsaw (☎22 529 3000; www.ambafrance-pl.org; ul Piękna 1); Kraków consulate (☎12 424 5300; www.cracovie.org.pl; ul Stolarska 15, Kraków)

Germany Warsaw (☎22 584 1700; www.warschau.diplo.de; ul Jazdów 12); Kraków consulate (☎12 424 3000; www.warschau.diplo.de; ul Stolarska 7, Kraków)

Ireland (☎22 849 6633; www.irlandia.pl; ul Mysia 5)

Japan (☎22 696 5000; www.pl.emb-japan.go.jp; ul Szwoleżerów 8)

Lithuania (☎22 625 3368; www.lietuva.pl; ul Ujazdowskie 14)

Netherlands (☎22 559 1200; www.nlembassy.pl; ul Kawalerii 10)

New Zealand (☎22 521 0500; www.nzembassy.com/poland; Al Ujazdowskie 51)

Russia (☎22 849 5111; http://warsaw.rus embassy.org; ul Belwederska 49)

Slovakia (☎22 525 8110; www.mzv.sk/varsava; ul Litewska 6)

South Africa (☎22 625 6228; warsaw.consular@foreign.gov.za; ul Koszykowa 54)

Ukraine (☎22 622 4797; www.ukraine-emb.pl; Al Szucha 7)

UK Warsaw (☎22 311 0000; http://ukinpoland.fco.gov.uk; ul Kawalerii 12); Kraków consulate (☎12 421 7030; http://ukinpoland.fco.gov.uk; ul Św Anny 9, Kraków)

USA Warsaw (☎22 504 2000; http://poland.us embassy.gov; Al Ujazdowskie 29/31); Kraków consulate (☎12 424 5100; http://poland.us embassy.gov; ul Stolarska 9, Kraków)

Food

Price ranges: budget (€; under 10zł), midrange (€€; 10zł to 25zł) and top end (€€€; over 25zł).

Gay & Lesbian Travellers

Since the change of government in 2007, overt homophobia from state officials has declined; though with the Church remaining influential in social matters, gay acceptance in Poland is still a work in progress. The gay community is becoming more visible, however, and in 2010 Warsaw hosted **EuroPride** (www.europride.com), the first time this major gay festival had been held in a former communist country.

In general though, the Polish gay and lesbian scene remains fairly discreet. Warsaw and Kraków are the best places to find gay-friendly bars, clubs and accommodation. The free tourist brochure, the *Visitor,* lists a few gay nightspots, as do the **In Your Pocket** (www.inyourpocket.com) guides.

A good source of information on gay Warsaw and Kraków is online at www.gay guide.net. **Lambda** (☎22 628 5222; www.lamb dawarszawa.org) is a national gay rights and information service.

Internet Access

Internet access is near universal in Polish accommodation: either as wireless access, via on-site computers, or both. As a result, individual accommodation with internet access has not been denoted as such in this chapter.

In the unlikely event that your lodgings are offline, you'll likely find an internet cafe nearby; expect to pay between 3zł and 5zł per hour. Also, some forward-thinking city councils have set up wireless access in their main market squares.

Internet Resources

Commonwealth of Diverse Cultures (www.commonwealth.pl) Outlines Poland's cultural heritage.

Poland.pl (www.poland.pl) News and a website directory.

Poland Tourism Portal (www.poland.travel) Useful official travel site.

Polska (www.poland.gov.pl) Comprehensive government portal.

VirtualTourist.com (www.virtualtourist. com) Poland section features postings by travellers.

Visit.pl (www.visit.pl) Accommodation booking service for Poland and beyond.

Media

The *Warsaw Business Journal* is aimed at the business community, while *Warsaw Insider* has more general-interest features, listings and reviews. *Warsaw Voice* is a weekly English-language news magazine with a business slant.

The free *Welcome to...* series of magazines covers Poznań, Kraków, Toruń, Zakopane and Warsaw monthly.

Recent newspapers and magazines from Western Europe and the USA are readily available at EMPiK bookshops, and at newsstands in the foyers of upmarket hotels.

Poland has a mix of privately owned TV channels, and state-owned nationwide channels. Foreign-language programs are painfully dubbed with one male voice covering all actors (that's men, women and children) and no lip-sync, so you can still hear the original language underneath.

Most hotels offer English-language news channels.

Money

Poland is obliged by the terms of its accession to the EU to adopt the euro as its currency at some point in the future; but it's not likely to happen until at least 2015.

In the meantime, the nation's currency is the złoty (*zwo*-ti), abbreviated to zł (international currency code PLN). It's divided into 100 groszy (gr). Denominations of notes are 10, 20, 50, 100 and 200 (rare) złoty, and coins come in one, two, five, 10, 20 and 50 groszy, and one, two and five złoty.

Bankomats (ATMs) accept most international credit cards and are easily found in the centre of all cities and most towns. Banks without an ATM may provide cash advances over the counter on credit cards.

Private *kantors* (foreign-exchange offices) are everywhere. They require no paperwork and charge no commission, though rates at *kantors* near tourist-friendly attractions or facilities can be poor.

Travellers cheques are more secure than cash, but *kantors* rarely change them, and banks that do will charge a commission. A better option is a stored value cash card, which can be used in the same manner as a credit card; ask your bank about this before leaving home.

Post

Postal services are operated by Poczta Polska; the Poczta Główna (Main Post Office) in each city offers the widest range of services.

The cost of sending a normal-sized letter (up to 20g) or a postcard to other European countries is 3zł, rising to 3.50zł for North America and 4.50zł for Australia.

Public Holidays

Poland's official public holidays:

New Year's Day 1 January

Easter Sunday March or April

Easter Monday March or April

State Holiday 1 May

Constitution Day 3 May

Pentecost Sunday Seventh Sunday after Easter

Corpus Christi Ninth Thursday after Easter

Assumption Day 15 August

All Saints' Day 1 November

Independence Day 11 November

Christmas 25 and 26 December

Telephone

Polish telephone numbers have nine digits, with no area codes. To call Poland from abroad, dial the country code ☑48, then the Polish number. The international access code when dialling out of Poland is ☑00. For help, try the operators for local numbers (☑913), national numbers and codes (☑912), and international codes (☑908), but don't expect anyone to speak English.

The three mobile-telephone providers are Orange, Era and Plus GSM. Prepaid accounts are cheap by Western European standards, and are easy to set up at local offices of these companies.

Most public telephones use magnetic phonecards, available at post offices and kiosks in units of 15 (9zł), 30 (15zł) and 60 (24zł). The cards can be used for domestic and international calls.

Travellers with Disabilities

Poland is not set up well for people with disabilities, although there have been significant improvements over recent years. Wheelchair ramps are only available at some upmarket hotels, and public transport will be a real challenge for anyone with mobility problems. However, many hotels now have at least one room especially designed for disabled access – book ahead for these. There are also some low-floor trams running on the Warsaw and Kraków public transport networks. Information on disability issues is available from **Integracja** (☑22 530 6570; www.integracja.org).

Visas

EU citizens do not need visas to visit Poland and can stay indefinitely. Citizens of Australia, Canada, Israel, New Zealand, Switzerland and the USA can stay in Poland up to 90 days without a visa.

However, since Poland's entry into the Schengen zone in December 2007, the 90-day visa-free entry period has been extended to all the Schengen countries; so if travelling from Poland through Germany and France, for example, you can't exceed 90 days in total. Once your 90 days is up, you must leave the Schengen zone for a minimum 90 days before you can once again enter it visa free.

South African citizens do require a visa. Other nationals should check with Polish embassies or consulates in their countries

for current visa requirements. Updates can be found at the website of the **Ministry of Foreign Affairs** (www.msz.gov.pl).

Getting There & Away

Air

The majority of international flights to Poland arrive at Warsaw's Okęcie airport, while other important airports include Kraków, Gdańsk, Poznań and Wrocław. The national carrier **LOT** (☑0801 703 703, 22 19572; www.lot.com) flies to all major European cities.

Other major airlines flying to/from Poland:

Aeroflot (☑22 650 2511; www.aeroflot.com)

Air France (☑22 556 6400; www.airfrance.com)

Alitalia (☑22 692 8285; www.alitalia.it)

British Airways (☑22 529 9000; www.ba.com)

easyJet (☑0703 203 025; www.easyjet.com)

KLM (☑22 556 6444; www.klm.pl)

Lufthansa (☑22 338 1300; www.lufthansa.pl)

Malév (☑22 697 7474; www.malev.hu)

Ryanair (☑0703 303 033; www.ryanair.com)

SAS (☑22 850 0500; www.flysas.com)

Wizz Air (☑0703 503 010; www.wizzair.com)

Land

Since Poland is now within the Schengen zone, there are no border posts or border-crossing formalities between Poland and Germany, the Czech Republic, Slovakia and Lithuania. Below is a list of major road border crossings with Poland's non-Schengen neighbours that accept foreigners and are open 24 hours.

Belarus (South to north) Terespol, Kuźnica Białostocka

Russia (West to east) Gronowo, Bezledy

Ukraine (South to north) Medyka, Hrebenne, Dorohusk

If you're going to Russia or Lithuania and your train/bus passes through Belarus, you need a Belarusian transit visa and you must get it in advance.

Bus

International bus services are offered by dozens of Polish and international companies. One of the major operators is **Eurolines Polska** (☑32 351 2020; www.eurolinespolska.pl), which runs buses in all directions.

Car & Motorcycle

To drive a car into Poland, EU citizens need their driving licence from home, while other nationalities must obtain an International Drivers Permit in their home country. Also required are vehicle registration papers and liability insurance (Green Card). If your insurance is not valid for Poland you must buy an additional policy at the border.

Train

Trains link Poland with every neighbouring country and beyond, but international train travel is not cheap. To save money on fares, investigate special train tickets and rail passes (see p634). Domestic trains in Poland are significantly cheaper, so you'll save money if you buy a ticket to a Polish border destination, then take a local train.

Do note that some international trains to/from Poland have been linked with theft. Keep an eye on your bags, particularly on the Berlin–Warsaw, Prague–Warsaw and Prague–Kraków overnight trains.

Sea

For ferry services from Gdańsk and Gdynia see p448 and p449, respectively. There are also car and passenger ferries from the Polish town of Świnoujście, operated by the following companies:

Polferries (www.polferries.pl) Offers daily services from Świnoujście to Ystad (eight hours) in Sweden, every Saturday to Rønne (5¼ hours) in Denmark, and four days a week to Copenhagen (12 hours).

Unity Line (www.unityline.pl) Runs daily ferries between Świnoujście and the Swedish ports of Ystad (seven hours) and Trelleborg (seven hours).

Any travel agency in Scandinavia will sell tickets for these services. In Poland, ask at any Orbis Travel office. In summer, passenger boats ply the Baltic coast from Świnoujście to Ahlbeck, Heringsdorf, Bansin and Zinnowitz in Germany.

Getting Around

Air

LOT (☎0801 703 703, 22 19572; www.lot.com) flies several times a day from Warsaw to Gdańsk, Kraków, Poznań and Wrocław. Another Polish airline, **Jet Air** (☎22 846 8661; www.jetair. pl), serves the same airports.

Bicycle

Cycling is not great for getting around cities, but is often a good way to travel between villages. If you get tired, it's possible to place your bike in the luggage compartment at the front or rear of slow passenger trains (these are rarely found on faster services). You'll need a special ticket for your bike from the railway luggage office.

Bus

Buses can be useful on short routes and through the mountains in southern Poland; but usually trains are quicker and more comfortable, and private minibuses are quicker and more direct.

Most buses are operated by the state bus company, PKS. It provides two kinds of service from its bus terminals *(dworzec autobusowy PKS)*: ordinary buses (marked in black on timetables); and fast buses (marked in red), which ignore minor stops.

Timetables are posted on boards, and additional symbols next to departure times may indicate the bus runs only on certain days or in certain seasons. Terminals usually have an information desk, but it's rarely staffed with English speakers. Tickets for PKS buses are usually bought at the terminal, but sometimes also from drivers. Note that the quoted bus frequencies in this chapter relate to the summer schedule.

The price of bus tickets is determined by the length, in kilometres, of the trip. Minibuses charge set prices for journeys, and these are normally posted in their windows or at the bus stop.

Car & Motorcycle
Fuel & Spare Parts

Petrol stations sell several kinds of petrol, including 94-octane leaded, 95-octane unleaded, 98-octane unleaded and diesel. Most petrol stations are open from 6am to 10pm (from 7am to 3pm Sunday), though some operate around the clock. Garages are plentiful. Roadside assistance can be summoned by dialling ☎981 or ☎22 9637.

Hire

Major international car-rental companies, such as **Avis** (www.avis.pl), **Hertz** (www.hertz. pl) and **Europcar** (www.europcar.com.pl), are represented in larger cities and have smaller offices at airports. Rates are comparable to full-price rental in Western Europe.

Rental agencies will need to see your passport, your local driving licence (which must be held for at least one year) and a credit card (for the deposit). You need to be at least 21 or 23 years of age to rent a car; sometimes 25 for a more expensive car.

Road Rules

The speed limit is 130km/h on motorways, 100km/h on two- or four-lane highways, 90km/h on other open roads and 50km/h in built-up areas. If the background of the sign bearing the town's name is white you must reduce speed to 50km/h; if the background is green there's no need to reduce speed (unless road signs indicate otherwise). Radar-equipped police are very active, especially in villages with white signs.

Unless signs state otherwise, cars may park on pavements as long as a minimum 1.5m-wide walkway is left for pedestrians. Parking in the opposite direction to traffic flow is allowed. The permitted blood alcohol level is a low 0.02%, so it's best not to drink if you're driving. Seat belts are compulsory, as are helmets for motorcyclists. Between October and February, all drivers must use headlights during the day (and night!).

Train

Trains will be your main means of transport. They're cheap, reliable and rarely overcrowded (except for July and August peak times). **Polish State Railways** (PKP; www.pkp.pl) operates trains to almost every place listed in this chapter. A private company, **Arriva** (www.arriva.pl), also operates local services in the eastern part of Pomerania.

Train Types

Express InterCity trains only stop at major cities and are the fastest way to travel by rail. These trains require seat reservations.

Down the pecking order are the older but cheaper **TLK trains** (*pociąg TLK*). They're slower and more crowded, but will likely be the type of train you most often catch. TLK trains do not normally require seat reservations, except at peak times.

InterRegio trains run services between adjoining regions of Poland, and often operate less frequently at weekends.

At the bottom of the hierarchy, slow **passenger trains** (*pociąg osobowy*) stop by every tree at the side of the track that could be imagined to be a station, and are best used only for short trips. Seats can't be reserved.

Classes & Fares

Express InterCity and TLK trains carry two classes: *druga klasa* (2nd class) and *pierwsza klasa* (1st class), which is 50% more expensive. Most 2nd-class and all 1st-class carriages have nonsmoking compartments.

Note that the quoted train fares in this chapter are for a second-class ticket on a TLK train, or the most likely alternative if the route is mainly served by a different type of train. Frequencies are as per the summer schedule.

In a couchette on an overnight train, compartments have four/six beds in 1st/2nd class. Sleepers have two/three people (1st/2nd class) in a compartment fitted with a washbasin, sheets and blankets. *Miejsca sypialne* (sleepers) and *kuszetki* (couchettes) can be booked at special counters in larger train stations; prebooking is recommended.

Timetables

Train *odjazdy* (departures) are listed at train stations on a yellow board and *przyjazdy* (arrivals) on a white board. Ordinary trains are marked in black print, fast trains in red. The letter 'R' in a square indicates the train has compulsory seat reservation.

The timetables also show which *peron* (platform) it's using. The number applies to *both* sides of the platform. If in doubt, check the platform departure board or route cards on the side of carriages, or ask someone.

Full timetable and fare information in English can be found on the PKP website.

Ticketing

If a seat reservation is compulsory on your train, you will automatically be sold a *miejscówka* (reserved) seat ticket. If you do not make a seat reservation, you can travel on *any* train (of the type requested) to the destination indicated on your ticket on the date specified.

Your ticket will list the *klasa* (class); the *poc* (type) of train; where the train is travelling *od* (from) and *do* (to); the major town or junction the train is travelling *prez* (through); and the total *cena* (price). If more than one place is listed under the heading *prez* (via), ask the conductor *early* if you have to change trains at the junction listed or be in a specific carriage (the train may separate later).

If you get on a train without a ticket, you can buy one directly from the conductor for a small supplement (7zł) – but do it right away. If the conductor finds you first, you'll be fined for travelling without a ticket. You can always upgrade from 2nd to 1st class for a small extra fee (7zł), plus the additional fare.

Slovakia

Includes »

Best Places to Eat

» Bratislavský Meštiansky Pivovar (p482)

» Kolkovna (p482)

» Salaš Krajinka (p492)

» Reštaurácia Bašta (p490)

Best Places to Stay

» Ginger Monkey Hostel (p501)

» Grand Hotel Kempinski (p499)

» Apartments Bratislava (p479)

» Hostel Blues (p479)

Why Go?

Ancient castle ruins, traditional villages and mountainous national parks: visiting Slovakia is about experiencing a place where age-old folkways and nature still hold sway. In this compact country you can hike beside a waterfall-filled gorge one day and see nailless wooden churches in a village museum the next. The small capital, Bratislava, may not have the superlative sights of nearby Prague or Budapest, but it's abuzz with development, each new riverfront dining and entertainment complex vying to outdo the next. The rabbit-warren Old Town centre is well worth a day or two of cafe hopping.

Just make sure you also venture east. In the countryside, fortresses tower over cities and rivers, hiking trails cover the hills and well-preserved medieval towns nestle below rocky peaks. Pull up a plate of *bryndzove halušky* (sheep's-cheese dumplings) with a glass of *slivovica* (firewater-like plum brandy) and drink a toast for us – *nazdravie*!

When To Go
Bratislava

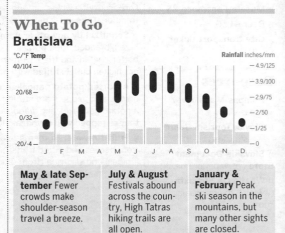

May & late September Fewer crowds make shoulder-season travel a breeze.	**July & August** Festivals abound across the country, High Tatras hiking trails are all open.	**January & February** Peak ski season in the mountains, but many other sights are closed.

Fast Facts

» **Area** 49,035 sq km

» **Capital** Bratislava

» **Telephone area code** 02

» **Emergency** 112

Exchange Rates

Australia	A$1	€0.72
Canada	C$1	€0.71
Japan	¥100	€0.82
New Zealand	NZ$1	€0.54
UK	UK£1	€1.12
USA	US$1	€0.69

Set Your Budget

» **Budget hotel room** €30-60

» **Two-course meal** €15

» **Museum entrance** €3

» **Beer** €1.50

» **City transport ticket** €0.70

Resources

» **Kompas Maps** (www.kompas.sk)

» **Slovak Tourism Board** (www.slovakia.travel)

» **Slovakia Document Store** (www.panorama.sk)

» **What's On Slovakia** (www.whatsonslovakia.com)

Connections

Though few airlines fly into Slovakia itself, Bratislava is just 60km from the well-connected Vienna International Airport. By train from Bratislava, Budapest (three hours) and Prague (five hours) are easy to reach. Travelling further east, buses become your best bet. Connect to Zakopane, Poland (two hours) from Poprad, and to Uzhgorod, Ukraine (2½ hours) through Košice.

ITINERARIES

Three Days

Two nights in Bratislava is enough time to wander the Old Town streets, stop at a new river-park restaurant and see a museum or two. The following day is best spent on a castle excursion, either to Devín or Trenčín. Or, better yet, spend all three days hiking in the rocky High Tatra mountains, staying central in the Starý Smokovec resort town or in more off-beat Ždiar in the Belá Tatras.

One Week

After a day or two in the capital, venture east. Spend at least four nights in and around the Tatras so you can both hike to a mountain hut and take day trips to the must-see Spiš Castle ruins and medieval Levoča. You might also make time for a gentle raft ride in Pieniny. Then, for the last night or two, continue on to Bardejov to see a complete Renaissance town square, icon art and the neighbouring folk village and wooden churches.

Essential Food & Drink

» **Sheep's cheese, and more sheep's cheese** *Bryndza*, sharp, soft and spreadable; *oštiepok*, solid and ball-shaped; *korbačik*, 'little whips' or long, smoked strands; *žinčina*, a traditional sheep's-whey drink (like sour milk)

» **Schnitzel by any other name** *Vyprážaný bravčový rezeň*, breaded, fried pork steak; *Černohorský rezeň*, potato batter-coated and fried, with cheese; *gordon blu*, fried pork or chicken cutlet stuffed with ham and cheese

» **Assorted potato pancakes** Various sautéed meats, onions and peppers are stuffed *v zemiakovej placke* (in a potato pancake), like *diabolské soté* (devil's sautée), or they're topped with bryndza cheese and sour cream

» **Fruit firewater** Homemade or store-bought liquor, made from berries and pitted fruits, such as *borovička* (from juniper) and *slivovica* (from plums)

Slovakia Highlights

1 Hike between mountain huts in one of Europe's smallest alpine mountain ranges, the **High Tatras** (p494)

2 Linger over drinks at one of the myriad sidewalk and riverfront cafes in Old Town **Bratislava** (p476).

3 Wander among the 4 hectare–long ruins of **Spiš Castle** (p505), among the biggest in Europe

4 Experience the folk culture in traditional villages like **Vlkolínec** (p492) and **Čičmany** (p492)

5 Gaze on Renaissance splendour and ancient icons in **Bardejov** (p512)

6 Travel back in time at the Unesco-noted mining town of **Banská Štiavnica** (p487)

7 Climb wooden ladders past crashing waterfalls in the dramatic and challenging gorges of **Slovenský Raj National Park** (p506)

BRATISLAVA

📞 02 / POP 428,800

Slovakia's capital city is a host of contrasts: the charming Starý Mesto (Old Town) sits across the river from a communist, concrete-block apartment jungle. The age-old castle shares a skyline with the startlingly UFO-like 'New Bridge' from the 1970s. Narrow pedestrian streets, pastel 18th-century buildings and sidewalk cafes galore make for a supremely strollable – if tiny – historic centre. You may want to pop into a museum or climb up to the castle for views, but the best thing to do with a day here is meander the alleyways, stopping in as many cafes as you dare. Be warned, you may have to dodge a German- or Italian-speaking tour group or two along the way. After that, if you haven't had enough to drink in the Old Town, one of the chichi new bar-restaurants at the up-and-coming riverfront-park complex will surely quench your thirst. Your choice; old or new, it's all part of the capital city's charm.

History

Founded in AD 907, by the 12th century Bratislava (then known as Poszony in Hungarian, or Pressburg in German) was a large city in greater Hungary. King Matthias Corvinus founded a university here, Academia Istropolitana, that is still evident today. Many of the imposing baroque palaces you see date to the reign of Austro-Hungarian empress Maria Theresa (1740–80), when the city flourished. Between the subsequent Turkish occupation of Budapest and emancipation in the mid-1800s, Hungarian parliament met locally and monarchs were crowned in St Martin's Cathedral.

'Bratislava' was officially born as the second city of a Czechoslovak state after WWI. Post WWII, the communists did a number on the town's architecture and spirit – razing a large part of the Old Town, including the

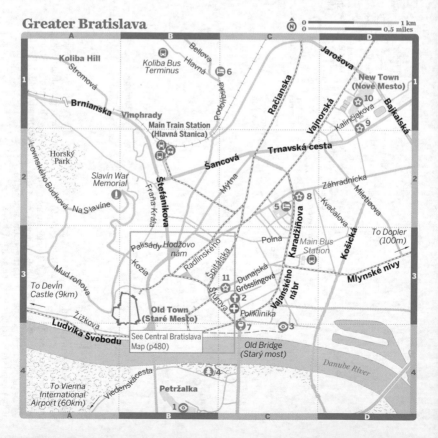

Greater Bratislava

synagogue, to make way for a new highway. Today, the city is under construction once again. Look for a new (and not so cheap) hotel opening shortly on a corner near you.

◉ Sights

In addition to those mentioned here, there are a number of galleries and small museums scattered about the Old Town.

Bratislava Castle CASTLE
(Map p480; www.snm.sk; grounds free, museum adult/child €2.50/1.25; ⊙grounds 9am-9pm, museum 10am-6pm Tue-Sun) Dominating the west side of the Old Town on a hill above the Danube, the castle's look is often likened to that of an upturned table. The base of what you see today is a 1950s reconstruction; an 1811 fire left the fortress in ruins for more than a century. Renovations, begun years ago, will continue for years to come. Nevertheless, a white coat of paint has done much to improve the castle's appearance. Most of the buildings contain administrative offices. At the time of research, only a temporary-exhibit museum space was open; more will follow. In the meantime, the walls, lawns and ramparts still provide a great vantage point for city viewing.

Museum of Jewish Culture MUSEUM
(Map p480; www.snm.sk; Židovská 17; adult/child €7/2; ⊙11am-5pm Sun-Fri) The most moving of the three floors of exhibits here focuses

---

FINDING A MAN AT WORK

The most photographed sight in Bratislava is not a church or a castle, it's the bronze statue called the **Watcher** (Map p480) peeping out of an imaginary manhole below a 'Man at Work' sign at the intersection of Panská and Rybárska. He's not alone. There are several other quirky statues scattered around the old town. Look out for the **Frenchman** who leans on a park bench, the **Photographer** who stalks paparazzi-style around a corner, and the **Schöner Náci**, who tips his top hat on a main square. Look up to find other questionable characters, like a timepiece-toting monk and a rather naked imp, decorating building facades around the pedestrian centre.

on the large Jewish community and buildings lost during and after WWII. Black-and-white photos show the neighbourhood and synagogue before it was ploughed under.

St Martin's Cathedral CHURCH
(Map p480; Dóm sv Martina; Rudnayovo nám; adult/child €2/free; ⊙9-11.30am & 1-5pm Mon-Sat, 1.30-4.30pm Sun) A relatively modest interior belies the elaborate history of St Martin's Cathedral: 11 Austro-Hungarian monarchs (10 kings and one queen, Maria Theresa) were crowned in this 14th-century church. The busy motorway almost touching St Martin's follows the moat of the former city walls.

Hviezdoslavovo námestie SQUARE
(Map p480) Embassies, restaurants and bars are the mainstay of the long, tree-lined plaza that anchors the southern end of the pedestrian zone. At the Hviezdoslavovo's east end, the ornate 1886 **Slovak National Theatre**, one of the city's opera houses, steals the show. Look also for 13th-century town ruins beneath the glass skylight just outside. The theatre is not open for tours, but ticket prices are not prohibitive. The nearby neo-baroque 1914 **Reduta Palace**, on Moštová, is under indefinite reconstruction.

Hlavné námestie SQUARE
(Map p480) Cafe tables outline Hlavné nám, or Main Sq, the sight of numerous festival performances and a permanent crafts fair that grows exponentially at Christmas time. **Roland's Fountain**, at the square's heart, is

Start the morning by climbing up the ramparts of **Bratislava Castle**. The museum is under long-term construction, but from the grounds you have a view of both the barrel-tile roofs of Old Town and the concrete jungle, Petržalka. On your way back down, stop at the excellent **Museum of Jewish Culture**, and **St Martin's Cathedral**, then spend the afternoon strolling through the Old Town. Later you could feel the beat at **Aligator Rock Pub** or dine waterfront at a restaurant like **Kolkovna** in the Eurovea river complex.

Day two, trip out to **Devín Castle** to see evocative buildings and ruins from the 9th to the 18th centuries. This nearby fortress, across the river from Austria, is much more impressive than Bratislava's own.

thought to have been built in 1572 as a fire hydrant of sorts. Flanking the northeast side of the square is the 1421 **Old Town Hall**; it and the city museum contained within are under indefinite reconstruction. You'll often find a musician in traditional costume playing a *fujira* (2m-long flute) on the steps of the **Jesuit Church**.

Eurovea NEIGHBOURHOOD
(Map p476; Pribinova) Sitting beneath a cafe umbrella or strolling along the grassy waterfront became the things to do after the Eurovea complex opened in 2010. Riverfront restaurants are the main attraction, but there's also a full shopping mall hidden within. The plaza adjoining the new Slovak National Theatre (New SND) often hosts concerts.

Apponyi Palace MUSEUM
(Map p480; www.muzeum.bratislava.sk; Radničná 1; adult/child €6/2; ⊙10am-6pm Tue-Sun) Explore the area's winemaking heritage in the cellar exhibits of a restored 1761 palace. Upstairs the museum rooms are outfitted with period furnishings. Both sections have excellent, interactive English-language audio.

Slovak National Gallery MUSEUM
(Map p480; Slovenská Národná Galéria; www.sng. sk; Rázusovo nábr 2; adult/child €3.50/2; ⊙10am-5pm Tue-Sun) A Stalinist modern building and an 18th-century palace make interesting co-hosts for the Slovak National Gallery. The nation's eclectic art collection contained here ranges from Gothic to graphic design.

New Bridge TOWER
(Nový most; Map p480; www.u-f-o.sk; Viedenská cesta; observation deck adult/child €8/5; ⊙10am-11pm) Colloquially called the UFO (pronounced ew-fo) bridge, this modernist marvel from 1972 has a viewing platform, an overhyped nightclub and a restaurant with out-of-this-world prices.

Slovak National Museum MUSEUM
(Map p480; www.snm.sk; Vajanského nábr 2; adult/child €3.50/1.50; ⊙9am-5pm Tue-Sun) Changing exhibits on the lower floors, natural history on top.

Primate's Palace MUSEUM
(Map p480; adult/child €2/1; ⊙10am-5pm Tue-Sun) Napoleon and Austrian emperor Franz I signed the Treaty of Pressburg on 26 December 1805 here in the glittery Hall of Mirrors.

🏃 Activities

From April through September, **Slovak Shipping & Ports** (Map p480; ☑5293 2226; www.lod. sk; Fajnorovo nábr 2) runs 45-minute Bratislava return boat trips (adult/child €4/2.50) on the Danube. Its Devín sightseeing cruise (adult/child return €5.50/3.50) plies the waters to the castle, stops for one to two hours and returns to Bratislava in 30 minutes.

You can rent bikes from **Bratislava Sightseeing** (Map p480; ☑0907683112; www. bratislavasightseeing.com; Fajnorovo nábr; per hr/day €4/18; ⊙10am-6pm mid-May-mid-Sep), located in a children's playground along the waterfront. Bike tours available, too.

☞ Tours

FREE **Be Free Tours** WALKING TOUR
(Map p480; www.befreetours.com; Hviezdoslavovo nám; tour free; ⊙11am & 4pm Tue-Sat, 4pm Sun & Mon) Lively, two-hour-plus English tour of the Old Town, including stories and legends, leave from in front of the historic Slovak National Theatre (Historic SND).

Bratislava Culture & Information Centre WALKING TOUR
(Map p480; ☑5443 4059; www.bkis.sk; Klobučnívcka 2; tour €14; ⊙2pm Apr-Oct, by appointment Nov-Mar) Official tourist office–run, one-hour walking tour of the Old Town in

ⓘ DEVÍN CASTLE

To see a more historically complete fortress, outfitted as in olden days, take the bus beneath the New Bridge (Nový Most) to **Devín Castle** (p486), 8km outside the city.

English or German. Segway tours also available by reservation.

Oldtimer   MOTORISED TOUR
(Prešporáčik; ☑0903302817; www.tour4u.sk; Hlavné nám; adult/child from €8/4; ⊙9am-7pm May-Oct, by appointment Nov-Mar) Old-fashioned cars take you around town or up to the castle; great for those who can't climb hills. Thirty- to 60-minute tours, with recorded audio in English and German.

Bratislava Pub Crawl   DRINKING TOUR
(www.befreetours.sk; Rock OK, Šafárikovo nám 4; ticket €13; ⊙9.30pm Tue-Sat) Visit four different bars and clubs in one night with this backpacker-oriented tour; drink specials included.

🎇 Festivals & Events

Cultural Summer Festival (www.bkis.sk) A smorgasbord of plays and performances comes to the streets and venues around town June through September.

Bratislava Jazz Days (www.bjd.sk) World-class jazz takes centre stage three days in October.

Christmas Market From 26 November, Hlavné nám fills with food and drink, crafts for sale and staged performances.

🛏 Sleeping

In recent years it's seemed as if a newer and pricier top-end hotel has opened every few minutes, including an exorbitant Kempinski. For a full accommodation listing, see www.bkis.sk. Getting a short-term rental flat in the old town (€65 to €120 per night) is a great way to stay super central without paying hotel prices; plus you can self cater. Family-run and friendly, the modern units of **Apartments Bratislava** (www.apartments bratislava.sk) are our top choice. **Bratislava Apartments** (www.bratislava-apartments.com) and **Bratislava Hotels** (www.bratislavahotels. com) are other options.

Unless noted, hostels listed have kitchen, laundry and sheets, beer and wine available, and no lockouts.

Penzión Virgo   PENSION €€
(Map p480; ☑3300 6262; www.penzionvirgo.sk; Panenská 14; s/d €65/78; ⊙@) Exterior-access rooms are arranged around a courtyard; each one feels light and airy despite dark-wood floors and baroque-accent wallpaper. Sip an espresso with the breakfast buffet (€5), or cook for yourself if you opt for an apartment (€100).

Hotel Avance   HOTEL €€
(Map p480; ☑5920 8400; www.hotelavance.sk; Medená 9; r incl breakfast €99-119; P❉@🛜) Thick carpeting and cushy duvets add to the comfort factor at this contemporary gem. Design-driven details include floating nightstands with cool underlighting and glass-tile mosaics in sleek bathrooms.

Sheraton Bratislava   HOTEL €€€
(Map p476; ☑3535 0000; http://www.sheraton bratislava.com; Eurovea, Pribinova 12; r €150-240, P❉@🛜) One of Bratislava's newer properties, the upscale Sheraton gets points for a prime, Eurovea riverfront location. Minuses include overpriced parking and wi-fi. Watch for weekend deals.

🏆 **Hostel Blues**   HOSTEL €
CHOICE (Map p480; ☑0905204020; www.hostel blues.sk; Špitálska 2; dm €15-20, d €52-63; ⊙@🛜) Friendly, professional staff not only help you plan your days, they offer free city sightsee-

---

DON'T MISS

THE SMALLER SIGHTS

» **Blue Church** (Modrý kostol; Map p476; Bezručova 2; admission free; ⊙dawn-dusk) Every surface of the 1911 Church of St Elizabeth, more commonly known as the Blue Church, is an art nouveau fantasy dressed in cool sky-blue and deeper royal blue.

» **Michael's Gate & Tower** (Map p480; Michalská brána & veža; www.muz eum.bratislava.sk; Michalská 24; adult/child €2/1; ⊙10am-6pm Tue-Sun) Climb past the five small storeys of medieval weaponry in the town's only remaining gate to a superior Old Town view from the top.

» **Museum of Clocks** (Map p480; www.muzeum.bratislava.sk; Židovská 1; adult/child €2/1; ⊙10am-5pm Tue-Sun) Random old clocks, but they're contained in an interestingly narrow building.

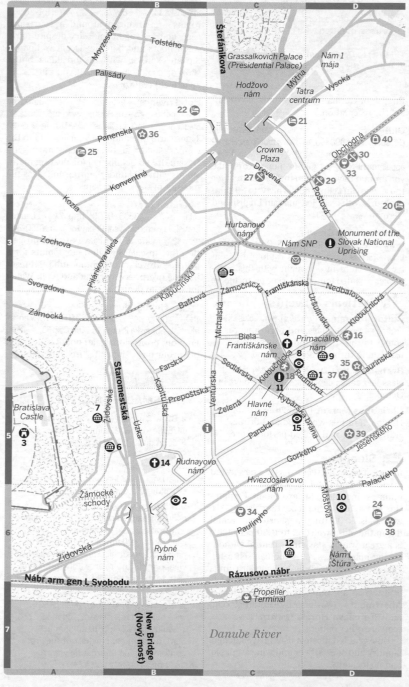

SLOVAKIA BRATISLAVA

ing tours. The coffeehouse-like communal space, which occasionally hosts concerts, adds to the urban apartment-living feel here. Choose from five- to 10-bed, single-sex or mixed dorms, or those with double bunk beds(!). Private rooms have their own bathrooms.

Tulip House Hotel
BOUTIQUE HOTEL €€€
(Map p480; ☑3217 1819; www.tuliphouse.sk; Štúrova 10; ste incl breakfast €150-300; P❄✳@☎) Exquisite art nouveau accents are the hallmark of this 1903 property. The decor – chocolate-brown suede headboards contrasting with plush white carpeting – is all modern elegance. Enjoy epicurean meals at pedestrian prices in the small cafe.

Hotel-Penzión Arcus
PENSION €€
(Map p476; ☑5557 2522; www.hotelarcus.sk; Moskovská 5; s/d incl breakfast €65/100; ❄☎) Because this family-run place was once an apartment building, the 13 rooms are quite varied (some with balcony, some with courtyard views). Flowery synthetic linens seem a bit outdated but bathrooms are new and sparkly white.

Downtown Backpackers
HOSTEL €
(☑5464 1191; www.backpackers.sk; Panenská 31; dm €13-20, d €45-60; ❄@☎) The first hostel in Bratislava, Backpackers is still a boozy (you enter through a bar) bohemian classic. Red-brick walls and tapestries add character, as does the fact that you have to walk through some dorm rooms to get to others.

Austria Trend
HOTEL €€
(Map p480; ☑5277 5817; www.austria-trend.sk; Vysoká 2a; r €120-150; P✳@) Newer business hotel on the edge of the Old Town.

A1 Hostel
HOSTEL €
(Map p480; ☑0944280288; http://a1hostelbratis lava.com/; Heydukova 1; dm/d €15/40; ❄☎) Little more than a super-clean, three-room flat, A1 offers quiet and camaraderie – but no kitchen.

✕ Eating

The pedestrian centre is chock-a-block with dining options priced for expense accounts and foreigners. If you want to splash out (from €20 a plate), choose a fancy-sounding foreign name (Le Monde, UpsideDown, Steakhouse etc) and go for it. What's harder to find is decent Slovak food; stick to our suggestions in the Old Town. Reasonable eateries, both sit-down and takeaway, line Obchodná street near the university. Note

Central Bratislava

that most restaurants offer lunch set menus, which can be a real steal.

TOP CHOICE **Kolkovna** CZECH & SLOVAK €€
(Map p476; ☎2091 5280; Eurovea, Pribinova 8; mains €7-12; ⊙11am-midnight) Topping the list of no less than a dozen restaurants and cafes at the riverfront Eurovea complex, Kolkovna has hearty portions and reasonable prices. Braised and roast meats are the mainstay, but there is lighter fare to go with your tank-imported draft Pilsner beer (no bottles, no preservatives). Book ahead for an outdoor table on weekend evenings.

TOP CHOICE **Bratislavský Meštiansky Pivovar**
SLOVAK €€-€€€
(Map p480; ☎0944512265; Drevená 8; mains €6-12; ⊙11am-midnight Sun-Thu, until 1am Sat & Sun) Not only does this stylish microbrewery serve Bratislava's freshest beer, it offers some of the city's most creative Slovak cooking. Both after work and at weekends, crowds of young professionals fill in beneath the vaulted ceilings and stylised Old Town artwork. Reservations are never a bad idea.

U Remeselníka SLOVAK €-€€
(Map p480; Obchodná 64; mains €5-11) Small and folksy, this cellar cafe associated with the traditional Úľuv craft store upstairs is a great place to try a trio of *halušky* (small dumplings) – with sheep's cheese and bacon, with kolbasa, and with cabbage.

Slovak Pub SLOVAK €-€€
(Map p480; Obchodná 62; mains €5-10; ⊙10am-midnight Mon-Thu, 10am-1am Fri & Sat, noon-midnight Sun) No denying that Slovak Pub, with its themed-rooms, is firmly on the tourist trail. But it does serve every traditional national dish you can think of, and the owners use cheese from their biofarm.

Divný Janko SLOVAK €-€€
(Jozefská 2; mains €4-7) A locally popular little hang-out: get your fill of tasty fried pork and chicken steaks – stuffed with pineapple,

sausage, you name it... Oh, and salads are available, too.

Čínska Panda
CHINESE €-€€

(Map p480; Vysoká 39; mains €5-8) And now for something completely different – an authentic and flavourful Chinese-run restaurant with solid vegetarian options. Great set lunch menus (€4).

Govinda
VEGETARIAN €

(Map p480; Obchodná 30; sandwiches & meals €2.50-4; ⊗11am-8pm Mon-Fri, 11.30am-5pm Sat) Indian-inspired vegetarian meals and takeaway.

U Jakubu
SLOVAK €

(Map p480; Nám SNP 24; mains €2-5; ⊗8am-6pm Mon-Fri) Self-service cafeteria with Slovak faves.

Tesco
SUPERMARKET

(Map p480; Kamenné nám 1; ⊗8am-9pm Mon-Fri, 9am-7pm Sat & Sun) Humongous grocery store below ground level.

🍷 Drinking

From mid-April to October, sidewalk cafe tables sprout up in every corner of pedestrian Old Town. Any one will do for a cocktail or a coffee (no dining required). For example, several places – look for names like Verne, Bar 17 and Slang Pub – are strung out along Hviezdoslavovo. But lately *the* place to drink is riverfront at one of the many bar-restaurant-cafes in the Eurovea complex. Slovak Pub and Bratislavský Meštiansky Pivovar are also good imbibing options, and music bars can be quiet enough for a casual sip on weekdays. See p479 for a pub-crawl tour.

TOP CHOICE Sky Bar
BAR

(Map p480; ☎5441 1244; Hviezdoslavovo nám 7) You'd never guess from the ground floor what an amazing view this seventh-storey, upscale, Old Town bar has. It's a don't-miss. Just reserve ahead for a table, or you'll be standing in tight quarters.

Kréma Gurmánov Bratislavy
BAR

(Map p480; Obchodná 52) A dark cellar bar called KGB could be just the place for a clandestine tryst.

☆ Entertainment

Check **Slovak Spectator** (www.slovakspectator.com), the **Bratislava Culture & Information Centre** (www.bkis.sk) and **Kam do Mesta** (www.kamdomesta.sk) for the latest events.

BRATISLAVA FOR CHILDREN

Little ones are rarely seen at restaurants, few of which have children's menus or playgrounds. Some lodgings do provide cribs or cots. Places for kid-focused fun:

» **Bibiana** (Map p480; www.bibiana.sk; Panská 41; admission free; ⊗10am-6pm Tue-Sun) This children's library/art gallery also sponsors frequent kid-focused performances.

» **Sad Janka Krála Park** (Map p476; Viedenská cesta, Petržalka; admission free; ⊗24hr) Across the Danube from the old town, the 22-hectare waterfront park and playgrounds have room for roaming.

Nightclubs & Live Music

Cover charges for Bratislava music bars and clubs are usually quite low (free to €5). On weekends, many upscale restaurants turn into discos after 10pm; listen for the beat.

Nu Spirit
BAR

(Map p480; Medená 16; ⊗10am-4am Mon-Fri, 5pm-4am Sat & Sun) Funky DJs, Brazilian rhythms, live blues drummers... this hip underground club dabbles in all the soulful sounds.

Aligator Rock Pub
CLUB

(Map p480; Laurinská 7; ⊗5pm-3am Mon-Sat) One of the few places that's packed even on weeknights. Live performances at this cellar club run the gamut from Pink Floyd covers to harder-core rock.

Café Štúdio Club
BAR

(Map p480; cnr Laurinská & Radničná; ⊗10am-1am Mon-Wed, to 3am Thu & Fri, 4pm-3am Sat) Bop to the oldies, or chill out to jazz; weekends there's always live music of some sort.

Apollon Club
GAY & LESBIAN

(Map p480; www.apollon-gay-club.sk; Panenská 24; ⊗6pm-3am Mon-Thu, 8pm-5am Fri & Sat, 8pm-1am Sun) THE gay disco in town has two bars and three stages. Monday is karaoke; Sunday is an underwear party.

The following are outside of the centre:

Dopler
CLUB

(Map p476; Prievozská 18; ⊗8pm-5am Fri & Sat) The city's biggest DJ-dance club; college-age and younger crowd.

PETER LIPA: SLOVAK JAZZ GREAT

For more than 30 years singer, songwriter, musician and producer Peter Lipa has been a star on the Slovak jazz scene. He performs internationally and is a founder of the Bratislava Jazz Days festival.

What is the state of live jazz in Bratislava today?

Unfortunately, though popular, jazz still struggles to found adequate standing in our society. Other kinds of 'stage art' have state-run organizations that support performances; jazz promotion is up to the skills of people who are doing it.

What are your favourite clubs and venues?

Club Hlava XXII has opened, traditional jazz is played in Café Štúdio Club, and sometimes there are good concerts in Aligator [Rock Pub] and Nu Spirit bar.

Who are some of the voices to listen for?

Slovak Jazz Society, a private association, organises the 'New faces of Slovak Jazz' show at the beginning of December. New talents are discovered there each year. I'd recommend these experienced musicians from the younger generation: Juraj Baros, Rado Tariska, Ondrej Krajnak and Klaudius Kovac.

Hlava XXII   CLUB
(Map p476; Bazová 9; ⊙3pm-3am Tue-Sat) Jam sessions, blues and world beat – live.

Sport

Bratislava's hallowed ice-hockey team, HC Slovan, plays at the **Ondrej Nepela Stadium** (Map p476; Odbojárov 9), which underwent a €40 million upgrade for the 2011 ice hockey world championship. The hometown football team plays at its namesake **SK Slovan Stadium** (Map p476; Tegelhoffa 4) nearby. Buy tickets for both online at www.ticketportal.sk.

Performing Arts

Folk dance and music ensembles, like **Šľuk** (www.sluk.sk) and **Lúčnica** (www.lucnica.sk), perform at various venues around town.

Slovak National Theatre   THEATRE
(Slovenské Národné Divadlo, SND; www.snd.sk) The national theatre company stages quality operas (Slavic and international), ballets and dramas in two venues. The gilt decorations of the landmark **Historic SND** (Map p480; Hviezdoslavovo nám; booking office cnr Jesenského & Komenského; ⊙8am-5.30pm Mon-Fri, 9am-1pm Sat) is a show worth seeing in itself. The modern **New SND** (Map p476; Pribinova 17; ⊙9am-5pm Mon- Fri) also contains a cafe and theatre offices.

Slovak Philharmonic   THEATRE
(www.filharmonia.sk) At the time of research the Philharmonic's home, Reduta Palace, was under indefinite reconstruction. Until finished, the state orchestra performs at the SND theatres.

🛍 Shopping

There are several crystal, craft and jewellery stores, as well as souvenir booths, in and around Hlavné nám. Artisan galleries tend to inhabit the small alleyways of Old Town streets.

Ú Ľuv   HANDICRAFTS
(Map p480; www.uluv.sk; Obchodná 64) For serious folk-art shopping head to the main outlet of ÚĽuv, the national handicraft cooperative, where there are two stores and a courtyard filled with artisans' studios.

ℹ Information

Emergency
Emergency (⊘112)
Main police station (⊘159; Gunduličova 10)

Internet Access

Many local cafes have wireless internet access; Hlavné and Hviezdoslavovo squares are free wi-fi zones.

Klar-i-net (Klariská 4; per 30min €2; ⊙10am-10pm Mon-Fri, 3-10pm Sat & Sun; ⊛) Numerous well-equipped terminals; office services and beverages available.

Media
Slovak Spectator (www.slovakspectator.sk) English-language weekly newspaper with current affairs and event listings.

Medical Services
Poliklinika Ruzinov (⊘4823 4113; Ružinovská 10) Hospital with emergency services and a 24-hour pharmacy.

ℹ WORTH THE DISCOUNT?

Bratislava City Card (1/2/3 days €10/12/15), sold at the Bratislava Culture & Information Centre, covers public transport and provides discounted museum admission. But unless you're going to take a tour or plan to see every single sight, it might not be worth it. Admission prices are cheap and the Old Town is small enough to walk.

Money

Bratislava has numerous banks and ATMs in the Old Town, with several branches on Poštova. There are also ATMs and exchange booths in the train and bus stations, and at the airport.

Tatra Banka (Dunajská 4) Staff speak excellent English.

Post

Main post office (Nám SNP 34-35)

Tourist Information

Bratislava Culture & Information Centre (BKIS; ☏16 186; www.bkis.sk; Klobučnícka 2; ⏰9am-6pm Mon-Fri, 9am-3pm Sat, 10am-3pm Sun) Official tourist office staff hoard brochures behind the counter, and seem uninterested, but keep pressing and they'll assist – a little. Small Bratislava guide available.

Bratislava Tourist Service (BTS; ☏2070 7501; www.bratislava-info.sk; Ventúrska 9; ⏰10am-8pm) A tiny, tiny place, but the young staff are obliging. Maps and knick-knacks for sale.

Websites

Bratislava City Guide (www.bratislava-city.sk) City info from the government.

Visit Bratislava (http://visit.bratislava.sk) Comprehensive city tourist board site.

ℹ Getting There & Away

Bratislava is the main hub for trains, buses and the few planes that head in and out of the country.

Air

For international airlines serving Bratislava, see p519. Keep in mind that Vienna's much busier international airport is only 60km west.

Airport Bratislava (BTS; www.airport bratislava.sk; Ivanská cesta) New terminal opened in 2010, 9km northeast of centre. Flights connect to Prague, Warsaw, UK cities and more.

Danube Wings (V5; www.danubewings.eu) The only airline with domestic service, has weekday, early-morning and evening flights to Košice.

Boat

From April through October, plying the Danube is a cruisey way to get from Bratislava to Vienna or Budapest.

Slovak Shipping & Ports (☏5293 2226; www.lod.sk; Hydrofoil Terminal, Fajnorova nábr 2) Several weekly hydrofoils to Vienna (€16 one way, 1¾ hours) and Budapest (€79 one way, four hours).

Twin City Liner (☏0903610716; www.twincity liner.com; Propeller Terminal, Rázusovo nábr) Up to four boats a day to Vienna (€17 to €28 one way, 1½ hours).

Bus

Direct destinations include cities throughout Slovakia and Europe, but the train is usually comparably priced and more convenient. For schedules, see http://cp.atlas.sk. The **Main Bus Station** (Autobusová stanica, AS; Mlynské Nivy) is 1.5km east of the old town; locals call it 'Mlynské Nivy' (the street name).

Eurobus (☏0972250305; www.eurobus.sk) Runs some international routes.

Eurolines (☏5556 7349; www.slovaklines.sk) Contact for most international buses.

Slovenská autobusová doprava (SAD; www.sad.sk) National bus company.

Train

Rail is the main way to get around Slovakia and to neighbouring countries. Intercity and Eurocity (IC/EC) trains, listed here, are the quickest. Note that *Rýclík* (R), or 'Fast' trains take longer, but run more frequently and cost less. *Osobný* (Ob)

INTERNATIONAL BUSES FROM BRATISLAVA

DESTINATION	COST (€)	DURATION (HR)	FREQUENCY (DAILY)
Vienna	8	1¼	12
Prague	16	4¼	4
Budapest	14	2½-4	8
London	81	23	1

DESTINATION	COST (€)	DURATION (HR)	FREQUENCY (DAILY)
Vienna	10	1	hourly
Prague	24	4¼	6
Budapest	14	2¾	5
Warsaw	58	10½	1
Moscow	110	37	1

trains are the milk runs. For schedules see www.cp.atlas.sk.

Main Train Station (Hlavná stanica; www.slovakrail.sk; Predštanicné nám)

❶ Getting Around

To/From the Airport

CITY BUS No 61 links Bratislava airport with the main train station (20 minutes).

SHUTTLE BUS A shuttle runs from the Bratislava airport to Mlynské Nivy bus station (€1) hourly weekdays from 9am to 6.50pm.

TAXI Standing taxis (over)charge about €20 to town; ask the price before you get in.

VIENNA BUS A regular bus (€9) connects Vienna airport with the Bratislava's main bus station.

Car

Numerous international car-hire companies like Hertz and Sixt have offices at the airport. Good smaller agencies include:

Advantage Car Rental (☑6241 0510; www.acr.sk) Reasonable prices include Bratislava-wide delivery.

Buchbinder (☑4363 7821; www.buchbinder.sk) In-town pick-up possible for a fee.

Car Rental 24 (☑4363 8335; www.carrental24.sk)

Public Transport

Bratislava has an extensive tram, bus and trolley-bus network; though the Old Town is small, so you

won't often need it. **Dopravný Podnik Bratislava** (DPB; www.dpb.sk; Hodžovo nám; ⊙6am-7pm Mon-Fri) is the public transport company; you'll find a route map online. The office is in the underground passage beneath Hodžovo nám.

Tickets cost €0.25/0.70/1.40 for 10/60/90 minutes. Buy at newsstands and validate on board (or risk a legally enforceable €50 fine). Passes cost €3.50/6.50/8/12 for one/two/three/seven days; buy at the DPB office, validate on board.

Important lines:

Tram 13 Main Train Station to Nám L Štúra

Bus 93 Main Train Station to Hodžovo nám

Bus 206 Main Bus Station to Hodžovo nám

Bus 310 Main Bus Station to Main Train Station

Taxi

Standing cabs compulsively overcharge foreigners; an around-town trip should not cost more than €10. To save, ask someone to help you order a taxi (not all operators speak English).

AA Euro Taxi (☑16 022)

Hello Taxi (☑16 321)

Trend Taxi (☑16 302)

AROUND BRATISLAVA

One of the best sights in Bratislava is actually 9km west of the city centre. **Devín Castle** (www.muzeum.bratislava.sk; Muranská; adult/child €3/1.50; ⊙10am-5pm Tue-Fri, to 6pm Sat & Sun) was once the military plaything of 9th-century warlord Prince Ratislav. The castle

DOMESTIC TRAINS FROM BRATISLAVA

DESTINATION	COST (€)	DURATION (HR)	FREQUENCY (DAILY)
Trenčín	9	1½	3
Žilina	11	2½	4
Poprad	16	4	4
Košice	19	5½	4

PIEŠŤANY

Thermal waters bubble under much of this country, but it's Slovakia's premier spa site, **Piešťany** (www.spa-piestany.sk) that attracts most visitors. On **Kúpelne ostrov** (Spa Island) you can swim in thermal pools, breathe seaside-like air in a salt cave and be wrapped naked in hot mud. Many of the 19th-century buildings sport a new coat of Maria-Theresa-yellow paint, others are more modern. Reserve online for a stay, or head to the *kasa* (cashier) at **Napoleon 1** (☏033-775 2198; ⊗7.30am-7pm) to book a day service. **Eva Pools** (adult/child €3/2; ⊗11am-5pm) and **Balnea Esplanade Hotel** (per day adult/child €15/10, 3hr €10/7; ⊗8am-10pm) have public swimming. From Bratislava (87km) the train takes 1¼ hours (€4, 12 daily) and you can continue on the same route to Trenčín (€2, 45 minutes).

withstood the Turks but then was blown up in 1809 by the French. Peer at older bits that have been unearthed and tour a reconstructed palace museum. Bus 29 links Devín with Bratislava's Nový Most (New Bridge) stop, under the bridge. Austria is just across the river.

SOUTHERN SLOVAKIA

Southern Slovakia was the mining centre for greater Hungary from the 14th to the 18th centuries, but its fortunes have long since dried up. Much of the region is industrially oriented today, but the ancient mining town of Banská Štiavnica is a gem.

Banská Štiavnica

☏045 / POP 10,700

Like a fossil preserved in amber, Banská Štiavnica is a medieval wonder frozen in time. In its 16th-century heyday the town was an architectural showcase. As the minerals ran out and the mines closed, progress stopped, leaving buildings wonderfully untouched. Walking up and down among the steeply terraced hillsides now you'll see many of the same Old Town burghers' houses, churches, alleys and stairways that you would have seen then. Unesco recognised the town way back in 1972. At a mere fraction of its peak population today, the town is primarily a holiday destination, with numerous mining-related museums and an old and new castle facing each other across the steep valley.

From the train station it's a 2km climb uphill through the factories and housing blocks to Nám sv Trojice, the main, Old Town square. Buses stop 500m closer, at a crossroads, Križovatka.

◉ Sights

Wandering the steep streets gazing at the detailed architectural designs is the main attraction. Buildings aren't all in pristine condition, but the overall effect is still arresting. The numerous affiliates of the **Slovak Mining Museum** (www.muzeumbs.sk) in town include:

Open-air Mining Museum MUSEUM
(JK Hella 12; adult/child €5/2.50; ⊗8am-4pm Tue-Sun by tour) Take a trip down into a former working mine, 2km west of the centre.

Old Castle MUSEUM
(Starozámocká 1; adult/child €3/1.50; ⊗8am-4pm Tue-Sun by tour) Town history exhibits in a 16th-century stronghold.

New Castle CASTLE
(Novozámocká 1; adult/child €3/1.50; ⊗8am-4pm Tue-Sun by tour) Constructed only five years after the Old Castle; it has exhibits on the historical struggle against Turkish invasion.

⛏ Sleeping & Eating

Penzión Kachelman PENSION €€
(☏6922 319; www.kachelman.sk; Kammerhofská 18; s/d incl breakfast €43/70; ☎) Several large Renaissance buildings combine to form a fine inn and restaurant with rustic touches. The long and varied Slovak menu (mains €5 to €12), including grilled specialties, is worth trying. It's close to the bus stop, below the Old Town centre.

Hostel 6 HOSTEL €
(☏0905106706; www.hostel6.sk; Andreja Slackovica 6; dm/d €14/30; ☎@) A hospitable little backpackers hostel with thoroughly modern amenities inside an old building. Choose from a private double, or five- or six-bed dorms. Great balcony views, full kitchen and laundry.

Penzión Príjemný Oddych PENSION €
(☏6921 301; www.prijemnyoddych.sk; Starozámocká 3; r €30-36) Yellow walls and framed

folk embroidery keep this pension up near the Old Castle feeling light and, indeed, *prijemný* (pleasing). Small on-site restaurant, playground and sauna.

Mešianka
CAFE **€**

(Andreja Kmeťa 2; pizzas €3-6) A place that's part pastry cafe, part pizzeria and part beer garden? May seem an odd combination, but the wood-fired pies are quite good.

ℹ Information

City Tourist Information Office (☑6949 653; www.banskastiavnica.sk; Nám sv Trojice 3; ◷8am-4pm) Semiprecious stones and minerals for sale in addition to info; beneath a branch of the mining museum. Two internet terminals (per hour €1).

ℹ Getting There & Away

Banská Štiavnica is not the easiest place to get to. Only one direct bus daily departs from Bratislava (€8, 3½ hours), at 1pm. Otherwise, all bus and train arrivals require a change in Zvolen or Banská Bystrica. Check schedules at http://cp.atlas.sk.

WEST SLOVAKIA

Snaking along the Small Carpathians on the main route northeast of Bratislava, watch for hilltop castle ruins high above the Váh River. Trenčín's magnificent reconstructed castle is one of the most impressive along this once heavily fortified stretch.

Trenčín

☑032 / POP 60.000

Looming high above the 18th- and 19th-century buildings of the Old Town, Trenčín's mighty castle has all the dark foreboding you'd want from a medieval fortress. Today's form dates from around the 15th century, but the city is much older than that. Roman legionnaires fancied the site and stationed here (they called it Laugaricio) in the 2nd century AD. You can read the inscription to prove it. Afterwards, enjoy the sidewalk cafes and lively nightlife fuelled by the town's university population. The entire centre – including two large, interlocking pedestrian squares – is easily walkable.

◉ Sights

Trenčín Castle
FORTRESS

(www.muzeumtn.sk; adult/child €5/3; ◷9am-5.30pm) First noted in a Viennese chronicle of 1069, Trenčín Castle developed through the centuries until 1790 when it was damaged by fire. Much of what you see is reconstruction, but there are remnants that date to the earliest days. From the town, climb ever more stairs to reach the lowest level of fortifications and commanding views of the Váh River plain. Two levels higher you enter the various towers and furnished palaces with one of the frequent tours (75 minutes, in Slovak only; call two days ahead to arrange an English-speaking guide). The most evocative time to visit is during festivals and on summer weekend evenings during two-hour, torchlight tours – complete with medieval sword fighting, minstrels and staged frolics.

Roman inscription
ANCIENT SITE

The town's unique claim to fame is a Roman inscription of AD 179; soldier's graffiti commemorating a battle against Germanic tribes. It is actually carved into the cliff behind the **Hotel Tatra** (Ul gen MR Štefánika 2) and can only be viewed through a window in the hotel's staircase; ask at reception. The translation reads: 'To the victory of the emperor and the army which, numbering 855 soldiers, resided at Laugaricio. By order of Maximianus, legate of the 2nd auxiliary legion.'

Galéria Bazovského
MUSEUM

(www.gmab.sk; Palackého 27; adult/child €2/1; ◷9am-5pm Tue-Sun) Temporary exhibits at the Galéria Bazovského represent some of the best of 20th-century Slovak and Czech art. The main collection contains works by local painter Miloš Bazovský (1899–1968).

Town Gate Tower
HISTORIC BUILDING

(Mestská veža; Sládkovičova; adult/child €1/0.50; ◷10am-8pm, closed Nov-Mar) An inconspicuous glass elevator leads to the town gate entry, and six really steep flights later you emerge at a 360-degree view of the Old Town.

A few other small museums around town hold some interest, and there are historic buildings like the **Piarist Church** (Mierové nám) and the former 1913 **Synagogue** (Štúrovo nám) for exterior viewing.

🏃 Activities

Ostrov
BEACH

(off Mládežnícka) Floating in the middle of the Váh river, the Ostrov (island) is Trenčín's playground. A freely accessible, small,

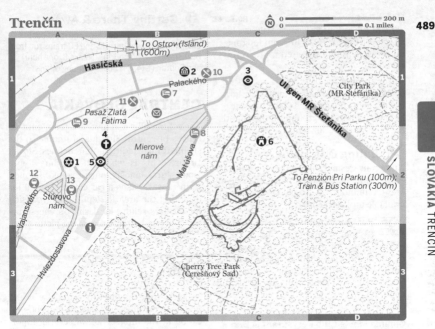

Trenčín

⊙ Sights
1 Former Synagogue.............................A2
2 Galéria Bazovského.........................B1
3 Hotel Tatra...C1
4 Piarist Church...................................A2
   Roman inscription.....................(see 3)
5 Town Gate Tower...............................A2
6 Trenčín Castle..................................C2

🛏 Sleeping
7 Grand Hotel.......................................B1
8 Hotel Pod Hradom.............................B2
9 Penzión Svorad.................................A1

🍴 Eating
10 Cinema Movie Club
   Restaurant & Bar..............................B1
11 Plzenská...B1

🍷 Drinking
12 Jamm Club...A2
13 Steps Bar...A2

sandy beach, volleyball court, swing sets and summer concessions are part of the attraction. At the time of research an outdoor pool with water slide was under construction here.

✨ Festivals & Events

World music, jazz, rock, techno, hip hop and alternative music are all represented in one weekend in July at the **Bazant Pohoda Festival** (www.pohodafestival.sk), the largest music festival in Slovakia.

🛏 Sleeping

Penzión pri Parku PENSION €
(☑0902979814; www.penzionpriparku.sk; Kragujevackých hrdinov 7; s/d €25/33; 🐾) Mod decor fills the eclectic nook-and-cranny rooms of this Victorian building in the park. Staying here you're near both train and bus stations.

Grand Hotel HOTEL €€
(☑7434 353; www.grand-hotel.sk; Palackého 34; s/d €63/70; 🌣@🐾) Perks at this super-central, contemporary hotel include free bike rental and whirlpool and sauna use. Rooms are awash in dark woods and upscale neutrals.

Penzión Svorad HOSTEL €
(☑7430 322; www.svorad-trencin.sk; Palackého 4; dm €18-32; 🐾) Peeling linoleum, thin mattresses – but oh, what castle views. This dormitory-like pension (with private bathrooms) resides in part of an old grammar school; maybe that's why the staff are so rule-obsessed.

Hotel Pod Hradom HOTEL €€
(☑7481 701; www.podhradom.sk; Matúšova 12; s €65-80, d €76-98; @) A 10-room lodging on a wee, winding street en route to the castle.

Autocamping na Ostrove CAMPING €
(☑7434 013; www.slovanet.sk/camping; Ostrov; tent site from €6, bungalow d €14) Riverside bungalow camping ground on the island has central space for tents.

✖ Eating & Drinking
Numerous restaurants and cafes line Mierové nám and Štúrovo nám; choose any one for imbibing al fresco. Quick eats are available on Palackého.

TOP CHOICE Reštaurácia Bašta SLOVAK €€
(Ostrove Zamarovce; mains €5-15; ⊙24hr) Some of the freshest, cooked-to-order Slovak faves we've ever tasted – pork stuffed with spicy *klobasa*, *bryndza* (sheep's cheese) cream soup... Breakfasts are tasty, too. Well worth the walk to the Ostrov (island).

Cinema Movie Club Restaurant & Bar
INTERNATIONAL €
(Palackého 33; mains €5-7; ☏) Chicken and risotto dishes at this student haunt are quite good, but the real deal is the weekday lunch set menu (under €4).

Plzenská SLOVAK €€
(Zlatá Fatima; mains €5-13) Dig into hearty Slovak fare in pub-like surrounds off the main square. Don't forget to get a frothy glass of Czech pilsner.

Steps Bar BAR
(Sládkovičova 4-6) Both the sidewalk cafe and the upstairs bar attract a hip, college-age crowd.

Jamm Club CLUB
(Štúrovo nám 5) Hosts occasional live jazz and blues (other nights are disco).

❶ Information
Cultural Information Centre (☑6504 294; www.visittrencin.sk; Sládkovičova 1; ⊙9am-6pm Mon-Fri, 8am-4pm Sat) Exceptionally helpful, well-informed staff give out handfuls of brochures for town and region. Good, free map available.

Library of Trenčín (Hasicska 1; ⊙7am-7pm Mon-Fri, 8am-1pm Sun) Free internet.

Main post office (Mierové nám 21)

VUB Bank (Mierové nám 37) ATM and exchange.

❶ Getting There & Away
Riding the rails is the quickest and most cost-efficient way to get here. IC and EC trains run from Bratislava (€9, 1½ hours), Žilina (€8, one hour) and Poprad (€14, 2¾ hours), among others.

CENTRAL SLOVAKIA

The rolling hills and low, forested mountain ranges of central Slovakia are home to the shepherding tradition that defines Slovak culture. This is where the nation's Robin Hood, Juraj Jánošík, once roamed. Limited train routes means a car can be helpful for exploring the area in depth. Look roadside for farmers selling local sheep's cheese before you head off into one of the picturesque valleys.

Žilina
☑041 / POP 85,300
A Slavic tribe in the 6th century was the first to recognise Žilina's advantageous location at the intersection of several important trade routes on the Váh River. Today it's still a transit point for exploring Malá Fatra National Park, surrounding fortresses and folksy villages. It's a pleasant little city, but there isn't much to see besides the old palace-like castle on the outskirts.

From the train station in the northeast, a walk along Národná takes you through Nám A Hlinku up to Mariánské nám, the main pedestrian square.

◉ Sights
Budatín Castle PALACE
(www.pmza.sk; Topoľová 1; adult/child €1/0.50; ⊙8am-5pm Tue-Sun) The small castle, 1½km north across the Váh River, is more palace than fortress. The museum inside contains exhibits of 18th- and 19th-century decorative arts as well as wire figures made by area tinkers.

🛏 Sleeping & Eating
The information office has a list of student dorms that take travellers in July and August. Interchangeable bars and cafes lie around Mariánske and Hlinka squares.

Hotel Dubna Skala HOTEL €€
(☑5079 100; www.hoteldubnaskala.sk; Hurbanova 8; s/d €95/105; ❄☏) Modern boutique interiors fit surprisingly well within an ornate 10th-century exterior. The well-regarded

BOJNICE & ORAVA CASTLES

Central Slovakia has numerous castles and ruins. Two of the more famous are a bit removed.

Bojnice Castle (Bojnice zámok; www.bojnicecastle.sk; adult/child €6/3; ☺9am-5pm Tue-Sun) is straight out of a fairy-tale dream, crowned with towers and turrets and crenulated mouldings. The original 12th-century fortification got an early-20th-century redo by the Pálffy family, who modelled it on French romantic castles. The time to visit is during the International Festival of Ghosts and Ghouls in May, when costumed guides put on shows throughout the castle and grounds. The palace also gets decked out for Christmas, Valentine's Day and various medieval events. The nearby city of Prievidza has bus connections to Žilina (€3, 1¼ hours, 10 daily), Bratislava (€8, 3¼ hours, eight daily) and others. From there take local bus 3 or 7 the 3km to Bojnice, a little town with lodging and restaurants.

The classic 1922 vampire film *Nosferatu* featured the pointed towers of **Orava Castle** (Oravský hrad; www.oravamuzeum.sk; Oravský Podzámok; adult/child €6/4; ☺8.30am-5pm, closed Apr), which rise from an impossibly narrow blade of rock. This, one of the most complete castles in Slovakia, dates from at least 1267. Later additions and reconstructions were, of course, made, most notably after a fire in 1800. The museum is chock full of weapons, folk art and period furniture. Legend has it that the castle contains one mirror where the reflection will make you beautiful, and another that will make you ugly – make sure to ask the difference. Below the castle in the tiny village of Oravsky Podzámok there's a pizza pub and a pension. Buses run at least hourly between there and Ružomberok (€2, 45 minutes), where you can transfer to the Bratislava–Košice train line. Buses run less frequently to Žilina (€2.50, 1½ hours, five daily). Another alternative is to transfer by train from the main line to a trunk line in Kraľovany (€1.50, 55 minutes, six daily).

wine-cellar restaurant here similarly juxtaposes old and new with clean white arches and stone wall accents.

Penzión Majovey HOTEL €€
(☑5624 152; www.slovanet.sk/majovey in Slovak; Jána Milca 3; s/d €35/60) The deep coral facade and central location are more interesting than the stark white rooms here, but the bathrooms are huge. Tile floors keep things cool throughout.

Kompas Café HOSTEL €
(☑0918481319; http://kompascafe.wordpress.com; Vojtecha Spanyola 37; dm €14) Pretty basic, two- to five-bed workers' dorms with a cafe and kitchen; 1km south of centre.

TOP CHOICE Voyage Voyage SLOVAK €€
(Mariánske nám 191; mains €5-12) A modernized Slovak menu here includes inventive dishes like chicken filet stuffed with peaches and cheese. Don't miss the ice-cream cocktails and milkshakes.

Pizzeria Carolina PIZZA €
(Národná 5; pizza & pasta €4-9) Outdoor cafe tables fill up fast at this student fave; dine downstairs to be near the salad bar.

ℹ Information

Main post office (Sládkovičova 1)

Tourist Information Office (TIK; ☑7233 186; www.zilina.sk; Republiky 1; ☺9am-5pm Mon-Fri, 9am-2pm Sat & Sun) Town and surrounding-area information available.

Volksbank (Národná 28) Bank and ATM near the train station.

ℹ Getting There & Away

Žilina is on the main railway line between Bratislava and Košice. Four daily IC (and many more, slower, 'fast') trains head to Bratislava (€11, 2½ hours), Trenčín (€8, one hour), Poprad (€11, 1½ hours) and Košice (€14, 2¾ hours).

Around Žilina

As well as nearby Malá Fatra National Park, a few folk-culture sights within an hour of Žilina are well worth exploring.

MARTIN

The town of Martin is primarily an industrial centre, but it has a number of small museums and the country's largest *skanzen* (open-air village museum). Traditional buildings from all over the region have been moved to the **Museum of the Slovak Village** (Múzeum Slovenské Dediny; www.snm-em.sk; adult/child €2/1; ☺9am-6pm Tue-Sun). It comes complete with working *krčma* (village pub). Contact the **Tourist Information Office** (☎4234776; www. tikmartin.sk; Štefánika 9A; ☺9am-5pm Mon-Fri) for more details. From Žilina it's easiest to take the bus the 35km to Martin (€1.50, 40 minutes, half-hourly). The village museum is 4km southeast of the city. Take local bus 10 from the main station to the last stop, Ľadovaň, and walk the remaining 1km up through the forest (or hail a taxi in town).

ČIČMANY

If you've seen a brochure or postcard of Slovakia, you've probably seen a photograph of **Čičmany** (www.cicmany.viapvt.sk); dark log homes painted with white geometric patterns fill the traditional village. This is no *skanzen*; most houses are private residences, but **Radenov House** (Čičmany 42; adult/child €2/1; ☺8am-4pm Tue-Sun) is a museum. There's a gift shop, a small restaurant and a pension in the long, narrow settlement. Buses run the 50 minutes south of Žilina (€2) five times a day; return times allow hours to wander and photograph.

VLKOLÍNEC

The folksy mountain village of **Vlkolínec** (www.vlkolinec.sk; adult/child €3/2; ☺9am-3pm), about 71km east and southeast of Žilina, is a Unesco-noted national treasure. The pastel paint and steep roofs on the 45 traditional plastered log cabins are remarkably well maintained. It's easy to imagine a *vlk* (wolf) wandering through this wooded mountainside settlement arranged along a small stream. You pay entry to walk around, and one of the buildings has been turned into a small house museum, but this is still a living village – if just barely. Of the approximately 40 residents, almost half are schoolchildren.

Three weekday-only buses make the 25-minute (€0.50) drive to Vlkolínec from the Ružomberok train station; last return is at 3:15pm. Otherwise, driving or hiking the 6km uphill from Ružomberok is the only way to get to the village. At least five direct trains a day stop in Ružomberok on their way from Bratislava (€12, 3½ hours) and Žilina (€3, one hour) to Poprad (€4, one hour).

Two kilometres west of Ružomberok, **Salaš Krajinka** (www.salaskrajinka.sk; E18; mains €4-11), is one of the country's best sheep dairy restaurants. Buy the *bryndza* and other products on-site, or sit down for a

full meal in the modern-rustic dining room with a glass wall looking into the barn.

Malá Fatra National Park

♫041

Sentinel-like formations stand watch at the rocky gorge entrance to the valley filled with pine-clad slopes above. The Malá Fatra National Park (Národný park Malá Fatra) incorporates a chocolate-box-pretty, 200-sq-km swathe of its namesake mountain range. The Vrátna Valley (Vrátna dolina), 25km east of Žilina, lies at the heart of the park. From here you can access the trailheads, ski lifts and a cable car to start your exploration. The long, one-street town of Terchová is at the lower end of the valley, Chata Vrátna is at the top. The village of Štefanová lies east of the main valley road, 1km uphill from Terchová.

◉ Sights

Statue of Juraj Jánošík   MONUMENT
Above the village of Terchová is an immense aluminium statue of Juraj Jánošík, Slovakia's Robin Hood. In early August, much dancing, singing and feasting go on beneath his likeness during the **Jánošík Days** folk festival.

Považké Museum   MUSEUM
(www.pmza.sk; Sv Cyrila a Metoda 96, Terchová; adult/child €2/1; ☺9am-3.30pm Tue-Sun) Check out the pictures, artefacts and drawings depicting the notorious highwayman Jánošík's exploits (and gruesome death) at the small museum above the town info office. Ask for the English-language narration.

Vrátna Valley   PARK
The road to **Vrátna Valley** (www.vratna.sk) in Malá Fatra National Park runs south from Terchová through the crags of **Tiesňavy Gorge**, past picnic sites and scenic stops. A **cable car** (Vratna Výtah; return adult/child €10/7; ☺9am-4.30pm mid-Jun-Sep & mid-Dec-mid-Apr) carries you from the top of the valley to **Snilovské saddle** (1524m) below two peaks, **Chleb** (1647m) and **Velký Kriváň** (1709m). Both are on the red ridge trail, one of the most popular in the park. A hike northeast from Chleb over **Hromové** (1636m), **Poludňový grúň** (1636m) and **Stoh** (1608m) to **Medziholie saddle** (1185m) takes about 5½ hours. From there you can descend for an hour on the green trail to Štefanová village where there's a bus stop, and places to stay and eat. Note that

the main summer season is July and August; during other months businesses may close for maintenance. For serious hiking, VKÚ's 1:50,000 Malá Fatra-Vrátna map (No 110) and Dajama's *Knapsacked Travel: Malá Fatra* are good.

🏃 Activities

The full complement of Vrátna Valley's 14 **ski tows and lifts** (⏱8am-4pm) are open from December to April. Shacks with **ski rental** (from €12 per day) keep the same hours and are located at Starý Dvor, where **ski passes** (per day adult/child €22/15) are also for sale.

In summer, in the same parking lot, the **Organization for Sport Activities** (📞0903546600; www.splavovanie.sk; Starý Dvor; ⏱9am-5pm Jul & Aug) rents mountain bikes and organises rafting trips.

🛏 Sleeping & Eating

Numerous private cottages are available for rent in the Terchová area, many listed on the information office websites. No camping is allowed in the park. The food situation in the valley isn't the best. There are a few food stands near the chairlifts and cable car, and most lodgings have restaurants. Otherwise, forage in Terchová.

Penzión Vŕšky PENSION €€
(📞5627 300; www.penzionvrsky.sk; Vŕšky, Terchová; r €48, cottages €138-199; ❄🤶) Built in 2010 on a hill above the road to Terchová, this log-cabin lodge may seem better situated for those with cars, but it does allow backdoor access to the park. Simple-but-spotless rooms have natural wood furnishings; roomy cottages sleep six. Don't miss the restaurant's original take on Slovak food (mains €6 to €13).

Penzión Sagan PENSION €
(📞0903744302; www.penzionsagan.sk; Štefanová 553; s/d incl breakfast €30/50; ❄🤶) Pine-clad rooms couldn't be more impeccably kept, nor could the smiling staff and fireplace in the little restaurant be more welcoming. Look for the homely guesthouse tucked way back into Štefanová village.

Hotel Boboty HOTEL €€
(📞5695 228; www.hotelboboty.sk; Nový Dvor; s/d €60/80; @🤶🏊) Services galore – sauna, massage, heated pool, billiards, free ski shuttle – are available at the valley's biggest lodging.

Chata Vrátna MOUNTAIN HUT €
(📞5695 739; http://chata.vratna.org; Vrátna vyťah; d/tr €22/30) Muddy hikers, giggling children and a fragrant wood-smoke aroma fill this well-worn, basic chalet near the cable car at the top of Vrátna Valley.

Reštaurácia Starý Majer SLOVAK €
(📞5695 419; mains €5-10; ⏱10am-9pm) Dig into well-done traditional sheepherders' dishes at rough-hewn outdoor tables, or inside among rustic farm implements.

Chata na Grúni MOUNTAIN HUT €
(📞5695 324; www.chatanagruni.sk; dm €11) Hiker's hut at the top of Gruni Ski Lift; four- to six-bed dorms and self-service restaurant.

Autocamping Belá CAMPING GROUND €
(📞5621 478; http://camping.bela.sk; camping site €4-9; ⏱May–mid-Oct; 🏊) A fine camping ground with 300 sites, a heated pool and food stand. There's a bus stop in front; 5km west of Terchová.

ℹ Information

Mountain Rescue Service (Horská Záchranná služba; 📞5695 232; http://his.hzs.sk/; Štefanová) Rescue service and weather info.

Terchová Tourist Information Centre (📞5695 307; www.ztt.sk; Sv Cyrila a Metoda 96, Terchová; ⏱8am-4pm Mon-Fri, 10am-1pm Sat & Sun) Knick-knacks and maps for sale; ATM in building.

Turistcko-Informačna Chalupa (📞0907534354; www.uteczmesta.sk; Vrátňanská cesta, Terchová; ⏱8am-8pm)

WORTH A TRIP

GOING LOCAL IN LIPTOV

From the high plain southeast of the Malá Fatra, you can see no fewer than five surrounding mountain ranges. The rolling hills and dales of the **Liptov** (www.liptov.sk) region make a lovely place to stay. From here you can easily reach most Central Slovak sights on a day trip – if you have a car (buses requires much transferring). **Jasna** (www.jasna.sk), in Low Tatras National Park, is a favourite winter playground with a relatively new summer–winter cable car. Several thermal spas are found in the area. Driving past all the farmer's stands in the region selling sheep chese, you'll know you've gone local.

Malá Fatra National Park

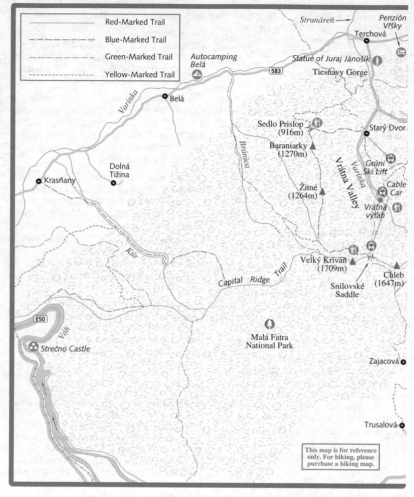

———————	Red-Marked Trail
—··—··—··—	Blue-Marked Trail
— — — — —	Green-Marked Trail
-----------	Yellow-Marked Trail

Strunáreň

Penzión Vŕšky

Terchová

Autocamping Belá

Statue of Juraj Jánošík

Tiesňavy Gorge

583

Belá

Varinka

Sedlo Prislop (916m)

Starý Dvor

Baraniarky (1270m)

Branica

Grúni Ski Lift

Žitné (1264m)

Vrátna Valley

Varinka

Cable Car

Vrátna výťah

Dolná Tižina

Krasňany

Velký Kriváň (1709m)

Capital Ridge Trail

Kŕ

Snilovské Saddle

Chleb (1647m)

E50

Strečno Castle

Váh

Malá Fatra National Park

Zajacová

Trusalová

This map is for reference only. For hiking, please purchase a hiking map.

Private office arranges lodging and sport activates, provides info and sells books and maps.

ℹ Getting There & Around

Almost hourly buses link Žilina with Terchová (€1.60, 40 minutes) and valley stops, terminating near Chata Vrátna at Vrátna výťah (€2, one hour). Or you can change in Terchová for local buses. Check schedules at www.cp.atlas.sk.

EAST SLOVAKIA

Alpine peaks in Slovakia? As you look upon the snow-strewn jagged mountains rising like an apparition east of Liptovský Mikuláš, you may think you're imagining things. But there they are indeed. Hiking the High Tatras is undoubtedly the highlight of the region, but in eastern Slovakia you can also admire ancient architecture, explore castle ruins, seek out small villages and visit the country's second city.

High Tatras

♪052

The High Tatras (Vysoké Tatry), the tallest range in the Carpathian Mountains, tower

Not that the fact has arrested development on the Slovak ski slopes, much to the chagrin of watchdog groups like International Union for Conservation of Nature.

Mid-mountain, three main resort towns string west to east. Štrbské Pleso is the traditional ski centre and is most crowded, with condos and construction galore. Eleven kilometres east, Smokovec is an amalgam of the Nový (New), Starý (Old) and Horný (upper) settlements. Here you still have some turn-of-the-20th-century heyday feel, plus numerous lodging options, eateries and the most services. Five kilometres further, Tatranská Lomnica is the quaintest and the quietest village. All have mountain access by cable car, funicular or chairlift. Poprad is the closest sizeable city (with mainline train station and airport), 14km south of central Starý Smokovec.

When planning your trip, keep in mind that the highest trails are closed to snow from November to mid-June. June and July can be especially rainy; July and August are the warmest (and most crowded) months. Hotel prices and crowds are at their lowest from October to April.

⊙ Sights & Activities

A 600km network of trails covers the alpine valleys and some peaks, with full-service mountain huts where hikers can stop for a meal or a rest along the way. Routes are colour coded and easy to follow. Pick up one of the numerous detailed maps and hiking guides available at bookstores and information offices. Park regulations require you to keep to the trails and refrain from picking flowers. Be aware that most of the trails are rocky and uneven, watch for sudden thunderstorms on ridges and peaks where there's no protection, and know that the assistance of the Mountain Rescue Service is not free.

SMOKOVEC RESORTS

From Starý Smokovec a **funicular railway** (www.vt.sk; adult/child return €7/5; ⊙7am-7pm Jul & Aug, 8am-5pm Sep-Jun) takes you up to **Hrebienok** (1280m). From here you have a great view of the **Veľká Studená Valley** and a couple of hiking options. The red **Tatranská Magistrála Trail** transects the southern slopes of the High Tatras for 65km start to finish. Bilíkova chata (p498), a log-cabin lodge and restaurant, is only a 10-minute hike from Hrebienok. Following the Magistrála east on an easy trail section to **Studený Potok** waterfalls takes about 30 minutes. Heading west instead, you could follow the

over most of Eastern Europe. Some 25 peaks measure above 2500m. The massif is only 25km wide and 78km long, but photo opportunities at higher elevations are enough to get you fantasising about a career with National Geographic – pristine snowfields, ultramarine mountain lakes, crashing waterfalls and rocky slopes... Down below, traditionally thick pine forests took a beating in a serious wind storm, but the newly formed meadows are making a comeback. Since 1949 most of this jagged range has been included in the Tatra National Park (Tanap), complementing a similar park across the peaks in Poland.

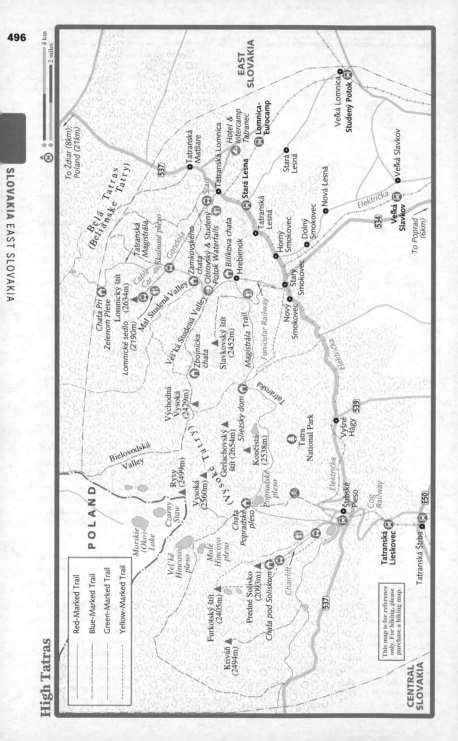

High Tatras

Legend:
- Red-Marked Trail
- Blue-Marked Trail
- Green-Marked Trail
- Yellow-Marked Trail

This map is for reference only. For hiking, please purchase a hiking map.

CENTRAL SLOVAKIA

EAST SLOVAKIA

POLAND

Belá Tatras (Belianske Tatry)

Vysoké Tatry (Vysoké Tatry)

Tatra National Park

To Ždiar (8km); Poland (21km)

To Poprad (6km)

Scale: 0 – 4 km / 0 – 2 miles

Locations and features:
- Tatranská Matliare
- Tatranská Lomnica
- Hotel & Intercamp Tatranec
- Stará Lesná
- Lomnica-Eurocamp
- Veľká Lomnica, Studený Potok
- Stará Lesná
- Veľká Slavkov
- Nová Lesná
- Tatranská Lesná
- Veľká Slavkov
- Horný Smokovec
- Dolný Smokovec
- Starý Smokovec
- Nový Smokovec
- Hrebienok
- Bílíkova chata
- Obrovský & Studený Potok Waterfalls
- Zamkovského chata
- Skalnaté pleso
- Chata Pri Zelenom Plese
- Lomnický sedlo (2190m)
- Lomnický štít (2634m)
- Malá Studená Valley
- Veľká Studená Valley
- Zbojnícka chata
- Slavkovský štít (2452m)
- Východná Vysoká (2429m)
- Sliezsky dom
- Gerlachovský štít (2654m)
- Končistá (2538m)
- Magistrála Trail
- Funicular Railway
- Tatranská
- Vyšné Hágy
- Bielovodská Valley
- Rysy (2499m)
- Vysoká (2560m)
- Čzarny Staw
- Morskie (Oko) Lake
- Veľká Hincovo pleso
- Malé Hincovo pleso
- Popradské pleso
- Chata Popradské pleso
- Štrbské Pleso
- Cog Railway
- Tatranská Lieskovec
- Tatranská Štrba
- Furkotský štít (2405m)
- Predné Solisko (2093m)
- Chata pod Soliskom
- Chairlift
- Kriváň (2494m)
- Električka

Roads: 537, 534, 539, E50

Magistrála to the lakeside **Sliezsky dom** hut (two hours), down a small green connector trail, to the yellow-marked trail back to Starý Smokovec (four hours total).

Mountain climbers scale to the top of **Slavkovský štít** (2452m) via the blue trail from Starý Smokovec (seven to eight hours return). To ascend the peaks without marked hiking trails (**Gerlachovský štít** included), you must hire a guide. Contact the **Mountain Guides Society Office** (☑4422 066; www.tatraguide.sk; Starý Smokovec 38; ☺10am-6pm Mon-Fri, noon-6pm Sat & Sun, closed weekends Oct-May); guides cost from €150, and the society runs classes too.

At the top of the funicular, tow-assist snow sledging and summer tubing are to be had at **Funpark** (Hrebienok; per ride €1.50; ☺10am-4pm July & Aug, 9am-4pm Dec-Feb).

Rent mountain bikes at **Tatrasport** (www.tatry.net/tatrasport; Starý Smokovec 38; per day €15; ☺8am-noon&1-6pm), above the bus-station parking lot.

TATRANSKÁ LOMNICA & AROUND

While in the Tatras, you shouldn't miss the ride to the precipitous 2634m summit of **Lomnický štít** (bring a jacket!). From Lomnica, a large **gondola** (www.vt.sk; adult/child return €13/9; ☺8.30am-7pm Jul & Aug, to 4pm Sep-Jun) pauses mid-station at **Štart** before it takes you to the winter sports area, restaurant and lake at **Skalnaté pleso**. From there, a smaller **cable car** (www.vt.sk; adult/child return €20/14; ☺8.30am-5.30pm Jul & Aug, to 3.30pm Sep-Jun) goes on to the summit. The second leg of the journey requires a time-reserved ticket. On sunny summer days time slots do sell out, so get in line early. You're given 50 minutes at the top to admire the views, walk the observation platforms and sip a beverage in the cafe before your return time.

One of the top Tatra day hikes starts from Skalnaté pleso, following the rocky Magistrála Trail west past amazingly open views back into the forest at **Zamkovského chata** (1½ hours), an atmospheric mountain hut and restaurant (p499). Continue down hill, along the even rockier, steeper path past the **Obrovský** and **Studený Potok** waterfalls on to Hrebienok (three hours total). From there the funicular takes you down to Starý Smokovec.

Get off the cable car at Štart and you're at **Funtools** (www.vt.sk; cable car plus 1 ride €9; ☺9am-6pm Jun-Sep), from where you can take a fast ride down the mountain on a two-wheeled scooter, a luge-like three-wheel cart or on a four-wheel modified skateboard.

DON'T MISS

HIGH TATRA HIKES

The 65km-long **Magistrála Trail** may start at the base of the Western (Zapadné) Tatras, but most of it runs beneath the peaks (between 1300m and 1800m) of the **High Tatras**. Because there's a relatively small elevation change, the trail is accessible by cable-assisted cars and lifts, and there are huts to stop and eat at, you need not be in peak mountaineering shape to experience it. Some of our favourite routes are Skalnaté pleso to Hrebienok, Štrbské Pleso to Popradské pleso, and Skalnaté pleso to Chata pri Zelenom plese.

In recent years much winter sport development has taken place on the slopes above Tatranská Lomnica; the area now counts about 30 skiable hectares. From Skalnaté pleso a high-speed winter **quad lift** (☺9am-4pm) hoists riders to **Lomnické sedlo**, a 2190m saddle below the summit, and access to an advanced 6km-long ski run (1300m drop). A multimillion-euro renovation also added a high-speed **six-seat chair lift** (☺9am-4pm) from the village up to Štart, snow-making capacity and a ski-in/ski-out car park. **Vysoké Tatry** (www.vt.sk; Tatranská Lomnica 7, Tatranská Lomnica; day lift ticket adult/child €24/17; ☺9am-3.30pm Dec-Apr) sells passes from the base of the cable car, where ski rental (from €12 per day) and lockers are also available.

ŠTRBSKÉ PLESO & AROUND

Condo and hotel development continue unabated in the village, but the namesake clear blue glacial lake (*pleso*) is surrounded by dark pine forest and rocky peaks and remains beautiful. **Row boats** (per 45min €10-15; ☺10am-6pm May-Sep) are for rent from the dock in front of the Grand Hotel Kempinski.

In good weather the streets are overrun, as one of the most popular day hikes departs from here. Follow the red-marked **Magistrála Trail** uphill from the train station on a rocky forest trail for about 1¼ hours to **Popradské pleso**, an even more idyllic lake at 1494m. The busy mountain hut there (p499) is like a hotel, with a large, self-service restaurant. You can return to the train line by following the paved road down to the Popradské pleso stop (45 minutes). Or the Magistrála zigzags dramatically up the

ℹ️ MULTI-RESORT SKI PASSES

Recently Park Snow and Vysoký Tatry resorts, the ski concessions in Štrbské Pleso and Tatranská Lomnica respectively, have joined forces to offer multi-day, multi-resort lift passes (three days €69 per adult). The **Super Slovak Ski Pass** (http://skipass.jasna.sk) covers not only the resorts listed here, but other smaller ski areas around the country.

mountainside from Popradské pleso and then traverses east towards Sliezsky dom and the Hrebienok funicular above Starý Smokovec (four hours).

There is also a year-round **chairlift** (www.parksnow.sk; adult/child return €7.50/5; ⊗8am-3.30pm) up to **Chata pod Soliskom** (p499), from where it's a one-hour walk north along a red trail to the 2093m summit of **Predné Solisko**.

Park Snow (www.parksnow.sk; Areál FIS; day lift ticket adult/child €24/17; ⊗8.30am-3.30pm), Štrbské Pleso's poplar ski and snowboard resort, has two chairlifts, four tow lines, 12km of easy to moderate runs, one jump and a snow-tubing area.

🛏️ Sleeping

For a full listing of Tatra lodgings, look online at www.tatryinfo.eu. Cheaper sleeps are available in small settlements like Nová Lesná down the hill or east over the ridge at Ždiar (p501) in the Belá Tatras. No wild/backcountry camping is permitted: there is a camping ground near Tatranská Lomnica. For the quintessential Slovak mountain experience, you can't beat hiking from one *chata* (a mountain hut; could be anything from a shack to a chalet) to the next, high up among the peaks. Food (optional meal service or restaurant) is always available. Beds fill up, so book ahead.

SMOKOVEC RESORTS

Look for reasonable, been-there-forever boarding houses with one-word names like 'Delta' just west of the Nový Smokovec electric train stop on the several no-name streets that run to the south.

TOP CHOICE **Penzión Tatra** PENSION €
(📞0903650802; www.tatraski.sk; Starý Smokovec 66; s/d incl breakfast €25/50; @🗗) Big

and colourful modern rooms fill the classic 1900 alpinesque building above the train station. It's super central. Choose to have your breakfast in the large common room, or out on the terrace. Billiard table and ski storage available.

Villa Siesta HOTEL €€
(📞4423 024; www.villasiesta.sk; Nový Smokovec 88; r €52-64, ste €64-113; 🗗) Light fills this airy, contemporary mountain villa furnished in natural hues. The full restaurant, sauna and Jacuzzi are a bonus.

Villa Mon Ami B&B €€
(📞4423 024; www.monami.sk; Nový Smokovec 31; r/apt incl breakfast €50/110; @🗗) Scrolled ironwork beds, chandeliers and lobby fireplace make Mon Ami a romantic option. The three-story, half-timber villa is set in a park on the main drag.

Grand Hotel HOTEL €€€
(📞4870 000; www.grandhotel.sk; Starý Smokovec 38; r €90-190; 🗗🞉) More than 100 years of history are tied up in Starý Smokovec's grande dame. Rooms could use an update.

Mountain huts above the resorts:

Bilíkova chata MOUNTAIN HUT €
(📞4422 439; www.bilikovachata.sk; Hrebienok; s/d without bathroom €25/50) Basic log-cabin hotel with full-service restaurant among the clouds; only a seven-minute walk from the Hrebienok funicular station.

Zbojnícka chata MOUNTAIN HUT €
(📞0903638000; www.zbojnickachata.sk; dm incl breakfast €15) Sixteen-bed dorm room, self-service eatery and small kitchen; at 1960m, four-plus hours' hike up from Hrebienok.

TATRANSKÁ LOMNICA & AROUND

Look for private rooms (*privat* or *zimmer frei*), from €15 per person, on the back streets south and east of the train station. You can book ahead online at www.tatry.sk and www.tanap.sk/homes.html.

Grandhotel Praha HOTEL €€
(📞4467 941; www.grandhotelpraha.sk; s/d incl breakfast €110/155; @🞉) Remember when travel was elegant and you dressed for dinner? Well, the 1899 Grandhotel's sweeping marble staircase and crystal chandeliers do. Rooms are appropriately classic, and there's a snazzy spa here, high above the village.

Penzión Encian PENSION €
(☑4467 520; www.tatry.sk/encian; Tatranská Lomnica 36; s/d €30/47; @) Steep roofs, overflowing flowerboxes and a small restaurant hearth give Encian an appropriate mountain appeal. No genuine nonsmoking rooms, and a mercurial owner.

More mountain huts and camping grounds in this area:

TOP CHOICE **Zamkovského chata** MOUNTAIN HUT €
(☑4422 636; www.zamka.sk; per person €15-20) Atmospheric wood chalet with four-bed bunk rooms and restaurant; great hike stop midway between Skalnaté Pleso and Hrebienok.

Chata pri Zelenom plese MOUNTAIN HUT €
(☑4467 420; www.zelenepleso.sk; dm €15) Fifty-bed lakeside lodging at 1540m; about 2½ hours hike east of Skalnaté Pleso, en route to the Belá Tatras.

Rijo Camping CAMPING GROUND €
(☑4467 493; www.rijocamping.eu; Stará Lesná 52; campsites €5-7.50; ☺May-Sep) Pine trees shade much of the field at this small, tent-only site, 1km north of Stará Lesná bus stop.

Hotel & Intercamp Tatranec CAMPING GROUND €
(☑4467 092; www.hoteltatranec.com; Tatranská Lomnica 202; campsites €6-9, r €40, cabin €60) Ageing six-person cabins, motel and restaurant – with an open tent field. North of the 'T Lomnica zast' stop on the train line to Studený Potok.

ŠTRBSKÉ PLESO & AROUND

Development and crowds make staying in this village our last choice, with one grand exception.

Grand Hotel Kempinski LUXURY HOTEL €€€
(☑3262 222; www.kempinski-hightatras.com; Kupelna 6; r €199-300; 割@≋) Far and away the swankiest Tatra accommodation: the classic, villa-like Kempinski entices high-end travellers with evening turndown service, heated marble bathroom floors and incredible lake views. Take a swim in the luxury spa and see the mountains stretch before you through two-storey glass.

Chata pod Soliskom MOUNTAIN HUT €
(☑0917655446; www.chatasolisko.sk; dm €16) Small log hostel (eight beds), nice terrace,

no hiking required; next to the chairlift terminus at 1800m.

Chata Popradské pleso MOUNTAIN HUT €
(☑4492 177; www.popradskepleso.sk; dm €16, r €36-70) Sizeable mountain hotel with restaurant and bar. It's a one-hour rugged hike up from the village or a paved hike up from Popradské pleso train stop.

✗ Eating & Drinking

The resort towns are close enough that it's easy to sleep in one and eat in another. There's at least a small grocery in each town. Nightlife is limited here; what's there is mostly in Starý Smokovec.

SMOKOVEC RESORTS

A couple of oft-changing discos are scattered around; ask for the latest when you arrive.

TOP CHOICE **Reštaurácia Svišť** SLOVAK €€
(☑4422 545; Nový Smokovec 30; mains €5-11) From hearty dumplings to beef filet with a wine reduction, this stylish Slovak restaurant does it all well – and surprisingly reasonably. At weekends you may want to reserve.

Pizzeria La Montanara ITALIAN €
(Starý Smokovec 22; mains €4-7) A local favourite, La Montanara serves good pies, pastas, soups and vegetables. It's above a grocery on the eastern edge of town.

Tatry Pub PUB
(Tatra Komplex, Starý Smokovec; ☺3pm-1am Sun-Thu, 3pm-3am Fri & Sat; ☎) The official watering hole of the Mountain Guide Club is a lively place to drink, with a full schedule of dart tournaments, concerts and the like.

Cafe Hoepfner CAFE €
(Hotel Smokovec, Starý Smokovec 22; cakes €1-3) Friendly, local cafe with cakes and coffees; live jazz summer Saturday evenings.

Koliba Smokovec SLOVAK €
(Starý Smokovec 5; mains €7-15; ☺3-10pm) A traditional rustic grill restaurant; some evening folk music.

TATRANSKÁ LOMNICA & AROUND
Hikers can carb-load at the predictable Slovak eateries by the train station.

Reštaurácia U Medveda CZECH & SLOVAK €€
(Tatranská Lomnica 88; mains €5-12) A good, off-the-beaten-track choice (south by the post office) for traditional cooking. Grilled specialties are a highlight.

Vila Park Reštaurácia SLOVAK €€
(Hotel Vila Park, Tatranská Lomnica 40; mains €8-12) What a treat to see fresh vegetables as main ingredients and sides. Slovak dishes here have a distinct international flair.

Humno BAR
(cable car station base; ⊙10am-midnight Sun-Thu, until 3am Fri & Sat) It's a club, it's cocktail bar, it's an après-ski... With a capacity of 300, one of Lomnica's newest ventures can afford to be a little of everything.

ŠTRBSKÉ PLESO & AROUND
Food stands line the road above the train station, on the way to Aréal FIS and the chair lift.

Koliba Patria SLOVAK €€
(southern lake shore, Štrbské pleso; mains €6-15) Come here for the lovely lakeside terrace and complex meat dishes. The trappings are definitely more refined than a typical *koliba* (rustic mountain restaurant serving Slovak sheepherder specialties).

Samoobslužná Reštaurácia SLOVAK €
(Hotel Toliar, Štrbské pleso 21; mains €2-6; ⊙7am-10pm) The self-service cafeteria has one-dish meals (goulash, chicken stir-fry etc) and vegetarian options.

ⓘ Information
All three main resort towns have ATMs on the main street.

Emergency
Mountain Rescue Service (✆emergency 18 300; http://his.hzs.sk/; Starý Smokovec 23)

Internet Access
Galérka Cafe (Hotel Toliar, Štrbské Pleso 21; per hr €2; ⊙8am-midnight; 🛜) Two terminals available for public rental.

Townson Travel (Tatranská Lomnica 94; per hr €2; ⊙9am-5pm Mon-Fri) A travel agency with one public computer.

U Michalka Café (Starý Smokovec 4; per hr €2; ⊙10am-10pm; 🛜) Pleasant cafe with four terminals, great tea and strudel.

Tourist Information
Note that information offices do not book rooms; they hand out a brochure listing some – not all – accommodation.

Tatra Information Office Starý Smokovec (TIK; ✆4423 440; Starý Smokovec 23; ⊙8am-8pm Mon-Fri, to 1pm Sat) Largest area info office, with the most brochures.

TIK Štrbské Pleso (✆4492 391; Štrbské Pleso; ⊙8am-4pm) Provides good trail info especially; uphill north from the Hotel Toliar.

TIK Tatranská Lomnica (✆4468 118; Cesta Slobody; ⊙10am-6pm Mon-Fri, 9am-1pm Sat) Has the most helpful staff; opposite Penzión Encian on the main street.

Travel Agencies
T-Ski Travel (✆4423 200; www.slovakiatravel. sk; Starý Smokovec 46; ⊙9am-4pm Mon-Thu, to 5pm Fri-Sun) Books lodging, arranges ski and mountain-bike programs, offers rafting and other outside-the-Tatras tours. Located at the funicular station.

Websites
High Tatras Tourist Trade Association (www. tatryinfo.eu) Comprehensive overview of area, including accommodation.

Tatra National Park (www.tanap.org) National park website.

Tatry.sk (www.tatry.sk) Official website of Tatra towns; look under 'Maps' for village layouts.

ⓘ Getting There & Around
To reach the Tatras by public transport, you'll need to switch in Poprad. From there a narrow-gauge electric train makes numerous stops in the resort towns along the main road; buses go to smaller, downhill villages as well. Either way, to get between Štrbské pleso and Tatranská Lomnica, you have to change in Starý Smokovec. Check schedules at www.cp.atlas.sk.

Train
During daylight hours, electric trains (TEZ) run at least every two hours. You can buy individual TEZ tickets at stations, and block tickets (one to three used) additionally at tourist offices. Validate all on board.

BUSES FROM THE TATRAS

ROUTE	COST (€)	DURATION (MIN)	FREQUENCY (DAILY)
Poprad–Starý Smokovec	0.85	20	every 30min
Poprad–Tatranská Lomnica	1.10	30	hourly
Poprad–Štrbské pleso	1.60	60	every 45min
Tatranská Lomnica–Ždiar	1	25	8

ROUTE	COST (€)	DURATION (MIN)
Poprad–Starý Smokovec	0.70	25
Poprad–Tatranská Lomnica	0.80	25
Poprad–Štrbské pleso	1.30	75
Štrbské pleso–Starý Smokovec	1	40
Štrbské pleso–Tatranská Lomnica	0.60	10

Belá Tatras

☑052

Travel east over the High Tatra mountain ridges and you start to hear Slovak spoken with a Polish accent. The Goral folk culture is an intricate part of the experience in the small Belianské Tatry (Belá Tatras). Traditional wooden cottages, some with striking red-and-white graphic designs, are still the building method of choice in the main village of Ždiar. A rustic, laid-back, much more local-oriented atmosphere pervades around town. From here it's an easy day trip or journey on to Poland; heck, it's almost close enough to walk.

ŽDIAR

Decorated timber cottages line long and narrow Ždiar, the oldest mountain settlement, inhabited since the 16th century. Goral traditions have been both bolstered and eroded by tourism. Several sections of the village are historical reservations, including the **Ždiar House Museum** (Ždiarsky dom; adult/child €3/1.50; ⊙10am-4pm Tue-Sun), a tiny, tiny place with colourful local costumes and furnishings.

Cross over the main road from the museum and a green trail skirts the river through **Monkova Valley** (880m), a level hike with very little elevation change. After 45 minutes the trail climbs up over **Širkové saddle** (1826m) and gets you to **Kopské saddle** (1750m) in about four hours total (seven hours return). Past this point you've crossed into the High Tatras; Chata pri Zelenom plese (p499) is an hour away and the cable car to Tatranská Lomnica is 2½ hours beyond that.

West of the main road there are two ski areas; in summer one becomes **Bikepark Bachledova** (www.skibachledova.sk; ⊙9am-4pm mid-Jul–mid-Sep). Here you can rent mountain bikes (from €5 per hour), chairlift them up the hill (€4 per ride) and thunder down.

🛏 Sleeping & Eating

Ždiar has a large number of pensions and *privaty* (here private rooms are sizeable lodgings with shared-facility rooms for rent, from €11 per person). Odds are pretty good if you just show up, or check www.zdiar.sk under *ubytovanie*.

TOP CHOICE **Ginger Monkey Hostel**   HOSTEL €
(☑4498 084; www.gingermonkey.eu; Ždiar 294; dm/d €13/30; @令) Crushing mountain views from a comfy old Goral-style house, hot tea at any hour, laundry, free breakfast, and a surprising sense of community... Clearly the world-travelling owner/managers have picked up a tip or two along the way. The place has a full kitchen, where a communal dinner may be cooking (by donation), or at the weekend the whole group might go out to a local eatery together. Don't just book one night; you'll end up extending. Cat, dog and chickens on site.

Penzión Kamzík   PENSION €
(☑4498 226; www.penzionkamzik.sk; Ždiar 513; s/d €13/30; 令) Staff at the Kamzík are every bit as cheerful as the pension's vibrant apricot exterior. Some of the modern rooms come with balconies. Small restaurant, table tennis, billiards and sauna.

Goral Krčma   SLOVAK €
(☑4498 138; Ždiar 460; mains €3-6) A traditional 'village pub' restaurant, this *krčma* serves all the regional specialities, like potato pancakes stuffed with a spicy sauté.

Rustika Pizzeria   ITALIAN €
(Ždiar 334; pizza €4-6; ⊙5-10pm) Wood-fired pizza in a rambling old log house midvillage.

Ždiarsky Dom   SLOVAK €
(Ždiar 55; mains €3-6) Rustic Slovak cooking next door to the little museum.

ⓘ Information

PLP Shop (☑0903642492; Ždiar 333; ⏰9am-noon & 3-6pm) Souvenir shop, info office, bicycle rental (from €10 per day) and internet use (€2 per hour).

ⓘ Getting There & Away

Bus is the only way to get to the Belá Tatras. Poland (open EU border) is 14km north of Žiar. For Slovak schedules, check www.cp.atlas.sk; for Polish, see also http://strama.eu. Buses from Ždiar connect directly with Poprad (€1, one hour, 11 daily), Starý Smokovec (€1.60, 40 minutes, 11 daily), Tatranská Lomnica (€1, 30 minutes, 21 daily) and Zakopane, Poland (€2.50, 50 minutes, two daily).

Poprad

☑052 / POP 55,000

The nearest sizeable city to the High Tatras, Poprad has all the major services and is an important transport hub. Otherwise, the modern city's attraction is limited to an interesting suburb and a thermal water park. From the adjacent train and bus stations, the central pedestrian square, Nám sv Egídia, is a five-minute walk south on Alžbetina.

⊙ Sights & Activities

Spišská Sobota   SQUARE
Sixteenth-century Spiš-style merchants' and artisans' houses line the Spišská Sobota town square. The suburb is 1.2km northeast of Poprad's train station.

Aqua City   BATHHOUSE
(www.aquacitypoprad.sk; Športová 1397; per day €15-30; ⏰9am-9pm) Sauna, swim, bubble and slide zones are all part of Poprad's thermal water park. Among the admirably green initiatives here, the heat and electricity derive from geothermal and solar sources.

🛏 Sleeping & Eating

There's a large Billa grocery store just east of the bus station.

Hotel Cafe Razy   PENSION €
(☑7764 101; www.hotelcaferazy.sk; Nám Sv Egídia 58; s/d €36/56) Sane and simple rooms upstairs (some wi-fi); semi-crazy pub and pizza cafe down. On the modern main square.

Penzión Sabato   B&B €€
(☑7769 580; www.sabato.sk; Sobotské nám 6, Spišská Sobota; r incl breakfast €70-110; 🛜) Exposed stone arches, cobblestone courtyard and open-hearth restaurant reveal this inn's 17th-century age – as do romantically decorated rooms.

Hotel Sobota   HOTEL €€
(☑4663 121; www.hotelsobota.sk; Kežmarská 15, Spišská Sobota; s/d incl breakfast €45/59; ✱@🛜) Modern construction with old slate-and-timber aesthetic. Full restaurant.

ⓘ Information

City Information Centre (☑7721 700; www.poprad.sk; Dom Kultúry Štefániková 72; ⏰8am-5pm Mon-Fri, 9am-noon Sat) Town info only, lists private rooms.

ⓘ Getting There & Away

AIR Poprad-Tatry International airport (www.airport-poprad.sk; Na Letisko 100) is 5km west of centre. Note that at the time of research it didn't receive any regular flights.

BUS Buses go to and from Levoča (€1.60, 30 minutes, hourly), Bardejov (€4.50, 2¼ hours, four daily) and Zakopane, Poland (€5, two hours, two daily).

CAR Pick-up around town is available by prearrangement from **Car Rental Tatran** (☑0903250255; www.autopozicovnatatry.sk).

TRAIN For more on the electric trains that traverse the 14km or so to the High Tatras resorts, see p519. Mainline trains run directly to Bratislava (€16, four hours, four IC trains daily), Trenčín (€14, 2¾ hours, four IC trains daily) and Košice (€5, 1½ hours, 12 daily).

Kežmarok

☑052 / POP 17,400

Snuggled beneath the broody peaks of the High Tatras, Kežmarok's pocket-sized Old Town square with distinct churches and small castle seems especially agreeable. Look for the influence of original 13th-century Germanic settlers in the architecture even today. During July the **European Folk Craft Market** – one of the nation's largest – comes to town.

From the adjacent bus and train stations, 1km northwest of the pedestrian centre, follow Dr Alexandra street to the main square, Hlavné nám. The red-and-green, pseudo-Moorish **New Evangelical Church** (cnr Toporcerova & Hviezdoslavovo; admission €2; ⏰10am-noon & 2-4pm Tue-Sat, closed Nov-Apr), c 1894, dominates the south end of town. Admission covers entry to the much more evocative **Old Wooden Evangelical Church**, built in 1717 without a single nail. It has an amazing interior of carved and painted wood, as well as an original organ.

At the other end of the square, the small, mansionlike **Kežmarok Castle** (Hradné nám 45; adult/child €3/2; ☺9am-4pm by tour) dates back to the 15th century. It's now a museum with period furniture and archaeology exhibits.

You'll find cafes aplenty around the pedestrian Hlavné nám. Our favourite *cukráreň* (pastry cafe) is 'Sweet Dream', **Sladký Sen** (Hlavné nám 90; cakes €1-3; ☺8am-6pm). The town's location makes this an easy day trip from the High Tatra resort towns or Levoča. If you decide to stay over, choose **Penzión U Jakubu** (☑4526 315; www.penzionujakuba.sk; Starý trh 39; r €30) for its folksy Slovakness, or **Hotel Club** (☑4524 051; www.hotelclubkez marok.sk; Dr Alexandra 24; s/d €34/47; @☜) for more contemporary flair. Both have good restaurants.

Kežmarok Information Agency (☑4492 135; www.kezmarok.sk; Hlavné nám 46; ☺9am-4pm) has loads more information if you need it. From here buses are the only way to go: connect directly to Poprad (€1, 30 minutes, 16 daily), Tatranská Lomnica (€1, 30 minutes, 12 daily), Ždiar (€1.30, 40 minutes, four daily) or Levoča (€2, one hour, six daily).

Pieniny National Park

☑052

People come to the 21-sq-km **Pieniny National Park** (www.pieniny.sk) to raft the river beneath impressive 500m-tall cliffs. Along with a Polish park on the north bank, Pieniny was created in 1967 to protect Dunajec Gorge, east of the Slovak village of Červený Kláštor.

At the mouth of the gorge, a few of the rooms in the fortified 14th-century **Red Monastery** (Červený Kláštor; adult/child €2/1; ☺10am-5pm, closed Nov-Apr) hold a diminutive museum, but you're here to float. There are two departure points for a **river float trip** (☑4282 840; www.pltnictvo.sk; adult/child €10/5; ☺9am-dusk May-Oct) on Rte 243: one opposite the monastery, and another 1km upriver west of the village. Most visitors pile into one of the continually launching, traditional – and dry – *pltě* (shallow, flat-bottom wood rafts). But for €40 to €50 per person you can be outfitted for a wet, and slightly wilder, rubber-raft ride. Don't be expecting Class V thrills though. The Dunajec River is a fairly sedate 1½-hour experience terminating near the Slovak village of Lesnica.

To return to Červený Kláštor you can hike back the way you came, along the riverside trail through the 9km-long gorge, in a little over two hours. It's an interesting walk even if rafting is not your thing. Alternatively, 500m southeast of the river trip terminus is **Chata Pieniny** (☑4397 530; www.chatapien iny.sk; Lesnica; dm €10, meals €3-10) in Lesnica. There you can rent a bicycle for a one-way ride (€4) back through the gorge, or board a minibus that will transport you the 22km back by road (€3). In summer, the log *chata* and its restaurant are continually abuzz. Folk musicians from this distinctive region often play to the crowds. Yes, it's a bit touristy, but in a fun, very Slovak way.

There's not a lot of reason to stay over unless you're stuck, but you could pitch a tent in the field outside **Hotel Pltník** (☑4822 525; www.hotelpltnik.sk; Červený Kláštor; campsite €4-6) or check into one of the copious private rooms (signed *privaty* or *zimmer frei*) on the road in Červený Kláštor.

Though Pieniny is only 42km north of Kežmarok, getting here is a challenge unless you have a vehicle. Travel agents in the High Tatras resort towns can help you arrange scheduled trips with transport. Public buses run to Červený Kláštor from Poprad (€3, 1¾ hours), via Kežmarok (€2, 1¼ hour), only once in the morning and once in the evening. Several pedestrian bridges lead from here into Poland.

Levoča

☑053 / POP 14,700

So this is what Slovakia looked like in the 13th century... Levoča is one of the few towns to still have its ancient defences largely intact. Here high medieval walls surround Old Town buildings and cobblestone alleyways. At the centre of it all stands the pride of the country's religious art and architecture collection, the Gothic Church of St Jacob. During the Middle Ages the king of Hungary invited Saxon Germans to colonise frontier lands. Levoča became central to the resulting Slavo-Germanic Spiš region. Unesco recognised the cultural significance of the Old Town by adding it to its list of World Heritage sites at Spiš (including Spiš Castle and Spiš Chapter, in Spišské Podhradie).

From the bus stop at Nám Štefana Kluberta, follow Košicka west two blocks to the main square.

◉ Sights

Church of St Jacob
CHURCH

(Chrám sv Jakuba; Nám Majstra Pavla; adult/child €3/1.50; ◎by tour 11am-4pm Mon, 8.30am-4pm Tue-Sat, 1-4pm Sun) The spindles-and-spires Church of St Jacob, built in the 14th and 15th centuries, elevates your spirit with its soaring arches, precious art and rare furnishings. Everyone comes to see the splendid 18m-high Gothic altar (1517) created by Master Pavol of Levoča. Not much is known about the sculptor, but his work is much revered. Cherubic representations of both the Last Supper and the Madonna and Child are carved into the wood-and-paint masterpiece. (This Madonna's face appeared on the original 100Sk banknote.) Buy tickets at the cashier inside the Municipal Weights House across the street from the north door. Entry is generally on the hour, but admissions are more frequent in July and August, and more sporadic off-season. The adjacent 16th-century **cage of shame** was built to punish naughty boys and girls.

Nám Majstra Pavla
SQUARE

Gothic and Renaissance eye candy abound on the main square, Nám Majstra Pavla. The private **Thurzov House** (1517), at No 7, has a characteristically frenetic Spiš Renaissance roofline. No 20 is the **Master Pavol Museum**, dedicated to the works of the city's most celebrated son. The 15th-century **Historic Town Hall** (Radnica) building, centre square, is really more interesting than the limited exhibits contained within. Temporary, town-related displays are on show at No 40, **Creative Culture in Spiš** (Výtarná Kultura na Spiši), originally a municipal building, then a school. One ticket gets you into all of the last three, as they are branches of the **Spiš Museum** (www.spisskemuzeum.com; adult/child €3/1.50; ◎9am-5pm Tue-Sun).

Church of Mariánska hora
CHURCH

From town you can see the Church of Mariánska hora, 2km north, where the largest Catholic pilgrimage in Slovakia takes place in early July.

🛏 Sleeping & Eating

Hotel U Leva
HOTEL €€

(☎4502 311; www.uleva.sk; Nám Majstra Pavla 24; s/d/apt €50/73/99; ◎◎) Spread across two Old Town buildings, each of the 23 cleanly contemporary rooms is unique. All have muted jewel-tone walls enlivening them, and apartments come with kitchens. The fine restaurant (mains €7 to €13) combines atypical ingredients (brie, spinach) with time-honoured Slovak techniques.

Hotel Arkáda
HOTEL €

(☎4512 372; www.arkada.sk; Nám Majstra Pavla 26; s/d €36/52; @◎) Furnishings in the Old Town building are mostly uninspired, but you can upgrade to a suite with antiques and arched ceilings for just €70. The cellar restaurant (mains €5 to €11) is much more atmospheric, with ancient brick vaults. Traditional and grilled dishes here attract quite a local following.

Oáza
PENSION €

(☎4514 511; www.ubytovanieoaza.sk; Nová 65; dm incl breakfast €10) Simple two-bed rooms with shared bathroom, and four-bed rooms with bath and kitchen, are just what the budget doctor ordered.

Reštaurácia Slovenka
SLOVAK €

(Nám Majstra Pavla 66; mains €3-7) The only place in town to get homemade *pirohy* (dumplings, somewhat akin to ravioli, stuffed with potato) topped with sheep's cheese and crackling.

Cukráren Oáza
CAFE €

(Nám Majstra Pavla 28; ◎8am-8pm) Creamy cakes, pastries and ice creams served in a tropical-themed 'oasis' is quite a treat.

❶ Information

Pretty much everything in town, including banks and post, is on the main square.

Levonet Internet Café (Nám Majstra Pavla 38; per hr €2; ◎10am-10pm)

Tourist information office (☎4513 763; www.levoca.sk; Nám Majstra Pavla 58; ◎9am-noon & 12.30-4pm) Ask for the free photocopied map.

❶ Getting There & Away

Levoča is on the main E50 motorway between Poprad (28km) and Košice (94km). Bus travel is most practical in the area. The local bus stop at Nám Štefana Kluberta is much closer to town than the bus station, which is 1km southeast of centre. Frequent coach services take you to:

Košice (€4.50, two hours, five daily)

Poprad (€1.60, 30 minutes, hourly) Has onward, mainline train connections best for travelling to Bratislava.

Spišská Nová Ves (€1, 20 minutes, every 30 minutes) For transferring to Slovenský Raj.

Spišské Podhradie (€1, 20 minutes, 11 daily) For Spiš Castle.

Spišské Podhradie

🎵053 / POP 3800

Stretching for 4 hectares above the village of Spišské Podhradie, the ruined Spiš Castle is undoubtedly one of largest in Europe. The ruins are certainly one of the most photographed sights in Slovakia. Two kilometres west, the medieval Spiš Chapter ecclesiastical settlement is also a Unesco World Heritage site. In between, the village itself has a few services, but not much else.

◉ Sights

Spiš Castle   CASTLE
(Spišský hrad; www.spisskemuzeum.com; adult/child €4.50/2.50; ⊙9am-7pm, closed Nov-Apr) From the E50 motorway you catch glimpses of eerie outlines and stony ruins crowning the ridge on the eastern side of Spišské Podhradie. Can it really be that big? Indeed, Spiš Castle seems to go on forever. If the reconstructed ruins are this impressive, imagine what the fortress was once like. Be sure to get the English audio tour that brings the past into focus through story and legend.

Chronicles first mention Spiš Castle in 1209, and the remaining central **residential tower** is thought to date from that time. From there defenders are said to have repulsed the Tatars in 1241. Rulers and noble families kept adding fortifications and palaces during the 15th and 16th centuries, but by 1780 the site had already lost military significance and much was destroyed by fire. It wasn't until the 1970s that efforts were made to salvage and fortify what remained. Few structures are whole, but there's a **cistern**, a **Romanesque palace** that contains the very small museum, and the **chapel** adjacent to it. Night tours and medieval festivals take place some summer weekends.

Spiš Castle is 1km east of Spišské Podhradie, a healthy, uphill hike above the spur rail station. The easiest approach to the castle by car is off the E50 highway on the east (Prešov) side.

Spiš Chapter   MONASTERY
(Spišská Kapitula; adult/child €2/1) On the west side of Spišské Podhradie, you'll find the still-active Spiš Chapter, a 13th-century Catholic complex encircled by a 16th-century wall. Charming private Gothic houses line the single street running between the two medieval gates. The highlight is the 1273 Romanesque **St Martin's Cathedral** (Spišská Kapitula 1; admission €1; ⊙10am-noon & 1-5pm Mon-Sat), with twin towers and an ornate sanctuary. Inside are several impressive trifold-painted Gothic altars from the 15th century. Buy tickets for the cathedral and pick up a guide from the information office at Spišská Kapitula 4. If you're travelling to Spiš Chapter by bus from Levoča, get off one stop (and 1km) before Spišské Podhradie, at Kapitula.

🛏 Sleeping & Eating

This is potentially a day trip from Levoča or the High Tatras, so there's not a lot of reason to stay over. The castle has a food stand, and the village has a little grocery store.

Penzión Podzámok   PENSION €
(☑4541 755; www.penzionpodzamok.sk; Podzámková 28; r with/without bathroom €30/20) Family houses have been cobbled together to create a simple 42-bed guesthouse with a backyard view of the castle. It's in the village, north across the bridge.

Spišsky Salaš   MOUNTAIN HUT €
(☑4541 202; www.spisskysalas.sk; Levočská cesta 11; mains €3-7) Dig into lamb stew in the folksy dining room or on the covered deck, and watch the kids romp on rough-hewn play sets. The rustic log complex also has three simple rooms for rent (per person €13). It's 3km west of Spiš Chapter, on the road toward Levoča.

❶ Getting There & Away

Spišské Podhradie is 15km east of Levoča and 78km northeast of Košice.

BUS Frequent buses connect with Levoča (€1, 20 minutes), Poprad (€2.50, 50 minutes) and Košice (€4, 1½ hours).

TRAIN An inconvenient spur railway line heads to Spišské Podhradie from Spišské Vlachy (€0.50, 10 minutes, five daily), a station on the main line. Check schedules at www.cp.atlas.sk.

Slovenský Raj & Around

🎵053

With rumbling waterfalls, steep gorges, sheer rockfaces, thick forests and hilltop meadows, Slovenský Raj lives up to the name of 'Slovak Paradise'. A few easier trails exist, but the one-way ladder-and-chain ascents make this a national park for the passionately outdoorsy. You cling to a metal rung headed straight up a precipice while an icy waterfall splashes and sprays you from a metre away. Oh, and that's after

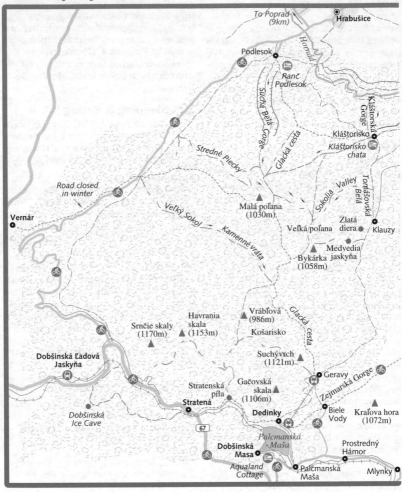

you've scrambled horizontally across a log ladder to cross the stream down below – pure exhilaration.

The nearest town of any size is the uninspiring Spišská Nová Ves, 23km southeast of Poprad. Of the three trailhead resort villages, Podlesok, outside of Hrabušice (16km southwest of Poprad), is our favourite – for its variety of hiking options, food stands, diverse lodging and sport possibilities. Čingov, 5km west of Spišská Nová Ves, also has good lodging. About 50km south, Dedinky is more of a regular village with a pub, supermarket and houses on a lake.

⊙ Sights & Activities

Before you trek, pick up VKÚ's 1:25,000 *Slovenský Raj* hiking map (No 4) or Dajama's *Knapsacked Travel: The Slovak Paradise* hiking book, available at many tourist offices and bookshops countrywide.

Slovenský Raj National Park   PARK
(Slovak Paradise; admission €1 Jul & Aug, free Sep-Jun) The national park has numerous trails that include one-way *roklina* (gorge) sections and take at least half a day. From Čingov a green trail leads up the Hornád River Gorge an hour to **Tomašovský výhľad**, a rocky outcropping and overlook that is a good short-

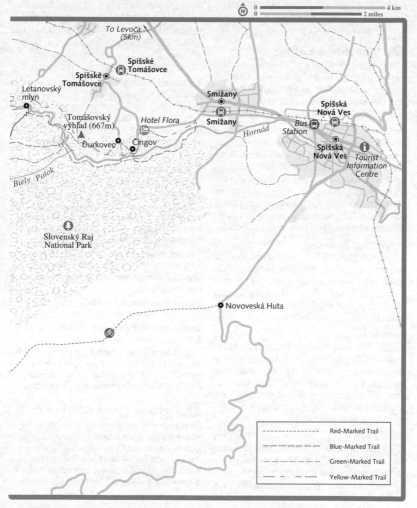

SLOVAKIA SLOVENSKÝ RAJ & AROUND

hike destination. Or continue to the green, one-way, technically aided **Kláštorisko Gorge trail**, allowing at least eight hours for the circuit.

You can also reach the Kláštorisko Gorge ascent from Podlesok (six hours). Another excellent alternative from Podlesok is to hike six to seven hours up the dramatic, ladder and technical-assist **Suchá Belá Gorge**, then east to Kláštorisko chata on a yellow then red trail. From there, take the blue trail down to the Hornád River, then follow the river gorge upstream to return to Podlesok.

One of the shortest, dramatic, technical-assist hikes starts at Biele Vody (15 minutes northeast of Dedinky via the red trail) and follows the blue-trail up **Zejmarská Gorge**. The physically fit can run, clamber and climb up in 50 minutes; others huff and puff up in 90 minutes. To get back, you can follow the green trail down to Dedinky, or there's a **chairlift** (adult/child €1/0.50; ⏱9am-5pm Jun-Aug) that works sporadically.

Dobšinská Ice Cave   CAVE
(www.ssj.sk; adult/child €7/3.50; ⏱9am-4pm Tue-Sun, closed Sep-May) The fanciful frozen formations in this Unesco-noted ice cave

are more dazzling in early June than late August. A 15-minute hike leads up to where tours begin every hour or so.

🛏 Sleeping & Eating

All the listed lodgings have restaurants. Numerous food stands and eateries and a small grocery are available in Podlesok. The biggest area supermarket is next to the bus station in Spišská Nová Ves.

Autocamp Podlesok CAMPING GROUND €
(☑4299 165; atcpodlesok@gmail.com; Podlesok; campsites €4-8, cottages & huts per person €10; 🗟) The always-busy office at this lively camping ground provides loads of trail info and a wi-fi hotspot to check email. Pitch a tent in the big field (600 capacity) or choose from fairly up-to-date A-frame cabins, small huts and cottages with two to 12 beds and a bathroom.

TOP CHOICE **Ranč Podlesok** PENSION €
(☑0918407077; www.rancpodlesok.sk; Podlesok 5; d/tr €30/45; 🗟) A blue park trail runs behind this stone-and-log lodge and restaurant at park's edge. Spacious rooms, a giant swing set and sand volleyball add to the attraction. It's 1km past the Podlesok village area.

Penzión Lesnica PENSION €
(☑449 1518; www.stefani.sk; Čingov 113; s/d incl breakfast €30/37) These nine simple, sunny-coloured rooms close to the trail fill up fast, so book ahead. Locals also know that the attached restaurant is one of the best local places for a Slovak repast (mains €3 to €7) – or an ice-cream sundae.

Hotel Flora HOTEL €
(☑449 1129; www.hotelfloraslovenskyraj.sk; Čingov 110; s/d incl breakfast €30/50; 🗟) With stonework fireplaces and leather chairs, the public spaces exude a mountain rusticicity; too

bad the rooms are plain. At least the restaurant (mains €6 to €14) has a large terrace.

Koliba Zuzana SLOVAK €-€€
(☑0905278397; www.kolibazuzana.szm.sk; Dedinky 127; mains €3-10) Lakeside restaurant with terrace; two suites (€80) for rent upstairs.

Aqualand Cottage HOSTEL €
(☑0948007735; www.aqualand.sk; Dobšinská Maša-Dedinky; dm €13, s/d without bathroom €25/32) A sprawling cottage-hostel with commonroom, fireplace and two kitchens across the lake from Dedinky proper.

ℹ Information

Outside Spišska Nová Ves, your lodging is often the best source of information; park info booths are open in July and August. Get cash before you arrive; there is an ATM and exchange at Spišska Nová train station. Helpful websites include www.slovenskyraj.sk and www.slovenskyraj.info.

@ve.net Internet Café (Zimná 58, Spišská Nová Ves; per hr €2; ⊙9am-6pm Mon-Fri)
Mountain Rescue Service (☑emergency 183 00; http://his.hzs.sk)
Tourist information booth (Čingov; ⊙9am-5pm, closed Sep-Jun)
Tourist information booth (Podlesok; ⊙10am-1pm, closed Sep-Jun)
Tourist Information Centre (☑4428 292; Letná 49, Spišská Nová Ves; ⊙8am-6pm Mon-Fri, 9am-1pm Sat, 2-6pm Sun May-Sep, 8am-5pm Mon-Fri Oct-Apr) Helps with accommodation.

ℹ Getting There & Around

Off season especially, you may consider hiring a car in Košice; connections to the park can be a chore. You'll have to transfer at least once, most likely in Spišský Štvrtok or Spišská Nová Ves. Buses run infrequently on weekends, more often in July and August. No buses run directly

BUSES FROM SPISŠKA NOVÁ VES

ROUTE	COST (€)	DURATION (MIN)	FREQUENCY (DAILY)
Poprad–Spišský Štvrtok	1	30	12 Mon-Fri
Levoča –Spišský Štvrtok	0.85	20	10 Mon-Fri
Spišský Štvrtok –Podlesok	0.85	20	2 Mon-Fri
Poprad –Spišska Nová Ves	2	45	11
Levoča –Spišska Nová Ves	0.85	20	18
Spišska Nová Ves –Čingov	0.50	15	6 Mon-Fri
Spišska Nová Ves –Podlesok	1.20	30	2 Mon-Fri
Spišska Nová Ves –Dedinky	2	90	3 Mon-Fri

between trailhead villages. Carefully check schedules at http://cp.atlas.sk.

Trains run from Spisšká Nová Ves to Poprad (€1, 20 minutes, 12 daily) and Košice (€3.80, one hour, 15 daily).

Košice

📞 055 / POP 235.300

An eclectic mix of Old Town architecture – modern hotels, Middle Ages churches, and art nouveau facades – lets you know this is a living city, not a relic. A handful of exhibits add to the attraction, but mostly you'll want to gather with locals on the benches near the musical fountain, or raise a glass at a sidewalk cafe. Visit during one of the summer street festivals, or enjoy the weekend nightlife, and you'll have plenty of opportunities to make new friends.

Košice received its city coat of arms in 1369 and for centuries was the eastern stronghold of the Hungarian kingdom. On 5 April 1945 the Košice Government Program – which made communist dictatorship in Czechoslovakia a virtual certainty – was announced here. Today US Steel forms the backbone of the city; you can't miss the company's influence, from the ice-hockey stadium it sponsors to the factory flare stacks on the industrial outskirts.

◉ Sights

At the time of research the East Slovak Museum was under reconstruction. Ask about it and other small exhibits at the tourist office.

Hlavná   SQUARE
Most all of the sights are in or around the town's long, plaza-like main square, Hlavná. Landscaped flowerbeds surround the central **musical fountain**, across from the 1899 **State Theatre**. To the north stands a large baroque **plague column** from 1723. Look for the turn-of-the-20th-century, art nouveau **Hotel Slaviá** at No 63. No 27, **Shire Hall** (1779), is where the Košice Government Program was proclaimed in 1945; today there's a minor art gallery inside.

Cathedral of St Elizabeth   CHURCH
(Dóm sv Alžbety, Hlavná; church free, attractions each €1; ⊙1-3pm Mon, 9am-5pm Tue-Fri, 9am-1pm Sat) The dark and brooding 14th-century Cathedral of St Elizabeth wins the prize for sight most likely to grace your Košice postcard home. You can't miss Europe's easternmost Gothic cathedral, which domi-

nates the square. Below the church, a **crypt** contains the tomb of Duke Ferenc Rákóczi, who was exiled to Turkey after the failed 18th-century Hungarian revolt against Austria. Don't forget to climb the 160 narrow, circular stone steps up the church's **tower** for city views. Climbing the **royal staircase** as the monarchs once did provides an interior perspective. Just to the south, the 14th-century **St Michael's Chapel** has limited entry hours.

Lower Gate Underground Museum   MUSEUM
(Hlavná; adult/child €1/0.50; ⊙10am-6pm Tue-Sun) The underground remains of medieval Košice – lower gate, defence chambers, fortifications and waterways – were only uncovered during construction work in 1996. Get lost in the mazelike passages and tunnels of the archaeological excavations at the south end of the square.

Wax Museum   MUSEUM
(www.waxmuseum.sk; Hlavná 3; adult/child €4/2.60; ⊙11am-3pm Mon-Fri, noon-3pm Sat, 1-3pm Sun) Fourteenth-century Urban Tower, rebuilt in the 1970s, now holds a fairly cheesy wax museum.

🛏 Sleeping

The City Information Centre has an annual town booklet that lists local accommodation, including university dorms open to the public in July and August.

Penzión Beryl   HOTEL €€
(📞6998 539; www.penzionberyl.sk; Mojmírová 2; incl breakfast s €55-69, d €65-80; ❀❄🛜) Modern rooms here have ecofriendly bamboo floors and earth-tone designs. A full, hot breakfast buffet includes both egg and sweet dishes. The accommodating staff can help arrange theatre tickets and car rental.

Chrysso Penzión   BOUTIQUE HOTEL €€
(📞6230 450; www.penzionchrysso.sk; Zvonárska 3; s/d/apt €58/68/78; ❄🛜) Think design-driven details, like silk throws and sleek leather chairs in chocolate and cream. A wine bar, terrace and restaurant downstairs are similarly stylish.

Hotel Zlatý Dukat   HOTEL €€€
(📞7279 333; www.hotelzlatydukat.sk; Hlavná 16; r incl breakfast €90-195; @🛜) Look through the glass floor near the reception to see the 13th-century foundations of this main-square hotel. Luxury touches include flatscreen TVs, flowers and room service.

Košice

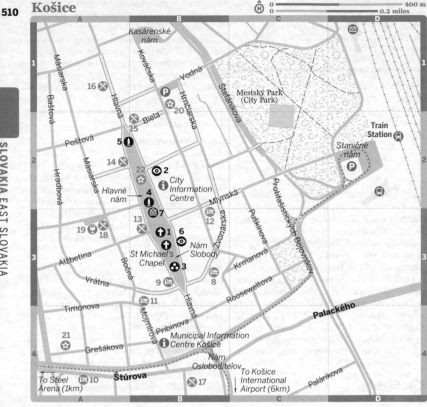

K2

HOSTEL €

(☎6255 948; Štúrova 32; s/d without bathroom €16/27) Dowdy singles and doubles, super close to the pedestrian centre. No common room or kitchen.

Penzión Slovakia

PENSION €

(☎7289 820; www.penzionslovakia.sk; Orliá 6; s/d €45/55; ✴️📶) Charming city guesthouse with grill restaurant downstairs.

✕ Eating

Stará Sýpka

SLOVAK €€

(Fejova 1; mains €5-11) Enjoy today's Slovak cooking in a pleasant cafe-restaurant-beer cellar that's quite popular. In summer, the courtyard terrace is the best.

Cafe Napoli

ITALIAN €-€€

(Hlavná 82; mains €4-11) Stylish young locals fill up this modern Italian restaurant, taking advantage of the long cocktail list and good wine selection.

Villa Regia

FINE DINING €€-€€€

(www.villaregia.sk; Dominikánske nám 3; mains €7-18) Steaks, seafood and vegetarian dishes get artistic treatment amid a rustic Old World atmosphere. The vaulted ceilings and stone walls extend to the upstairs pension rooms as well.

Karczma Mlyn

SLOVAK €

(Hlavná 82; mains €3-8) A pubby place, Mlyn is good for a pint and for heaping portions of cheap and hearty traditional fare. Enter through the courtyard.

Cukráreň Aida

CAFE €

(Hlavná 81; cakes €1-3; ⊙8am-10pm) The most popular ice-cream and cake shop in town; several branches on the main square.

Bagéteria

CAFE €

(Hlavná 36; sandwiches €1-3) Baguette sandwiches to eat in or take out.

Sights
1 Cathedral of St Elizabeth....................B3
2 Hotel Slávia....................................B2
3 Lower Gate Underground
   Museum.......................................B3
4 Musical Fountain.............................B2
5 Plague Column................................A2
6 Shire Hall......................................B3
   State Theatre...........................(see 22)
7 Wax Museum..................................B3

Sleeping
8 Chrysso Penzión.............................B3
9 Hotel Zlatý Dukát............................B3
10 K2..A4
11 Penzión Beryl...............................B3
12 Penzión Slovakia...........................B3

Eating
13 Bageteria....................................B3
14 Cafe Napoli..................................A2
15 Cukráreň Aida..............................B2
16 Karczma Mlyn...............................A1
17 Stará Sýpka..................................B4
18 Villa Regia...................................A3

Drinking
19 HC Pub 21....................................A3

Entertainment
20 Jazz Club.....................................B1
21 State Philharmonic Košice.................A4
22 State Theatre................................B2

Drinking & Entertainment

Any of the sidewalk cafes on the main square are fine places to drink on a warm evening. The free monthly publication *Kam do Mesta* (www.kamdomesta.sk) lists in Slovak the whats, wheres and whens of the entertainment scene.

HC Pub 21   PUB
(Dominikánske nám 9) Live folk-rock plays Tuesday evenings. Otherwise, it's a convivial hockey-themed pub.

Jazz Club   CLUB
(Kováčska 39) DJs spin here most nights, but there are also occasional live concerts.

State Theatre   THEATRE
(Štátne Divadlo Košice; www.sdke.sk; Hlavná 58; box office 9am-5.30pm Mon-Fri, 10am-1pm Sat) Local opera and ballet companies stage performances in the 1899 neo-baroque theatre from September to May.

State Philharmonic Košice   LIVE MUSIC
(Štátna Filharmónia Košice; www.sfk.sk; House of the Arts, Moyzesova 66) The spring musical festival is a good time to catch performances of the city's philharmonic at the House of the Arts, but concerts take place year-round.

Steel Aréna   SPORTS
(www.steelarena.sk; Nerudova 12) A co-host venue for the 2011 ice hockey world championships; the hometown's revered team, HC Košice, plays here. Buy tickets at www.ticketportal.sk.

Information

City Information Centre (6258 888; www.kosice.sk; Hlavná 59; 9am-6pm Mon-Fri, 9am-1pm Sat, 1-5pm Sun Jun-Sep, closed Sun Oct-May) Ask for both the free annual town guide and the full-size colour brochure of historic sites. Good info on cultural events.

Ľudová Banka (Mlynská 29) ATM and exchange; well located between the train station and centre.

Municipal Information Centre (MIC; 16 168; www.mickosice.sk; Dargov Department Store; Hlavná 2; 9am-8pm Mon-Sat) Souvenir and tickets sales, hidden mid-department store.

Net Club (Hlavná 9; per hr €1.60; 9am-10pm) Large internet/gaming cafe.

Police station (159; Pribinova 6)

Getting There & Away

Check bus and train schedules at http://cp.atlas.sk.

Air

Košice International Airport (KSC; www.airportkosice.sk) is 6km southwest of the centre. For international airlines serving Košice, see p519). **Danube Wings** (V5; www.danubewings.eu) has two daily flights to Bratislava, on weekdays only.

Bus

You can book ahead on some Ukraine-bound buses through **Eurobus** (www.eurobus.sk). Getting to Poland is easier from Poprad. Destinations include Bardejov (€4, 1¾ hours, 12 daily), Levoča (€4.50, two hours, five daily) and Uzhgorod (Ukraine; €7, two to three hours, three daily).

TRAINS FROM KOŠICE

DESTINATION	COST (€)	DURATION (HR)	FREQUENCY (DAILY)
Bratislava	19	5½	4 (IC)
Poprad (High Tatras)	5	1½	12
Spišska Nová Ves (Slovenský Raj)	3.80	1	15
Miskolc, Hungary	5	1¼	2
Lviv, Ukraine	60	12¾	1

Car

Several of the big international car-hire firms like Avis and Eurocar have representatives at the airport. It is often cheaper to rent in Bratislava, even with the added kilometres.

Buchbinder (☑0911 582 200; www.buch binder.sk) Smaller firm with good rates. Crackerjack staff arrange gratis pick-up in the city.

❶ Getting Around

The Old Town is small, so you probably can walk everywhere. Transport tickets (€0.60 one zone) cover most buses and trams; buy them at newsstands and validate on board. Bus 23 between the airport and the train station requires a two-zone ticket (€1).

Bardejov

☑054 / POP 33,400

The steep roofs and flat fronts of the burghers' houses on Bardejov's Renaissance Old Town square appear strikingly homogeneous at first. Look closer and you notice an ethereal sgraffito decoration or a pastel hue and plaster detail setting each apart. Unesco must have been impressed too, as it included the quiet square on its World Heritage list. Bardejov received its royal charter in 1376, and grew rich on trade between Poland and Russia into the 16th century. A few local museums shed light on this region's Eastern-facing art and culture, and this is a good base for exploring further. Wooden churches in the area reflect the Carpatho-Rusyn heritage that the area shares with neighbouring parts of Ukraine and Poland. A few kilometres north in Bardejovské Kúpele you can take a cure at a thermal spa or see these churches in a traditional open-air village museum. In late 1944 heavy WWII fighting took place at the Dukla Pass on the Polish border, 54km northeast of Bardejov. Tanks still stand in the area today as a memorial.

◉ Sights

The main square, **Radičné nám** is a sight in itself, and you can walk along the old **town walls and bastions** along Na Hradbách.

Šariš Museum
MUSEUM

(www.muzeumbardejov.sk; ◷8am-noon & 12.30-4pm Tue-Sun) There are two local branches of the Šariš Museum worth seeing. Centre square, the **Town Hall** (Radnica; Radničné nám 48; adult/child €1.50/1) contains altarpieces and a historical collection. Built in 1509, it was the first Renaissance building in Slovakia. At the **Icon Exposition** (Radničné nám 27; adult/child €1.50/1), more than 130 dazzling icons and iconostases from the 16th to 19th centuries are on display. This is an excellent opportunity to see the religious art that originally decorated Greek Catholic and Orthodox wooden churches east of Bardejov.

Basilica of St Egídius
CHURCH

(Bazilika Sv Egídia; Radničné nám; adult/child €1.50/1; ◷9.30am-5pm Mon-Fri, 10am-3pm Sat, 11.30am-3pm Sun) The interior of this 15th-century basilica is packed with 11 Gothic altarpieces, built from 1460 to 1510. Each has a thorough explanation in English.

🛏 Sleeping & Eating

Cafes can be found around Radničné nám.

Penzion Hradby
PENSION €

(☑0918349229; www.penzion-hradby.sk; Stöcklova 8; s/d/tr €20/28/40; 🐾) Budget digs in the heart of the Old Town: basic rooms provide all you need, in view of the town walls. Rooms share a fully equipped kitchen.

el. Restaurant & Lodging
PENSION €-€€

(☑4728 404; www.el-restaurant.sk; Stöcklova 43; s/d/apt incl breakfast €30/40/70; 🐾) A myriad of chicken dishes are on the menu of the modern Slovak restaurant downstairs. Upstairs, three bright and cheery rooms are for

Bardejov

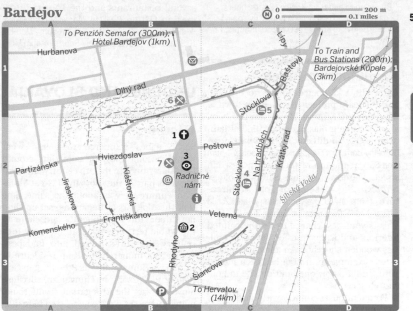

SLOVAKIA BARDEJOV

Bardejov

◉ Sights

1 Basilica of St Egídius	B2
2 Šariš Museum Icon Exposition	B3
3 Sariš Museum -Town Hall	B2

🛏 Sleeping

4 el. Restaurant & Lodging	C2
5 Penzión Hrady	C1

✖ Eating

6 La Bello	B1
7 Pohoda Café	B2

rent. It's very central; paid garage parking only.

La Bello　　　　　　ITALIAN　€-€€
(Radničné nám 50; mains €4-11) An atmospheric, Italianesque restaurant is the local fave. The thin-crust pizzas are all wood-fired, and grilled meat platters are equally as good.

Pohoda Café　　　　　　SLOVAK　€
(Radničné nám 39; mains €3-8) This cellar restaurant is a solid choice for Slovak specialities; the bar is quite popular on weekends.

Hotel Bardejov　　　　　　HOTEL　€-€€
(☑4883 487; www.hotelbardejov.sk; Toplianska ul 23; s/d/apt incl breakfast €38/50/70; 🛜) Fairly

utilitarian rooms by the stream on the Old Town outskirts, but they're clean and quiet.

Penzión Semafor　　　　　　PENSION　€
(☑0905830984; www.penzionsemafor.sk; Kellerova 13; s/d €30/40) Five bright doubles and an apartment in a family-run guesthouse.

ℹ Information

ČSOB (Radničné nám 7) Bank exchange and ATM.

Golem Internet Café (Radničné nám 35; per hr €2; ☺9.30am-10.30pm Mon-Thu, 9.30am-midnight Fri, 4.30-11pm Sat & Sun)

Main post office (Dlhý rad 14)

Tourist information centre (☑4723 013; www.bardejov.sk; Radničné nám 21; ☺9am-5.30pm Mon-Fri, 11.30am-3.30pm Sat & Sun, closed Sat & Sun Oct-Apr) Info, maps, souvenirs and guide services.

ℹ Getting There & Away

Bardejov is on a small spur train line, so buses to here are most convenient. Though you're close to Poland here, you're not near an international bus route. For those with a car, the E371 crosses into Poland north of Svidník, a town 35km east of Bardejov.

Buses go to and from Košice (€4, 1¾ hours, 12 daily), Poprad (€4.50, 2¼ hours, five daily) and Bardejovské Kúpele (€0.55, 10 minutes, 12 daily).

Bardejovské Kúpele

Three short kilometres to the north you'll find the leafy, promenade-filled spa town of **Bardejovské Kúpele**. If you want to book a service like a massage or a mineral bath (from €10), go directly to the **Spa House** (Kúpelny dom; ☎4774 225; ☺8am-noon & 1-5pm Mon-Sat) at the top of the main pedestrian street. The town also has Slovakia's oldest *skanzen*, the **Museum of Folk Architecture** (Múzeum ľudovej architektúry; adult/child €1.30/0.70; ☺9am-5pm Tue-Sun, to 3pm Oct-Apr). This is your best chance to see the painted interiors and iconostases of the area's nailless wooden churches. An ancient (Unescolisted) example from Zboj has been moved here, and a larger one built on site to hold church services.

Frequent buses connect with Bardejov. If you have a car, park in the lot by the bus station at the base of the town and walk uphill; the whole place is pedestrian-only. At the base near the colonnade, there are several restaurants and the **Tourist Information Office** (☎4744 744; www.bardejovske -kupele.sk; Kino Žriedlo; ☺8am-5pm Mon-Fri, 10.30am-4pm Sat & Sun May-Sep, 9am-4pm Mon-Fri Oct-Apr).

UNDERSTAND SLOVAKIA

History

Slavic tribes wandered west into what would become Slovakia sometime around the 5th century; in the 9th century, the territory was part of the short-lived Great Moravian empire. It was about the same time that the Magyars (Hungarians) set up shop next door and subsequently laid claim to the whole territory. When in the early 16th century the Turks moved into Budapest, Hungarian monarchs took up residence in Bratislava (known then as Pressburg in German, and Pozsony in Hungarian). Because Slovakia was the Hungarian frontierland, many fortresses were constructed here during the Middle Ages, and can still be seen today.

It wasn't until the turn of the 20th century that the Slovak intellectuals cultivated

---

WOODEN CHURCHES

Travelling east from Bardejov, you come to a crossroads of Western and Eastern Christianity. From the 17th to the 19th centuries, nearly 300 dark-wood, onion-domed churches were built in the region. Of the fewer than 50 that remain, eight have been recognised by Unesco. A handful celebrate the Roman Catholic or Protestant faiths, but most belong to the Eastern rites of Greek Catholicism and Orthodoxy. Typically they honour the Holy Trinity with three domes, three architectural sections and three doors on the icon screen. Richly painted icons and venerated representations of Christ and the saints decorate the iconostases, and usually every inch of the churches' interiors have also been handpainted. These can be quite the sight to behold, but it's not easy to get inside. Most of these rural village churches are remote, with extremely limited bus connections, and the doors are kept locked. Sometimes there's a map posted showing where the keeper of the key lives; sometimes he's next door, and sometimes you're out of luck. The way to guarantee seeing icons and an interior is to go to the Icon Exhibition in Bardejov, and the *skanzen* in Bardejovské Kúpele, 3km north. The church in Hervatov (c 1500) is one of the closest to Bardejov. If you're up for a further adventure, numerous resources can aid your search:

Carpathian Wooden Pearls (www.drevenechramy.sk) An illustrated map of 27 wooden churches designated national cultural treasures.

Cultural Heritage of Slovakia: Wooden Churches A comprehensive, full-colour book by Miloš Dudas with photos and church descriptions; for sale at bookstores.

Wooden Architecture in Prešovsky Kraj (www.po-kraj.sk/en) Government website that lists all the wooden churches in the Prešov prefecture (under 'Facts').

Wooden Churches near Bardejov An English-language booklet for sale at the Bardejov tourist office.

ties with neighbouring Czechs and took their nation into the united Czechoslovakia post-WWI. The day before Hitler's troops invaded Czechoslovakia in March 1939, Slovak leaders declared Slovakia a German protectorate, and a brief period of sovereignty ensued. This was not a popular move and in August 1944 Slovak partisans instigated the ill-fated Slovak National Uprising (Slovenské Národné Povstanie, or SNP), a source of ongoing national pride (and innumerable street names).

After the reunification and communist takeover in 1948, power was centralised in Prague until 1989 when the Velvet Revolution brought down the iron curtain here. Elections in 1992 saw the left-leaning, nationalist Movement for a Democratic Slovakia (HZDS) come to power with Vladimír Mečiar, a former boxer, as prime minister. Scarcely a year later, without referendum, the Czechoslovak federation dissolved peacefully on 1 January 1993, bringing Slovakia its first true independence.

Despite changing government leadership that alternately rejected and embraced economic and social reforms, Slovakia was accepted into NATO and the EU by 2004, became a Schengen member state in 2007 and adopted the euro as the national currency in January 2009. Bratislava and the High Tatras were the first areas to bounce back from the subsequent global economic downturn. Investment and development are once again going strong there, but the provinces have been plagued with a series of floods that have hampered recovery.

The People of Slovakia

A deeply religious and familial people, Slovaks have strong family ties and a deep sense of folk traditions. Today Roman Catholics form the majority (about 69%), but evangelicals are also numerous and east Slovakia has many Greek Catholic and Orthodox believers. The young are warm and open, but there can be residual communist reserve within older generations. Generosity and warmth lurk just behind this stoicism. If you make friends with a family, the hospitality (and free-flowing liquor) may just knock you out. Thankfully, in the tourist industry, surly service is now the exception rather than the rule.

Government statistics estimate that Slovakia's population is 86% Slovak, 10% Hungarian and 1.7% Roma. This last figure is in some dispute as some groups estimate the Roma population to be as high as 4%, most of whom live in eastern Slovakia. The Roma are viewed by the general populace with an uncompromising suspicion – at best.

Folk Arts & Architecture

A few Slovak city-dwellers may have been put off by the clichéd image of the communist-era 'happy peasant', but traditional folk arts – from music to architecture – are still celebrated across the country. Indeed, attending one of the many village folk festivals in July and August can be the highlight of a visit: colourful costumes, upbeat traditional music (punctuated by stomps and squeals) and hearty *klobasa* and beer are all part of the fun. Two of the biggest are the Východná Folk Festival (www.obec-vychodna.sk), in the small namesake village 32km west of Poprad, and Terchová's Janošik Days, in the Malá Fatra National Park.

Traditional Slovak folk instruments include the *fujara* (a 2m-long flute), the *konkovka* (a shepherd's flute), drums and cimbalom. Today you'll likely still see a folk troupe accompanied by fiddle, bass, clarinet and sometimes trumpet or accordion. National folk companies like Lučnica (www.lucnica. sk) and Šľuk (www.sluk.sk) perform across the country. But each microregion has its own particular melodies and costumes.

Outside of festivals, the best place to experience folk culture is at a *skanzen*, an open-air museum where examples of traditional wooden cottages and churches have been gathered in village form. The houses are fully furnished in traditional style and frequent activates, especially around holidays, focus on folk culture. The largest *skanzen*, in Martin, represents several regions and the village of Vlkolínec is like a living *skanzen*. A hillside open-air village museum in Bardejovské Kúpele sheds light on that area's far-eastern, Orthodox-leaning culture. The *skanzen* there has two good examples of the nailless wooden churches for which the area is known.

Several more of these architectural gems – built from the 16th to the 19th century with wooden onion domes outside and ornately painted walls and iconostasis inside – can be found around Bardejov; many more are further east. For more see the boxed text on p514.

TO BUILD OR NOT TO BUILD

Slovak national parks have long been mixed-use, with residential and recreational zones sharing space with more pristine areas. In some ways, this can be good. The elaborate system of cable cars, funiculars and hiker lodging in the High Tatras make the upper altitudes accessible. But recent years have seen increased development in those mountains: new high-speed chairlifts and ski runs in Tatranská Lomnica, never-ending resort construction in Štrbské Pleso... Watchdog groups like the International Union for the Conservation of Nature have protested, suggesting that national park status should be in question. But so far the government doesn't see a problem. Though the parks are less crowded than the Alps or the Rockies, tens of thousands of hikers pass through every year. Try to do your bit to keep things clean; pack out what you pack in, stay on trails and don't pick the flowers.

The Landscape

A hilly, forested country for the most part, Slovakia sits at the heart of Europe, straddling the northwestern end of the Carpathian Mountains. With such great scenery, it's not surprising that most Slovaks spend their weekends outdoors. National parks and protected areas comprise 20% of the territory and the entire country is laced with a network of trails. You will doubtless run into a backpack-toting Slovak wherever you walk out in nature.

Not to be missed is the High Tatras (Vysoké Tatry) National Park, protecting a 12km-long rocky mountain range that seems to rise out of nowhere. The tallest peak, Gerlachovský štít, reaches an impressive 2654m, and snow could blanket the upper reaches any month. The lesser pine-clad ridges of Malá Fatra National Park are popular with local hikers and skiers. In Slovenský Raj National Park, ladders, chain assists and other technical aids make the challenging, narrow gorges and waterfalls accessible to those seeking a challenge.

Unlike the mountainous north, southwestern Slovakia is a fertile lowland stretching from the foothills of the Carpathians down to the Danube River, which forms the border with Hungary. Rivers across the country are prone to spring and autumn flooding, so pay attention to the news when travelling.

Food & Drink

Slovakia isn't known for its 'cuisine' as much as for its home cooking. Soups like *cesnaková polievka* (garlic soup), clear with croutons and cheese, and *kapust-*

nica (cabbage soup), with a paprika-and-pork base, start most meals. The national dish is *bryndzové halušky*, gnocchi-like dumplings topped with soft, sharp sheep's cheese and bits of bacon fat. You'll also find *bryndza* sheep cheese on potato pancakes, in *pirohy* (dumplings) and served as a *natierka* (spread) with bread and raw onions. Don't pass up an opportunity to eat in a *salaš* or a *koliba* (rustic eateries named for traditional parts of a sheepherder's camp), where these traditional specialities are the mainstay.

Much of what you'll see on regular menus is basic central European fare: various fried meat schnitzels, hearty pork dishes and paprika-infused stews. It's all very meaty, but most towns have at least one (vegetarian-friendly) pizza place. For dessert, try *palacinka* (crepes), usually stuffed with berries and chocolate or *ovocné knedličky* (fruit dumplings).

Spirits of Slovakia

Though removed from the office setting in recent years, the Slovak drinking tradition is still going strong at home. It would be impolite to begin any visit or meal without a toast. So expect to be served a shot of *slivovica* (plum-based firewater), *borovička* (a potent berry-based clear liquor), Demänovka (a herbal liquor related to Czech Becherovka) or something of the sort.

Unlike its neighbour to the north, Slovakia is not known for its *pivo* (beer). But the full-bodied Zlatý Bažant and dark, sweet Martiner are decent.

Wine is really much more the thing here. What do oenophiles say? Oh, yes, it's highly drinkable (ie good and cheap). The Modra region squeezes out dry medium-bodied reds, like Frankovka and Kláštorné. Slovak reisling and Müller Thurgau varietals are fruity but on the dry side. Tokaj, a white dessert wine from the east, is trying (not terribly successfully, marketingwise) to give the Hungarian version of the same wine a run for its money.

SURVIVAL GUIDE

Directory A–Z

Accommodation

Bratislava has more hostels and five-star hotels than midrange accommodation. Outside the capital, you'll find a whole host of reasonable *penzióny* (guesthouses or pensions). Breakfast is usually available (sometimes included) at all lodgings, and wi-fi is common and usually free. Unless otherwise noted, all lodgings listed offer nonsmoking rooms; those with only nonsmoking are indicated with a ⊝. Parking is widely available outside Bratislava.

PRICE RANGES

Note that prices listed in this chapter are for tourist season.

Budget (€) Under €60 (hostel dorms and shared-bathroom rooms, provincial guesthouses).

Midrange (€€) From €60 to €150 (pensions and hotels with restaurants or bars).

Top end (€€€) From €150 to much higher (upscale and international hotels, mostly in Bratislava).

SEASONS

May to September Tourist season countrywide; prices reflected in this guide.

October to April Off-season, rates drop dramatically (10% to 50%).

January to March Additional tourist/ski season in the mountains.

Christmas, New Year and Easter Prices 20% to 30% higher than in tourist season; reservations essential.

BOOKING RESOURCES

Lodge Yourself (www.ubytujsa.sk)

Bratislava Hotels (www.bratislavahotels.com)

Slovakia Tourist Board (www.slovakia.travel)

AN ICE-HOCKEY OBSESSION

Enter any bar or restaurant during puck-pushing season (September to April) and 12 large men and an ice rink will probably be on the TV screen, even at fancy restaurants. The national team usually ranks among the world's 10 strongest, but they haven't managed to break into the Olympic top three yet. (The team was only created when Czechoslovakia dissolved in 1993.) Local club rivalries are quite heated, with the most popular teams being HC Slovan in Bratislava and HC Košice in Košice (go figure). Stoking the obsessive fires is the fact that these teams' two stadiums co-hosted the IIHF world championships in spring of 2011. Bratislava's Ondrej Nepela Arena got a big-money overhaul for the event, so it doesn't seem like the ice-hockey fever will cool down anytime soon.

Activities

Hiking The **Mountain Rescue Service** (Horská záchranná služba; ☎18 300; http://his.hzs.sk) provides hiking and weather information in addition to aid.

Skiing Check out the snow conditions at **Ski Info** (www.ski.sk).

Business Hours

Sight and attraction hours vary throughout the year; we've listed the opening times for tourist season, May through September, only. Schedules vary October through April; check ahead.

Unless otherwise noted within reviews, these are the standard hours for service listings in this guide.

Banks 8am-5pm Mon-Fri

Bars 11am-midnight Mon-Thu, 11am-2am Fri & Sat, 4pm-midnight Sun

Grocery stores 6.30am-6pm Mon-Fri, 7am-noon Sat

Post offices 8am-5pm Mon-Fri, 8-11am Sat

Nightclubs 4pm-4am Wed-Sun

Restaurants 10.30am-10pm

Shops 9am-6pm Mon-Fri, 9am-noon Sat

Embassies & Consulates

Australia and New Zealand do not have embassies in Slovakia; the nearest are in Vienna and Berlin respectively. The following are in Bratislava.

Canada (☎02-5920 4031; http://www.canadainternational.gc.ca/czech-tcheque/; Carlton-Savoy Building, Mostová 2)

France (☎02-5934 7111; www.france.sk; Hlavné nám 7)

Germany (☎02-5920 4400; www.pressburg.diplo.de; Hviezdoslavovo nám 10)

Ireland (☎02-5930 9611; www.embassyofireland.sk; Carlton-Savoy Bldg, Mostová 2)

Netherlands (☎02-5262 5081; www.holandskoweb.com; Frana Krála 5)

UK (☎02-5998 2000; http://ukinslovakia.fco.gov.uk; Panská 16)

USA (☎02-5443 0861; http://slovakia.usembassy.gov; Hviezdoslavovo nám 4)

Food

Restaurant review price indicators are based on the cost of a main course.

Budget (€) Under €6.

Midrange (€€) From €6 to €12.

Top end (€€€) From €12 up.

Gay & Lesbian Travellers

Homosexuality has been legal here since the 1960s, but this is a conservative, mostly Catholic country. The GLBT scene is small in Bratislava, and all but nonexistent elsewhere. Check out www.gay.sk.

Holidays

New Year's & Independence Day 1 January

Three Kings Day 6 January

Good Friday & Easter Monday March/April

Labour Day 1 May

Victory over Fascism Day 8 May

SS Cyril & Methodius Day 5 July

SNP Day 29 August

Constitution Day 1 September

Our Lady of Sorrows Day 15 September

All Saints' Day 1 November

Christmas 24 to 26 December

Internet Access

Wi-fi is widely available at lodgings and cafes across the country. Towns will usually have one internet cafe where the laptopless can log on.

Money

ATMs Quite common even in smaller towns, but shouldn't be relied upon in villages.

Credit cards Visa and Mastercard are accepted at most hotels and restaurants (though only if you announce before requesting the bill that you plan to pay by card).

Currency Since January 2009, Slovakia's legal tender has been the euro. But you'll still hear reference to the former currency, the Slovak crown, or Slovenská koruna (Sk).

Tipping 10% is fairly standard, though some locals tip less.

Post

Post office service is reliable, but be sure to hand your outgoing mail to a clerk; your postcard may languish in a box for quite some time.

Telephone

Landline numbers can have either seven or eight digits. Mobile phone numbers (10 digits) are often used for businesses; they start with ☎09. When dialling from abroad, you need to drop the zero from both city area codes and mobile phone numbers. Purchase local and international phone cards at newsagents.

MOBILE PHONES

The country has GSM (900/1800MHz) and 3G UMTS networks operated by providers Orange, T-Mobile and O2.

PHONE CODES

Dial out of Slovakia ☎00

Country code ☎421

Tourist Information

Association of Information Centres of Slovakia (AICES; ☎16 186; www.aices.sk) Runs an extensive network of city information centres.

Slovak Tourist Board (www.slovakia.travel) No Slovakia-wide information office exists; your best bet is to go online.

Travellers With Disabilities

Slovakia lags behind many EU states in accommodation for disabled travellers. **Slovak Union for the Disabled** (www.sztp.sk) works to change the status quo. Hotels and restaurants have few ramps or barrier-free rooms. There's some accessibility on public transport, including buses that lower, and special seating.

Visas

For a full list of visa requirements, see www.mzv.sk (under 'Ministry' and then 'Travel').

No visa required EU citizens.

Visa-free for up to 90 days Visitors from Australia, New Zealand, Canada, Japan and the US.

Visa required South African nationals, among others.

Getting There & Away

For more travel specifics see the appropriate destination section; Bratislava and Košice are the country's main bases of entry/exit. Flights, tours and rail tickets can be booked online at lonelyplanet.com/booking.

Entering Slovakia from the EU, indeed from most of Europe, is a breeze. Lengthy custom checks make arriving from the Ukraine a bit more tedious.

Air

Bratislava's intra-European airport is small. Unless you're coming from the UK, which has a fair number of direct flights, your arrival will likely be by train. Vienna, Austria, has the nearest international air hub.

AIRPORTS

Airport Bratislava (BTS; www.airportbratislava.sk) Two dozen European destinations.

Košice International Airport (KSC; www.airportkosice.sk) Flights to Prague and Vienna.

Vienna International Airport (VIE; Schwechat; www.viennaairport.com) Austrian airport with regular bus connections to Bratislava, 60km west. Worldwide connections.

AIRLINES

The main airlines operating in Slovakia:

Austrian Airlines (OS; www.aua.com) Connects Košice with Vienna.

Czech Airlines (OK; www.czechairlines.com) Connects Prague with Bratislava and Košice.

Danube Wings (V5; www.danubewings.eu) Connects regularly with Basel, Switzerland; has summer flights to Italian and Croatian holiday destinations.

LOT Airlines (WAW; www.lot.com) Flies four days a week between Bratislava and Warsaw.

Ryanair (FR; www.ryanair.com) Connects Bratislava with numerous destinations across the UK and Italy, coastal Spain, Paris, Brussels and Stockholm.

Land

Border posts between Slovakia and fellow EU Schengen member states, Czech Republic, Hungary, Poland and Austria are nonexistent. You can come and go at will. This makes checks at the Ukrainian border all the more strident, as you will be entering the EU. By bus expect one to two hours wait; by car, much more.

BUS

Local buses connect Poprad and Ždiar with Poland. **Eurobus** (www.eurobus.sk) and **Eurolines** (www.slovaklines.sk) handle international routes across Europe from Bratislava and heading east to the Ukraine from Košice.

CAR & MOTORCYCLE

Private vehicle requirements for driving in Slovakia are registration papers, 'green card' (proof of third-party liability insurance), nationality sticker, first-aid kit and warning triangle.

TRAIN

See http://cp.atlas.sk for international and domestic train schedules. Direct trains connect Bratislava to Austria, the Czech Republic, Poland and Hungary; from Košice, trains connect to the Czech Republic, Poland, Ukraine and Russia.

River

During spring and summer, Danube riverboats offer an alternative way to get between Bratislava and Vienna or Budapest.

Getting Around

Air

Danube Wings (V5; www.danubewings.eu) offer the only domestic air service; weekdays only, between Bratislava and Košice.

Bicycle

Roads are often narrow and potholed, and in towns cobblestones and tram tracks can prove dangerous for bike riders. Bike rental is uncommon outside mountain resorts. The cost of transporting a bike by rail is usually 10% of the train ticket.

Bus

Read timetables carefully; fewer buses operate on weekends and holidays.

Cestovné poriadky (http://cp.atlas.sk) Up-to-date bus and train schedules on line.

Slovenská autobusová doprava (SAD; www.sad.sk) Comprehensive national bus network; most useful in the mountains.

Car & Motorcycle

Licences Foreign driving licences with photo ID are valid in Slovakia.

Motorway stickers (*nálepka*) Toll stickers are required on *all* green-signed motorways. Fines for not having them can be hefty. Buy at petrol stations (rental cars usually have them).

Parking City streetside parking restrictions are eagerly enforced. Always buy a ticket from a machine, attendant or newsagent in Old Town centres.

Rental Car hire is available in Bratislava and Košice primarily.

Local Transport

Towns all have good bus systems; villages have infrequent service. Bratislava and Košice additionally have trams.

Hours Public transport generally operates from 4.30am to 11.30pm daily.

Tickets City transport tickets are good for all local buses, trams and trolleybuses. Buy at newsstands and validate on board or risk serious fines (this is not a scam).

Train

Train is the way to travel in Slovakia; most places listed in this chapter are off the main Bratislava–Košice line. No online reservations.

Cestovné poriadky (http://cp.atlas.sk) Up-to-date bus and train schedules online.

Slovak Republic Railways (ŽSR; ☑18 188; www.slovakrail.sk) Far-reaching, efficient national rail service.

Slovenia

Best Places to Stay

» Antiq Hotel (p525)
» Hotel Mitra (p553)
» Hotel Triglav Bled (p537)
» Max Piran (p549)
» Celica Hostel (p529)

Best Places to Eat

» Špajza (p530)
» Pri Mari (p549)
» Restavracija
Topli Val (p543)
» Restavracija
Pungaršek (p538)

Why Go?

It's a pint-sized place, with a surface area of just more than 20,000 sq km and 2 million people. But 'good things come in small packages', and never was that old chestnut more appropriate than in describing Slovenia.

Slovenia has been dubbed a lot of different things by its PR machine – 'Europe in Miniature', 'The Sunny Side of the Alps', 'The Green Piece of Europe' – and they're all true. Slovenia has everything, from beaches, snowcapped mountains, hills awash in grape vines and wide plains blanketed in sunflowers to Gothic churches, baroque palaces and art nouveau public buildings. Its incredible mixture of climates brings warm Mediterranean breezes up to the foothills of the Alps, where it can snow in summer. And with more than half of its total area covered in forest, Slovenia really is one of the 'greenest' countries in the world. In recent years, it has taken on the role as Europe's activities playground.

Come for all these things but come too for the Slovenes themselves – generous, broad-minded and welcoming.

When To Go

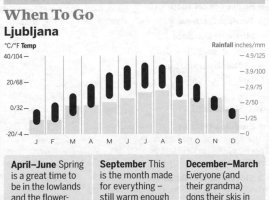

Ljubljana

April–June Spring is a great time to be in the lowlands and the flower-carpeted valleys of Gorenjska.

September This is the month made for everything – still warm enough to swim and tailor-made for hiking.

December–March Everyone (and their grandma) dons their skis in this winter-sport mad country.

Fast Facts

» **Area** 20,273 sq km

» **Capital** Ljubljana

» **Telephone country code** 386

» **Emergency** 112

Exchange Rates

Australia	A$1	€0.72
Canada	C$1	€0.71
Japan	¥100	€0.82
New Zealand	NZ$1	€0.54
UK	UK£1	€1.12
USA	US$1	€0.69

Set Your Budget

» **Budget hotel room** €40

» **Two-course meal** €20

» **Museum entrance** €3

» **Beer in shop/bar** €1/3

» **100km by train/bus** €6.03/9.20

Resources

» **E-uprava** (http://e-uprava.gov.si/e-uprava/en/portal.euprava) Official portal with info on everything

» **Slovenian Tourist Board** (www.slovenia.info) Ambitious tourist site

Connections

Border formalities with Slovenia's three European Union neighbours – Italy, Austria and Hungary – are nonexistent and all are accessible by train and (less frequently) bus. Venice can also be reached by boat from Izola and Piran. Expect a somewhat closer inspection of your documents when travelling to/from non-EU Croatia.

ITINERARIES

One Week

Spend a couple of days in Ljubljana, then head north to unwind in Bohinj or romantic Bled beside idyllic mountain lakes. Depending on the season, take a bus or drive over the hair-raising Vršič Pass into the valley of the vivid blue Soča River and take part in some adventure sports in Bovec or Kobarid before returning to Ljubljana.

Two Weeks

Another week will allow you to see just about everything in this chapter: all of the above as well as the Karst caves at Škocjan and Postojna and the Venetian ports of Koper, Izola and Piran on the Adriatic.

Essential Food & Drink

» **Pršut** Air-dried, thinly sliced ham from the Karst region not unlike Italian prosciutto

» **Žlikrofi** Ravioli-like parcels filled with cheese, bacon and chives

» **Žganci** The Slovenian stodge of choice – groats made from barley or corn but usually *ajda* (buckwheat)

» **Potica** A kind of nut roll eaten at teatime or as a dessert

» **Wine** Distinctively Slovenian tipples include peppery red Teran from the Karst region and Malvazija, a straw-colour white wine from the coast

LJUBLJANA

♪ 01 / POP 257,675

Ljubljana (lyoob-*lya*-na) is by far Slovenia's largest and most populous city. It is also the nation's political, economic and cultural capital. As such, virtually everything of national importance begins, ends or is taking place in Ljubljana.

But it can be difficult to get a grip on the place. In many ways the city whose name *al-*

most means 'beloved' (*ljubljena*) in Slovene does not feel like an industrious municipality of national importance but a pleasant, self-contented small town. You might think that way too, especially in spring and summer when cafe tables fill the narrow streets of the Old Town and along the Ljubljanica River and street musicians entertain passers-by on pedestrian Čopova ul and Prešernov trg. Then Ljubljana becomes a little Prague or Kraków

Slovenia Highlights

1 Experience the architecture, hilltop castle, green spaces and cafe life of **Ljubljana** (p523), Slovenia's beloved capital

2 Wax romantic in picture-postcard **Bled** (p535), with a lake, an island and a castle as backdrop

3 Get into the outdoors or in the bluer-than-blue Soča in the majestic mountain scenery at **Bovec** (p541), one of the country's major outdoor-activities centres

4 Explore the Karst caves at **Škocjan** (p544), with scenes straight out of Jules Verne's *A Journey to the Centre of the Earth*

5 Swoon at the wonderful Venetian architecture of the romantic port of **Piran** (p548)

without the crowds. And you won't be disappointed with the museums and galleries, atmospheric bars and varied nightlife either.

History

Legacies of the Roman city of Emona – remnants of walls, dwellings, early churches, even a gilded statuette – can be seen everywhere. Ljubljana took its present form in the mid-12th century as Laibach under the Habsburgs, but it gained regional prominence in 1809, when it became the capital of Napoleon's short-lived 'Illyrian Provinces'. Some fine art nouveau buildings filled up the holes left by a devastating earthquake in 1895, and architect Jože Plečnik continued the remake of the city up until WWII. In recent years the city's dynamic mayor, Zoran Janković, has doubled the number of pedestrian streets, extended a great swathe of the river embankment and spanned the Ljubljanica River with two new footbridges.

⊙ Sights

The oldest part of town, with the most important historical buildings and sights (including Ljubljana Castle) lies on the right (east) bank of the Ljubljanica. Center, which has the lion's share of the city's museums and galleries, is on the left (west) side of the river.

CASTLE AREA

Ljubljana Castle CASTLE
(⌖306 4293; www.ljubljanafestival.si; admission free; ⊙9am-11pm summer, 10am-9pm winter) Ljubljana Castle crowns a wooded hill that is the city's focal point. It's an architectural mishmash, including fortified walls dating from the early 16th century, a late-15th-century chapel and a 1970s concrete cafe. The best views are from the 19th-century **watchtower** (adult/child €5/2; ⊙9am-9pm summer, 10am-6pm winter); admission includes a visit to the **Virtual Museum**, a 23-minute, 3D video tour of Ljubljana though the centuries. More interesting is the new **Slovenia History Exhibition** (with tower & Virtual Museum adult/child €8/4.80) next door, which guides you through the past via iconic objects and multimedia exhibits. The fastest way to reach the castle is via the **funicular** (vzpenjača; return adult/child €3/2; ⊙9am-11pm summer, 10am-9pm winter), which ascends from Krekov trg every 10 minutes, though you can also take the hourly **tourist train** (adult/child €3/2; ⊙up 9am-9pm, down 9.20am-9.20pm) from south of the tourist informa-

tion centre (TIC) on Stritarjeva ul. It takes about 15 minutes to walk to the castle via Reber ul from the Old Town.

PREŠERNOV TRG & OLD TOWN

Prešernov Trg SQUARE
This central square is dominated by the **Prešeren monument** (1905), honouring national poet France Prešeren, and the salmon pink, 17th-century **Franciscan Church of the Annunciation** (⊙6.40am-noon & 3-8pm). Wander north of the square along Miklošičeva c to admire the fine **art nouveau buildings**, including the landmark Grand Hotel Union at No 1, built in 1905; the former People's Loan Bank (1908) at No 4; and the colourful erstwhile Cooperative Bank from 1922 at No 8.

Triple Bridge BRIDGE
Leading southward from Prešernov trg is the small but perfectly formed Triple Bridge; prolific architect Jože Plečnik added two side bridges to the 19th-century span in 1931 to create something truly unique.

Old Town HISTORIC AREA
Ljubljana's oldest and most important district is made up of three elongated 'squares': **Mestni trg**, 'City Square' containing a copy of the baroque **Robba Fountain** (the original is now in the National Gallery) in front of the Gothic **town hall** (1718); **Stari trg** (Old Sq); and **Gornji trg** (Upper Sq).

CENTRAL MARKET AREA

Central Market MARKET
East of Prešernov trg is a lively open-air market (p531). Walk eastward along the magnificent riverside **Plečnik Colonnade** past the new **Butchers' Bridge**, with wonderful sculptures by Jakov Brdar and miniature padlocks left behind by lovers, to **Dragon Bridge** (Zmajski Most; 1901), a span guarded by four of the mythical creatures that are now the city's mascots.

Cathedral of St Nicholas CHURCH
(Dolničarjeva ul 1; ⊙10am-noon & 3-6pm) Bordering the market, the 18th-century city's main church is filled with pink marble, white stucco, gilt and a panoply of baroque frescos. Check out the magnificent bronze doors (1996) on the west and south sides.

TRG FRANCOSKE REVOLUCIJE AREA

City Museum of Ljubljana MUSEUM
(⌖241 25 00; www.mestnimuzej.si; Gosposka ul 15; adult/child €4/2.50; ⊙10am-6pm Tue & Wed, Fri-Sun, 10am-9pm Thu) This excellent museum focuses on Ljubljana's history, culture and

politics via imaginative multimedia and interactive displays. The reconstructed Roman street dating back to the 1st century AD is worth a visit alone.

National & University Library HISTORIC BUILDING
(☎200 11 09; Turjaška ul 1; ⏰9am-6pm Mon-Fri, 9am-2pm Sat) Diagonally opposite is the National & University Library, Plečnik's masterpiece completed in 1941, with its distinctive horse-head doorknobs and staircase of black marble that leads to a stunning reading room.

MUSEUM AREA

National Museum of Slovenia MUSEUM
(☎241 44 00; www.nms.si; Prešernova c 20; adult/child €3/2.50, free 1st Sun of month; ⏰10am-6pm Fri-Wed, 10am-8pm Thu) Housed in an elegant 1888 building, the country's most important depository of historical items has rich archaeological and coin collections, including a Roman lapidarium and a Stone Age bone flute discovered near Cerkno in western Slovenia in 1995.

Slovenian Museum of Natural History MUSEUM
(☎241 09 40; www2.pms-lj.si; adult/student €3/2.50, inc national museum €5/4) Housed in the same building and keeping the same hours, this museum contains the usual reassembled mammoth and whale skeletons, stuffed birds, reptiles and mammals as well as an excellent mineral collections from the 19th century.

National Gallery MUSEUM
(☎241 54 18; www.ng-slo.si; Prešernova c 24 & Cankarjeva c 20; adult/child €7/5, free 1st Sun of month; ⏰10am-6pm Tue-Sun) Slovenia's foremost assembly of fine art is housed over two floors both in an old building dating to 1896 and an impressive modern wing.

Ljubljana Museum of Modern Art MUSEUM
(☎241 68 00; www.mg-lj.si; Tomšičeva ul 14; adult/student €5/2.50; ⏰10am-6pm Tue-Sun) Founded in 1948, this fine space has been given a massive facelift and is now largely given over to temporary exhibits of modern and contemporary art.

Tours

Two-hour **walking tours** (adult/child €10/5; ⏰10am, 2pm & 5pm Apr-Oct), combined with a ride on the funicular or the tourist train up to the castle or a cruise on the Ljubljanica, are organised by the TIC (p534). They depart daily from the town hall on Mestni trg.

Festivals & Events

There is plenty going on in and around the capital, including **Druga Godba** (www.drugagodba.si), a week-long festival of alternative and world music at the Križanke in May; the **Ljubljana Festival** (www.ljubljanafestival.si), the nation's premier cultural event (music, theatre and dance) held from early July to late August; and the **International Ljubljana Marathon** (www.ljubljanskimaraton.si) in late October.

Sleeping

The TIC (p534) has comprehensive details of private rooms (from s/d €30/50) and apartments (from d/q €55/80) though only a handful are central.

TOP CHOICE **Antiq Hotel** BOUTIQUE HOTEL **€€€**
(☎421 35 60; www.antiqhotel.si; Gornji trg 3; s €61-133, d €77-168; ❄@) Ljubljana's original boutique hotel, cobbled together from a series of townhouses in the heart of the Old Town, has 16 rooms and apartments, most of which are very spacious, and a multilevel back garden. The decor is kitsch with a smirk and there are fabulous little nooks and touches everywhere. A short distance west across the Ljubljanica is its sister, the new **Antiq Palace** (☎08-389 67 00; www.antiqpalace.com; Gosposka ul 10 & Vegova ul 5a; s/d €180/210; ❄@ᯤ), with 13

LJUBLJANA IN TWO DAYS

From central **Prešernov trg** (p524), walk to Krekov trg and take the funicular up to **Ljubljana Castle** (p524) to get an idea of the lay of the land. After a seafood lunch at **Ribca** (p531), explore the Old Town then cross the Ljubljanica River via St James Bridge and walk north along bust-lined Vegova ul to Kongresni trg. Over a cup of something hot and a slice of something sweet at **Zvezda** (p532), plan your evening: low key at **Jazz Club Gajo** (p533), chichi at **Top: Eat & Party** (p533) or alternative at **Metelkova Mesto** (p532).

On your second day check out some of the city's excellent **museums** (p525), and then stroll or cycle through Park Tivoli, stopping for an oh-so-local horse burger at **Hot Horse** (p531) along the way.

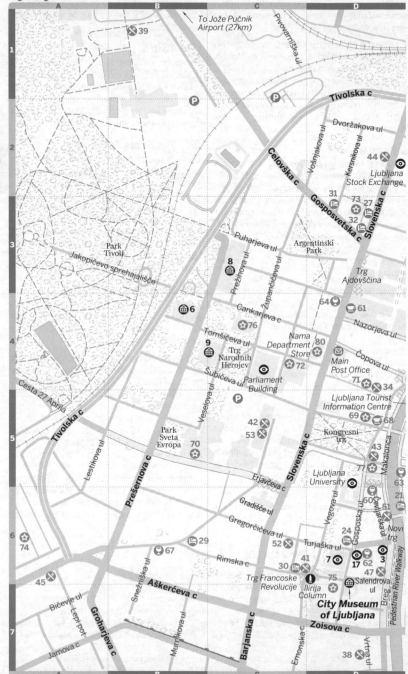

To Jože Pučnik
Airport (27km)

Pivovarniška ul

Tivolska c

Dvoržakova ul

Vošnjakova ul

Kersnikova ul

44

Ljubljana
Stock Exchange

Celovška c

Gosposvetska c

Slovenska c

31

73

27

32

Puharjeva ul

Argentinski
Park

Trg
Ajdovščina

Park
Tivoli

Jakopičevo sprehajališče

Prežihova ul

Župančičeva ul

8

Čankarjeva c

64

61

Nazorjeva ul

6

76

Tomšičeva ul

9

Trg
Narodnih
Herojev

Nama
Department
Store

80

Čopova ul

Main
Post Office

71

34

Šubičeva ul

72

Parliament
Building

Ljubljana Tourist
Information Centre

69

68

Veselova ul

42

53

Kongresni
trg

43

77

Makalonca

Cesta 27 Aprila

Tivolska c

Prešernova c

Park
Sveta
Evropa

70

Erjavčeva c

Ljubljana
University

63

Vegova ul

600

21

51

Gosposka ul

Čevljarška ul

Gradišče ul

Novi
trg

Lestikova ul

Gregorčičeva ul

24

74

67

52

Turjaška ul

7

17

62

3

45

30

41

75

47

Rimska c

Trg Francoske
Revolucije

Ilirija
Column

Salendrova
ul

**City Museum
of Ljubljana**

Bičevje ul

Lepi pot

Snežniška ul

Aškerčeva c

Murnikova ul

Barjanska c

Zoisova c

Jamova c

Ernonska ul

38

Vrtna ul

Breg

Pedestrian River Walkway

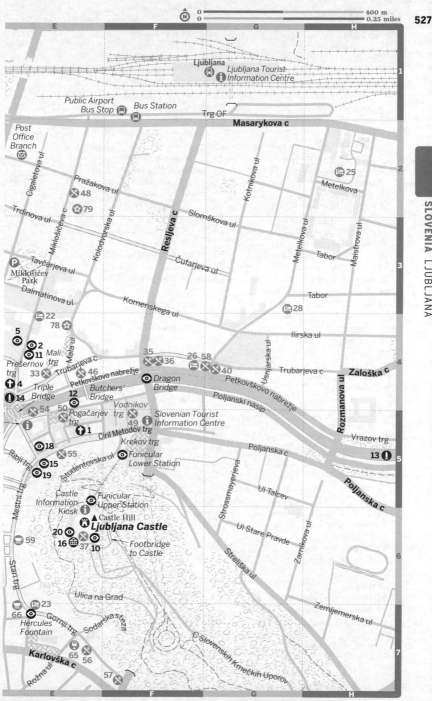

0 — 400 m
0 — 0.25 miles

Ljubljana

Ljubljana Tourist
Information Centre

Public Airport
Bus Stop

Bus Station

Trg OF

Masarykova c

Post
Office
Branch

Olgaletova ul

Pražakova ul

48

79

Trdinova ul

Miklošičeva c

Kolodvorska ul

Resljeva c

Slomškova ul

Kotnikova ul

25

Metelkova

Metelkova ul

Majstrova ul

Tavčarjeva ul

Miklošičev
Park

Dalmatinova ul

Čufarjeva ul

Tabor

Komenskega ul

Tabor

28

Ilirska ul

22

78

5

2

11

Mali
trg

Mala ul

Trubarjeva c

Usnjarska ul

Trubarjeva c

Zaloška c

Prešernov
trg

33

46

Petkovškovo nabrežje

35

26 58

36

40

Dragon
Bridge

4

Triple
Bridge

14

Butchers'
Bridge

12

Petkovškovo nabrežje

Poljanski nasip

Rozmanova ul

54

50

Pogačarjev
trg

1

Vodnikov
trg

49

Slovenian Tourist
Information Centre

Vrazov trg

13

Ciril Metodov trg

Krekov trg

Poljanska c

Poljanska c

18

55

Studentovska ul

Funicular
Lower Station

Ribji trg

15

19

Castle
Information
Kiosk

Funicular
Upper Station

Mestni trg

▲Castle Hill

Ljubljana Castle

Stari trg

59

20

16

37 10

Footbridge
to Castle

Strossmayerjeva

Ul Talcev

Ul Stare Pravde

Streliška ul

Zamlinkova ul

Ulica na Grad

66

23

Gornji trg

Sodarska steza

Hercules
Fountain

Zemljemerska ul

Karlovška c

65

56

Rožna ul

57

C Slovenskih Kmečkih Uporov

residential suites surrounding two courtyards of a former palace, parts of which date back to the 16th century. The suites are enormous, many retain their original features and are equipped with a full kitchen. The in-house spa facilities over two floors are the flashiest in Ljubljana.

Slamič B&B
PENSION €€

(☏433 82 33; www.slamic.si; Kersnikova ul 1; s €65-75, d €95-100; P❄@) It's a titch away from the action but Slamič, a B&B above a famous cafe and teahouse, offers 11 bright rooms with antique(ish) furnishings and parquet floors. Choice rooms include the ones looking onto a back garden and Nos 9 and 11 just off an enormous terrace.

Penzion Pod Lipo
PENSION €€

(☏031-809 893; www.penzion-podlipo.com; Borštnikov trg 3; d/tr/q €64/75/100; @) Sitting atop one of Ljubljana's oldest *gostilne* and by a 400-year-old linden tree along Rimska c, this 10-room inn offers excellent value in a part of the city that is filling up with bars and restaurants. We love the communal kitchen, the original hardwood floors, the computer in each room and the east-facing terrace that catches the morning sun.

TOP CHOICE ✦ Celica Hostel
HOSTEL €€

(☏230 97 00; www.hostelcelica.com; Metelkova ul 8; dm €17-21, s/d/tr cell €53/56/66, 3- to 5-bed r per person €21-26, 7-bed r per person €19-23; P@☎) This stylishly revamped former prison (built in 1882) in Metelkova has 20 'cells', designed by as many different architects and complete with their original bars; it also has nine rooms and apartments with three to seven beds; and a packed, popular 12-bed dorm. The ground floor is home to cafes (set lunch €4.10 to €6.40; open 7am to midnight), and the hostel boasts its own gallery where everyone can show their own work. Laundry costs €7.

Ljubljana Resort
CAMPING GROUND €

(☏568 39 13; www.ljubljanaresort.si/eng; Dunajska c 270; camping adult €7-13, child €5.25-9.75; P❄@⛱) This attractive 6-hectare camping ground-cum-resort 5km north of the centre also offers a 62-room hotel (singles €60 to €75, doubles €75 to €90) and a dozen stationery mobile homes (€84 to €158) accommodating up to five people. Next door is **Laguna** (www.laguna.si, adult/child from €14/10, ☺May-to Sep), a water park with the works. Take bus 6 or 11 to the Ježica stop.

Zeppelin Hostel
HOSTEL €

(☏051-637 436; www.zeppelinhostel.com; 2 fl, Slovenska c 47; dm €18-24, d €49-60; @☎) Located in the historic Evropa building on the corner of Gosposvetska c, this hostel with three large and bright dorm rooms (four to eight beds) and three doubles (one en suite) is run by an affable Slovenian-Spanish couple.

Pri Mraku
HOTEL €€

(☏421 96 00; www.daj-dam.si; Rimska c 4; s €70-86, d €106-116; P❄@☎) Although it calls itself a *gostilna*, 'At Twilight' is really just a smallish hotel with 35 rooms in an old building with a garden. Rooms on the 1st and 4th floors have air-con. It's near the Križanke on Trg Francoske Revolucije – ideal for culture vultures.

Hotel Park
HOTEL €€

(☏300 25 00; www.hotelpark.si; Tabor 9; s €55-90, d €70-130; P❄@) A recladding outside and a facelift within has turned this 243-room tower-block hotel an even better-value central mid-range choice. The 200 pleasant 'standard' and 'comfort' (air-conditioned) rooms are bright and unpretentiously well equipped. Cheaper 'hostel' rooms on the 7th and 12th floors, some of which have shared facilities (but always a toilet), cost €20 to €23 per person in a double and €17 to €19 in a quad. Students with ISIC cards get a 10% discount.

Alibi Hostel
HOSTEL €

(☏251 12 44; www.alibi.si; Cankarjevo nabrežje 27; dm €15-18, d €40-50; @☎) This well-situated 106-bed hostel on the Ljubljanica has brightly painted, airy dorms with four to eight wooden bunks and a dozen doubles. There's a private apartment at the top for six people. Just south of Miklošičev Park, its sister property, the smaller **Alibi M14 Hostel** (☏232 27 70; www.alibi.si; 2 fl, Miklošičeva c 14; dm €18-20, d €50-60; ❄@☎), has six rooms, including a 10-bed dorm.

H2O
HOSTEL €€

(☏041-662 266; info@simbol.si; Petkovškovo nabrežje 47; dm/d/q €17/50/68; @☎) Also along the Ljubljanica, this six-room hostel wraps around a tiny courtyard, and one room has views of the castle. Rooms, with two to six beds, have their own kitchens.

Hotel Center
PENSION €€

(☏520 06 40, 041 263 347; www.hotelcenter.si; Slovenska c 51; s €45-55, d €60-66; @) The decor is simple and functionally modern at this new eight-room pension, but everything is spotless and you can't beat the central location.

The owners run the popular Cafe Compañeros (p532) below.

✗ Eating

Špajza
TOP CHOICE

SLOVENIAN €€

(☑425 30 94; Gornji trg 28; mains €14.60-22; ⊘noon-11pm) A favourite in the Old Town, the 'Pantry' is a nicely decorated rabbit warren of a restaurant with rough-hewn tables and chairs, wooden floors, frescoed ceilings and nostalgic bits and pieces. Try the stupendous *žlikrofi* (pasta stuffed with cheese, bacon and chives; €9 to €12), mushroom dishes in season or the *kozliček iz pečiče* (oven-roasted kid; €14.60). Wines from a dozen different producers from Goriška Brda in Primorska are served.

Pri Škofu
SLOVENIAN €€

(☑426 45 08; Rečna ul 8; mains €8-22; ⊘10am-midnight Mon-Fri, noon-midnight Sat & Sun) This wonderful little place in tranquil Krakovo, south of the city centre, serves some of the best prepared local dishes and salads in Ljubljana from an ever-changing menu. Weekday set lunches are €8.

Most
TOP CHOICE

INTERNATIONAL €€

(☑232 81 83; www.restavracija-most.si; Petkovškovo nabrežje 21; mains €13-23) This tastefully decorated, very welcoming restaurant at the foot of Butchers' Bridge serves international dishes that lean toward the Mediterranean. Try the saffron risotto with shrimps and porcini.

Taverna Tatjana
SEAFOOD €€

(☑421 00 87; Gornji trg 38; mains €8.50-25; ⊘5pm-midnight Mon-Sat) A wooden-beamed cottage pub with a nautical theme, this is actually a rather exclusive fish restaurant with a lovely back courtyard for the warmer months.

Čompa
SLOVENIAN €

(☑040-542 552; Trubarjeva c 40; mains €10-18; ⊘noon-3pm & 7pm-1am Mon-Sat) This new favourite Slovenian restaurant with outside seating along pedestrian Trubarjeva c serves massive platters of meats, cheese and vegetables *na žaru* (on the grill) to happy, very hungry punters.

Gostilna na Gradu
SLOVENIAN €

(☑08-205 19 30; www.nagradu.si; Grajska planota 1; dishes €4.50-10) After a wait of what seemed to be forever, the comfortable Inn at the Castle has opened in Ljubljana Castle and – joy of joys – it's serving affordable local dishes such as *jelenov golaž* (venison goulash),

skutni njoki (gnocchi with curd cheese) and *bobiči* (Istrian-style vegetarian soup).

Le Petit Restaurant
FRENCH €€

(☑426 14 88; Trg Francoske Revolucije 4; mains €12-20; ⊘7.30am-1am) Opposite the Križanke, what has always been a popular French-style cafe on French Revolution Sq has now opened a wonderful restaurant on the 1st floor with a provincial decor and menu. The pleasant, boho cafe still offers great coffee and a wide range of breakfast goodies (€2.20 to €6.50) and lunches (sandwiches €2.90 to €4.50).

Harambaša
BALKAN €

(☑041-843 106; Vrtna ul 8; dishes €4.50-6; ⊘10am-10pm Mon-Fri, noon-10pm Sat, to 6pm Sun) You'll find authentic Bosnian – Sarajevan to be precise – dishes here such as *čevapčiči* (spicy meatballs) and *pljeskavica* (meat patties) served at low tables in a charming modern cottage.

Zhong Hua
CHINESE €

(☑230 16 65; Trubarjeva c 50; mains €5.80-12.10; ⊘11am-10.30pm) This place just up from the Ljubljanica is just about the most authentic Chinese restaurant in town. Name a dish and they'll make it – and pretty authentically too. The less adventurous will to stick with rice and noodle dishes (€4.90 to €6.50).

Sokol
SLOVENIAN €

(☑439 68 55; Ciril Metodov trg 18; mains €7-20; ⊘7am-11pm Mon-Sat, 10am-11pm Sun) In an old vaulted house, traditional Slovenian food is served on heavy tables by costumed waiters. Along with traditional dishes such as *obara* (veal stew, €7) and Krvavica sausage with cabbage and turnips (€8.50), there's more exotic fare such as grilled stallion steak (€16).

Namasté
INDIAN €€

(☑425 01 59; www.restavracija-namaste.si; Breg 8; mains €6.30-17.90; ⊘11am-midnight Mon-Sat, to 10pm Sun) Should you fancy a bit of Indian, head for this place on the left bank of the Ljubljanica. You won't get high street quality curry but the thalis (from €8) and tandoori dishes (from €9) are good.

Cantina Mexicana
MEXICAN €€

(☑426 93 25; www.cantina.si; Knafljev prehod 3; mains €7.90-18.80; ⊘11am-midnight Sun-Thu, to 1am Fri & Sat) The capital's most stylish Mexican restaurant has an eye-catching red-and-blue exterior and hacienda-like decor inside. The fajitas (€8.70 to €14.30) are great.

Quick Eats

Ribca
SEAFOOD €

(☑425 15 44; Adamič-Lundrovo nabrežje 1; dishes €3.30-7.60; ☺8am-4pm Mon-Fri, to 2pm Sat) This basement seafood bar, below the Plečnik Colonnade in Pogačarjev trg, serves tasty fried squid, sardines and herrings to hungry market-goers. Set lunch is €7.50.

Restavracija 2000
SELF-SERVICE €

(☑476 69 25; Trg Republike 1; dishes €2.15-3.70; ☺9am-7pm Mon-Fri, to 3pm Sat) In the basement of the Maximarket department store, this self-service eatery is surprisingly upbeat, and just the ticket if you want something quick while visiting the museums.

Paninoteka
SANDWICH BAR €

(☑059-018 455; Jurčičev trg 3; soups & toasted sandwiches €3-6; ☺8am-1am Mon-Sat, 9am-11pm Sun) Healthy sandwich creations on a lovely little square by the river with outside seating.

Ajdovo Zrno
VEGETARIAN €

(☑040-482 446; www.satwa.si; Trubarjeva c 7; soups & sandwiches €2-4, set lunch €6; ☺10am-7pm Mon-Fri) 'Buckwheat Grain' serves soups, sandwiches, fried vegetables and lots of different salads (self-service, €3 to €10) and casseroles (€3.50). And it has terrific, freshly squeezed juices. Enter from little Mali trg.

Hot Horse
BURGERS €

(☑031-709 716; www.hot-horse.si; Park Tivoli, Celovška c 25; snacks & burgers €2.80-6; ☺9am-6am Tue-Sun, 10am-6am Mon) This kiosk in the city's largest park supplies *Ljubljančani* with one of their favourite treats: horse burgers (€4).

Falafel
STREET FOOD €

(☑041-640 166; Trubarjeva c 40; dishes €3.50-4.50, daily menu €4.50; ☺11am-midnight Mon-Fri, noon-midnight Sat, 1-10pm Sun) Sandwiches, salads and the eponymous falafel – ideal for veggies on the hoof (though there are meat dishes).

Nobel Burek
STREET FOOD €

(Miklošičeva c 30; burek €2, pizza slices €1.40; ☺24hr) This hole-in-the-wall serves Slovenian-style fast food round-the-clock.

As in all European capitals, Ljubljana is awash in pizzerias (€5 to €8.50).

Pizzeria Foculus (☑421 92 95; www.foculus. com; Gregorčičeva ul 3; ☺11am-midnight) Pick of the crop, which boasts a vaulted ceiling painted with spring and autumn leaves.

Kavalino (☑232 09 90; www.kavalino.si; Trubarjeva c 52; ☺8am-10pm Mon-Thu, to 11pm Fri & Sat)

Trta (☑426 50 66; www.trta.si; Grudnovo nabrežje 21; ☺11am-10pm Mon-Fri, noon-10.30pm Sat) On the right bank of the Ljubljanica.

Mirje (☑426 60 15; Tržaška c 5; ☺10am-10pm Mon-Fri, noon-10pm Sat) Southwest of the city centre.

Self-Catering

Handy supermarkets include a large **Mercator** (Slovenska c 55; ☺7am-9pm) southwest of the train and bus stations and a smaller, more central **Mercator branch** (Kongresni trg 9; ☺7am-8pm Mon-Fri, 8am-3pm Sat & Sun) just up from the river.

The **Maximarket supermarket** (Trg Republike 1; ☺9am-9pm Mon-Fri, 8am-5pm Sat) in the basement of the department store of the same name has the largest selection of food and wine in the city centre.

The **open-air market** (Pogačarjev trg & Vodnikov trg; ☺6am-6pm Mon-Fri, to 4pm Sat summer, 6am-4pm Mon-Sat winter), held across two squares north and east of the cathedral, sells mostly fruit and vegetables and dry goods.

🍷 Drinking

Few cities of this size have central Ljubljana's concentration of inviting cafes and bars, the vast majority with outdoor seating in the warmer months.

Bars & Pubs

Nebotičnik
CAFE-BAR

(☑059-070 395; 12th fl, Štefanova ul 1; ☺8am-3am) After a decade-long hibernation this cafe-bar with its breathtaking terrace atop Ljubljana's famed art deco Skyscraper (1933) has awakened, and the 360-degree views are still spectacular.

Pri Zelenem Zajcu
BAR

(☑031-632 992; Rožna ul 3; ☺9am-midnight Mon-Wed & Sun, to 1am Thu & Sat, to 2am Fri) Ljubljana's only absinthe bar, 'At the Green Rabbit' to you, has its own label and relaxed vibe. It's a bit of a warren of a place (as it would be) but we're sure you'll feel comfortably frisky here.

Open Cafe
GAY & LESBIAN

(☑041-391 371; www.open.si; Hrenova ul 19; ☺4pm-midnight) This very stylish gay cafe south of the Old Town has become the meeting point by Ljubljana's burgeoning gay culture.

Makalonca
CAFE-BAR

(☑030-362 450; Hribarjevo nabrežje 19; ☺8am-1am Mon-Sat, 10am-10pm Sun) This cafe-bar with a 100m-long terrace within the columns of the Ljubljanica embankment is the perfect place to nurse a drink and watch the river roll by.

Žmavc
CAFE-BAR

(☎251 03 24; Rimska c 21; ◷7.30am-1am Mon-Fri, from 10am Sat, from 6pm Sun) This super popular student hang-out west of Slovenska c, with *manga* comic-strip scenes and graffiti decorating the walls, is always voted tops in cafe-bar polls here.

Dvorni Bar
WINE BAR

(☎251 12 57; www.dvornibar.net; Dvorni trg 2; ◷8am-1am Mon-Sat, 9am-midnight Sun) This wine bar is an excellent place to taste Slovenian vintages; it stocks more than 100 varieties and has wine tastings every second or third Wednesday of the month (check the website).

Maček
CAFE-BAR

(☎425 37 91; Krojaška ul 5; ◷9am-12.30am Mon-Sat, to 11pm Sun) *The* place to be seen in Ljubljana on a summer afternoon, the 'Cat' is the most popular venue on the right bank of the Ljubljanica.

LP Bar
CAFE-BAR

(☎041-846 457; Novi trg 2; ◷8am-midnight Mon-Wed & Sat, to 1am Thu & Fri, 9am-3pm Sun) Within the Academy of Arts and Sciences, LP (no relation to us!) is a civilised place for a libation, with cafe-bar, bookshop and heated seats outside. Great views of the castle.

Cafes & Teahouses

Zvezda
CAFE

(☎421 90 90; Kongresni trg 4 & Wolfova ul 14; ◷7am-11pm Mon-Sat, 10am-8pm Sun) The 'Star' has all the usual varieties of coffee and tea but is celebrated for its shop-made cakes, especially *skutina pečena* (€2.90), an eggy cheesecake.

Čajna Hiša
TEAHOUSE

(☎421 24 44; Stari trg 3; ◷9am-10.30pm Mon-Fri, 9am-3pm & 6-10pm Sat; ☏) If you take your cuppa seriously, come here; the appropriately named 'Tea House' offers a wide range of green and black teas and fruit tisanes (pot €2 to €3.60)

Juice Box
JUICE BAR

(☎051-614 545; Slovenska c 38; juices & smoothies €3.60-4.90; ◷7am-8pm Mon-Fri, 8am-3pm Sat; ☏) Of the new crop of juice bars, this is the best, with some excellent fruit and vegetable combinations.

Slaščičarna Pri Vodnjaku
ICE-CREAM PARLOUR

(☎425 07 12; Stari trg 30; ◷8am-midnight) For ice cream, the 'Confectionery by the Fountain' will surely satisfy – there are almost three-dozen flavours (per scoop €1.20), as well as teas (€2) and fresh juices (from €1.40).

☆ Entertainment

The free bimonthly **Ljubljana in Your Pocket** (www.inyourpocket.com) is your best source of information though the **Ljubljana.info** (www.ljubljana.info) has practical information and listings as well.

Nightclubs

Metelkova Mesto
CLUB

(www.metelkova.org; Masarykova c 24) 'Metelkova Town', an ex-army garrison taken over by squatters after independence, is now a free-living commune. In this two-courtyard block, idiosyncratic clubs, bars and art spaces hide behind brightly tagged doorways, coming to life generally after midnight, daily in summer and at weekends the rest of the year. Venues come in and go out; try to wade though the website or just stroll over and have a look yourself. It's just behind the Celica Hostel (p529).

Cafe Compañeros
CLUB

(☎520 06 40; Slovenska c 51; ◷11am-5am) Raucous studenty hang-out with a lounge and terrace bar on the ground floor and a wild and crazy club with live music below.

Klub K4
CLUB

(☎438 02 61; www.klubk4.org; Kersnikova ul 4; ◷10pm-2am Tue, 11pm-4am Wed & Thu, 11pm-6am Fri & Sat, 10pm-4am Sun) This evergreen venue in the basement of the Student Organisation of Ljubljana University (ŠOU) headquarters features rave-electronic music on Fridays and Saturdays, with other styles of music on weeknights, and a popular gay and lesbian night, K4 Roza, on Sundays. It closes in summer.

KMŠ
CLUB

(☎425 74 80; www.klubkms.si; Tržaška ul 2; ◷8am-5am Mon-Fri, 9pm-5am Sat) Located in the deep recesses of a former tobacco factory complex, the 'Maribor Student Club' is comatose till Saturday when it turns into a lively dance place.

Bachus Center Club
CLUB

(☎241 82 40; www.bachus-center.com; Kongresni trg 3; ◷8pm-5am Tue-Sat) This place has something for everyone, including a restaurant and bar-lounge, and attracts a mainstream crowd.

Club As
CLUB

(☎425 88 22; www.gostilnaas.si; Čopova 5a, enter from Knafljev prehod; ◷9am-3am Wed-Sat) DJs transform this candlelit basement bar into a pumping, crowd-pulling nightclub four nights a week.

Top: Eat & Party
CLUB

(☎040-667 722; www.klubtop.si; Tomšičeva ul 2; ⏰11pm-5am) This retro restaurant and cocktail bar on the 6th floor of the Nama department store becomes a popular dance venue nightly and attracts a very chi-chi crowd. Take the glass-bubble lift from along Slovenska c or the lift in the passageway linking Cankarjeva ulica and Tomšičeva ulica.

Live Music

Orto Bar
LIVE MUSIC

(☎232 16 74; www.orto-bar.com; Graboličeva ul 1; ⏰9pm-4am Tue & Wed, to 5am Thu-Sat) A popular bar-club for late-night drinking and dancing with occasional live music, Orto is just five minutes from Metelkova Mesto.

Hugo Barrera Club
LIVE MUSIC

(☎040-177 477; Adamič Lundrovo nabrežje 5; ⏰7am-2am Mon-Wed, to 3am Thu-Sat, 10am-2am Sun) Below the Plečnik Colonnade at the foot of Butchers' Bridge this new venue offers live music from the '60s, '70s and '80s four nights a week.

Sax Pub
LIVE MUSIC

(☎283 9009; Eipprova ul 7; ⏰noon-1am Mon, 10am-1am Tue-Sat, 4-10pm Sun) Over two decades in Trnovo, the colourful Sax has live jazz at around 9pm on Thursday or Sunday from late August to December and February to June. Canned stuff rules at other times.

Jazz Club Gajo
LIVE MUSIC

(☎425 32 06; www.jazzclubgajo.com; Beethovnova ul 8; ⏰7pm-2am Mon-Sat) Established in 1994, Gajo is the city's premier venue for live jazz and attracts both local and international talent. Jam sessions are at 9pm on Monday.

Roxly Cafe Bar
LIVE MUSIC

(☎430 10 21, 041-399 599; www.roxly.si; Mala ul 5; ⏰8am-2am Mon-Wed, to 3am Thu & Fri, 10am-3am Sat) This cafe, bar and restaurant north of the Ljubljanica features live rock music (mostly blues and rock) from 10pm two or three nights a week.

Performing Arts

Cankarjev Dom
LIVE MUSIC

(☎241 71 00, box office 241 72 99; www.cd-cc.si; Prešernova c 10) is Ljubljana's premier cultural centre and has two large auditoriums (the Gallus Hall has perfect acoustics) and a dozen smaller performance spaces.

Križanke
LIVE MUSIC

(☎241 60 00, box office 241 60 26; www.festival-lj. si; Trg Francoske Revolucije 1-2) Hosts concerts of the Ljubljana Festival (p525) and other events at a former 18th-century monastic complex.

Opera House
OPERA, LIVE MUSIC

(☎241 17 40, box office 241 17 66; www.opera.si; Župančičeva ul 1) Opera and ballet are performed at the renovated and extended neo-Renaissance Opera House (1882).

Philharmonic Hall
LIVE MUSIC

(Slovenska Filharmonija; ☎241 08 00; www.filharmonija.si; Kongresni trg 10) This concert hall dating from 1891 is home to the Slovenian Philharmonic Orchestra.

Cinema

Slovenska Kinoteka
CINEMA

(☎434 25 20; www.kinoteka.si; Miklošičeva c 28) The 'Slovenian Cinematheque' screens archival art and classic films in their original languages.

ℹ Information

Discount Cards

The new **Urbana-Ljubljana Tourist Card** (www.visitljubljana.si/en/ljubljana-and-more/ljubljana-tourist-card), available from the tourist offices for 24/48/72 hours (€23/30/35), offers free admission to most museums and galleries, walking and boat tours and unlimited city bus travel.

Internet Access

Web connection is available at virtually every hostel and hotel, the Slovenia Tourist Information Centre (p534; per 30min €1), the STA Travel Cafe (p534; per 20min €1) and the Student Organisation of the University of Ljubljana (p534; free). In addition:

Cyber Cafe Xplorer (☎430 19 91; Petkovškovo nabrežje 23; per 30min/hr €2.50/4; ⏰10am-10pm Mon-Fri, 2-10pm Sat & Sun) Some 10 computers, wi-fi and cheap international phone calls.

DrogArt (☎439 72 70; Kolodvorska ul 20; 1st 15min free, then per 30min/hr €1/1.80; ⏰10am-4pm Mon-Fri) Opposite the train station; three computers.

Portal.si Internet (☎234 46 00; Trg OF 4; per hr €4.20; ⏰5.30am-10.30pm Sun-Fri, 5am-10pm Sat) In the bus station (get code from window 4); three computers.

Internet Resources

City of Ljubljana (www.ljubljana.si) Comprehensive information portal on every aspect of life and tourism.

Left Luggage

Bus station (Trg OF 4; per day €2; ☺5.30am-10.30pm Sun-Fri, 5am-10pm Sat) Window 3.

Train station (Trg OF 6; per day €2-3; ☺24hr) Coin lockers on platform 1.

Maps

Excellent free maps are available from the tourist offices. The more detailed 1:20,000-scale *Mestni Načrt Ljubljana* (Ljubljana City Map; €7.70) from **Kod & Kam** (☑600 50 80; www.kod-kam.si; Miklošičeva c 34) is available at newsstands and bookshops.

Medical Services

Central Pharmacy (Centralna Lekarna; ☑244 23 60; Prešernov trg 5; ☺7.30am-7.30pm Mon-Fri, 8am-3pm Sat)

Health Centre Ljubljana (Zdravstveni Dom Ljubljana; www.zd-lj.si; ☑472 37 00; Metelkova ul 9; ☺7.30am-7pm) For nonemergencies.

University Medical Centre Ljubljana (Univerzitetni Klinični Center Ljubljana; ☑522 50 50; www3.kclj.si; Zaloška c 2; ☺24hr) A&E service.

Money

There are ATMs at every turn, including a row of them outside the main TIC office. At the train station you'll find a **bureau de change** (☺7am-8pm) changing cash (but not travellers cheques) for no commission.

Abanka (Slovenska c 50; ☺9am-5pm Mon-Fri)

Nova Ljubljanska Banka (Trg Republike 2; ☺8am-6pm Mon-Fri)

Post

Main post office (Slovenska c 32; ☺8am-7pm Mon-Fri, to 1pm Sat) Holds poste restante for 30 days and changes money.

Post office branch (Pražakova ul 3; ☺8am-7pm Mon-Fri, to noon Sat) Just southwest of the bus and train stations.

Tourist Information

Tourist Information Centre Ljubljana Old Town (TIC; ☑306 12 15; www.visitljubljana.si; Kresija Bldg, Stritarjeva ul; ☺8am-9pm Jun-Sep, 8am-7pm Oct-May); train station (☑433 94 75; Trg OF 6; ☺8am-10pm Jun-Sep, 10am-7pm Mon-Fri, 8am-3pm Sat Oct-May) Knowledgeable and enthusiastic staff dispense information, maps and useful literature and help with accommodation.

Slovenia Tourist Information Centre (STIC; ☑306 45 76; www.slovenia.info; Krekov trg 10; ☺8am-9pm Jun-Sep, 8am-7pm Oct-May) Good source of information for the rest of Slovenia, with internet and bicycle rental also available.

Student Organisation of the University of Ljubljana

(Študentska Organizacija Univerze Ljubljani; ŠOU; ☑433 03 20, 051-373 999; www.sou-lj.si; Trubarjeva c 7; ☺9am-6pm Mon-Thu, 9am-3pm Fri) Information and free internet.

Travel Agency

STA Ljubljana (☑439 16 90, 041-612 711; www.staljubljana.com; 1st fl, Trg Ajdovščina 1; ☺10am-5pm Mon-Fri) Discount airfares for students; go online at the **STA Travel Cafe** (☺8am-midnight Mon-Sat).

❶ Getting There & Away

The bus and train stations are 800m north-east of Prešernov trg up Miklošičeva c. Ljubljana's Jože Pučnik Airport is 27km north of the city at Brnik near Kranj.

Bus

The **bus station** (☑234 46 00, information 090-934 230; www.ap-ljubljana.si; Trg OF 4; ☺5.30am-10.30pm Sun-Fri, 5am-10pm Sat) opposite the train station has bilingual info-phones. Buses serve Bohinj (€8.70, 2¼ hours, 91km, hourly) via Bled (€6.30, 1¼ hours, 57km, hourly). Those to Piran (€12, 2½ to three hours, 140km, up to five daily) go via Koper (€11.10, 1¾ to 2½ hours, 122km) and Postojna (€6, one hour, 54km, half-hourly). There's also service to Maribor (€12.40, three hours, 141km, between two and four daily).

International bus services from Ljubljana include Belgrade (€35, 7¾ hours, 537km, three times daily); Florence (€38, eight hours, 480km, 5.10am daily); Frankfurt (€86, 14 hours, 777km, 6.30pm daily) via Munich (€44, 6¾ hours, 344km); Pula (€22, 4½ hours, 249km, once daily) via Poreč (€21, three hours, 202km) and Rovinj (€21, 2½ hours, 182km); Sarajevo (€38, 10 hours, 566km, twice daily); Skopje (€50, 16 hours, 978km, twice daily); Split (€44, 10½ hours, 528km, daily in summer) via Rijeka (€17, 2½ hours, 136km); Trieste (€11.60, 2¼ hours, 106km, twice daily); and Venice–Mestre (€25, five hours, 230km, three daily).

Train

Ljubljana's **train station** (☑291 33 32; www.slo-zeleznice.si; Trg OF 6; ☺5am-10pm) has services to Koper (€10, 2½ hours, 153km, up to five daily). Alternatively you can take one of the more frequent Sežana-bound trains and change at Divača (€6.85, 1½ hours, 104km).

Ljubljana–Vienna trains (€63.20, 6¼ hours, 385km, one direct, four via Maribor daily) via Graz (€34.20, 200km, 3½ hours) are expensive, although Spar Schiene fares go as low as €29 on certain trains at certain times.

Three trains depart daily for Munich (€72, six hours, 405km). The 11.50pm departure has sleeping carriages available.

A Venice train (one way/return €25/40, four hours, 244km) via Sežana departs at 2.28am. But it's cheaper to go first to Nova Gorica (€8.50, 3½ hours, 153km, five daily), cross over on foot to the train station in Gorizia and then take an Italian train to Venice (about €9, 2½ hours).

For Zagreb (€13.40, 2½ hours, 154km) there are seven trains daily via Zidani Most. Two trains from the capital at 6.20am and 2.53pm serve Rijeka (€13.80, 2½ hours, 136km) via Postojna.

Trains to Budapest (€53.40, 8¾ hours, 451km, twice daily) go via Ptuj and Hodoš; there are 'Budapest Spezial' fares available for as low as €29 on certain trains at certain times. Belgrade (€25 to €44, 10 hours, 535km) is served by four trains a day.

Getting Around

The cheapest way to/from Ljubljana's **Jože Pučnik Airport** (LJU; ☎04-206 19 81; www.lju-airport.si) at Brnik is by city bus (€4.10, 45 minutes, 27km) from stop 28 at the bus station. These run at 5.20am and hourly from 6.10am to 8.10pm Monday to Friday; on weekends there's a bus at 6.10am and then one every two hours from 9.10am to 7.10pm. A **private airport van** (☎040-771 771, 051- 321 414; www.airport-shuttle.si) also links Trg OF near the bus station (€5) or your hotel (€9) with the airport (30 minutes) up to 11 times daily between 5.10am and 10.30pm. A **taxi** (☎031-216 111; 059-060 777) from Center in Ljubljana will cost €40.

Ljubljana's city buses operate every five to 15 minutes from 5am (6am on Sunday) to 10.30pm, though some start as early as 3.15am and go until midnight and a couple run overnight. The flat fare (€0.80) is paid with a stored-value magnetic Urbana Card (www.jh-lj.si/urbana) which can be purchased at newsstands, tourist offices and the **LPP Information Centre** (☎430 51 75; Slovenska c 56; ⏲7am-7pm Mon-Fri) for €2; credit can then be added for from €1 to €50. The central area is perfectly walkable, though, so buses are really only necessary if you're staying way out of town.

Ljubljana Bike (per 2hr/day €1/5; ⏲8am-7pm or 9pm Apr-Oct) has two-wheelers available from locations around the city, including outside the STIC and opposite the Antiq Hotel.

JULIAN ALPS

The Julian Alps form Slovenia's dramatic northwest frontier with Italy. Triglav National Park, established in 1924, includes almost all of the Alps lying within Slovenia. The centrepiece of the park is, of course, Mt Triglav (2864m), Slovenia's highest and most sacred mountain, but there are many other peaks here reaching above 2000m. Along with an abundance of fauna and flora, the area offers a wide range of outdoor activities.

Kranj

☎04 / POP 34,620

At the foot of the Kamnik-Savinja Alps, with the snowcapped peak of Storžič (2132m) and others in full view to the north, Kranj is Slovenia's fourth-largest city. The attractive Old Town, perched on an escarpment above the confluence of the Sava and Kokra Rivers, barely measures 250m wide by 1km long.

The frequent buses between Kranj and Ljubljana's airport at nearby Brnik (€1.80, 10 minutes, 10km) make it possible to head straight to the Julian Alps without first going to the capital. While waiting for your onward bus to Bled (€3.60, 40 minutes, 29km), have a look at the **Old Town**, a 600m walk south from the bus station. On your way you'll pass the 87-room **Hotel Creina** (☎281 75 00; www.hotel-creina.si; Koroška c 5; s €60-80, d €80-100; P❄@🛜), expensive but the only game in town with bikes for rent (per hour/day €1/12). The **tourist office** (☎238 04 50; www.tourism-kranj.si; Glavni trg 2; ⏲8am-7pm Mon-Sat, 9am-6pm Sun) can find you a private room from €20 or, in summer, a bed in a student dormitory (from €15).

Pedestrianised streets lead to the **Church of St Cantianus**, with impressive frescos and stained glass. Another 300m further south, the Old Town dead-ends at the Serbian Orthodox **Plague Church**, built during a time of pestilence in 1470, and the 16th-century **defence tower** behind it. Ask the TIC about guided tours of the **tunnels** (adult/child €3/2.50; ⏲5pm Tue & Fri, 10am Sat & Sun) under the Old Town built as air-raid shelters during WWII. **Mitnica** (☎040-678 778; Tavčarjeva ul 35; ⏲7am-11pm Mon-Wed, 7am-1am Thu, 7am-2am Fri & Sat, 10am-11pm Sun) is a relaxing cafe-bar in a 16th-century toll house with a huge terrace overlooking the river.

Bled

☎04 / POP 5460

With an emerald-green lake, a picture-postcard church on a tiny island, a medieval castle clinging to a rocky cliff, and some of Slovenia's highest peaks as backdrops, Bled seems to have been designed by some god of tourism. Bled can get crowded in season, but it's always an excellent base from which to explore the mountains.

Bled

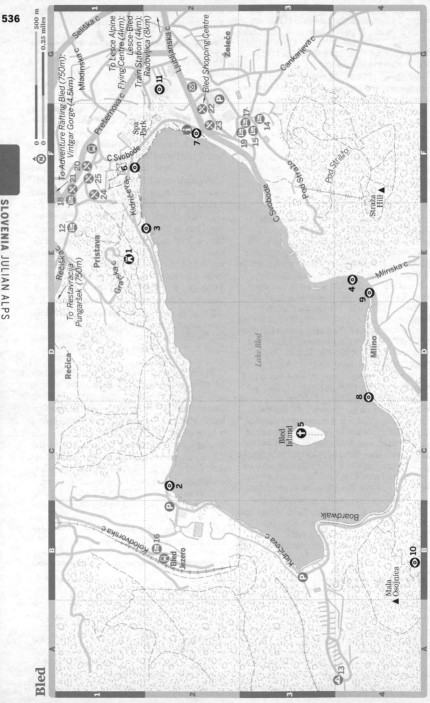

Želječe

Lake Bled

Bled Island

Mlino

Rečica

Pristava

Spa Park

Bled Jezero

Straža Hill

Mala Osojnica

Bled

⊙ Sights

Lake Bled LAKE

A relaxed stroll around the 2km-by-1.4km lake shouldn't take more than a couple of hours, including the short climb to the **Osojnica viewing point** in the southwest. If you prefer, jump aboard the **tourist train** (adult/child €3/2; ⊙9am-9pm May-Oct) just south of the TIC for the 40-minute twirl around the lake.

Bled Island ISLAND, CHURCH

This tiny, tear-shaped islet is where you'll find Bled's icon, the baroque **Church of the Assumption** (⊙9am-dusk). The trip by piloted **gondola** (pletna; ☎041-427 155; per person €12) allows enough time on the island to look around and ring the 'lucky' bell; all in all, it's about 1½ hours. Do-it-yourself rowing boats for four/six people cost €10/15 per hour.

Bled Castle CASTLE, MUSEUM

(☎572 9782; www.blejski-grad.si; Grajska c 25; adult/child €7/3.50; ⊙8am-8pm summer, to 6pm

winter) Perched atop a 100m-high cliff, this castle, first mentioned a millennium ago, offers the perfect backdrop to a lake view. One of the easiest ways up on foot leads from behind Bledec Hostel. Admission includes entry to several attractions including the **museum collection** and 16th-century **chapel**.

Vintgar Gorge GORGE

(adult/child €4/2; ⊙8am-7pm mid-May–Oct) The highlight of visiting the gorge, an easy walk 4km to the northwest of the centre, is the 1600m-long wooden walkway (1893) that criss-crosses the swirling Radovna River for the first 700m or so. Thereafter the scenery becomes tamer and ends at the 16m-high **Šum Waterfall**. From June to September, a daily bus (one way/return €3.50/6.30) leaves Bled bus station for Vintgar at 10am daily, arriving at 10.30am and returning at 12.30pm. Otherwise reach it on foot via the Gostilna Vintgar, an inn just 3km away on quiet roads from the Bledec Hostel.

🏃 Activities

Agencies organise a wide range of outdoor activities in and around Bled, offering everything from mountain biking (from €28) and canyoning (€50) to paragliding (€85). One of the best trips is the Emerald River Adventure (€55), an 11-hour hiking and swimming foray into Triglav National Park and along the Soča River available from **3glav adventures** (☎041-683 184; www.3glav-adventures.com; Ljubljanska c 1; ⊙9am-noon & 4-7pm Apr-Oct). **Adventure Rafting Bled** (☎574 40 41, 051-676 008; www.adventure-rafting.si; Grajska c 21; Hrastova ul 2; ☎Apr-Oct) also organises rafting and canyoning. Both the TIC and Kompas (p539) rent bikes for €3.5/11 per hour/day.

🛏️ Sleeping

Kompas (p539) has a list of private rooms and farmhouses, with singles/doubles starting at €24/38.

TOP CHOICE **Hotel Triglav Bled** BOUTIQUE HOTEL €€€
(☎575 26 10; www.hoteltriglavbled.si; Kolodvorska c 33; s €89-159, d €99-179, ste €139-209; P ❄ @ 🛜 🏊) This bijou of a boutique hotel is in a painstakingly restored caravanserai that opened in 1906 opposite Bled Jezero train station. Many of the 22 rooms are furnished with antiques, there's an enormous sloped garden that grows the vegetables served in the 1906 terrace restaurant and the views of the lake from everywhere (including the indoor pool) are breathtaking.

Penzion Mayer
PENSION €€

(②576 10 58; www.mayer-sp.si; Želeška c 7; s €55, d €75-80, apt €120-150; P@) This flower bedecked 12-room inn in a renovated 19th-century house has a lovely stand-alone cottage with apartments for two to four people. The Mayer's inhouse restaurant is excellent.

Garni Hotel Berc
PENSION €€

(②576 56 58; www.berc-sp.si; Pod Stražo 13; s €45-50, d €70-80; P@☎) This purpose-built place, reminiscent of a Swiss chalet, has 15 rooms on two floors in a quiet location above the lake. Just opposite is a smaller branch, **Garni Penzion Berc** (②574 18 38; Želeška c 15; s €35-40, d €60-65), with 11 rooms.

Camping Bled
CAMPING GROUND €

(②575 20 00; www.camping-bled.com; Kidričeva c 10c; adult €8.50-12.50, child €5.95-8.75, huts d €30-40; P@☎) This popular 6.5-hectare site fills a small valley at the western end of the lake. The new all-natural A-frame huts on a terrace above the site have become one of Bled's most sought-after addresses.

Traveller's Haven
HOSTEL €

(②041-396 545; www.travellers-haven.si; Riklijeva c 1; dm/d €19/48; @) This uber-popular hostel in a converted old villa has six rooms with between two and six beds, a great kitchen, laundry, free bikes and a chilled vibe.

Vila Gorenka
PENSION €

(②574 47 22, 040-958 624; http://freeweb.siol.net/mz2; Želeška c 9; per person €17-25; P@) This budget establishment has 10 double rooms with washbasins – toilets and showers are shared – in a charming old two-story villa dating back to 1909. Some rooms on the 2nd floor have wooden balconies gazing on the lake.

Bledec Hostel
HOSTEL €

(②574 52 50; www.youth-hostel-bledec.si; Grajska c 17; HI members/nonmembers dm €18/20, d €48/52; P@☎) This well-organised HI-affiliated hostel in the shadow of the castle has dorms with four to eight beds with bathrooms, a bar and an inexpensive restaurant. A laundry service (€8.50) is available and bicycle rental is free.

✖ Eating

You'll find a **Mercator** (Ljubljanska c 4; ☉7am-8pm Mon-Sat, 8am-noon Sun) at the eastern end of Bled Shopping Centre. There's a smaller **Mercator branch** (Prešernova c 48; ☉7am-8pm Mon-Sat, 8am-4pm Sun) close to the hostels.

TOP Restavracija Pungaršek
CHOICE
SLOVENIAN, MEDITERRANEAN €€

(②059-059 136; www.pungarsek.si; Kolodvorska c 2; mains €13.50-22.50; ☉11am-10.30pm Mon-Sat, to 6pm Sun) North of the lake and equidistant from the Hotel Triglav Bled and hostels, this upmarket restaurant is arguably Bled's finest. Mushrooms dishes are exquisite and desserts to die for. Outside seating under the pines in the warmer months.

Gostilna Pri Planincu
SLOVENIAN, BALKAN €

(②574 16 13; Grajska c 8; mains €7-22; ☉10am-10pm) 'At the Mountaineers' is a homey pub-restaurant just down the hill from the hostels, with Slovenian mains and grilled Balkan specialities such as *čevapčiči* (€8.30) and *pljeskavica z kajmakom* (Serbian-style meat patties with mascarpone-like cream cheese; €9). There's pizza upstairs.

Ostarija Peglez'n
SEAFOOD €€

(②574 42 18; C Svobode 19a; mains €8.50-27; ☉noon-midnight) The most colourful restaurant in Bled, the 'Iron Inn' is just opposite the landmark Grand Hotel Toplice, with at-

---

WORTH A TRIP

RADOVLJICA

A short distance southeast of Bled and well served by bus (€1.80, 15 minutes, 8km), the sleepy town of Radovljica (pop 6025) has a particularly delightful square called **Linhartov trg** in its Old Town, where there are restored and painted houses, an interesting gallery, the fascinating **Beekeeping Museum** (②532 05 20; Linhartov trg 1; adult/child €3/2; ☉10am-6pm Tue-Sun summer, 8am-3pm Tue, Thu & Fri, 10am-noon & 3-5pm Wed, Sat & Sun winter) and a **tourist office** (②531 53 00; www.radovljica.si; Gorenjska c 1; 9am-1pm & 2-6pm Mon-Sat summer, 9am-4pm Mon-Fri, to 1pm Sat winter). Have a meal or a drink at **Gostilna Augustin** (②531 41 63; Linhartov trg 15; mains €9-17), a delightful restaurant and bar with a back terrace affording views of Mt Triglav itself. The square lies 400m southeast of the bus station via Gorenjska c or just 100m up narrow Kolodvorska ul from the train station to the south.

The Julian Alps offer some of Europe's finest hiking. In summer 174 mountain huts (*planinska koča* or *planinski dom*) cater to hikers and none is more than five hours' walk from the next. These huts get very crowded, especially on weekends, so booking ahead is wise.

At €27 per person in a room with up to four beds or €18 in a dormitory in a Category I hut (Category II huts charge €20 and €12 respectively), the huts aren't cheap, but as they serve meals (a simple meal should cost between €4.70 and €6.20 in a Category I hut, and €3.50 and €5 in a Category II hut) you can travel light. Sturdy boots and warm clothes are indispensable, even in midsummer. Trails are generally well marked with a white-centred red circle, but you can still get lost and it's very unwise to trek alone.

For information and maps contact the area's tourist offices or the Alpine Association of Slovenia (p556) in Ljubljana.

tractively retro decor and some of the best fish dishes in town.

Pizzeria Rustika   PIZZA €
(☑576 89 00; Riklijeva c 13; pizza €5.70-9.50; ⏱noon-11pm) A marble-roll down the hill from the hostels, this place has its own wood-burning oven and seating on two levels plus an outside terrace.

Slaščičarna Šmon   CAFE €
(☑574 16 16; Grajska c 3; ⏱7.30am-10pm) This is the place for Bled's sweet of choice: *kremna rezina* (€2.40), a layer of vanilla custard topped with whipped cream and sandwiched neatly between two layers of flaky pastry.

ⓘ Information

A Propos Bar (☑574 40 44; Bled Shopping Centre, Ljubljanska c 4; per 15/30/60min €1.25/2.10/4.20; ⏱8am-midnight Sun-Thu, to 1am Fri & Sat) Internet access.

Gorenjska Banka (C Svobode 15) Just north of the Park Hotel.

Kompas (☑572 75 00; www.kompas-bled.si; Bled Shopping Centre, Ljubljanska c 4; ⏱8am-7pm Mon-Sat, 8am-noon & 4-7pm Sun) Private rooms and bicycles.

Post office (Ljubljanska c 10)

Tourist Information Centre Bled (☑574 11 22; www.bled.si; C Svobode 10; ⏱8am-9pm Mon-Sat, 10am-6pm Sun Jul & Aug, 8am-7pm Mon-Sat, 11am-5pm Sun Mar-Jun & Sep-Oct, 8am-6pm Mon-Sat, noon-4pm Sun Nov, 8am-6pm Mon-Fri, 8am-1pm Sun Dec-Feb) Free internet access for 15 minutes or €2.50/4 per 30/60 minutes.

ⓘ Getting There & Around

Frequent buses to Bohinj (€3.60, 40 minutes, 29km, hourly), Ljubljana (€6.30, 1¼ hours, 57km, hourly) and Kranj (€3.60, 40 minutes, 29km, half-hourly) via Radovljica (€1.80, 15 minutes, 7km) leave from the central bus station.

Trains to Bohinjska Bistrica (€1.70, 20 minutes, 18km, eight daily) and Nova Gorica (€5.90, 1¾ hours, 79km, eight daily) use little Bled Jezero train station, which is 2km west of central Bled – handy for the Hotel Triglav Bled and the camping ground. Trains for Ljubljana (€4.50 to €6.10, 45 minutes to one hour, 51km, up to 19 daily) use Lesce-Bled train station, 4km to the east of town.

Book a taxi on ☑031-705 343.

Bohinj
☑04 / POP 5275

Lake Bohinj, a larger and less-developed glacial lake 26km to the southwest, is a world apart from Bled. Mt Triglav is visible from here and there are activities galore – from kayaking and mountain biking to hiking up Triglav via one of the southern approaches.

Bohinjska Bistrica, the area's largest village, is 6km east of the lake and only interesting for its train station. The main tourist hub on the lake is **Ribčev Laz** at the eastern end, with a supermarket, post office with an ATM and **tourist office** (☑574 60 10; www.bohinj-info.com; Ribčev Laz 48; ⏱8am-8pm Mon-Sat, to 6pm Sun summer, 8am-6pm Mon-Sat, 9am-3pm Sun winter), which can help with accommodation and sells fishing licences (€25 per day for the lake, €42 catch and release in the Sava Bohinjka). Central **Alpinsport** (☑572 34 86, 041-596 079; www.alpinsport.si; Ribčev Laz 53; ⏱9am or 10am-6pm or 8pm) organises a range of activities, and hires out kayaks, canoes, bikes (per hour/day €4/13.50) and other equipment from a kiosk near the stone bridge. Next door is the delightful **Church of St John the Baptist** (⏱10am-noon & 4-7pm summer, by appointment other times), which contains splendid 15th- and 16th-century frescos.

The nearby village of **Stara Fužina** has an appealing little **Alpine Dairy Museum** (☑577 01 56; Stara Fužine 181; adult/child €2.50/2; ⊙11am-7pm Tue-Sun Jul & Aug, 10am-noon & 4-6pm Tue-Sun Jan-Jun, Sep & Oct). Just opposite is a cheesemonger called **Planšar** (☑572 30 95; Stara Fužina 179; ⊙noon-8pm summer, by appointment other times), which specialises in homemade dairy products such as hard Bohinj cheese, cottage cheese and curd pie. Just 2km east is **Studor**, a village famed for its *toplarji*, the double-linked hayrack with barns or storage areas at the top, some of which date from the 18th and 19th centuries.

One of the reasons people come to Bohinj is to hike to **Savica Waterfall** (adult/child €2.50/1.25, parking €3; ⊙8am-8pm Jul & Aug; 9am-6pm Apr-Jun, Sep & Oct), which cuts deep into a gorge 60m below and is the source of Slovenia's longest river. It's a 4km hike from Camp Zlatorog in Ukanc at the lake's western end.

From early April to October, the inventively named **Tourist Boat** (☑041-434 986; adult/child 1 way €8.50/6, return €10/7; ⊙10am-6pm) departs from the pier just opposite the Alpinsport kiosk every 40 minutes (between four and six times a day at other times), terminating a half-hour later at the Ukanc jetty.

The **Cows' Ball** in September is a zany weekend of folk dance, music, eating and drinking to mark the return of the cows from their high pastures down to the valleys. The **International Wildflower Festival** over two weeks in late May/early June includes guided walks and tours, traditional craft markets and concerts. For details on both, go to www.bohinj.si.

🛏 Sleeping & Eating

The tourist office can help arrange accommodation in **private rooms** (per person €13-15) and **apartments** (d €42.50-48.50, q €75-86).

Penzion Gasperin PENSION €€
(☑059-920 382, 041-540 805; www.bohinj.si/gasperin; Ribčev Laz 36a; per person €25-35; ⓟ@☎) This spotless chalet-style guesthouse with 23 rooms is just 350m east of the tourist office and run by a friendly British-Slovenian couple. Most rooms have balconies.

Hotel Jezero HOTEL €€€
(☑572 91 00; www.bohinj.si/alpinum/jezero; Ribčev Laz 51; s €60-80, d €100-140; ⓟ@☎☼) Further renovations have raised the standards even higher at this 76-room place just across from the lake. It has a lovely indoor swimming pool, two saunas and a fitness centre.

Hostel Pod Voglom HOSTEL €
(☑572 34 61; www.hostel-podvoglom.com; Ribčev Laz 60; dm €17-19, r per person with bathroom € 23-26, without bathroom € 20-22; ⓟ@) This budget accommodation 3km west of the centre has 122 beds in 46 somewhat frayed rooms in two buildings. The so-called Hostel Building has doubles, triples and dormitory accommodation with up to four beds and shared facilities; rooms in the Rodica Annexe, with between one and four beds, are en suite.

Camp Zlatorog CAMPING GROUND €
(☑572 30 64; www.hoteli-bohinj.si/en; Ukanc 2; per person €7-19, tent/campervan €11/23; ⊙May-Sep) This pine-shaded 2.5-hectare camping ground accommodating 500 guests is at the lake's western end, 4.5km from Ribčev Laz.

Restavracija Triglav SLOVENIAN €€
(☑572 35 38; Stara Fužina 23; mains €10.50-17) This country-style place in nearby Stara Fužina serves up hearty Slovenian favourites like lamb and whole pig cooked on the spit and mushrooms on the grill. There's live music from 6pm daily in summer.

Center Bohinj Pizzerija PIZZA €
(☑572 3170; www.bohinj.si/center; Ribčev Laz 50; pizza €6-10, mains €8.50-14; ⊙9am-10pm) This cheap and kinda cheerful jack-of-all-trades just down from the tourist office is the only eatery in the very centre of Ribčev Laz.

ⓘ Getting There & Around

Buses run regularly from Ukanc ('Bohinj Zlatorog' on most schedules) to Ljubljana (€8.70, 2¼ hours, 91km, hourly) via Ribčev Laz, Bohinjska Bistrica and Bled (€4.10, 50 minutes, 34km), with six extra buses daily between Ukanc and Bohinjska Bistrica (€2.30 20 minutes, 12km). From Bohinjska Bistrica, passenger trains to Nova Gorica (€5.20, 1¼ hours, 61km, up to nine daily) make use of a century-old tunnel under the mountains that provides the only option for reaching the Soča Valley. In addition there are daily auto trains (*avtovlaki*) from Bohinjska Bistrica to Podbrdo (€8.20, 10 minutes, 7km, five daily) and Most na Soči (€12.50, 40 minutes, 28km, three daily).

Kranjska Gora

☑04 / POP 1510

Nestling in the Sava Dolinka Valley about some 40km northwest of Bled, Kranjska Gora is Slovenia's largest and best-equipped ski resort. It's at its most perfect under a blanket of snow, but at other times there are endless possibilities for hiking and mountaineering in Triglav National Park, which is right on the town's doorstep to the south. Few travellers will be unimpressed by a trip over the hair-raising Vršič Pass (1611m), the gateway to the Soča Valley.

◉ Sights & Activities

Borovška c, 400m south of where the buses stop, is the heart of the village, with the endearing **Liznjek House** (🖉588 19 99; Borovška 63; adult/child €2.50/1.70; ☉10am-6pm Tue-Sat, to 5pm Sun summer, 9.30am-4pm Tue-Fri, 10am-5pm Sat & Sun winter), an 18th-century museum house with a good collection of household objects and furnishings peculiar to Gorenjska. At its western end is the **Tourist Information Centre Kranjska Gora** (🖉580 94 40; www.kranjska-gora.si; Tičarjeva c 2; ☉8am-7pm Mon-Sat, 9am-6pm Sun Jun-Sep & mid-Dec–Mar, 8am-3pm Mon-Sat Apr, May & Oct–mid-Dec). If you have time (and your own wheels), visit the new **Slovenian Mountaineering Museum** (🖉583 35 01; www.planinskimuzej.si; Savska c 1; adult/child €5/3.50; ☉9am-7pm summer, to 5pm winter) in a startlingly modern structure in Mojstrana, a village 14km to the east.

Kranjska Gora has lots of places offering ski tuition and hiring out equipment, including **ASK Kranjska Gora Ski School** (🖉588 53 02; www.ask-kg.com; Borovška c 99a) in the same building as SKB Banka. Rent bikes from one of several **Sport Point** (🖉588 48 83; www.sport-point.si; Borovška c 74; per hr/day €3.50/10) outlets. The men's and giant slalom **Vitranc Cup** (www.pokal-vitranc.com) are held here in early March, and the **Ski-Jumping World Cup Championships** (www.planica. info) at nearby Planica later that month.

🛏 Sleeping & Eating

Accommodation costs peak from December to March and in midsummer. **Private rooms** (per person €14-24) and **apartments** (d €34-50, q €68-108) can be arranged through the tourist office.

Hotel Kotnik HOTEL €€
(🖉588 15 64; www.hotel-kotnik.si; Borovška c 75; s €54-64, d €68-88; @) If you're not into sprawling hotels with hundreds of rooms, choose this charming, bright yellow low-rise property. It has 15 cosy rooms, a great restaurant and pizzeria, and it couldn't be more central.

Brezov Gaj PENSION €€
(🖉588 57 90; www.brezov-gaj.si; Koroška c 7; per person €25-34; P@) The 'Birch Grove' offers some of the best value in Kranjska Gora. Some of the half-dozen rooms have balco-

nies, there's a fitness room and a place to store bikes and skis.

🌿 Natura Eco Camp Kranjska Gora
CAMPING GROUND €
(🖉064-121 966; www.naturacamp-kranjskagora.si; adult €8-10, child €5-7, cabin & tree tent €25-30) This wonderful new site some 300m from the main road on an isolated horse ranch in a forest clearing is as close to paradise as we've been for a while. Pitch a tent or stay in one of the little wooden cabins or the unique tree tents, great pouches with air mattresses suspended from the branches.

Hostel Nika HOSTEL €
(🖉588 10 00, 031-644 209; www.porentov-dom. si; Bezje 16; dm €10-11 d €26; P@) This atmospheric, very cheap place on the Sava Dolinka with 23 rooms and 68 beds in Čičare is about 800m northeast of the centre and just across the main road from the TGC Shopping Centre. It's a great starting point for walks into the mountains.

Gostilna Pri Martinu SLOVENIAN €€
(🖉582 03 00; Borovška c 61; mains €6.50-12.50) This atmospheric tavern-restaurant in an old house just beyond Liznjek House is one of the best places to try local specialities such as *telečja obara* (veal stew; €4) and *ričet* (barley stew with smoked pork ribs; €6). Lunch is a snip at just under €7.

❶ Getting There & Away

Buses run hourly to Ljubljana (€8.70, two hours, 91km) via Jesenice (€3.10, 25 minutes, 22m), where you can change for Bled (€3.10, 30 minutes, 21km) as there's just one direct departure to Bled (€4.70, one hour, 40km) on weekdays at 9.15am. A service to Bovec (€6.70, 2¼ hours, 46km) via the Vršič Pass departs five times daily (six at the weekend) from late June to early September.

Soča Valley

The Soča Valley region is defined by the 96km-long Soča River coloured a deep, almost artificial turquoise. The valley has more than its share of historical sights, most of them related to one of the costliest battles of WWI, but the majority of visitors are here for the rafting, hiking, skiing and other active sports.

BOVEC
🖉05 / POP 1810
Effectively the capital of the Soča Valley, Bovec has a great deal to offer adventure-sports

enthusiasts. With the Julian Alps above, the Soča River below and Triglav National Park all around, you could spend a week here hiking, kayaking, mountain biking and, in winter, skiing at Mt Kanin (2587m), Slovenia's highest ski station, without ever doing the same thing twice.

The compact village square, Trg Golobarskih Žrtev, has everything you'll need. There are cafes, a hotel, the **Tourist Information Centre Bovec** (☑389 64 44; www.bovec.si; Trg Golobarskih Žrtev 8; ⊗8.30am-8.30pm summer, 9am-6pm winter) and a half-dozen adrenaline-raising adventure-sports companies.

🏃 Activities

Organised adventure sports (all prices per person) on offer include **canyoning** (from €45 for two hours) or **caving** (from €40 with guide). Or you could try your hand at **hydrospeed** (like riding down a river on a boogie board); you'll pay €45 to €52 for a 6km to 8km ride. A guided 10km **kayaking** tour costs from €42, or a one-day training course at €70.

From April to October, you can go **rafting** (€37/49 for a 10/20km trip). And in winter you can take a **tandem paraglider flight** (ie as a passenger accompanied by a qualified pilot; €110) from atop the Kanin cable car, 2000m above the valley floor.

The choice of operators is dizzying but the three most experienced are: **Bovec Rafting Team** (☑388 61 28, 041-338 308; www.bovec-rafting-team.com; Mala Vas 106); **Soča Rafting** (☑389 62 00, 041-724 472; www.socarafting.si; Trg Golobarskih Žrtev 14); and **Top Extreme** (☑041-620 636; www.top.si; Trg Golobarskih Žrtev 19).

🛌 Sleeping & Eating

Private rooms (per person €15-30) are easy to come by in Bovec through the TIC.

Martinov Hram PENSION €€
(☑388 62 14; www.martinov-hram.si; Trg Golobarskih Žrtev 27; s €33-48, d €54-70; P🐾) This lovely guesthouse just 100m east of the centre has a dozen nicely furnished rooms and an excellent restaurant with an emphasis on game, trout and mushroom dishes.

Alp Hotel HOTEL €€
(☑388 40 00; www.alp-hotel.si; Trg Golobarskih Žrtev 48; s €48-66, d €78-98; P@🐾) This 103-room hotel is fairly good value and as central as you are going to find in Bovec. Guests get to use the swimming pool at the nearby Hotel Kanin.

Kamp Palovnik CAMPING GROUND €
(☑388 60 07; www.kamp-polovnik.com; Ledina 8; adult €6.50-7.50, child €5-5.75; ⊗Apr-mid-Oct; P) Camping facilities are generally better in Kobarid, but this site about 500m southeast of the town centre is much more convenient.

Gostišče Vančar SLOVENIAN €
(☑389 60 76, 031-312 742; www.penzionvancar.com; Čezsoča 43; mains €ri6-8) This inn 3km south of Bovec is where local people go to taste such local specialities as *kalja* (a sweetcorn pudding) and *bovški krafni* ('raviolis' stuffed with dried pears, raisins and walnuts).

ℹ️ Getting There & Away

Buses to Nova Gorica (€7.50, two hours, 77km, up to five a day) go via Tolmin (€3.10, 30 minutes, 22km). A service to Kranjska Gora (€6.70, 2¼ hours, 46km) via Vršič Pass departs five times daily (six at the weekend) from late June to early September.

KOBARID
☑05 / POP 1230

Some 21km south of Bovec, quaint Kobarid (Caporetto in Italian) lies in a broad valley on the west bank of the Soča River. Although it's surrounded by mountain peaks higher than 2200m, Kobarid somehow feels more Mediterranean than alpine. The Italian border is a mere 9km to the west.

⊙ Sights

Kobarid Museum MUSEUM
(☑389 00 00; www.kobariski-muzej.si; Gregorčičeva ul 10; adult/child €5/2.50; ⊗9am-6pm Mon-Fri, to 7pm Sat & Sun summer, 10am-5pm Mon-Fri, 9am-6pm Sat & Sun winter) A couple of hundred metres to the southeast is this award-winning museum, devoted almost entirely to the Isonzo (Soča) Front of WWI, which formed the backdrop to Ernest Hemingway's *A Farewell to Arms*.

🏃 Activities

A free pamphlet and map titled *The Kobarid Historical Trail* outlines a 5km-long route that will take you past remnants of WWI troop emplacements to the impressive **Kozjak Stream Waterfalls** and **Napoleon Bridge** built in 1750. More ambitious is the hike outlined in the free *Pot Miru/Walk of Peace* brochure.

There are several outfits on or just off the town's main square that can organise **rafting** (€29 to €37), **canyoning**, **canoeing** and **paragliding** from April to October. They include:

A2 Rafting (📞041-641 899; www.a2rafting.eu) in a kiosk outside Apartma-Ra.

XPoint (📞388 53 08, 041-692 290; www.xpoint.si; Trg Svobode 6)

Positive Sport (📞040-654 475; www.positive-sport.com; Markova ul 2)

🛏 Sleeping

TOP
CHOICE **Hotel Hvala**   HOTEL
(📞389 93 00; wwww.hotel-hvala.si; Trg Svobode 1; s €72-76, d €104-112; P❋@) The best place to stay in town. It has 31 splendid rooms and a unique lift that takes you on a vertical tour of Kobarid.

Kamp Koren   CAMPGROUND
(📞389 13 11; www.kamp-koren.si; Drežniške Ravne 33; per person pitch €9.50-11; P@🛜) The oldest (and, some would say, friendliest) camping ground in the valley. It's a 4-hectare site about 500m northeast of Kobarid on the left bank of the Soča River and just beyond the Napoleon Bridge with 100 pitches and six **chalets** (d/tr from €55/60).

Apartma-Ra   APARTMENTS
(📞041-641899; apartma-ra@siol.net; Gregorčičeva ul 6c; per person €15-25; P❋@) This welcoming little place lies between the museum and Trg Svobode and has five rooms and apartments.

🍴 Eating

In the centre of Kobarid you'll find one of Slovenia's best restaurants, which specialises in fish and seafood.

Restavracija Topli Val (📞389 93 00; wwww.hotel-hvala.si; Trg Svobode 1; mains €9.50-25; ⊗noon-10pm) Incomparable.

Hiša Franko (📞389 41 20; www.hisafranko.com; Staro Selo 1; mains €20-24; ⊗noon-3pm & 6-11pm Tue-Sun) Another slow-food phenomenon in these parts in the village of Staro Selo some 3km west of town.

ℹ Information

Tourist Information Centre Kobarid (📞380 04 90; www.dolina-soce.com; Trg Svobode 16; ⊗9am-8pm Jul & Aug, 9am-1pm & 2-6pm Mon-Fri, 10am-1pm & 3-6pm Sat & Sun Sep-Jun) In the centre of town.

ℹ Getting There & Around

Buses, which arrive at and depart from in front of the Cinca Marinca bar on Trg Svobode, link Kobarid with Nova Gorica (€6, 1¼ hours, 55km, up to five daily) and Ljubljana (€11.60, three hours, 131km, up to four daily) passing Most na Soči train station, which is good for Bled and Bohinj.

Buses crossing over the spectacular Vršič Pass to Kranjska Gora (€6.90, three hours, 68km) depart a couple of times a day in July and August.

NOVA GORICA
📷05 / POP 12,240

When the town of Gorica, capital of the former Slovenian province of Goriška, was awarded to the Italians after WWII, the new socialist government in Yugoslavia set out to build a model town on the eastern side of the border. They called it New Gorica and erected a chain-link barrier between the two towns. This rather flimsy 'Berlin Wall' was pulled down to great fanfare in 2004, leaving Piazza della Transalpina (or Trg z Mozaikom on the Slovenian side) straddling the border right behind Nova Gorica's train station. The latter now contains the esoteric **Museum of the Border in Gorica 1945-2004** (📞333 44 00; admission free; ⊗1-5pm Mon-Fri, 9am-5pm Sat, 10am-5pm Sun).

The helpful **Tourist Information Centre Nova Gorica** (📞330 46 00; www.novagorica-turizem.com; Bevkov trg 4; ⊗8am-8pm Mon-Fri, 9am-1pm Sat & Sun summer, 8am-6pm Mon-Fri, 9am-1pm winter) is in the Kulturni Dom (Cultural House).

One of the few inexpensive central options for overnighting, **Prenočišče Pertout** (📞330 75 50, 041-624 452; www.prenocisceper tout.com; Ul 25 Maja 23; s/d €24/34; P@) is a five-room B&B in Rožna Dolina, south of the town centre and scarcely 100m northeast of the Italian border. Some 2km east of the centre along the road to Ajdovščina, the **Siesta** (📞333 12 30; www.hotel-siesta.si; Industrijska c 5; s/d €39/49; P@) is a modern-ish 20-room hotel with bargain-basement rates.

Marco Polo (📞302 97 29; Kidričeva ul 13; mains €6-17; ⊗11am-midnight), an Italian eatery with a delightful back terrace about 250m east of the tourist office, is one of the town's best places to eat, serving pizza (€5.50 to €7.60), pasta (€6 to €12) and more-ambitious dishes.

Buses travel hourly between Nova Gorica and Ljubljana (€10.70 2½ hours, 116km) via Postojna (€6.70, 1½ hours, 63km), and up to five times daily to Bovec (€7.50, two hours, 77km) via Tolmin (€4.70, one hour, 39km).

Trains link Nova Gorica with Bohinjska Bistrica (€5.20, 1½ hours, 61km, up to seven daily), a springboard for Bled, with Postojna (€6.25, two hours, 61km, six daily) via Sežana and Divača, and with Ljubljana (€8.50, 3½ hours, 153km, five daily) via Jesenice.

KARST & COAST

Slovenia's short coast (47km) is an area for both history and recreation. The southernmost resort town of Portorož has some decent beaches, but three important towns famed for their Venetian Gothic architecture – Koper, Izola and Piran – are the main drawcards here. En route from Ljubljana or the Soča Valley, you'll cross the Karst, a huge limestone plateau and a land of olives, ruby-red Teran wine, *pršut* (air-dried ham), old stone churches and deep subterranean caves, including Postojna and Škocjan.

Postojna

[↗]05 / POP 8910

Slovenia's single most-popular tourist attraction, **Postojna Cave** ([↗]700 01 00; www.postojnska-jama.si; Jamska c 30; adult/child €20/12; ⊙tours hourly 9am-6pm summer, 3 or 4 times from 10am daily winter) is about 1.5km northwest of the town of that name. The 5.7km-long cavern is visited on a 1½-hour tour – 4km of it by electric train and the rest on foot. Inside, impressive stalagmites and stalactites in familiar shapes stretch almost endlessly in all directions.

Just steps south of the cave's entrance is **Proteus Vivarium** (www.turizem-kras.si; adult/child €7/4.20 with cave €25/15; ⊙9.30am-5.30pm May-Sep, 10.30am-3.30pm Oct-Apr), a speliobiological research station with a video introduction to underground zoology. A 45-minute tour then leads you into a small, darkened cave to peep at some of the endemic *Proteus anguinus*, a shy (and miniscule) salamander unique to Slovenia.

🛏 Sleeping & Eating

Kompas Postojna　　PRIVATE ROOMS €
([↗]721 14 80; www.kompas-postojna.si; Titov trg 2a; r per person €17-24; ⊙8am-7pm Mon-Fri, 9am-1pm Sat summer, 8am-5pm Mon-Fri, 9am-1pm Sat winter) Private rooms in town and down on the farm.

Hotel Sport　　HOTEL, HOSTEL €€
([↗]720 22 44; www.sport-hotel.si; Kolodvorska c 1; dm €25, s/d from €55/70; P@�) A hotel of some sort or another since 1880, the Sport offers reasonable value for money, with 37 spic-and-span and very comfortable rooms, including five with nine dorm beds each. There's a kitchen with small eating area. It's 300m north of the centre.

Špajza　　SLOVENIAN €€
([↗]726 45 06; Ul 1 Maja 1; mains €11-16) A welcome new addition to Postojna's limited eating scene, this attractively decorated *gostilna* 100m southeast of Kompas serves excellent local specialities.

ℹ Getting There & Away

Buses from Ljubljana to Koper, Piran and Nova Gorica all stop in Postojna (€6, one hour, 54km, half-hourly). The train is less useful, as the station is 1km east of town (ie almost 3km from the caves).

Buses bound for Postojna Cave and Predjama Castle leave Postojna's train station five times a day between 9.20am and 4.10pm. The bus is free but those with train tickets take precedence. The last bus from the castle is 4.40pm and from the cave at 5.05pm. A taxi to/from the castle, including an hour's wait, will cost €30.

Škocjan Caves

[↗]05

The immense system of **Škocjan Caves** ([↗]708 21 10; www.park-skocjanske-jame.si; Škocjan 2; adult/child €14/6), a Unesco World Heritage site since 1986, is far more captivating than the larger one at Postojna, and for many travellers a visit here will be a highlight of their trip to Slovenia. With relatively few stalactites, the attraction is the sheer depth of the awesome underground chasm, which you cross by a dizzying little footbridge. To see this you must join a guided walking tour, lasting 1½ to two hours and involving hundreds of steps and a funicular ride at the end. Tours depart hourly from 10am to 5pm from June to September, at 10am, 1pm and 3.30pm in April, May and October, and at 10am and 1pm (with an additional one at 3pm on Sunday) from November to March.

The nearest town with accommodation is **Divača** (population 1325), 5km to the northwest. **Gostilna Malovec** ([↗]763 12 25; Kraška 30a; s/d €32/48) has a half-dozen basic but renovated rooms in a building beside its traditional **restaurant** (mains €8-15; ⊙8am to 10pm) and flashy new 20-room **hotel** ([↗]763 33 33; www.hotel-malovec.si; s/d €54/80; P@�). The nearby **Orient Express** ([↗]763 30 10; Kraška c 67; pizza €4.60-14; ⊙11am-11pm Sun-Fri, to 2am Sat) is a popular pizzeria and pub.

Bus services running from Ljubljana to Koper and the coast stop at Divača (€7.90, 1½ hours, 82km, hourly) as do trains (€6.85, 1½ hours, 104km, hourly). A van meets incoming trains at 10am, 11.04am, 2pm and

PREDJAMA

The tiny village of Predjama (population 85), some 10km northwest of Postojna, is home to remarkable **Predjama Castle** (☑700 01 00; www.turizem-kras.si; Predjama 1; adult/child €8/5; ☉9am-7pm summer, 10am-4pm winter), which appears to grow out of a gawping cave. The partly furnished interior spread over four floors boasts costumed wax mannequins, one of which dangles from the dripping rock-roofed torture chamber. Beneath are stalactite-adorned **caves** (adult/child €7/4.20, with castle €13/8; ☉1-hour tours 11am-5pm May-Sep), which lack Postojna's crowds but also much of its grandeur.

3.10pm and will transport those with bus or train tickets to the caves for free. Otherwise there is a large map indicating the walking route posted outside the station.

Lipica

☑05 / POP 100

Lipica is where Austrian Archduke Charles, son of Ferdinand I, established a stud farm in 1580 to breed horses for the Spanish Riding School in Vienna. The snow-white beauties are still raised at the **Lipica Stud Farm** (☑739 15 80; www.lipica.org; Lipica 5; adult/child €10/5), which offers equestrian fans a large variety of tours and riding presentations as well as lessons and carriage rides. Tour times are complicated; see the website for details.

The 85-room **Hotel Klub** (☑739 15 80; s/d €32/49; [P] [@] [❷]) near the stud farm has a sauna and fitness centre. The nearby **Hotel Maestoso** (☑739 15 80; s/d €80/120; [P] [❷] [❷]) has 68 more modern rooms.

Most people visit Lipica as a day trip from Sežana, 5km to the north, or Divača, 10km to the northeast, which are on the Ljubljana–Koper rail line. There is no public transport from either station to Lipica; a taxi will cost between €7 and €15.

Koper

☑05 / POP 24,830

Coastal Slovenia's largest town, Koper (Capodistria in Italian) at first glance appears to be a workaday city that scarcely gives tourism a second thought. Yet its central core is delightfully medieval and far less overrun than its ritzy cousin Piran, 18km down the coast. Known as Aegida to the ancient Greeks, Koper grew rich as a key port trading salt and was the capital of Istria under the Venetian Republic during the 15th and 16th centuries. It remains Slovenia's most important port.

⊙ Sights

Turn back the clock as you pass through **Muda Gate** (1516) leading into Prešernov trg and the bridge-shaped **Da Ponte Fountain** (1666). Carry on north up Župančičeva ul and then Čevljarska ul, the narrow commercial artery, to reach **Titov trg**. This fine square is dominated by the 15th-century **City Tower** (adult/child €2/1.50; ☉9am-2pm & 4-9pm), which can be reached via 204 steps. It is attached to the part-Gothic, part-Renaissance **Cathedral of the Assumption**. The Venetian Gothic and Renaissance **Praetorian Palace** (Titov trg 3; admission free; ☉9am-8pm) contains the town hall, with an old pharmacy and the tourist office on the ground floor and a ornate ceremonial hall on the 1st floor. Opposite, the splendid 1463 **Loggia**, with attached gallery. Next to it is the circular Romanesque **Rotunda of St John the Baptist**, a baptistery with ceiling fresco dating from the 12th century.

The **Koper Regional Museum** (☑663 35 70; www.pmk-kp.si; Kidričeva ul 19; adult/child €2/1.50; ☉9am-7pm Tue-Fri, to 1pm Sat & Sun), inside the Belgramoni-Tacco Palace, contains an Italianate sculpture garden. Kidričeva ul, with its multicoloured **medieval houses**, leads west into Carpacciov trg, the former fish market with a 15th-century **salt warehouse**.

🛏 Sleeping

Museum Hostel   HOSTEL, APARTMENTS **€**
(☑626 18 70, 041-504 466; bozic.doris@siol.net; Muzejski trg 6; per person €20-25; [❷]) This excellent-value place is more a series of bright apartments with modern kitchens and bathrooms than a hostel. Reception is at the little Museum Bife, a cafe-bar on Muzejski trg; the rooms are actually at Mladinska ul 7 and Kidričeva ul 34.

Hotel Koper   HOTEL **€€€**
(☑610 05 00; www.terme-catez.si; Pristaniška ul 3; s €76-92, d €120-150; [❄] [@] [❷]) This 65-room property on the very edge of the historic Old Town is the only central hotel in Koper.

Koper

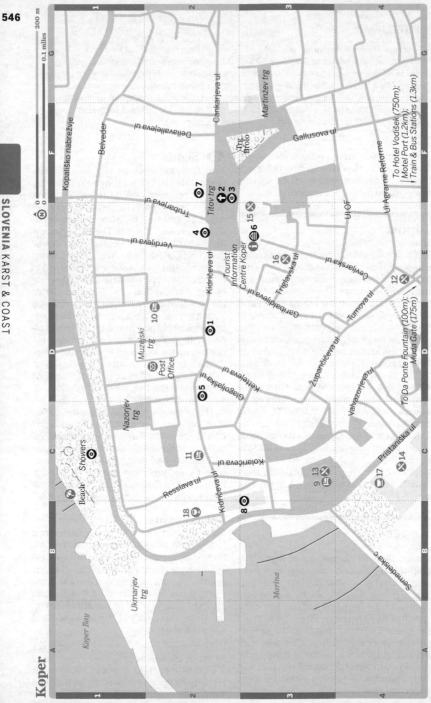

SLOVENIA KARST & COAST

200 m
0.1 miles

Koper Bay

Kopališko nabrežje

Belveder

Dellavallejeva ul

Cankarjeva ul

Martinzev trg

Trg Brolo

Gallusova ul

Ul OF

Ul Agrarne Reforme

To Hotel Vodišek (750m);
Motel Port (1.2km);
Train & Bus Stations (1.3km)

Trubarjeva ul

Titov trg

Verdijeva ul

Kidričeva ul

Tourist Information Centre Koper

Triglavska ul

Gevljarska ul

Garibaldijeva ul

Tumova ul

Županićeva ul

12

16

15

6

2
3

7

4

1

10

Muzejski trg

Post Office

Nazorjev trg

Ketteljeva ul

Glagoljaška ul

5

Valvazorjeva ul

Pristaniška ul

Beach
Showers

Resslava ul

Kolarjeva ul

11

18

8

9 13

17

14

Kidričeva ul

Ukmarjev trg

Marina

Semedelska c

To Da Ponte Fountain (100m);
Muda Gate (175m)

Koper

Hotel Vodišek   HOTEL €€
(📞639 24 68; www.hotel-vodisek.com; Kolodvorska c 2; s €48-60, d €72-90; P✴@📶) With 35 small but reasonably priced rooms, this place is in a shopping centre halfway between the Old Town and the train and bus stations. Bicycle use is free for guests.

Motel Port   HOTEL, HOSTEL €
(📞611 75 44; www.motel-port.si; Ankaranska c 7; dm €22, s €36/49.50; ⊙Jul-Aug; P✴@📶) On the 2nd floor of a shopping centre southeast of the Old Town, this student house, open to visitors in summer, only has 30 rooms, some of them en suite and air-conditioned and others dorm rooms with four to six beds.

🍴 Eating

You'll find a small branch of the **Mercator** (Titov trg 2; ⊙7am-8pm Mon-Fri, 7am-1pm Sat, 8am-noon Sun) supermarket giant in the Old Town.

Istrska Klet Slavček   ISTRIAN, SLOVENIAN €
(📞627 67 29; Župančičeva ul 39; dishes €3-12; ⊙7am-10pm Mon-Fri) The 'Istrian Cellar' below an 18th-century palace is one of the most colourful places for a meal in Koper's Old Town. Filling set lunches go for less than €8,

and there's local Malvazija and Teran wine from the barrel.

La Storia   ITALIAN €€€
(📞626 20 18; www.lastoria.si; Pristaniška ul 3; mains €8.50-25) This Italian-style *trattoria* with sky-view ceiling frescos inside and a delightful covered terrace outside focuses on salads, pasta and fish dishes.

Pizzeria Atrij   PIZZA €€
(📞627 22 55; Čevljarska ul 8, enter from Triglavska ul 2; pizza €3-6.50; ⊙9am-9pm Mon-Fri, 10am-10pm Sat) A popular pizzeria down an alleyway no wider than your average quarterback's shoulder spread, the Atrij has a small covered garden out back.

Drinking

Kavarna Kapitanija   CAFE
(📞040-799 000; Ukmarjev trg 8; ⊙7am-midnight Mon-Fri, 8am-midnight Sat & Sun) This attractive space, with its wide-open terrace and wicker lounges, would be even more inviting if the tacky souvenir kiosks and parked cars across the grassy strip didn't block the harbour view.

Forum   CAFE-BAR
(Pristaniška ul 2; ⊙7am-11pm; 📶) Cafe-bar at the northern side of the market and facing a little park and the sea; a popular local hang-out.

ℹ Information

Banka Koper (Kidričeva ul 14)

Pina Internet Cafe (📞627 80 72; Kidričeva ul 43; per hr adult/student €4.20/1.20; ⊙noon-10pm Mon-Fri, from 4pm Sat & Sun) Central internet cafe with 10 terminals.

Post office (Muzejski trg 3)

Tourist Information Centre Koper (📞664 64 03; www.koper.si; Praetorian Palace, Titov trg 3; ⊙9am-8pm Jul & Aug, 9am-5pm Sep-Jun)

ℹ Getting There & Away

The joint bus and train station is about 1.5km southeast of central Titov trg. To walk into town, just head north along Kolodvorska c in the direction of the cathedral's distinctive campanile (bell tower).

Buses run to Piran (€2.70, 30 minutes, 18km) every 20 minutes on weekdays and 40 minutes at weekends. Up to five daily buses daily head for Ljubljana (€11.10, 1¾ to 2½ hours, 122km), though the train is more comfortable, with four local services and two faster IC ones (€10, 2¼ hours) at 5.23am and 2.45pm.

Buses to Trieste (€3, 45 minutes, 23km, up to eight per day) run along the coast via Ankaran and Muggia between 6am and 7.30pm from Monday to Saturday. Destinations in Croatia include Rovinj (€11, three hours, 129km, 6.30pm Monday and Friday, 11am Saturday and Sunday, 3.50pm daily June to September) via Poreč (€10, two hours, 88km).

You can order a taxi on ☑040-671 086.

Izola

☑05 / POP 11,545

Overshadowed by more genteel Piran, Izola (Isola in Italian) has a certain Venetian charm, narrow old streets, and excellent (and uncrowded) waterfront restaurants. Ask the helpful **Tourist Information Centre Izola** (☑640 10 50; www.izola.eu; Sončno nabrežje 4; ☺9am-9pm Jun-Sep, 9am-5pm Mon-Fri, 10am-5pm Sat Oct-May) about **private rooms** (s €19-26, d €30-36) or, in July and August, check out the 174-bed **Riviera** (☑662 1740; branko.miklobusec@ guest.arnes.si; Prekomorskih Brigad ul 7; dm €25), a student dormitory overlooking the marina. At the other end of the price range is the 52-room **Hotel Marina** (☑660 41 00; www.hotelmarina.si; Veliki trg 11; s €59-126, d €79-156; P✳@⍩) on the main square and fronting the harbour. **Ribič** (☑641 83 13; www.ribic.biz; Veliki trg 3; mains €9-25; ☺8am-midnight Mon-Sat, to 10pm Sun) is a landmark seafood restaurant on the waterfront much loved by locals. Out in Izola's industrial suburbs, **Ambasada Gavioli** (☑641 8212, 041-353 722; www.myspace.com/ambasadagavioli; Industrijska c 10; ☺11pm-6am Fri & Sat) remains coastal Slovenia's top club, showcasing a procession of international and local DJs.

Frequent buses between Koper (€1.80, 15 minutes, 8km) and Piran (€2.30, 20 minutes, 10km) go via Izola.

The **Prince of Venice** (☑05-617 80 00; www.kompas-online.net) catamaran serves Venice (€50 to €70, 2½ hours) from Izola at 7.30am or 8am between one and three times a week (days vary) from April to October.

Piran

☑05 / POP 4515

Picturesque Piran (Pirano in Italian), sitting at the tip of a narrow peninsula, is everyone's favourite coastal town in Slovenia. The Old Town is a gem of Venetian Gothic architecture, but it can be a mob scene at the height of summer. Still, it's hard not to fall in love with the winding Venetian Gothic alleyways and tempting seafood restaurants. It is believed that the town's name comes from the *pyr*, Greek for fire, as fires were once lit at Punta, the tip of the peninsula, to guide ships to the port at Aegida (now Koper).

◉ Sights

Cathedral of St George　　　CHURCH
(Adamičeva ul 2) Piran is watched over by the hilltop cathedral mostly dating from the 17th century. If time allows, visit the attached **Parish Museum of St George** (☑673 34 40; admission €1; ☺10am-1pm & 5-7pm Mon-Fri, 11am-7pm Sat & Sun), which contains church plate, paintings and a lapidary in the crypt. The cathedral's free-standing **bell tower** (admission €2; ☺10am-2pm & 5-8pm) dates back to 1609 and can be climbed. The octagonal **baptistery** (1650) has imaginatively recycled a 2nd-century Roman sarcophagus as a baptismal font. To the east is a 200m-long stretch of the 15th-century **town wall** complete with loopholes.

Minorite Monastery　　　MONASTERY
(☑673 44 17; Bolniška ul 20) Parts of this monastery to the east of Tartinijev trg date back to the 14th century; go up the steps and check out the wonderful cloister enlivened with Gregorian chant. Opposite, the **Church of Our Lady of the Snows** has a superb 15th-century arch painting of the Crucifixion.

Sergej Mašera Maritime Museum　　MUSEUM
(☑671 00 40; www.pommuz-pi.si; Cankarjevo nabrežje 3; adult/student & senior/child €3.50/2.50/2.10; ☺9am-noon & 5-9pm Tue-Sun summer, 9am-5pm Tue-Sun winter) The exhibits here focus on the sea, sailing and saltmaking – all crucial to Piran's development over the centuries. Check out the 2000-year-old Roman amphorae under glass on the ground floor and the impressive antique ships' models and figureheads upstairs.

Aquarium Piran　　　AQUARIUM
(☑673 25 72; www.aquariumpiran.com; Kidričevo nabrežje 4; adult/child €7/5; ☺9am-7pm summer, to 5pm winter) About 100m south of Tartinijev trg and facing the marina, the town's recently renovated aquarium may be on the small side, but there's a tremendous variety of sea life packed into its two-dozen tanks.

Tartinijev trg　　　SQUARE
At No 4 of this historic central square is the attractive 15th-century **Venetian House**, with its tracery windows and stone lion relief. When built this would have overlooked Piran's inner port, which was filled in 1894 to form the square. Tartinijev trg is named in honour of the 18th-century violinist and composer Giuseppe Tartini (1692–1770), whose statue stands in the centre.

Trg 1 Maja
SQUARE

The name of this square (1st May Sq) may sound like a socialist parade ground, but in fact it's one of Piran's most attractive squares, with a cistern dating from the late 18th century. Rainwater from the surrounding roofs flows into it through the fish borne by the stone putti in the corners.

Punta
HISTORIC AREA

Punta, the historical 'snout' of Piran, still has a lighthouse, but today's version is small and modern. Attached to it, the round, serrated tower of 18th-century Church of St Clement evokes the ancient beacon from which Piran got its name.

🏃 Activities

Most water-related activities take place in Portorož, but if you want to try **diving** Noriksub (☎673 22 18, 041-590 746; www.sku pinanoriksub.si; Prešernovo nabrežje 24; shore/boat dive €30/40; ⊙10am-noon & 2-6pm Tue-Sun summer, 10am-4pm Sat & Sun winter) organises shore and boat-guided dives and hires out equipment. A 'taster' course is €50.

Bicycles are available for rent from a shop in the Old Town called Gaastra (☎040-255 400; Vidalijeva ul 3; per day €7; ⊙9am-1pm & 5-8pm summer, to 5pm Mon-Sat winter).

🛏 Sleeping

Private rooms (s €18-31.50, d €26-48) and apartments (d €40-50, q €65-75) are available through the Maona Tourist Agency (p551) and the Turist Biro (☎673 25 09; www.turistbiro -ag.si; Tomažičeva ul 3; ⊙9am-1pm & 4-7pm Mon-Sat, 10am-1pm Sun), opposite the Hotel Piran.

TOP CHOICE Max Piran
B&B €€

(☎673 34 36, 041-692 928; www.max piran.com; Ul IX Korpusa 26; d €60-70; ❄@⑦) Piran's most romantic accommodation option has just six rooms – each bearing a woman's name rather than a number – in a delightful coral-coloured 18th-century townhouse. It's a short walk from the cathedral.

Miracolo di Mare
B&B €€

(☎921 76 60, 051-445 511; www.miracolodimare.si; Tomšičeva ul 23; s €50-55, d €60-70; @⑦) A favourite B&B, the 'Wonder of the Sea' has a dozen charming (though smallish) rooms, some of which give on to the most charming raised back garden in Piran.

Hotel Tartini
HOTEL €€€

(☎671 10 00; www.hotel-tartini-piran.com; Tartinijev trg 15; s €62-86, d €84-124; P❄@) This attractive, 45-room property faces Tartinijev trg

and manages to catch a few sea views from the upper floors. The staff are especially friendly and helpful. If you've got the dosh, splash out on the eyrie-like suite 40a.

Alibi B11
HOSTEL €

(☎031-363 666; www.alibi.si; Bonifacijeva ul 11; per person €20-22; ⊙Apr-Dec; @⑦) The flagship of the Alibi stable is not its nicest property but has mostly doubles in eight rooms over four floors and a roof terrace in an ancient townhouse on a narrow street. Reception for all three hostels is here and there's a washing machine. Diagonally opposite is Alibi B14 (Bonifacijeva ul 14; per person €20-22), an upbeat and colourful four-floor party place with seven rooms, each with two to four beds. More subdued is Alibi T60 (Trubarjeva ul 60; per person €25; ❄) to the east with a fully equipped double on each of five floors. The view from the terrace of the top room is priceless. The new Vista Apartment (Trg 1 Maja 4; per person €25) is a two-room duplex apartment with sea views that sleeps up to eight people.

Val Hostel
HOSTEL €

(☎673 25 55; www.hostel-val.com; Gregorčičeva ul 38a; per person €22-27; @⑦) This central, partially renovated hostel has 20 rooms, with two to four beds, shared shower, kitchen and washing machine. It's a great favourite with backpackers.

Kamp Fiesa
CAMPING GROUND €

(☎674 62 30; autocamp.fiesa@siol.net; adult/child €12/4; ⊙May-Sep; P) The closest camping ground to Piran is at Fiesa, 4km by road but less than 1km by coastal trail east from the Cathedral of St George. It's tiny and crowded but right on the beach.

🍴 Eating & Drinking

There's an outdoor fruit and vegetable market (Zelenjavni trg; ⊙7am-2pm Mon-Sat) in the small square behind the town hall. Mercator (Levstikova ul 5; ⊙7am-8pm Mon-Sat, 8am-noon Sun) has a branch in the Old Town. Ham Ham (Cankarjevo nabrežje 19; ⊙7am-midnight) is a convenience store opposite the bus station.

TOP CHOICE Pri Mari
MEDITERRANEAN, SLOVENIAN €€

(☎673 47 35, 041-616 488; Dantejeva ul 17; mains €8.50-16; ⊙noon-11pm Tue-Sun summer, noon-10pm Tue-Sat, noon-6pm Sun winter) This stylish and welcoming restaurant run by an Italian-Slovenian couple serves the most inventive Mediterranean and Slovenian dishes in town. Be sure to book ahead.

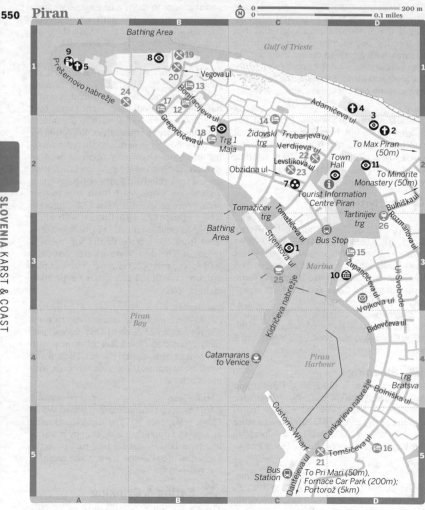

Riva Piran   SEAFOOD €€
(☑673 22 25; Gregorčičeva ul 46; mains €8-28; ⊙11.30am-midnight) The best waterfront seafood restaurant and worth patronising is this classy place with the strip's best decor and sea views.

Galeb   SEAFOOD €
(☑673 32 25; Pusterla ul 5; mains €8-11; ⊙11am-4pm & 6-11pm or midnight Wed-Mon) This excellent family-run restaurant, which has some seafront seating, is located east of the Punta lighthouse. The food is good but takes no risks.

Flora   PIZZA €
(☑673 12 58; Prešernovo nabrežje 26; pizza €4-8; ⊙10am-1am summer, 10am-10pm winter) The terrace of this simple pizzeria east of the lighthouse has great views of the Adriatic.

Cafe Teater   CAFE-BAR
(☑051-694 100; Stjenkova ul 1; ⊙8am-3am) Anyone who's anyone in Piran can be found at this cafe with a waterfront terrace and faux antique furnishings.

Žižola Kantina   BAR
(Tartinijev trg 10; ⊙9am-2am) This simple, nautically themed bar named after the jujube

Piran

(Chinese date) that grows prolifically along the Adriatic has tables right on the main square and serves 15 different flavours of *žganje* (fruit brandy).

❶ Information

Banka Koper (Tartinijev trg 12)

Caffe Neptun (☑041-724 237; www.caffe neptun.com; Dantejeva ul 4; per 20min €1; ⊘7am-1am) Modern cafe near bus station with internet access; free with drink.

Maona Tourist Agency (☑673 45 20; www. maona.si; Cankarjevo nabrežje 7; ⊘9am-8pm Mon-Sat, 10am-1pm & 5-7pm Sun) Rents private rooms, organises activities and cruises.

Post office (Leninova ul 1)

Tourist Information Centre Piran (☑673 02 20, 673 44 40; www.portoroz.si; Tartinijev trg 2; ⊘9am-8pm summer, 9am-5pm winter) Housed in the impressive town hall.

❶ Getting There & Away

Buses from everywhere except Portorož arrive at the bus station, a 300m stroll south along the portside Cankarjevo nabrežje from Tartinijev trg. Trying to drive a car into Piran is insane; vehicles are stopped at a toll gate 200m south of the bus station, where the sensible choice is to use the huge Fornače car park (per hour/day €1.20/12) and ride the frequent shuttle bus into town.

Buses run every 20 to 40 minutes to Koper (€2.70, 30 minutes, 18km) via Izola, while five head for Trieste in Italy (€10, 1¾ hours, 36km) between 6.45am and 6.55pm Monday to Saturday. Between three and five daily buses go to Ljubljana (€12, 2½ to three hours, 140km) via Divača and Postojna.

From the southern end of Tartinijev trg, a shuttle bus (€1) goes every 15 minutes to Portorož.

Venezia Lines (☑05-674 71 60; www.venezia lines.com) catamarans sail to Venice (one way €45-55, return €64-69, 2¼ hours) at 8.30am on Wednesday from May to September. A service run by **Trieste Lines** (www.triestelines.it; one way/return €8.50/15.70) links Piran and Trieste most days during the same period.

Book a taxi on ☑031-730 700.

Portorož

☑05 / POP 2900

Portorož (Portorose in Italian), the biggest coastal resort in Slovenia, is actually quite classy for a seaside town, even along Obala, the main drag. Portorož's sandy beaches are relatively clean, and there are pleasant spas and wellness centres where you can take the waters or cover yourself in curative mud.

At the same time, the vast array of accommodation options makes Portorož a useful fallback if everything's full in Piran; the **Tourist Information Centre Portorož** (☑674 22 20; www.portoroz.si; Obala 16; ⊘9am-8pm summer, 9am-5pm winter) has listings. On the way into Portorož, the summer-only hostel **Prenočišča Korotan** (☑674 54 00; www.sd.upr. si/sdp/prenocisca; Obala 11; s/d €36/49.50; ⊘Jul & Aug; ℗@) has good-sized en-suite rooms but there's a supplement for stays of one or two nights. At the other end of the scale, the 181-room **Kempinski Palace Portorož** (☑692 70 00; www.kempinski.com/portoroz; Obala 45; s/d from €135/185; ℗❋@🅿🍽), the art nouveau hotel that put Portorož on the map, has arisen phoenix-like after a protracted renovation and is now the classiest hotel in Slovenia.

There are dozens of pizzerias along Obala, but the venue of choice is **Pizzeria Figarola** (☑031-313 415; Obala 18; pizza €5.50-8.90), with a huge terrace just up from the main pier. For seafood you won't do better than at **Staro Sidro** (☑674 50 74; Obala 55; mains €8-19; ☻noon-11pm Tue-Sun) next to the lovely (and landmark) Vila San Marco.

Kavarna Cacao (☑674 10 35; Obala 14; ☻8am-1am Sun-Thu, to 3am Fri & Sat) wins the award as the most stylish cafe-bar on the coast and boasts a fabulous waterfront terrace. For live music on Tuesday and Friday from 10pm head for the **Kanela Bar** (☑674 61 81; Obala 14; ☻11am-3am), a workhorse of a rock 'n' roll bar secreted between the beach and the Kavarna Cacao.

Portorož is served every 15 minutes by shuttle bus (€1) to/from Piran. Catch it along Obala.

EASTERN SLOVENIA

The rolling vine-covered hills of eastern Slovenia are attractive but much less dramatic than the Julian Alps or, indeed, the coast. If you're heading by train to Vienna via Graz in Austria it saves money to stop in lively Maribor, Slovenia's second-largest city; international tickets are very expensive per kilometre, so doing as much travelling as possible on domestic trains saves cash. While there, consider visiting postcard-perfect Ptuj less than 30km down the road.

Maribor

☑02 / POP 87,275

Slovenia's second city, chosen as the European Capital of Culture in 2012, really has no unmissable sights but oozes with charm thanks to its delightful (but tiny) Old Town. Pedestrianised central streets buzz with cafes and student life, and in late June/early July the old, riverside Lent district hosts the **Festival Lent** (http://lent.slovenija.net), a two-week extravaganza of folklore and culture.

Maribor Castle (Grajski trg 2), on the main square's northeast corner, contains a magnificent 18th-century **rococo staircase** visible from the street and the **Maribor Regional Museum** (☑228 35 51; www.pmuzej-mb.si; adult/child €3/2; ☻9am-4pm Tue-Sat, 9am-2pm Sun), one of Slovenia's richest archaeological and ethnographical collections. To the

southwest, the **cathedral** (Slomškov trg) sits in an oasis of fountain-cooled calm. Follow little Poštna ul southward into **Glavni trg** with its 16th-century **town hall** (Glavni trg 14) and extravagant **plague pillar** erected by townspeople in gratitude for having survived the plague. A block further south down Mesarski prehod and along the Drava River's northern bank is the **Stara Trta** (Vojašniška 8), the world's oldest living grapevine. It's been a source of a dark red wine called Žametna Črnina (Black Velvet) for more than four centuries.

The **Tourist Information Centre Maribor** (☑234 66 11; www.maribor-pohorje.si; Partinzanska c 6a; ☻9am-7pm Mon-Fri, to 6pm Sat & Sun) is in a kiosk opposite the Franciscan church. For budget accommodation, try the **Lollipop Hostel** (☑040-243 160; lollipophostel@yahoo.com; Maistrova ul 17; dm €20; @), with 13 beds in two rooms a short distance from the train station and run by an affable Englishwoman. A short distance to the southeast is the **Grand Hotel Ocean** (☑234 36 73; www.hotelocean.si; Partizanska c 39; s/d €118/152; P☼@), a stunning 22-room boutique hotel named after the first train to pass through the city in 1846.

Gril Ranca (☑252 55 50; Dravska ul 10; dishes €4.80-7.50; ☻8am-11pm Mon-Sat, noon-9pm Sun) along the Drava in Lent serves simple but scrumptious Balkan grills. For something spicier try nearby **Takos** (☑252 71 50; Mesarski prehod 3; mains €6.50-12; ☻11am-11pm Mon-Thu, to 2.30am Fri & Sat), an atmospheric Mexican restaurant that turns into a snappy little night spot at the weekend.

Buses run to Ljubljana (€12.40, three hours, 141km) two to four times a day. Also served are Celje (€6.70, 1½ hours, 65km, four a day) and Ptuj (€3.60, 45 minutes, 27km, hourly). There are daily buses to Munich (€46, 7½ hours, 453km) at 6.30pm and 9.50pm, and one to Vienna (€29, 4½ hours, 258km) at 7.45pm. Of the two-dozen daily trains to/from Ljubljana (€8.50, 2½ hours, 156km), some seven are IC express trains costing €14.40 and taking just under two hours.

Ptuj

☑02 / POP 19,010

Rising above a wide, fairly flat valley, compact Ptuj – Poetovio to the Romans – forms a symphony of red-tile roofs best viewed from the other side of the Drava River.

☉ Sights

Ptuj Castle   CASTLE
(Na Gradu 1) Ptuj's pinnacle is well-preserved, containing the fine **Ptuj Regional Museum** (🖉787 92 30; www.pok-muzej-ptuj.si; adult/child €4/2.50; ⊙9am-6pm Mon-Fri, 9am-8pm Sat & Sun summer, 9am-5pm daily winter).

🎭 Festivals

Kurentovanje   CARNIVAL
(www.kurentovanje.net) In February the crowds come to spot the shaggy straw men at Slovenia's foremost traditional carnival. A 'rite of spring', it is celebrated for 10 days up to Mardi Gras, or Shrove Tuesday (February or early March); the museum has some excellent Kurentovanje-related exhibits.

🛏 Sleeping

Hostel Eva   HOSTEL €
(🖉771 24 41, 040-226 522; www.bikeek.si; Jadranska ul 22; per person €12-17) If you're looking for budget accommodation, head for this a welcoming place that's connected to a bike shop (rental per hour/day €3.80/11) with six rooms containing two to four beds and a large, light-filled kitchen.

TOP CHOICE **Hotel Mitra**   HOTEL €€
(🖉787 74 55, 051-603 069; www.hotel-mitra.si; Prešernova ul 6; s €56-68, d €96-103; P✱@🛜) If you'd like more comfort, continue walking west on Prešernova ul past a parade of cafes and bars to one of provincial Slovenia's more interesting hotels, with 26 generous-sized guestrooms and three humongous suites, lovely Oriental carpets on the original wooden floors and a wellness centre in an old courtyard cellar.

🍴 Eating

Next to the town's open-air **market** (Novi trg; ⊙7am-3pm) you'll find a large **Mercator** (Novi trg 3; ⊙7.30am-7.30pm Mon-Fri, to 1pm Sat) supermarket.

Amadeus   GOSTILNA €€
(🖉771 70 51; Prešernova ul 36; mains €6.50-20; ⊙noon-10pm Mon-Thu, noon-11pm Fri & Sat, noon-4pm Sun) A very pleasant *gostilna* above a cafe-bar, it serves *štruklji* (dumplings with herbs and cheese, €4.50), steak and pork dishes.

Gostilna Ribič   GOSTILNA €€
(🖉749 06 35; Dravska ul 9; mains €9.50-20; ⊙10am-11pm Sun-Thu, to midnight Fri & Sat) The best restaurant in Ptuj has a great riverside terrace and is the ideal spot to have fish.

ℹ Information

Tourist Information Centre Ptuj (🖉779 60 11; www.ptuj.info; Slovenski trg 5; ⊙8am-8pm summer, 9am-6pm winter) Facing a medieval tower in the Old Town, it has reams of information and lists of places to stay.

ℹ Getting There & Away

Buses to Maribor (€3.60, 45 minutes, 27km) run at hourly on weekdays but are less frequent on weekends. You can reach Ptuj up to nine times a day by train from Ljubljana (€8 to €10.50, 2½ hours, 155km) direct or via Zidani Most and Pragersko.

UNDERSTAND SLOVENIA

History

Slovenes can make a credible claim to having invented democracy. By the early 7th century, their Slavic ancestors had founded the Duchy of Carantania (Karantanija), based at Krn Castle (now Karnburg in Austria). Ruling dukes were elected by ennobled commoners and invested before ordinary citizens. This unique model was noted by the 16th-century French political philosopher Jean Bodin, whose work was a key reference for Thomas Jefferson when he wrote the American Declaration of Independence in 1776. Carantania (later Carinthia) was fought over by the Franks and Magyars from the 8th to 10th centuries, and later divided up among Austro-Germanic nobles and bishops. Between the late 13th and early 16th centuries, almost all the lands inhabited by Slovenes, with the exception of the Venetian-controlled coastal towns, came under the control of the Habsburgs.

Indeed, Austria ruled what is now Slovenia until 1918, apart from a brief interlude between 1809 and 1813 when Napoleon created six so-called Illyrian Provinces from Slovenian and Croatian regions and made Ljubljana the capital. Napoleon proved a popular conqueror as his relatively liberal regime de-Germanised the education system. Slovene was taught in schools for the first time, leading to an awakening of national consciousness. In tribute, Ljubljana still has a French Revolution Sq (Trg Francoske Revolucije) with a column bearing a likeness of the French emperor.

Fighting during WWI was particularly savage along the Soča Valley – the so-called Isonzo Front – which was occupied by Italy then dramatically retaken by German-led Austro-Hungarian forces. The war ended with the collapse of Austria-Hungary, which handed western Slovenia to Italy as part of postwar reparations. Northern Carinthia, including the towns of Beljak and Celovec (now Villach and Klagenfurt), voted to stay with Austria in a 1920 plebiscite. What remained of Slovenia joined fellow south (*jug*) Slavs in forming the Kingdom of Serbs, Croats and Slovenes, later Yugoslavia.

Nazi occupation in WWII was for the most part resisted by Slovenian partisans, though after Italy capitulated in 1943 the anti-partisan Slovenian Domobranci (Home Guards) were active in the west. To prevent their nemeses the communists from taking political control in liberated areas, the Domobranci threw their support behind the Germans. The war ended with Slovenia regaining Italian-held areas from Piran to Bovec, but losing Trst (Trieste) and part of Gorica (Gorizia).

In Tito's Yugoslavia, Slovenia, with only 8% of the national population, was the economic powerhouse, creating up to 20% of the national GDP. But by the 1980s the federation had become increasingly Serb-dominated, and Slovenes feared they would lose their political autonomy. In free elections, Slovenes voted overwhelmingly to break away from Yugoslavia and did so on 25 June 1991. A 10-day war that left 66 people dead followed; Yugoslavia swiftly signed a truce in order to concentrate on regaining control of coastal Croatia.

Slovenia was admitted to the UN in May 1992 and became a member of the EU in May 2004. It replaced the tolar with the euro as the national currency in January 2007.

In the national elections of October 2008, Janez Janša's coalition government was narrowly defeated by the Social Democrats under Borut Pahor, who was able to form a coalition with three minority parties. Since 2004, Slovenia has been moving towards a two-party system, with the Social Democrats and Janša's Slovenian Democratic Party as the major political forces.

The Slovenes

The population of Slovenia is largely homogeneous. Just over 83% are ethnic Slovenes, with the remainder Serbs, Croats, Bosnians, Albanians and Roma; there are also small enclaves of Italians and Hungarians, who have special deputies looking after their interests in parliament. Slovenes are ethnically Slavic, typically hardworking, multilingual and extrovert. Just under 58% of Slovenes identify themselves as Catholics.

The Arts

Slovenia's most cherished writer is the Romantic poet France Prešeren (1800–49). His patriotic yet humanistic verse was a driving force in raising Slovene national consciousness. Fittingly, a stanza of his poem 'Zdravljica' (A Toast) forms the lyrics of the national anthem.

Many of Ljubljana's most characteristic architectural features, including its recurring pyramid motif, were added by celebrated Slovenian architect Jože Plečnik (1872–1957), whose work fused classical building principles and folk-art traditions.

Postmodernist painting and sculpture were more or less dominated from the 1980s by the multimedia group Neue Slowenische Kunst (NSK) and the artists' cooperative Irwin. It also spawned the internationally known industrial-music group Laibach, whose leader, Tomaž Hostnik, died tragically in 1983 when he hanged himself from a *kozolec*, the traditional (and iconic) hayrack found only in Slovenia. Slovenia's vibrant music scene embraces rave, techno, jazz, punk, thrash-metal and *chanson* (torch songs from the likes of Vita Mavrič); the most popular local rock group is Siddharta, still going strong after 15 years. There's also been a folk-music revival: keep an ear out for the groups Katice and Katalena, who play traditional Slovenian music with a modern twist, and the vocalist Brina.

Well-received Slovenian films in recent years include *Kruh in Mleko* (Bread & Milk, 2001), the tragic story by Jan Cvitkovič of a dysfunctional small-town family, and Damjan Kozole's *Rezerni Deli* (Spare Parts, 2003) about the trafficking of illegal immigrants through Slovenia from Croatia to Italy by a couple of embittered misfits living in the southern town of Krško, site of the nation's only nuclear power plant. Much lighter fare is *Petelinji Zajtrk* (Rooster's Breakfast, 2007), a romance by Marko Naberšnik set in Gornja Radgona on the Austrian border in northeast Slovenia, and the bizarre US-made documentary *Big River Man* (John Maringouin, 2009) about an overweight dyspeptic marathon swimmer who takes on – wait for it – the Amazon and succeeds.

Environment

Slovenia is amazingly green; indeed, 58% of its total surface area is covered in forest and it's growing. Slovenia is home to almost 3200 plant species – some 70 of which are indigenous. Triglav National Park is particularly rich in native flowering plants. Among the more peculiar endemic fauna in Slovenia is a blind salamander called *Proteus anguinus* that lives deep in Karst caves, can survive for years without eating and has been called a 'living fossil'.

Slovenian Cuisine

Slovenia boasts an incredibly diverse cuisine, but except for a few national favourites such as *žlikrofi* (pasta stuffed with cheese, bacon and chives) and *jota* (hearty bean soup) and incredibly rich desserts like *gibanica*, you're not likely to encounter many of these regional specialities on menus. Dishes like *brodet* (fish soup) from the coast, *ajdovi žganci z ocvirki* (buckwheat 'porridge' with savoury pork crackling) and salad greens doused in *bučno olje* (pumpkinseed oil) are generally eaten at home.

A *gostilna* or *gostišče* (inn) or *restavracija* (restaurant) more frequently serves *rižota* (risotto), *klobasa* (sausage), *zrezek* (cutlet/steak), *golaž* (goulash) and *paprikaš* (piquant chicken or beef 'stew'). *Riba* (fish) is usually priced by the *dag* (100g). *Postrv* (freshwater trout) generally costs half the price of sea fish, though grilled squid *(lignji na žaru)* doused in garlic butter is usually a bargain.

Common in Slovenia are such Balkan favourites as *cevapčiči* (spicy meatballs of beef or pork) and *pljeskavica* (spicy meat patties), often served with *kajmak* (a type of clotted cream).

You can snack cheaply on takeaway pizza slices or pieces of *burek* (€2), flaky pastry stuffed with meat, cheese or apple. Alternatives include *štruklji* (cottage-cheese dumplings) and *palačinke* (thin sweet pancakes).

Some restaurants have *dnevno kosilo* (set lunches), including *juha* (soup), *solata* (salad) and a main course, for as low as €7.

Wine, Beer & Brandy

Distinctively Slovenian wines include peppery red Teran made from Refošk grapes in the Karst region, Cviček, a dry light red – almost rosé – wine from eastern Slovenia, and Malvazija, a straw-colour white from the coast that is light and dry. Slovenes are justly proud of their top vintages, but cheaper barstandard 'open wine' (*odprto vino*) sold by the decilitre (100mL) is just so-so.

Pivo (beer), whether *svetlo* (lager) or *temno* (porter), is best on *točeno* (draught) but always available in cans and bottles too.

There are dozens of kinds of *žganje* (fruit brandy) available, including *češnjevec* (made with cherries), *sadjevec* (mixed fruit), *brinjevec* (juniper), *hruška* (pears, also called *viljamovka*) and *slivovka* (plums).

Like many other countries in Europe, Slovenia bans smoking across the board in all public places, including restaurants, bars and hotels.

SURVIVAL GUIDE

Directory A–Z

Accommodation

Very roughly, budget accommodation in Slovenia means a double room under €50. Midrange is €50 to €100 and top end is anything over €100. Accommodation can be a bit more expensive in Ljubljana. Unless otherwise indicated, rooms include toilet and bath or shower and breakfast. Smoking is banned in all hotels and hostels.

Camping grounds generally charge per person, whether you're in a tent or caravan. Almost all sites close from mid-October to mid-April. Camping 'rough' is illegal in Slovenia, and this law is enforced, especially around Bled and on the coast. Seek out the Slovenian Tourist Board's *Camping in Slovenia*.

Slovenia's ever-growing stable of hostels includes Ljubljana's trendy Celica and the Alibi chain found both in the capital and in Piran. Throughout the country there are student dormitories (residence halls) moonlighting as hostels for visitors in July and August. Unless stated otherwise hostel rooms share bathrooms. Hostels usually cost from €17 to €22; prices are at their highest in July and August.

Tourist information offices can usually help you find private rooms, apartments and tourist farms, or they can recommend private agencies that will. Such accommodation can appear misleadingly cheap if you overlook the 30% to 50% surcharge levied on stays of less than three nights. Also be aware that many such properties are in outlying villages with minimal (or no) public transport, and that the cheapest one-star category rooms with shared bathroom are actually very rare, so you'll usually pay well above the quoted minimum. Depending on the season you might save a little money by going directly to any house with a sign reading *sobe* or *Zimmer frei* (indicating 'rooms available' in Slovene and German). For more information check out the STB's *Friendly Countryside* pamphlet listing some 200 farms with accommodation.

Guesthouses, known as a *penzion*, *gostišče*, or *prenočišča*, are often cosy and better value than full-blown hotels. Beware that locally listed rates are usually quoted per person assuming double occupancy. A tourist tax – routinely from €1 per person per day – is usually not included.

Activities

EXTREME SPORTS

Several areas specialise in adrenalin-rush activities – rafting, hydro-speed, kayaking and canyoning – including Bovec (p542) and Bled (p537). Bovec is also a great place for paragliding. Gliding costs are very reasonable from Lesce near Bled. Scuba diving from Piran (p549) is also good value.

HIKING

Hiking is extremely popular, with the **Alpine Association of Slovenia** (www.pzs.si) counting more than 58,000 members and *Ljubljančani* flocking in droves to Triglav National Park (p539) on weekends. There are some 10,000km of marked trails and paths – 8250km of which are mountain trails – and more than 170 mountain huts offer comfortable trailside refuge. Ask for the STB's exhaustive *Hiking in Slovenia*.

SKIING

Skiing is a Slovenian passion, with slopes particularly crowded over the Christmas holidays and in early February. See the STB's *Slovenia Skiing* for more details.

Kranjska Gora (up to 1291m; p540) has some challenging runs, and the world record for ski-jumping was set at nearby Planica, 4km to the west. Above Lake Bohinj, Vogel (up to 1800m) is particularly scenic, as is Kanin (up to 2300m) above Bovec, which can have snow into late spring. Being relatively close to Ljubljana, Krvavec (up to 1971m), northeast of Kranj, can have particularly long lift queues.

Just west of Maribor in eastern Slovenia is a popular choice and the biggest downhill skiing area in the country. Although relatively low (336m to 1347m), the Mariborsko Pohorje is easily accessible, with very varied downhill pistes and relatively short lift queues.

OTHER ACTIVITIES

Mountain bikes are available for hire from travel agencies and some hotels at Bled, Bohinj, Bovec, Kranjska Gora and Postojna.

The Soča River near Kobarid and the Sava Bohinjka near Bohinj are great for fly-fishing April to October. Catch-and-release licences for the latter cost €42 and are sold at the tourist office.

Spas and wellness centres are very popular in Slovenia; the STB publishes a useful brochure called *Health Resorts*. Many towns (eg Portorož) have some spa complexes, and hotels often offer free or low-rate entry to their guests.

Business Hours

Most businesses post their opening times (*delovni čas*) on the door. Many shops close Saturday afternoons. A handful of grocery stores open on Sundays, including some branches of the ubiquitous Mercator supermarket chain. Most museums close on Mondays. Banks often take lunch breaks from noon or 12.30pm to 2pm or 3pm and some open on Saturday mornings. Post offices are generally open from 8am to 6pm weekdays and till noon on Saturday.

Restaurants typically open from 10pm or 11am to 10pm or 11pm. Bars stay open to midnight, though they usually have longer hours on weekends and shorter ones on Sundays.

Embassies & Consulates

Following are among the embassies and consulates in Slovenia. They are all in Ljubljana unless otherwise stated:

Australia (☎01-234 86 75; Železna c 14; ☺9am-1pm Mon-Fri)

Austria (☎01-479 07 00; Prešernova c 23; ☺8am-noon Mon-Thu, 8-10am Fri) Enter from Veselova ul.

Canada (☎01-252 44 44; 12th fl, Trg Republike 3; ☺9am-noon Mon-Fri)

Croatia Ljubljana (☎01-425 62 20; Gruberjevo nabrežje 6; ☺9am-1pm Mon-Fri); Maribor (☎02-234 66 80; Trg Svobode 3; ☺10am-1pm Mon-Fri)

France (☎01-479 04 00; Barjanska c 1; ☺8.30am-12.30pm Mon-Fri) Enter from Zoisova c 2.

Hungary ([☎]01-512 18 82; ul Konrada Babnika 5; ⊙8am-5pm Mon-Fri)

Ireland ([☎]01-300 89 70; Palača Kapitelj, Poljanski nasip 6; ⊙9.30am-12.30pm & 2.30-4pm Mon-Fri)

Italy Ljubljana ([☎]01-426 21 94; Snežniška ul 8; ⊙9-11am Mon-Fri); Koper ([☎]05-627 37 49; Belvedere 2; ⊙9-11am Mon-Fri)

Netherlands ([☎]01-420 14 61; Palača Kapitelj, Poljanski nasip 6; ⊙9am-noon Mon-Fri)

New Zealand ([☎]01-580 30 55; Verovškova ul 57; ⊙8am-3pm Mon-Fri)

South Africa ([☎]01-200 63 00; Pražakova ul 4; ⊙3-4pm Tue) In the Kompas building.

UK ([☎]01-200 39 10; 4th fl, Trg Republike 3; ⊙9am-noon Mon-Fri)

USA ([☎]01-200 55 00; Prešernova c 31; ⊙9-11.30am & 1-3pm Mon-Fri)

Festivals & Events

Major cultural and sporting events are listed under 'Upcoming Events' on the home page of the of the **Slovenian Tourist Board** (www.slovenia.info) website and in the STB's comprehensive *Calendar of Major Events in Slovenia*, issued annually.

Food

Price ranges are: budget (€; under €15), midrange (€€; €15 to €30) and top end (€€€; over €30).

Gay & Lesbian Travellers

Roza Klub ([☎]01-430 47 40; Kersnikova ul 4) in Ljubljana is made up of the gay and lesbian branches of **ŠKUC** (www.skuc.org), which stands for Študentski Kulturni Center (Student Cultural Centre) but is no longer student-oriented as such.

A more or less monthly publication called **Narobe** (Upside Down; www.narobe.si) is in Slovene only, though you might be able to at least glean from the listings.

Holidays

Slovenia celebrates 14 holidays (*prazniki*) a year. If a holiday falls on a Sunday, then the following Monday becomes the holiday.

New Year 1 & 2 January

Prešeren Day (Slovenian Culture Day) 8 February

Easter & Easter Monday March/April

Insurrection Day 27 April

Labour Day holidays 1 & 2 May

National Day 25 June

Assumption Day 15 August

Reformation Day 31 October

All Saints Day 1 November

Christmas Day 25 December

Independence Day 26 December

Internet Access

Virtually every hostel and hotel now has internet access – a computer for guests' use (free or for a nominal fee), wi-fi, or both. Most cities and towns have at least one internet cafe but they usually only have a handful of terminals. The useful **e-točka** (e-points; www.e-tocke.gov.si) website lists free access terminals, wi-fi hotspots and commercial internet cafes across Slovenia.

Internet Resources

The website of the **Slovenian Tourist Board** (www.slovenia.info) is tremendously useful, as is that of **Mat'Kurja** (www.matkurja.com), a directory of Slovenian web resources. Most Slovenian towns and cities have a website accessed by typing www.town.si (or sometimes www.town-tourism.si). Especially good are **Ljubljana** (www.ljubljana.si), **Maribor** (www.maribor.si) and **Piran/Portorož** (www.portoroz.si).

Money

The official currency is the euro. Exchanging cash is simple at banks, major post offices, travel agencies and *menjalnice* (bureaux de change), although many don't accept travellers cheques. Major credit and debit cards are accepted almost everywhere, and ATMs are ubiquitous.

Post

Local mail costs €0.33 for up to 20g, while an international airmail stamp costs €0.49. Poste restante is free; address it to and pick it up from the main post office at Slovenska c 32, 1101 Ljubljana.

Telephone

Slovenia's country code is [☎]386. Public telephones require a phonecard (*telefonska kartica* or *telekartica*), available at post offices and some newsstands. The cheapest card (€3, 25 units) gives about 20 minutes' calling time to other European countries; the highest value is €14.60 with 300 units. Local SIM cards with €5 credit are available for €12 from **SiMobil** (www.simobil.si), for €15 from **Mobitel** (www.mobitel.si) and for just €3.99 from

EMERGENCY NUMBERS

» **Ambulance** ☏112
» **Fire Brigade** ☏112
» **Police** ☏113
» **Roadside Assistance** ☏1987

new-kid-on-the-block **Tušmobil** (www.tusmo bil.si). Mobile numbers in Slovenia are identified by the prefix ☏030 and ☏040 (SiMobil), ☏031, ☏041, ☏051 and ☏071 (Mobitel) and ☏070 (Tušmobil).

Tourist Information

The Ljubljana-based **Slovenian Tourist Board** (☏01-589 85 50; www.slovenia.info; Dimičeva ul 13) has dozens of tourist information centres (TICs) in Slovenia, and seven branches abroad. See 'STB Representative Offices Abroad' on its website for details.

Visas

Citizens of virtually all European countries, as well as Australia, Canada, Israel, Japan, New Zealand and the USA, do not require visas to visit Slovenia for stays of up to 90 days. Holders of EU and Swiss passports can enter using a national identity card.

Those who do require visas (including South Africans) can get them for up to 90 days at any Slovenian embassy or consulate – see the website of the **Ministry of Foreign Affairs** (www.mzz.gov.si) for a full listing. They cost €35 regardless of the type of visa or length of validity. You'll need confirmation of a hotel booking plus one photo, and you may have to show a return or onward ticket.

Women Travellers

In the event of an emergency call the **police** (☏113) any time or the **SOS Helpline** (☏080 11 55; www.drustvo-sos.si; ☉noon-10pm Mon-Fri, 6-10pm Sat & Sun).

Getting There & Away

Air

Slovenia's only international airport receiving regular scheduled flights at present – Aerodrom Maribor does limited charters only – is Ljubljana's **Jože Pučnik Airport** (LJU; ☏04-206 1981; www.lju-airport.si) at Brnik, 27km north of Ljubljana. From there, the Slovenian flag-carrier, **Adria Airways** (JP; ☏080 13 00, 01-369 10 10; www.adria-airways.

com), serves some 30 European destinations on regularly scheduled flights, with just as many holiday spots served by charter flights in summer. Adria can be remarkably good value and includes useful connections to places like İstanbul, Pristina (Kosovo) and Tirana (Albania).

Other airlines with regularly scheduled flights to and from Ljubljana:

Air France (AF; ☏01-244 34 47; www.airfrance. com) Daily flights to Paris (CDG).

Austrian Airlines (OS; ☏04-202 01 00; www. aua.com) Multiple daily flights with Adria to Vienna.

Brussels Airlines (SN; ☏04-206 16 56; www. brusselsairlines.com) Daily flights with Adria to Brussels.

ČSA Czech Airlines (OK; ☏04-206 17 50; www.czechairlines.com) Flights to Prague.

easyJet (EZY; ☏04-206 16 77; www.easyjet. com) Low-cost daily flights to London Stansted.

Finnair (AY; ☏080 13 00; www.finnair.com) Flights to Helsinki.

JAT Airways (JU; ☏01-231 43 40; www.jat. com) Daily flights to Belgrade.

Turkish Airlines (TK; ☏04-206 16 80; www. turkishairlines.com) Flights to İstanbul.

Land

BUS

International bus destinations from Ljubljana include Serbia, Germany, Croatia, Bosnia & Hercegovina, Macedonia, Italy and Scandinavia; see p559. You can also catch buses to Italy and Croatia from coastal towns, including Piran (p551) and Koper (p547).

TRAIN

It is possible to travel to Italy, Austria, Germany, Croatia and Hungary by train; Ljubljana (p559) is the main hub, although you can, for example, hop on international trains in certain cities like Maribor and Ptuj). International train travel can be expensive. It is sometimes cheaper to travel as far as you can on domestic routes before crossing any borders.

Sea

Piran despatches ferries to Trieste daily and catamarans to Venice at least once a week in season; see p551 for details. There's also a catamaran between nearby Izola and Venice in summer months; see p548.

Getting Around

Bus

Book long-distance buses ahead of time, especially when travelling on Friday afternoons. If your bag has to go in the luggage compartment below the bus, it will cost about €1.50 extra. Check the online bus timetable on the **Avtobusna Postaja Ljubljana** (www.ap-ljubljana.si) website.

Bicycle

Bicycle rental places are generally concentrated in the more popular tourist areas such as Ljubljana, Bled, Bovec and Piran though a fair few cycle shops and repair places hire them out as well.

Car

Daily rates usually start at around €40/210 per day/week, including unlimited mileage, collision-damage waiver and theft protection. Unleaded petrol *(bencin)* costs €1.19 (95 octane) and €1.22 (98 octane), with diesel at €1.13. You must keep your headlights illuminated throughout the day. If you'll be doing a lot of driving consider buying Kod & Kam's 1:100,000 *Avtoatlas Slovenija* (€29).

Tolls are no longer paid separately on the motorways. Instead all cars must display a *vinjeta* (road-toll sticker) on the windscreen. They cost €15/30 for a week/month for cars and €7.50/25 for motorcycles and are available at petrol stations, post offices, some newsstands and tourist information centres. These stickers will already be in place on a rental car, but if you are driving your own vehicle, failure to display such a sticker risks a fine of up to €800.

Further information is available from the **Automobile Association of Slovenia** (☑ 01-530 52 00; www.amzs.si).

Hitching

Hitchhiking is fairly common and legal everywhere in Slovenia except on motorways and a few major highways. But it's never totally safe and Lonely Planet doesn't recommend it.

Train

Slovenian Railways (Slovenske Železnice; ☑ 01-291 33 32; www.slo-zeleznice.si) has a useful online timetable that's easy to use. Buy tickets before boarding or you'll incur a €2.50 supplement. Be aware that EuroCity (EC) and InterCity (IC) trains carry a surcharge of €1.60 on top of standard quoted fares, while InterCity Slovenia ones cost €9.50/6.30 extra in 1st/2nd class.

Switzerland

Includes »

Best Places to Eat

» Atrio Vulcanelli (p599)
» Lötschberg AOC (p582)
» Osteria Chiara (p603)

Best Places to Stay

» Pension für Dich (p595)
» Hôtel Masson (p575)
» Mountain Hostel (p589)

Why Go?

What giddy romance Zermatt, St Moritz and other glitterati-encrusted names evoke.

This is *Sonderfall Schweiz* ('special case Switzerland'), a privileged neutral country set apart from others, proudly idiosyncratic, insular and unique. Blessed with gargantuan cultural diversity, its four official languages alone say it all.

The Swiss don't do half-measures: Zürich, their most gregarious urban centre, has cutting-edge art, legendary nightlife and one of the world's highest living standards. The national passion for sweat, stamina and clingy Lycra takes 65-year-olds across 2500m-high mountain passes for Sunday strolls, sees giggly three-year-olds skiing rings around grown-ups, prompts locals done with 'ordinary' marathons to sprint backwards up mountains – all in the name of good old-fashioned fun.

So don't depend just on your postcard images of Bern's chocolate-box architecture, the majestic Matterhorn or the thundering Rheinfall – Switzerland is a place that's so outrageously beautiful it simply must be seen to be believed.

When to Go

Geneva

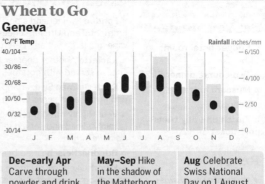

Dec–early Apr Carve through powder and drink glühwein at an alpine resort

May–Sep Hike in the shadow of the Matterhorn and be wowed by its mesmerising stance

Aug Celebrate Swiss National Day on 1 August and witness Swiss national pride in full force

Fast Facts

» **Area** 41,285 sq km

» **Population** 7.8 million

» **Capital** Bern

» **Telephone** country code ☏41; international access code ☏00

» **Emergency** police ☏117; fire ☏118; ambulance ☏144

Exchange Rates

Australia	A$1	Sfr0.95
Canada	C$1	Sfr0.93
Euro Zone	€1	Sfr1.29
Japan	¥100	Sfr1.12
New Zealand	NZ$1	Sfr0.68
UK	UK£1	Sfr1.46
USA	US$1	Sfr0.87

Set Your Budget

» **Budget hotel room** Sfr80–100

» **Two-course dinner** Sfr25

» **Museum entrance** Sfr15

» **Beer** Sfr5

» **Zurich one-day transport ticket** Sfr8.20

Resources

» **swissinfo** (www.swissinfo.ch)

» **MySwitzerland** (www.myswitzerland.com)

Connections

Landlocked between France, Germany, Austria, Liechtenstein and Italy, Switzerland's a doddle to move on from. Geneva city buses run as far as the French border (a couple cross into France, continuing along the southern shore of Lake Geneva) and there are plenty of direct train connections from Geneva and Zurich to Paris, as well as Hamburg, Milan and Barcelona. There are also TGV links from Geneva and Zurich. Cosmopolitan Zürich enjoys as many international rail connections, including daily trains to/from Stuttgart, Munich and Innsbruck. In northern Switzerland, Basel is the major European rail hub, with separate train stations serving France and Germany. Then, of course, there is Italy, a mere hop and a skip from Locarno in Italianate Ticino.

ITINERARIES

One Week

Starting in vibrant Zürich, shop famous Bahnhofstrasse and hit the bars of Züri-West. Next, head to the Jungfrau region to explore some kick-ass alpine scenery (think James Bond racing an avalanche down a sheer snowy rock face). Take a pit stop in beautiful Lucerne before finishing up in country capital Bern.

Two Weeks

As above, then head west for French-immersion lessons in Geneva or lakeside Lausanne. Explore the Neuchâtel and Fribourg cantons, stopping in Gruyères to dip into a cheesy fondue and overdose on meringues drowned in thick double cream. Zip to Zermatt or across to St Moritz to frolic in snow or green meadows, then loop east to taste the Italian side of Switzerland.

Essential Food & Drink

» **Fondue** Switzerland's best-known dish, in which melted Emmental and Gruyère cheese are combined with white wine in a large pot and eaten with bread cubes.

» **Raclette** Another popular artery-hardener of melted cheese served with potatoes.

» **Rösti** German Switzerland's national dish of fried shredded potatoes is served with everything.

» **Veal** Highly rated throughout the country; in Zürich, veal is thinly sliced and served in a cream sauce (*Gschnetzeltes Kalbsfleisch*).

» **Bündnerfleisch** Dried beef, smoked and thinly sliced.

» **Wurst** Like their northern neighbours, the Swiss also munch on a wide variety of sausages.

GENEVA

POP 185,700

Supersleek, slick and cosmopolitan, Geneva (Genève in French, Genf in German) is a rare breed of city. It's one of Europe's priciest. Its people chatter in every language under the sun (184 nationalities comprise 45% of the city's population) and it's constantly thought of as the Swiss capital – which it isn't. This gem of a city superbly strung around the sparkling shores of Europe's largest alpine lake is, in fact, only Switzerland's second-largest city.

Yet the whole world is here: the UN, International Red Cross, International Labour Organization, World Health Organization – 200-odd governmental and nongovernmental international organisations fill the city's plush hotels with big-name guests, feast on an incredulous choice of cuisine and help prop up the overload of banks, jewellers and chocolate shops for which Geneva is known. Strolling manicured city parks, lake sailing and skiing next door in the Alps are weekend pursuits.

⊙ Sights & Activities

The city centre is so compact it's easy to see many of the main sights on foot.

Lake Geneva   LAKE

Begin your exploration of Europe's largest alpine lake by having a coffee on **Île Rousseau**, where a statue honours the celebrated freethinker. Cross to the southern side of the lake and walk west to the **Horloge Fleurie** (Flower Clock; Quai du Général-Guisan) in the Jardin Anglais. Geneva's most photographed clock, crafted from 6500 flowers, has ticked since 1955 and sports the world's longest second hand (2.5m).

The 140m-tall **Jet d'Eau** on the lake's southern shore is impossible to miss. At any one time there are 7 tonnes of water in the air, shooting up with incredible force – 200km/h, 1360 horsepower – to create its sky-high plume, kissed by a rainbow on sunny days.

Old Town   HISTORIC AREA

The main street, Grand-Rue, shelters the **Espace Rousseau** at No 40, where the 18th-century philosopher was born.

Nearby, the part-Romanesque, part-Gothic **Cathédrale de St-Pierre** is where Protestant John Calvin preached from 1536 to 1564. Beneath the cathedral is the **site archéologique** (☏022 311 75 74; www.site-ar cheologique.ch; Cour St-Pierre 6; adult/child Sfr8/4; ⊙10am-5pm Tue-Sun), an interactive space safeguarding fine 4th-century mosaics and a 5th-century baptismal font.

You can trace Calvin's life in the neighbouring **Musée Internationale de la Réforme** (International Museum of the Reformation; ☏022 310 24 31; www.musee-reforme.ch; Rue du Clootre 4; adult/student/child Sfr8/3/2; ⊙10am-5pm Tue-Sun).

Palais des Nations   LANDMARK

(☏022 907 48 96; www.unog.ch; Ave de la Paix 14; tours Sfr10; ⊙10am-noon & 2-4pm Apr-Oct, to 5pm Jul & Aug, 10am-noon & 2-4pm Mon-Fri Nov-Mar) The art deco Palais des Nations is the European arm of the UN and the home of 3000 international civil servants. You can see where decisions about world affairs are made on the hour-long tour. Afterwards check out the extensive gardens – don't miss the towering grey monument coated with heat-resistant titanium donated by the USSR to commemorate the conquest of space. An ID or passport is obligatory for admission.

FREE **International Red Cross & Red Crescent Museum**   MUSEUM

(Musée Internationale de la Croix Rouge et du Croissant-Rouge; ☏022 748 95 25; www.micr.org; Ave de la Paix 17; ⊙10am-5pm Wed-Mon) A compelling multimedia trawl through atrocities perpetuated by humanity in recent history. Against the long litany of war and nastiness, documented in films, photos, sculptures and soundtracks, are set the noble aims of the organisation.

Other Museums   MUSEUMS

Konrad Witz's *La pêche miraculeuse* (c 1440–44) portraying Christ walking on water on Lake Geneva is a highlight of the **Musée d'Art et d'Histoire** (☏022 418 26 00; http://mah.ville-ge.ch; Rue Charles Galland 2; permanent collection free, temporary exhibition fees vary; ⊙10am-5pm Tue-Sun). The particularly

GENEVA IN TWO DAYS

Explore the left-bank **parks**, **gardens** and **Jet d'Eau**, then hit the **Old Town** for lunch and a stroll. Tummy full, take in a **museum**, followed by a dip in the water and an aperitif at **Bains des Pâquis**. On day two, plan a tour of **CERN** or **Palais des Nations**, followed by another stroll along the lake.

Switzerland Highlights

1 Hit the hip bars of **Zurich** (p591) and relax the next day with a stroll along the city's sublime lake.

2 Be wowed by the Eiger's monstrous north face on a ride to the 'top of Europe', 3471m **Jungfraujoch** (p591).

3 Get wet with a fountain dash beneath Geneva's **Jet d'Eau** (p563) or a soak in a white-chocolate bath.

SCHAFFHAUSEN

Schaffhausen

Lake Constance (Bodensee)

GERMANY

Stein am Rhein

A4

THURGAU

Frauenfeld

ARGAU

Baden

Limmat River

A1

Winterthur

A1

ZÜRICH

St Gallen

A1

Uetliberg

Zürich

Adliswil

Lake Zürich

Herisau

ST GALLEN

Appenzell

A13

AUSTRIA

ST GALLEN

Buchs

VADUZ

Liechtenstein

A2

A14

Lucerne

ZUG

Zug

SCHWYZ

Rigi

Schwyz

Glarus

Sargans

Mt Pilatus (2120m)

Stans

Lake Lucerne (Vierwaldstättersee)

GLARUS

Chur

Klosters

Sarnen

Altdorf

Flims-Laax

Davos

Scuol

A8

Engelberg

Mt Titlis (3239m)

Arosa

Guarda

Meiringen

Oberalp Pass

Rhine River

Zernez

URI

GRAUBÜNDEN

Zuoz

Swiss National Park

St Gotthard Pass

San Bernardino Pass

A13

St Moritz

TICINO

A2

Maloja

Bernina Pass

Locarno

Bellinzona

ITALY

Lugano

Lake Lugano

Lake Maggiore

④ Be surprised by Swiss capital **Bern** (p579): think medieval charm, folkloric fountains and a pulsating party scene.

⑤ Sleep in hay in the mysterious green hills and thick, dark forests of the clover-shaped **Jura canton** (p577).

⑥ Gape at the iconic Matterhorn and wander around the car-free alpine village of **Zermatt** (p577).

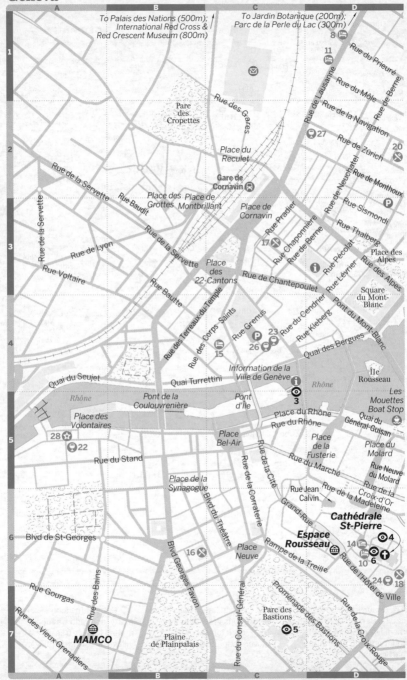

To Palais des Nations (500m);
International Red Cross &
Red Crescent Museum (800m)

To Jardin Botanique (200m);
Parc de la Perle du Lac (300m)

Parc des Cropettes

Rue des Gares

Place du Reculet

Gare de Cornavin

Place des Grottes

Place de Montbrillant

Place de Cornavin

Rue de la Servette

Rue Baudit

Rue de la Servette

Rue de Lyon

Rue Voltaire

Rue de la Servette

Rue Bautte

Place des 22-Cantons

Rue de Chantepoulet

Rue Pradier

Rue Chaponnière

Rue de Berne

Rue de la Navigation

Rue du Môle

Rue de Lausanne

Rue du Prieuré

Rue de Berne

Rue de Monthoux

Rue de Zürich

Rue de Neuchâtel

Rue Sismondi

Rue Thalberg

Place des Alpes

Rue des Alpes

Square du Mont-Blanc

Rue Pécolat

Rue Lévrier

Pont du Mont-Blanc

Rue des Terreaux-du-Temple

Rue des Corps Saints

Rue Grenus

Rue du Cendrier

Rue Kleberg

Quai des Bergues

Île Rousseau

Rhône

Les Mouettes Boat Stop

Quai du Général-Guisan

Quai du Seujet

Rhône

Quai Turrettini

Pont de la Coulouvrenière

Pont d'Île

Information de la Ville de Genève

Place du Rhône

Rue du Rhône

Place de la Fusterie

Place du Molard

Place des Volontaires

Place Bel-Air

Rue du Stand

Rue de la Cité

Rue de la Corraterie

Rue du Marché

Rue Neuve du Molard

Rue de la Croix-d'Or

Place de la Synagogue

Blvd du Théâtre

Rue Jean Calvin

Rue de la Madeleine

Grand-Rue

Cathédrale St-Pierre

Espace Rousseau

Blvd de St-Georges

Blvd Georges Favon

Place Neuve

Rampe de la Treille

Rue de l'Hôtel de Ville

Rue Gourgas

Rue des Bains

Rue du Conseil-Général

Promenade des Bastions

Rue de la Croix-Rouge

Rue des Vieux Grenadiers

MAMCO

Plaine de Plainpalais

Parc des Bastions

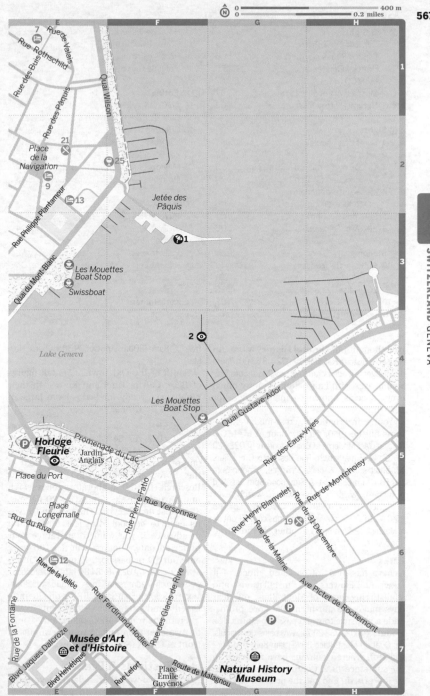

SWITZERLAND GENEVA

0   400 m
0   0.2 miles

Rue de Valais
7
Rue Rothschild
Rue des Buis
Rue des Pâquis
Quai Wilson

Place
de la
Navigation
21
25
9
13

Jetée des
Pâquis

Rue Philippe Plantamour

1

Quai du Mont-Blanc

Les Mouettes
Boat Stop
Swissboat

Lake Geneva

2

Les Mouettes
Boat Stop

Quai Gustave-Ador

Horloge
Fleurie
Promenade du Lac
Jardin
Anglais
Place du Port

Rue des Eaux-Vives

Place
Longemalle
Rue du Rive

Rue Pierre-Fatio
Rue Versonnex

Rue Henri Blanvalet
Rue de Montchoisy
Rue du 31 Décembre
19
Rue de la Mairie

12
Rue de la Vallée

Rue Ferdinand-Hodler
Rue des Glacis de Rive

Ave Pictet de Rochemont

Rue de la Fontaine

Musée d'Art
et d'Histoire

Blvd Jacques Dalcroze
Blvd Helvétique
Rue Lefort
Place
Émile
Guyénot
Route de Malagnou

Natural History
Museum

well thought-out **Natural History Museum** (Musée d'Histoire Naturelle; ☎022 418 63 00; Route de Malagnou 1; admission free; ⊙9.30am-5pm Tue-Sun) buzzes with kids ogling at pretty much every species known to man, stuffed for perpetuity.

Young, international, cross-media exhibitions fill the 1950s factory floor at **MAMCO** (Musée d'Art Moderne et Contemporain; ☎022 320 61 22; www.mamco.ch; Rue des Vieux-Grenadiers 10; adult/student & child Sfr8/free; ⊙noon-6pm Tue-Fri, 11am-6pm Sat & Sun, noon-9pm 1st Wed of month), while every Swatch watch ever designed ticks inside **La Cité du Temps** (☎022 818 39 00; www.citedutemps.com; 1 Pont de la Machine; ⊙9am-6pm), another old industrial space.

Parks   PARKS
Geneva has loads of parkland, much of it lakefront. Flowers, art installations and soul-stirring views of Mont Blanc on clear days make the northern lakeshore promenade a pleasure to walk: pass hip **Bains des Pâquis** (☎022 732 29 74; www.bains-des-paquis. ch; Quai du Mont-Blanc 30; ⊙9am-8pm mid-Apr–mid-Sep), where Genevans have frolicked in the sun since 1872. Continue north to **Parc de la Perle du Lac** and the peacock-studded lawns of the **Jardin Botanique** (admission

free; ⊙8am-7.30pm Apr-Oct, 9.30am-5pm Nov-Mar).

South of the Old Town, 4.5m-tall figures of Bèze, Calvin, Farel and Knox – in their nightgowns ready for bed – loom large in **Parc des Bastions**.

FREE **CERN**   LABORATORY
(☎022 767 84 84; www.cern.ch; ⊙tours 10.30am Mon-Sat) The World Wide Web was one of the many creations to come out of the European Organisation for Nuclear Research (CERN), a laboratory for research into particle physics funded by 20 nations, 8km west near Meyrin. The free guided visits need to be booked at least one month in advance if you want to guarantee your preferred date, and you will need to present your ID or passport. Equally riveting is **Microcosm** (☎022 767 84 84; http://microcosm. web.cern.ch; admission free; ⊙8.15am-5.30pm Mon-Fri, 8.30am-5pm Sat), CERN's on-site multimedia and interactive visitors centre.

From the train station, take tram 14 or 16 to Avanchet then bus 56 to its terminus in front of CERN (Sfr3, 40 minutes).

🎇 Festivals & Events
August's two-week **Fêtes de Genève** (www. fetes-de-geneve.ch) ushers in parades, open-

air concerts, lakeside merry-go-rounds and fireworks. On 11 December, the **Escalade** celebrates the foiling of an invasion by the Duke of Savoy in 1602 with a costumed parade, the smashing and eating of chocolate cauldrons, and a day of running races around the Old Town.

🛏 Sleeping

When checking-in, ask for your free public transport ticket covering unlimited bus travel for the duration of your hotel stay.

Hôtel de la Cloche   HOTEL $
(☎022 732 94 81; www.geneva-hotel.ch/cloche; Rue de la Cloche 6; s/d from Sfr95/110, without bathroom from Sfr65/98; ☻☎) Elegant fireplaces, bourgeois furnishings, wooden floors and the odd chandelier add a touch of grandeur to this old-fashioned one-star hotel.

Hôme St-Pierre   HOSTEL $
(☎022 310 37 07; www.homestpierre.ch; Cour St-Pierre 4; dm Sfr31, s/d without bathroom Sfr48/72; ☺reception 9am-noon & 4-8pm Mon-Sat, 9am-noon Sat; ☻@) This boarding house was founded by the German Lutheran Church in 1874. Women are its primary clientele – just six dorm beds are up for grabs for six lucky guys – and the rooftop terrace that crowns the place is magical.

Hotel St-Gervais   HOTEL $$
(☎022 732 45 72; www.stgervais-geneva.ch; Rue des Corps-Saints 20; d from Sfr140, s/d without bathroom from Sfr105/119; ☺reception 7am-11pm) Travellers with jumbo-sized suitcases beware: scaling the seven floors in the pocket-handkerchief lift of this quaint choice near the train station is a squash and a squeeze. Renovated rooms are on the 1st and 7th floors.

Hôtel Bel'Esperance   HOTEL $$
(☎022 818 37 37; www.hotel-bel-esperance.ch; Rue de la Vallée 1; s/d from Sfr105/154; ☺reception 7am-10pm; ☻@☎) This two-star hotel is a two-second flit to the Old Town. Rooms are quiet and cared for, and those on the 1st floor share a kitchen. Ride the lift to the 5th floor to flop on a chair on a flower-filled rooftop terrace. Free wi-fi.

La Cour des Augustins   HOTEL $$$
(☎022 322 21 00; www.lacourdesaugustins.com; s/d from Sfr175/250; Rue Jean-Violette 15; P@☎) South of the centre and disguised by a 19th-century facade, the crisp white interior of this 'boutique gallery hotel' sports the latest technology and screams cutting edge.

Edelweiss   HOTEL $$$
(☎022 544 51 51; www.manotel.com; Place de la Navigation 2; d from Sfr290; ☎) Plunge yourself into the heart of the Swiss Alps *en ville* at this Heidi-style hideout, with its big cuddly St Bernard, fireplace and chalet-styled restaurant.

Hôtel Auteuil   HOTEL $$$
(☎022 544 22 22; www.manotel.com; Rue de Lausanne 33; d from Sfr350; P☻✳@☎) The star of this design-driven hotel near the station is its collection of B&W photos of 1950s film stars in Geneva. Grab *The Book* from reception to find out precisely who's who where. Free wi-fi.

Hôtel Les Armures   HOTEL $$$
(☎022 310 91 72; www.hotel-les-armures.ch; Rue du Puits-St-Pierre 1; s/d from Sfr450/720; P☻✳@☎) This slumbering 17th-century beauty oozes history from every last ceiling beam. Beautifully placed in the heart of Geneva's Old Town, it has an intimate and refined atmosphere.

FREE THRILLS

Bags of fabulous things to see and do in Geneva don't cost a cent. Our favourite freebies:

» Dashing like mad under the iconic **Jet d'Eau**

» Getting lost in the **Old Town**

» Commiserating over the dark side of humanity at the **International Red Cross & Red Crescent Museum**

» Admiring every species of tiger known to man in the **Natural History Museum**

» Hobnobbing with big-bang scientists at **CERN**

» Going green in the **Jardin Botanique**

» Flopping on the beach on the **Bains de Pâquis** jetty

» **Pedalling** along the lake into France or towards Lausanne

WANT MORE?

Head to **Lonely Planet** (www.lonely planet.com/switzerland/geneva) for planning advice, author recommendations, traveller reviews and insider tips.

City Hostel HOSTEL $
(☑022 901 15 00; www.cityhostel.ch; Rue de Ferrier 2; dm from Sfr32, s/d from Sfr61; ⊙reception 7.30am-noon & 1pm-midnight; P⊙@) Spanking clean is the trademark of this well-organised hostel, where two-bed dorms give travellers a chance to double up cheaply. Rates include sheets, towels and use of the kitchen, TV room and a free locker.

Auberge de Jeunesse HOSTEL $
(☑022 732 62 60; www.yh-geneva.ch; Rue Rothschild 28-30; dm Sfr29, d from Sfr85; ⊙6.30-10am & 2pm-1am Jun-Sep, 6.30-10am & 4pm-midnight Oct-May; @) Dorms max out at 12 beds.

✕ Eating

Geneva flaunts ethnic food galore. For the culinary curious with no fortune to blow, the Pâquis area cooks up cuisine from most corners of the globe in cheapish eateries. In the Old Town, terrace cafes and restaurants crowd Geneva's oldest square, medieval Place du Bourg-de-Four. Near the station, Scandale is a hot lunchtime spot. For quintessential Swiss fondue (Sfr32) and yodelling, **Edelweiss** (☑022 544 51 51; www.manotel.com; Place de la Navigation 2) is *the* address.

Chez Ma Cousine INTERNATIONAL $
(☑022 310 96 96; www.chezmacousine.ch; Place du Bourg-de-Four 6; mains Sfr14-17; ⊙lunch & dinner) *'On y mange du poulet'* (we eat chicken) is the strap line of this student institution that appeals for one good reason – generously handsome, homely portions of chicken, potatoes and salad at an unbeatable price.

Omnibus INTERNATIONAL $$
(☑022 321 44 45; www.omnibus-cafe.ch; Rue de la Coulouvrenière 23; mains Sfr19-45; ⊙lunch & dinner Mon-Fri, dinner Sat & Sun) Don't be fooled by the graffiti-plastered facade of this Rhôneside space. Inside, a maze of retro rooms seduces on first sight. Its business card is a recycled bus ticket.

L'Adresse INTERNATIONAL $$
(☑022 736 32 32; www.ladresse.ch; Rue du 31 Decembre 32; mains Sfr24-37; ⊙lunch & dinner Tue-Sat) An urban loft with rooftop terrace and hybrid lifestyle boutique–contemporary bistro, this hip address is at home in converted artist workshops. *The* address for lunch, brunch or (in their words) Saturday slunch…

Au Grütli INTERNATIONAL $$
(☑022 328 98 68; www.cafedu grutli.ch; Rue du Général Dufour 16; mains Sfr28-36; ⊙breakfast, lunch & dinner Mon-Fri, dinner Sat & Sun) Indonesian lamb, moussaka, scallops with ginger and citrus fruits or Provençal chicken are among the international flavours at this razor-sharp theatre restaurant.

Café de Paris FRENCH $$
(rue du Mont Blanc 26; mains Sfr40; ⊙lunch & dinner) A memorable dining experience since 1930. Everyone goes for the same thing here: green salad, beef steak with a killer-calorie herb and butter sauce, and as many fries as you can handle.

Les 5 Portes FRENCH $
(☑022 731 84 38; Rue de Zürich 5; mains Sfr16-22; ⊙breakfast, lunch & dinner Mon-Fri, lunch & dinner Sat & Sun) The Five Doors is a fashionable Pâquis port of call that embraces every mood and moment.

Mikado JAPANESE $
(☑022 732 47 74; Rue de l'Ancien Port 9; sushi Sfr2.50, mains Sfr6.50; ⊙lunch & dinner Tue-Sat) If it's authenticity, speed and tasty fast food on a red lacquered tray you want, this Japanese delicatessen hits the spot.

☍ Drinking & Entertainment

Pâquis, the district in between the train station and lake, is particularly well endowed with bars. In summer the **paillote** (Quai du Mont-Blanc 30; ⊙to midnight), with wooden tables inches from the water, gets crammed.

Scandale BAR
(☑022 731 83 73; www.scandale.ch; Rue de Lausanne 24; ⊙11am-2am Tue-Fri, 5pm-2am Sat) Retro 1950s furnishings in a cavernous interior with comfy sofas ensures this lounge bar is never empty. Happenings include art exhibitions, Saturday-night DJs and bands.

Buvette des Bains BAR
(☑022 738 16 16; www.bains-des-paquis.ch; Quai du Mont-Blanc 30; ⊙8am-10pm) Meet Genevans at this earthy beach bar at Bains des Pâquis. Dining is on trays and in summer alfresco.

La Bretelle BAR
(☑022 732 75 96; Rue des Étuves 17; ⊙6pm-2am) Little has changed since the 1970s, when

this legendary bar opened. Live accordion accompanies French chansons most nights.

La Clémence
BAR

(☏022 312 24 98; www.laclemence.ch; Place du Bourg-de-Four 20; ☺7am-1am Mon-Thu & Sun, to 2am Fri & Sat) Indulge in a glass of local wine or an artisanal beer at this venerable cafe-bar located on Geneva's loveliest square.

La Plage
BAR

(☏022 342 20 98; Rue Vautier 19; ☺11am-1am Mon-Thu, 10am-2am Fri & Sat, 5pm-1am Sun) With bare wood tables, checked lino floor, green wooden shutters and tables outside, the Beach in Carouge is a timeless drinking hole.

L'Usine
CLUB

(☏022 781 34 90; www.usine.ch; Place des Volontaires 4) This grungy and youthful converted gold-roughing factory entertains with dance nights, art happenings, theatre, cabaret and club nights.

Piment Vert
BAR

(☏022 731 93 03; www.pimentvert.ch; Place De-Grenus 4; ☺11.30am-2.45pm & 5.30-10pm Mon-Fri, noon-4pm Sat) Fast, fresh, and trendy sums up this hybrid Indian-Sri Lankan bar.

Le Chat Noir
LIVE MUSIC

(☏022 343 49 98; www.chatnoir.ch, in French; Rue Vautier 13; ☺Tue-Sat) Nightly jazz, rock, funk and salsa gigs.

Le Déclic
CLUB

(☏022 320 59 40; www.ledeclic.ch; Blvd du Pont d'Arve 28; ☺5pm-2am Mon-Fri, 9pm-2am Sat) Gay nightclub.

Ciné Lac
CINEMA

(www.cinelac.ch, in French; adult/under 14yr Sfr17/14; ☺Jul & Aug) Glorious summertime open-air cinema with a screen set up on the lakeside.

❶ Information

Cantonal Hospital (☏022 372 33 11; emergency 022 372 81 20; www.hug-ge.ch; Rue Micheli du Crest 24)

Police station (☏117; Rue de Berne 6)

Post office (Rue du Mont-Blanc 18; ☺7.30am-6pm Mon-Fri, 9am-4pm Sat)

SOS Médecins à Domicile (☏022 748 49 50; www.sos-medecins.ch, in French) Home/hotel doctor calls.

Tourist office (☏022 909 70 00; www.geneve-tourisme.ch; Rue du Mont-Blanc 18; ☺10am-6pm Mon, 9am-6pm Tue-Sat)

❶ Getting There & Away

AIR Aéroport International de Genève (GVA; ☏0900 57 15 00; www.gva.ch), 4km from town, has connections to major European cities and many others worldwide. It is also an easyJet hub.

BOAT CGN (Compagnie Générale de Navigation; ☏0848 811 848; www.cgn.ch) operates a steamer service from its Jardin Anglais jetty to other villages on Lake Geneva. Many only sail May to September, including those to/from Lausanne (Sfr37.60, 3½ hours). Eurail and Swiss Pass holders are valid on CGN boats or there is a one-day CGN boat pass (Sfr49).

BUS International buses depart from the **bus station** (☏0900 320 320, 022 732 02 30; www.coach-station.com; Place Dorcière).

TRAIN Trains run to most Swiss towns including at least hourly to/from Lausanne (Sfr20.60, 40 minutes), Bern (Sfr46, 1¾ hours) and Zürich (Sfr80, 2¾ hours).

International daily rail connections from Geneva include Paris (TGV from Sfr130, 3½ hours),

---

WORTH A TRIP

ZEN OUT IN GRYON & LEYSIN

Trek off the beaten track to lap up Swiss alpine charm in untouched **Gryon** (1130m), with great meadow hiking trails and **Chalet Martin** (☏024 498 33 21; Chalet Martin; www.gryon.com; dm/d from Sfr25/70; ℗@), a Swiss-Australian-run hostel that travellers give rave reviews. The vibe is strictly laid-back and the place organises dozens of activities – paragliding, skiing and chocolate tasting included. Take a train from Lausanne to Bex (Sfr17.40, 40 minutes, hourly), then the cogwheel train to Gryon (Sfr6.20, 30 minutes, hourly). The hostel is a five-minute signposted walk from the train stop.

Equally Zen is **Leysin**, a hub for skiers, boarders and hikers who can't sing the praises highly enough of **Hiking Sheep** (☏024 494 35 35; www.hikingsheep.com; dm/d Sfr30/80; ℗✿@). The tall, art deco house has a kitchen, great communal facilities, a pine-forested backyard and breathtaking views from its balconies. Find it a two-minute walk from Leysin-Grand Hôtel train station. Ride the cogwheel train from Aigle (Sfr10.80, 30 minutes, hourly), in turn linked by train with Lausanne (Sfr14.80, 30 minutes, hourly).

Hamburg (from Sfr278, 9½ hours), Milan (from Sfr97, 4½ hours) and Barcelona (from Sfr125, 10 hours).

ℹ️ Getting Around

TO/FROM THE AIRPORT Getting from the airport is easy with regular trains into Gare de Cornavin (Sfr3, eight minutes). Slower bus 10 (Sfr3) does the same 5km trip. A metered taxi costs Sfr30 to Sfr50.

Bicycle Pick up a bike at Genève Roule (%022 740 13 43; www.geneveroule.ch; Place de Mont-brillant 17; h8am-6pm Mon-Sat) or its seasonal Jetée des Pâquis pick-up point for Sfr12/20 per day/weekend. May to October, borrow a bike (with advertisements on it) for free.

PUBLIC TRANSPORT Buses, trams, trains and boats service the city, and ticket dispensers are found at all stops. Tickets cost Sfr2 (within one zone, 30 minutes) or Sfr3 (two zones, one hour), and a city/canton day pass is Sfr7/12. The same tickets are also valid on the yellow shuttle boats known as Les Mouettes (the seagulls) that criss-cross the lake every 10 minutes between 7.30am and 6pm.

LAKE GENEVA REGION

East of Geneva, Western Europe's biggest lake stretches like a giant liquid mirror be-tween French-speaking Switzerland on its northern shore and France to the south. Known as Lake Geneva by many and Lac Léman to Francophones, the Swiss side of the lake cossets the elegant city of Lausanne, the pretty palm tree–studded Riviera resort of Montreux, and the marvellous emerald spectacle of vines marching up steep hill-sides in strict unison.

Lausanne

POP 125,900

In a fabulous location overlooking Lake Geneva, Lausanne is an enchanting beauty with several distinct personalities: the for-mer fishing village of Ouchy, with its sum-mer beach-resort feel; Place St-François, with stylish, cobblestone shopping streets; and Flon, a warehouse district of bars, gal-leries and boutiques. It's also got a few amazing sights. One of the country's grand-est Gothic cathedrals dominates its medi-eval centre.

The **tourist office** (☑021 613 73 21; www.lausanne-tourisme.ch; Place de la Navigation 4; ☺9am-6pm Oct-Mar, to 8pm Apr-Sep) neighbours Ouchy metro station and has a **branch** **office** (Place de la Gare 9; ☺9am-7pm) at the train station.

👁 Sights & Activities

Musée de l'Art Brut MUSEUM
(☑021 315 25 70; www.artbrut.ch; Ave des Bergières 11-13; adult/student/child Sfr10/5/free, 1st Sat of month free; ☺11am-6pm Tue-Sun Sep-Jun, daily Jul & Aug) This alluring museum showcases a fascinating amalgam of 15,000 works of art created by untrained artists – psychi-atric patients, eccentrics and incarcerated criminals. The works offer a striking variety, at times a surprising technical capacity and in some cases an inspirational world view. Biographies and explanations are in Eng-lish. The museum is about 600m northwest of Place St François; take bus 2 or 3 to the Beaulieu stop.

Musée Olympique MUSEUM
(☑021 621 65 11; www.museum.olympic.org; Quai d'Ouchy 1; adult/student/child Sfr15/10/free; ☺9am-6pm Apr-Oct, 9am-6pm Tue-Sun Nov-Mar) Lausanne is home to the International Olympic Committee, and sports aficionados can immerse themselves in archival footage, interactive computers and memorabilia at the information-packed Musée Olympique.

Cathédrale de Notre Dame CHURCH
(☺7am-7pm Mon-Fri, 8am-7pm Sat & Sun Apr-Aug, 7am-5.30pm Sep-Mar) This glorious Gothic ca-thedral is arguably the finest in Switzerland. Built in the 12th and 13th centuries, high-lights include the stunningly detailed carved portal, vaulted ceilings and archways, and carefully restored stained-glass windows.

🛏 Sleeping

Hotel guests get a Lausanne Transport Card covering unlimited use of public transport for the duration of their stay.

Lausanne Guest House GUEST HOUSE $
(☑021 601 80 00; www.lausanne-guesthouse.ch; Chemin des Épinettes 4; dm Sfr36, s/d Sfr96/125, without bathroom Sfr86/105; P☻@☎) An at-tractive mansion converted into quality backpacking accommodation near the train station. Many rooms have lake views and some of the building's energy is solar.

Hôtel du Port HOTEL $$$
(☑021 612 04 44; www.hotel-du-port.ch; Place du Port 5; s/d from Sfr165/195; ☻☎) A perfect location in Ouchy, just back from the lake, makes this a good choice. The best doubles peep at the lake and suites slumber on the 3rd floor.

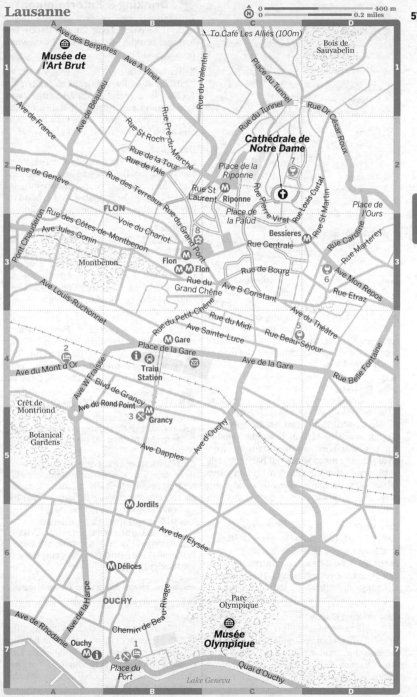

0   400 m
0   0.2 miles

To Café Les Alliés (100m)

Bois de Sauvabelin

Musée de l'Art Brut

Ave des Bergières

Ave A Vinet

Rue du Valentin

Place du Tunnel

Rue du Tunnel

Rue Dr César Roux

Ave de France

Ave de Beaulieu

Rue St Roch

Rue Pré-du-Marché

Cathédrale de Notre Dame

Rue de Genève

Rue de la Tour

Rue de l'Ale

Rue des Terreaux

Rue du Grand Pont

Place de la Riponne

Rue St Laurent

Riponne

Place de la Palud

Rue Pierre Viret

Rue Louis Curtat

Rue St Martin

Place de l'Ours

FLON

Voie du Chariot

Flon

Rue des Côtes-de-Montbenon

Ave Jules Gonin

Pont Chauderon

Montbenon

Flon

Rue Centrale

Bessières

Rue Caroline

Rue Marterey

Rue du Grand Chêne

Ave B Constant

Rue de Bourg

Ave Mon Repos

Rue Etraz

Ave Louis-Ruchonnet

Rue du Petit-Chêne

Rue du Midi

Rue Sainte-Luce

Ave du Théâtre

Rue Beau-Séjour

Rue Belle Fontaine

Gare

Place de la Gare

Ave de la Gare

Ave du Mont d'Or

Train Station

Ave W Fraisse

Blvd de Grancy

Ave du Rond Point

Crêt de Montriond

Botanical Gardens

Grancy

Ave Dapples

Ave d'Ouchy

Jordils

Ave de l'Elysée

Délices

Ave de la Harpe

OUCHY

Parc Olympique

Ave de Rhodanie

Chemin de Beau-Rivage

Musée Olympique

Ouchy

Place du Port

Quai d'Ouchy

Lake Geneva

Lausanne

Camping de Vidy   CAMPING GROUND **$**
(☏021 622 50 00; www.camping lausannevidy.ch; Chemin du Camping 3; campsites per adult Sfr8.50, per tent from Sfr12) This camping ground is on the lake just to the west of the Vidy sports complex. Sites are well maintained and it's popular with families in summer. Get off bus 2 at Bois de Vaux.

🍴 Eating

Café Les Alliés   FRENCH **$$**
(☏021 648 69 40; www.lesallies.ch; Rue de la Pontaise 48; mains Sfr19-40; ◷lunch & dinner Mon-Fri) It's not much to look at from the outside but inside a cosy, warm restaurant with creaky timber floors winds out back towards a pleasant summer garden. Imaginative salads precede mains like *steak de veau poêlé au jus d'abricots* (pan-cooked steak in apricot sauce).

Café de Grancy   INTERNATIONAL **$$**
(☏021 616 86 66; www.cafédegrancy.ch; Ave du Rond Point 1; mains Sfr18-36; ◷breakfast, lunch & dinner; 🛜) An old-time bar resurrected with flair by young entrepreneurs, this spot is a hip hang-out with comfy lounges, weekend brunch and a tempting restaurant out back.

Café du Vieil Ouchy   SWISS **$$**
(☏021 616 21 94; Place du Port 3, Ouchy; mains Sfr18-39; ◷Thu-Mon) A simple but charming location for fondue (Sfr24.50), rösti and other classics. Follow up with a meringue smothered in thick double Gruyère cream.

🍷 Drinking & Entertainment

Lausanne is one of Switzerland's busier night-time cities. Look for the handy free listings booklet *What's Up* (www.whats upmag.ch) in bars.

XIIIeme Siècle   PUB
(☏021 312 40 64; Rue Cité-Devant 10; ◷10pm-4am Tue-Sat) In a grand medieval setting with stone vaults and huge timber beams, this cosy stalwart is a great place for a beer or six and has a laid-back, convivial atmosphere.

Bar Tabac   BAR
(☏021 312 33 16; Rue Beau Séjour 7; ◷7am-9pm Mon-Wed, to 1am Thu & Fri, 9am-2am Sat, 9am-3pm Sun) Squeaky timber floors lend warmth and punters engage in animated chat around the bar at this spruced corner tavern of old.

Le Bleu Lézard   BAR
(☏021 321 38 30; www.bleu-lezard.ch; Rue Enning 10; ◷7am-1am Mon-Thu, to 2am Fri, 8am-2am Sat, 9.30am-1am Sun; 🛜) An oldie but a goodie, this corner bar-eatery cooks up Sunday brunch and has a chatty atmosphere and a club-styled dance floor in the cellar.

D-Club   CLUB
(☏021 351 51 40; www.dclub.ch; Place de Centrale; admission Sfr10-25; ◷11pm-5am Wed-Sat) DJs spin funk to house at this heaving club. Take the stairs down from Rue du Grand Pont, turn right and descend to Place de Centrale.

ℹ Getting There & Around

BOAT The **CGN** (Compagnie Générale de Navigation; www.cgn.ch) steamer service runs May to September to/from Geneva (Sfr37.60, 3½ hours).

BUS Buses service most destinations (up to three stops Sfr1.90, one hour unlimited travel in central Lausanne Sfr3). The m2 metro line connects Ouchy with the train station and costs the same as the buses.

TRAIN There are trains to/from Geneva (Sfr20.60, 33 to 51 minutes, up to six hourly), Geneva airport (Sfr25, 42 to 58 minutes, up to four hourly) and Bern (Sfr31, 70 minutes, one or two hourly).

Montreux

POP 24,600

In 1971 Frank Zappa was doing his thing in the Montreux casino when the building caught fire, casting a pall of smoke over Lake Geneva and inspiring the members of Deep Purple to pen their classic rock number 'Smoke on the Water'.

The showpiece of the Swiss Riviera has been an inspiration to writers, artists and musicians for centuries. Famous one-time residents include Lord Byron, Ernest Hemingway and the Shelleys. It's easy to see why: Montreux boasts stunning Alp views, tidy rows of pastel buildings and Switzerland's most extraordinary castle.

Each year crowds throng to the **Montreux Jazz Festival** (www.montreuxjazz.com) for a fortnight in early July. Free concerts take place every day, but big-name gigs cost (Sfr40 to Sfr100).

⊙ Sights

Château de Chillon   CASTLE
(☎021 966 89 10; www.chillon.ch; Ave de Chillon 21; adult/student/child Sfr12/10/6; ⊙9am-7pm Apr-Sep, 9.30am-6pm Mar & Oct, 10am-4pm Nov-Feb, last entry 1hr before close) Originally constructed on the shores of Lake Geneva in the 11th century, Château de Chillon was brought to the world's attention by Lord Byron and the world has been filing past ever since. Spend at least a couple of hours exploring its numerous courtyards, towers, dungeons and halls filled with arms, period furniture and artwork.

The castle is a 45-minute lakefront walk from Montreux. Otherwise trolley bus 1 (Sfr2.30) passes every 10 minutes.

🛏 Sleeping & Eating

Hôtel Masson   HOTEL **$$**
(☎021 966 00 44; www.hotelmasson.ch; Rue Bonivard 5; d from Sfr120; **P**🐾) In 1829, this vintner's mansion was converted into a hotel. Its old charm has remained intact and the hotel, set in magnificent grounds, is on the Swiss Heritage list of most beautiful hotels in the country. Find it in the hills southeast of Montreux.

Auberge de Jeunesse   HOSTEL **$**
(☎021 963 49 34; Passage de l'Auberge 8, Territet; dm from Sfr33; ⊙mid-Feb–mid-Nov; @) This chirpy hostel is a 30-minute walk along the lake clockwise from the tourist office (or take the local train to Territet or bus 1).

Hôtel La Rouvenaz   HOTEL **$$**
(☎021 963 27 36; Rue du Marché 1; s/d from Sfr130/190; @🐾) A simple, family-run spot with 12 rooms and its own Italian restaurant, you cannot get any closer to the lake or the heart of the action.

Montagnard   SWISS **$$**
(☎021 964 83 49; www.montagnard.ch; mains Sfr22-28; ⊙Wed-Sun) For a taste of country fare in a timber farmhouse with gardens, head to this restaurant in the village of Villard-sur-Chamby, a 9.5km taxi ride from central Montreux.

FAIRYLAND ABSINTHE

It was in the deepest darkest depths of the Val de Travers – dubbed the Pays des Fées (Fairyland) – that the magical green drink absinthe was first distilled in 1740; it was first produced commercially in 1797 (although it was a Frenchman called Pernod who made the first known bitter green liqueur just a few kilometres across the French–Swiss border in Pontarlier).

From 1910, following Switzerland's prohibition of the wickedly alcoholic and ruthlessly bitter aniseed drink, distillers of the so-called 'devil in the bottle' in the Val de Travers moved underground. In 1990 the great-grandson of a preprohibition distiller in Môtiers came up with Switzerland's first legal aniseed liqueur since 1910 – albeit one which was only 45% proof alcohol (instead of 50% to 75%) and which scarcely contained thujone (the offensive chemical found in wormwood, said to be the root of absinthe's devilish nature). An *extrait d'absinthe* (absinthe extract) quickly followed and in 2005, following Switzerland's lifting of its absinthe ban, the **Blackmint – Distillerie Kübler & Wyss** (☎032 861 14 69; www.blackmint.ch; Rue du Château 7) in Môtiers distilled its first true and authentic batch of the mythical *fée verte* (green fairy) from valley-grown wormwood. Mix one part crystal-clear liqueur with five parts water to make it green (and wait for light and floaty feelings to hit, as was the case after the first glass we shared with friends back home!).

Swilling the green fairy, aka absinthe, at the bar aboard an old steam train as it puffs the length of the Val de Travers is particularly evocative. Jump aboard in Neuchâtel with **Vapeur Val de Travers** (☎032 863 24 07; www.rvt-historique-ch; Rue de la Gare 19, Travers; day trips with lunch Sfr75).

Café du Grütli SWISS $$
(☎021 963 42 65; Rue du Grand Chêne 8; mains Sfr18-30; ☺Wed-Mon) This cheerful little eatery is hidden in the old part of town and provides good home cooking. Think rösti with ham, hearty meat dishes, salads and the inevitable fondue.

ⓘ Getting There & Away

There are trains to Geneva (Sfr28, 70 minutes, hourly) and Lausanne (Sfr10.20, 25 minutes, three hourly). Make the scenic journey to Interlaken via the GoldenPass Panoramic, with changes at Zweisimmen and Spiez (Sfr80, three hours, daily; rail passes valid).

Gruyères

With its riot of 15th- to 17th-century houses, cobbled heart, and menus of cheese and featherweight meringues drowned in thick cream, Gruyères is so dreamy even Sleeping Beauty wouldn't wake up.

⊙ Sights & Activities

Maison du Gruyère CHEESERY
(☎026 921 84 00; www.lamaisondugruyere.ch; adult/under 12yr Sfr7/3; ☺9am-7pm Apr-Sep, to 6pm Oct-Mar) The beans about Gruyères' hard name-protected cheese, made for centuries in its surrounding alpine pastures, are spilled

here in Pringy, 1.5km away. The cheese-making takes place several times daily and can be watched through glass windows.

FREE **Fromagerie d'Alpage de Moléson**
CHEESERY
(☎026 921 10 44; ☺9.30am-10pm mid-May–mid-Oct) At this 17th-century mountain chalet, 5km southwest of Gruyères in Moléson-sur-Gruyères (elevation 1100m), cheese is made a couple of times a day in summer using old-fashioned methods.

Musée HR Giger MUSEUM
(☎026 921 22 00; adult/child Sfr10/5; ☺10am-6pm Apr-Oct, to 5pm Tue-Sun Nov-Mar) Fans of the *Alien* movies will relish this shrine to HR Giger's expansive imagination in a 16th-century mansion. Finish with a drink in the Giger-style bar opposite.

Sentier des Fromageries WALK
For more cheese-making, hike through green Gruyères pastures to a couple of tiny mountain huts where shepherds make cheese in summer along the Sentier des Fromageries (7km to 8km, two hours). The **tourist office** (☎026 921 10 30; www.gruyeres.ch, in French; Rue du Bourg 1; ☺10.30am-noon & 1.30-4.30pm Mon-Fri, plus 9am-5pm Sat & Sun Jul–mid-Sep) has details.

Château CASTLE
(☎026 921 21 02; www.chateau-gruyeres.ch; adult/child Sfr9.50/3; ☺9am-6pm Apr-Oct, 10am-

---

WORTH A TRIP

NEUCHÂTEL

Its Old Town sandstone elegance, the airy Gallic nonchalance of its cafe life and the gay lakeside air that breezes along the shoreline of its glittering lake make Neuchâtel disarmingly charming. The small university town, complete with its own spirited *comune libre* (free commune), is compact enough to discover on foot, while the French spoken here is said to be Switzerland's purest. Not just that: Neuchâtel's town observatory gives the official time-check for all of Switzerland.

The pedestrian zone and Place Pury (the local bus hub) are about 1km from the train station; walk down the hill along Ave de la Gare. The lakeside **tourist office** (☎032 889 68 90; www.neuchateltourism.ch; Hôtel des Postes, Place du Port; ☺9am-noon & 1.30-5.30pm Mon-Fri, to noon Sat Sep-Jun, 9am-6.30pm Mon-Fri, 9am-4pm Sat, 10am-2pm Sun Jul & Aug) is next to the post office.

The 15th-century **Chateau de Neuchâtel** (☎032 889 60 00; guided tours free; ☺10am-noon & 2-4pm Mon-Sat, 2-4pm Sun Apr-Sep) and the adjoining **Collegiate Church** are the centrepieces of the Old Town. The striking cenotaph of 15 statues dates from 1372. Scale the nearby **prison tower** (☎032 717 71 02; Rue Jehanne de Hochberg 5; admission Sfr1; ☺8am-6pm Apr-Sep) for broad views of town and lake.

Visit the **Musée d'Art et d'Histoire** (☎032 717 79 25; www.mahn.ch, in French; Esplanade Léopold Robert 1; adult/under 16yr Sfr8/free, Wed free; ☺11am-6pm Tue-Sun) to see beloved 18th-century clockwork figures.

Trains serve Geneva (Sfr38, 70 minutes, hourly), Bern (Sfr18.20, 35 minutes, hourly) and other destinations.

THE JURA

The grandest towns in this clover-shaped canton are little more than enchanting villages. Deep, mysterious forests and impossible green clearings succeed one another across the low mountains of the Jura and some 1200km of marked paths across the canton give hikers plenty of scope. This is the place to escape.

Its capital is **Delémont**, though there is little reason to linger. Head instead 12km northwest to stroll around contemporary art and installations at the open-air sculpture park **La Balade de Séprais** (www.balade-seprais.ch). Or feast on thin crisp *tartes flambées* and apple cake to die for at **Hôtel-Restaurant de la Demi Lune** (📞032 461 35 31; Place Roger Schaffter; s/d from Sfr95/100) in **St Ursanne**, a drop-dead-gorgeous medieval village with a 12th-century Gothic church, 16th-century town gate, clusters of ancient houses and a lovely stone bridge crossing the Doubs River.

The **tourist office** (📞032 420 47 73; Place Roger Schaffter; ⊙10am-noon & 2-5pm Mon-Fri, 10am-4pm Sat & Sun) offers up heaps of information on river kayaking, canoeing and walking.

From Delémont there are trains heading to St Ursanne (Sfr6.80, 20 minutes, hourly), from where you can continue to Porrentuy (Sfr4.80, 12 minutes).

4.30pm Nov-Feb) The ab fab turreted castle is Gruyères' crowning glory.

✕ Eating

Chalet de Gruyères SWISS $$
(📞026 921 21 54; www.chalet-gruyeres.ch, in French; Rue du Château 53; fondues & raclettes Sfr30; ⊙lunch & dinner) Dip into a *moitié-moitié* (mix of Gruyère and soft local vacherin) at this cosy, cowbell-strewn restaurant where fondue is the star of every menu, irrespective of season (locals only eat fondue in winter).

❶ Getting There & Away

Gruyères can be reached by hourly bus or train (Sfr17.20, 40 minutes to one hour) from Fribourg to Bulle, then another hourly bus or train (Sfr3.50, 15 to 20 minutes). The village is a 10-minute walk uphill from the train station.

VALAIS

Matterhorn country: an intoxicating land that seduces the toughest of critics with its endless panoramic vistas and breathtaking views. This is an earthy part of southern Switzerland where farmers were so poor a century ago they didn't have two francs to rub together, yet today it's a jet-set land where celebrities sip Sfr10,000 champagne cocktails from ice-carved goblets.

An area of extraordinary natural beauty, the outdoors here is so great it never goes out of fashion. Switzerland's 10 highest mountains – all over 4000m – rise to the sky here, while snow fiends ski and board in one of Europe's top resorts, Zermatt. When snows melt and valleys turn lush green, hiking opportunities are boundless.

Zermatt

POP 5800

Since the mid-19th century, Zermatt has starred among Switzerland's glitziest resorts. Today it attracts intrepid mountaineers and hikers, skiers who cruise at snail's pace, spellbound by the scenery, and style-conscious darlings flashing designer togs in the lounge bars. But all are smitten with the Matterhorn (4478m), the Alps' most famous peak and an unfathomable monolith synonymous with Switzerland that you simply can't quite stop looking at.

◉ Sights & Activities

Gornergrat MOUNTAIN
Alpine views of Gornergrat (3090m) from the cable cars and gondolas are uniformly breathtaking, especially from the **cogwheel train** (one way Sfr38), which takes 35 to 45 minutes with two to three departures per hour. Sit on the right-hand side to gawp at the Matterhorn. Alternatively, hike from Zermatt to Gornergrat in five hours.

Cemetery CEMETERY
A walk in Zermatt's cemetery is a sobering experience for any would-be mountaineer, as numerous monuments tell of untimely deaths on Monte Rosa and the Matterhorn.

Matterhorn Museum
MUSEUM

(☑027 967 41 00; www.matterhornmuseum. ch; Kirchplatz; adult/student/10-16yr/under 10yr Sfr10/8/5/free; ⊙11am-6pm mid-Dec–Sep, 2-6pm Oct, closed Nov–mid-Dec) On 13 July 1865 Edward Whymper led the first successful ascent of the mountain. The climb took 32 hours but the descent was marred by tragedy when four team members crashed to their deaths in a 1200m fall down the North Wall. Visit the museum to see the infamous rope that broke.

Alpin Center
SKI SCHOOL

(☑027 966 24 60; www.alpincenter-zermatt.ch; Bahnhofstrasse 58; ⊙8.30am-noon & 3-7pm mid-Nov–Apr & Jul-Sep) Climbs led by mountain guides can be arranged to major 4000ers, including Breithorn (Sfr165), Riffelhorn (Sfr257) and, for experts willing to acclimatise for a week, Matterhorn (Sfr998). The program also covers multiday hikes, glacier hikes to Gorner (Sfr120), snowshoeing (Sfr140) and ice-climbing (Sfr175).

Skiing
SKIING

For skiers and snowboarders, Zermatt is cruising heaven, with mostly long, scenic red runs, plus a scattering of blues for ski virgins and knuckle-whitening black runs for experts. The three main skiing areas are **Rothorn**, **Stockhorn** (good for mogul fans) and **Klein Matterhorn** (snowboarding freestyle park and half-pipe) – holding 300km of ski runs in all, with free buses shuttling skiers between areas. February to April is peak time. Snow can be sketchy in early summer but lifts are significantly quieter.

A day pass covering all ski lifts in Zermatt (excluding Cervinia) costs Sfr67/57/34 per adult/student/child and Sfr75/64/38 including Cervinia.

Klein Matterhorn
SKIING

Klein Matterhorn is topped by Europe's highest cable-car station (3820m), providing access to Europe's highest skiing, Switzerland's most extensive summer skiing (25km of runs) and deep powder at the Italian resort of **Cervinia**. Broad and exhilarating, the No 7 run down from the border is a must-ski. Don't forget your passport.

If the weather is fine, take the lift up to the summit of Klein Matterhorn (3883m) for top-of-the-beanstalk views over the Swiss Alps (from Mont Blanc to Aletschhorn) and deep into Italy.

🛏 Sleeping & Eating

Most places close May to mid-June and again from October to mid-November.

Berggasthaus Trift
HOSTEL $

(☑079 408 70 20; dm/d with half-board Sfr66/152; ⊙Jul-Sep) It's a trudge to this 2337m-high mountain hut but the hike is outstanding. The alpine haven is run by Hugo (a whiz on the alphorn) and Fabienne, who serve treats such as home-cured beef and oven-warm apple tart on the terrace. Get the camera ready for when the sun sets over Monte Rosa.

Hotel Bahnhof
HOTEL $$

(☑027 967 24 06; www.hotelbahnhof.com; Bahnhofstrasse; dm Sfr40, s/d Sfr70/110; ☎) Opposite the station, these spruce budget digs have a lounge, a snazzy open-plan kitchen and proper beds that are a godsend after scaling or schussing down mountains all day. Free wi-fi.

Zermatt SYHA Hostel
HOSTEL $

(☑027 967 23 20; Staldenweg 5; dm/d from Sfr48/110; @) Question: how many hostels have the Matterhorn peeking through the window in the morning? Answer: one. And if that doesn't convince you, the modern dorms, sunny terrace and first-rate facilities should.

Whymper Stube
SWISS $$

(☑027 967 22 96; Bahnhofstrasse 80; mains Sfr23-42) The mantra at this alpine classic serving the tastiest fondue in Zermatt (including variations with pears and gorgonzola): gorge today, climb tomorrow.

Bayard Metzgerei
SWISS $

(☑027 967 22 66; Bahnhofstrasse 9; sausages from Sfr6; ⊙noon-6.30pm Jul-Sep, 4-6.30pm Dec-Mar) Follow your nose to this butcher's grill for to-go bratwurst, chicken and other carnivorous bites.

🍷 Drinking

Papperla Pub
PUB

(☑027 967 40 40; Steinmattstrasse 34; ⊙11am-11.30pm; ☎) Rammed with sloshed skiers, this pub blends pulsating music with lethal Jägermeister bombs and good vibes. Squeeze in, slam shots, then shuffle downstairs to Schneewittchen club (open to 4am) for more of the same.

Hennu Stall
BAR

(☑027 966 35 10; Klein Matterhorn; ⊙2-7pm) Last one down to this snow-bound 'chicken run' is a rotten egg. Hennu is the wildest après-ski shack on Klein Matterhorn. A metre-long 'ski' of shots will make you cluck all the way down to Zermatt.

Igloo Bar
BAR

(Gornergrat; www.iglu-dorf.ch; ☉10am-4pm) Sub-zero sippers sunbathe, stare wide-mouthed at the Matterhorn and guzzle glühwein amid the ice sculptures at this igloo bar. It's on the run from Gornergrat to Riffelberg.

ⓘ Information

The **tourist office** (☏027 966 81 00; www.zermatt.ch; Bahnhofplatz 5; ☉8.30am-6pm Mon-Sat, 8.30am-noon & 1.30-6pm Sun mid-Jun–Sep, 8.30am-noon & 1.30-6pm Mon-Sat, 9.30am-noon & 4-6pm Sun Oct–mid-Jun) has all the bumph.

ⓘ Getting There & Around

CAR Zermatt is car-free, and dinky electric vehicles are used to transport goods and serve as taxis around town. Drivers have to leave their vehicles in one of the garages or the open-air car park in Tδsch (Sfr13.50 per day) and take the train (Sfr7.60, 12 minutes) into Zermatt.

TRAIN Trains depart roughly every 20 minutes from Brig (Sfr35, 1½ hours), stopping at Vispen route. Zermatt is also the starting point of the *Glacier Express* to Graubünden, one of the most spectacular train rides in the world.

BERN

POP 123,400

One of the planet's most underrated capitals, Bern is a fabulous find. With the genteel old soul of a Renaissance man and the heart of a high-flying 21st-century gal, the riverside city is both medieval and modern. The 15th-century Old Town is gorgeous enough to sweep you off your feet and make you forget the century (it's definitely worthy of its 1983 Unesco World Heritage site protection order). But the edgy vintage boutiques, artsy-intellectual bars and Renzo Piano's futuristic art museum crammed with Paul Klee pieces slam you firmly back into the present.

⊙ Sights

Old Town
HISTORIC AREA

Bern's flag-bedecked medieval centre is an attraction in its own right, with 6km of covered arcades and cellar shops/bars descending from the streets. After a devastating fire in 1405, the wooden city was rebuilt in today's sandstone.

Bern's **Zytglogge** (clock tower) is a focal point; crowds congregate around to watch its revolving figures twirl at four minutes before the hour, after which the actual chimes begin. Tours enter the tower to see the clock mechanism from May to October; contact the tourist office for details.

Equally enchanting are the 11 decorative **fountains** (1545) depicting historical and folkloric characters. Most are along Marktgasse as it becomes Kramgasse and Gerechtigkeitsgasse, but the most famous lies in Kornhausplatz: the **Kindlifresserbrunnen** (Ogre Fountain) of a giant snacking…on children.

Inside the 15th-century Gothic **Münster** (cathedral; www.bernermuenster.ch; tower adult/7-16yr Sfr5/2, audioguide Sfr5; ☉10am-5pm Mon-Sat, 11.30am-5pm Sun summer, noon-4pm Mon-Fri, 10am-5pm Sat, 11.30am-4pm winter, tower closes 30min earlier), a 344-step hike up the lofty spire – Switzerland's tallest – is worth the climb.

Paul Klee Centre
MUSEUM

(☏031 359 01 01; www.zpk.org; Monument in Fruchtland 3; adult/6-16yr Sfr18/6, audioguides Sfr5; ☉10am-5pm Tue-Sun) Bern's Guggenheim, the fabulous Zentrum Paul Klee is an eye-catching 150m-long building designed by Renzo Piano 3km east on the outskirts of town. Inside the three-peak structure, the middle 'hill' showcases 4000 rotating works from Paul Klee's prodigious and often playful career. Interactive computer displays built into the seating mean you can get the low-down on all the Swiss-born artist's major pieces, and music audioguides (Sfr5) take visitors on one-hour DIY musical tours of his work.

In the basement of another 'hill' is **Kindermuseum Creaviva**, an inspired children's museum where kids can experiment with hands-on art exhibits (included in admission price) or sign up for a one-hour art workshop (Sfr15).

In the grounds, a walk through fields takes visitors past a stream of modern and contemporary sculptures, including works by Yoko Ono and Sol Lewitt; the walk also affords views of the museum's wave-like living roof sections.

Take bus 12 from Bubenbergplatz to Zentrum Paul Klee (Sfr3.80; sit on the right for the best views of the city on your way out there). By car the museum is right next to the Bern-Ostring exit of the A6.

Einstein Museum
MUSEUM

(☏031 312 00 91; www.einstein-bern.ch; Kramgasse 49; adult/student Sfr6/4.50; ☉10am-7pm Mon-Fri, to 4pm Sat Feb-Dec) The world's most famous

Bern

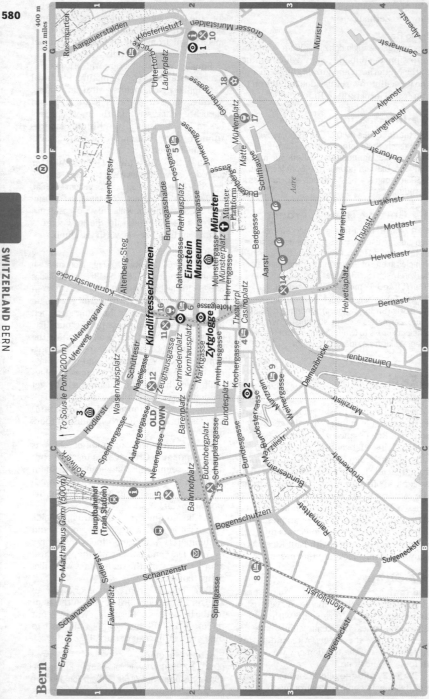

N

0   400 m
0   0.2 miles

Bern

scientist developed his theory of relativity in Bern in 1905. Find out more at the Einstein Haus, in the humble apartment where Einstein lived between 1903 and 1905 while working as a low-paid clerk in the Bern patent office. Multimedia displays now flesh out the story of the subsequent general equation – $E=MC^2$, or energy equals mass times the speed of light squared – that fundamentally changed humankind's understanding of space, time and the universe. Upstairs, a 20-minute biographical film tells Einstein's life story.

FREE **Houses of Parliament** HISTORIC SITE
(☏031 332 85 22; www.parliament.ch; Bundesplatz; ⊙hourly tours 9am-4pm Mon-Sat) The 1902 Bundeshäuser, home of the Swiss Federal Assembly, is impressively ornate, with statues of the nation's founding fathers, a stained-glass dome adorned with cantonal emblems and a huge 214-bulb chandelier.

Tours are offered when parliament is in recess; otherwise watch from the public gallery. Bring your passport to get in.

Bärengraben BEAR PARK
(www.baerenpark-bern.ch, in German; ⊙9.30am-5pm) Bern was founded in 1191 by Berchtold V and named for the unfortunate bear (*bärn* in local dialect) that was his first hunting victim. The bear remains the city's heraldic mascot, hence the bear pits. Since 2009 the bears live in a new, spacious, riverside park. Beware: don't feed the bears anything random, but do buy a paper cone of fresh fruit (Sfr3).

Kunstmuseum MUSEUM
(☏031 328 09 44; www.kunstmuseumbern.ch, in German; Hodlerstrasse 8-12; adult/student main collection Sfr8/5, temporary exhibitions Sfr8-18; ⊙10am-9pm Tue, to 5pm Wed-Sun) The permanent collection at the Museum of Fine Arts includes works by Italian artists such as Fra Angelico, Swiss artists such as Ferdinand Hodler, and works by Picasso and Dalí.

🛏 Sleeping

The tourist office makes hotel reservations (for free) and has information on 'three nights for the price of two' deals.

Marthahaus Garni HOTEL $
(☏031 332 41 35; www.marthahaus.ch; Wyttenbachstrasse 22a; s/d Sfr115/145, without bathroom from Sfr70/105; ◈@?) Plum in a leafy residential location, this five-storey building feels like a friendly boarding house. Clean, simple rooms are very white with a smattering of modern art, plus there's a kitchen.

Hotel Landhaus HOTEL $$
(☏031 331 41 66; www.landhausbern.ch; Altenbergstrasse 4; dm from Sfr33, d from Sfr160, without bathroom from Sfr120; P◈@?) Backed by the grassy slope of a city park and fronted by the river and Old Town spires, this historic hotel oozes character. Its soulful ground-floor restaurant, a tad bohemian, draws a staunchly local crowd.

Bellevue Palace HOTEL $$$
(☏031 320 45 45; www.bellevue-palace.ch; Kochergasse 3-5; s/d from Sfr360/390; P◈✳@?) Bern's power brokers and international statesmen such as Nelson Mandela gravitate towards Bern's only five-star hotel. Near the parliament, it's *the* address to impress. Cheaper weekend rates.

Hotel National HOTEL $
(☏031 381 19 88; www.nationalbern.ch, in German; Hirschengraben 24; s/d Sfr100/140, without bath-

room from Sfr60/120; @) The quaint, charming National wouldn't be out of place in Paris, with its wrought-iron lift, lavender sprigs and Persian rugs over creaky wooden floors.

Hotel Innere Enge   HOTEL $$$
(☎031 309 61 11; www.zghotels.ch; Engestrasse 54; d from Sfr240; P⊖@⊛) It might not be city centre, but this jazz hotel north of the city centre is unique. Run with passion by Bern Jazz Festival organiser Hans Zurbrügg and wife Marianne Gauer, a top Swiss hotel-interior designer, the place oozes panache. Don't miss its cellar jazz bar.

Hotel Belle Epoque   HOTEL $$$
(☎031 311 43 36; www.belle-epoque.ch; Gerechtigkeitsgasse 18; s/d from Sfr250/350; ⊖@⊛) Standards are so exacting at this romantic hotel with art deco furnishings that modern aberrations are cleverly hidden – dig the TV in the steamer-trunk-style cupboard – so as not to spoil the look.

Hotel Glocke Backpackers Bern   HOSTEL $
(☎031 311 37 71; www.bernbackpackers.com; Rathausgasse 75; dm Sfr34-45; ⊗reception 8-11am & 3-10pm; ⊖@⊛) Its Old Town location makes this many backpackers' first choice, although street noise might irritate light sleepers.

SYHA Hostel   HOSTEL $
(☎031 326 11 11; www.youthhostel.ch/bern; Weihergasse 4; dm from Sfr33; ⊗reception 7am-noon & 2pm-midnight; ⊖@⊛) Prettily set across from the river, this well-organised hostel sports clean dorms and a leafy terrace with red seating and ping-pong table. Free bike rental May to October (Sfr20 deposit).

✗ Eating
Waterside or Old Town, Bern cooks up a delicious choice of dining handy for all budgets.

Lötschberg AOC   SWISS $$
(☎031 311 34 55; Zeughausgasse 16; mains Sfr14-28) Take an all-Swiss wine and beer list, add cheese specialities from the Valais (including fondue and raclette, of course), decorate the cheerful yellow walls with circular, wood wine racks, add chequered tablecloths and you have one of the most dynamic Swiss restaurants in the country. This popular, casual spot, favoured by locals and visitors alike, serves exceptional Swiss fare without the kitsch and is as great for a bite and a glass of wine as it is for a full sit-down meal.

Altes Tramdepot   SWISS $
(☎031 368 14 15; Am Bärengraben; mains Sfr16-20; ⊗lunch & dinner) Even locals recommend this cavernous microbrewery by the bear pits. Swiss specialities snuggle up to wok-cooked stir-fries, pasta and international dishes on its bistro-styled menu.

Du Nord   INTERNATIONAL $$
(☎031 332 23 38; www.dunord-bern.ch; Lorrainestrasse 2; mains Sfr20-36; ⊗closed Sun) This gay-friendly space with good-value international kitchen and bar buzzes with Bern's hippest and the occasional gig. Find it crowned by a pretty pink, fairy-tale turret.

TOP QUICK EATS

This student-busy city has some super quick-eat options, oozing atmosphere and even a table thrown in for a highly affordable price. You'll pay less than Sfr15 for a full meal.

Munch between meals on a *brezel* (pretzel; around Sfr3) smothered in salt crystals or sunflower, pumpkin or sesame seeds from kiosks at the train station; or a bag of piping-hot chestnuts crunched to the tune of the astronomical clock striking.

Markthalle (Bubenbergplatz 9; ⊗6.30am-11.30pm Mon-Wed, to 12.30am Thu & Fri, 7.30am-12.30am Sat; ✗) Buzzing in atmosphere and quick-snack action, this covered market arcade is jam-packed with eateries from around the world: curries, vegetarian, wok stir-fries, *bruschette,* noodles, pizza, south Indian, Turkish, Middle Eastern...you name it, it's here. Eat standing at bars or around plastic tables.

Sous le Pont (www.souslepont.ch) Grab fries, falafel or a *schnitzelb* from the graffiti-covered hole-in-the-wall next to the eponymous cafe-bar and dine at the graffiti-covered table in the graffiti-covered courtyard. Beer costs Sfr3.80/5.20 per 300/500dL glass.

Tibits (☎031 312 91 11; Bahnhofplatz 10; ⊗6.30am-11.30pm Mon-Wed, 6.30am-midnight Thu-Sat, 8am-11pm Sun; ✗) This vegetarian buffet restaurant inside the train station is just the ticket for a quick healthy meal, any size, any time of day. Serve yourself, get it weighed and pay accordingly.

Terrasse & Casa
ITALIAN $$

(☏031 350 50 01; www.schwellenmaetteli.ch; Dam-aziquai 11; mains Sfr29-44; ☺Terrasse open daily, Casa closed Mon) Dubbed 'Bern's Riviera', this twinset of classy hang-outs on the Aare is an experience. Terrasse is a glass shoebox with wooden decking over the water and sun-loungers overlooking a weir, while Casa serves Italian food in a country-styled tim-ber-framed house.

Kornhauskeller
SWISS $$$

(☏031 327 72 72; Kornhausplatz 18; mains Sfr32-52; ☺lunch & dinner Mon-Sat, dinner Sun) Dress well and dine fine beneath vaulted frescoed arches at Bern's former granary, where beau-tiful people sip cocktails alongside historic stained-glass on the mezzanine above.

🍷 Drinking & Entertainment

For an earthy drink with old-generation lo-cals, order one at the marble-topped bar in-side the **Markthalle** (Bubenbergplatz 9).

Sous le Pont
BAR

(☏031 306 69 55; www.souslepont.ch; Neubrück-strasse 8; ☺11.30am-2.30pm & 6pm-2.30am Tue-Thu, 11.30am-2.30pm & 7pm-2am Fri, 7pm-2.30am Sat) Delve into the grungy underground scene around the station in the bar of semi-chaotic alternative-arts centre, Reitschule. Find it in an old stone, graffiti-covered build-ing – an old riding school built in 1897 – by the railway bridge.

Silo Bar
BAR

(☏031 311 54 12; www.silobar.ch, in German; Müh-lenplatz 11; ☺10pm-3.30am Thu-Sat) By the water in the hip Matte quarter, Bern's monumental 19th-century corn house throbs with main-stream hits and a lively predominantly stu-dent set – *the* place to drink, dance and party.

Café des Pyrénées
BAR

(☏031 311 30 63; Kornhausplatz 17; ☺Mon-Sat) With its mix of wine-quaffing trendies and beer-loving students, this Bohemian joint feels like a Parisian cafe-bar.

Wasserwerk
CLUB

(☏031 312 12 31; www.wasser werkclub.ch; Wasserwerkgasse 5; ☺10pm-late Thu-Sat) Bern's main techno venue with bar, club and oc-casional live music.

🛈 Information

BernCard (per 24/48/72hr Sfr20/31/38) Discount card providing admission to perma-nent collections at 27 museums, free public transport and city-tour discounts.

Bern Tourismus (☏031 328 12 12; www.berninfo.com; Bahnhoftplatz; ☺9am-8.30pm Jun-Sep, 9am-6.30pm Mon-Sat, 10am-5pm Sun Oct-May) Street-level floor of the train station. City tours, free hotel bookings, internet access (per hour Sfr12).

Post office (Schanzenstrasse 4; ☺7.30am-9pm Mon-Fri, 8am-4pm Sat, 4-9pm Sun)

Tourist office (☏031 328 12 12; Bärengraben; ☺9am-6pm Jun-Sep, 10am-4pm Mar-May & Oct, 11am-4pm Nov-Feb) By the bear pits.

🛈 Getting There & Around

AIR Bern-Belp airport (BRN; ☏031 960 21 21; www.alpar.ch), 9km southeast of the city centre, is a small airport with direct flights to/from Munich (from where there are onward connections pretty much everywhere) with Lufthansa and Southampton in the UK with Fly Be. **Airport shuttles** (☏031 971 28 88, 079 651 70 70) coordinated with flight departures pick up/drop off at the train station (Sfr15, 20 minutes).

BICYCLE Pedal around with a bike, micro-scooter or skateboard from **Bern Rollt** (☏079 277 28 57; www.bernrollt.ch; 1st 4hr free, then per hr Sfr1; ☺7.30am-9.30pm May-Oct), which has kiosks inside the train station, at the west-ern end of Zeughausgasse and just off Buben-bergplatz on Hirschengrasse.

PUBLIC TRANSPORT Bus and tram tickets are available from ticket machines at stops, and cost Sfr2 (maximum six stops) or Sfr3.80 for a single journey within zones 1 and 2. **Moonliner** (☏031 321 88 12; www.moonliner.ch, in German) night buses transport night owls from Bahnhofplatz two or three times between midnight and 3.30am on Friday and Saturday nights. Fares start at Sfr5.

TRAINS Hourly trains connect to most Swiss towns, including Geneva (Sfr46, 1¾ hours), Basel (Sfr37, 70 minutes) and Zürich (Sfr46, one hour).

CENTRAL SWITZERLAND & BERNESE OBERLAND

The Bernese Oberland should come with a health warning – caution: may cause trem-bling in the north face of Eiger, uncontrol-lable bouts of euphoria at the foot of Jung-frau, 007 delusions at Schilthorn and A-list fever in Gstaad. Mark Twain wrote that no opiate compared to walking through this landscape – and he should know – and even when sober, the electric-green spruce forests, mountains so big they'll swallow you up, surreal china-blue skies, swirling glaciers and turquoise lakes seem hallucinatory. Up at Europe's highest station, Jungfraujoch, husky yapping mingles with Bollywood beats. Yet just paces away, the serpentine Aletsch Glacier flicks out its tongue and you're surrounded by 4000m turrets and frosty stillness.

Lucerne

POP 59,500

Recipe for a gorgeous Swiss city: take a cobalt lake ringed by mountains of myth, add a medieval Old Town and sprinkle with covered bridges, sunny plazas, candy-coloured houses and waterfront promenades. Lucerne is bright, beautiful and has been little Miss Popular since the likes of Goethe, Queen Victoria and Wagner savoured her views in the 19th century. Legend has it that an angel with a light showed the first settlers where to build a chapel in Lucerne, and today it still has amazing grace.

◉ Sights

Old Town   HISTORIC AREA

Your first port of call should be the medieval Old Town, with its ancient rampart walls and towers, 15th-century buildings with painted facades and the two much-photographed covered bridges. **Kapellbrücke** (Chapel Bridge), dating from 1333, is Lucerne's best-known landmark. It's famous for its distinctive water tower and the spectacular 1993 fire that nearly destroyed it. Though it has been rebuilt, fire damage is still obvious on the 17th-century pictorial panels under the roof. In better condition, but rather dark and dour, are the *Dance of Death* panels under the roofline of **Spreuerbrücke** (Spreuer Bridge).

Sammlung Rosengart   MUSEUM

(☏041 220 16 60; www.rosengart.ch; Pilatusstrasse 10; adult/student Sfr18/16; ◷10am-6pm Apr-Oct, 11am-5pm Nov-Mar) Lucerne's blockbuster cultural attraction is the Rosengart Col-

Lucerne

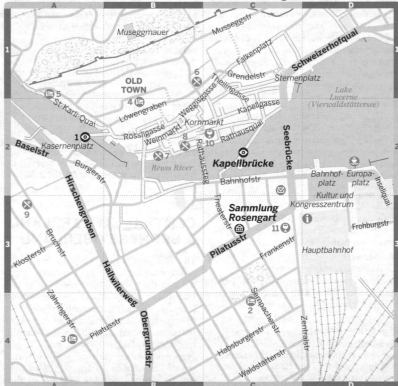

lection, occupying a graceful neoclassical pile. It showcases the outstanding stash of Angela Rosengart, a Swiss art dealer and close friend of Picasso. Alongside works by the great Spanish master are paintings and sketches by Cézanne, Klee, Kandinsky, Miró, Matisse and Monet. Standouts include Joan Miró's electric-blue *Dancer II* (1925) and Paul Klee's childlike *X-chen* (1938).

Complementing this collection are some 200 photographs by David Douglas Duncan of the last 17 years of Picasso's life with his family in their home on the French Riviera. It's a uniquely revealing series and principally a portrait of the artist as an impish craftsman, lover and father.

Verkehrshaus   MUSEUM
(☑041 370 44 44; www.verkehrshaus.ch; Lidostrasse 5; adult/child Sfr24/12; ☉9am-6pm Apr-Oct, 10am-5pm Nov-Mar) Planes, trains and automobiles are the name of the game in the huge, family-oriented Transport Museum, east of the city centre, which is devoted to Switzerland's proud transport history. Space rockets, a communications display, simulators, a planetarium, an **IMAX cinema** (www.imax.ch; adult/child Sfr18/14) and the **Swiss Arena** – a gigantic 1:20,000 walkable map of Switzerland, taken from aerial photos, where you can delight in leaping over the Alps – all help make this Switzerland's most popular museum. Take bus 6, 8 or 24 from Bahnhofplatz.

Strandbad Lido   SWIMMING
(☑041 370 38 06; www.lido-luzern.ch; Lidostrasse 6a; adult/child Sfr6/3; ☉9am-8pm mid-May–Sep) Perfect for a splash or sunbathe, this lakefront beach has a playground, volleyball court and heated outdoor pool. Or swim for free on the other bank of the lake by Seepark, off Alpenquai.

Outventure   ADVENTURE SPORTS
(☑041 611 14 41; www.outventure.ch; Stans) Outventure tempts adrenalin junkies with pursuits including tandem paragliding (Sfr150), canyoning (from Sfr110), glacier trekking (Sfr150) and canoeing on Lake Lucerne (Sfr115).

Bike Rental   CYCLING
(☑041 51 227 32 61; half-/full day Sfr25/33) Bikes can be rented at the train station. Check out the routes circumnavigating the lake; an easygoing and scenic option is the 16km pedal to Winkel via Kastanienbaum.

🎉 Festivals & Events

Lucerne's six-day **Fasnacht** celebrations are more boisterous and fun than Basel's carnival. The party kicks off on 'Dirty Thursday' with the emergence of the character 'Fritschi' from a window in the town hall, when bands of musicians and revellers take to the streets. The carnival moves through raucous celebrations climaxing on Mardi Gras (Fat Tuesday), and is over on Ash Wednesday.

June's **Jodler Fest Luzern** (www.jodlerfest luzern.ch) is a classic alpine shindig: think 12,000 Swiss yodellers, alphorn players and flag throwers.

🛏 Sleeping

Backpackers Lucerne   HOSTEL $
(☑041 360 04 20; www.backpackerslucerne.ch; Alpenquai 42; dm/d from Sfr33/70; ☉reception 7-10am & 4-11pm; @🛜) It's backpacker heaven: right on the lake, this soulful place has art-slung walls, bubbly staff, a well-equipped kitchen and immaculate dorms with balconies. It's a 15-minute walk southeast of the station.

Hotel Alpha   HOTEL $
(☑041 240 42 80; www.hotelalpha.ch; Zähringerstrasse 24; s/d from Sfr75/110; @🛜) Easy on the eye and wallet, this hotel is in a quiet residential area 10 minutes' walk from the centre. Rooms are simple, light and spotlessly clean.

Bed and Breakfast
B&B **$**

(☎041 310 15 14; www.thebandb.ch; Taubenhausstrasse 34; s/d Sfr80/120; ☺Mar-Oct; P☺☺ⓢ) This friendly B&B feels like a private home, with stylish, contemporary rooms – crisp white bedding, scatter cushions and hot pink and lime accents. Unwind in the flowery garden or with a soak in the old-fashioned tub. Free wi-fi is another bonus. Take bus 1 to Eichof.

Tourist Hotel
HOTEL **$$**

(☎041 410 24 74; www.touristhotel.ch; St-Karli-Quai 12; dm from Sfr40, s/d Sfr140/220, without bathroom from Sfr80/120; P☺☺@ⓢ) Don't be put off by the uninspired name and pease-pudding green facade of this central, riverfront cheapie. Dorms are basic, but rooms cheery, with bold paint jobs, parquet floors and flat-screen TVs.

Jailhotel Löwengraben
HOTEL **$$**

(☎041 410 78 30; www.jailhotel.ch; Löwengraben 18; s/d from Sfr120/150; ☺ⓢ) This former prison has novelty value, but you might get a jailhouse shock when you enter your cell to find barred windows, bare floorboards and a prefab bathroom. It's fun for a laugh and its location is stellar, but it ain't great for quality shut-eye with thumping techno in Alcatraz club downstairs to 3am.

The Hotel
HOTEL **$$$**

(☎041 226 86 86; www.the-hotel.ch; Sempacherstrasse 14; ste from Sfr420; ✱@ⓢ) Streamlined and jet black, 10 vampy suites reveal stainless-steel fittings, open-plan bathrooms peeking through to garden foliage, and stills from movie classics gracing the ceilings at this Jean Nouvel creation. Downstairs Bam Bou is one of Lucerne's hippest restaurants.

SYHA hostel
HOSTEL **$**

(☎041 420 88 00; www.youthhostel.ch/luzern; Sedelstrasse 12; dm/d from Sfr33/82; ☺check-in 2pm-midnight summer, from 4pm winter; P@) These HI digs are modern, well run and clean, and value-for-money meals are available throughout the day. Take bus 18 from the train station to Jugendherberge.

✗ Eating & Drinking

Many places in Lucerne double as bars and restaurants. Places open for breakfast and stay open until late in the evening. Self-caterers should head to Hertensteinstrasse, where cheap eats are plentiful from snack stands (and frankly, you won't find much in the way of cheap sit-down eats in this town).

Restaurant Schiff
SWISS **$$**

(☎041 418 52 52; Unter der Egg 8; mains Sfr20-45) Under the waterfront arcades and lit by tea lights at night, this restaurant has bags of charm. Try fish from Lake Lucerne and some of the city's most celebrated *Chögalipaschtetli* (vol-au-vents stuffed with meat and mushrooms).

Jazzkantine
ITALIAN **$**

(☎041 410 73 73; Grabenstrasse 8; mains Sfr15-22; ☺7am-12.30am Mon-Sat, 4pm-12.30am Sun) Stainless-steel bar, sturdy wooden tables and chalkboard menus – this is an arty haunt. Go for tasty *bruschette* or more ambitious dishes like penne vodka. Saturday-night gigs follow weeknight jazz workshops.

La Terraza
ITALIAN **$$**

(☎041 410 36 31; Metzgerrainle 9; mains Sfr18-45) Set in a 12th-century building that has housed fish sellers, dukes and scribes over the years, La Terraza oozes atmosphere. Think *bella* Italia with an urban edge. When the sun's out, sit on the riverfront terrace for favourites like clam-and-rocket spaghetti.

Schützengarten
INTERNATIONAL **$$**

(☎041 240 01 10; Bruchstrasse 20; mains Sfr19-45; ☺Mon-Sat; ✎) As well as a cracking sense of humour, Schützengarten has smiley service, wood-panelled surrounds, appetising vegetarian and vegan dishes, and organic wine. Sit on the vine-strewn terrace in summer.

Rathaus Bräuerei
PUB

(☎041 410 52 57; Unter den Egg 2; ☺8am-midnight Mon-Sat, to 11pm Sun) Sip home-brewed beer under the vaulted arches of this buzzy tavern, or nab a pavement table and watch the river flow.

Roadhouse
BAR

(☎041 220 27 27; www.roadhouse.ch; Pilatusstrasse 1; ☺11am-4am) Roadhouse plays solid rock to a young, fun crowd. Check out Wednesday night's jam sessions, where anyone with an instrument or voice (preferably both) can take the stand.

ⓘ Information

Lucerne Card (24/48/72hr Sfr19/27/33) If you are planning to visit several museums, it's worth buying a Lucerne Card, available at the tourist office. It gets you 50% discount on museum admissions, unlimited use of public transport and other reductions.

Luzern Tourism (☎041 227 17 17; www.luzern.com; Zentralstrasse 5; ☺8.30am-7.30pm Mon-Fri, 9am-7.30pm Sat & Sun mid-Jun–mid-Sep,

9am-6.30pm daily May–mid-Jun & mid-Sep–Oct, 8.30am-5.30pm Mon-Fri, 9am-1pm Sat & Sun Nov-Apr) Accessed from platform 3 of the train station.

Surfers Island (☑041 412 00 44; Weinmarkt 15; per hr Sfr10; ☺10am-7pm Mon-Fri, to 4pm Sat) Internet access.

❶ Getting There & Away

Frequent trains connect Lucerne to Interlaken West (Sfr33.40, two hours, via the scenic Brünig Pass), Bern (Sfr35, 1¾ hours), Lugano (Sfr55, 2¾ hours), Geneva (Sfr72, 3¾ hours, via Olten or Langnau) and Zürich (Sfr23, one hour).

Interlaken

POP 5300

Once Interlaken made the Victorians swoon with its dreamy mountain vistas, viewed from the chandelier-lit confines of its grand hotels. Today it makes daredevils scream with its adrenalin-loaded adventures. Straddling the glittering Lakes Thun and Brienz, and dazzled by the pearly whites of Eiger, Mönch and Jungfrau, the scenery here is mind-blowing. Particularly, some say, if you're abseiling waterfalls, thrashing white water or gliding soundlessly above 4000m peaks.

Though the streets are filled with enough yodelling kitsch to make Heidi cringe, Interlaken still makes a terrific base for exploring the Bernese Oberland. Its adventure capital status has spawned a breed of funky bars, party-mad hostels and restaurants serving flavours more imaginative than fondue.

🏃 Activities

Tempted to hurl yourself off a bridge, down a cliff or along a raging river? You're in the right place. Switzerland is the world's second-biggest adventure-sports mecca, nipping at New Zealand's sprightly heels, and Interlaken is its busiest hub.

Almost every heart-stopping pursuit you can think of is offered here (although the activities take place in the greater Jungfrau Region). You can white-water raft on the Lütschine, Simme and Saane Rivers; go canyoning in the Saxetet, Grimsel or Chli Schliere gorges; and canyon-jump at the Gletscherschlucht near Grindelwald. If that doesn't grab you, there's paragliding, glacier bungee jumping, skydiving, ice-climbing, hydro-speeding and zorbing, where you're strapped into a giant plastic ball and sent spinning down a hill.

Prices are from Sfr90 for rock climbing, Sfr95 for zorbing, Sfr110 for rafting or canyoning, Sfr120 for hydro-speeding, Sfr130 for bungee jumping, Sfr160 for paragliding, Sfr195 for hang-gliding and Sfr430 for skydiving. Most excursions are without incident, but there's always a small risk and it's wise to ask about safety records and procedures. Major operators able to arrange most sports:

Alpin Center   ADVENTURE SPORTS
(☑033 823 55 23; www.alpincenter.ch; Hauptstrasse 16)

Alpinraft   ADVENTURE SPORTS
(☑033 823 41 00; www.alpinraft.ch; Hauptstrasse 7)

Outdoor Interlaken   ADVENTURE SPORTS
(☑033 826 77 19; www.outdoor-interlaken.ch; Hauptstrasse 15)

Swissraft   ADVENTURE SPORTS
(☑033 821 66 55; www.swissraft-activity.ch; Obere Jungfraustrasse 72)

🛏 Sleeping

Hotel Rugenpark   B&B $
(☑033 822 36 61; www.rugenpark.ch; Rugenparkstrasse 19; s/d from Sfr85/130, without bathroom from Sfr65/105; ☺closed Nov–mid-Dec; ℗☺@) Chris and Ursula have worked magic to transform this into a sweet B&B. Rooms are humble, but the place is spotless and has been enlivened with colourful butterflies, beads and travel trinkets. Quiz your knowledgeable hosts for help and local tips.

Funny Farm   GUESTHOUSE $
(☑033 828 12 81; www.funny-farm.ch; Hauptstrasse 36; ℗@☎) Funny Farm is halfway between a squat and an island shipwreck. The ramshackle art nouveau house, surrounded by makeshift bars and a swimming pool, is patrolled by Spliff, the lovably dopey St Bernard. Dorms are a bit faded and musty, but guests don't care; they're here for the party and revel in such anarchism. Closed during 2011; check the website for details.

Schlaf im Stroh   FARMSTAY $
(☑033 822 04 31; www.uelisi.ch; Lanzenen 30; ☺May-Sep; ℗) Our readers have been singing the praises of this friendly farm for years. Bring your sleeping bag to snooze in the straw and wake up to a hearty breakfast. Kids adore the resident cats, goats and rabbits. It's 15 minutes' walk from Interlaken Ost station along the Aare River (upstream). Closed during 2011; check the website for details.

RiverLodge & Camping TCS

CAMPING GROUND **$**

(☎033 822 44 34; Brienzstrasse 24; campsites per adult/tent Sfr10/9; ☻May–mid-Oct; ☜) Facing the Aare River and handy for Interlaken Ost train station, this camping ground and hostel duo offer first-class facilities, including a communal kitchen and laundry. Rent bikes and kayaks here.

Victoria-Jungfrau Grand Hotel & Spa

HOTEL **$$$**

(☎033 828 28 28; www.victoria-jungfrau.ch; Höheweg 41; s/d from Sfr560/680, d with Jungfrau views from Sfr780; ℗☻@☜☒) The reverent hush and impeccable service evoke an era when only royalty and the seriously wealthy travelled. A perfect melding of well-preserved Victorian features and modern luxury make this Interlaken's answer to Raffles.

Balmer's Herberge

HOSTEL **$**

(☎033 822 19 61; www.balmers.ch; Hauptstrasse 23; dm from Sfr29, s/d Sfr45/78; ℗@☜) Adrenalin junkies hail Balmer's for its fun frat-house vibe. These party-mad digs offer beer-garden happy hours, wrap lunches, pumping bar with DJs, and chill-out hammocks for nursing a hangover.

Backpackers Villa Sonnenhof

HOSTEL **$**

(☎033 826 71 71; www.villa.ch; Alpenstrasse 16; dm from Sfr35; ☻reception 7am-11pm; @) While most Interlaken hostels are charged with more energy than a Duracell bunny, this homely place recharges your batteries. The olive-fronted villa exudes Victorian flair with stucco and vintage steamer trunks, immaculate dorms, well-equipped kitchen and leafy garden.

Post Hardmannli

HOTEL **$$**

(☎033 822 89 19; www.post-hardermannli.ch; s/d Sfr100/155; ℗) An affable Swiss-Kiwi couple, Andreas and Kim, run this rustic chalet. Rooms are simple yet comfy, decorated with pine and chintzy pastels. Cheaper rooms forgo balconies and Jungfrau views. The home-grown farm produce at breakfast is a real treat.

✖ Eating & Drinking

Am Marktplatz is scattered with bakeries and bistros with alfresco seating. The bars at Balmer's and Funny Farm are easily the liveliest drinking holes for revved-up 20-something travellers. You'll find a mixed crowd in the Happy Inn.

Benacus

SWISS **$$**

(☎033 821 20 20; www.benacus.ch; Stadthausplatz; mains Sfr20-33; ☻closed Sun, lunch Sat) Supercool Benacus is a breath of urban air with its glass walls, slick wine-red sofas, lounge music and street-facing terrace. The TV show 'Funky Kitchen Club' is filmed here. The menu stars creative flavours like potato and star anise soup, and Aargau chicken with caramelised pak choi.

Belvéderè Brasserie

SWISS **$$**

(☎033 828 91 00; Höheweg 95; mains Sfr17-36) Yes it's attached to the rather boring-looking Hapimag, but this brasserie has an upbeat modern decor and a terrace with Jungfrau views. It serves up international favourites such as veal in merlot sauce, alongside a handful of Swiss stalwarts such as fondue and rösti.

Goldener Anker

INTERNATIONAL **$$**

(☎033 822 16 72; www.anker.ch, in German; Marktgasse 57; mains Sfr18-41; ☻dinner) This beamed restaurant, locals will whisper in your ear, is the best in town. Globetrotters include everything from sizzling fajitas to red snapper and ostrich steaks. It also has a roster of live bands.

Sandwich Bar

SWISS **$**

(☎033 821 63 25; Rosenstrasse 5; snacks Sfr4-9; ☻7.30am-7pm Mon-Fri, 8am-5pm Sat) This snack bar is an untouristy gem. Choose your bread and get creative with fillings (our favourite is *Bündnerfleisch* with sundried tomatoes and parmesan). Otherwise try soups, salads and locally made ice cream.

❶ Information

The **post office** (Postplatz; ☻8am-noon & 1.45-6pm Mon-Fri, 8.30-11am Sat) and **tourist office** (☎033 826 53 00; www.interlakentourism.ch; Höheweg 37; ☻8am-7pm Mon-Fri, 8am-5pm Sat, 10am-noon & 5-7pm Sun Jul–mid-Sep, 8am-noon & 1.30-6pm Mon-Fri, 9am-noon Sat rest of year) are near Interlaken West.

❶ Getting There & Away

The only way south for vehicles without a detour around the mountains is the car-carrying train from Kandersteg, south of Spiez.

Trains to Grindelwald (Sfr10.20, 40 minutes, hourly), Lauterbrunnen (Sfr7, 20 minutes, hourly) and Lucerne (Sfr30, two hours, hourly) depart from Interlaken Ost. Trains to Brig (Sfr41, 1½ hours, hourly) and Montreux via Bern or Visp (Sfr57 to Sfr67, 2¾ hours, hourly) leave from either Interlaken West or Ost.

Jungfrau Region

If the Bernese Oberland is Switzerland's Alpine heart, the Jungfrau region is where yours will skip a beat. Presided over by glacier-encrusted monoliths Eiger, Mönch and Jungfrau (Ogre, Monk and Virgin), the scenery stirs the soul and strains the neck muscles. It's a magnet for skiers and snowboarders with its 200km of pistes; a one-day ski pass for Kleine Scheidegg-Männlichen, Grindelwald-First, or Mürren-Schilthorn costs Sfr59. Come summer, hundreds of kilometres of walking trails allow you to capture the landscape from many angles, but it never looks less than astonishing.

The Lauterbrunnen Valley branches out from Interlaken with sheer rock faces and towering mountains on either side, attracting an army of hikers and mountain bikers. Cowbells echo in the valley and every house and hostel has a postcard-worthy view. Many visitors choose to visit this valley on a day trip from Interlaken.

GRINDELWALD
POP 3800

Once a simple farming village nestled in a valley under the north face of the Eiger, Grindelwald's charms were discovered by skiers and hikers in the late 19th century, making it one of Switzerland's oldest and the Jungfrau's largest resorts. It has lost none of its appeal over the decades, with archetypal alpine chalets and verdant pastures set against an Oscar-worthy backdrop.

Grindelwald tourist office (☑ 033 854 12 12; www.grindelwald.ch; Dorfstrasse; ☉ 8am-noon & 1.30-6pm Mon-Fri, 9am-noon & 1.30-5pm Sat & Sun summer & winter, 8am-noon & 1.30-5pm Mon-Fri, 9am-noon Sat rest of year) is at the Sportzentrum, 200m from the train station.

Hourly trains link Grindelwald with Interlaken Ost (Sfr10.20, 40 minutes, hourly).

◉ Sights & Activities

Oberer Gletscher   GLACIER
(Upper Glacier; adult/child Sfr6/3; ☉ 9am-6pm mid-May–Oct) The shimmering, slowly melting Oberer Gletscher is a 1½-hour hike from the village, or catch a bus (marked Terrasen Weg-Oberer Gletscher) to Hotel-Restaurant Wetterhorn. Walk 10 minutes from the bus stop, then pant up 890 log stairs to reach a terrace offering dramatic vistas. A crowd-puller is the vertiginous hanging bridge spanning the gorge.

Gletscherschlucht   GLACIER
(Glacier Gorge; admission Sfr7; ☉ 10am-5pm May-Oct, to 6pm Jul & Aug) Turbulent waters carve a path through the craggy Gletscherschlucht, a 30-minute walk south of the centre. A footpath weaves through tunnels hacked into cliffs – a popular spot for canyon- and bungee-jumping expeditions.

Grindelwald-First   SKIING
First is the main skiing area, with runs stretching from **Oberjoch** at 2486m to the village at 1050m. In the summer it caters to **hikers** with 90km of trails at about 1200m, 48km of which are open year-round.

Catch the longest **cable car** (☑ 033 854 80 80; www.maennlichen.ch) in Europe from Grindelwald-Grund to Männlichen (single/return Sfr31/Sfr51), where there are more extraordinary views and hikes.

🛏 Sleeping & Eating

Mountain Hostel   HOSTEL $
(☑ 033 854 38 38; www.mountainhostel.ch; dm Sfr37-42, d Sfr92-102; ☐) Near the Männlichen cable-car station, this is a good base for sports junkies. Cyclists are especially welcome. Rates include free ice-skating and swimming at a nearby facility.

SYHA Hostel   HOSTEL $
(☑ 033 853 10 09; www.youthhostel.ch/grindelwald; Terrassenweg; dm Sfr31.50-38.50, d Sfr108, d without bathroom Sfr80; ☉ reception 7.30-10am & 4-10pm; @) This excellent hostel is in a cosy wooden chalet perched high on a hill, with magnificent views. Avoid the 20-minute slog from the train station by taking the Terrassenweg-bound bus to the Gaggi Säge stop.

SLEEP SUSTAINABLY

Perched above Grindelwald village, eco-friendly chalet **Naturfreundehaus** (☑ 033 853 13 33; www.naturfreundehaeuser.ch; Terrassenweg; dm/s/d Sfr36/46/72; ☉ closed low season; ☐), whose name suitably translates as the House of Friends of Nature, is a green gem. Most folk have a cat or dog; Vreni and Heinz have Mono the trout as family pet. Creaking floors lead up to cute pine-panelled rooms, including a shoebox single – Switzerland's smallest, so they say. Try an Eiger coffee with amaretto or a homemade mint cordial in the quirky cafe downstairs. The garden has wonderful views to Eiger and Wetterhorn.

Memory SWISS **$$**
(☑033 854 31 31; Dorfstrasse; mains Sfr16-28; ◷11.30am-10.30pm) Always packed, the Eiger Hotel's unpretentious restaurant rolls out tasty Swiss grub such as rösti and fondue. Try to bag a table on the street-facing terrace.

C & M SWISS **$$**
(☑033 853 07 10; mains Sfr20-35; ◷Wed-Mon) Just as appetising as the menu are the stupendous views to Unterer Gletscher from this gallery-style cafe's sunny terrace. Enjoy a salad, coffee and cake, or seasonally inspired dishes such as venison stew with dumplings and bilberry-stuffed apple.

GIMMELWALD
POP 118

Decades ago some anonymous backpacker scribbled these words in the guestbook at the Mountain Hostel: 'If heaven isn't what it's cracked up to be, send me back to Gimmelwald.' Enough said. When the sun is out in Gimmelwald, this pipsqueak of a village will simply take your breath away. Once a secret bolthole for hikers and adventurers keen to escape the region's worst tourist excesses, Gimmelwald gets a fair whack of foot traffic these days – though even the presence of crowds can't diminish its scintillating, classic Swiss scenery and outdoorsy charm.

The surrounding hiking trails include one down from Mürren (30 to 40 minutes) and one up from Stechelberg (1¼ hours). Cable cars are also an option (Mürren or Stechelberg Sfr5.60).

After a long summer hike, bed down at **Pension Berggeist** (☑033 855 17 30; www. berggeist.ch; dm/d Sfr15/40), a dead-simple and rustic place with bargain rooms, priceless views and sandwiches sold by the centimetre to please every pocket. Book all kinds of activities here, from skydiving to llama trekking.

Or there's the backpacking legend **Mountain Hostel** (☑033 855 17 04; www.mountain hostel.com; dm Sfr20; ◷reception 8.30am-noon & 6-11pm Apr-Nov; @) A soak in its outdoor whirlpool with stunning views hits the spot every time. (And don't forget to sign the guestbook!) **Esther's Guest House** (☑033 855 54 88; www.esthersguesthouse.ch; s/d Sfr45/100; @) is a sweet B&B with a tiny shop inside, where you can stock up on local goodies like Gimmelwald salami and Stechelberg honey.

MÜRREN
POP 438

Arrive on a clear evening when the sun hangs low on the horizon, and you'll think you've died and gone to heaven. Car-free Mürren *is* storybook Switzerland.

In summer, the **Allmendhubel funicular** (single/return Sfr12/7.40) takes you above Mürren to a panoramic restaurant. From here, you can set out on many walks, including the famous **Northface Trail** (1½ hours) via Schiltalp to the west, with spellbinding views of the Lauterbrunnen Valley and monstrous Eiger north face – bring binoculars to spy intrepid climbers. There's also a kid-friendly **Adventure Trail** (one hour).

The **tourist office** (☑033 856 86 86; www. wengen-muerren.ch; ◷8.30am-7pm Mon-Sat, to 8pm Thu, to 6pm Sun high season, to 7pm Mon-Sat, to 5pm Sun shoulder seasons, 8.30am-noon & 1-5pm Mon-Fri low season) is in the sports centre.

Sleeping options include **Eiger Guesthouse** (☑033 856 54 60; www.eigerguesthouse. com; dm Sfr40-70, d Sfr160, without bathroom Sfr120; @), by the train station, with the downstairs pub serving tasty grub; and **Hotel Jungfrau** (☑033 856 64 64; www.hoteljung frau.ch; s Sfr88-110, d Sfr270-300; @), overlooking the nursery slopes from its perch above Mürren. It dates to 1894 and has a beamed lounge with open fire. Ten out of 10 to muchlauded chalet **Hotel Alpenruh** (☑033 856 88 00; www.alpenruh-muerren.ch; s/d Sfr145/270; ◷@), for service, food and unbeatable views to Jungfrau massif.

Tham's (☑033 856 01 10; mains Sfr15-28; ◷dinner) serves Asian fare cooked by a former five-star chef who's literally taken to the hills to escape.

SCHILTHORN

There's a tremendous 360-degree panorama available from the 2970m **Schilthorn** (www. schilthorn.ch). On a clear day, you can see from Titlis to Mont Blanc and across to the German Black Forest. Yet you may find that some visitors seem more preoccupied with practising their delivery of the immortal line, 'The name's Bond – James Bond' than they are in taking in the 200 or so peaks before them. Don't be surprised: this is where some scenes from *On Her Majesty's Secret Service* were shot in the 1960s, as the fairly tacky **Touristorama** below the Piz Gloria revolving restaurant reminds you.

Buy a Sfr116 excursion trip (Half-Fare Card and Eurail Pass 50% off, Swiss Pass 65% off) going to Lauterbrunnen, Grütschalp, Mürren, Schilthorn and returning through Stechelberg to Interlaken. A return from Lauterbrunnen (via Grütschalp) and Mürren costs about Sfr100, as does the return journey via the Stechelberg cable car.

JUNGFRAUJOCH

Sure, the world wants to see Jungfraujoch (3471m) and yes, tickets are expensive, but don't let that stop you. It's a once-in-a-lifetime trip and there's a reason why two million people a year visit this Holy Grail, Europe's highest train station. The icy wilderness of swirling glaciers and 4000m turrets that unfolds is truly enchanting.

Clear good weather is essential for the trip; check www.jungfrau.ch or call ☏033 828 79 31 and don't forget warm clothing, sunglasses and sunscreen. Up top, when you tire of the view (is this possible?), dash downhill on a snow disc (free), zip across the frozen plateau on a flying fox (Sfr20), enjoy a bit of tame skiing or boarding (Sfr33), drive a team of Greenland dogs or do your best Tiger-Woods-in-moon-boots impersonation with a round of glacier golf. It isn't cheap at Sfr10 a shot, but get a hole-in-one and you win the Sfr100,000 jackpot (which, mysteriously, nobody has yet won).

From Interlaken Ost, journey time is 2½ hours each way (Sfr177.80 return, Swiss Pass/Eurail Sfr133). The last train back is at 5.50pm in summer, 4.40pm in winter. However, there's a cheaper 'good morning' ticket of Sfr153.80 (Swiss/Eurail Pass discounts available) if you take the first train (6am from Interlaken Ost) and leave the summit by 12.30pm. Between 1 November and 30 April the reduction is valid for both the 6am and 7.05am trains, and the 12.30pm restriction doesn't apply.

ZÜRICH

POP 365,400

Zürich used to be Europe's best-kept secret. Conservative bankers and perfect, medieval landmarks stood at the forefront, with no hint that a city as cool and hip as Berlin or Amsterdam lurked within this financial centre's impeccably clean streets. But somewhere between ranking as the top city in the world for quality life seven years running, hosting Europe's largest street party and

Head to **Lonely Planet** (www.lonely planet.com/switzerland/zurich) for planning advice, author recommendations, traveller reviews and insider tips.

erecting a flagship store made entirely of 16 stacked shipping containers, the secret got out and the international press started writing about the real Zürich: a cool, stylish and surprising city.

You can eat a traditional wurst while pondering a swim in the postcard-perfect lake dotted with majestic swans, inspect Le Corbusier's last architectural construction, get lost in cobbled streets lined with half-timbered, sloping landmarks, sip a cocktail atop an ancient tower with a view of the Alps or go clubbing in a former powdered-milk warehouse.

◉ Sights

Old Town   HISTORIC AREA

Explore the cobbled streets of the pedestrian Old Town lining both sides of the river.

The bank vaults beneath **Bahnhofstrasse**, the city's most elegant street, are said to be crammed with gold and silver. Indulge in affluent Züricher-watching and ogle at the luxury shops selling watches, clocks, chocolates, furs, porcelain and fashion labels galore.

On Sundays all of Zürich strolls around the lake – the locals are on to something, and one short meander tells you why (it's simply sublime, relaxing and on a clear day you'll glimpse the Alps in the distance).

Fraumünster   CHURCH

(www.fraumuenster.ch; Münsterplatz; ⊙9am-6pm May-Sep, 10am-5pm Oct-Apr) On the west bank of the Limmat River, the 13th-century Fraumünster is Zürich's most noteworthy attraction, with some of the most distinctive and attractive stained-glass windows in the world.

Grossmünster   CHURCH

(Grossmünsterplatz; www.grossmuenster.ch; ⊙9am-6pm mid-Mar–Oct, 10am-5pm Nov–mid-Mar, tower closed Sun morning mid-Mar–Oct & Sun Nov–mid-Mar) Across the river, the dual-towered Grossmünster was where, in the 16th century, the Protestant preacher Huldrych Zwingli first spread his message of 'pray and work' during the Reformation – a

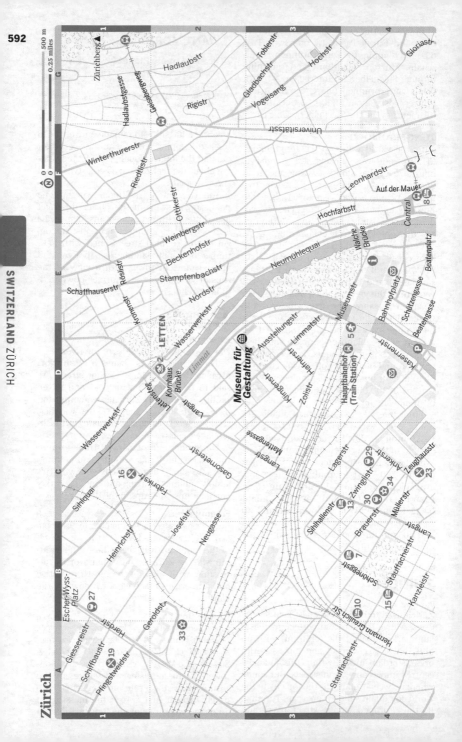

Zürich

SWITZERLAND ZÜRICH

500 m
0.25 miles

Map labels:

Zürichberg

Hadlaubstr

Hadlaubstgasse

Geissbergstr

Rigistr

Gladbachstr

Toblerstr

Hochstr

Gloriastr

Vogelsang

Universitätstr

Winterthurerstr

Riedtlistr

Ottikerstr

Leonhardstr

Auf der Mauer

Central

Weinbergstr

Beckenhofstr

Hochfarbstr

Schaffhauserstr

Rösslistr

Kronenstr

Stampfenbachstr

Nordstr

Wasserwerkstr

Neumühlequai

Walche Brücke

Museumstr

Bahnhofplatz

Beatenplatz

Schützengasse

Beatengasse

LETTEN

Wasserwerkstr

Limmat

Kornhaus Brücke

Lettensteg

Langstr

Ausstellungsstr

Hafnerstr

Limmatstr

Klingenstr

Zollstr

Kasernenstr

Museum für Gestaltung

Hauptbahnhof (Train Station)

Sihlquai

Fabrikstr

Gasometerstr

Langstr

Mattengasse

Lagerstr

Zwinglistr

Ankerstr

Zeughausstr

Heinrichstr

Josefstr

Neugasse

Sihlhallenstr

Brauerstr

Müllerstr

Langstr

Schöneggstr

Stauffacherstr

Kanzleistr

Escher-Wyss-Platz

Giessereistr

Hardstr

Schiffbaustr

Geroldstr

Hermann Greulich Str

Stauffacherstr

Pfingstweidstr

Sihlamtstr

27

19

16

33

29

13

30

34

23

7

10

15

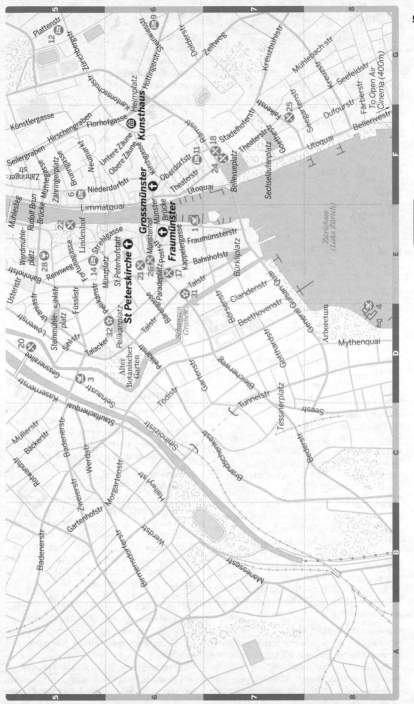

seminal period in Zürich's history. The figure glowering from the south tower of the cathedral is Charlemagne, who founded the original church at this location.

St Peterskirche CHURCH
(St Peter's Church; St Peterhofstatt; ⊘8am-6pm Mon-Fri, to 4pm Sat, 11am-5pm Sun) From any position in the city, it's impossible to overlook the 13th-century tower of St Peterskirche. Its prominent clock face, 8.7m in diameter, is Europe's largest.

Kunsthaus MUSEUM
(☑044 253 84 84; www.kunsthaus.ch; Heimplatz 1; adult/student/child Sfr18/8/free, Sun free; ⊘10am-8pm Wed-Fri, to 6pm Tue & Sat & Sun) Zürich's impressive Fine Arts Museum boasts a rich collection of Alberto Giacometti stick-figure sculptures, Monets, Van Goghs, Rodin sculptures and other 19th- and 20th-century art. Swiss artist Ferdinand Hodler is also represented.

Museum für Gestaltung MUSEUM
(☑043 446 67 67; www.museum-gestaltung. ch; Ausstellungsstrasse 60; adult/student Sfr9/6; ⊘10am-8pm Tue-Thu, to 5pm Fri-Sun) The exhibitions at this Design Museum are consistently impressive and wide-ranging –

anything from Bollywood to photographic short stories.

🏃 Activities
Zürich comes into its own in summer when its green lakeshore parks buzz with bathers, sun-seekers, in-line skaters, footballers, lovers, picnickers, party animals, preeners and police patrolling on rollerblades!

Swimming Areas SWIMMING
(admission Sfr6; ⊘9am-7pm May & Sep, to 8pm Jun-Aug) From May to mid-September, outdoor swimming areas – think a rectangular wooden pier partly covered by a pavilion – open around the lake and up the Limmat River. Many offer massages, yoga and saunas, as well as snacks. Our favourites are trendy **Seebad Enge** (☑044 201 38 89; www. seebadenge.ch; Mythenquai 95), where the bar opens until midnight in fine weather; and **Letten** (☑044 362 92 00; Lettensteg 10; admission free), where hip Züri-Westers swim, barbecue, skateboard, play volleyball or just drink and hang out on the grass and concrete.

Along the river, 19th-century **Frauenbad** (Stadthausquai) is open to women only during the day, and **Männerbad** (Schanzengraben) is men-only. Both open their trendy bars to both sexes at night – leave shoes at the entrance and drink with feet dipped in the water!

✨ Festivals & Events

Zürich celebrates spring with **Sechseläuten** (www.sechselaeuten.ch), which sees guild members in historical costume parade down the streets on the third Monday in April, climaxing with the burning of a fireworks-filled 'snowman' (Böögg) to mark winter's end.

August's **Street Parade** (www.street-parade.ch) is Europe's largest street party in any given year, attracting well over half a million ravers.

🛏 Sleeping

Pension für Dich PENSION **$**
(☑044 317 91 60; www.fuerdich.ch; Stauffacherstrasse 141; d without bathroom from Sfr95; ☺🛜) These simple but fabulous apartments have been converted into comfy rooms – think retro furnishings meets Ikea. A number of rooms have balconies, and breakfast can be had for a steal at its cafe downstairs, plus you're smack in the centre of the Kreis 4 nightlife action. There's no reception – just head to the bar in the cafe.

Hotel Widder HOTEL **$$$**
(☑044 224 25 26; www.widderhotel.ch; Rennweg 7; s/d from Sfr530/725; P✹@🛜) A stylish hotel in the equally grand Augustiner district, the Widder is a pleasing fusion of modernity and traditional charm. Rooms and public areas across the eight town houses that make up this place are stuffed with art and designer furniture.

ONCE A TRUCK TARPAULIN, NOW A BAG

Freitag (☑043-3669520; Geroldstrasse 17; 11am-7.30pm Mon-Fri, 11am-5pm Sat), run by two ambitious Swiss dudes, proves everything can have a second life. Choose an industrial-looking messenger bag, travelling tote or women's purse made from 100% recycled materials (truck tarps, seat belts etc) in this flagship store housed in a 26m-high stack of retired shipping containers in Züri-West. Even if you can't afford the pricey bags, hike up to the alfresco viewing platform in the top container.

Camping Seebucht CAMPING GROUND **$**
(☑044 482 16 12; www.camping-zurich.ch; Seestrasse 559; campsites per adult/tent Sfr7.50/11; ☺May-Sep) On the western shore of the lake, 4km from the city centre, this camping ground has good facilities. Take bus 161 or 165 from Bürkliplatz.

Hotel Foyer Hottingen HOTEL **$**
(☑044 256 19 19; www.hotel-foyer-hottingen.ch; Hottingerstrasse 31; dm from Sfr45, s from Sfr130, without bathroom from Sfr115; ☺) Rooms are clinical but excellent value; some have a balcony. Each floor has showers and communal kitchen, and on the top floor is a dorm for women only, with a roof terrace.

SYHA hostel HOSTEL **$**
(☑043 399 78 00; www.youthhostel.ch; Mütschellenstrasse 114, Wollishofen; dm from Sfr42, s/d from Sfr107/127; @) This bulbous, purple-red hostel features a swish 24-hour reception/dining hall, flat-screen TVs and sparkling modern bathrooms. Dorms are small. Take tram 7 to Morgental, or S-Bahn to Wollishofen.

Dakini B&B **$**
(☑044 291 42 20; www.dakini.ch; Brauerstrasse 87; s/d from Sfr80/140; ☺@) This relaxed B&B attracts a bohemian crowd of artists and performers, academics and trendy tourists who don't bat an eyelid at its location near the red-light district. Take tram 8 to Bäckeranlange.

Hotel Rothaus HOTEL **$$**
(☑043 322 10 58; www.hotelrothaus.ch; Sihlhallenstrasse 1; s/d from Sfr100/130; ☺🛜) Smack in the middle of the Langstrasse action, you'd never guess this cheerful red brick place was once a brothel. A variety of fresh, airy rooms are complemented by a busy little eatery-bar downstairs.

Hotel Otter HOTEL **$$**
(☑044 251 22 07; www.wueste.ch; Oberdorfstrasse 7; s/d/apt from Sfr125/155/200; 🛜) A true gem, the Otter has 17 rooms variously decorated with pink satin sheets and plastic beads, raised beds, wall murals and in one instance a hammock. A popular bar, the Wüste, is downstairs.

Hotel du Thèâtre HOTEL **$**
(☑044-2672670; www.hotel-du-theatre.ch; Seilergraben 69; s/d from Sfr100/110; 🛜) Located in the lively Niederdorf and within walking distance to the train station, this friendly boutique hotel is decorated with designer furniture and old film stills (an ode to the hotel's past – in the 1950s it was a combined

theatre and hotel). Tranquillity prevails here and the staff are more than happy to give guests insider tips on local restaurants and bars.

Hotel Greulich
HOTEL $$$

(☑043 243 42 43; www.greulich.ch; Hermann Greulich Strasse 56; s/d from Sfr190/255; ☺🖥) The curving blue-grey walls lend these designer digs in a quieter part of Kreis 4 a retro art deco touch. Minimalist off-white rooms are laid out in facing bungalows along two sides of an austere courtyard.

Hotel Plattenhof
HOTEL $$$

(☑044 251 19 10; www.plattenhof.ch; Plattenstrasse 26; s/d from Sfr190/255; 🅿🖥) This place manages to be cool without looking pretentious. It features a youthful, vaguely Japanese style, with low beds and mood lighting in its newest rooms. Even the older rooms are stylishly minimalist. Take tram 6 to Platte.

City Backpacker
HOSTEL $

(☑044 251 90 15; www.city-backpacker.ch; Niederdorfstrasse 5; dm Sfr35, s/d from Sfr75/115; ☺reception closed noon-3pm; @) This youthful party hostel is friendly and well equipped, if a trifle cramped. Overcome the claustrophobia in summer by hanging out on the roof terrace – the best spot in Zürich to wind down at sunset with a few cold beers.

✗ Eating

Zürich has a thriving cafe culture and hundreds of restaurants – explore Niederdorfstrasse and its nearby backstreets.

Zeughauskeller
SWISS $$

(☑044 211 26 90; www.zeughauskeller.ch; Bahnhofstrasse 28a; mains Sfr18-35; ☺11.30am-11pm; ✑) The menu at this huge, atmospheric beer hall – set inside a former armoury (look for the shields and various protective antiques hanging from the walls) – offers 20 different kinds of sausages in eight languages, as well as numerous other Swiss specialities of a carnivorous and vegetarian variety. It's a local institution and well loved by the lunch crowd, so expect queues during the week between noon and 2pm.

Cafe für Dich
CAFE $

(☑044 317 91 60 Stauffacherstrasse 141; Zähringerplatz 11; snacks Sfr5-9; ☺6pm-midnight Mon, 9am-midnight Tue-Sun) This laid-back cafe in Kreis 4 could easily be in San Francisco or Brooklyn, with its no-nonsense come-and-hang-out vibe. Occasional one-man-band live music and poetry readings keep the

atmosphere serious but fun, and it's a fab spot to grab a tea, single malt, local beer or a small snack (olives, quiches) throughout the day and eve.

Restaurant Zum Kropf
SWISS $$

(☑044 221 18 05; www.zumkropf.ch; In Gassen 16; mains Sfr23-48; ☺closed Sun) Notable for its historic interior, with marble columns, stained glass and ceiling murals, Kropf has been favoured by locals since 1888 for its hearty Swiss staples and fine beers.

Les Halles
INTERNATIONAL $$

(☑044 273 11 25; www.les-halles.ch; Pfingstweidstrasse 6; mains Sfr22-31; ☺11am-midnight Mon-Wed, to 1am Thu-Sat) One of several chirpy barrestaurants in revamped factory buildings, this is the best place in town to tuck into *moules mit frites* (mussels and fries). Hang at the bustling bar and shop at the market.

Reithalle
INTERNATIONAL $$

(☑044 212 07 66; www.restaurant-reithalle.ch; Gessnerallee 8; mains Sfr22-35; ☺lunch & dinner Mon-Fri, dinner Sat & Sun) Fancy dining in stables in a former barracks complex? The walls at this boisterous, convivial spot are still lined with the cavalry horses' feeding and drinking troughs. Cuisine is copious Swiss and international, and tables are cleared at 11.30pm when the place morphs into a dance club.

Alpenrose
SWISS $$

(☑044 271 39 19; Fabrikstrasse 12; mains Sfr24-42; ☺Mon-Sat) With its timber-clad walls, 'no polka dancing' warning and fine cuisine from regions all over Switzerland, this place makes for an inspired meal out. Try risotto from Ticino, *pizokel* (a kind of long and especially savoury *spätzli,* or dumpling) from Graubünden or freshly fished local perch filets. Reservations essential.

Seidenspinner
MODERN EUROPEAN $$$

(☑044 241 07 00; www.seidenspinner.ch; Ankerstrasse 120; mains Sfr29-55; ☺lunch & dinner Tue-Fri, dinner Sat) A favourite with the media and fashion crowd, Silk-spinner boasts an extravagant interior with huge flower arrangements and shards of mirrored glass. European cooking dominates.

Kronenhalle
SWISS $$$

(☑044 251 66 69; Rämistrasse 4; mains Sfr32-87; ☺lunch & dinner) Haunt of city movers and shakers in suits, with an old-world feel, the Crown Hall is a brasserie where impeccably mannered waiters move discreetly beneath Chagall, Miro, Matisse and Picasso originals.

Café Sprüngli   SWISS $

(☑044 224 47 31; www.spruengli.ch; Bahnhofstrasse 21; mains Sfr9-15; ◷7am-6.30pm Mon-Fri, 8am-6pm Sat, 9.30am-5.30pm Sun) Indulge in cakes, chocolate and coffee at this epicentre of sweet Switzerland, in business since 1836. You can have a light lunch too but whatever you do, don't fail to check out the chocolate shop heaven around the corner on Paradeplatz.

Tibits by Hiltl   INTERNATIONAL $

(☑044 260 32 22; www.tibits.ch; Seefeldstrasse 2; meals per 100g Sfr3.80, mains from Sfr10; ◷6.30am-midnight Mon-Fri, 8am-midnight Sat, 9am-midnight Sun; ☑) Tibits is where with-it, health-conscious Zürichers eat light. Think tasty vegetarian buffet, fresh fruit juices, coffees and cake – take your pick and pay at the counter.

Sternen Grill   SWISS $

(Theatrestrasse 22; snacks from Sfr6; ◷11.30am-midnight) This is the city's most famous – and busiest – sausage stand; just follow the crowds streaming into Bellevueplatz for a tasty greasefest.

Schipfe 16   INTERNATIONAL $

(☑044 211 21 22; Schipfe 16; menus Sfr17-20; ◷lunch Mon-Fri) Overlooking the Limmat River from the historic Schipfe area, Schipfe 16 is a good-natured canteen-style spot for a humble speed lunch.

♟ Drinking & Entertainment

Buzzing drinking options congregate in the happening Kreis 4 district (the former red light district known as the Langstrasse area – it's safe to wander though you may be offered drugs or sex – with loads of popular bars quietly humming off its side streets) and Kreis 5 district, together known as Züri-West. Mid-May to mid-September, Wednesday to Sunday, the trendy water bars at the **lake baths** are hot places to hang bare-footed. Clubbers should dress well and be prepared to cough up Sfr15 to Sfr30 admission.

For a month from mid-July, there's an extremely popular waterside **open-air cinema** (☑0800 078078; www.orangecinema.ch; Zürichhorn).

Jules Verne Panorama Bar   BAR

(☑044-8886666; Uraniastrasse 9; ◷11am-midnight Mon-Fri, 11.30am-midnight Sat, 4-11pm Sun) Served on the top floor of a round observatory tower, the jumbo cocktails are almost as impressive as the 360-degree view. Best for an early drink around sunset – later in the evening elbow-room is non-existent.

Longstreet Bar   BAR

(☑044 241 21 72; www.longstreetbar.ch; Langstrasse 92; ◷8pm-3am Tue-Thu, to 4am Fri & Sat, to 2am Sun) Run by the guy seemingly behind half Zürich's nightlife, this purple-felt lined one-time cabaret is now a throbbing music bar with DJs. Count the thousands of light bulbs.

Liquid   CLUB

(☑079 446 73 66; www.liquid-bar.ch; Zwinglistrasse 12; ◷5pm-1am Mon-Thu, to 3am Fri, 7pm-3am Sat) With its striped wallpaper and plastic chairs moulded in the shape of boiled eggs broken in half, this is kitsch at its best – a hip backdrop for lounge-oriented music nights.

Hard One   BAR

(☑044 444 10 00; www.hardone.ch; Hardstrasse 260; admission free-Sfr15; ◷6pm-2am Tue-Thu, to 4am Fri & Sat) The punters flock to this glass cube of a lounge bar for great views and weekend gigs.

Zukunft   CLUB

(www.zukunft.ch; Dienerstrasse 33; ◷11pm-late Thu-Sat) Look for a modest queue (there's no name) and head downstairs to this literally underground dance bar, where a broad range of electro and other dance music keep a mixed crowd happy.

Supermarket   CLUB

(☑044 440 20 05; www.supermarket.li; Geroldstrasse 17; ◷11pm-late Thu-Sat) Looking like an innocent little house, Supermarket boasts three cosy lounge bars around the dance floor, a covered back courtyard and an interesting roster of DJs playing house. The crowd is mid-20s.

Kaufleuten   CLUB

(☑044-2253322; Pelikanplatz 18; ◷from 11pm Thu-Sat) Two floors, four bars and a dance floor adjacent to the art deco stage of this former theatre keep this a perennial favourite among all age groups year after year. Dress to impress.

Alte Börse   CLUB

(www.alteboerse.com; Bleicherweg 5; ◷10pm-late Thu-Sat) Hundreds of dance fanatics cram into this club in a respectable town-centre building for intense electronic sessions with DJs from all over the world. It also gets in occasional live acts.

ⓘ Information

Police station (☑044 216 71 11; Bahnhofquai 3)
Post office (train station; ◷7am-9pm)

University Hospital (☎044 255 11 11, 044 255 21 11; www.usz.ch; Rämistrasse 100) Casualty medical service.

Zürich Tourism (☎044 215 40 00, hotel reservations 044 215 40 40; www.zuerich.com; train station; ☺8am-8.30pm Mon-Sat, 8.30am-6.30pm Sun May-Oct, 8.30am-7pm Mon-Sat, 9am-6.30pm Sun Nov-Apr)

ZürichCard (per 24/72hr Sfr17/24) Discount card available from the tourist office and airport train station; provides free public transport, free museum admission and more.

ℹ Getting There & Away

AIR Zürich airport (ZRH; ☎043 816 22 11; www.zurich-airport.com), 10km north of the centre, is a small international hub with two terminals.

CAR The A3 approaches Zürich from the south along the shore of Lake Zürich. The A1 is the fastest route from Bern and Basel.

TRAIN Direct daily trains run to Stuttgart (Sfr76, three hours), Munich (Sfr104, 4½ hours) and Innsbruck (Sfr79, four hours) plus many other international destinations. There are regular direct departures to most major Swiss towns, such as Lucerne (Sfr23, 46 to 50 minutes), Bern (Sfr46, 57 minutes) and Basel (Sfr31, 55 minutes).

ℹ Getting Around

TO/FROM THE AIRPORT Up to nine trains an hour yo-yo between the airport and main train station between 6am and midnight (Sfr6, nine to 14 minutes).

BICYCLE City bikes (www.zuerirollt.ch) can be picked up at **Velogate** (train station; ☺8am-9.30pm) for free if you bring the bike back after six hours or pay Sfr5 per day.

BOAT April to October **lake steamers** (☎044 487 13 33; www.zsg.ch) depart from Bürkliplatz.

PUBLIC TRANSPORT There is a comprehensive, unified bus, tram and S-Bahn service in the city, which includes boats plying the Limmat River. Short trips under five stops are Sfr2.40. A 24-hour pass for the centre is Sfr7.80. For unlimited travel within the canton, including extended tours of the lake, a day pass costs Sfr30.40.

NORTHERN SWITZERLAND

This region is left off most people's Switzerland itineraries – precisely why you should visit! Sure, it is known for industry and commerce, but it also has some great attractions. Breathe in the sweet (OK slightly stinky) odours of black-and-white cows as you roll through the bucolic countryside. Take time to explore the tiny rural towns set among green rolling hills, and on Lake Constance (Bodensee) and the Rhine (Rhein) River on the German border.

Basel

POP 165,100

Strangely, given its northerly location, Basel has some of the hottest weather in the country, so you should visit in the summer. When the mercury starts rising the city sheds its notorious reserve and just cuts loose. As locals bob along in the fast-moving Rhine River, cool off in the city's numerous fountains, whiz by on motor scooters, and dine and drink on overcrowded pavements, you could almost be in Italy, rather than on the dual border with France and Germany.

Basel's (Bâle in French) idyllic Old Town and many enticing galleries and museums are top draws any time of year. The famous Renaissance humanist Erasmus of Rotterdam was associated with the city and his tomb rests in the cathedral.

◉ Sights & Activities

Old Town   HISTORIC AREA

With its cobbled streets, colourful fountains, medieval churches and stately buildings, the Old Town is a wonderful place to wander. In Marktplatz check out the impressive rust-coloured **Rathaus** (Town Hall), with frescoed courtyard. The 12th-century **Münster** (cathedral; ☺10am-5pm), southeast from Marktplatz, is another highlight, with Gothic spires and Romanesque St Gallus doorway.

Theaterplatz is a crowd-pleaser, with a curious **fountain**, designed by Swiss sculptor Jean Tinguely. His madcap scrap-metal machines perform a peculiar water dance, delighting children and weary travellers alike. Also check out the 700-year-old **Spalentor** gate tower, a remnant of the town's old city walls, with a massive portal and grotesque gargoyles.

Kunstmuseum   ART MUSEUM

(Museum of Fine Arts; ☎061 206 62 62; www.kunstmuseumbasel.ch; St Alban-Graben 16; adult/student/child Sfr12.50/5/free, 1st Sun of month free; ☺10am-5pm Tue-Sun) Art lovers can ogle at Switzerland's largest art collection, including works by Klee and Picasso.

Fondation Beyeler   ART MUSEUM

(☎061 645 97 00; www.beyeler.com; Baselstrasse 101, Riehen; adult/student/child Sfr25/12/6;

☺10am-6pm, to 8pm Wed) The art space to really knock your socks off is the Fondation Beyeler, in an open-plan building by Italian architect Renzo Piano. The quality of its 19th- and 20th-century paintings is matched only by the way Miró and Max Ernst sculptures are juxtaposed with similar tribal figures. Take tram 6 to Riehen.

★ Festivals & Events

Basel's huge **Fasnacht** spring carnival kicks off at 4am on the Monday after Ash Wednesday with the **Morgestraich**: streetlights are extinguished and a procession of masked, costumed revellers wends its way through town. Restaurants and bars stay open all night and the streets positively throb with festivities.

🛏 Sleeping

Hotels are often full during Basel's trade fairs and conventions; book ahead. Guests receive a free Mobility Pass upon checking in, meaning free travel on public transport.

Hotel Stadthof   HOTEL $

(✆061 261 87 11; www.stadthof.ch; Gerbergasse 84; s/d from Sfr75/125) Book ahead to snag a room at this spartan but decent central hotel, located above a pizzeria on an Old Town square. The cheaper rooms share toilet and shower.

Au Violon   HOTEL $

(✆061 269 87 11; www.au-violon.com; Im Lohnhof 4; s/d from Sfr120/140; ❀🐾) Quaint, atmospheric Au Violon was a prison from 1835 to 1995. Most of the rooms are two cells rolled into one and overlook a cobblestone courtyard or the cathedral. Sitting atop a leafy hilltop, its restaurant is equally appealing.

Hotel Krafft   HOTEL $

(✆061 690 91 30; www.hotelkrafft.ch; Rheingasse 12; s/d from Sfr75/125; 🐾) Design-savvy urbanites adore this place. Sculptural chandeliers dangle in the creaky-floored dining room (for fine food) overlooking the Rhine, and stainless-steel water bars adorn each landing of the spiral stairs.

Basel Backpack   HOSTEL $

(✆061 333 00 37; www.baselbackpack.ch; Dornacherstrasse 192; dm Sfr32, s/d from Sfr80/100; ❀@) Converted from a factory, this independent hostel south of the main train station has cheerful, colour-coded eight-bed dorms and more sedate doubles and family rooms.

SYHA Basel City Youth Hostel   HOSTEL $

(✆061 365 99 60; www.youthhostel.ch/basel.city; Pfeffingerstrasse 8; dm Sfr35.50, s/d Sfr79/95; ☺reception 7am-noon & 3-11pm; @) A convenient hostel in former post office buildings, it's across from the train station. Rooms have up to four beds and there's space aplenty – including a summertime interior courtyard.

✕ Eating

Atrio Vulcanelli   INTERNATIONAL $$

(✆061 683 06 80; www.vulcanelli.ch; Erlenmattstrasse 5; mains Sfr16-36; ☺dinner Wed-Sat) Nautical and cabaret meets bohemian in this vast, high-ceilinged space-cum-bistro north of the Old Town. Its hodgepodge of creaky wood tables and decadent candelabras keeps things cosy and the seasonal cuisine is spot on. In summer after dinner, head over to the open-air **beach bar** (☺10pm-5am Fri & Sat) down the street, which morphs into a club in the wee hours.

Acqua   ITALIAN $$

(✆061 564 66 66; www.acquabasilea.ch; Binningerstrasse 14; mains Sfr17-42; ☺lunch & dinner Tue-Fri, dinner Sat) For a glam postindustrial experience, head to these converted waterworks. Cuisine is Tuscan and Basel's beautiful people drink in the attached lounge bar or on the summer terrace.

Druck Punkt   BISTRO $$

(✆061 261 50 22; St Johanns Vorstadt 19; mains Sfr17-25; ☺Mon-Fri) This converted print shop makes an unpretentious bistro, with chalky walls and heavy wooden tables.

Parterre   INTERNATIONAL $$

(✆061 695 89 98; www.parterre.net; Klybeckstrasse 1b; mains Sfr16-38; ☺dinner Mon-Sat) Unusual dishes such as lake salmon in saffron sauce with potato gratin and cabbage stud the menu in this slightly alternative place overlooking a park. Snacks and light meals are served throughout the day.

Oliv   MEDITERRANEAN $$

(✆061 283 03 03; www.restaurantoliv.ch; Bachlettenstrasse 1; mains Sfr25-39; ☺lunch & dinner Tue-Fri, dinner Sat) A trendy hang-out not far from the zoo, Oliv leans towards fresh and varied Mediterranean cooking. Unusually, dainty appetites can order half portions.

St Alban Stübli   SWISS $$$

(✆061 272 54 15; www.st-alban-stuebli.ch; St Alban Vorstadt 74; mains Sfr40-59; ☺Mon-Fri) Set in a lovely quiet street, this is your quintessential cosy local tavern with dim yellow lighting,

Basel

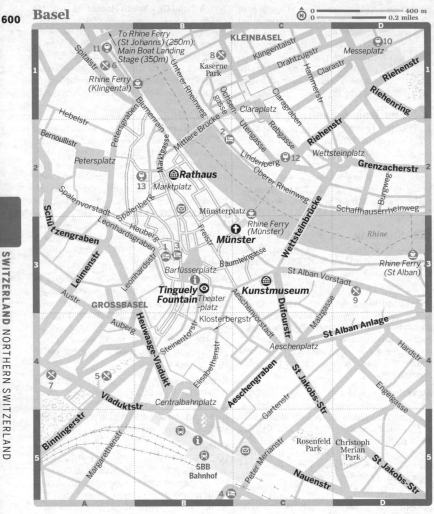

plenty of timber and fine linen. Food fuses local with French.

🍷 Drinking & Entertainment

Steinenvorstadt and Barfüsserplatz teem with teens and 20-somethings on the weekends. A faint whiff of grunge floats around Kleinbasel, the area around Rheingasse and Utengasse, with a few watering holes and something of a red-light zone to lend it edge.

Bar Rouge
BAR

(☎061 361 30 21; www.barrouge.ch; Level 31, Messeplatz 10; ☺5pm-1am Mon-Wed, to 2am Thu, to 4am Fri & Sat) This plush red bar with panoramic views from the 31st floor of the ugly glass Messeturm (trade fair tower) is the city's most memorable. Hipsters, and a few suits early on weekday evenings, come to appreciate the regular DJs and films.

Hirscheneck
BAR

(☎061 692 73 33; Lindenberg 23; ☺9am-midnight Sun-Thu, 10am-2am Fri & Sat) A relaxed, grungy, almost knockabout place with an urban vibe (try to spot someone *without* piercings), this corner bar has tables on the footpath and regular gigs and DJs.

Basel

Zum Roten Engel   CAFE-BAR
(☏061 261 20 08; Andreasplatz 15; ☺9am-midnight Mon-Sat, 10am-10pm Sun) Spilling onto an irresistible, tiny cobblestone square, this student haunt is perfect for a latte by day or glass of wine come dusk.

Cargo-Bar   CLUB
(☏061 321 00 72; www.cargobar.ch; St Johanns Rheinweg 46; ☺4pm-1am Sun-Thu, to 2.30am Fri & Sat) A nice halfway house between cool and alternative, located in a tucked-away spot on the river. There are lots of art installations, live gigs, video shows and DJs.

❶ Information

Post office (Rüdengasse 1; ☺7.30am-6.30pm Mon-Wed, to 7pm Thu-Fri, 8am-5pm Sat)

Tourist office (☏061 268 68 68; www.basel. com; Stadt-Casino, Barfüsserplatz, Steinenberg 14; ☺8.30am-6.30pm Mon-Fri, 9am-5pm Sat, 9am-4pm Sun)

❶ Getting There & Away

AIR The **EuroAirport** (BSL or MLH; ☏061 325 31 11; www.euroairport.com), 5km northwest of town in France, is the main airport for Basel.

TRAIN Basel is a major European rail hub, with two main train stations: the Swiss-French SBB (south bank) and the BBF (north bank) for trains to/from Germany.

Destinations include Paris (from Sfr70, 3½ to five hours). Local trains to the Black Forest stop only at BBF, though fast EC services stop at SBB too. Main destinations along this route are Amsterdam (from Sfr180, eight hours, daily), Frankfurt (from Sfr137, three hours, daily) and Hamburg (from Sfr220, 6½ to 7½ hours, daily).

Services within Switzerland from SBB include Geneva (Sfr69, 2¾ hours, twice hourly) and Zürich (Sfr31, 55 minutes to 1¾ hours, twice hourly).

❶ Getting Around

Bus 50 links the airport and SBB train station (Sfr6.60, 20 minutes). The trip by **taxi** (☏061 691 77 88) costs around Sfr40.

Appenzellerland

The Appenzellers are the butt of many a cruel joke by their fellow Swiss, a little like Tasmanians in Australia or Newfoundlanders in Canada. As Swiss Germans say, Appenzellers *hätte ä langi Laitig* (have a very long cable). It takes a while after you tug for them to get the message. And indeed, there's no denying that the Appenzell canton is still firmly rooted in tradition: Innerrhoden continues to hold a yearly open-air parliament and didn't permit women to vote until 1991.

Such devotion to rural tradition has an upside: locals go to great lengths to preserve their heritage. This area of impossibly green valleys, thick forests and mighty mountains is dotted with timeless villages and crisscrossed by endless hiking and cycling paths.

The pastel-hued village of **Appenzell** is a feast for the eyes and the stomach. Behind the gaily decorative coloured facades of its traditional buildings lie cafes, cake shops, cheese shops, delicatessens, butchers and restaurants all offering local specialities. Don your lazy hat and enjoy a long slow lunch and wander!

The train station is 400m from the town centre, home to the **tourist office** (☏071 788 96 41; www.appenzell.ch; Hauptgasse 4; ☺9am-noon & 1.30-6pm Mon-Fri, 10am-noon & 2-5pm Sat & Sun Apr-Oct, 9am-noon & 2-5pm Mon-Fri, 2-5pm Sat & Sun Nov-Mar).

Hotel Appenzell (☏071 788 15 15; www. hotel-appenzell.ch; Landsgemeindeplatz; s/d Sfr130/220; ☜) sits in a brightly decorated, typical Appenzeller building and is a solid choice to both sleep and sample seasonal cuisine, including vegetarian dishes and the local strong-smelling Appenzell cheese.

There is a train to St Gallen (Sfr10.80, 50 minutes, twice hourly).

SHAFFHAUSEN & THE RHINE

Schaffhausen is the kind of quaint medieval town one more readily associates with Germany (perhaps no coincidence given how close the border is). Ornate frescos and oriel windows adorn pastel-coloured houses in the pedestrian-only Altstadt (Old Town), home to the **tourist office** (☑052 632 40 20; www.schaffhausen-tourismus.ch, www.shtotal.info; Herrenacker 15; ⊙9.30am-6pm Mon-Fri, to 4pm Sat Jun-Sep, to 2pm Sun Jun-Aug, to 5pm Mon-Fri, to 1pm Sat Oct-May).

Prime views preen their feathers atop the 16th-century **Munot fortress** (admission free; ⊙8am-8pm May-Sep, 9am-5pm Oct-Apr), a 15-minute uphill walk through vineyards from town.

Westward along the river on foot (40 minutes) or aboard bus 1 to Neuhausen is **Rheinfall** (Rhine Falls), waterfalls that, though only 23m tall, are deemed Europe's largest. The amount of water thundering down is extraordinary.

The 45km **boat trip** (☑052 634 08 88; www.urh.ch or www.riverticket.ch; Freier Platz; single/return Sfr21/30; ⊙Mar-Oct) from Schaffhausen to Konstanz sails past one of the Rhine's more beautiful stretches. It passes meadows, castles and ancient villages, including **Stein am Rhein**, 20km to the east, where you could easily wear out your camera snapping pictures of the buildings in the picture-perfect Rathausplatz.

Direct hourly trains run to/from Schaffhausen and Zürich (Sfr18.20, 40 minutes).

TICINO

This is the Switzerland that Heidi never mentioned: the summer air is rich, hot (and smokefree thanks to a cantonwide ban on smoking in public places since 2007) and the peacock-proud posers propel their scooters in and out of traffic. Italian weather, Italian style. And that's not to mention the Italian ice cream, Italian pizza, Italian architecture and Italian language.

South of the Alps, Ticino (Tessin in German and French) has a distinct look. The canton manages to perfectly fuse Swiss cool with Italian passion, as evidenced by a lusty love for Italian comfort food and full-bodied wines that's balanced by a healthy respect for rules and regulations.

Locarno

POP 15,600

The rambling red enclave of Italianate town houses, piazzas and arcades ending at the northern end of Lake Maggiore, coupled with more hours of sunshine than anywhere else in Switzerland, give this laid-back town a summer resort atmosphere. The lowest town in Switzerland, it seemed like a soothing spot to host the 1925 peace conference that was intended to bring stability to Europe after WWI.

Five minutes' walk west of the train station is the town's heart, Piazza Grande, and

the **tourist office** (☑091 791 00 91; www.maggiore.ch; Largo Zorzi 1; ⊙9am-6pm Mon-Fri, 10am-6pm Sat, 10am-1.30pm & 2.30-5pm Sun mid-Mar–Oct, 9.30am-noon & 1.30-5pm Mon-Fri, 10am-noon & 1.30-5pm Sat Nov–mid-Mar) nearby.

⊙ Sights & Activities

Madonna del Sasso   SANCTUARY

Don't miss the formidable Madonna del Sasso, located up on the hill, with panoramic views of the lake and town. The sanctuary was built after the Virgin Mary allegedly appeared in a vision in 1480. It features a church with 15th-century paintings, a small museum and several distinctive statues.

There is a funicular from the town centre, but the 20-minute climb is not demanding (take Via al Sasso off Via Cappuccini) and you pass some shrines on the way.

✯ Festivals & Events

In August more than 150,000 film buffs hit town for the two-week **International Film Festival** (www.pardo.ch). Cinemas are used during the day but at night films are shown in the open-air on a giant screen in the Piazza Grande.

🛏 Sleeping

Camping Delta   CAMPING GROUND $

(☑091 751 60 81; www.campingdelta.com; Via Respini 7; campsites Sfr47-57, plus per adult/senior & student/child Sfr20/17/6; ⊙Mar-Oct) Although pricey, this camping ground has great facilities and is brilliantly located between the shores of Lago Maggiore and the Maggia River.

Vecchia Locarno
HOTEL $

(☑091 751 65 02; www.hotel-vecchia-locarno. ch; Via della Motta 10; s/d without bathroom from Sfr55/100) Rooms are gathered around a sunny internal courtyard, evoking a Mediterranean mood, and some have Old Town views. Digs are simple but comfortable.

✗ Eating & Drinking

Lake Maggiore has a great variety of fresh and tasty fish, including *persico* (perch) and *corigone* (whitefish).

Osteria Chiara
ITALIAN $$

(☑091 743 32 96; Vicolo della Chiara 1; mains Sfr16-30; ⊗Tue-Sat) Tucked away on a cobbled lane, this has all the cosy feel of a grotto. Sit at granite tables beneath the pergola or at timber tables by the fireplace for chunky pasta and mostly meat dishes. From the lake follow the signs up Vicolo dei Nessi.

Bar Sport
BAR

(Via della Posta 4; ⊗8am-1am Mon-Fri, 10am-1am Sat, 2pm-1am Sun) A run-of-the-mill place by day, this rough-and-tumble bar with red-walled dance space out the back and beer garden is a huge hit with night owls. A few other bars loiter nearby.

❶ Getting There & Away

The St Gotthard Pass provides the road link (A2) to central Switzerland. There are trains from Brig (Sfr51, 2½ hours, hourly) that pass through Italy en route; change trains at Domodossola across the border and bring your passport.

THESE BOOTS ARE MADE FOR WALKING...NOT

Hiking trails abound around Appenzell. One more unusual one is the **Barefoot Path** from Gonten, 5km west of Appenzell, to Gontenbad (one hour), for which you really don't need shoes – think lush green moors and meadows. In Gontenbad, dip in mud-laden water from the moors at **Natur-Moorbad** (☑071 795 31 23; www.naturmoorbad.ch; admission Sfr20; Gontenbad), a moor bath dating to 1740, whose wholly natural products relieve stress or skin conditions (adding in nettles, ferns and other plants) or simply serve to luxuriate loved ones with sweet rose baths (Sfr86 for two).

Lugano

POP 51.900

There is a distinct vibrant snappiness in the air in Lugano, Switzerland's southernmost tourist town, where visitors unravel the spaghetti maze of cobblestone streets while locals toil in stuffy banks – this is the country's third-most important banking centre.

A sophisticated slice of Italian life with colourful markets, upmarket shops, interlocking *piazze* and lakeside parks, lucky Lugano lounges on the northern shore of Lake Lugano, at the feet of Mounts San Salvatore and Bré. Read: a superb base for lake trips, water sports and hillside hikes.

The Centro Storico (Old Town) is a 10-minute walk downhill from the train station; take the stairs or the funicular (Sfr1.10). The **tourist office** (☑091 913 32 32; www.lugano-tourism.ch; ⊗9am-7pm Mon-Fri, to 5pm Sat, 10am-5pm Sun Apr-Oct, 9am-noon & 2-5.30pm Mon-Fri, 10am-12.30pm & 1.30-5pm Sat Nov-Mar) runs a **booth** (⊗2-7pm Mon-Sat) at the station.

◉ Sights & Activities

Wander through the mostly porticoed lanes woven around the busy main square, Piazza della Riforma (which is even more lively when the Tuesday- and Friday-morning markets are held). Via Nassa is the main shopping street and indicates there is no shortage of cash in this town.

Chiesa di Santa Maria degli Angioli CHURCH
(St Mary of the Angels; Piazza Luini; ⊗8am-5pm) The simple Romanesque Chiesa di Santa Maria degli Angioli, against which a now-crumbling former hotel was built, contains two frescos by Bernardino Luini dating from 1529. Covering the entire wall that divides the church in two is a grand didactic illustration of the Crucifixion. The closer you look, the more scenes of Christ's Passion are revealed, along with others of Christ being taken down from the Cross and the Resurrection. The power and vivacity of the colours are astounding.

Museo del Cioccolato Alprose MUSEUM
(☑091 611 88 88; www.alprose.ch; Via Rompada 36, Caslano; adult/child Sfr3/1; ⊗9am-5.30pm Mon-Fri, to 4.30pm Sat & Sun) Chomp on a chocolate-coated history lesson: watch the sweet substance being made and taste it for free. Get there by the Ferrovia Ponte Tresa train (Sfr7).

WORTH A TRIP

BELLINZONA'S UNESCO CASTLES

Ticino's capital is a quiet stunner. Strategically placed at the conversion point of several valleys leading down from the Alps, Bellinzona is visually unique. Inhabited since Neolithic times, it is dominated by three grey-stone, fairy-tale medieval castles. But Bellinzona has a surprisingly low tourist profile, in spite of its castles together forming a Unesco World Heritage site.

The **tourist office** (☑091 825 21 31; www.bellinzonaturismo.ch; Piazza Nosetto; ☺9am-6pm Mon-Fri, to noon Sat, reduced hours in winter), in the restored Renaissance town hall, can provide information on Bellinzona and the whole canton.

You can roam the ramparts of the two larger castles, **Castelgrande** or **Castello di Montebello**, both of which are still in great condition and offer panoramic views of the town and countryside. **Castello di Sasso Corbaro** is situated 230m above town and can easily be reached by road from Castello di Montebello or by Via Ospedale.

Alternatively, seize the rare opportunity to dine in a Unesco World Heritage site at medieval **Castelgrande** (☑091 826 23 53; www.castelgrande.ch; Castelgrande; mains Sfr35-60; ☺Tue-Sun).

Bellinzona is on the train route connecting Locarno (Sfr8.20, 20 to 25 minutes) and Lugano (Sfr11.80, 26 to 30 minutes).

Boat Trips

BOAT TRIPS

Take a boat trip to one of the photogenic villages hugging the shoreline – car-free **Gandria** is popular – and feast on traditional Ticinese dishes in your pick of quintessential Ticinese grottos.

🛏 Sleeping

Many hotels close for part of the winter.

Hotel Pestalozzi HOTEL **$$**
(☑091 921 46 46; www.pestalozzi-lugano.ch; Piazza Indipendenza 9; s/d Sfr108/190, without bathroom Sfr68/112; ✻🔊) This renovated art nouveau building is home to rooms with reds, blues and creams dominating the decor. Cheaper ones have a shared bathroom in the corridor.

Hotel Montarina HOTEL **$$**
(☑091 966 72 72; www.montarina.ch; Via Montarina 1; s/d from Sfr85/125; 🅿🔊🏊) Behind the train station, this charming hotel has airy rooms, timber floors and antiques. Some rooms have kitchens and the garden is pool-clad.

Hostel Montarina HOSTEL **$**
(☑091 966 72 72; www.montarina.ch; Via Montarina 1; dm from Sfr34) Hostel Montarina has simple rooms with four to 16 bunk beds. A buffet breakfast is available for Sfr12.

SYHA hostel HOSTEL **$**
(☑091 966 27 28; www.luganoyouth hostel.ch; Via Cantonale 13, Savosa; dm/s/d Sfr29/70/98; ☺mid-Mar–Oct; 🏊) Housed in Villa Savosa, this is one of Switzerland's more enticing youth hostels. Take bus 5 to Crocifisso.

🍴 Eating

For pizza or overpriced pasta, any of the places around Piazza della Riforma are pleasant and lively enough.

Bottegone del Vino ITALIAN **$$**
(☑091 922 76 89; Via Magatti 3; mains Sfr27-42; ☺Mon-Sat) Favoured by the local banking brigade at lunchtime, this is a great place to taste fine local wines over a well-prepared meal. The menu changes daily and knowledgeable waiters fuss around the tables, only too happy to suggest the perfect Ticino tipple.

Grand Café Al Porto INTERNATIONAL **$$$**
(☑091 910 51 30; Via Pessina 3; mains Sfr31-48; ☺8am-6.30pm Mon-Sat) This cafe, which began life way back in 1803, has several fine rooms for dining inside. Be sure to head upstairs to take a peek into the frescoed Cenacolo Fiorentino, once a monastery dining hall.

Al Lido INTERNATIONAL **$$**
(☑091 971 55 00; Viale Castagnola; snacks Sfr9-15, mains Sfr19-32; ☺brunch & dinner Wed-Sat) Lugano's lakeside beach restaurant is hot for Sunday buffet brunch (Sfr37) and its Wednesday-evening version (same price), with DJ thrown in.

L'Antica Osteria del Porto REGIONAL **$$**
(☑091 971 42 00; Via Foce 9; mains Sfr22-41; ☺Wed-Mon) Set back from the sailing club, this is the place to savour local fish and Ticinese dishes.

Drinking & Entertainment

Soho Café COCKTAIL BAR
(☎091 922 60 80; Corso Pestalozzi 3; ⏰7am-1am Mon-Fri, 4pm-1am Sat) Good-looking Lugano townies crowd into this long, orange-lit bar for cocktails. Chilled DJ music creates a pleasant buzz. The problem might be squeezing through to the bar!

New Orleans Club CLUB
(☎091 921 44 77; www.neworleansclublugano.com; Piazza Indipendenza 1; ⏰5pm-1am Mon-Sat) A lively spot Thursday to Saturday night with Latin, hip-hop and disco nights.

ⓘ Getting There & Around

AIR From **Agno airport** (☎091 612 11 11; www.lugano-airport.ch), **Darwin Airline** (www.darwinairline.com) flies to Rome (Fiumicino), Geneva and Olbia (in Sardinia). **Flybaboo** (www.flybaboo.com) flies regularly to Geneva and **Swiss** (www.swiss.com) to Zürich.

BUS To St Moritz, one postal bus runs direct via Italy at least Friday to Sunday (Sfr69, four hours, daily late June to mid-October and late December to early January). Reserve at the bus station, the train station information office or on ☎091 807 85 20. All postal buses leave from the main bus depot at Via Serafino Balestra, but you can pick up the St Moritz and some other buses outside the train station 15 minutes later.

TRAIN Lugano is on the same road and rail route as Bellinzona.

GRAUBÜNDEN

Don't be fooled by Graubünden's diminutive size on a map. This is topographic origami at its finest. Unfold the rippled landscape to find an outdoor adventurer's paradise riddled with more than 11,000km of walking trails, 600-plus lakes and 1500km of down-

hill ski slopes – including super swanky St Moritz and backpacker mecca Flims-Laax. Linguistically wired to flick from Italian to German to Romansch, locals keep you guessing too.

Flims-Laax

They say if the snow ain't falling anywhere else, you'll surely find some around Flims-Laax. These towns, along with tiny Falera, 20km west of Chur, form a single ski area known as the **Weisses Arena** (White Arena), with 220km of slopes catering for all levels. Laax in particular is a mecca for snowboarders, who spice up the local nightlife too. The resort is barely two hours by train and bus (less by car) from Zürich airport.

The main **tourist office** (☎081 920 92 00; www.flims.com in summer, www.laax.com in winter; Via Nova; ⏰8am-6pm Mon-Fri, to noon Sat mid-Jun–mid-Aug, to 5pm Mon-Sat mid-Dec–mid-Apr) is in Flims-Dorf.

⊙ Activities

Skiing SKIING
The ski slopes range as high as 3000m and are mostly intermediate or easy, although there are some 45km of more challenging runs. A one-day ski pass includes ski buses and costs Sfr62 (plus Sfr5 for the KeyCard that you use to access the lifts).

Laax SNOWBOARDING
Laax was the first Swiss resort to allow snowboarders to use the lifts back in 1985, and remains a mecca for snowsurfers, with two huge half-pipes (one said to be the biggest in the world) and a freestyle park huddled around the unfortunately named Crap Sogn Gion peak. The season starts in late October

---

KIRSCH & KISSES

It is just melted cheese and bread, right? Wrong. You'll find two variations of fondue dominating most menus: *moitié-moitié*, a mix of vacherin and Gruyère cheeses (a slightly nutty concoction) or pure vacherin (smooth and creamy). In both versions, the finely grated cheese is added to a *caquelon* (a special ceramic pot) with a clove of garlic rubbed along its sides. White wine and a touch of kirsch (cherry schnapps) are carefully added until the cheese reaches an ideal consistency – not too thin, not too thick. Then you begin dipping bread into the mixture.

A common error is frequently made by foreigners who drink beer with the dish – this is a bad idea. Beer simply sits on top of the cheese in your stomach, resulting in an unpleasant (and often sleepless) night holding your belly. Do as the locals do and drink hot tea or wine, or better yet, dip the cubes of bread into kirsch before hitting the cheese. But make sure you stir carefully, unless you have a crush on one of your dinner companions that is: per Swiss tradition, if you lose your bread in the pot, you must kiss the person seated on your left.

on the glacier and, depending on snowfalls, in mid-December elsewhere.

Vorderrhein
RIVER RAFTING

In summer try river rafting on a turbulent 17km stretch of the Vorderrhein between Ilanz and Reichenau. It will take you through the **Rheinschlucht** (Rhine Gorge), somewhat optimistically dubbed Switzerland's Grand Canyon, but impressive enough for all that. **Swissraft** (☑081 911 52 50; www.swissraft.ch) offers half-/full-day rafting for Sfr109/160.

🛏 Sleeping & Eating

Sleep? Dream on.

Riders Palace
HOTEL $$

(☑081 927 97 00; www.riderspalace.ch; Laax Murschetg; dm Sfr30-60, d Sfr180-280) It may resemble an oversized Rubik's cube, but Riders Palace is a curious slice of designer cool with bare concrete walls and fluorescent lighting. Choose between basic five-bed dorms, slick rooms with Philippe Starck tubs or hi-tech suites complete with PlayStation and Dolby surround. Find it 200m from the Laax lifts.

La Vacca
SWISS $$$

(☑081 927 99 62; Plaun Station, Laax-Murschetg lifts; mains Sfr40-70; ☺late Dec–mid-Apr) Experience the raw funk of La Vacca, a tipi where cowhide-draped chairs surround a roaring open fire. Forget stringy fondue; the menu is as exciting as the design – think melt-in-your-mouth bison steaks paired with full-bodied Argentine wines.

🍷 Drinking

In the drinking stakes, there's the too-cool lobby bar with DJs at **Riders Palace** (☺4pm-4am) or the **Crap Bar** (☑081 927 99 45; Laax-Murschetg lifts; ☺4pm-2am), the place to slam shots, check your email and shimmy in your snow-boots after a day pounding powder.

ℹ Getting There & Away

Postal buses run to Flims and the other villages in the White Arena area hourly from Chur (Sfr12.80 to Flims Dorf, 30 minutes). A free local shuttle bus connects the three villages.

St Moritz

POP 5100

Switzerland's original winter wonderland and the cradle of Alpine tourism, St Moritz (San Murezzan in Romansch) has been luring royals, the filthy rich and moneyed wannabes since 1864. With its smugly perfect lake and aloof mountains, the town looks a million dollars. Still waiting to make your first billion? Stay in St Moritz Bad.

Yet despite the Gucci set propping up the bars and celebs bashing the pistes (A-listers such as Kate Moss and George Clooney included), this resort isn't all show. The real riches lie outdoors with superb carving on Corviglia, hairy black runs on Diavolezza and miles of hiking trails when the powder melts.

🏃 Activities

Skiers and snowboarders will revel in the 350km of runs in three key areas. Avid cross-country skiers can glide through snow-dusted woodlands and plains on 160km of groomed trails. See www.skiengadin.ch for the complete skiing low-down.

You can also hike or try your hand at golf (including on the frozen lake in winter), tennis, in-line skating, fishing, horse riding, sailing, windsurfing and river rafting, to mention just a few activities. The tourist office has a list of prices and contacts.

Corviglia & Signal
SKIING

For groomed slopes with big mountain vistas, head to Corviglia (2486m), accessible by funicular from Dorf. From Bad a cable car goes to Signal (shorter queues), giving access to the slopes of Piz Nair. A ski pass for both areas costs Sfr67 (child/youth Sfr23/45) for one day.

Diavolezza
SKIING

Silhouetted by glaciated 4000ers, Diavolezza (2978m) is a must-ski for free-riders and fans of jaw-dropping descents.

🛏 Sleeping & Eating

Chesa Chantarella
HOTEL $$

(☑081 833 33 55; www.chesachantarella.ch; Via Salastrains; s/d from Sfr120/210; ☺Jun-Sep & Dec-Apr; ℗) Sitting above the town, this is a lively choice with bright, modern rooms. Sip hot chocolate on the terrace, venture down to the wine cellar or dine on hearty local fare in the restaurant.

Hotel Waldhaus am See
HOTEL $$$

(☑081 836 60 00; www.waldhaus-am-see.ch; s/d from Sfr180/330; ℗@�) Overlooking the lake, this friendly pad has light-flooded rooms with pine furnishings and floral fabrics, many with enticing lake and mountain views. There's a sauna and a restaurant serving appetising grill specialities.

Jugendherberge St Moritz
HOSTEL $

(☑081 836 61 11; www.youthhostel.ch/st.moritz; Stille Via Surpunt 60; dm/d from Sfr55/140; @) Budget beds are gold-dust rare in St Moritz, but you'll find one at this hostel edging the forest. The four-bed dorms and doubles are quiet and clean. There's a kiosk, games room and laundrette.

Hatecke
SWISS $$

(☑081 864 11 75; www.hatecke.ch; snacks & mains Sfr16-28; ◎9am-6.30pm Mon-Fri, to 6pm Sat) Edible art is the only way to describe the organic, locally sourced delicacies at Hatecke. *Bündnerfleisch* and venison ham are carved into wafer-thin slices on a century-old slicing machine in this speciality shop. Sit on a sheepskin stool in the funky cafe next door to lunch on delicious Engadine beef carpaccio or *Bündnerfleisch* with truffle oil.

Engiadina
SWISS $$

(☑081 833 32 65; Plazza da Scuola 2; fondue Sfr29-46; ◎Mon-Sat) A proper locals' place, Engiadina is famous for fondue, and that's the best thing to eat here. Champagne gives the melted cheese a kick. It's open year-round.

🍷 Drinking

Around 20 bars and clubs pulsate in winter. While you shuffle to the beat, your wallet might also waltz itself wafer-thin: nights out in St Moritz can be nasty on the banknotes.

Roo Bar
BAR

(☑081 837 50 50; Via Traunter Plazzas 7; ◎2-8pm Dec-Apr) After a hard day's skiing or boarding, snow bums fill the terrace of this après-ski joint at Hauser's Hotel. Hip hop, techno and copious quantities of schnapps fuel the party.

Bobby's Pub
PUB

(☑081 834 42 83; Via dal Bagn 50a; ◎9.30am-1.30am) This laid-back and friendly English-style watering hole serves 30 different brews and attracts young snowboarders in season. It's among the few places open year-round.

❶ Information

The **tourist office** (☑081 837 33 33; www. stmoritz.ch; Via Maistra 12; ◎9am-noon & 1.30-6pm Sat, 4-6pm Sun Dec-Easter & mid-Jun–mid-Sep, 9am-noon & 2-6pm Mon-Fri, 9am-noon Sat rest of year) has all the usual traveller info.

❶ Getting There & Away

BUS The *Palm Express* postal bus runs to Lugano (Sfr69 or Sfr20 with Swiss Travel pass,

four hours, daily summer; Friday, Saturday and Sunday winter); advance reservations are obligatory(☑058 386 31 66).

TRAIN The **Glacier Express** (www.glacier express.ch) plies one of Switzerland's most famous scenic train routes, connecting St Moritz to Zermatt (Sfr138 plus Sfr15 or Sfr30 reservation fee in summer, 7½ hours, daily) via the 2033m Oberalp Pass. It covers 290km and crosses 291 bridges. Novelty drink glasses in the dining car have sloping bases to compensate for the hills – remember to keep turning them around!

Swiss National Park

The road west from Müstair stretches 34km over the Ofenpass (Pass dal Fuorn, 2149m), through the thick woods of Switzerland's only **national park** (www.nationalpark.ch; ◎Jun-Oct) and on to **Zernez** and the hands-on **Swiss National Park Centre** (☑081 851 41 41; www.nationalpark.ch; adult/child Sfr7/3; ◎8.30am-6pm Jun-Oct, 9am-noon & 2-5pm Nov-May), where you can explore a marmot hole, eyeball adders in the vivarium and learn about conservation and environmental change.

The national park was established in 1914 – the first such park in Europe – and spans 172 sq km. 'Nature gone wild' pretty much sums it up: think dolomite peaks, shimmering glaciers, larch woodlands, gentian-flecked pastures, clear waterfalls, and high moors strung with topaz lakes. Zernez **tourist office** (☑081 856 13 00; Chasa Fuchina) has hike details, including the three-hour hike from S-chanf to Trupchun (popular in autumn when you might spy rutting deer) and the Naturlehrpfad circuit near **Il Fuorn**, where bearded vultures can be sighted.

Entry to the park and its car parks is free. Walkers can enter by trails from Zernez, S-chanf and Scuol. Conservation is paramount here, so stick to footpaths and respect regulations prohibiting camping, littering, lighting fires, cycling, picking flowers and disturbing the animals.

🛏 Sleeping & Eating

There are several hotels and restaurants in Zernez and a couple in the park itself.

Hotel Bär & Post
HOTEL $

(☑081 851 55 00; www.baer-post.ch; dm/s/d from Sfr19/88/70) Welcoming all-comers since 1905, these central digs have inviting rooms with lots of stone, pine and downy duvets, plus basic bunk rooms. There's also a sauna and a rustic restaurant, dishing up good steaks and pasta.

Chamanna Cluozza HOSTEL $
(☑081 856 12 35; dm/d with half-board Sfr60/138; ☺late Jun–mid-Oct) For peace and a cracking location, you can't beat this forest hideaway. Dorms are great for walkers eager to hit the trail first thing. It's a three-hour-odd hike from Zernez.

Il Fuorn HOTEL $$
(☑081 856 12 26; www.ilfuorn.ch; s/d Sfr120/199, without bathroom Sfr95/150; half-board extra Sfr30; ☺May-Oct) In the heart of the national park, this guesthouse has light, comfy rooms with loads of pine. Trout and game are big on the *stübli* (cosy Swiss bistro) menu.

ℹ Getting There & Away

Trains run regularly from Zernez to St Moritz (Sfr17.40, 50 minutes), stopping at S-chanf, Zuoz and Celerina. For the latter and St Moritz, change at Samedan.

UNDERSTAND SWITZERLAND

History

The region's first inhabitants were a Celtic tribe, the Helvetii. The Romans arrived in 107 BC via the Great St Bernard Pass, but were gradually driven back by the Germanic Alemanni tribe, which settled in the region in the 5th century AD. Burgundians and Franks also came to the area, and Christianity was gradually introduced.

The territory was united under the Holy Roman Empire in 1032, but central control was never tight, and neighbouring nobles fought each other for local influence. Rudolph I spearheaded the Germanic Habsburg expansion and gradually brought the squabbling nobles to heel.

The Swiss Confederation

Upon Rudolph's death in 1291, local leaders saw a chance to gain independence. The forest communities of Uri, Schwyz and Nidwalden formed an alliance on 1 August 1291, which is seen as the origin of the Swiss Confederation (their struggles against the Habsburgs are idealised in the legend of William Tell). This union's success prompted other communities to join: Lucerne (1332),

followed by Zürich (1351), Glarus and Zug (1352), and Bern (1353).

Encouraged by successes against the Habsburgs, the Swiss acquired a taste for territorial expansion and more land was seized. Fribourg, Solothurn, Basel, Schaffhausen and Appenzell joined the confederation, and the Swiss gained independence from the Holy Roman Emperor Maximilian I after their victory at Dornach in 1499.

Eventually, the Swiss over-extended themselves when they took on a superior force of French and Venetians at Marignano in 1515 and lost. Realising they could no longer compete against better-equipped larger powers, they declared their neutrality. Even so, Swiss mercenaries continued to serve in other armies for centuries, and earned an unrivalled reputation for skill and courage.

The Reformation during the 16th century caused upheaval throughout Europe. The Protestant teachings of Luther, Zwingli and Calvin spread quickly, although the inaugural cantons remained Catholic. This caused internal unrest that dragged on for centuries.

The French Republic invaded Switzerland in 1798 and established the Helvetic Republic. The Swiss vehemently resisted such centralised control, causing Napoleon to restore the former confederation of cantons in 1803. Yet France still retained overall jurisdiction. Following Napoleon's defeat by the British and Prussians at Waterloo, Switzerland finally gained independence.

The Modern State

Throughout the gradual move towards one nation, each canton remained fiercely independent, to the extent of controlling coinage and postal services. The cantons lost these powers in 1848, when a new federal constitution was agreed upon, with Bern as the capital. The Federal Assembly was set up to take care of national issues, but the cantons retained legislative (Grand Council) and executive (States Council) powers to deal with local matters.

Having achieved political stability, Switzerland could concentrate on economic and social matters. Poor in mineral resources, it developed industries dependent on highly skilled labour. A network of railways and roads was built, opening up previously inaccessible regions of the Alps and helping the development of tourism.

The Swiss carefully guarded their neutrality in the 20th century. Their only involvement in WWI was organising units of the Red Cross (founded in Geneva in 1863 by Henri Dunant). Switzerland did join the League of Nations after peace was won, but only on the condition that its involvement was financial and economic rather than military. Apart from some accidental bombing, WWII left Switzerland largely unscathed.

While the rest of Europe was still recovering from the war, Switzerland was able to forge ahead from an already powerful commercial, financial and industrial base. Zürich developed as an international banking and insurance centre, while the World Health Organization (WHO) and many other international bodies set up headquarters in Geneva. Switzerland's much-vaunted neutrality led it to decline joining either the UN or EU, but the country became one of the world's richest and most respected.

Then, in the late 1990s, a series of scandals forced Switzerland to begin reforming its famously secretive banking industry. In 1995, after pressure from Jewish groups, Swiss banks announced that they had discovered millions of dollars lying in dormant pre-1945 accounts, belonging to Holocaust victims and survivors. Three years later, amid allegations they'd been sitting on the money without seriously trying to trace its owners, the two largest banks, UBS and Credit Suisse, agreed to pay US$1.25 billion in compensation to Holocaust survivors and their families.

New Millennium

The year 2001 was truly Switzerland's *annus horribilis*. The financial collapse of the national airline Swissair, a canyoning accident in the Bernese Oberland killing 21 tourists, an unprecedented gun massacre in the Zug parliament and a fatal fire in the Gotthard Tunnel within 12 months all prompted intense soul-searching. Four years on, devastating floods prompted a more pragmatic debate on what should be done.

Since the new millennium, historically isolated Switzerland has recognised the universal challenges it faces and has slowly but surely started reaching out to the world. In 2002 it became the 190th member of the UN and in 2005 it finally joined Europe's 'Schengen' passport-free travel zone, a move that did not actually come into effect until December 2008 for overland arrivals and March 2009 for airport arrivals. Yet few expect the country to even consider joining either the EU – something French-speaking cantons would welcome – or the euro single currency any time soon (if ever).

Banking confidentiality, dating to the Middle Ages here, was enshrined in law in 1934 when numbered (rather than named) bank accounts were introduced. However, in 2004, the country made another concession to that veil of secrecy when it agreed to tax accounts held in Switzerland by EU citizens.

In late 2008, the country's privileged banking sector even gave itself a scare. As

IT ALL HAPPENED IN SWITZERLAND

» Albert Einstein came up with his theories of relativity and the famous formula $E=MC^2$ in Bern in 1905.

» Switzerland gave birth to the World Wide Web at the acclaimed CERN (European Centre for Nuclear Research) institute outside Geneva.

» The first acid trip took place in Switzerland. In 1943 chemist Albert Hofmann was conducting tests for a migraine cure in Basel when he accidentally absorbed the lysergic acid diethylamide, or LSD, compound through his fingertips.

» Of the 800 or so films produced by India's huge movie-making industry each year, more are shot in Switzerland than in any other foreign country. 'For the Indian public, Switzerland is the land of their dreams,' film star Raj Mukherjee has said. Favourite destination shoots include the Bernese Oberland, Central Switzerland and Geneva.

» Switzerland's central Alpine region possesses one of Europe's richest traditions of myth and legend. Pontius Pilate is said to rise out of the lake on Mt Pilatus, near Lucerne, every Good Friday (the day he condemned Jesus Christ) to wash blood from his hands – and anybody who witnesses this event will allegedly die within the year. Tiny 'wild folk' with supernatural powers, called Chlyni Lüüt, were once reputed to inhabit Mt Rigi, also near Lucerne. Their children's spleens were removed at birth, giving them the ability to leap around mountain slopes.

the subprime mortgage scandal fired shock waves through the world's financial markets, Switzerland's two largest banks – UBS and Credit Suisse – were forced to admit heavy losses too. The government waded in with a US$60 billion package to bail out UBS, to the horror of most Swiss, who howled in protest at the huge bonuses paid in preceding years to those very bank managers who'd risked all – and cocked up.

Switzerland Today

In keeping with Western European trends, the Swiss banned smoking on public transport in 2005 and in 2007 Ticino became the first canton to outlaw smoking in all public places. In 2009 smoking was banned in all restaurants and bars across the country. In November of the same year, Switzerland again made headlines when 57% of the country voted to ban the construction of all new minarets in Switzerland. The move – backed by the Swiss Peoples Party (SVP) but opposed by the government – was ultimately accepted in the end by the Swiss government and implemented into law. In 2010, voters also approved a referendum initiative to deport all foreigners who had committed a serious crime.

People

Switzerland's name may stand for everything from knives to watches, but don't expect this nation to take a stand for anyone other than itself. Militarily neutral for centuries, and armed to the teeth to make sure it stays that way, in Switzerland it's the Swiss Way or the highway.

With a population of almost 7.8 million, Switzerland averages 176 people per sq km. Zürich is the largest city, followed by Geneva, Basel and Bern. Most people are of Germanic origin, as reflected in the breakdown of the four national languages (see p614). Around 20% of residents in Switzerland are not Swiss citizens.

The Swiss are polite, law-abiding people who usually see no good reason to break the rules. Living quietly with your neighbours is a national obsession. Good manners infuse the national psyche, and politeness is the cornerstone of all social intercourse. Always shake hands when being introduced to a Swiss, and kiss on both cheeks to greet and say goodbye to friends. Don't forget to greet shopkeepers when entering shops. When

drinking with the Swiss, always wait until everyone has their drink and toast each of your companions, looking them in the eye and clinking glasses. Drinking before the toast is unforgivable, and will lead to seven years of bad sex...or so the superstition goes. Don't say you weren't warned.

In a few mountain regions such as Valais, people still wear traditional rural costumes, but dressing up is usually reserved for festivals. Yodelling, playing the alphorn and Swiss wrestling are also part of the alpine tradition.

Religion

The split between Roman Catholicism (42%) and Protestantism (35%) roughly follows cantonal lines. Strong Protestant areas include Zürich, Geneva, Vaud, Bern and Neuchâtel; Valais, Ticino, Fribourg, Lucerne and the Jura are predominantly Catholic.

Just over 4% of the population is Muslim.

Arts

Many foreign writers and artists, including Voltaire, Byron, Shelley and Turner, have visited and settled in Switzerland. Local and international artists pouring into Zürich during WWI spawned its Dadaist movement.

Paul Klee (1879–1940) is the best-known native painter. He created bold, hard-lined abstract works. The writings of Genevan philosopher Jean-Jacques Rousseau (1712–78) played an important part in the development of democracy. Critically acclaimed postwar dramatists and novelists Max Frisch (1911–91) and Friedrich Dürrenmatt (1921–90) entertained readers with their dark satire, tragi-comedies and morality plays. On the musical front, Arthur Honegger (1892–1955) is Switzerland's most recognised composer.

The Swiss have made important contributions to graphic design and commercial art. Anyone who's ever used a computer will have interacted with their fonts, from Helvetica to Frutiger to Univers.

The father of modern architecture, Le Corbusier (1887–1965), who designed Notre Dame du Haut chapel at Ronchamps in France, Chandigarh in India and the UN headquarters in New York, was Swiss. One of the most-acclaimed contemporary architectural teams on earth, Jacques Herzog and Pierre de Meuron, live and work in Basel. Winners of the prestigious Pritzker Prize in

2001, this pair created London's acclaimed Tate Modern museum building.

Gothic and Renaissance architecture are prevalent in urban areas, especially Bern. Rural Swiss houses vary according to region, but are generally characterised by ridged roofs with wide, overhanging eaves, and balconies and verandahs enlivened by colourful floral displays, especially geraniums.

To the chagrin of many, Switzerland also sports some pretty artistic graffiti. Giant intricately spray-painted patterns (along with less savoury pieces) grace buildings scattered along railway tracks near train stations.

Environment

Mountains make up 70% of Switzerland's 41,285 sq km. Farming is intensive and cows graze on the upper slopes as soon as the retreating snow line permits.

Europe's highest elevations smugly sit here. The Dufourspitze (4634m) of Monte Rosa in the Alps is Switzerland's highest point, but the Matterhorn (4478m), with its Toblerone-shaped cap is better known. Then of course there's Mont Blanc (4807m), a hulk of a mountain – Europe's highest – shared with France and Italy.

Switzerland's 1800 glaciers cover a 2000-sq-km area, but global warming means they're melting rapidly. The country's most famous mass of ice, rock and snow – the 23km-long Aletsch Glacier – shrunk 114.6m in 2006 alone and could shrink 80% by 2100

if things don't change, say experts: 600 people posed nude on the glacier in 2007 for a photo by New Yorker Spencer Tunick as part of a Greenpeace campaign calling for governments worldwide to act quickly.

The St Gotthard Mountains in central Switzerland are the source of many lakes and rivers, including the Rhine and the Rhône. The Jura Mountains straddle the border with France, and peak at around 1700m. Between the two is the Mittelland, a region of hills also known as the Swiss Plateau, criss-crossed by rivers, ravines and winding valleys.

The ibex, with its huge curved ridged horns is the most distinctive alpine animal. In all some 12,000 of this type of mountain goat roam Switzerland and prime ibex-spotting terrain is the country's only national park (169 sq km), unimaginatively called the Swiss National Park.

Switzerland is extremely environmentally friendly: its citizens produce less than 400kg of waste each per year (half the figure for the USA), are diligent recyclers and are actively encouraged to use public transport. Moreover, pioneering green travel networks integrate the country's nonmotorised traffic routes: **SwitzerlandMobility** (www.switzerlandmobility.ch) maps out 169 routes for walkers (6300km), cyclists (8500km), mountain bikers (3300km), roller-bladers or -skaters (1000km) and canoeists (250km) countrywide – all perfectly signposted and easy to follow.

GOIN' GREEN WITH THE ECO-ANGELS

Many Swiss resorts have been polishing their eco-halos recently in a bid to offset the impact of skiing. To further plan your environmentally friendly ski trip and reduce your carbon snowprint, see **Save Our Snow** (www.saveoursnow.com) and the **Association of Car-Free Swiss Resorts** (www.gast.org, in German).

Whiter-than-white ski resorts in Graubünden include **Arosa** (www.arosa.ch), a one-hour train journey from Chur, which runs on nearly 100% renewable energy, operates free shuttle buses and boasts Switzerland's first carbon offsetting policy; **Flims-Laax** (p605), which makes snow using hydroelectricity and recycled water; and **St Moritz** (p606), with its clean-energy policy, pedestrian zones and efficient public transport network.

Gstaad (www.gstaad.ch) has a pedestrianised centre, excellent public transport and makes huge efforts to preserve its natural surroundings in the Bernese Oberland. Valais skiers can carve with a clear conscience in **Verbier** (www.verbier.ch), where energy-efficient snow-grooming machines use biodiesel fuel. In the Jungfrau region, **Zermatt** (p577) is a whiter-than-white green classic with its car-free and eco-sound building policies, free shuttle buses and 60% hydroelectricity. Other notable wholly car-free resorts include **Saas Fee** (www.saas-fee.ch) near Zermatt, **Wengen** and **Mürren** (p590) near Lauterbrunnen, and Valais' **Bettmeralp** (www.bettmeralp.ch).

Reinventing the Alps is the hot topic at higher altitudes. Most pressing is not so much how to be green, how to be ecological, how to burn clean energy – Swiss eco-angels have that sorted. Rather, it is what must be done to keep ski resorts sustainable as the globe warms: experts say you can forget sure-thing snow below 1500m by 2050.

Food & Drink

Staples & Specialities

Lactose intolerants will struggle in this dairy-obsessed country, which makes some of the world's most delectable chocolate and where cheese is a way of life. The best-known Swiss dish is fondue, in which melted Emmental and Gruyère are combined with white wine in a large pot and eaten with bread cubes. Another popular artery-hardener is raclette, melted cheese served with potatoes. Rösti (fried shredded potatoes) is German Switzerland's national dish, and is served with everything.

Many dishes are meaty, and veal is highly rated throughout the country. In Zürich it is thinly sliced and served in a cream sauce (*Gschnetzeltes Kalbsfleisch*). *Bündnerfleisch* is dried beef, smoked and thinly sliced. Like their northern neighbours, the Swiss also munch on a wide variety of *wurst* (sausage).

Wine is considered an essential accompaniment to lunch and dinner. Local vintages are generally good quality, but you might not have heard of them, as they are rarely exported. The main growing regions are Italian- and French-speaking areas, particularly in Valais and by Lakes Neuchâtel and Geneva.

Where to Eat & Drink

Buffet-style restaurant chains, such as Manora, have a huge selection of freshly cooked food at low prices. Migros and Coop are the main supermarket chains. Street stalls are a good place to pick up cheap eats – you'll find kebabs and sandwiches everywhere. Bratwurst and pretzel stands (sometimes the pretzels are even stuffed with meats and cheeses) also abound in German cantons.

Restaurants sometimes close between meals (generally from 3pm to 5pm), although this is becoming rare in large cities, and tend to have a closing day, often Monday. Cafes usually stay open all day. Bars are open from lunchtime until at least midnight. Clubs get going after 10pm and close around 4am.

In cities and larger towns there are dedicated vegetarian restaurants. Most eateries offer a small selection of meatless options too, including large salad plates.

SURVIVAL GUIDE

Directory A–Z

Accommodation

From palatial palaces and castles to mountain refuges, nuclear bunkers, icy igloos or simple haylofts, Switzerland sports traditional and creative accommodation in every price range. Moreover, an increasing number of places are green when it comes to eco-friendly heating, lighting, waste disposal and so on. Online, www.myswitzerland.com is a great resource for tracking down accommodation.

The prices may seem steep – even the most inexpensive places are pricey compared with other parts of Europe. The upside is that hostels, hotels and B&Bs almost always include a generous breakfast in their price and the standard of accommodation is high, divine fluffy feather duvet included.

In both Switzerland and Lichtenstein, many budget hotels have cheaper rooms with shared toilet and shower facilities, and more expensive rooms with private bathroom. For a budget double with bathroom expect to pay up to Sfr150; midrange places will set you back anywhere from Sfr150 to Sfr250, while top-end places priced from Sfr250 offer pure, unadulterated, time-honoured Swiss luxury, with gasp-worthy price tag to match.

Rates in cities and towns stay constant most of the year. In mountain resorts prices are seasonal:

Low season mid-September to mid-December, mid-April to mid-June

Mid-season January to mid-February, mid-June to early July, September

High season July to August, Christmas, mid-February to Easter

PRICE RANGES

Our reviews refer to double rooms with a private bathroom, except in hostels or where otherwise specified. Quoted rates are for high season.

$$$	more than Sfr250
$$	Sfr150 to Sfr250
$	less than Sfr150

HAY BARNS

If you're looking for a way to experience life on a Swiss farm, **Aventure sur la Paille/ Schlaf im Stroh** (☑041 678 12 86; www. abenteuer-stroh.ch) offers the ultimate adventure. When their cows are out to pasture in summer, or indeed even after they've been brought in for the winter come early October, farmers charge travellers Sfr20 to Sfr30 per adult and Sfr10 to Sfr20 per child to sleep on straw in their hay barns or lofts (listen to the jangle of cow or goat bells beneath your head!). Farmers provide cotton undersheets (to avoid straw pricks) and woolly blankets for extra warmth, but guests need their own sleeping bags and pocket torch. Nightly rates include a farmhouse breakfast; shower and evening meals are extras.

HOSTELS

Switzerland has two types of hostels: **Swiss Youth Hostels** (SYHA; www.youthhostel.ch), affiliated with Hostelling International (HI), where nonmembers pay an additional 'guest fee' of Sfr6, and independent hostels which can be more charismatic. Prices listed in this book for SYHA hostels do not include the guest fee. On average a dorm bed in either type costs Sfr30 to Sfr40, including sheets.

There are another 80 hostels in the shape of alpine chalet or rural farmhouse that offer hostel-style accommodation under the green umbrella group **Naturfreundehaus** (Friends of Nature; www.nfhouse.org).

Activities

There are dozens of ski resorts throughout the Alps, pre-Alps and Jura, and 200-odd different ski schools. Equipment hire is available at resorts, and ski passes allow unlimited use of mountain transport.

There is simply no better way to enjoy Switzerland's spectacular scenery than to walk through it. There are 50,000km of designated paths, often with a convenient inn or cafe located en route. Yellow signs marking the trail make it difficult to get lost, and each provides an average walking time to the next destination. Slightly more strenuous mountain paths have white-red-white markers. The **Schweizer Alpen-Club** (SAC;

☑031 370 1818; www.sac-cas.ch, in German; Monbijoustrasse 61, Bern) maintains huts for overnight stays at altitude and can also help with extra information.

You can water-ski, sail and windsurf on most lakes, and rafting on many Alpine rivers, including the Rhine and the Rhône. And there are more than 350 lake beaches.

Bungee jumping, paragliding, canyoning and other high-adrenalin sports are widely available throughout Switzerland, especially in the Interlaken area.

Business Hours

Reviews in this guidebook won't list business hours unless they differ from the following standards:

Banks 8.30am to 5pm Monday to Fri; 8am to noon Saturday

Clubs from roughly 9pm to late

Pubs & cafes 5pm to midnight; to 2am on weekends

Restaurants 11am to 2.30pm, 5pm to 11pm

Shops 8am to noon & 2pm to 6.30pm Monday to Friday , to 9pm Thursday or Friday in towns, 8am to 5pm Saturday

Electricity

Swiss sockets are recessed, hexagonally shaped and incompatible with most plugs from abroad (including 'universal' adapters).

Embassies & Consulates

Embassies are in Bern while cities such as Zürich and Geneva have several consulates. Neither Australia nor New Zealand has an embassy in Switzerland, but each has a consulate in Geneva. For a comprehensive list, see www.eda.admin.ch.

Australia (☑022 799 91 00; www.australia.ch; Chemin des Fins 2, Geneva)

Canada Bern (☑031 357 32 00; www.canada -ambassade.ch; Kirchenfeldstrasse 88); Geneva (☑022 919 92 00; 5 Ave de l'Ariana)

New Zealand (☑022 929 03 50; Chemin des Fins 2, Grand-Saconnex, Geneva)

UK Bern (☑031 359 77 00; http://ukin switzerland.fco.gov.uk/en; Thunstrasse 50); Geneva (☑022 918 24 00; Ave Louis Casai 50); Zürich (☑01 383 65 60; Hegibachstrasse 47)

USA Bern (☑031 357 70 11; http://bern.us embassy.gov; Sulgeneckstrasse 19); Geneva (☑022 840 51 60; Rue François Versonnex 7); Zürich (☑043 499 29 60; Dufourstrasse 101)

✯✯ Festivals & Events

There are more events than we could possibly list; check www.switzerland.com for a complete listing.

February

Fasnacht A lively spring carnival of wild parties and parades is celebrated countrywide, but with particular enthusiasm in Basel and Lucerne.

March

Combats de Reines March to October, the lower Valais stages traditional cow fights known as the Combats de Reines.

April

Landsgemeinde On the last Sunday in April, the people of Appenzell gather in the main square to take part in a unique open-air parliament.

July

Montreux Jazz Festival (www.montreuxjazz. com) Big-name rock/jazz acts hit town for this famous festival, held during the first two weeks of July.

August

National Day On 1 August celebrations and fireworks mark the country's National Day.

Street Parade (www.streetparade.ch) Zürich lets its hair down in the second week of August with an enormous techno parade with 30 lovemobiles and more than half a million excited ravers.

October

Vintage Festivals Down a couple in wine-growing regions such as Neuchâtel and Lugano in early October.

November

Onion Market Bern takes on a carnival atmosphere for a unique market day held on the fourth Monday of November.

December

L'Escalade (www.escalade.ch) This historical festival in Geneva (11 December) celebrates deliverance from would-be conquerors.

Gay & Lesbian Travellers

Attitudes toward homosexuality are reasonably tolerant in Switzerland. Zürich and Geneva have particularly lively gay scenes.

Online listing guides:

Cruiser magazine (www.cruiser.ch)

Pink Cross (www.pinkcross.ch)

Food

The following price indicators for the cost of a main course are used in the listings:

$$$ more than Sfr40

$$ Sfr20 to Sfr40

$ less than Sfr20

Internet Resources

Switzerland has a strong presence on the internet, with most tourist-related businesses having their own website; a good place to start is **Switzerland Tourism** (www.myswitzerland.com), with many useful links. Tune into the latest beat on **Glocals** (www.glocals.com), Switzerland's savviest urbanites tell you where the party is!

Language

Located in the corner of Europe where Germany, France and Italy meet, Switzerland is a linguistic melting pot with three official federal languages: German (spoken by 64% of the population), French (19%) and Italian (8%). Swiss 'German' speakers write standard or 'high' German, but speak their own language: Schwyzertütsch has no official written form and is mostly unintelligible to outsiders.

A fourth language, Romansch, is spoken by less than 1% of the population, mainly in the canton of Graubünden. Derived from Latin, it's a linguistic relic that has survived in the isolation of mountain valleys. Romansch was recognised as a national language by referendum in 1938 and given federal protection in 1996.

English-speakers will have few problems being understood in the German-speaking parts. However, it is simple courtesy to greet people with the Swiss-German *grüezi* and to enquire *Sprechen Sie Englisch?* (Do you speak English?) before launching into English.

In French Switzerland you shouldn't have too many problems either, unlike in Italian-speaking Switzerland, where few speak anything other than Italian and some French and/or German.

Money

Swiss francs are divided into 100 centimes (*Rappen* in German-speaking Switzerland).

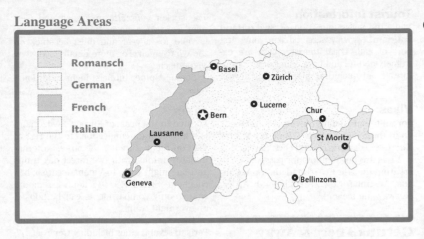

Romansch

German

French

Italian

Basel · Zürich

· Lucerne

Chur

★ Bern

St Moritz

Lausanne

· Bellinzona

Geneva

There are notes for 10, 20, 50, 100, 200 and 1000 francs, and coins for five, 10, 20 and 50 centimes, as well as for one, two and five francs.

All major travellers cheques and credit cards are accepted. Nearly all train stations have currency-exchange facilities open daily and ATMs are everywhere.

There's no need to tip in Switzerland, unless you feel the service was superlative. Tips are included in meal prices.

Post

Postcards and letters sent to Europe cost Sfr1.30/1.20 priority/economy; to elsewhere they cost Sfr1.80/1.40.

Post office opening times vary. Typically they open 7.30am to noon and 2pm to 6.30pm Monday to Friday and until 11am Saturday.

Public Holidays

New Year's Day 1 January

Easter March/April (Good Friday, Easter Sunday and Monday)

Ascension Day 40th day after Easter

Whit Sunday & Monday Seventh week after Easter

National Day 1 August

Christmas Day 25 December

St Stephen's Day 26 December

Telephone

Area codes do not exist in Switzerland or Liechtenstein. Although the numbers for a particular city or town share the same three-digit prefix (for example Bern 031, Geneva 022), numbers always must be dialled in full, even when calling from next door – literally.

Mobile phone numbers start with the code 079. To find a phone number in Switzerland, check the phone book (http://tel.local.ch/en); dial ✍1812 (connection charge 80c plus 10c a minute) to speak to a machine; or ✍1811 (connection charge Sfr1.50, Sfr0.70 for the first minute and Sfr0.22 per minute thereafter) for a real person; the latter also finds international telephone numbers.

National telephone provider **Swisscom** (http://fr.swisscom.ch) operates the world's densest network of public phone booths. Minimum charge for a call is Sfr0.50 and phones take Swiss franc or euro coins, and phonecards, sold at post offices, newsagencies etc. Many booths also accept major credit cards.

The normal/cheap tariff for international dialling to fixed-line phones is Sfr0.12/0.10 per minute for several countries, including Australia, Britain, Canada, New Zealand and the USA; and Sfr0.25/0.20 to countries including Ireland, Japan and the Netherlands.

Save money by buying a prepaid Swisscom card worth Sfr10, Sfr20, Sfr50 and Sfr100. Or look for prepaid cards from rival operators such as **Mobile Zone** (www.mobilezone.ch, in German, French & Italian).

Prepaid local SIM cards (Sfr30 to Sfr100) are available from the three network operators (you'll need your passport when you buy):

Orange (www.orange.ch)

Sunrise (www.sunrise.ch)

Swisscom Mobile (www.swisscom-mobile.ch)

Tourist Information

Make the Swiss tourist board Switzerland Tourism (www.myswitzerland.com) your first port of call. Local tourist offices are extremely helpful and have reams of literature to give out, including maps (nearly always free).

Visas

For up-to-date details on visa requirements, go to the Swiss Federal Office for Migration (www.eda.admin.ch) and click 'Services'.

Visas are not required for passport holders from the UK, EU, Ireland, the USA, Canada, Australia, New Zealand, South Africa, Norway and Iceland.

Getting There & Away

Air

The main international airports:

EuroAirport (MLH or BSL; +33 3 89 90 31 11; www.euroairport.com) France-based, serving Basel as well as Mulhouse in France and Freiburg, Germany.

Geneva International airport (GVA; 0900 57 15 00; www.gva.ch)

Zürich airport (ZRH; 043 816 22 11, SMS 9292 message ZRH plus flight number for flight information; www.zurich-airport.com)

Lake

Switzerland can be reached by steamer from several lakes.

Lake Constance (Switzerland (071 466 78 88; www.sbsag.ch); Austria (05574 42868; www.bodenseeschifffahrt.at); Germany (07531 3640 389; www.bsb-online.com) From Germany.

Lake Geneva (0848 811 848; www.cgn.ch) From France.

Lago Maggiore (091 751 61 40; www.navigazionelaghi.it) From Italy.

Land

CAR & MOTORCYCLE

Roads into Switzerland are good despite the difficulty of the terrain, but special care is needed to negotiate mountain passes.

Upon entering Switzerland you will need to decide whether you wish to use the motorways: there is a one-off charge of Sfr40 payable in cash, including euros, at the border or, better still, in advance through Switzerland Tourism or a motoring organisation.

The sticker (*vignette* in French and German, *contrassegno* in Italian) you receive is valid for a year and must be stuck on the windscreen. For more details, see www.vignette.ch.

Some Alpine tunnels incur additional tolls.

TRAIN

Located in the heart of Europe, Switzerland is a hub of train connections to the rest of the Continent. Zürich is the busiest international terminus, with two direct day trains and one night train to Vienna (seat/six-bed couchette Sfr123/148, 9½ hours); separate women-only compartments can be booked on overnight trains.

There are several TGV trains daily from Paris to several cities including Geneva (€77, 3½ hours), Lausanne (€92 to €120, 3½ to four hours), Bern (€106 to €132, 4½ hours), Basel (€91, 3¾ hours) and Zurich (from €140; 4½ hours). Most connections from Germany, including from Frankfurt and Berlin, pass though Zürich or Basel.

Trains between Switzerland and Italy are operated by both Swiss and Italian national railways. Eurail and Interail passes are valid, and Swiss Pass holders get 20% discount. Nearly all connections to/from Italy pass through Milan before branching off to Zürich (Sfr97, 3¾ hour), Lucerne (Sfr97, 3½ hour), Bern (Sfr87.80, 3½ hour) or Lausanne (Sfr84, 3¾ hour).

Getting Around

Air

Swiss International Air Lines (www.swiss.com) serves the major hubs of EuroAirport (Basel), Geneva and Zürich airports, with return fares fluctuating wildly in price – anything from Sfr70 to Sfr300; and Swiss no-frills carrier Fly Baboo (www.flybaboo.com) flies Geneva-Lugano.

Bicycle

You can hire bikes from most train stations with Rent-a-Bike (041 925 11 70; www.rent-a-bike.ch, in French & German; per day Sfr33) and return to any station with a rental office. Bikes can be transported on most trains; station-rented bikes travel free (maximum five bikes per train), otherwise you need a bike pass (one day Sfr15, with Swiss travel pass Sfr10). Bern, Geneva and Zürich offer free bike loans from their train stations.

Local tourist offices often have good cycling information.

Bus

Yellow postal buses are a supplement to the rail network, following postal routes and linking towns to the more inaccessible regions in the mountains. In all, routes cover some 8000km of terrain. Services are regular, and departures tie in with train arrivals. Postbus stations are next to train stations and offer destination and timetable information.

Car

The **Swiss Touring Club** (Touring Club der Schweiz; ☎022 417 24 24; www.tcs.ch), Switzerland's largest motoring organisation, is affiliated with the AA in Britain and has reciprocal agreements with motoring organisations worldwide.

You do not need an International Driving Permit to operate a vehicle in Switzerland. A licence from your home country is sufficient. There are numerous petrol stations and garages throughout Switzerland if you break down.

For the best deals on car hire, prebook; particularly competitive rates are often found on **Auto Europe** (www.autoeurope.com).

When driving in Switzerland, be prepared for winding roads, high passes and long tunnels. Normal speed limits are 50km/h in towns, 120km/h on motorways, 100km/h on semimotorways (designated by roadside rectangular pictograms showing a white car on a green background) and 80km/h on other roads. Mountain roads are well maintained but you should stay in low gear whenever possible and remember that ascending traffic has the right of way over descending traffic, and postbuses always have right of way. Snow chains are recommended during winter. Use dipped lights in *all* road tunnels. Some minor Alpine passes are closed from November to May – check with the local tourist offices before setting off.

Switzerland is tough on drink-driving; your blood alcohol level is over 0.05% you face a large fine or imprisonment.

Train

The Swiss rail network consists of a combination of state-run and private lines, and

---

PASSES & DISCOUNTS

Swiss public transport is an efficient, fully integrated and comprehensive system, which incorporates trains, buses, boats and funiculars. Convenient discount passes make the system even more appealing – on extensive travel within Switzerland the following national travel passes generally offer betters savings than Eurail or Inter Rail passes. Find comprehensive information on all of them at http://traintickets.myswitzerland.com.

The **Swiss Pass** (www.swisstravelsystem.ch) is the best deal for big travellers, allowing unlimited travel on almost every train, boat and bus service in the country, and on trams and buses in 38 towns. Reductions of 50% apply on funiculars, cable cars and private railways, such as Jungfrau Railways. These passes are available for four days (Sfr260), eight days (Sfr376), 15 days (Sfr455), 22 days (Sfr525) and one month (Sfr578); prices are for 2nd-class tickets. If you are under 26, buy the **Swiss Youth Pass** equivalent, 25% cheaper in each instance. The **Swiss Flexi Pass** allows free, unlimited trips for three to six days within a month and costs Sfr249 to Sfr397 (2nd class). With either pass, two people travelling together get 15% off. Passes also allow you free admission to all Swiss museums, making them an even better bargain.

The **Swiss Card** allows a free return journey from your arrival point to any destination in Switzerland, 50% off rail, boat and bus excursions, and reductions on mountain railways. It costs Sfr182 (2nd class) or Sfr255 (1st class) and it is valid for a month. The **Half-Fare Card** is a similar deal, minus the free return trip. It costs Sfr99 for one month.

The **Family Card** gives free travel for children aged under 16 if they're accompanied by a parent and is available free to pass purchasers.

All these passes are best purchased online before arrival in Switzerland at www.swisstravelsystem.com or in the UK from the **Swiss Travel Centre** (☎0207 420 49 00; 30 Bedford St, London WC2E 9ED). In Switzerland larger train-station offices sell travel passes.

covers 5000km. Trains are clean, reliable and frequent, and are as fast as the terrain will allow. Prices are high, and if you plan on taking more than one or two train trips it's best to purchase a travel pass. All fares quoted in this chapter are for 2nd class; 1st-class fares are about 65% higher. All major stations are connected by hourly departures, but services stop from around midnight to 6am.

Most train stations offer luggage storage at a counter (around Sfr5 per piece) or in 24hr lockers (Sfr3 to Sfr10), and have excellent information counters. Train schedules are revised yearly; double-check details before travelling either online with **Swiss Federal Railways** (www.rail.ch, www.sbb.ch/en), abbreviated to SBB/CFF/FFS in German/French/Italian. Or call its **Rail Service** (☑0900 300 300, per min Sfr1.19).

Survival Guide

Directory A–Z

Directory A–Z answers questions about Central Europe as a whole. For more detailed, country-specific information, look in the Directory at the end of each destination chapter. Note that facilities can vary based on whether you travel in the more westerly (Germany, Austria, Switzerland, Liechtenstein) or more easterly (Slovakia, Slovenia, Czech Republic, Poland, Hungary) countries of the region.

Accommodation

From splashy five-star hotels to homey pensions, Central Europe has a full range of accommodation. Hostels and student dormitories are more prevalent in cities, while hikers' huts are found only in the mountains. Top-end digs are rarely found outside cities or mountain resorts in the east but are more common in smaller towns of the west.

Accommodation can fill up at popular tourist destinations and during Christmas, New Year and Easter especially; it's advisable to book ahead in those cases. Tourist offices often have extensive accommodation lists and a few will

help you book (sometimes for a small fee). Agencies offering short-stay apartments can provide good value.

Reviews in this book are ordered by author preference, prices are quoted at high-season rates. Unless otherwise noted, all lodgings come with a private bathroom. More and more accommodation is going smoke-free inside, but a few pensions to the east and south may not have any non-smoking rooms.

Prices

Individual price range breakdowns are listed in the respective country directories. In general:

Budget (€) Camping, hostel dorms and shared bathrooms; some provincial guesthouses and inns without catering.

Midrange (€€) Pensions and guesthouses, some with

bars or restaurants, and small hotels.

Top end (€€€) Upscale boutique properties, business hotels, international chain hotels, ski resorts and almost anything in Switzerland...

Seasons

May to September Main tourist season prices quoted in this book's reviews.

July to August Peak travel time; expect crowds and book ahead.

October to April Off-season, rates drop dramatically (10% to 50%).

January to March Additional tourist/high season in the mountains.

Christmas, New Year and Easter Prices 20% to 30% higher than tourist season; reservations essential.

Camping

Camping provides the cheapest accommodation across the region, but, in cities, most camping grounds will be some distance from the centre, possibly with limited access by public transport.

» Expect a charge per tent or site, plus per person and per vehicle.

» In the west, well-maintained grounds exist for tents and some campsites offer bungalows, wooden cabins and caravan spaces.

» Campsites are especially well catered for in Germany and Austria.

» In the east, minimal services are the norm; spartan cabins often ring a small open ground for pitching a tent.

» If you're on foot, the money you save by camping can quickly be eaten up by

---

BOOK YOUR STAY ONLINE

For more accommodation reviews by Lonely Planet authors, check out hotels.lonelyplanet.com/Europe. You'll find independent reviews, as well as recommendations on the best places to stay. Best of all, you can book online.

EMERGENCY NUMBERS

The EU-wide general emergency number is ☑112; Liechtenstein and Switzerland also use this number. See the Fast Facts section at the start of the destination chapters for more details.

the cost of commuting to and from a town centre.

» It is illegal to camp anywhere but in designated areas in national parks or, with permission, on private property.

» Camping grounds may be open April to October, May to September, or June to August; a few private operations are open year-round.

FARMHOUSES

Villages or agrotourism (staying at a farmhouse) offer a distinctly local experience, often in picturesque rural areas. Some work may or may not be expected; in return, you might get fresh milk straight from the cow. In Switzerland, you can also stay in a hay barn. Reaching these remote outposts almost always requires having your own transport. Resources:

European Centre for Eco Agro Tourism (www.eceat. org) Thousand-plus network of small-scale lodges and ecofriendly farms.

Country Holidays in Europe (www.eurogites.org) Lists rural options.

World Wide Opportunities on Organic Farms (www. wwoof.org) Super work-stay opportunities in Austria, Germany, Switzerland and the Czech Republic.

Centre for Rural Tourism (www.falutur.hu) In Hungary.

Federation for Village Tourism (www.agroturystyka.pl) In Poland.

Guesthouses & Pensions

Small pensions and guesthouses are common in big cities and small villages across Central Europe.

» Priced lower than most hotels, they usually have loads more character. Think flower-fronted chalet or trendy apartment building.

» Typically, more personal service is available at a pension than a hotel.

» Most are small with less than a dozen rooms, but some are larger with saunas and other amenities.

» Small restaurants or bars are not uncommon.

» Some sort of breakfast is usually available.

» Wi-fi is widely available.

» More and more places have nonsmoking rooms.

Homestays & Private Rooms

Renting a room in a private home is becoming less common regionwide. You'll find fewer opportunities in the westerly countries than in the easterly ones.

» Tourist offices and town websites have contacts of available options; travel agencies can sometimes book accommodation in local homes.

» If you're approached at train and bus stations with offers of a room, ask lots of questions or visit the place before you agree.

» In holiday villages around parks, lakes and mountains look for houses with '*Zimmer frei*', '*sobe*', '*privat*' or '*szoba kiadó*' (in German, Slovene, Slovak or Hungarian); just knock on the door and ask what's available.

International private home and apartment resources include:

Home Away Holiday Rentals (www.holiday-rentals.co.uk)
Sublet.com (www.sublet.com)

Vacation Rental By Owner (www.vrbo.com)

Hostels

Hostels offer the cheapest (secure) roof over your head in Central Europe and you do not have to be a youngster to take advantage of them. What to expect:

» Four to 10 bunks per co-ed room from €15.

» Single and double rooms, where available, often cost as much as a pension.

» Amenities usually include internet access, a common room, kitchen, personal lockers and shared bathrooms.

» Polskie Towarzystwo Schronisk Młodzieżowych (PTSM) hostels in Poland still have daytime lock-outs.

» Big city hostels may offer organised tours.

» Local tourist offices list universities that open student dormitories as hostels in July and August.

Resources:
Europe's Famous Hostels (www.famoushostels.com)
Hostel Planet (www.hostel planet.com)
Hostelling International (HI; www.hihostels.com)
Hostel World (www.hostel world.com)
Hostels.com (www.hostels. com)
Hostelz (www.hostelz.com)

Hotels

Categorisation varies from country to country and the hotels recommended in this book cater to a range of budgets.

» In general, the more facilities (restaurant, swimming pool etc), the higher the rate.

» Wi-fi access is widespread, air-conditioning less so (look for the 🛜 or ❄ symbols in reviews).

» Hotel parking may be tight or nonexistent in cities.

» Breakfast is often available, if not included. Ask before

you check in; the repast may cost extra but be mandatory.

» Discounts may be available for long stays or large groups.

» Single rooms (one twin bed), when available, cost less.

» In larger places, inquire if there are less-expensive rooms with a washbasin in-room and toilet and shower down the hall.

» Off-season, in the eastern countries in particular, hotel owners may be open to a little bargaining.

Rental Accommodation

Short-term apartment rental is an increasingly popular and affordable option, particularly in the eastern part of Central Europe. Corporate apartments are more upscale, with laundry facilities, parking, daily cleaning services and a concierge. What to expect, in general:

» an unoccupied apartment

» at least a kitchenette, if not a full kitchen

» rates from €40 to €150 per day

» room for two to five persons in prime locations

» limited, if any, internet access

Listings may be available on general hotel booking-agency sites; see individual destination chapters for business specifics.

Activities

While the cities of Central Europe offer nonstop entertainment, it's in the region's forests, on its lakes and rivers, and atop its mountains where you'll find some of the biggest thrills – and lungfuls of fresh air.

General tours:

Backroads (www.backroads. com) Ecosensitive tour company offering a range of biking, hiking, multisport, single and multicountry trips in the region.

Adventure Finder (www.ad venturefinder.com) Single and multisport trips in Austria, Slovakia, Czech Republic and Germany.

Bird & Animal Watching

The countries of central Europe may not be the world's

premier destinations for wildlife watching, but there are a few good sites – especially in Hungary.

Tours:

Ecotours (www.ecotours. hu) Birding, butterfly and wildlife tours in Hungary, Austria, Slovenia, Slovakia and Poland.

Probirder (www.probirder. com) Bird-watching tours in the Czech Republic, Slovakia, Slovenia, Poland and Hungary.

Wings (www.wingsbirds.com) Single-country birding tours in Germany, Austria and the Czech Republic.

Resources:

» *Birds of Europe* by Lars Svennson

» *Central and Eastern European Wildlife* by Gerard Gorman

» *Birding in Eastern Europe* by Gerard Gorman

Cycling

Cycling allows you to get up close to the scenery and the local people, keeping you fit in the process. Look under the Getting Around sections in each destination chapter for specifics on riding and renting bicycles. Most airlines and long-distance bus companies transport bicycles. Note that bicycle theft can be an issue in cities, and in the mountainous regions it can be heavy going, but this is offset by the dense concentration of things to see.

Tours:

Backroads (www.backroads. com) Bicycle itineraries for Slovenia, across Poland, Hungary, Slovakia and through the Czech Republic and Austria.

First Light Bicycle Tours (www.firstlightbicycletours. com) Cycling tours in the Czech Republic and an epic journey from Kraków to Budapest. Self-guided trips also available.

Top Bicycle (www.topbicycle. com) Multicountry cycle tours

SCENE-SETTING MOVIES

Watching films based in Central Europe can provide background for an upcoming trip.

» **Goodbye Lenin** (2003) Comedy set in East Berlin; when a girl awakes from a coma postcommunism, her family pretends the Wall never fell.

» **The Sound of Music** (1965) Sure, you've seen it, but you need to practise your lines before prancing around Salzburg.

» **Schindler's List** (1993) *The* film to see about the Holocaust.

» **Kafka** (1991) Not much to do with the real Kafka, but Prague and its castle look beautiful in this black-and-white writer's mystery.

» **Latcho Drom** (1993) Haunting musical documentary following the historical migration of the Roma into modern-day Central Europe.

» **The Third Man** (1939) Trying to find some remnants of post-WWII Vienna will become an obsession after this great film noir by Carol Reed.

through combinations of Germany, Austria, the Czech Republic, Poland, Slovakia and Hungary.

Velo Touring (www.velo-touring.hu) Budapest company offering tours of Austria and Hungary.

Hiking

Keen hikers can spend a lifetime exploring Central Europe's many trails. The mountains in Switzerland, Austria, Slovenia, Slovakia and Poland, especially, are criss-crossed with clearly marked paths and offer rewarding challenges for everyone from beginners to experts. **Ramblers Holidays** (www.ramblersholidays.co.uk) offers single-country hiking tours in Germany, Austria, Switzerland, Poland and Hungary.

Getting there Public transport and cable cars will often get you to trailheads.

Accommodation Lodging and basic meals are often available at hikers' huts (may be a dorm-filled shack or hotel-like chalet).

Best months For high mountain hiking, July to early September; in lower ranges and forests, May through October.

Difficulty indicators

» **Red-white-red marker** You need sturdy hiking boots and a pole.

» **Blue-white-blue marker** Indicates the need for mountaineering equipment.

Skiing & Snowboarding

Central Europe is the continent's ski capital. The destination chapters in this book are brimming with details on how to get your downhill fix. Ski resorts in the Swiss Alps offer world-class facilities – and vistas that are incomparable in the region – but they are also the most expensive. Austria is generally slightly cheaper than Germany and Switzerland. A general rule of

thumb is that the further east you travel, the less expensive the skiing.

Ski season Early December to late March; at higher altitudes it may extend an extra month either way.

Snow conditions Vary greatly from year to year and region to region, but January and February tend to be the best (and busiest). For conditions in Austria, Switzerland and Germany, log onto www.onthesnow.com.

Business Hours

For country-specific hours in Central Europe, see the individual Directory sections for guidance. In general:

Offices Closed Saturday and Sunday (including some tourist offices off-season).

Museums & castles Closed Monday; may be closed additional days or completely from October through to April.

Banks & post offices Open 9am to 5pm Monday to Friday; may also be open on Saturday mornings.

Shops Open until 6pm or 7pm, some closed Sundays; megamarts such as Tesco never shut their doors.

Children

Central Europe is a great place to bring the young ones. It has well-established attractions geared towards children of all ages, especially in the more western countries. Lonely Planet's *Travel with Children* is an excellent general resource and includes topics ranging from children's health to games that will keep the kids amused. Typical facilities:

Restaurants Highchairs, kids' menus and play areas are more common in the western countries of the region than the eastern.

Hotels & pensions Cribs and cots are widely available.

Safety seats Most car-hire firms provide children's safety seats for a fee; they must be booked in advance.

Supplies Selection of baby food, infant formulas, soy and cow's milk, disposable nappies (diapers) and the like is better in large cities than smaller ones.

Customs Regulations

Unless you cross the border into non-EU countries, you are generally unlikely to be subjected to a search. Duty-free goods are no longer sold to those travelling from one EU country to another.

For duty-free goods that are purchased at airports or on ferries outside the EU, the usual allowances apply:

Tobacco (200 cigarettes, 50 cigars or 250g of loose tobacco)

Alcohol (1L of spirits or 2L of liquor with less than 22% alcohol by volume; and 2L of wine)

Perfume (50g of perfume and 250ml of eau de toilette).

Allowances for duty-*paid* items bought for personal use at normal shops and supermarkets:

Tobacco (800 cigarettes, 200 cigars or 1kg of loose tobacco)

Alcohol (10L of spirits, 20L of fortified wine or aperitif, 90L of wine or 110L of beer)

Perfume (unlimited quantities).

Discount Cards

Note that seniors aged over 60 or 65 and students with ID may receive a discount at museums, sights and recreational facilities.

Camping Card International (CCI; www.campingcardinternational.com) Discount of 5% to 10% at affiliated camping grounds.

Issued by camping federations, automobile associations and some campsites. May eliminate the need to leave your passport at reception.

Hostelling International Card (www.hihostels.com) Provides discounts at affiliated hostels, rarely mandatory, usually may be bought on-site.

International Student Identity Card (ISIC; www.isic.org) ID-style card with photograph, provides discounts on various transport, sight admissions and inexpensive meals in some student cafeterias and restaurants. Teachers can get the International Teachers Identity Card (ITIC).

International Youth Travel Card (IYTC; www.myisic.com) and **Euro26 Card** (www.euro26.org) Similar discounts and benefits as ISIC for non-students under age 26.

Railplus Senior Card For European residents over 65, provides discounts of around 25% for international train travel. Check at your domestic train station.

Electricity

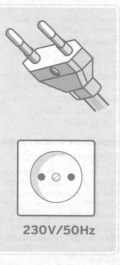

230V/50Hz

Check the voltage and cycle (usually 50Hz) used in your home country and your appliance. Modern battery chargers and computer power supplies will *usually* adjust voltage automatically. Otherwise, don't mix 110/125V with 220/240V without a transformer.

Embassies & Consulates

See the individual destination chapters for the addresses of embassies and consulates in Central Europe. Note that it's important to realise what your embassy can and cannot do for you while abroad. If you have all your money and documents stolen, it might assist with getting a new passport, but a loan for onward travel is almost always out of the question. Generally speaking, they won't be much help if you're in trouble that is remotely your own fault; you are bound by the laws of the country you are visiting.

Gay & Lesbian Travellers

Homosexual activities are legal in every country covered by this book. Local attitudes towards public displays of same-sex affection vary widely among them, and between large, urban centres and smaller, rural areas. Berlin, Munich and Vienna have vibrant and active gay scenes. It's a different story in the eastern countries of the region: most capital cities there have small gay scenes centred on one or two bars or clubs. Gay and lesbian venues are almost nonexistent outside urban centres.

Resources:

Gay Journey (www.gayjourney.com) A mishmash of travel-related forums, booking engines, travel packages, bar and club reviews, and write-ups of gay-friendly destinations.

International Gay & Lesbian Travel Association (www.iglta.org) Worldwide gay- and lesbian-friendly business listings (including accommodation and services); travel agent.

Mi Casa Su Casa (www.gayhometrade.com) Paid-membership international home-exchange service for gay and lesbian travellers.

Spartacus International Gay Guide (www.spartacusworld.com) A male-only directory of gay entertainment venues.

Health

It is unlikely that you will encounter unusual health problems in Central Europe. The tap water is potable, though taste varies. If you have serious health issues, or are travelling for an extended period, it is always wise to remember the following tips:

» Bring a copy of your prescriptions, including generic names, so you can get replacements.

» Bring a spare set of contact lenses, glasses or your eye prescription.

Recommended Vaccinations

Though no vaccinations are specifically required for Central Europe, the World Health Organization (WHO) recommends that all travellers should be covered for diphtheria, tetanus, measles, mumps, rubella and polio. Be aware that most vaccines don't produce immunity until at least two weeks after they're given.

Availability & Cost of Health Care

Good, basic health care is readily available.

Hospitals In the east of the region, hospitals are most common in major cities.

Pharmacies Provide valuable advice on small issues, sell over-the-counter medicine and advise when more specialised help is required.

Dental care The standard of dental care is usually good.

Doctors Embassies, consulates, tourist offices and five-star hotels can usually recommend doctors or clinics with English-speaking staff.

Insurance

Worldwide travel insurance is available at www.lonelyplanet.com/travel_services. You can buy, extend and claim online anytime – even if you're already on the road. For information on car insurance, see p632.

Health Insurance

If you're an EU citizen, the European Health Insurance Card (EHIC) covers you for most medical care. The form is available from health centres. Note the EHIC will not cover you for non-emergencies or emergency repatriation. Citizens from other countries should find out if there are reciprocal arrangements for free medical care between their country and the countries they are visiting.

Note that some insurance policies will specifically exclude 'dangerous activities'. Check that the policy covers ambulances and also an emergency flight home.

Supplementary policies:

STA Travel (www.statravel.com) Good-value student polices; wide variety available, so check the fine print.

Travel Guard (www.travelguard.com) Emergency health insurance for those who have home coverage that doesn't extend to Central Europe.

Travel Insurance

More and more airline companies and booking agencies are offering trip-cancellation insurance when you get your tickets. Check conditions before you sign; some policies only refund for cancellation under specific circumstances. Insure My Trip (www.insuremytrip.com) compares travel policies.

Internet Access

As computer ownership has become the norm across the region, the number of internet cafes has decreased and the availability of wi-fi has increased. Make sure you have a web-based email account so that you can send and receive email on the road if you don't have a laptop or other web-enabled device with you. In general:

» Most cities have at least one internet or gaming cafe, smaller towns and villages may not.

» Hostels are reliable places to find computer internet access.

» Free wi-fi (known as WLAN in Germany) is common at lodgings, in restaurants and cafes, and even in some town squares. Train stations and airport wi-fi access usually require payment.

» To find wi-fi hot spots, search sites such as www.jiwire.com or paid providers like www.t-mobile.com.

Legal Matters

You are required by law to prove your identity if asked by police, so always carry your passport or an identity card if you're an EU citizen. Most regional authorities are friendly and helpful, especially if you have been a victim of a crime.

Maps

Buying a good regional map will make things easier if you are planning a trip across more than a couple of countries. When driving or cycling, an atlas can be invaluable.

Central Europe Road Atlas, Freytag & Berndt Good for road trips, available worldwide.

Media

Newspaper *International Herald Tribune* is sold in larger towns; most capitals have their own English-language weekly papers.

Radio English-language radio stations BBC World Service and Voice of America (VOA) are rebroadcast on local AM or FM radio stations.

TV CNN International and Eurosport are often found on regional cable and satellite TV systems.

Money

At the time of publication, the countries in Central Europe using the euro as their currency are Austria, Germany, Slovenia and Slovakia. The other countries use their own currencies, which are easily convertible, stable and reliable. Major international currencies such as the euro and the US dollar are easy to exchange. Hungary, Poland and the Czech Republic are expected to convert to the euro in years to come. A useful internet site for calculating exchange rates is www.xe.com/ucc.

For security and flexibility, diversify your source of funds: carry an ATM card, credit card and some cash.

ATMs

ATMs connected to international networks such as Cirrus are widely available in cities and towns, including at transport arrival halls. Find a money machine before travelling to villages. Other points to consider:

» Withdrawal fees are usually charged by both your domestic bank and the ATM operator.

» Check to see that there are no ancillary devices attached

to the ATM and cover the key pad when entering your code to discourage theft.

» A few people report problems with their pin codes while abroad, so have a back-up card or plan.

Credit Cards

Note that separate systems for processing the bill may be used for cash and charge, especially in the eastern countries. Announce that you intend to pay by card before requesting the cheque; once the bill arrives, it may be too late.

» **Visa and MasterCard** Commonly accepted at hotels, pensions, larger restaurants, train stations; occasionally accepted at smaller restaurants.

» **American Express, Discover, Diners Club etc** Accepted only rarely, at larger establishments.

Tipping

Adding 5% to 10% to a bill for service is common across Europe. See the destination-specific Directories for details.

Travellers Cheques

International ATMs have all but eliminated the need for travellers cheques. Finding a place to cash these can be difficult and commissions are generally high.

Wire Transfers

Western Union (www.western union.com) enables you to wire money to thousands of offices across the region. The sender will be given a code that they then communicate to you and you take to the nearest office, along with your passport, to receive your cash.

Photography

» Museums, castles and other Central European attractions may charge a fee for camera use (roughly equivalent to an additional ticket price).

GETTING YOUR TAX BACK

Sales tax applies to many goods and services in Europe; the amount – 10% to 20% – is already built into the price of the item. Luckily, when non-EU residents spend more than a certain amount (around €75) they can usually reclaim that tax when leaving the country. Note that none of this applies to EU residents. Even a US citizen living in London is not entitled to a rebate on items bought in Frankfurt. Conversely, an EU passport holder living in New York is.

Making a tax-back claim is straightforward:

» Check that the shop offers duty-free sales; often a sign will read 'Tax-Free Shopping'.

» When purchasing, ask the shop attendant for a tax-refund voucher, filled in with the correct amount and the date.

» Claim a refund directly at international airports (beware of very long lines), or have your claim documents stamped at ferry ports or border crossings and mailed back for a refund.

» It is never a good idea, and may be illegal, to take pictures of military installations or at airport immigration.

» Memory cards and sticks are expensive to buy in Central Europe.

» Some internet cafes will download your photos to a CD for a fee.

Lonely Planet's *Travel Photography,* by Richard I'Anson, is a useful guide for people who want to get their shots just right.

Post

Postal services can be considered reliable throughout Central Europe. See the individual country Directory chapter for specific details.

Public Holidays

For specific public holidays, please see the Directory in each destination chapter.

Safe Travel

Central Europe is as safe – or unsafe – as any other part

---

of the developed world. If you can handle yourself in the big cities of Western Europe, North America or Australia, you'll have little trouble dealing with the less pleasant sides of travel here. A few tips:

» If possible, work out a list of places where you can be contacted.

» When hiking or skiing alone or in the back country, leave a note at your hotel or park headquarters stating your departure time, intended route and anticipated return.

Scams

Overall the region is quite safe, but there are a few scams to watch out for:

» Men, be wary of the attention of uber-gorgeous women who invite you to a club in eastern cities; the drinks may be absurdly priced (€100-plus) and enforcers may appear at the end of the night to walk you to the ATM. (Did you really think it was your charming good looks that attracted them?) Be careful and pay attention to your surroundings.

» There have been a few reports of unscrupulous people making quick, hi-tech duplicates of credit- or debit-card information. Be alert if your card leaves your possession for longer than necessary and check your charges from the road if possible.

Theft

Petty crime is as common here as elsewhere in Europe and your wariness should extend to other travellers. Theft-thwarting tips:

» Make copies of all important documents, such as passport and driver's licence.

» Be aware of your belongings in tourist centres; pickpockets target anywhere you'll be distracted – from crowded transport to busy attractions.

» Be especially vigilant on overnight trains; keep your bags locked and avoid those neck-hanging travel wallets that can be cut off easily.

» Avoid leaving luggage and other items in plain view in parked cars.

» In case of theft or loss, always report the incident to the police and ask for a statement; otherwise, your travel-insurance company won't pay.

Telephone

For individual country codes and dialling instructions see the Directory at the end of each destination chapter. Towns with a local area code have it listed directly underneath its heading.

Mobile Phones

Mobile phones have become essential communication devices throughout Central Europe – don't be surprised to see a Slovenian farmer chatting on a mobile while leaning on a haystack.

Networks In general, Central Europe has GSM (900/1800MHz) and 3G UMTS networks.

Local SIM cards Widely available (from €10) at mobile phone dealers and some supermarkets; make sure your phone is unlocked.

Roaming If your phone supports local networks, it will usually switch to roaming automatically. Check costs with your provider, they can be crazily high.

Phonecards

You may ring abroad from almost any phone box in Central Europe. Public telephones accepting stored-value phonecards (available from news-stands and retail outlets) are the norm now. Both domestic rate phonecards and international discount cards are available.

Time

Time zone Countries covered in this book are GMT+1 hour.

Daylight saving Central European countries employ daylight saving; usually pushing forward an hour on the last Sunday in March, setting back one hour on the last Sunday in October.

Clocks The 24-hour time system is usually used.

Tourist Information

Tourist information is widely available with booths or tourist offices located in main city and town centres, and sometimes at airports and train stations. Services offered vary and smaller town offices may close on weekends off-season. Tourist contacts are provided under specific city, town and village sections.

Official country tourism bureaus:

Austria (www.austria.info)
Czech Republic (www. czechtourism.com)
Germany (www.cometo germany.com)

Liechtenstein (www.tour ismus.li)
Poland (www.poland.travel)
Slovakia (www.slovakia.travel)
Slovenia (www.slovenia.info)
Switzerland (www.myswit zerland.com)

Travellers with Disabilities

Access varies depending on where you travel in the region.

In western countries:

» Wheelchair ramps are common at midrange hotels and upmarket hotels, most museums and many restaurants and cafes.

» Public transport often has accessibility features.

» Trains that accept Eurail passes in Germany and Switzerland are fitted for wheelchair access; these require (free) prebooking.

In eastern countries:

» Few hotels are equipped for the disabled traveller.

» Ramps are rare; some train stations have staircases only.

» Some buses have lowering capability for wheelchair access.

Useful international resources:

Disability World (www. disabilityworld.com)

Royal Association for Disability & Rehabilitation (RADAR; www.radar.org.uk)

Access-Able Travel Source (www.access-able.com)

Society for Accessible Travel & Hospitality (www. sath.org)

Visas

Detailed visa regulations are given in the Directory section of each destination chapter, but it is unlikely that you will need to hassle with them. Although Switzerland and Liechtenstein are not members of the EU, all countries in this book are part of the Schengen Agreement. Therefore all of Central Europe is considered one 'country' in terms of your 90-day or visa length of stay. In general:

Visa-free for up to 90 days Visitors from Australia, New Zealand, Canada, Japan and the US; valid passport required.

No visa required EU citizens; identity card required.

Visa sometimes required South African nationals, among others.

Note that:

» Many – but not all – of the border posts between the countries of the region have disappeared.

» Some countries require that your passport remain valid for at least three months beyond your expected departure; in practice, this is rarely checked.

» For those who do require visas, it's important to remember that these will have a 'use-by' date; you'll be refused entry after that period.

» Most countries do not issue visas on their borders, but you may be able to apply in a neighbouring country.

Volunteering

A volunteer work placement is a great way to gain deeper insight into local culture. Lonely Planet's *Volunteer: A Traveller's Guide* is an overall introduction to the subject.
Resources:

Coordinating Committee for International Voluntary Service (www.unesco.org/ccivs) Umbrella organisation with more than 140 members worldwide.

International Willing Workers on Organic Farms (WWOOF; www.wwoof.org) Arrange to live and work on a host's organic farm.

Serve Your World (www.serveyourworld.com) Volunteering search engine that includes Europe.

Weights & Measures

The metric system is in use throughout Central Europe. In Germany, cheese and other food items are often sold per *Pfund* (500g).

Women Travellers

Women travellers, in general, will find Central Europe relatively enlightened and should have no more problems travelling solo here than at home.

Work

European bosses aren't keen on giving jobs to foreigners when unemployment rates are high. Officially, EU citizens are allowed to work in any other EU country. For long-term employment, workers will probably need to apply for a residency permit. Other nationalities require work permits that can be very difficult to arrange.

The market for teaching English is saturated in places such as Prague and Budapest. You may be more successful in the smaller towns and cities of the former communist countries. Other typical jobs for tourists (for example, washing dishes in Alpine resorts) may come with board and lodging. If you do find a temporary job in Central Europe, the pay is likely to be abysmally low. For more details, look under Work in the individual destination chapter Directory sections.
Resources:

Transitions Abroad (www.transitionsabroad.com) Publishes work-abroad books, lists job opportunities.

Childcare International (www.childint.co.uk) Au-pair and nanny jobs tending to little Europeans.

International Cooperative Education (www.icemenlo.com) Jobs for those with Teaching English as a Foreign Language (TEFL) credentials.

Jobs in the Alps (www.jobs-in-the-alps.com) Mainly service jobs like chambermaids, bar staff and porters. Some language skills required.

Season Workers (www.seasonworkers.com) Ski-resort and summer work; also English-teaching jobs.

Transport

Though things are equalising, transport can vary depending on whether you travel the more westerly (Germany, Austria, Switzerland, Liechtenstein) or more easterly (Slovakia, Slovenia, the Czech Republic, Poland, Hungary) countries in the region.

GETTING THERE & AWAY

Central Europe is well connected to the wider world by air, and competition among low-cost carriers has made short air hops available from Europe and the UK. Taking the train (northwards from Turkey or Greece, for example, or eastwards from England, France or Spain) is a scenic and ecofriendly alternative.

The westernmost countries have the best connections, but from Europe you can get pretty much everywhere in this book by rail with a switch or two. Bus, bicycle and car are other possible modes of transport that can be used to enter the region. Refer to the individual destination chapters for specific details. Note that flights, tours and rail tickets can be booked online at lonelyplanet.com/bookings.

Entering Central Europe

There is little hassle when entering the region through gateway airports or from EU border states. Crossings to take note of:

From Belarus or Ukraine To Poland, Slovakia or Hungary; expect time delays and tighter-than-ever immigration and customs controls. Have necessary visas for Belarus and/or Ukraine, and no more than the permitted number of cigarettes.

From Romania, Serbia or Croatia To Hungary or Slovenia; involves no great problems as long as you have the necessary visas and documents.

Air

Frankfurt and Zürich are major international air hubs linked to points across the globe; Vienna is only slightly less connected. You can also reach major cities like Munich, Prague, Budapest and Warsaw from abroad. Airports in Ljubljana and Bratislava host intra-European flights only, tiny

Liechtenstein has no airport. For airport specifics, see the Transport sections at the end of each destination chapter.

Airlines

National carriers take you to and from a host of world cities, and a web of low-cost carrier routes connects across Western Europe. The rule of thumb is the further east you go, the fewer regional airports there are.

Central European national airlines (Slovakia has none):

Adria Airways (JP; www. adria-airways.com) Slovenia

Austrian Airlines (OS; www. aua.com)

ČSA (OK; www.czechairlines. com) Czech Republic

LOT Polish Airlines (LO; www.lot.com)

Lufthansa (LH; www. lufthansa.com) Germany

Malév Hungarian Airlines (MA; www.malev.hu)

Swiss International Air Lines (LX; www.swiss.com)

The following low-cost carriers offer the biggest selection of flights to and from Central Europe:

Air Berlin (AB; www.airberlin. de) Germany-based, serves Western Europe (including Italy, Spain, Austria), North America and Southeast Asia.

Danube Wings (V5; www. danubewings.eu) Connecting Vienna or Bratislava with Italy or Croatia.

easyJet (U2; www.easyjet. com) Connects most of Central Europe with the UK; some intra-European flights, too.

germanwings (4U; www. germanwings.com) Connects across Europe from multiple points in Germany, Switzer land, Austria, Budapest, Prague and Kraków.

Ryanair (1l; www.ryanair. com) Dozens of sometimes remote, secondary airport destinations across the UK and Europe (excluding Switzerland).

Vueling (VY; www.vueling. com) Connects Spanish

hubs with Prague, Vienna and Zürich.

Wizzair (W6; www.wizzair. com) Connects multiple Polish and German destinations, Prague and Budapest with Europe.

Additional airlines serving the region:

Air Canada (AC; www. aircanada.ca)

Air France (AF; www.air france.com)

American Airlines (AA; www.aa.com)

British Airways (BA; www. britishairways.com)

Delta Air Lines (DL; www. delta.com)

Continental Airlines (CO; www.continental.com)

KLM (KL; www.klm.nl)

Qantas (QF; www.qantas. com.au)

Singapore Airlines (SQ; www.singaporeair.com)

Tickets

You'll find cheaper fares are often available if you travel midweek, stay away at least one Saturday night or take advantage of promotional offers. Sign up for sales alerts at individual airline websites or at **Airfare Watchdog** (www.airfarewatchdog.co.uk or www.airfarewatchdog.com).

AIR PASSES

Before departure, travellers from countries such as the USA, Canada, Australia and New Zealand can buy the **Europebyair FlightPass** (www.europebyair.com), which offers flexible one-way US$99 intra-European flights with no blackout dates.

The three major airline alliances have various passes that include flights within Europe – if you fly to Europe with one of the member carriers. Typically segments cost €55 to €240.

OneWorld (www.oneworld.com)

Sky Team (www.skyteam.com)

Star Alliance (www.star alliance.com)

STUDENT & YOUTH FARES

Full-time students and those aged under 26 sometimes have access to better deals than other travellers. These may not always be cheaper fares but can include more flexibility to change flights and/or routes. You have to show a document proving your date of birth and a valid International Student Identity Card (ISIC) or an International Youth Travel Card (IYTC). See **International Student Travel Confederation** (www. istc.org) or **STA Travel** (www. statravel.com) for more details.

Land

Bicycle

Transporting a bicycle by plane is possible (taken apart or whole); check with the airline for regulations and fees.

SEARCHING THE SKIES

International powerhouse search engines like www.expedia.com and www.orbitz.com can help you find airfares on major airlines. Tracking down a budget carrier deal in Europe is a wee bit trickier; some of the low-cost airlines opt out of consolidator websites. We recommend searching these websites:

» **FlyBudget.com** (www.flybudget.com)

» **Fly Cheapo** (www.flycheapo.com)

» **Kayak** (www.kayak.com)

» **Skyscanner** (www.skyscanner.net)

» **Vayama** (www.vayama.com)

Bus

Major urban centres are well connected by bus to European destinations. However, budget air and rail prices rival bus fares, so these slow, long-distance routes are not popular. See the Transport and Getting There & Away sections of individual destination chapters for specific routes and prices.

Car & Motorcycle

No special requirements exist for driving into Central Europe. If you've hired a car elsewhere, make sure all the countries you plan to visit are insured by the rental agency.

Train

Regular train services connect Central Europe with practically every corner of the European continent. To get here by rail from Central Asia is possible but will require several days and/or transfers. In general:

Germany, Switzerland, Austria and Slovenia Connected by direct train with some Western European capitals, require transfers from Eastern Europe and Moscow.

Poland, Hungary, Slovakia and the Czech Republic Direct routes to Eastern Europe, may require transfers to Western Europe.

Liechtenstein Requires transfer through Austrian or Swiss border towns.

Sea

Though it's not the most common way of arriving, a few ferries do run to Central Europe. For specifics, see individual destination chapters. Compare prices and check routes at **Ferry Savers** (www. ferrysavers.com).

Routes:

Germany To Scandinavia and Baltic states.

Poland To Denmark and Sweden.

Slovenia To Italy.

GETTING AROUND

Air

If you're travelling without checked luggage, booking at least two weeks ahead and willing to travel to alternative airports, European air flights can be quite affordable. Both national and low-cost carriers fly within the region; check the prices of both. For a list of major airlines see p629; for carriers with more limited service, see the specific destination chapters. Germanwings and Air Berlin have the most extensive intra–Central European networks. Note that smaller nations, such as Hungary, have no internal flights.

Bicycle

Crossing Central Europe by bicycle is certainly doable. Just remember that in addition to flat river plains, the region encompasses Europe's highest mountain peaks.

» Cycling is allowed on roads and highways, not on limited-access motorways or autobahns.

» Numerous proper bike routes exist in western countries; further east you'll be relying on roadsides and rural routes.

» Helmets are not compulsory, but are advised.

» Rental outlets are more common in western than eastern countries; some are listed in this book, otherwise check with tourist offices.

» All but the fastest, ICE trains allow bicycle transport; some bus transport is available.

Boat

Seasonal boat travel on Central Europe's riverways is a cruisey, scenic – and very slow – way to get around. You won't save any money

plying the waters, but you will gain a unique perspective on the region. Organised boat tours are also available, see p633.

Danube River (April to October) Ferries run from southern Germany to Austria, within Austria, and from Austria to Slovakia and into Hungary. Most popular route: Vienna–Bratislava–Budapest.

Moselle and Rhine Rivers Varying length routes within Germany.

Bus

Buses generally have a slight edge over trains and planes in terms of cost, but are slower and much less comfortable. They tend to be best for getting around mountainous areas and for reaching remote rural villages. International services link major cities only. Note that even if two towns in different countries appear close on the map, there's often no direct international service between them.

Eurolines (www.eurolines. com) Umbrella agency for international European bus lines; multicountry passes available (15 days from €205, 30 days from €310).

Busabout (www.busabout. com) Offers a 'hop-on, hop-off' bus (six to nine stops, from €320) that travels through northern Germany, the Czech Republic, Austria, southern Germany and Switzerland – in that order. Prebooking recommended.

Car & Motorcycle

Travelling by motor vehicle allows great flexibility compared to other transport; you can get further off the beaten track and away from cities. But it does consume more carbon. Note that a car can be a major inconvenience in the region's urban centres, which have enthusiasticallly enforced parking restrictions and many one-way streets. **ViaMichelin** (www.viamichelin. com) is an excellent map source for route planning.

Automobile Associations

Ask your motoring organisation for details about free and reciprocal services offered by affiliated organisations around Europe. Some rental agreements include roadside assistance.

Independent breakdown-assistance policies:

European residents European Five Star Service offered by **AA** (www.theaa. com); European Motoring Assistance offered by **RAC** (www.rac.co.uk).

Non-Europeans Often it's less expensive to arrange international coverage with your home-country national motoring organisation before departure.

Driving Licence & Documentation

Requirements include the following:

» Proof of insurance and of vehicle ownership or rental.

CLIMATE CHANGE & TRAVEL

Every form of transport that relies on carbon-based fuel generates CO_2, the main cause of human-induced climate change. Modern travel is dependent on aeroplanes, which might use less fuel per kilometre per person than most cars but travel much greater distances. The altitude at which aircraft emit gases (including CO_2) and particles also contributes to their climate change impact. Many websites offer 'carbon calculators' that allow people to estimate the carbon emissions generated by their journey and, for those who wish to do so, to offset the impact of the greenhouse gases emitted with contributions to portfolios of climate-friendly initiatives throughout the world. Lonely Planet offsets the carbon footprint of all staff and author travel.

» EU, North American and Australian driving licences generally acceptable.

» For any other type of licence, obtain an International Driving Permit (IDP) from your local motoring organisation.

» Every vehicle travelling across an international border should display a sticker that shows the country of registration.

Fuel

Fuel prices can vary enormously from country to country, but in general are similar to those in the UK and higher than in the US. Unleaded petrol of 95 or 98 octane, and diesel, are widely available throughout Central Europe. **Automobile Association** (www.aaroadwatch. ie/eupetrolprices) is a useful webpage tracking European fuel prices.

Hire

Hiring a vehicle is a relatively straightforward procedure across the region; you will find most rental options near airports and in capital cities. What to expect:

» Minimum rental age between 21 and 25.

» Credit card required.

» Standard manual transmission; you'll pay more for automatic.

» Price inclusions vary (unlimited mileage? collision waiver? taxes?); be sure to ask ahead.

» Daily rates from €25 to €75, in general.

» Big international firms may allow drop-off in a different town or country (for a fee).

» Local firms may charge less.

» Booking ahead will always save you money.

International companies and consolidators:

Autos Abroad (www.autos abroad.com)

Auto Europe (www.auto europe.com)

Avis (www.avis.com)

Budget (www.budget.com)

Europcar (www.europcar. com)

Hertz (www.hertz.com)

Kemwel Holiday Autos (www.kemwel.com)

Insurance

» Third-party motor accident insurance is compulsory throughout the region.

» It is usually included with rental, covered by your private auto insurance or by some major credit cards.

» Europeans driving a private vehicle should get a Green Card, an internationally recognised proof of insurance, from their insurer.

» Check that the Green Card lists all the countries you intend to visit. If it doesn't, you will have to take out separate third-party cover in the country in question.

» You'll need this cover in the event of an accident outside the country where the vehicle is insured.

» Obtain a European Accident Statement from your insurance company.

» Never sign statements you can't read or understand – insist on a translation and sign it only if it's acceptable.

Motorcycle

Motorcycle and moped rental is not very common in Central Europe. Wearing of helmets for riders and passengers is compulsory. Resources:

Ride the World (www.ride theworld.com)

Horizons Unlimited (www. horizonsunlimited.com)

Road Conditions

Conditions and types of roads vary across the region, but it is possible to make some generalisations.

Motorways (autobahns, autoroutes etc) Provide the most direct routes and best-condition roads; usually four- to six-lanes, 100km/h-plus speed limits and require a tariff (a motorway sticker or pass) for usage.

Highways Good-condition roads, more extensive coverage than motorways; speed limit may slow down through towns.

Minor routes Normally more than adequate, with many stops in towns and villages. Far-eastern Poland, Slovakia and Hungary have a few less-than-perfect rural roads.

Night driving Horse-drawn conveyances, cyclists, pedestrians and domestic animals can be night-time hazards on narrow rural roads.

Road Rules

See the individual destination chapters for more details, or contact an automobile association for the specific rules of each nation. In many countries, driving infringements are subject to an on-the-spot fine; always ask for a receipt.

In general:

» Drive on the right-hand side of the road.

» Keep right except when overtaking, and use your indicators for any change of lane and when pulling away from the kerb.

» Speed limits are sign-posted, generally: no speed limit on German autobahns unless marked, 110km/h or 120km/h on motorways, 100km/h on other highways, 80km/h on secondary and tertiary roads, and 50km/h or 60km/h in built-up areas.

» Use of seatbelts is mandatory; in most countries, children aged under 12 are not permitted in the front seat.

» Driving after drinking any alcohol is a very serious offence, with legal blood-alcohol limits between 0% (that's ZERO) and 0.08%.

» It's prohibited to turn right against a red light, even after coming to a stop.

» In case of an accident, carrying and using a red reflector warning triangle is mandatory.

» Never pass a tram on the left or stop within 1m of tram tracks.

Hitching

Hitching is never entirely safe in any country, and we don't recommend it. Travellers who decide to hitch should understand that they are taking a small but potentially serious risk. You will occasionally see someone catching a ride in the eastern part of the eastern Central European countries. If you do decide to stick out a thumb, look presentable and cheerful, make a sign indicating your intended destination in the local language and remember the following:

» Travelling in pairs and letting someone know where you plan to go is safer.

» Women travelling alone should never hitch.

» Never let your pack be put in the boot.

» Only sit next to a door that can be opened.

» Don't hesitate to refuse a ride if you feel at all uncomfortable, and insist on being let out at the first sign of trouble.

» Hitching is usually illegal on motorways – stand on the slip roads or approach drivers at petrol stations and truck stops.

It is sometimes possible to arrange a lift in advance: scan student noticeboards in colleges, contact car-sharing agencies or click onto either of the following:

BUG – the Backpackers Ultimate Guide to Europe (www.bugeurope.com)

Hitchhikers (www.hitchhikers.org)

Local Transport

Central European cities and towns have extensive and safe public transport networks; villages may have limited access. In general, in the larger cities you'll need to buy tickets at newsagents, vending machines or public transport offices and validate on board. See destination chapters' Transport sections for specifics.

Local buses Travel around cities and to outlying towns and villages.

Metros Exist in Berlin, Vienna, Budapest and Prague; transfers between lines or zones may require additional tariffs.

Taxis Often prohibitively expensive, especially from airports, and train and bus stations; calling ahead will always save money over hailing on the street.

Trams & trolleybuses (electric buses) Available in many cities across the region; some sleek new cars have electronic readouts, stop indicators and air-conditioning.

Tours

Central Europe is easy to explore independently – a package holiday may be worth considering if you have a specific interest or time is extremely limited. Examples of major and multi-country operators are listed below; search online for more limited-focus operators (history tours, archaeology tours etc). For information on cycling, hiking and bird-watching tours see p622. Tour prices are generally for double occupancy; singles have to share or pay a supplement.

Land Tours

Contiki (www.contiki.com) Weeks-long, party-oriented, Europe-wide bus tours (ages 18 to 35).

Elder Hostel (www.elderhostel.org) Educational tours for people aged over 50.

Homeric Tours (www.homerictours.com) First-class multicapital tours in Central Europe.

Regent Holidays (www.regent-holidays.co.uk) Experienced operator offers city-break tours in Germany, Austria, Poland, Hungary, the Czech Republic and Slovakia.

Smithsonian Institution (www.smithsonianjourneys.org) Cultural-oriented itineraries, including 'Old World' tours through Poland, Slovakia, Hungary, Austria and the Czech Republic.

Tauck Tours (www.tauck.com) Alpine, capital, Christmas market, Germanic and other multicountry theme tours in the region.

River Tours

River cruiseships generally hold 100 to 300 passengers,

meals are included and rooms can be posh – if small – with their own river views.

AMA Waterways (www.ama waterways.com) Superluxe ships cruising the Danube and Rhine; land detours available.

Cruise Locators (www. cruiselocators.com) Consolidator, can help compare and contrast companies.

Viking River Cruises (www. vikingrivercruises.com) Danube, Rhine and multisided itineraries in Central Europe, including an eight-day cruise to Budapest, Bratislava, Vienna, the Danube Valley and Nuremburg.

Train

For our money, trains are the most atmospheric, comfortable and fun way to make tracks in Central Europe. All of the major, and most of the minor, cities are on the rail network. It's perfectly feasible for train travel to be your only form of intercity transport. Overnight trains have the added benefit of saving you a night's accommodation. Think before you schedule, however – a daytime train journey through the Alps is a trip highlight.

Useful resources:

Deutsche Bahn (www.bahn. de) German national rail site, covers the schedules of all the nations of Central Europe (but only has prices for Germany).

European Rail Guide (www. europeanrailguide.com) Current timetables.

The Man in Seat 61 (www. seat61.com) Invaluable train descriptions, rail passes and details of journeys to the far reaches of the continent.

Thomas Cook (www.thomas cookpublishing.com) Publishes the *Thomas Cook European Timetable* book, which has long been the long-term travellers' bible. Comprehensive listing of train schedules and supplement and reservation requirements.

Classes

Train cars in Central Europe come in 1st- and 2nd-class flavours. What to expect:

» Most train cars have a modern, aeroplane-like layout.

» 1st-class chairs are larger, often near laptop outlets, and cost roughly twice as much as 2nd class.

» Cabin compartments (four to eight seats facing each other) are found on some trains in the easternmost countries.

» Longer routes and overnight trains often have dining cars, but these are slowly being replaced by snack bars and mobile carts.

» On busy routes, and during the peak summer season, reserve a seat in advance.

» In the east, it often pays to stick to the faster and generally newer IC (Intercity) or EC (Eurocity) trains, especially if you're concerned about the condition of the bathrooms.

» Supplements apply on IC and EC express trains. Reservations are often obligatory.

» German ICE (Intercity Express) international trains are among the quickest, and the priciest, in the region.

» Note that long-distance Central European trains sometimes split en route; make sure you're in the correct carriage.

Rail Passes

European rail passes are worth buying only if you plan on doing a whole lot of travelling in the more expensive westernmost countries. If buying a pass, up-front planning will help you make the

---

OVERNIGHT TRAINS

You can take advantage of a night's lodging saved when travelling by rail between the west and the east of the region. (Even intercountry distances are relatively small in Central Europe.) On an overnight train:

» Reservations are always advisable.

» A bed space costs extra (from about €20 to €100 additional to the ticket).

» Carry your valuables on you at all times as a petty-theft preventative.

Western Central Europe

If you don't fancy sleeping in your seat with somebody else's elbow in your ear, options include the following:

» **Couchettes** Comfortable enough, four bunks per compartment in 1st class or six in 2nd class.

» **Sleepers** Most comfortable option, beds for one or two passengers in 1st class, and two or three passengers in 2nd class.

Eastern Central Europe

Some trains in these countries offer three classes of sleeping accommodation.

» **First class** Two berths per compartment; you're usually paying for space rather than decor or service.

» **Second class** Four berths in a closed compartment.

» **Third class** Six basic bunks per compartment; not available everywhere.

SAMPLE RAIL PASS RATES

See below for details of the countries covered by each pass.

Eurail

PASS NAME	AGE	CLASS	DURATION	PRICE (USD)
Global – all countries	12-25	2nd	10 days in 2 months	$565
Global – all countries	12-25	2nd	15 days	$480
Global – all countries	over 26	1st	10 days in 2 months	$869
Global – all countries	over 26	1st	15 days	$735
Select – 3 contiguous countries	12-25	2nd	5 days in 2 months	$299
Select – 3 countries	over 26	1st	5 days in 2 months	$465
Select – 5 countries	12-25	2nd	5 days in 2 months	$369
Select – 5 countries	over 26	1st	5 days in 2 months	$569

Inter-Rail

PASS NAME	AGE	CLASS	DURATION	PRICE (EURO)
Global – all countries	12-25	2nd	10 days in 22 days	€249
Global – all countries	12-25	2nd	15 days	€289
Global – all countries	over 26	1st	10 days in 22 days	€559
Global – all countries	over 26	1st	15 days	€619
Global – all countries	over 26	2nd	10 days in 22 days	€369
Global – all countries	over 26	2nd	15 days	€409

most of your investment. Note that not all countries in Central Europe are covered by all rail passes.

EURAIL

There are so many different **Eurail** (www.eurail.com) passes covering such a wide variety of areas and time periods that you need to have a good idea of your itinerary before purchasing. Two or more people travelling together can get a 'saver' version of passes at a discount.

Who? Can only be bought by residents of non-European countries; supposed to be purchased before European arrival (but you generally buy online...).

Where? Valid for travel on national railways and some private lines in Switzerland, Austria, Germany, the Czech Republic, Poland, Hungary and Slovenia.

EUROPEAN EAST PASS

Who? Can be purchased at travel agencies by anyone not permanently resident in Europe (including the UK).

Where? Valid for travel in Austria, Hungary, the Czech Republic, Slovakia and Poland.

How much? For five days of 1st- or 2nd-class travel within one month, **Rail Europe** (www.raileurope -world.com) charges US$214 or US$179; extra rail days (maximum five), US$36 each. No student discount.

INTER-RAIL

Terms and conditions vary from country to country, but there is a discount of around 50% on normal fares using the **Inter-Rail pass** (www. interrailnet.com).

Who? Available to European residents (and to nationals of Turkey, Morocco, Tunisia and Algeria) of more than six months' standing; passport identification is required.

Where? Valid in all Central European countries except Liechtenstein; not valid on some high-speed services, when travelling in the country where the pass was bought. Special rules apply for night-time train travel.

NATIONAL RAIL PASSES

Some discounted single-country rail passes are available from Eurail and Inter-Rail, as well as from the national train service itself. These are not always great value, but they do save the time and hassle of having to buy individual tickets. In a large or expensive country such as Germany or Switzerland, a pass can make sense; in a small, relatively inexpensive country such as Slovakia, it makes none whatsoever.

Language

WANT MORE?

For in-depth language information and handy phrases, check out Lonely Planet's *Central Europe Phrasebook*. You'll find it at **shop.lonelyplanet.com**, or you can buy Lonely Planet's iPhone phrasebooks at the Apple App Store.

This chapter offers basic vocabulary to help you get around Central Europe. If you read our coloured pronunciation guides as if they were English, you'll be understood. Note that the stressed syllables are indicated with italics.

Some of the phrases in this chapter have both polite and informal forms (indicated by the abbreviations 'pol' and 'inf' respectively). Use the polite form when addressing people you're meeting for the first time, who are older than you, officials and service staff. The abbreviations 'm' and 'f' indicate masculine and feminine gender respectively.

CZECH

An accent mark over a vowel in written Czech indicates it's pronounced as a long sound.

Note that air is pronounced as in 'hair', aw as in 'law', oh as the 'o' in 'note', ow as in 'how', uh as the 'a' in 'ago', kh as in the Scottish *loch,* and zh as the 's' in 'pleasure'. Also, r is a rolled sound in Czech and the apostrophe (') indicates a slight y sound after a consonant.

Basics

Hello.	*Ahoj.*	uh·hoy
Goodbye.	*Na shledanou.*	nuh·skhle·duh·noh
Excuse me.	*Promiňte.*	pro·min'·te
Sorry.	*Promiňte.*	pro·min'·te
Please.	*Prosím.*	pro·seem
Thank you.	*Děkuji.*	dye·ku·yi
Yes./No.	*Ano./Ne.*	uh·no/ne

What's your name?
Jak se jmenujete/jmenuješ? (pol/inf) — yuhk se *yme*·nu·ye·te/*yme*·nu·yesh

My name is ...
Jmenuji se ... — *yme*·nu·yi se ...

Do you speak English?
Mluvíte anglicky? — mlu·vee·te uhn·glits·ki

I don't understand.
Nerozumím. — ne·ro·zu·meem

Accommodation

campsite	*tábořiště*	ta·bo·rzhish·tye
guesthouse	*penzion*	pen·zi·on
hotel	*hotel*	ho·tel
youth hostel	*mládežnická ubytovna*	mla·dezh·nyits·ka u·bi·tov·nuh

Do you have a ... room?	*Máte ... pokoj?*	ma·te ... po·koy
single	*jednolůžkový*	yed·no·loozh·ko·vee
double	*dvoulůžkový*	dvoh·loozh·ko·vee

How much is it per ...?	*Kolik to stojí ...?*	ko·lik to sto·yee ...
night	*na noc*	nuh nots
person	*za osobu*	zuh o·so·bu

Eating & Drinking

What would you recommend?
Co byste doporučil/   tso *bis*·te do·po·ru·chil/
doporučila? (m/f)   do·po·ru·chi·luh

Do you have vegetarian food?
Máte vegetariánská   *ma*·te ve·ge·tuh·ri·ans·ka
jídla?   *yeed*·luh

I'll have ...	Dám si ...	dam si ...
Cheers!	Na zdraví!	nuh zdruh·vee

I'd like the ...,	Chtěl/	khtyel/
please.	Chtěla bych	khtye·luh bikh
	..., prosím. (m/f)	... pro·seem
bill	účet	oo·chet
menu	jídelníček	yee·del·nyee·chek

(bottle of) beer	(láhev) piva	(la·hef) pi·vuh
(cup of) coffee/tea	(šálek) kávy/čaje	(sha·lek) ka·vi/chuh·ye
water	voda	vo·duh
(glass of) wine	(skleničku) vína	(skle·nyich·ku) vee·nuh
breakfast	snídaně	snee·duh·nye
lunch	oběd	o·byed
dinner	večeře	ve·che·rzhe

Emergencies

Help!	Pomoc!	po·mots
Go away!	Běžte pryč!	byezh·te prich

Call ...!	Zavolejte ...!	zuh·vo·ley·te ...
a doctor	lékaře	lair·kuh·rzhe
the police	policii	po·li·tsi·yi

I'm lost.
Zabloudil/   zuh·bloh·dyil/
Zabloudila jsem. (m/f)   zuh·bloh·dyi·luh ysem

Signs – Czech

Vchod	Entrance
Východ	Exit
Otevřeno	Open
Zavřeno	Closed
Zakázáno	Prohibited
Záchody/Toalety	Toilets

Numbers – Czech

1	jeden	ye·den
2	dva	dvuh
3	tři	trzhi
4	čtyři	chti·rzhi
5	pět	pyet
6	šest	shest
7	sedm	se·dm
8	osm	o·sm
9	devět	de·vyet
10	deset	de·set

I'm ill.
Jsem nemocný/   ysem ne·mots·nee/
nemocná. (m/f)   ne·mots·na

Where are the toilets?
Kde jsou toalety?   gde ysoh to·uh·le·ti

Shopping & Services

I'm looking for ...
Hledám ...   hle·dam ...

How much is it?
Kolik to stojí?   ko·lik to sto·yee

That's too expensive.
To je moc drahé.   to ye mots druh·hair

bank	banka	buhn·kuh
post office	pošta	posh·tuh
tourist office	turistická informační kancelář	tu·ris·tits·ka in·for·muhch·nyee kuhn·tse·larzh

Transport & Directions

Where's the ...?
Kde je ...?   gde ye ...

What's the address?
Jaká je adresa?   yuh·ka ye uh·dre·suh

Can you show me (on the map)?
Můžete mi to   moo·zhe·te mi to
ukázat (na mapě)?   u·ka·zuht (nuh muh·pye)

One ... ticket to (Telč), please.	... jízdenku do (Telče), prosím.	... yeez·den·ku do (tel·che) pro·seem
one-way	Jedno-směrnou	yed·no·smyer·noh
return	Zpáteční	zpa·tech·nyee
bus	autobus	ow·to·bus
plane	letadlo	le·tuhd·lo
train	vlak	vluhk

GERMAN

German is spoken in Germany, Austria, Liechtenstein, Belgium, Switzerland and Luxembourg.

Vowels in German can be short or long, which influences the meaning of words. Note that air is pronounced as in 'fair', aw as in 'saw', eu as the 'u' in 'nurse', ew as ee with rounded lips, ow as in 'now', kh as in the Scottish *loch* (pronounced at the back of the throat), r is also a throaty sound, and zh is pronounced as the 's' in 'pleasure'.

Basics

Hello.

(Austria)	*Servus.*	zer·vus
(Germany)	*Guten Tag.*	goo·ten taak
(Switzerland)	*Grüezi.*	grew·e·tsi
Goodbye.	*Auf Wiedersehen.*	owf vee·der·zey·en
Excuse me.	*Entschuldigung.*	ent·shul·di·gung
Sorry.	*Entschuldigung.*	ent·shul·di·gung
Please.	*Bitte.*	bi·te
Thank you.	*Danke.*	dang·ke
Yes.	*Ja.*	yaa
No.	*Nein.*	nain

What's your name?
Wie ist Ihr Name?   vee ist eer naa·me

My name is ...
Mein Name ist ...   main naa·me ist ...

Do you speak English?
Sprechen Sie Englisch?   shpre·khen zee eng·lish

I don't understand.
Ich verstehe nicht.   ikh fer·shtey·e nikht

Accommodation

campsite	*Campingplatz*	kem·ping·plats
guesthouse	*Pension*	paang·zyawn
hotel	*Hotel*	ho·tel
youth hostel	*Jugend-herberge*	yoo·gent·her·ber·ge

Signs – German

Eingang	Entrance
Ausgang	Exit
Offen	Open
Geschlossen	Closed
Verboten	Prohibited
Toiletten	Toilets

Do you have a ... room?	*Haben Sie ein ...?*	haa·ben zee ain ...
single	*Einzelzimmer*	ain·tsel·tsi·mer
double	*Doppelzimmer mit einem Doppelbett*	do·pel·tsi·mer mit ai·nem do·pel·bet

How much is it per ...?	*Wie viel kostet es pro ...?*	vee feel kos·tet es praw ...
night	*Nacht*	nakht
person	*Person*	per·zawn

Eating & Drinking

What would you recommend?
Was empfehlen Sie?   vas emp·fey·len zee

Do you have vegetarian food?
Haben Sie vegetarisches Essen?   haa·ben zee ve·ge·taa·ri·shes e·sen

I'll have ...
Ich hätte gern ...   ikh he·te gern ...

Cheers!
Prost!   prawst

I'd like the ..., please.	*Bitte bringen Sie ...*	bi·te bring·en zee ...
bill	*die Rechnung*	dee rekh·nung
menu	*die Speise-karte*	dee shpai·ze·kar·te

beer	*Bier*	beer
coffee	*Kaffee*	ka·fey
tea	*Tee*	tey
water	*Wasser*	va·ser
wine	*Wein*	vain

breakfast	*Frühstück*	frew·shtewk
lunch	*Mittagessen*	mi·taak·e·sen
dinner	*Abendessen*	aa·bent·e·sen

Emergencies

Help!	*Hilfe!*	hil·fe
Go away!	*Gehen Sie weg!*	gey·en zee vek

Call ...!	*Rufen Sie ...!*	roo·fen zee ...
a doctor	*einen Arzt*	ai·nen artst
the police	*die Polizei*	dee po·li·tsai

I'm lost.
Ich habe mich verirrt.   ikh haa·be mikh fer·irt

I'm ill.
Ich bin krank.   ikh bin krangk

Where are the toilets?
Wo ist die Toilette?   vo ist dee to·a·le·te

Numbers – German		
1	*eins*	ains
2	*zwei*	tsvai
3	*zdrei*	drai
4	*vier*	feer
5	*fünf*	fewnf
6	*sechs*	zeks
7	*sieben*	zee·ben
8	*acht*	akht
9	*neun*	noyn
10	*zehn*	tseyn

Shopping & Services

I'm looking for ...
Ich suche nach ...   ikh *zoo*·khe nakh ...

How much is it?
Wie viel kostet das?   vee feel *kos*·tet das

That's too expensive.
Das ist zu teuer.   das ist tsoo *toy*·er

market	*Markt*	markt
post office	*Postamt*	*post*·amt
tourist office	*Fremden-verkehrs-büro*	*frem*·den·fer·kairs·bew·raw

Transport & Directions

Where's ...?
Wo ist ...?   vaw ist ...

What's the address?
Wie ist die Adresse?   vee ist dee a·*dre*·se

Can you show me (on the map)?
Können Sie es mir (auf der Karte) zeigen?   *keu*·nen zee es meer (owf dair *kar*·te) *tsai*·gen

One ...ticket to (Berlin), please.	*Einen ... nach (Berlin), bitte.*	*ai*·nen ... naakh (ber·*leen*), *bi*·te
one-way	*einfache Fahrkarte*	*ain*·fa·khe *faar*·kar·te
return	*Rückfahr-karte*	*rewk*·faar·kar·te

boat	*Boot*	bawt
bus	*Bus*	bus
plane	*Flugzeug*	*flook*·tsoyk
train	*Zug*	tsook

HUNGARIAN

A symbol over a vowel in written Hungarian indicates it's pronounced as a long sound. Double consonants should be drawn out a little longer than in English.

Note that aw is pronounced as in 'law', eu as in 'nurse', ew as ee with rounded lips, and zh as the 's' in 'pleasure'. Also, r is rolled in Hungarian and the apostrophe (') indicates a slight y sound.

Basics

Hello.	*Szervusz.* (sg)	*ser*·vus
	Szervusztok. (pl)	*ser*·vus·tawk
Goodbye.	*Viszlát.*	*vis*·lat
Excuse me.	*Elnézést kérek.*	*el*·ney·zeysht *key*·rek
Sorry.	*Sajnálom.*	*shoy*·na·lawm
Please.	*Kérem.* (pol)	*key*·rem
	Kérlek. (inf)	*keyr*·lek
Thank you.	*Köszönöm.*	*keu*·seu·neum
Yes.	*Igen.*	*i*·gen
No.	*Nem.*	nem

What's your name?
Mi a neve/ neved? (pol/inf)   mi o *ne*·ve/ *ne*·ved

My name is ...
A nevem ...   o *ne*·vem ...

Do you speak English?
Beszél/Beszélsz angolul? (pol/inf)   be·*seyl*/be·*seyls on*·gaw·lul

I don't understand.
Nem Értem.   nem *eyr*·tem

Accommodation

campsite	*kemping*	*kem*·ping
guesthouse	*panzió*	*pon*·zi·āw
hotel	*szálloda*	*sal*·law·do
youth hostel	*ifjúsági szálló*	*if*·yū·sha·gi *sal*·lāw

Signs – Hungarian	
Bejárat	Entrance
Kijárat	Exit
Nyitva	Open
Zárva	Closed
Tilos	Prohibited
Toalett	Toilets

Numbers – Hungarian

1	*egy*	ej
2	*kettő*	ket·tēū
3	*három*	ha·rawm
4	*négy*	neyj
5	*öt*	eut
6	*hat*	hot
7	*hét*	heyt
8	*nyolc*	nyawlts
9	*kilenc*	ki·lents
10	*tíz*	teez

Do you have a ... room?	*Van Önnek kiadó egy ... szobája?*	von eun·nek ki·o·dāw ed' ... saw·ba·yo
single	*egyágyas*	ej·a·dyosh
double	*duplaágyas*	dup·lo·a·dyosh

How much is it per ...?	*Mennyibe kerül egy ...?*	men'·nyi·be ke·rewl ej ...
night	*éjszakára*	ey·so·ka·ro
person	*főre*	fēū·re

Eating & Drinking

What would you recommend?
Mit ajánlana? — mit o·yan·lo·no

Do you have vegetarian food?
Vannak Önöknél vegetáriánus ételek? — von·nok eu·neuk·neyl ve·ge·ta·ri·a·nush ey·te·lek

I'll have ...
... kérek. — ... key·rek

Cheers! (to one person)
Egészségedre! — e·geys·shey·ged·re

Cheers! (to more than one person)
Egészségetekre! — e·geys·shey·ge·tek·re

I'd like the ...	*... szeretném.*	... se·ret·neym
bill	*A számlát*	o sam·lat
menu	*Az étlapot*	oz eyt·lo·pawt

(bottle of) beer	*(üveg) sör*	(ew·veg) sheur
(cup of) coffee/tea	*(csésze) kávé/tea*	(chey·se) ka·vey/te·o
water	*víz*	veez
(glass of) wine	*(pohár) bor*	(paw·har) bawr

breakfast	*reggeli*	reg·ge·li
lunch	*ebéd*	e·beyd
dinner	*vacsora*	vo·chaw·ro

Emergencies

Help!	*Segítség!*	she·geet·sheyg
Go away!	*Menjen innen!*	men·yen in·nen
Call a doctor!	*Hívjon orvost!*	heev·yawn awr·vawsht
Call the police!	*Hívja a rendőrséget!*	heev·yo o rend·ēūr·shey·get

I'm lost.
Eltévedtem. — el·tey·ved·tem

I'm ill.
Rosszul vagyok. — raws·sul vo·dyawk

Where are the toilets?
Hol a vécé? — hawl o vey·tsey

Shopping & Services

I'm looking for ...
Keresem a ... — ke·re·shem o ...

How much is it?
Mennyibe kerül? — men'·nyi·be ke·rewl

That's too expensive.
Ez túl drága. — ez tūl dra·go

market	*piac*	pi·ots
post office	*postahivatal*	pawsh·to·hi·vo·tol
tourist office	*turistairoda*	tu·rish·to·i·raw·do

Transport & Directions

Where's the ...?
Hol van a ...? — hawl von o ...

What's the address?
Mi a cím? — mi o tseem

Can you show me (on the map)?
Meg tudja mutatni nekem (a térképen)? — meg tud·yo mu·tot·ni ne·kem (o teyr·key·pen)

One ... ticket to (Eger), please.	*Egy ... jegy (Eger)be.*	ej ... yej (e·ger)·be
one-way	*csak oda*	chok aw·do
return	*oda-vissza*	aw·do·vis·so

bus	*busz*	bus
plane	*repülőgép*	re·pew·lēū·geyp
train	*vonat*	vaw·not

POLISH

Polish vowels are generally pronounced short. Nasal vowels are pronounced as though you're trying to force the air through your nose, and are indicated with n or m following the vowel.

Note that ow is pronounced as in 'how', kh as in the Scottish *loch*, and zh as the 's' in 'pleasure'. Also, r is rolled in Polish and the apostrophe (') indicates a slight y sound.

Basics

Hello.	*Cześć.*	cheshch
Goodbye.	*Do widzenia.*	do vee·*dze*·nya
Excuse me.	*Przepraszam.*	pshe·*pra*·sham
Sorry.	*Przepraszam.*	pshe·*pra*·sham
Please.	*Proszę.*	*pro*·she
Thank you.	*Dziękuję.*	jyen·*koo*·ye
Yes.	*Tak.*	tak
No.	*Nie.*	nye

What's your name?
Jak się pan/pani   yak shye pan/*pa*·nee
nazywa? (m/f pol)   na·*zi*·va
Jakie się nazywasz? (inf)   yak shye na·*zi*·vash

My name is ...
Nazywam się ...   na·*zi*·vam shye ...

Do you speak English?
Czy pan/pani mówi   chi pan/*pa*·nee *moo*·vee
po angielsku? (m/f)   po an·*gyel*·skoo

I don't understand.
Nie rozumiem.   nye ro·*zoo*·myem

Accommodation

campsite	*kamping*	*kam*·peeng
guesthouse	*pokoje gościnne*	po·*ko*·ye gosh·*chee*·ne
hotel	*hotel*	*ho*·tel
youth hostel	*schronisko młodzieżowe*	skhro·*nees*·ko mwo·jye·*zho*·ve

Do you have a ... room?	*Czy jest pokój ...?*	chi yest *po*·kooy ...
single	*jedno-osobowy*	yed·no-o·so·*bo*·vi
double	*z podwójnym łóżkiem*	z pod·*vooy*·nim *woozh*·kyem

Signs – Polish	
Wejście	Entrance
Wyjście	Exit
Otwarte	Open
Zamknięte	Closed
Wzbroniony	Prohibited
Toalety	Toilets

How much is it per ...?	*Ile kosztuje za ...?*	ee·le kosh·*too*·ye za ...
night	*noc*	nots
person	*osobę*	o·*so*·be

Eating & Drinking

What would you recommend?
Co by pan polecił? (m)   tso bi pan po·*le*·cheew
Co by pani poleciła? (f)   tso bi *pa*·nee po·le·*chee*·wa

Do you have vegetarian food?
Czy jest żywność   chi yest *zhiv*·noshch
wegetariańska?   ve·ge·tar·*yan'*·ska

I'll have ...	*Proszę ...*	*pro*·she ...
Cheers!	*Na zdrowie!*	na *zdro*·vye

I'd like the ..., please.	*Proszę o ...*	*pro*·she o ...
bill	*rachunek*	ra·*khoo*·nek
menu	*jadłospis*	ya·*dwo*·spees

(bottle of) beer	*(butelka) piwa*	(boo·*tel*·ka) *pee*·va
(cup of) coffee/tea	*(filiżanka) kawy/herbaty*	(fee·lee·*zhan*·ka) *ka*·vi/her·*ba*·ti
water	*woda*	*vo*·da
(glass of) wine	*(kieliszek) wina*	(kye·lee·*shek*) *vee*·na

breakfast	*śniadanie*	shnya·*da*·nye
lunch	*obiad*	*o*·byad
dinner	*kolacja*	ko·*la*·tsya

Emergencies

Help!	*Na pomoc!*	na *po*·mots
Go away!	*Odejdź!*	o·*deyj*

Call ...!	*Zadzwoń po ...!*	*zad*·zvon' po ...
a doctor	*lekarza*	le·*ka*·zha
the police	*policję*	po·*lee*·tsye

I'm lost.
Zgubiłem/   zgoo·*bee*·wem/
Zgubiłam się. (m/f)   zgoo·*bee*·wam shye

I'm ill.
Jestem chory/a. (m/f)   yes·tem *kho*·ri/a

Where are the toilets?
Gdzie są toalety?   gjye som to·a·*le*·ti

Numbers – Polish

1	jeden	ye·den
2	dwa	dva
3	trzy	tshi
4	cztery	chte·ri
5	pięć	pyench
6	sześć	sheshch
7	siedem	shye·dem
8	osiem	o·shyem
9	dziewięć	jye·vyench
10	dziesięć	jye·shench

Shopping & Services

I'm looking for ...
Szukam ...   shoo·kam

How much is it?
Ile to kosztuje?   ee·le to kosh·too·ye

That's too expensive.
To jest za drogie.   to yest za dro·gye

market	targ	tark
post office	urząd	oo·zhond
	pocztowy	poch·to·vi
tourist office	biuro	byoo·ro
	turystyczne	too·ris·tich·ne

Transport & Directions

Where's the ...?
Gdzie jest ...?   gjye yest ...

What's the address?
Jaki jest adres?   ya·kee yest ad·res

Can you show me (on the map)?
Czy może pan/pani   chi mo·zhe pan/pa·nee
mi pokazać   mee po·ka·zach
(na mapie)? (m/f)   (na ma·pye)

One ... ticket	Proszę bilet	pro·she bee·let
(to Katowice),	... (do	... (do
please.	Katowic).	ka·to·veets)
one-way	w jedną	v yed·nom
	stronę	stro·ne
return	powrotny	po·vro·tni

boat	łódź	wooj
bus	autobus	ow·to·boos
plane	samolot	sa·mo·lot
train	pociąg	po·chonk

SLOVAK

An accent mark over a vowel in written Slovak indicates it's pronounced as a long sound.

Note that air is pronounced as in 'hair', aw as in 'law', oh as the 'o' in 'note', ow as in 'how', uh as the 'a' in 'ago', dz as the 'ds' in 'adds', kh as in the Scottish *loch,* and zh as the 's' in 'pleasure'. The apostrophe (') indicates a slight y sound.

Basics

Hello.	Dobrý deň.	do·bree dyen'
Goodbye.	Do videnia.	do vi·dye·ni·yuh
Excuse me.	Prepáčte.	pre·pach·tye
Sorry.	Prepáčte.	pre·pach·tye
Please.	Prosím.	pro·seem
Thank you.	Ďakujem	dyuh·ku·yem
Yes.	Áno.	a·no
No.	Nie.	ni·ye

What's your name?
Ako sa voláte?   uh·ko suh vo·la·tye

My name is ...
Volám sa ...   vo·lam suh ...

Do you speak English?
Hovoríte po   ho·vo·ree·tye po
anglicky?   uhng·lits·ki

I don't understand.
Nerozumiem.   nye·ro·zu·myem

Accommodation

campsite	táborisko	ta·bo·ris·ko
guesthouse	penzión	pen·zi·awn
hotel	hotel	ho·tel
youth hostel	nocľaháreň	nots·lyuh·ha·ren'
	pre mládež	pre mla·dyezh

Do you have a single room?
Máte jedno-   ma·tye yed·no-
posteľovú izbu?   pos·tye·lyo·voo iz·bu

Do you have a double room?
Máte izbu s   ma·tye iz·bu s
manželskou   muhn·zhels·koh
postelou?   pos·tye·lyoh

Signs – Slovak

Vchod	Entrance
Východ	Exit
Otvorené	Open
Zatvorené	Closed
Zakázané	Prohibited
Záchody/Toalety	Toilets

How much is it per ...?	Koľko to stojí na ...?	kolʹ·ko to sto·yee nuh ...
night	noc	nots
person	osobu	o·so·bu

Eating & Drinking

What would you recommend?
Čo by ste mi odporučili?	cho bi stye mi od·po·ru·chi·li

Do you have vegetarian food?
Máte vegetariánske jedlá?	ma·tye ve·ge·tuh·ri·yan·ske yed·la

I'll have ...	Dám si ...	dam si ...
Cheers!	Nazdravie!	nuhz·druh·vi·ye

I'd like the ..., please.	Prosím si ...	pro·seem si ...
bill	účet	oo·chet
menu	jedálny lístok	ye·dal·ni lees·tok

(bottle of) beer	(fľaša) piva	(flyuh·shuh) pi·vuh
(cup of) coffee/tea	(šálka) kávy/čaju	(shal·kuh) ka·vi/chuh·yu
water	voda	vo·duh
(glass of) wine	(pohár) vína	(po·har) vee·nuh

breakfast	raňajky	ruh·nyai·ki
lunch	obed	o·bed
dinner	večera	ve·che·ruh

Emergencies

Help!	Pomoc!	po·mots
Go away!	Choďte preč!	khodʹ·tye prech

Call ...!	Zavolajte ...!	zuh·vo·lai·tye ...
a doctor	lekára	le·ka·ruh
the police	políciu	po·lee·tsi·yu

I'm lost.
Stratil/Stratila som sa. (m/f)	struh·tyil/struh·tyi·luh som suh

I'm ill.
Som chorý/chorá. (m/f)	som kho·ree/kho·ra

Where are the toilets?
Kde sú tu záchody?	kdye soo tu za·kho·di

Numbers – Slovak

1	jeden	ye·den
2	dva	dvuh
3	tri	tri
4	štyri	shti·ri
5	päť	petʹ
6	šesť	shestʹ
7	sedem	se·dyem
8	osem	o·sem
9	deväť	dye·vetʹ
10	desať	dye·suhtʹ

Shopping & Services

I'm looking for ...
Hľadám ...	hlyuh·dam ...

How much is it?
Koľko to stojí?	kolʹ·ko to sto·yee

That's too expensive.
To je príliš drahé.	to ye pree·lish druh·hair

market	trh	trh
post office	pošta	posh·tuh
tourist office	turistická kancelária	tu·ris·tits·ka kuhn·tse·la·ri·yuh

Transport & Directions

Where's the ...?
Kde je ...?	kdye ye ...

What's the address?
Aká je adresa?	uh·ka ye uh·dre·suh

Can you show me (on the map)?
Môžete mi ukázať (na mape)?	mwo·zhe·tye mi u·ka·zuhtʹ (nuh muh·pe)

One ... ticket (to Poprad), please.	Jeden ... lístok (do Popradu), prosím.	ye·den ... lees·tok (do pop·ruh·du) pro·seem
one-way	jedno-smerný	yed·no-smer·nee
return	spiatočný	spyuh·tochʹ·nee

bus	autobus	ow·to·bus
plane	lietadlo	li·ye·tuhd·lo
train	vlak	vluhk

SLOVENE

We've used the symbols oh (as the 'o' in 'note') and ow (as in 'how') to help you pronounce vowels followed by the letters *l* and v in written Slovene – at the end of a syllable these combinations produce a sound similar to the 'w' in English.

Note also that uh is pronounced as the 'a' in 'ago', zh as the 's' in 'pleasure', r is rolled, and the apostrophe (') indicates a slight y sound.

Basics

Hello.	*Zdravo.*	zdra·vo
Goodbye.	*Na svidenje.*	na svee·den·ye
Excuse me.	*Dovolite.*	do·vo·lee·te
Sorry.	*Oprostite.*	op·ros·tee·te
Please.	*Prosim.*	pro·seem
Thank you.	*Hvala.*	hva·la
Yes.	*Da.*	da
No.	*Ne.*	ne

What's your name?
Kako vam/ti   ka·ko vam/tee
je ime? (pol/inf)   ye ee·me

My name is ...
Ime mi je ...   ee·me mee ye ...

Do you speak English?
Ali govorite   a·lee go·vo·ree·te
angleško?   ang·lesh·ko

I don't understand.
Ne razumem.   ne ra·zoo·mem

Accommodation

campsite	*kamp*	kamp
guesthouse	*gostišče*	gos·teesh·che
hotel	*hotel*	ho·tel
youth hostel	*mladinski hotel*	mla·deen·skee ho·tel

Do you have a ... room?	*Ali imate ... sobo?*	a·lee ee·ma·te ... so·bo
single	*enoposteljno*	e·no·pos·tel'·no
double	*dvoposteljno*	dvo·pos·tel'·no

Signs – Slovene	
Vhod	Entrance
Izhod	Exit
Odprto	Open
Zaprto	Closed
Prepovedano	Prohibited
Stranišče	Toilets

How much is it per ...?	*Koliko stane na ...?*	ko·lee·ko sta·ne na ...
night	*noč*	noch
person	*osebo*	o·se·bo

Eating & Drinking

What would you recommend?
Kaj priporočate?   kai pree·po·ro·cha·te

Do you have vegetarian food?
Ali imate   a·lee ee·ma·te
vegetarijansko   ve·ge·ta·ree·yan·sko
hrano?   hra·no

I'll have ...	*Jaz bom ...*	yaz bom ...
Cheers!	*Na zdravje!*	na zdrav·ye

I'd like the ..., please.	*Želim ..., prosim.*	zhe·leem ... pro·seem
bill	*račun*	ra·choon
menu	*jedilni list*	ye·deel·nee leest

(bottle of) beer	*(steklenica) piva*	(stek·le·nee·tsa) pee·va
(cup of) coffee/tea	*(skodelica) kave/čaja*	(sko·de·lee·tsa) ka·ve/cha·ya
water	*voda*	vo·da
(glass of) wine	*(kozarec) vina*	(ko·za·rets) vee·na

breakfast	*zajtrk*	zai·tuhrk
lunch	*kosilo*	ko·see·lo
dinner	*večerja*	ve·cher·ya

Emergencies

Help!	*Na pomoč!*	na po·moch
Go away!	*Pojdite stran!*	poy·dee·te stran

Call ...!	*Pokličite ...!*	pok·lee·chee·te ...
a doctor	*zdravnika*	zdrav·nee·ka
the police	*policijo*	po·lee·tsee·yo

I'm lost.
Izgubil/   eez·goo·beew/
Izgubila sem se. (m/f)   eez·goo·bee·la sem se

I'm ill.
Bolan/Bolna sem. (m/f)   bo·lan/boh·na sem

Where are the toilets?
Kje je stranišče?   kye ye stra·neesh·che

Shopping & Services

I'm looking for ...
Iščem ...   *eesh·*chem ...

How much is this?
Koliko stane?   *ko·*lee·ko *sta·*ne

That's too expensive.
To je predrago.   to ye pre·dra·*go*

market	*tržnica*	*tuhrzh·*nee·tsa
post office	*pošta*	*posh·*ta
tourist office	*turistični urad*	too·*rees·*teech·nee oo·*rad*

Transport & Directions

Where's the ...?
Kje je ...?   kye ye ...

What's the address?
Na katerem naslovu je?   na ka·*te·*rem nas·*lo·*voo ye

Can you show me (on the map)?
Mi lahko pokažete (na zemljevidu)?   mee lah·*ko* po·*ka·*zhe·te (na zem·lye·*vee·*doo)

Numbers – Slovene

1	*en*	en
2	*dva*	dva
3	*trije*	*tree·*ye
4	*štirje*	*shtee·*rye
5	*pet*	pet
6	*šest*	shest
7	*sedem*	*se·*dem
8	*osem*	*o·*sem
9	*devet*	de·*vet*
10	*deset*	de·*set*

One ... ticket to (Koper), please.	*... vozovnico do (Kopra), prosim.*	*... vo·zov·*nee·tso do (ko·*pra*) *pro·*seem
one-way	*Enosmerno*	e·no·*smer·*no
return	*Povratno*	pov·*rat·*no
boat	*ladja*	*lad·*ya
bus	*avtobus*	*av·*to·boos
plane	*letalo*	le·*ta·*lo
train	*vlak*	vlak

behind the scenes

SEND US YOUR FEEDBACK

We love to hear from travellers – your comments keep us on our toes and help make our books better. Our well-travelled team reads every word on what you loved or loathed about this book. Although we cannot reply individually to postal submissions, we always guarantee that your feedback goes straight to the appropriate authors, in time for the next edition. Each person who sends us information is thanked in the next edition – and the most useful submissions are rewarded with a free book.

Visit **lonelyplanet.com/contact** to submit your updates and suggestions or to ask for help. Our award-winning website also features inspirational travel stories, news and discussions.

Note: We may edit, reproduce and incorporate your comments in Lonely Planet products such as guidebooks, websites and digital products, so let us know if you don't want your comments reproduced or your name acknowledged. For a copy of our privacy policy visit lonelyplanet.com/privacy.

OUR READERS

Many thanks to the travellers who used the last edition and wrote to us with helpful hints, useful advice and interesting anecdotes:
Pam Ames, Emma Antrobus, Asher Frankfurt, James French, Alex Joseph, Philipp Kirchmeir, Megan Kwong, Dalibor Micka, William Parnell, Paula J. Swiatkowski, Noreen Tai, Marstin Tallant

AUTHOR THANKS

Lisa Dunford

I'm grateful to Dora Whitaker, Kirsten Rawlings and all the others at LP that helped make this book what it is. Heartfelt thanks go to my dear friends Saša, Fero, Šimon and Sara Petriska, Edita and Anton Augustin. It means so much to me being a part of your 'family.' I appreciate the hospitality and guidance of everyone along the road, including Andrea Sarkany, Miro, Vera & Jan Zachar, Jennifer Josifek and Jess McMurray.

Brett Atkinson

Thanks to my Czech friends and drinking partners who again conspired to make a globetrotting Kiwi feel right at home. Special thanks to Greg and Francie in Olomouc. Finally, love and special thanks to Carol and to Mum and Dad.

Mark Baker

On the ground in Hungary, my gratitude goes out to the helpful people at Tourinform and to my friend in Pécs, Krisztina Koncz, who introduced me to Villány's wonderful wines and even took the day off to show me around Szeged.

Kerry Christiani

Special thanks go to my husband Andy for being with me every step of the way on this book. I'd also like to thank all the tourism professionals who made the road to research silky smooth, especially Sabine Günterseder (Upper Austria Tourism), Monika Reichel (Salzburg Information) and Nicholas Boekdrukker (Innsbruck Tourism).

Steve Fallon

Thanks to Tatjana Radovič and Petra Stušek at the Ljubljana Tourist Board and Lucija Jager at the Slovenian Tourist Board. Slovenian Railways' Marino Fakin, Tone Plankar at the Ljubljana bus station and Tomaž Škofic of Adria Airways helped with transport and Dušan Brejc of the Wine Association of Slovenia with the right vintage(s). It was wonderful catching up with mates Domen Kalajžič of 3glav Adventures, Bled, and Aleš Hvala of Hotel Hvala, Kobarid. As always, my efforts here are dedicated to my partner, Michael Rothschild.

Tim Richards

As always, I'm indebted to the professional staff of Poland's tourist offices, who perform their jobs with enthusiasm and skill. I also give thanks to the national train company PKP; their trains aren't always fast, but they're usually on time. Much love to my Polish friends – particularly Ewa, Magda, Gosia and Andrzej – for their continued good company. Thanks to artist Tomasz Moczek and his friends Marcin and Kuba, with whom I spent a pleasant hour drinking beer in the sunshine within a crumbling former brewery in Wrocław, while talking about gnomes; and to Belarusian sailor Aleksandr, who kept me company on a train journey between Giżycko and Białystok. Cheers also to Ania and Jaime, who I met via Twitter and shared a drink with at a Lublin pub. Finally, to the unseen hotel staff who prepared my packed breakfasts when (often) catching an insanely early train – I salute you!

Caroline Sieg

Thanks to my parents for instilling in me a lifelong zest for travel. Thanks *mucho* to Lucy Monie for giving me this gig and *merci viel mal* to all my friends – old and new – for wining and dining with me across the country.

And last but not least, thanks to Jules and Thresher, for all those memories that never go out of style.

Ryan Ver Berkmoes

Thanks to all the authors who worked so hard on this LP guidebook. Great job all! Meanwhile in Germany, Angela Cullen was a dear as always and I'm happy to see she still prefers Harry over a chihuahua. It was good to get back on track with Alan Wissenburg. Thanks to Birgit Borowski and Dr Eva Missler in Stuttgart. And thanks to Claudia Stehle as always for taking me to the dark depths of the BF. Samuel L Bronkowitz gets a nod as does Erin, the Kona-Denny's girl.

ACKNOWLEDGMENTS

Climate map data adapted from Peel MC, Finlayson BL & McMahon TA (2007) 'Updated World Map of the Köppen-Geiger Climate Classification', *Hydrology and Earth System Sciences*, 11, 1633–44.

Cover photograph: Sculpture of cockerel on roof of St Vitus Cathedral, Czech Republic, Gavin Gough/Lonely Planet Images. Many of the images in this guide are available for licensing from Lonely Planet Images: www.lonelyplanetimages.com.

THIS BOOK

Central Europe is part of Lonely Planet's Europe series, which includes *Western Europe, Eastern Europe, Mediterranean Europe, Scandinavia* and *Europe on a Shoestring*. This guidebook was commissioned in Lonely Planet's London office, and produced by the following:

Commissioning Editors
Joe Bindloss, Paula Hardy, Dora Whitaker

Coordinating Editor
Sonya Mithen

Coordinating Cartographer Anita Banh

Coordinating Layout Designer Paul Iacono

Managing Editors Brigitte Ellemor, Tasmin Waby McNaughtan, Kirsten Rawlings

Managing Cartographers Adrian Persoglia, Herman So

Managing Layout Designer Jane Hart

Assisting Editor Andi Lien

Cover Research Mazzy Prinsep

Internal Image Research Aude Vauconsant

Language Content Annelies Mertens, Branislava Vladislavljevic

Thanks to Ryan Evans, Lisa Knights, Gerard Walker

index

how to use this book

These symbols will help you find the listings you want:

- 👁 Sights
- 🏃 Activities
- 🍃 Courses
- 👉 Tours
- 🎎 Festivals & Events
- 🛏 Sleeping
- ✕ Eating
- 🍷 Drinking
- ☆ Entertainment
- 🛍 Shopping
- ℹ Information/ Transport

Look out for these icons:

- **TOP CHOICE** Our author's recommendation
- **FREE** No payment required
- 🌱 A green or sustainable option

Our authors have nominated these places as demonstrating a strong commitment to sustainability – for example by supporting local communities and producers, operating in an environmentally friendly way, or supporting conservation projects.

These symbols give you the vital information for each listing:

- ☎ Telephone Numbers
- ⊙ Opening Hours
- P Parking
- ⊖ Nonsmoking
- ❄ Air-Conditioning
- @ Internet Access
- 📶 Wi-Fi Access
- 🏊 Swimming Pool
- 🥗 Vegetarian Selection
- 📖 English-Language Menu
- 👪 Family-Friendly
- 🐾 Pet-Friendly
- 🚌 Bus
- ⛴ Ferry
- S Subway
- ⊖ London Tube
- 🚊 Tram
- 🚆 Train

Reviews are organised by author preference.

Map Legend

Sights
- 🏖 Beach
- 🔴 Buddhist
- 🟠 Castle
- 🟢 Christian
- 🔵 Hindu
- 🔵 Islamic
- 🔵 Jewish
- 🟠 Monument
- 🔵 Museum/Gallery
- 🟢 Ruin
- 🟢 Winery/Vineyard
- 🟢 Zoo
- 🟢 Other Sight

Activities, Courses & Tours
- ⊖ Diving/Snorkelling
- 🔵 Canoeing/Kayaking
- 🔵 Skiing
- 🔵 Surfing
- 🔵 Swimming/Pool
- 🔵 Walking
- 🔵 Windsurfing
- 🔵 Other Activity/ Course/Tour

Sleeping
- 🛏 Sleeping
- 🔵 Camping

Eating
- ✕ Eating

Drinking
- 🔵 Drinking
- ⊖ Cafe

Entertainment
- ✕ Entertainment

Shopping
- 🔵 Shopping

Information
- 🔵 Post Office
- 🔵 Tourist Information

Transport
- 🔵 Airport
- ⊗ Border Crossing
- 🔵 Bus
- ++⊕++ Cable Car/ Funicular
- -⊖- Cycling
- -⊖- Ferry
- Ⓜ Metro
- 🔵 Monorail
- P Parking
- 🔵 S-Bahn
- 🔵 Taxi
- ++⊙++ Train/Railway
- 🔵 Tram
- ⊖ Tube Station
- Ⓤ U-Bahn
- • Other Transport

Routes
- Tollway
- Freeway
- Primary
- Secondary
- Tertiary
- Lane
- Unsealed Road
- Plaza/Mall
- Steps
-)= = Tunnel
- Pedestrian Overpass
- Walking Tour
- Walking Tour Detour
- Path

Boundaries
- International
- State/Province
- Disputed
- Regional/Suburb
- Marine Park
- Cliff
- Wall

Population
- ◉ Capital (National)
- ◉ Capital (State/Province)
- ● City/Large Town
- ○ Town/Village

Geographic
- 🔵 Hut/Shelter
- 🔵 Lighthouse
- 🔵 Lookout
- ▲ Mountain/Volcano
- 🔵 Oasis
- 🔵 Park
-)(Pass
- 🔵 Picnic Area
- 🔵 Waterfall

Hydrography
- River/Creek
- Intermittent River
- Swamp/Mangrove
- Reef
- Canal
- Water
- Dry/Salt/ Intermittent Lake
- Glacier

Areas
- Beach/Desert
- + + + Cemetery (Christian)
- × × × Cemetery (Other)
- Park/Forest
- Sportsground
- Sight (Building)
- Top Sight (Building)

Kerry Christiani

Austria Born in Essex, Kerry now lives in the Black Forest, Germany. On her second visit to Austria for Lonely Planet she discovered the truth about the von Trapps in Salzburg, sweated out a rare heatwave in the Alps and climbed (almost) every mountain – and in doing so fell for the country and its great outdoors all over again. Kerry's wanderlust has taken her to six continents, inspiring numerous articles and some 20 guidebooks, including Lonely Planet's *Germany*, *Switzerland* and *France*.

Read more about Kerry at:
lonelyplanet.com/members/kerrychristiani

Steve Fallon

Slovenia Steve has been travelling to Slovenia since the early 1990s, when most everyone but the Slovenes had never heard of the place. Never mind, it was his own private Idaho for over a decade. Though *on še govori slovensko kot jamski človek* (he still speaks Slovene like a caveman), Steve considers part of his soul to be Slovenian and returns as often as he can for a glimpse of the Julian Alps in the sun, a dribble of *bučno olje* and a dose of the dual.

Tim Richards

Poland Tim spent a year teaching English in Kraków in 1994-95, having transferred with an international teaching organisation from a two-year stint in Egypt. He was fascinated by the massive post-communism transition affecting every aspect of Polish life, and by surviving remnants of the Cold War days. He's since returned to Poland repeatedly for Lonely Planet, deepening his continued relationship with this beautiful, complex country. When he's not on the road for Lonely Planet, Tim is a freelance journalist living in Melbourne, Australia, writing on various topics, particularly travel and the arts. You can see more of his writing at www.iwriter.com.au, and in his collection of essays about his Polish experiences as a Kindle e-book, *We Have Here the Homicide*.

Caroline Sieg

Germany, Liechtenstein, Switzerland Half –Swiss, half-American, Caroline's relationship with Switzerland began when she and her family first moved to Lucerne at age five. Several moves back and forth across the Atlantic ended when she resided in Zurich throughout high-school and beyond, including working a season in a ski resort in the Valais. These days, Caroline heads to Switzerland as often as possible – to ski, indulge in cheese and chocolate or to simply meander along Lake Zürich.

Read more about Caroline at:
lonelyplanet.com/members/carolinesieg

Ryan Ver Berkmoes

Germany Ryan Ver Berkmoes once lived in Germany. Three years in Frankfurt during which time he edited a magazine until he got a chance for a new career: with Lonely Planet. One of his first jobs was working on the Germany chapter of the fourth edition of this very book. Later he worked on the first edition of Lonely Planet's *The Netherlands*, a country where they pronounce his name better than he can. He continues to write about both. These days he lives in Portland, Oregon. Follow him at ryanverberkmoes.com. He tweets at @ryanvb.

Read more about Ryan at:
lonelyplanet.com/members/ryanverberkmoes

OUR STORY

A beat-up old car, a few dollars in the pocket and a sense of adventure. In 1972 that's all Tony and Maureen Wheeler needed for the trip of a lifetime – across Europe and Asia overland to Australia. It took several months, and at the end – broke but inspired – they sat at their kitchen table writing and stapling together their first travel guide, *Across Asia on the Cheap*. Within a week they'd sold 1500 copies. Lonely Planet was born.

Today, Lonely Planet has offices in Melbourne, London and Oakland, with more than 600 staff and writers. We share Tony's belief that 'a great guidebook should do three things: inform, educate and amuse'.

OUR WRITERS

Lisa Dunford

Coordinating author, Slovakia A fascination with Central Europe has gripped Lisa since childhood, probably because her grandfather emigrated from the Carpathian mountains that were a part of Hungary, then Czechoslovakia and now are just over the border in the Ukraine. She studied in Budapest junior year at university and, post graduation, worked for the Agency for International Development at the US embassy in Bratislava. While living in Slovakia, Lisa explored the region extensively: skiing in Switzerland, hefting a *weizen* beer or two in Austria and Germany, spelunking in Slovenia and admiring old towns in Poland and the Czech Republic. She returns often both for freelance assignments and to visit friends and cousins. Lisa has contributed to numerous Lonely Planet books, including *Czech & Slovak Republics*, *Hungary*, *Eastern Europe* and *Discover Europe*.

Read more about Lisa at:
lonelyplanet.com/members/lisa_dunford

Brett Atkinson

Czech Republic Brett Atkinson has been travelling to Eastern Europe for more than 20 years, honeymooning in Bosnia, Croatia and Hungary, writing about the legacy of the communist era, and enjoying more than a few local beers. For his fourth extended research trip to the Czech Republic, he dived into Prague's emerging visual arts scene, trekked the spectacular valleys of the Bohemian Switzerland region, and continued to marvel at sunsets above Prague Castle. When he's not on the road for Lonely Planet, Brett's at home in Auckland, planning his next overseas sojourn with wife Carol. He's contributed to more than 20 Lonely Planet titles, and travelled to more than 60 countries. See www.brett-atkinson.net for details of his latest writing and travels.

Mark Baker

Hungary Mark first came to Eastern Europe in the mid-'80s as a grad student in International Affairs. Those were the dark days of the dying communist regimes, yet even then he was hooked by the region's quirky history, beauty and cheap booze. He's lived in Prague for the better part of 20 years, and is a frequent traveller throughout the region (and now has a special fondness for Hungary). After working as a fulltime journalist for The Economist Group and Radio Free Europe, he's found permanent employment as a freelance travel writer and is co-author of Lonely Planet *Prague* and Lonely Planet *Romania*, among other titles.

OVER PAGE MORE WRITERS

Published by Lonely Planet Publications Pty Ltd
ABN 36 005 607 983
9th edition – Oct 2011
ISBN 978 1 74179 682 7
© Lonely Planet 2011   Photographs © as indicated 2011
10 9 8 7 6 5 4 3 2 1
Printed in China